WALTER KITONA

RYERSON   B721

979 5000   X 1-6711

RYERSON   B721

Management Accounting

Canadian Fifth Edition

Management Accounting

Canadian Fifth Edition

Don R. Hansen
Oklahoma State University

Maryanne M. Mowen
Oklahoma State University

Nabil S. Elias
University of Manitoba

David W. Senkow
University of Regina

NELSON

THOMSON LEARNING

Australia • Canada • Mexico • Singapore • Spain • United Kingdom • United States

NELSON
THOMSON LEARNING

Management Accounting,
Canadian Fifth Edition

by Don R. Hansen, Maryanne M. Mowen,
Nabil S. Elias, and David W. Senkow

Editorial Director and Publisher:
Evelyn Veitch

Acquisitions Editor:
Paul Manley

Marketing Manager:
Anthony Rezek

Developmental Editor:
Karina TenVeldhuis

Production Editor:
Bob Kohlmeier

Production Coordinator:
Hedy Sellers

Copy Editor:
Riça Night

Proofreader:
Marg Bukta

Art Director:
Angela Cluer

Interior Design:
Liz Harasymczuk

Cover Design:
Peggy Rhodes

Cover Image:
PhotoDisc

Compositor:
Susan Calverley

Indexer:
Dennis A. Mills

Printer:
Quebecor World

Canadian Cataloguing in Publication Data

Main entry under title:

Management accounting

Canadian 5th ed.
Includes bibliographical references and index.
ISBN 0-17-616844-3

1. Managerial accounting.
I. Hansen, Don R.

HF5657.4.M35 2000   658.15'11
C00-931932-8

Brief Contents

Contents

PART 3
PLANNING AND CONTROL 551

Preface

The Canadian Fifth Edition of *Management Accounting* introduces students to the fundamentals of management accounting. Though it is assumed that students have been introduced to the basics of financial accounting, extensive knowledge of financial accounting is not needed. Our emphasis is on the use of accounting information. Thus, the text should be of value to students with a variety of backgrounds. Although written to serve undergraduates, the text has been used successfully at the graduate level. There is sufficient variety in the assignment material to accommodate both undergraduate and graduate students.

Many business students who are required to take a course in management accounting are not accounting majors. For these students, it is often difficult to appreciate the value of the concepts being taught. *Management Accounting*, Canadian Fifth Edition, overcomes this attitude by using introductory chapter scenarios based on real-world settings and by presenting realistic examples illustrating the concepts within the chapters. Seeing that effective management requires a sound understanding of how to use accounting information should enhance the interest of both accounting and nonaccounting majors.

ACTIVITY-BASED MANAGEMENT

Management accounting continues to evolve and respond to changes in the manufacturing and service sectors of today's business world. One significant response has been the development of activity-based management. The effect of the activity-based management model on management accounting has been dramatic. The widespread acceptance and practice of activity concepts demands treatment of activity-based methods in an integrated, comprehensive framework. To respond to this need, we have developed such a framework. Within this framework, we offer extensive coverage of such topics as activity-based costing, kaizen costing, Balanced Scorecard, environmental cost management, activity-based budgeting, process value analysis, quality, productivity, life-cycle cost management, target costing, and international management accounting issues.

FUNCTIONAL-BASED CONCEPT COVERAGE

To provide balance, the Canadian Fifth Edition continues to provide extensive coverage of traditional topics. There is still widespread usage of costing models that rely on production functions and control models that focus on functional organizational units. Covering these functional-based models is essential not just because they are used but because the significant differences between the activity-based and functional-based approaches can be brought to light. This helps students determine when it is appropriate to use the different approaches. This coverage also exposes the limitations of functional-based costing and control and highlights the advantages of activity-based costing and control. The understanding that comes from the integrated approach of this text should help future managers bring about change when it is merited. Furthermore, perhaps the realization that management accounting is not a static discipline will itself contribute to additional innovative developments.

Take a few minutes to review the table of contents. You will see a balanced, integrative presentation of the activity-based and functional-based management accounting concepts.

ORGANIZATION OF THE TEXT

The sequence of chapters essentially follows that of the Canadian Fourth Edition. This presentation is used to facilitate integration of the activity-based concepts throughout the text. Changes to specific chapters are listed below.

Chapter 1: An introduction to the concepts of strategic cost management and strategic positioning was added.

Chapter 2: Discussion of activity cost behavior was moved to Chapter 3. The section on cost tracing was rewritten to simplify the concepts. The concept of drivers for tracing is introduced, while discussion of specific types of drivers, such as activity and resource drivers, is deferred until later chapters. Finally, the functional-based management accounting systems are introduced, defined, and compared briefly with activity-based management accounting systems.

Chapter 3: This activity cost behavior chapter has dropped the manual computation of regression coefficients in favor of an explanation of the use of popular computer spreadsheet regression routines.

Chapter 4: A section has been added that shows how activities are identified and assigned costs. Coverage of normal costing is reduced.

Chapter 13: A section on activity-based budgeting has been added.

Chapter 14: The discussion of the fixed overhead denominator variance has been simplified and expanded to include the concept of capacity management.

Chapter 15: Discussion of activity-based budgeting has been moved to the budgeting chapter. A section on the Balanced Scorecard has been added. Furthermore, kaizen costing concepts have been added and the section on target costing expanded.

Chapter 16: A section on gain-sharing has been added.

Chapter 17: This is a new chapter that deals with environmental cost management. This chapter defines and classifies environmental costs, assigns them to products, describes life-cycle cost assessment, and discusses control approaches, including an environmental perspective as part of the Balanced Scorecard.

CHAPTER ORGANIZATION AND STRUCTURE

Each chapter is carefully structured to help students focus on important concepts and retain them. Components found in each chapter include:

Learning Objectives. Each chapter begins with a set of learning objectives to guide students in their study of the chapter. These objectives outline the organizational flow of the chapter and serve as points of comprehension and evaluation. Learning objectives are tied to specific sections of topic coverage within the chapter. They are repeated in the margin at the beginning of the corresponding chapter coverage and are summarized at the end of the chapter.

Scenario. An interesting real-world scenario opens each chapter. The scenario ties directly to concepts covered in the chapter and helps students relate chapter topics to actual business happenings. "Questions to Think About," critical-thinking questions that appear at the end of each scenario, are designed to pique student interest in the chapter and stimulate class discussion.

Summary of Learning Objectives. Each chapter concludes with a comprehensive summary of the learning objectives. Students can review and test their knowledge of key concepts and evaluate their ability to complete chapter objectives.

Key Terms. Throughout each chapter, key terms are highlighted in colour for quick identification. A list of key terms, with page references, is presented at the end of each chapter to provide additional reinforcement. All key terms are defined in a comprehensive glossary at the end of the text.

Review Problems. Each chapter contains at least one review problem with the accompanying solution provided. These review problems demonstrate the application of major concepts and procedures covered in the chapter.

Questions for Writing and Discussion. Approximately 15 to 25 short-answer questions appear at the end of each chapter to test students' knowledge of chapter concepts. Many of the questions call for students to use critical thinking and written and oral communication skills. Several questions can be used to stimulate class participation and discussion.

Exercises. Exercises usually emphasize one or two chapter concepts and can be completed fairly quickly (30 minutes maximum). Exercises require basic application and computation and often ask students to interpret and explain their results.

Problems. Each chapter contains many end-of-chapter problems, with varying degrees of length and difficulty. Problems generally take longer to complete than exercises and probe for a deeper level of understanding. Problems usually have more than one issue and present challenging situations, complex computations, and interpretations.

Managerial Decision Cases. Most chapters contain at least two cases. Cases have greater depth and complexity than problems. They are designed to help students integrate multiple concepts and further develop their analytical skills. Several cases deal with ethical behavior.

Research Assignments. Research assignments appear in all chapters, allowing students to expand their research and communication skills beyond the classroom. One research assignment in each chapter, labelled "Cybercase," requires the student to research information on the Internet.

ADDITIONAL FEATURES OF THE CANADIAN FIFTH EDITION

Coverage of Environmental Costing. A full chapter (Chapter 17) has been added on this current and relevant topic.

International Coverage. To emphasize the importance of international issues, we provide a full chapter on this topic (Chapter 19) as well as examples integrated throughout the text.

Ethics. We continue to emphasize in the Canadian Fifth Edition the study of ethical conduct for management accountants. The role of ethics is discussed in Chapter 1. Examples of ethical conduct relative to management accounting issues are provided in other chapters as well. Chapter 19, dealing with international issues in management accounting, also has a section that discusses ethics in the international environment. Chapter 1 has several substantive problems on ethics, and subsequent chapters have at least one problem or case involving an ethical dilemma. These problems allow the instructor to introduce value judgments into management accounting decision making.

Real-World Emphasis. The Canadian Fifth Edition incorporates many real-world applications of management accounting concepts, making the study of these concepts more familiar and interesting to the student. Opening scenarios introduce chapter topics within the context of realistic business examples. Real-company examples are incorporated throughout many chapters.

Increased Coverage of Service Industry. Service businesses are experiencing unprecedented growth in today's economy. Managers of service businesses often use the same management accounting models as manufacturers, but they must adapt them to their own unique situations of providing intangibles to consumers. To address this need, we have increased the coverage of service industry applications in the Canadian Fifth Edition. In addition, many real-company examples of service businesses are given.

ANCILLARIES

Check Figures. Key figures for solutions to selected problems and cases are provided as an aid to students as they prepare their answers.

Study Guide (prepared by Donna Ulmer, St. Louis Community College at Meramec, and Deborah Mortimer, University of Manitoba). The study guide provides a detailed review of each chapter and allows students to check their understanding of the material through quizzes and exercises. Specifically, students are provided with a key terms test, a chapter quiz, and practice exercises. Answers are provided for all assignment material. Learning organizers help students compare and contrast key concepts and aid in visual learning.

Instructor's Manual (prepared by Marvin Bouillon, Iowa State University, and Nabil Elias, University of Manitoba). The instructor's manual contains a complete set of lecture notes for each chapter and a listing of all exercises and problems with estimated difficulty and time required for solution.

Solutions Manual (prepared by Don Hansen and Maryanne Mowen, Oklahoma State University, and Dave Kennedy, Lethbridge Community College). The solutions manual contains the solutions for all end-of-chapter questions, exercises, problems, and cases. Solutions have been error-checked to ensure their accuracy and reliability.

Solutions Transparencies. Transparency masters for selected solutions are available to adopters of the Canadian Fifth Edition.

Test Bank. Extensively revised for the Canadian Fifth Edition, the test bank offers multiple-choice problems, short problems, and essay problems. Designed to make exam preparation as convenient as possible for the instructor, each test bank chapter contains enough questions and problems to permit the preparation of several exams without repetition of material.

The test bank is available in computerized format, allowing instructors to design and edit their own tests.

Spreadsheet

Spreadsheet Templates. Spreadsheet templates using Microsoft Excel® and Lotus 1-2-3® provide outlined formats of solutions for selected end-of-chapter exercises and problems. These exercises and problems are identified with a margin symbol. The templates allow students to develop spreadsheet and "what-if" analysis skills.

PowerPoint Slides. Selected transparencies of key concepts and exhibits from the text are available in PowerPoint presentation software.

Web Site (www.caccounting.nelson.com). A Web site designed specifically for *Management Accounting*, Canadian Fifth Edition, includes on-line and downloadable instructor and student resources.

BusinessLink Videos. A series of five videos illustrates key management accounting concepts, including activity-based costing, product costing, and total quality management. These videos feature companies such as Archway Cookies, World Gym, and Symbios Logic. A student workbook and an instructor's manual are available to accompany the videos.

Cases in Management Accounting. These forty cases require students to think critically and strategically as well as apply technical accounting analysis to familiar scenarios and settings. The cases are also integrative in that they involve aspects of manufacturing and service operations, organizational design, and data analysis. The casebook includes Excel spreadsheet applications and Microsoft Access cost accounting/management databases. Case topics include process value analysis, the DuPont method, activity-based costing (ABC), activity-based management (ABM), break-even analysis, budgeting, performance measurement (including the Balanced Scorecard approach), and transfer pricing. Photos that accompany the case provide the student with a contextual perspective that facilitates learning.

California Car Company Case. This 144-page, award-winning simulation forms the foundation of management accounting. Using construction block cars, students learn about the manufacturing process and management accounting by simulating their own production line. Students benefit from a manufacturing production line simulation while exploring key management accounting topics.

ACKNOWLEDGMENTS

We would like to express our appreciation to all who have provided helpful comments and suggestions. The reviewers of the prior editions helped make it a successful product. Many valuable comments from instructors and students have helped us make significant improvements in the Canadian Fifth Edition. In particular, we would like to thank the following individuals, who provided formal comments. Their input was deeply appreciated.

For the Canadian Fifth Edition:

Ibrahim Aly, Concordia University
D.H. Drury, McGill University
Anamitra Shome, Brock University
Rashmi Thakkar, University of Calgary

For the Fifth U.S. Edition:

Wagby M. Abdallah, Seton Hall University
Janice Ammons, Quinnipiac College
Larry Bitner, Hood College
Jon A. Booker, Tennessee Technological University
Frank Cicalease, Kean University
Michael L. Costigan, Southern Illinois University—Edwardsville
Wilbur L. Garland, Coastal Carolina University
Sanjay Gupta, Valdosta State University
Kathryn A. Hansen, California State University—Los Angeles
Jay S. Holmen, University of Wisconsin—Eau Claire
Paul Jensen, University of Central Arkansas
William B. Joyce, Michigan Technological University
Celina L. Jozsi, University of South Florida
John P. Keithley, St. Louis University
Rajabali Kiani-Aslani, California State University—Northridge
Noel McKeon, Florida Community College—Jacksonville
Paul H. Mihalek, University of Hartford
B. Radhakrishna, University of Minnesota
David A. Remmele, University of Wisconsin—Whitewater
Alicia Rieffel, Louisiana State University—Baton Rouge
Elaine Sanders, University of Texas—San Antonio

We would like to thank our verifier—Dave Kennedy, Lethbridge Community College, who served as the error-checker for the text. His careful editing helped us produce a text and ancillary package of higher quality and accuracy.

We also want to express our gratitude to the Society of Management Accountants of Canada and the Institute of Management Accountants for their permission to use adapted problems from past CMA examinations. Extracts from Management Accounting 1 (MA1), published by the the Certified General Accountants Association of Canada (© CGA-Canada, 1991, 1992, 1993, 1995), are reprinted by permission. The Society of Management Accountants of Manitoba and the Institute of Management Accountants have also given us permission to reprint the ethical standards of conduct for management accountants.

Finally, we should offer special thanks to all the Nelson Thomson Learning and South-Western College Publishing staff. They have been most helpful and have carried out their tasks with impressive expertise and professionalism. We especially wish to thank Paul Manley and Karina TenVeldhuis at Nelson and Leslie Kauffman at South-Western for their exceptionally insightful comments and dedicated work.

Nabil S. Elias
David W. Senkow
Don R. Hansen
Maryanne M. Mowen

About the Authors

Nabil S. Elias is Professor of Accounting at the Asper School of Business, The University of Manitoba. He received his Ph.D. from the University of Minnesota in 1970. He is a Fulbright scholar and both a CMA and an FCMA. He taught at the American Graduate School of International Management "Thunderbird," INSEAD, HEC, and ESCP. Dr. Elias also served on the Accounting Standards Board and as president of the Canadian Academic Accounting Association. His research interests are in environmental accounting, accounting for human capital, and information and conflict resolution. He has published in such journals as *The Journal of Accounting Research, The Accounting Review, Contemporary Accounting Research, Management Accounting*, and *CMA Magazine*, and is co-author of *Environmental Management and Reporting*. Dr. Elias has conducted seminars or consulted for such organizations as Boeing Technology, James Richardson International, Palliser, Cangene, the CIBC, and national and local CA, CMA, and CGA organizations. He has led several delegations of MBA students to Mexico, China, Hong Kong, and Japan.

David W. Senkow is Assistant Professor of Accounting in the Faculty of Administration, University of Regina. He received his Ph.D. from the University of Minnesota in 1992. His research interests include experimental economics and the effects of information characteristics and institutional structures on management decision behaviour. He has published in *The Accounting Review* and *The Economic Journal*. Dr. Senkow has served the accounting profession through committees of CMA-Canada (Saskatchewan) and the Institute of Chartered Accountants of Saskatchewan and on the board of the Accounting Education Foundation of Saskatchewan. He is currently a vice-president of the Canadian Academic Accounting Association. His outside interests include walking, watching a variety of sports, and drag racing his 1967 Mustang.

Don R. Hansen is Professor of Accounting at Oklahoma State University. He received his Ph.D. from the University of Arizona in 1977. He has an undergraduate degree in mathematics from Brigham Young University. His research interests include productivity measurement, activity-based costing, and mathematical modelling. He has published articles in both accounting and engineering journals, including *The Accounting Review, The Journal of Management Accounting Research, Accounting Horizons*, and *IIE Transactions*. Dr. Hansen has served on the editorial board of *The Accounting Review* and is currently serving as an associate editor of the *Journal of Accounting Education*. His outside interests include playing basketball, watching sports, and studying Spanish and Portuguese.

Maryanne M. Mowen is Associate Professor of Accounting at Oklahoma State University. She received her Ph.D. from Arizona State University in 1979. Dr. Mowen brings an interdisciplinary perspective to teaching and writing in cost and management accounting, with degrees in history and economics. In addition, she does scholarly research in behavioural decision theory. She has published articles in journals such as *Decision Science, The Journal of Economics and Psychology*, and *The Journal of Management Accounting Research*. Dr. Mowen's interests outside the classroom include reading, playing golf, travelling, and working crossword puzzles.

CHAPTER 1

Introduction: The Role, History, and Direction of Management Accounting

Learning Objectives

After studying Chapter 1, you should be able to:

1. Explain the need for management accounting information.

2. Explain the differences between management accounting and financial accounting.

3. Provide a brief historical description of management accounting.

4. Identify and explain the current focus of management accounting.

5. Describe the role of management accountants in an organization.

6. Explain the importance of ethical behaviour for managers and management accountants.

7. Identify the different professional accounting designations available for management accountants.

Scenario

Consider the following comments made by individuals from several different organizations:

A. **Manager of a For-Profit Water-Testing Facility:** "I have just received a request to bid on the lab work for a large water-bottling company. The competition for this job is intense. Given the specifications described in the written request and the level of competition we are facing, I need an accurate assessment of cost for each lab test that will be performed. Once I have the unit cost for each type of lab test, I can obtain the total cost based on the expected volume of tests. With this cost information, I can then calculate the minimum bid that will provide a reasonable dollar return." (Product costing and pricing decision)

B. **Local Operator:** "I am confident that replacing the tooling in our machines and redesigning the grinding process will improve quality and decrease the time required to perform the operation. However, I would like to know if the number of defective units really drops and by how much. I also need to know if cycle time actually decreases because of the changes. Furthermore, do these changes reduce the cost of performing the work we do? I also need to know the cost of resources used before and after the proposed changes to see if cost improvement is really taking place." (Continuous improvement)

C. **Bank Manager:** "This is incredible! The no-equity loans were supposed to be our most profitable new product. Yet costs exceeded expectations by

$150,000. What happened? Did we spend too much time with each client? Was there less demand for the product than expected? Were processing costs greater than budgeted? Did more loans go into default than expected? I need information that reveals what happened so that corrective action can be taken." (Operational control)

D. **Chief Executive Officer (of an airline):** "Our profits are being squeezed by the intense competition we are facing. My marketing vice-president argues that we can improve our financial position by reducing our airfares. She claims that if we reduce fares by 20 percent and simultaneously increase advertising expenditures by $500,000, we can increase the number of passengers by 20 percent. I need to decide whether the price decrease coupled with an increase in advertising costs and

passenger volume will be profitable." (Cost–volume–profit decision)

E. **Hospital Administrator:** "I am not at all pleased with the performance of the emergency room. This latest performance report seems to reveal a total disregard for cost control. The actual costs incurred for almost every category are higher than the planned costs. Additionally, the revenues are lower than they should be for the number of patients treated. I think I need to meet with the assistant administrator of that area." (Managerial control)

F. **Manager:** "We must soon decide whether the acquisition of the computer-aided manufacturing equipment is in our best interest or not. This is a critical decision involving enormous amounts of capital, and it carries with it some long-term implications regarding

the type of labour we employ. To help us in that decision, our controller has estimated the cost of capital and the increase in after-tax cash flow that would be expected over the life of the equipment." (Capital investment decision and strategic planning)

Questions to Think About

1. Who are the users of management accounting information?

2. What is management accounting information used for?

3. Should a management accounting system provide both financial and nonfinancial information?

4. What organizations need a management accounting information system?

MANAGEMENT ACCOUNTING INFORMATION SYSTEM

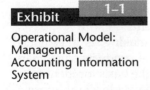

Objective 1

Explain the need for management accounting information.

The **management accounting information system** is an information system that produces outputs using inputs and processes needed to satisfy specific management objectives. Processes are the heart of a management accounting information system and are used to transform the inputs into outputs that satisfy the system's objectives. Processes are described by activities such as collecting, measuring, storing, analyzing, reporting, and managing information. Outputs include special reports, product costs, customer costs, budgets, performance reports, and even personal communication. The operational model of a management accounting information system is illustrated in Exhibit 1–1.

The management accounting information system is not bound by any formal criteria that define the nature of the inputs or processes—or even the output. The criteria are flexible and based on management objectives. The management accounting system has three broad objectives:

Exhibit 1–1

Operational Model: Management Accounting Information System

1. to provide information for costing out services, products, and other objects of interest to management;
2. to provide information for planning, controlling, evaluation, and continuous improvement; and
3. to provide information for decision making.

These three objectives reveal that managers and other users need management accounting information and need to know how to use it. Management accounting information can help managers identify opportunities and problems, solve problems, and evaluate performance (accounting information is needed and used in all phases of management, including planning, controlling, and decision making). Furthermore, the need for management accounting information is not limited to manufacturing organizations but is present in all organizations: manufacturing, merchandising, and service.

Information Needs of Managers and Other Users

The opening scenarios can be used to illustrate each of the management accounting system objectives. Scenario A (the manager of a for-profit water-testing facility), for example, shows the importance of determining the cost of products (illustrating objective 1). Scenario B emphasizes the importance of tracking costs and nonfinancial measures of performance over time. Thus Scenario A emphasizes the importance of accuracy in product costing, while Scenario B underscores the importance of tracking efficiency measures—both financial and nonfinancial (illustrating objective 2). Trends in these measures can suggest ways of improving a company's operations. For example, Milliken & Company, a leading textile manufacturer, began to use trend charts to track the change time for its dye nozzles. These charts provided the incentive for engineering and production personnel to reduce change time from 22 minutes to 8.2 minutes—a dramatic improvement.[1] Accuracy in cost assignments and the use of nonfinancial information by both managers and nonmanagers have emerged as fundamental requirements for many organizations. These and other related issues have led to the development of an improved management accounting information system known as an **activity-based cost management** information system.

Scenarios B, C, E, and F illustrate planning, control, evaluation, and continuous improvement (objective 2). Managers, executives, and workers need an information system that will identify problems, such as the possibility of cost overruns (Scenario C) or the inability of a manager in a subunit to implement a plan properly (Scenario E). Once problems are known, actions can be taken to identify and implement solutions. Scenario B also illustrates that both financial and nonfinancial information are needed so that workers can evaluate and monitor the effects of decisions that are intended to improve operational and unit performance. Informing workers about operational and financial performance allows workers to assess the effectiveness of their efforts to improve their work. Workers and managers should be committed to continuously improving the activities they perform. **Continuous improvement** means searching for ways to increase the overall efficiency and productivity of activities by reducing waste, increasing quality, and reducing costs. Thus, information is needed to help identify opportunities for improvement and to evaluate the progress made in implementing actions designed to create improvement.

The third objective, providing information for decision making, is intertwined with the first two. For example, information about the costs of products, customers, processes, and other objects of interest to management can be the basis for identifying problems and alternative solutions. Similar observations can be made about information pertaining to planning, control, and evaluation. Examples include using product

---

1. James Don Edwards, "How Milliken Stays on Top," *Journal of Accountancy* (April 1989): pp. 63–74 (see especially pp. 72–74).

cost to prepare a bid (Scenario A), helping a manager decide whether to reduce prices and increase advertising to improve profitability (Scenario D), or helping a manager decide whether to automate (Scenario F). This last scenario also underscores the importance of **strategic decision making**, which is defined as the process of choosing among alternative strategies with the goal of selecting one or more strategies that provide a company with a reasonable assurance of long-term growth and survival.

The Management Process

The management process is defined by the following activities: (1) planning, (2) controlling, and (3) decision making. The management process describes the functions carried out by managers and empowered workers. Empowering workers to participate in the management process means giving them a greater say in how the plant operates. Thus, **employee empowerment** is simply authorizing operational personnel to plan, control, and make decisions without explicit authorization from middle- and higher-level management.

Employee empowerment is justified by the belief that the employees closest to the work can provide valuable input in terms of ideas, plans, and problem solving. Workers are allowed to shut down production to identify and correct problems, and their input is sought and used to improve production processes. Two examples illustrate the power of this concept. First, empowered workers at Duffy Tool and Stamping saved $14,300 per year by redesigning a press operation.[2] In one department, completed parts (made by a press) came down a chute and fell into a parts tub. When the tub became full, press operators had to stop operation while the stock operator removed the full tub and replaced it with an empty one. Empowered workers redesigned the operation so that each press had a chute with two branches—each leading to a tub. Now completed parts are routed into one branch of the chute. When the tub associated with the active branch becomes full, the completed parts are routed to the other branch and its tub while the full tub is being removed and replaced with an empty tub. This new design avoids machine downtime and produces significant savings. Second, GR Spring and Stamping implemented an employee empowerment program in 1991. From 1991 to 1995, the number of ideas implemented increased from 0.67 per employee to 11.22 per employee.[3] Increased involvement in managing the company through employee empowerment is a key element in enhancing continuous improvement efforts.

Planning   The detailed formulation of action to achieve a particular end is the management activity called planning. **Planning**, therefore, requires setting objectives and identifying methods of achieving those objectives. For example, a firm may have the objective of increasing its short-term and long-term profitability by improving the overall quality of its products. By improving product quality, the firm should be able to reduce scrap and rework, decrease the number of customer complaints, reduce the amount of warranty work, reduce the resources currently assigned to inspection, and so on, thus increasing profitability. But how is this to be accomplished? Management must develop some specific methods that, when implemented, will lead to the achievement of the desired objective. A plant manager, for example, may initiate a supplier evaluation program that has the objective of identifying and selecting suppliers who are willing and able to supply defect-free parts. Empowered workers, on the other hand, may be able to identify production causes of defects and create new methods for producing a product that will reduce scrap and rework and the need for inspection. The new methods should be clearly specified and detailed.

---

2. George F. Hanks, "Excellence Teams in Action," *Management Accounting* (February 1995): p. 35.

3. Joseph F. Castellano, Donald Klein, and Harper Roehm, "Minicompanies: The Next Generation of Employee Empowerment," *Management Accounting* (March 1998): pp. 22–30.

Controlling Planning is only half the battle. Once a plan is created, it must be implemented and its implementation monitored by managers and workers to ensure that the plan is being carried out as intended. The managerial activity of monitoring a plan's implementation and taking corrective action as needed is referred to as **controlling**. Control is usually achieved with the use of feedback. **Feedback** is information that can be used to evaluate or correct the steps being taken to implement a plan. Based on the feedback, a manager (or worker) may decide to let the implementation continue as is, take corrective action of some type to put the actions back in harmony with the original plan, or do some midstream replanning.

Feedback is a critical facet of the control function. It is here that management accounting once again plays a vital role. Feedback can be financial or nonfinancial in nature. For example, the chute redesign at Duffy Tool and Stamping saved more than $14,000 per year—financial feedback. But the redesign also eliminated machine downtime and increased the number of units produced per hour (operational feedback). Both measures convey important information. Often financial and nonfinancial feedback take the form of formal reports that compare the actual data with planned data or benchmarks (internal, external, or historical). These reports are referred to as **performance reports**.

Decision Making The process of choosing among competing alternatives is **decision making**. This pervasive managerial function is intertwined with planning and control. A manager cannot plan without making decisions. Managers must choose among competing objectives and methods for carrying out the chosen objectives. Only one of numerous competing plans can be chosen. Similar comments can be made concerning the control function.

Decisions can be improved if information about the alternatives is gathered and made available to managers. One of the major roles of the management accounting information system is to supply information that facilitates decision making. For example, the manager in Scenario A was faced with the prospect of submitting a bid on laboratory tests for a water-bottling company. A large number of possible bids could be submitted, but the manager must choose one and only one to submit to the prospective customer. The manager requested information concerning the expected manufacturing costs of the laboratory tests. This cost information, along with the manager's knowledge of competitive conditions, should improve his or her ability to select a bid price. Imagine having to submit a bid without some idea of the production costs.

Organization Type

The use of accounting information by managers is not limited to manufacturing organizations. Regardless of the organizational form, managers must be proficient in using accounting information. The basic concepts taught in this text apply to a variety of settings. The six scenarios at the beginning of this chapter involved manufacturing, health care, transportation, profit, and not-for-profit organizations. Hospital administrators, presidents of corporations, dentists, educational administrators, and city managers can all improve their managerial skills by being well-grounded in the basic concepts and use of accounting information.

Conceptual Framework of Management Accounting

We can gain a better understanding of the link between management accounting information and management processes by referring to a conceptual framework. Management accounting is a discipline with both theoretical and practical roots. Its theoretical foundations are found in such disciplines as economics, finance, organization theory, management, and psychology. Its practical applications are found in all organizations where decisions are based on financial and other quantitative information. From routine decision making (for example, how many units to produce on a production run) to strategic decisions (for example, how best to redesign the organizational structure to meet the new global competitive pressures of producing a wider variety of products at a lower cost), effective decisions depend on a thorough understanding of management accounting concepts and techniques. The following sections set out the conceptual framework that will be followed in the text.

Cost Accumulation and Product Costing   Decision making in all organizations must consider costs, and systems of cost accumulation and cost assignment are found in all types of organizations. A basic understanding of the capabilities and limitations of cost accounting systems is crucial for good decision making. This material is covered in Part 1, Cost Accumulation and Product Costing. Economics provides the theoretical foundation of cost accumulation and cost allocation. In a simple economy, with few exceptions, most costs can easily be traced to the primary product. Today, the bulk of costs are often not directly traceable to the wide variety of products or services an organization offers. Indirect or overhead costs have increasingly become a major component of total costs in many organizations, and the largest single cost component in some organizations. The challenge of relating costs to products or services (and other cost objects) can be met only by understanding the economics of overhead. Management accounting attempts to apply economic concepts of cost in practical settings, where costs must be accumulated and allocated to (1) products and services, (2) departments (subunits of the organization), or (3) activities.

Managerial Decision Making   Management accounting concepts and techniques are useful for decision making, which involves making choices between competing alternatives. This area is the domain of decision theory, and an understanding of the basic concepts of decision theory is important to making good choices. This material is covered in Part 2, Managerial Decision Making.

In Part 2, the emphasis is on operating decisions. We will come to understand that accounting information produced for one economic purpose may not necessarily be useful for another purpose; the nature of the decision determines the relevance of the information. The application of decision theory also requires a number of logical steps:

1. identify the problem that requires a decision,
2. determine the set of feasible alternative courses of action,
3. measure or estimate the effects of these alternative courses of action,
4. assess the possible outcomes, and
5. make the choice that best satisfies the objectives of the organization.

By necessity, decision making affects future outcomes, and questions of uncertainty about the future are important and require particular attention.

We make two basic assumptions in Part 2. First we will assume that decision makers make rational choices in the traditional economic sense. That is, if alternative A is more profitable (or less expensive) than alternative B, other things being equal, A should be accepted and B rejected. The validity of the assumption of rational choice will be examined briefly in Part 2, but a fuller discussion of it lies outside the scope of this text. The second assumption we make is that what is good for a subunit of the organization is good for the organization as a whole. The effects of relaxing the second assumption are dealt with in Part 3.

Planning and Control Systems   A major reason many organizations, particularly large ones, run as well as they do is the existence of a planning and control system. In Part 3, we explore the requirements for effective planning and control. For a single decision maker, the theoretical foundation of planning and control is embedded in the concept of feedback and corrective action, as discussed earlier. Where there are multiple decision makers, additional problems arise. Different managers may have different objectives, resulting in conflict. Domains of accountability (that is, responsibility for actions, outputs, or outcomes) are often blurred, and the information available to one manager may not be shared with other managers within an organization; that is, there is information asymmetry. These factors contribute to problems for planning and control.

Information asymmetry often also exists between managers and owners. A manager is delegated specific activities to perform with specific objectives and makes decisions on behalf of the owner. The success of this manager's decisions may be due to good effort or to good fortune, but information asymmetry prevents direct observation of the cause. Monitoring of managerial performance and the use of incentives to encourage a harmony of objectives or goal congruence are some of the issues that we will consider in Part 3.

Modern organizations rely on delegation of authority and on accountability for actions or results or both. As with other systems, we can achieve a fuller understanding of planning and control systems by studying their structure and process. For example, the responsibilities of various positions within the organization (structure) are identified, in general terms, in a typical organization chart. A more specific understanding of the way the organization works, however, might be obtained by examining how people actually make decisions and how products and documents flow within the organization (process). In terms of structure, organizations usually assign responsibilities for cost, revenue, profit, or investment performance. In terms of process, managers usually formulate plans and budgets, compile actual performance records, track differences between budgeted and actual performance, examine the reasons for these differences, and take corrective actions if required. In this sense, a manager of a subunit is primarily concerned with his or her own performance. Suboptimization results from actions that are best from the subunit's (or its manager's) point of view but may not be best from the organization's point of view. It raises a number of planning and control issues. Some of these will be dealt with in Part 3.

MANAGEMENT ACCOUNTING AND FINANCIAL ACCOUNTING

Objective 2

Explain the differences between management accounting and financial accounting.

The accounting information system within an organization has two major subsystems: a management accounting system and a financial accounting system. The accounting information system is, itself, a subsystem of a firm's overall management information system. The two accounting subsystems differ in their objectives, the nature of their inputs, and the type of processes used to transform inputs into outputs. The **financial accounting information system** is primarily concerned with producing outputs for external users. It uses well-specified economic events as inputs and processes that meet certain rules and conventions. For financial accounting, the nature of the inputs and the rules and conventions governing processes are defined by the financial accounting standards established by the **Accounting Standards Board** of the Canadian Institute of Chartered Accountants.[4] The overall objective is to prepare external reports (financial statements) for investors, creditors, government agencies, and other outside users. This information is used for such things as investment decisions, stewardship evaluation, monitoring activity, and regulatory measures.

The management accounting system produces information for internal users, such as managers, executives, and workers. Thus, management accounting could be

---

4. The *Canada Business Corporations Act* specifically refers to the *CICA Handbook*, and the provincial securities commissions require compliance with it. Although the provincial securities commissions (e.g., the Ontario Securities Commission [OSC] and the Quebec Securities Commission [QSC], etc.) play a less predominant role in standard setting than does the Securities and Exchange Commission [SEC] in the United States, they do influence the direction of standard setting. The OSC specifically has become more directly involved in standard setting.

properly called internal accounting, and financial accounting could be called external accounting. Specifically, management accounting identifies, collects, measures, classifies, and reports information that is useful to internal users in planning, controlling, and decision making.

When comparing management accounting to financial accounting, several differences can be identified. Some of the more important differences follow and are summarized in Exhibit 1–2.

- *Targeted Users* As mentioned, management accounting focuses on providing information for internal users, whereas financial accounting focuses on providing information for external users.
- *Restrictions on Inputs and Processes* Management accounting is not subject to the requirements of generally accepted accounting principles. The Accounting Standards Board sets the accounting policies that must be followed for financial reporting. The inputs and processes of financial accounting are well-defined and, in fact, restricted. Only certain kinds of economic events qualify as inputs, and processes must follow generally accepted methods. Unlike financial accounting, management accounting has no official body that prescribes the format, content, and rules for selecting inputs and processes and preparing accounting reports. Managers are free to choose whatever information they want—provided that it can be justified on a cost–benefit basis. The Society of Management Accountants of Canada issues **Management Accounting Guidelines** to assist management accountants in fulfilling their responsibilities, but management accountants are under no obligation to follow any set of standards except as related to external reporting.
- *Type of Information* The restrictions imposed by financial accounting tend to produce objective and verifiable financial information. For management accounting, information may be financial or nonfinancial and may be much more subjective in nature.
- *Time Orientation* Financial accounting has a historical orientation. It records and reports events that have already happened. Although management accounting too records and reports events that have already occurred, it also exhibits a very strong emphasis on providing information about future events. Management, for example, may want to know not only what it cost to produce a product in the past, but also what it will cost to produce a product in the future. Knowing what it will cost helps in planning material purchases and making pricing decisions, among other things. This future orientation is demanded because of the need to support the managerial functions of planning and decision making.
- *Degree of Aggregation* Management accounting provides measures and internal reports used to evaluate the performance of entities, product lines, departments, and managers. Essentially, very detailed information is needed and provided. Financial accounting, on the other hand, focuses on overall firm performance, providing a more aggregated viewpoint.

Exhibit 1–2

Comparision of Management and Financial Accounting

Management Accounting	Financial Accounting
1. Internally focused	1. Externally focused
2. No mandatory rules	2. Must follow externally imposed rules
3. Financial and nonfinancial information; subjective information possible	3. Objective financial information
4. Emphasis on the future	4. Historical orientation
5. Internal evaluation and decisions based on very detailed information	5. Information about the firm as a whole
6. Broad, multidisciplinary	6. More self-contained

- *Breadth* Management accounting is much broader than financial accounting. It includes aspects of managerial economics, industrial engineering, and management science, as well as numerous other areas.

It should be emphasized, however, that both the management accounting information system and the financial accounting information system are part of the total accounting information system. Unfortunately, all too often the content of the management accounting system is driven by the needs of the financial accounting system. The reports of both management and financial accounting are frequently derived from the same database, which usually was originally established to support the reporting requirements of financial accounting. Many organizations need to redesign this database in order to satisfy more fully the needs of the internal users. For example, a firm's profitability is of interest to investors, but managers need to know the profitability of individual products. The accounting system should therefore be designed to provide both total profits and profits for individual products. The key point here is flexibility—the accounting system should be able to supply different information for different purposes.

A BRIEF HISTORICAL PERSPECTIVE ON MANAGEMENT ACCOUNTING

Objective 3

Provide a brief historical description of management accounting.

Most of the product-costing and management accounting procedures used in the twentieth century were developed between 1880 and 1925.[5] Interestingly, many of the early developments (until about 1914) concerned managerial product costing—tracing a firm's profitability to individual products and using this information for strategic decision making. By 1925, however, most of this emphasis had been abandoned in favour of inventory costing—assigning manufacturing costs to products so that the cost of inventories could be reported to external users of a firm's financial statements.

Financial reporting became the driving force for the design of cost accounting systems. Managers and firms were willing to accept aggregated average cost information about individual products. Apparently, more detailed and accurate cost information about individual products was not needed. As long as a company had relatively homogeneous products that consumed resources at about the same rate, the average cost information supplied by a financially driven costing system was good enough. Furthermore, for some firms, even as product diversity increased, the need to have more accurate cost information was offset by the high cost of the processing required to provide the information. For many firms, the cost of a more detailed cost system apparently exceeded its benefits.

Some effort to improve the managerial usefulness of conventional cost systems took place in the 1950s and 1960s. Users discussed the shortcomings of information supplied by a system designed to prepare financial reports. Efforts to improve the system, however, essentially centred on making the financial accounting information more useful to users rather than on producing an entirely new set of information and procedures apart from the external reporting system.

In the 1980s and 1990s, many recognized that some management accounting practices were no longer serving managerial needs. Some even claimed that existing management accounting systems were obsolete and virtually useless. More accurate product costing and more useful and detailed input were needed to allow managers to improve quality and productivity and reduce costs. In response to the perceived failure of the traditional management accounting system, efforts were made to develop a new management accounting system—one that satisfied the demands of the current economic environment.

---

5.   The historical information in this section is based on H. Thomas Johnson and Robert Kaplan, *Relevance Lost: The Rise and Fall of Management Accounting* (Boston: Harvard Business School Press, 1987).

CURRENT FOCUS OF MANAGEMENT ACCOUNTING

Objective 4

Identify and explain the current focus of management accounting.

Thus, the economic environment has required the development of innovative and relevant management accounting practices. Consequently, activity-based management accounting systems have been developed and implemented in many organizations. Additionally, the focus of management accounting systems has been broadened to enable managers to better serve the needs of customers and manage the firm's value chain. Furthermore, to secure and maintain a competitive advantage, managers must emphasize time, quality, and efficiency, and accounting information must be produced to support these three fundamental organizational goals.

Activity-Based Management

The demand for more accurate and relevant management accounting information has led to the development of activity-based management. **Activity-based management** is an integrated systemwide approach that focuses management's attention on activities with the objective of improving customer value and the resulting profit. Activity-based management emphasizes activity-based costing (ABC) and process value analysis. Activity-based costing improves the accuracy of assigning costs by tracing costs first to activities and then to the products or customers that consume these activities. Process value analysis, on the other hand, emphasizes activity analysis—trying to determine why activities are performed and how well they are performed. The objective is to find ways to perform necessary activities more efficiently and to eliminate those that do not create customer value. Peter Drucker, an internationally respected management guru, points out the growing importance of activity-based costing (management):

> Traditional cost accounting in manufacturing does not record the cost of nonproducing such as the cost of faulty quality, or of a machine being out of order, or of needed parts not being on hand. Yet these unrecorded and uncontrolled costs in some plants run as high as the costs that traditional accounting does record. By contrast, a new method of cost accounting developed in the last ten years—called "activity-based" accounting—records all costs. And it relates them, as traditional accounting cannot, to value-added. Within the next 10 years it should be in general use, and then we will have operational control in manufacturing.[6]

Activity-based management has become an accepted and widely used practice, substantiating to a large degree the foresight of Peter Drucker.

Customer Orientation

Activity-based management has the objective of increasing customer value by managing activities. Customer value is a key focus because firms can establish a competitive advantage by creating better customer value for the same cost as, or for a lower cost than, that of competitors or by creating equivalent value for a lower cost than that of competitors. **Customer value** is the difference between what a customer receives (customer realization) and what the customer gives up (customer sacrifice). What is received is called the total product. The **total product** is the complete range of tangible and intangible benefits that a customer receives from a purchased product. Thus, customer realization includes basic and special product features, service, quality, instructions for use, reputation, brand name, and any other factors deemed important by customers. Customer sacrifice includes the cost of purchasing the product, the time and effort spent acquiring and learning to use the product, and **postpurchase costs**, which are defined as the costs of using, maintaining, and

---

6. Peter F. Drucker, "We Need to Measure, Not Count," *The Wall Street Journal* (13 April 1993): p. A14.

disposing of the product. Increasing customer value means increasing customer realization or decreasing customer sacrifice, or both.

Strategic Positioning Increasing customer value to create a sustainable competitive advantage is achieved through judicious selection of strategies. Cost information plays a critical role in this process and does so through a process called *strategic cost management*. **Strategic cost management** is the use of cost data to develop and identify superior strategies that will produce a sustainable competitive advantage. Generally, firms choose a strategic position corresponding to one of two general strategies: (1) cost leadership (2) superior products through differentiation.[7] The objective of the cost leadership strategy is to provide the same or better value to customers at a *lower* cost than competitors do. Thus, a low-cost strategy has the objective of increasing customer value by reducing sacrifice. For example, reducing the cost of making a product by improving a process would allow the firm to reduce the product's selling price, thus reducing customer sacrifice. A differentiation strategy, on the other hand, strives to increase customer value by increasing realization. Providing something to customers that is not provided by competitors creates a competitive advantage. For example, a retailer of computers could offer on-site repair service, a feature not offered by other rivals in the local market. Of course, for a differentiation strategy to be viable, the value added to the customer by the differentiation must exceed the firm's cost of providing the differentiation. Also, different strategies usually require different cost information, implying that the cost systems may differ according to the strategy adopted by a firm.

Value-Chain Framework A focus on customer value means that the management accounting system should produce information about both realization and sacrifice. Collecting information about customer sacrifice means gathering information outside the firm. But there are even deeper implications. Successful pursuit of cost leadership and/or differentiation strategies requires an understanding of a firm's *internal* and *industrial* value chains. Effective management of the internal **value chain** is fundamental to increasing customer value, especially if maximizing customer realization at the lowest possible cost (to the firm) is a goal. The **internal value chain** is the set of activities required to design, develop, produce, market, and deliver products and services to customers. Thus, emphasizing customer value forces managers to determine which activities in the value chain are important to customers. A management accounting system should track information about a wide variety of activities that span the internal value chain. Consider, for example, the delivery segment. Timely delivery of a product or service is part of the total product, and thus of value to the customer. Customer value can be increased by increasing the speed of delivery and response. Federal Express exploited this part of the value chain and successfully developed a service that was not being offered by the postal service. Today, many customers believe that a delivery delayed is a delivery denied. This seems to indicate that a good management accounting system ought to develop and measure indicators of customer satisfaction.

The industrial value chain is also critical for strategic cost management. The **industrial value chain** is the linked set of value-creating activities from basic raw materials to the disposal of the final product by end-use customers. Exhibit 1–3 illustrates a possible value chain for the apple industry. A given firm operating within the industry may not—and likely will not—span the entire value chain. The exhibit illustrates that different firms participate in different segments of the chain. Understanding the industrial value chain is critical to understanding a firm's strategically important activities. Breaking down a firm's value chain into its strategically

7. The Japanese have also shown that it is possible for a firm to pursue a strategy that combines the two: a differentiation with cost advantage strategy.

important activities is basic to successful implementation of cost leadership and differentiation strategies. Fundamental to a value-chain framework is the recognition of existing complex linkages and interrelationships among activities both within and external to the firm. Thus, there are two types of linkages: *internal* and *external*. **Internal linkages** are relationships among activities that are performed within a firm's portion of the industrial value chain (the internal value chain). **External linkages** are activity relationships between the firm and the firm's suppliers and customers. Thus, we can talk about *supplier linkages* and *customer linkages*. Using these linkages to bring about a win–win outcome for the firm, its suppliers, and its customers is the key to successful strategic cost management. The objective, of course, is to manage these linkages better than competitors do, thus creating a competitive advantage.

It is important to note that companies have internal customers as well. For example, the procurement process acquires and delivers parts and materials to producing departments. For the procurement department, providing high-quality parts on a timely basis to managers of producing departments is just as vital as it is for the company as a whole to provide high-quality goods to external customers. The emphasis on managing the internal value chain and servicing internal customers has revealed the importance of a cross-functional perspective.

Exhibit 1–3

Value Chain: Apple
Industry

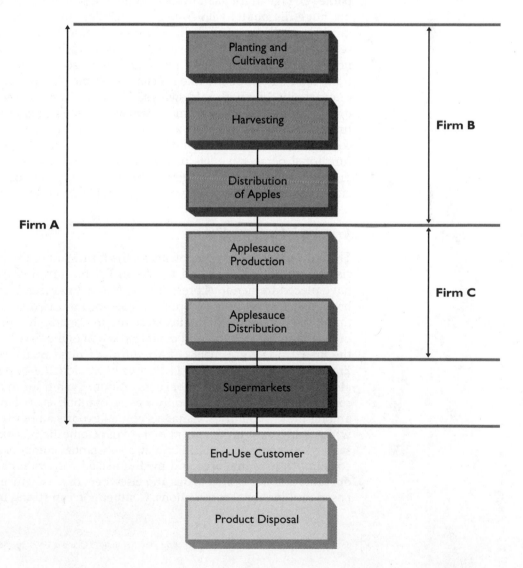

Cross-Functional Perspective

Managing the value chain means that a management accountant must understand many functions of the business, from manufacturing to marketing to distribution to customer service. This need is magnified when the company is involved in international trade. We see this, for example, in the varying definitions of product cost. Activity-based management accounting has moved beyond the traditional manufacturing cost definition of product cost to more inclusive definitions. These contemporary approaches to product costing may include initial design and engineering costs, as well as manufacturing costs and the costs of distribution, sales, and service. An individual who is well-schooled in the various definitions of product cost, and who understands the shifting definitions of cost from the short run to the long run, can be invaluable in determining what information is relevant in decision making. For example, strategic decisions may require a product cost definition that assigns the costs of all value-chain activities, whereas a short-run decision that is concerned with whether a special order should be accepted or rejected may require a product cost that assigns only marginal or incremental costs.

Why try to relate management accounting to marketing, management, engineering, finance, and other business functions? When a value-chain approach is taken and customer value is emphasized, we see that these disciplines are interrelated; a decision affecting one affects the others. For example, many manufacturing companies engage in frequent trade loading, the practice of encouraging (often by offering huge discounts) wholesalers and retailers to buy more product than they can quickly resell. As a result, inventories become bloated, and the wholesalers and retailers stop purchasing for a time. This looks like a marketing problem, but it is not—at least not entirely. When selling stops, so does production. Thus in the past, trade-loading companies like Procter & Gamble, Bristol-Myers Squibb, and Duracell found themselves with wild swings in production. Sometimes the factories were producing around the clock to meet demand for the heavily discounted product; other times the factories were idle and workers were laid off. In effect, the sales ended up costing the companies millions of dollars of added production cost.[8] A cross-functional perspective lets us see the forest, not just one or two of the trees. This broader vision allows managers to increase quality, reduce the time required to serve customers (both internal and external), and improve efficiency.

Global Perspective

The current global trend in business, the formation of the European Union, and the rising fortunes of Japan and the Asian Pacific Rim countries (until the late 1990s) have placed tremendous pressures on North American businesses. These pressures have also opened up new opportunities for increased economy and efficiency. No doubt the revamping of the tax structure in Canada that resulted in the elimination of the manufacturing tax and the introduction of the Goods and Services Tax in 1991, the Free Trade Agreement (FTA) with the United States, and the North American Free Trade Agreement (NAFTA) between Canada, the United States, and Mexico are all reactions to increased global competition. Even prior to these reactions, Canada's role in the international economy was substantial, as evidenced by its representation among the G7 countries. Canada's annual exports amounted to $268 billion in 1994, which is in excess of 33 percent of its Gross Domestic Product; and its imports for the same year amounted to $233 billion, a substantial component of its annual domestic consumption. Many large and medium-sized corporations in Canada have foreign operations in the United States and elsewhere or are themselves divisions of foreign-based multinational corporations. Competition can spring up overnight from unsus-

8. Patricia Sellers, "The Dumbest Marketing Ploy," *Fortune* (5 October 1992): pp. 88–94.

pected sources. Because of intense global competitive pressures, the cost of making bad decisions based on low-quality information has increased significantly. Thus, increasing global competition has created a demand for improved management accounting information.

Environmental Perspective

An increased awareness of the environmental pressures facing society has highlighted the need for accountability for the environmental costs of doing business. Environmental factors are increasingly becoming an integral part of the decision-making process and of the management control system. Reasons for this development include trends involving environmental regulation, potential hefty fines that may result if environmental factors are ignored, or a genuine concern for the environment by management.[9]

The emphasis on environmental issues poses a threat to companies that are thought to be unconcerned with the environment. That was certainly the case with calls in Europe for boycotting Canadian lumber and with logging blockades by environmentalists concerned with the effects of MacMillan Bloedel's clear-cut foresting practices. (A new management was brought in that made the company more responsive to sustainable development.) At the same time, it also provides an opportunity for environmentally minded Canadian entrepreneurs to respond to environmental challenges around the world.

Total Quality Management

Continuous improvement is fundamental for establishing a state of manufacturing excellence. Manufacturing excellence is the key to survival in today's world-class competitive environment. Producing products with little waste that actually perform according to specifications are the twin objectives of world-class firms. A philosophy of **total quality management**, in which manufacturers strive to create an environment that will enable workers to manufacture perfect (zero-defect) products, has replaced the "acceptable quality" attitudes of the past. This emphasis on total quality has also created a demand for a management accounting system that provides financial and nonfinancial information about quality.

Service industries are also dedicated to improving quality. Service firms present special problems because quality may differ from employee to employee. As a result, service firms are emphasizing consistency through the development of systems that support employee efforts. For example, USAA, a financial services company specializing in insurance for current and former military officers, invested heavily in information technology in the mid-1980s. Incoming documents (for example, policy applications, cheques, and appraisals) are scanned electronically and stored on optical disks. When a customer calls USAA to see if a policy application for a new house has been received, a service representative can check the customer's file on the computer and answer the question immediately. This is in contrast to the old system, which required USAA representatives to search a warehouse or others' desks for the relevant files—a process that could take up to two weeks.[10]

---

9. Recent discussion of these issues includes Nabil Elias, "Environmental Issues in Accounting," 16th Annual Congress of the European Accounting Association, Turku, Finland, April 1993; Deloitte Touche Tohamatsu International Institute for Sustainable Development and Sustainability, *Coming Clean*, Deloitte Touche Tohamatsu International, 1993; *Accounting for the Environment*, Management Accounting Issues Paper #1, Society of Management Accountants of Canada, 1992; Leonard Eckel and Kathryn Fisher, "Being accountable for the environment," *CMA Magazine* (December/January 1992): 10; Daniel Ruch and Janice John Roper, "The greening of corporate Canada," *CMA Magazine* (December/January 1992): 15–18.

10. Myron Magnet, "Who's Winning the Information Revolution?" *Fortune* (30 November 1992): pp. 110–117.

Quality cost measurement and reporting are key features of a management accounting system for both manufacturing and service industries. In both cases, the management accounting system should be able to provide both operational and financial information about quality, including such information as the number of defects, quality cost reports, quality cost trend reports, and quality cost performance reports.

Time as a Competitive Element

Time is a crucial element in all phases of the value chain.[11] World-class firms reduce time to market by compressing their design, implementation, and production cycles. These firms deliver products or services quickly by eliminating nonvalue-added time—time that is of no value to the customer (for example, the time a product spends on the loading dock). Interestingly, decreasing nonvalue-added time appears to go hand in hand with increasing quality. The USAA example given in the previous section demonstrates the improvement in service quality that resulted from the insightful management of time. The overall objective, of course, is to increase customer responsiveness.

What about the relationship between time and product life cycles? The rate of technological innovation has increased for many industries, and the life of a particular product can be quite short. Managers must be able to respond quickly and decisively to changing market conditions. Information that allows them to accomplish this must be available. For example, Hewlett-Packard has found that it is better to be 50 percent over budget in new product development than to be six months late. This correlation between cost and time is the kind of information that should be available from a management accounting information system.

Efficiency

While quality and time are important, improving these dimensions without corresponding improvements in profit performance may be futile, if not fatal. Improving efficiency is also a vital concern. Both financial and nonfinancial measures of efficiency are needed. Cost is a critical measure of efficiency. Trends in costs over time and measures of productivity changes can provide important measures of the efficacy of continuous improvement decisions. For these efficiency measures to be of value, costs must be properly defined, measured, and assigned; furthermore, production of output must be related to the inputs required, and the overall financial effect of productivity changes should be calculated.

THE ROLE OF THE MANAGEMENT ACCOUNTANT

Objective 5

Describe the role of management accountants in an organization.

Today's business press writes about world-class firms. These are firms at the cutting edge of customer support. They know their market and their product. They strive to continually improve product design, manufacture, and delivery. These companies can compete with the best of the best in a global environment. Management accountants must also be world-class. They must be intelligent, well-prepared, and up to date with new developments. They also must be familiar with the customs and practices of the countries in which their firms operate.

The role of management accountants in an organization is one of support. They assist those individuals who are responsible for carrying out an organization's basic objectives. Positions that have direct responsibility for the basic objectives of an organization are referred to as **line positions**. Positions that are supportive in nature and

---

11. An excellent analysis of time as a competitive element is contained in A. Faye Borthick and Harold P. Roth, "Accounting for Time: Reengineering Business Processes to Improve Responsiveness," *Journal of Cost Management* (Fall 1993): pp. 4–14.

have only indirect responsibility for an organization's basic objectives are called **staff positions**.

For example, assume that the basic mission of an organization is to produce and sell laser printers. The vice-presidents of manufacturing and marketing, the factory manager, and the assemblers are all line positions. The vice-presidents of finance and human resources, the cost accountant, and the purchasing manager are all staff positions.

The partial organization chart shown in Exhibit 1–4 illustrates the organizational positions for production and finance. Because one of the basic objectives of the organization is to produce, those directly involved in production hold line positions. Although management accountants, such as controllers and cost accounting managers, may wield considerable influence in the organization, they have no authority over the managers in the production area. The managers in line positions are the ones who set policy and make the decisions that impact production. However, by supplying and interpreting accounting information, management accountants can have significant input into policies and decisions.

The **treasurer** is responsible for the finance function. Specifically, the treasurer raises capital and manages cash and investments. The treasurer may also be in charge of credit and collection and insurance. As shown in Exhibit 1–4, the treasurer reports to the financial vice-president.

The **controller**, the chief accounting officer, supervises all accounting departments. Because of the critical role that management accounting plays in the operation of an organization, the controller is often viewed as a member of the top management team and is encouraged to participate in planning, controlling, and decision-making activities. As the chief accounting officer, the controller has responsibility for both internal and external accounting requirements. This charge may include direct responsibility for internal auditing, cost accounting, financial accounting (including reports to securities commissions and financial statements), systems accounting (including analysis, design, and internal controls), and taxes. The duties and organization of the controller's office vary from firm to firm. For example, in some firms the internal audit department may report directly to the financial vice-president; similarly, the systems department may report directly to the financial vice-president or some other vice-president. A possible organization of a controller's office is also shown in Exhibit 1–4.

Exhibit   1–4   Partial Organization Chart, Manufacturing Company

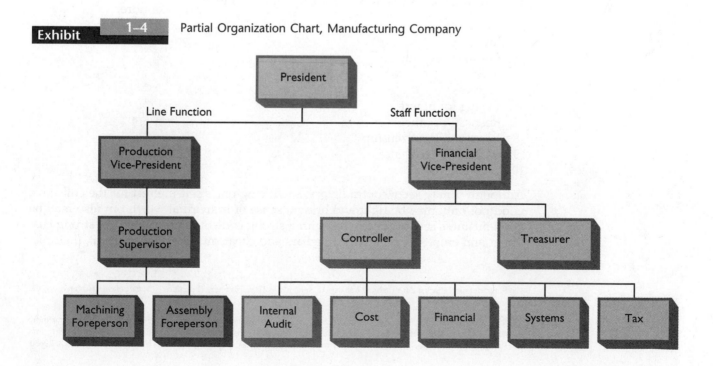

MANAGEMENT ACCOUNTING AND ETHICAL CONDUCT

Objective 6

Explain the importance of ethical behaviour for managers and management accountants.

Virtually all management accounting practices were developed to assist managers in maximizing profits. Traditionally, the economic performance of the firm has been the overriding concern. Yet managers and management accountants should not become so focused on profits that they develop a belief that the *only* goal of a business is maximizing its net worth. The objective of profit maximization should be constrained by the requirement that profits be achieved through legal and ethical means. While this assumption has always been implicit in management accounting, it should be made explicit. To help achieve this objective, many of the problems in this text force explicit consideration of ethical issues.

Ethical Behaviour

Ethical behaviour involves choosing actions that are right, proper, and just. Our behaviour can be right or wrong; it can be proper or improper; and the decisions we make can be just or unjust. People often differ in their views of the meaning of the ethical terms cited; however, there seems to be a common principle underlying all ethical systems. This principle is expressed by the belief that each member of a group bears some responsibility for the well-being of other members. Willingness to sacrifice one's self-interest for the well-being of the group is the heart of ethical action.[12]

This notion of sacrificing one's self-interest for the well-being of others produces some core values—values that describe what is meant by right and wrong in more concrete terms. James W. Brackner, writing for the "Ethics" column in *Management Accounting*, made the following observation:

> For moral or ethical education to have meaning, there must be agreement on the values that are considered "right." Ten of these values are identified and described by Michael Josephson in "Teaching Ethical Decision Making and Principled Reasoning." The study of history, philosophy, and religion reveals a strong consensus as to certain universal and timeless values essential to the ethical life.
>
> These ten core values yield a series of principles that delineate right and wrong in general terms. Therefore, they provide a guide to behavior.[13]

The ten core values referred to in the quotation follow:

1. Honesty
2. Integrity
3. Promise keeping
4. Fidelity
5. Fairness
6. Caring for others
7. Respect for others
8. Responsible citizenship
9. Pursuit of excellence
10. Accountability

Although it may seem contradictory, sacrificing one's self-interest for the collective good not only may be right and bring a sense of individual worth but also may be good business sense. Companies with a strong code of ethics can create strong customer and employee loyalty. While liars and cheats may win on occasion, their vic-

---

12. For a detailed discussion of ethical behaviour, see LaRue Tone Hosmer, *The Ethics of Management* (Homewood, Ill.: Irwin, 1987).

13. James W. Brackner, "Consensus Values Should Be Taught," *Management Accounting* (August 1992): 19. For a more complete discussion of the ten core values, see also Michael Josephson, "Teaching Ethical Decision Making and Principled Reasoning," *Ethics Easier Said Than Done* (Los Angeles, Ca.: The Josephson Institute, Winter 1988), 29–30.

tories are often short-term ones. Companies in business for the long term find that it pays to treat all of their constituents honestly and loyally.

Standards of Ethical Conduct for Management Accountants

Organizations commonly establish standards of conduct for their managers and employees. Professional associations also establish ethical standards. For example, the Society of Management Accountants in each province has formulated a code of ethics for its members. Although the details vary from one province to another, the common themes are similar to those expressed by the Management Accounting Practices Committee of the Institute of Management Accountants (IMA) in the United States in a statement outlining standards of ethical conduct for management accountants.[14] In this statement, management accountants are told that "they shall not commit acts contrary to these standards nor shall they condone the commission of such acts by others in their organizations." The standards of competence, confidentiality, integrity, and objectivity are typical of those used in the codes of professional ethics in each of the Canadian provinces. The recommended resolution of ethical conflicts is unique to the statement by the IMA. The standards and recommended resolution of ethical conflicts are presented in Exhibit 1–5. In addition, an example of a provincial Certified Management Accountant code of ethical conduct is included in the Appendix for this chapter.

Exhibit 1–5

Standards of Ethical Conduct for Practitioners of Management Accounting and Financial Management

Practitioners of management accounting and financial management have an obligation to the public, their profession, the organizations they serve, and themselves, to maintain the highest standards of ethical conduct. In recognition of this obligation, the Institute of Management Accountants has promulgated the following standards of ethical conduct for practitioners of management accounting and financial management. Adherence to these standards, both domestically and internationally, is integral to achieving the *Objectives of Management Accounting*. Practitioners of management accounting and financial management shall not commit acts contrary to these standards, nor shall they condone the commission of such acts by others within their organizations.

Competence

Practitioners of management accounting and financial management have a responsibility to:
- Maintain an appropriate level of professional competence by ongoing development of their knowledge and skills.
- Perform their professional duties in accordance with relevant laws, regulations, and technical standards.
- Prepare complete and clear reports and recommendations after appropriate analysis of relevant and reliable information.

Confidentiality

Practitioners of management accounting and financial management have a responsibility to:
- Refrain from disclosing confidential information acquired in the course of their work except when authorized, unless legally obligated to do so.
- Inform subordinates as appropriate regarding the confidentiality of information acquired in the course of their work and monitor their activities to assure the maintenance of that confidentiality.
- Refrain from using or appearing to use confidential information acquired in the course of their work for unethical or illegal advantage either personally or through third parties.

(continued)

11. "Standards of Ethical Conduct for Management Accountants," *Statement on Management Accounting No. 1C* (Montvale, N.J.: Institute of Management Accountants, 1983).

Integrity

Practitioners of management accounting and financial management have a responsibility to:

- Avoid actual or apparent conflicts of interest and advise all appropriate parties of any potential conflict.
- Refrain from engaging in any activity that would prejudice their ability to carry out their duties ethically.
- Refuse any gift, favor, or hospitality that would influence or would appear to influence their actions.
- Refrain from either adversely or passively subverting the attainment of the organization's legitimate and ethical objectives.
- Recognize and communicate professional limitations or other constraints that would preclude responsible judgment or successful performance of an activity.
- Communicate unfavorable as well as favorable information and professional judgments or opinions.
- Refrain from engaging in or supporting any activity that would discredit the profession.

Objectivity

Practitioners of management accounting and financial management have a responsibility to:

- Communicate information fairly and objectively.
- Disclose fully all relevant information that could reasonably be expected to influence an intended user's understanding of the reports, comments, and recommendations presented.

Resolution of Ethical Conflict

In applying the standards of ethical conduct, practitioners of management accounting and financial management may encounter problems in identifying unethical behavior or in resolving an ethical conflict. When faced with significant ethical issues, practitioners of management accounting and financial management should follow the established policies of the organization bearing on the resolution of such conflict. If these policies do not resolve the ethical conflict, such practitioners should consider the following courses of action:

- Discuss such problems with the immediate superior except when it appears that the superior is involved, in which case the problem should be presented initially to the next higher managerial level. If a satisfactory resolution cannot be achieved when the problem is initially presented, submit the issues to the next higher managerial level. If the immediate superior is the chief executive officer, or equivalent, the acceptable reviewing authority may be a group such as the audit committee, executive committee, board of directors, board of trustees, or owners. Contact with levels above the immediate supervisor should be initiated only with the superior's knowledge, assuming the superior is not involved. Except where legally prescribed, communication of such problems to authorities or individuals not employed or engaged by the organization is not considered appropriate.
- Clarify relevant ethical issues by confidential discussion with an objective advisor (e.g., IMA Ethics Counseling Service) to obtain a better understanding of possible courses of action.
- Consult your own attorney as to legal obligations and rights concerning the ethical conflict.
- If the ethical conflict still exists after exhausting all levels of internal review, there may be no other recourse on significant matters than to resign from the organization and to submit an informative memorandum to an appropriate representative of the organization. After resignation, depending on the nature of the ethical conflict, it may also be appropriate to notify other parties.

Source: *Statement on Management Accounting, No. 1C*, "Standards of Ethical Conduct for Practitioners of Management Accounting and Financial Management." Copyright 1997, Institute of Management Accountants, 10 Paragon Drive, Montvale, N.J. Reprinted with permission.

To illustrate an application of the code, suppose a manager's bonus is linked to reported profits, with the bonus increasing as profits increase. Thus, the manager has an incentive to find ways to increase profits, including unethical approaches. For example, a manager could increase profits by delaying promotions of deserving employees or by using cheaper parts to produce a product. In either case, if the motive is simply to increase the bonus, the behaviour could be labelled unethical. Neither action is in the best interest of the company or its employees. Yet where should the blame be assigned? After all, the reward system strongly encourages the manager to increase profits. Is the reward system at fault or is the manager who chooses to increase profits? Or both?

In reality, both are probably at fault. It is important to design the evaluation and reward system so that incentives to pursue undesirable behaviour are minimized. Yet designing a perfect reward system is not a realistic expectation. Managers also have an obligation to avoid abusing the system. Standard III-3 of the IMA code makes this clear: "Management accountants have a responsibility to refuse any gift, favor, or hospitality that would influence their actions." Similarly, Section 2.1 in the Appendix specifies that a CMA shall "subordinate personal interest to those of the public, the employer, or the Society and profession." Manipulating income to increase a bonus can be interpreted as a violation of this standard. Basically, the prospect of an increased bonus (that is, a favour) should not influence a manager to engage in unethical actions.

PROFESSIONAL DESIGNATIONS

Objective 7

Identify the different professional accounting designations available for management accountants.

Three different Canadian professional designations are available to management accountants. They are issued by the provincial arms of national accounting organizations: Certified Management Accountant (CMA—issued by the Society of Management Accountants), Chartered Accountant (CA—issued by the Institute of Chartered Accountants), and Certified General Accountant (CGA—issued by the Certified General Accountants Association). Each designation offers particular advantages to a management accountant. In each case, an applicant must meet specific educational and experience requirements and pass a qualifying examination[15] to become certified. Thus, all three certifications offer evidence that the holder has achieved a minimum level of professional competence. Furthermore, all three designations either require or encourage the holders to engage in continuing professional education. Because certification reveals a commitment to professional competency, most organizations encourage their management accountants to hold a professional designation.

The CMA

One of the main purposes of the **Certified Management Accountant (CMA)** designation[16]—and its predecessor designation, the RIA (Registered Industrial Accountant)—was to establish management accounting as a recognized professional discipline, separate from the profession of public accounting. The CMA designation was adopted across Canada in the mid-1980s to replace the RIA designation. The RIA designation had become increasingly less descriptive of the work of many management accountants, who are found not only in the manufacturing but also in the service, resource, not-for-profit, and government sectors of the Canadian economy. With the introduction of the CMA professional program in the early 1990s and the strategic leadership program in 2000, the CMA designation's reputation has grown.

---

15. Starting in Fall 1997, the CGA program began requiring a certification examination (since replaced by the CMA Strategic Leadership program). Students already enrolled in the program in Fall 1997 were required to pass a series of course examinations.

16. There is also a CMA designation in the United States that has different requirements (e.g., the passing of four examinations, the absence of an equivalent to the professional program).

A management accountant with the CMA designation has passed the CMA entrance examination and has satisfied other essential requirements (for example, experience). The entrance examination to the strategic leadership program is a key element of the CMA accreditation process. It tests general knowledge and technical competence in management, management accounting, economics, and financial accounting. A candidate must then enroll for two years in the CMA strategic leadership program while at the same time acquiring management accounting work experience. The strategic leadership program emphasizes issues of professional competence, including strategy, judgment, communication, leadership, and ethics. Entrance to the CMA program used to require a postsecondary certificate or diploma. Starting in 2000, students are required to possess a university degree.

The CA

The **Chartered Accountant (CA)** designation is the oldest and best-known accounting designation in Canada. Although the CA designation's primary orientation is external reporting and auditing, not management accounting, many management accountants are CAs. Approximately 40 percent of CAs are in public practice, and a good percentage of those are not auditors. The remaining 60 percent occupy positions in management, management accounting, or other branches of accounting in business, not-for-profit, or government organizations.

In order to become a CA, one must have a university degree. Preparation for the Uniform Final Examination (UFE) is administered by provincial institutes. Requiring candidates to pass the UFE prior to qualification as a CA ensures that they have met the minimum standards for the designation. In addition, CAs must train in an approved public accounting office for a period determined by the provincial institutes. The average length of time required is 30 working months.

The Certified Public Accountant (CPA) designation is the parallel certification in the United States. It also requires the passing of examinations and public accounting experience. A reciprocal agreement facilitates CAs' moving to work in the United States or CPAs' assuming employment in Canada.

The CGA

The **Certified General Accountant (CGA)** designation is the fastest-growing accounting designation in Canada. The CGA program offers a great deal of flexibility, since a candidate can choose an area of specialization: management accounting is one such area. The requirements of the CGA include a number of national course examinations, a certification examination, and an experience requirement in an accounting-related job. Although a CGA was not required to have a university degree to enter the program, a university degree or equivalent is now required prior to certification—a change that took effect in 1998. A joint CGA–University of Calgary program facilitates the simultaneous completion of a university degree and the CGA designation.

Other

The **Certified Internal Auditor (CIA)** is another designation available to internal accountants. This certification was first administered in the United States but is now administered in Canada as well. The forces that led to the creation of this certification in 1974 are similar to those that resulted in the CMA designation in the United States. Internal auditing is different from both external auditing and management accounting, and many internal auditors felt a need for a specialized certification.

SUMMARY OF LEARNING OBJECTIVES

1. Explain the need for management accounting information.

Managers, workers, and executives use management accounting information to identify problems, solve problems, and evaluate performance. Essentially, management accounting information helps managers carry out their roles of planning, controlling, and decision making. Planning is the detailed formulation of action to achieve a particular end. Controlling is the monitoring of a plan's implementation. Decision making is choosing among competing alternatives.

2. Explain the differences between management accounting and financial accounting.

Management accounting differs from financial accounting in several ways. Management accounting information is intended for internal users, whereas financial accounting information is directed toward external users. Management accounting is not bound by the externally imposed rules of financial reporting. Furthermore, it tends to be more subjective and uses both financial and nonfinancial measures, whereas financial accounting provides audited, objective financial information. Finally, management accounting provides more detail than financial accounting, and it tends to be broader and multidisciplinary.

3. Provide a brief historical description of management accounting.

Most of the product-costing and internal accounting procedures used in the 20th century were developed between 1880 and 1925. By 1925, management accounting procedures emphasized inventory costing, stemming from the emphasis on external reporting. In the 1950s and 1960s, some effort was made to improve the managerial usefulness of traditional cost systems. In recent years, significant efforts have been made to radically change the nature and practice of management accounting, largely in response to some dramatic changes in the competitive environment.

4. Identify and explain the current focus of management accounting.

Management accounting must provide information that allows managers to focus on customer value, total quality management, and time-based competition. To this end, information about value-chain activities and customer sacrifice (such as postpurchase costs) must be collected and made available. Activity-based management is a major innovative response to the demand for more accurate and relevant manage-ment accounting information. Additionally, managers must decide on the strategic position of the firm. One of two positions is usually emphasized—either cost leadership or product differentiation. Which position is chosen can affect the nature of the management accounting information system.

5. Describe the role of management accountants in an organization.

Management accountants are responsible for identifying, collecting, measuring, analyzing, preparing, interpreting, and communicating information used by management to achieve the basic objectives of the organization. Management accountants need to be sensitive to the information needs of managers. Management accountants serve as staff members of the organization and are responsible for providing information; they are usually intimately involved in the management process as valued members of the management team.

6. Explain the importance of ethical behaviour for managers and management accountants.

Management accounting aids managers in their efforts to improve the economic performance of the firm. Unfortunately, some managers have overemphasized the economic dimension and have engaged in unethical and illegal actions. Many of these actions have relied on the management accounting system to bring about and even support that unethical behaviour. To emphasize the importance of the ever-present constraint of ethical behaviour on profit-maximizing behaviour, this text presents ethical issues in many of the problems appearing at the end of each chapter.

7. Identify the different professional accounting designations available for management accountants.

There are three certifications available in Canada: the CMA, the CA, and the CGA. The CMA is a certification designed especially for management accountants. The prestige of the CMA has increased significantly over the years, and this certification is now highly regarded in business. The CA is primarily intended for those practising public accounting; however, since this certification is so highly regarded, it is held by many leading management accountants. Holders of the CGA designation include both public and management accountants, and CGA-Canada is the fastest-growing professional accounting body in Canada.

APPENDIX: AN EXAMPLE OF A PROVINCIAL CODE OF ETHICS FOR MANAGEMENT ACCOUNTANTS

Each provincial professional accounting organization has a code of ethics. While these codes differ in detail, they are generally based on the qualities of professionalism, integrity, and honesty. As an example, excerpts from the Code of Ethics of the Society of Management Accountants of Manitoba are provided.

Standards for Ethical Conduct for Management Accountants

This "Code of Ethics," while dealing with many issues regarding Society Members in Public Practice, is intended to be a code for those members in management accounting as well. [*Authors' note:* Public practice refers to public accounting and management consulting services and, in Manitoba, external auditing as well. At the time of writing, public accounting and auditing is not regulated in Manitoba.]

1. Definitions [*Authors' note:* This section defines member, practice of accounting, public practice, and review and audit.]
2. General
2.1 A Member will, in exercising his professional responsibilities, in all professional matters, subordinate personal interest to those of the public, the employer, or the Society and profession, as the nature of the case may require. A Member will in all respects conduct the Practice of Accounting:
   (a) with integrity, honesty, courtesy, fairness and good faith; and
   (b) with dignity and demeanour, upholding the professional status and good repute of the profession of accounting.
2.2 A Member will perform all services rendered in the Practice of Accounting with the degree of care, diligence and skill that would be exercised in comparable circumstances by a reasonably prudent Certified Member, suitably trained and experienced for the competent performance of the services.
2.3 Confidentiality
   Information concerning the business and affairs of a client or employer of a Member will be kept in strict confidence and not directly or indirectly used or disclosed by the Member, otherwise than as necessary for performance of the services for which the Member was engaged or employed, unless:
   (a) the client or employer has expressly consented to the use or disclosure;
   (b) the information is, at the time of use or disclosure, in the public domain through no fault of the Member;
   (c) the disclosure is required by law; or
   (d) the disclosure is necessary in connection with any practice review or legal or disciplinary action.
2.4 Conflict of Interest
   (a) A Member will not directly or indirectly undertake, engage in or maintain any relationship, business activity, or make or maintain any investment which adversely affects or may reasonably be expected to adversely affect the independence or quality of any services in the Practice of Accounting which the Member was engaged or employed to provide.
   (b) Except as provided in section 3.10, a client or employer may expressly consent in writing to a business, activity, investment or relationship which would otherwise be in contravention of subsection (a), hereof.
   (c) If circumstances arise which are prohibited under subsection (a), the Member will promptly disclose the same to his client or employer and take the steps necessary to comply with subsection (a) or subsection (b), hereof.
2.5 Improper Activities
   A Member will not directly or indirectly associate himself or permit himself to be associated with any:

(a) act, business or enterprise which he knows or has reason to believe is illegal or otherwise improper; or

(b) written document or verbal statement which he knows or has reason to believe is materially false or misleading or otherwise tending to materially misrepresent the actual situation, whether or not the association is under disclaimer.

3.1   Registration of the Practice of Public Accounting [*Authors' note:* Sections 3.1 to 3.6 deal with rules regarding registration, communication with the CMA Canada Manitoba Partner's office, firm names, legal form of the practice, standards of practice, and qualification.]

3.6.1 A Member will not accept or continue to perform any services in the Practice of Public Accounting unless he has:

(a) Successfully completed within one year of public accounting registration, the educational requirements as determined by the Board from time to time, unless on good or sufficient grounds the Board will exempt him therefrom. Currently the educational requirements are attendance at:

(i) "CMA in Public Practice"; and

(ii) "File Preparation and Documentation"; and

(iii) Where the Member is performing audits, a course on audit techniques; and

(b) Participated in the Society's mentoring process which is comprised of:

(i) the assignment of a mentor by the Society; and

(ii) a review of any financial or accounting related statements by the mentor, prior to its release to the public.

The mentoring process will conclude upon either the successful review by the Public Practice Review Committee, or as otherwise determined by the Public Practice Review Committee.

[*Authors' note:* The remainder of the document deals with insurance, trust funds, penalties for nonadherence to the standards, fees, contingency fees, advertising, confidentiality, compliance, appeals of public practice review decisions, and other matters related to public practice. It is worthy to note that other provinces place stricter control over the provision of auditing services, particularly in Ontario and Quebec, where CMAs have little right, if any, to perform public audits. However, there is no restriction on providing management consulting services or other nonaudit-type services.]

KEY TERMS

Accounting Standards Board, 8
Activity-based cost management, 4
Activity-based management, 11
Certified General Accountant (CGA), 22
Certified Internal Auditor (CIA), 22
Certified Management Accountant (CMA), 21
Chartered Accountant (CA), 22
Continuous improvement, 4
Controller, 17
Controlling, 6
Customer value, 11

Decision making, 6
Employee empowerment, 5
Ethical behaviour, 18
External linkages, 13
Feedback, 6
Financial accounting information system, 8
Industrial value chain, 12
Internal linkages, 13
Internal value chain, 12
Line positions, 16
Management Accounting Guidelines, 9

Management accounting information system, 3
Performance reports, 6
Planning, 5
Postpurchase costs, 11
Staff positions, 17
Strategic cost management, 12
Strategic decision making, 5
Total product, 11
Total quality management, 15
Treasurer, 17
Value chain, 12

QUESTIONS FOR WRITING AND DISCUSSION

1. What is a management accounting information system?

2. Describe the inputs, processes, and outputs of a management accounting information system.

3. What are the three objectives of a management accounting information system?

4. What organizations need management accounting information systems?

5. Who are the users of management accounting information?

6. What is management accounting information used for?

7. Should a management accounting system provide both financial and nonfinancial information? Explain.

8. What is meant by continuous improvement?

9. Describe what is meant by employee empowerment.

10. Explain why operational (nonmanagement) workers need management accounting information.

11. Describe the connection between planning, feedback, and controlling.

12. What role do performance reports play with respect to the control function?

13. How do management accounting and financial accounting differ?

14. Explain the role of financial reporting in the development of management accounting. Why has this role changed in recent years?

15. What is activity-based management? Why is it important?

16. Explain the meaning of customer value. How is focusing on customer value changing management accounting?

17. What is the internal value chain? Why is it important?

18. What is the industrial value chain? Why is it important?

19. Explain why today's management accountant must have a cross-functional perspective.

20. Discuss the relationship of time-based competition and management accounting information.

21. What is the difference between a staff position and a line position?

22. The controller should be a member of the top management staff. Do you agree or disagree? Explain.

23. What is the role of the controller in an organization? Describe some of the activities over which he or she has control.

24. What is ethical behaviour? Is it possible to teach ethical behaviour in a management accounting course?

25. Firms with higher ethical standards will experience a higher level of economic performance than firms with lower or poor ethical standards. Do you agree? Why or why not?

26. Review either of the codes of ethical conduct for management accountants. Do you believe that the code you reviewed will have an effect on the ethical behaviour of management accountants? Explain.

27. What are the three accounting designations in Canada? Can holders of all these designations practise management accounting? What do these designations indicate about the distinctions between management accounting and financial accounting?

28. Management accounting concepts apply only to manufacturing operations. Do you agree with this statement? Explain.

EXERCISES

1–1

**Management
Accounting
Information System**
LO1

The items that follow are associated with a management accounting information system.

a. Surveying customers to assess postpurchase costs
b. Incurrence of postpurchase costs
c. Costing out products
d. Assigning the cost of labour to a product

Spreadsheet

e. Report showing the cost of a product
f. Measuring the cost of quality
g. Repairing a defective part
h. Providing information for planning and control
i. Designing a product
j. Measuring the cost of design
k. A budget that shows how much should be spent on design activity
l. Using output information to make a decision
m. Usage of materials
n. A report comparing the actual costs of quality with the expected costs of quality

Required:

Classify the items into one of the following categories:

1. Inputs
2. Processes
3. Outputs
4. System objectives

1–2

Employee Empowerment

LO1

Duffy Tool and Stamping has formed "excellence teams" made up of production line employees. These teams have been given the charge to improve production processes and enhance employee safety. The teams follow a very structured problem-solving methodology and have managed to make numerous improvements in production as well as safety. During a six-year period, pretax profits increased each year. Duffy's management largely credits the excellence teams for the cost reductions and increased profits.

Another company, Grand Rapids Spring and Wire Products, has formed minicompanies within its factory. The objective of minicompanies is to have each employee assume ownership of his or her work. Each minicompany has its own suppliers and customers (all within the factory). Furthermore, each minicompany is assigned its own support people: accountants, engineers, marketing people, and so on. The individuals within the minicompany are given responsibility for developing and maintaining good relations with their suppliers and customers, identifying problems, and developing and implementing solutions to those problems. The focus of each minicompany is on quality, cost, delivery, safety, and morale. The company has successfully created a quality culture, achieved a reputation for being a competitive, world-class manufacturer, and has become "a learning organization."

Required:

1. What are the objectives of excellence teams and minicompanies? Did the companies achieve these objectives?
2. Do you think that employee empowerment is a good idea? Explain your answer. If yes, do you see any disadvantages? Explain.
3. What role, if any, does management accounting information have in employee empowerment?
4. What do you suppose is meant by the phrase "quality culture"? What is meant by "a learning organization?"

1–3

The Managerial Process

LO1

Each of the following scenarios requires the use of accounting information to carry out one or more of the following managerial activities: planning, control (including performance evaluation), or decision making. Identify the managerial activity or activities that are applicable for each scenario, and indicate the role of accounting information in the activity.

A. Water-bottling Company Manager: "A water-testing facility approached me recently and offered us its entire range of tests. It provided a price list revealing the amount it is willing to receive for each test. In many cases, the prices are below our costs. I need to know the costs of the individual tests to assess the feasibility of accepting its offer and perhaps suggest some price adjustments on some of the tests."

B. Operating Manager: "This report indicates that we have 30 percent more defects than originally targeted. An investigation into the cause has revealed the problem. We were using a lower-quality material than expected, and the waste has been higher than normal. By switching to the quality level originally specified, we can reduce the defects to the planned level."

C. Divisional Manager: "Our market share has increased because of higher-quality products. Current projections indicate that we should sell 25 percent more units than last year. I want a projection of the effect this increase in sales will have on profits. I also want to know our expected cash receipts and cash expenditures on a month-by-month basis. I have a feeling that some short-term borrowing may be necessary."

D. Plant Manager: "Foreign competitors are producing goods with lower costs and delivering them more rapidly than we can to customers in our markets. We need to decrease the cycle time and increase the efficiency of our manufacturing process. There are two proposals that should help us accomplish these goals, both of which involve investing in computer-aided manufacturing. I need to know the future cash flows associated with each system and the effect each system has on unit costs and cycle time."

E. Manager: "At the last board meeting, we established an objective of earning a 25 percent return on sales. I need to know how many units of our product we need to sell to meet this objective. Once I have the estimated sales in units, we need to outline a promotional campaign that will take us where we want to be. However, in order to compute the targeted sales in units, I need to know the expected unit price and a lot of cost information."

F. Manager (Health Minister): "Perhaps the Victoria Hospital should be closed since health care costs are mounting and we cannot support all the health facilities in the province. While other hospitals in the city have had a tough time breaking even, Victoria's deficit has been larger than most. I want to know what costs can be avoided if Victoria shuts down. I want some assessment of the impact on the other health services we offer and on other hospitals."

1–4

Customer Value; Strategic Positioning LO4

Nadira Persaud has decided to purchase a personal computer. She has narrowed the choices to two: Drantex and Confiar. Both brands have the same processing speed, 6.4 gigabytes of hard-disk capacity, a 3.5-inch disk drive, and a CD-ROM drive, and each comes with the same basic software support package. Both come from mail-order companies with good reputations. The selling price for each is identical. After some review, Nadira discovers that the cost of operating and maintaining a Drantex computer over a three-year period is estimated to be $300. For the Confiar machine, the operating and maintenance cost is $600. The sales agent for Drantex emphasized the lower operating and maintenance costs. The agent for Confiar, however, emphasized the service reputation of the product and the faster delivery time (a Confiar can be purchased and delivered one week sooner than a Drantex). Based on all the information, Nadira has decided to buy Confiar.

Required:

1. What is the total product purchased by Nadira?
2. How does the strategic positioning differ for the two companies?
3. When asked why she decided to buy the Confiar machine, Nadira responds, "I think that Confiar offers more value than Drantex." What are the possible sources of this greater value? What implications does this have for the management accounting information system?
4. Suppose that Nadira's decision was prompted mostly by the desire to receive the computer quickly. Informed that it was losing sales because of the longer time it was taking to produce and deliver its products, the management of the compa-

ny producing the Drantex PC decided to improve delivery performance by improving its internal processes. These improvements decreased the number of defective units and the time required to produce its product. Consequently, delivery time and costs both decreased, and the company was able to lower its prices for the Drantex. Explain how these actions translate into strengthening the competitive position of the Drantex PC relative to the Confiar PC. Also discuss the implications for the management accounting information system.

1–5

Role of Management Accountants

LO5

Management accountants are actively involved in the process of managing the entity. This process includes making strategic, tactical, and operating decisions while helping to coordinate the efforts of the entire organization. To fulfill these objectives, the management accountant accepts certain responsibilities that can be identified as (1) planning, (2) controlling, (3) evaluating performance, (4) ensuring accountability of resources, and (5) external reporting.

Required:

Describe each of these responsibilities of the management accountant and identify examples of practices and techniques. (US CMA adapted)

1–6

Line versus Staff

LO5

The job responsibilities of two employees of Barney Manufacturing follow.

Joan Dennison, Cost Accounting Manager. Joan is responsible for measuring and collecting costs associated with the manufacture of the garden hose product line. She is also responsible for preparing periodic reports comparing the actual costs with planned costs. These reports are provided to the production line managers and the plant manager. Joan helps explain and interpret the reports.

Steven Swasey, Production Manager. Steven is responsible for the manufacture of the high-quality garden hose. He supervises the line workers, helps develop the production schedule, and is responsible for seeing that production quotas are met. He is also held accountable for controlling manufacturing costs.

Required:

Identify Joan and Steven as line or staff and explain your reasons.

1–7

Ethical Behaviour

LO6

Consider the following scenario:

Manager: "If I can reduce my costs by $40,000 during this last quarter, my division will show a profit that is 10 percent above the planned level, and I will receive a $10,000 bonus. However, given the projections for the fourth quarter, that does not look promising. I really need that $10,000. I know one way I can qualify. All I have to do is lay off my three most expensive salespeople. After all, most of the orders are in for the fourth quarter, and I can always hire new sales personnel at the beginning of the next year."

Required:

What is the right choice for the manager to make? Why did the ethical dilemma arise? Is there any way to redesign the accounting reporting system to discourage the type of behaviour that this manager is contemplating?

1–8

Ethical Issues

LO6

Assess and comment on each of the following statements that have appeared in newspaper editorials:

a.   Business students come from all segments of society. If they have not been taught ethics by their families and by their elementary and secondary schools, there is little effect a business school can have.

b.   Sacrificing self-interest for the collective good won't happen unless a majority of Canadians also accept this premise.

   c. Competent executives manage people and resources for the good of society. Monetary benefits and titles are simply the byproducts of doing a good job.
   d. Unethical firms and individuals, like high rollers in Las Vegas, are eventually wiped out financially.

1–9

Ethical Issues

LO6

The Alert Company is a closely held investment service group that has been very successful over the past five years, consistently providing most members of the top management group with bonuses equivalent to 50 percent of their salaries (commonly called "50 percent bonuses"). In addition, both the chief financial officer and the chief executive officer have received 100 percent bonuses. Alert expects this trend to continue.

Recently, Alert's top management group, which holds 35 percent of the outstanding shares of common stock, has learned that a major corporation is interested in acquiring Alert. Alert's management is concerned that this corporation may make an attractive offer to the other shareholders and that management would be unable to prevent the takeover. If the acquisition occurs, this executive group is uncertain about continued employment in the new corporate structure. As a consequence, the management group is considering changes to several accounting policies and practices that, although not in accordance with generally accepted accounting principles, would make the company a less attractive acquisition. Management has told Roger Deerling, Alert's controller, to implement some of these changes. Roger has also been informed that Alert's management does not intend to disclose these changes immediately to anyone outside the top management group.

Required:

Using the IMA's code of ethics for management accountants (see Exhibit 1–5), evaluate the changes that Alert's management is considering and discuss the specific steps that Roger should take to resolve the situation. (US CMA adapted)

1–10

Ethical Issues

LO6

Webson Manufacturing Company produces component parts for the airline industry and has recently undergone a major computer system conversion. Michael Darwin, the controller, has established a troubleshooting team to alleviate accounting problems that have occurred since the conversion. Michael has chosen Maureen Hughes, assistant controller, to head the team that will include Bob Randolph, cost accountant; Cynthia Wells, financial analyst; Marjorie Park, general accounting supervisor; and George Crandall, financial accountant.

The team has been meeting weekly for the last month. Maureen insists on being part of all the team conversations in order to gather information, make the final decision on any ideas or actions that the team develops, and prepare a weekly report for Michael. She has also used this team as a forum to discuss issues and disputes about him and other members of Webson's top management team. At last week's meeting, Maureen told the team that she thought a competitor might purchase Webson's common stock because she had overheard Michael talking about this on the telephone. As a result, most of Webson's employees now informally discuss the sale of Webson's common stock and how it will affect their jobs.

Required:

Is Maureen Hughes's discussion with the team about the prospective sale of Webson unethical? Discuss, citing specific standards from the IMA's code of ethical conduct (see Exhibit 1–5) to support your position. (US CMA adapted)

1–11

Ethical Responsibilities

LO6

JLA Electronics is a Canadian high-tech company that manufactures and distributes computer and telecommunications equipment. JLA has developed a lightweight handheld fax system, Porto-Fax, that will allow the user total freedom in receiving and transmitting information. Marketing research studies indicate that the potential market for this item is large, and immediate action in test marketing the product is recommended.

Although JLA has excess capacity at its current manufacturing facility, the company has decided to build a new manufacturing plant to accommodate the Porto-Fax and is in the process of deciding where to locate the plant. The current unionized employees believe that this move is being made to eliminate union involvement in the Porto-Fax manufacturing process. The management team that was formed to oversee the site selection process has already received bids from several locales, both domestic and foreign, offering a wide range of incentives to encourage the company to select particular sites.

Some of the incentives are personal in nature, such as housing at reduced cost for the selection team, reduced property taxes, open accounts at certain restaurants, and free tickets to local sporting events. Other incentives offered affect corporate profitability and include reduced tax rates, low-interest or no-interest loans, outright grants, and low-cost property. The marketing research team has reported that product price will have a major effect on the sale of Porto-Fax and recommends that the selection team pick a site that minimizes costs.

Required:

1. What is meant by the term "corporate social responsibility"?
2. Should JLA Electronics consider its social responsibility when making the final decision regarding the site selection?
3. Describe the ethical responsibilities of the individuals on the site selection team.
4. Discuss the responsibilities that the union at the current manufacturing facility may have in this situation. (US CMA adapted)

1–12

Not-for-Profit
Organization
LO5

The Board of Directors of the Royal Montreal Orchestra was grappling with potential budget cuts and their impact on the orchestra's devoted fans. At a special meeting of the Board, one of the directors commented that no one on the Board had extensive management accounting training and recommended that they bring in a management accounting consultant.

Another member of the Board stated the following:

Keep those accountants out. First, this is a cultural organization, and accountants don't understand what we are grappling with: they only understand the numbers. Second, it is important to keep our organization dominated by our strategy, and accountants do not understand strategy. Third, we are not here to make a profit, and the training of accountants has to do with profit and how to measure it. We would probably have had to shut down many years ago if accountants were involved in our difficult decision-making process.

I suggest that we keep our orchestra at last year's size. We cannot afford to have a substandard orchestra. If we cut salaries this year, we risk losing our best talents. Let's keep our expenditure side untouched, and hope that our revenue side will catch up.

Required:

1. Comment on the role of management accountants in cultural and not-for-profit organizations. Do you agree with the Board member's statement regarding management accountants?
2. Comment on the Board member's statement regarding budgeted expenditures and revenues. Do you agree with her point of view?

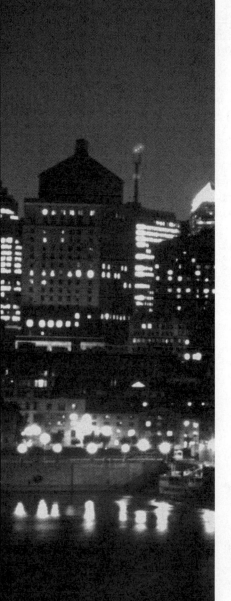

PART 1

Cost Accumulation and Product Costing

Part I deals with cost accumulation and product costing. Systems of cost accumulation and product costing are concerned with the determination of costs for different purposes. The purposes of cost accumulation and product costing are:

Decision Making Cost information is crucial in decisions such as product pricing. The selection of a price may affect the volume of sales, which in turn could also affect costs (since generally, the higher the volume, the higher the total cost). Other decisions, such as product line addition or deletion, bidding, make or buy, accepting a special order, etc., should also be based on relevant cost information.

Planning and Control Cost information is also crucial for short- and long-term planning and for setting budgets. Appropriate corrective action for control purposes is also dependent on accurate and relevant cost information. The assignment of responsibility for performance requires relevant cost information that enhances control and facilitates corrective action and accountability.

Product Costing Product cost information is necessary for decision making and strategic cost management. It is also necessary for assigning costs to inventories (on the balance sheet) and to cost of goods sold (on the income statement).

Basic cost and management accounting concepts are introduced in Chapter 2. Determination of costs is based on an attempt to trace the cost to its most logical cause or driver. Two central concerns are how costs change with activity levels and how they can be identified with particular activities, departments, processes, or products. One of the more obvious reasons for cost increases or decreases is a change in volume or activity level. Chapter 2 deals with a classification of costs based on variability with respect to volume (variable costs versus fixed costs). Some costs are more difficult than others to trace to activities, departments, processes, or products. The problem of overhead cost allocation is briefly discussed in Chapter 2 and discussed further in the remaining chapters in Part 1. A solid understanding of Chapter 2 is essential for all the topics that follow.

Activity cost behaviour provides the basis for many costing decisions and is at the core of decision making and of planning and control. It is discussed in Chapter 3.

The economics of overhead, briefly mentioned in the discussion of the conceptual framework in Chapter 1, involves two concepts: common cost allocation and fixed costs. For example, costs not directly traceable to a particular product can be assigned in many different ways if there is no predominant cause and effect relationship between cost and product. Some methods of cost assignment are more useful than others; some methods can be downright misleading. If such common costs are fixed and insensitive to changes in volume, as is the case in many high-tech environments, any cost allocation may be arbitrary.

Many companies with multiple products and joint facilities have adopted activity-based costing (ABC) systems. Chapter 4 provides a full discussion of ABC and its application to the service sector. The chapter also examines when activity-based costing is more applicable.

Chapters 5 and 6 deal with specific cost systems: job costing and process costing. These costing systems are special cases of cost accumulation and allocation. Chapter 7 examines more involved allocation questions and several approaches for cost allocatation. Chapters 5 to 7 provide a more or less conventional view of cost accounting systems.

The Problem of Cost Allocation

Consider the following examples:

- A company installed a product deletion program for unprofitable products. As some unprofitable products were deleted, some profitable products gradually showed lower profits and eventually losses. Why did this happen? As common costs were allocated among products, the elimination of apparently unprofitable products did not eliminate the allocated common costs. These common costs now had to be spread over fewer products, making the remaining products less profitable.
- A company found that it could not compete on price for a particular product against smaller, less efficient manufacturers. Why? The cost accounting department was producing cost figures that were used for decision-making purposes (including price setting) based on an allocation method that apparently overcharged common costs to this particular product and undercharged for other products not produced by the competition.
- A heavy-equipment manufacturer found that, during a severe recession, its costs (per unit) were much higher than during a boom period. Why? It became clear that costs that were insensitive to volume changes, that is, fixed costs, were spread over fewer units during the recession, which resulted in a substantially higher per unit cost. Yet prices had to be lower in order to attract sales during the recession. Conversely, the fixed costs were spread over a large volume of products during boom periods, and the fixed cost per unit was much lower. Yet prices could be set much higher since the company could not cope with the demand during the boom.

In all the above examples, product costing was a problem. Allocation problems due to common costs, coupled with the increase in nonvariable (fixed) costs in modern business organizations, require a careful approach to cost accumulation and allocation. Chapters 2 and 4 emphasize the *why*, *when*, and *how* of cost allocation. Chapters 5 to 7 focus on the *how* of allocation in conventional cost accounting systems.

CHAPTER 2

Basic Management Accounting Concepts

Learning Objectives

After studying Chapter 2, you should be able to:

1. Explain the cost assignment process.

2. Define tangible and intangible products, and explain why there are different product cost definitions.

3. Prepare income statements for manufacturing and service organizations.

4. Explain the differences between functional-based and activity-based management accounting systems.

Scenario

Kaylin Johnson, manager of Perry Electronics Division, scheduled a visit with the division's controller, Randy McManus, to address some issues recently brought to her attention. The following conversation was recorded.[1]

Kaylin: "Randy, you've been my controller for ten years. You, more than anyone, should be able to respond to some of the concerns that are surfacing in our company. Specifically, I have engineers, production managers, and marketing managers who are no longer comfortable with our cost accounting system. I look at our reports and I see product costs reported to the fourth decimal place, which seems to imply great accuracy. Yet I have

managers who are saying that these costs are almost useless. The costs don't reflect the differences in product attributes such as colours, features, packaging, and service. Prices for these new products and technology seem to be continually decreasing. Does our cost accounting system really allow us to assess product-line profitability properly?"

Randy: "Well, I am pretty comfortable that in the aggregate our product costs are accurate. What we report on our balance sheet and income statements is pretty much on target. However, I'm not as confident that our cost assignment procedures allow us to make strong statements about individual product profitability. Many of the costs are assigned using assumed

relationships and may not reflect a cause-and-effect relationship."

Kaylin: "If what you're saying is right, how can we rely on the individual costs for decision making? For example, can we use them to help us price our products or to bid on potential jobs? Can they be used to help us improve product designs? This also brings up another set of issues. We have six customer distribution channels and a variety of customers within each channel. Are there significant cost differences in servicing these channels and customers?"

Randy: "Well, the points you make are good. First, we shouldn't mistake precision for accuracy. Reporting a number to the fourth decimal place doesn't mean that the costs have been assigned correctly. And if these costs are not assigned correctly, relying on them for pricing and design decisions could be disastrous. We don't know the real costs of the product differences you mention, nor do we know the real cost differences between distribution channels and customers."

Kaylin: "Well, Randy, something must be done. Can we improve the accuracy of our product costing? We must know how much each product is costing. It is also vital to have accurate cost information about our distribution channels and customers. It seems to me that we need to learn more about costs

and then make decisions that bear directly on the costs. Understanding the nature of costs is fundamental to good management, and I need your help. After all, if we are going to pursue continuous improvement, we must know where we are and what we can do to make things better."

1. Many of the issues described in the scenario were confronted by Hewlett-Packard's North American Distribution Organization. Their experience is described in the following two articles: SAM Project Team, "Hewlett-Packard Knows What It Takes and What It Costs," *As Easy As ABC*, Issue No. 21, Summer 1995; Cathie Wier and SAM Project Team, "Hewlett-Packard: Asking the Right Questions—Getting the Right Answers," *As Easy As ABC*, Issue

No. 22, Fall 1995. These articles can be read on-line at **www.abctech.com**.

Questions to Think About

1. What is meant by product-costing accuracy?

2. How will increasing the accuracy of product costing improve decision making?

3. Why does Randy feel that the division's product costs are not very accurate?

4. Is assigning costs accurately as important for services as it is for tangible products?

COST ASSIGNMENT: DIRECT TRACING, DRIVER TRACING, AND ALLOCATION

Objective 1

Explain the cost assignment process.

To study management accounting, it is necessary to understand the meaning of *cost* and the associated cost terminology. Assigning costs to products, services, and other objects of managerial interest is one of the principal objectives of a management accounting information system. Increasing the accuracy of assignments produces higher-quality information, which can then be used to make better decisions. For example, Lord Corporation, a producer of products that reduce vibration and noise, found that more accurate cost assignments produced better pricing decisions and significant increases in profits.[2] However, before discussing the cost assignment process, we first need to define what we mean by "cost" and more fully describe its managerial importance.

Cost

Cost is the cash or cash-equivalent value sacrificed for goods and services that are expected to bring a current or future benefit to the organization. We say *cash equivalent* because noncash resources can be exchanged for the desired goods or services. For example, it may be possible to exchange equipment for materials used in production. In effect, we can think of cost as a dollar measure of the resources used to achieve a given benefit. In striving to produce a current or future benefit, managers should make every effort to minimize the cost required to achieve this benefit. Reducing the cost required to achieve a given benefit means that a firm is becoming more efficient. Managers should have the objective of providing the same (or greater) customer value for a lower cost than their competitors. Why? Doing so means that a firm has achieved a competitive advantage.

Managers should also understand what is meant by opportunity cost. **Opportunity cost** is the benefit given up or sacrificed when one alternative is chosen over another. For example, a firm may invest $100,000 in inventory for a year

2.   Alan W. Rupp, "ABC: A Pilot Approach," *Management Accounting* (January 1995): 50–55.

instead of investing the capital in a productive investment that would yield a 12 percent rate of return. The opportunity cost of the capital tied up in inventory is $12,000 (0.12 × $100,000) and is part of the cost of carrying the inventory.

Costs are incurred to produce future benefits. In a profit-making firm, future benefits usually mean revenues. As costs are used up in the production of revenues, they are said to expire. Expired costs are called **expenses.** In each period, expenses are deducted from revenues in the income statement to determine the period's profit. For a company to remain in business, revenues must consistently exceed expenses; moreover, the income earned must be large enough to satisfy the owners of the firm. Thus, cost and price are related in the sense that price must exceed cost such that sufficient income is earned.

Furthermore, lowering price increases customer value by lowering customer sacrifice, and the ability to lower price is connected to the ability to lower costs. Hence, managers need to know cost and trends in cost. Usually, however, knowing cost really means knowing what *something* or some *object* costs. Assigning costs to determine the cost of this object is therefore critical in providing this information to managers.

Cost Objects

Management accounting systems are structured to measure and assign costs to entities, called cost objects. A **cost object** is any item—such as a product, a customer, a department, a project, an activity, and so on—for which costs are measured and assigned. For example, if we want to determine what it costs to produce a bicycle, then the cost object is the bicycle. If we want to determine the cost of operating a maintenance department within a plant, then the cost object is the maintenance department. If the objective is to determine the cost of developing a new toy, then the cost object is the new toy development project.

In recent years, activities have emerged as important cost objects. An **activity** is a basic unit of work performed within an organization. It can also be defined as an aggregation of actions within an organization useful to managers for purposes of planning, controlling, and decision making. Activities not only act as cost objects but also play a prominent role in assigning costs to other cost objects. Examples of activities include setting up equipment for production, moving materials and goods, purchasing parts, billing customers, paying bills, maintaining equipment, expediting orders, designing products, and inspecting products. Notice that an activity is described by an action verb (for example, paying and designing) joined with an object (for example, bills and products) that receives the action. Notice also that the action verb and the object reveal very specific goals.

Accuracy of Assignments

Assigning costs *accurately* to cost objects is crucial. Our notion of accuracy is not evaluated based on knowledge of some underlying "true" cost. Rather, it is a relative concept and has to do with the reasonableness and logic of the cost assignment methods used. The objective is to measure and assign as well as possible the cost of the resources consumed by a cost object. Some cost assignment methods are clearly more accurate than others. For example, suppose you want to determine the cost of lunch for Elaine Day, a student who frequents Hideaway, an off-campus pizza parlour. One cost assignment approach is to count the number of customers Hideaway has between noon and 1:00 p.m. and then divide the total receipts earned during this period by this number of customers. Suppose that this comes out to $6.179 per lunchtime customer (note the three-decimal precision). Thus, based on this approach we would conclude that Elaine spends $6.179 per day for lunch. Another approach is to go with Elaine and *observe* how much she spends. Suppose that she has a slice of pizza and a medium drink each day, costing $3.49. It is not difficult to see which cost assignment is more accurate. The $6.179 cost assignment is distorted (despite its three-decimal precision) by the consumption patterns of other customers (cost objects). As it turns out, most lunchtime clients order the luncheon special for $6.99 (a mini-pizza, salad, and medium drink).

Distorted cost assignments can produce erroneous decisions and bad evaluations. For example, if a plant manager is trying to decide whether to continue producing power internally or to buy it from a local utility company, then an accurate assessment of how much it is costing to produce the power is fundamental to the analysis. An overstatement of the cost of power production could suggest to the manager that the internal power department should be shut down in favour of external purchase, whereas a more accurate cost assignment might suggest the opposite. It is easy to see that bad cost assignments can prove to be costly. As the pizza example suggests, establishing a cause-and-effect relationship between the cost to be assigned and the cost object is the key to creating a reasonably accurate cost assignment.

Traceability   The relationship of costs to cost objects can be exploited to help increase the accuracy of cost assignments. Costs are directly or indirectly associated with cost objects. **Indirect costs** are costs that cannot be easily and accurately traced to a cost object. **Direct costs** are those costs that can be easily and accurately traced to a cost object.[3] "Easily traced" means that the costs can be assigned in an economically feasible way, and "accurately traced" means that the costs are assigned using a *cause-and-effect relationship*. Thus, **traceability** is simply the ability to assign a cost to a cost object in an economically feasible way by means of a cause-and-effect relationship. The more costs that can be traced to the object, the greater the accuracy of the cost assignments. Establishing traceability is a key element in building accurate cost assignments.

It is possible for a particular cost item to be classified as both a direct cost and an indirect cost. Management accounting systems typically deal with many cost objects. It all depends on which cost object is the point of reference. For example, if a manufacturing plant is the cost object, then the cost of heating and cooling the manufacturing plant is a direct cost; however, if the cost object is a product produced in the manufacturing plant, then this utility cost is an indirect cost.

Methods of Tracing   Traceability means that costs can be assigned easily and accurately, whereas **tracing** is the actual assignment of costs to a cost object using an *observable* measure of the resources consumed by the cost object. Tracing costs to cost objects can occur in one of two ways: (1) direct tracing, or (2) driver tracing. **Direct tracing** is the process of identifying and assigning costs that are specifically or physically associated with a cost object to that cost object. This is most often accomplished by *physical observation*. The pizza example illustrates the concept. The cost object is Elaine Day's lunch. By observing that she has a slice of pizza and a medium drink, we can assign the cost of $3.49. The cost is directly traceable to her. As a second example, let the cost object be a product: bicycles. The product uses both materials and labour. It is easy to observe how many wheels and other parts are used by the product and how many hours of labour it takes to produce each bicycle. Both material and labour usage are physically observable; therefore, their costs can be directly charged to a bicycle. In both examples, the cost objects are the exclusive consumers of the resources in question. Ideally, all costs should be charged to cost objects using direct tracing. Unfortunately, it is often the case that cost objects are not the exclusive consumers of resources. In such cases, we appeal to driver tracing to assign costs.

Driver tracing is the use of drivers to assign costs to cost objects. In a cost assignment context, **drivers** are observable causal factors that measure a cost object's resource consumption. Therefore, drivers are factors that cause changes in resource usage and thus have a cause-and-effect relationship with the costs associated with a

3. This definition of direct costs is based on the glossary of terms prepared by Computer Aided Manufacturing-International, Inc. (CAM-I). See Norm Raffish and Peter B. B. Turney, "Glossary of Activity-Based Management," *Journal of Cost Management* (Fall 1991): 53–63.

cost object. For example, assume that Elaine Day and Martin Small go to lunch together. Elaine and Martin agree to share the cost of the lunch. They order a large pizza (divided into ten slices) for $11 and a pitcher of root beer (containing five glasses) for $2.50; Elaine also orders a small salad for $1.25. How much cost should be assigned to each person? Note that the two share the pizza and root beer, whereas the salad is a "resource" exclusive to Elaine. The cost of the salad is assigned by direct tracing ($1.25 to Elaine and $0 to Martin). To assign the costs of the pizza and root beer, drivers are chosen: slices of pizza and glasses of root beer, respectively. A rate is calculated per unit of resource (as measured by the drivers): $1.10 per slice of pizza ($11/10) and $0.50 per glass of root beer ($2.50/5). Next, usage of the driver is observed for each person (cost object). Assume that Martin eats six slices of pizza and drinks three glasses of root beer, with Elaine consuming the remainder. The cost per person is then calculated as follows:

	Elaine	Martin
Salad (direct tracing)	$1.25	$0.00
Pizza (driver tracing)		
4 slices @ $1.10	4.40	—
6 slices @ $1.10	—	6.60
Root Beer (driver tracing)		
2 glasses @ $0.50	1.00	—
3 glasses @ $0.50	—	1.50
Totals	$6.65	$8.10

It is also important to understand that this simple pizza example of a shared resource directly extends into more complex business settings. Inspecting products may be the "pizza" shared by precision surgical instruments produced in a plant. The cost of inspection can be assigned to individual instruments (the cost objects) using the number of inspection hours ("slices of pizza") consumed by each type of instrument. Consider as a second example the cost of a heart monitor used by cardiac patients (the cost object). The heart monitor is the "pizza," and monitoring hours used could be the "slices of pizza" chosen to assign the costs to cardiac patients. Thus, the tracing principles used in the pizza example relate directly to costing in realistic business environments.

Driver tracing is usually less precise than direct tracing. However, if the cause-and-effect relationship is sound, then a high degree of accuracy can be expected. Consider, for example, the driver: number of pizza slices. Suppose that the slices are not exactly equal in size and that Elaine chose to eat four of the smaller slices. Thus, her cost for pizza is really less than $4.40. Even so, if the difference in the size of the slices is not great, then we can still say that the cost is accurate. Nonetheless, this illustrates the importance of how we select, specify, and measure drivers. These issues are explored in greater depth in Chapters 3 and 4. For now, it is sufficient to understand their role in cost assignment and that they can produce somewhat less accurate assignments than direct tracing. Of more immediate concern is the situation where cost objects are not exclusive consumers of resources and where no cause-and-effect relationship can be defined (or where defining a causal relationship would be cost-prohibitive).

Assigning Indirect Costs   Indirect costs are those costs that cannot be assigned to cost objects using either direct tracing or driver tracing. This occurs either when no causal relationship exists between the cost and the cost object or when tracing is not economically feasible. Assignment of indirect costs to cost objects is called **allocation**. Since no causal relationship exists, allocating indirect costs is based on *convenience* or some *assumed* linkage. For example, consider the cost of heating and lighting a manufacturing plant in which five products are manufactured. Suppose that this utility cost is to be assigned to the five products. Clearly, it is difficult to see any causal relationship. A convenient way to allocate this cost is simply to assign it in

Exhibit   2–1

Cost Assignment
Methods

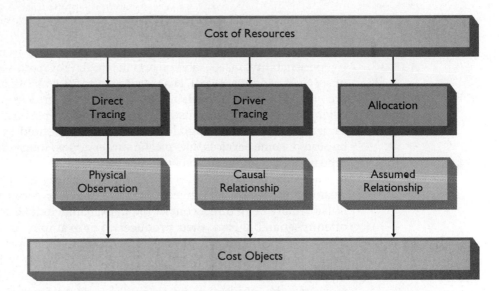

proportion to the direct labour hours used by each product. Arbitrarily assigning indirect costs to cost objects reduces the overall accuracy of the cost assignments. Accordingly, the best costing policy may be assigning only direct (traceable) costs to cost objects. However, allocations of indirect costs may serve other purposes besides accuracy. For example, allocating indirect costs to products (a cost object) may be required to satisfy external reporting conventions. Nonetheless, most managerial uses of cost assignments are better served by accuracy; thus, at the very least tracing and allocation cost assignments should be reported separately.

Cost Assignment Summarized   The foregoing discussion reveals three methods of assigning costs to cost objects: direct tracing, driver tracing, and allocation. These methods are illustrated in Exhibit 2–1. Of the three methods, direct tracing is the most accurate; it relies on physically observable, exclusive causal relationships. Direct tracing is followed by driver tracing in terms of cost assignment accuracy. Driver tracing relies on causal factors, called drivers, to assign costs to cost objects. The accuracy of driver tracing depends on the quality of the causal relationship described by the driver. Identifying drivers and assessing the quality of the causal relationship are much more costly than either direct tracing or allocation. In fact, one advantage of allocation is its simplicity and low cost of implementation. However, allocation is the least accurate cost assignment method: its use should therefore be minimized, and it should be avoided where possible. In many (maybe most) cases, the benefits of increased accuracy outweigh the additional measurement cost associated with driver tracing. This cost–benefit issue is discussed more fully later in the chapter. What it really entails is choosing among competing management accounting information systems.

PRODUCT AND SERVICE COSTS

Objective 2

Define tangible and intangible products, and explain why there are different product cost definitions.

The output of organizations represents one of the most important cost objects. There are two types of output: *tangible products* and *services*. **Tangible products** are goods produced by converting raw materials through the use of labour and capital inputs, such as plant, land, and machinery. Televisions, hamburgers, automobiles, computers, clothes, and furniture are examples of tangible products. **Services** are tasks or activities performed for a customer or an activity performed by a customer using an organization's products or facilities. Services are also produced using materials, labour, and capital inputs. Insurance coverage, medical care, dental care, funeral care, and accounting are examples of service activities performed for customers. Car rental, video rental, and skiing are examples of services where the customer uses an organization's products or facilities.

Services differ from tangible products on four important dimensions: intangibility, perishability, inseparability, and heterogeneity. **Intangibility** means that buyers of services cannot see, feel, hear, or taste a service before it is bought. Thus, services are *intangible products*. **Perishability** means that services cannot be stored for future use by a consumer but must be consumed when performed. (There are also a few unusual cases where tangible goods cannot be stored.) Although services cannot be stored, some services, like plastic surgery, have long-term effects and need not be repeated for a given customer. Other services have short-term effects and generate repeat customers. Examples of repetitive services are janitorial services and dry cleaning. **Inseparability** means that producers of services and buyers of services must usually be in direct contact for an exchange to take place. In effect, services are often inseparable from their producers. For example, an eye examination requires both the patient and the optometrist to be present. However, producers of tangible products need not have direct contact with the buyers of their goods. Thus, buyers of automobiles never need to have contact with the engineers and assembly line workers who produce their automobiles. **Heterogeneity** means that there is a greater chance of variation in the performance of services than in the production of products. Service workers can be affected by the job they undertake, the mix of other individuals with whom they work, their education and experience, and personal factors such as home life.

These factors make providing a consistent level of service more difficult. The measurement of productivity and quality in a service company must be ongoing and sensitive to these factors. These differences affect the types of information needed for planning, control, and decision making. Exhibit 2–2 illustrates the features associated with services, some of their derived properties, and how they interface with the management accounting system. Notice that accurate cost assignments, quality, and productivity are concerns shared by producers of services and producers of tangible products.

Exhibit 2–2	Feature	Derived Properties	Impact on Management Accounting
Interface of Services with Management Accounting	Intangibility	Services cannot be stored	No inventories
		No patent protection	Strong ethical code*
		Cannot display or communicate services	
		Prices difficult to set	Demand for more accurate cost assignment*
	Perishability	Service benefits expire quickly	No inventories
		Services may be repeated often for one customer	Need for standards and consistent high quality*
	Inseparability	Customer directly involved with production of service	Costs often accounted for by customer type*
		Centralized mass production of services difficult	Demand for measurement and control of quality to maintain consistency*
	Heterogeneity	Wide variation in service product possible	Productivity and quality measurement and control must be ongoing*
			Total quality management critical*

* Many of these effects are also true of tangible products.

Organizations that produce tangible products are called *manufacturing* organizations. Those that produce intangible products are called *service* organizations. Managers of both types of organizations need to know how much individual products cost. Accurate product costs are vital for profitability analysis and for strategic decisions concerning product design, pricing, and product mix. Individual product cost can refer to either a tangible or an intangible product. Thus, when we discuss product costs, we are referring to both intangible and tangible products.

Different Costs for Different Purposes

Product cost is a cost assignment that supports a well-specified managerial objective. Thus, what "product cost" means depends on the managerial objective being served. The product cost definition illustrates a fundamental cost management principle: "different costs for different purposes." As a first example, suppose that management is interested in strategic profitability analysis. To support this objective, management needs information about all the revenues and costs associated with a product. In this case, a *value-chain product cost* is appropriate, because it accounts for all the costs necessary to assess strategic profitability. A firm's *internal value chain* is the set of all activities required to design, develop, produce, market, distribute, and service a product. The internal value chain is illustrated in Exhibit 2–3. A value-chain product cost is obtained by first assigning costs to the set of activities that define the value chain and then assigning the cost of these activities to products.

As a second example, suppose that the managerial objective is short-run or tactical profitability analysis. In this case, the costs of designing and developing may not be relevant—especially for existing products. A decision, for example, to accept or reject an order for an existing product would depend on the price offered by the potential customer and the costs of producing, marketing, distributing, and servicing the special order. Thus, only the operating activities within the value chain would be important. The assignment of the costs of these activities to the product defines an *operating product cost*. As a third example, suppose that the managerial objective is external financial reporting. In this case, *traditional product costs* are needed. The rules and conventions that govern external financial reporting mandate that only

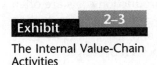

Exhibit 2–3

The Internal Value-Chain Activities

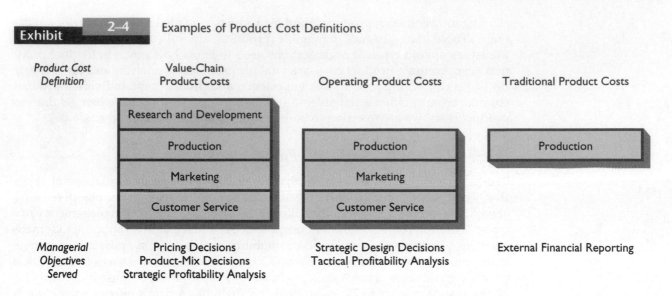

Exhibit 2–4   Examples of Product Cost Definitions

production costs can be used in calculating product costs. Exhibit 2–4 summarizes the three product cost examples. Other objectives may use still other product cost definitions.

Product Costs and External Financial Reporting

One of the central objectives of a cost management system is the calculation of product costs for external financial reporting. For product-costing purposes, externally imposed conventions dictate that costs be classified in terms of the special purposes, or functions, they serve. Costs are subdivided into two major functional categories: production and nonproduction. **Production costs** are those costs associated with the manufacture of goods or the provision of services. **Nonproduction costs** are those costs associated with the functions of designing, developing, marketing, distribution, customer service, and general administration. The costs of marketing, distribution, and customer service are often placed into one general category called *selling costs*. The costs of designing, developing, and general administration are placed into a second general category called *administrative costs*. For tangible goods, production and nonproduction costs are often referred to as *manufacturing costs* and *nonmanufacturing costs*, respectively. Production costs can be further classified as *direct materials*, *direct labour*, and *overhead*. Only these three cost elements are assigned to products for external financial reporting.

Direct Materials   **Direct materials** are those materials that are directly traceable to the goods or services being produced. The cost of these materials can be directly charged to products because physical observation can be used to measure the quantity consumed by each product. Materials that become part of a tangible product or those that are used in providing a service are usually classified as direct materials. Examples of direct materials include steel in an automobile, wood in furniture, alcohol in cologne, denim in jeans, braces for correcting teeth, surgical gauze and anesthesia for an operation, a casket for a funeral service, and food on an airline.

Direct Labour   **Direct labour** is the labour that is directly traceable to the goods or services being produced. As with direct materials, physical observation can be used to measure the quantity of labour used to produce a product or service. Those employees who convert raw materials into a product or who provide a service to customers are classified as direct labour. Examples of direct labourers include workers on an assembly line at General Motors, a chef in a restaurant, a surgical nurse attending an open-heart operation, and a pilot for Air Canada.

Overhead   All production costs other than direct materials and direct labour are lumped into one category called **overhead.** In a manufacturing firm, overhead is also known as *factory burden* or *manufacturing overhead.* The overhead cost category contains a wide variety of items. Many inputs other than direct labour and direct materials are needed to produce products. Examples include amortization on buildings and equipment, maintenance, supplies, supervision, material handling, power, property taxes, landscaping of factory grounds, and plant security. **Supplies** are generally those materials necessary for production that do not become part of the finished product or that are not used in providing a service. Dishwasher detergent in a fast-food restaurant and oil for production equipment are examples of supplies.

Direct materials that form an insignificant part of the final product are usually lumped into the overhead category as a special kind of indirect material. This approach is justified on the basis of cost and convenience. The cost of the tracing is greater than the benefit of increased accuracy. The glue used in furniture or toys is an example.

The cost of overtime for direct labourers is usually assigned to overhead as well. The rationale for doing so is that typically no particular production run can be identified as the cause of the overtime. Accordingly, overtime cost is common to all production runs and is therefore an indirect manufacturing cost. Note that only the overtime cost is treated this way. If workers are paid an $8 regular rate and a $4 overtime premium, then only the $4 overtime premium is assigned to overhead. The $8 regular rate is still regarded as a direct labour cost. In certain cases, however, overtime is associated with a particular production run—for example, when a special order is taken while production is at 100 percent capacity. In such cases, it is appropriate to treat overtime premiums as a direct labour cost.

Selling and Administrative Costs   There are two broad categories of nonproduction costs: selling costs and administrative costs. For external financial reporting, selling and administrative costs are *noninventoriable* or *period costs.* **Noninventoriable (period) costs** are expensed in the period in which they are incurred. Thus, none of these costs can be assigned to products or appear as part of the reported values of inventories on the balance sheet. In a manufacturing organization, the level of these costs can be significant (often greater than 25 percent of sales revenue), and controlling them may bring greater cost savings than the same effort exercised in controlling production costs. For service organizations, the relative importance of selling and administrative costs depends on the nature of the service produced. Physicians and dentists, for example, do very little marketing and thus have very low selling costs. A grocery chain, on the other hand, may incur substantial marketing costs, especially if the stores experiment with alternative shopping and delivery technologies. For example, Netherlands-based retailer Albert Heijn implemented a home shopping program in which consumers order products via fax, telephone, or interactive-CD technology. For a small charge, the orders are delivered to the customers' homes.[4]

Those costs necessary to market, distribute, and service a product or service are **marketing (selling) costs.** They are often referred to as *order-getting* and *order-filling costs.* Examples of selling costs include salaries and commissions of sales personnel, advertising, warehousing, shipping, and customer service. The first two items are examples of order-getting costs; the last three are order-filling costs.

All costs associated with research, development, and the general administration of the organization that cannot be reasonably assigned to either marketing or production are **administrative costs.** General administration has the responsibility of ensuring that the various activities of the organization are properly integrated so that the overall mission of the firm is realized. The president of the firm, for example, is concerned with the efficiency of selling, production, and research and development as their respective roles are carried out. Proper integration of these functions is essential to maximize the overall

4.   James Fallon, "Worldwide Connections," *Supermarket News* (25 September 1995): 15–16.

profits of a firm. Examples of general administrative costs are top executive salaries, legal fees, printing the annual report, and general accounting. Research and development costs are the costs associated with designing and developing new products.

Prime and Conversion Costs   The production and nonproduction classifications give rise to some related cost concepts. The functional delineation between non-manufacturing and manufacturing costs is essentially the basis for the concepts of noninventoriable costs and inventoriable costs—at least for the purposes of external reporting. Combinations of different production costs also produce the concepts of conversion costs and prime costs.

Prime cost is the sum of direct materials cost and direct labour cost. **Conversion cost** is the sum of direct labour cost and overhead cost. For a manufacturing firm, conversion cost can be interpreted as the cost of converting raw materials into a final product.

EXTERNAL FINANCIAL STATEMENTS

Objective 3

Prepare income statements for manufacturing and service organizations.

For external reporting, costs are usually classified according to function. In preparing an income statement, production costs and selling and administrative costs are segregated from each other. They are segregated because production costs are viewed as product costs, and selling and administrative costs are viewed as period costs. Thus, production costs attached to the products sold are recognized as an expense (cost of sales) on the income statement. Production costs that are attached to products that are not sold are reported as inventory on the balance sheet. Selling and administrative expenses are viewed as costs of the period and must be deducted each and every period as expenses; therefore, they would not appear on the balance sheet.

Income Statement: Manufacturing Firm

The income statement based on a functional classification for a manufacturing firm is displayed in Exhibit 2–5. This income statement follows the traditional format taught in an introductory financial accounting course. Income computed by following a functional classification is frequently referred to as **absorption-costing (full-costing) income,** because all manufacturing costs are fully assigned to the product.

Under the absorption-costing approach, expenses are segregated according to function and then deducted from revenues to arrive at income before taxes. As can be seen in Exhibit 2–5, there are two major functional categories of expense: *cost of goods sold* and *operating expenses*. These categories correspond, respectively, to a

Exhibit   2–5

Income Statement for a Manufacturing Organization

Income Statement: Manufacturing Organization For the Year Ended December 31, 2001		
Sales		$2,800,000
Less cost of goods sold:		
Beginning finished goods inventory	$ 500,000	
Add: Cost of goods manufactured	1,200,000	
Goods available for sale	$1,700,000	
Less: Ending finished goods inventory	300,000	1,400,000
Gross margin		$1,400,000
Less operating expenses:		
Selling expenses	$ 600,000	
Administrative expenses	300,000	900,000
Income before taxes		$ 500,000

firm's manufacturing and nonmanufacturing expenses. **Cost of goods sold** is the cost of direct materials, direct labour, and overhead attached to the units sold. To compute the cost of goods sold, it is first necessary to determine the cost of goods manufactured.

Cost of Goods Manufactured   The **cost of goods manufactured** represents the total cost of goods completed during the current period. The only costs assigned to goods completed are the manufacturing costs of direct materials, direct labour, and overhead. The details of this cost assignment are given in a supporting schedule, called the *statement of cost of goods manufactured*. An example of this supporting schedule for the income statement in Exhibit 2–5 is shown in Exhibit 2–6.

Notice in Exhibit 2–6 that the total manufacturing costs added during the period are added to the manufacturing costs found in beginning work in process, yielding total manufacturing costs to account for. The costs found in ending work in process are then deducted from total manufacturing costs to arrive at the cost of goods manufactured. If the cost of goods manufactured is for a single product, then the average unit cost can be computed by dividing the cost of goods manufactured by the units produced. For example, assume that the statement in Exhibit 2–6 was prepared for the production of bottles of perfume and that 480,000 bottles were completed during the period. The average unit cost is $2.50 per bottle ($1,200,000/480,000).

Work in process consists of all partly completed units found in production at a given point in time. Beginning work in process consists of the partly completed units on hand at the beginning of a period. Ending work in process consists of those on hand at the period's end. In the statement of cost of goods manufactured, the cost of these partly completed units is reported as the cost of beginning work in process and the cost of ending work in process. The cost of beginning work in process represents the manufacturing costs carried over from the prior period; the cost of ending work in process represents the manufacturing costs that will be carried over to the next period. In both cases, additional manufacturing costs must be incurred to complete the units in work in process.

Exhibit 2–6

Statement of Cost of Goods Manufactured

Statement of Cost of Goods Manufactured
For the Year Ended December 31, 2001

Direct materials:		
Beginning inventory	$200,000	
Add: Purchases	450,000	
Materials available	$650,000	
Less: Ending inventory	50,000	
Direct materials used		$ 600,000
Direct labour		350,000
Manufacturing overhead:		
Indirect labour	$122,500	
Amortization	177,500	
Rent	50,000	
Utilities	37,500	
Property taxes	12,500	
Maintenance	50,000	450,000
Total manufacturing costs added		$1,400,000
Add: Beginning work in process		200,000
Total manufacturing costs		$1,600,000
Less: Ending work in process		400,000
Cost of goods manufactured		$1,200,000

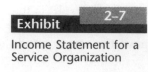

Exhibit   2-7

Income Statement for a
Service Organization

Income Statement: Service Organization For the Year Ended December 31, 2001			
Sales			$300,000
Less expenses:			
Cost of services sold:			
Beginning work in process		$ 5,000	
Service costs added:			
Direct materials	$ 40,000		
Direct labour	80,000		
Overhead	100,000	220,000	
Total		$225,000	
Less: Ending work in process		10,000	215,000
Gross margin			$ 85,000
Less operating expenses:			
Selling expenses		$ 8,000	
Administrative expenses		22,000	30,000
Income before taxes			$ 55,000

Income Statement: Service Organization

An income statement for a service firm is shown in Exhibit 2–7. In a service organization, the cost of services sold is computed differently from the cost of goods sold in a manufacturing firm. As the income statement reveals, there are no beginning or ending finished goods inventories. Unlike a manufacturing firm, the service firm has no finished goods inventories—it is not possible to store services. Thus, in a direct comparison with manufacturing firms, cost of services sold would always correspond to cost of goods manufactured. Furthermore, as Exhibit 2–7 reveals, the cost of services sold during a period (equivalent to cost of goods manufactured) can be computed following the same format shown in Exhibit 2–6. Exhibit 2–7 reveals that it is possible to have work in process for services. For example, an architect may have drawings in process and an orthodontist may have numerous patients in various stages of process for braces.

TYPES OF MANAGEMENT ACCOUNTING SYSTEMS: A BRIEF OVERVIEW

Objective 4

Explain the differences between functional-based and activity-based management accounting systems.

Management accounting systems can be broadly classified as *functional-based* and *activity-based*. Both functional-based and activity-based approaches are found in practice. **Functional-based management (FBM) accounting systems** were used throughout the 1900s and are still widely used in both the manufacturing and the service sectors. **Activity-based management (ABM) accounting systems** are much newer (developed within the final two decades of the 20th century). Activity-based cost management systems are also extensively used, and their use is increasing—particularly among organizations faced with product and customer diversity, more product complexity, shorter product life cycles, increased quality requirements, and intense competitive pressures.

FBM versus ABM Accounting Systems

The general models for functional-based and activity-based management accounting systems are displayed in Exhibits 2–8 and 2–9. Notice that both models have two dimensions. The vertical dimension of the models describes how costs are assigned to cost objects like products and customers, whereas the horizontal dimension is concerned with how the systems try to improve operational efficiency and control costs. The central element or heart of the FBM model is functions; the corresponding element of the ABM model is activities. Functions are usually grouped into organizational units, such as departments or plants (for example, engineering, quality control, and assembly are functions organized as departments). Activities with a common objective group together to form **processes**. For example, purchasing goods, receiving goods, and paying for goods received are major activities that define the procurement process. Comparing each dimension provides significant insight into how the two management accounting models differ.

FBM Cost View In an FBM accounting system, resource costs are assigned to functional units and then to products. In assigning costs, both direct tracing and driver tracing are used, although in an FBM system, driver tracing uses only **production drivers** (also called **unit-level drivers**)—measures of consumption that are highly correlated with production output. Thus units of product or drivers that are highly correlated with units produced—such as direct labour hours, direct materials, and machine hours—are

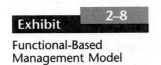

Exhibit 2–8

Functional-Based
Management Model

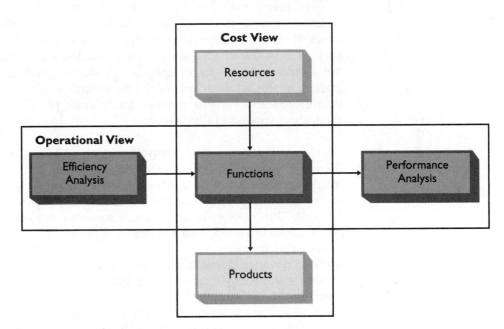

Exhibit 2–9

Activity-Based
Management Model

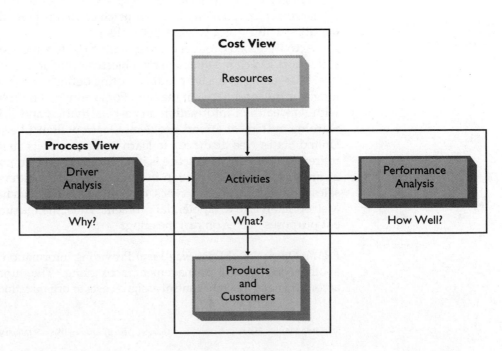

the only activity drivers assumed to be of importance. Because FBM systems use only drivers related to the production function to assign costs, this cost assignment approach is referred to as production- or **functional-based costing (FBC)**. The production or unit-level drivers on which FBC relies are often not the only drivers that explain cause-and-effect relationships. Drivers other than production drivers that explain cause-and-effect relationships are referred to as **nonunit-level drivers**. For example, production drivers like units produced or direct labour hours may have nothing to do with the cost of purchasing raw materials. In reality, the number of purchase orders might be the appropriate measure of consumption by each product. Yet in an FBC system, purchasing costs would be assigned using a measure like units produced or direct labour hours. Cost assignments made in these cases must be classified as allocation (recall that allocation is cost assignment based on *assumed* linkages or convenience). Furthermore, if nonunit-level costs—such as purchasing—are significant, functional-based costing can be described as allocation-intensive.

The product-costing objective of a functional-based costing system is typically satisfied by assigning production costs to inventories and cost of goods sold for purposes of external financial reporting. More comprehensive product cost definitions, such as the value-chain and operating cost definitions illustrated in Exhibit 2–4, are not available for management use. However, production-based costing systems often furnish useful variants of the traditional product cost definition. For example, prime costs and variable manufacturing costs per unit may be reported (variable costs are discussed in Chapter 3).

ABM Cost View In **activity-based costing (ABC)**, costs are traced to activities and then to products. As with functional-based costing, both direct tracing and driver tracing are used; however, the role of driver tracing is significantly expanded by identifying and using drivers unrelated to the volume of product produced (nonunit-level drivers). Thus activity-based cost assignments emphasize tracing over allocation; in fact, it could be called tracing-intensive. The use of both unit-level and nonunit-level activity drivers increases both the accuracy of cost assignments and the overall quality and relevance of cost information. For example, consider the activity "moving raw materials and partly finished goods from one point to another within a factory." The number of moves required for a product is a much better measure of the product's demand for the material-handling activity than the number of units produced. In fact, the number of units produced may have nothing to do with measuring products' demands for material handling. (A batch of 10 units could require as much material-handling activity as a batch of 100 units.)

Activity-based product costing tends to be flexible. Cost information is produced to support a variety of managerial objectives, including the financial reporting objective. More comprehensive product-costing definitions are emphasized for better planning, control, and decision making. For example, a more flexible accounting system, with its wealth of information on costs, activities, and drivers, could act as an early warning system of ethical problems. Metropolitan Life Insurance Company in the United States was dismayed to learn that some of its agents were selling policies as retirement plans. This practice is illegal, and cost the company more than $20 million in fines as well as $50 million in refunds to policyholders.[5] Comprehensive data on sales, individual agents, types of policies, and policyholders could have alerted Metropolitan Life to a potential problem. Thus, the maxim "different costs for different purposes" takes on real meaning.

FBM's Operational Efficiency View Providing information for planning and control is another objective of management accounting. The functional-based management accounting approach to control assigns costs to organizational units and then holds the

---

5. Chris Roush, "Fields of Green—and Disaster Areas," *Business Week*, 9 January 1995, 94.

Exhibit 2–10	Functional-Based	Activity-Based
Comparison of Functional-Based and Activity-Based Cost Management Systems	1. Unit-level drivers 2. Allocation-intensive 3. Narrow, rigid product costing 4. Focus on managing costs 5. Sparse activity information 6. Maximization of individual unit performance 7. Use of financial measures of performance	1. Unit- and nonunit-level drivers 2. Tracing-intensive 3. Broad, flexible product costing 4. Focus on managing activities 5. Detailed activity information 6. Systemwide performance maximization 7. Use of both financial and nonfinancial measures of performance

organizational unit manager responsible for controlling the assigned costs. Performance is measured by comparing actual outcomes with standard or budgeted outcomes. The emphasis is on financial measures of performance (nonfinancial measures are usually ignored). Managers are rewarded based on their ability to control costs. Thus, the functional-based approach traces costs to individuals who are responsible for incurring costs. The reward system is used to motivate these individuals to manage costs by increasing the operating efficiency of their organizational units. This approach assumes that maximizing the performance of the overall organization is achieved by maximizing the performance of individual organizational subunits (referred to as responsibility centres).

ABM's Operational Efficiency View Activity-based control subsystems also differ significantly from functional-based systems. The functional-based emphasis is on managing costs. The emerging consensus, however, is that management of activities, not costs, is the key to successful control. **Activity-based management** focuses on the management of activities with the objective of improving the value received by the customer and the profit received by providing this value. It includes driver analysis, activity analysis, and performance evaluation and draws on activity-based costing as a major source of information.[6] The process view is concerned with identifying factors that cause an activity's cost (explaining *why* costs are incurred), assessing *what* work is done (identifying activities), and evaluating the work performed and the results achieved (looking at *how well* the activity is performed). Thus, activity-based control requires detailed information on activities.

This new approach focuses on accountability for activities rather than costs and emphasizes the maximization of systemwide performance instead of individual performance. Activities cut across functional and departmental lines, are systemwide in focus, and require a global approach to control. Essentially, this form of control admits that maximizing the efficiency of individual subunits does not necessarily lead to maximum efficiency for the system as a whole. Another significant difference should also be mentioned. In an activity-based management accounting information system, both financial and nonfinancial measures of performance are important. Exhibit 2–10 compares the characteristics of the functional-based and activity-based cost management systems.

Choice of a Management Accounting System

Activity-based management accounting offers significant benefits, including improved product-costing accuracy, improved decision making, enhanced strategic planning, and better ability to manage activities. Furthermore, the activity-based system is particularly suited for supporting the goal of continuous improvement—an

---

6. This definition of activity-based management and the illustrative model in Exhibit 2–9 are based on Norm Raffish and Peter B. B. Turney, "Glossary of Activity-Based Management," *Journal of Cost Management* (Fall 1991): 53–63. Many other terms throughout the text relating to activity-based management are also drawn from this source.

objective that is critical for firms competing on a global basis. These benefits, however, are not obtained without costs. An activity-based management accounting system is more complex, and it requires a significant increase in measurement activity—and measurement can be costly. However, with the advances in information technology, the costs of measurement have declined, making activity-based systems more attractive. Simultaneously, the cost of making bad decisions has increased (because of more intense competition resulting from the emergence of a worldwide economy, deregulation of services, and so on). The need to improve the quality of decision making has also increased the appeal of activity-based approaches.

For many firms, the benefits of replacing an FBM system with an ABM system outweigh the costs. As a result, the use of activity-based costing and activity-based management is spreading, and interest in activity-based management accounting is high. Firms like J. M. Schneider, Inc., Volkswagen Canada, Royal Bank of Canada, Hughes Aircraft, Caterpillar, Xerox, National Semiconductor, Tektronix, Dayton Extruded Plastics, Armistead Insurance, and Zytec have adopted activity-based costing and management systems.[7] Furthermore, this is only a very small listing of firms that are using activity-based systems.

SUMMARY OF LEARNING OBJECTIVES

1.   Explain the cost assignment process.
Costs are assigned to cost objects such as products, projects, plants, and customers. There are three methods of cost assignment: direct tracing, driver tracing, and allocation. Direct and driver tracing offer more accuracy because they are based on cause-and-effect relationships. Direct tracing relies on physical observation to assign costs. Driver tracing relies on the use of causal factors called drivers to assign costs. Allocation relies on assumed relationships and convenience to assign costs. Allocation is essentially an arbitrary assignment and should be avoided as much as possible.

2. Define tangible and intangible products, and explain why there are different product cost definitions.
There are two types of output: tangible products and services. Tangible products are goods that are produced by converting raw materials through the use of labour and capital inputs such as plant, land, and machinery. Services are tasks or activities performed for a customer or an activity performed by a customer using an organization's products or facilities. Product cost is defined as cost assigned to a product that satisfies a particular managerial objective. Since managerial objectives can differ, product cost definitions can differ—each depending on the managerial objective being served.

3. Prepare income statements for manufacturing and service organizations.
If expenses are grouped according to function and then deducted from revenues, we have absorption-costing income statements. Absorption-costing income statements are generally used for external financial reporting. For manufacturing firms, the major functional classifications are manufacturing and nonmanufacturing; for service organizations, the categories are production and nonproduction. For manufacturing firms, the cost of goods manufactured must be calculated. No such requirement exists for a services firm.

4. Explain the differences between functional-based and activity-based management accounting systems.
A functional-based management accounting system uses only unit-level drivers, tends to be more allocation-intensive, uses narrow product cost definitions, focuses on managing costs, provides little activity information, emphasizes individual organizational unit performance, and uses financial measures of performance. An activity-based management accounting system uses both unit-level and nonunit-level drivers, is tracing-intensive, allows flexible product-costing definitions, focuses on managing activities, provides detailed activity information, emphasizes systemwide performance, and uses both financial and nonfinancial measures of performance.

---

7. *Activity-Based Management*, Management Accounting Issues Paper 10, The Society of Management Accountants of Canada, 1995, Hamilton, Ontario; Peter B. B. Turney, "Activity-Based Management," *Management Accounting* (January 1992): 20–25; Jack Hedicke and David Feil, "Hughes Aircraft," *Management Accounting* (February 1991): 29–33; and Lou F. Jones, "Product Costing at Caterpillar," *Management Accounting* (February 1991): 34–42.

KEY TERMS

REVIEW PROBLEMS

I. MANUFACTURING, COST CLASSIFICATION, AND INCOME STATEMENT

Pop's Burger Heaven produces and sells quarter-pound hamburgers. Each burger sells for $1.50. During December, Pop's sold 10,000 burgers (the average amount sold each month). The restaurant employs cooks, servers, and one supervisor (the owner, John Peterson). All cooks and servers are part-time employees. Pop's maintains a pool of part-time employees so that the number of employees scheduled can be adjusted to the changes in demand. Demand varies on a weekly as well as a monthly basis.

A janitor is hired to clean the building on a weekly basis. The building is leased from a local real estate company. The building has no seating capabilities. All orders are filled on a drive-through basis.

The supervisor schedules work, opens the building, counts the cash, advertises, and is responsible for hiring and firing. The following costs were incurred during December:

Hamburger meat	$1,600	Utilities		500
Lettuce	300	Amortization		
Tomatoes	250	Cooking equipment		200
Buns	300	Cash register		50
Other ingredients	20	Advertising		100
Cooks' wages	2,550	Rent		800
Servers' wages	2,032	Janitorial supplies		50
Supervisor's salary	2,000	Janitor's wages		120

Required:

1. Classify the costs for Pop's December operations in one of the following categories: direct materials, direct labour, overhead, or selling and administrative.

2. Prepare an absorption-costing income statement for the month of December.

Solution

1.   Classification:
     Direct materials: Hamburger meat, lettuce, tomatoes, and buns
     Direct labour: Cooks' wages
     Overhead: Utilities, amortization on the cooking equipment, rent, janitor's wages, janitorial supplies, and other ingredients
     Selling and administrative: Servers' wages, supervisor's salary, amortization on the cash register, and advertising

Explanation of Classification:
Cooks are direct labourers because they make the hamburgers. "Other ingredients" are overhead because of cost and convenience, even though technically they are direct materials. Because the primary purpose of the building is production (cooking hamburgers), all of the rent and building-related costs are classified as indirect production costs. (An argument could be made that the building also supports the selling and administrative functions and, consequently, a portion of the rent and building-related costs should be classified as selling and administrative costs.) Servers are responsible for taking and filling orders and are, therefore, classified as sales personnel. The cash register is used to support the sales function. The supervisor is responsible for overseeing the business as a whole and for coordinating the sales and production functions, so salary is an administrative cost.

2.   Income Statement:

Sales ($1.50 × 10,000)		$15,000
Less cost of goods sold:		
Direct materials	$2,450	
Direct labour	2,550	
Overhead	1,690	6,690
Gross profit		$ 8,310
Less operating expenses:		
Selling expenses	$2,182	
Administrative expenses	2,000	4,182
Net income		$ 4,128

II. SERVICES, COST SYSTEMS, AND INCOME STATEMENT

Celestial Funeral Home offers a full range of services. Based on past experience, Celestial uses the following formula to describe its total overhead costs: $Y = \$100,000 + \$25X$, where Y = total overhead costs and X = number of funerals. Overhead costs are assigned by dividing the total overhead by the number of funerals. For a given funeral, the cost of direct materials ranges from $750 to $5,000, depending on the family's selection of a coffin. The average is $2,000. Direct labour averages $500 per funeral. During 2001, Celestial conducted 1,000 funerals. The average price charged for each funeral is $3,500. Celestial incurs annual selling expenses of $25,000 and administrative expenses of $75,000.

Required:

1.   Does Celestial sell a tangible or an intangible product? Explain.
2.   Does Celestial use a functional-based or an activity-based management accounting system? Explain. Do you think this is a good choice? Explain.
3.   What is the total overhead cost incurred by Celestial for the year?
4.   What is the overhead cost per funeral for the year?
5.   Calculate the unit product cost for the year.
6.   Prepare an income statement for Celestial.

Solution

1.   Funerals are intangible products. They are services: as such, they cannot be stored and are connected to the producer (inseparability).

2. The use of a unit-level driver (number of funerals) to assign overhead costs (and, apparently, direct materials and direct labour) suggests a functional-based system. A functional-based system will probably work quite well for a local funeral home business. There is very little product diversity, selling and administrative expenses represent a small portion of total costs, and there are virtually no pre-production costs (research and development costs are absent). Thus, product cost is essentially defined by production costs. Furthermore, the absence of a great variety of products coupled with the fact that overhead costs represent a small percentage of product costs makes driver tracing much less important (direct materials and direct labour can be assigned using direct tracing).

3. $Y = \$100,000 + \$25(1,000)$
   $Y = \$125,000$

4. $\$125,000/1,000 = \$125$

5. Unit product cost:

Direct materials	$2,000
Direct labour	500
Overhead	125
	$2,625

6. Income Statement:

Sales		$3,500,000
Less cost of goods sold:		
Direct materials	$2,000,000	
Direct labour	500,000	
Overhead	125,000	2,625,000
Gross profit		$ 875,000
Less operating expenses:		
Selling expenses	$ 25,000	
Administrative expenses	75,000	100,000
Net income		$ 775,000

QUESTIONS FOR WRITING AND DISCUSSION

1. What is meant by "product-costing accuracy"?

2. What is a cost object? Give some examples.

3. What is an activity? Give some examples of activities within a manufacturing firm.

4. What is a direct cost? an indirect cost?

5. What does traceability mean? What is tracing?

6. What is allocation?

7. What are drivers? Give an example of a driver.

8. Explain the difference between direct tracing and driver tracing.

9. Explain how driver tracing works.

10. What is a tangible product?

11. What is a service?

12. Explain how services differ from tangible products.

13. Give three examples of product cost definitions. Why do we need different product cost definitions?

14. Identify the three cost elements that determine the cost of making a product (for external reporting).

15. How do the income statements of a manufacturing firm and a service firm differ?

16. Describe some of the major differences between a functional-based cost management system and an activity-based cost management system.

17. When would a company choose an activity-based cost management system over a functional-based system? What forces are moving firms to implement activity-based cost management systems?

EXERCISES

2–1

**Direct Tracing and
Driver Tracing**

LO1

Harry Whipple, owner of an inkjet printer, has agreed to allow Mary and Natalie, two friends who are pursuing master's degrees in English, to print several papers for their graduate English courses. However, he has imposed two conditions. First, they must supply their own paper. Second, they must pay Harry a fair amount for the usage of the ink cartridge. Cartridges for the printer cost $80 and usually provide a printing capacity of 4,000 normal pages before replacement (normal means a page without graphs). Paper is bought in reams of 500 units at $4 per ream. Mary's printing requirements are for 500 pages, while Natalie's are for 1,000 pages.

Required:

1. Calculate the cost per page for the papers produced by Mary. Repeat for Natalie.
2. In computing the cost per page, which cost was assigned through direct tracing? through driver tracing?
3. Suppose that Natalie uses a lot of graphs in her writing, whereas Mary uses hardly any. Explain how this difference could affect the accuracy of the ink cost assigned to Natalie. What recommendation would you make for improving the cost assignment? Explain.

2–2

**Direct Tracing and
Driver Tracing**

LO1, LO2

Shellbrook General Hospital has two types of patients: normal care and intensive care. On a daily basis, both types of patients consume resources necessary for their care. For example, they occupy beds; receive nursing care; use care supplies (lotion, gauze, tissues, etc.); have bedding, towels, and clothes laundered; eat meals, and so on. Bill Simons, the hospital administrator, wants to calculate the cost per patient day for each type of patient.

To illustrate how daily care costs can be assigned to each type of patient, information has been gathered for nursing care. There are always four nurses on duty. There are three shifts, each lasting 8 hours. Nurses work 40 hours per week and are paid an average of $40,000 per year, including benefits. Full-time nurses work 50 weeks per year. The hospital employs only one part-time nurse, who is paid $20,000 for the hours worked during the year (only the amount needed to ensure that the four-nurse coverage policy is satisfied). Assume that a year is exactly 52 weeks. During the year, normal care patients accounted for 8,000 patient days and intensive care patients accounted for 2,000 patient days. Intensive care patients use half of the nursing care hours.

Required:

1. Calculate the nursing cost per patient day for each patient type, using patient days to assign the cost.
2. Calculate the nursing cost per patient day for each patient type, using nursing hours used to assign the cost. Is this cost assignment more accurate than the one using patient days? Explain your reasoning.
3. Suppose that one nurse each shift is dedicated to the intensive care unit and that the other three nurses provide additional help as needed. What additional information would you like to have in order to assign nursing costs so that a cost per patient day can be calculated for each patient type? Which of the three assignment methods are you using?

2–3

**Cost Assignment
Methods**

LO1

Hummer Company uses manufacturing cells to produce its products (a cell is a manufacturing unit dedicated to the production of subassemblies or products). One manufacturing cell produces small motors for lawn mowers. Suppose that the small-motor manufacturing cell is the cost object. Assume that all or a portion of the following costs must be assigned to the cell:

a. Salary of cell supervisor
b. Power to heat and cool the plant in which the cell is located
c. Materials used to produce the motors
d. Maintenance for the cell's equipment (provided by the maintenance department)
e. Labour used to produce motors
f. Cafeteria that services the plant's employees
g. Amortization on the plant
h. Amortization on equipment used to produce the motors
i. Ordering costs for materials used in production
j. Engineering support (provided by the engineering department)
k. Cost of maintaining the plant and grounds
l. Cost of the plant's personnel office
m. Property tax on the plant and land

Required:

Identify which cost assignment method would likely be used to assign the costs of each activity to the small-motor manufacturing cell: direct tracing, driver tracing, or allocation. When driver tracing is selected, identify a potential activity driver that could be used for the tracing.

2–4

Value-Chain Activity

LO2

The following activities are performed within a manufacturing firm. Classify each activity according to its value-chain activity category (for example, activity: grinding parts; value-chain activity category: producing).

a. Advertising products
b. Repairing goods under warranty
c. Designing a new process
d. Assembling parts
e. Shipping goods to a wholesaler
f. Inspecting incoming raw materials and parts
g. Storing finished goods in a warehouse
h. Creating a new computer chip
i. Answering product-use questions using a customer "hot line"
j. Moving partly finished goods from one department to another
k. Building a prototype of a new product
l. Creating plans for a new model of an automobile
m. Conducting a sales campaign by phone
n. Picking goods from a warehouse
o. Setting up equipment

2–5

Product Cost Definitions

LO2

Three possible product cost definitions were introduced: value-chain, operating, and traditional. Identify which of the three best fits the following situations (justify your choice):

a. Setting the price for a new product
b. Valuation of finished goods inventories for external reporting
c. Choosing among different products in order to maintain a product mix that will provide the company with a long-term sustainable competitive advantage
d. Choosing among competing product designs
e. Calculating cost of goods sold for external reporting
f. Deciding whether to increase the price of an existing product
g. Deciding whether to accept or reject a special order, where the price offered is lower than the normal selling price
h. Determining which of several potential new products should be developed, produced, and sold

2–6

Cost of Goods Manufactured and Sold

LO3

Spreadsheet

Lawton Company manufactures sleeping bags. At the beginning of September, the following information was supplied by their accountant:

Raw materials inventory	$37,000
Work-in-process inventory	18,000
Finished goods inventory	20,200

During September, direct labour cost was $40,500, raw materials purchases were $61,500, and the total overhead cost was $105,750. The inventories at the end of September were as follows:

Raw materials inventory	$16,800
Work-in-process inventory	29,500
Finished goods inventory	19,100

Required:

1. Prepare a statement of cost of goods manufactured for September.
2. Prepare a statement of cost of goods sold for September.

2–7

Preparation of Income Statement: Manufacturing Firm

LO3

Bohanan manufactures a stuffed bear called Smokee. Last year 100,000 bears were made and sold for $30 each. The actual unit cost for a stuffed bear follows:

Direct materials	$ 4.00
Direct labour	6.00
Overhead	13.00
Total unit cost	$23.00

The only selling expenses were a commission of $2 per unit sold and advertising totalling $50,000. Administrative expenses equalled $150,000. There were no beginning or ending finished goods inventories.

Required:

1. Prepare an income statement for external users. Did you need to prepare a supporting statement of cost of goods manufactured? Explain.
2. Suppose 100,000 bears were produced (and 100,000 sold) but that the company had a beginning finished goods inventory of 5,000 bears produced in the previous year at a cost of $20 per unit. The company follows a first-in, first-out policy for its inventory (meaning that the units produced first are sold first for purposes of cost flow). What effect does this have on the income statement? Show the new statement.

2–8

Functional-Based versus Activity-Based Management Accounting Systems

LO4

Iquitos Manufacturing produces two different models of cameras. One model has an automatic focus; the other requires the user to focus manually. The two products are produced in batches (an equal number of batches is used for each product). Each time a batch is produced, the equipment must be configured (set up) for the specifications of the camera model being produced. The machine configuration required for the automatic-focus model is more complex and consumes more of the setup activity resources than that for the manual-focus camera. Total setup costs are $100,000 per year. Total setup hours are 10,000, with 7,000 hours needed for the automatic model and 3,000 hours needed for the manual model.

The manual model is more labour-intensive, requiring much more assembly time and less machine time. Total direct labour hours used for both products are 100,000, with 70,000 hours used for the manual model and 30,000 hours used for the automatic model. Iquitos produces 40,000 units of the manual model and 60,000 units of the automatic model each year. The company currently assigns only manufacturing costs to the two products. Overhead costs are assigned to the two products in proportion to the direct labour hours used by each product. All other costs are viewed as period costs.

Iquitos budgets costs for all departments within the plant—both support departments (like maintenance and purchasing) and production departments (like machining and assembly). Departmental managers are evaluated and rewarded on their ability to control costs. Individual managerial performance is assessed by comparing actual costs with budgeted costs.

Required:

1. Is Iquitos using a functional-based or an activity-based management accounting system? Explain.
2. Setup costs are overhead costs. What is the setup cost assigned per unit for each model using Iquitos's current method of assigning overhead costs to products? Would you classify this cost assignment as direct tracing, driver tracing, or allocation? Explain.
3. Can you suggest a better way of assigning setup costs? Provide calculations, and explain why you think the method is better. Is this method compatible with production-based costing or with activity-based costing? Explain.

2–9

Cost of Goods Manufactured and Sold

LO3

Spreadsheet

Hayward Company, a manufacturing firm, has supplied the following information from its accounting records for 2001 (in 1,000s):

Direct labour cost	$10,500
Purchases of raw materials	15,000
Supplies used	675
Factory insurance	350
Commissions paid	2,500
Factory supervision	2,225
Advertising	800
Material handling	3,745
Work-in-process inventory, December 31, 2000	12,500
Work-in-process inventory, December 31, 2001	14,250
Materials inventory, December 31, 2000	3,475
Materials inventory, December 31, 2001	9,500
Finished goods inventory, December 31, 2000	6,685
Finished goods inventory, December 31, 2001	4,250

Required:

1. Prepare a statement of cost of goods manufactured.
2. Prepare a statement of cost of goods sold.

2–10

Income Statement; Cost Concepts; Service Company

LO2, LO3

Lance Peckam owns and operates three Confiable Muffler outlets in Red Deer, Alberta. Confiable Muffler specializes in replacing mufflers; the replacement mufflers have a lifetime guarantee. Confiable is a franchise popular throughout western Canada. In April, purchases of materials equalled $200,000, the beginning inventory of material was $26,300, and the ending inventory of material was $14,250. Payments to direct labour during the month totalled $53,000. Overhead incurred was $120,000. The Red Deer outlets also spent $15,000 on advertising during the month. A franchise fee of $3,000 per outlet is paid every month. Revenues for April were $500,000.

Required:

1. What was the cost of materials used for muffler-changing services during April?
2. What was the prime cost for April?
3. What was the conversion cost for April?
4. What was the total service cost for April?
5. Prepare an income statement for the month of April.
6. Confiable purchases all its mufflers from Remington Company, a muffler manufacturer. Discuss the differences between the products offered by Remington and Confiable.

2–11

Cost Assignment; Product Cost Definitions

LO1, LO2

Halverson Company produces chemicals used in the mining industry. Each plant is dedicated to producing a single industrial chemical. One of its plants produces an electrolyte used in the copper industry's solvent extraction process. During the most recent year, the electrolyte plant produced and sold 2,000,000 kilograms of electrolyte. No inventories of the chemical are carried. The chemical sells for $2 per kilogram. Annual manufacturing costs for the electrolyte plant totalled $2,800,000. The plant is also responsible for packaging and shipping its products. Distribution and packaging costs for the electrolyte plant were $200,000. Research and development costs are incurred centrally and assigned to each plant in proportion to its sales revenues. The revenues of the electrolyte plant were 25 percent of the company's total revenues. For the year just completed, the company reported $1.2 million for research and development. The company also reported $320,000 in sales commissions. Commissions are also assigned to plants in proportion to their sales.

Required:

1. Compute the unit product cost that must be used for external financial reporting purposes (cost per kilogram of electrolyte). How would the other costs be treated for external financial reporting?
2. Compute the unit operating product cost. What purpose might this cost serve?
3. Compute the unit value-chain product cost. Why would management want to know this product cost?
4. Classify the cost assignments for the value-chain product cost as direct tracing, driver tracing, or allocation. For any cost classified as allocation, is it possible to change that assignment to direct tracing or driver tracing? Explain.

PROBLEMS

2–12

Driver Tracing

LO1

Listed below are costs that are to be assigned to certain cost objects. For each case, identify possible drivers that could be used for the cost assignment. Example: *Cost:* setting up equipment; *Object:* Products; *Driver:* Number of setups used by each product

	Cost	Cost Object
a.	Processing cheques in a bank	Customer accounts
b.	Unloading shipments of raw materials	Products
c.	Shipping goods	Customers
d.	Ordering supplies	Departments
e.	Reworking products	Products
f.	Moving materials	Products
g.	Nursing care	Patients
h.	Processing insurance claims	Claims
i.	Special product testing	Products
j.	Physical therapy in a hospital	Patients

2–13

Cost Identification

LO2

Following are a list of cost items described in the chapter and a list of brief settings that describe the items. Match the items with the settings. There may be more than one cost classification associated with each setting; however, select the setting that seems to fit the item best.

Cost items:

a. Opportunity cost
b. Period cost
c. Product cost
d. Direct labour cost
e. Selling cost

    f.   Conversion cost
    g. Prime cost
    h. Direct materials cost
    i.   Overhead cost
    j.   Administrative cost

Settings:

1. Marcus Armstrong, manager of Timmins Optical, estimated that the cost of plastic, the wages of the technician producing the lenses, and overhead totalled $30 per pair of single-vision lenses.
2. Linda was having a hard time deciding whether to return to school. She was concerned about the good salary she would have to give up for the next four years.
3. Randy Harris is the finished goods warehouse manager for a medium-sized manufacturing firm. He is paid a salary of $90,000 per year. As he studied the financial statement prepared by the local CA firm, he wondered how his salary was treated.
4. Jamie Young is in charge of the legal department at company headquarters. Her salary is $95,000 per year. She reports to the chief executive officer.
5. All factory costs that are not classified as direct materials or direct labour.
6. A new product required machining, assembly, and painting. The design engineer asked the accounting department to estimate the labour cost for each of the three operations. The engineer supplied the estimated labour hours for each operation.
7. After obtaining the estimate of direct labour cost, the design engineer estimated the cost of the materials that would be used for the new product.
8. The design engineer totalled the costs of materials and direct labour for the new product.
9. The design engineer also estimated the cost of converting the raw materials into their final form.
10. The auditor pointed out that the amortization on the corporate jet had been incorrectly assigned to finished goods inventory (the jet was primarily used to fly the CEO and other staff to various company sites). Accordingly, the amortization charge was reallocated to the income statement.

2–14

Functional-Based versus Activity-Based Management Accounting Systems

LO4

The following actions are associated with either functional-based management accounting or activity-based management accounting.

a. Budgeted costs for the maintenance department are compared with the actual costs of the maintenance department.
b. The maintenance department manager receives a bonus for "beating" the budget.
c. The costs of resources are traced to activities and then to products.
d. The purchasing department is evaluated on a departmental basis.
e. Activities are identified and listed.
f. Activities are categorized as adding value or not adding value to the organization.
g. A standard for a product's material usage cost is set and compared with the product's actual material usage cost.
h. The cost of performing an activity is tracked over time.
i. The distance between moves is identified as the cause of material-handling cost.
j. A purchasing agent is rewarded for buying parts below the standard price set by the company.
k. The cost of the material-handling activity is reduced dramatically by redesigning the plant layout.
l. An investigation is undertaken to find out why the actual labour cost for the production of 1,000 units is greater than the labour standard allowed.

m. The percentage of defective units is calculated and tracked over time.
n. Engineering has been given the charge to find a way to reduce setup time by 75 percent.
o. The manager of the receiving department lays off two receiving clerks so that the fourth-quarter budget can be met.

Required:

Classify these actions as belonging to either a functional-based management accounting system or an activity-based management accounting system. Explain your classification.

2–15

Income Statement; Cost of Services Provided; Service Attributes

LO2, LO3

Spreadsheet

Berry Company is an architectural firm. The firm is located in Windsor, Ontario, and employs ten professionals and five staff. The firm does design work for small and medium-sized construction businesses. The following data are provided for the year ended July 31, 2001:

Designs processed	2,000
Designs in process, August 1, 2000	$ 60,000
Designs in process, July 31, 2001	100,000
Cost of services sold	890,000
Beginning direct materials inventory	20,000
Purchases, direct materials	40,000
Direct labour	800,000
Overhead	100,000
Administrative	50,000
Selling	60,000

Required:

1. Prepare a statement of cost of services sold.
2. Refer to the statement prepared in Requirement 1. What is the dominant cost? Will this always be true of service organizations? If not, provide an example of an exception.
3. Assume that the average fee for a design is $700. Prepare an income statement for Berry Company.
4. Discuss three differences between services and tangible products. How do these differences affect the computations in Requirement 1?

2–16

Income Statement; Cost of Goods Manufactured

LO3

W. W. Phillips Company produced 4,000 leather recliners during 2001. These recliners sell for $400 each. Phillips had 500 recliners in finished goods inventory at the beginning of the year. At the end of the year, there were 700 recliners in finished goods inventory. Phillips's accounting records provide the following information:

Purchases of raw materials	$320,000
Raw materials inventory, January 1, 2001	46,800
Raw materials inventory, December 31, 2001	66,800
Direct labour	200,000
Indirect labour	40,000
Rent, factory building	42,000
Amortization, factory equipment	60,000
Utilities, factory	11,956
Salary, sales supervisor	90,000
Commissions, salespersons	180,000
General administration	300,000
Work-in-process inventory, January 1, 2001	13,040
Work-in-process inventory, December 31, 2001	14,996
Finished goods inventory, January 1, 2001	80,000
Finished goods inventory, December 31, 2001	114,100

Required:

1. Prepare a statement of cost of goods manufactured.
2. Compute the average cost of producing one unit of product in 2001.
3. Prepare an income statement for external users.

2–17

Cost Identification and Analysis; Income Statement

LO2, LO3

Melissa Southern has decided to open a printing shop. She has secured two contracts. One is a five-year contract to print a popular regional magazine. The contract calls for 5,000 copies each month. The second contract is a three-year agreement to print tourist brochures for the province. The provincial tourism office requires 10,000 brochures per month.

Melissa has rented a building for $1,400 per month. Her printing equipment was purchased for $40,000 and has a life expectancy of 20,000 hours with no salvage value. Amortization is calculated for a period based on the hours of usage. Melissa has scheduled the delivery of the products so that two production runs are needed. In the first run, the equipment is prepared for the magazine printing. In the second run, the equipment is reconfigured for brochure printing. It takes twice as long to configure the equipment for the magazine setup as it does for the brochure setup. The total setup costs per month are $600.

Insurance costs for the building and equipment are $140 per month. Power to operate the printing equipment is strongly related to machine usage. The printing equipment causes virtually all of the power costs. Power costs will run $350 per month. Printing materials will cost $0.40 per copy for the magazine and $0.08 per copy for the brochure. Melissa will hire workers to run the presses as needed (part-time workers are easy to hire). She must pay $10 per hour. Each worker can produce 20 copies of the magazine per printing hour or 100 copies of the brochure. Distribution costs are $500 per month. Melissa will receive a salary of $1,500 per month. She is responsible for personnel, accounting, sales, and production—in effect, she is responsible for coordinating and managing all aspects of the business.

Required:

1. What are the total monthly manufacturing costs?
2. What are the total monthly prime costs? total monthly prime costs for the regional magazine? for the brochure? Did you use direct tracing, driver tracing, or allocation to assign costs to each product?
3. What are the total monthly conversion costs? Suppose that Melissa wants to determine monthly conversion costs for each product. Assign monthly conversion costs to each product using direct tracing and driver tracing whenever possible. For those costs that cannot be assigned using a tracing approach, you may assign them using direct labour hours.
4. If Melissa receives $1.80 per copy of the magazine and $0.45 per brochure, how much will her income be for the first month of operations? (Prepare an income statement.)

2–18

Cost of Goods Manufactured; Cost of Inventories

LO3

On January 30, 2001, the manufacturing facility of a medium-sized company was severely damaged by an accidental fire. As a result, the company's direct materials, work-in-process, and finished goods inventories were destroyed. The company did have access to certain incomplete accounting records, which revealed the following:

1. Beginning inventories, January 1, 2001:
   Direct materials $32,000
   Work-in-process   68,000
   Finished goods   30,000
2. Key ratios for the month of January 2001:
   Gross profit = 20% of sales
   Prime costs = 70% of manufacturing costs *for the month.*
   Factory overhead = 40% of conversion costs
   Ending work-in-process is always 10% of the monthly manufacturing costs

3. All costs are incurred uniformly in the manufacturing process.
4. Actual operations data for the month of January 2001:

Sales	$900,000
Direct materials purchases	320,000
Direct labour incurred	360,000

Required:

1. From the above data, reconstruct a statement of cost of goods manufactured.
2. Calculate the total cost of inventory lost, identifying each category where possible (i.e., direct materials, work-in-process, and finished goods), at January 30, 2001. (CMA Canada adapted)

2–19

Cost of Goods Manufactured; Cost of Goods Sold

LO3

In January 2001, Sayers Manufacturing incurred the following costs in manufacturing Detecto, its only product:

Direct materials purchased	$900,000
Direct labour incurred	710,000
Benefits	75,000
Overtime premium	50,000
Supervisory salaries	125,000
Utility expenses	92,500
Amortization (equipment)	22,800
Supplies (factory)	10,000
Factory rent	31,300

An analysis of the accounting records showed the following balances in the inventory accounts at the beginning and end of January:

	January 1	January 31
Direct materials	$ 80,000	$ 90,000
Work in process	110,000	74,600
Finished goods	95,000	108,000

Sayers treats overtime premium and benefits as indirect costs.

Required:

1. Determine the cost of goods manufactured for January 2001.
2. What was the cost of goods sold for January 2001? (CMA Canada adapted)

MANAGERIAL DECISION CASES

2–20

Cost Classification; Income Statement; Unit-Based Cost Behaviour; Service Organization

LO2, LO3

Gateway Construction Company is a family-operated business that was founded in 1950 by Samuel Gateway. In the beginning, the company consisted of Gateway and three employees laying gas, water, and sewage pipelines as subcontractors. Currently, the company employs 25 to 30 people; Jack Gateway, Samuel's son, directs it. The company's main business specialty continues to be laying pipeline.

Most of Gateway's work comes from contracts with city and municipal agencies. All of the company's work is located in Saskatchewan. The company's sales volume averages $3 million, and profits vary between 0 and 10 percent of sales.

Sales and profits have been somewhat below average for the past three years due to a recession and intense competition. Because of this competition, Jack Gateway is constantly reviewing the prices that other companies bid for jobs; when a bid is lost, he makes every attempt to analyze the reasons for the differences between his bid and that of his competitors. He uses this information to increase the competitiveness of future bids.

Jack has become convinced that Gateway's current accounting system is deficient. Currently, all expenses are simply deducted from revenues to arrive at net income. No effort is made to distinguish among the costs of laying pipe, obtaining contracts, and administering the company. Yet all bids are based on the costs of laying pipe.

With these thoughts in mind, Jack began a careful review of the income statement for the previous year (see below). First, he noted that jobs were priced on the basis of equipment hours, with an average price of $165 per equipment hour. However, when it came to classifying and assigning costs, he decided that he needed some help. One thing that really puzzled him was how to classify his own salary of $114,000. About half of his time was spent in bidding and securing contracts, and the other half was spent in general administrative matters.

Gateway Construction
Income Statement
For the Year Ended December 31, 2001

Sales (18,200 equipment hours at $165)		$3,003,000
Less expenses:		
Utilities	$ 24,000	
Machine operators	218,000	
Rent (office building)	24,000	
CA fees	20,000	
Other direct labour	265,700	
Administrative salaries	114,000	
Supervisor salaries	70,000	
Pipe	1,401,340	
Tires and fuel	418,600	
Amortization, equipment	198,000	
Salaries of mechanics	50,000	
Advertising	15,000	
Total expenses		2,818,640
Net income		$ 184,360

Required:

1. Classify the costs in the income statement as (1) costs of laying pipe (production costs); (2) costs of securing contracts (selling costs); or (3) costs of general administration. For production costs, identify direct materials, direct labour, and overhead costs. The company never has significant work in process: most jobs are started and completed within a day.
2. Using the functional classification developed in Requirement 1, prepare an absorption-costing income statement. What is the average cost per equipment hour for laying pipe?
3. Assume that a significant cost driver is equipment hours. Identify the costs that would likely be traced to jobs using this driver. Explain why you think that these costs are traceable using equipment hours. What is the cost per equipment hour for these traceable costs?

2–21

Cost Information and Ethical Behaviour; Service Organization

LO1

Jean Erickson, manager and owner of an advertising company in Winnipeg, Manitoba, had arranged a meeting with Leroy Gee, the chief accountant for a large local competitor. The two were lifelong friends. They had grown up together in a small town and attended the same university. Leroy was a competent, successful accountant but was currently experiencing some personal financial difficulties. The problems were created by some investments that had turned sour, leaving him with a $15,000 personal loan to pay off—just at the time that his oldest son was scheduled to enter university.

Jean, on the other hand, was struggling to establish a successful advertising business. She had recently acquired the rights to open a branch office of a large regional advertising firm headquartered in Edmonton, Alberta. During her first two years, she had managed to build a small, profitable practice; however, her chance to gain a significant foothold in the Winnipeg advertising community hinged on her successfully winning a bid to represent the province of Manitoba in a major campaign aimed at attracting new industry and tourism. The meeting she had scheduled with Leroy concerned the bid she planned to submit.

Jean: "Leroy, I'm at a critical point in my business venture. If I can win the bid for the province's advertising dollars, I'll be set. Winning the bid will bring $600,000 to $700,000 in revenues into the firm. On top of that, I estimate that the publicity will bring in another $200,000 to $300,000 in new business."

Leroy: "I understand. My boss is anxious to win that business as well. It would mean a huge increase in profits for my firm. It's a competitive business, though. As new as you are, I doubt that you'll have much chance of winning."

Jean: "You may be wrong. You're forgetting two very important considerations. First, I have the backing of all the resources and talent of a regional firm. Second, I have some political connections. Last year, I was hired to run the publicity side of the premier's campaign. He was impressed with my work and would like me to have this business. I am confident that the proposals I submit will be very competitive. My only concern is to submit a bid that beats your firm. If I come in with a lower bid and with good proposals, the premier can see to it that I get the work."

Leroy: "Sounds promising. If you do win, however, there will be a lot of upset people. After all, they are going to claim that the business should have been given to local advertisers, not to some out-of-province firm. Given the size of your office, you'll have to get support from Edmonton. You could take a lot of heat."

Jean: "True. But I am the owner of the branch office. That fact alone should blunt most of the criticism. Who can argue that I'm not a local? Listen, with your help, I think I can win this bid. Furthermore, if I do win it, you can reap some direct benefits. With that kind of business, I can afford to hire an accountant, and I'll make it worthwhile for you to transfer jobs. I can offer you an up-front bonus of $15,000. On top of that, I'll increase your annual salary by 20 percent. That should solve most of your financial difficulties. After all, we have been friends since day one—and what are friends for?"

Leroy: "Jean, my wife would be ecstatic if I were able to improve our financial position as quickly as this opportunity affords. I certainly hope that you win the bid. What kind of help can I provide?"

Jean: "Simple. To win, all I have to do is beat the bid submitted by your firm. Before I submit my bid, I would like you to review it. With the financial skills you have, it should be easy for you to spot any excessive costs that I may have included. Or perhaps I will have included the wrong kind of costs. By cutting excessive costs and eliminating costs that may not be directly related to the project, I should be able to make my bid competitive enough to meet or beat your firm's bid."

Required:

1. What would you do if you were Leroy? Fully explain the reasons for your choice.
2. What is the likely outcome if Leroy agrees to review the bid? Is there much risk to him personally if he reviews the bid? Should the degree of risk have any bearing on his decision?
3. Assume that Leroy is a CMA. Apply the code of ethics for management accountants to the proposal given to Leroy (see Chapter 1). What standards would be violated if he agrees to review the bid?

RESEARCH ASSIGNMENTS

2–22

Cybercase

LO1, LO3, LO4

Obtain copies of financial statements for a manufacturing firm and a service firm from the Internet. Write a memo discussing the differences and similarities of the two statements.

2–23

Research Assignment

LO1, LO3, LO4

Interview an accountant who works for either a manufacturing firm or a service firm (preferably one who works in cost accounting). Ask that person the following questions, and write up his or her responses:

a. What product or products does your firm produce?
b. What costs are assigned to the product or products produced?
c. For a particular product, what direct materials are used?
d. What percentage of total manufacturing costs is direct labour? materials? overhead?
e. How is overhead assigned to the products?
f. Do you use or plan to use an activity-based management accounting system? Why or why not?

CHAPTER 3

Activity Cost Behaviour

Learning Objectives

After studying Chapter 3, you should be able to:

1. Define and describe cost behaviour for fixed, variable, and mixed costs.

2. Explain the role of the resource usage model in understanding cost behaviour.

3. Separate mixed costs into their fixed and variable components using the high–low method, the scatterplot method, and the method of least squares.

4. Evaluate the reliability of a cost equation.

5. Explain the role of multiple regression in assessing cost behaviour.

6. Describe the use of managerial judgment in determining cost behaviour.

Scenario

"I have just been told that our quality costs make up about 20 percent of divisional sales revenues. I was also told that quality costs are incurred because poor quality exists or may exist. Twenty percent seems high to me. All this time I thought that we were spending money to create better quality, not because we had poor quality. Rick, what am I missing here?" asked Patricia Fernandez, manager of a small-appliance division. "What do we need to do to increase our efficiency?"

Rick Anderson, divisional controller, pondered the questions a moment and then responded.

Rick: "Patricia, based on some recent seminars that I have attended, I now realize that managing costs and increasing efficiency have a lot to do with managing the activities that we perform inside the division. But to manage activities, we really need to understand how the costs of activities change as activity output changes. Consider our rework activity. When our inspection activity detects a bad appliance, we tear it apart and redo the work so that the product functions as it should. Some costs, such as the amortization on the equipment used, do not change as the number of reworked products increases. Other costs, like materials and power, do increase with the num-ber of units reworked. And some costs will change only with fairly large changes in activity output."

Patricia: "This is interesting, but how will understanding this cost behaviour help me increase my division's efficiency?"

Rick: "Simple. If it is really true that the cost of the rework activity is a function of the number of units reworked, then you can manage costs by focusing on what drives rework costs: reworked units. If we can find ways to reduce the num-ber of defective units, then the cost of the rework activity should decrease, increasing our overall effi-ciency. And it would be interest-ing—in fact, essential—to know how the cost of resources used changes as the activity output changes. For example, we may need to spend more in preventing bad units to reduce rework. If the increase in prevention costs is less than the reduction in rework costs, then we would want to increase our prevention activity."

Questions to Think About

1. Suppose that the division reduces the demand for rework

activity. Will resource spending be reduced by the same proportion for this activity? Is there a difference between resource spending and resource usage?

2. Suppose that I know the total cost of rework activity and the total number of units reworked. Given this information, can I determine how much of this total cost is vari-

able? How much is fixed? Is knowing fixed- and variable-cost behaviour important?

3. What role does management play in determining cost behaviour?

4. Can you think of reasons other than those suggested by the scenario that make it important for managers to understand cost behaviour?

THE BASICS OF COST BEHAVIOUR

Objective 1

Define and describe cost behaviour for fixed, variable, and mixed costs.

In Chapter 2, we looked at the way costs can be used to determine the cost of goods sold and the value of ending inventory. These costs are important for preparing external financial reports—namely, the income statement and the balance sheet. The costs that are reported on these statements are organized by function. That is, all of the company's costs are put into one of three categories: production or manufacturing (in the cost of goods sold account), marketing expenses, and administrative expenses. This organization is fine for external reporting: in fact, it is required. However, the functional groupings are not helpful at all for budgeting, control, and decision making. For these purposes, we need to understand cost behaviour.

Suppose that a new company is expanding rapidly. Last year, the company made and sold 10,000 units; in the coming year, it expects to sell 20,000 units. Could we say that costs in the coming year will double? No, probably not. In fact, we would expect that the cost of making 20,000 units would be less than twice the cost of making 10,000 units. The reason is that, while some costs are *variable* and will double as output doubles, other costs are *fixed* and will not change as output doubles. In order to answer what will happen to costs as output doubles, we need to know about cost behaviour.

Cost behaviour is the general term for describing whether costs change as output changes. There are many different ways that cost reacts to output changes. We will begin by looking at the simplest possibilities—fixed costs, variable costs, and mixed costs.

Fixed Costs

A cost that stays the same as output changes is a fixed cost. More formally, a **fixed cost** is a cost that, *in total*, remains constant within a relevant range as the level of activity output changes. To illustrate fixed-cost behaviour, consider Reddy Heaters, a company that produces heater inserts for coffeepots. Although there are many activities performed within the plant, we will look at only one: the pipe-cutting activity. Here machines are used to cut thin metal pipe into 8-centimetre segments. Since one pipe segment is used in each heater insert, we can use the number of heaters produced as the output measure for the cutting activity.

For simplicity, assume that the cutting activity uses two inputs: (1) the cutting machine and (2) power to operate the cutting machine. Consider the cutting machines: they are leased for $60,000 per year and have the capacity to produce up to 240,000 pipe segments for heater inserts. The cost of leasing the cutting machines is a fixed cost: it stays at $60,000 total cost per year no matter how many segments are cut. This behaviour is illustrated by the following example:

	Reddy Heaters	
Lease of Machines	Number of Heater Inserts	Unit Cost
$60,000	0	N/A
60,000	60,000	$1.00
60,000	120,000	0.50
60,000	180,000	0.33
60,000	240,000	0.25

Two parts of the fixed-cost definition need further discussion: relevant range and the phrase "in total." **Relevant range** is the range over which the assumed cost/output relationship is valid. For the cutting activity, the cutting machines currently leased can produce up to 240,000 heater inserts per year. Thus the relevant range is from 0 units to 240,000 units—the output for which the total cost of leasing remains constant. Reddy Heaters pays $60,000 per year for leasing the equipment regardless of whether it produces 0, 60,000, 120,000, or 240,000 units.

We can gain additional insight into the nature of fixed costs by portraying them graphically (Exhibit 3–1). As can be seen, for the relevant range, fixed-cost behaviour is illustrated by a horizontal line. Notice that at 120,000 units produced, the leasing cost is $60,000; at 240,000 units produced, the leasing cost is still $60,000. This line visually demonstrates that this cost remains unchanged as the output varies. Total fixed costs can be represented by the following linear equation:

$$\text{Total fixed costs} = \$60,000$$

Notice that total fixed costs do not depend on the output measure (number of heater inserts). They are $60,000 no matter what the output.

While the total cost of leasing remains unchanged, the cost per segment (the unit cost) does change as more units are produced. As the table shows, within the range of 60,000 to 240,000 units, the unit cost of leasing the pipe-cutting machines decreases

Exhibit 3–1

Fixed-Cost Behaviour

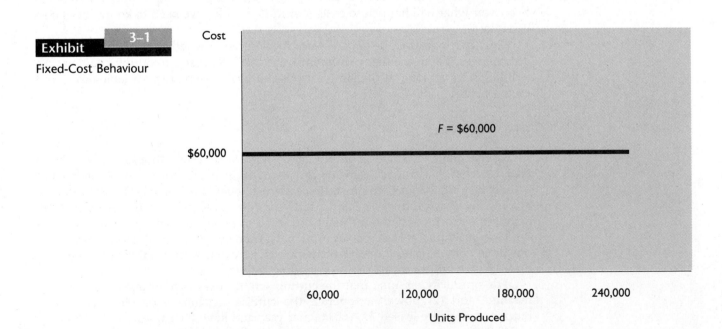

from \$1 to \$0.25. Thus, while fixed costs *in total* remain unchanged as output increases, the *unit fixed cost* changes (because the fixed costs are being spread out over more output).

A final note on fixed costs is that they can change—but that change does not depend on changes in output. For example, suppose that the company leasing the cutting machines to Reddy Heaters increases the lease payment from \$60,000 to \$65,000 per year. The cost of the machines would still be fixed, but at the new higher amount. In the graph, the entire cost curve would shift up to \$65,000. The relevant range would still be from 0 units to 240,000 units. Thus, at 120,000 units produced, the leasing cost is \$65,000; at 240,000 units produced, the leasing cost is still \$65,000. Again, the cost remains unchanged as the level of output varies.

Variable Costs

While fixed costs do not change as output varies, variable costs do change as output changes. A **variable cost** is a cost that, in total, varies in direct proportion to changes in activity output. That is, a variable cost goes up as output goes up and goes down as output goes down.

Let's expand the Reddy Heaters example to include the other resource used by the cutting activity: power. Power cost behaves differently from the cost of the cutting machines. Power is consumed only if output is produced; therefore, as more output is produced, more power is used. Assume that each time a segment is cut, the machine uses 0.1 kilowatt-hour at \$2 per kilowatt-hour. The cost of power per pipe segment is \$0.20 (\$2 × 0.1). The cost of power for various levels of activity output follows:

Reddy Heaters		
Cost of Power	Number of Heater Inserts	Unit Cost
\$ 0	0	N/A
12,000	60,000	\$0.20
24,000	120,000	0.20
36,000	180,000	0.20
48,000	240,000	0.20

As more heater inserts are produced, the total cost of power increases in direct proportion. For example, as activity output doubles from 60,000 to 120,000 units, the total cost of power doubles from \$12,000 to \$24,000. Notice also that the unit cost of power is constant.

Variable costs can also be represented by a linear equation. Here total variable costs depend on the level of the driver. This relationship can be described by the following equation:

Total variable costs = Variable cost per unit × Number of units

In the Reddy Heaters example, the cost of power is described by the following equation:

Total variable costs = \$0.20 × Number of heater inserts

Exhibit 3–2 graphically illustrates a variable cost. Notice that variable-cost behaviour is a straight line starting at the origin. At zero units processed, total variable cost is zero. However, as units produced increase, the total variable cost also increases. For example, at 120,000 units, the total variable cost is \$24,000. We can see that total cost increases in direct proportion to increases in the number of units; the rate of increase is measured by the slope of the line. Here, the slope of the line is 0.20.

Exhibit   3–2

Variable-Cost Behaviour

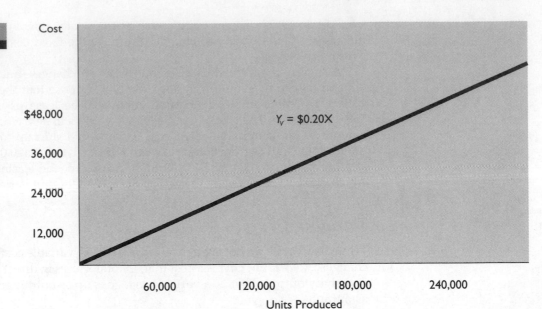

Mixed Costs

A **mixed cost** is a cost that has both a fixed and a variable component. For example, sales representatives are often paid a salary plus a commission on their sales. Suppose that Reddy Heaters has three sales representatives, each earning a salary of $10,000 per year plus a commission of $0.50 per heater insert sold. The activity is selling inserts, and the driver is units sold. If 100,000 heater inserts are sold, then the total selling cost (associated with the sales representatives) is $80,000—the sum of the fixed salary cost of $30,000 (3 × $10,000) and the variable cost of $50,000 ($0.50 × 100,000). The linear equation for a mixed cost is given by the following:

$$\text{Total cost} = \text{Fixed cost} + \text{Total variable cost}$$

For Reddy Heaters, the selling cost is represented by the following equation:

$$\text{Total cost} = \$30,000 + (\$0.50 \times \text{Units sold})$$

The following table shows the selling cost for different levels of sales activity:

	Reddy Heaters			
Inserts Sold	Fixed Cost of Selling	Variable Cost of Selling	Total Cost	Selling Cost per Unit
40,000	$30,000	$ 20,000	$ 50,000	$1.25
80,000	30,000	40,000	70,000	0.88
120,000	30,000	60,000	90,000	0.75
160,000	30,000	80,000	110,000	0.69
200,000	30,000	100,000	130,000	0.65

The graph for our mixed-cost example given in Exhibit 3–3 assumes that the relevant range is 0 units to 200,000 units. Mixed costs are represented by a line that intercepts the vertical axis (at $30,000 for this example). The intercept corresponds to the fixed-cost component, and the slope of the line gives the variable cost per unit of the cost driver (the slope is $0.50 for this example).

Classifying Costs According to Behaviour

In our discussion of fixed, variable, and mixed costs, we concentrated on the definitions and took for granted a number of factors that are important for determining

Mixed-Cost Behaviour

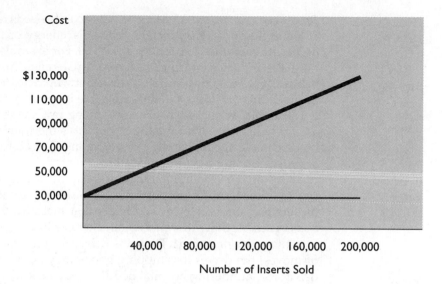

Number of Inserts Sold

whether a cost is fixed or variable. Now it is time to look more closely at the way we can classify costs according to behaviour. To assess cost behaviour, we must first consider the time horizon. Then we must identify the resources needed and output of the activity. Finally, we must measure the inputs and outputs and determine the impact of output changes on the activity cost.

Time Horizon   Determining whether a cost is fixed or variable depends on the time horizon. According to economics, in the **long run**, all costs are variable; in the **short run,** some costs may be fixed. But how long is the short run? In the Reddy Heaters example, the leasing cost of the cutting machines was fixed for a year, so a year was the length of the short run for that cost. The length of the short run may differ from one cost to another cost.

Consider a process that takes materials and moulds them into the shape of a garden hose. The output is the number of metres of hose. As the amount of hose changes, the direct materials used are relatively easy to adjust (acquiring more as the output increases and less as it decreases). For all practical purposes, the firm may treat direct materials as strictly variable, even though for the next few hours (or days) the amount of materials already purchased may be fixed.

What about direct labour? In some settings, a company may be able to hire and lay off its labour relatively quickly—in which case direct labour could be treated as a variable cost. In other cases, circumstances may prevent laying off labour for short-term drops in production. For example, there may be contracts with labour unions that make such layoffs impossible, even when there have been permanent changes in the need for labour. Only when the contract is renegotiated can the level of labour be adjusted. In this case, direct labour is a fixed cost rather than a variable cost. The same observation can be made for other forms of labour. For example, salaries of moulding production line supervisors are also difficult to adjust as the activity output varies. It could take months, or even years, to determine whether a drop in production output is permanent and whether there is therefore a need to reduce the number of supervisory jobs. Accordingly, this cost is typically seen as fixed.

The length of the short-run period depends to some extent on management judgment and on the purpose for which cost behaviour is being estimated. For example, submitting a bid on a one-time, special order may span only a month, long enough to create a bid and produce the order. Other types of decisions, such as product discontinuance or product-mix decisions, will affect a much longer period of time. In this case, the costs that must be considered are long-run variable costs, including product design and development, market development, and market penetration.

Resources and Output Measures   Every activity needs resources to accomplish the task at hand. Resources may include materials, energy or fuel, labour, and capital. These inputs are combined to produce an output. For example, if the activity is moving materials, the inputs could include crates (materials), fuel (energy), a forklift operator (labour), and forklifts (capital). The output would be moved materials. But how do we measure this output? One measure is the number of times the activity is performed. For example, suppose that we are moving raw materials from the storeroom to the assembly line. A good measure of output is the number of moves. The more moves that are made, the higher the cost of moving. Therefore, we could say that the number of moves is a good output measure for material handling. Exhibit 3-4 illustrates the relationship between inputs, activities, output, and cost behaviour.

Another term for output measure is driver. Recall from Chapter 2 that activity drivers are observable causal factors that measure the amount of resources a cost object uses. Activity drivers explain changes in activity costs by measuring changes in activity use or output. Thus, the driver for material handling may be the number of moves; the driver for shipping goods may be the number of units sold; and the driver for laundering hospital bedding may be kilograms of laundry. The choice of driver is tailored not only to the particular firm but also to the particular activity or cost being measured. Therefore, in order to understand the behaviour of costs, we must first determine the underlying activities and associated drivers that measure activity capacity and usage. The need to understand this cost-activity relationship leads us to determine an appropriate measure of activity output, or activity driver.

There are two general categories of activity drivers: production (or unit-level) drivers and nonunit-level drivers. Production drivers explain changes in costs as the number of units produced changes. Kilograms of direct materials, kilowatt-hours used to run production machinery, and direct labour hours are examples of production drivers. In other words, as kilograms of materials used, kilowatt-hours, and direct labour hours increase, output also increases.

Nonunit-Level Drivers   Nonunit-level drivers explain changes in cost as factors other than units change. For example, setups are a nonunit-level activity. Every time the factory has to stop producing one product in order to set up the production line to produce a different product, setup costs are incurred. No matter how many units are produced in the new batch, the setup cost remains the same. You have probably run into this type of activity in your personal life. Let's consider a common household production activity—making chocolate chip cookies. Suppose you decide to make two dozen cookies. First you have to set up for cookie baking by taking out a bowl, a

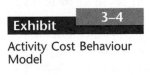

Exhibit   3-4

Activity Cost Behaviour Model

spoon, a baking sheet, and the ingredients. Another time, you might decide to make four dozen cookies. You still have to set up, and that activity will probably take the same amount of effort as it took you to set up for two dozen cookies. The point is that setting up is not related to the number of units (cookies). Instead, it is a nonunit-level activity. Other examples of nonunit-level activities include amortization on the factory, the salary of the factory manager, and the cost of running the purchasing department.

In a functional-based costing system, cost behaviour is assumed to be described by unit-level drivers only. In an activity-based system, both unit-level and nonunit-level drivers are used. Thus the ABC system produces a much richer view of cost behaviour than a functional-based system.

ACTIVITIES, RESOURCE USAGE, AND COST BEHAVIOUR

Objective 2

Explain the role of the resource usage model in understanding cost behaviour.

Short-run costs often do not adequately reflect all the costs necessary to design, produce, market, distribute, and support a product. Recently, there have been some new insights into the nature of long-run and short-run cost behaviour.[1] These insights relate to activities and the resources needed to perform them.

Capacity is simply the actual or potential ability to do something. So when we talk about capacity for an activity, we are describing the amount of the activity the company can perform. How much capacity is needed depends on the level of performance. Usually, we can assume that the capacity needed corresponds to the level where the activity is performed efficiently. This efficient level of activity performance is called **practical capacity**. On occasion there is excess capacity. To see how this happens and how it affects cost behaviour, we need to look at flexible and committed resources.

Flexible Resources

It would be nice if a company could purchase only those resources it needed and could purchase them precisely at the time they were needed. Sometimes that happens. For example, direct materials are frequently purchased at the time and in the amount needed. This kind of a resource is called a *flexible resource*. **Flexible resources** are supplied as needed and used; they are acquired from outside sources, where the terms of acquisition do not require any long-term commitment for any particular amount of the resource. Thus, the company is free to buy only the amount needed. As a result, the quantity of the resource supplied equals the quantity required for production. Materials and energy are examples. There is no unused capacity for this category of resources, since the amount of the resource used just equals the amount acquired.

Since the cost of the resources supplied as needed equals the cost of the resources used, the total cost of the resources increases as the amount of the activity increases (the demand for the resource). So the cost of flexible resources is a variable cost.

Committed Resources

Other resources must be purchased before they are needed. A factory building is a good example. The building must be planned and built before production takes place. **Committed resources** are resources that are supplied in advance of usage; they are acquired by the use of either explicit or implicit contract to obtain a given quantity of resource, regardless of whether the amount of resource available is fully used or not. Committed resources may have unused capacity, since more may be available than are actually used.

---

1. The concepts presented in the remainder of this section are based on Alfred M. King, "The Current Status of Activity-Based Costing: An Interview with Robin Cooper and Robert S. Kaplan," *Management Accounting* (September 1991): 22–26; Robin Cooper and Robert S. Kaplan, "Activity-Based Systems: Measuring the Costs of Resource Usage," *Accounting Horizons* (September 1992): 1–13; and Robert S. Kaplan and Anthony A. Atkinson, *Advanced Management Accounting* (3rd ed.), Prentice-Hall, 1998.

Let's look further at committed resources. Many resources are acquired to be used for particular time periods, and before the actual demands for the resource are realized. For example, organizations acquire many multiperiod service capacities by paying cash up front or by entering into an explicit contract that requires periodic cash payments. Buying or leasing buildings and equipment is an example of this form of advance resource acquisition. The annual expense associated with the multiperiod category is independent of actual usage; thus, these costs can be defined as **committed fixed costs** and they provide long-term activity capacity.

A second important example of committed resources concerns organizations that acquire resources in advance through implicit contracts, usually with their salaried and hourly employees. The implicit understanding is that the organization will maintain employment levels even though there may be temporary downturns in the quantity of activity used. As a result, the cost associated with this category of resources is independent of the quantity used—at least in the short run. Thus, in the short run, the amount of the resource cost remains unchanged even though the quantity used may vary, and this resource category can be treated (cautiously) as a fixed cost. We may call these short-term committed resources **discretionary fixed costs.** They are costs incurred for the acquisition of short-term activity capacity.

An example of implicit contracting is hiring three receiving clerks, for $90,000, who can supply the capacity of processing 9,000 receiving orders ("receiving orders" is the driver used to measure the receiving activity's capacity and usage).[2] Certainly, none of the three clerks would expect to be laid off if only 6,000 orders were actually processed—unless, of course, the downturn in demand is viewed as permanent. This implicit contracting raises ethical issues. Many companies today are turning to contingent employment to handle variation in demand for labour services. A key reason for the increase in contingent employment includes "buffering core workers against job loss." Apparently, many companies attempt to shield long-time workers from market fluctuations.[3] Suppose that the drop is permanent. In this case, we have an activity with too much capacity; until we reduce the capacity, resource spending will not be reduced. Thus, resource spending changes lag changes in permanent activity output demands.

Step-Cost Behaviour

In our discussion of cost behaviour, we have assumed that the cost function is continuous. In reality, some cost functions may be discontinuous, as shown in Exhibit 3–5. This type of cost function is known as a step function. A **step cost** displays a constant level of cost for a range of output and then jumps to a higher level of cost at some point, where it remains for a similar range of output. In Exhibit 3–5, the cost is $100 as long as the output is between 0 and 10 units. If the output is between 10 and 20 units, the cost jumps to $200.

Items that display step-cost behaviour must be purchased in chunks. The width of the step defines the range of activity usage for which that amount of the resource must be acquired. The width of the step in Exhibit 3–5 is 10 units of output. If the width of the step is narrow, as in Exhibit 3–5, the cost of the resource changes in response to fairly small changes in usage. Some step costs display narrow steps. An example of a cost with narrow steps is copier paper. The paper is not purchased sheet by sheet. Instead, it is purchased in boxes of 10 reams (5,000 sheets) each. A typical company would use many boxes a year, so the step is narrow. If the width of the step is narrow, we can approximate these costs with a strictly variable-cost assumption.

2.   Receiving refers to the activities involved in bringing purchased materials into the plant. The activities may include inspecting, unpacking, creating a receiving order to match to the invoice, and moving the materials to the storeroom.

3.   "Contingent Employment on the Rise," *Deloitte & Touche Review* (4 September 1995): 1–2.

Activity Output (units)

Other types of step costs have fairly wide steps. In reality, many so-called fixed costs are probably best described by a step-cost function. Many committed resources, particularly those that involve implicit contracting, follow a step-cost function. Suppose, for example, that a company hires three sustaining engineers; these are engineers responsible for redesigning existing products to meet customer requirements. Each engineer is paid a salary of $50,000 per year and can process 2,500 engineering change orders per year. The company has acquired the capacity to process 7,500 (3 × 2,500) change orders per year at a total cost of $150,000 (3 × $50,000). The nature of the resource requires that the capacity be acquired in chunks (one engineer hired at a time). The cost function for this example is displayed in Exhibit 3–6. Notice that the width of the steps is 2,500 units—a much wider step than the cost function displayed in Exhibit 3–5.

Activity Usage: Number of Engineering Change Orders

Step costs with wide steps are assigned to the fixed-cost category. Most of these costs are fixed over the normal operating range of a firm. If that range is 5,000 to 7,500 change orders (as shown in Exhibit 3–6), then the firm will spend $150,000 on engineering resources. Only if the firm wants to increase its capacity for engineering above the 7,500-order level will it increase its spending on engineers.

Frequently, there is excess capacity for activities that are characterized by this type of step behaviour. For example, during the year the company may not actually process 7,500 change orders: that is, all of the available change order-processing capacity may not be used. Assume that 6,000 change orders were processed during the year. We can see that 80 percent (6,000/7,500) of the engineering capacity is actually being used. The engineering department has 20 percent unused or excess capacity. The cost of this unused capacity is $30,000 (0.20 × $150,000). Note that the cost of unused activity occurs because the resource (engineering redesign) must be acquired in lumpy (whole) amounts. Even if the company had anticipated the need for only 6,000 change orders, it would have been difficult to hire the equivalent of 2.4 engineers (6,000/2,500).

The example illustrates that when resources are acquired in advance, there may be a difference between the amount purchased and the amount actually used. This can occur only for activities that require committed resources, with costs that display a fixed-cost behaviour. To show this, let's expand our engineering example to include both flexible and committed resources. Recall that there are three engineers, each paid $50,000 and each capable of processing 2,500 change orders. Assume that $90,000 was spent on supplies for the engineering activity and that these supplies are a flexible resource. What is the total cost of one change order?

The cost of a single change order is a combination of its fixed cost (the committed resource—engineering) and its variable cost (the flexible resource—supplies). To calculate the fixed cost per unit, we need to calculate the fixed activity rate. The **fixed activity rate** is simply the total committed cost divided by the *total capacity*.

Fixed engineering rate = $150,000/7,500 = $20 per change order

Of course, the **variable activity rate** is the total cost of the flexible resources divided by the *capacity used*.

Variable engineering rate = $90,000/6,000 = $15 per change order

Therefore, the total cost of one change order is $35. Notice the difference between the 7,500 change orders used to compute the fixed activity rate and the 6,000 orders used to compute the variable activity rate. Because the fixed rate is based on committed resources, we use the capacity available. After all, the three engineers could have processed as many as 7,500 orders. For the variable rate, we use the actual capacity used. This is because the flexible resources are purchased as necessary, so that the $90,000 of supplies relate to the 6,000 change orders actually processed.

Typically, the functional-based management accounting system provides information only about the cost of the resources purchased. An activity-based management accounting system, on the other hand, tells us how much of the activity is used and the cost of its usage. The relationship between resources supplied and resources used is expressed by the following equation:

Resources available = Resources used + Unused capacity

This equation can be expressed in both physical and financial terms. For the engineering order example, the relationship takes the following form when expressed in physical terms:

Available orders = Orders used + Orders unused
7,500 orders = 6,000 orders + 1,500 orders

When the relationship is expressed in financial terms, we simply attach dollar amounts. For the engineering example, this takes the following form:

Cost of orders supplied = Cost of orders used + Cost of unused orders
$240,000 = $210,000 + $30,000

The cost of orders used is $210,000 [($20 + $15) × 6,000]. Of course, the $240,000 is equal to the $150,000 spent on engineers and the $90,000 spent on supplies.

Why is this formulation important? It is important because it gives managers crucial information about their ability to expand or contract production. The $30,000 of excess engineering capacity means that, for example, a new product could be introduced without increasing current spending on engineering, provided that the new product uses no more than 1,500 orders.

Implications for Control and Decision Making

The activity-based model just described can improve both managerial control and decision making. Operational control systems encourage managers to pay more attention to controlling resource use and spending. For example, a well-designed operational control system allows managers to assess the changes in resource demands that occur from new product-mix decisions. Adding new, customized products may increase the demands for various overhead activities. If sufficient unused activity capacity does not exist, then resource spending must increase. Similarly, if activity management brings about excess capacity (by finding ways to reduce resource usage), managers must carefully consider what to do with the excess capacity. Eliminating the excess capacity may decrease resource spending and thus improve overall profits. Alternatively, the excess capacity could be used to increase the number and type of products, thereby increasing revenues without increasing resource spending. How resource usage and spending are affected is more fully explored in Chapter 15.

The activity-based resource usage model also allows managers to calculate the changes in resource supply and demand resulting from implementing such decisions as whether to make or buy a part, to accept or reject special orders, and to keep or drop product lines. Additionally, the model increases the power of a number of traditional management accounting decision-making models. The impact on decision making is explored in the decision-making chapters found in Part 2. Most of the decision-making models in those chapters depend heavily on knowledge of cost behaviour.

METHODS FOR SEPARATING MIXED COSTS INTO FIXED AND VARIABLE COMPONENTS

Objective 3

Separate mixed costs into their fixed and variable components using the high–low method, the scatterplot method, and the method of least squares.

While some costs can be fairly easily classified as strictly variable, fixed, or step-fixed, others fall into the mixed-cost category. It is necessary to separate such costs into fixed and variable components.

Often the only information available is the total cost of an activity and a measure of activity usage. For example, the accounting system will usually record both the total cost of the maintenance activity for a given period and the number of maintenance hours provided during that period. The accounting records do not reveal how much of the total maintenance cost represents a fixed charge and how much represents a variable charge. Often the total cost is simply recorded with no attempt to segregate the fixed and variable costs.

Since accounting records may reveal only the total cost and the associated activity usage of a mixed-cost item, it is necessary to separate the total cost into its fixed and variable components. Only through a formal effort to separate costs can all costs be classified into the appropriate cost behaviour categories.

There are three widely used methods of separating a mixed cost into its fixed and variable components: the high–low method, the scatterplot method, and the method of least squares. Each method requires us to make the simplifying assumption of a linear cost relationship. Therefore, before we examine each of these methods more closely, let's review the concept of linearity.

Linearity Assumption

The definition of variable cost assumes a linear relationship between the cost of an activity and its associated driver. For example, suppose that Star Company produces personal computers. Each personal computer uses one floppy disk drive, each of which costs $40. The total variable cost of disk drives can be expressed as:

$$\text{Total variable cost} = \$40 \times \text{Units produced}$$

If 100 computers are produced, the total cost of floppy drives is $4,000 ($40 × 100). If 200 computers are produced, the total cost is $8,000 ($40 × 200). As production doubles, the cost of the drives doubles. In other words, cost increases in direct proportion to the number of units produced. The linear relationship for the computer example is portrayed in Exhibit 3–7. How reasonable is this assumption that costs are linear? Do variable activity costs really increase in direct proportion to increases in the level of the activity driver? If not, then how closely does this assumed linear cost function approximate the underlying cost function?

Economists usually argue that variable costs increase at a decreasing rate up to a certain volume, at which point they increase at an increasing rate. This type of nonlinear behaviour is displayed in Exhibit 3–8. Here variable costs increase as the num-

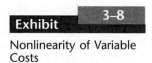

Exhibit 3–7

Linearity of Variable Costs

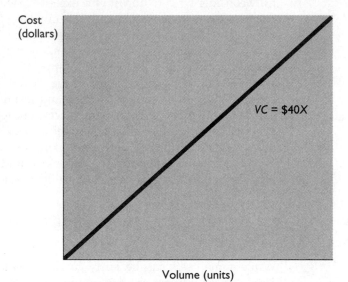

Cost (dollars)

VC = $40X

Volume (units)

Exhibit 3–8

Nonlinearity of Variable Costs

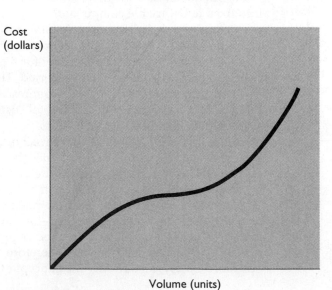

Cost (dollars)

Volume (units)

ber of units increases, but not in direct proportion. For example, a power supplier that initially has ample capacity may offer prices that decrease per kilowatt-hour to encourage consumption; yet once the power plant capacity has been met, any further demands may produce higher prices to ration a now scarce input among users. What if the nonlinear view more accurately portrays reality? What do we do then? One possibility is to determine the actual cost function. But every activity could have a different cost function, and this approach could be very time consuming and expensive (if it can even be done). It is much simpler to assume a linear relationship.

If the linear relationship is assumed, then the main concern is how closely this assumption approximates the underlying cost function. Exhibit 3–9 gives us some idea of the consequences of assuming a linear cost function. Recall that the relevant range is the range of activity output for which the assumed cost relationships are valid. Here validity refers to how closely the linear cost function approximates the underlying cost function. Note that for units outside the relevant range, the approximation appears to break down.

The equation for a linear (or straight-line) cost function is as follows:

$$\text{Total cost} = \text{Fixed cost} + (\text{Variable rate} \times \text{Output})$$

This equation is a **cost formula.** Let's take a closer look at each term in the cost formula. A **dependent variable** is a variable whose value depends on the value of another variable. Total cost is the dependent variable: it is the cost we are trying to predict. Its value depends on the values of the parameters and variable on the right-hand side of the equation. An **independent variable** is a variable that measures output and explains changes in the cost. It is an activity driver. The choice of an independent variable is related to its economic plausibility. That is, the manager will attempt to find an independent variable that causes or is closely associated with the dependent variable. The **intercept parameter** corresponds to the fixed cost. Graphically, the intercept parameter is the point at which the mixed-cost line intercepts the cost (vertical) axis (see Exhibit 3–10). The **slope parameter** corresponds to the variable cost per unit of activity. Graphically, this represents the slope of the mixed-cost line.

Since accounting records reveal only the total cost and the amount of activity output, those values must be used to estimate the intercept and slope parameters (the fixed cost and the variable rate). With estimates of the fixed cost and the variable rate, the behaviour of the mixed cost can be predicted as activity usage changes.

Exhibit 3–9

Linear Approximation

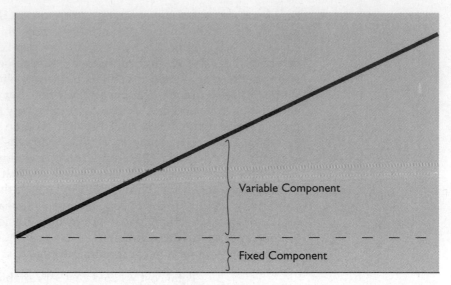

Three methods will be described for estimating the fixed cost and the variable rate: the high–low method, the scatterplot method, and the method of least squares.[4] The same data will be used to illustrate each method so that comparisons can be made among them. The data have been accumulated for the setup activity of Larson Company's Moncton, New Brunswick, plant. The plant manager believes that setup hours is a good driver for the activity of setting up the production line. Assume that the plant's accounting records show the following setup costs and setup hours for the past five months:

Month	Setup Cost	Setup Hours
January	$1,000	100
February	1,250	200
March	2,250	300
April	2,500	400
May	3,750	500

The High–Low Method

From basic geometry, we know that two points are sufficient to determine a line. Once we know two points on a line, then we can determine its equation. Given two points, the slope and the intercept can be determined. The **high–low method** is a method of determining the equation of a straight line by specifying the two points that will be used to compute the slope and intercept parameters. Specifically, the method uses the high and low points. The *high point* is defined as the point with the highest output or activity level. The *low point* is defined as the point with the lowest output or activity level.

The equations for determining the variable rate (slope) and fixed cost (intercept) are, respectively, as follows:

Variable rate = Change in cost/Change in activity
Variable rate = (High cost – Low cost)/(High output – Low output)

and

Fixed cost = Total cost for high point – (Variable rate × High output)

4. For additional discussion of cost estimation, see Anthony A. Atkinson, *Cost Estimation in Management Accounting—Six Case Studies* (Hamilton, Ontario: Society of Management Accountants of Canada, 1987).

or

$$\text{Fixed cost} = \text{Total cost for low point} - (\text{Variable rate} \times \text{Low output})$$

Notice that the fixed-cost component can be computed using the total cost at either the high point or the low point.

For Larson, the high point is 500 setup hours at a setup cost of \$3,750, or (500, \$3,750). The low point is 100 setups at a setup cost of \$1,000, or (100, \$1,000). Once the high and low points are defined, the values of the variable rate and the fixed cost can be computed:

$$\text{Variable rate} = (\$3,750 - \$1,000)/(500 - 100) = \$2,750/400 = \$6.875$$

and

$$\text{Fixed cost} = \$3,750 - (\$6.875 \times 500) = \$312.50$$

The cost formula using the high–low method is as follows:

$$\text{Total cost} = \$312.50 + (\$6.875 \times \text{Setup hours})$$

If the number of setup hours for June is expected to be 350, this cost formula will predict a total cost of \$2,718.75, with fixed costs of \$312.50 and variable costs of \$2,406.25.

The high–low method has the advantage of objectivity. That is, any two people using the high–low method on a particular data set will arrive at the same answer. In addition, the high–low method allows a manager to get a quick fix on a cost relationship using only two data points. For example, a manager may have only two years' worth of data. Sometimes this will be enough to get a crude approximation of the cost relationship.

The high–low method is usually not as good as the other methods. Why? First, the high and low points may be *outliers*. Outliers represent atypical cost-activity relationships. If so, the cost formula computed using these two points will not represent what usually takes place. The scatterplot method can help a manager avoid this trap by selecting two points that appear to be representative of the general activity cost pattern. Second, even if these points are not outliers, other pairs of points may clearly be more representative. Again, the scatterplot method allows the choice of the more representative points.

The Scatterplot Method

The **scatterplot method** is a method of determining the equation of a line by plotting the data on a graph. The first step in applying the scatterplot method is to plot the data points so that the relationship between setup costs and activity level can be seen. This plot is referred to as a **scattergraph** and is shown in Exhibit 3–11. The vertical axis is the total setup cost, and the horizontal axis is the number of setup hours. Inspecting Exhibit 3–11 gives us increased confidence that the assumption of a linear relationship between setup costs and setup hours is reasonable for the indicated range of activity. Thus, one purpose of a scattergraph is to see whether or not the assumed linear relationship is reasonable. Additionally, inspecting the scattergraph may reveal any points that do not seem to fit the general pattern of behaviour. Upon investigation, it may be discovered that these points (the outliers) were due to some unusual occurrences. This knowledge can provide justification for their elimination from the analysis and perhaps lead to a better estimate of the underlying cost function.

A scattergraph can help provide insight concerning the relationship between cost and activity usage. In fact, a scattergraph allows one to visually fit a line to the points on the scattergraph. In doing so, the line should be chosen that appears to fit the points the best. In making that choice, a manager or cost analyst is free to use past experience with the behaviour of the cost item. Experience may provide a good intuitive sense of

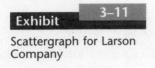

Exhibit   3–11

Scattergraph for Larson
Company

how setup costs behave; the scattergraph then becomes a useful tool for quantifying this intuition. Fitting a line to the points in this way is how the scatterplot method works. Keep in mind that the scattergraph and other statistical aids are tools that can help managers improve their judgment. Using the tools does not restrict the manager from also using judgment to alter any of the estimates produced by formal methods.

Examine Exhibit 3–11 carefully. Based only on the information contained in the graph, how would you fit a line to the points in it? Suppose that you decide that a line passing through points 1 and 3 provides the best fit. Note that the line you decide fits the points does *not* have to pass through any of the plotted points, but the line should best fit all of the points.

The variable rate can be computed in the following way. First, let point 1 be designated by (100, $1,000) and point 3 by (300, $2,250). Next, use these two points to compute the slope:

$$\text{Variable rate} = (\$2,250 - \$1,000)/(300 - 100) = \$1,250/200 = \$6.25$$

Thus, the variable cost per setup hour is $6.25. Given the variable rate, the final step is to compute the fixed-cost component. If we use point 3, the following equation results:

$$\text{Fixed cost} = \$2,250 - (\$6.25 \times 300) = \$375$$

Of course, the fixed-cost component can also be computed using point 1, which produces the same result:

$$\text{Fixed cost} = \$1,000 - (\$6.25 \times 100) = \$375$$

The fixed and variable components of setup cost have now been identified. The cost formula for the setup activity can be expressed as follows:

$$\text{Total cost} = \$375 + (\$6.25 \times \text{Setup hours})$$

With this formula, the total cost of setups for activity output between 100 and 500 can be predicted and then broken down into fixed and variable components. For example, assume that 350 setup hours are planned for June. Using the cost formula, the predicted cost is $2,562.50 [$375 + ($6.25 × 350)]. Of this total cost, $375 is fixed and $2,187.50 is variable.

The cost formula for the setup activity was obtained by fitting a line to points 1 and 3 in Exhibit 3–11. Judgment was used to select the line. Whereas one person may decide, by inspection, that the best-fitting line is the one that passes through points 1 and 3, others, using their own judgment, may decide that the line should pass through points 2 and 4—or points 1 and 5, or none of the plotted points at all.

A significant advantage of the scatterplot method is that it affords a cost analyst the opportunity to see the data. Exhibit 3–12 gives examples of cost behaviour situations that are not appropriate for the simple application of the high–low method. Graph A shows a nonlinear relationship between activity cost and activity usage. An example of such a relationship might be a volume discount given on direct materials or evidence of learning by workers (for example, as more hours are worked, the total

Exhibit **3–12**

Cost Behaviour Patterns

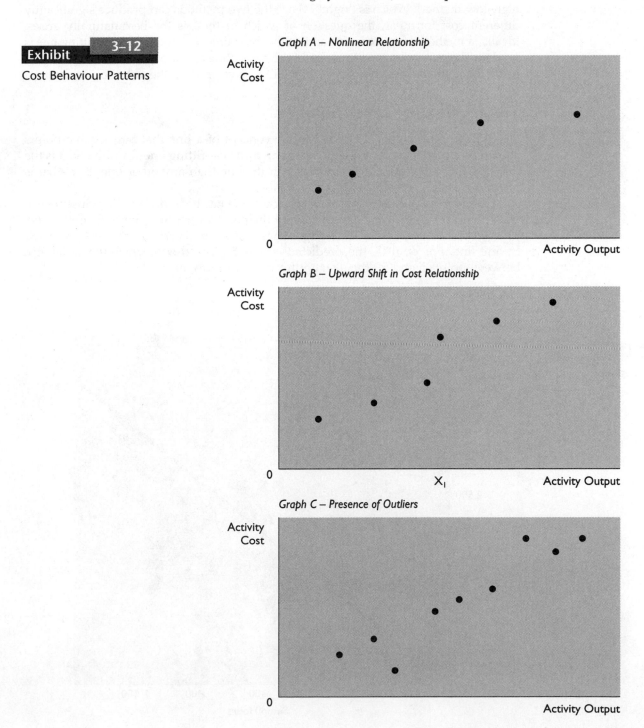

Graph A – Nonlinear Relationship

Graph B – Upward Shift in Cost Relationship

Graph C – Presence of Outliers

cost increases at a decreasing rate due to the increased efficiency of the workers). Graph B shows an upward shift in cost if more than X_1 units are made. Perhaps this could mean that an additional supervisor must be hired or a second shift run. Graph C shows outliers that are not representative of the overall cost relationship.

The scatterplot method suffers from the lack of any objective criterion for choosing the best-fitting line. The quality of the cost formula depends on the quality of the analyst's subjective judgment. The high–low method removes the subjectivity in the choice of the line. Regardless of who uses the method, the same line will result.

There is a large difference between the fixed-cost components and the variable rates from the high–low and the scatterplot methods. The predicted setup cost for 350 setup hours is $2,562.50 according to the scatterplot method and $2,718.75 according to the high–low method. Which is "right"? Since the two methods can produce significantly different cost formulas, the question of which method is the best naturally arises. Ideally, a method that is objective and, at the same time, produces the best-fitting line is needed. The method of least squares defines best-fitting and is objective in the sense that using the method for a given set of data will always produce the same cost formula.

The Method of Least Squares

Up to this point, we have alluded to the concept of a line that best fits the points shown on a scattergraph. What do we mean by a best-fitting line? Intuitively, it is the line in which the data points are closer to the line than any other line. But what is meant by closer?

Consider Exhibit 3–13. Here an arbitrary line has been drawn. The closeness of each point to the line can be measured by the point's vertical distance from the line. This vertical distance is the difference between the actual cost and the cost predicted by the line. For point 5, the predicted cost is 5*. The **deviation** is the difference between points 5 and 5* (the distance from the point to the line).

Exhibit 3–13

Line Deviations

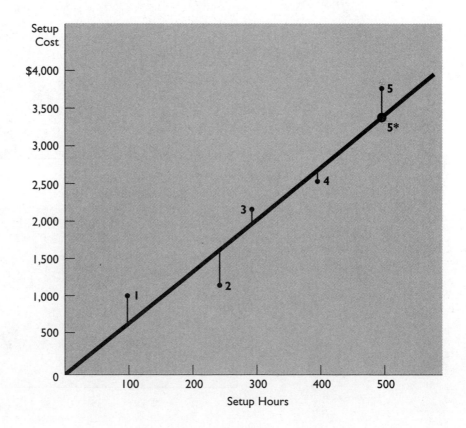

The vertical distance measures the closeness of a single point to the line, but we need a measure of closeness of all points to the line. One possibility is to measure the deviation of all points from the line and then to add all the single deviation measures to obtain an overall measure. However, this overall measure may be misleading. For example, the sum of small positive deviations could result in an overall measure greater than the sum of large positive deviations and large negative deviations, because of the cancelling effect of positive and negative numbers. To correct for this problem, the method of least squares first squares each single deviation and then sums these squared deviations as the overall measure of closeness. Squaring the deviations results in only positive numbers, thus avoiding the cancellation problem caused by a mix of positive and negative numbers.

Since the measure of closeness is the sum of the squared deviations of the points from the line, the smaller the measure, the better the line fits the points. For example, the scatterplot method line has a closeness measure of 343,750. A similar calculation produces a closeness measure of 523,438 for the high–low line. Thus, the scatterplot line fits the points better than the high–low line. This outcome supports our earlier claim that the use of judgment in the scatterplot method is superior to the high–low method.

In principle, comparing closeness measures can produce a ranking of all lines from best to worst. The line that fits the points better than any other line is called the **best-fitting line.** It is the line with the smallest (least) sum of squared deviations. The **method of least squares** identifies the best-fitting line. You can learn the manual calculations for the least-squares formula from a statistics textbook. For our purposes, we can use a computer regression program to do the calculations.

Using the Regression Programs

Computing the regression formula manually is tedious, even with only five data points. As the number of data points increases, manual computation becomes impractical. Fortunately, spreadsheet packages such as Lotus 1-2-3®, Quattro Pro®, and Microsoft Excel® have regression routines that will perform the computations.[5] All you need to do is input the data points. The spreadsheet regression programs supply more than the estimates of the coefficients. They also provide information that can be used to assess the reliability of the cost equation, a feature that is not available for the scatterplot and high–low methods.

The first step in using the computer to calculate regression coefficients is to enter the data. Exhibit 3–14 shows the computer screen you would see if you entered the Larson Company data on setups into a spreadsheet. It is a good idea to label your variables as is done here. The next step is to run the regression. This step will vary depending on the program you are using, but in Excel and Quattro Pro, the regression routine is located under the "tools" menu.

Exhibit 3–14

Spreadsheet Data for Larson Company

Month	Setup Costs	Setup Hours
Jan	1,000	100
Feb	1,250	200
Mar	2,250	300
Apr	2,500	400
May	3,750	500

5. Quattro Pro is a registered trademark of Novell, Inc. Excel is a registered trademark of Microsoft Corporation. Any reference to Quattro Pro or Excel refers to this footnote.

Exhibit   3–15

Regression Output for
Larson Company

	A	B	C	D
1		Regression Output:		
2	Constant			125
3	Std Err of Y Est			299.304749934466
4	R Squared			0.9443005181347I5
5	No. of Observation			5
6	Degrees of Freedom			3
7				
8	X Coefficient(s)		6.75	
9	Std Err of Coef.		0.9464847243	
10				

Sheet1 / Sheet2 / Sheet3 /

When the "regression" screen pops up, you can tell the program where the dependent and independent variables are located. Then, you need to tell the program where to place the regression output. In less than a blink of an eye, the regression output is complete. The regression output for the setup costs is shown in Exhibit 3–15.

Let's look at the information in Exhibit 3–15. First, let's locate the fixed cost and variable rate coefficients. These are highlighted in the exhibit. The fixed cost is the constant—in this case, 125. The variable rate is the X coefficient—here, 6.75. Now we can construct the setup cost formula for the method of least squares:

$$\text{Setup costs} = \$125 + (\$6.75 \times \text{Setup hours})$$

We can use this formula to predict setup costs for future months, as we did with the formulas for the high–low and scatterplot methods.

Since the regression cost formula is the best-fitting line, it should produce better predictions of setup costs. For 350 setup hours, the setup cost predicted by the least-squares line is $2,487.50 [$125 + ($6.75 × 350)], with a fixed component of $125 and a variable component of $2,362.50. Using this prediction as a standard, the scatterplot line most closely approximates the least-squares line.

RELIABILITY OF COST FORMULAS

Objective 4

Evaluate the reliability of a cost equation.

While the computer output in Exhibit 3–15 can give the fixed- and variable-cost coefficients, its major usefulness is its ability to provide information about how reliable the estimated cost formula is. This feature is not provided by either the scatterplot method or the high–low method. We will use the printout in Exhibit 3–15 as the basis for discussing a statistical assessment of a cost formula's reliability: *goodness of fit*. Although the printout provides other useful information for assessing statistical reliability, we will just look at **goodness of fit**. This measure is important because the method of least squares identifies the best-fitting line, but it does not reveal how good the fit is. The best-fitting line may not be a good-fitting line. It may perform miserably when it comes to predicting costs.

R^2—The Coefficient of Determination

Initially, we assume that a single activity driver explains changes (or variability) in activity cost. Our experience with the Larson Company example suggests that setup hours can explain changes in setup costs. The scattergraph shown in Exhibit 3–11 confirms this belief because it reveals that setup cost and setup hours seem to move together. Thus, it seems reasonable that setup hours would explain much of the variability in setup costs. We can determine statistically just how much variability is explained by looking at the **coefficient of determination** or R^2. R^2 is the percentage of variability in the dependent variable explained by an independent variable. This percentage is a goodness-of-fit measure. The higher the percentage of cost variability explained, the better the fit. Since the coefficient is the percentage of variability explained, it always has a value between 0 and 1.0. In the printout in Exhibit 3–15, the coefficient of determination is labelled "R Squared" and highlighted. The value given is 0.9443, which means that about 94 percent of the variability in setup cost is explained by the number of setup hours. This result tells us that the least-squares line is a good-fitting line.

There is no cutoff point for a good versus a bad coefficient of determination. Clearly, the closer R^2 is to 1, the better. However, is 89 percent good enough? How about 73 percent? Or even 46 percent? The answer is that it depends. If your cost equation yields a coefficient of determination of 75 percent, you know that your independent variable explains three-fourths of the variability in cost. You also know that some other factor or combination of factors explains the remaining one-fourth. Depending on your tolerance for error, you may want to improve the equation by trying different independent variables (for example, number of setups rather than setup hours) or by trying multiple regression (which is explained in a later section of this chapter).

Coefficient of Correlation

A related measure of goodness of fit is the **coefficient of correlation**, which is the square root of the coefficient of determination. Since square roots can be negative, the value of the coefficient of correlation can range between –1 and +1. If the coefficient of correlation is positive, then the two variables (in this example, setup cost and setup hours) move together in the same direction, and positive correlation exists. Perfect positive correlation would yield a value of 1.00 for the coefficient of correlation. If, on the other hand, the coefficient of correlation is negative, then the two variables move in a predictable fashion but in opposite directions. Perfect negative correlation would yield a coefficient of correlation of –1.00. A coefficient of correlation value close to 0 indicates no correlation. That is, knowledge of the movement of one variable gives us no clue as to the movement of the other variable. Exhibit 3–16 illustrates the concept of correlation. For the Larson Company example, the coefficient of correlation (r) is simply the square root of R^2 or 0.97.

The square root is positive because the correlation between setup hours and setup cost is positive. In other words, as the number of setup hours increases, the total setup cost also increases. This positive correlation is reflected by a positive sign on the X coefficient shown in Exhibit 3–15. If cost decreases as activity usage increases, then the coefficient of correlation (and the value of the X coefficient) is negative. The sign of the X coefficient reveals the sign of the coefficient of correlation. In the Larson Company example, the very high positive correlation between setup cost and setup hours indicates that setup hours is a good choice for a cost driver.

Exhibit	3–16

Correlation Illustrated

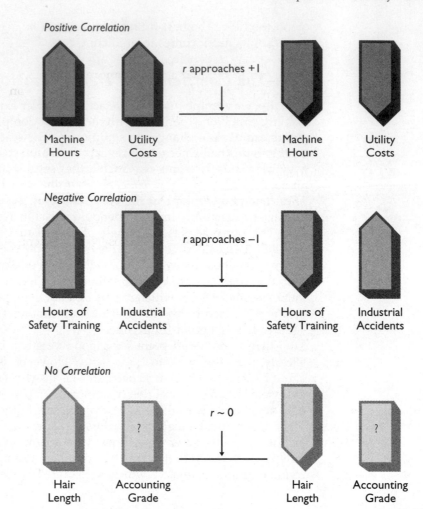

MULTIPLE REGRESSION

Objective 5

Explain the role of multiple regression in assessing cost behaviour.

Sometimes obtaining the best cost equation is more complicated than simply identifying one activity driver and regressing activity cost on this driver. The outcome may not produce a cost equation that is good enough for managerial use. In the Larson Company example, 94 percent of the variability in setup cost was explained by changes in setup hours, and that is an excellent result. In other cases, however, a single independent variable may explain much less of the variability in the dependent variable. Then, one possible solution is to search for additional explanatory variables.

In the case of two or more explanatory variables, the linear equation is expanded to include the additional variables:

$$\text{Total cost} = b_0 + b_1 X_1 + b_2 X_2 + \ldots$$

where

b_0 is the fixed cost (intercept)
b_1 is the variable rate (slope) for the first independent variable
X_1 is the first independent variable
b_2 is the variable rate (slope) for the second independent variable
X_2 is the second independent variable

and so on.

When there are two or more explanatory variables, neither the high–low method nor the scatterplot methods can be used. Fortunately, the extension of the method of least squares is straightforward. Whenever least squares is used to fit an equation involving two or more explanatory variables, the method is called **multiple regression.** Any practical application of multiple regression requires the use of a computer program.

For example, suppose that the accountant for a factory that produces laser printers in Scarborough, Ontario, is analyzing factory utilities cost. The accountant knows that electricity is used to power the machines and suspects that machine hours would be a good cost driver. Electricity is also used to power the air conditioning; for this reason, the utilities cost rises significantly in the summer. Thus, utilities cost is explained by more than one variable and needs a more complex cost equation:

$$\text{Utilities cost} = \text{Fixed cost} + (b_1 \times \text{Machine hours}) + (b_2 \times \text{Summer})$$

In this equation, machine hours is a continuous variable that takes on values much like those for setup hours in the Larson Company example. "Summer" is a dichotomous or dummy variable; it takes on the values zero and one. That is, a particular month either is or is not in the summer. In Scarborough, summer lasts from May through September. Exhibit 3–17 illustrates 12 months of data for the utilities regression.

Let's take a closer look at the data in Exhibit 3–17. In January, there were 1,340 machine hours, and utilities cost $1,688. January is not a summer month—hence, the variable "summer" takes the value 0. In June, there were 1,432 machine hours, it is a summer month (so "summer" takes the value 1), and total utilities cost was $2,304. The other 10 months of data can be interpreted in the same manner.

Exhibit 3–17

Data for Scarborough Factory Utilities Cost Regression

Month	Mhrs	Summer	Utilities Cost
Jan	1340	0	$1,688
Feb	1298	0	1636
Mar	1376	0	1734
April	1405	0	1770
May	1500	1	2390
June	1432	1	2304
July	1322	1	2166
August	1416	1	2284
Sept	1370	1	1730
Oct	1580	0	1991
Nov	1460	0	1840
Dec	1455	0	1833

Exhibit   3–18

Exhibit   3–18

Multiple Regression
Results for Scarborough
Factory Utilities Cost

	A	B	C	D
	Multiple Regression Results for Scarborough Factory Utilities Cost.xls			
1	Constant		243.1114997159	
2	Std Err of Y Est		55.5082829356447	
3	R Squared		0.96717927255452	
4	No. of Observation		12	
5	Degrees of Freedom		9	
6				
7	X Coefficient(s)	1.09715750519456	510.49073361447	
8	Std Err of Coef.	0.2102263321 15593	32.5489645352191	

When multiple regression is run on these data, the results in Exhibit 3–18 are obtained. The results give rise to the following equation:

Utilities cost = \$243.11 + (\$1.097 × Machine hours) + (\$510.49 × Summer)

This equation can be used to predict the cost of utilities for future months. Suppose that the accountant wants to predict the cost of utilities for the following April and anticipates 1,350 machine hours. The predicted or budgeted cost would be \$1,724 [\$243.11 + (1.097 × 1,350) + (\$510.49 × 0)]. If, instead, the cost of utilities for May were to be predicted based on 1,350 machine hours, the predicted or budgeted cost would be \$2,235 [\$243.11 + (1.097 × 1,350) + (\$510.49 × 1)].

Notice that R^2 is 0.967, or 96.7 percent. You might try running the regression using just machine hours as the independent variable. The R^2 for that regression is much lower, clearly indicating the value of adding the second driver.

MANAGERIAL JUDGMENT

Objective 6

Describe the use of
managerial judgment
in determining cost
behaviour.

Managerial judgment is critically important in determining cost behaviour, and is by far the most widely used method in practice.[6] Many managers simply use their experience and past observation of cost relationships to determine fixed and variable costs. This method, however, may take a number of forms. Some managers simply assign particular activity costs to the fixed category and others to the variable category, ignoring the possibility of mixed costs. Thus, a chemical firm may regard materials and utilities as strictly variable with respect to kilograms of chemical produced and all other costs as fixed. Even labour, a traditional and common example of a unit-based variable cost, may be fixed for this firm. The appeal of this method is simplicity. Before opting for this course, however, management would do well to make sure that each cost is predominantly fixed or variable and that the decisions being made are not highly sensitive to errors in classifying costs. To illustrate the use of judgment in assessing cost behaviour, consider Elgin Sweeper Company, a leading manufacturer of motorized street sweepers. Using production volume as the cost

---

6. Maryanne M. Mowen, *Accounting for Costs as Fixed and Variable* (Montvale, N.J.: National Association of Accountants, 1986), 19–20. This practice of using managerial judgment to assign costs to cost behaviour categories has continued in more advanced cost accounting systems.

driver, Elgin revised its chart of accounts to organize costs into fixed and variable components. Elgin's accountants used their knowledge of the company to assign costs, using a decision rule that categorized a cost as fixed if it was fixed 75 percent of the time, and variable if it was variable 75 percent of the time.[7]

Management may instead identify mixed costs and divide these costs into fixed and variable components by deciding just what the fixed and variable parts are—that is, using experience to say that a certain amount of a cost is fixed and that the rest must therefore be variable. For example, a factory may put lease payments for a photocopier into one account and the cost of paper and toner into another. The result is that it is easy to group the lease cost with other fixed costs and to treat the variable costs separately. The variable component can then be computed using one or more cost/volume data points. This approach has the advantage of accounting for mixed costs but is subject to a similar type of error as the strict fixed/variable dichotomy. That is, management may be wrong in its assessment.

Finally, management may use experience and judgment to refine statistical estimation results. The experienced manager might "eyeball" the data and throw out several points as being highly unusual or might revise the estimation results to take into account projected changes in cost structure or technology. Recently, Martin Color-Fi, a recycler, found that it was paying top prices for discarded plastics. Demand for recyclable plastics has mushroomed, and prices have tripled in the space of a year. The reason for the growth in demand? A run-up in the price of cotton due to poor crops in China, Pakistan, and India. The cotton shortage led Asian mills to substitute polyester and other synthetics. These synthetic fabrics are made from PET (the polyethylene-terephthalate found in recyclable plastic bottles). Companies like Martin must look forward, not back, to predict the impact of demand for substitute products on prices and profits.[8] Statistical techniques are highly accurate in depicting the past, but they cannot foresee the future—which is, of course, what management really wants.

The advantage of using managerial judgment to separate fixed and variable costs is its simplicity. In situations in which the manager has a deep understanding of the firm and its cost patterns, this method can give good results. However, if the manager does not have good judgment, errors will occur. Therefore, it is important to consider the experience of the manager, the potential for error, and the effect that error could have on related decisions.

SUMMARY OF LEARNING OBJECTIVES

1. Define and describe cost behaviour for fixed, variable, and mixed costs.

Cost behaviour is the way in which a cost changes in relation to changes in activity usage. The time horizon is important in determining cost behaviour because costs can change from fixed to variable depending on whether the decision takes place over the short run or the long run. Variable costs are those that change in total as activity usage changes. Usually, we assume that variable costs increase in direct proportion to increases in activity usage. Fixed costs are those that do not change in total as activity usage changes. Mixed costs have both a variable and a fixed component.

2. Explain the role of the resource usage model in understanding cost behaviour

The resource usage model adds to our understanding of cost behaviour. Resources acquired in advance of usage are categorized as committed resources. Resources acquired as used and needed are flexible resources. Some costs, especially discretionary fixed

7.   John P. Callan, Wesley N. Tredup, Randy S. Wissinger, "Elgin Sweeper Company's Journey Toward Cost Management," *Management Accounting* (July 1991): 24–27.

8.   Stephanie Anderson Forrest, "There's Gold in Those Hills of Soda Bottles," *Business Week*, 11 September 1995, 48.

costs, tend to follow a step-cost function. These resources are acquired in lumpy amounts. If the width of the step is sufficiently large, then the costs are viewed as fixed; otherwise, they are approximated by a variable-cost function.

3. Separate mixed costs into their fixed and variable components using the high–low method, the scatterplot method, and the method of least squares.
There are three formal methods of decomposing mixed costs: the high–low method, the scatterplot method, and the method of least squares. In the high–low method, the two points chosen from the scattergraph are the high and the low points with respect to activity level. These two points are then used to compute the intercept and the slope of the line on which they lie. The high–low method is objective and easy. However, if either the high point or the low point is not representative of the true cost relationship, the relationship will be estimated incorrectly.

The scatterplot method involves inspecting a scattergraph (a plot showing total mixed cost at various activity levels) and selecting two points that seem to best represent the relationship between cost and activity. Since two points determine a line, the two selected points can be used to determine the intercept and the slope of the line on which they lie. The intercept gives an estimate of the fixed-cost component, and the slope an estimate of the variable cost per unit of activity. The scatterplot method is a good way to identify nonlinearity, the presence of outliers, and the presence of a shift in the cost relationship. Its disadvantage is that it is subjective.

The method of least squares uses all of the data points (except outliers) on the scattergraph and produces a line that best fits all of the points. The line is best fitting in the sense that it is closest to all the points as measured by the sum of the squared deviations of the points from the line. The method of least squares produces the line that best fits the data points and is therefore recommended over the high–low and scatterplot methods.

4. Evaluate the reliability of a cost equation.
The least-squares method has the advantage of offering methods of assessing the reliability of cost equations. The coefficient of determination allows an analyst to compute the amount of cost variability explained by a particular cost driver. The correlation coefficient also measures the strength of the association but has the additional advantage of indicating the direction of the relationship.

5. Explain the role of multiple regression in assessing cost behaviour.
One driver may not be sufficient in explaining enough of the variability in activity cost behaviour. In such a case, adding additional variables to the equation may increase its ability to predict activity costs as well as provide insights on how activity costs can be managed.

6. Describe the use of managerial judgment in determining cost behaviour.
Managerial judgment can be used alone or in conjunction with the high–low, scatterplot, or least-squares method. Managers use their experience and knowledge of cost and activity-level relationships to identify outliers, understand structural shifts, and adjust parameters due to anticipated changing conditions.

KEY TERMS

REVIEW PROBLEMS

I. RESOURCE USAGE AND COST BEHAVIOUR

Kaylin Manufacturing Company has three accounts payable clerks who are responsible for processing purchase invoices. Each clerk is paid a salary of $30,000 and is capable of processing 5,000 invoices per year when working efficiently. In addition to the salaries, Kaylin spends $9,000 per year for forms, postage, cheques, and so on (assuming that 15,000 invoices are processed). During the past year, 12,500 invoices were processed.

Required:

1. Calculate the activity rate for the purchase order activity. Break the activity into fixed and variable components.
2. Compute the total activity availability and break this into activity usage and unused activity.
3. Calculate the total cost of resources supplied and break this into activity usage and unused activity.

Solution

1. Activity rate = [(3 × $30,000) + $9,000]/15,000
        = $6.60 per invoice
    Fixed rate = $90,000 / 15,000 = $6.00 per invoice
    Variable rate = $9,000 / 15,000 = $0.60 per invoice
2. Activity availability = Activity usage + Unused capacity
        15,000 invoices = 12,500 invoices + 2,500 invoices
3. Cost of activity supplied = Cost of activity used + Cost of unused activity
    $90,000 + ($0.60 × 12,500) = ($6.60 × 12,500) + ($6.00 × 2,500)
            $97,500 = $82,500 + $15,000

II. HIGH–LOW AND METHOD OF LEAST SQUARES

Kim Wilson, controller for Max Enterprises, has decided to estimate the fixed and variable components associated with the company's shipping activity. She has collected the following data for the past six months:

Packages Shipped	Total Shipping Costs
10	$ 800
20	1,100
15	900
12	900
18	1,050
25	1,250

Required:

1. Estimate the fixed and variable components for the shipping costs using the high–low method. Using the cost formula, predict the total cost of shipping if 14 packages are shipped.
2. Estimate the fixed and variable components using the method of least squares. Using the cost formula, predict the total cost of shipping if 14 packages are shipped.
3. For the method of least squares, explain what the coefficient of determination is, and compute the coefficient of correlation.

Solution

1. The estimate of fixed and variable costs using the high–low method is as follows:

   High point is (25, $1,250); Low point is (10, $800)

   Variable rate = ($1,250 – $800)/(25 – 10) = $450/15 = $30 per package
   Fixed cost= $1,250 – ($30 × 25) = $500

   Total cost= $500 + ($30 × Packages shipped)

   Total cost (14 packages shipped) = $500 + ($30 ×14)
   = $920

2. The computer output using the method of least squares is as follows:

   Constant = $509.912; X Coefficient = $29.405; R-Squared = 0.969

   Total cost = $509.83 + ($29.41 × Packages shipped)

   Total cost (14 packages shipped) = $509.83 + ($29.41 × 14)
   = $921.57

3. The coefficient of determination (R^2) tells us that about 96.9 percent of the variability in the shipping cost is explained by the number of packages shipped. The correlation coefficient (r) is the square root of the coefficient of determination, or 0.984.

QUESTIONS FOR WRITING AND DISCUSSION

1. Why is knowledge of cost behaviour important for managerial decision making? Give an example to illustrate your answer.

2. How does the length of the time horizon affect the classification of costs as fixed or variable? What is the meaning of short run? long run?

3. What is the relationship between flexible resources and cost behaviour?

4. What is the relationship between committed resources and cost behaviour?

5. Explain the difference between committed and discretionary fixed costs. Give examples of each.

6. Describe the difference between a variable cost and a step cost with narrow steps.

7. When is it reasonable to treat step costs as if they were variable costs?

8. What is the difference between a step cost with narrow steps and a step cost with wide steps?

9. What is an activity rate?

10. Why do mixed costs pose a problem when it comes to classifying costs into fixed and variable categories?

11. Why is a scattergraph a good first step in decomposing mixed costs into their fixed and variable components?

12. Describe how the scatterplot method breaks out the fixed and variable costs from a mixed cost. Now describe how the high–low method works. How do the two methods differ?

13. What are the advantages of the scatterplot method over the high–low method? the high–low method over the scatterplot method?

14. Describe the method of least squares. Why is this method better than either the high–low method or the scatterplot method?

15. What is meant by the "best-fitting line"?

16. Is the best-fitting line necessarily a good-fitting line? Explain.

17. Describe what is meant by "goodness of fit." Explain the meaning of the coefficient of determination.

18. What is the difference between the coefficient of determination and the coefficient of correlation? Which of the two measures of goodness of fit do you prefer? Why?

19. When is multiple regression required to explain cost behaviour?

20. Some firms assign mixed costs to either the fixed or variable cost categories without using any formal methodology to separate them. Explain how this practice can be defended.

EXERCISES

3–1

Cost Behaviour

LO1

The salary paid to a plant supervisor is $80,000 per year. The plant is capable of producing 80,000 kilograms of a chemical per year.

Required:

1. Prepare a table that shows how the cost of plant supervision behaves in total and on a per-unit basis as production increases from 0 to 80,000 kilograms, using 20,000-kilogram increments.
2. How would you classify the behaviour of this supervision cost?

3–2

Cost Behaviour

LO1

Kilroy Company has determined that the best driver for its material-moving activity is "kilometres travelled." The company also discovered that the cost of fuel for forklifts doubled as the kilometres travelled doubled. The cost for 10,000 kilometres was $20,000 and that for 20,000 kilometres was $40,000.

Required:

1. Prepare a table that shows the total cost of fuel and unit cost for kilometres travelled ranging from 0 to 80,000 kilometres, using increments of 20,000 kilometres.
2. How would you describe the behaviour of the material-moving cost?

3–3

Cost Behaviour

LO1, LO2

The University of Saskatchewan Huskies had just won a berth in the Vanier Cup finals, and the students and alumni were excited. Holiday Travel Agency, located close to campus, decided to put together a championship game package. For $16,000, a 737 jet could be chartered to take up to 170 people to and from Toronto, where the game would be played. A block of 75 hotel rooms could be confirmed for $400 each (with a three-night commitment); Holiday Travel must pay for all the rooms in advance and cannot cancel any of them. On the day of the game, a pregame buffet will be catered at $20 per person; each person will receive a game favour package consisting of a sweatshirt, a T-shirt, a commemorative pin with the university and Vanier Cup logos, and two pompoms in the team colours). All items in the favour package can be purchased by Holiday Travel before the trip and will cost the agency $75 per set. Buses will be chartered in Toronto to take the participants to and from the airport and the game. Each bus holds 50 people and can be chartered for $500.

Required:

List the resources that are mentioned in the above scenario. Then, for each resource, (1) determine whether it is a flexible resource or a committed resource, and (2) the type of cost behaviour displayed (variable, fixed, mixed, step cost).

3–4

Cost Behaviour

LO1

Action Figure, Inc., is a manufacturer of moulded plastic action figures that fast-food restaurants purchase to include in children's meal packs. Each action figure is moulded in a mould and takes about 50 grams of plastic costing $6.00 per kilogram. Every month or so, Action Figures contracts with an outside supplier to develop new moulds based on current movie and cartoon characters. Each mould could be used indefinitely but, practically speaking, has a life of only about three months. After that, children are tired of those figures and want to move on to others.

Required:

1. Is the plastic a flexible or committed resource? Are the moulds flexible or committed resources?
2. What is the cost behaviour of the plastic? the moulds?

3–5

Cost Behaviour

LO1

Jackson Company manufactures air-conditioning compressors. Based on past experience, Jackson has found that its total cost of moving materials can be represented by the following formula: Cost of moving materials = $90,000 + $0.20 × kilograms of material moved. The activity of moving materials uses forklifts, forklift operators, crates, and fuel (for the forklifts). During 2001, Jackson moved 200,000 kilograms of materials.

Required:

1. Identify the activity, its resources (inputs), and its driver (output measure).
2. Identify which resources are likely to vary with the driver over the relevant range. Assume that the relevant range is 150,000 to 250,000 kilograms of materials.
3. What is the total cost of moving materials incurred by Jackson in 2001? the total fixed cost? the total variable cost?
4. What is the cost of moving materials per kilogram moved?
5. What is the fixed cost per kilogram moved?
6. What is the variable cost of moving materials per kilogram moved?
7. Recalculate Requirements 4, 5, and 6 for the following levels of activity: (a) 150,000 kilograms moved and (b) 250,000 kilograms moved. Explain this outcome.

3–6

Resource Use and Cost Behaviour

LO2

For the following activities and their associated resources, identify: (1) an activity driver and (2) whether that driver is a flexible resource or a committed resource. Also, label each resource as one of the following with respect to the cost driver: (1) variable, (2) committed fixed, or (3) discretionary fixed.

Activity	Resource Description
Maintenance	Equipment, labour, parts
Inspection	Test equipment, inspectors (each inspector can inspect five batches per day), units inspected (process requires destructive sampling)*
Packing	Materials, labour (each packer places five units in a box), conveyor belt
Processing payables	Clerks, materials, equipment, and facility
Assembly	Conveyor belt, supervision (one supervisor for every three assembly lines), direct labour, materials

* Destructive sampling occurs whenever it is necessary to destroy a unit as inspection occurs.

3–7

Resource Supply and Usage; Activity Rates; Service Organization

LO2

Alva Community Hospital has five laboratory technicians who are responsible for doing a series of standard blood tests. Each technician is paid a salary of $30,000 and is capable of processing 4,000 tests per year. The lab facility represents a recent addition to the hospital and cost $300,000. It is expected to last 20 years. Equipment used for the testing cost $10,000 and has a life expectancy of 5 years. Both facility and equipment are amortized on a straight-line basis. In addition to the salaries, facility, and equipment, Alva expects to spend $200,000 for chemicals, forms, power, and other supplies (assuming that 20,000 tests are processed). During the year, 16,000 blood tests were run.

Required:

1. Classify the resources associated with the blood-testing activity into one of the following: (1) committed resources or (2) flexible resources.
2. Calculate the fixed activity rate and the variable activity rate for the blood-testing activity. What is the total cost of one blood test?
3. Compute the total activity availability, and break this into activity usage and unused activity.
4. Calculate the total cost of resources supplied, and break this into the cost of activity used and the cost of unused activity.

3–8

Separating Fixed and Variable Costs; Service Setting

LO3, LO4

Betty Yeager has been operating a dental practice for the past five years. As part of her practice, she provides a dental hygiene service. She has found that her costs for this service increase with patient load. Costs for this service over the past eight months are as follows:

Spreadsheet

Month	Patients Served	Total Cost
May	320	$2,000
June	480	2,500
July	600	3,000
August	200	1,900
September	720	4,500
October	560	2,900
November	630	3,400
December	300	2,200

Required:

1. Prepare a scattergraph based on these data. Use cost for the vertical axis and number of patients for the horizontal. Based on an examination of the scattergraph, does there appear to be a linear relationship between the cost of dental hygiene services and patients served?
2. Compute the cost formula for dental hygiene services using the high–low method. Using the formula, calculate the predicted cost of dental hygiene services for January for 450 patients.
3. Compute the cost formula for dental hygiene services using the method of least squares. Using the regression cost formula, find the predicted cost of dental hygiene services for January for 450 patients. What does the coefficient of determination tell you about the cost formula computed by regression?
4. Which cost formula—the one computed using the high–low method or the one using the least-squares coefficients—do you think is better? Explain.

3–9

Separation of Mixed Costs; High–Low and Least Squares

LO3, LO4

Spreadsheet

Suppose that you have the following data:

Inspection Cost	Inspection Hours
$120	10
220	20
320	30
440	40
500	50

Required:

1. Using the high–low method, prepare a cost formula for inspection cost.
2. Using the method of least squares, prepare a cost formula for inspection cost.
3. Comment on the usefulness of the coefficient of determination in evaluating the reliability of the least-squares equation.

3–10

High–Low Method; Managerial Judgment

LO3, LO6

You have been asked to budget the overhead costs for the month of June 2001. The budget will be based on the costs incurred during the months of May 2000 and September 2000. 2001's fixed costs are expected to be 4 percent higher than in 2000, whereas variable costs will increase by 6 percent. The data for May 2000 and September 2000 are as follows:

	May 2000	September 2000
Units produced	20,000	13,000
Units sold	18,000	16,000
Bad debts expense	$ 1,800	$ 1,600
Amortization of factory equipment	5,000	5,000
Direct labour cost	200,000	130,000
Direct materials used	120,000	78,000
Factory rent	12,000	12,000
Heat, light, and power	17,000	11,400
Indirect labour	60,000	49,500
Insurance on factory	2,500	2,500
President's salary	16,000	16,000
Sales commissions	18,000	16,000
Supplies used	40,000	26,000

Required:

1. For 2000, prepare a cost formula for overhead cost using the high–low method.
2. Prepare a budget of overhead costs for the month of June 2001 if 17,000 units are expected to be produced and 15,000 are expected to be sold. (CGA Canada adapted)

3–11

Scatterplot; Method of Least Squares

LO3

The following data represent the dollar values of the total cost (fixed plus variable) for different machine hours in a particular division of a manufacturing company.

Machine Hours	Total Costs
60	$100
40	80
80	120
20	45
50	90

Required:

1. Draw a scattergraph for these data using machine hours as the independent variable. Does a linear assumption of cost behaviour seem appropriate?
2. Fit a least-squares regression line to these data, and interpret the Y-intercept and the slope of the equation.
3. What is the value of R^2 for this least-squares equation? Interpret it.
4. What total cost would you predict for 75 machine hours? Explain.
5. What total cost would you predict for 200 machine hours? Explain. (CGA Canada adapted)

3–12

High–Low Method; Cost Formulas

LO3

During the past year, the high and low levels of resource usage occurred in April and October, respectively (for three different resources). The three resources are associated with the machining activity. Machine hours is the activity driver. The total costs of the three resources, and the activity output, as measured by machine hours for the two different levels, follow:

Activity	Machine Hours	Total Cost
Machine amortization		
Low	10,000	$130,000
High	25,000	130,000
Power usage		
Low	10,000	13,000
High	25,000	32,500
Drilling labour		
Low	10,000	22,000
High	25,000	37,000

Required:

1. Determine the cost behaviour of each resource. Use the high–low method to assess the fixed and variable components.
2. Using your knowledge of cost behaviour, predict the cost of each item for an activity output level of 15,000 machine hours.
3. Construct a cost formula that can be used to predict the total cost of the three resources combined. Using this formula, predict the total machining cost if activity usage (output) is 18,000 direct labour hours. In general, when can cost formulas be combined to form a single cost formula?

3–13

Method of Least Squares; Evaluation of Cost Equation

LO3, LO4

The method of least squares was used to develop a cost equation to predict the cost of purchasing goods. Eighty data points were used for the regression. The following computer output was received:

Intercept	$30,500
Slope	$10
Coefficient of correlation	0.85
Standard error	$1,500

The driver used was "number of purchase orders."

Required:

1. What is the cost formula?
2. Using the cost formula, predict the cost of purchasing if 10,000 orders are processed.
3. What percentage of the variability in purchasing cost is explained by the number of purchase orders? Do you think the equation will predict well? Why or why not?

3–14

Multiple Regression

LO5

Materhorn, a manufacturer of VCRs, is interested in determining the cost of its warranty repair activity. Two cost drivers have been identified that are believed to be important in explaining the cost of this activity: the number of defective products produced and the hours of inspection. To see if the belief is valid, the company's cost analysts gather 100 weeks of data and run a multiple regression analysis. The following printout is obtained:

Parameter	Estimate	t for H_0 Parameter $= 0$	$Pr > t$	Standard Error of Parameter
Intercept	$2,000	80.00	0.0001	25.000
Number of defects	60	2.58	0.0050	23.256
Inspection hours	−10	−1.96	0.0250	5.103

$R^2 = 0.88$
$S_e = 150$
Observations: 100

Required:

1. Write out the cost equation for Materhorn's warranty repair activity.
2. If Materhorn expects to have 100 defects per week and to spend 150 hours on inspection, what are the anticipated warranty repair costs?
3. Is number of defects positively or negatively correlated with warranty repair costs? Are inspection hours positively or negatively correlated with quality control costs?
4. What does R^2 mean? Overall, what is your evaluation of the cost equation that was developed for the warranty repair activity?

3–15

Cost Behaviour Patterns

LO1

The following graphs represent cost behaviour patterns that might occur in a company's cost structure. The vertical axis represents total cost, and the horizontal axis represents activity output.

Required:

For each of the following situations, choose the graph that best illustrates the cost pattern involved. Also, for each situation identify the driver that measures activity usage.

1. The cost of power when a fixed fee of $500 per month is charged plus an additional charge of $0.12 per kilowatt-hour used.
2. Commissions paid to sales representatives. Commissions are paid at the rate of 5 percent of sales made up to total annual sales of $500,000, and 7 percent of sales above $500,000.
3. A part purchased from an outside supplier costs $12 per part for the first 3,000 parts and $10 per part for all parts purchased in excess of 3,000 units.
4. The cost of surgical gloves purchased in increments of 100 units (gloves come in boxes of 100 pairs).

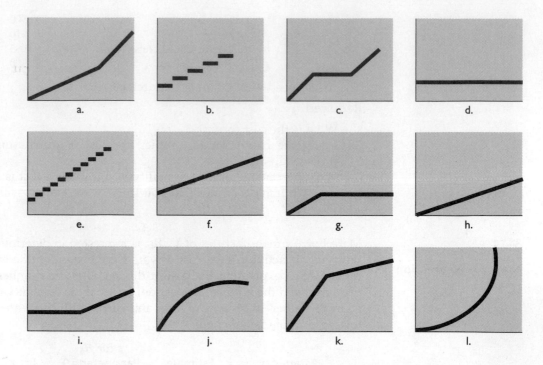

5. The cost of tuition at a university that charges $250 per credit hour up to 15 credit hours. Hours taken in excess of 15 are free.

6. The cost of tuition at another university that charges $4,500 per semester for any course load ranging from 12 to 15 credit hours. Students taking fewer than 12 credit hours are charged $375 per credit hour. Students taking more than 15 credit hours are charged $4,500 plus $300 per credit hour in excess of 15.

7. A beauty shop's purchase of soaking solution to remove artificial nails. Each jar of solution can soak off approximately 50 nails before losing effectiveness.

8. The purchase of diagnostics equipment by a company for inspection of incoming orders.

9. Use of disposable gowns by patients in a hospital.

10. The cost of labour at a local fast-food restaurant. Three employees are always on duty during working hours; more employees can be called in during periods of heavy demand to work on an "as-needed" basis.

11. A manufacturer found that the maintenance cost of its heavy machinery was tied to the age of the equipment. Experience indicated that the maintenance cost increased at an increasing rate as the equipment aged.

PROBLEMS

3–16

Cost Behaviour; Resource Usage Model

LO1, LO2

Rolertyme Company manufactures roller skates. With the exception of the rollers, all parts of the skates are produced internally. Neeta Booth, Rolertyme's president, has decided to make the rollers instead of buying them from external suppliers. The company needs 100,000 sets per year; currently it pays $1.90 per set of rollers.

The rollers can be produced using an available area within the plant. However, equipment for production of the rollers would need to be leased (at $30,000 per year). Additionally, it would cost $0.50 per machine hour for power, oil, and other operating expenses. The equipment will provide 60,000 machine hours per year. Direct materials costs will average $0.75 per set of four, and direct labour costs will average $0.25 per set. Since only one type of roller would be produced, no additional demands would be made on the setup activity. Other overhead activities (besides machining and setups), however, would be affected. The company's cost management system provides the following information about the current status of the overhead activities that would be affected (the supply and demand figures do not include the effect of roller production on these activities). The lumpy quantity indicates how much capacity must be purchased should any expansion of activity supply be needed. The purchase price is the cost of acquiring the capacity represented by the lumpy quantity. This price also represents the cost of current spending on the existing activity supply (for each block of activity).

Activity	Activity Driver	Supply	Usage	Lumpy Quantity	Purchase Price
Purchasing	Orders	25,000	22,000	5,000	$25,000
Inspection	Hours	10,000	9,000	2,000	30,000
Material handling	Moves	4,500	4,300	2,500	15,000

Production of rollers would place the following demands on the overhead activities:

Activity	Resource Demands
Machine	50,000 machine hours
Purchasing	2,000 purchase orders (associated with raw materials used to make the rollers)
Inspection	750 inspection hours
Material handling	500 moves

Producing the rollers also means that the purchase of outside rollers will cease. Because rollers are no longer being purchased, the number of purchase orders (associated with the outside acquisition of rollers) will drop by 5,000. Similarly, the moves for the handling of incoming orders will decrease by 200. The company has not inspected the rollers purchased from outside suppliers.

Required:

1. Classify all resources associated with the production of rollers as flexible resources or committed resources. For committed resources, label them as short-term and long-term commitments. How should we describe the cost behaviour of these short-term and long-term resource commitments? Explain.
2. Calculate the total annual resource spending (for all overhead activities except for setups) that the company will incur after production of the rollers begins. Break this cost into fixed and variable activity costs. In calculating these figures, assume that the company will spend no more than necessary. What is the effect on resource spending caused by production of the rollers (include the effect of materials and labour)?
3. Refer to Requirement 2. For each activity, break down the cost of activity supplied into the cost of activity usage and the cost of unused activity.

3–17

High–Low Method; Scatterplot Method; Method of Least Squares

LO3

You have been given the following information about the heat, light, and power costs for the Lily Company.

Month	Machine Hours	Heat, Light, and Power
January	2,800	$16,100
February	2,600	15,500
March	2,880	16,500
April	2,760	16,100
May	2,840	16,350
June	2,320	14,300
July	1,840	12,400
August	1,640	11,560
September	2,920	16,700
October	3,400	18,600
November	3,280	18,100
December	2,960	16,850

Required:

1. Using the high–low method, predict what the heat, light, and power cost would be for a month in which 2,500 machine hours are worked.
2. Using the scatterplot method, predict what the heat, light, and power cost would be for a month in which 2,500 machine hours are worked.
3. Using the method of least squares, predict what the heat, light, and power cost would be for a month in which 2,500 machine hours are worked.
4. Compare and evaluate your answers to Requirements 1, 2, and 3. (CGA Canada adapted)

3–18

High–Low Method; Method of Least Squares; Correlation LO3, LO4, LO5

Farnsworth Company has gathered data on its overhead activities and associated costs for the past 10 months. Tracy Heppler, a member of the controller's department, has convinced management that overhead costs can be better estimated and controlled if the fixed and variable components of each overhead activity are known. Tracy has identified 150 different activities and has grouped them into sets based on her belief that they share a common driver. (This classification process has reduced the number of cost formulas needed from 150 to 25.) For example, she has decided that unloading incoming goods, counting goods, and inspecting goods can be grouped together as a more general receiving activity, based on her belief that the costs of the three related activities are all driven by the same driver: number of receiving orders. To confirm her activity classification and driver assignment, she has gathered 10 months of data on the number of receiving orders and on the cost of receiving. Just in case receiving orders is not a good driver, she has also collected data on the kilograms of material received.

Month	Number of Receiving Orders	Kilograms of Materials Received	Receiving Cost
1	1,000	300,000	$18,000
2	700	250,000	15,000
3	1,500	450,000	28,000
4	1,200	320,000	17,000
5	1,300	440,000	25,000
6	1,100	280,000	18,000
7	1,600	550,000	30,000
8	1,400	390,000	24,000
9	1,700	230,000	21,000
10	900	230,000	15,000

Required:

1. Using the high–low method, prepare a cost formula for the receiving activity using the number of receiving orders as the driver.
2. Using the method of least squares, prepare a cost formula for the receiving activity using the number of receiving orders as the driver. What does the coefficient of determination tell us about the use of receiving orders as the independent variable?
3. Using the method of least squares, prepare a cost formula for the receiving activity using the number of kilograms of material received as the driver. What does the coefficient of determination tell us about the use of kilograms of material received as the independent variable?
4. Run a multiple regression using both the number of receiving orders and the kilograms of material as independent variables. Which of the three regression equations do you think is best? Why?

3–19

Cost Formulas; Single and Multiple Cost Drivers; Coefficient of Correlation

LO3, LO4, LO5

Kimball Company has developed the following cost formulas using the method of least squares:

Material cost = $80 × Direct labour hours, r = 0.95
Labour cost (direct) = $20 × Direct labour hours, r = 0.96
Overhead cost = $350,000 + $100 × Direct labour hours, r = 0.75 —
Selling cost = $50,000 + $10 × Direct labour hours, r = 0.93

The company has a policy of producing on demand and keeps very little, if any, finished goods inventory (thus, units produced = units sold).

The president of Kimball Company has recently implemented a policy that any special orders will be accepted if they cover the costs that the orders cause. This policy was implemented because Kimball's industry is in a recession, and the company is producing well below capacity (and expects to continue doing so for the coming year). The president is willing to accept orders that at least cover their variable costs so that the company can keep its employees and avoid layoffs. Also, any orders above variable costs will increase the company's overall profitability.

Required:

1. Compute the total unit variable cost. Suppose that Kimball has an opportunity to accept an order for 20,000 units at $220 per unit. Each unit uses one direct labour hour for production. Should Kimball accept the order? (The order would not displace any of Kimball's regular orders.)
2. Explain the significance of the coefficient of correlation measures (r) for the cost formulas. Did these measures have a bearing on your answer in Requirement 1? Should they have a bearing? Why?   *ont only . 75*
3. Suppose that the following multiple regression equation is developed for overhead costs:

$$\text{Overhead cost} = \$100{,}000 + (\$100 \times \text{Direct labour hours}) +$$
$$(\$5{,}000 \times \text{Number of setups}) + (\$300 \times \text{Engineering hours})$$

The correlation coefficient for the equation is 0.94. Assume that the order of 20,000 units requires 12 setups and 600 engineering hours. Given this new information, should the company accept the special order referred to in Requirement 1? Is there any other information about cost behaviour that you would like to have? Explain.

3–20

High–Low Method; Regression; Multiple Regression

LO3, LO4, LO5

Weber Valley Regional Hospital has collected data on all of its activities for the past seven months. Data for cardiac nursing care follow:

Month	Cost	Hours of Nursing Care
May 2000	$ 66,000	1,600
June 2000	76,500	1,900
July 2000	78,100	1,950
August 2000	73,180	1,800
September 2000	69,500	1,700
October 2000	64,250	1,550
November 2000	52,000	1,200
December 2000	66,000	1,600
January 2001	110,000	1,800
February 2001	86,485	1,330
March 2001	105,022	1,700
April 2001	100,000	1,600
May 2001	120,000	2,000
June 2001	109,500	1,790

Required:

1. Using the high–low method, calculate the variable rate per hour and the fixed cost for the nursing-care activity. Comment on your results.
2. Prepare a scatterplot for the nursing-care activity using the given data. Use one symbol, perhaps an "*x*," for observations occurring in 2000, and another symbol, perhaps a "*y*," for observations occurring in 2001.
3. Upon looking into the events that happened at the end of 2000, you find that the cardiology ward bought a cardiac-monitoring machine for the nursing station. A decision was also made to add a new supervisory position for the evening shift. Monthly amortization on the monitor and the salary of the new supervisor total $10,000. In addition, the rest of the nursing staff received a raise, and the cost of supplies has increased. Run the following regressions:
    a. Run a regression on the data from 2000 and 2001 using nursing hours as the single independent variable.
    b. Run a regression on the data from 2000 using nursing hours as the single independent variable.
    c. Run a regression on the data from 2001 using nursing hours as the single independent variable.
    d. Create a dummy variable called "changes" that takes the value "0" for observations in 2000 and the value "1" for observations in 2001. Run a multiple regression using nursing hours and "changes" as the independent variables.
    Which of the four cost formulas should be used to budget the cost of the cardiac nursing-care activity for the remainder of 2001? Explain.

3–21

Comparison of Regression Equations

LO1, LO3, LO4, LO5

Loving Toys Company is attempting to determine cost behaviour of its overhead activities for its Truro, Nova Scotia, plant. One of the major activities is the setup activity. Two possible drivers have been mentioned: setup hours and number of setups. The plant controller has accumulated the following data for the setup activity to be analyzed using the method of least squares:

Month	Setup Costs	Setup Hours	Number of Setups
February	$ 7,700	2,000	70
March	7,650	2,100	50
April	10,052	3,000	50
May	9,400	2,700	60
June	9,584	3,000	20
July	8,480	2,500	40
August	8,550	2,400	60
September	9,735	2,900	50
October	10,500	3,000	90

Required:

1. Estimate a cost equation with setup hours as the only independent variable. If the Truro plant forecasts 2,600 setup hours for the next month, what will the budgeted setup cost be?
2. Estimate an equation with number of setups as the only independent variable. If the Truro plant forecasts 80 setups for the next month, what will the budgeted setup cost be?
3. Which of the two regression equations do you think does a better job of predicting setup costs? Explain.
4. Run a multiple regression analysis using both setup hours and number of setups as independent variables. Calculate the budgeted cost using the multiple regression equation. Would you recommend using the multiple-driver equation over a single-driver equation? Explain.

MANAGERIAL DECISION CASES

3–22

Scattergraph; Method of Least Squares; Choice of Independent Variable
LO3, LO4, LO5

Grace Fahran, the executive director of a hospital in Thunder Bay, is preparing a budget for the hospital's finance committee. As part of the budget submission, Grace wants to include an analysis of the overhead cost data over a 30-month period. Total overhead costs include all costs such as supplies, pharmaceutical, and labour costs (including administrative staff and nurses but excluding doctors' salaries). The number of patient admissions includes all patients who are admitted into the hospital, but excluding emergencies and outpatients. The number of administrative staff includes all department heads and support, but excludes nurses and doctors. The following data were obtained for a preliminary analysis:

Month	Overhead Costs	Patient Admissions	Administrative Staff
1	$1,969,000	414	48
2	1,973,000	423	48
3	1,975,000	419	48
4	1,978,000	426	48
5	1,990,000	450	46
6	2,014,000	432	46
7	1,997,000	464	47
8	2,012,000	432	48
9	2,023,000	458	48
10	2,050,000	455	47
11	2,040,000	469	47
12	2,063,000	475	46
13	2,058,000	481	46
14	2,078,000	467	49
15	2,050,000	480	49
16	2,081,000	476	49
17	2,093,000	483	48
18	2,086,000	479	48
19	2,085,000	500	48
20	2,090,000	488	47
21	2,090,000	495	48
22	2,096,000	460	48
23	2,098,000	478	47
24	2,105,000	482	50
25	2,148,000	497	50
26	2,120,000	474	50
27	2,099,000	511	50
28	2,130,000	497	49
29	2,135,000	509	51
30	2,132,000	516	51

Required:

1. Prepare a scattergraph of overhead costs using the number of administrative staff as the independent variable.
2. Prepare a scattergraph of overhead costs using the number of patient admissions as the independent variable.
3. Based on the scattergraphs prepared in Requirements 1 and 2, which would be the more appropriate choice of independent variable? Explain.
4. Determine an overhead cost equation using the method of least squares with the number of administrative staff as the independent variable.
5. Determine an overhead cost equation using the method of least squares with the number of patient admissions as the independent variable.

6. Compare the goodness of fit for the equations in Requirements 4 and 5.
7. Discuss one factor that would limit the usefulness of the cost equations determined in Requirements 4 and 5. (CGA Canada adapted)

3–23

Simple and Multiple Regression; Evaluating Reliability

LO3, LO4, LO5

The Lockit Company manufactures doorknobs for residential houses and apartments. Lockit is considering the use of simple (single-driver) and multiple regression analysis to forecast annual sales because previous forecasts have been inaccurate. The sales forecast will be used to initiate the budgeting process and to better identify the underlying process that generates sales.

Larry Husky, Lockit's controller, has considered many possible independent variables and equations to predict sales and has narrowed his choices to four equations. Larry used annual observations from 20 prior years to estimate each of the four equations. Following are the variables used in the four equations and a statistical summary of these equations:

S_t = Forecasted sales in dollars for Lockit in period t
S_{t-1} = Actual sales in dollars for Lockit in period $t-1$
G_t = Forecasted U.S. gross domestic product in period t
G_{t-1} = Actual Canadian gross domestic product in period $t-1$
N_{t-1} = Lockit's net income in period t-1

SUMMARY OF FOUR EQUATIONS

Equation	Dependent Variable	Independent Variable	Intercept	Independent Variable (Rate)	R^2
1	S_t	S_{t-1}	$ 500,000	$ 1.10	0.94
2	S_t	G_t	1,000,000	0.00001	0.90
3	S_t	G_{t-1}	900,000	0.000012	0.81
4	S_t	N_{t-1}	600,000	10.00	0.96
		G_t		0.000002	
		G_{t-1}		0.000003	

Required:

1. Write Equations 2 and 4 in the form $Y = F + VX$.
2. If actual sales are $1,500,000 in 2000, what would be the forecasted sales for Lockit in 2001?
3. Explain why Larry Husky might prefer Equation 3 to Equation 2.
4. Explain the advantages and disadvantages of using Equation 4 to forecast sales. (US CMA adapted)

3–24

Suspicious Acquisition of Data; Ethical Issues

LO1

Bill Lewis, manager of the Thomas Electronics Division, called a meeting with his controller, Brindon Peterson, CMA, and his marketing manager, Patty Fritz. The following is a transcript of the conversation that took place during the meeting.

Bill: "Brindon, the variable-costing system that you developed has proved to be a big plus for our division. Our success in winning bids has increased, and as a result, our revenues have increased by 25 percent. However, if we intend to meet this year's profit targets, we are going to need something extra—am I not right, Patty?"
Patty: "Absolutely. While we have been able to win more bids, we still are losing too many, particularly to our major competitor, Kilborn Electronics. If I knew more about their bidding strategy, I imagine we could be more successful competing with them."
Bill: "Would knowing their variable costs help?"
Patty: "Certainly. It would give me their minimum price. With that knowledge, I'm sure we could find a way to beat them on several jobs, particularly for those jobs where we are at least as efficient. It would also help us identify where we are not cost-competitive. With this information, we might be able to find ways to increase our efficiency."

Bill: "Well, I have good news. I have some data here in these handouts that reveal bids that Kilborn made on several jobs. I have also been able to obtain the direct labour hours worked for many of these jobs. But that's not all. I have monthly totals for manufacturing costs and direct labour hours for all their jobs for the past ten months. Brindon, with this information, can you estimate what the variable manufacturing cost per hour is? If you can, we can compute the variable costs for each job and the markup that Kilborn is using."

Brindon: "Yes, an analysis of the data you're requesting is possible. I have a question, though, before I do this. How did you manage to acquire these data? I can't imagine that Kilborn would willingly release this information."

Bill: "What does it matter how the data were acquired? The fact is, we have them, and we have an opportunity to gain a tremendous competitive advantage. With that advantage, we can meet our profit targets, and we will all end the year with a big bonus."

After the meeting, in a conversation with Patty, Brindon learned that Bill was dating Jackie Wilson, a cost accountant (and CMA) who happened to work for Kilborn. Patty speculated that Jackie might be the source of the Kilborn data. Upon learning this information, Brindon expressed some strong reservations to Patty about analyzing the data.

Required:

1. Assume that Bill did acquire the data from Jackie Wilson. Comment on Jackie's behaviour. Which of the standards of ethical conduct outlined in Chapter 1 did she violate?

2. Were Brindon's instincts correct—should he have felt some reservations about analyzing the data? Would it be ethical to analyze the data? Do any of the standards of ethical conduct apply? What would you do if you were Brindon? Explain.

RESEARCH ASSIGNMENT

3–25

Cybercase

LO2, LO6

Use the World Wide Web to gather information on one of the theme parks at Walt Disney World: Magic Kingdom, Epcot, Disney-MGM Studios, or Disney's Animal Kingdom (see **asp.disney.go.com/disneyworld/db/seetheworld/themeparks/ index.asp**).

Once you have selected your park, list as many resources as possible and classify them as flexible or committed. Discuss the cost behaviour of each. How do you think cost behaviour affected the planning for the theme park?

CHAPTER 4

Activity-Based Costing

Learning Objectives

After studying Chapter 4, you should be able to:

1. Discuss the importance of unit costs.

2. Describe functional-based costing approaches.

3. Explain why functional-based costing approaches may produce distorted costs.

4. Explain how an activity-based costing system works.

5. Provide a detailed description of how activities can be grouped into homogeneous sets to reduce the number of activity rates.

6. Describe the role of activity-based costing for organizations with only one product, homogeneous products, or a JIT structure.

Scenario

Ryan Chesser, president and owner of Sharp Paper, Inc., was reviewing the most recent financial reports. Profits had once again declined. The company had failed to achieve its targeted return for the third consecutive year. The company's inability to improve its profits frustrated Chesser. After all, Sharp Paper had been a dominant factor in the industry for more than two decades. The company owns three paper mills, which produce coated and uncoated specialty printing papers. Customers have access to a variety of papers differing in finish, colour, weight, and packaging. More than 400 individual products were marketed by the company.[1]

To ascertain the reasons for the company's declining fortunes, Ryan had asked his vice-presidents of production (Jeff Clark) and marketing (Jennifer Woodruff) to do some research on why the competition was winning bids on some major product lines despite aggressive pricing by Sharp. Four weeks after giving the assignment, he received the following report:

MEMO

To: Ryan Chesser, President
From: Jeff Clark and
Jennifer Woodruff

Subject: Competitive Position
of Sharp
Date: February 12, 2001

Our investigation has revealed some rather interesting information—information that we believe can benefit our company. We began by contacting some customers who have switched some of their purchases to competitors. We discovered that the switch usually involved our high-volume products. We have been losing bids on these products even when they were aggressively priced. Often the loss of business was to smaller competitors with less diverse product lines. Their prices were significantly lower than ours, and, in fact, seemed unrealistically low.

Our next effort was focused on determining whether competitors were employing a new technology that might provide significant cost advantages. Virtually all of our small competitors use the same manufacturing processes that we use. No evidence of significant differences in efficiency emerged.

Curiously, our low-volume products appear to be the most profitable. In some cases, we are the only company that produces these specialty products. At times, we even receive referrals from some of our competitors. But some of our operational managers have urged us to drop some of these low-volume products, arguing that they're more bother than they're worth. Yet these products are being reported as highly profitable. Our initial discussions with Jan Booth, our controller, failed to reveal any logical reasons explaining why the profit margins on the low-volume products were so much greater than those on our high-volume products, which seems counterintuitive given the special processes and handling required for the low-volume products. We were even told that we could increase our margin on the low-volume products by increasing prices. Recent price increases were readily accepted by customers—without any complaints.

Yesterday Jan approached us and indicated that she had given some thought to our questions and concerns. She mentioned the possibility that many of our problems may be rooted in the way we are currently assigning costs to products. She noted that we are using a traditional, functional-based costing system and that it may be causing distortions in product costs. Given the results of our other inquiries, this possibility may be worth further investigation.

---

1. The setting and the issues in this introductory case are based in part on the following three articles: James P. Borden, "Review of Literature on Activity-Based Costing," *Journal of Cost Management for the Manufacturing Industry* (Spring 1990); John K. Shank and Vijay Govindarajan, "Transaction-Based Costing for the Complex Product Line: A Field Study," *Journal of Cost Management for the Manufacturing Industry* (Summer 1988): 31–38; and Robin Cooper, "Does Your Company Need a New Cost System?" *Journal of Cost Management for the Manufacturing Industry* (Spring 1987): 45–49.

Questions to Think About

1. What are product costs?

2. What role do product costs play in bids?

3. If product costing is the root of the bidding difficulties, why are the smaller, less diverse firms having more success?

4. Why wasn't the controller's office able to explain the high-profit margins on the low-volume products?

5. What is meant by a traditional, functional-based costing system? Why might it cause distortions in product costs?

6. Assuming that Sharp's problems are founded in the way costs are assigned to products, what can Sharp do to solve the problem?

UNIT COSTS

Objective 1

Discuss the importance of unit costs.

Functional-based and activity-based costing assign costs to cost objects such as products, customers, materials, and marketing channels. Once costs are assigned to a cost object, a unit cost is computed by dividing the total assigned cost by the amount of the particular cost object. Because of their importance, calculation of unit product costs will be discussed first. We will discuss other cost objects later. Conceptually, computing the unit product cost is simple. The **unit cost** is the total cost associated with the units produced divided by the number of units produced. For example, if a construction company builds 100 subdivision homes of the same size and quality and the total cost for these homes is $6 million, then the cost of each home is $60,000 ($6 million/100 homes). Similarly, if Jiffy-Change, a service firm that specializes in changing oil, works on 400 autos per month and total costs are $4,000, then the cost per car serviced is $10. Although the concept is simple, the practical reality of the computation can be somewhat more complex. First, what is meant by "total cost"? Does this consist only of production costs? Or production costs plus marketing costs? Or all costs of the organization? Second, how do we measure the costs to be assigned? Do we use actual costs incurred or estimated costs? Third, how do we associate costs with the product? When only one product is produced, this question is trivial, because all costs incurred are traceable to that one product. But when more than one product is produced, the answer is more complex.

The first question is answered by defining what is meant by "product cost." Recall that the product cost definition depends on the managerial objective being served. For example, product cost is often defined as production costs: direct materials, direct labour, and overhead. This product cost definition is used for external financial reporting. But it is also useful for making certain decisions. For example, it can serve as a critical input for establishing bid prices. Furthermore, this common product cost definition can be used to illustrate the differences between functional-based and activity-based approaches for assigning costs. This is the definition of product cost that will be used in this chapter. The second and third questions are concerned with how costs are measured and assigned to products. Total manufacturing costs must be measured, and then these costs must be associated with the units produced. **Cost measurement** consists of determining the dollar amounts of direct materials, direct labour, and overhead used in production. The dollar amounts may be the actual amounts expended for the manufacturing inputs, or they may be estimated amounts. Often, estimated amounts are used to ensure timeliness of cost information or to control costs. The process of associating the costs, once measured, with the units produced is called **cost assignment**. Functional-based and activity-based approaches are alternative ways of assigning costs to products.

Importance of Unit Product Costs

A cost accounting system measures and assigns costs so that the unit cost of a product or service can be determined. Unit cost is a critical piece of information for manufacturing and service firms. Unit costs are essential for valuing inventory, determining income, and making a number of important decisions. For example, bidding is a common requirement in the markets for specialized products and services. It is virtually impossible to submit a meaningful bid without knowing the unit costs of the products or services to be produced. Unit product cost information is vital in a number of other areas as well. Decisions concerning product design and the introduction of new products and services are affected by expected unit costs. Decisions to make or buy a product or service, accept or reject a special order, or keep or drop a product or service require unit cost information. Because unit cost information is so vital, its accuracy is essential. Distorted unit product costs are not acceptable.

Production of Unit Cost Information

To produce unit cost information, a product cost definition, cost measurement, and cost assignment are required. As already mentioned, we will use the traditional product cost definition in this chapter. There are also a number of different ways to measure and assign costs. Two possible measurement systems are *actual costing* and *normal costing*.

Actual costing assigns the actual costs of direct materials, direct labour, and overhead to products. In practice, strict actual-cost systems are rarely used, because they cannot provide accurate unit cost information on a timely basis. Interestingly, per-unit computation of the direct materials and direct labour costs is not the source of the difficulty. The amount of actual direct materials and direct labour used for a product can be physically observed as the units are produced. Thus, actual prime costs can be assigned using direct tracing, and they can be assigned on a timely basis. For these two manufacturing inputs, there are no significant problems with either accuracy or timeliness. The main problem with using actual costs for the calculation of unit cost is with manufacturing overhead.

Assigning actual overhead costs creates a conflict between timeliness and accuracy. For example, consider a firm that produces a single product. In this case, we know that all the year's overhead costs belong to the units produced during the year. Thus, if we wait until the end of the year, we can compute an accurate cost per unit simply by dividing the year's overhead costs by the year's production. Unfortunately, waiting until the end of the year to compute an overhead rate is unacceptable. A company needs unit cost information throughout the year. Most decisions requiring unit cost information cannot wait until the end of the year.

It is possible to provide more timely unit cost information by using the same procedure for a shorter period—say, a week or a month (for example, by dividing a month's overhead by a month's output). This approach, however, tends to produce unit costs that fluctuate from month to month. This outcome occurs for two major reasons: (1) nonuniform incurrence of overhead, and (2) changes in production volume. Many overhead costs are not incurred uniformly throughout the year: they can differ significantly from one period to the next. Similarly, per-unit overhead costs can fluctuate dramatically because of changes in production volume.

Normal costing assigns the actual costs of direct materials and direct labour to products; however, overhead costs are assigned using predetermined rates. A **predetermined overhead rate** is a rate based on estimated data and calculated using the following formula:

$$\text{Overhead rate} = \frac{\text{Estimated overhead cost}}{\text{Estimated activity usage}}$$

Virtually all firms assign overhead to production on a predetermined basis. How overhead rates are used to assign costs to products will become clear as we discuss functional-based costing and activity-based costing. Since functional-based costing can be viewed as a special case of activity-based costing, we will discuss it first. Furthermore, by discussing functional-based costing first, we will see the potential advantages of activity-based costing much more clearly.

FUNCTIONAL-BASED PRODUCT COSTING

Objective 2

Describe functional-based costing approaches.

Functional-based product costing assigns the cost of direct materials and direct labour to products using direct tracing. Overhead costs, on the other hand, pose a different challenge. The physically observable input–output relationship that exists between direct labour, direct materials, and products is simply not available for overhead. Therefore, overhead costs are assigned using driver tracing and allocation.

Specifically, functional-based costing uses only *unit-level* activity drivers to assign overhead costs to products. **Unit-level activity drivers** are factors that cause changes in cost as the units produced change. The use of only unit-based drivers to assign overhead costs to products assumes that the overhead consumed by products is highly correlated with the number of units produced. For those overhead costs for which this assumption is valid, the unit-based assignment corresponds to driver tracing; for those overhead costs that do not fit the assumption, the cost assignment is an allocation.

A functional-based predetermined overhead rate requires specification of a unit-level driver, an estimate of the capacity measured by the driver, and an estimate of the expected overhead cost. Examples of unit-level drivers commonly used to assign overhead include the following:

1. Units produced
2. Direct labour hours
3. Direct labour dollars
4. Machine hours
5. Direct material dollars

After we have identified the unit-level driver, the next step is to determine the activity capacity that the driver measures. Although any reasonable capacity could be chosen, the four usual candidates are expected capacity, normal capacity, theoretical capacity, and practical capacity. **Expected activity capacity** is the activity

Exhibit   4–1

Activity Capacity
Measures

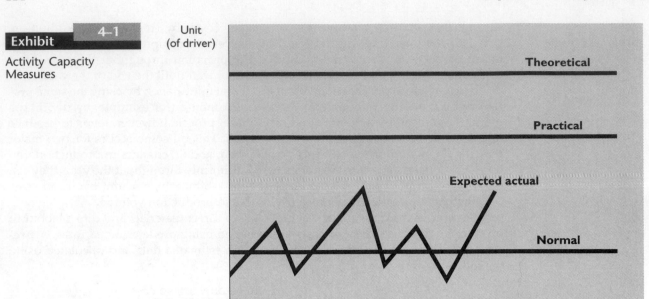

output the firm expects to attain for the coming year. **Normal activity capacity** is the average activity output that a firm experiences in the long term (normal volume is computed over more than one year). **Theoretical activity capacity** is the absolute maximum activity output that can be realized if everything operates *perfectly*. **Practical activity capacity** is the maximum output that can be realized if everything operates *efficiently*. Of the four choices, the last three have the advantage of using the same activity level period after period. As a result, they each produce less period-to-period fluctuation of the per-unit overhead cost than a rate based on expected annual capacity.

Using practical or theoretical capacity is often recommended because it avoids assigning unused capacity costs to products and encourages management of any excess capacity. Exhibit 4–1 illustrates these four measures of activity capacity.

Plantwide Rates

Exhibit 4–2 illustrates how plantwide overhead rates are computed. This calculation consists of two stages. Overhead costs are first accumulated in one large plantwide pool (first-stage cost assignment). Overhead costs are assigned to the pool simply by adding all the overhead costs expected to be incurred within the plant for a year. In a sense, we could argue that the costs are assigned to a very broad macro activity: production. Once costs are accumulated in this pool, we then compute a plantwide rate using a single unit-level driver (often direct labour hours). In the second stage, overhead costs are assigned to products, multiplying the plantwide rate by the actual amount of the unit-level driver used by each product.

Computation of a Plantwide Rate The computation of a plantwide rate is best illustrated with an example. Belring produces two telephones: a cordless phone and a regular model. The company has the following estimated and actual data for 2001:

Budgeted overhead	$360,000
Expected activity (in direct labour hours)	100,000
Actual overhead	$380,000
Actual activity (in direct labour hours)	100,000

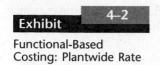

Exhibit 4-2

Functional-Based
Costing: Plantwide Rate

Suppose that Belring bases its predetermined overhead rate on expected direct labour hours (DLH) as follows:

Predetermined overhead rate = Budgeted overhead/Expected activity
$$= \$360,000/100,000 \text{ direct labor hours (DLH)}$$
$$= \$3.60 \text{ per DLH}$$

Applied Overhead The total overhead assigned to actual production at any point in time is called **applied overhead**. Applied overhead is computed using the following formula:

Applied overhead = Overhead rate × Actual activity output

Using the overhead rate, we see that the applied overhead for 2001 is:

Applied overhead = Overhead rate × Actual activity
$$= \$3.60 \times 100,000 \text{ DLH}$$
$$= \$360,000$$

The difference between the actual overhead and the applied overhead is called an **overhead variance**. For Belring, the overhead variance is $20,000 ($380,000 − $360,000). If the actual overhead is greater than the applied overhead, the variance is called **underapplied overhead**. For the Belring example, the overhead is $20,000 underapplied. If the actual overhead is less than the applied overhead, the variance is called **overapplied overhead**. Usually, at the end of the year, underapplied overhead is added to cost of goods sold and overapplied overhead is subtracted from cost of goods sold.

Per-Unit Cost A product's unit cost is computed as the sum of total prime costs and applied overhead costs and then dividing this total cost by the number of units produced. To illustrate unit-cost computation, assume that the following actual data were collected for each product:

	Cordless	Regular
Units produced	10,000	100,000
Prime costs	$78,000	$738,000
Direct labour hours	10,000	90,000

The unit-cost calculations are summarized in Exhibit 4–3. Notice the role played by the predetermined rate of $3.60 per DLH in calculating the unit cost.

Exhibit 4–3

Unit-Cost Computation: Plantwide Rate

	Cordless	Regular
Prime costs	$ 78,000	$ 738,000
Applied overhead costs:		
$3.60 × 10,000	36,000	—
$3.60 × 90,000	—	324,000
Total manufacturing costs	$114,000	$1,062,000
Units produced	÷ 10,000	÷ 100,000
Unit cost (total costs/units)	$ 11.40	$ 10.62

Departmental Rates

Exhibit 4–4 illustrates a two-stage conceptual framework for departmental overhead rates. In the first stage, the plantwide overhead costs are divided up and assigned to individual production departments, creating departmental overhead cost pools. In this first-stage cost assignment, departments are the cost objects, and overhead costs are assigned using a combination of direct tracing, driver tracing, and allocation. We describe in detail in Chapter 7 how this first-stage cost assignment is done. Once costs are assigned to individual production departments, then unit-based drivers—such as direct labour hours (for labour-intensive departments) and machine hours (for machine-intensive departments)—are used to compute departmental rates. Products passing through the departments are assumed to consume overhead resources in proportion to the department's unit-based drivers (such as machine hours or direct labour hours used). Thus, in the second stage, overhead is assigned to products by multiplying the departmental rates by the amount of the driver used in the respective departments. The total overhead assigned to products is simply the sum of the amounts applied in each department.

Exhibit 4–4

Functional-Based Costing: Departmental Rates

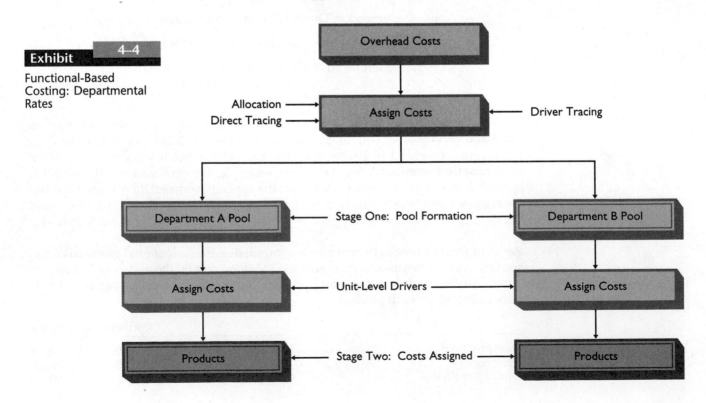

Exhibit 4–5	Fabrication	Assembly
Budgeted overhead	$252,000	$108,000
Expected and actual usage (direct labour hours):		
Cordless	7,000	3,000
Regular	13,000	77,000
	20,000	80,000
Expected and actual usage (machine hours):		
Cordless	4,000	1,000
Regular	36,000	9,000
	40,000	10,000

Exhibit 4–5

Departmental Data

The rationale for departmental rates is simple. Some producing departments may be more "overhead-intensive" than other producing departments. Thus, products that spend more time in overhead-intensive departments should be assigned more overhead cost than those that spend less time in these departments. Departmental rates pick up these possible effects, while plantwide rates lose them through averaging.

Computation of Departmental Rates   Assume that Belring has two production departments: fabrication and assembly. In fabrication, the major electronic component is made. Other parts are purchased from suppliers and sister divisions. Data relating to the departments for 2001 are given in Exhibit 4–5. Notice that fabrication is machine-intensive (compare expected machine hours), whereas assembly tends to be labour-intensive. Observing this, Belring bases its departmental overhead rates on machine hours in fabrication and on direct labour hours in assembly. Two overhead rates are calculated:

$$\text{Fabrication rate} = \text{Budgeted overhead}/\text{Expected machine hours}$$
$$= \$252,000/40,000$$
$$= \$6.30 \text{ per machine hour}$$

$$\text{Assembly rate} = \text{Budgeted overhead}/\text{Expected direct labour hours}$$
$$= \$108,000/80,000$$
$$= \$1.35 \text{ per direct labour hour}$$

Applied Overhead   Total applied overhead for the year is simply the sum of the amounts applied in each department:

$$\text{Applied overhead} = (\$6.30 \times \text{Actual machine hours}) + (\$1.35 \times \text{Actual direct labour hours})$$
$$= (\$6.30 \times 40,000) + (\$1.35 \times 80,000)$$
$$= \$252,000 + \$108,000$$
$$= \$360,000$$

Notice that the applied overhead equals the budgeted overhead. This happens only when the actual usage is the same as the expected usage, as in this example.

Per-Unit Cost   Using the departmental rates, the data from Exhibit 4–5, and the earlier information on prime costs and units produced, we show the computation of the unit cost in Exhibit 4–6.

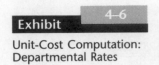

Exhibit 4-6

Unit-Cost Computation:
Departmental Rates

	Cordless	Regular
Prime costs	$ 78,000	$ 738,000
Applied overhead costs:		
($1.35 × 3,000) + ($6.30 × 4,000)	29,250	—
($1.35 × 77,000) + ($6.30 × 36,000)	—	330,750
Total manufacturing costs	$107,250	$1,068,750
Units produced	÷ 10,000	÷ 100,000
Unit cost (total costs/units)	$ 10.73	$ 10.69

LIMITATIONS OF FUNCTIONAL-BASED COST ACCOUNTING SYSTEMS

Objective 3

Explain why functional-based costing approaches may produce distorted costs.

Plantwide and departmental rates have been used for decades and continue to be used successfully by many organizations. In some settings, however, they do not work well and may actually cause severe product cost distortions. For some companies—particularly those characterized by intense or increasing competition (usually on a worldwide level), continuous improvement, total quality management, total customer satisfaction, and sophisticated technology—product cost distortions can be damaging. As firms operating in this competitive environment adopt new strategies for achieving competitive excellence, their cost accounting systems must often change to keep pace. Specifically, the need for more accurate product costs has forced many companies to take a serious look at their costing procedures. Cost systems that worked reasonably well in the past may no longer be acceptable.

Often organizations experience certain symptoms indicating that their cost accounting system is outdated. Many of these symptoms were described in this chapter's opening scenario involving Sharp Paper Inc. For example, if costs are distorted and severe overcosting of a major high-volume product is the outcome, then bids will be systematically lost, even when the company feels that it is pursuing an aggressive bidding strategy. This can be especially puzzling when the company is confident that it is operating as efficiently as its competitors. Thus, one symptom of an outdated cost system is the inability to explain the outcome of bids. On the flip side, if competitors' prices seem unrealistically low, it should cause managers to wonder about the accuracy of their cost system. Similarly, if somehow an organization's cost system is systematically understating the cost of low-volume specialty products—products that require special processes and handling—then the organization may find that it has a seemingly profitable niche all to itself. Yet it may find operational managers wanting to drop some of these "niche" products. These symptoms of an outdated cost system, along with several others, are listed in Exhibit 4–7.[2]

Organizations that have experienced some or all of these symptoms have found that their plantwide or departmental rates are simply no longer capable of accurately assigning overhead costs to individual products. At least two major factors impair the ability of unit-based plantwide and departmental rates to assign overhead costs accurately: (1) the proportion of nonunit-related overhead costs to total overhead costs is large, and (2) the degree of product diversity is great.

---

2.   The list of warning signals is based on Robin Cooper, "You Need a New Cost System When...," *Harvard Business Review* (January–February 1989): 77–82.

Exhibit	4–7

Symptoms of an Outdated Functional-Based Costing System

1. The outcome of bids is difficult to explain.
2. Competitors' prices appear unrealistically low.
3. Products that are difficult to produce show high profits.
4. Operational managers want to drop products that appear profitable.
5. Profit margins are difficult to explain.
6. The company has a highly profitable niche all to itself.
7. Customers do not complain about price increases.
8. The accounting department spends a lot of time supplying cost data for special projects.
9. Some departments are using their own accounting system.
10. Product costs change because of changes in financial reporting regulations.

Nonunit-Related Overhead Costs

The use of either plantwide rates or departmental rates assumes that a product's consumption of overhead resources is related strictly to the number of units produced. For activities that are performed each time a unit of product is produced, this assumption makes sense. But what if there are nonunit-level activities—(activities that are unrelated to the number of units produced? Setup costs, for example, are incurred each time a batch of products is produced. A batch may consist of 1,000 or 10,000 units, but the cost of setup is the same. Yet as more setups are done, setup costs increase. The number of setups, not the number of units produced, is a much better measure of the consumption of the setup activity. Product reengineering costs may depend on the number of different engineering work orders rather than on the number of units produced of any given product. Thus, *nonunit-level drivers* such as setups and engineering hours are needed for accurate cost assignment of nonunit-level activities. **Nonunit-level activity drivers** are factors that measure the consumption of nonunit-level activities by products and other cost objects.

Using only unit-based activity drivers to assign nonunit-related overhead costs can create distorted product costs. The severity of this distortion depends on what proportion of total overhead costs these nonunit-based costs represent. For many companies, this percentage can be significant. Schrader Bellows and John Deere Component Works, for example, experienced nonunit-based overhead cost ratios of about 50 percent and 40 percent, respectively.[3] This suggests that some care should be exercised in assigning nonunit-based overhead costs. If nonunit-based overhead costs are only a small percentage of total overhead costs, the distortion of product costs would be quite small. In such a case, using only unit-based activity drivers to assign overhead costs would be acceptable.

Product Diversity

The presence of significant nonunit overhead costs is a necessary but not sufficient condition for problems to arise with plantwide and departmental rates. If products consume the nonunit overhead activities in the same proportion as the unit-level overhead activities, then no product-costing distortion will occur (with the use of traditional overhead assignment methods). The presence of product diversity is also necessary. **Product diversity** simply means that products consume overhead activities in different proportions. There are several reasons that products might consume overhead in different proportions. For example, differences in product size, product complexity, setup time, and size of batches can all cause products to consume overhead at different rates. Regardless of the nature of the product diversity, product cost will be distorted whenever the quantity of unit-based overhead that a product con-

3. See Robin Cooper, "Cost Classification in Unit-Based and Activity-Based Manufacturing Cost Systems," *Journal of Cost Management for the Manufacturing Industry* (Fall 1990): 4–14.

sumes does not vary in direct proportion to the quantity of nonunit-based overhead that it consumes. The proportion of each activity consumed by a product is defined as the **consumption ratio**. How nonunit overhead costs and product diversity can produce distorted product costs is best illustrated with an example.[4]

An Example Illustrating the Failure of Unit-Based Overhead Rates

To illustrate how traditional unit-based overhead rates can distort product costs, we will return to the Belring example, this time providing more detailed information about the overhead activities that define their total overhead cost. The detailed data are provided in Exhibit 4–8: assume that the expected and actual outcomes are the same. Because the quantity of regular phones produced is 10 times greater than that of cordless phones, we can label the regular phones a high-volume product and the cordless phones a low-volume product. The phones are produced in batches.

For simplicity, only four types of overhead activities, performed by four distinct support departments, are assumed: setting up the equipment for each batch (different configurations are needed for the electronic components associated with each phone), moving a batch, machining, and testing. Testing is performed after each department's operations. After fabrication, each component is tested to ensure functionality. After assembly, the entire unit is tested to ensure that it is operational.

Problems with Costing Accuracy The activity usage data in Exhibit 4–8 reveal some serious problems with either plantwide or departmental rates for assigning overhead costs. The main problem with either procedure is the assumption that machine hours or direct labour hours drive or cause all overhead costs.

From Exhibit 4–8, we know that producing regular phones, the high-volume product, uses nine times as many direct labour hours as producing cordless phones, the low-volume product (90,000 hours versus 10,000 hours). Thus, if a plantwide rate is used, the regular phones will be assigned nine times more overhead cost than the

Exhibit 4–8

Product-Costing Data

ACTIVITY USAGE MEASURES

	Cordless	Regular	Total
Units produced per year	10,000	100,000	110,000
Prime costs	$78,000	$738,000	$816,000
Direct labour hours	10,000	90,000	100,000
Machine hours	5,000	45,000	50,000
Production runs	20	10	30
Number of moves	60	30	90

ACTIVITY COST DATA (Overhead Activities)

Activity	Activity Cost
Setup	$120,000
Material handling	60,000
Machining	100,000
Testing	80,000
Total	$360,000

4. See the following publications by Anthony A. Atkinson, "Manage Activities Instead of Costs," *CMA Magazine*, Vol. 63, No. 4, May 1989: 25; "Activity Costing and Efficiency," *CMA Magazine*, Vol. 63, No. 5, June 1989: 8; and "Diagnosing Costing Problems," *CMA Magazine*, Vol. 63, No. 3, April 1989: 20. See also John A. Miller, "Manage Costs? Manage Activities," *CMA Magazine*, March 1992: 35; and Paul A. Sharman, "Activity-Based Management: A Growing Practice," *CMA Magazine*, Vol. 67, No. 2, March 1993: 17–22.

cordless phones. But is this reasonable? Do unit-based drivers explain the consumption of all overhead activities? In particular, can we reasonably assume that each product's consumption of overhead increases in direct proportion to the direct labour hours used? Let's look at the four overhead activities and see if unit-based drivers accurately reflect the demands of regular and cordless phone production.

Examination of the data in Exhibit 4–8 suggests that a significant portion of overhead costs is not driven or caused by direct labour hours. For example, each product's demands for setup and material-handling activities are more logically related to the number of production runs and the number of moves, respectively. These nonunit activities represent 50 percent ($180,000/$360,000) of the total overhead costs—a significant percentage. Notice that the low-volume product, cordless phones, uses twice as many runs (20/10) and twice as many moves (60/30) as the regular phones. However, use of direct labour hours, a unit-based activity driver, and a plantwide rate assigns nine times more setup and material-handling costs to the regular phones than to the cordless ones. Thus, product diversity exists, and we should expect product cost distortion because the quantity of unit-based overhead that each product consumes does not vary in direct proportion to the quantity of nonunit-based overhead that it consumes.

The consumption ratios for the two products are illustrated in Exhibit 4–9. Consumption ratios are simply the proportion of each activity consumed by a product. The consumption ratios suggest that a plantwide rate based on direct labour hours will overcost the regular phones and undercost the cordless phones.

The problem is aggravated when departmental rates are used (refer to Exhibit 4–5). In the assembly department, regular phones consume 25.67 times as many direct labour hours as cordless phones do (77,000/3,000). In the fabrication department, regular phones consume 9 times as many machine hours as cordless phones do (36,000/4,000). Thus, the regular phones receive about 25.67 times more overhead than the cordless phones in the assembly department, and in the fabrication department they receive 9 times more overhead. As Exhibit 4–6 shows, with departmental rates, the unit cost of the cordless phones decreases to $10.73, and the unit cost of the regular phones increases to $10.69. This change is in the wrong direction, which emphasizes the failure of unit-based activity drivers, at either the plant level or the departmental level, to accurately reflect each product's demands for setup and material-handling costs.

Solving the Problem of Cost Distortion   The cost distortions just described can be solved using activity rates. That is, rather than assigning the overhead costs to departmental or plantwide pools, why not calculate a rate for each overhead activity and then use this activity rate to assign overhead costs? Using the drivers indicated in Exhibit 4–9 and the data provided in Exhibit 4–8, activity rates are computed below:

Setup rate:	$120,000/30 runs = $4,000.00 per run
Material-handling rate:	$60,000/90 moves = $666.67 per move
Machining rate:	$100,000/50,000 machine hours = $2.00 per machine hour
Testing rate:	$80,000/100,000 direct labour hours = $0.80 per direct labour hour

Exhibit 4–9	Overhead Activity	Cordless Phones	Regular Phones	Activity Driver
Product Diversity: Consumption Ratios	Setups	0.67[a]	0.33[a]	Production runs
	Material handling	0.67[b]	0.33[b]	Number of moves
	Power	0.10[c]	0.90[c]	Machine hours
	Testing	0.10[d]	0.90[d]	Direct labour hours

a   20/30 (cordless) and 10/30 (regular)
b   60/90 (cordless) and 30/90 (regular)
c   5,000/50,000 (cordless) and 45,000/50,000 (regular)
d   10,000/100,000 (cordless) and 90,000/100,000 (regular)

To assign overhead costs, the amount of activity consumed by each product is needed. These amounts are found in Exhibit 4–8. The calculation of the unit for each product using activity rates is given in Exhibit 4–10.

Comparison of Functional-Based and Activity-Based Product Costs   In Exhibit 4–11, the unit cost from activity-based costing is compared with the unit costs produced by functional-based costing using either a plantwide or a departmental rate. This comparison clearly illustrates the effects of using only unit-based activity drivers to assign overhead costs. The activity-based cost assignment reflects the pattern of overhead consumption and is therefore the most accurate of the three costs shown in Exhibit 4–11. Activity-based product costing reveals that the functional-based costing undercosts the cordless phones and overcosts the regular phones. In fact, the ABC assignment almost doubles the cost of the cordless phones and decreases the cost of the regular phones by almost $1 per unit—a movement in the right direction, given the pattern of overhead consumption. In a diverse product environment, ABC promises greater accuracy, and given the importance of making decisions based on correct information, a detailed look at ABC is certainly merited.

Exhibit 4–10		Cordless	Regular
Unit-Cost Computation: Activity Rates	Prime costs	$ 78,000	$ 738,000
	Applied overhead costs:		
	Setups:		
	($4,000 × 20)	80,000	
	($4,000 × 10)		40,000
	Material handling:		
	($666.67 × 60)	40,000	
	($666.67 × 30)		20,000
	Machining:		
	($2 × 5,000)	10,000	
	($2 × 45,000)		90,000
	Testing:		
	($0.80 × 10,000)	8,000	
	($0.80 × 90,000)		72,000
	Total manufacturing costs	$216,000	$ 960,000
	Units produced	÷ 10,000	÷100,000
	Unit cost (total costs/units)	$ 21.60	$ 9.60

Exhibit 4–11		Cordless	Regular	Source
Comparison of Unit Costs	Activity-based cost	$21.60	$ 9.60	Exhibit 4–10
	Funcional-based cost:			
	Plantwide rate	11.40	10.62	Exhibit 4–3
	Departmental rate	10.73	10.69	Exhibit 4–6

ACTIVITY-BASED PRODUCT COSTING: DETAILED DESCRIPTION

Objective 4

Explain how an activity-based costing system works.

In Exhibits 4–1 and 4–2, we saw that functional-based overhead costing involves two stages: first, overhead costs are assigned to an organizational unit (plant or departments), and second, overhead costs are then assigned to products. As Exhibit 4–12 illustrates, an **activity-based costing (ABC) system** traces costs first to activities and then to products. The underlying assumption is that activities consume resources and that products, in turn, consume activities. Thus, activity-based costing is also a two-stage process.[5] An ABC system, however, emphasizes direct tracing and driver tracing (exploiting cause-and-effect relationships), whereas a functional-based costing system tends to be allocation-intensive (largely ignoring cause-and-effect relationships). As the Exhibit 4–12 model reveals, the focus of activity-based costing is activities. Thus, identifying activities must be the first step in designing an activity-based costing system.

ABC: Two-Stage Assignment

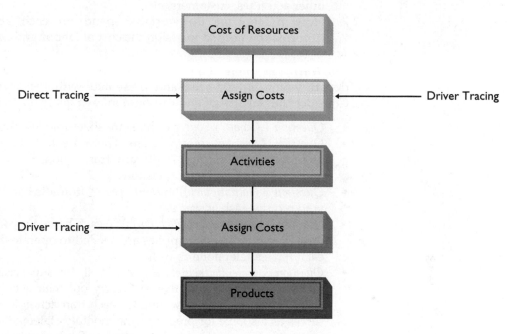

Identifying Activities and Their Attributes

Since an activity is an action taken or work performed by equipment or people for other people, identifying activities is usually accomplished by interviewing managers or representatives of functional work areas (departments). A set of key questions is asked whose answers provide much of the data needed for an activity-based costing system. This interview-derived data is used to prepare an *activity dictionary*. An **activity dictionary** lists the activities in an organization along with some critical activity attributes. **Activity attributes** are financial and nonfinancial information items that describe individual activities. What attributes are used depends on the purpose. Examples of activity attributes associated with a costing objective include types of resources consumed, amount (percentage) of time spent on an activity by workers, cost objects that consume the activity output (reason for performing the activity), a measure of activity output (**activity driver**), and the activity name.

Key Set of Questions   Interview questions can be used to identify activities and activity attributes needed for costing purposes. The information derived from these questions serves as the basis for constructing an activity dictionary as well as providing data helpful for assigning resource costs to individual activities. The following list is not exhaustive, but will serve to illustrate the nature of the information gathering process.

1. How many employees are in your department? (Activities consume labour.)
2. What do they do (please describe)? (Activities are people doing things for other people.)

5. The two-stage description is a simplification for both the functional-based and the activity-based models. In reality, multiple stages are possible. Chapter 7 explores these issues in greater detail for both models.

3. Do customers outside your department use any equipment? (Activities also can be equipment doing work for other people.)
4. What resources (equipment, materials, energy) are used by each activity? (Activities consume resources in addition to labour.)
5. What are the outputs of each activity? (Helps identify activity drivers.)
6. Who and what uses the activity output? (Identifies the cost object: products, other activities, customers, etc.)
7. How much time do workers spend on each activity? by equipment? (Information needed to assign the cost of labour and equipment to activities.)

Illustrative Example Suppose, for example, that a manager of a bank's credit card department is interviewed and presented with the seven questions just listed. Consider the purpose of and response to each question, in the order indicated.

- *Question 1 (labour resource):* There are six employees, including me.
- *Question 2 (activity identification):* There are four major activities: supervising employees, processing credit card transactions, issuing customer statements, and answering customer questions.
- *Question 3 (activity identification):* Yes. Automatic bank tellers service customers who require cash advances.
- *Question 4 (resource identification):* We each have our own computer, printer, and desk. Paper and other supplies are needed to operate the printers. Of course, we each have a telephone as well.
- *Question 5 (potential activity drivers):* Well, for supervising, I manage employees' needs and try to ensure that they carry out their activities efficiently. Processing transactions produces a posting for each transaction in our computer system and serves as a source for preparing the monthly statements. The number of monthly customer statements has to be the product for the issuing activity, and I suppose that customers served is the output for the answering activity. And I guess the number of cash advances would measure the product of the automatic teller activity, although the teller really generates more transactions for other products, such as chequing accounts. So perhaps the number of teller transactions is the real output.
- *Question 6 (identifying potential cost objects):* We have three products: classic, gold, and platinum credit cards. Transactions are processed for these three types of cards, and statements are sent to clients holding these cards. Similarly, answers to questions are all directed to clients who hold these cards. As far as supervising, I spend time ensuring the proper coordination and execution of all activities, except for the automatic teller: I really have no role in managing that particular activity.
- *Question 7 (identifying resource drivers):* I just completed a work survey and have the percentage of time calculated for each worker. All five clerks work on each of the three departmental activities. About 40 percent of their time is spent processing transactions, with the rest of their time split evenly between preparing statements and answering questions. Phone time is used only for answering client questions, and computer time is 70 percent transaction processing, 20 percent statement preparation, and 10 percent answering questions. Furthermore, my own time and that of my computer are 100 percent administrative.

Activity Dictionary Based on the answers to the survey, an activity dictionary can now be prepared. Exhibit 4–13 illustrates the dictionary for the credit card department. The activity dictionary names the activity (usually by combining an action verb and an object that receives the action), describes the tasks that make up the activity, classifies the activity as primary or secondary, lists the users (cost objects), and identifies a measure of activity output (activity driver). A **primary activity** is an activity that is consumed by a product or customer. A **secondary activity** is one that is consumed by other primary and secondary activities. Ultimately, secondary activities are consumed by a primary activity. For example, the supervising activity is consumed

Exhibit   4–13

Activity Dictionary:
Credit Card Department

Activity Name	Activity Description	Activity Type	Cost Object(s)	Activity Driver
Supervising employees	Scheduling, coordinating, and evaluating performance	Secondary	Activities within department	Total labour time for each activity
Processing transactions	Sorting, keying, and verifying	Primary	Credit cards	Number of transactions
Preparing statements	Reviewing, printing, stuffing, and mailing	Primary	Credit cards	Number of statements
Answering questions	Answering, logging, reviewing database, and making callbacks	Primary	Credit cards	Number of calls
Providing automatic tellers	Accessing accounts, withdrawing funds	Primary	Credit cards, chequing, and savings accounts	Number of teller transactions

by the following primary activities: processing transactions, preparing statements, and answering phones. The three products—classic, gold, and platinum credit cards—in turn, consume the primary activities. It is not unusual for a typical organization to produce an activity dictionary containing 200 to 300 activities.

Assigning Costs to Activities

Once activities are identified and described, the next task is determining how much it cost to perform each activity. This requires the identification of the resources being consumed by each activity. Activities consume resources such as labour, materials, energy, and capital. The costs of these resources are found in the general ledger, but how much is spent on each activity is not revealed. It therefore becomes necessary to assign the resource costs to activities using direct tracing and driver tracing. For labour resources, a *work distribution matrix* is often used. A work distribution matrix simply identifies the amount of labour consumed by each activity and is derived from the interview process (or a written survey). For example, the manager of the credit card department disclosed the following about labour usage by the individual activities (see Question 7):

	Percentage of Time on Each Activity	
Activity	Supervisor	Clerks
Supervising employees	100%	0%
Processing transactions	0%	40%
Preparing statements	0%	30%
Answering questions	0%	30%

The time spent on each activity is the basis for assigning the labour costs to the activity. If the time is 100 percent, then labour is exclusive to the activity and direct tracing can be used to assign the cost (such would be the case for the supervisory labour cost). If the resource is shared by several activities (as is the case for the clerical resource), then driver tracing is used to assign the labour cost. These drivers are called resource drivers. A **resource driver** is a factor that measures the consumption of a resource by activities. Once resource drivers are identified, then the costs of the resource can be assigned to the activities. Assume, for example, that the supervisor's salary is $50,000, and each clerk is paid a salary of $30,000 ($150,000 total clerical cost for five clerks). The amount of labour cost assigned to each activity is given below:

Supervising employees	$50,000	(by direct tracing)
Processing transactions	$60,000	(40% × $150,000)
Preparing statements	$45,000	(30% × $150,000)
Answering questions	$45,000	(30% × $150,000)

Labour, of course is not the only resource consumed by activities. The interview, for example, reveals that the credit card department uses computers (capital), phones (capital), desks (capital), and paper (materials). The automatic teller activity uses the automatic teller (capital) and energy. The costs of these resources must also be assigned to the various activities. They are assigned in the same way as described for labour (using direct tracing and resource drivers). The cost of computers could be assigned using direct tracing for the supervising activity and hours of usage for the remaining activities. From the interview, we know the relative usage of computers for each activity. Suppose the general ledger reveals that the cost per computer is $1,200 per year. Thus, an additional $1,200 would be assigned to the supervising activity, and $6,000 (5 × $1,200) would be assigned to the other activities based on relative usage—70 percent ($4,200) to processing transactions, 20 percent ($1,200) to preparing statements, and 10 percent ($600) to answering questions. Repeating this process for all resources, the total cost of each activity can be calculated. Exhibit 4–14 gives the cost of the activities for the credit card department under the assumption that all resource costs have been assigned (these numbers are assumed because not all the data are given for their calculation).

Exhibit 4–14

Credit Card Department Activity Costs: First Stage

Supervising employees	$ 75,000
Processing transactions	100,000
Preparing statements	79,500
Answering questions	69,900
Providing automatic tellers	250,000

Assigning Activity Costs to Other Activities

Assigning costs to activities completes the first stage of activity-based costing. In this first stage, activities are classified as primary and secondary. If there are secondary activities, then intermediate stages exist. In an intermediate stage, the costs of secondary activities are assigned to the activities that consume their output. For example, supervising employees is a secondary activity. The output measure is the total employee time used by each activity (see the activity dictionary, Exhibit 4–13). From the work distribution matrix prepared earlier, we know that the three primary departmental activities use clerical labour in the proportions 40 percent, 30 percent, and 30 percent, respectively. The cost of supervising employees would be assigned to each consuming primary activity using these ratios (which now function as an activity driver). The new costs using the activity driver and the activity costs from Exhibit 4–14 are shown in Exhibit 4–15.

Exhibit 4–15

Credit Card Department Activity Costs: Intermediate Stage

Processing transactions	$130,000 [$100,000 + (0.4 × $75,000)]
Preparing statements	102,000 [$ 79,500 + (0.3 × $75,000)]
Answering questions	92,400 [$ 69,900 + (0.3 × $75,000)]
Providing automatic tellers	250,000

Assigning Costs to Products

Once the costs of primary activities are determined, then these costs can be assigned to products in proportion to their usage of the activity, as measured by activity drivers. This assignment is accomplished by calculating a predetermined activity rate and multiplying this rate by the actual usage of the activity. From Exhibit 4–13, the activity drivers are identified for each of the four primary activities: number of transactions for processing transactions, number of statements for preparing statements, number of calls for answering questions, and number of teller transactions for the activity of providing automatic tellers. To calculate an activity rate, the practical capacity of each activity must be determined. To assign costs, we must also determine the amount of each activity consumed by each product. For our purposes, we will assume that total activity usage for all products is equal to the practical activity capacity. For the credit card example, the following data have been collected:

	Classic	Gold	Platinum	Total
Number of cards	5,000	3,000	2,000	10,000
Transactions processed	600,000	300,000	100,000	1,000,000
Number of statements	60,000	36,000	24,000	120,000
Number of calls	10,000	12,000	8,000	30,000
Number of teller transactions*	15,000	3,000	2,000	20,000

* The number of teller transactions for the cards is 10 percent of the total transactions from all sources. Thus, teller transactions total 200,000 (10 × 20,000).

Using these data and the costs from Exhibit 4–15, the activity rates can be calculated:

Rate calculations:

Processing transactions:	$130,000/1,000,000 = $0.13 per transaction
Preparing statements:	$102,000/120,000 = $0.85 per statement
Answering questions:	$92,400/30,000 = $3.08 per call
Providing automatic tellers:	$250,000/200,000 = $1.25 per transaction

Using these rates, costs are assigned as shown in Exhibit 4–16. As should be evident, the assignment process is the same as the one used in the Belring example illustrated in Exhibit 4–10. However, we now know the full story behind the development of the

Exhibit 4–16

Credit Card Department Activity Costs: Final Stage

	Classic	Gold	Platinum
Processing transactions:			
$0.13 × 600,000	$ 78,000		
$0.13 × 300,000		$ 39,000	
$0.13 × 100,000			$13,000
Preparing statements:			
$0.85 × 60,000	51,000		
$0.85 × 36,000		30,600	
$0.85 × 24,000			20,400
Answering questions:			
$3.08 × 10,000	30,800		
$3.08 × 12,000		36,960	
$3.08 × 8,000			24,640
Providing automatic tellers:			
$1.25 × 15,000	18,750		
$1.25 × 3,000		3,750	
$1.25 × 2,000			2,500
Total costs	$178,550	$110,310	$60,540
Units	÷ 5,000	÷ 3,000	÷ 2,000
Unit cost (Total costs/Units)	$ 35.71	$ 36.77	$ 30.27

activity rates and usage measures. Furthermore, the banking setting emphasizes the usefulness of activity-based costing in service organizations.

HOMOGENEOUS ACTIVITY POOLS

In the first stage of activity-based costing, activities are identified, costs are associated with individual activities, and activities are classified as primary and secondary. In the intermediate stage, costs of secondary activities are reassigned to primary activities. In the final stage, costs of primary activities are assigned to products and customers. Assigning costs to other activities (intermediate stage) or assigning costs to products and customers (final stage) requires the use of activity rates. In principle, an activity rate is calculated for each activity. A firm may have hundreds of different activities, and thus hundreds of activity rates. Although information technology is certainly capable of handling this volume, there may be some merit to reducing the number of rates, if possible. For example, fewer rates may produce more readable and manageable product cost reports. Fewer rates may also reduce the perceived complexity of an activity-based costing system.

Process for Reducing the Number of Rates

To reduce the number of overhead rates required and streamline the process, activities can be grouped into homogeneous sets based on similar characteristics: (1) they are logically related, and (2) they have the same consumption ratios for all products. Costs are associated with each of these homogeneous sets by summing the costs of the individual activities belonging to the set. The collection of overhead costs associated with each set of activities is called a **homogeneous cost pool**. Since the activities within a homogeneous cost pool have the same consumption ratio, the activity drivers of *each* activity assign costs to products in exactly the same proportions. This means that only one driver is needed to assign the pool's costs, and thus the number of rates can be reduced.

Once a cost pool is defined, the cost per unit of the chosen activity driver is computed by dividing the pool costs by the activity driver's practical capacity. The result of this calculation is called the **pool rate**.

To illustrate this process, consider once again the Belring example. Four overhead activities have been identified: setups, material handling, machining, and testing. The first criterion for homogeneity requires the existence of logical relationships. Setup activities and material-handling activities are performed each time a batch of products is produced. Thus, these two activities are logically related by the more general batch-level production activity. Similarly, testing and machining activities are performed each time a unit of product is produced (recall that each unit is tested). Thus, these two activities are logically related by the more general activity of producing a unit of product. Moreover, from Exhibit 4–9 we know that the setups and material-handling grouping and the power and testing grouping have the same consumption ratios for both products (0.33 and 0.67 for the first group and 0.10 and 0.90 for the second group). Thus, we are able to reduce four activities to two homogeneous sets of activities. These two sets can now be used to form homogeneous cost pools. Let's call the set with setups and material handling the batch-level pool and the set with machining and testing the unit-level pool. The total cost associated with each pool is simply the sum of the related activities. The pool rate is the total cost divided by a driver chosen from an activity in the set. Assume that the number of runs is the driver chosen for the batch-level pool and that machine hours is the driver chosen for the unit-level pool. Using the data from Exhibit 4–8, the pool costs and rates follow:

Batch-Level Pool			Unit-Level Pool	
Setups	$120,000		Machining	$100,000
Material handling	60,000		Testing	80,000
Total	$180,000		Total	$180,000
Driver quantity	÷ 30 runs			÷ 50,000 machine hours
Pool rate	$ 6,000 per run			$ 3.60 per machine hour

The unit product costs for regular and cordless phones, using these pool rates to assign the overhead costs, will be the same as those we calculated earlier using individual activity rates (see Exhibit 4–10). This result is shown in Exhibit 4–17.

Exhibit   4–17

Unit Costs Activity-Based Costing: Pool Rates

	Cordless	Regular
Prime costs	$ 78,000	$738,000
Overhead costs:		
Batch-level pool:		
($6,000 × 20)	120,000	
($6,000 × 10)		60,000
Unit-level pool:		
($3.60 × 5,000)	18,000	
($3.60 × 45,000)		162,000
Total manufacturing costs	$216,000	$960,000
Units of production	10,000	100,000
Unit cost (Total costs/Units)	$21.60	$9.60

Detailed Classification of Activities

In building sets of related activities, activities are classified into one of the following four general activity categories: (1) unit level, (2) batch level, (3) product level, and (4) facility level. Classifying activities into these general categories facilitates product costing because the costs of activities associated with the different levels respond to different types of cost drivers (cost behaviour differs by level). The definition of the activities belonging to each general category clearly illustrates this feature. **Unit-level activities** are those performed each time a unit is produced. For example, machining and assembly are activities performed each time a unit is produced. The costs of unit-level activities vary with the number of units produced. **Batch-level activities** are those performed each time a batch of goods is produced. The costs of batch-level activities vary with the number of batches, but they are fixed with respect to the number of units in each batch. Setups, inspections (unless each unit is inspected), production scheduling, and material handling are examples of batch-level activities. **Product-level (sustaining) activities** are those performed as needed to support the various products produced by a company. These activities consume inputs that develop products or allow products to be produced and sold. These activities and their costs tend to increase as the number of different products increases. Engineering changes, development of product-testing procedures, marketing a product, process engineering, and expediting are examples of product-level activities. **Facility-level activities** are those that sustain a factory's general manufacturing processes. These activities benefit the organization at some level but do not provide a benefit for any specific product. Examples include plant management, landscaping, support of community programs, security, property taxes, and plant amortization.

Of the four general levels, the first three—unit level, batch level, and product level—contain product-related activities. For these three levels, it is possible to measure the demands placed on the activities by individual products. Activities within these three levels can be further subdivided on the basis of consumption ratios.

Activities with the same consumption ratios can use the same activity driver to assign costs. Thus, in effect, all activities within each of the first three levels that have the same activity driver are grouped together. This final grouping creates a homogeneous set of activities: a collection of activities that are at the same level and use the same activity driver. Exhibit 4–18 illustrates the activity classification model that creates homogeneous sets of activities. Notice that facility-level activities do not undergo the driver classification.

The fourth general category, facility-level activities, poses a problem for the ABC philosophy of tracing costs to products. Tracing activity costs to individual products depends on the ability to identify the amount of each activity consumed by a product (product demands for activities must be measured). Facility-level activities (and their costs) are common to a variety of products, and it is not possible to identify how individual products consume these activities. A pure ABC system, therefore, would not assign these costs to products. They would be treated as period costs. In effect, these costs are fixed costs—costs that are not driven by any of the cost drivers found in any of the first three categories. In practice, companies that adopt ABC systems usually implement a full-costing (or absorption-costing) approach and allocate these facility-level costs to individual products.[6] Unit-level, batch-level, or product-level cost drivers are often used for the allocation. As a practical matter, assigning these costs may not significantly distort product costs, because they are likely to be small relative to the total costs that are appropriately traced to individual products.

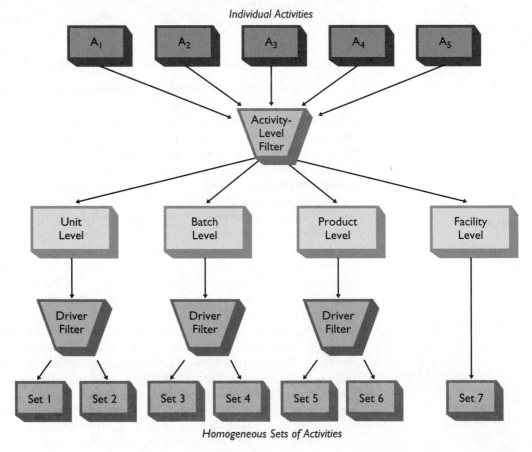

Exhibit 4–18

Formation of Homogeneous Sets of Activity

---

6. A study of 31 companies and 51 cost systems revealed that all companies using an ABC system allocated facility-level costs to products. See Robin Cooper, "Cost Classification in Unit-Based and Activity-Based Manufacturing Systems."

There is, however, a possible exception to this observation about facility-level costs and activity drivers. When a company has organized its production facilities around product lines, then it can be argued that space drivers measure the consumption of facility-level costs. This is because floor space within a plant is dedicated to the production of a single product or subassembly. In this case, area occupied can be viewed as a possible activity driver for facility costs. Assigning facility-level costs on the basis of space drivers can also serve to motivate managers to reduce the space needed for production, thus reducing facility-level costs over time.

Comparison with Functional-Based Costing

The hierarchical classification of activities allows us to illustrate the fundamental differences between activity-based and functional-based costing systems. In a functional-based system, the consumption of overhead by products is assumed to be explained only by unit-based activity drivers. In a sophisticated functional system, overhead costs are classified as fixed or variable with respect to unit-based drivers. Unit-based costing systems allocate fixed overhead to individual products using fixed overhead rates, and assign variable overhead using variable overhead rates. From the perspective of activity-based costing, the variable overhead is appropriately traced to individual products (for this category, overhead consumption increases as units produced increase). However, assigning fixed overhead costs using unit-based activity drivers can be arbitrary, and may not reflect the activities actually consumed by the products. Many of the costs assigned in the fixed overhead category are in reality batch-level, product-level, and facility-level costs that vary with drivers other than unit-level drivers.

Activity-based costing systems improve product-costing accuracy by recognizing that many of the so-called fixed overhead costs actually vary in proportion to changes other than production volume. If we understand what causes these costs to increase or decrease, we can trace them to individual products. This cause-and-effect relationship allows managers to improve product-costing accuracy, which can significantly improve decision making. Additionally, this large pool of fixed overhead costs is no longer so mysterious. Knowing the underlying behaviour of many of these costs allows managers to exert more control over the activities that cause the costs.[7]

ABC, JIT, AND PRODUCT COSTING

Objective 6

Describe the role of activity-based costing for organizations with only one product, homogeneous products, or a JIT structure.

In an activity-based costing system, product-costing accuracy is improved by tracing activity costs to the products that consume the activities. Because of the large number of overhead activities that are shared by products, the effort and expense of an activity-based costing system can be considerable. Single-product firms and multiple-product firms that choose to dedicate entire facilities to the production of a single product have no problems with costing accuracy. All overhead activities and costs are directly traceable to a single product.

Firms that install a JIT (just-in-time) manufacturing system achieve some of the same product-costing benefits found in a single-product environment. These benefits are realized because JIT manufacturing adopts a more focused approach than that found in traditional manufacturing. Installing a JIT system affects product costing because it affects the traceability of costs, enhances product-costing accuracy, diminishes the need for allocation of service-centre costs, and changes the behaviour

7. See *Implementing Activity-Based Costing, Management Accounting Guidelines #17*, Society of Management Accountants of Canada, 1993. For more discussion of ABC and its potential application to service organizations, see John Antos, "Activity-Based Management for Service, Not-for-Profit, and Governmental Organizations," *Journal of Cost Management* (Summer 1992): 13–23; and William Rotch, "Activity-Based Costing in Service Industries," *Journal of Cost Management* (Summer 1990): 4–14. For an example of an application of ABC in a partnership that provides a wide range of engineering and architectural consulting services, see Beth M. Chaffman and John Talbot, "Activity-Based Costing in a Service Organization," *CMA Magazine*, Vol. 64, No. 10, December/January 1991: 15–18.

and relative importance of direct labour costs. To understand and appreciate these effects, we need a fundamental understanding of what JIT manufacturing is and how it differs from traditional manufacturing.[8]

Basic Features of JIT

JIT manufacturing is a demand-pull system. The objective of **JIT manufacturing** is to eliminate waste by producing a product only when it is needed and only in the quantities demanded by customers. Demand pulls products through the manufacturing process. Each operation produces only what is necessary to satisfy the demand of the succeeding operation. No production takes place until a signal from a succeeding process indicates a need to produce. Parts and materials arrive just in time to be used in production. JIT assumes that all costs other than direct materials are driven by time and space drivers. JIT then focuses on eliminating waste by compressing time and space. Successful implementation of JIT has brought about significant improvements such as better quality, increased productivity, reduced lead times, major reductions in inventories, reduced setup times, lower manufacturing costs, and increased production rates. For example, Oregon Cutting Systems (OCS), a manufacturer of cutting chain (for chain saws), timber harvesting equipment, and sporting equipment, within a period of three to five years, reduced defects by 80 percent, waste by 50 percent, setup times from hours to minutes (one punch press had setup time reduced from 3 hours to 4.5 minutes), lead times from 21 days to 3 days, and manufacturing costs by 35 percent.[9] J. M. Schneider, Inc., of Kitchener, Ontario, brought itself back into the black in the face of declining demand in the meat-packing industry. In one year, JIT reduced inventory levels by over $6 million; yield, labour, and material cost reductions were in excess of $8 million; customer returns were down by 43 percent, water usage was down by 30 percent, and landfill charges were reduced by 50 percent.[10] Syncrude Canada Ltd. uses a JIT approach to operations to improve efficiency and increase capacity.[11] JIT techniques have also been implemented by the following companies:

AT&T	General Motors	Motorola
Black & Decker	Harley-Davidson	Toys "R" Us
Borg Warner	Hewlett-Packard	Wal-Mart
Chrysler	John Deere	Westinghouse
Ford	Intel	Xerox
General Electric	Mercury Marine	

A survey of Canadian manufacturers indicates that JIT is being implemented by relatively large firms and that the ability to acquire supplies in a timely fashion is important in JIT adoption.[12] Managers in companies that did not adopt JIT cited several reasons, including incapable suppliers, fluctuation in demand, and inadequate support by senior management. The survey reports that the major reasons for adopting JIT are reductions in inventory, costs, and the production time cycle; and improvements in quality and on-time delivery.

---

8. For more discussion of JIT in manufacturing and service organizations, see: Il-woon Kim, Hai G. Park, and Lance J. Besser, "Are You Ready for JIT?" *CMA Magazine*, Vol. 66, No. 2, July–August 1988, 44–48; Al Bhimani and Michael Bromich, "Accounting for Just-in-Time Manufacturing Systems," *CMA Magazine*, Vol. 65, No. 1, February 1991, 31–34; and John Y. Lee, "JIT Works for Services Too," *CMA Magazine*, Vol. 64, No. 6, July–August 1990, 20–23.

9. Jack C. Bailes and Ilene K. Kleinsorge, "Cutting Waste with JIT," *Management Accounting* (May 1992): 28–32.

10. Douglas W. Dodds, "Making It Better and Better," *CMA Magazine*, Vol. 66, No. 2, February 1992, 16–21.

11. John A. Clarke, "Fuel Efficient," *CA Magazine*, December 1999, 18–25.

12. Murray Lindsay and Suresh S. Kalagnanam, *The Adoption of Just-In-Time Production Systems in Canada and Their Association with Management Control Practices*. A Research Publication by the Society of Management Accountants of Canada, Hamilton, Ontario, 1993.

Inventory Effects   **JIT purchasing** requires suppliers to deliver parts and materials just in time to be used in production. Supplier linkages are vital. Supply of parts must be linked to production, which is linked to demand. JIT exploits supplier linkages by negotiating long-term contracts with a few chosen suppliers located as close to the production facility as possible and establishing more extensive supplier involvement. One effect of successful exploitation of these linkages is to reduce all inventories to much lower levels. For example, Mercedes-Benz U.S., to save both time and money, pared its supplier list to 100 (versus 1,000 for the E-class sedan). Mercedes-Benz has offered suppliers multiyear contracts in exchange for 5 percent price cuts.[13]

Contrast this with the traditional push-through system of manufacturing. In traditional manufacturing, materials are supplied and parts produced and transferred to the succeeding process in an effort to meet customer demand and delivery schedules. However, in a traditional push-through environment, slow or delayed reaction time is often a problem, which, in turn, creates a demand for finished goods inventories (otherwise, customers would grow old waiting for the firm to produce and deliver the needed goods). In a push-through environment, finished goods inventories are also needed to serve as a buffer when production, for whatever reason, is less than demand. Usually, the push-through system produces significantly higher levels of finished goods inventory than a JIT system does.

Plant Layout   The type and efficiency of plant layout is managed differently under JIT manufacturing. In traditional job and batch manufacturing, products are moved from one group of identical machines to another. Typically, machines with identical functions are located together in an area referred to as a department or process. Workers who specialize in the operation of a specific machine are located in each department. JIT replaces this traditional plant layout with a pattern of manufacturing cells. Cell structure is directly related to some of the efficiencies cited earlier for Oregon Cutting Systems, such as reduced lead times and lower manufacturing costs. The cellular manufacturing design can also affect plant size and number of plants, because it typically requires less space. Compaq Computer Corp., for example, cut its space requirement by 23 percent and increased output per square metre by 16 percent at its plant in Scotland. Space savings like these can reduce the demand to build new plants and will affect the size of new plants when they are needed.

Manufacturing Cells   **Manufacturing cells** contain machines that are grouped in families, usually in a semicircle. The machines are arranged so that they can be used to perform a variety of operations in sequence. Each cell is set up to produce a particular product or product family. Products move from one machine to another from start to finish. Workers are assigned to cells and are trained to operate all machines within the cell. Thus, labour in a JIT environment is multiskilled, not specialized. Each manufacturing cell is essentially a minifactory, and cells are often referred to as a factory within a factory. Exhibit 4–19 compares JIT's plant layout with the traditional pattern.

Grouping of Employees   Another major structural difference between JIT and traditional organizations relates to how employees are grouped. As just indicated, each cell is viewed as a minifactory; thus, each cell requires easy and quick access to support services, which means that centralized service departments must be scaled down and their personnel reassigned to work directly with manufacturing cells. For example, with respect to raw materials, JIT calls for multiple stock points, each one near where the material will be used. There is no need for a central store location—in fact, such an arrangement actually hinders efficient production. A purchasing agent can be

13. David Woodruff and Karen Lowry Miller, "Mercedes' Maverick in Alabama," *Business Week*, 11 September 1995, 64–65.

4–19   Plant Layout Pattern: Traditional versus JIT

Traditional Manufacturing Layout

Each product passes through departments that specialize in one process. Departments process multiple products.

JIT Manufacturing Layout

Notice that each product passes through its own cell. All machines necessary to process each product are placed within the cell. Each cell is dedicated to the production of one product or one subassembly.

assigned to each cell to handle material requirements. Similarly, other service personnel, such as manufacturing and quality engineers, can be assigned to cells.

Other support services may be relocated to the cell by training cell workers to perform the services. For example, in addition to direct production work, cell workers may perform setup duties, move partly completed goods from station to station within the cell, perform preventive maintenance and minor repairs, conduct quality inspections, and perform janitorial tasks. This multiple-task capability is directly related to the demand-pull or pull-through production approach. Producing on demand means that *production workers* (formerly direct labourers) may often have "free" time. This nonproduction time can be used to perform some of the other support activities.

Employee Empowerment A major procedural difference between traditional and JIT environments is the degree of participation allowed workers in the management of the organization. According to the JIT view, increasing the degree of participation increases productivity and overall cost efficiency. Workers are allowed a say in how the plant operates. For example, workers are allowed to shut down production to identify and correct problems. Input is sought and used to improve production processes. Workers, as at Saturn and Southwest Airlines, are often involved in interviewing and hiring other employees, sometimes even including prospective bosses. The reason? If the "chemistry is right," then the workforce will be more efficient—and will work together better. Employee empowerment calls for a different style of management: managers in the JIT environment need to act as facilitators more than as supervisors. Their role is to develop people and their skills so that they can make value-adding contributions.

Exhibit 4–20

Comparison of JIT
Approach with
Traditional
Manufacturing

JIT	Traditional
1. Pull-through system	1. Push-through system
2. Insignificant inventories	2. Significant inventories
3. Small supplier base	3. Large supplier base
4. Long-term supplier contracts	4. Short-term supplier contracts
5. Cellular structure	5. Departmental structure
6. Multiskilled labuor	6. Specialized labour
7. Decentralized services	7. Centralized services
8. High employee involvement	8. Low employee involvement
9. Facilitating management style	9. Supervisory management style
10. Total quality control	10. Acceptable quality level

Total Quality Control JIT necessarily carries with it a much stronger emphasis on managing quality. A defective part brings production to a grinding halt. Poor quality simply cannot be tolerated in a manufacturing environment that operates without inventories. Simply put, JIT cannot be implemented without a commitment to total quality control (TQC). TQC is essentially a never-ending quest for perfect quality, the striving for a defect-free product design and manufacturing process. This approach to managing quality is diametrically opposed to the traditional doctrine, called **acceptable quality level (AQL)**. AQL permits or allows defects to occur provided they do not exceed a predetermined level.[14]

The major differences between JIT manufacturing and traditional manufacturing are summarized in Exhibit 4–20. These differences have some fairly direct implications for product costing and for the role of ABC in a JIT environment.

Traceability of Overhead Costs

A cost system uses three methods to assign costs to individual products: direct tracing, driver tracing, and allocation. Of the three methods, the most accurate is direct tracing; it is therefore preferred over the other two methods. In a JIT environment, many overhead costs formerly assigned to products using either driver tracing or allocation are now directly attributable to products. Cellular manufacturing, multiskilled labour, and decentralized service activities are the major JIT features that are responsible for this change in traceability.

In a departmental structure, many different products may be subjected to a process located in a single department (for example, grinding). After completion of the process, the products are then transferred to other processes located in different departments (for example, assembly, painting, and so on). Although a different set of processes is usually required for each product, most processes are applicable to more than one product. For example, 30 different products may need grinding. Because more than one product is processed in a department, the costs of that department are common to all products passing through it and, therefore, must be assigned to products using activity drivers or allocation. In a manufacturing-cell structure, however, all processes necessary for the production of each product or major subassembly are collected in one area called a cell. The costs of operating that cell can be assigned to the cell's product or subassembly using direct tracing. (However, if a family of products uses a cell, then we must resort to drivers and allocation to assign costs.)

Equipment formerly located in other departments, for example, is now reassigned to cells, where it may be dedicated to the production of a single product or subassembly. In this case, amortization is now a directly attributable product cost.

---

14. Paul A. Sharman, "World Class Productivity at Standard Aero," *CMA Magazine*, Vol. 65, No. 3, April 1991, 7–12, describes how Standard Aero of Winnipeg, Manitoba, through improved productivity and total quality management (TQM), increased its earnings by 45 percent in one year on a sales increase of 4.5 percent.

Exhibit   4–21

Product Cost Assignment:
Traditional versus JIT
Manufacturing

Manufacturing Cost	Traditional Environment	JIT Environment
Direct labour	Direct tracing	Direct tracing
Direct materials	Direct tracing	Direct tracing
Material handling	Driver tracing	Direct tracing
Repairs and maintenance	Driver tracing	Direct tracing
Energy	Driver tracing	Direct tracing
Operating supplies	Driver tracing	Direct tracing
Supervision (department)	Allocation	Direct tracing
Insurance and taxes	Allocation	Allocation
Plant amortization	Allocation	Allocation
Equipment amortization	Driver tracing	Direct tracing
Custodial services	Allocation	Direct tracing
Cafeteria services	Driver tracing	Driver tracing

Multiskilled workers and decentralized services add to the effect. Workers in the cell
are trained to set up, maintain, and operate the equipment in that cell. Cell workers
may also be used to move a partly finished piece from one machine to the next and
to perform maintenance, setups, and material handling—all of which are support
functions that were previously done by a different set of labourers for all product
lines. Additionally, people with specialized skills (for example, industrial engineers
and production schedulers) are assigned directly to manufacturing cells. Thus,
because of multitask assignments and redeployment of other support personnel,
many support costs can now be assigned to a product using direct attribution.
Exhibit 4–21 compares the traceability of some selected costs in a traditional manufacturing environment with their traceability in the JIT environment (assuming single-
product cells). Comparisons are based on the three cost assignment methods.

Product Costing and ABC

One consequence of increasing directly attributable costs is to increase the accuracy
of product costing. Directly attributable costs are physically and exclusively associated with the product and can safely be said to belong to it. Other costs, however, are
common to several products and must be assigned to these products using activity
drivers and allocation. Because of cost and convenience, activity drivers that are less
than perfectly correlated with the consumption of overhead activities may be chosen.
JIT manufacturing reduces the need for this difficult type of assessment by converting many common costs to directly traceable costs. While activity-based costing
offers significant improvement in product-costing accuracy, focusing offers even
more potential improvement.

Exhibit 4–21 illustrates that JIT does not convert all costs into directly traceable costs.
Even with JIT in place, some overhead activities remain common to the manufacturing cells. These remaining support activities are mostly facility-level activities. In a
JIT system, the batch size is one unit of product. Thus, all batch-level activities convert into unit-level activities. Additionally, many of the batch-level activities are
reduced or eliminated. For example, material handling may be significantly reduced
because of reorganizing from a departmental structure to a cellular structure.
Similarly, for single-product cells, there is no setup activity. Even for cells that produce a family of products, setup times are minimal. Furthermore, it is likely that the
need to use activity drivers for the cost of product-level activities is significantly
diminished because of decentralizing these support activities to the cell level. Is
there, then, a role for ABC in a JIT firm?

Although JIT diminishes the value of ABC for tracing manufacturing costs to
individual products, an activity-based costing system has much broader application

than just tracing manufacturing costs to products. For many strategic and tactical decisions, the product cost definition needs to include nonmanufacturing costs. Thus, knowing and understanding general and administrative, research, development, marketing, customer service, and postpurchase activities and their cost drivers is essential for sound cost analysis. Oregon Cutting Systems, the firm whose JIT experience we described earlier, in 1990 appointed a special multidisciplinary team to explore the possibility of implementing an activity-based costing system. The team was given the charge to identify cost drivers for the organization's service areas (value-chain activities other than manufacturing). The objective was to exploit activities and their drivers to achieve efficiency gains comparable to the manufacturing area. Furthermore, we should keep in mind that managers are interested in more than just products as cost objects. Thus, although JIT may diminish the importance of ABC for product costing, it may actually provide impetus for using ABC for other applications, such as customer cost analysis.

Activity-Based Customer Costing

Customers, distribution channels, and markets are also cost objects of fundamental interest. This is true for both JIT and non-JIT environments. For example, consider customers. It is possible to have customer diversity, just as it is possible to have product diversity. Customers can consume customer-driven activities in different proportions. Sources of customer diversity include such things as order frequency, delivery frequency, geographic distance, sales and promotional support, and engineering support requirements. Knowing how much it costs to service different customers can be vital information for such purposes as pricing, determining customer mix, and improving profitability. Furthermore, because of diversity of customers, distribution channels, and so on, multiple drivers are needed to trace costs accurately. ABC can therefore be useful to organizations that may have only one product, homogeneous products, or a JIT structure where direct tracing diminishes the value of ABC for product costing.

Customer Costing versus Product Costing Assigning the costs of customer service to customers is done in the same way that manufacturing costs are assigned to products. Customer-driven activities such as order entry, order picking, shipping, making sales calls, and evaluating a client's credit are identified and listed in an activity inventory. The cost of the resources consumed is assigned to activities, and the cost of the activities is assigned to individual customers. The same model and procedures apply to customers as apply to products. Although we will not define them, it is also possible to have different levels of customer-driven activities, such as order level, customer level, and channel level.[15] Thus, in principle, it is possible to build homogeneous customer-driven cost pools using level and driver attributes. A simple example will illustrate the basics of activity-based customer costing.

Example Suppose that Milan Company produces precision parts for 11 major buyers. ABC is used to assign production costs to products. Of the 11 customers, one accounts for 50 percent of the sales, with the other 10 accounting for the remainder of the sales. The 10 smaller customers purchase parts in roughly equal quantities. Orders placed by the smaller customers are about the same size. Data concerning Milan's customer activity follow:

---

15. A detailed discussion of customer-driven costs, including formal definitions of customer-level activities, can be found in Michael C. O'Guin and Stephen A. Rebishke, "Customer-Driven Costs Using Activity-Based Costing," in *Handbook of Cost Management*, ed. Barry Brinker (New York: Warren Gorham Lamont, 1993), B5–1 and B5–29.

	Large Customer	Ten Smaller Customers
Units purchased	500,000	500,000
Orders placed	2	200
Number of sales calls	10	210
Manufacturing costs	$3,000,000	$3,000,000
Order-filling costs allocated*	$202,000	$202,000
Sales-force costs allocated*	$110,000	$110,000

* Allocated based on sales volume.

Currently, customer-driven costs are assigned to customers based on units sold, a unit-level driver. ABC improves the assignment by using drivers that better reflect the consumption of the activities by customers: number of orders and number of sales calls. The activity rates are $2,000 per order ($404,000/202 orders) for order filling and $1,000 per call ($220,000/220 calls) for the sales-force activity. Using this information, the customer-driven costs can be assigned to each group of customers as follows:

	Large Customer	Ten Smaller Customers
Order-filling costs	$ 4,000	$400,000
Sales-force costs	$10,000	$210,000

This reveals a much different picture of the cost of servicing each type of customer. The smaller customer is costing more, a difference that is attributable to smaller, more frequent orders and to the evident need of the sales force to engage in more negotiation to make a sale.

What does this tell management that it didn't know before? First, the large customer costs much less to service than the smaller customers and perhaps should be charged less. Second, it raises some significant questions relative to the smaller customers. Is it possible, for example, to encourage these customers to put in larger, less frequent orders? Perhaps offering discounts for larger orders would be appropriate. Why are the smaller customers more difficult to sell to? Why are more calls needed? Are they less informed about the products than the larger customer is?

This example illustrates ABC's power and value even for firms that have implemented JIT. It also shows ABC's potential value in areas other than manufacturing, and this value is also available for non-JIT firms.

SUMMARY OF LEARNING OBJECTIVES

1. Discuss the importance of unit costs.
Unit costs are important for inventory valuation, income determination, and providing input to a variety of decisions such as pricing, making or buying, and accepting or rejecting special orders. Because of their importance, their accuracy becomes a critical issue.

2. Describe functional-based costing approaches.
Functional-based costing assigns direct materials and direct labour using direct tracing; overhead is assigned using a two-stage process. In the first stage, overhead costs are collected in pools, at either the plant level or the departmental level. Once the pools are defined, the costs of the overhead pools are assigned to products using unit-level drivers, the most common being direct labour hours.

3. Explain why functional-based costing may produce distorted costs.
Overhead costs have increased in significance over time and in many firms represent a much higher percentage of product costs than direct labour. At the same time, many overhead activities are unrelated to the number of units produced. Functional-based costing systems are not able to assign the costs of these nonunit-related overhead activities properly. These overhead activities are consumed by products in different proportions than unit-based overhead activities are consumed. Because of this difference, assigning overhead using only unit-based drivers can distort product costs. This can be a serious matter if the nonunit-based overhead costs are a significant proportion of total overhead costs.

4. Explain how an activity-based costing system works.

Activities are identified and defined through interviews and surveys. This information allows an activity dictionary to be constructed. The activity dictionary lists activities and potential activity drivers, classifies activities as primary and secondary, and provides any other attributes deemed to be important. Resource costs are assigned to activities by using direct tracing and resource drivers. The costs of secondary activities are ultimately assigned to primary activities using activity drivers. Finally, the costs of primary activities are assigned to products, customers, and other cost objects. Thus, the cost assignment process is described by the following general steps: (1) identifying the major activities and building an activity dictionary, (2) determining the cost of each activity, (3) identifying a measure for consumption for activity costs (activity drivers), (4) calculating an activity rate, (5) measuring the demands placed on activities by each product, and (6) calculating product costs.

5. Provide a detailed description of how activities can be grouped into homogeneous cost pool sets to reduce the number of activity rates.

Homogeneous sets of activities are collections of activities that have the same activity-level classification and the same activity-driver classification. Classifying by level places activities into one of four categories: unit level, batch level, product level, or facility level. Unit-level activities occur each time a unit of product is produced. Batch-level activities occur when batches of products are produced. Product-level activities are incurred to enable production of each different type of product. Facility-level activities sustain a facility's general manufacturing processes. Finally, level-classified activities with the same consumption ratio are combined to form homogeneous sets. Summing the costs associated with activities within homogeneous sets defines homogeneous cost pools. An activity driver for one of the activities in the set is chosen to compute pool rates and assign costs to individual products.

6. Describe the role of activity-based costing for organizations with only one product, homogeneous products, or a JIT structure.

In a JIT environment, more costs become directly traceable to the products being produced. Batch-level activities either convert to unit-level activities or are eliminated. The net effect is to diminish the need for ABC to trace production costs to products. This outcome is similar to environments where only a single product or homogeneous products are produced. But ABC is still very useful in other areas of the company. The need for tracing costs to other objects, such as customers, still exists. Tracing customer-driven costs to customers, markets, and distribution channels can provide significant information to managers, allowing them to make better pricing decisions, customer-mix decisions, and decisions that improve profitability.

KEY TERMS

Acceptable quality level (AQL), 135
Activity attributes, 123
Activity-based costing (ABC) system, 122
Activity dictionary, 123
Activity drivers, 123
Actual costing, 112
Applied overhead, 115
Batch-level activities, 129
Consumption ratio, 120
Cost assignment, 112
Cost measurement, 112

Expected activity capacity, 113
Facility-level activities, 129
Homogeneous cost pool, 128
JIT manufacturing, 132
JIT purchasing, 133
Manufacturing cells, 133
Nonunit-level activity drivers, 119
Normal activity capacity, 114
Normal costing, 113
Overapplied overhead, 115
Overhead variance, 115
Pool rate, 128

Practical activity capacity, 114
Predetermined overhead rate, 113
Primary activity, 124
Product diversity, 119
Product-level (sustaining) activities, 129
Resource driver, 125
Secondary activity, 124
Theoretical activity capacity, 114
Underapplied overhead, 115
Unit cost, 111
Unit-level activities, 129
Unit-level activity drivers, 113

REVIEW PROBLEMS

I. PLANTWIDE RATES

Nabors Company produces two types of stereos. For the most recent year, Nabors reports the following data:

Budgeted overhead		$180,000
Expected activity (in direct labour hours)		50,000
Actual activity (in direct labour hours)		51,000
Actual overhead		$200,000

	Deluxe	Regular
Units produced	5,000	50,000
Prime costs	$40,000	$300,000
Direct labour hours	5,000	46,000

Required:

1. Calculate a predetermined overhead rate based on direct labour hours.
2. What is the applied overhead?
3. What is the underapplied or overapplied overhead?
4. Calculate the unit cost of each stereo unit.

Solution:

1. Rate = $180,000/50,000 = $3.60 per direct labour hour
2. Applied overhead = $3.60 × 51,000 = $183,600
3. Overhead variance = $200,000 − 183,600 = $16,400 underapplied
4. Unit cost:

	Deluxe	Regular
Prime costs	$ 40,000	$ 300,000
Applied overhead costs:		
$3.60 × 5,000	18,000	
$3.60 × 46,000		165,600
Total manufacturing costs	$ 58,000	$ 465,600
Units produced	÷5,000	÷50,000
Unit cost (total costs/Units)	$ 11.60	$ 9.31

II. DEPARTMENTAL RATES

Nabors Company gathers the following departmental data for a second year. Two types of stereos are produced: deluxe and regular.

	Departmental Data	
	Fabrication	Assembly
Budgeted overhead	$120,000	$60,000
Expected and actual activity (direct labour hours):		
Deluxe	3,000	2,000
Regular	8,000	43,000
Total direct labour hours	11,000	45,000
Expected and actual activity (machine hours):		
Deluxe	2,000	5,000
Regular	18,000	5,000
Total machine hours	20,000	10,000

In addition to the departmental data, the following information is provided:

	Deluxe	Regular
Units produced	5,000	50,000
Prime costs	$40,000	$300,000

Required:

1. Calculate departmental overhead rates, using machine hours for fabrication and direct labour hours for assembly.
2. Calculate the applied overhead by department.
3. Calculate the applied overhead by product.
4. Calculate unit costs.

Solution:

1. Departmental rates:
   Fabrication: $120,000/20,000 = $6.00 per machine hour
   Assembly: $60,000/45,000 = $1.333 per labour hour
2. Applied overhead (by department)
   Fabrication: $6.00 × 20,000 = $120,000
   Assembly: $1.333 × 45,000 = $59,985
3. Applied overhead (by product)
   Deluxe: ($6.00 × 2,000) + ($1.333 × 2,000) = $14,666
   Regular: ($6.00 × 18,000) + ($1.333 × 43,000) = $165,319
4. Unit cost:
   Deluxe: ($40,000 + 14,666)/5,000 = $10.93
   Regular: ($300,000 + $165,319)/50,000 = $9.31

III. ACTIVITY-BASED RATES

Nabors Company produces two types of stereos. Activity data follow:

	Product-Costing Data		
Activity Usage Measures	Deluxe	Regular	Total
Units produced per year	5,000	50,000	55,000
Prime costs	$39,000	$369,000	$408,000
Direct labour hours	5,000	45,000	50,000
Machine hours	10,000	90,000	100,000
Production runs	10	5	15
Number of moves	120	60	180

	Activity Cost Data (overhead activities)
Activity	Activity Cost
Setting up equipment	$ 60,000
Material handling	30,000
Machining	50,000
Testing	40,000
Total	$180,000

Required:

1. Calculate the consumption ratios for each activity.
2. Group activities based on the consumption ratios and activity level.
3. Calculate a rate for each pooled group of activities.
4. Using the pool rates, calculate unit product costs.

Solution:

1. Consumption ratios:

Overhead Activity	Activity Driver	Deluxe	Regular
Setups	Production runs	0.67	0.33
Material handling	Number of moves	0.67	0.33
Machining	Machine hours	0.10	0.90
Testing	Direct labour hours	0.10	0.90

2. Batch-level: setups and material handling
   Unit-level: machining and testing

3.

Batch-Level Pool		Unit-Level Pool	
Setups	$60,000	Machining	$ 50,000
Material handling	30,000	Testing	40,000
Total	$90,000	Total	$ 90,000
Runs	÷ 15	Machine hours	÷100,000
Pool rate	$ 6,000 per run	Pool rate	$ 0.90 per mach. hr.

4. Unit Costs: Activity-Based Costing

	Deluxe	Regular
Prime costs	$ 39,000	$369,000
Applied overhead costs:		
Batch-level pool:		
($6,000 × 10)	60,000	
($6,000 × 5)		30,000
Unit-level pool:		
($0.90 × 10,000)	9,000	
($0.90 × 90,000)		81,000
Total manufacturing costs	$108,000	$480,000
Units produced	÷ 5,000	÷ 50,000
Unit cost (Total costs/Units)	$ 21.60	$ 9.60

QUESTIONS FOR WRITING AND DISCUSSION

1. Explain why knowing the unit cost of a product or service is important.

2. What is cost measurement? cost assignment? What is the difference between the two?

3. Explain why an actual overhead rate is rarely used for product costing.

4. Describe the two-stage process associated with plantwide overhead rates.

5. Describe the two-stage process for departmental overhead rates.

6. Explain why departmental rates might be chosen over plantwide rates.

7. Explain how a plantwide overhead rate, using a unit-based cost driver, can produce distorted product costs. In your answer, identify two major factors that impair the ability of plantwide rates to assign cost accurately.

8. Explain how low-volume products can be undercosted and high-volume products overcosted if only unit-based cost drivers are used to assign overhead costs.

9. Explain how undercosting low-volume products and overcosting high-volume products can affect a firm's competitive position.

10. What are nonunit-related overhead activities? nonunit-based cost drivers? Give some examples.

11. What is meant by "product diversity"?

12. What is an overhead consumption ratio?

13. Explain how departmental overhead rates can produce product costs that are more distorted than those computed using a plantwide rate.

14. Overhead costs are the source of product cost distortions. Do you agree? Explain.

15. What is activity-based product costing?

16. What is an activity dictionary?

17. What is the difference between a primary and a secondary activity?

18. Explain how costs are assigned to activities.

19. Explain how homogeneous sets of activities are produced. Why are they produced?

20. What is a homogeneous cost pool?

21. What are unit-level activities? batch-level activities? product-level activities? facility-level activities?

22. What is JIT manufacturing? List four ways in which JIT manufacturing differs from traditional manufacturing.

23. What are manufacturing cells? Explain how they differ from production departments.

24. Explain why some indirect manufacturing costs in traditional manufacturing become direct costs in JIT manufacturing. Give some examples of costs that change in this way.

25. In JIT manufacturing, direct labour costs are less important and largely fixed in nature. Do you agree? Explain.

26. Without inventories, there is no distinction between product and period costs. Do you agree? Explain.

27. How does JIT manufacturing increase product-costing accuracy?

28. Why might ABC be useful in a company with only one product? with JIT manufacturing?

EXERCISES

4–1

Normal versus Actual Costing

LO1

Nublado Company produces ski boots. At the beginning of the year, the cost manager estimated that overhead costs would be $2,910,000 and that 300,000 units would be produced. Actual data concerning production for the past year follow:

	Quarter 1	Quarter 2	Quarter 3	Quarter 4	Total
Units produced	100,000	40,000	20,000	140,000	300,000
Prime costs	$2,000,000	$800,000	$400,000	$2,800,000	$6,000,000
Overhead costs	$800,000	$600,000	$900,000	$700,000	$3,000,000

Required:

1. Calculate the unit cost for each quarter and for the year using the following costs:
   a. Actual prime costs
   b. Actual overhead costs
   c. Actual total manufacturing costs
2. What do the calculations in Requirement 1 tell you about actual costing?
3. Using supporting calculations, describe how normal costing would work.

4–2

Plantwide Rates; Overhead Variance

LO1, LO2

Hite Manufacturing uses a normal costing system. Budgeted overhead for the coming year is $1,500,000. Expected actual activity is 400,000 direct labour hours. During the year, Hite worked a total of 384,000 direct labour hours, and actual overhead totalled $1,400,000.

Required:

1. Compute the predetermined overhead rate for Hite Manufacturing.
2. Compute the applied overhead.
3. Compute the overhead variance and label the variance as underapplied or overapplied overhead.
4. Explain why predetermined rates are used.

4–3

Unit Cost; Plantwide Overhead Rate; Applied Overhead

LO1, LO2

Spreadsheet

Computer Systems Design, which develops specialized software for companies, uses a normal costing system. The following data are available for 2001:

Budgeted

Overhead	$600,000
Machine hours	25,000
Direct labour hours	80,000

Actual

Units produced	100,000
Overhead	$595,500
Prime costs	$900,000
Machine hours	25,050
Direct labour hours	78,000

Overhead is applied on the basis of direct labour hours.

Required:

1. What is the predetermined overhead rate?
2. What is the applied overhead for 2001?
3. Was overhead overapplied or underapplied, and by how much?
4. What is the unit cost for the year?

4–4

Unit Overhead Cost; Predetermined Plantwide Overhead Rate; Applied Overhead

LO1, LO2

Using the information from 4–3, suppose Computer Systems Design applied overhead to production on the basis of machine hours instead of direct labour hours.

Required:

1. What is the predetermined overhead rate?
2. What is the applied overhead for 2001?
3. Is overhead overapplied or underapplied, and by how much?
4. What is the unit cost?
5. How can Computer Systems Design decide whether to use direct labour hours or machine hours as the basis for applying factory overhead?

4–5

Unit Overhead Cost; Predetermined Departmental Overhead Rates; Overhead Variance

LO1, LO2

Spreadsheet

Kildoz Pharmaceutical uses a predetermined overhead rate to apply overhead. Overhead is applied on the basis of direct labour hours in the mixing department and on the basis of machine hours in the tableting department. At the beginning of 2001, the following estimates are provided for the coming year:

	Mixing	Tableting
Direct labour hours	100,000	10,000
Machine hours	10,000	140,000
Direct labour cost	$900,000	$190,000
Overhead cost	$300,000	$196,000

Actual results reported for 2001 are as follows:

	Mixing	Tableting
Direct labour hours	98,000	12,000
Machine hours	11,000	144,000
Direct labour cost	$882,400	$168,000
Overhead cost	$301,000	$206,000

Required:

1. Compute the predetermined overhead rate for each department.
2. Compute the applied overhead for 2001. What is the underapplied or overapplied overhead for each department? for the firm?

3. Suppose a batch of pills used 2,000 direct labour hours in mixing and 800 machine hours in tableting. If the batch size is 40,000 units, what is the overhead cost per pill?

4–6

Product-Costing Accuracy; Consumption Ratios

LO3

Gator Company has traditionally produced a handcrafted ladies' purse (sold under the label Gator Elegant). A marketing consultant has recommended that a second purse be produced—using lower-quality materials and automation so that it can be produced in larger quantities. This purse will be sold under the label Gator Eminent. Gator decides to produce the second purse. The company buys the equipment for automated production and installs it in a currently unused part of its plant. Gator discovers that a small part of the operation associated with the handcrafted purse can be automated (using the same equipment just purchased) without compromising its claim that the purse is essentially handcrafted. However, the settings on the equipment must be adjusted before it can be used for this purpose (and changed back for production of the other purse). The cost of setting up the equipment is $3,000 per year.

The production equipment is expected to last five years, with a capacity of supplying a total of 25,000 machine hours. The costs associated with the equipment follow:

Amortization $10,000*
Operating costs   8,000

* Amortization is computed on a straight-line basis; book value at the beginning of the year was $50,000.

The controller has collected the expected annual prime costs for each purse, the machine hours, the setup hours, and the expected production.

	Elegant	Eminent
Direct labour	$9,000	$3,000
Direct materials	$3,000	$3,000
Units	3,000	3,000
Machine hours	500	4,500
Setup hours	100	100

Required:

1. Do you think that the direct labour costs and direct materials costs are accurately traced to each purse? Explain.
2. The controller has suggested that overhead costs be assigned to each product using a plantwide rate based on direct labour costs. Assume that the setup and machine costs are the only overhead costs. For each purse, calculate the overhead cost per unit that would be assigned using this approach. Do you think that machine costs are traced accurately to each purse? setup costs? Explain.
3. Now calculate the overhead cost per unit for each purse using an overhead rate based on machine hours. Do you think machine costs are traced accurately to each purse? setup costs? Explain.

4–7

Formation of an Activity Dictionary

LO4

A hospital is in the process of implementing an ABC system. A pilot study is being done to assess the effects of the costing change on specific treatments. Of particular interest is the cost of caring for patients who receive inpatient recovery treatment for illness, surgery (noncardiac), and injury. These patients are housed on the hospital's third and fourth floors. These two floors are dedicated to patient care and have only nursing stations and patient rooms. A partial transcript of an interview with the hospital's nursing supervisor is provided below.

1. How many nurses are in the hospital?
   There are 101 nurses, including me.
2. Of these 100 nurses, how many are assigned to the third and fourth floors?
   Fifty nurses are assigned to these two floors.

3. What do these nurses do (please describe)?
    Provide nursing care for patients, which, as you know, means answering questions, changing bandages, administering medicine, changing clothes, etc.
4. And what do you do?
    I supervise and coordinate all the nursing activity in the hospital. This includes surgery, maternity, the emergency room, and the two floors you mentioned.
5. What other lodging and care activities are done for the third and fourth floors by persons other than nurses?
    The patients must be fed. The hospital cafeteria delivers meals. The laundry department picks up dirty clothing and bedding once each shift. The floors also have a physical therapist assigned to provide care on a physician-directed basis.
6. Does patient care involve the use of any equipment?
    Yes. Mostly monitoring equipment.
7. Who or what uses the activity output?
    Patients. But there are different kinds of patients. On these two floors, we classify patients into three categories according to severity: intensive care, intermediate care, and normal care. The more severe the illness, the more activity used. Nurses spend much more time with intermediate-care patients than with normal-care patients. The more severe patients tend to use more of the laundry service as well. Their clothing and bedding need to be changed more frequently. On the other hand, severe patients use less food. They eat fewer meals. Typically, we measure each patient type by the number of days of hospital stay. And you have to realize that the same patient contributes to each type of treatment.

Required:

Prepare an activity dictionary with four categories: activity name, activity description, primary or secondary classification, and activity driver.

4–8

Activity versus Plantwide Overhead Rates: Resource Drivers; Activity Drivers

LO3, LO4

Milan Machining Company has identified the following overhead activities, costs, and activity drivers for the coming year:

Activity	Expected Cost	Activity Driver	Activity Capacity
Setting up	$60,000	Number of setups	300
Inspecting	$45,000	Inspection hours	4,500
Grinding	$90,000	Machine hours	18,000
Receiving	$25,000	Number of parts	50,000

The company produces several different machine subassemblies used by other manufacturers. Information on separate batches for two of these subassemblies follows:

	Subassembly A	Subassembly B
Direct materials	$850	$950
Direct labour	$600	$600
Units completed	100	50
Number of setups	1	1
Inspection hours	4	2
Machine hours	20	30
Parts used	20	40

The company's normal activity is 4,000 direct labour hours. Each batch uses 50 hours of direct labour.

Required:

1. Upon investigation, you discover that Receiving employs one worker, who spends half her time on the receiving activity and half her time on inspecting products. Her salary is $40,000. Receiving also uses a forklift, at a cost of $5,000

per year for amortization and fuel. The forklift is used only in receiving. Verify the cost of the receiving activity given above. What resource driver was used?

2. Determine the unit cost for each product using direct labour hours to apply overhead.
3. Determine the unit cost for each product using the four activity drivers.
4. Which method produces the more accurate cost assignment? Why?

4–9

Activity Classification

LO5

Colbie Components produces two types of wafers: wafer A and wafer B. A wafer is a thin slice of silicon used as a base for integrated circuits or other electronic components. The dies on each wafer represent a particular configuration designed for use by a particular end product. Colbie makes wafers in batches, with each batch corresponding to a particular type of wafer (A or B). In the wafer inserting and sorting process, dies are inserted and the wafers are tested to ensure that the dies are not defective. Materials are ordered and received just in time for production. Terms for payment for materials are 2/10, n/30. Discounts are always taken (payment occurs on the last date possible).

The following activities are listed in Colbie's activity dictionary:

1. Developing test programs
2. Making probe cards
3. Testing products
4. Setting up batches
5. Engineering design
6. Handling wafer lots
7. Inserting dies
8. Purchasing materials
9. Receiving materials
10. Paying suppliers
11. Providing utilities (heat, lighting, and so on)
12. Providing space

Required:

1. What activities are done each time a wafer is produced (unit-level activities)?
2. What activities are done each time a batch is produced (batch-level activities)?
3. Which activities are done to enable production to take place (product-level activities)?
4. Which activities are done to sustain production processes (facility-level activities)?

4–10

Activity-Based Costing: Homogeneous Cost Pools; Activity Drivers

LO4, LO5

Tristar Manufacturing produces two types of battery-operated toy cars: sports and police. The cars are produced using one continuous process. Four activities have been identified: machining, setups, receiving, and packing. Resource drivers have been used to assign costs to each activity. The overhead activities, activity costs, and other related data are as follows:

Product	Machine Hours	Setups	Receiving Orders	Packing Orders
Sports	20,000	200	200	1,600
Police	20,000	100	400	800
Costs	$80,000	$24,000	$18,000	$30,000

Required:

1. Classify the overhead activities as unit level, batch level, product level, or facility level.
2. Create homogeneous cost pools. Identify the activities that belong to each pool.
3. Identify the activity driver for each pool, and compute the pool rate.
4. Assign the overhead costs to each product using the pool rates computed in Requirement 3.

4–11

Functional-Based Costing; Activity-Based Costing; Pricing

LO2, LO3, LO4

Spreadsheet

Hammer Company produces a variety of electronic equipment. One of its plants produces two laser printers: the deluxe and the regular. At the beginning of the year, the following data were prepared for this plant:

	Deluxe	Regular
Quantity	100,000	800,000
Selling price	$900.00	$750.00
Unit prime cost	$529.00	$482.75
Unit overhead cost	$47.00	$117.25

Overhead is applied using direct labour hours.

Upon examining the data, the vice-president of marketing was particularly impressed with the per-unit profitability of the deluxe printer and suggested that more emphasis be placed on producing and selling this product. The plant manager objected to this strategy, arguing that the cost of the deluxe printer was understated. He argued that overhead costs could be assigned more accurately by using activity drivers—factors that reflected each product's demands for overhead activities. To convince higher management that overhead rates using activity drivers could produce a significant difference in product costs, he obtained the following projected information from the controller for the production output given:

Pool Name[a]	Activity Driver	Pool Rate[b]	Deluxe	Regular
Setups	Number of setups	$3,000	300	200
Machining	Machine hours	200	100,000	300,000
Engineering	Engineering hours	40	50,000	100,000
Packing	Packing orders	20	100,000	400,000
Providing space	Machine hours	1	200,000	800,000

[a] Pools are named according to the nature of the activities found within each pool. Providing space is a collection of facility-level activities. Packing and setups are collections of batch-level activities. Engineering is a collection of product-level activities, and machining is a collection of unit-level activities.
[b] Cost per unit of activity driver

Required:

1. Using the projected data based on functional-based costing, compute gross profit as a percentage of sales, gross profit per unit, and total gross profit for each product.
2. Using the pool rates, compute the overhead cost per unit for each product. Using this new unit cost, compute gross profit percentage, gross profit per unit, and total gross profit for each product.
3. In view of the outcome in Requirement 2, evaluate the suggestion by the vice-president of marketing to switch the emphasis to the deluxe model.

4–12

Two-Stage Procedure; Activity-Based Costing

LO5

Mendoza Company has recently decided to convert from functional-based product costing to an activity-based system. The company produces two types of clocks: small and large. The clocks are produced in batches. Information concerning these two products follows:

	Small Clock	Large Clock
Quantity produced	100,000	200,000
Machine hours	50,000	50,000
Direct labour hours	100,000	100,000
Material handling (number of moves)	2,000	4,000
Engineering (hours)	10,000	5,000
Receiving (number of orders processed)	250	500
Setups	60	20
Maintaining (hours used)	4,000	2,000
Kilowatt-hours	25,000	25,000
Inspecting (number of hours)	3,000	1,000

Additionally, the following overhead costs are reported for the activities associated with the two products:

Material handling	$120,000
Maintaining equipment	80,000
Producing power	30,000
Amortization (machines)*	60,000
Engineering	100,000
Receiving	30,000
Setups	96,000
Inspecting	60,000

* Amortization is straight line; book value at the beginning of the year was $600,000. The machine hours reported represent the normal activity level. The remaining life of the machinery is 10 years or 1 million machine hours.

Required:

1. Classify activities by level and then by driver.
2. Group all overhead costs into homogeneous cost pools. Select an activity driver for each cost pool and compute a pool rate.
3. Using the pool rates calculated in Requirement 2, assign all overhead costs to the two products and compute the overhead cost per unit for each.

4–13

Classification of Activities

LO5

Classify the following activities as unit level, batch level, product level, or facility level. Also identify a potential activity driver for each activity.

1. Setting up equipment
2. Receiving materials
3. Inspecting goods
4. Shipping goods
5. Ordering supplies
6. Ordering production
7. Administering parts
8. Moving materials
9. Processing customer orders
10. Supervising plant
11. Welding subassemblies
12. Assembling components
13. Testing special products
14. Providing heating and air conditioning in the plant
15. Expediting goods
16. Providing plant space

4–14

Changing to an ABC System

LO3

In 1991, Sterling Company changed its cost system. It went from using a single, plantwide overhead rate based on direct labour hours to a system using departmental overhead rates. The departmental overhead rates used direct labour hours, machine hours, and direct material dollars to assign overhead to products.

In 2001, Sterling's president, Pamela Jones, was mulling over the possibility of changing to an ABC system. She had heard that the life of a cost system is about 10 years and was worried that the current system was no longer serving the company's needs. She was also convinced, however, that a change to ABC simply because it was a "hot" topic was not the right approach. Any change had to be in the company's best economic interests.

Required:

As a consultant to Pamela, identify the factors that should be considered in changing to an ABC system. In your discussion, include a definition of an outmoded or obsolete cost system.

4–15

JIT and Product-Costing Accuracy

LO6

Before installing a JIT system, Rumple Company used machine hours to assign maintenance costs to its three products (small, medium, and large tablecloths). The maintenance costs totalled $280,000 per year. The machine hours used by each product and the quantity of each product produced are as follows:

	Machine Hours	Quantity Produced
Small	30,000	7,500
Medium	30,000	7,500
Large	40,000	10,000

After installing JIT, three manufacturing cells were created, and cell workers were trained to perform maintenance. Maintenance costs for the three cells still totalled $280,000; however, these costs are now traceable to each cell as follows:

Cell, small tablecloths	$ 76,000
Cell, medium tablecloths	84,000
Cell, large tablecloths	120,000

Required:

1. Compute the pre-JIT maintenance cost per tablecloth for each type.
2. Compute maintenance cost per unit for each type of tablecloth after installing JIT.
3. Explain why the JIT maintenance cost per unit is more accurate than the pre-JIT cost.

4–16

JIT: Traceability of Costs; Product-Costing Accuracy

LO6

The manufacturing costs assigned to an electronic component before and after installing JIT follow:

	Before	After
Direct materials	$ 60,000	$ 60,000
Direct labour	40,000	50,000
Maintenance	50,000	30,000
Power	10,000	8,000
Amortization	12,500	10,000
Material handling	8,000	4,000
Engineering	9,600	8,000
Setups	15,000	8,500
Building and grounds	11,800	12,400
Supplies	4,000	3,000
Supervision (plant)	8,200	8,200
Cell supervision	0	30,000
Departmental supervision	18,000	0
Total	$247,100	$232,100

In both the pre- and the post-JIT setting, 100,000 units of the component are manufactured. In the JIT setting, manufacturing cells are used to produce each product.

Required:

1. Compute the unit cost of the product before and after JIT. Explain why the JIT unit cost is more accurate.
2. Identify the costs in the JIT environment that are directly traceable to the electronic component. Classify the remaining costs as those that must be traced using drivers or allocated if truly indirect. Discuss the role of ABC in a JIT environment.

4–17

Customer-Driven Costs

LO6

Emery Company has two classes of customers: JIT firms and non-JIT firms. The JIT customer category places small, frequent orders, and the non-JIT customer category tends to place larger, less frequent orders. Both types of customer are buying the same product. Emery charges manufacturing cost plus 25 percent for a given order. The 25 percent markup is set large enough to cover nonmanufacturing costs and provide a reasonable return for Emery. Both customer types generated the same sales in units, so Emery's management had assumed that the customer support costs were about the same and priced the goods the same for each customer. Emery recently received some complaints from some of the non-JIT customers. Several of these customers are threatening to take their business to other suppliers who allegedly charge less. For example, one customer said that he could buy the same 5,000 units from a competitor for $3 per unit less than Emery's price. This customer wanted a price concession.

A recently hired cost accountant suggested that the problem might have to do with unfair cost assignments and suggested that customer costs be assigned to each customer category using activity-based costing. She collected the following information about customer-related activities and costs for the most recent quarter:

	JIT Customers	Non-JIT Customers
Sales orders	200	20
Sales calls	20	20
Service calls	100	50
Average order size	500	5,000
Manufacturing cost/unit	$100	$100
Customer costs:		
Processing sales orders	$ 880,000	
Selling goods	320,000	
Servicing goods	300,000	
Total	$1,500,000	

Required:

1. Calculate the total revenues per customer category and assign the customer costs to each customer type using revenues as the allocation base.
2. Calculate the customer cost per customer type using activity-based cost assignments. Discuss the merits of offering the non-JIT customers a $3 price decrease.
3. Assume that the JIT customers are simply imposing the frequent orders on Emery. There has been no formal discussion between JIT customers and Emery regarding supply of goods on a just-in-time basis. The sales pattern has simply evolved over time. As an independent consultant, what would you suggest to Emery's management?

PROBLEMS

4–18

Functional-Based versus Activity-Based Costing

LO2, LO3, LO4

Janeiro Company for years produced only one product: backpacks. Recently, the company decided to add a line of duffel bags. With this addition, the company began to assign overhead costs using departmental rates. Before adopting this approach, the company used a predetermined plantwide overhead rate based on units produced. Departmental rates meant that overhead costs had to be assigned to each producing department to create overhead pools. Predetermined departmental rates could then be calculated for each overhead cost pool. Surprisingly, after the addition of the duffel-bag line and the switch to departmental rates, the costs of producing the backpacks increased and their profitability dropped.

The marketing manager and the production manager both complained about the increase in the production cost of backpacks. The marketing manager was concerned because the increase in unit costs led to pressure to increase the backpacks' unit selling price. She was resisting this pressure because she was certain that the increase would harm the company's market share. The production manager was also receiving pressure to cut costs, yet he was convinced that nothing different was being done in the way the backpacks were produced. He was also convinced that further efficiency in the manufacture of the backpacks was unlikely. After some discussion, the two managers decided that the problem had to be connected with the addition of the duffel-bag line.

Upon investigation, they were informed that the only real change in product-costing procedures had been in the way overhead costs were assigned. A two-stage procedure was now in use. First, overhead costs are assigned to the two producing departments, patterns and finishing. Some overhead costs are assigned to producing departments using direct tracing and some using driver tracing. For example, the salaries of the producing department's supervisors are assigned using direct tracing, whereas the costs of the factory's accounting department are assigned using driver tracing (the driver being the number of transactions processed for each department). Second, the costs accumulated in the producing departments are assigned to the two products using direct labour hours as a driver (the rate in each department is based on direct labour hours). The managers were assured that great care was being taken to associate overhead costs with individual products. So that they could construct their own example of cost assignment, the controller provided the following information to show how accounting costs are assigned to products:

	Department		
	Pattern	Finishing	Total
Accounting cost	$48,000	$72,000	$120,000
Transactions processed	32,000	48,000	80,000
Total direct labour hours	25,000	50,000	75,000
Direct labour hours per backpack*	0.10	0.20	0.30
Direct labour hours per duffel bag*	0.40	0.80	1.20

* Hours required to produce one unit of each product

The controller remarked that the cost of operating the accounting department had doubled with the addition of the new product line. The increase came because of the need to process additional transactions, which had also doubled in number.

During the first year of producing duffel bags, the company produced and sold 150,000 backpacks and 25,000 duffel bags. The 150,000 backpacks matched the previous year's output for that product.

Required:

1. Compute the amount of accounting cost assigned to each backpack and duffel bag using the departmental rates based on direct labour hours.
2. Compute the amount of accounting cost assigned to a backpack before the duffel-bag line was added using a plantwide rate based on units produced. Is this assignment accurate? Explain.
3. Suppose that the company decided to assign the accounting costs directly to the product lines using the number of transactions as the activity driver. What is the accounting cost per unit of backpacks? per unit of duffel bags?
4. Which way of assigning overhead does the best job, the functional-based approach using departmental rates or the activity-based approach using transactions processed for each product? Explain. Discuss the value of activity-based costing before the duffel-bag line was added.

4–19

Plantwide versus Departmental Rates

LO2

The Cheetah Company produces custom-made stuffed toy animals and competes in a very competitive marketplace. The company establishes its selling prices as being equal to the cost of production plus a 30 percent markup. The production process consists of two departments:

- The Skins Department, where the outside liners (skins) for each toy animal are handmade from specially ordered materials.

- The Stuffing Department, where the skins are filled by machine with a standard stuffing material to complete the toys.

   The two production departments (the Skins and Stuffing Departments) are both served by two other departments (the Purchasing Department and the Cleaning and Maintenance Department). Descriptions of the operations of these departments, and of how their costs are assigned, are given below:

Purchasing

- This department purchases all materials and supplies required for all departments.
- Its costs are assigned to the two production departments based on the total amount of materials ordered by each producing department.

Cleaning and Maintenance

- This department cleans the entire building and maintains all the equipment in the company.
- Its costs are assigned to the two production departments on the basis of the total square metres each producing department occupies.

Required:

1. Should the company use a plantwide overhead rate or departmental overhead rates? Explain your answer.
2. Comment on the company's cost assignment policy and, where necessary, suggest improvements. Justify fully any suggested improvements that you make. (CMA Canada adapted)

4–20

Plantwide versus Departmental Rates; Product-Costing Accuracy; Pool Rates

LO2, LO3, LO4

Spreadsheet

Maxwell Company produces small engines for model boats (Engine A and Engine B). Both products pass through two producing departments. Engine A's production is much more labour-intensive than Engine B's. Engine B is by far the more popular of the two engines. The following data have been gathered for these two products:

	Product Data	
	Engine A	Engine B
Units produced per year	30,000	300,000
Prime costs	$100,000	$1,000,000
Direct labour hours	140,000	300,000
Machine hours	20,000	200,000
Production runs	40	60
Inspection hours	800	1,200

	Departmental Data	
	Department 1	Department 2
Direct labour hours:		
Engine A	10,000	130,000
Engine B	30,000	270,000
Total	40,000	400,000
Machine hours:		
Engine A	10,000	10,000
Engine B	170,000	30,000
Total	180,000	40,000
Overhead costs:		
Setup costs	$ 90,000	$ 90,000
Inspection costs	70,000	70,000
Machining	120,000	40,000
Maintenance	140,000	40,000
Total	$420,000	$240,000

Required:

1. Compute the overhead cost per unit for each product using a plantwide rate based on direct labour hours.
2. Compute the overhead cost per unit for each product using departmental rates. In calculating departmental rates, use machine hours for Department 1 and direct labour hours for Department 2. Repeat, using direct labour hours for Department 1 and machine hours for Department 2. Of the two approaches, which would most likely be chosen? Explain why.
3. Compute the overhead cost per unit for each product using activity-based costing. Form homogeneous cost pools where possible.
4. Using the activity-based product costs as the standard, comment on the ability of departmental rates to improve the accuracy of product costing.

4–21

Production-Based Costing versus Activity-Based Costing; Assigning Costs to Activities; Resource Drivers

LO3, LO4, LO5

Willow Company produces lawn mowers. One of its plants produces two versions of mowers: a basic model and a deluxe model. The deluxe model has a sturdier frame, a higher-horsepower engine, a wider blade, and mulching capability. At the beginning of the year, the following data were prepared for this plant:

	Basic Model	Deluxe Model
Expected quantity	40,000	20,000
Selling price	$180	$360
Prime costs	$80	$160
Machine hours	5,000	5,000
Direct labour hours	10,000	10,000
Engineering support (hours)	1,500	4,500
Receiving (orders processed)	250	500
Material handling (number of moves)	2,000	4,000
Purchasing (number of requisitions)	100	200
Maintenance (hours used)	1,000	3,000
Paying suppliers (invoices processed)	250	500
Setting up batches (number of setups)	20	60

Additionally, the following overhead activity costs are reported:

Maintaining equipment	$114,000
Engineering support	120,000
Material handling	?
Setting up equipment	96,000
Purchasing materials	60,000
Receiving goods	40,000
Paying suppliers	30,000
Providing space	20,000
Total	$?

Facility-level costs are allocated in proportion to machine hours (an approach that provides a measure of the time the facility is used by each product).

Material handling uses three inputs: two forklifts, propane to operate the forklifts, and three operators. The three operators are paid salaries of $40,000 each. The operators spend 25 percent of their time on the receiving activity and 75 percent on moving goods (material handling). Propane costs $3 per move. Amortization amounts to $6,000 per forklift per year.

Required:

1. Calculate the cost of the material-handling activity. Label the cost assignments as driver tracing or direct tracing. Identify the resource drivers.
2. Calculate the cost per unit for each product using direct labour hours to assign all overhead costs.

3. Form homogeneous cost pools and calculate pool rates. Explain why you group activities in pools.
4. Using the pool rates computed in Requirement 3, calculate the cost per unit for each product. Compare these costs with those calculated using functional-based costing. Which cost is the most accurate? Explain.

4–22

ABC Costing and Cost Behaviour

LO4, LO5

Underwood Company produces several different models of a stereo system. The company has recently adopted an ABC system. The unit cost expected for one model follows:

Model B

Unit-level costs (includes materials and labour)	$ 60
Batch-level costs	40
Product-level costs	20
Facility-level costs	10
Total unit cost	$130

The unit cost is based on an expected volume of 10,000 units. These units will be produced in ten equal batches. The product-level costs are all from engineering support. The product-level costs are driven by engineering orders. The $20 cost assignment is based on five orders. Facility-level costs are allocated on the basis of direct labour hours (one hour per unit produced).

Required:

1. Calculate the total manufacturing cost to produce 10,000 units of model B. Present the total cost for each activity category.
2. Now assume that the company has revised its forecast for model B and expects to produce 15,000 units. A decision has been made to handle the increased production by increasing batch size to 1,500 units. The increased production will not require an increase in engineering support. Calculate the total cost to produce the 15,000 units of model B. Present the total cost for each activity category. Explain the outcome.
3. Assume that the revised forecast of 15,000 units is made. Now, however, a decision is made to handle the extra production by increasing the number of batches from 10 to 15. Also, the sales of the extra 5,000 units are possible only if an engineering modification is made. This increases the expected engineering orders from 5 to 6. Explain why the costs changed from those predicted in Requirement 2.
4. Discuss the value of classifying and reporting costs by activity category.

4–23

Activity-Based Costing; Assigning Resource Costs; Primary and Secondary Activities

LO3, LO4

Longridge Hospital has identified three activities for daily maternity care: occupancy and feeding, nursing, and nursing supervision. The nursing supervisor oversees 150 nurses, 25 of whom are maternity nurses (the other nurses are located in other care areas, such as the emergency room and intensive care). The nursing supervisor has three assistants, a secretary, several offices, computers, phones, and furniture. The three assistants spend 75 percent of their time on the supervising activity and 25 percent of their time as surgical nurses. They each receive a salary of $48,000. The nursing supervisor is paid a salary of $70,000. She spends 100 percent of her time supervising. The secretary receives a salary of $22,000 per year. Other costs directly traceable to the supervisory activity (amortization, utilities, phone, etc.) average $100,000 per year.

Daily care output is measured as "patient days." The hospital has traditionally assigned the cost of daily care by using a daily rate (a rate per patient day). There are actually different kinds of daily care, and rates are structured to reflect these differences. For example, a higher rate is used for an intensive care unit than for a maternity care unit. Within units, however, the daily rates are the same for all patients. Under the traditional, functional approach, the daily rate is computed by dividing the annual costs of occupancy and feeding, nursing, and a share of supervision by the unit's capacity (expressed in patient days). The cost of supervision is assigned to each care area based on the number of nurses. A single cost driver (patient days) is used to assign the costs of daily care to each patient.

A pilot study has revealed that the demands for nursing care vary within the maternity unit, depending on the severity of a patient's case. Specifically, demand for nursing services per day increases with severity. Assume that within the maternity unit there are three levels of increasing severity: normal patients, cesarean patients, and patients with complications. The pilot study provided the following activity and cost information:

Activity	Annual Cost	Activity Driver	Activity Quantity
Occupancy and feeding	$1,000,000	Patient days	10,000
Nursing care (maternity)	950,000	Nursing hours	50,000
Nursing supervision	?	Number of nurses	6,000

The pilot study also revealed the following information concerning the three types of patients and their annual demands:

Patient Type	Patient Days	Nursing Hours
Normal	7,000	17,500
Cesarean	2,000	12,500
Complications	1,000	20,000
Total	10,000	50,000

Required:

1. Calculate the cost per patient day using a functional-based approach.
2. Calculate the cost per patient day using an activity-based approach.
3. The hospital processes 1,000,000 kilograms of laundry per year. The cost for the laundry activity is $500,000 per year. In a functional-based costing system, the cost of the laundry department is assigned to each user department in proportion to the kilograms of laundry produced. Typically, maternity produces 200,000 kilograms per year. How much would this change the cost per patient day calculated in Requirement 1? Describe what information you would need to modify the activity-based calculation in Requirement 2. Under what conditions would an activity-based calculation provide a more accurate cost assignment?

4–24

Product-Costing Accuracy; Corporate Strategy; Activity-Based Costing

LO3, LO4, LO5

Pearson Manufacturing produces chemicals for industrial use. One plant specializes in the production of chemicals used in the copper industry. Two compounds are produced: compound X-12 and compound S-15. Compound X-12 was originally developed by Pearson's chemists and played a key role in extracting copper from low-grade ore. The patent for X-12 has expired, and competition for this market has intensified dramatically. Compound X-12 produced the highest volume of activity, and for many years X-12 was the only chemical compound produced by the plant. Five years ago, S-15 was added. Compound S-15 was more difficult to manufacture and required special handling and setups. For the first three years after the addition of the new product, profits increased. In the last two years, however, the plant has faced intense competition, and its sales of X-12 have dropped. In fact, the plant showed a small loss in the most recent reporting period. The plant manager is convinced that competing producers have been guilty of selling X-12 below the cost to produce it—perhaps with the objective of expanding market share. The following conversation between Diane Woolridge, the plant's manager, and Rick Dixon, the divisional marketing manager, reflects the division's concerns about the future of the plant and its products.

Rick: "You know, Diane, the divisional manager is very concerned about the plant's trend. He indicated that in this budgetary environment, we can't afford to carry plants that don't show a profit. We shut one down just last month because it couldn't handle the competition."

Diane: "Rick, our compound X-12 has a reputation for quality and value—we have a very pure product. It has been a mainstay for years. I don't understand what's happening."

Rick: "I just received a call from one of our major customers concerning X-12. He said that a sales representative from another firm had offered the chemical at $10 per kilogram—about $6 less than what we ask. It's hard to compete with a price like that. Perhaps the plant is simply obsolete."

Diane: "No. I don't agree. We have good technology. I think that we are efficient. And it's costing a little more than $10 per kilogram to produce X-12. I don't see how these companies can afford to sell it so cheaply. I'm not convinced that we should meet the price. Perhaps we should emphasize producing and selling more S-15. Our margin is high on that product, and we have virtually no competition for it. We recently raised the price per kilogram, and our customers didn't blink an eye."

Rick: "You may be right. I think we can increase the price even more and not lose business. I called a few customers to see how they would react to a 25 percent increase in price, and they all said that they would still purchase the same quantity as before."

Diane: "It sounds promising. However, before we make a major commitment to S-15, I think we had better explore other possible explanations. The market potential is much less than that for X-12. I want to know how our production costs compare to our competitors' costs. Perhaps we could be more efficient and find a way to earn our normal return on X-12. Besides, my production people hate producing S-15. It's very difficult to produce."

After meeting with Rick, Diane requested an investigation of the production costs and comparative efficiency. Independent consultants were hired. After a three-month assessment, the consulting group provided the following information on the plant's production activities and the costs associated with the two products:

	X-12	S-15
Production (kilograms)	1,000,000	200,000
Selling price	$15.93	$12.00
Overhead per unit*	$6.41	$2.89
Prime cost per kilogram	$4.27	$3.13
Number of production runs	100	200
Receiving orders	400	1,000
Machine hours	125,000	60,000
Direct labour hours	250,000	22,500
Engineering hours	5,000	5,000
Material handling	500	400

* Calculated using a plantwide rate based on direct labour hours, which is
  the current way of assigning the plant's overhead to its products.

The consulting group recommended switching the overhead assignment to an activity-based approach. They maintained that activity-based cost assignment is more accurate and will provide better information for decision making. To facilitate this recommendation, they grouped the plant's activities into homogeneous sets based on common processes, activity levels, and consumption ratios. The costs of these pooled activities follow:

Overhead Pool:*

Setup costs	$ 240,000
Machine costs	1,750,000
Receiving costs	2,100,000
Engineering costs	2,000,000
Material-handling costs	900,000
Total	$6,990,000

* The pools are named for the major activities found within them.
  All overhead costs within each pool can be assigned using a single
  driver (based on the major activity after which the pool is named).

Required:

1. Verify the overhead cost per unit reported by the consulting group using direct labour hours to assign overhead. Compute the per-unit gross margin for each product.
2. Recompute the unit cost of each product using activity-based costing. Compute the per-unit gross margin for each product.
3. Should the company switch its emphasis from the high-volume product to the low-volume product? Comment on the validity of the plant manager's concern that competitors are selling below the cost of producing compound X-12.
4. Explain the apparent lack of competition for S-15. Comment also on the willingness of customers to accept a 25 percent increase in price for this compound.
5. Describe what actions you would take based on the information provided by the activity-based unit costs.

4–25

JIT and Traceability of Costs

LO6

Assume that a company has just recently switched to JIT manufacturing. Each manufacturing cell produces a single product or major subassembly. Cell workers have been trained to perform a variety of tasks. Additionally, many services have been decentralized. Costs are assigned to products using direct tracing, driver tracing, and allocation. For the costs that follow, indicate the most likely product cost assignment method used *before JIT* and *after JIT*. Use three columns: Cost Item, Before JIT, and After JIT. You may assume that direct tracing is used whenever possible, followed by driver tracing, with allocation being the method of last resort.

a.   Inspection costs
b.   Power to heat, light, and cool plant
c.   Minor repairs on production equipment
d.   Salary of production supervisor (department/cell)
e.   Oil to lubricate machinery
f.   Salary of plant supervisor
g.   Costs to set up machinery
h.   Salaries of janitors
i.   Power to operate production equipment
j.   Amortization on production equipment
k.   Raw materials
l.   Salary of industrial engineer
m.   Parts for machinery
n.   Pencils and paper clips for production supervisor (department/cell)
o.   Insurance on plant and equipment
p.   Overtime wages for cell workers
q.   Plant amortization
r.   Material handling
s.   Preventive maintenance

4–26

Cost Assignment and JIT

LO6

Lisboa Company produces two types of lamp bases (modern and traditional). Both pass through two producing departments: moulding and painting. The firm also has a maintenance department, which services and repairs the equipment used in each producing department. Budgeted data for the three departments follow:

	Maintenance	Moulding	Painting
Overhead	$200,000	$330,000	$238,000
Maintenance hours	—	7,500	2,500
Machine hours	—	24,000	2,000
Direct labour hours	—	2,000	12,000

In the moulding department, the modern lamp base requires 1 hour of machine time, and the traditional lamp base requires 2 hours. In the painting department, the modern lamp base requires 0.5 hour of direct labour, and the traditional lamp base requires 1 hour. Production of 8,000 modern units and 8,000 traditional units is expected. Before calculating departmental overhead rates, maintenance costs are assigned to moulding and painting in proportion to the maintenance hours used. Maintenance costs are added to the direct overhead costs found in each department to form departmental overhead pools. An overhead rate is then calculated for each producing department using machine hours for moulding and direct labour hours for painting.

Immediately after preparing the budgeted data, a consultant suggests that two manufacturing cells be created: one for the manufacture of the modern model and the other for the manufacture of the traditional model. Cell workers would be trained to perform maintenance; hence, the maintenance department would be decentralized. The total direct overhead costs estimated for each cell are $200,000 for cell M (modern) and $184,000 for cell T (traditional).

Required:

1. Assign the maintenance costs to each producing department, and compute the overhead cost per unit for each lamp base.
2. Compute the overhead cost per unit if manufacturing cells are created. Which unit overhead cost do you think is the more accurate—the one computed with a departmental structure or the one computed using a cell structure? Explain.
3. Explain why the total overhead costs are less under JIT than under traditional manufacturing.

4–27

Customers as a Cost Object

LO6

A bank has requested an analysis of chequing account profitability by customer type. Customers are categorized according to the size of their account: low balances, medium balances, and high balances. The activities associated with the three different customer categories, and their associated annual costs, are given below.

Opening and closing accounts	$ 200,000
Issuing monthly statements	300,000
Processing transactions	2,050,000
Customer inquiries	400,000
Providing ATM services	1,120,000
Total cost	$4,070,000

Additional information concerning the usage of the activities by the various customers is also provided:

	Account Balance		
	Low	Medium	High
Number of accounts opened/closed	15,000	3,000	2,000
Number of statements issued	450,000	100,000	50,000
Number of transactions processed	18,000,000	2,000,000	500,000
Number of ATM transactions	1,000,000	600,000	400,000
Number of chequing accounts	38,000	8,000	4,000

Required:

1. Calculate a cost per account per year by dividing the total cost of processing and maintaining chequing accounts by the total number of accounts. What is the average fee per month that the bank should charge to cover the costs incurred because of chequing accounts?
2. Calculate a cost per customer by customer category using activity rates.
3. Currently the bank offers free chequing to all its customers. The interest revenues average $90 per account; however, the interest revenues earned per account by category are $80, $100, and $165 for the low, medium, and high balance accounts, respectively. Calculate the average profit per account (average revenue less average cost from Requirement 1). Now calculate the profit per

account using the revenue per customer type and the unit cost per customer type calculated in Requirement 2.

4. After reviewing the analysis from Requirement 3, a bank vice-president recommended eliminating the free chequing feature for low-balance customers. The president expressed reluctance to do so, arguing that the low-balance customers more than make up the loss through cross-sales. He presented a survey showing that 50 percent of the customers would switch banks if a chequing fee were imposed. Explain how you could verify the president's argument using activity-based costing.

4–28

ABC and Customer-Driven Costs

LO6

Sorensen Manufacturing produces several types of bolts used in aircraft. The bolts are produced in batches according to customer order. Although there are a variety of bolts, they can be grouped into three product families. Because the product families are used in different kinds of aircraft, customers can also be grouped into three categories, corresponding to the product family they purchase. The number of units sold to each customer class is the same. The selling prices for the three product families range from $0.50 to $0.80 per unit. Historically, the costs of order entry, processing, and handling were expensed and not traced to individual customer groups. These costs are not trivial: they totalled $4,500,000 for the most recent year. Furthermore, these costs have been increasing over time. Recently, the company started to emphasize a cost reduction strategy; however, any cost reduction decisions had to contribute to the creation of a competitive advantage.

Because of the magnitude and growth of order-filling costs, management decided to explore the causes of these costs. They discovered that order-filling costs were driven by the number of customer orders processed. Further investigation revealed the following cost behaviour for the order-filling activity:

Fixed step-cost component: $50,000 per step (2,000 orders define a step)*
Variable cost component: $20 per order

* Sorensen currently has sufficient steps to process 100,000 orders.

The expected customer orders for the year total 100,000. The expected usage of the order-filling activity and the average size of an order by customer category follow:

	Category I	Category II	Category III
Number of orders	50,000	30,000	20,000
Average order size	600	1,000	1,500

As a result of the cost behaviour analysis, the marketing manager recommended the imposition of a charge per customer order. The president of the company concurred. The charge was implemented by adding the cost per order to the price of each order (computed using the projected ordering costs and expected orders). This ordering cost was then reduced as the size of the order increased and eliminated as the order size reached 2,000 units (the marketing manager indicated that any penalties imposed for orders greater than this size would result in a loss of sales from some of the smaller customers). Within a short time after communicating this new price information to customers, the average order size for all three product families increased to 2,000 units.

Required:

1. Sorensen has traditionally expensed order-filling costs. What is the most likely reason for this practice?
2. Calculate the cost per order for each customer category.
3. Calculate the reduction in order-filling costs produced by the change in pricing strategy (assume that resource spending is reduced as much as possible and that the total units sold remain unchanged). Explain how exploiting customer activity information produced this cost reduction. Are there any other internal activities that might benefit from this pricing strategy?

MANAGERIAL DECISION CASES

4–29

Activity-Based
Costing;
Consideration of
Customer-Driven
Costs

LO4, LO6

Sharp Paper, Inc., has three paper mills, one of which is located in Kamloops, British Columbia. The Kamloops mill produces 300 different types of coated and uncoated specialty printing papers. This large variety of products was the result of a full-line marketing strategy adopted by Sharp's management. Management was convinced that the value of variety more than offset the extra costs of the increased complexity.

During 2001, the Kamloops mill produced 120,000 tons of coated paper and 80,000 tons of uncoated. Of the 200,000 tons produced, 180,000 were sold. Sixty products account for 80 percent of the tons sold. Thus, 240 products are classified as low-volume products.

Lightweight lime hopsack in cartons (LLHC) is one of the low-volume products. LLHC is produced in rolls, converted into sheets of paper, and then sold in cartons. In 2001, the cost to produce and sell one ton of LLHC was as follows:

Raw materials:

Furnish (3 different pulps)	2,225 pounds	$ 450
Additives (11 different items)	200 pounds	500
Tub size	75 pounds	10
Recycled scrap paper	(296 pounds)	(20)
Total raw materials		$ 940
Direct labour		$ 450
Overhead:		
Paper machine ($100/ton × 2,500 pounds)		$ 125
Finishing machine ($120/ton × 2,500 pounds)		150
Total overhead		$ 275
Shipping and warehousing		$ 30
Total manufacturing and selling cost		$1,695

Overhead is applied using a two-stage process. First, overhead is allocated to the paper and finishing machines using the direct method of allocation with carefully selected cost drivers. Second, the overhead assigned to each machine is divided by the budgeted tons of output. These rates are then multiplied by the number of pounds required to produce one good ton.

In 2001, LLHC sold for $2,400 per ton, making it one of Sharp Paper's most profitable products. A similar examination of some of the other low-volume products revealed that they also had very respectable profit margins. Unfortunately, the performance of the high-volume products was less impressive, with many showing losses or very low profit margins. This situation led Ryan Chesser to call a meeting with his marketing vice-president, Jennifer Woodruff, and his controller, Jan Booth.

Ryan: "The above-average profitability of our low-volume specialty products and the poor profit performance of our high-volume products make me believe that we should switch our marketing emphasis to the low-volume line. Perhaps we should drop some of our high-volume products, particularly those showing a loss."
Jennifer: "I'm not convinced that the solution you are proposing is the right one. I know our high-volume products are of high quality, and I am convinced that we are as efficient in our production as other firms. I think that somehow our costs are not being assigned correctly. For example, the shipping and warehousing costs are assigned by dividing these costs by the total tons of paper sold. Yet—"
Jan: "Jennifer, I hate to disagree, but the $30 per ton charge for shipping and warehousing seems reasonable. I know that our method of assigning these costs is identical to that used by a number of other paper companies."
Jennifer: "Well, that may be true, but do these other companies have the variety of products that we have? Our low-volume products require special handling and processing, but when we assign shipping and warehousing costs, we average these

special costs across our entire product line. Every ton produced in our mill passes through our mill shipping department and is sent either directly to the customer or to our distribution centre and then eventually to customers. My records indicate quite clearly that virtually all the high-volume products are sent directly to customers, whereas most of the low-volume products are sent to the distribution centre. Now all the products passing through the mill shipping department should receive a share of the $2,000,000 annual shipping costs. I am not convinced, however, that all products should receive a share of the receiving and shipping costs of the distribution centre as currently practised."

Ryan: "Jan, is this true? Does our system allocate our shipping and warehousing costs in this way?"

Jan: "Yes, I'm afraid it does. Jennifer may have a point. Perhaps we need to re-evaluate our method to assign these costs to the product lines."

Ryan: "Jennifer, do you have any suggestions concerning how the shipping and warehousing costs ought to be assigned?"

Jennifer: "It seems reasonable to make a distinction between products that spend time in the distribution centre and those that do not. We should also distinguish between the receiving and shipping activities at the distribution centre. All incoming shipments are packed on pallets and weigh 1 ton each (there are 14 cartons of paper per pallet). In 2001, receiving processed 56,000 tons of paper. Receiving employs 15 people at an annual cost of $600,000. Other receiving costs total about $500,000. I would recommend that these costs be assigned using tons processed.

Shipping, however, is different. There are two activities associated with shipping: picking the order from inventory and loading the paper. We employ 30 people for picking and 10 for loading, at an annual cost of $1,200,000. Other shipping costs total $1,100,000. Picking and loading are more concerned with the number of shipping items than with tonnage. That is, a shipping item may consist of two or three cartons instead of pallets. Accordingly, the distribution centre's shipping costs should be assigned using the number of items shipped. In 2001, for example, we handled 190,000 shipping items."

Ryan: "These suggestions have merit. Jan, I would like to see what effect Jennifer's suggestions have on the per-unit assignment of shipping and warehousing for LLHC. If the effect is significant, then we will expand the analysis to include all products."

Jan: "I'm willing to compute the effect, but I'd like to suggest one additional feature. Currently, we have a policy to carry about 25 tons of LLHC in inventory. Our current cost system totally ignores the cost of carrying this inventory. Since it costs us $1,665 to produce each ton of this product, we are tying up a lot of money in inventory—money that could be invested in other productive opportunities. In fact, the return lost is about 16 percent per year. This cost should also be assigned to the units sold."

Ryan: "Jan, that also sounds good to me. Go ahead and include the carrying cost in your computation."

To help in the analysis, Jan gathered the following data for LLHC for 2001:

Tons sold	10
Average cartons per shipment	2
Average shipments per ton	7

Required:

1. Identify the flaws associated with the current method of assigning shipping and warehousing costs to Sharp's products.
2. Compute the shipping and warehousing cost per ton of LLHC sold using the new method suggested by Jennifer and Jan.
3. Using the new costs computed in Requirement 2, compute the profit per ton for LLHC. Compare this with the profit per ton computed using the old method. Do

you think that this same effect would be realized for other low-volume products? Explain.

4. Comment on Ryan's proposal to drop some high-volume products and place more emphasis on low-volume products. Discuss the role of the accounting system in supporting this type of decision making.

5. After receiving the analysis of LLHC, Ryan decided to expand the analysis to all products. He also had Jan re-evaluate the way in which mill overhead was assigned to products. After the restructuring was completed, Ryan took the following actions: (a) the prices of most low-volume products were increased, (b) the prices of several high-volume products were decreased, and (c) some low-volume products were dropped. Explain why his strategy changed so dramatically.

4–30

Activity-Based Product Costing and Ethical Behaviour
LO4, LO5, LO6

Consider the following conversation between Leonard Bryner, president and manager of a firm engaged in job manufacturing, and Chuck Davis, CMA, the firm's controller.

Leonard: "Chuck, as you know, our firm has been losing market share over the past three years. We have been losing more and more bids, and I don't understand why. At first I thought that other firms were undercutting us simply to gain business, but after examining some of the public financial reports, I believe that they are making a reasonable rate of return. I am beginning to believe that our costs and costing methods are at fault."

Chuck: "I can't agree with that. We have good control over our costs. Like most firms in our industry, we use a normal job-costing system. I really don't see any significant waste in the plant."

Leonard: "After talking with some other managers at a recent industrial convention, I'm not so sure that waste by itself is the issue. They talked about activity-based management, activity-based costing, and continuous improvement. They mentioned the use of something called activity drivers to assign overhead. They claimed that these new procedures can help produce more efficiency in manufacturing, better control of overhead, and more accurate product costing. A big deal was made of eliminating activities that added no value. Maybe our bids are too high because these other firms have found ways to decrease their overhead costs and to increase the accuracy of their product costing."

Chuck: "I doubt it. For one thing, I don't see how we can increase product-costing accuracy. So many of our costs are indirect costs. Furthermore, everyone uses some measure of production activity to assign overhead costs. I imagine that what they are calling activity drivers is just some new buzzword for measures of production volume. Fads in costing come and go. I wouldn't worry about it. I'll bet that our problems with decreasing sales are temporary. You might recall that we experienced a similar problem about twelve years ago—it was two years before it straightened out."

Required:

1. Do you agree with Chuck Davis and the advice that he gave Leonard Bryner? Explain.

2. Was there anything wrong or unethical in the behaviour that Chuck Davis displayed? Explain your reasoning.

3. Do you think that Chuck was well informed—that he was aware of the accounting implications of activity-based costing and that he knew what was meant by cost drivers? Should he have been? Review (in Chapter 1) the first category of the standards of ethical conduct for management accountants. Do any of these apply to Chuck's case?

RESEARCH ASSIGNMENT

4–31

Cybercase
LO4, LO5, LO6

There are numerous examples of ABC applications in the real world. A good source of ABC case studies for various industries is found at **www.abctech.com.** Access the site and select *industry cases*. Within this category, select *transportation* and click on *U.S. Airways*. Read this case. Next, return to *industry cases*, select *manufacturing*, and click on *Michelman*. Read this case. Answer the following questions about the two cases:

1. What reasons were offered for implementing ABC?
2. Describe the implementation procedures.
3. How many activities were identified?
4. What type of benefits (results) did each company achieve?
5. What problems, if any, were mentioned?

CHAPTER 5

Job-Order Costing

Learning Objectives

After studying Chapter 5, you should be able to:

1. Describe the differences between job-order costing and process costing, and identify the types of firms that would use each method.

2. Describe the cost flows and prepare the journal entries associated with job-order costing.

3. Identify and set up the source documents used in job-order costing.

Scenario

The Applegate Construction Company[1] was established in 1957. For more than 40 years, the company specialized in building subdivisions. The company could be described as a small, successful business with a good reputation for building quality homes. Recently, Walter Applegate, the founder and owner of the company, retired and his son, Jay Applegate, assumed control of the company.

Jay decided that the company needed to expand into custom-built homes and nonresidential construction. As he began to explore these possibilities, he encountered some problems with the company's current accounting system. Accordingly, he requested a meeting with his aunt, Bonnie Barlow, the financial manager. She was responsible for bookkeeping and payroll. A local CGA firm prepared all financial reports and filed the company's tax returns.

Jay: "Bonnie, as you know, I want our company to become one of the largest in this region. To accomplish this, I am convinced that we need to expand our operations to include both custom homes and industrial buildings. I think we can gain business in both of these areas by capitalizing on our reputation for quality. However, I am afraid that as we enter these markets, we are going to have to change our accounting system. I'm going to need your help in making the changes."

Bonnie: "I'm not sure why you want to change our accounting procedures. They are simple, and they've worked well for 40 years."

Jay: "In the past, our company has built homes in subdivisions that were basically the same. We've had slight variations in design so that they weren't carbon copies, but each home has required essentially the same work and materials. The cost of each home has been computed by simply accumulating the actual costs incurred over the period of time it took to build all the homes and then dividing this total by the number of units constructed. But this approach will not work when we enter the market for custom-built homes or industrial units."

Bonnie: "I think I see the problem. Custom-built homes, for example, may each require different cement work and different carpentry work, and may use more expensive materials, like a spa tub instead of a regular bathtub. They may also differ significantly in size from our standard units. If we simply divide the total construction costs for a period by the number of units produced, we won't get a very accurate representation of what it's costing to build any individual home. Additionally, the cost of our standard units could be distorted. Industrial units would cause even worse problems. It sounds like we do need a different method of accumulating our construction costs."

Jay: "I agree. We need some way of tracking the labour, materials, and overhead used by each job. In addition, by moving into custom home building, we'll be working much more closely with the customers and their architects. I know there will be times when the customer doesn't go through with building the house, but we will have spent a considerable amount of time on design. How will we measure the cost of our consulting service?"

Bonnie: "Jay, these costing issues are more complicated than what we are used to dealing with. Let me talk to our accountant and see what advice she can give us. I am sure that she can suggest a cost system that will address these issues."

1.   This scenario is based on the actual experiences of a mid-sized construction firm. The names of

the company and people involved have been changed to preserve confidentiality.

Questions to Think About

1. Does Applegate Construction Company produce a product or provide a service? Would the buyer of a typical subdivision house answer this question differently than a custom house buyer would?

2. List some examples of direct materials, direct labour, and overhead for Applegate's typical subdivision home. List some examples of each for custom homes. Is Jay Applegate right—will the accounting system need to change? How?

UNIT COST IN THE JOB-ORDER ENVIRONMENT

Objective 1

Describe the differences between job-order costing and process costing, and identify the types of firms that would use each method.

We have seen that companies keep track of total and unit costs for a number of reasons, including the generation of financial statements, the determination of profitability, and the making of decisions (for example, what price to charge). However, we have not yet given much thought to the way that the kinds of products or services produced might affect the kind of accounting system to be used.

Manufacturing and service firms can be divided into two major types depending on whether or not their products/services are unique. Consider Applegate Construction Company. At first, the company built houses in subdivisions. These houses were quite similar to one another, and the basic cost of each was the same. Certainly the houses looked somewhat different—one might have red brick, another multicoloured brick, and still another white brick. However, these cosmetic differences did not affect *cost* to any great extent. Therefore, Applegate could treat each house as an identical unit for accounting purposes. However, as Jay Applegate noted, this accounting system would not work with custom houses. Custom houses vary significantly, and more importantly from our standpoint, their costs vary significantly. The cost of a custom house with 250 square metres, three bathrooms, and aluminum-clad windows will be quite different from the cost of a custom house with 375 square metres, four bathrooms, three fireplaces, and wood-trimmed windows. As a result, Applegate Construction Company must tailor its accounting system to its production.

Job-Order Production and Costing

Firms operating in job-order industries produce a wide variety of products or jobs that are usually quite distinct from each other. Customized or built-to-order products fit into this category, as do services that vary from customer to customer. Examples of job-order processes include printing, construction, furniture making, automobile repair, and beautician services. In manufacturing, a job may be a single unit (such as a house) or a batch of units (such as eight tables). Improved technology enables companies to produce even more products to special order. For example, Israeli firm Indigo Ltd. has developed a new printing system that makes it economical to print very small batches of cans, bottles, labels, and so on. Thus, this process would make it feasible to produce 500 beverage cans for the year-end party for a campus organization.[2]

Job-order systems may be used to produce goods for inventory that are subsequently sold in the general market. Often, however, a job is associated with a particular customer order. The key feature of job-order costing is that the cost of one job differs from that of another job, and must be kept track of separately. For job-order production systems, costs are accumulated by job. This approach to assigning costs is called a **job-order costing system.** In a job-order firm, collecting costs by job provides vital information for management. For example, frequently prices are based on costs in a job-order environment.

Process Production and Costing

Firms in process industries mass-produce large quantities of similar or homogeneous products. Examples of process manufacturers include food, cement, petroleum, and chemical firms. One litre of paint is the same as another litre; one tube of toothpaste is the same as another tube. The important point here is that the cost of one unit of a product is identical to the cost of another. Service firms can also use a process-costing approach. For example, a bank's cheque-clearing department incurs a uniform cost to clear each cheque, no matter the size of the cheque or the name of the person to whom it is written.

Process firms accumulate production costs by process or by department for a given time period. The output for the process for that period is measured. Unit costs are computed by dividing the process costs for the given period by the output of the period. This approach to cost accumulation is known as a **process-costing system.** Exhibit 5–1 summarizes and contrasts the characteristics of job-order and process costing.

Calculating Unit Cost with Job-Order Costing

While the variety of product cost definitions discussed in Chapter 2 apply to both job-order and process costing, we will use the traditional product-costing definition to illustrate job-order costing procedures. That is, production costs consist of direct materials, direct labour, and overhead. Overhead can be assigned using an activity-based approach or functional-based approaches, depending on the need for product-costing accuracy found within a particular job-order company. It should be understood that the functional-based unit-level approaches to assigning overhead are simply special cases of the more general ABC system. Unit-level systems can be used effectively whenever one of three conditions is met: (1) the nonunit-level overhead is a small percentage of the total overhead, (2) the products produced in the job envi-

Exhibit 5–1

Comparison of Job-Order and Process Costing

Job-Order Costing	Process Costing
1. Wide variety of distinct products	1. Homogeneous products
2. Costs accumulated by job	2. Costs accumulated by process or department
3. Unit cost computed by dividing total job costs by units produced on that job	3. Unit cost computed by dividing process costs for a period by units produced in the period

2. Peter Coy and Neal Sandler, "A Package for Every Person," *Business Week*, 6 February 1995, 44.

ronment have the same overhead consumption ratios, or (3) the cost of using both unit-level and nonunit-level drivers exceeds the benefits. It is also important in a job-order environment to use predetermined overhead rates, since the completion of a job rarely coincides with the completion of a fiscal year. Therefore, in the remainder of this chapter, we will use normal costing. Recall that normal costing requires us to cost units of production using actual direct materials cost, actual direct labour cost, and overhead applied using one or more predetermined rates.

The unit cost of a job is simply the total cost of materials used on the job, labour worked on the job, and overhead assigned using one or more activity drivers. Although the concept is simple, the practical reality of the computation can be somewhat more complex, especially when there are products that differ from one another. Initially, to illustrate the unit-cost computation, we use only a single unit-level driver to assign overhead. Later, job-order costing procedures are illustrated using the multiple-driver approach of activity-based costing.

Suppose that Stan Johnson forms a new company, Johnson Leathergoods, which specializes in the production of custom leather products. Stan believes that there is a market for one-of-a-kind leather purses, briefcases, and backpacks. In his company's first month of operation, he obtains two orders: the first is for 20 leather backpacks for a local sporting goods store, and the second is for 10 distinctively tooled briefcases for the coaches of a local football team. Stan agrees to provide these orders at a price of cost plus 50 percent.

Let's look at the computation of unit cost for Stan's first order. The backpacks will require direct materials (leather, thread, buckles), direct labour (cutting, sewing, assembling), and overhead. Assume that overhead is assigned using a single unit-level driver, direct labour hours (a plantwide rate). Suppose that the materials cost $1,000 and the direct labour costs $1,080 (120 hours at $9 per hour). If the predetermined overhead rate is $2 per direct labour hour, then the overhead applied to this job is $240 (120 hours at $2 per hour). Now we can see that the total cost of the backpacks is $2,320, and the unit cost is $116, computed as follows:

Direct materials	$1,000
Direct labour	1,080
Overhead	240
Total cost	$2,320
÷ number of units	÷ 20
Unit cost	$ 116

This example, with the total cost of materials, labour, and overhead for a single job, is the simplest example of a **job-order cost sheet** (sometimes shortened to "job cost sheet"). The job-order cost sheet is prepared for every job. It is subsidiary to the work-in-process account and is the primary document for accumulating all costs related to a particular job. Of course, there is much more information that could be presented on a job-order cost sheet, and this will be discussed in a later section of this chapter.

Since cost is so closely linked to price in this case, it is easy to see that Stan will charge the sporting goods store $3,480 (cost of $2,320 plus 50 percent of $2,320), or $174 per backpack.

THE FLOW OF COSTS THROUGH THE ACCOUNTS

Objective 2

Describe the cost flows and prepare the journal entries associated with job-order costing.

When we talk about cost flow, we are talking about the way we account for costs from the point at which they are incurred to the point at which they are recognized as an expense on the income statement. Of principal interest in a job-order system is the flow of manufacturing costs. Accordingly, we begin with a description of exactly how the three manufacturing cost elements—direct materials, direct labour, and overhead—flow through the following accounts: Raw Materials, Work in Process, Overhead Control, Finished Goods, and Cost of Goods Sold.

Let's continue to use the simplified job-shop environment provided by our example of Johnson Leathergoods. To start the business, Stan leased a small building and bought the necessary production equipment. Recall that he finalized two orders for January: one for 20 backpacks for a local sporting goods store, and a second for 10 briefcases for the coaches of a local football team. Both orders must be delivered January 31 and will be sold for manufacturing cost plus 50 percent. Stan expects to average two orders per month for the first year of operation.

Stan created two job-order cost sheets, one for each order. The first job-order cost sheet is for the backpacks, the second is for the briefcases.

Accounting for Materials

Since the company is just beginning business, it has no beginning inventories. To produce the orders in January and have a supply of materials on hand at the beginning of February, Stan purchases, on account, $2,500 of raw materials. This purchase is recorded as follows:

1.	Raw Materials	2,500	
	Accounts Payable		2,500

Raw Materials is an inventory account. It is also the controlling account for all raw materials. When materials are purchased, the cost of these materials "flows" into the raw materials account through the debit to Raw Materials.

When the production supervisor needs materials for a job, materials are removed from the storeroom. The cost of the materials is removed from the materials account and added to the Work in Process account. Of course, in a job-order environment, the materials moved from the storeroom to work in process must be "tagged" with the appropriate job name. Suppose that Stan needs $1,000 of materials for the backpacks and $500 for the briefcases. The following entry would then be made:

2.	Work in Process	1,500	
	Raw Materials		1,500

This second entry captures the notion of raw materials flowing from the storeroom to work in process. All such flows are summarized in the Work in Process account as well as being posted individually to the respective jobs on their job-order cost sheets. Recall that Work in Process is a controlling account, and the job cost sheets are the subsidiary accounts. Therefore, the job-order cost sheet for backpacks would show $1,000 for direct materials, and the job-order cost sheet for the briefcases would show $500 for direct materials. Exhibit 5–2 summarizes the raw materials cost flows.

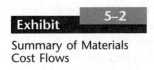

Exhibit 5–2

Summary of Materials Cost Flows

Exhibit 5–3

Summary of Direct
Labour Cost Flows

Accounting for Direct Labour Cost

Since two jobs were in progress during January, Stan must determine not only the total number of direct labour hours worked, but also the time worked on each job. The backpacks required 120 hours at an average wage rate of $9 per hour, for a total direct labour cost of $1,080. For the briefcases, the total was $450, based on 50 hours at an average hourly wage of $9. In addition to the postings to each job's cost sheet, the following summary entry would be made:

3.	Work in Process	1,530	
	Wages Payable		1,530

The summary of the labour cost flows is given in Exhibit 5–3. Notice that the direct labour costs assigned to the two jobs exactly equal the total assigned to Work in Process. Remember that the labour cost flows reflect only direct labour cost. Indirect labour is assigned as part of overhead.

Accounting for Overhead

The use of normal costing means that actual overhead costs are never assigned directly to jobs. Overhead is applied to each individual job using a *predetermined* rate or rates. The more general case, of course, is the application of overhead using activity-based costing. The use of a single, plantwide overhead rate is a specialized case of ABC. Finally, actual overhead costs incurred must be accounted for as well, but on an overall (not job-specific) basis. First, we will describe how to account for applied overhead using ABC; next we will look at the application of overhead using a plantwide rate; and then we will discuss accounting for actual overhead.

ABC and Job-Order Costing Recall that activity-based costing requires the firm to identify production activities and related activity drivers. Then a rate is computed for each activity (or homogeneous sets of activities). Suppose that Stan estimates annual overhead of $9,600, and that this amount can be broken down into three categories: purchasing (locating vendors, preparing purchase documents, and purchasing materials), machining (power, lubricants, and use of machines), and a pool of unit-level activities called "other." Purchasing cost is driven by the number of purchase orders, machining cost is driven by machine hours, and the unit-level pool costs are assigned using number of direct labour hours. The budgeted cost for each activity pool and the expected demands for each driver are as follows:

Activity Pool	Cost	Cost Driver	Demand
Purchasing	$3,000	Purchase orders	100
Machining	$4,200	Machine hours	2,800
Other	$2,400	Direct labour hours	4,800

Activity-based rates would be:

Purchasing: $3,000/100 = $30 per purchase order
Machining: $4,200/2,800 = $1.50 per machine hour
Other: $2,400/4,800 = $0.50 per direct labour hour

In order to assign overhead costs to each job, we must know the demand each job places on the three activity drivers. The demands of the two jobs follow:

	Backpacks	Briefcases
Purchase orders	3	1
Machine hours	60	30
Direct labour hours	120	50

Overhead assigned to each job is calculated as follows:

	Backpacks	Briefcases
Purchasing		
(3 × $30); (1 × $30)	$ 90	$ 30
Machining		
(60 × $1.50); (30 × $1.50)	90	45
Other		
(120 × $0.50); (50 × $0.50)	60	25
Total overhead applied	$240	$100

Overhead applied using ABC is credited to the overhead account in the amount of $340: $240 for the backpack job and $100 for the briefcase job. The summary entry reflects a total of $340 (assigning all overhead to jobs worked on in January):

4.	Work in Process	340	
	Overhead Control		340

The credit balance in the Overhead Control account equals the total applied overhead at a given point in time. In normal costing, only applied overhead ever enters the Work in Process account.

Applying Overhead Using Functional Approaches   Overhead costs can also be assigned using plantwide overhead rates or departmental overhead rates. Typically, direct labour hours is the measure used to calculate a plantwide overhead rate, whereas departmental overhead rates are based on unit-level drivers, such as direct labour hours, machine hours, and direct materials dollars. The use of a plantwide rate has the virtue of being simple and reduces data collection requirements. To illustrate these two features, recall that total estimated overhead costs for Johnson Leathergoods are $9,600. Assume that the budgeted direct labour hours total 4,800 hours. Accordingly, the predetermined overhead rate is:

Overhead rate = $9,600/4,800 = $2 per direct labour hour

For the backpacks, with a total of 120 hours worked, the amount of overhead cost posted to the Work in Process account is $240 ($2 × 120). For the briefcases, the overhead cost is $100 ($2 × 50). Compared to the ABC assignments, there are fewer calculations. Note also that assigning overhead to jobs requires only a rate and the direct labour hours used by the job. Since direct labour hours are already being collected to assign direct labour cost to jobs, overhead assignment would not demand any additional data collection.

Unfortunately, use of a plantwide rate may also significantly reduce the accuracy of cost assignment. The use of a single unit-level driver may not reflect the actual consumption of resources by individual jobs. For example, a third job that requires 6 purchase orders, 200 machine hours, and 100 direct labour hours would have an overhead assignment of $530 [(6 × $30) + (200 × $1.50) + (100 × $0.50)] using ABC, but only $200 (100 × $2) using a unit-level rate. Clearly this job would be undercosted using a single rate, because the impact of increased machine usage and purchasing is ignored when direct labour hours alone is used as the driver. This increased cost could have a significant effect on product-mix decisions and pricing decisions (among others).

Accounting for Actual Overhead Costs   To illustrate how actual overhead costs are recorded, assume that Johnson Leathergoods incurred the following indirect costs for January:

Lease payment	$200
Utilities	50
Equipment amortization	100
Indirect labour	65
Total overhead costs	$415

Notice that these overhead costs reflect what is spent by account category, not by activity. These resources were used to enable the three activities—purchasing, machining, and other (unit-level) activities—to be performed. For an ABC system, determining the actual cost of activities requires that these costs be unbundled and assigned to individual activities. For example, how much of the indirect labour cost belongs to purchasing? When separate support departments exist, activity costs are traced to them and then assigned to products on the basis of usage. This is discussed in Chapter 7. What is important at this point is to understand that the actual overhead costs never enter the Work in Process account. The usual procedure is to record actual overhead costs on the debit side of the Overhead Control account. For example, the actual overhead costs would be recorded as follows:

5.	Overhead Control	415	
	Lease Payable		200
	Utilities Payable		50
	Accumulated Amortization–Equipment		100
	Wages Payable		65

The debit balance in the Overhead Control account gives the total actual overhead costs at a given point in time. Since actual overhead costs are on the debit side of this account and applied overhead costs are on the credit side, the balance in the Overhead Control account is the overhead variance at a given point in time. For Johnson Leathergoods at the end of January, the actual overhead of $415 and applied overhead of $340 produce underapplied overhead of $75 ($415 − $340).

The flow of overhead costs is summarized in Exhibit 5–4. Notice that the total overhead applied from all jobs is entered in the Work in Process account. Therefore, the information in Exhibit 5–4 is pertinent to both ABC and a plantwide overhead rate.

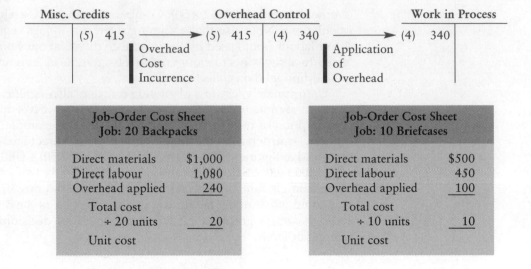

Exhibit 5–4

Summary of Overhead Cost Flows

Accounting for Finished Goods

We have already seen what takes place when a job is completed. The direct materials, direct labour, and applied overhead amounts are totalled to yield the manufacturing cost of the job. This job cost sheet is then transferred to a finished goods file. Simultaneously, the costs of the completed job are transferred from the Work in Process account to the Finished Goods account.

For example, assume that the backpacks were completed in January with the completed cost sheet shown in Exhibit 5–5. Since the backpacks are completed, the total manufacturing costs of $2,320 must be transferred from the Work in Process account to the Finished Goods account. This transfer is described by the following entry:

6.	Finished Goods	2,320	
	Work in Process		2,320

A summary of the cost flows occurring when a job is finished is shown in Exhibit 5–5.

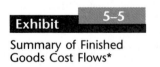

Exhibit 5–5

Summary of Finished Goods Cost Flows*

* There is no reason to show the job-order cost sheet for the briefcases, since they are still in process.

Exhibit 5–6

Statement of Cost of
Goods Manufactured

Johnson Leathergoods Company Statement of Cost of Goods Manufactured For the Month Ended January 31, 2001		
Direct materials:		
Beginning raw materials inventory	$ 0	
Purchases of raw materials	2,500	
Total raw materials available	$2,500	
Ending raw materials	1,000	
Total raw materials used		$1,500
Direct labour		1,530
Overhead:		
Lease	$ 200	
Utilities	50	
Amortization	100	
Indirect labour	65	
Total actual overhead	$ 415	
Less: Underapplied overhead	75	
Overhead applied		340
Current manufacturing costs		$3,370
Add: Beginning work in process		0
Total manufacturing costs		$3,370
Less: Ending work in process		1,050
Cost of goods manufactured		$2,320

The completion of a job is an important step in the flow of manufacturing costs. The cost of the completed job must be removed from work in process, added to finished goods, and, eventually, added to the cost of goods sold expense on the income statement. To ensure accuracy in computing these costs, a cost of goods manufactured statement is prepared. The statement of cost of goods manufactured presented in Exhibit 5–6 summarizes the production activity of Johnson Leathergoods for January. It is important to note that applied overhead is used to arrive at the cost of goods manufactured. Both work-in-process and finished goods inventories are carried at normal cost rather than actual cost.

Notice that ending work in process is $1,050. Where did we obtain this figure? Of the two jobs, the backpacks were finished and transferred to finished goods. The briefcases are still in process, however, and the manufacturing costs assigned thus far are direct materials, $500; direct labour, $450; and overhead applied, $100. The total of these costs gives the cost of ending work in process. You may want to check these figures against the job-order cost sheet for briefcases given in Exhibit 5–4.

Accounting for Cost of Goods Sold

In a job-order firm, units can be produced for a particular customer or they can be produced for inventory and later sales. If a job is produced specially for a customer (as with the backpacks), then when that job is shipped to the customer, the cost of the finished job becomes the cost of the goods sold. When the backpacks are completed, the following entries would be made (recall that the selling price is 150 percent of manufacturing cost).

7.	Cost of Goods Sold	2,320	
	Finished Goods		2,320
8.	Accounts Receivable	3,480	
	Sales Revenue		3,480

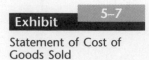

Exhibit   5–7

Statement of Cost of
Goods Sold

Statement of Cost of Goods Sold	
Beginning finished goods inventory	$ 0
Cost of goods manufactured	2,320
Goods available for sale	$2,320
Less: Ending finished goods inventory	0
Normal cost of goods sold	$2,320
Add: Underapplied overhead	75
Adjusted cost of goods sold	$2,395

In addition to these entries, a statement of cost of goods sold is usually prepared at the end of each reporting period (for example, monthly and quarterly). Exhibit 5–7 presents such a statement for Johnson Leathergoods for January. Typically, the overhead variance is not significant and, therefore, is closed to the Cost of Goods Sold account. Cost of goods sold before adjustment for an overhead variance is called **normal cost of goods sold.** After adjustment for the period's overhead variance takes place, the result is called the **adjusted cost of goods sold.** It is this latter figure that appears as an expense on the income statement.

However, closing the overhead variance to the Cost of Goods Sold account is often not done until the end of the year. Variances are expected each month because of nonuniform production and nonuniform actual overhead costs. As the year unfolds, these monthly variances should, by and large, offset each other so that the year-end variance is small, assuming that the predetermined overhead rate is reasonable. Nonetheless, to illustrate how the year-end overhead variance would be treated, we will close out the overhead variance experienced by Johnson Leathergoods in January.

Closing the underapplied overhead to cost of goods sold requires the following entry:

9.	Cost of Goods Sold	75	
	Overhead Control		75

Notice that debiting Cost of Goods Sold is equivalent to adding the underapplied amount to the normal cost of goods sold figure. If the overhead variance had been overapplied, the entry would reverse and Cost of Goods Sold would be credited (reduced).

If the backpacks had not been ordered by a customer but had been produced for inventory to be sold through a subsequent marketing effort, then all 20 units might not be sold at the same time. Assume that on January 31, 15 backpacks were sold. In this case, the cost of goods sold figure is the unit cost times the number of units sold, or $1,740 ($116 × 15). The remainder, or $580 ($116 × 5), would be recorded in Ending Inventory. The unit-cost figure is found on the cost sheet in Exhibit 5–5.

Closing out the overhead variance to Cost of Goods Sold completes the description of manufacturing cost flows. To facilitate a review of these important concepts, Exhibit 5–8 shows a complete summary of the manufacturing cost flows for Johnson Leathergoods. Notice that these entries summarize information from the underlying job-order cost sheets. Although the description in this exhibit is specific to the example, the pattern of cost flows shown would be found in any manufacturing firm that uses a normal job-order cost system.

Manufacturing cost flows, however, are not the only cost flows experienced by a firm. Nonmanufacturing costs are also incurred. A description of how we account for these costs follows.

Exhibit 5-8 Summary of Manufacturing Cost Flows

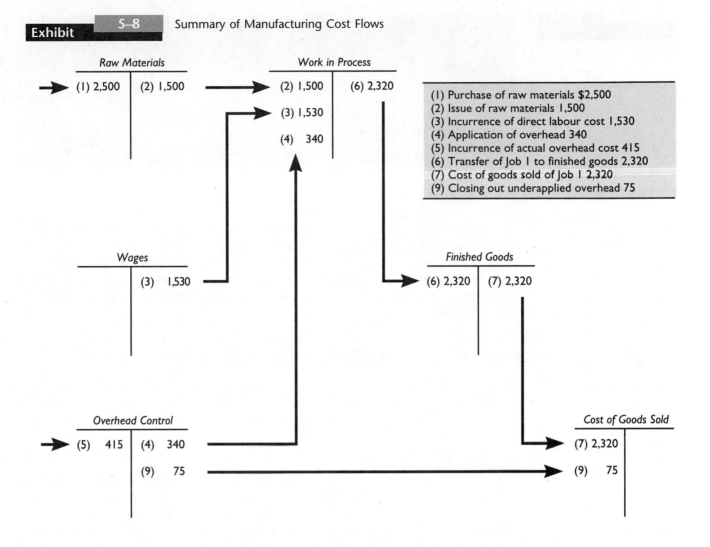

Accounting for Nonmanufacturing Costs

Recall that costs associated with selling and general administrative activities are classified as nonmanufacturing costs. According to the traditional product cost definition, these costs are period costs and are never assigned to the product. They are not part of the manufacturing cost flows. They do not belong to the overhead category and are treated as a totally separate category.

To illustrate how these costs are accounted for, assume that Johnson Leathergoods had the following additional transactions in January:

Advertising circulars	$ 75
Sales commission	125
Office salaries	500
Amortization, office equipment	50

The following compound journal entry could be used to record these costs:

Selling Expense Control	200	
Administrative Expense Control	550	
Accounts Payable		75
Wages Payable		625
Accumulated Amortization—Office Equipment		50

Exhibit　5–9

Income Statement

Johnson Leathergoods Company Income Statement For the Month Ended January 31, 2001		
Sales		$3,480
Less: Cost of goods sold		2,395
Gross margin		$1,085
Less selling and administrative expenses:		
Selling expenses	$200	
Administrative expenses	550	750
Net income		$ 335

Control accounts accumulate all of the selling and administrative expenses for a period. At the end of the period, all of these costs flow to the period's income statement. An income statement for Johnson Leathergoods is shown in Exhibit 5–9.

With the description of the accounting procedures for selling and administrative expenses completed, the basic essentials of a normal job-order costing system are also complete.

SOURCE DOCUMENTS: KEEPING TRACK OF INDIVIDUAL COSTS

Objective 3

Identify and set up the source documents used in job-order costing.

We have seen how costs for each job flow through the accounts and onto the financial statements. Now let's take a closer look at the accounting for job-order production by focusing on the source documents that support the job-order cost sheet.

Job-Order Cost Sheet

Every time a new job is started, a job-order cost sheet is prepared. As you recall, the job-order cost sheet is subsidiary to the Work in Process account, and contains all information pertinent to a job. For our simple example, the job-order cost sheet was quite brief, containing only the job description (backpacks) and cost of materials, labour, and overhead. However, a real company typically has many more orders and has to keep track of much more information.

Johnson Leathergoods had only two jobs in January, and these could be easily identified by calling them "backpacks" and "briefcases." Some companies find that the customer's name is sufficient to identify a job. For example, Applegate Construction Company may identify its custom houses as the "Smith residence" or the "Malkovich residence." As more and more jobs are produced, a company will usually find it most convenient to number them. Thus, you will see Job 13, Job 22, and Job 44. Perhaps the job number starts with the year, so that the first job of 2001 is 2001-1, the second is 2001-2, and so on. The key point is that each job is unique and must have a uniquely identifiable name. This name, or job-order number, heads the job-order cost sheet.

In a manual accounting system, the job-order cost sheet is a paper document. In today's world, however, most accounting systems are automated. The cost sheet usually corresponds to a record in a work-in-process master file. The collection of all job cost sheets defines a **work-in-process file.** In a manual system, the file would be located in a filing cabinet, whereas in an automated system it is stored electronically. In either system, the file of job-order cost sheets serves as a subsidiary work-in-process ledger.

Both manual and automated systems require the same kind of data in order to accumulate costs and track the progress of a job. A job cost system must have the ability to identify the quantity of direct materials, direct labour, and overhead consumed by each job. In other words, documentation and procedures are needed to associate the manufacturing inputs used by a job with the job itself. This need is satisfied through the use of materials requisitions for direct materials, time tickets for direct labour, and source documents for other activity drivers that might be used in applying overhead.

Materials Requisitions

The cost of direct materials is assigned to a job by the use of a source document known as a **materials requisition form**, illustrated in Exhibit 5–10. Notice that the form asks for the type, quantity, and unit cost of the direct materials issued and, most importantly, for the job number. Using this form, the cost accounting department can enter the cost of direct materials onto the correct job-order cost sheet.

If the accounting system is automated, this posting may entail directly entering the data at a computer terminal, using the materials requisition forms as source documents. A program enters the cost of direct materials into the record for each job.

In addition to providing essential information for assigning direct materials costs to jobs, the materials requisition form may also have other data items, such as a requisition number, a date, and a signature. These data items are useful for maintaining proper control over a firm's inventory of direct materials. The signature, for example, transfers responsibility for the materials from the storage area to the person receiving the materials, usually a production supervisor.

No attempt is made to trace the cost of other materials, such as supplies, lubricants, and so on, to a particular job. You will recall that these indirect materials are assigned to jobs through the predetermined overhead rate.

Job Time Tickets

Direct labour also must be associated with each particular job. The means by which direct labour costs are assigned to individual jobs is the source document known as a **time ticket** (see Exhibit 5–11). When an employee works on a particular job, he or she fills out a time ticket that identifies the employee's name and wage rate, the hours worked on this job, and job number. These time tickets are collected daily and transferred to the cost accounting department, where the information is used to post

Exhibit 5–10

Materials Requisition Form

			Material Requisition Number 12
Date	April 8, 2001		
Department	Grinding		
Job Number	16		

Description	Quantity	Cost/Unit	Total Cost
Casing	100	$3	$300

Authorized Signature _____ Jim Lawson _____

Exhibit 5–11

Job Time Ticket

Employee Number	45			Job Time Ticket Number 68	

Name   Ed Wilson

Date   April 12, 2001

Start Time	Stop Time	Total Time	Hourly Rate	Amount	Job Number
8:00	10:00	2	13	$26	16
10:00	11:00	1	13	13	17
11:00	12:00	1	13	13	16
1:00	5:00	4	13	52	16

Approved by _Jim Lawson_
Department Supervisor

the cost of direct labour to individual jobs. Again, in an automated system, posting involves entering the data into the computer.

Time tickets are used only for direct labourers. Since indirect labour is common to all jobs, these costs belong to overhead and are allocated using one or more predetermined overhead rates.

Other Source Documents

The use of activity-based costing to assign overhead to jobs clearly requires the company to keep track of more than one activity driver. These other bases must be accounted for as well. That is, the actual amount used of the other drivers (for example, machine hours, number of purchase orders, number of setups) must be collected and posted to the job cost sheets. If the amount of the driver is already accounted for (for example, number of purchase orders), no new source document is needed. However, if the driver is not currently being kept track of, a new source document must be developed. For example, a source document that will track the machine hours used by each job can be modelled on job time tickets.

All completed job-order cost sheets of a firm can serve as a subsidiary ledger for the finished goods inventory. In a manual accounting system, the completed sheets would be transferred from the work-in-process files to the finished goods inventory file. In an automated accounting system, an updating run would delete the finished job from the work-in-process master file and add this record to the finished goods master file. In either case, adding the totals of all completed job-order cost sheets gives the cost of finished goods inventory at any point in time. As finished goods are sold and shipped, the cost records would be pulled (or deleted) from the finished goods inventory file. These records then form the basis for calculating a period's cost of goods sold.

SUMMARY OF LEARNING OBJECTIVES

1. Describe the differences between job-order costing and process costing, and identify the types of firms that would use each method.
Job-order costing and process costing are two major cost assignment systems. Job-order systems are used for firms that produce a wide variety of heteroge-

neous (unique) products. Process costing is used by firms that mass-produce a homogeneous product.

2. Describe the cost flows and prepare the journal entries associated with job-order costing.
In job-order costing, materials and direct labour are

charged to the Work in Process account (Raw Materials and Payroll are credited, respectively). Overhead costs are assigned to Work in Process using a predetermined rate. The cost of completed units is credited to Work in Process and debited to Finished Goods. When goods are sold, the cost is debited to Cost of Goods Sold and credited to Finished Goods.

3. Identify and set up the source documents used in job-order costing.
In job-order costing, the key document or record for accumulating manufacturing costs is the job-order cost sheet. Materials requisition forms (for direct materials), time tickets (for direct labour), and source documents for manufacturing activities are the source documents needed to assign manufacturing costs to jobs.

KEY TERMS

Adjusted cost of goods sold, 176
Job-order cost sheet, 169
Job-order costing system, 168

Materials requisition form, 179
Normal cost of goods sold, 176
Process-costing system, 168

Time ticket, 179
Work-in-process file, 178

REVIEW PROBLEMS

I. JOB COST USING PLANTWIDE AND DEPARTMENTAL OVERHEAD RATES

Timter Company uses a normal job-order costing system. The company has two departments through which most jobs pass. Selected budgeted and actual data for the past year follow:

	Department A	Department B
Budgeted overhead	$100,000	$500,000
Actual overhead	$110,000	$520,000
Expected activity (direct labour hours)	50,000	10,000
Expected machine hours	10,000	50,000
Actual direct labour hours	51,000	9,000
Actual machine hours	10,500	52,000

During the year, several jobs were completed. Data pertaining to one such job, Job 10, follow:

Direct materials	$20,000
Direct labour cost:	
Department A (5,000 hours × $9)	$45,000
Department B (1,000 hours × $9)	$ 9,000
Machine hours used:	
Department A	100
Department B	1,200
Units produced	10,000

Timter Company uses a plantwide predetermined overhead rate to assign overhead to jobs. Direct labour hours (DLH) is used to compute the predetermined overhead rate.

Required:

1. Compute the predetermined overhead rate.
2. Using the predetermined rate, compute the per-unit manufacturing cost for Job 10.
3. Recalculate the unit manufacturing cost for Job 10 using departmental overhead rates. Use direct labour hours for Department A and machine hours for Department B. Explain why this approach provides a more accurate unit cost.

Solution

1. The predetermined overhead rate is $600,000/60,000 = $10 per DLH. Add the budgeted overhead for the two departments and divide by the total expected direct labour hours (DLH = 50,000 + 10,000).

2.
Direct materials	$ 20,000
Direct labour	54,000
Overhead ($10 × 6,000 DLH)	60,000
Total manufacturing cost	$134,000
Unit cost ($134,000/10,000)	$ 13.40

3. The predetermined rate for Department A is $100,000/50,000 = $2 per DLH. The predetermined rate for Department B is $500,000/50,000 = $10 per machine hour.

Direct materials	$20,000
Direct labour	54,000
Overhead:	
Department A ($2 × 5,000)	10,000
Department B ($10 × 1,200)	12,000
Total manufacturing costs	$96,000
Unit cost ($96,000/10,000)	$ 9.60

Overhead assignment using departmental rates is more accurate because there is a higher correlation with the overhead assigned and the overhead consumed. Notice that Job 10 spends most of its time in Department A, the least overhead-intensive of the two departments. Departmental rates reflect this differential time and consumption better than plantwide rates do.

II. CALCULATION OF WORK IN PROCESS AND COST OF GOODS SOLD WITH MULTIPLE JOBS

Greenthumb Landscape Design designs landscape plans and plants the material for clients. On April 1, there were three jobs in process: Jobs 68, 69, and 70. During April, two more jobs were started: Jobs 71 and 72. By April 30, Jobs 69, 70, and 72 were completed and sold. The following data were gathered:

	Job 68	Job 69	Job 70	Job 71	Job 72
April 1, Balance	$540	$1,230	$990	—	—
Direct material	700	560	75	$3,500	$2,750
Direct labour	500	600	90	2,500	2,000

Overhead is applied at the rate of 120 percent of direct labour cost. Jobs are sold at cost plus 40 percent. Operating expenses for April totalled $3,670.

Required:

1. Prepare job-order cost sheets for each job as of April 30.
2. Calculate the ending balance in work in process (as of April 30) and cost of goods sold for April.
3. Construct an income statement for Greenthumb Landscape Design for the month of April.

Solution

1.
	Job 68	Job 69	Job 70	Job 71	Job 72
April 1, Balance	$ 540	$1,230	$ 990	—	—
Direct material	700	560	75	$3,500	$2,750
Direct labour	500	600	90	2,500	2,000
Applied overhead	600	720	108	3,000	2,400
Totals	$2,340	$3,110	$1,263	$9,000	$7,150

2. Ending balance in work in process (Jobs 68 and 71) = $2,340 + 9,000 = $11,340
    Cost of goods sold for April (Jobs 69, 70, and 72) = $3,110 + 1,263 + 7,150 = $11,523

3.
Greenthumb Landscape Design
Income Statement
For the Month Ended April 30, 20xx

Sales ($11,523 × 140%)	$16,132
Cost of goods sold	11,523
Gross margin	$ 4,609
Less: Operating expenses	3,670
Operating income	$ 939

QUESTIONS FOR WRITING AND DISCUSSION

1. Explain the differences between job-order costing and process costing.

2. Explain the role of cost drivers in assigning overhead costs to jobs.

3. Explain how overhead is assigned to production when a predetermined overhead rate is used.

4. Wilson Company has a predetermined overhead rate of $5 per direct labour hour. The job-order cost sheet for Job 145 shows 1,000 direct labour hours costing $10,000 and materials requisitions totalling $7,500. Job 145 had 500 units completed and transferred to finished goods. What is the cost per unit for Job 145?

5. Why are the accounting requirements for job-order costing more demanding than those for process costing?

6. Give some examples of service firms that might use job-order costing, and explain why they would do so.

7. Suppose that you and a friend decide to set up a lawnmowing service next summer. Describe the source documents that you would need to account for your activities.

8. How is job-order costing related to profitability analysis? to pricing?

9. What are some differences between a manual job-order costing system and an automated job-order costing system?

10. What is the role of materials requisition forms in a job-order costing system? time tickets? predetermined overhead rates?

EXERCISES

5–1

Job-Order Costing versus Process Costing

LO1

Identify each of the following types of businesses as either job-order or process.

a. paint manufacturing
b. auto manufacturing
c. toy manufacturing
d. custom cabinet making
e. airplane manufacturing (e.g. 767s)
f. personal computer assembly
g. furniture making
h. custom furniture making
i. dental services
j. hospital services
k. paper manufacturing
l. auto repair
m. architectural services
n. landscape design services
o. light bulb manufacturing

5–2

Job-Order versus Process Costing

LO1

For each of the following types of industries, give an example of a firm that would use job-order costing. Then give an example of a firm that would use process costing.

1. auto manufacturing
2. dental services
3. auto repair
4. costume making

5–3

Applying Overhead to Jobs; Costing Jobs

LO2, LO3

Corbin Company is an engineering design firm that builds computer-controlled machinery to client specifications. On May 1, Jobs 345 and 346 were in process with the following costs:

	Job 345	Job 346
Direct materials	$ 6,700	$24,500
Direct labour	8,000	22,000
Applied overhead	6,800	18,700
May 1 balance	$21,500	$65,200

During May, Jobs 347 and 348 were started. Data on May costs for all jobs are as follows:

	Job 345	Job 346	Job 347	Job 348
Direct materials	$15,000	$ 9,000	$ 500	$3,450
Direct labour	13,800	10,000	1,500	4,000

Job 346 was completed on May 28, and the client was billed at cost plus 30 percent. All other jobs remained in process.

Required:

1. Calculate the overhead rate based on direct labour cost.
2. Calculate the overhead applied to each job during the month of May.
3. Prepare job-order cost sheets for each job as of the end of May.
4. Calculate the balance in Work in Process on May 31.
5. What is the selling price of Job 346?

5–4

Job Cost Calculation

LO2

Carol Taylor, owner of the Sewing Room, does alterations and sews clothing to order. She just completed making 26 dance costumes for a tap class at Encore Dance Studio. The job required materials costing $234, as well as 39 direct labour hours at $10 per hour. Overhead is applied on the basis of direct labour hours at a rate of $4 per hour.

Required:

1. What is the total cost of the job? the unit cost?
2. If Carol charges a price that is 1.5 times cost, what price is charged to each member of the dance class?

5–5

Balance of Work in Process and Finished Goods

LO2

Patton Company uses job-order costing. At the end of the month, the following information was gathered:

Job Number	Total Cost	Complete?	Sold?
101	$450	no	no
102	300	yes	yes
103	500	yes	no
104	670	no	no
105	800	no	no
106	230	yes	no
107	150	yes	yes
108	700	no	no

The beginning balance of Finished Goods was zero.

Required:

1. Calculate the balance in Work in Process at the end of the month.
2. Calculate the balance in Finished Goods at the end of the month.
3. Calculate the Cost of Goods Sold for the month.

5–6

Type of Costing System; Unit Cost; Job Cost

LO1, LO2

Jackson Jewellers has two departments. Department 1 makes class rings for high-school students. Each ring is essentially the same. Department 2 makes custom jewellery to order for clients. Department 2 creates a unique design for each piece and produces it using a variety of gemstones and gold.

On May 14, John Calvin met with Dave Jackson to discuss having a special pin designed for his wife in celebration of their 20th wedding anniversary. Dave created a butterfly design that would take advantage of a pair of matched watermelon tourmalines. To make the pin, gold backing was poured; the tourmalines and several small diamonds were then set into it. In all, direct materials cost $500, direct labour was $250, and overhead was applied at the rate of 100 percent of direct labour cost.

Required:

1. Which type of costing is used by Department 1? by Department 2?
2. What was the total cost of the pin for John Calvin's wife?

5–7

Job-Order Costing Using ABC

LO2

Refer to 5–6. Several months later, Dave met with his accountant to look at a new activity-based costing system. Two activities were identified: security (for gold and gems—includes insurance, amortization on safes, security alarms) and machining (power and amortization on machinery). Other overhead costs were grouped together as "other."

Activity	Cost	Driver	Driver Amount
Security	$50,000	Materials cost	$500,000
Machining	35,000	Machine hours	2,000
Other	74,000	Direct labour cost	$160,000

Dave wondered how this system would affect the costs he had been charging, so he used the Calvin job as an example. This job required direct materials of $500, direct labour of $250, and two machine hours.

Required:

1. Calculate the activity rates for security, machining, and other overhead.
2. Using these activity rates, what would the total cost of the Calvin job have been?

5–8

ABC and Job-Order Costing

LO2, LO3

Spreadsheet

Trent Company, a job-order costing firm, worked on four jobs in July. Data are as follows:

	Job 14	Job 15	Job 16	Job 17
Balance, July 1	$12,450	$3,770	0	0
Direct materials	$6,000	$7,900	$15,350	$1,000
Direct labour	$10,000	$8,500	$23,000	$900
Machine hours	200	150	1,000	10
Material moves	50	10	200	5
Purchase orders	10	40	10	20

ABC is used to apply overhead to jobs. The power rate is $3 per machine hour; the material-handling rate is $25 per move; the purchasing rate is $40 per purchase order. By July 31, Jobs 14 and 15 were completed, and Job 15 was sold. All others remain in process.

Required:

1. Prepare job-order cost sheets for each job, showing all costs through July 31.
2. Calculate the balance in Work in Process on July 31.

3. Calculate the cost transferred to Finished Goods during July.
4. Calculate the Cost of Goods Sold for July.

5–9

Income Statement for a Job-Order Costing Firm

LO2

Refer to 5–8. Trent prices its jobs at cost plus 50 percent. During July, marketing expenses were $2,000, and administrative expenses were $3,500.

Required:

Prepare an income statement for Trent Company for the month of July.

5–10

Journal Entries; Job Costs

LO3

Spreadsheet

The following transactions occurred during the month of April for Kearney Company.

a. Materials costing $3,000 were purchased on account.
b. Materials totalling $1,700 were requisitioned for use in production: $500 for Job 443 and the remainder for Job 444.
c. During the month, direct labour worked 50 hours on Job 443 and 100 hours on Job 444. Direct labour is paid at a rate of $8 per hour.
d. Overhead is applied using a plantwide rate of $7.50 per direct labour hour.
e. Actual overhead for the month was $1,230 and was paid in cash.
f. Job 443 was completed and transferred to Finished Goods.
g. Job 442, which had been completed and transferred to Finished Goods in March, was sold on account for cost ($2,000) plus 25 percent.

Required:

1. Prepare journal entries for transactions (a) through (e).
2. Prepare job-order cost sheets for Jobs 443 and 444. Prepare journal entries for transactions (f) and (g).
3. Prepare a statement of cost of goods manufactured for April. Assume that the beginning balance in the Raw Materials account was $1,400, and the beginning balance in the Work in Process account was zero.

5–11

Overhead Application; Journal Entries; Job Cost

LO2

At the beginning of the year, Paxton Company budgeted overhead of $180,000 and budgeted 15,000 direct labour hours. During the year, Job K456 was completed with the following information: direct materials cost was $2,340, and direct labour cost was $3,600. The average wage for Paxton Company is $10 per hour.

By the end of the year, 15,400 direct labour hours had actually been worked, and Paxton Company had incurred the following actual overhead costs for the year:

Equipment lease	$ 5,000
Amortization on building	20,000
Indirect labour	100,000
Utilities	15,000
Other overhead	45,000

Required:

1. Calculate the overhead rate for the year.
2. Calculate the total cost of Job K456.
3. Prepare the journal entries to record actual overhead, and to apply overhead to production for the year.
4. Is overhead overapplied or underapplied? by how much?
5. Assume that the normal cost of goods sold for the year is $700,000. What is the adjusted cost of goods sold?

5–12

Cost Flows

LO2

For each of the following independent jobs, fill in the missing data. Factory overhead is applied in Department 1 at the rate of $6 per direct labour hour (DLH). Factory overhead is applied in Department 2 at the rate of $8 per machine hour. Direct labour wages average $10 per hour in each department.

	Job 213	Job 214	Job 217	Job 225
Total sales revenue	$?	$4,375	$5,600	$1,150
Price per unit	12	?	14	5
Material used in production	365	?	488	207
Direct labour cost, Department 1	?	700	2,000	230
Machine hours, Department 1	15	35	50	12
Direct labour cost, Department 2	50	100	?	0
Machine hours, Department 2	25	50	?	?
Overhead applied, Department 1	90	?	1,200	138
Overhead applied, Department 2	?	400	160	0
Total manufacturing cost	855	3,073	?	575
Number of units	?	350	400	?
Unit cost	8.55	?	9.87	?

5–13

Job Cost, Source Documents

LO2, LO3

Spade Millhone Detective Agency performs investigative work for a variety of clients. Recently, Reliance Insurance Company asked Spade Millhone to investigate a series of suspicious claims for whiplash. In each case, the claimant was driving on a highway and was suddenly rear-ended by a Reliance-insured car. The claimants were all driving old, uninsured vehicles. The Reliance clients reported that the claimants suddenly changed lanes in front of them and the accidents were unavoidable. Reliance suspected that these "accidents" were the result of insurance fraud: the claimants cruised the highways in virtually worthless cars, attempting to cut in front of other cars. Reliance believed that the injuries were faked.

S. Spade spent 40 hours shadowing the fake claimants and taking pictures as necessary. His surveillance methods located the office of a doctor used by all the claimants. Spade took pictures of the claimants performing tasks that they had sworn they could no longer perform, due to their whiplash injuries. K. Millhone spent 25 hours using the Internet to research court documents in other provinces to locate the names of the claimants and their doctor. She found a pattern of similar insurance claims for each of the claimants.

The Spade Millhone Detective Agency bills clients for detective time at $100 per hour. Mileage is charged at $0.40 per kilometre. The agency logged 430 kilometres on the Reliance job. The film and developing costs amounted to $80.

Required:

1. Prepare a job-order cost sheet for the Reliance job.
2. Why is overhead not specified in the charges? How does Spade Millhone charge clients for the use of overhead (e.g., the ongoing costs of their office—supplies, paper for notes and reports, telephone, utilities)?
3. The mileage is tallied from a source document. Design a source document for this use, and make up data for it that would total the 430 kilometres driven on the Reliance job.

5–14

Calculating Ending Work in Process, Income Statement

LO2, LO3

Brandt Company produces unique metal sculptures. On January 1, there were three jobs in process with the following costs:

	Job 35	Job 36	Job 37
Direct materials	$100	$ 340	$ 780
Direct labour	350	700	1,050
Applied overhead	420	840	1,260
Total	$870	$1,880	$3,090

During January, two more jobs were started: Job 38 and Job 39. Direct materials and direct labour costs incurred by each job in process in January are as follows:

	Direct Materials	Direct Labour
Job 35	$400	$300
Job 36	150	200
Job 37	260	150
Job 38	800	650
Job 39	760	700

Jobs 37 and 38 were completed and sold by January 31.

Required:

1. If overhead is applied on the basis of direct labour dollars, what is the overhead rate?
2. Prepare simple job-order cost sheets for each of the five jobs in process during January.
3. What is the ending balance of Work in Process on January 31? What is the Cost of Goods Sold in January?
4. Suppose that Brandt Company prices its jobs at cost plus 50 percent. In addition, during January selling and administrative costs of $1,200 were incurred. Prepare an income statement for the month of January.

5–15

Journal Entries; T-Accounts

LO2

Spreadsheet

Parish, Inc., builds custom equipment for manufacturing firms. During May, the following events occurred:

a. Direct materials were purchased on account for $32,475.
b. Direct materials totalling $27,000 were requisitioned for use in production: $15,000 for Job 644 and the remainder for Job 648.
c. Direct labour payroll for the month was $26,250, with an average wage of $12.50 per hour. Job 644 required 1,000 direct labour hours; Job 648 required 1,100 direct labour hours.
d. Actual overhead of $19,950 was incurred and paid.
e. Overhead is charged to production at the rate of $10 per direct labour hour.
f. Job 644 was completed and transferred to finished goods.
g. Job 648, which was started during May, remained in process at the end of the month.
h. Job 640, which had been completed in March, was sold on account for cost plus 25 percent.

Beginning balances as of May 1 were as follows:

Direct Materials	$ 6,070
Work in Process (for Job 644)	10,000
Finished Goods (for Job 640)	6,240

Required:

1. Prepare the journal entries for events (a) through (e).
2. Prepare simple job-order cost sheets for Jobs 644 and 648.
3. Prepare the journal entries for events (f) and (h).
4. Calculate the ending balances of the following:
    a. Direct Materials
    b. Work in Process
    c. Finished Goods

5–16

Journal Entries; T–Accounts

LO2

Dearinger Company uses job-order costing. During January, the following data were reported:

a. Materials purchased: direct materials, $62,000; indirect materials, $8,500
b. Materials issued: direct materials, $62,100; indirect materials, $4,000

c. Labour costs incurred: direct labour, $44,000; indirect labour, $12,250
d. Other manufacturing costs incurred (all payables): $59,000
e. Overhead is applied on the basis of 130 percent of direct labour cost.
f. Work finished and transferred to finished goods cost $150,000.
g. Finished goods costing $140,000 were sold on account for 120 percent of cost.

Required:

1. Prepare journal entries to record these transactions.
2. Prepare a T-account for Overhead Control. Post all relevant information to this account. What is the ending balance in this account? What does the ending balance represent?
3. Prepare a T-account for Work in Process. Assume a beginning balance of $10,000, and post all relevant information to this account. Did you assign any actual overhead costs to Work in Process? Why or why not?

5–17

**Overhead
Assignment: Actual
and Normal Activity
Compared**

LO2

Reynolds Printing Company specializes in wedding announcements. Reynolds uses an actual job-order cost system. An actual overhead rate is calculated at the end of each month using actual direct labour hours and overhead for the month. Once the actual cost of a job is determined, the customer is billed at actual cost plus 50 percent.

During April, Mrs. Lucky, a good friend of owner Jane Reynolds, ordered three sets of wedding announcements to be delivered May 10, June 10, and July 10, respectively. Reynolds scheduled production for each order on May 7, June 7, and July 7, respectively. The orders were assigned job numbers 115, 116, and 117, respectively.

Reynolds assured Mrs. Lucky that she would attend each of her daughters' weddings. Out of sympathy and friendship, she also offered a lower price. Instead of cost plus 50 percent, she gave Mrs. Lucky a special price of cost plus 25 percent. Additionally, she agreed to wait until the final wedding to bill for the three jobs.

On August 15, Reynolds asked her accountant to bring the completed job-order cost sheets for Jobs 115, 116, and 117. She also gave instructions to lower the price, as had been agreed upon. The cost sheets revealed the following information:

	Job 115	Job 116	Job 117
Cost of direct materials	$250.00	$250.00	$250.00
Cost of direct labour (5 hours)	25.00	25.00	25.00
Cost of overhead	200.00	400.00	400.00
Total cost	$475.00	$675.00	$675.00
Total price	$593.75	$843.75	$843.75
Number of announcements	500	500	500

Reynolds could not understand why the overhead costs assigned to Jobs 116 and 117 were so much higher than those for Job 115. She asked for an overhead cost summary sheet for the months of May, June, and July, which showed that actual overhead costs were $20,000 for each month. She also discovered that direct labour hours worked on all jobs were 500 hours in May and 250 hours each in June and July.

Required:

1. How do you think Mrs. Lucky will feel when she receives the bill for the three sets of wedding announcements?
2. Explain how the overhead costs were assigned to each job.
3. Assume that Reynolds's average activity is 500 hours per month and that the company usually experiences overhead costs of $240,000 each year. Can you recommend a better way to assign overhead costs to jobs? Recompute the cost of each job and its price given your method of overhead cost assignment. Which method do you think is best? Why?

5–18

Overhead Applied to Jobs; Departmental Overhead Rates

LO2

Watson Products, Inc. uses a normal job-order costing system. Currently, a plantwide overhead rate based on machine hours is used. Marlon Burke, the plant manager, has heard that departmental overhead rates can offer significantly better cost assignments than a plantwide rate can offer. Watson has the following data for its two departments for the coming year:

	Department A	Department B
Overhead costs (expected)	$50,000	$22,000
Normal activity (machine hours)	20,000	16,000

Required:

1. Compute a predetermined overhead rate for the plant as a whole based on machine hours.
2. Compute predetermined overhead rates for each department using machine hours. (Carry your calculations out to three decimal places.)
3. Job 73 used 20 machine hours from Department A and 50 machine hours from Department B. Job 74 used 50 machine hours from Department A and 20 from Department B. Compute the overhead cost assigned to each job using the plantwide rate computed in Requirement 1. Repeat the computation using the departmental rates found in Requirement 2. Which of the two approaches gives the fairer assignment? Why?
4. Repeat Requirement 3, this time assuming that the expected overhead cost for Department B is $40,000. For this company, would you recommend departmental rates over a plantwide rate?

5–19

Unit Cost; Ending Work in Process; Journal Entries

LO2

During October, Harrison Company worked on two jobs. Data relating to these two jobs follow:

	Job 34	Job 35
Units in each order	60	100
Units sold	60	—
Materials requisitioned	$640	$530
Direct labour hours	370	550
Direct labour cost	$3,145	$4,950

Overhead is assigned on the basis of direct labour hours at a rate of $5. During October, Job 34 was completed and transferred to finished goods. Job 35 was the only unfinished job at the end of the month.

Required:

1. Calculate the per-unit cost of Job 34.
2. Compute the ending balance in the Work in Process account.
3. Prepare the journal entries reflecting the completion and sale of Job 34. The selling price is 140 percent of cost.

5–20

Predetermined Overhead Rates; Variances; Cost Flows

LO2

Barrymore Costume Company, located in Toronto, sews costumes for plays and musicals. Barrymore considers itself primarily a service firm, because it never produces costumes without a preexisting order and because it purchases materials to the specifications of the particular job. Any finished goods ending inventory is temporary and is zeroed out as soon as the show producer pays for the order. Overhead is applied on the basis of direct labour cost. During the first quarter of 2001, the following activity took place in each of the accounts that follow:

Work in Progress			
Bal	17,000	245,000	
DL	80,000		
OH	140,000		
DM	40,000		
Bal	32,000		

Finished Goods			
Bal	40,000	210,000	
	245,000		
Bal	75,000		

Overhead		
138,500	140,000	
	Bal	1,500

Cost of Goods Sold	
210,000	

Job 32 was the only job in progress at the end of the first quarter. A total of 1,000 direct labour hours at $10 per hour was charged to Job 32.

Required:

1. Assume that overhead is applied on the basis of direct labour cost. What was the overhead rate used during the first quarter of 2001?
2. What was the applied overhead for the first quarter? the actual overhead? the underapplied or overapplied overhead?
3. What was the cost of goods manufactured for the quarter?
4. Assume that the overhead variance is closed to the Cost of Goods Sold account. Prepare the journal entry to close out the Overhead account. What is the adjusted balance in Cost of Goods Sold?
5. For Job 32, identify the costs incurred for direct materials, direct labour, and overhead.

PROBLEMS

5–21

Activity-Based Costing and Overhead Rates; Unit Costs

LO2, LO3

Courtney Company manufactures specialty tools to customer order. Budgeted overhead for the coming year is as follows:

Purchasing	$30,000
Setups	15,000
Engineering	20,000
Other	25,000

Previously, Jennifer Langston, Courtney Company's controller, had applied overhead on the basis of machine hours. Expected machine hours for the coming year are 10,000. Jennifer has been reading about activity-based costing, and she wonders whether it might offer some advantages to her company. She decided that appropriate drivers for overhead activities are purchase orders for purchasing, number of setups for setup cost, engineering hours for engineering cost, and machine hours for other. Budgeted amounts for these drivers are 5,000 purchase orders, 1,000 setups, and 500 engineering hours.

Jennifer has been asked to prepare bids for two jobs with the following information:

	Job 1	Job 2
Direct materials	$4,500	$8,600
Direct labour	$1,000	$2,000
Number of setups	2	3
Number of purchase orders	15	20
Number of engineering hours	25	10
Number of machine hours	200	200

The typical bid price includes a 30 percent markup over full manufacturing cost.

Required:

1. Calculate a plantwide rate for Courtney Company based on machine hours. What is the bid price of each job using this rate?
2. Calculate activity rates for the four overhead activities. What is the bid price of each job using these rates?
3. Which bids are more accurate? Why?

5–22

Activity-Based Costing and Overhead Rates; Unit Costs

LO2, LO3

Mueller Custom Designs makes cabinets to custom order. Mark Mueller identified the following budgeted overhead activities and drivers:

Activity	Cost	Cost Driver	Amount
Machine operation	$40,000	Machine hours	10,000
Setups	$10,000	Number of setups	2,000
Designing costs	$30,000	Design hours	5,000

Frank and Sally Willis were building a large custom house and wanted "lots of storage." Their job had the following data:

Direct materials	$6,210
Direct labour wages	$5,000
Machine hours	600
Number of setups	100
Design hours	225

Cindy and Ray Gordon were remodelling an older house. They needed some basic cabinets for the kitchen. Mark Mueller suggested a basic design he had built numerous times before. The Gordon job had the following data:

Direct materials	$1,500
Direct labour wages	$1,750
Machine hours	60
Number of setups	1
Design hours	0

Required:

1. Calculate a unit-based overhead rate based on machine hours. What is the total cost of the Willis job using this rate? What is the total cost of the Gordon job using this rate?
2. Calculate activity rates. What is the cost of the Willis job using the three activity rates? What is the cost of the Gordon job using the three activity rates?
3. Of the two costing approaches (unit-based or ABC), which is more accurate and why?

5–23

Activity-Based Costing; Accuracy of Unit Costs; Multiple Overhead Rates Using Activity Drivers versus Single Overhead Rates; Pricing Decisions

LO2

Ferguson Equipment, Inc., produces custom-designed manufacturing equipment. Ferguson recently received a request to manufacture 40 units of a specialized machine at a price lower than it normally accepts. Marketing manager Emily Dorr indicated that if the order were accepted at that price, the company could expect additional orders from the same customer. In fact, if the company could offer this price in the market generally, she believed that sales of this machine would increase by 50 percent.

Cleon Skowesen, president of Ferguson, was skeptical about accepting the order. The company had a policy of refusing to accept any order that did not provide revenues at least equal to its full manufacturing cost plus 10 percent. The price offered was $2,500 per unit. However, before a final decision was made, Cleon decided to request information on the estimated cost per unit. He was concerned because the company was experiencing increased competition, and the number of new orders was dropping. Also, the controller's office had recently researched the possibility of using activity-based, multiple overhead rates instead of the single rate currently in use. The controller had promised more accurate product costing, and Cleon was curious about how this approach would affect the pricing of this particular machine.

Within 24 hours, the controller assembled the following data:

a. The plantwide overhead rate is based on an expected volume of 450,000 direct labour hours and the following budgeted overhead (all figures are yearly):

Amortization, building	$600,000
Amortization, equipment	300,000
Material handling	800,000
Power (machine usage)	700,000
Rework costs	250,000
Purchasing	118,000
Supervision (plantwide)	200,000
Cost of scrapped units	640,000
Other plantwide overhead	460,000
Total	$4,068,000

b. Expected activity for selected activity drivers (for the year) follows:

Material moves	10,000
Kilowatt-hours	100,000
Units reworked	2,000
Units scrapped	1,000
Machine hours	100,000
Purchase orders	20,000

c. Estimated data for the potential job (based on the production of 40 units) follow:

Direct labour (4,100 hours)	$36,900
Direct materials	$24,000
Number of material moves	6
Number of kilowatt-hours	1,000
Number of units reworked	2
Number of units scrapped	3
Number of machine hours	1,000
Number of purchase orders	20

Required:

1. Compute the estimated unit cost for the potential job using the current method to assign overhead on a plantwide basis. Given this unit cost, compute the total gross margin earned by the job. Would the job be accepted under normal operating conditions?
2. Classify overhead activities as unit level, batch level, product level (sustaining), or facility level. Calculate pool rates using the activity drivers in (b). The rate for facility-level overhead is based on direct labour hours.
3. Compute the estimated unit cost for the potential job using the pool rates computed in Requirement 2. Report per-unit costs by activity category. Given this cost per unit, compute the total gross margin earned by the job. Should the job be accepted?
4. Which approach—the plantwide rate or the multiple overhead rate with activity drivers—is best for the company? Explain.

5–24

Job Cost Sheets; Journal Entries; Inventories

LO2, LO3

On July 1, Polk Company had the following balances in its inventory accounts:

Raw Materials	$22,000
Work in Process	7,905
Finished Goods	25,000

Work in Process is made up of three jobs with the following costs:

	Job 17	Job 18	Job 19
Raw materials	$1,100	$910	$1,415
Direct labour	900	850	1,050
Applied overhead	540	510	630

During July, Polk experienced the following transactions:

a. Materials purchased on account: $13,000
b. Materials requisitioned: Job 17, $8,500; Job 18, $7,200; Job 19, $12,300
c. Job time tickets collected and summarized: Job 17, 175 hours at $10 per hour; Job 18, 165 hours at $11 per hour; and Job 19, 225 hours at $10 per hour
d. Overhead is applied on the basis of direct labour cost.
e. Actual overhead: $3,500
f. Jobs 17 and 18 were completed and transferred to the finished goods warehouse.
g. Job 18 was shipped; the customer was billed for 160 percent of the cost.

Required:

1. Prepare job-order cost sheets for Jobs 17, 18, and 19. Post the beginning inventory data, and then update the cost sheets for the July activity.
2. Prepare journal entries for the July transactions.
3. Prepare a schedule of inventories on July 31.

5–25

Job-Order Costing: Housing Construction

LO2, LO3

Butter, Inc., is a privately held, family-founded corporation that builds single- and multiple-unit housing. Most projects Butter undertakes involve the construction of multiple units. Butter has adopted a job-order costing system for determining the cost of each unit. The costing system is fully computerized. Each project's costs are divided into the following five categories:

a. General conditions, including construction site utilities, project insurance, permits and licences, architect's fees, decorating, field office salaries, and cleanup costs.
b. Hard costs, such as subcontractors, direct materials, and labour.
c. Finance costs, including title and registration fees, inspection fees, and taxes and discounts on mortgages.
d. Land costs, which refer to the purchase price of the construction site.
e. Marketing costs, such as advertising, sales commissions, and appraisal fees.

Recently, Butter purchased land for the purpose of developing 20 new single-family houses. The cost of the land was $250,000. Lot sizes vary from 0.25 acre to 0.5 acre. The 20 lots occupy a total of 8 acres.

General condition costs for the project totalled $120,000. This $120,000 is common to all 20 of the units that were constructed on the building site.

Job 3, the third house built in the project, occupied a quarter-acre lot and had the following hard costs:

Direct materials	$ 8,000
Direct labour	6,000
Subcontractor	14,000

For Job 3, finance costs totalled $4,765 and marketing costs $800. General condition costs are allocated on the basis of units produced. Each unit's selling price is determined by adding 40 percent to the total of all costs.

Required:

1. Identify all production costs that are directly traceable to Job 3. Are all remaining production costs equivalent to overhead found in a manufacturing firm? Are there nonproduction costs that are directly traceable to the housing unit? Which ones?

2. Develop a job-order cost sheet for Job 3. What is the cost of building this house? Did you include finance and marketing costs in computing the unit costs? Why or why not? How did you determine the cost of land for Job 3?
3. Which of the five cost categories corresponds to overhead? Do you agree with the way in which this cost is allocated to individual housing units? Can you suggest a different allocation method?
4. Calculate the selling price of Job 3. Calculate the profit made on the sale of this unit.

5–26

Job-Order Costing: Service Organization

LO2

Price-Gordon Architectural Consultants Ltd. uses a modified job-order costing system to keep track of project costs. During April, the firm worked on four projects. The following table provides a summary of the cost of materials used and the number of consulting hours worked on each of the four projects in April:

Project Number	Cost of Materials	Consulting Hours Worked
480	$120	138
484	85	145
485	100	160
486	150	187

The records for March showed that 20 hours had been worked and $68 worth of materials had been used on Project 480. Projects 480 and 486 were completed in April, and bills were sent to the clients.

Consultants at Price-Gordon billed clients at $100 per consulting hour. The actual labour cost to the firm (based on salary cost) was $40 per hour. Overhead is charged to projects on the basis of the consultants' time spent on the project. Total overhead for the current fiscal year at an expected activity of 10,000 consulting hours is estimated to be $267,000. This total overhead cost included a fixed portion of $84,000, which covered rent, amortization, and so on. Actual overhead for April was $21,455. Price-Gordon closes overapplied or underapplied overhead to Cost of Goods Sold at month end.

Required:

1. Determine the product costs associated with Project 480.
2. Determine the balance in work in process as at April 30.
3. Prepare the income statement for April, including the appropriate amount of overapplied or underapplied overhead. Other expenses for April were $2,340.94. (CMA Canada adapted)

5–27

Plantwide Overhead Rate; Departmental Rates; Effects on Job-Pricing Decisions

LO2, LO3

Alden Peterson, marketing manager for Retlief Company, was puzzled by the outcome of two recent bids. The company's policy was to bid 150 percent of the full manufacturing cost. One job (labelled Job SS) had been turned down by a prospective customer who had indicated that the proposed price was $3 per unit higher than the winning bid. A second job (Job TT) has been accepted by a customer who was amazed that Retlief could offer such favourable terms. This customer revealed that Retlief's price was $43 per unit lower than the next lowest bid.

Alden had been informed that the company was more than competitive in terms of cost control. Accordingly, he began to suspect that the problem was related to cost assignment procedures. Upon investigating, Alden was told that the company uses a plantwide overhead rate based on direct labour hours. The rate is computed at the beginning of the year using budgeted data. Selected budgeted data follow:

	Department A	Department B	Total
Overhead	$500,000	$2,000,000	$2,500,000
Direct labour hours	200,000	50,000	250,000
Machine hours	20,000	120,000	140,000

Alden also discovered that the overhead costs in Department B were higher than those in Department A because B has more equipment, higher maintenance, higher power consumption, higher amortization, and higher setup costs. In addition to the general procedures for assigning overhead costs, Alden was supplied with the following specific manufacturing data on Job SS and Job TT:

Job SS

	Department A	Department B	Total
Direct labour hours	5,000	1,000	6,000
Machine hours	200	500	700
Prime costs	$100,000	$20,000	$120,000
Units produced			14,400

Job TT

	Department A	Department B	Total
Direct labour hours	400	600	1,000
Machine hours	200	3,000	3,200
Prime costs	$10,000	$40,000	$50,000
Units produced			1,500

Required:

1. Using a plantwide overhead rate based on direct labour hours, develop the bid prices for Job SS and Job TT. (Express the bid price on a per-unit basis.)
2. Using departmental overhead rates (use direct labour hours for Department A and machine hours for Department B), develop per-unit bids for Job SS and Job TT.
3. Compute the difference in gross margin that would have been earned had the company used departmental rates in its bids instead of the plantwide rate.
4. Explain why the use of departmental rates in this case provides a more accurate product cost.

5–28

ABC, Departmental Rates, and Pricing Decisions

LO2, LO3

(A continuation of 5–27 with activity data added.) Alden Peterson, marketing manager for Retlief Company, was puzzled by the outcome of two recent bids. The company's policy was to bid 150 percent of the full manufacturing cost. One job (Job SS) had been turned down by a prospective customer who had indicated that the proposed price was $3 per unit higher than the winning bid. A second job (Job TT) has been accepted by a customer who was amazed that Retlief could offer such favourable terms. This customer revealed that Retlief's price was $43 per unit lower than the next lowest bid.

Alden knew that the company was more than competitive in terms of cost control. Accordingly, he suspected that the problem was related to cost assignment procedures. Upon investigating, he discovered that a plantwide overhead rate, based on direct labour hours, had been used to assign overhead costs to the jobs. With some help from the controller, the bids were recalculated using departmental rates. Alden knew that this approach could improve the accuracy of the cost assignment, because one of the two departments was labour-intensive and the other was machine-intensive. Both jobs spent time in each department, although Job TT spent most of its time in the machine-intensive department. The per-unit bid prices for the different approaches follow:

	Job SS	Job TT
Plantwide rate:		
Bid price:	$18.75	$ 60.00
Departmental rates:		
Bid price	14.67	101.01

Alden had been reading about the increased accuracy of an ABC system and convinced the controller to help in obtaining the following information:

Overhead Activities	Cost	Activity Category	Activity Driver
Maintenance	$500,000	Product sustaining	Machine hours
Power	225,000	Unit level	Kilowatt-hours
Setups	150,000	Batch level	Setup hours
General factory	625,000	Facility level	Machine hours*

* This is an arbitrary allocation. The controller argued that machine hours used by a job would be correlated with the area occupied by the producing departments.

The expected levels of the activity drivers for the year follow:

Machine hours	140,000
Kilowatt-hours	100,000
Setup hours	20,000

The following activity data for each job are also provided:

	Job SS	Job TT
Machine hours	700	3,200
Kilowatt-hours	400	2,500
Setup hours	20	100
Prime costs	$120,000	$50,000
Units	14,400	1,500

Required:

1. Calculate the cost of each job using activity-based costing. List the costs of each job by activity category.
2. Calculate the bid price for each job using the normal markup. How do these bid prices compare with the bids that use plantwide and departmental rates? Does this approach offer any real improvement? Explain.
3. Suppose that the best competing bid for Job SS was $4.20 lower than Retlief's original bid (the one based on a plantwide rate). Also assume that the bid on Job TT was $25 lower than the next-lowest bid. Now compare the ABC bids with the bids based on departmental rates. What does this comparison imply about the value of ABC as price competition intensifies?
4. Discuss the importance of having the facility-level costs listed separately as the job costs are detailed. Should these costs be included in the base for calculating the bid?

5–29

Job-Order Costing, Comprehensive Manufacturing

LO2

Avid Assemblers uses job-order costing to assign costs to products. The company assembles and packages 20 different products to customer specifications. Products are worked on in batches of 30 to 50 units. Each batch is designated a job.

On October 1, the company had the following balances recorded.

Raw materials	$ 7,800
Work in process	45,726
Finished goods	23,520

Work in process consisted of the following jobs:

	Job 202	Job 204	Job 205
Direct materials	$ 4,200	$ 3,190	$ 2,800
Direct labour	8,500	7,210	6,500
Applied overhead	5,100	4,326	3,900
Total	$17,800	$14,726	$13,200
Number of units	30	50	35

Finished goods consisted of Job 203, with the following costs:

Direct materials	$ 7,200
Direct labour	10,200
Applied overhead	6,120
Total	$23,520
Number of units	50

Shown below are the direct cost data related to jobs started in October:

	Job 206	Job 207	Job 208	Total
Direct materials	$4,180	$3,600	$1,200	$ 8,980
Direct labour	9,200	8,340	2,910	20,450
Number of units	40	50	40	

Other information:

1. Direct materials and direct labour added to beginning work in process in October were as follows:

	Job 202	Job 204	Job 205	Total
Direct materials	$ 950	$ 410	$1,200	$ 2,560
Direct labour	2,000	3,500	4,500	10,000

2. Overhead is applied at a predetermined rate on the basis of direct labour cost.
3. Actual expenses for October were as follows:

Supervisory salaries	$4,000
Factory rent	2,000
Amortization (machines)	3,000
Indirect labour	5,000
Supplies (factory)	1,100
Selling expenses	8,500
Property tax, insurance	1,250
CPP, EI, and other benefits*	3,200

* 80 percent of employer contributions and benefits relates to factory personnel.

4. Purchases of direct materials (raw materials) during October amounted to $8,500. Indirect materials (supplies) are handled in a separate account.
5. Only Jobs 207 and 208 are still in process at closing on October 31. Finished goods consisted only of Job 205 at month end.
6. Avid writes off any over- or underapplied overhead to Cost of Goods Sold in the month it is incurred.

Required:

1. What is the predetermined overhead rate used by Avid to apply overhead to jobs?
2. What is the unit cost of Job 204 in October?
3. What are the October 31 balances for the following inventory accounts?
    a. Raw Materials
    b. Work in Process
    c. Finished Goods
4. What is the cost of goods manufactured in October? (You do not have to prepare a statement as part of this Requirement.)
5. Determine the over- or underapplied overhead for October and prepare the journal entry required to dispose of this amount. (CMA Canada adapted)

5–30

Predetermined Overhead Rate; Journal Entries

LO2

The following data were taken from the records of Cougar Enterprises, a Canadian manufacturer that uses a job-order costing system:

Work in Process, December 1

Job Number	170	175	180
Direct materials	$1,800	$2,400	$1,500
Direct labour	1,200	2,400	600
Applied overhead	600	1,350	450
Total	$3,600	$6,150	$2,550

During December, jobs numbered 170 through 190 were worked on, and the following costs were incurred:

Job Number	170	175	180	185	190	Total
Direct materials	$600	$ 900	$1,200	$1,350	$1,500	$ 5,550
Direct labour	$750	$1,500	$3,000	$2,250	$6,000	$13,500
Direct labour hours	50	100	200	150	400	900

Additional information:

1. Total overhead costs are applied to jobs on the basis of direct labour hours worked. At the beginning of the year, the company estimated that total overhead costs for the year would be $150,000, and the total labour hours worked would be 12,500.
2. The balance in the Departmental Overhead Control account on December 1 was $160,010. Actual direct labour hours for the previous 11 months (January through November) were 11,250.
3. There were no jobs in finished goods on December 1.
4. Expenses for December were as follows (not yet recorded in the books of account):

Direct materials purchased	$ 7,500
Salaries:	
Production clerk	1,500
Supervisor	2,200
Amortization (plant and equipment)	2,490
Factory supplies	1,500
Sales staff salaries	9,200
Utilities (factory)	1,800
Administrative expenses	9,500
	$35,690

5. The company writes off all over- or underapplied overhead to Cost of Goods Sold at the end of the year.
6. Jobs numbered 170, 180, 185, and 190 were completed during December. Only job 190 remained in finished goods on December 31.
7. The company charges its customers 250 percent of total manufacturing cost.
8. Cost of goods sold to December 1 was $358,750.

Required:

1. Using the information given, calculate the following amounts:
    a. the predetermined overhead rate used to apply overhead to products.
    b. the cost of ending work-in-process inventory.
    c. the cost of goods manufactured in December.
    d. the unadjusted gross margin for December.

2. Prepare the summary journal entries to the control accounts required to record all the transactions for December that relate to production. (*Note:* you should not make entries for individual jobs.)
3. Calculate the over- or underapplied overhead for the year. What effect would this amount have on net income? (CMA Canada adapted)

5–31

Activity-Based Costing; Job Costs and Prices

LO2

Mountain View Rentals, located in Banff, Alberta, rents bikes to tourists for bike hiking in the Rocky Mountains. The rental price is tied to cost, so it is important to know the cost of the bikes, labour, and overhead. The bikes can be categorized into three levels, depending on sophistication and anticipated use. The cost per bike-rental-day (the rental of one bike for one day) for the three levels is as follows:

Level 1 $ 7.50
Level 2   12.00
Level 3   20.00

Since each worker performs a number of tasks (for example, answering the phone, renting bikes, cleaning the shop, and maintaining bikes), there is no separate category for direct labour. Labour is included in overhead. Overhead for last year was $50,000, and it was applied to the jobs based on a unit-level rate of $5 per bike-rental-day. The rental rate is calculated by adding a 40 percent markup to total cost.

Recently, Mountain View Rentals added a picnic catering service that lets customers call the day before to order a picnic lunch to be taken on the bike hike. As a result, budgeted annual overhead increased to $100,000, while budgeted bike-rental-days remained at 10,000.

The addition of the picnic catering service rendered the unit-based overhead application method obsolete, so Mountain View Rentals decided to use a modified activity-based costing system. Major overhead activities identified are purchasing (based on number of purchase orders); power (based on number of kilowatt-hours); maintenance (based on number of maintenance hours); and other (based on direct labour hours).

Budgeted activity levels for the coming year are as follows:

Activity	Cost	Cost Driver	Quantity
Purchasing	$30,000	Purchase orders	10,000
Power	20,000	Kilowatt-hours	50,000
Maintenance	6,000	Maintenance hours	600
Other	44,000	Direct labour hours	22,000

Usage by the two different departments of Mountain View Rentals is as follows:

	Bike Rental	Picnic Catering
Purchase orders	7,000	3,000
Kilowatt-hours	5,000	45,000
Maintenance hours	500	100
Direct labour hours	11,000	11,000

Once the overhead is assigned to the bike rental segment, an overhead rate based on bike-rental-days is computed. Initially for the catering operation, overhead assigned to catering, using activity rates, is totalled and a single rate based on direct labour hours is computed.

Required:

1. Ignoring the desired shift to an activity-based costing system, calculate a single unit-based rate for last year and this year based on bike-rental-days. Suppose

that the Carson family vacations in Banff each year and rents five bikes from Mountain View Rental for a two-day period. Maria and Fred Carson rent Level 3 bikes, while the Carson children rent Level 2 bikes. What was the cost of the Carson family rental last year? this year? What price was charged last year? this year? How do you suppose Maria and Fred feel about this?

2. Calculate activity-based rates for the four activities. How much total overhead is assigned to the bike rental operation? to the catering operation?
3. Suppose that the overhead allocated to the bike rental operation is then applied to jobs on the basis of bike-rental-days, as before. Now, what are this year's cost and price for the Carson rental?
4. Carol and Thurman Estes are honeymooning in Banff and decide to spend one day biking in the mountains. They rent two Level 1 bikes and order a picnic lunch for two. The materials for the picnic cost $12, and it takes one hour to make and pack the picnic. Using the overhead assigned to the catering operation in Requirement 2, calculate a catering overhead rate based on direct labour hours. What is the total cost of the Estes job?
5. Mountain View Rentals is considering adding Level 4 bikes to its lineup. However, these bikes are high-performance racing bikes and require considerably more maintenance and specialized parts ordering than the Level 1 through 3 bikes. How can activity-based costing help Mountain View decide what the cost of the Level 4 bikes is and whether or not the firm should add these bikes to its rental list?

5–32

Job-Order Costing

LO2

Handy Widget Company does a wide variety of metal work on a custom basis. During the month of June 2001, six jobs were worked on. A summary of the job cost sheets on these jobs is given below:

Job Number	Direct Materials	Direct Labour	Applied Overhead	Total Cost
1243	$ 410	$ 360	$ 288	$ 1,058
1244	850	790	632	2,272
1245	110	85	68	263
1246	1,500	1,140	912	3,552
1247	950	850	680	2,480
1248*	270	115	92	477
	$4,090	$3,340	$2,672	$10,102

* ending work in progress

Handy Widget has used the same overhead rate on all jobs. Job 1243 was the only job in process at the beginning of the month. At that time, Job 1243 had incurred direct labour costs of $150 and total costs of $570.

Required:

1. What is the apparent predetermined overhead rate being used by Handy Widget?
2. Assume that during June, the factory overhead was overapplied by $600. What was the actual factory overhead cost incurred during the month?
3. What was the total amount of direct materials placed into production during June?
4. How much direct labour cost was incurred during June?
5. What was the cost of goods manufactured for June? (CGA Canada adapted)

MANAGERIAL DECISION CASES

5–33

Assigning Overhead to Jobs; Ethical Issues

LO2

Tonya Martin, CMA, who is the controller of the Parts Division of Gunderson, Inc., was meeting with Doug Adams, the division's manager. The topic of discussion was the assignment of overhead costs to jobs and their impact on the division's pricing decisions. Their conversation follows:

Tonya: "Doug, as you know, about 25 percent of our business is based on government contracts, with the other 75 percent being based on jobs from private sources that we have won through bidding. During the last several years, our private business has declined. We have been losing more bids than usual. After some careful investigation, I have concluded that we are overpricing some jobs because of improper assignment of overhead costs. Some jobs are also being underpriced. Unfortunately, the jobs being overpriced are coming from our higher-volume, labour-intensive products; thus, we are losing business."

Doug: "I think I understand. Jobs associated with our high-volume products are being assigned more overhead than they should be receiving. Then, when we add our standard 40 percent markup, we end up with a higher price than our competitors, who assign costs more accurately."

Tonya: "Exactly. We have two producing departments, one labour-intensive and the other machine-intensive. The labour-intensive department generates much less overhead than the machine-intensive department does. Furthermore, virtually all of our high-volume jobs are labour-intensive. We have been using a plantwide rate based on direct labour hours to assign overhead to all jobs. As a result, the high-volume, labour-intensive jobs receive a greater share of the machine-intensive department's overhead than they deserve. This problem can be greatly alleviated by switching to departmental overhead rates. For example, an average high-volume job would be assigned $100,000 of overhead using a plantwide rate and only $70,000 using departmental rates. The change would lower our bidding price on high-volume jobs by an average of $42,000 per job. By increasing the accuracy of our product costing, we can make better pricing decisions and win back much of our private-sector business."

Doug: "Sounds good. When can you implement the change in overhead rates?"

Tonya: "It won't take long. I can have the new system working within four to six weeks—certainly by the start of the new fiscal year."

Doug: "Hold it. I just thought of a possible complication. As I recall, most of our government contract work is done in the labour-intensive department. This new overhead assignment scheme will push down the cost on the government jobs, and we will lose revenues. They pay us full cost plus our standard markup. This business is not threatened by our current costing procedures, but we can't switch our rates for only the private business. Government auditors would question the lack of consistency in our costing procedures."

Tonya: "You do have a point. I thought of this issue also. According to my estimates, we will gain more revenues from the private sector than we will lose from our government contracts. Besides, the costs of our government jobs are distorted; in effect, we are overcharging the government."

Doug: "They don't know that—and never will, unless we switch our overhead assignment procedures. I think I have the solution. Officially, let's keep our plantwide overhead rate. All of the official records will reflect this overhead-costing approach for both our private and our government business. Unofficially, I want you to develop a separate set of books that can be used to generate the information we need to prepare competitive bids for our private-sector business."

Required:

1. Do you believe that the solution proposed by Doug Adams is ethical? Explain.

2. Suppose that Tonya Martin decides that Doug's solution is not right. In your opinion, is Tonya supported in this view by the standards of ethical conduct described in Chapter 1? Explain.

3. Suppose that, despite Tonya's objections, Doug insists strongly on implementing the action. What should Tonya do?

5–34

Job-Order Costing: Dental Practice

LO2, LO3

Dr. Sherry Bird is employed by Dental Associates. Dental Associates recently installed a computerized job-order costing system to help monitor the cost of its services. Each patient is treated as a job and assigned a job number when he or she checks in with the receptionist. The receptionist/bookkeeper notes the time the patient enters the treatment area and when the patient leaves the area. The difference between the entry and exit times is the patient hours used and is the direct labour time assigned to the dental assistant (a dental assistant is constantly with the patient). Fifty percent of the patient hours is the direct labour time assigned to the dentist (the dentist typically splits her time between two patients).

The chart filled out by the dental assistant provides additional data that are entered into the computer. For example, the chart contains service codes that identify the nature of the treatment, such as whether the patient received a crown, a filling, or a root canal. The chart identifies not only the type of service but also its level. For example, if a patient receives a filling, the dental assistant indicates (by a service-level code) whether the filling involved one, two, three, or four surfaces. The service and service-level codes are used to determine the rate to be charged to the patient. The costs of providing different services at different levels also vary.

Costs assignable to a patient consist of materials, labour, and overhead. The type and quantity of materials used are identified by the assistant and entered into the computer by the bookkeeper. Material prices are kept on file and accessed to provide the necessary cost information. Overhead is applied on the basis of patient hours. The rate used by Dental Associates is $20 per patient hour. Direct labour cost is also computed using patient hours and the wage rates of the direct labourers. Dr. Bird is paid an average of $36 per hour for her services. Dental assistants are paid an average of $12 per hour. Given the treatment time, the software program calculates and assigns the labour cost for the dentist and her assistant; overhead cost is also assigned using the treatment time and the overhead rate.

The overhead rate does not include a charge for any X-rays. The X-ray department is separate from dental services; X-rays are billed and costed separately. The cost of an X-ray is $3.50 per film; the patient is charged $5 per film. If cleaning services are required, cleaning labour costs $9 per patient hour.

Glen Johnson, a patient (Job 267), spent 30 minutes in the treatment area and had a two-surface filling. He received two Novocain shots and used three ampoules of amalgam. The cost of the shots was $1. The cost of the amalgam was $3. Other direct materials used were insignificant in amount and were included in the overhead rate. The rate charged to the patient for a two-surface filling is $45. One X-ray was taken.

Required:

1. Prepare a job-order cost sheet for Glen Johnson. What is the cost for providing a two-surface filling? What is the gross margin earned? Is the X-ray a direct cost of the service? Why are the X-rays costed separately from the overhead cost assignment?

2. Suppose that the patient time and associated patient charges are as given below for four types of fillings:

	One Surface	Two Surfaces	Three Surfaces	Four Surfaces
Time	20 minutes	30 minutes	40 minutes	50 minutes
Charge	$35	$45	$55	$65

Compute the cost for each filling and the gross margin for each type of filling. Assume that the cost of Novocain is $1 for all fillings. Ampoules of amalgam start at $2 and increase by $1 for each additional surface. Assume also that only one X-ray film is needed for all four cases. Does the increase in billing rate appear to be fair to the patient? Is it fair to the dental corporation?

5–35

Job-Order Costing and Pricing Decisions

LO2

Nutratask, Inc., is a pharmaceutical manufacturer of amino-acid-chelated minerals and vitamin supplements. The company was founded in 1974 and is capable of performing all manufacturing functions, including packaging and laboratory functions. Currently, the company markets its products in the United States, Canada, Australia, Japan, and Belgium.

Mineral chelation enhances the mineral's availability to the body, making the mineral a more effective supplement. Most of the chelates supplied by Nutratask are in powder form, but the company has the capability to make tablets or capsules.

The production of all chelates follows a similar pattern. Upon receiving an order, the company's chemist prepares a load sheet (a bill of materials that specifies the product, the theoretical yield, and the quantities of raw materials that should be used). Once the load sheet is received by production, the materials are requisitioned and sent to the blending room. The chemicals and minerals are added in the order specified and blended for two to eight hours, depending on the product. After blending, the mix is put on long trays and sent to the drying room, where it is allowed to dry until the moisture content is 7 to 9 percent. Drying time for most products is from one to three days.

After the product is dry, several small samples are taken and sent to a laboratory to be checked for bacteria levels and to see whether the product meets customer specifications. If the product is not fit for human consumption or if it fails to meet customer specifications, additional materials are added under the chemist's direction to bring the product up to standard. Once the product passes inspection, it is ground into a powder of different meshes (particle sizes) according to customer specifications. The powder is then placed in heavy cardboard drums and shipped to the customer (or, if requested, put in tablet or capsule form and then shipped).

Since each order is customized to meet the special needs of its customers, Nutratask uses a job-order costing system. Recently, Nutratask received a request for a 300-kilogram order of potassium aspartate. The customer offered to pay $8.80 per kilogram. Upon receiving the request and the customer's specifications, Lanny Smith, the marketing manager, requested a load sheet from the company's chemist. The load sheet indicated the following material requirements:

Material	Amount Required
Aspartic acid	195.00 kg
Citric acid	15.00 kg
K_2CO_3 (50%)	121.50 kg
Rice	30.00 kg

The theoretical yield is 300 kilograms.

Lanny also reviewed past jobs that were similar to the requested order and discovered that the expected direct labour time was 16 hours. The production workers at Nutratask earn an average of $6.50 per hour, plus $6 per hour for taxes, insurance, and additional benefits.

Purchasing sent Smith a list of prices for the materials needed for the job.

Material	Price per kg
Aspartic acid	$5.75
Citric acid	2.02
K_2CO_3	4.64
Rice	0.43

Overhead is applied using a companywide rate based on direct labour costs. The rate for the current period is 110 percent of direct labour costs.

Whenever a customer requests a bid, Nutratask usually estimates the manufacturing costs of the job and then adds a markup of 30 percent. This markup varies depending on the competition and general economic conditions. Currently, the industry is thriving, and Nutratask is operating at capacity.

Required:

1. Prepare a job cost sheet for the proposed job. What is the expected per-unit cost? Should Nutratask accept the price offered by the prospective customer? Why or why not?

2. Suppose Nutratask and the prospective customer agree on a price of cost plus 30 percent. What is the gross margin that Nutratask expects to earn on the job?

3. Suppose that the actual costs of producing 300 kilograms of potassium aspartate were as follows:

Direct materials:		
Aspartic acid	$1,170	
Citric acid	30	
K₂CO₃	577	
Rice	13	
Total material cost		$1,790
Direct labour		225
Overhead		247

What is the actual per-unit cost? The bid price is based on expected costs. How much did Nutratask gain (or lose) because the actual costs differed from the expected costs? Suggest some possible reasons why the actual costs differed from the projected costs. How can management use this information for dealing with future jobs?

4. Assume that the customer had agreed to pay actual manufacturing costs plus 30 percent. Suppose the actual costs are as described in Requirement 3, with one addition: an underapplied overhead variance is allocated to Cost of Goods Sold and spread across all jobs sold in proportion to their total cost (unadjusted cost of goods sold). Assume that the underapplied overhead cost added to the job in Requirement 3 is $30. Upon seeing the addition of the underapplied overhead in the itemized bill, the customer calls and complains about having to pay for Nutratask's inefficient use of overhead costs. If you were assigned to deal with this customer, what kind of response would you prepare? How would you explain and justify the addition of the underapplied overhead cost to the customer's bill?

RESEARCH ASSIGNMENTS

5–36

Research Assignment
LO1, LO2, LO3

Interview an accountant who works for a service organization that uses job-order costing. For a small firm, you may need to talk to an owner or a manager. Examples are a funeral home, insurance firm, repair shop, medical clinic, and dental clinic. Write a paper that describes the job-order cost system used by the firm. Some of the questions that the paper should address are:

a. What service or services does the firm offer?
b. What document or procedure do you use to collect the costs of the services performed for each customer?
c. How do you assign the cost of direct labour to each job?
d. How do you assign overhead to individual jobs?
e. How do you assign the cost of direct materials to each job?

f.   How do you determined what to charge each customer?

g.   How do you account for a completed job?

As you write the paper, state how the service firm you investigated has adapted the job-order accounting procedures described in this chapter to its particular circumstances. Were the adaptations justified? Explain why or why not. Also, offer any suggestions you might have for improving the approach that you observed.

5–37

Cybercase

LO1, LO3

Healtheon Corporation (**www.healtheon.com**) is involved in creating Internet solutions for medical recordkeeping. Given that clinics and doctors' offices use a job-order costing system, discuss how the Healtheon software may improve productivity and efficiency. In addition, what problems remain to be solved? Use the Healtheon Web site as well as the following article: George Anders, "Healtheon Struggles in Efforts to Remedy Doctors' Paper Plague," *The Wall Street Journal*, October 2, 1998, pp. A1 and A6.

CHAPTER 6

Process Costing

Learning Objectives

After studying Chapter 6, you should be able to:

1. Describe the basic characteristics and cost flows associated with process manufacturing.

2. Define equivalent units, and explain their role in process costing. Explain the differences between the weighted average method and the FIFO method of accounting for process costs.

3. Prepare a departmental production report using the weighted average method.

4. Explain how process costing is affected by nonuniform application of manufacturing inputs and the existence of multiple processing departments.

5. Prepare a departmental production report using the FIFO method. (Appendix)

Scenario

Makenzie Gibson, owner of Healthblend Nutritional Supplements, was reviewing last year's income statement. Net income was up 33 percent over the previous year's, and Makenzie was pleased. The idea for the company was the result of her recovery from some personal health problems. By working with health care professionals, she had learned to blend a number of different herbs into therapeutic formulas that had brought about an amazing recovery. Hoping to share her discoveries, Makenzie had begun producing some of these same therapeutic formulas in the basement of her home. Now, 10 years later, she was the owner of a multimillion-dollar business housed in a modern facility with more than 60 employees.

Despite her business success, Makenzie was convinced that she could not afford to be complacent. Recently, the owner of a health food store had told her that some other suppliers had dropped competing lines because they were no longer profitable. He had asked Makenzie if all of her products were profitable or if she simply offered the full range as a marketing strategy. She had been forced to admit that she did not know whether all of her products were profitable—in fact, she didn't even know the manufacturing cost of each individual product. All she knew was that overall profits were high.

After some reflection, she decided that knowing individual product costs would be useful for decisions regarding production methods, prices, and the mix of products. So, she contacted Judith Manesfield, manager of a regional CA firm's small business practice section, for help. After several visits by Judith and her staff, Makenzie received the following preliminary report:

Makenzie Gibson
Healthblend Nutritional
  Supplements
Saskatoon, Saskatchewan

Dear Ms. Gibson:
As you know, your current accounting system does not collect the necessary data for costing out the various products that you produce. You currently manufacture three major product lines: mineral, herb, and vitamin. Each product, regardless of its type, passes through three processes: picking, encapsulating, and bottling. In picking, the ingredients are measured, sifted, and blended. In encapsulating, the powdered mix from the first process is put into capsules. The capsules are then transferred to the bottling department, where they are bottled, after which the bottles are labelled and fitted with safety seals and lids.

Each bottle contains 50 capsules, and the capsules are of equal size for all three product lines. The cost of materials among the three product lines differs, but within a product line, the cost of materials for different products is not significantly different. The layout of the plant is structured so that all three product lines are produced simultaneously; thus, there are three different picking departments, one for each major product line.

Based on the nature of the manufacturing processes, our tentative recommendation is to accumulate costs of manufacturing by process for a given time period and measure the output for that same period. By dividing the costs accumulated for the period by the output for the period, you can obtain a good measure of individual product cost.

The cost system we recommend will require a minimal increase in your bookkeeping activities. With your permission, we will proceed with the development of the cost system. As part of this development, we will conduct several training seminars so that your financial staff can operate the system once it is implemented.

Questions to Think About

1. Why do you suppose that Makenzie did not originally implement an accounting system that would give individual product costs?

2. Using a separate work-in-process account for each producing department, describe the flow of costs through Healthblend's plant.

3. Makenzie recognized that unit-cost information for each product was important in determining individual product profitability. What other managerial decisions would be facilitated by having this type of information?

CHARACTERISTICS OF PROCESS MANUFACTURING

Objective 1

Describe the basic characteristics and cost flows associated with process manufacturing.

Makenzie Gibson hired the consultant to help her decide how best to cost out Healthblend's products. The consultant first studied Healthblend's methods of production. This is vital, since the production process helps determine the best way of accounting for costs. The study showed that a large number of similar products pass through an identical set of processes. Since each product within a product line passing through the three processes would receive similar "doses" of materials, labour, and overhead, Judith Manesfield saw no need to accumulate costs by batches (a job-costing system). Instead, she recommended accumulating costs by process.

Process costing works well whenever relatively homogeneous products pass through a series of processes and receive similar amounts of manufacturing costs. Large manufacturing plants, such as chemical, food, and tire manufacturers, use process costing.

Let's consider the Healthblend example in more detail. From the consultant's letter, we know that there are three processes, each centred in a producing department. In the picking department, direct labour selects the appropriate herbs, vitamins, minerals, and inert materials (typically some binder, such as cornstarch) for the product to be manufactured. Then the materials are measured and combined in a mixer to blend them thoroughly. When the mix is complete, the resulting mixture is sent to the encapsulation department. In encapsulation, the vitamin, mineral, or herb blend is loaded into a machine that fills half of a gelatin capsule. The filled half is matched to the capsule's other half capsule, and a safety seal is applied. This process is entirely mechanized. Overhead in this department consists of amortization on machinery, maintenance of machinery, supervision, fringe benefits, light, and power. The final department is bottling. Filled capsules are transferred to this department, loaded into a hopper, and automatically counted into bottles. Filled bottles are mechanically capped, and direct labour then manually packs the correct number of bottles into boxes to ship to retail outlets.

Now let's look at Healthblend from an accounting perspective. Suppose that Healthblend has only one picking department, through which all three major product lines pass. Since the product lines differ significantly in the cost of their material inputs, accumulating material costs by process no longer makes any sense. More accurate product costing can be achieved by accumulating material costs by batch. In this case, labour and overhead could still be accumulated by process, but raw materials would be assigned to batches using the usual job-costing approach. Note, however, that even with this change, process costing could still be used for the encapsulating department and the bottling department. In these two departments, each product receives the same amount of material, labour, and overhead.

This example illustrates that some manufacturing settings may need to use a blend of job and process costing. Using job-order procedures to assign material costs to products and a process approach to assign conversion costs is known as **operation costing.** Other blends are possible as well. The example also shows that it is possible to use more than one form of costing within the same firm. This is the case if Healthblend uses operation costing for the picking department and process costing for the other two departments.

The fundamental point is that the cost accounting system should be designed to fit the nature of operations. Job-order and process-costing systems fit pure job and pure process production environments, respectively. There are many settings, however, in which blends of the two costing systems may be suitable. By studying the pure forms of job-order and process costing, we can develop the ability to understand and use any hybrid form.

Types of Process Manufacturing

In a process firm, units typically pass through a series of manufacturing or producing departments; in each department or process is an operation that brings the product one step closer to completion. In each department, materials, labour, and overhead may be needed. When a particular process is completed, the partly completed goods are transferred to the next department. After passing through the final department, the completed goods are transferred to the warehouse.

Production at Healthblend Nutritional Supplements is an example of **sequential processing**. In a sequential process, units must pass through one process before they can be worked on in later processes. Exhibit 6–1 shows the sequential pattern of the manufacture of Healthblend's minerals, herbs, and vitamins.

Another processing pattern is **parallel processing**, in which two or more sequential processes are required in order to produce a finished good. Partly completed units (for example, two subcomponents) can be worked on simultaneously in different processes and then brought together in a final process for completion. Consider, for example, the manufacture of hard disk drives for personal computers. In one series of processes, write-heads and cartridge disk drives are produced,

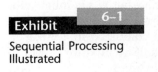

Exhibit 6–1

Sequential Processing
Illustrated

Exhibit 6–2

Parallel Processing Illustrated

Process 1: Production and assembly of write-head and disk drive
Process 2: Testing of write-head and disk drive
Process 3: Production of circuit board
Process 4: Testing of circuit board

assembled, and tested. In a second series of processes, printed circuit boards are produced and tested. These two major subcomponents then come together for assembly in the final process. Exhibit 6–2 portrays this type of processing pattern. Notice that processes 1 and 2 can occur independently of (or parallel to) processes 3 and 4.

Other forms of parallel processing also exist. However, regardless of which processing pattern exists within a firm, all units produced share a common property. Since units are homogeneous and subjected to the same operations for a given process, each unit produced in a period should receive the same unit cost. Understanding how unit costs are computed requires an understanding of the manufacturing cost flows that take place in a process-costing firm.

How Costs Flow Through the Accounts in Process Costing

The manufacturing cost flows for a process-costing system are generally the same as those for a job-order costing system. As raw materials are purchased, the cost of these materials flows into a Raw Materials inventory account. Similarly, raw materials, direct labour, and applied overhead costs flow into a Work in Process account. When goods are completed, the cost of the completed goods is transferred from Work in Process to the Finished Goods account. Finally, as goods are sold, the cost of the finished goods is transferred to the Cost of Goods Sold account. The journal entries generally parallel those described in a job-order costing system.

Although job-order and process cost flows are generally similar, some differences exist. In process costing, each producing department has its own Work in Process account. As goods are completed in one department, they are transferred to the next department. Exhibit 6–3 illustrates this process for Healthblend. Notice that a product (let's say, multivitamins) starts out in the picking department, where the proper amounts of vitamin, mineral, and inert materials are mixed. Picking direct labour and applied overhead are recognized and added to the picking Work in Process account.

Exhibit 6–3

Flow of Manufacturing Cost through the Accounts of a Process-Costing Firm

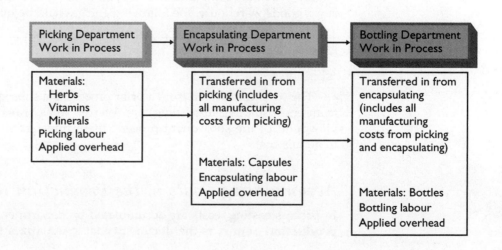

When the mixture is properly blended, it is transferred to the encapsulating department, where capsules are filled. The filled capsules are then transferred to the bottling department. There, the capsules are bottled and then the bottles are packaged. The important point is that as the product is transferred from one department to another, so are all of the costs attached to the product. By the end of the process, all manufacturing costs end up in the final department (bottling, in this case) with the final product.

Let's attach some costs to the various departments and follow them through the accounts. For example, suppose that Healthblend decides to produce 2,000 bottles of multivitamins, with the following costs:

	Picking	Encapsulating	Bottling
Direct materials	$1,700	$1,000	$ 800
Direct labour	50	60	300
Applied overhead	450	500	600
Total	$2,200	$1,560	$1,700

When the multivitamin mixture is transferred to the encapsulating department from the picking department, it takes $2,200 of cost along with it. This $2,200 is *transferred-in cost* to the encapsulating department and is treated as another type of direct materials cost. You could think of the encapsulating department as "buying" the mixture from the picking department. Then encapsulating adds $1,560 of cost from its process and transfers completed capsules plus $3,760 of cost ($2,200 from picking and $1,560 added in encapsulating) to the bottling department. Again, bottling treats the $3,760 of transferred-in cost as a direct materials cost and adds its own cost of $1,700 to come up with a total cost of $5,460. The completed bottles of multivitamins are transferred to the finished goods warehouse along with the $5,460 of manufacturing cost. If there were 2,000 bottles manufactured, each would have a manufacturing cost of $2.73 ($5,460/2,000).

When the mixture is transferred from picking to encapsulating, the following journal entry would occur:

Work in Process (Encapsulating)	2,200	
Work in Process (Picking)		2,200

Similarly, the journal entry to record the transferred-in costs from encapsulating to bottling would be:

Work in Process (Bottling)	3,760	
Work in Process (Encapsulating)		3,760

Finally, when the completed multivitamins leave the bottling department for the finished goods warehouse, the following entry would be made:

Finished Goods	5,460	
Work in Process (Bottling)		5,460

The costs transferred from a prior process to a subsequent process (for example, from encapsulating to bottling) are referred to as **transferred-in costs**. From the viewpoint of the subsequent process, these transferred-in costs are a type of raw materials cost.

Accumulating Costs in the Production Report

In process costing, costs are accumulated by department for a period of time. The **production report** is the document that summarizes the manufacturing activity that takes place in a process department for a given time period. A production report contains information on costs transferred in from prior departments as well as costs added in the current department, such as direct materials, direct labour, and overhead; it is subsidiary to the Work in Process account, just as the job-order cost sheet is subsidiary to the Work in Process account in a job-order costing system.

A production report provides information about the physical units processed in a department and about the manufacturing costs associated with them. Thus, a production report is divided into a unit information section and a cost information section. The unit information section has two major subdivisions: (1) units to account for, and (2) units accounted for. Similarly, the cost information section has two major subdivisions: (1) costs to account for, and (2) costs accounted for. A production report traces the flow of units through a department, identifies the costs charged to the department, shows the computation of unit costs, and reveals the disposition of the department's costs for the reporting period.

Service and Manufacturing Firms

Any product or service that is basically homogeneous and repetitively produced can take advantage of a process-costing approach. Let's look at three possibilities: services, manufacturing firms with a JIT orientation, and traditional manufacturing firms.

Cheque processing in a bank, teeth cleaning by a dental hygienist, air travel between Calgary and Winnipeg, sorting mail by postal code, and laundering and pressing shirts are examples of homogeneous services that are repetitively produced. Although services cannot be stored, it is possible for firms engaged in service production to have work-in-process inventories. For example, a batch of tax returns can be partly completed at the end of a period. However, many services are provided so quickly that there are no work-in-process inventories. Tooth cleaning, funerals, surgical operations, sonograms, and carpet cleaning are a few examples where work-in-process inventories would be virtually nonexistent. Therefore, process costing for services is relatively simple. The total costs for the period are divided by the number of services provided to compute unit cost.

Manufacturing firms may also operate without significant work-in-process inventories. Specifically, firms that have adopted a JIT approach to manufacturing view the carrying of unnecessary inventories as wasteful. These firms try to reduce work-in-process inventories to very low levels. Furthermore, JIT firms usually structure their manufacturing so that process costing can be used to determine product costs.

In many JIT firms, work cells are created that produce a product or subassembly from start to finish. Costs are collected by cell for a time period, and output for the cell is measured for the same period. Unit costs are computed by dividing the costs for the period by the output for the period. There is no ambiguity concerning what costs belong to the period and how output is measured. One of the objectives of JIT manufacturing is simplification. Keep this in mind as you study the process-costing requirements of manufacturing firms that carry work-in-process inventories. The impressive difference between the two settings illustrates one of JIT's significant benefits.

Finally, traditional manufacturing firms may have significant beginning and ending work-in-process inventories. It is the presence of these inventories that leads to much of the complication surrounding process costing. These complications are due to several factors: the presence of beginning and ending work-in-process inventories; different approaches to the treatment of beginning inventory cost; and nonuniform application of manufacturing costs. We will discuss the treatment of these complicating factors in the following sections.

THE IMPACT OF WORK-IN-PROCESS
INVENTORIES ON PROCESS COSTING

Objective 2

Define *equivalent units*, and explain their role in process costing. Explain the differences between the weighted average method and the FIFO method of accounting for process costs.

The computation of unit cost for the work performed during a period is a key part of the production report. This unit cost is needed both to compute the cost of goods transferred out of a department and to value ending work-in-process inventory.[1] You might think that this is easy—just divide total cost by the number of units produced. However, the presence of work-in-process inventories causes problems. First, defining a unit of production, given that some units produced during a period are complete while those in ending work-in-process inventory are not, is a problem. This is handled through the concept of equivalent units of production. Second, how should the costs of beginning work in process be treated? Should they be pooled with current-period costs or separated and transferred out first? Two methods have been developed to handle this problem: the weighted average method and the FIFO method.

Equivalent Units of Production

By definition, ending work in process is not complete. Thus, a unit completed and transferred out during the period is not identical (or equivalent) to one in ending work-in-process inventory, and the cost attached to the two units should not be the same. In computing the unit cost, the output of the period must be defined. A major problem of process costing is making this definition.

To illustrate the output problem of process costing, assume that Department A had the following data for October:

Units, beginning work in process	—
Units completed	1,000
Units, ending work in process (25% complete)	600
Total manufacturing costs	$11,500

What is the output in October for this department? 1,000? 1,600? If we say 1,000 units, we ignore the effort expended on the units in ending work in process. Furthermore, the manufacturing costs incurred in October belong both to the units completed and to the partly completed units in ending work in process. On the other hand, if we say 1,600 units, we ignore the fact that the 600 units in ending work in process are only partly completed. Somehow, output must be measured so that it reflects the effort expended on both completed and partly completed units.

The solution is to calculate equivalent units of output. **Equivalent units of output** are the complete units that could have been produced given the total amount of manufacturing effort expended for the period under consideration. Determining equivalent units of output for transferred-out units is easy: a unit would not be transferred out unless it was complete. Thus, every transferred-out unit is an equivalent unit. Units remaining in ending work-in-process inventory, however, are not complete. Thus, someone in production must "eyeball" ending work in process to estimate its degree of completion. In the example, the 600 units in ending work in process are 25 percent complete; this is equivalent to 150 fully completed units (600 × 25%). Therefore, the equivalent units for October would be the 1,000 completed units plus 150 equivalent units in ending work in process—a total of 1,150 units of output. Exhibit 6–4 illustrates the concept of equivalent units of production.

Knowing the output for a period and the manufacturing costs for the department for that period ($11,500 in this example), we can calculate a unit cost, which in

---

1. While both manufacturing and service firms can use process costing, typically only manufacturing firms have problems with the valuation of ending inventories of work in process and finished goods. As a result, much of the discussion in this chapter illustrates process manufacturing.

Exhibit   6–4

Equivalent Units of
Production

Concept:

100 units completed   = 100 equivalent units

200 units, 50% complete   =   = 100 equivalent units

Example:
1,000 units completed, 600 units, 25% complete

1,000 units completed   = 1,000 equivalent units

600 units, EWIP, 25% complete   =   150 equivalent units

                                                        Total = 1,150 equivalent units

this case is $10 ($11,500/1,150). The unit cost is used to assign a cost of $10,000 ($10 × 1,000) to the 1,000 units transferred out and a cost of $1,500 ($10 × 150) to the 600 units in ending work in process. This unit cost is $10 per equivalent unit. Thus, when valuing ending work in process, the $10 unit cost is multiplied by the equivalent units, not the actual number of partly completed units.

Two Methods of Treating Beginning Work-in-Process Inventory

The presence of beginning work-in-process inventories also complicates the computation of the unit cost. The work done on these partly completed units represents prior-period work, and the costs assigned to them are prior-period costs. In computing a current-period unit cost for a department, two approaches have evolved for dealing with the prior-period output and prior-period costs found in beginning work in process: the weighted average method and the first-in, first-out (FIFO) method. Basically, the **weighted average costing method** combines beginning inventory costs with current-period costs to compute unit cost. In essence, the costs are pooled, and only one average unit cost is computed and applied to both units transferred out and units remaining in ending inventory.

The **FIFO costing method**, on the other hand, separates units in beginning inventory from those produced during the current period. It is assumed that units from beginning inventory are completed first, and then transferred out (along with all of the prior-period costs as well as the current-period costs for completing those units). Only then is current-period production started and either completed (and transferred out, along with current costs) or left incomplete as ending work-in-process inventory.

If product costs do not change from period to period, or if there is no beginning work-in-process inventory, the FIFO and weighted average methods yield the same results. The weighted average method is discussed in more detail in the next section. Further discussion of the FIFO method is found in the Appendix.

WEIGHTED AVERAGE COSTING

The weighted average costing method treats beginning inventory costs and the accompanying equivalent output as if they belong to the current period. This is done for costs by adding the manufacturing costs in beginning work in process to the manufacturing costs incurred during the current period. The total cost is treated as if it were the current period's total manufacturing cost. Similarly, beginning inventory output and current-period output are merged in the calculation of equivalent units. Under the weighted average method, equivalent units of output are computed by adding units completed to equivalent units in ending work in process. Notice that the equivalent units in beginning work in process are included in the computation. Consequently, these units are counted as part of the current period's equivalent units of output.

Five Steps in Preparing a Production Report

Recall that the production report summarizes cost and manufacturing activity for a producing department for a given time period. The general pattern is described by the following five steps:

1. Analysis of the flow of physical units
2. Calculation of equivalent units
3. Computation of unit cost
4. Valuation of inventories (goods transferred out and ending work in process)
5. Cost reconciliation

We will follow the five steps in the following example. Doing so gives some structure to the method of accounting for process costs and makes it easier to learn and remember.

Example of the Weighted Average Method

To illustrate the weighted average method, let's use cost and production data for Healthblend's picking department for July (assume that units are measured in litres):

Production:	
Units in process, July 1 (75% complete)	20,000
Units completed and transferred out	50,000
Units in process, July 31 (25% complete)	10,000
Costs:	
Work in process, July 1	$3,525
Costs added during July	$10,125

Using the data for the picking department, Exhibit 6–5 illustrates the use of the weighted average method to allocate manufacturing costs to units transferred out and to units remaining in ending work in process. Notice that costs from beginning work in process (BWIP) are pooled with costs added to production during July. These total pooled costs ($13,650) are averaged and assigned to units transferred out and to units in ending work in process (EWIP). On the units side, we concentrate on the degree of completion of all units at the end of the period. We do not care about the percentage of completion of beginning work-in-process inventory. We care only

Exhibit 6–5 Weighted Average Method

Costs:

BWIP Cost

July Cost

$3,525

$10,125

$13,650

Total Manufacturing Cost

Output for July:

60,000 Total Physical Units   Become 52,500
BWIP   Equivalent Units

                                    20,000

+

Units Started and Completed

                                    30,000

+

EWIP, 25% Complete

                                    2,500
                                   ───────
                                    52,500

Cost Assignment:

Cost/Unit = $13,650 ÷ 52,500 = $0.26
Transferred Out ($0.26 X 50,000) $13,000
EWIP ($0.26 X 2,500)   650
    Total Cost Assigned $13,650

Key:

■ = 10,000 Units Completed

□ = 10,000 Units, 25% Completed

about whether these units are complete or not by the end of July. Thus, equivalent units are computed by pooling manufacturing effort from June and July.

Let's take a closer look at the July production in Healthblend's picking department by focusing on the five steps of the weighted average method.

Step 1: Physical Flow Analysis The purpose of Step 1 is to trace the physical units of production. Physical units are not equivalent units; they are units that may be in any stage of completion. We can see in Exhibit 6–5 that there are 60,000 physical units.[2] In this example, 20,000 are from beginning inventory. Another 40,000 were started in July. From those 40,000, 10,000 remain in ending inventory, 25 percent complete. The analysis of physical flow of units is usually accomplished by preparing a **physical flow schedule** like the one shown in Exhibit 6–6. To construct the schedule from the information given in the example, two calculations are needed. First, units started and completed in this period are obtained by subtracting the units in beginning work in process from the total units completed. Next, the units started are obtained by adding the units started and completed to the units in ending work in process. Notice that the "total units to account for" must equal the "total units accounted for." The physical flow schedule in Exhibit 6–6 is important because it contains the information needed for calculating equivalent units (Step 2).

---

2. In Exhibit 6–5, each box represents 10,000 units. The key point to remember is that a unit may be in any stage of completion. We can see that output for July consists of six boxes: two for BWIP, three for units started and completed, and one for EWIP. Hence there are 60,000 physical units to account for.

Exhibit   6–6

Physical Flow Schedule

Units to account for:		
Beginning work in process (75% complete)		20,000
Started during the period		40,000
Total units to account for		60,000
Units accounted for:		
Completed and transferred out:		
Started and completed	30,000	
From beginning work in process	20,000	50,000
Ending work in process (25% complete)		10,000
Total units accounted for		60,000

Step 2: Calculation of Equivalent Units Given the information in the physical flow schedule, you can calculate the weighted average equivalent units for July. This calculation is shown in Exhibit 6–7. Notice that July's output is measured as 52,500 units: 50,000 units completed and transferred out, and 2,500 equivalent units from ending inventory (10,000 × 25%). What about beginning inventory? There were 20,000 units in beginning inventory, 75 percent complete. These units are included in the 50,000 units completed and transferred out during the month. Thus, beginning inventory units are treated as if they were started and completed during the current period.

Exhibit   6–7

Equivalent Units of
Production: Weighted
Average Method

Units completed	50,000
Add: Units in ending work in process × fraction completed	
10,000 units × 25%	2,500
Equivalent units of output	52,500

Step 3: Computation of Unit Cost In addition to July output, July manufacturing costs are needed to compute a unit cost. The weighted average method rolls back and includes the manufacturing costs associated with the units in beginning work in process. Thus, the total manufacturing cost for July is defined as $13,650 ($3,525 + $10,125). The manufacturing costs carried over from the prior period ($3,525) are treated as if they were current-period costs. Given the manufacturing costs for July and the output for the month, we can calculate the unit cost and use it to determine the cost of goods transferred out and the cost of ending work in process. For July, the weighted average method gives the following unit cost:

$$\text{Unit cost} = \$13,650/52,500 = \$0.26 \text{ per equivalent unit}$$

Step 4: Valuation of Inventories With the unit cost of $0.26, the cost of goods transferred to the encapsulating department is $13,000 (50,000 units × $0.26 per unit), and the cost of ending work in process is $650 (2,500 equivalent units × $0.26 per unit). Notice that units completed (from Step 1), equivalent units in ending work in process (from Step 2), and the unit cost (from Step 3) were all needed to value both goods transferred out and ending work in process.

Step 5: Cost Reconciliation The total manufacturing costs assigned to inventories are as follows:

Cost of goods transferred out	$13,000
Cost of goods, ending work in process	650
Total costs accounted for	$13,650

Exhibit   6–8

Production Report—
Weighted Average
Method (July 2001)

Healthblend Company
Picking Department
Production Report for July 2001
(Weighted Average Method)

UNIT INFORMATION

Physical Flow

Units to account for:		Units accounted for:	
Beginning work in process	20,000	Completed	50,000
Started	40,000	Ending work in process	10,000
Total units to account for	60,000	Total units accounted for	60,000

Equivalent Units

Completed	50,000
Ending work in process	2,500
Total equivalent units	52,500

COST INFORMATION

Cost to account for:

Beginning work in process	$ 3,525
Incurred during the period	10,125
Total costs to account for	$13,650

Cost per equivalent unit	$0.26

Cost accounted for:	Transferred Out	Ending Work in Process	Total
Goods transferred out ($0.26 × 50,000)	$13,000	—	$13,000
Goods in ending work in process ($0.26 × 2,500)	—	$650	650
Total costs accounted for	$13,000	$650	$13,650

The manufacturing costs to account for are also $13,650.

Cost of beginning work in process	$ 3,525
Costs incurred during the period	10,125
Total costs to account for	$13,650

Thus, the costs to account for are exactly assigned to inventories, and we have the necessary **cost reconciliation.** Remember, the total costs assigned to goods transferred out and to ending work in process must agree with the total costs in beginning work in process and the manufacturing costs incurred during the current period.

Production Report   Steps 1 through 5 provide all of the information needed to prepare a production report for the picking department for July. This report is given in Exhibit 6–8.

Evaluation of the Weighted Average Method

The major benefit of the weighted average method is simplicity. If we treat units in beginning work in process as belonging to the current period, all equivalent units belong to the same category when it comes to calculating unit costs. Thus, unit-cost computations are simplified. The main disadvantage of this method is reduced accuracy in computing unit costs for current-period output and for units in beginning work in process. If the unit cost in a process is relatively stable from one period to the next, the weighted average method is reasonably accurate. However, if the price of manufacturing inputs increases significantly from one period to the next, the unit cost of current output is understated, and the unit cost of beginning work-in-process units is overstated. If greater accuracy in computing unit costs is desired, a company should use the FIFO method to determine unit costs.

MULTIPLE INPUTS AND MULTIPLE DEPARTMENTS

Objective 4

Explain how process costing is affected by nonuniform application of manufacturing inputs and the existence of multiple processing departments.

Accounting for production under process costing is complicated by nonuniform application of manufacturing inputs and by the presence of multiple processing departments. We will now discuss how process-costing methods address these complications.

Nonuniform Application of Manufacturing Inputs

Up to this point, we have assumed that work in process being 60 percent complete meant that 60 percent of the materials, labour, and overhead needed to complete the process have been used and that another 40 percent are needed to finish the units. In other words, we have assumed that manufacturing inputs are applied uniformly as the manufacturing process unfolds.

Assuming uniform application of conversion costs (direct labour and overhead) is not unreasonable. Direct labour input is usually needed throughout the process, and overhead is often assigned on the basis of direct labour hours. Direct materials, on the other hand, are not as likely to be applied uniformly. In many instances, materials are added either at the beginning or near the end of the process.

For example, look at the differences in Healthblend's three departments. In the picking and encapsulating departments, all materials are added at the beginning of the process. However, in the bottling department, materials are added both at the beginning (filled capsules and bottles) and at the end (bottle caps and boxes).

Work in process in the picking department that is 50 percent complete with respect to conversion inputs would be 100 percent complete with respect to the material inputs. But work in process in bottling that is 50 percent complete with respect to conversion would be 100 percent complete with respect to bottles and transferred-in capsules, but zero percent complete with respect to bottle caps and boxes.

Different percentage-of-completion figures for manufacturing inputs pose a problem for the calculation of equivalent units. Fortunately, the solution is relatively simple. Equivalent-unit calculations are done for each category of manufacturing input. Thus, there are equivalent units calculated for each category of materials and for conversion cost. The conversion cost category can be broken down into direct labour and overhead, if desired. If direct labour and overhead are applied uniformly, however, this serves no useful purpose.

To illustrate, assume that Healthblend's picking department has the following data for September:

Production:
Units in process, September 1, 50% complete*	10,000
Units completed and transferred out	60,000
Units in process, September 30, 40% complete*	20,000

Costs:
Work in process, September 1:	
Materials	$1,600
Conversion costs	200
Total	$1,800
Current costs:	
Materials	$12,000
Conversion costs	3,200
Total	$15,200

* With respect to conversion costs

Exhibit   6–9

Physical Flow Schedule:
Nonuniform Inputs

Units to account for:		
Units in beginning work in process (50% complete)		10,000
Units started during September		70,000
Total units to account for		80,000
Units accounted for:		
Units completed and transferred out:		
Started and completed	50,000	
From beginning work in process	10,000	60,000
Units in ending work in process (40% complete)		20,000
Total units accounted for		80,000

If Healthblend uses the weighted average method for process costing, we can easily illustrate the effect of nonuniform application of manufacturing inputs. Exhibit 6–9 illustrates Step 1—creating the physical flow schedule. Accounting for the flow of physical units is not affected by the nonuniform application of manufacturing inputs, because physical units may be in any stage of completion.

But nonuniform application of inputs does affect the computation of equivalent units (Step 2). Exhibit 6–10 illustrates this computation. Notice that two categories of input are used to calculate equivalent units. Since all materials are added at the beginning of the process, all units are 100 percent complete with respect to materials. Thus, there are 20,000 equivalent units of materials in ending work in process. However, since only 40 percent of the conversion costs have been applied, there are only 8,000 conversion equivalent units in ending work in process.

When different categories of equivalent units exist, a unit cost for each category must be computed. The cost per completed unit (Step 3) is the sum of these individual unit costs. The computations for the example are as follows:

$$\text{Unit materials cost} = (\$1,600 + \$12,000)/80,000$$
$$= \$0.17$$
$$\text{Unit conversion cost} = (\$200 + \$3,200)/68,000$$
$$= \$0.05$$
$$\text{Total unit cost} = \text{Unit materials cost} + \text{Unit conversion cost}$$
$$= \$0.17 + \$0.05$$
$$= \$0.22 \text{ per completed unit}$$

Valuation of goods transferred out (Step 4) is accomplished by multiplying the unit cost by the number of units completed:

$$\text{Cost of goods transferred out} = \$0.22 \times 60,000$$
$$= \$13,200$$

Valuation of ending work in process is done by obtaining the cost of each manufacturing input and then summing these individual input costs. For the example, this requires adding the cost of the materials in ending work in process to the conversion costs in ending work in process.

Exhibit   6–10

Equivalent Units of
Production: Nonuniform
Application

	Materials	Conversion
Units completed	60,000	60,000
Add: Units in ending work in process × Fraction completed		
20,000 × 100%; 20,000 × 40%	20,000	8,000
Equivalent units of output	80,000	68,000

The cost of materials is the unit materials cost multiplied by the material equivalent units in ending work in process. Similarly, the conversion cost in ending work in process is the unit conversion cost multiplied by the conversion equivalent units. Thus, the cost of ending work in process is as follows:

Materials: $0.17 × 20,000 $3,400
Conversion: $0.05 × 8,000   400
Total cost $3,800

Step 5 reconciles the costs to ensure that the computations are correct.

Costs to account for:
  Costs from beginning work in process $ 1,800
  Costs incurred during the period   15,200
    Total costs to account for $17,000

Costs accounted for:
  Cost of goods transferred out $13,200
  Cost of goods in ending work in process   3,800
    Total costs accounted for $17,000

Exhibit 6-11

Production Report—Weighted Average Method (September 2001)

Healthblend Company
Picking Department
Production Report for September 2001
(Weighted Average Method)

UNIT INFORMATION

Units to account for:		Units accounted for:	
Beginning work in process	10,000	Completed	60,000
Started	70,000	Ending work in process	20,000
Total units to account for	80,000	Total units accounted for	80,000

Equivalent Units

	Materials	Conversion Cost
Completed	60,000	60,000
Ending work in process	20,000	8,000
Total equivalent units	80,000	68,000

COST INFORMATION

	Materials	Conversion Cost	Total
Costs to account for:			
Beginning work in process	$ 1,600	$ 200	$ 1,800
Incurred during the period	12,000	3,200	15,200
Total costs to account for	$13,600	$3,400	$17,000
Cost per equivalent unit	$0.17	$0.05	$0.22

	Transferred Out	Ending Work in Process	Total
Costs accounted for:			
Goods transferred out ($0.22 × 60,000)	$13,200	—	$13,200
Goods in ending work in process:			
Materials ($0.17 × 20,000)	—	$3,400	3,400
Conversion ($0.05 × 8,000)	—	400	400
Total costs accounted for	$13,200	$3,800	$17,000

Using the information generated from the five steps, you can prepare a production report (see Exhibit 6–11). As the example has shown, applying manufacturing inputs at different stages of a process poses no serious problems. However, the effort required to compute the costs has increased.

Multiple Departments

In process manufacturing, some departments receive partly completed goods from prior departments. The usual approach is to treat transferred-in goods as a separate material category when calculating equivalent units.

In dealing with transferred-in goods, two important points should be remembered. First, the cost of this material is the cost of the goods transferred out as computed in the prior department. Second, the units started in the subsequent department correspond to the units transferred out from the prior department (assuming that there is a one-to-one relationship between the output measures of both departments).

For example, let's consider the month of September for Healthblend, restricting our attention to the transferred-in category. Assume that the encapsulating department had 15,000 units in beginning inventory (with transferred-in costs of $3,000) and completed 70,000 units during the month. Further, the picking department completed and transferred out 60,000 units at a cost of $13,200 in September. In constructing a physical flow schedule for the encapsulating department, consider its dependence on the picking department:

Units to account for:	
Beginning work in process	15,000
Transferred in during September	60,000
Total units to account for	75,000
Units accounted for:	
Completed and transferred out:	
Started and completed	55,000
Beginning work in process	15,000
Ending work in process	5,000
Total units accounted for	75,000

Equivalent units for the transferred-in category are calculated as follows (ignoring other input categories):

Units completed	70,000
Add: Units in ending work in process × Fraction completed (5,000 × 100%*)	5,000
Equivalent units of output	75,000

* Remember that the EWIP is 100 percent complete with respect to transferred-in costs, not to all costs of the encapsulating department.

To compute the unit cost, we add the cost of the units transferred in from picking in September to the transferred-in costs in beginning work in process and divide by transferred-in equivalent units:

$$\text{Unit cost (transferred-in category)} = (\$13{,}200 + \$3{,}000)/75{,}000$$
$$= \$16{,}200/75{,}000$$
$$= \$0.216$$

The only additional complication introduced in the analysis for a subsequent department is the presence of the transferred-in category. As has just been shown, dealing with this category is similar to handling any other category. However, it must be remembered that the current cost of this special type of raw material is the cost of the units transferred in from the prior process and that the units transferred in are the units started.

APPENDIX: PRODUCTION REPORT—FIFO COSTING

Objective 5

Prepare a departmental production report using the FIFO method.

Under the FIFO costing method, the equivalent units and manufacturing costs in beginning work in process are excluded from the current-period unit-cost calculation. This method recognizes that the work and costs carried over from the prior period legitimately belong to that period.

If changes occur in the prices of the manufacturing inputs from one period to the next, then FIFO produces a more accurate (that is, more current) unit cost than does the weighted average method. A more accurate unit cost means better cost control, better pricing decisions, and so on. Keep in mind that if the period is as short as a week or a month, however, the unit costs calculated under the two methods are not likely to differ much. In that case, the FIFO method has little, if anything, to offer over the weighted average method. Perhaps for this reason, many firms use the weighted average method.

Since FIFO excludes prior-period work and costs, we need to create two categories of completed units. FIFO assumes that units in beginning work in process are completed first, before any new units are started. Thus, one category of completed units is beginning work-in-process units. The second category is for those units started and completed during the current period.

For example, assume that a department had 20,000 units in beginning work in process and that it completed and transferred out a total of 50,000 units. Of the 50,000 completed units, 20,000 are the units initially found in beginning work in process. The remaining 30,000 were started and completed during the current period.

These two categories of completed units are needed in the FIFO method so that each category can be costed correctly. For the units started and completed, the unit cost is obtained by dividing total current manufacturing costs by the current-period equivalent output. However, for the beginning work-in-process units, the total associated manufacturing costs are the sum of the prior-period costs plus the costs incurred in the current period to finish the units. As can be seen in Exhibit 6–12, costs from the current period and from beginning inventory are not pooled. Instead, current-period cost is added to beginning inventory cost in order to complete the units on hand at the start of the period.

The computations in Exhibit 6–12 are based on the same Healthblend data used for the weighted average method when we assumed uniform use of manufacturing inputs (see Exhibit 6–5). Using the same data highlights the differences between the two methods. The five steps in costing out production follow.

Production:
Units in process, July 1 (75% complete)	20,000
Units completed and transferred out	50,000
Units in process, July 31 (25% complete)	10,000

Costs:
Work in process, July 1	$ 3,525
Costs added during July	10,125

Step 1: Physical Flow Analysis   The purpose of Step 1 is to trace the physical units of production. As with the weighted average method, in the FIFO method, a physical flow schedule is prepared. This schedule, shown in Exhibit 6–13, is identical for both methods.

Step 2: Calculation of Equivalent Units   Exhibit 6–14 illustrates the calculation of equivalent units under the FIFO method. From the equivalent-unit computation in Exhibit 6–14, one difference between weighted average and FIFO becomes immediately apparent. Under FIFO, the equivalent units in beginning work in process, work done in the prior period, are not counted as part of the total equivalent work. Only the equivalent work *to be completed* this period is counted. The equivalent work to be

Exhibit 6–12   FIFO Method

Costs:

BWIP Cost

July Cost

Costs to
Complete BWIP

$3,525

$10,125

BWIP Units

Current-Period
Units

Output for July:

60,000 Total Physical Units   Become 37,500
Equivalent Units

BWIP

→ 5,000

+

Units Started and Completed

→ 30,000

+

EWIP

→ 2,500

37,500

Cost Assignment:

Unit Cost = $10,125 ÷ 37,500 = $0.27
Transferred Out:
  From BWIP $ 3,525
  Complete BWIP ($0.27 X 5,000)   1,350
  Start & Complete in July
    ($0.27 X 30,000)   8,100
EWIP ($0.27 x 2.500)   675
  Total Cost Accounted For $13,650

Key:

= 10,000 Units, 100% Completed in July

= 10,000 Units, 25% Completed in July

Exhibit 6–13

Physical Flow Schedule

Units to account for:		
Beginning work in process (75% complete)		20,000
Started during July		40,000
Total units to account for		60,000
Units accounted for:		
Completed and transferred out:		
Started and completed	30,000	
From beginning work in process	20,000	50,000
Ending work in process (25% complete)		10,000
Total units accounted for		60,000

completed for the units from the prior period is computed by multiplying the number of units in beginning work in process by the percentage of work remaining. Since in this example the percentage of work done in the prior period is 75 percent, the percentage left to be completed this period is 25 percent, or an equivalent of 5,000 additional units of work.

Exhibit   6–14

Equivalent Units of
Production: FIFO
Method

Units started and completed	30,000
Add: Units in beginning work in process × Fraction	
to be completed (20,000 × 25%)	5,000
Add: Units in ending work in process × Fraction	
complete (10,000 × 25%)	2,500
Equivalent units of output	37,500

The effect of excluding prior-period effort is to produce the current-period equivalent output. Recall that under the weighted average method, 52,500 equivalent units were computed for this month. Under FIFO, only 37,500 units are calculated for the same month. These 37,500 units represent current-period output. The difference, of course, is explained by the fact that the weighted average method rolls back and counts the 15,000 equivalent units of prior-period work (20,000 units BWIP × 75%) as belonging to this period.

Step 3: Computation of Unit Cost The additional manufacturing costs incurred in the current period are $10,125. Thus, the current-period unit manufacturing cost is $10,125/37,500, or $0.27. Notice that the costs of beginning inventory are excluded from this calculation. Only current-period manufacturing costs are used.

Step 4: Valuation of Inventories Since all equivalent units in ending work in process are current-period units, the cost of ending work in process is simply $0.27 × 2,500, or $675. However, when it comes to valuing goods transferred out, another difference emerges between the weighted average method and FIFO.

Under weighted average, the cost of goods transferred out is simply the unit cost multiplied by the units completed. Under FIFO, however, there are two sources of completed units: 20,000 units from beginning inventory, and 30,000 units started and completed. The cost of the 30,000 units that were started and completed in the current period and transferred out is $8,100 ($0.27 × 30,000). For these units, the use of the current-period unit cost is entirely appropriate.

However, the cost of the beginning work-in-process units that were transferred out is another matter. These units started the period with $3,525 of manufacturing costs already incurred and 15,000 units of equivalent output already completed. To finish these units, the equivalent of 5,000 units were needed. The cost of finishing the units in beginning work in process is $1,350 ($0.27 × 5,000). Adding this $1,350 to the $3,525 in cost carried over from the prior period gives a total manufacturing cost for these units of $4,875. The unit cost of these 20,000 units, then, is about $0.244 ($4,875/20,000).

Step 5: Cost Reconciliation With the completion of Step 5, the production report can be prepared. This report is shown in Exhibit 6–15. The total costs assigned to production are as follows:

Goods transferred out:	
Units in beginning work in process	$ 4,875
Units started and completed	8,100
Goods in ending work in process	675
Total costs accounted for	$13,650

The total manufacturing costs to account for during the period are as follows:

Beginning work in process	$ 3,525
Incurred during the period	10,125
Total costs to account for	$13,650

Exhibit 6–15

Production Report—
FIFO Method (July 2001)

Healthblend Company
Picking Department
Production Report for July 2001
(FIFO Method)

UNIT INFORMATION

Units to account for:

Beginning work in process	20,000
Started	40,000
Total units to account for	60,000

Units accounted for:	Physical Flow	Equivalent Units
Started and completed	30,000	30,000
Completed from beginning inventory	20,000	5,000
Ending work in process	10,000	2,500
Total units accounted for	60,000	37,500

COST INFORMATION

Costs to account for:

Beginning work in process	$ 3,525
Incurred during the period	10,125
Total costs to account for	$13,650
Cost per equivalent unit	$0.27

Costs accounted for:	Transferred Out	Ending Work in Process	Total
Units in beginning work in process:			
From prior period	$ 3,525	—	$ 3,525
From current period ($0.27 × 5,000)	1,350	—	1,350
Units started and completed ($0.27 × 30,000)	8,100	—	8,100
Goods in ending work in process			
($0.27 × 2,500)	—	$675	675
Total costs accounted for	$12,975	$675	$13,650

Often the total costs accounted for do not precisely equal the costs to account for, due to rounding error. An easy way to bring the amounts into balance is to adjust the cost of goods transferred out by the amount of the rounding error.

The differences between the weighted average method and the FIFO method consist of the way that equivalent units and unit costs are calculated, and the way unit costs are used to assign costs to the finished goods and work-in-process inventories. In the example, the difference is small; the cost for goods transferred out is $13,000 for the weighted average method (see Exhibit 6–8) and $12,975 for the FIFO method (see Exhibit 6–15). The ending work-in-process inventories are $650 (weighted average) and $675 (FIFO). This reflects the slightly higher current-period unit cost that is applied to a greater extent to ending work-in-process inventory under FIFO. If the difference between current-period and prior-period costs was greater, the difference in the assigned costs would also be greater.

SUMMARY OF LEARNING OBJECTIVES

1. Describe the basic characteristics and cost flows associated with process manufacturing.
Cost flows under process costing are similar to those under job-order costing. Raw materials are purchased and debited to the Materials account. Direct materials used in production, direct labour, and overhead applied are charged to the Work in Process account. In a production process with several processes, there is a Work in Process account for each department or process. Goods completed in one department are transferred out to the next department. When units are completed in the final department or process, their cost is credited to Work in Process and debited to Finished Goods.

2. Define *equivalent units*, and explain their role in process costing. Explain the difference between the weighted average method and the FIFO method of accounting for process costs.
Equivalent units of production are the complete units that could have been produced given the total amount of manufacturing effort expended during the period. The number of physical units is multiplied by the percentage of completion to calculate equivalent units. Two approaches have evolved for dealing with beginning work-in-process inventory costs. The weighted average costing method combines beginning inventory costs with current-period costs to compute unit costs. The FIFO costing method separates units in beginning inventory from those produced during the current period.

3. Prepare a departmental production report using the weighted average method.
The production report summarizes the manufacturing activity occurring in a department for a given period. It discloses information concerning the physical flow of units, equivalent units, unit costs, and the disposition of the manufacturing costs associated with the period.

4. Explain how process costing is affected by nonuniform application of manufacturing inputs and the existence of multiple processing departments.
Nonuniform application of productive inputs requires the determination of separate percentage-of-completion figures for each input. This, in turn, requires the computation of separate equivalent units and unit costs. When a company has more than one processing department, the output of one department becomes the raw material of a succeeding department. The usual method is to handle the transferred-in units and costs as another form of material.

5. Prepare a departmental production report using the FIFO method. (Appendix)
A production report prepared according to the FIFO method separates the cost of beginning work in process from the cost of the current period. BWIP is assumed to be completed and transferred out first. Cost from BWIP is not pooled with current-period cost in computing unit cost. Additionally, equivalent units of production exclude work done in the prior period.

KEY TERMS

Cost reconciliation, 219
Equivalent units of output, 214
FIFO costing method, 215
Operation costing, 210

Parallel processing, 210
Physical flow schedule, 217
Production report, 212
Sequential processing, 210

Transferred-in costs, 212
Weighted average costing
   method, 215

REVIEW PROBLEM

Payson Company, which uses the weighted average method, produces a product that passes through two departments: mixing and cooking. In the mixing department, all materials are added at the beginning of the process. All other manufacturing inputs are added uniformly. The following information pertains to the mixing department for February:

a. Beginning work in process (BWIP), February 1: 100,000 kilograms, 40 percent complete with respect to conversion costs. The costs assigned to this work are as follows:

Materials	$20,000
Labour	10,000
Overhead	30,000

b. Ending work in process (EWIP), February 28: 50,000 kilograms, 60 percent complete with respect to conversion costs.

c. Units started: 320,000 kilograms. The following costs were added during the month:

Materials	$211,000
Labour	100,000
Overhead	270,000

Required:

1. Prepare a physical flow schedule.
2. Prepare a schedule of equivalent units.
3. Compute the cost per equivalent unit.
4. Compute the cost of goods transferred out and the cost of ending work in process.
5. Prepare a cost reconciliation.

Solution

1. Physical flow schedule:

Units to account for:		Units accounted for:	
Units, BWIP	100,000	Units completed and transferred out	370,000*
Units started	320,000	Units, EWIP	50,000
Total	420,000	Total	420,000

* 270,000 units started and completed, plus 100,000 units from BWIP

2. Schedule of equivalent units:

	Materials	Conversion
Units completed	370,000	370,000
Units, EWIP × Fraction completed:		
50,000 × 100%; 50,000 × 60%	50,000	30,000
Equivalent units of output	420,000	400,000

3. Cost per equivalent unit:

Direct materials unit cost = ($20,000 + $211,000)/420,000 = $0.55
Conversion unit cost = ($40,000 + $370,000)/400,000 = $1.025
Total unit cost = $1.575 per equivalent unit

4. Cost of goods transferred out and cost of ending work in process:

Cost of goods transferred out = $1.575 × 370,000 = $582,750
Cost of EWIP = ($0.55 × 50,000) + ($1.025 × 30,000)
= $58,250

5. Cost reconciliation:

Costs to account for:		Costs accounted for:	
BWIP	$ 60,000	Goods transferred out	$582,750
Costs added	581,000	EWIP	58,250
Total to account for	$641,000	Total costs accounted for	$641,000

QUESTIONS FOR WRITING AND DISCUSSION

1. Distinguish between sequential processing and parallel processing.

2. Describe the differences between process costing and job-order costing.

3. What are equivalent units? Why are they needed in a process-costing system?

4. Under the weighted average method, how are prior-period costs and output treated? How are they treated under the FIFO method?

5. Under what conditions will the weighted average and FIFO methods give essentially the same results?

6. How is the equivalent-unit calculation affected when materials are added at the beginning or end of the process rather than uniformly throughout the process?

7. Explain why transferred-in costs are a special type of raw material for the receiving department.

8. What are the similarities in and differences between the manufacturing cost flows for job-order firms and process firms?

9. What journal entry would be made as goods are transferred out from one department to another department? from the final department to the warehouse?

10. Describe the five steps in accounting for the manufacturing activity of a processing department, and explain how they interrelate.

11. What is a production report? What purpose does this report serve?

12. In assigning costs to goods transferred out, how do the weighted average and FIFO methods differ?

13. Describe the effect of automation on the process accounting system.

14. How does the adoption of a JIT approach to manufacturing affect process costing?

15. How would process costing for services differ from process costing for manufactured goods?

EXERCISES

6–1

Basic Cost Flows

LO1

Jumpin Jeans produces a variety of styles of jeans in three departments: cutting, sewing, and packaging. During one month, the three departments recorded the following costs:

	Cutting	Sewing	Packaging
Direct materials	$1,800	$ 300	$ 75
Direct labour	50	600	300
Applied overhead	250	1,200	300

Three hundred pairs of jeans were completed during the month.

Required:

1. Prepare a schedule showing, for each department, the cost of direct materials, direct labour, applied overhead, product transferred in from a prior department, and total manufacturing.
2. Prepare the journal entries to transfer costs from the (a) cutting to sewing departments, (b) sewing to packaging departments, (c) packaging department to finished goods.
3. What is the total unit cost of a pair of jeans?

6–2

Equivalent Units

LO2

Department B had the following data for November:

Units in beginning work in process	—
Units completed	500
Units in ending work in process, 30% complete	300
Total manufacturing cost	$1,652

Required:

1. Calculate equivalent units of production in ending work-in-process inventory. Calculate total equivalent units of production for Department B for November.
2. What is the unit manufacturing cost for Department B for November?
3. What is the cost of goods transferred out? What is the cost of ending work-in-process inventory?

6–3

Physical Flow; Equivalent Units

LO1, LO2, LO3

Spreadsheet

Jadlow Company manufactures a product that passes through two processes. The following information was obtained for the first department for May:

a. All materials are added at the beginning of the process.
b. Beginning work in process had 9,000 units, 30 percent complete with respect to conversion costs.
c. Ending work in process had 5,400 units, 25 percent complete with respect to conversion costs.
d. Jadlow started in process 11,000 units.

Required:

1. How many units were transferred out during the month of May?
2. How many units were started and completed during the month of May?
3. Prepare a physical flow schedule for the month of May.
4. Compute equivalent units for the month of May.

6–4

Weighted Average Method; Valuation of Goods Transferred Out and Ending WIP

LO3

Happy Toddler, Inc., manufactures products that pass through two or more processes. Happy Toddler uses the weighted average method to compute unit costs. During April, equivalent units were computed as follows:

	Materials	Conversion Cost
Units completed	6,000	6,000
Units in ending work in process × Fraction completed:		
4,000 × 0%; 4,000 × 60%	0	2,400
Equivalent units of output	6,000	8,400

The unit cost was computed as follows:

Materials	$1.30
Conversion cost	0.50
Total	$1.80

Required:

1. Determine the cost of ending work in process and the cost of the goods transferred out.
2. If possible, prepare a physical flow schedule.

6–5

Basic Flows; Equivalent Units

LO1, LO2

Shannon Company produces a product that passes through two departments.

Data for June on Department 1 were as follows: beginning work in process was zero; ending work in process had 300 units, 50 percent complete with respect to conversion costs; and 540 units were started. Materials are added at the beginning of the process in Department 1.

Data for June on Department 2 were as follows: beginning work in process was 100 units, 20 percent complete with respect to conversion costs; and ending work in process was 50 units, 40 percent complete with respect to conversion costs. All materials are added at the end of the process in Department 2.

Required:

1. For Department 1 for June, calculate the following:
    a. Number of units transferred to Department 2.
    b. Equivalent units of production for materials and for conversion costs.
2. For Department 2 for June, calculate the following:
    a. Number of units transferred out to Finished Goods.
    b. Equivalent units of production for materials and for conversion costs.

6–6

**Steps in Preparing
Cost of Production
Report**

LO3

Spreadsheet

Palomino Paints, Inc., manufactures a variety of paints in three departments: grinding, mixing, and canning. Palomino uses the weighted average method. The following are cost and production data for the grinding department for March (assume that units are measured in kilograms):

Production:
Units in process, March 1 (60% complete)	40,000
Units completed and transferred out	100,000
Units in process, March 31 (20% complete)	20,000

Costs:
Work in process, March 1	$187,200
Costs added during March	$629,200

Required:

1. Prepare a physical flow analysis for the grinding department for the month of March.
2. Calculate equivalent units of production for the grinding department for the month of March.
3. Calculate unit cost for the grinding department for the month of March.
4. Calculate the cost of units transferred out and the cost of ending work-in-process inventory.
5. Prepare a cost reconciliation for the grinding department for the month of March.

6–7

**Cost of Production
Report**

LO3

Refer to 6–6. Prepare a cost of production report for the grinding department for the month of March.

6–8

**Production Report,
No Beginning
Inventory**

LO3

Gilroy, Inc., produces key chains. The key chains are produced in two departments. The data for Department 1 are as follows:

Beginning work in process	0
Units started	43,000
Units transferred out	35,500
Raw materials cost	$16,340
Direct labour cost	$27,126
Overhead applied	$63,294

Materials are added at the beginning of the process. Ending inventory is 80 percent complete with respect to labour and overhead.

Required:

Prepare a production report for Department 1.

6–9

**Physical Flow;
Equivalent Units;
Unit Costs; Cost
Assignment**

LO3

Kirlen Company manufactures soluble plant fertilizer. Department 1 mixes the chemicals required for the fertilizer. The following data are for the year:

Beginning work in process	0
Units started	92,500
Raw materials cost	$277,500
Direct labour cost	$50,680
Overhead applied	$76,020
Units in ending work in process	5,000

Ending work in process is 100 percent complete with respect to materials and 60 percent complete with respect to conversion.

Required:

1. Prepare a physical flow schedule.
2. Calculate equivalent units of production for:
   a. Raw materials
   b. Conversion
3. Calculate unit costs for:
   a. Raw materials
   b. Conversion costs
   c. Total manufacturing costs
4. What is the total cost of units transferred out? What is the cost assigned to units in ending inventory?

6–10

Physical Flow; Equivalent Units; Unit Costs; Cost Assignment

LO3

For the month of December 2001, Pacific Rim Company's records show the following information:

a. The beginning work-in-process inventory consisted of 6,000 units that were 20 percent complete with respect to both direct materials and conversion costs. The balance in the account was $36,820, comprising $18,000 in direct materials and $18,820 in conversion costs.
b. The ending work-in-process inventory consisted of 4,000 units that were 70 percent complete with respect to direct materials and 50 percent complete with respect to conversion costs.
c. Costs incurred during December amounted to $156,925 for direct materials and $124,180 for conversion costs. During December, 20,000 units were transferred to finished goods.
d. Pacific Rim uses the weighted average method.

Required:

1. Prepare a physical flow schedule.
2. Calculate the equivalent units of production for:
   a. Direct materials
   b. Conversion
3. Calculate unit costs for:
   a. Direct materials
   b. Conversion
   c. Total manufacturing
4. What is the total cost of units transferred out? What is the cost assigned to units in ending work-in-process inventory? (CGA Canada adapted)

6–11

Equivalent Units— Weighted Average Method

LO2

The following are data for four independent process-costing departments.

	A	B	C	D
Beginning inventory	3,200	1,000	0	30,000
Percent completed	30%	40%	0%	75%
Units started	17,000	23,000	40,000	40,000
Ending inventory	4,000	0	9,000	10,000
Percent completed	25%	0%	10%	25%

Required:

Compute the equivalent units of production for each of the four departments using the weighted average method.

6–12

Appendix: Equivalent Units—FIFO Method

LO5

Using the data from 6–11, compute the equivalent units of production for each of the four departments using the FIFO method.

6–13

Nonuniform Inputs

LO4

Terry Linens, Inc., manufactures bed and bath linens. The bath linens department sews terry cloth into towels of various sizes. Terry Linens uses the weighted average method. All materials are added at the beginning of the process. The following data are for the bath linens department for June:

Production:

Units in process, June 1, 25% complete*	10,000
Units completed and transferred out	60,000
Units in process, June 30, 60% complete*	20,000

Costs:

Work in process, June 1:

Materials	$ 49,000
Conversion costs	2,625
Total	$ 51,625

Current costs:

Materials	$351,000
Conversion costs	78,735
Total	$429,735

* With respect to conversion costs

Required:

1. Prepare a physical flow analysis for the bath linens department for the month of June.
2. Calculate equivalent units of production for the bath linens department for the month of June.
3. Calculate unit cost for materials, for conversion, and in total for the bath linens department for the month of June.
4. Calculate the cost of units transferred out and the cost of ending work-in-process inventory.
5. Prepare a cost reconciliation for the bath linens department for the month of June.

6–14

Cost of Production Report; Nonuniform Inputs

LO3, LO4

Refer to 6–13. Prepare a cost of production report for the bath linens department for the month of June using the weighted average method.

6–15

Nonuniform Inputs; Transferred-In Cost

LO4

Drysdale Dairy produces a variety of dairy products. In Department 12, cream (transferred in from Department 6) and other materials (sugar and flavourings) are mixed and churned to make ice cream. The following data are for Department 12 for August:

Production:

Units in process, August 1, 25% complete*	40,000
Units completed and transferred out	120,000
Units in process, August 31, 60% complete*	30,000

Costs:

Work in process, August 1:

Transferred-in from Department 6	$2,100
Materials	1,500
Conversion costs	3,000
Total	$6,600

Current costs:

Transferred-in from Department 6	$30,900
Materials	22,500
Conversion costs	45,300
Total	$98,700

* With respect to conversion costs

Drysdale Dairy uses weighted average costing.

Required:

1. How many units were transferred in during the month?
2. Calculate equivalent units for the following categories: transferred-in, materials, and conversion.
3. Calculate unit costs for the following categories: transferred-in, materials, and conversion. Calculate total unit cost.

6–16

Appendix: FIFO Equivalent Units; Unit Cost

LO5

Halligan Company manufactures a product in four departments. Data for the first department follow:

Production:
Units in process, July 1, 75% complete	60,000
Units completed and transferred out	150,000
Units in process, July 31, 25% complete	30,000

Costs:
Work in process, July 1	$193,500
Costs added during the month	500,625

Halligan uses FIFO costing.

Required:

1. Prepare a physical flow analysis for the first department for the month of July.
2. Calculate equivalent units of production for the first department for the month of July.
3. Calculate unit cost for materials, for conversion, and in total for the first department for the month of July.
4. Calculate the cost of units transferred out and the cost of ending work-in-process inventory for the first department.
5. Prepare a cost reconciliation for the first department for the month of July.

6–17

Appendix: FIFO Cost of Production Report

LO5

Refer to 6–16. Prepare a cost of production report for the first department of Halligan Company for the month of July.

6–18

Appendix: FIFO Method; Valuation of Goods Transferred Out and Ending Work in Process

LO5

Bijan Company uses FIFO to account for the costs of production. For the first processing department, the following equivalent-unit schedule has been prepared:

	Materials	Conversion Cost
Started and completed	45,000	45,000
Beginning work in process × Fraction to be completed:		
8,000 × 0%; 8,000 × 40%	0	3,200
Ending work in process × Fraction completed:		
16,000 × 100%; 16,000 × 75%	16,000	12,000
Equivalent units of output	61,000	60,200

The cost per equivalent unit for the period was as follows:

Materials	$1.00
Conversion cost	2.50
Total	$3.50

The cost of beginning work in process was materials, $10,000; conversion costs, $18,000.

Required:

1. Determine the cost of ending work in process and the cost of goods transferred out.
2. If possible, prepare a physical flow schedule.

6–19

Weighted Average Method; Valuation of Goods Transferred Out and Ending Work in Process

LO3

Refer to the data in 6–18.

Required:

Compute the cost of ending work in process and the cost of goods transferred out using the weighted average method.

6–20

Weighted Average Method; Unit Cost; Valuation of Goods Transferred Out and Ending Work in Process

LO3

Poston Products, Inc., produces a chemical product that passes through three departments. For the month of May, the following equivalent-unit schedule was prepared for the first department:

	Materials	Conversion Cost
Units completed	5,000	5,000
Units, ending work in process × Fraction completed:		
6,000 × 100%; 6,000 × 50%	6,000	3,000
Equivalent units of output	11,000	8,000

Costs assigned to beginning work in process were materials, $30,000; conversion, $5,000. Manufacturing costs incurred during the month of May were materials, $25,000; conversion, $65,000. Poston Products uses the weighted average method.

Required:

1. Compute the unit cost for the month of May.
2. Determine the cost of ending work in process and the cost of goods transferred out.

6–21

Appendix: FIFO Method; Unit Cost; Valuation of Goods Transferred Out and Ending Work in Process

LO5

Tolliver Company is a manufacturer that uses FIFO to account for its production costs. The product Tolliver makes passes through two processes. Tolliver's controller prepared the following equivalent-unit schedule:

	Materials	Conversion Cost
Units started and completed	8,000	8,000
Units, beginning work in process × Fraction to be completed:		
2,000 × 0%; 2,000 × 50%	0	1,000
Units, ending work in process × Fraction completed:		
4,000 × 100%; 4,000 × 25%	4,000	1,000
Equivalent units of output	12,000	10,000

Costs in beginning work in process were materials, $6,000; conversion costs, $24,000. Manufacturing costs incurred during October were materials, $72,000; conversion costs, $96,000.

Required:

1. Prepare a physical flow schedule for the month of October.
2. Compute the cost per equivalent unit for the month of October.
3. Determine the cost of ending work in process and the cost of goods transferred out.

6–22

Weighted Average Method; Equivalent Units; Unit Cost; Multiple Departments

LO2, LO3, LO4

Hogarth, Inc., manufactures a product that passes through three processes. During July, the first department transferred 12,000 units to the second department. The cost of the units transferred into the second department was $20,500. Materials are added uniformly in the second process.

The second department had the following physical flow schedule for July:

Units to account for:	
Units in beginning work in process (40% complete)	2,000
Units started	?
Total units to account for	?
Units accounted for:	
Units in ending work in process (50% complete)	4,000
Units completed	?
Total units accounted for	?

Costs in beginning work in process for the second department were materials, $3,200; conversion costs, $3,120; transferred in, $4,000. Costs added during the month were materials, $16,000; conversion costs, $24,960; transferred in, $20,500.

Required:

1. Assuming the use of the weighted average method, prepare a schedule of equivalent units.
2. Compute the unit cost for the month of July.

6–23

Appendix: FIFO Method, Equivalent Units; Unit Cost; Multiple Departments

LO2, LO4, LO5

Using the same data found in 6–22, assume that the company uses the FIFO method.

Required:

Prepare a schedule of equivalent units and compute the unit cost for the month of July.

6–24

Journal Entries; Cost of Ending Inventories

LO1

Naylor Company has two processing departments: assembly and finishing. A predetermined overhead rate of $6 per DLH is used to assign overhead to production. The company experienced the following operating activity for November:

a. Raw materials issued to assembly, $15,200
b. Direct labour cost: assembly, 550 hours at $9.50 per hour; finishing, 400 hours at $8.80 per hour
c. Overhead is applied to production
d. Goods transferred to finishing, $21,340
e. Goods transferred to finished goods warehouse, $25,500
f. Actual overhead incurred, $6,000

Required:

1. Prepare the required journal entries for these transactions.
2. Assuming that assembly and finishing have no beginning work-in-process inventories, determine the cost of each department's ending work-in-process inventories.

6–25

Process Costing, Food Manufacturing

LO1, LO2

Wholesome Bread makes and supplies bread throughout eastern Canada. Six operations describe the production process:

a. Flour, milk, yeast, salt, butter, and so on are mixed in a large vat.
b. A conveyor belt transfers the dough to a machine that weighs it and shapes into loaves.
c. The individual loaves are allowed to sit and rise.

d.   The dough is moved to a 30-metre-long funnel oven (the dough enters the oven on racks and spends 20 minutes moving slowly through the oven).
e.   The bread is removed from the oven, sucked from the pan by a vacuum, and allowed to cool.
f.   The bread is sliced and wrapped.

During one week, 4,500 loaves of bread were produced. The total cost of materials (ingredients and wrapping material) was $675. The cost of direct labour and overhead totalled $1,575. There were no beginning or ending work-in-process inventories.

Required:

1.   Compute the unit cost for the 4,500 loaves of bread produced during the week.
2.   Would Wholesome Bread ever need to worry about using the FIFO method or the weighted average method? Why or why not? What implication does this have for the food industry in general?
3.   Assume that Wholesome Bread also produces rolls and buns. Also assume that the only difference is that the machine is set to shape the dough differently. What adjustments would need to be made to cost out the three different bread products?

6–26

Weighted Average Method; Physical Flow; Equivalent Units; Unit Costs; Cost Assignment

LO1, LO2, LO3

Spreadsheet

Funnifaces, Inc., manufactures various Halloween masks. Each mask is shaped from a piece of rubber in the moulding department. The masks are then transferred to the finishing department, where they are painted and have elastic bands attached. In April, the moulding department reported the following data:

a.   In moulding, all materials are added at the beginning of the process.
b.   Beginning work in process consisted of 6,000 units, 20 percent complete with respect to direct labour and overhead. Cost in beginning inventory included direct materials, $1,800; and conversion costs, $552.
c.   Costs added to production during the month were direct materials, $3,800; and conversion costs, $8,698.
d.   At the end of the month, 18,000 units were transferred out to finishing. Then, 2,000 units remained in ending work in process, 25 percent complete.

Required:

1.   Prepare a physical flow schedule.
2.   Calculate equivalent units of production for direct materials and conversion cost.
3.   Compute unit cost.
4.   Calculate the cost of goods transferred to finishing at the end of the month. Calculate the cost of ending inventory.

6–27

Appendix: FIFO Method; Physical Flow; Equivalent Units; Unit Costs; Cost Assignment

LO5

Refer to the data in 6–26. Calculate the following using the FIFO method:

Required:

1   Prepare a physical flow schedule.
2.   Calculate equivalent units of production for direct materials and conversion cost.
3.   Compute unit cost.
4.   Calculate the cost of goods transferred to finishing at the end of the month. Calculate the cost of ending inventory.

PROBLEMS

6–28

Weighted Average Method; Single-Department Analysis; One Cost Category

LO3

Ellis Company produces a product that passes through two processes: assembly and finishing. All manufacturing costs are added uniformly for both processes. The following information was obtained for the assembly department for November:

a. Work in process, November 1, had 6,000 units (60 percent completed) and the following costs:

Direct materials	$23,282
Direct labour	8,108
Overhead applied	4,300

b. During November, 17,300 units were completed and transferred to the finishing department, and the following costs were added to production:

Direct materials	$33,440
Direct labour	35,160
Overhead applied	14,688

c. On November 30, there were 2,700 partly completed units in process. These units were 70 percent complete.

Required:

Prepare a production report for the assembly department for November using the weighted average method of costing. The report should disclose the physical flow of units, equivalent units, and unit costs and should track the disposition of manufacturing costs.

6–29

Appendix: FIFO Method; Single-Department Analysis; One Cost Category

LO5

Refer to the data in 6–28.

Required:

Prepare a production report for the assembly department for November using the FIFO method of costing. The report should contain the same schedules described in 6–28. (*Hint:* Carry the unit-cost computation to four decimal places.)

6–30

Weighted Average Method; Single-Department Analysis; Three Cost Categories

LO3

Tyrone Company produces a variety of stationery products. One product, sealing wax sticks, passes through two processes: blending and moulding. The weighted average method is used to account for production costs. Two ingredients, paraffin and pigment, are added at the beginning of the blending process and are heated and mixed for several hours. After blending, the resulting product is sent to the moulding department, where it is poured into moulds and cooled. The following information relates to the blending process for August:

a. Work in process, August 1, had 20,000 kilograms, 20 percent complete with respect to conversion costs. Costs associated with partly completed units were:

Paraffin	$12,000
Pigment	10,000
Direct labour	3,000
Overhead applied	10,000

b. Work in process, August 31, had 30,000 kilograms, 70 percent complete with respect to conversion costs.

c. Units completed and transferred out totalled 500,000 kilograms. The following costs were added during the month:

Paraffin	$ 306,000
Pigment	255,000
Direct labour	387,750
Overhead applied	129,250

Required:

1. Prepare the following: (a) a physical flow schedule, and (b) an equivalent-unit schedule with cost categories for paraffin, pigment, and conversion cost.
2. Calculate the unit cost for each cost category.
3. Compute the cost of ending work in process and the cost of goods transferred out.
4. Prepare a cost reconciliation.

6–31

Physical Flow; Equivalent Units; Unit Costs, Cost Assignment

LO3, LO4

Timepeace Company manufactures a special type of fast-drying paint. You are attempting to verify the following balances, which have been recorded on the Timepeace books at the end of the year:

	Units	Cost
Work in process	450,000	$ 991,440
Finished goods	300,000	1,514,700

Materials are added at the beginning of the manufacturing process. Overhead is applied at 50 percent of direct labour costs. There is no beginning finished goods inventory. Beginning and ending work-in-process inventories are 50 percent complete with respect to conversion costs. A physical count revealed that the ending physical units are correct.

Additional information:

		Costs	
	Units	Materials	Labour
Beginning work in process	300,000	$ 300,000	$ 472,500
Units started	1,500,000	—	—
Units completed	1,350,000	—	—
Material costs added	—	$1,950,000	—
Labour costs added	—	—	$2,992,500

Required:

1. Prepare a physical flow schedule.
2. Using the weighted average method, calculate the equivalent units of production.
3. Calculate unit costs for: (a) direct materials, (b) direct labour, and (c) applied overhead.
4. What is the total cost of units transferred out? What is the cost assigned to units in ending work-in-process inventory? What is the cost assigned to units in ending finished goods inventory?
5. Prepare the necessary journal entry to correctly state the ending inventories of finished goods and work in process, assuming that Timepeace's books have not been closed. (CGA Canada adapted)

6–32

Weighted Average Method, Production Report

LO3, LO4

The Chang Manufacturing Company makes wood-finishing stain. The production of stain begins with the blending of various chemicals and ends with the canning of the stain. Canning occurs when the mixture reaches the 90 percent stage of completion. After canning, the cans are transferred to the shipping department. Here the cans are crated and shipped to various customers. Conversion costs are added uniformly throughout the process. Overhead is applied at the rate of $4.00 per direct labour hour. The following are the actual production data for April:

April Production Costs

Work in process, April 1:
Direct materials—chemicals	$ 68,400
Direct labour ($15 per hour)	18,750
Applied overhead	5,000

Costs added in April:
Direct materials—chemicals	342,600
Direct materials—cans	10,500
Direct labour ($15 per hour)	105,000
Applied overhead	28,000

Units for April:
Work-in-process inventory, April 1 (25% complete)	8,000 litres
Transferred to shipping department during April	40,000 litres
Started during April	42,000 litres
Work-in-process inventory, April 30 (80% complete)	10,000 litres

Required:

Prepare a production report using the weighted average method.
(CGA Canada adapted)

6–33

Appendix: FIFO Method, Production Report

LO4, LO5

Using the same data as in 6–32, assume that Chang uses the FIFO method.

Required:

1. Prepare a production report using the FIFO method.
2. What are the advantages and disadvantages of using the weighted average method versus the FIFO method? Under what circumstances is it appropriate to use each method? (CGA Canada adapted)

6–34

Weighted Average Method; Single-Department Analysis; Transferred-In Goods

LO3, LO4

Keating Company manufactures a product that passes through three departments. In Department C, materials are added at the end of the process. Conversion costs are incurred uniformly throughout the process. During January, Department C received 20,000 units from Department B. The transferred-in cost of the 20,000 units was $70,350.

The following costs were added by Department C during January:

Direct materials	$40,635
Direct labour	58,500
Overhead applied	29,400

On January 1, Department C had 4,000 units in inventory; these units were 30 percent complete with respect to conversion costs. On January 31, 3,000 units were in inventory, one-third complete with respect to conversion costs. The costs associated with the 4,000 units in beginning inventory were as follows:

Transferred in	$14,970
Direct labour	7,560
Overhead applied	4,200

Required:

Prepare a production report using the weighted average method. In preparing the report, follow the five steps outlined in this chapter.

6–35

Appendix: FIFO Method; Single-Department Analysis; Transferred-In Goods

LO4, LO5

Merrifield, Inc., manufactures a single product that passes through several processes. During the first quarter of the year, the mixing department received 45,000 litres of liquid from the cooking department (transferred in at $28,800). Upon receiving the liquid, the mixing department adds a powder and allows blending to take place for 30 minutes. The product is then passed on to the bottling department.

There were 9,000 litres in process at the beginning of the quarter, 75 percent complete with respect to conversion costs. The costs attached to the beginning inventory were as follows:

Transferred in	$5,700
Powder	804
Conversion costs	1,800

Costs added by the mixing department during the first quarter were as follows:

Powder	$4,200
Conversion costs	9,080

There were 7,875 litres in ending inventory, 20 percent complete with respect to conversion costs.

Required:

Prepare a production report using the FIFO method. In preparing the report, follow the five steps outlined in this chapter. Carry unit costs out to three decimal places. Round to the nearest dollar in the production report.

6–36

Weighted Average Method, Transferred-In Goods

LO3, LO4

Refer to 6–35.

Required:

Prepare a production report for the mixing department using the weighted average method.

6–37

Weighted Average Method, Journal Entries

LO1, LO3

Seacrest Company uses a process-costing system. The company manufactures a product that is processed in two departments, A and B. In Department A, materials are added at the beginning of the process; in Department B, additional materials are added at the end of the process. In both departments, conversion costs are incurred uniformly throughout the process. As work is completed, it is transferred out. The following summarizes the production activity and cost for November:

	Department A	Department B
Beginning inventories:		
Physical units	5,000	8,000
Costs:		
Transferred in	—	$45,320
Direct materials	$10,000	—
Conversion costs	$6,900	$16,800

Current production:	Department A	Department B
Units started	25,000	?
Units transferred out	28,000	33,000
Costs:		
Transferred in	—	?
Direct materials	$57,800	$37,950
Conversion costs	$95,220	$128,100
Percentage completion:		
Beginning inventory	40%	50%
Ending inventory	80%	50%

Required:

1. Using the weighted average method, prepare the following for Department A:
   a. A physical flow schedule
   b. An equivalent-units calculation
   c. Calculation of unit costs
   d. Cost of ending work in process and cost of goods transferred out
   e. A cost reconciliation
2. Prepare journal entries that show the flow of manufacturing costs for Department A.
3. Repeat Requirements 1 and 2 for Department B.

6–38

Appendix: FIFO Method, Two-Department Analysis

LO4, LO5

Refer to the data in 6–37.

Required:
Repeat the Requirements in 6–37 using the FIFO method.

6–39

Weighted Average Method, Two-Department Analysis

LO3, LO4

Benson Pharmaceuticals uses a process-costing system to compute the unit costs of the over-the-counter cold remedies that it produces. It has three departments: picking, encapsulating, and bottling. In picking, the ingredients for the cold capsules are measured, sifted, and blended. The mix is transferred out in litre containers. The encapsulating department takes the powdered mix and places it in capsules. One litre of powdered mix converts into 1,500 capsules. After the capsules are filled and polished, they are transferred to bottling where they are placed in bottles, which are then affixed with a safety seal and a lid and labelled. Each bottle receives 50 capsules.

During March, the following results are available for the first two departments:

	Picking	**Encapsulating**
Beginning inventories:		
Physical units	10 litres	4,000
Costs:		
Materials	$252	$ 32
Labour	$282	$ 20
Overhead applied	$?	$?
Transferred in	—	$ 140
Current production:		
Transferred out	140 litres	208,000
Ending inventory	20 litres	6,000
Costs:		
Materials	$3,636	$1,573
Labour	$4,618	$1,944
Overhead applied	$?	$?
Transferred in	—	$?

	Picking	**Encapsulating**
Percentage of completion:		
Beginning inventory	40%	50%
Ending inventory	50%	40%

Overhead in both departments is applied as a percentage of direct labour costs. In the picking department, overhead is 200 percent of direct labour. In the encapsulating department, the overhead rate is 150 percent of direct labour.

Required:

1. Prepare a production report for the picking department using the weighted average method. Follow the five steps outlined in this chapter.
2. Prepare a production report for the encapsulating department. Follow the five steps outlined in this chapter.

6–40

Appendix: FIFO Method, Two-Department Analysis

LO4, LO5

Refer to the data in 6–39.

Required:

Prepare a production report for each department using the FIFO method.

6–41

Weighted Average Method, Multiple-Department Analysis

LO3, LO4

Strathmore, Inc., manufactures educational toys using a weighted average process-costing system. Plastic is moulded into the appropriate shapes in the moulding department. Moulded components are transferred to the assembly department, where the toys are assembled and additional materials (for example, fasteners, decals) are applied. Completed toys are then transferred to the packaging department, where each toy is boxed.

Strathmore showed the following data on toy production for February:

	Moulding	Assembly	Packaging
Beginning inventory:			
Units	500	—	150
Costs:			
Prior department	—	—	$1,959.00
Direct materials	$2,500.00	—	$ 375.00
Conversion cost	$1,050.00	—	$ 225.00
Started or transferred in:			
Units	1,000	?	?
February costs:			
Prior department	—	$14,950.00	$11,754.00
Direct materials	$5,000.00	$ 487.60	$ 2,407.50
Conversion cost	$7,660.00	$ 1,166.00	$ 2,977.50
Ending inventory, units	200	400	—

Beginning and ending work in process for the three departments showed the following degree of completion:

	Moulding	Assembly	Packaging
Degree of completion:			
BWIP, direct materials	100%	—	100%
BWIP, conversion costs	30%	—	50%
EWIP, direct materials	100%	40%	—
EWIP, conversion costs	20%	40%	—

Required:

1. Prepare a physical flow schedule for February for each of the following:
   a. Moulding department
   b. Assembly department
   c. Packaging department
2. Compute equivalent units of production for direct materials and for conversion costs for each of the following:

a. Moulding department
b. Assembly department
c. Packaging department

3. Complete the following unit-cost chart:

	Moulding	Assembly	Packaging
Unit prior-department cost*			
Unit direct material cost			
Unit conversion cost	_____	_____	_____
Total unit cost			

* Cost transferred in from prior department

4. Determine the cost of ending work in process and the cost of goods transferred out for each of the three departments.
5. Reconcile the costs for each department.

6–42

Appendix: FIFO Method, Multiple-Department Analysis

LO4, LO5

Refer to the data in 6–41.

Required:
Repeat Requirements 2 through 5 using the FIFO method.

6–43

Production Report

LO3

Susan Manners, cost accountant for Lean Jeans, Inc., spent the weekend completing a production report for the inspection department for the month of December. Inspection is the final department in the production of fashion jeans. In that department, each pair of jeans is carefully inspected for quality workmanship. At the end of the inspection process, a slip of paper with "Inspected by _____" is slipped into a back pocket; then the jeans are placed in a bin to be transferred to finished goods.

First thing Monday morning, Susan returned to work and found that someone had accidentally spilled coffee on her report, partly obliterating some of the figures. Susan has only one hour to reconstruct her report.

Inspection Department
Production Report
For the Month of December
(Weighted Average Method)

UNIT INFORMATION

Units to account for:	
Beginning inventory	?
Transferred in from assembly	4,000
Total units to account for	4,700

	Equivalent Units			
	Physical Flow	Prior Department	Materials	Conversion Costs
Units accounted for:				
Units completed	?	?	?	?
Units in ending WIP	900	?	—	?
Total units accounted for	4,700	?	3,800	4,250

COST INFORMATION

	Prior Department	Materials	Cost Conversion	Total
Costs to account for:				
Beginning WIP	$11,900	?	$ 210	$12,110
Incurred in December	?	?	4,040	72,097
Total cost to account for	$79,900	$57	$4,250	$84,207
Unit cost	$17.00	?	$1.00	?

	Transferred Out	Ending WIP	Total
Costs accounted for:			
Goods transferred out	?	—	?
Ending inventory:			
Prior department	—	?	?
Materials	—	—	—
Conversion cost	—	?	?
Total costs accounted for	$?	$15,750	$84,207

Required:

Help Susan meet the deadline by filling in the appropriate number for each question mark.

6–44

Weighted Average Method, Incomplete Records

LO3, LO4

Wentworth Processing manufactures a single product in a continuous processing environment. All materials are added at the beginning of the process, and conversion costs are applied uniformly throughout the process. Wentworth has perfected its process to the point that no spoilage occurs. To assign costs to inventories, the company uses weighted average process costing.

During a recent conversion from a manual to a computerized system, Wentworth used a number of part-time clerks to enter data into the new system. As a result of inadequate supervision, certain records were misplaced, causing some accounting information for 2001 to be incomplete. As the accounting supervisor, you must piece together the information to produce the financial reports for 2001. The following information was found on a scrap of paper wedged under the computer:

Wentworth Processing Information for 2001

Sales (selling price per unit, $40)	$4,080,000
Actual manufacturing overhead	660,000
Selling and administrative expenses	328,000
Unit costs of production:	
Direct materials (1 kilogram)	$ 5.00
Direct labour (1/2 hour)	6.00
Overhead	9.00
Total	$20.00
Units transferred to finished goods	140,000 units
Materials purchased	125,000 kilograms
Materials used in process	136,000 kilograms

An inventory count at year end (December 31, 2001) revealed that the inventories had the following balances in units:

Raw materials	8,000 kilograms
Work in process (35% complete)	22,000 units
Finished goods	45,000 units

No record of the opening balance of raw materials or finished goods could be found. Although the January 1, 2001, balance of physical units in work in process was unavailable, it was known that those units were 60 percent complete. The unit cost of production was the same in 2001 as it was in 2000.

Required:

Given the preceding information, calculate the following amounts for Wentworth Processing:

1. The opening (January 1, 2001) balance in units and costs of (a) raw materials, (b) work in process, and (c) finished goods.
2. Equivalent units for 2001 for (a) materials and (b) conversion costs.
3. Total cost for 2001 for (a) materials used and (b) conversion applied.
4. Cost of ending work in process, 2001.
5. Cost of units completed and transferred. (CMA Canada adapted)

MANAGERIAL DECISION CASES

6–45

Production Report, Ethical Behaviour

LO3

Consider the following conversation between Gary Means, manager of a division that produces industrial machinery and his controller, Donna Simpson, a CMA and CA:

Gary: "Donna, we have a real problem. Our operating cash is too low, and we are in desperate need of a loan. As you know, our financial position is marginal, and we need to show as much income as possible—and our assets need bolstering as well."

Donna: "I understand the problem, but I don't see what can be done at this point. This is the last week of the fiscal year, and it looks like we'll report income just slightly above breakeven."

Gary: "I know all this. What we need is some creative accounting. I have an idea that might help us, and I wanted to see if you would go along with it. We have 200 partly finished machines in process, about 20 percent complete. That compares with the 1,000 units that we completed and sold during the year. When you computed the per-unit cost, you used 1,040 equivalent units, giving us a manufacturing cost of $1,500 per unit. That per-unit cost gives us cost of goods sold equal to $1.5 million and ending work in process worth $60,000. The presence of the work in process gives us a chance to improve our financial position. If we report the units in work in process as 80 percent complete, this will increase our equivalent units to 1,160. This, in turn, will decrease our unit cost to about $1,345 and cost of goods sold to $1.345 million. The value of our work in process will increase to $215,200. With those financial stats, getting the loan would be a cinch."

Donna: "Gary, I don't know. What you're suggesting is risky. It wouldn't take much auditing skill to catch this one."

Gary: "You don't have to worry about that. The auditors won't be here for at least six to eight more weeks. By that time, we can have those partly completed units completed and sold. I can bury the labour cost by having some of our loyal employees work overtime for some bonuses. The overtime will never be reported. And as you know, bonuses come out of the corporate budget and are assigned to overhead—next year's overhead. Donna, this will work. If we look good and get the loan to boot, corporate headquarters will treat us well. If we don't do this, we could lose our jobs."

Required:

1. Should Donna agree to Gary's proposal? Why or why not? To assist in deciding, review the standards of ethical conduct for management accountants described in Chapter 1. Do any apply?
2. Assume that Donna refuses to cooperate and that Gary accepts this decision and drops the matter. Does Donna have any obligation to report the divisional manager's behaviour to a superior? Explain.
3. Assume that Donna refuses to cooperate; however, Gary insists that the changes be made. Now what should she do? What would *you* do?
4. Suppose that Donna is 63 and that the prospects for employment elsewhere are bleak. Assume again that Gary insists that the changes should be made. Donna also knows that his supervisor, the owner of the company, is his father-in-law. Under these circumstances, would your recommendations for Donna differ? If you were Donna, what would you do?

6–46

Process Costing versus Alternative Costing Methods, Impact on Resource Allocation Decision

LO1, LO3

Golding Manufacturing, a division of Farnsworth Sporting, Inc., produces two different models of bows and eight models of knives. The bow-manufacturing process involves the production of two major subassemblies: the limbs and the handle. The limbs pass through four sequential processes before reaching final assembly: layup, moulding, fabricating, and finishing. In the layup department, limbs are created by laminating layers of wood. In moulding, the limbs are heat-treated, under pressure, to form a strong, resilient limb. In the fabricating department, any protruding glue or other processing residue is removed. Finally, in finishing, the limbs are cleaned with acetone, dried, and sprayed with the final finishes.

The handles pass through two processes before reaching final assembly: pattern and finishing. In the pattern department, blocks of wood are fed into a machine that is set to shape the handles. Different patterns are possible, depending on the machine's setting. After coming out of the machine, the handles are cleaned and smoothed. They then pass to the finishing department, where they are sprayed with the final finishes. In final assembly, the limbs and handles are assembled into different models using purchased parts such as pulley assemblies, weight adjustment bolts, side plates, and string.

Since its inception, Golding has used process costing to assign product costs. A predetermined overhead rate is used, based on direct labour dollars (80 percent of direct labour dollars). Recently, Golding hired a new controller, Karen Jenkins. After reviewing the product-costing procedures, Karen requested a meeting with the divisional manager, Aaron Suhr. The following is a transcript of their conversation.

Karen: "Aaron, I have some concerns about our cost accounting system. We make two different models of bows and are treating them as if they were the same product. Now I know that the only real difference between the models is the handle. The processing of the handles is the same, but the handles differ significantly in the amount and quality of wood used. Our current costing does not reflect this difference in material input."

Aaron: "Your predecessor is responsible. He believed that tracking the difference in material cost wasn't worth the effort. He simply didn't believe that it would make much difference in the unit cost of either model."

Karen: "Well, he may have been right, but I have my doubts. If there is a significant difference, it could affect our views of which model is the more important to the company. The additional bookkeeping isn't very stringent. All we have to worry about is the pattern department. The other departments fit what I view as a process-costing pattern."

Aaron: "Why don't you look into it? If there is a significant difference, go ahead and adjust the costing system."

After the meeting, Karen decided to collect cost data on the two models: the Deluxe model and the Econo model. She tracked the costs for one week. At the end of the week, she had collected the following data from the pattern department:

a. There were a total of 2,500 bows completed: 1,000 Deluxe models and 1,500 Econo models.
b. There was no beginning work in process; however, there were 300 units in ending work in process: 200 Deluxe and 100 Econo models. Both models were 80 percent complete with respect to conversion costs and 100 percent complete with respect to materials.
c. The pattern department experienced the following costs:

Direct materials	$114,000
Direct labour	45,667

d. On an experimental basis, the requisition forms for materials were modified to identify the dollar value of the materials used by the Econo and Deluxe models:

Econo model	$30,000
Deluxe model	84,000

Required:

1. Compute the unit cost for the handles produced by the pattern department, assuming that process costing is totally appropriate.
2. Compute the unit cost of each handle using the separate cost information provided on materials.
3. Compare the unit costs computed in Requirements 1 and 2. Is Karen justified in her belief that a pure process-costing approach is not appropriate? Describe the costing system that you would recommend.
4. In the past, the marketing manager has requested more money for advertising the Econo line. Aaron has repeatedly refused to grant any increase in this product's advertising budget because its per-unit profit (selling price less manufacturing cost) is so low. Given the results in Requirements 1 through 3, was Aaron justified in his position?

RESEARCH ASSIGNMENT

6–47

Cybercase

LO1, LO4

Go to the Web site for Crayola, Inc. (**www.crayola.com**). There is a "factory tour" that you can take. Take the factory tours for both crayons and markers. List the departments for each product. Trace the flow of costs through each department to come up with a listing of total manufacturing costs for each of the finished products.

CHAPTER 7

Support Department Cost Allocation

Learning Objectives

After studying Chapter 7, you should be able to:

1. Describe the difference between support departments and producing departments.

2. Calculate single charging rates for a support department.

3. Allocate support-department costs to producing departments using the direct, sequential, and reciprocal methods.

4. Calculate departmental overhead rates.

Scenario

Hamilton and Barry, a large regional public accounting firm, consists of three major departments: audit, tax, and management advisory services (MAS). Gary Premark, head of management advisory services, is talking with Jan McAndrews, partner in charge.

Jan: "So far, this has been a good year for MAS, Gary. We're very pleased with the way you increased your client base and billing hours. Our only remaining problem is profitability. As you can see, the total costs of your department rose at a faster pace last year than the year before."

Gary: "My profitability is just fine—or would be if I weren't forced to use the inefficient services of this firm. Look at my photocopying costs! These are way out of line! I'd be better off using Kopykats a block away."

Jan: "Gary, as you know, we went to an in-house photocopying department to provide convenience and security. If it costs a little more, so be it. Besides, the convenience of just walking down the hall to get your reports and bids copied outweighs any small increase in cost allocation."

Gary: "Look, Jan, I don't mind paying a little extra for convenience, but this allocation is much more than a little extra. My department's

going to boycott photocopying until this problem gets resolved."

Jan: "Don't take that step just yet. Carol Morton is in charge of photocopying. Let's get some answers from her first."

Two days later Gary, Jan, and Carol Morton, executive assistant in charge of the photocopying service, meet in Jan's office.

Carol: "Gary, I understand you have some questions about the way photocopying is run. Let me assure you that we work very hard to keep costs down while providing topnotch service. Your department was charged only for the copies you made."

Gary: "Carol, I took my total cost allocation and divided by the number of copies. Do you realize that it comes to $0.12 per page? Why is your department so much higher than outside services?"

Carol: "Gary, you have to realize that we bought machinery for peak usage. In our firm, that's the month of April—when Tax runs most of its copies. Other months are slower, but I can't trade in the copier on a month-to-month basis. Also, we need at least one person ready to handle your copies or you'll really hit the ceiling. As a result, the per-page charges are higher."

Gary: "I think I'm beginning to see what's happening. Still, I'd like to explore different charging systems."

Jan: "If there's a problem here, it's a firmwide problem. I can assign Cynthia Bowles, our firm's new co-op student from the University of Regina, to take this on as a special project."

Questions to Think About

1. Why do you think that the copying department charges amount to $0.12 per page? List the types of costs incurred for photocopying, and divide them into fixed and variable categories.

2. Jan mentioned the security and convenience of in-house photo-copying. How do you think the firm might weigh these factors in deciding whether or not the cost of in-house copying is "worth it"?

3. Since the firm as a whole has decided to have an in-house copying department, why are copying costs charged to the individual departments? What purpose does the practice of developing support depart-ment charging rates serve?

In earlier chapters, we focused on product costs and the way they are assigned to products. The complexity of many modern firms leads the accountant to focus on the assignment of overhead. In Chapter 4, we studied a variety of ways to assign overhead: plantwide rates, departmental rates, and activity-based costing. In this chapter, we explain further the way that support department costs are assigned to producing departments for the calculation of departmental overhead rates.

Allocation is simply a means of dividing a pool of cost and assigning it to various subunits. It is important to realize that allocation does not affect the total cost. Total cost is neither reduced nor increased by allocation. However, the amounts of cost assigned to the subunits can be affected by the allocation procedure chosen. Because cost allocation can affect bid prices, the profitability of individual products, and the behaviour of managers, it is an important topic.

AN OVERVIEW OF COST ALLOCATION

Objective 1

Describe the difference between support departments and producing departments.

Mutually beneficial costs, which occur when the same resource is used in the output of two or more services or products, are called **common costs**. While these common costs may pertain to periods of time, individual responsibilities, sales territories, and classes of customers, this chapter will concentrate on the costs common to departments and to products. For example, the wages paid to security guards at a factory are a common cost of all of the different products manufactured there. The benefits of security are applicable to each product, yet the assignment of security cost to the individual products is an arbitrary process. In other words, while it is clear that the products (or services) require the common resource, and that the resource cost should be assigned to these cost objects, it is often unclear how best to go about assigning the cost. Usually, common cost assignment is made through a series of consistent allocation procedures.

Types of Departments

The first step in cost allocation is to determine just what the cost objects are. In the functional model, they are departments. There are two categories of departments: producing departments and support departments. **Producing departments** are directly responsible for creating the products or services sold to customers. In the opening scenario's public accounting firm, examples of producing departments are auditing, tax, and management advisory services. In a manufacturing setting, producing departments are those that work directly on the products being manufactured (for example, grinding and assembly). **Support departments** provide essential support services for producing departments. These departments are indirectly connected with an organization's services or products. Examples include maintenance, grounds, engineering, housekeeping, personnel, and stores. Of course, the Hamilton and Barry photocopying department is a support department.

Once the producing and support departments have been identified, the overhead costs incurred by each department can be determined. Note that this involves tracing costs to the departments, not allocating costs, because the costs are directly associated with the individual department. A factory cafeteria, for example, would have food costs, salaries of cooks and servers, amortization on dishwashers and stoves, and supplies (for example, napkins, plastic forks). Overhead directly associated with a producing department, such as assembly in a furniture-making plant, would include utilities (if measured in that department), supervisory salaries, and amortization on equipment used in that department. Overhead that cannot be easily assigned to a producing or support department is assigned to a catchall department, such as general factory. General factory might include amortization on the factory building, rental of a Santa Claus suit for the factory Christmas party, the cost of restriping the factory parking lot, the plant manager's salary, and telephone service. In this way, all costs are assigned to a department.

Exhibit 7–1

Examples of Departmentalization for a Manufacturing Firm and a Service Firm

MANUFACTURING FIRM: FURNITURE MAKER	
Producing Departments	**Support Departments**
Assembly	Materials storeroom
Supervisory salaries	Clerk's salary
Small tools	Amortization on forklift
Indirect materials	Cafeteria
Amortization on machinery	Food
Finishing	Cooks' salaries
Sandpaper	Amortization on stoves
Amortization on sanders and buffers	Maintenance
	Janitors' salaries
	Cleaning supplies
	Machine oil and lubricants
	General factory
	Amortization on building
	Security and utilities

SERVICE FIRM: BANK	
Producing Departments	**Support Departments**
Auto loans	Drive through
Loan processors' salaries	Tellers' salaries
Forms and supplies	Amortization on equipment
Commercial lending	Data processing
Lending officers' salaries	Personnel salaries
Amortization on office equipment	Software
Bankruptcy prediction software	Amortization on hardware
Personal banking	Bank administration
Supplies and postage for statements	Salary of CEO
	Receptionist's salary
	Telephone costs
	Amortization on bank vault

Exhibit   7–2

Steps in Allocating
Support-Department
Costs to Producing
Departments

1. Departmentalize the firm.
2. Classify each department as a support or producing department.
3. Trace all overhead costs in the firm to a support department or producing department.
4. Allocate support-department costs to the producing departments.
5. Calculate predetermined overhead rates for producing departments.
6. Allocate overhead costs to the units of individual products through the predetermined overhead rates.

Exhibit 7–1 shows how a manufacturing firm and a service firm can be divided into producing and support departments. The manufacturing plant, which makes furniture, may be departmentalized into two producing departments (assembly and finishing) and four support departments (materials storeroom, cafeteria, maintenance, and general factory). The service firm, a bank, might be departmentalized into three producing departments (auto loans, commercial lending, and personal banking) and three support departments (drive through, data processing, and bank administration). Overhead costs are traced to each department. Note that each kind of factory or service overhead cost must be assigned to one, and only one, department.

Once the company has been departmentalized, and all overhead costs have been traced to the individual departments, support-department costs are assigned to producing departments and overhead rates are developed to cost product. Although support departments do not work directly on the products or services that are sold, the costs of providing these support services are part of the total product costs and must be assigned to the products. This assignment of costs consists of a two-stage allocation: (1) allocation of support-department costs to producing departments, and (2) assignment of these allocated costs to individual products. The second-stage allocation, achieved through the use of departmental overhead rates, is necessary because there are multiple products being worked on in each producing department. If there were only one product within a producing department, all the support service costs allocated to that department would belong to that product. Recall that a predetermined overhead rate is computed by taking total estimated overhead for a department and dividing it by an estimate of an appropriate base. Now we see that a producing department's overhead consists of two parts: overhead directly traced to a producing department, and overhead allocated to the producing department from the support departments. A support department cannot have an overhead rate that assigns overhead costs to units produced, because it does not make a salable product. That is, products do not pass through support departments. The purpose of support departments is to service producing departments, not the products that pass through the producing departments. For example, maintenance personnel repair and maintain the equipment in the assembly department, not the furniture that is assembled in that department. Exhibit 7–2 summarizes the steps involved.

Types of Allocation Bases

Producing departments cause services; therefore, the costs of support departments are also caused by the activities of the producing departments. **Causal factors** are variables or activities within a producing department that provoke the incurrence of support service costs. In choosing a basis for allocating support-department costs, every effort should be made to identify appropriate causal factors (cost drivers). Using causal factors results in product costs' being more accurate; furthermore, if the causal factors are known, managers are more able to control the consumption of support services.

To illustrate the types of cost drivers that can be used, consider the following three support departments: power, personnel, and materials handling. For power

Exhibit 7-3

Examples of Possible Cost Drivers for Support Departments

Accounting
　Number of transactions

Cafeteria
　Number of employees

Data processing
　Number of lines entered
　Number of hours of service

Engineering
　Number of change orders
　Number of hours

Maintenance
　Machine hours
　Maintenance hours

Materials storeroom
　Number of material moves
　Kilograms of material moved
　Number of different parts

Payroll
　Number of employees

Personnel
　Number of employees
　Number of firings or layoffs
　Number of new hires
　Direct labour cost

Power
　Kilowatt-hours
　Machine hours

Purchasing
　Number of orders
　Cost of orders

Shipping
　Number of orders

costs, a logical allocation base is kilowatt-hours, which can be measured by separate meters for each department. If separate meters do not exist, perhaps machine hours used by each department would provide a good proxy, or means of approximating power usage. For personnel costs, both the number of producing-department employees and the labour turnover (for example, number of new hires) are possible cost drivers. For materials handling, the number of material moves, the hours of material handling used, and the quantity of material moved are all possible cost drivers. Exhibit 7–3 lists some possible cost drivers that can be used to allocate support-department costs. When competing cost drivers exist, managers need to assess which provides the most convincing relationship.

While the use of a causal factor to allocate common cost is the best, sometimes an easily measured causal factor cannot be found. In that case, the accountant looks for a good proxy. For example, the common cost of plant amortization may be allocated to producing departments on the basis of area occupied. Area occupied does not cause amortization; however, it can be argued that the area occupied by a department is a good proxy for the services provided to it by the factory building. The choice of a good proxy to guide allocation depends on the company's objectives for allocation.

Objectives of Allocation

A number of important objectives are associated with the allocation of support-department costs to producing departments and ultimately to specific products. In a study of cost allocation, Atkinson surveyed practice in Canada and the literature related to allocation. He found that the goals served by allocations, including the allocation of costs of support departments, are diverse, covering such economic and managerial purposes as coordination of decisions and motivation and evaluation of decision makers.[1] These purposes parallel the conceptual themes introduced in Chapter 1 of managerial decisions and planning and control systems. It is critical to keep these themes in mind while you study the issues of cost accumulation and cost

1.　See A. A. Atkinson, *Intra-firm Cost and Resource Allocations: Theory and Practice* (Toronto: The Canadian Academic Accounting Association, 1987).

determination involving support departments. This view is also reflected in the following objectives that have been identified by the IMA.[2]

1. To obtain a mutually agreeable price
2. To compute product-line profitability
3. To predict the economic effects of planning and control
4. To value inventory
5. To motivate managers

Competitive pricing requires an understanding of costs. Only by knowing the costs of each service or product can the firm create meaningful bids. If costs are not accurately allocated, the costs of some services could be overstated, resulting in bids that are too high and a loss of potential business. Alternatively, if the costs are understated, bids could be too low, producing losses on these services.

Good estimates of individual product costs also allow a manager to assess the profitability of individual products and services. Multiproduct companies need to be sure that all products are profitable, and that the firm's overall profitability is not disguising the poor performance of individual products.

By assessing the profitability of various services, a manager may evaluate the mix of services offered by the firm. From this evaluation, it may be decided to drop some services, reallocate resources from one service to another, reprice certain services, or exercise greater cost control in some areas. The validity of any evaluation, however, depends to a great extent on the accuracy of the cost assignments made to individual products.

For a service organization, such as a hospital, inventory valuation is not relevant. For manufacturing organizations, however, this objective must be given special attention. Rules of financial reporting (GAAP)[3] require that both direct and indirect manufacturing costs be assigned to the products produced unless indirect costs are insignificant. The procedure of allocating support department costs to producing departments and then reassigning those costs to products going through the producing departments is in keeping with this requirement. Inventories and cost of goods sold are normally reported on a full-cost basis.

Allocations can be used to motivate managers. If the costs of support departments are not allocated to producing departments, managers may treat these support services as free and overconsume these services. Consumption of a support service may continue until the marginal benefit of the service equals zero. In reality, of course, the marginal cost of a support service is usually greater than zero. By allocating the costs and holding the managers of producing departments responsible for the economic performance of their units, the organization ensures that managers will use a support service until the marginal benefit of the service equals its cost. Thus, allocating support department costs helps each producing department select the correct level of support service consumption.

There are other behavioural benefits. Allocating support-department costs to producing departments encourages managers of those departments to monitor the performance of support departments. Since the costs of the support departments affect the economic performance of their own departments, those managers have an incentive to control support service costs through means other than simple usage of the service. We can see this happening in the opening scenario, as Gary compared the cost of in-house copying with external copy companies. If a support department is not as cost-effective as an outside source, perhaps the company should not continue to supply the support service internally. For example, many university libraries are moving toward the use of outside contractors for photocopying services. They have found

2. Statements of Management Accounting (Statement 4B), *Allocation of Service and Administrative Costs* (Montvale, N.J.: NAA, 1985). The NAA is now known as the Institute of Management Accountants (IMA).

3. Generally accepted accounting principles.

that these contractors are more cost-efficient and provide a higher level of service to library users than did the previous method of using professional librarians to make change, keep the copy machines supplied with paper, fix paper jams, and so on. This possibility of comparison should result in a more efficient internal support department. Monitoring by managers of producing departments will also encourage managers of support departments to be more sensitive to the needs of the producing departments.

Clearly, then, there are good reasons for allocating support-department costs. The validity of these reasons, however, depends on the accuracy and fairness of the cost assignments made.

In determining how to allocate support-department costs, the guideline of cost–benefit must be considered. In other words, the costs of implementing a particular allocation scheme must be compared to the benefits to be derived. As a result, companies try to use easily measured and easily understood bases for allocation.

ALLOCATING ONE DEPARTMENT'S COSTS TO ANOTHER DEPARTMENT

Objective 2

Calculate single charging rates for a support department.

Frequently, the costs of a support department are allocated to another department through the use of a charging rate. In this case, we focus on the allocation of one department's costs to other departments. For example, a company's data processing department may serve various other departments. The cost of operating the data processing department is then allocated to the user departments.

A Single Charging Rate

Let's return to the case of Hamilton and Barry, the public accounting firm from this chapter's opening scenario. Recall that the firm developed an in-house photocopying department to serve its three producing departments (audit, tax, and management advisory systems or MAS). The costs of the photocopying department include fixed costs of $26,190 per year (salaries and machine rental) and variable costs of $0.023 per page copied (paper and toner). Estimated usage (in pages) by the three producing departments is as follows:

Audit department	94,500
Tax department	67,500
MAS department	108,000
Total	270,000

If a single charging rate is used, the fixed costs of $26,190 will be combined with estimated variable costs of $6,210 (270,000 × $0.023). Total costs of $32,400 are divided by the estimated 270,000 pages to be copied, to yield a rate of $0.12 per page. The amount charged to the producing departments is solely a function of the number of pages copied. Suppose that the actual usage is audit, 92,000 pages; tax, 65,000 pages; and MAS, 115,000 pages. The total photocopying department charges would be as shown.

	Number of Pages	× Charge per Page =	Total Charges
Audit	92,000	$0.12	$11,040
Tax	65,000	0.12	7,800
MAS	115,000	0.12	13,800
Total	272,000		$32,640

Notice that the use of a single rate results in the fixed cost being treated as if it were variable. In fact, to the producing departments, photocopying is strictly variable. Did the photocopying department need $32,640 to copy 272,000 pages? No, it needed only $32,446 [$26,190 + (272,000 × $0.023)]. The extra amount charged is due to the treatment of a fixed cost in a variable manner.[4]

Budgeted versus Actual Usage

When we allocate support-department costs to the producing departments, should we allocate actual or budgeted costs? The answer is budgeted costs. There are two basic reasons for allocating support-department costs. One is to assign costs to the units produced. In this case, the budgeted support-department costs are allocated to producing departments as a preliminary step in forming the overhead rate. Recall that the overhead rate is calculated at the beginning of the period, when actual costs are not known. Thus, budgeted costs must be used. The second usage of allocated support-department costs is for performance evaluation. In this case, too, budgeted support-department costs are allocated to producing departments.

Managers of support and producing departments are usually held accountable for the performance of their units. Their ability to control costs is an important factor in their performance evaluation. This ability is usually measured by comparing actual costs with planned or budgeted costs. If actual costs exceed budgeted costs, the department may be operating inefficiently, with the difference between the two costs the measure of that inefficiency. Similarly, if actual costs are less than budgeted costs, the unit may be operating efficiently.

A general principle of performance evaluation is that managers should not be held responsible for costs or activities over which they have no control. Since managers of producing departments have significant input regarding the level of support service consumed, they should be held responsible for their share of service costs. This statement, however, has an important qualification: a department's evaluation should not be affected by the degree of efficiency achieved by another department.

This qualifying statement has an important implication for the allocation of support-department costs. Actual costs of a support department should not be allocated to producing departments, because they include efficiencies or inefficiencies achieved by the support department. Managers of producing departments have no control over the degree of efficiency achieved by a support-department manager. By allocating budgeted costs instead of actual costs, no inefficiencies or efficiencies are transferred from one department to another.

Whether budgeted usage or actual usage is used depends on the purpose of the allocation. For product costing, the allocation is done at the beginning of the year on the basis of budgeted usage so that a predetermined overhead rate can be computed. If the purpose is performance evaluation, however, the allocation is done at the end of the period and is based on actual usage. The use of cost information for performance evaluation is covered in more detail in a later chapter.

Let's return to our photocopying example. Recall that annual budgeted fixed costs were $26,190, and the budgeted variable cost per page was $0.023. The three producing departments—audit, tax, and MAS—estimated usage at 94,500 copies, 67,500 copies, and 108,000 copies, respectively. Given these data, we show the cost allocated to each department at the beginning of the year in Exhibit 7–4.

When the allocation is done for the purpose of budgeting the producing departments' costs, then of course the budgeted support-department costs are used. The photocopying costs allocated to each department would be added to other producing-department costs, including those directly traceable to each department plus other support-department allocations, to compute each department's anticipated spending. In a manufacturing plant, the allocation of budgeted support-department costs to the producing departments would precede the calculation of the predetermined overhead rate.

---

4. Note that the photocopying department would have charged out less than the cost needed if the number of pages copied had been less than the budgeted number of pages. You might calculate the total cost charged for 268,000 pages ($0.12 × 268,000 = $32,160) and compare it with the cost incurred of $32,354 [$26,190 + ($0.023 × 268,000)].

Exhibit   7–4

Use of Budgeted Data
for Product Costing

	Number of Copies	×	Total Rate	=	Allocated Cost
Audit	94,500		$0.12		$11,340
Tax	67,500		0.12		8,100
MAS	108,000		0.12		12,960
Total	270,000				$32,400

During the year, each producing department would also be responsible for actual charges incurred based on the actual number of pages copied. Going back to the actual usage assumed previously, we now make a second allocation to measure the actual performance of each department against its budget. The actual photocopying costs allocated to each department for performance evaluation purposes are shown in Exhibit 7–5.

Exhibit   7–5

Use of Actual Data for
Performance Evaluation
Purposes

	Number of Copies	×	Total Rate	=	Allocated Cost
Audit	92,000		$0.12		$11,040
Tax	65,000		0.12		7,800
MAS	115,000		0.12		13,800
Total	272,000				$32,640

Dual Charging Rates

While the use of a single rate is simple, it ignores the differential impact of changes in usage on costs. The variable costs of a support department increase as the level of support service increases. For example, the cost of paper and toner for the photocopying department increases as the number of pages copied increases. Fixed costs, on the other hand, do not vary with the level of support service. For example, the rental payment for photocopying machines does not change as the number of pages increases or decreases. The use of a single charging rate makes a support department's fixed costs appear variable to the user department, because the cost charged will vary directly with the amount of support service used. We can avoid the treatment of fixed costs as variable by developing two rates: one for fixed costs and one for variable costs. Often fixed support service costs are assigned using rates based on the long-term needs of the producing departments. Either the normal activity or the peak activity of the producing departments provides reasonable measures of original service needs. Variable costs are assigned based on usage, either budgeted or actual.

CHOOSING A SUPPORT DEPARTMENT COST ALLOCATION METHOD

Objective 3

Allocate support-
department costs to
producing depart-
ments using the
direct, sequential, and
reciprocal methods.

So far, we have considered cost allocation from one support department to several producing departments. We used the direct method of support department cost allocation, in which support-department costs are allocated only to producing departments. This was appropriate in the earlier example because no other support departments existed, and there was no possibility of interaction among support departments. Many companies, however, have multiple support departments, and they frequently interact. For example, in a factory, personnel and cafeteria serve each other and other support departments as well as the producing departments.

Ignoring these interactions and allocating service costs directly to producing departments may produce unfair and inaccurate cost assignments. For example, power, although a support department, may use 30 percent of the services of the maintenance department. The maintenance costs caused by the power department belong to the power department. Unless these costs are assigned to the power department, its costs are understated. In effect, some of the costs caused by power are "hidden" in the maintenance department, because maintenance costs would be lower if the power department did not exist. As a result, a producing department that is a heavy user of power and an average or below-average user of maintenance may then receive, under the direct method, a cost allocation that is understated.

In determining which support department cost allocation method to use, companies must determine the extent of support-department interaction. In addition, they must weigh the costs and benefits associated with three methods of allocating costs. In the next three sections, the direct, sequential, and reciprocal methods are described and illustrated.

Direct Method of Allocation

When companies allocate support-department costs only to the producing departments, they are using the **direct method** of allocation. The direct method is the simplest and most straightforward way to allocate support-department costs. Variable support service costs are allocated directly to producing departments in proportion to each department's usage of the service. Fixed costs are also allocated directly to the producing department, but in proportion to the producing department's normal or practical capacity.

Exhibit 7–6 illustrates the lack of support-department reciprocity on cost allocation using the direct method. In Exhibit 7–6, we see that by using the direct method,

Exhibit 7–6

Allocation of Support-Department Costs to Producing Departments: Direct Method

Suppose there are two support departments, power and maintenance, and two producing departments, grinding and assembly, each with a "bucket" of directly traceable overhead cost.
Objective: Distribute all maintenance and power costs to grinding and assembly using the direct method.

Direct method—Allocate maintenance and power costs only to grinding and assembly.

After allocation—zero cost in maintenance and power; all overhead cost is in grinding and assembly.

we allocate support-department cost to producing departments only. No cost from one support department is allocated to another support department. Thus, no support-department interaction is recognized.

To illustrate the direct method, consider the data in Exhibit 7–7 that show the budgeted activity and budgeted costs of two support departments and two producing departments. Assume that the causal factor for power costs is kilowatt-hours, and the causal factor for maintenance costs is maintenance hours. These causal factors are used as the bases for allocation. In the direct method, only the kilowatt-hours and the maintenance hours in the producing departments are used to compute the allocation ratios. The direct method allocation ratios and the support department cost allocations based on the data given in Exhibit 7–7 are shown in Exhibit 7–8. (To simplify the illustration, no distinction is made between fixed and variable costs.)

Exhibit 7–7

Data for Illustrating Allocation Methods

	Support Departments		Producing Departments	
	Power	Maintenance	Grinding	Assembly
Direct costs*	$250,000	$160,000	$100,000	$ 60,000
Normal activity:				
Kilowatt-hours	—	200,000	600,000	200,000
Maintenance hours	1,000	—	4,500	4,500

*For a producing department, direct costs refer only to overhead costs that are directly traceable to the department.

Exhibit 7–8

Direct Allocation Illustrated

STEP 1: CALCULATE ALLOCATION RATIOS		
	Grinding	Assembly
Power[a]	0.75	0.25
Maintenance[b]	0.50	0.50

STEP 2: ALLOCATE SUPPORT-DEPARTMENT COSTS USING THE ALLOCATION RATIOS				
	Support Departments		Producing Departments	
	Power	Maintenance	Grinding	Assembly
Direct costs	$250,000	$160,000	$100,000	$ 60,000
Power[c]	(250,000)	—	187,500	62,500
Maintenance[d]	—	(160,000)	80,000	80,000
	$ 0	$ 0	$367,500	$202,500

[a] 600,000/(600,000 + 200,000); 200,000/(600,000 + 200,000)
[b] 4,500/(4,500 + 4,500); 4,500/(4,500 + 4,500)
[c] Allocation of power based on allocation ratios from Step 1: 0.75 × $250,000; 0.25 × $250,000
[d] Allocation of maintenance based on allocation ratios from Step 1: 0.50 × $160,000; 0.50 × $160,000

Sequential Method of Allocation

The **sequential (or step) method** of allocation recognizes that interactions among the support departments occur. However, the sequential method does not fully recognize support-department interaction. Cost allocations are performed in step-down fashion, following a predetermined ranking procedure. Usually, the sequence is defined by ranking the support departments in order of the amount of support service rendered, from the greatest to the least. Degree of support service is usually measured by the direct costs of each support department: the department with the highest cost is seen as rendering the greatest service.

Exhibit 7–9 illustrates the sequential method. First, the support departments are ranked; here power is first, then maintenance. Then, power costs are allocated to maintenance and the two producing departments. Then, the costs of maintenance are allocated only to producing departments.

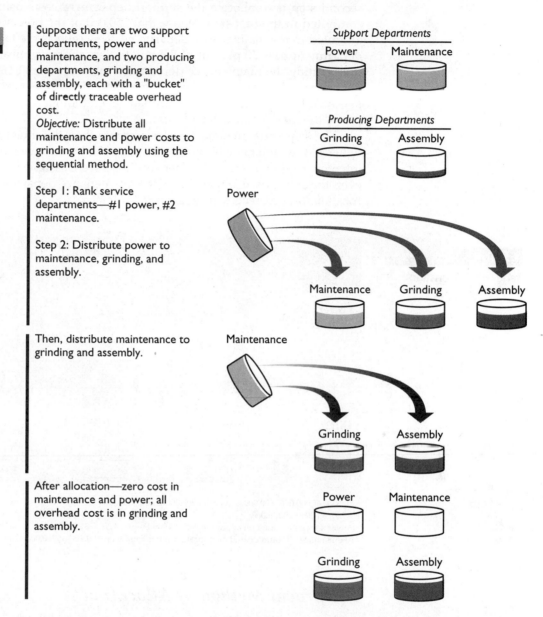

Exhibit 7–9

Allocation of Support-Department Costs to Producing Department: Sequential Method

Suppose there are two support departments, power and maintenance, and two producing departments, grinding and assembly, each with a "bucket" of directly traceable overhead cost.
Objective: Distribute all maintenance and power costs to grinding and assembly using the sequential method.

Step 1: Rank service departments—#1 power, #2 maintenance.

Step 2: Distribute power to maintenance, grinding, and assembly.

Then, distribute maintenance to grinding and assembly.

After allocation—zero cost in maintenance and power; all overhead cost is in grinding and assembly.

The costs of the first support department are allocated to all support departments after it in the sequence and to all producing departments. Then the costs of the support department next in sequence are similarly allocated, and so on. In the sequential method, once a support department's costs are allocated, it never receives a subsequent allocation from another support department. In other words, a given support department's costs are never allocated to support departments before it in the sequence. Also, note that the costs allocated from a support department are its direct costs plus any costs it receives in allocations from other support departments. A department's direct costs, of course, are those that are directly traceable to the department.

To illustrate the sequential method, consider the data provided in Exhibit 7–7. Using cost as a measure of service, we see that the support department rendering more service is power. Thus, its costs will be allocated first, followed by those for maintenance.

The allocations obtained with the sequential method are shown in Exhibit 7–10. The first step is to compute the allocation ratios. Note that the allocation ratios for the maintenance department ignore the usage by the power department since its costs cannot be allocated to a support department before it in the allocation sequence. The second step is to allocate the support-department costs using the allocation ratios computed in the first step. Notice that $50,000 of the power department's costs are allocated to the maintenance department. This reflects the fact that the maintenance department uses 20 percent of the power department's output. As a result, the cost of operating the maintenance department increases from $160,000 to $210,000. Also notice that when the costs of the maintenance department are allocated, no costs are allocated back to the power department, even though it uses 1,000 hours of the output of the maintenance department.

The sequential method is more accurate than the direct method because it recognizes some interactions among the support departments. It does not recognize all interactions, however: no maintenance costs were assigned to the power department even though it used 10 percent of the maintenance department's output. The reciprocal method corrects this deficiency.

Exhibit 7–10

Sequential Allocation Illustrated

STEP 1: CALCULATE ALLOCATION RATIOS			
	Maintenance	Grinding	Assembly
Power[a]	0.20	0.60	0.20
Maintenance[b]	—	0.50	0.50

STEP 2: ALLOCATE SUPPORT-DEPARTMENT COSTS USING THE ALLOCATION RATIOS			
	Support Departments		Producing Departments	
	Power	Maintenance	Grinding	Assembly
Direct costs	$250,000	$160,000	$100,000	$ 60,000
Power[c]	(250,000)	50,000	150,000	50,000
Maintenance[d]	—	(210,000)	105,000	105,000
	$ 0	$ 0	$355,000	$215,000

[a] 200,000/1,000,000; 600,000/1,000,000; 200,000/1,000,000
[b] 4,500/9,000; 4,500/9,000
[c] Power allocation based on allocation ratios from Step 1: 0.20 × $250,000; 0.60 × $250,000; 0.20 × $250,000
[d] Maintenance allocation based on allocation ratios from Step 1: 0.50 × $210,000; 0.50 × $210,000

Reciprocal Method of Allocation

The **reciprocal method** of allocation recognizes all interactions among support departments. Under the reciprocal method, one support department's use by another figures in determining the total cost of each support department, where the total cost reflects interactions among the support departments. Then, the new total of support-department costs is allocated to the producing departments. This method fully accounts for support-department interaction.

Total Cost of Support Departments To determine the total cost of a support department, so that it reflects interactions with other support departments, we must solve a system of simultaneous linear equations. Each equation, which is a cost equation for a support department, is defined as the sum of the department's direct costs plus the proportion of support service received from other support departments:

$$\text{Total cost} = \text{Direct costs} + \text{Allocated costs}$$

The method is best described using an example, employing the same data used to illustrate the direct and sequential methods (see Exhibit 7–11). The allocation ratios needed for the simultaneous equations are interpreted as follows: maintenance receives 20 percent of power's output; power receives 10 percent of maintenance's output. Now let P equal the total cost of the power department and M equal the total cost of the maintenance department. As previously indicated, the total cost of a support department is the sum of its direct costs plus the proportion of support service received from other support departments. Using the data and allocation ratios from Exhibit 7–11, we can express the cost equation for each support department as follows:

$$P = \text{Direct costs} + \text{Share of maintenance's cost} \tag{7.1}$$
$$= \$250,000 + 0.10M \text{ (power's cost equation)}$$
$$M = \text{Direct costs} + \text{Share of power's costs} \tag{7.2}$$
$$= \$160,000 + 0.2P \text{ (maintenance's cost equation)}$$

The direct cost components of each equation are taken from Exhibit 7–11, as are the allocation ratios.

The power cost equation (7.1) and the maintenance cost equation (7.2) can be solved simultaneously to yield the total cost for each support department. Substituting Equation 7.1 into Equation 7.2 gives the following:

$$M = \$160,000 + 0.20(\$250,000 + 0.10M)$$
$$M = \$160,000 + \$50,000 + 0.02M$$
$$0.98M = \$210,000$$
$$M = \$214,286$$

Substituting this value for M into Equation 7.1 yields the total cost for power:

$$P = \$250,000 + 0.1(\$214,286)$$
$$= \$250,000 + \$21,429$$
$$= \$271,429$$

After the equations are solved, the total costs of each support department are known. These total costs, unlike the direct or sequential methods, reflect all interactions between the two support departments.

Allocation to Producing Departments Once the total costs of each support department are known, the allocations to the producing departments can be made. These allocations, which are based on the proportion of output used by each producing

Exhibit 7–11

Data for Illustrating Reciprocal Method

	Support Departments		Producing Departments	
	Power	Maintenance	Grinding	Assembly
Direct costs:	$250,000	$160,000	$100,000	$ 60,000
Normal activity:				
Kilowatt-hours	—	200,000	600,000	200,000
Maintenance hours	1,000	—	4,500	4,500

Proportion of Output Used by Department				
	Power	Maintenance	Grinding	Assembly
Allocation ratios:				
Power	—	0.20	0.60	0.20
Maintenance	0.10	—	0.45	0.45

Exhibit 7–12	Support Departments		Producing Departments	
	Power	Maintenance	Grinding	Assembly
Direct costs:	$250,000	$160,000	$100,000	$ 60,000
Power[a]	(271,429)	54,286	162,857	54,286
Maintenance[b]	21,429	(214,286)	96,429	96,429
Total	$ 0	$ 0	$359,286	$210,715

Exhibit 7–12
Reciprocal Allocation Illustrated

[a] Power: 0.20 × $271,429; 0.60 × $271,429; 0.20 × $271,429
[b] Maintenance: 0.10 × $214,286; 0.45 × $214,286; 0.45 × $214,286

department, are shown in Exhibit 7–12. Notice that the total costs allocated to the producing departments from power and maintenance equal $410,000, the total direct costs of the two support departments ($250,000 + $160,000). (Actually, the total allocated costs equal $410,001, but the difference is due to a rounding error.)

Comparison of the Three Methods

Exhibit 7–13 gives the cost allocations from the power and maintenance departments to the grinding and assembly departments using the three support department cost allocation methods. How different are the results? Does it really matter which method is used? Depending on the degree of interaction among the support departments, the three allocation methods can give radically different results. In this particular example, the direct method allocated $12,500 more to the grinding department (and $12,500 less to the assembly department). Surely the manager of the assembly department would prefer the direct method, and the manager of the grinding department would prefer the sequential method. Because allocation methods affect the cost responsibilities of managers, it is important for the accountant to understand the consequences of the different methods and to have good reasons for the eventual choice.

It is important to keep a cost–benefit perspective in choosing an allocation method. The accountant must weigh the advantages of better allocation against the increased cost of using a more theoretically preferred method, such as the reciprocal method. For example, about 20 years ago, the controller for an IBM plant decided that the reciprocal method of cost allocation would do a better job of allocating support-department costs. He identified more than 700 support departments and solved the system of equations using a computer. Computationally, he had no problems. However, the producing-department managers did not understand the reciprocal method. They were sure that extra cost was being allocated to their departments; they just were not sure how. After months of meetings with the line managers, the controller threw in the towel and returned to the sequential method—which everyone did understand. Another factor in

Exhibit 7–13

Comparison of Support Department Cost Allocations Using the Direct, Sequential, and Reciprocal Methods

	Direct Method		Sequential Method		Reciprocal Method	
	Grinding	Assembly	Grinding	Assembly	Grinding	Assembly
Direct costs	$100,000	$ 60,000	$100,000	$ 60,000	$100,000	$ 60,000
Allocated from power	187,500	62,500	150,000	50,000	162,857	54,286
Allocated from maintenance	80,000	80,000	105,000	105,000	96,429	96,429
Total cost	$367,500	$202,500	$355,000	$215,000	$359,286	$210,715

allocating support-department cost is the rapid change in technology. Many firms currently find that support department cost allocation is useful for them. However, the move toward activity-based costing and just-in-time manufacturing can virtually eliminate the need for support department cost allocation. In the case of the JIT factory with manufacturing cells, much of the service (for example, maintenance, material handling, and setups) is performed by cell workers. Allocation is not necessary.

DEPARTMENTAL OVERHEAD RATES AND PRODUCT COSTING

Objective 4

Calculate departmental overhead rates.

After allocating all support costs to producing departments, we can then compute an overhead rate for each department. This rate is computed by adding the allocated support-department costs to the overhead costs that are directly traceable to the producing department and dividing this total by some measure of activity, such as direct labour hours or machine hours.

For example, from Exhibit 7–10, the total overhead costs for the grinding department after allocation of support costs under the sequential method are $355,000. Assume that machine hours are the base for assigning overhead costs to products passing through the grinding department and that the normal level of activity is 71,000 machine hours. The overhead rate for the grinding department is computed as follows:

Overhead rate = $355,000/71,000 machine hours = $5 per machine hour

Similarly, assume that the assembly department uses direct labour hours to assign its overhead. With a normal level of activity of 107,500 direct labour hours, the overhead rate for the assembly department is as follows:

Overhead rate = $215,000/107,500 direct labour hours = $2 per direct labour hour

Using these rates, we can determine the product's unit cost. To illustrate, suppose a product requires two machine hours of grinding per unit produced and one hour of assembly. The overhead cost assigned to one unit of this product would be $12 [(2 × $5) + (1 × $2)]. If the same product uses $15 of materials and $6 of labour (totalled from grinding and assembly), then its unit cost is $33 ($12 + $15 + $6).

One might wonder, however, just how accurate this $33 cost is. Is this really what it costs to produce the product in question? Since materials and labour are directly traceable to products, the accuracy of product costs depends largely on the accuracy of the assignment of overhead costs. This, in turn, depends on the degree of correlation between the factors used to allocate support service costs to departments and the factors used to allocate the department's overhead costs to the products. For example, if power costs are highly correlated with kilowatt-hours while machine hours are highly correlated with a product's consumption of the grinding department's overhead costs, then we can have some confidence that the $5 overhead rate accurately assigns costs to individual products. However, if the allocation of support service costs to the grinding department or the use of machine hours is faulty—or both—then product costs will be distorted. The same reasoning can be applied to the assembly department. To ensure accurate product costs, great care should be used in identifying and using causal factors for both stages of overhead assignment.

SUMMARY OF LEARNING OBJECTIVES

1. Describe the difference between support departments and producing departments.
Producing departments create the products or services that the firm is in business to manufacture and sell. Support departments provide support for the producing departments but do not themselves create a salable product. Because support departments exist to support a variety of producing departments, the costs of the support departments are common to all producing departments.

The reasons for support-department cost allocations include inventory valuation, product-line profitability, pricing, and planning and control. Allocation can also be used to encourage favourable managerial behaviour.

2. Calculate single charging rates for a support department.
When the costs of one support department are allocated to other departments, a charging rate must be developed. A single rate combines variable and fixed costs of the support department to generate a charging rate.

Budgeted, not actual, costs should be allocated so that the efficiencies or inefficiencies of the support departments themselves are not passed on to the producing departments.

3. Allocate support-department costs to producing departments using the direct, sequential, and reciprocal methods.

Three methods can be used to allocate support costs to producing departments: the direct method, the sequential method, and the reciprocal method. They differ in the degree of support-department interaction considered. By considering support-department interactions, you can achieve more accurate product costing. The result can be improved planning, control, and decision making. Two methods of allocation recognize interactions among support departments: the sequential (or step) method and the reciprocal method. These methods allocate support service costs among some (or all) interacting support departments before allocating costs to the producing departments.

4. Calculate departmental overhead rates.
Departmental overhead rates are calculated by adding direct departmental overhead costs to those costs allocated from the support departments and dividing the sum by the budgeted departmental base.

KEY TERMS

Causal factors, 253
Common costs, 251
Direct method, 259

Producing departments, 251
Reciprocal method, 262
Sequential (or step) method, 260

Support departments, 252

REVIEW PROBLEM

Antioch Manufacturing produces machine parts on a job-order basis. Most business is obtained through bidding. Most firms competing with Antioch bid full cost plus a 20 percent markup. Recently, with the expectation of gaining more sales, Antioch reduced its markup from 25 percent to 20 percent. The company operates two support departments and two producing departments. The budgeted costs and the normal activity levels for each department follow.

	Support Departments		Producing Departments	
	A	B	C	D
Overhead costs	$100,000	$200,000	$100,000	$50,000
Number of employees	8	7	30	30
Maintenance hours	2,000	200	6,400	1,600
Machine hours	—	—	10,000	1,000
Labour hours	—	—	1,000	10,000

The direct costs of Department A are allocated on the basis of employees; those of Department B, on the basis of maintenance hours. Departmental overhead rates are used to assign costs to products. Department C uses machine hours, and Department D uses labour hours.

The firm is preparing to bid on a job (Job K) that requires three machine hours per unit produced in Department C and no time in Department D. The expected prime costs (direct materials and direct labour) per unit are $67.

Required:

1. Allocate the support costs to the producing departments using the direct method.
2. What will the bid be for Job K if the direct method of allocation is used?
3. Allocate the support costs to the producing departments using the sequential method.
4. What will the bid be for Job K if the sequential method is used?
5. Allocate the support costs to the producing departments using the reciprocal method.
6. What will the bid be for Job K if the reciprocal method is used?

Solution

1.

	Support Departments		Producing Departments	
	A	B	C	D
Direct costs	$100,000	$200,000	$100,000	$ 50,000
Department A[a]	(100,000)	—	50,000	50,000
Department B[b]	—	(200,000)	160,000	40,000
Total	$ 0	$ 0	$310,000	$140,000

[a] 30/60 × $100,000; 30/60 × $100,000
[b] 6,400/8,000 × $200,000; 1,600/8,000 × $200,000

2. Department C: Overhead rate = $310,000/10,000 = $31 per machine hour. Product cost and bid price:

Prime costs	$ 67.00
Overhead (3 × $31)	93.00
Total unit cost	$160.00
Bid price ($160 × 1.2)	$192.00

3.

	Support Departments		Producing Departments	
	A	B	C	D
Direct costs	$100,000	$200,000	$100,000	$ 50,000
Department B[a]	40,000	(200,000)	128,000	32,000
Department A[b]	(140,000)	—	70,000	70,000
Total	$ 0	$ 0	$298,000	$152,000

[a] 2,000/10,000 × $200,000; 6,400/10,000 × $200,000; 1,600/10,000 × $200,000
[b] 30/60 × $140,000; 30/60 × $140,000

4. Department C: Overhead rate = $298,000/10,000 = $29.80 per machine hour. Product cost and bid price:

Prime costs	$ 67.00
Overhead (3 × $29.80)	89.40
Total unit cost	$156.40
Bid price ($156.40 × 1.2)	$187.68

5. Allocation ratios:

	Proportion of Output Used by Department			
	A	B	C	D
Department A	—	0.1045	0.4478	0.4478
Department B	0.2000	—	0.6400	0.1600

$$A = \$100,000 + 0.2000B$$
$$B = \$200,000 + 0.1045A$$

$$A = \$100,000 + 0.2(\$200,000 + 0.1045A)$$
$$A = \$100,000 + \$40,000 + 0.0209A$$
$$0.9791A = \$140,000$$
$$A = \$142,988$$

$$B = \$200,000 + 0.1045(\$142,988)$$
$$B = \$214,942$$

	Support Departments		Producing Departments	
	A	B	C	D
Direct costs	$100,000	$200,000	$100,000	$ 50,000
Department B	42,988	(214,942)	137,563	34,391
Department A	(142,988)*	14,942	64,030	64,030
Total	$ 0	$ 0	$301,593	$148,421

* Note: $14 difference is the result of rounding.

6. Department C: Overhead rate = $301,593/10,000 = $30.16 per machine hour. Product cost and bid price:

Prime costs	$ 67.00
Overhead (3 × $30.16)	90.48
Total unit cost	$157.48
Bid price ($157.48 × 1.2)	$188.98

QUESTIONS FOR WRITING AND DISCUSSION

1. Describe the two-stage allocation process for assigning support department costs to products in a functional manufacturing environment.

2. Explain how allocating support department costs can be helpful in making pricing decisions.

3. Why must support department costs be assigned to products for purposes of inventory valuation?

4. Explain how allocating support department costs is useful for planning and control.

5. Assume that a company has decided not to allocate any support department costs to producing departments. Describe the likely behaviour of the managers of the producing departments. Would this be good or bad? Explain why allocation would correct this type of behaviour.

6. Explain how allocating support department costs will encourage support departments to operate more efficiently.

7. Why is it important to identify and use causal factors to allocate support department costs?

8. Identify some possible causal factors for the following support departments:
   a. Cafeteria
   b. Custodial services
   c. Laundry
   d. Receiving, shipping, and stores
   e. Maintenance
   f. Personnel
   g. Accounting

9. Explain why it is better to allocate budgeted support department costs rather than actual support department costs.

10. Explain the difference between the direct method and the sequential method.

11. The reciprocal method of allocation is more accurate than either the direct or sequential methods. Do you agree? Explain.

EXERCISES

7–1

**Classifying
Departments as
Producing or Support**

LO1

Classify each of the following departments in a factory as a producing department or a support department:

a. Power
b. Maintenance
c. Finishing
d. Landscaping
e. Payroll
f. Quality control of suppliers
g. Cooking
h. Blending
i. General factory
j. Timekeeping
k. Packaging
l. Data processing
m. Engineering
n. Drilling
o. Cutting

7–2

**Identifying Causal
Factors**

LO1

For the following support departments, identify one or more causal factors that might be useful for support department cost allocation purposes.

a. Supervision
b. Data processing
c. Quality control
d. Purchasing
e. Receiving
f. Shipping
g. Vending (stocking snack machines throughout the plant)
h. Grounds
i. Building amortization
j. Power and light
k. Employee benefits
l. Housekeeping
m. Equipment repair
n. Heating and cooling

7–3

Single Charging Rate

LO2

J&L Sound recently established a centralized purchasing department to handle all purchasing for its four retail stores. The costs of the purchasing department include fixed costs of $42,000 per year (salaries, office equipment, and computers) and variable costs of $2.76 per purchase order (supplies, long-distance phone calls, and so on). Estimated usage in terms of number of purchase orders by the four retail stores is as follows:

Charlottetown	1,750
Fredericton	700
Halifax	3,000
Saint John	4,550
Total	10,000

By the end of the first year, the actual usage of the purchasing department was Charlottetown, 1,900 purchase orders; Fredericton, 500 purchase orders; Halifax, 3,100 purchase orders, and Saint John, 4,850 purchase orders.

Required:

1. Calculate a single charging rate per purchasing order for purchasing services.
2. At the end of the year, what were the purchasing department charges for each of the four retail stores? What was the total amount charged by the purchasing department to the stores?
3. Based on the fixed and variable amounts budgeted, how much should it have cost the purchasing department to provide 10,350 purchase orders? Is this amount different from the amount calculated in Requirement 2? Why or why not?

7–4

Single Charging Rate

LO2, LO3

Morton Auto Sales has three producing departments: new car sales, used car sales, and service. The service department provides service both to outside customers and to the new and used car sales departments. Morton wants to charge the new and used car sales departments for their use of the service department. It seems fair to charge each department for the cost of actual direct materials used (e.g., oil, engine parts) and to develop a single charging rate for direct labour and overhead.

Assume the following budgeted amounts for the year:

Direct labour cost	$360,000
Direct labour hours	24,000
Overhead cost	$240,000

Actual materials and direct labour hours incurred by the service department during the year are as follows:

	Materials	Actual DLH
New car sales department	$ 2,100	1,300
Used car sales department	7,890	4,700
Service department	86,300	19,100
Total	$96,290	25,100

Required:

1. Calculate the single charging rate per hour of labour.
2. Suppose that the used car sales department gets a 1994 Festiva as a trade-in that needs some general maintenance and some transmission work. The service department spends 8 hours working on the car and uses $478 of parts. Calculate the charge to the used car sales department by the service department.
3. Calculate the total costs charged by the service department to each of the "producing" departments for the year.

7–5

Single Charging Rate

LO2

Dottori Company charges all of its departments and manufacturing cells for the use of engineering services. Budgeted engineering costs for the year are $160,000, and budgeted engineering hours are 5,000. By the end of the year, total actual engineering hours equal 5,060, and actual cost is $160,600.

Required:

1. Calculate the billing rate for engineering.
2. If the small-motor cell required 344 engineering hours during the year, what was the cell charged for engineering services?
3. Were the departments and cells (taken as a whole) over- or undercharged for the actual costs of engineering—and if so, by how much?

7–6

Allocating Support-Department Cost Using the Direct Method

LO3

Spreadsheet

Quillen Company manufactures a product in a factory that has two producing departments (cutting and polishing) and two support departments (maintenance and human resources). The activity driver for maintenance is machine hours, and the activity driver for human resources is number of employees. The following data pertain to Quillen Company:

	Support Departments		Producing Departments	
	Human Resources	Maintenance	Cutting	Polishing
Direct costs	$200,000	$130,000	$112,400	$83,400
Normal activity:				
Number of employees	—	10	35	35
Maintenance hours	600	—	8,000	2,000

Required:

1. Calculate the allocation ratios to be used under the direct method for the human resources and maintenance departments. (Each support department will have two allocation ratios—one for cutting and the other for polishing.)
2. Allocate the support-department costs to the producing departments using the direct method.

7–7

Allocating Support-Department Cost Using the Sequential Method

LO3

Spreadsheet

Refer to 7–6. Under the sequential method, the human resource department costs are allocated first.

Required:

1. Calculate the allocation ratios to be used under the sequential method for the human resources and maintenance departments. Carry your calculations out to four digits. (The human resource department will have three allocation ratios—one each for maintenance, cutting, and polishing. The maintenance department will have two allocation ratios—one for each producing department.)
2. Allocate the support-department costs to the producing departments using the sequential method.

7–8

Allocating Support-Department Cost Using the Reciprocal Method

LO3

Refer to 7–6.

Required:

1. Calculate the allocation ratios to be used under the reciprocal method for the human resources and maintenance departments. Carry your calculations out to four digits. (The human resource department will have three allocation ratios—one each for maintenance, cutting, and polishing. The maintenance department will have three allocation ratios—one each for human resources, cutting, and polishing.)
2. Develop a cost equation for each support department and solve for the total support-department costs.
3. Based on the calculations in Requirement 1, allocate the support-department costs to the producing departments using the reciprocal method.

7–9

Direct Method and Overhead Rates

LO3, LO4

Gordon Company manufactures a product in two producing departments: P1 and P2. Three support departments—SA, SB, and SC—support the production departments. Budgeted data on the five departments follow:

	Support Departments			Producing Departments	
	SA	SB	SC	P1	P2
Overhead	$130,000	$240,000	$120,000	$60,000	$116,000
Kilowatt-hours	—	13,000	25,000	30,000	70,000
Square metres	2,000	—	6,000	24,000	8,000
Machine hours	—	—	—	4,000	6,000

SA's costs are allocated on the basis of kilowatt-hours; SB's costs are allocated on the basis of square metres; and SC's costs are allocated on the basis of machine hours. The company does not break overhead into fixed and variable components.

Required:

1. Allocate the overhead costs to the producing departments using the direct method.
2. Using machine hours, compute departmental overhead rates.

7–10

Sequential Method and Overhead Rates

LO3, LO4

Refer to the data in 7–9. The company has decided to use the sequential method of allocation instead of the direct method.

Required:

1. Allocate the overhead costs to the producing departments using the sequential method.
2. Using machine hours, compute departmental overhead rates.

7–11

Reciprocal Method and Overhead Rates

LO3, LO4

Mandelbrot Company produces fractals in two producing departments (generating and colouring) and two support departments (human resources and power). The following budgeted data pertain to these four departments:

	Support Departments		Producing Departments	
	Human Resources	Power	Generating	Colouring
Overhead	$144,000	$130,000	$50,000	$80,000
Payroll	—	$80,000	$160,000	$160,000
Kilowatt-hours	50,000	—	200,000	150,000
Direct labour hours	—	—	20,000	30,000

Costs of the human resources department are allocated on the basis of payroll, and costs of the power department are allocated on the basis of kilowatt-hours.

Required:

1. Allocate the overhead costs of the support departments to the producing departments using the reciprocal method.
2. Using direct labour hours, compute departmental overhead rates (to the nearest penny).

7–12

Direct Method and Overhead Rates

LO3, LO4

Refer to the data in 7–11. The company has decided to simplify its method of allocating support-department costs by switching to the direct method.

Required:

1. Allocate the costs of the support departments to the producing departments using the direct method.
2. Using direct labour hours, compute departmental overhead rates (to the nearest penny). Which rate do you consider more accurate—the one using the reciprocal method or the one using the direct method? Explain.

7–13

Sequential Method and Overhead Rates

LO3, LO4

Refer to the data in 7–11.

Required:

1. Allocate the costs of the support departments using the sequential method.
2. Using direct labour hours, compute departmental overhead rates (to the nearest penny). Explain why these rates are generally more accurate than those computed using the direct method.

7–14

Reciprocal Method

LO3

Trinity Medical Clinic has two support departments and two revenue-producing departments. The clinic's controller has decided to use the reciprocal method to allocate the costs of the support departments (A and B) to the revenue-producing departments (C and D). She has prepared the following cost equations for the two support departments. *A* equals the total cost for the first support department, and *B* equals the total cost for the second support department:

$$A = \$35,000 + 0.30B$$
$$B = \$40,000 + 0.20A$$

Before the controller was able to complete the allocation, she had to leave to take care of an emergency. In addition to these equations, she left a hastily scribbled note indicating that Department C uses 20 percent of A's output and 40 percent of B's output.

Required:

Allocate the costs of the two support departments to each of the two revenue-producing departments using the reciprocal method.

7–15

Choice of Allocation Method

LO3

Crusher Manufacturing has two support departments, power and maintenance. The company is trying to decide whether to use a direct allocation method or a reciprocal allocation method to distribute costs to its two producing departments, assembly and finishing. Shown below is the usage of each of the four departments for a normal month before any allocation.

Usage of Support Departments: Normal Month

	Provider of Support Service	
User of Service	Power (kilowatt-hours)	Maintenance (hours)
Power	1,000	800
Maintenance	2,000	—
Assembly	4,000	2,500
Finishing	3,000	1,700
	10,000	5,000

The direct costs of power and maintenance are as follows:

Power	$20,000
Maintenance	12,000
	$32,000

As the assistant to the controller, you have been asked to provide some data analysis to help him make his decision on the appropriate allocation method to use.

Required:

1. If the company chose to allocate the support-department costs directly to assembly and finishing, how much cost would be allocated to assembly? to finishing? (Show separately the amount allocated from each support department to each producing department in your answer.)

2. Using the reciprocal method, allocate the support-department costs to the appropriate departments, showing the amount allocated from each support department to each of its users.
3. Prepare a short memo to the controller discussing the two possible methods of allocating Crusher's support-department costs. Recommend the best method to be used, and defend your choice. (CMA Canada adapted)

7–16

Direct Method, Overhead Rates, Unit Cost

LO3, LO4

Morris Machine Works has two support departments—power and general factory—and two producing departments—grinding and assembly. Budgeted data for each follows:

	Power	General Factory	Grinding	Assembly
Direct costs	$60,000	$100,000	$103,000	$85,000
Machine hours	—	1,000	8,000	2,000
Square metres	4,000	—	2,000	6,000
Direct labour hours	600	12,000	20,000	40,000

Power is allocated on the basis of machine hours; general factory is allocated on the basis of square metres.

Required:

1. Allocate the support-department costs to producing departments using the direct method.
2. Calculate departmental overhead rates, using machine hours for grinding and direct labour hours for assembly.
3. If a unit has prime costs of $17.50 and spends one hour in grinding and two hours in assembly, what is the unit cost?

7–17

Sequential Method, Overhead Rates, Unit Cost

LO3, LO4

Refer to the data in 7–16.

Required:

1. Allocate the support-department costs to producing departments using the sequential method.
2. Calculate departmental overhead rates, using machine hours for grinding and direct labour hours for assembly.
3. If a unit has prime costs of $17.50 and spends one hour in grinding and two hours in assembly, what is the unit cost?

7–18

Comparison of Direct, Sequential, and Reciprocal Methods

LO3

The Sedgwick Company has one factory with two production departments (fabricating and assembly) and two support departments (SDX and SDY). The following table provides cost and production/service data:

	SDX	SDY	Fabricating	Assembly
Direct costs	$6,300	$5,600	$20,000	$37,500
SDX hours used	—	150	300	450
SDY hours used	100	—	500	200
Direct labour hours	—	—	1,000	1,500

Required:

1. Determine the amount of support-department costs that would be allocated to fabricating and assembly for each of the following methods (round your answer to the nearest dollar): (a) direct allocation, (b) sequential allocation (allocating SDX first), and (c) reciprocal allocation.
2. Which method, if any, do you think most appropriately allocates the support-departments costs to the products? Explain why. (CMA Canada adapted)

7–19

Direct Method, Job-Order Costing

LO3, LO4

Osaka Company uses the direct method of allocating support-department costs to production departments. Costs of Department S1 are allocated on the basis of number of employees. Costs of Department S2 are allocated on the basis of machine hours. In Department P1, machine hours are used to assign overhead costs to jobs. In Department P2, direct labour hours are used to assign overhead costs to jobs. The following information is available:

	S1	S2	P1	P2
Direct overhead costs	$50,000	$25,000	$200,000	$300,000
Number of employees	50	20	60	120
Machine hours	—	—	40,000	10,000
Direct labour hours	—	—	20,000	60,000

Job 49	Department P1	Department P2
Materials cost	$60	$45
Direct labour hours	1	2
Machine hours	3	1

Required:

Calculate the overhead cost of Job 49. (CGA Canada adapted)

7–20

Sequential Method, Job-Order Costing

LO3, LO4

Refer to the data in 7–19. Assume that Osaka uses the sequential method.

Required:

Calculate the overhead cost of Job 49. (CGA Canada adapted)

PROBLEMS

7–21

Comparison of Methods of Allocation

LO3

Spreadsheet

Powell-Morgan, Inc., is divided into two operating divisions: the Western Division and the Eastern Division. The company allocates personnel and accounting costs to each operating division. Personnel costs are allocated on the basis of employees; accounting costs, on the basis of the number of transactions processed. No effort is made to separate fixed and variable costs; however, only budgeted costs are allocated. Allocations for the coming year are based on the following data:

	Support Departments		Operating Divisions	
	Personnel	Accounting	Western	Eastern
Overhead costs	$340,000	$260,000	$170,000	$140,000
Number of employees	20	60	60	80
Transactions processed	2,000	200	3,000	5,000

Required:

1. Allocate the support-department costs using the direct method.
2. Allocate the support-department costs using the sequential method.
3. Allocate the support-department costs using the reciprocal method.

7–22

Comparison of Methods of Allocation

LO3, LO4

Gojar Uniform Company manufactures a variety of uniforms for city police services. Gojar has two producing departments, cutting and sewing. Usually, the uniforms are ordered in batches of 100.

Two support departments provide support for Gojar's operating units: maintenance and power. Budgeted data for next quarter follow. The company does not separate fixed and variable costs.

	Support Departments		Producing Departments	
	Maintenance	Power	Cutting	Sewing
Overhead costs	$240,000	$380,000	$65,000	$87,000
Machine hours	—	30,000	40,000	10,000
Kilowatt-hours	20,000	—	18,000	162,000
Direct labour hours	—	—	5,000	30,000

The predetermined overhead rate for cutting is computed on the basis of machine hours; direct labour hours are used for sewing.

Recently, the company was asked to bid on a three-year contract for uniforms for the Calgary Police Service. The prime costs for a batch of 100 sets of uniforms total $1,817.50. It takes two machine hours to produce a batch in the cutting department and 50 direct labour hours to sew the 100 uniforms in the sewing department.

Gojar Uniform Company policy is to bid full manufacturing cost plus 25 percent.

Required:

1. Prepare bids for Gojar Uniform Company using each of the following allocation methods: (a) the direct method, and (b) the reciprocal method.
2. Which method most accurately reflects the cost of producing the uniforms? Why?

7–23

Comparison of Ranking of Support Departments Using the Sequential Method

LO3, LO4

Refer to the data in 7–22.

Required:

1. Prepare bids for Gojar Uniform Company using each of the following allocation methods:
   a. Sequential method, allocating maintenance first, then power.
   b. Sequential method, allocating power first, then maintenance.
2. Was there a difference in the bids calculated in Requirement 1? Why?

7–24

Sequential and Direct Methods

LO3, LO4

Lilly Candies has three producing departments (mixing, cooking, and packaging) and five support departments. The following is the basic information on all departments (bases represent practical annual levels):

	Number of Items Processed	Number of Employees	Square Metres Occupied	Machine Hours	Labour Hours
Cafeteria	300	5	5,000	—	—
Personnel	1,000	10	7,000	—	—
Custodial services	200	7	2,000	—	—
Maintenance	2,500	15	16,000	—	—
Cost accounting	—	13	5,000	—	—
Mixing	2,800	20	40,000	4,000	30,000
Cooking	2,700	10	30,000	10,000	20,000
Packaging	3,000	20	20,000	6,000	50,000
Total	12,500	100	125,000	20,000	100,000

The budgeted overhead costs for the department are as follows for the coming year:

	Fixed	Variable	Total
Cafeteria	$ 20,000	$ 40,000	$ 60,000
Personnel	70,000	20,000	90,000
Custodial services	80,000	—	80,000
Maintenance	100,000	100,000	200,000
Cost accounting	130,000	16,500	146,500
Mixing	120,000	20,000	140,000
Cooking	60,000	10,000	70,000
Packaging	25,000	40,000	65,000

Required:

1. Allocate the support-department costs to the producing departments using the direct method.
2. Compute a predetermined fixed overhead rate and a predetermined variable overhead rate. Assume that overhead is applied using direct labour hours for mixing and packaging and machine hours for cooking.
3. Allocate the support-department costs to the producing departments using the sequential method. (*Hint:* Allocate fixed costs in order of descending magnitude of direct fixed costs. Allocate variable costs in order of descending magnitude of direct variable costs.)
4. Compute predetermined fixed and variable overhead rates based on Requirement 3. Overhead is applied using direct labour hours for mixing, and packaging and machine hours for cooking.
5. Assume that the prime costs for a batch of chocolate bars total $60,000. The batch requires 1,000 direct labour hours in mixing, 1,500 machine hours in cooking, and 5,000 direct labour hours in packaging. Assume that the selling price is equal to full manufacturing cost plus 30 percent. Compute the selling price of the batch assuming that costs are allocated using the direct method. Repeat, using the sequential method. Comment on the implications of using different allocation methods, assuming that a markup of 30 percent is typical for the industry. Which allocation method do you think should be used?

7–25

Reciprocal Method, Cost of Operating a Support Department

LO3

Watterman Company has two producing departments (machining and assembly) and two support departments (power and maintenance). The budgeted costs and normal usage are as follows for the coming year:

	Power	Maintenance	Machining	Assembly
Overhead costs*	$50,000	$40,000	$120,000	$60,000
Kilowatt-hours	—	100,000	300,000	100,000
Machine hours	5,000	—	10,000	5,000

* All overhead costs are variable.

Watterman's president was approached by the electric power company and offered the opportunity to buy power for $0.11 per kilowatt-hour. The president has asked you to determine the cost of producing the power internally so that a response to the offer can be made.

Required:

1. Compute the unit cost of kilowatts for overall plant usage. Based on this computation, how would you respond to the offer to buy the kilowatts externally?
2. Now use the reciprocal method to compute the cost of operating the power department. Divide this total cost by the total kilowatts produced by the power department to find a cost per kilowatt-hour. Based on this computation, how would you respond to the offer to buy kilowatts externally?
3. Show that the decision associated with the reciprocal method (Requirement 2) is correct by following two steps: (a) computing the savings realized if the power department is eliminated, and (b) computing the cost per kilowatt-hour saved by dividing the total savings by the kilowatts needed if the power department is eliminated. (*Hint:* Total savings include the direct costs of the power department plus any costs avoided by the maintenance department since it no longer needs to serve the power department. The total kilowatt-hours consumed by the company need to be adjusted since the maintenance department's power needs decrease when it decreases the amount of service it offers.)

7–26

**Direct Method,
Sequential Method,
Overhead Rates**

LO3, LO4

Bright, Inc., has two producing departments and four support departments. It currently uses the direct method of support department cost allocation. Data for the company follow:

	Producing Departments		Support Departments			
	PD1	PD2	SD1	SD2	SD3	SD4
Overhead	$183,000	$212,400	$30,000	$35,000	$40,000	$100,000
Square metres	2,000	2,000	400	5,000	600	—
Employees	15	45	—	12	20	3
Direct labour hours	30,000	90,000	—	24,000	20,000	6,000
Machine hours	10,000	20,000	—	—	—	—

Original Allocation Base
SD1   Machine hours
SD2   Number of employees
SD3   Direct labour hours
SD4   Square metres

Cara James, controller of Bright, Inc., is considering changing to a more accurate method of support department cost allocation. She has discovered the following:

1. SD1 provides its services only to the producing departments, based on machine hours.
2. SD2 provides services to both producing and support departments, based on the number of employees.
3. SD3 provides 15 percent of its service to SD1 and the remainder to PD1 and PD2, based on direct labour hours.
4. SD4 provides services to all other departments, based on area occupied.

Cara has decided to rank the support departments in the following order for purposes of cost allocation: SD4, SD2, SD3, SD1.

Required:

1. Allocate support-department costs using the direct method and the original allocation bases.
2. Allocate support-department costs using the sequential method as outlined by Cara James.
3. Calculate overhead rates for PD1 (based on machine hours) and PD2 (based on direct labour hours) using total departmental overhead costs as determined by the:
   a. Direct method.
   b. Sequential method.

7–27

**Fixed and Variable-
Cost Allocation**

LO2

El Greco's is a chain of restaurants serving Mediterranean (Greek, Italian, and Spanish) food in a family-type atmosphere. The chain has grown from one restaurant in 1989 to five restaurants located in Manitoba and Northwestern Ontario. In 2001, the owner of the company decided to set up a centralized purchasing department to purchase food and other supplies, and to coordinate inventory decisions. The purchasing department was opened in January 2001 by renting space adjacent to corporate headquarters in Winnipeg. All restaurants have been supplied with personal computers and modems by which to transfer information to central purchasing on a daily basis.

The purchasing department has budgeted fixed costs of $50,000 per year. Variable costs are budgeted at $16 per hour. Actual costs in 2001 equalled budgeted costs. Further information is as follows:

| | Actual Revenues | | Actual Hours of Purchasing |
	2000	2001	Used in 2001
Kenora	$337,500	$390,500	1,475
Brandon	360,000	375,000	938
Portage la Prairie	450,000	456,000	400
Winnipeg (West)	562,500	549,000	375
Winnipeg (South)	540,000	550,000	562

Required:

1. Suppose that the total costs of the purchasing department are allocated on the basis of 2001 sales revenue. How much will be allocated to each restaurant?
2. Suppose that El Greco's views 2000 sales figures as a proxy for budgeted capacity of the restaurants. Thus, fixed purchasing department costs are allocated on the basis of 2000 sales, and variable costs are allocated according to 2001 usage multiplied by the variable rate. How much purchasing department cost will be allocated to each restaurant?
3. Comment on the two allocation schemes. Which is better? Explain.

7–28

Single Charging Rate, Evaluation of Method

LO2

The Davis Company has a computer department that provides its services to two other departments (accounting and research). The computer department was designed with a capacity of 160 hours per month to meet the demands of accounting (50 percent of capacity) and research (50 percent of capacity).

The computer department is expected to incur costs of $180,000 per month plus $200 per hour of usage. During January, the computer department actually incurred costs of $243,750 while providing 70 hours of service to accounting and 80 hours to research.

The company's controller has indicated that she feels the costs of the computer department must be charged to the two departments using its services in order to control the total costs incurred by each department manager and to evaluate the managers' performance. The controller has therefore prepared the following cost allocation:

$$\text{Rate} = \text{Cost of computer department/Total hours used}$$
$$= \$243,750/150 = \$1,625 \text{ per hour}$$

Cost Allocation:
Accounting department (70 hours @ $1,625)	$113,750
Research department (80 hours @ $1,625)	130,000
Total cost of computer department	$243,750

Required:

1. As manager of the research department, comment on the validity and fairness of the method used to allocate the computer department's costs to your department.
2. Describe a more appropriate method of allocating the computer department's costs that might help to alleviate any problems inherent in the method used. (CMA Canada adapted)

7–29

Support Department Cost Allocations, Plantwide Overhead Rate versus Departmental Rates, Effects on Pricing Decisions

LO3, LO4

Alden Peterson, marketing manager for Retlief Company, was puzzled by the outcome of two recent bids. The company's policy was to bid 150 percent of the full manufacturing cost. One job (labelled Job SS) had been turned down by a prospective customer, who had indicated that the proposed price was $3 per unit higher than the winning bid. A second job (Job TT) had been accepted by a customer, who was amazed that Retlief could offer such favourable terms. This customer revealed that Retlief's price was $43 per unit lower than the next lowest bid.

Alden knew that Relief Company was more than competitive in terms of cost control. Accordingly, he suspected that the problem was related to cost assignment procedures. Upon investigating, Alden was told that the company used a plantwide overhead rate based on direct labour hours. The rate was computed at the beginning of the year using budgeted data. Selected budgeted data follow:

	Department A	Department B	Total
Overhead	$500,000	$2,000,000	$2,500,000
Direct labour hours	200,000	50,000	250,000
Machine hours	20,000	120,000	140,000

These data led to a plantwide overhead rate of $10 per direct labour hour. In addition, the following specific manufacturing data on Job SS and Job TT were given:

JOB SS

	Department A	Department B	Total
Direct labour hours	5,000	1,000	6,000
Machine hours	200	500	700
Prime costs	$100,000	$20,000	$120,000
Units produced	14,400	14,400	14,400

JOB TT

	Department A	Department B	Total
Direct labour hours	400	600	1,000
Machine hours	200	3,000	3,200
Prime costs	$10,000	$40,000	$50,000
Units produced	1,500	1,500	1,500

This information led to the original bid prices of $18.75 per unit for Job SS and $60 per unit for Job TT.

Then Alden discovered that the overhead costs in Department B were higher than those of Department A because Department B has more equipment, higher maintenance, higher power consumption, higher amortization, and higher setup costs. So he tried reworking the two bids by using departmental overhead rates. Department A's overhead rate was $2.50 per direct labour hour; Department B's overhead rate was $16.67 per machine hour. These rates resulted in unit prices of $14.67 for Job SS and $101.01 for Job TT.

Alden was still not satisfied, however. He did some reading on overhead allocation methods and learned that proper support department cost allocation can lead to more accurate product costs. He decided to create four support departments and recalculate departmental overhead rates. Information on departmental costs and related items follows:

	Maintenance	Power	Setups	General Factory	Dept. A	Dept. B
Overhead	$500,000	$225,000	$150,000	$625,000	$200,000	$800,000
Maintenance hours	—	1,500	500	—	1,000	7,000
Kilowatt-hours	4,500	—	500	15,000	10,000	50,000
Direct labour hours	10,000	12,000	6,000	8,000	200,000	50,000
Number of setups	—	—	—	—	40	160
Square metres	25,000	40,000	5,000	15,000	35,360	94,640

The following allocation bases (cost drivers) seemed reasonable:

Support Department	Allocation Base
Maintenance	Maintenance hours
Power	Kilowatt-hours
Setups	Number of setups
General factory	Square metres

Required:

1. Using the direct method, verify the original departmental overhead rates.
2. Using the sequential method, allocate support-department costs to the producing departments. Calculate departmental overhead rates using direct labour hours for Department A and machine hours for Department B. What would the bids for Job SS and Job TT have been if these overhead rates had been in effect?
3. Which method of overhead cost assignment would you recommend to Alden? Why?
4. Suppose that the best competing bid was $4.10 lower than the original bid price (based on a plantwide rate). Does this affect your recommendation in Requirement 3? Explain.

7–30

Service Organization: Direct and Reciprocal Methods

LO3

In January, a group of Quebec City lawyers and accountants decided to join efforts to provide "one-stop shopping" legal and accounting consulting services to industry and the government. The group established a consulting company, rented office space, and hired both professional and clerical staff.

Following several initial organizational meetings, the partners decided to divide the operation into three parts: the consulting department, the legal department, and the accounting department. The consulting department dealt directly with the clients, providing two distinct services, accounting consulting (AC) and legal consulting (LC). In its first full month of operations, this department recorded its own identifiable costs as $20,000, with 30 percent attributable to accounting consultants and 70 percent to legal consultants. Billings to clients amounted to $30,000 and $20,500 for accounting and legal consulting, respectively. This department made use of the other departments' services in preparing work for the external clients.

The accounting and legal departments provided professional services for each other and for the consulting department on the basis of hours worked according to the following schedule:

	Accounting Department	Legal Department	Consulting AC	LC
Accounting services	—	20%	60%	20%
Legal services	50%	—	10%	40%

The accounting department incurred $8,000 in direct costs in the first month, and the legal department incurred $10,000. Neither department directly bills external clients.

Having completed the first month's activity, the partners are ready to evaluate the performance of the group and of the individual areas. The managing partner is concerned that his organizational structure may be a major determinant of success and has asked you, as an outside consultant, to prepare some performance information for him.

Required:

1. Prepare an income statement for each consulting branch separately under each of the following approaches for allocating the support-department costs:
    a. Direct method
    b. Reciprocal method
2. Prepare a brief memorandum to the managing partner on the performance of the group and individual areas. (CMA Canada adapted)

MANAGERIAL DECISION CASES

7–31

Allocation, Pricing, Ethical Behaviour

LO1, LO2

Emma Hanks, manager of a division that produces valves and castings on a special-order basis, was excited about an order received from a new customer. The customer, a friend of Bob Johnson, Emma's supervisor, had placed an order for 10,000 valves. The customer agreed to pay full manufacturing cost plus 25 percent. The order was timely since business was sluggish, and Emma had some concerns about her division's ability to meet its targeted profits. Even with the order, the division would likely fall short in meeting the target by at least $50,000. After examining the cost sheet for the order, however, Emma thought she saw a way to increase the profitability of the job. Accordingly, she called Larry Smith, CMA, the controller of the division.

Emma: "Larry, this cost sheet for the new order reflects an allocation of maintenance costs to the grinding department based on maintenance hours used. Currently, 60 percent of our maintenance costs are allocated to grinding on that basis. Can you tell me what the allocation ratio would be if we used machine hours instead of maintenance hours?"

Larry: "Sure. Based on machine hours, the allocation ratio would increase from 60 percent to 80 percent."

Emma: "Excellent. Now tell me what would happen to the unit cost of this new job if we used machine hours to allocate maintenance costs."

Larry: "Hold on. That'll take a few minutes.... The cost would increase by $10 per unit."

Emma: "And with the 25 percent markup, the revenues on that job would jump by $12.50 per unit. That would increase the division's profitability by $125,000. Larry, I want you to change the allocation base from maintenance hours worked to machine hours."

Larry: "Are you sure? After all, if you recall, we spent some time assessing the causal relationships, and we found that maintenance hours reflect the consumption of maintenance cost much better than machine hours. I'm not sure that would be a fair cost assignment. We've used this base for years now."

Emma: "Listen, Larry, allocations are arbitrary anyway. Changing the allocation base for this new job will increase its profitability and allow us to meet our targeted profit goals for the year. If we meet or beat those goals, we'll be more likely to get the capital we need to acquire some new equipment. Furthermore, by beating the targeted profit, we'll get our share of the bonus pool. Besides, this new customer has a prosperous business and can easily afford to pay somewhat more for this order."

Required:

1. Evaluate Emma's position. Do you agree with her reasoning? Explain. What should Emma do?
2. If you were the controller, what would you do? Do any of the standards for ethical conduct for management accountants apply to the controller (see Chapter 1)? Explain.
3. Suppose Larry refused to change the allocation scheme. Emma then issued the following ultimatum: "Either change the allocation or look for another job!" Larry then made an appointment with Bob Johnson and disclosed the entire affair. Bob, however, was not sympathetic. He advised Larry to do as Emma had requested, arguing that the request represented good business sense. Now what should Larry do?
4. Refer to Requirement 3. Larry decided that he cannot comply with the request to change the allocation scheme. Appeals to higher-level officials have been in vain. Angered, Larry submitted his resignation and called the new customer affected by the cost reassignment. In his phone conversation, Larry revealed Emma's plans to increase the job's costs in order to improve the division's profits. The new customer expressed her gratitude and promptly cancelled her order for 10,000 valves. Evaluate Larry's action. Should he have informed the customer about Emma's intent? Explain.

7–32

Direct Method, Settlement of a Contract Dispute

LO3, LO4

A government agency contracted with FlyRite Helicopters to provide helicopter services on a requirements contract. After six months, FlyRite discovered that the agency's original estimates of the number of flying hours needed were grossly overstated. FlyRite Helicopters is now making a claim against the agency for defective specifications. The agency has been advised by its legal advisers that its chances in court on this claim would not be strong, and that an out-of-court settlement is therefore in order. As a result of the legal advice, the agency has hired a local CA firm to analyze the claim and prepare a recommendation for an equitable settlement.

The particulars on which the original bid was based follow. The contract was for three different types of helicopters and had a duration of one year. Thus, the data reflect the original annual expectations. Also, the costs and activity pertain only to the contract.

	Aircraft Type		
	Hughes 500D	206B Jet Ranger	206L–1 Long Ranger
Flying hours	1,200	1,600	900
Direct costs:			
Fixed:			
Insurance	$32,245	$28,200	$55,870
Lease payments	31,000	36,000	90,000
Pilot salaries	30,000	30,000	30,000
Variable:			
Fuel	$24,648	$30,336	$22,752
Minor servicing	6,000	8,000	4,500
Lease	—	—	72,000

In addition to the direct costs, the following indirect costs were expected:

	Fixed Costs	Variable Costs
Maintenance	$26,000	$246,667
Hangar rent	18,000	—
General administrative	110,000	—

Maintenance costs and general administrative costs are allocated to each helicopter on the basis of flying hours; hangar rent is allocated on the basis of the number of helicopters. The company has one of each type of aircraft.

During the first six months of the contract, the actual flying hours were as follows:

Type	Flying Hours
500D	299
206B	160
206L–1	204

The agency's revised projection of total hours for the year follows:

Type	Flying Hours
500D	450
206B	600
206L-1	800

Required:

1. Assume that FlyRite won the contract with a bid of cost plus 15 percent, where cost refers to cost per flying hour. Compute the original bid price per flying hour for each type of helicopter. Next, compute the original expected profit of the contract.

2. Compute the profit (or loss) earned by FlyRite for the first six months of activity. Assume that the planned costs were equal to the actual costs. Also assume that 50 percent of the fixed costs for the year have been incurred. Compute the profit that FlyRite should have earned during the first six months, assuming that 50 percent of the hours originally projected (for each aircraft type) had been flown.

3. Compute the profit (or loss) that the contract would provide FlyRite assuming the original price per flying hour and using the agency's revised projection of hours needed.

4. Assume that the agency has agreed to pay what is necessary so that FlyRite receives the profit originally expected in the contract. This will be accomplished by revising the price paid per flying hour based on the revised estimates of flying hours. What is the new price per flying hour?

7–33

Design of Cost Allocation System

LO1, LO2, LO3, LO4

The Taubner Company manufactures customized office furniture, and each contract is drafted to meet the needs of the individual client. Contracts are obtained through a competitive system of bidding for new jobs.

The company's production facilities consist of the following departments:

Production Departments
1. Machining Department: Departmental costs are $600,000 per year, of which 60 percent are fixed costs consisting mainly of amortization of the machinery.
2. Fabrication Department: Departmental costs are $300,000 per year, of which 10 percent are fixed costs. This department assembles the various parts of product and is very labour-intensive due to the wide variety of products produced.

Support Departments
1. Computer Facilities: Departmental costs are $200,000 per year, of which 80 percent are fixed costs of the equipment and staff.
2. Product Design Department: Departmental costs are $100,000 per year. The department uses 70 percent of the computer facilities for CAD programs to design the various products and production methods.
3. Purchasing Department: Departmental costs are $40,000 per year, of which 40 percent are fixed costs. The department's main duty is the purchase of materials for the machining department to make furniture.

Karen Bains, Taubner's president, has asked you to prepare a report to her addressing the following issues:

a. Should the company use plantwide or departmental rates for applying the manufacturing overhead to the products?
b. Should the support-department costs be allocated using the direct, the sequential, or the reciprocal method?
c. Should the support-department costs be allocated using variable- and fixed-cost pools or total departmental costs?
d. What would be the most logical base(s) for allocating each support-department cost? What would be the most logical base(s) for allocating the costs of each of the production departments?

Required:
Prepare a report to the president addressing the main issues for each case. Where there are alternative methods, be sure to identify the main characteristics of each alternative and to justify your recommended course of action. (CMA Canada adapted)

RESEARCH ASSIGNMENT

7–34

Research Assignment

LO1, LO2

Contact the controller of a local hospital and arrange an interview. Ask the hospital controller the following questions and write up his or her responses:

a. How many support departments do you have in the hospital? Will you describe several for me?
b. How many different revenue-producing departments are there in the hospital? Will you describe several for me?
c. How do you assign support-department costs to revenue-producing departments?
d. How many different products are there in the hospital?
e. How do you assign the costs of the support departments to individual products?
f. How many different products are costed in your hospital?
g. How do you determine the cost of a particular product?

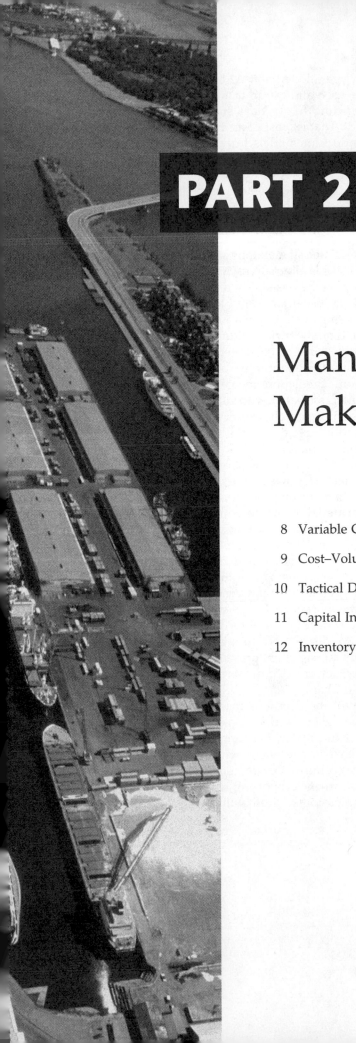

PART 2

Managerial Decision Making

Managers make decisions daily. Many of their decisions are obvious and require little more than being informed and using common sense. Some decisions have strategic implications, however, and require more consultation and participation by others in the organization. Some decisions have primarily short-term implications, while others require substantial long-term investments, as when establishing new plants, stores, product or service lines, or processes. The combined forces of intense global competition and rapid technological change have accelerated the frequency of these types of decisions. Almost all major decisions, whether they affect the short term or the long term, deal with a large number of factors. Some of these factors can be easily quantified, for example, the potential impact a decision will have on profit or cash flow, while other more qualitative factors defy quantification, for example, customer satisfaction, quality of products, and competitive posture. The emphasis in Part 2 is primarily, but not exclusively, related to the quantitative aspects of decisions. Quantification on a common measurement base reduces the number of factors or aspects of a decision that require management judgment. It allows the decision maker to focus more on those aspects of the decision that require judgment. However, it is important to note that quite often qualitative factors can be as important as quantitative aspects in reaching the ultimate decision.

The focus of the decision maker in this part of the book is the organization as a whole. The assumption is made that what is good for a subunit of the organization, for example, a division, is also good for the organization as a whole. This assumption is not always valid, however, and will be examined in more detail in Part 3 of the book.

Accounting Information and Decision Making

In making any decision, a manager must consider the future consequences of the alternatives available. The information available from traditional accounting records, largely kept for purposes of financial reporting, tends to be historical and irrelevant (past, sunk) for managerial decisions. Past data, however, can often be used and can in fact be relevant as the basis for predicting future data such as future costs and revenues. That is, past costs may not be directly relevant for decision models, but they may be relevant for prediction models. Historical information can also be useful for purposes of evaluating past performance, as will be discussed in Part 3 of the book.

Differential Cash-Flow Analysis

Managerial decision making involves making choices among feasible alternatives. Most, if not all, decisions are made on the basis of two types of criteria: financial criteria (usually referred to as quantitative), such as increasing cash inflows or decreasing cash outflows, and nonfinancial criteria (usually referred to as qualitative), such as customer satisfaction and product quality. The quantitative aspects of decision making require predictions related to the differences in cash flows associated with different choices. That is, to make informed choices, a manager must make a determination of differential cash flow. This is true regardless of the time horizon covered by the specific decision. When the time horizon of the anticipated differential cash flows is short, the interest factor does not enter into the analysis since it would be negligible and immaterial to the decision. However, when the time horizon is long, the compounded interest effects can be substantial. Chapters 8–10 (especially Chapters 9 and 10) are concerned with decisions over relatively short time horizons, where the interest factor can be ignored. Chapter 11 is concerned with cash flows over long time horizons. It covers the topic of capital investment decisions and focuses primarily on issues related to discounted future cash flows. Because inventory management presents a unique set of problems, decisions related to this topic are dealt with separately in Chapter 12.

Many of the decisions made by management are related to the interaction of costs, prices, and volume. Chapter 8 introduces a costing and internal reporting system that is consistent with, and highlights, the effects of volume changes on income. It also deals with performance reporting related to segments and assessing customer profitability using activity-based costing. Chapter 9 deals directly with short-term decisions and focuses on the interaction of costs, prices, and volume, all of which have an impact on profit and cash flow. In particular, the impact of volume on profit and cash flow is highlighted. Chapter 10 covers a more general case. It treats the different cash flows associated with different choices, whether or not these choices affect volume. Its focus is that generic information can be misleading and that managers must use different costs for different purposes.

Chapter 11 deals with differential cash flows that result from capital investment decisions, and with the unique considerations that result from long-term cash flows. These considerations include discounting, income tax effects of capital cost allowance, uncertainty, and inflation. Chapter 12 deals with the unique problems and decisions related to inventory management.

Decision Examples

The following brief cases provide examples of the types of decision situations that are addressed in Part 2:

- A company owner continued to increase his personal and financial investments in his company in anticipation of increased sales volume and in view of the tight cash flow his business was experiencing. Upon examination, a consultant pointed out that as the owner increased sales volume, his losses also increased. The owner was operating the business with a negative contribution margin. He was not aware of this problem since he had not analyzed costs into fixed and variable components and did not understand the relationships between costs, prices, and volume.
- During the last economic recession, a manager at first refused to sell her product below its full cost, including its average fixed cost, so as not to lose money on the product. She later discovered that she was actually losing many profitable opportunities because of her pricing strategy. She could not significantly decrease her fixed costs in the short run, but she was rejecting a number of special orders, priced below average full cost but above

average variable cost, that would not affect her regular customers. When she began to accept these special orders, her total contribution margins dramatically increased while her fixed costs remained relatively unaffected, thus increasing her income. Had she continued with her full cost pricing policy, her business probably would not have been able to survive the recession, let alone produce profits.
- The Continuing Education Division of a major Canadian university was required to be financially self-supporting as a result of university funding cuts. Each program in the division had been evaluated financially on the basis of total contribution margin. It was subsequently discovered that some programs, with higher total contribution margins, were actually driving overhead costs quite high. By applying ABC, the division controller was able to relate each major type of cost to its cost driver and draw a more accurate picture of the financial performance of each program. As a result, the division recommended corrective actions, including program and course fee changes and the elimination of some less profitable programs.
- A company decided to close down a department because the accounting records showed it to be unprofitable. Before the decision was implemented, however, a thorough analysis of differential cash flows was undertaken. The company's accountants found that many of the costs that had been considered departmental costs would not be eliminated if the department was closed down. These costs would continue because they were allocations from other departments and from the general overhead cost. Contractual obligations of the company also limited the extent of wage savings that would result from the elimination of the department. These factors were not apparent from the accounting records alone but became obvious when differential cash-flow analysis was performed.

The first three cases require careful consideration of the interdependencies of cost, price, and volume and of their effect on profit and cash flow. All of the cases require a full understanding of differential cash-flow analysis in general.

CHAPTER 8

Variable Costing: Segmented Reporting and Performance Evaluation

Learning Objectives

After studying Chapter 8, you should be able to:

1. Explain the differences between variable and absorption costing.

2. Explain how variable costing is useful in evaluating the performance of managers.

3. Prepare a segmented income statement based on a variable-costing approach, and explain how this format can be used with activity-based costing to assess customer profitability.

4. Explain how variable costing can be used in planning and control.

Scenario

Kathy Wise had been the manager of the Medical Supplies Division for three years. In the first year, the division's net income had shown a substantial increase over the prior year. Her second year saw an even greater increase. Kathy's boss, the vice-president for operations, was extremely pleased and promised her a $5,000 bonus if the division showed a similar increase in profits for the upcoming year. Kathy was elated. She was completely confident that the goal could be met. Sales contracts were already well ahead of last year's performance, and she knew that there would be no increases in costs.

At the end of the third year, Kathy received the data regarding operations for the first three years. Upon examining the operating data, Kathy was pleased. Sales had increased by 20 percent over the previous year, and costs had been kept stable. However, when she saw the yearly income statements, she was dismayed and perplexed. Instead of seeing a significant increase in income for the third year, she saw a small decrease. Surely, she thought, the accounting department had made an error.

Freda Mathews, controller for the Medical Supplies Division, met with Kathy to explain the anomalous results.

Freda: "Kathy, there's been no mistake here. Net income is lower this year than in the past two years. It's easily explained by looking at the changes in inventory."

Kathy: "Inventory? What's that got to do with income? We did a terrific job managing inventory this year. It had built up in the past two years, and I got sales up and inventory down. That's good, not bad!"

Freda: "Sure, Kathy, from an operating perspective. But you have to realize that inventory carries cost with it. That cost doesn't appear on the income statement until the stuff is sold. Then it flows through income and reduces it."

Kathy: "That's crazy! Do you mean that I'm going to lose my bonus even though we sold off our inventory and met cost and revenue projections?"

Freda: "Well, Kathy, I'm sorry about your bonus, but the income figures are solid. I'd be happy to spend a little time with you explaining how we account for income. We use absorption costing; it's recommended by GAAP. There is another possibility, variable costing, and it sounds to me like you are implicitly using that method."

Kathy: "There are two ways to figure income? Does it make a difference?"

Freda: "Oh yes. Variable costing doesn't permit inventory changes to affect income. So your income this year would be higher under variable costing. However, your income the past couple of years would have been lower. So over the long run, it evens out."

Kathy: "Hmmm. I wonder if I could get the VP to take a look at variable costing?"

Questions to Think About

1. Why do firms calculate income? What information does it provide?

2. What costs go into inventory? How can they affect income?

3. What is GAAP, and how does it affect the income statement of the Medical Supplies Division?

4. Why doesn't Kathy understand accounting? Should she?

5. What do you suppose Kathy's chances are for getting the vice-president to consider evaluating her performance on the basis of variable, instead of absorption, costing?

VARIABLE COSTING AND ABSORPTION COSTING: AN ANALYSIS AND COMPARISON

Objective 1

Explain the differences between variable and absorption costing.

In the opening scenario, two methods of computing income are identified: one based on variable costing and the other based on full, or absorption, costing. These are costing methods because they refer to the way in which product costs are determined. Recall that *product costs* are inventoried, whereas *period costs* are expensed in the period incurred. The difference between variable and absorption costing hinges on the treatment of fixed overhead.

Variable costing stresses the difference between fixed and variable manufacturing costs. This distinction is critical for many decision and control models that are used in management accounting. Studying variable costing provides a good foundation for the application of other important management accounting topics, such as cost–volume–profit analysis, relevant costing, and flexible budgeting.

Variable costing assigns only variable manufacturing costs to the product; these costs include direct materials, direct labour, and variable overhead. Fixed overhead is excluded from the product cost. Under variable costing, fixed overhead for a period is seen as expiring that period and is charged in total against the revenues of the period.[1]

Absorption costing assigns *all* manufacturing costs to the product. Direct materials, direct labour, variable overhead, and fixed overhead define the cost of a product. Thus, under absorption costing, fixed overhead is viewed as a *product* cost, not a period cost. Under this method, fixed overhead is assigned to the product through the use of a predetermined fixed overhead rate and does not expire until the product is sold. In other words, fixed overhead is an inventoriable cost. Exhibit 8–1 illustrates the classification of costs as product or period costs under absorption and variable costing. From Exhibit 8–1, it is clear that the only difference is in the treatment of fixed overhead.

1. Variable costing is more commonly known as direct costing. Direct costing, however, is a misnomer. Not all variable manufacturing costs are direct product costs. For example, variable overhead, by definition, consists of *indirect* manufacturing costs. Clearly, the more descriptive name for this method is variable costing, which is the term that is used in this text.

Exhibit   **8–1**

Classification of Costs as
Product or Period Costs
under Absorption and
Variable Costing

	Absorption Costing	Variable Costing
Product Costs	Direct materials (DM)	Direct materials (DM)
	Direct labour (DL)	Direct labour (DL)
	Variable overhead (VOH)	Variable overhead (VOH)
	Fixed overhead (FOH)	
Period Costs	Selling expense	Fixed overhead (FOH)
	Administrative expense	Selling expense
		Administrative expense

Currently, absorption costing is the most commonly used product-costing method for external reporting.[2] Yet as the dialogue between Kathy and Freda suggests, variable costing can supply vital cost information for decision making and control, information not supplied by absorption costing. For internal application, variable costing is an invaluable managerial tool. Let's look at the way the two costing methods affect inventory valuation and income determination.

Inventory Valuation

Different product-costing methods will affect the cost of goods stored in inventory. An example will make the inventory valuations of absorption and variable costing more concrete. During the most recent year, Fairchild Company had the following data associated with the product it makes:

Units, beginning inventory	—
Units produced	10,000
Units sold (@ $300 per unit)	8,000
Normal volume[a]	10,000
Variable costs per unit:	
Direct labour	$100
Direct materials	50
Variable overhead[b]	50
Variable selling and administrative	10
Fixed costs:	
Fixed overhead[b]	$250,000
Fixed selling and administrative	100,000

[a] This is the average activity level that a firm experiences over more than one fiscal period, and is often used as a denominator volume in the allocation of fixed manufacturing overhead.

[b] Assume that estimated and actual overhead are equal.

Recall that the unit product cost obtained under each method differs. Variable costing inventories only variable manufacturing costs, so each unit of product for Fairchild costs $200. Absorption costing includes all manufacturing costs, so each unit of product costs $225. The computations follow:

2. Section 3030.06 of the *CICA Handbook* requires that inventories of work in process and finished goods include the cost of materials, direct labour, and an appropriate share of overhead. This is usually interpreted as requiring absorption costing, but Section 3030.03 allows for some fixed overhead to be excluded if net income would otherwise be distorted because of fluctuations in production volume. This could be viewed as support for variable costing in some circumstances, and is different from the requirements in the United States and in the International Accounting Standards that only absorption costing be used in external financial reporting.

  Although variable costing is not acceptable in the United States for income tax purposes, it is acceptable in Canada provided that it is also used for accounting purposes (see Interpretation Bulletin IT–473 from the Canada Customs and Revenue Agency [CCRA], formerly known as—and sometimes still informally called—Revenue Canada).

	Variable Costing	Absorption Costing
Direct labour	$100	$100
Direct materials	50	50
Variable overhead	50	50
Fixed overhead ($250,000/10,000)	—	25
Total per unit cost	$200	$225

Of course, the difference in unit costs affects the amount shown on the balance sheet. Fairchild had no beginning inventory and produced 2,000 units more than it sold. Therefore, ending inventory is 2,000 units (10,000 – 8,000). Under variable costing, the value of ending inventory is $400,000 ($200 × 2,000). Under absorption costing, the value of ending inventory is $450,000 ($225 × 2,000). Note that the only difference between the two approaches is the treatment of fixed overhead. Thus, the unit product cost under absorption costing is always greater than the unit product cost under variable costing.

Income Statements: Analysis and Reconciliation

Because unit product costs are the basis for cost of goods sold, the variable- and absorption-costing methods can lead to different net income figures. The difference arises because of the amount of fixed overhead recognized as an expense under the two methods. Income statements for the Fairchild example appear in Exhibits 8–2 and 8–3. These income statements reveal that absorption-costing income is $50,000 higher than variable-costing income. As the following analysis shows, this difference is due to some of the period's fixed overhead flowing into inventory when absorption costing is used.

For variable costing (Exhibit 8–2), the variable cost of goods sold is $1.6 million ($200 × 8,000 units sold). The fixed overhead deducted as an expense is $250,000. Thus, the total manufacturing expenses deducted are $1.85 million. The total selling and administrative expenses deducted are $180,000 ($80,000 variable and $100,000 fixed).

Exhibit 8–2

Variable-Costing Income Statement

Fairchild Company Variable-Costing Income Statement			
Sales			$2,400,000
Less variable expenses:			
Variable cost of goods sold		$1,600,000	
Variable selling and administrative		80,000	1,680,000
Contribution margin			$ 720,000
Less fixed expenses:			
Fixed overhead		$ 250,000	
Fixed selling and administrative		100,000	350,000
Net income			$ 370,000

Exhibit 8–3

Absorption-Costing Income Statement

Fairchild Company Absorption-Costing Income Statement	
Sales	$2,400,000
Less: Cost of goods sold	1,800,000
Gross margin	$ 600,000
Less: Selling and administrative expenses	180,000
Net income	$ 420,000

For absorption costing (Exhibit 8–3), the cost of goods sold is $1.8 million ($225 × 8,000 units sold). Of this amount, $200,000 ($25 × 8,000) represents the fixed overhead that was recognized as an expense. The total selling and administrative expenses deducted are still $180,000 ($80,000 variable and $100,000 fixed).

Exhibits 8–2 and 8–3 show that sales, selling expenses, and administrative expenses are always the same. Variable cost of goods sold is always the same. However, the amount of fixed overhead that is expensed differs. Thus, income determined with variable costing is $50,000 less than income determined with absorption costing. For absorption costing, where did the other $50,000 of fixed overhead go?

Under absorption costing, each unit produced was assigned fixed overhead of $25. Of the 10,000 units produced, 2,000 units were not sold. These 2,000 units went into inventory and carried with them $50,000 ($25 × 2,000) of the period's fixed overhead. Only when these 2,000 units are sold will that $50,000 of fixed overhead be recognized as an expense. Thus, under absorption costing, $50,000 of the period's fixed overhead flows into inventory, and its recognition as an expense is deferred to a future period.

Note that none of the selling and administrative costs, either variable or fixed, are assigned to the product under either method. Both methods treat these costs as period costs. Therefore, marketing and administrative costs are never inventoried and never appear on the balance sheet.[3]

Production, Sales, and Income Relationships

The relationship between variable-costing income and absorption-costing income changes as the relationship between production and sales changes. If more is sold than was produced, variable-costing income is usually greater than absorption-costing income.[4] The reason is just the opposite of that for the Fairchild example. Selling more than was produced means that inventory is being used. Under absorption costing, units coming out of inventory have attached to them fixed overhead from a prior period. In addition, units produced and sold have all of the current period's fixed overhead attached. Thus, the amount of fixed overhead expensed by absorption costing is greater than the current period's fixed overhead by the amount of fixed overhead flowing out of inventory. Accordingly, variable-costing income is greater than absorption-costing income by the amount of fixed overhead flowing out of beginning inventory.

If production and sales are equal, of course, no difference exists between the two reported incomes. Since the units produced are all sold, absorption costing, like variable costing, will recognize the total fixed overhead of the period as an expense. No fixed overhead flows into or out of inventory.

The relationships between production, sales, and the two reported incomes are summarized in Exhibit 8–4. Note that if production is greater than sales, then inventory has increased. If production is less than sales, inventory must have decreased. If production is equal to sales, beginning inventory is equal to ending inventory.

To illustrate these relationships, consider the following example based on the operating data of Belnip, Inc., in the years 1999, 2000, and 2001.

Variable costs per unit:
Direct materials	$4.00
Direct labour	1.50
Variable overhead (estimated and actual)	0.50
Variable selling and administrative	0.25

---

3. What is Fairchild's variable cost per unit? $210. What is Fairchild's variable *product* cost per unit? $200. Note the difference; variable product cost does not include the $10 of variable selling and administrative expenses. Total variable cost per unit does include the selling and administrative expenses.

4. The fixed overhead rate also affects the difference between variable-costing and absorption-costing income. If the fixed overhead rate does not change, then variable-costing income is always greater than absorption-costing income when more is sold than produced. If the fixed overhead rate changes from period to period, the relationship may be reversed in some cases.

Exhibit 8–4

Production, Sales, and Income Relationships

	If		Then
1.		Production > Sales	Absorption net income > Variable net income
2.		Production < Sales	Absorption net income < Variable net income
3.		Production = Sales	Absorption net income = Variable net income

Estimated fixed overhead was $150,000 each year. Actual fixed overhead also was $150,000. Normal production volume is 150,000 units per year. The sales price each year was $10 per unit. Fixed selling and administrative expenses were $50,000 per year. Other operating data (in units) were as follows:

	1999	2000	2001
Beginning inventory	—	—	50,000
Production	150,000	150,000	150,000
Sales	150,000	100,000	200,000
Ending inventory	—	50,000	—

Income statements prepared under variable costing are shown in Exhibit 8–5. Exhibit 8–6 gives the income statements for absorption costing.

Exhibit 8–5

Variable-Costing Income Statements (in thousands of dollars)

	1999	2000	2001
Sales	$1,500.0	$1,000	$2,000
Less variable expenses:			
Variable cost of goods sold[a]	900.0	600	1,200
Variable selling and administrative[b]	37.5	25	50
Contribution margin	$ 562.5	$ 375	$ 750
Less fixed expenses:			
Fixed overhead	150.0	150	150
Fixed selling and administrative	50.0	50	50
Net income	$ 362.5	$ 175	$ 550

[a] Beginning inventory	—	—	$ 300
Variable cost of goods manufactured	$900	$900	900
Goods available for sale	$900	$900	$1,200
Less: Ending inventory	—	300	—
Variable cost of goods sold	$900	$600	$1,200

[b] $0.25 per unit × Units sold

Exhibit 8–6

Absorption-Costing Income Statements (in thousands of dollars)

	1999	2000	2001
Sales	$1,500.0	$1,000	$2,000
Less: Cost of goods sold*	1,050.0	700	1,400
Gross margin	$ 450.0	$ 300	$ 600
Less: Selling and administrative expenses	87.5	75	100
Net income	$ 362.5	$ 225	$ 500

[a] Beginning inventory	—	—	$ 350
Cost of goods manufactured	$1,050	$1,050	1,050
Goods available for sale	$1,050	$1,050	$1,400
Less: Ending inventory	—	350	—
Cost of goods sold	$1,050	$ 700	$1,400

In 1999, the net incomes for each method are identical. This means that both methods expensed the same amount of fixed overhead. Under variable costing, we know that the period's total fixed overhead of $150,000 was expensed. Under absorption costing, the fixed overhead is unitized and becomes part of the product cost. Estimated fixed overhead was $150,000 each year. The fixed overhead rate is $1 per unit ($150,000/150,000 units produced) for all three years. The applied fixed overhead is $150,000 ($1 × 150,000) for all three years. Since the actual fixed overhead in every year is also $150,000, there is no fixed overhead variance in any year. Thus, the fixed overhead expensed for any year is simply the overhead rate times the number of units sold. For 1999, the total fixed overhead expensed under absorption costing is $150,000 ($1 × 150,000 units sold). Both methods did indeed recognize the same amount of fixed overhead expense.

In 2000, however, the story is different. From Exhibits 8–5 and 8–6, we see that the absorption-costing income is $50,000 greater than the variable-costing income ($225,000 – $175,000). The difference between the two incomes exists because there is $50,000 less fixed overhead expensed under the absorption-costing method.

Under absorption costing, each unit produced is assigned $1 of fixed overhead. Since 150,000 units were produced but only 100,000 units were sold, 50,000 units were placed in inventory. These 50,000 units carried with them $1 of fixed overhead each, for a total of $50,000. This $50,000 of the current period's fixed overhead will not be recognized as an expense until the units in inventory are sold. Thus, under absorption costing, the period's $150,000 of fixed overhead can be broken down into two categories: $100,000 is expensed, and $50,000 is inventoried.

Under variable costing, however, the total fixed overhead of $150,000 is expensed since it is viewed as a period cost. Because variable costing recognizes $150,000 of fixed overhead expense and absorption costing recognizes only $100,000 of fixed overhead expense, the income reported by absorption costing is $50,000 more.

In 2001, the relationship between the two incomes reverses. The difference is now $50,000 in favour of variable costing. The favourable difference occurs because absorption costing not only recognizes $150,000 of fixed overhead expense for units produced and sold in this period but also recognizes the $50,000 of fixed overhead attached to the units in inventory that were produced in 2000 but sold in 2001. Thus, the total fixed overhead recognized as an expense is $200,000 under absorption costing versus only $150,000 under variable costing.

The key to explaining the difference between the two incomes is an analysis of the flow of fixed overhead. Variable costing always recognizes the period's total fixed overhead as an expense. Absorption costing, on the other hand, recognizes only the fixed overhead attached to the units sold. If production is different from sales, fixed overhead will either flow into or out of inventory. If the amount of fixed overhead in inventory increases, then absorption-costing income is greater than variable-costing income by the amount of the net increase. If the fixed overhead in inventory decreases, then variable-costing income is greater than absorption-costing income by the amount of the net decrease.

The change in fixed overhead in inventory is exactly equal to the difference between the two incomes. This change can be computed by multiplying the fixed overhead rate times the change in total units in the beginning and ending inventories (which is the difference between production and sales). The difference between absorption-costing net income (I_A) and variable-costing net income (I_V) can be expressed as:

$$I_A - I_V = \text{FOH rate} \times (\text{Units produced} - \text{Units sold})$$

Exhibit 8–7 shows how this shortcut approach can be used to explain the differences.

Exhibit 8-7		1999	2000	2001
Reconciliation of Variable and Absorption Costing (in thousands of dollars)	Net income:			
	Absorption costing	$362.5	$225	$500
	Variable costing	362.5	175	550
	Difference	$ 0	$ 50	$ (50)
	Explanation:			
	Units produced	150	150	150
	Units sold	150	100	200
	Change in inventory	0	50	(50)
	Fixed overhead rate	× $1	× $1	× $1
	Difference explained*	$ 0	$ 50	$ (50)

* In 1999, absorption costing recognized only the period's fixed manufacturing overhead as an expense. No fixed overhead flowed into or out of inventory. In 2000, $50,000 of fixed overhead flowed into inventory, and its recognition as an expense was deferred to a future period. In 2001, $50,000 of fixed manufacturing overhead flowed out of inventory and was recognized as an expense.

The Treatment of Fixed Overhead in Absorption Costing

The difference between absorption and variable costing centres on the recognition of expense associated with fixed overhead. Under absorption costing, fixed overhead must be assigned to units produced. This presents two problems that we have not yet explicitly considered. First, how do we convert overhead applied on the basis of direct labour hours or machine hours into overhead applied to units produced? Second, what is done when actual overhead does not equal applied overhead?

The first problem is solved relatively easily. Suppose that overhead is applied on the basis of direct labour hours. Further suppose that it takes 0.25 direct labour hours to produce one unit. If the fixed overhead rate is $12 per direct labour hour, then the fixed overhead per unit is $3 (0.25 × $12).

The solution to the second problem requires more thought. First we must calculate the applied fixed overhead and assign it to units produced. Then the total applied amount is compared to actual fixed overhead. If the over- or underapplied amount is immaterial, it is closed to Cost of Goods Sold. Any units going into ending inventory take with them the applied fixed overhead. Variable overhead (which can also be over- or underapplied) is treated in the same fashion. Review Problem II at the end of this chapter illustrates the handling of over- and underapplied fixed and variable overhead.

If the over- or underapplied amount is material, then it is allocated among ending Work in Process, Finished Goods, and Cost of Goods Sold. This complication is beyond the scope of this text.

VARIABLE COSTING AND PERFORMANCE EVALUATION OF MANAGERS

Objective 2

Explain how variable costing is useful in evaluating the performance of managers.

The evaluation of managers is often tied to the profitability of the units they control. How income changes from one period to the next and how actual income compares to planned income are frequently used as signals of managerial ability. To be a meaningful signal, however, income should reflect managerial effort. For example, if a manager has worked hard and increased sales while holding costs in check, income should increase over the prior period, signalling success. In general terms, if income performance is expected to reflect managerial performance, then managers have the right to expect the following:

1.   As sales revenue increases from one period to the next, all other things being equal, income should increase.

2. As sales revenue decreases from one period to the next, all other things being equal, income should decrease.

3. As sales revenue remains unchanged from one period to the next, all other things being equal, income should remain unchanged.

Interestingly, income under variable costing always follows this expected association between sales and income; but under absorption costing, at times, it does not. To illustrate, assume that a division of Myers, Inc., has the following operating data for its first two years. For simplicity, we assume no selling and administrative costs.

	2000	2001
Variable manufacturing costs per unit	$10	$10
Production (expected and actual units)	10,000	5,000
Units sold ($25 per unit)	5,000	10,000
Fixed overhead (estimated and actual)	$100,000	$100,000

The product cost under variable costing is $10 per unit for both years. If we assume that expected actual volume is used to compute a predetermined fixed overhead rate, the product cost under absorption costing is $20 per unit in 2000 and $30 per unit in 2001 ($10 + $100,000/10,000 for 2000; $10 + $100,000/5,000 for 2001).

The variable-costing and absorption-costing income statements are shown in Exhibit 8–8. Sales increased from 5,000 to 10,000 units. Total fixed costs, the variable manufacturing cost per unit, and the unit sales price are the same for both periods. Thus, the doubling of sales represents the only change from one period to the next. Under variable costing, income increased by $75,000 from 2000 to 2001 (from a loss of $25,000 to a profit of $50,000). However, under absorption costing, despite the increase in sales, net income decreased by $25,000 (from a profit of $25,000 to a profit of $0)!

The firm improved its sales performance from 2000 to 2001 (twice as many units were sold), fixed costs remained the same, and the unit variable cost was the same; yet absorption costing fails to reveal this improved performance. Variable costing, on the other hand, produces an increase in income corresponding to the improved sales performance. If you were the manager, which income approach would you prefer?

Exhibit 8–8

Variable- and Absorption-Costing Income Statements

VARIABLE-COSTING INCOME	2000	2001
Sales	$125,000	$250,000
Less variable expenses:		
Variable cost of goods sold[a]	50,000	100,000
Contribution margin	$ 75,000	$150,000
Less fixed expenses:		
Fixed overhead	100,000	100,000
Net income (loss)	$ (25,000)	$ 50,000

ABSORPTION-COSTING INCOME	2000	2001
Sales	$125,000	$250,000
Less cost of goods sold[b]	100,000	250,000
Net income (loss)	$ 25,000	$ 0

[a] $10 × 5,000 in 2000 and $10 × 10,000 in 2001

[b]		
Beginning inventory	$ —	$100,000
Cost of goods manufactured	200,000	150,000
Goods available for sale	$200,000	$250,000
Less: Ending inventory	100,000	—
Cost of goods sold	$100,000	$250,000

In order to use variable costing internally and absorption costing for external financial reporting purposes, many firms use variable costing (or a variation thereof) for internal purposes and add one line at the bottom of the variable-costing statement to adjust variable-costing income to absorption-costing income. The adjustment is the amount of the change in inventoried fixed manufacturing overhead for the period.

VARIABLE COSTING AND SEGMENTED REPORTING

Objective 3

Prepare a segmented income statement based on a variable-costing approach, and explain how this format can be used with activity-based costing to assess customer profitability.

The usefulness of variable costing for performance evaluation extends beyond evaluating managers. Managers need to be able to evaluate the activities over which they have responsibility. For example, managers must continually evaluate the profit contributions of plants, product lines, and sales territories.[5]

The separation of fixed and variable costs basic to variable costing is critical for making accurate evaluations. Implicit in an evaluation is an associated decision—for example, whether to continue to operate a plant or not, or whether to keep or drop a product line. Without a distinction between fixed and variable costs, the evaluation of profit-making activities and the resulting decision may both be erroneous.

Reporting the profit contributions of activities or other units within an organization is called **segmented reporting**. Segmented reports prepared on a variable-costing basis produce better evaluations and decisions than those prepared on an absorption-costing basis.

To evaluate many different activities within a firm, a manager needs more than the summary information that appears in a firm's income statement. For example, in a company with several divisions operating in different markets, the manager would certainly want to know how profitable each division has been. This knowledge may lead to greater overall profit by eliminating unprofitable divisions, giving special attention to problem divisions, allocating additional funds to the more profitable divisions, and so on. Divisional income statements, however, are not all that a good managerial accounting system should supply. Even finer segmentation is needed for managers to carry out their responsibilities properly. Divisions are made up of different plants. Plants produce products, and information on product profitability is critical. Some products may be profitable; some may not be. Similarly, profit information on sales territories, special projects, individual salespersons, and so on is important.

Managers need to know the profitability of various segments within a firm to be able to make evaluations and decisions concerning each segment's continued existence, level of funding, and so on. A **segment** is any profit-making entity within the organization. A report for a segment can provide valuable information on costs that are controllable by the segment's manager. Controllable costs are those costs whose level can be influenced by a manager. A manager who has no responsibility for a cost should not be held accountable for that cost. For example, divisional managers have no power to authorize corporate-level costs such as research and development and salaries of top managers. Therefore, divisional managers should not be held accountable for the incurrence of those costs. If noncontrollable costs are included in a segment report, they should be separated from controllable costs and labelled as noncontrollable. For example, fixed costs common to two or more plants within a division would not be allocated to each plant but instead would be shown as a common cost for the division.

---

5.   This form of disaggregated information is not necessarily the same as that required for publicly listed Canadian companies for external reporting purposes in accordance with the *CICA Handbook*. There are certain rules or guidelines that must be followed for external reporting purposes. The only rule for managerial accounting purposes is that of balancing out the cost and benefit of information.

     A joint project between the CICA's Accounting Standards Board and the FASB (Financial Accounting Standards Board) in the United States is aimed at producing revised financial accounting standards in this area. Preliminary conclusions from this project indicate a leaning toward publishing disaggregated information along the lines of that used for internal purposes, which is in turn determined by management based on cost and benefit considerations.

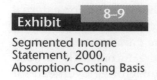

Exhibit 8–9

Segmented Income Statement, 2000, Absorption-Costing Basis

	Elcom, Inc. Segmented Income Statement, 2000 Absorption-Costing Basis		
	Stereos	Video Recorders	Total
Sales	$400,000	$290,000	$690,000
Less: Cost of goods sold	350,000	300,000	650,000
Gross margin	$ 50,000	$ (10,000)	$ 40,000
Less: Selling and administrative expenses	30,000	20,000	50,000
Net income (loss)	$ 20,000	$ (30,000)	$ (10,000)

Segmented Reporting: Absorption-Costing Basis

Should segmented reporting be on a variable-costing basis or an absorption-costing basis? To help answer this question, consider Elcom, Inc., a firm that manufactures stereos and video recorders in a single plant and uses absorption costing for both external and internal reporting. Exhibit 8–9 gives the absorption-costing income statements by product line and in total for 2000.

Devon relied on cost information collected by the external financial reporting system. However, the information needed for internal purposes often differs significantly from that required for external reporting. Cost behaviour and the traceability of costs may not be critical concerns for reporting results to external parties, but they are vital to managers who are attempting to make strategic decisions.

Devon discovered that many fixed costs that had been allocated to the video recorders were not eliminated when that product line was dropped. Since both stereos and video recorders were produced in the same plant, much of the fixed overhead was common to the two products. This includes amortization on the plant, taxes, insurance, and the plant manager's salary, among other items. When the video recorders were dropped, all these common fixed overhead costs were loaded entirely on the stereo product line. Similarly, some fixed selling and administrative costs previously assigned to the video recorder line were then fully assigned to the stereo line.

Upon seeing the product-line performance, Devon Lauffer, Elcom's president, decided to stop producing video recorders, reasoning that profits would increase by $30,000. A year later, however, the result was quite different. As the income statement for 2001 in Exhibit 8–10 shows, income actually decreased by $55,000. Why was the outcome so different from what Devon anticipated?

Exhibit 8–10

Income Statement, 2001, Absorption-Costing Basis

	Elcom, Inc. Income Statement, 2001 Absorption-Costing Basis
Sales	$400,000
Less: Cost of goods sold	430,000
Gross margin	$ (30,000)
Less: Selling and administrative expenses	35,000
Net income (loss)	$ (65,000)

Segmented Reporting: Variable-Costing Basis

A segmented income statement using variable costing provides the essential cost information for assessing the role of the video recorder line. Exhibit 8–11 gives the segmented income statement using variable costing for 2000.

Exhibit   8–11

Segmented Income
Statement, 2000,
Variable-Costing Basis

Elcom, Inc. Segmented Income Statement, 2000 Variable-Costing Basis			
	Stereos	Video Recorders	Total
Sales	$400,000	$290,000	$690,000
Less variable expenses:			
Variable cost of goods sold	300,000	200,000	500,000
Variable selling and administrative	5,000	10,000	15,000
Contribution margin	$ 95,000	$ 80,000	$175,000
Less direct fixed expenses:			
Direct fixed overhead	30,000	20,000	50,000
Direct selling and administrative	10,000	5,000	15,000
Segment margin	$ 55,000	$ 55,000	$110,000
Less common fixed expenses:			
Common fixed overhead			100,000
Common selling and administrative			20,000
Net income (loss)			$ (10,000)

Segmented income statements using variable costing have one feature in addition to the variable-costing income statements already shown. Fixed expenses are broken down into two categories: direct fixed expenses and common fixed expenses. This additional subdivision highlights controllable versus noncontrollable costs and enhances the manager's ability to evaluate each segment's contribution to overall firm performance.

Direct fixed expenses are fixed expenses that are directly traceable to a segment (a product line in this example). These are sometimes referred to as *avoidable fixed expenses* or *traceable fixed expenses*, because they vanish if the segment is eliminated. These fixed expenses are caused by the existence of the segment itself. In the Elcom example, amortization on equipment used in producing video recorders and the salary of the production supervisor of the video recorder production line are examples of direct fixed expenses.

Common fixed expenses are jointly caused by two or more segments. These expenses persist even if one of the segments to which they are common is eliminated. In the Elcom example, plant amortization and the salary of the plant supervisor are common fixed expenses. Elimination of the video recorder line did not eliminate the plant and its associated amortization. Similarly, the plant supervisor was still needed to oversee the production of the stereo product line.

Fixed costs that are direct for one segment definition may be indirect, or common, for another definition. For example, suppose that the stereo product line is segmented into two sales territories. In that case, the amortization on the equipment used to produce stereos is common to both territories but directly traceable to the product segment itself.

Now let's examine Exhibit 8–11 to see whether this form of segmented income statement is more useful than the absorption-costing format. Notice that both stereos and video recorders have large positive contribution margins ($95,000 for stereos and $80,000 for video recorders). Both products are providing revenue above variable costs that can be used to help cover the firm's fixed costs. However, some of the firm's fixed costs are caused by the segments themselves. Thus, the real measure of each segment's profit contribution is what is left over after these direct fixed costs are covered.

The profit contribution each segment makes toward covering a firm's common fixed costs is called the **segment margin**. A segment should at least be able to cover both its own variable costs and its own direct fixed costs. A negative segment margin drags down the firm's total profit, making it time to consider dropping the product. Ignoring any effect a segment may have on the sales of other segments, we see that the segment margin measures the change in a firm's profits that would occur if the segment were eliminated.

From Exhibit 8–11, we see that the video recorder line contributes $55,000 toward covering Elcom's common fixed costs. If the line is dropped, total profit decreases by $55,000—exactly what happened, as shown in Exhibit 8–10. Dropping the video recorder line was a disastrous decision, and Exhibit 8–11 shows why.

The correct decision is to retain both product lines. Both are making equal contributions to the firm's profitability. Dropping either product simply aggravates the problem, unless the dropped product is replaced by a product with a higher segment margin. Since both products have large positive contribution margins, other solutions to the net loss are needed. Accounting can help by focusing on a more detailed analysis of costs using activity-based costing.

Segmented Reporting: Activity-Based Costing Approach

An activity-based costing approach, with its insight into unit-, batch-, product-, and facility-level costs, may give management a more accurate feel for profits attributable to different product lines and for the existence of nonvalue-added costs. Elcom's overhead costs can be further analyzed by determining activities and drivers.

Suppose that the common fixed overhead includes material handling and maintenance. Direct fixed overhead includes setups. Elcom figures that the annual cost of each activity is as follows:

Material handling	$20,000
Maintenance costs	8,000
Setups	18,000

Now Elcom has some idea of where to focus attention. Material handling is a nonvalue-added activity, as are setups. Any reduction in these can go directly to the bottom line. Perhaps a reconfiguration of the plant will lead to lower material-handling costs, or perhaps a new agreement with suppliers can lead to having materials delivered directly to the line. Similarly, a change in the configuration of the assembly process might lead to quicker, cheaper setups. Finally, noticing that maintenance costs $8,000 might lead to a re-examination of the way in which maintenance is done. A JIT approach to manufacturing could lead to having maintenance done by line workers during downtime.

An activity-based approach shows the complexity of the manufacturing operation and reminds managers that a decrease in power costs can be achieved only with a decrease in machine usage (perhaps by the use of more efficient machinery). Similarly, a decrease in setup costs can come about only through streamlining or eliminating setup activity. Reducing activities reduces actual costs and leads to increased profits.

Customer Profitability

While customers are clearly important to profit, some are more profitable than others. Companies that assess the profitability of various customer groups can more accurately target their markets and increase profits. The first step in determining customer profitability is to identify the customer. The second step is to determine which customers add value to the company.

The identification of a company's customer may seem obvious. Grocery stores and automobile repair shops can easily identify their customers, and may even know them by name. However, frequently the company is part of a complex chain of customer relationships. For example, Weldcraft Products, Inc., produces welding torches, which are sold to distributors, retail stores, and, eventually, companies and individuals who use the torches to weld. Weldcraft determined that its main customer is distributors and redistributed its activities so that Weldcraft salespeople now spend much of their time with distributors.[6]

Once customer groups have been identified, the second step is to determine which customer groups are most profitable, eliminate the unprofitable customers, and retain and add to the base of profitable customers.

Some customers are so unprofitable that they should not be kept. Rice Lake Products, Inc., manufactures movable owl and geese decoys. The company sold both to specialty stores and to Wal-Mart. However, the Wal-Mart sales, at $19 each, infuriated the specialty stores that charged $20. Even worse from the viewpoint of Rice Lake Products was that the profit on a Wal-Mart sale averaged just $0.50, whereas the profit on a specialty store sale amounted to $4. The reason for the difference was that Wal-Mart required special packaging and promotion, and returned product that did not sell. Rice Lake Products chose to concentrate on sales to specialty stores.[7]

Sometimes, a company may need to add an initially unprofitable customer group, and then increase efficiency to make the group profitable. The highly competitive personal computer industry is finding that out. Gateway 2000, Inc., was initially very successful selling personal computing systems to technically inclined customers. Such customers know the difference between RAM and ROM and can easily assemble their own components into a working computer. However, the company's explosive growth has meant that less technically inclined customers have become a large proportion of the customer base. This new type of customer causes Gateway to incur additional costs. The early computer-savvy customer required relatively little technical support. The new customer base knows how to operate a computer, but wants the hardware preselected and configured in a package, wants the software installed by the company, and wants one-on-one help in troubleshooting problems. An important part of keeping these customers happy—so that they will continue to upgrade within the Gateway line—is good technical support. Consequently, Gateway has had to greatly increase the number of technical support personnel who work with buyers who call the firm's toll-free number.[8] Just as important in keeping the profits up in this environment is finding ways to keep the costs down, by improving quality control and simplifying the written instructions that accompany the new computer.

It is generally more costly to win a customer than to keep a customer. Originating a customer may require advertising, sales calls, the drafting of proposals, and the generation of prospective customer lists. All of these activities are costly. Keeping existing customers happy also requires effort. For example, many stores provide free gift wrapping as a service to the customer who has already made a purchase. Firms must have profitability data to understand the profit contribution of customer relationships, to match the costs of increased service with the benefits. Many companies are now taking a customer life-cycle approach, by recognizing that a loyal customer will yield significant revenue over the years. For example, the lifetime revenue stream of a pizza eater can be $8,000. For more expensive products, like a Cadillac, the amount approaches $332,000.[9]

Relational databases and improved accounting systems can greatly assist the effort to track customer profitability. Profitability analysis of various customer classes requires information on the product, marketing, and administrative activities used to serve each class. Let's analyze Barton, Inc., a manufacturer of highly realistic

6. Ellen Graham, "Meat and Potatoes: Sometimes the Most Successful Courses Are the Most Basic," *The Wall Street Journal*, 10 September 1993, R5.

7. Christie Brown, "A Great Way to Retire," *Forbes*, 9 October 1995, 96–97.

8. Lois Therrien, "Why Gateway Is Racing to Answer on the First Ring," *Business Week*, 13 September 1993, 92–94.

9. James L. Heskett, Thomas O. Jones, Gary W. Loveman, W. Early Sasser, Jr., and Leonard A. Schlesinger, "Putting the Service-Profit Chain to Work," *Harvard Business Review* (March/April 1994): 164–174.

model horses sold to three classes of customer: large discount chains, small independent toy stores, and hobbyists. Each model is made of high-density plastic, from a detailed mould. A team of designers ensures that the design is accurate for the breed depicted. Colour pigments are deep and rich. While Barton produces many designs, they all incur roughly the same manufacturing costs. Exhibit 8–12 provides manufacturing and marketing data.

Each class of customer places different demands on Barton. The large toy chains purchase 63 percent of the output. They receive price discounts averaging $1.25 per unit and are linked to Barton through electronic data interchange (EDI). As a result, when supplies at the chains run low, an order is transmitted electronically to Barton's factory and another shipment of models dispatched. No commissions are paid on chain store sales. However, Barton must pay each chain store outlet $1,500 per year for shelf space (this ensures premium shelf position within the stores). There are 75 outlets. Barton pays shipping costs. The chain stores are not particular about which models are shipped; therefore, Barton typically sends whatever is in stock at the time. There is no special packaging involved.

The independent toy stores are smaller and typically stock upscale toys with a heavily educational flavour. About 35 percent of Barton's production is sold to them. No price discounts are given to these stores, and no shelf space is paid for. However, a sales commission of $0.75 per unit sold is paid to the independent wholesale jobbers who sell to the stores. The stores pay any shipping costs from Barton's factory. The independent toy stores prefer models with a story attached. For example, a series of models of Indian war horses with accompanying explanatory booklets and special packaging are quite popular. Therefore, Barton attempts to ship all models with special packaging to the independents.

The final 2 percent of Barton's sales take place at summer fairs. Each summer Barton stages five model fairs around the United States. Fun and colourful, the fairs are designed to display the Barton models, to provide a meeting opportunity for model horse hobbyists, and to generate interest in the Barton product. Barton reserves meeting rooms at a hotel for two days, invites local area hobbyists to put on shows and demonstrations, and sets up a series of trading booths for model horse fanciers. Several of Barton's staff (designers, the president, and the vice-president of marketing) attend to chat with customers, answer questions, and display (and sell) the latest models. To generate additional interest in the fairs, a special model available only at that summer's fairs is designed and produced. The special model requires 150 hours of design time (at $14 per hour) and one setup (costing $1,000).

Exhibit 8–12

Cost Information for Barton, Inc.

Manufacturing expenses:	
Units produced	500,000
Average price per model	$15
Direct materials per unit	$5
Direct labour cost	$2
Overhead per unit	$1
Marketing expenses:	
Commissions (per model sold)	$0.75
Special packaging per unit	$0.20
EDI costs per year	$100,000
Fair expense	$75,000
Shipping	$157,500
Shelf space charges	$112,500

Exhibit **8–13**

Customer Analysis for
Barton, Inc.

Profit for Chain Stores	
Sales	$4,725,000
Less: Discounts	393,750
Net sales	$4,331,250
Less: Cost of goods sold	2,520,000
Gross profit	$1,811,250
Less: Shelf space	112,500
Shipping	157,500
EDI	100,000
Profit	$1,441,250

Profit for Independent Toy Stores	
Sales	$2,625,000
Less: Cost of goods sold	1,400,000
Gross profit	$1,225,000
Less: Commissions	131,250
Special packaging	35,000
Profit	$1,058,750

Profit for Fairs	
Sales	$150,000
Less: Cost of goods sold	80,000
Gross profit	$ 70,000
Less: Fair expense	75,000
Design time	2,100
Setup	1,000
Loss	$ (8,100)

Given this information, Barton can analyze profitability by customer class. Exhibit 8–13 provides profit statements for each class of customer. The chain stores yield the most revenue, but it must be adjusted for discounts. Expenses directly attributable to the chain store outlets include shelf space payments, shipping charges, and the cost of the EDI equipment and personnel. The independent toy stores receive no price discount, but do require special packaging and the payment of commissions. The fairs have the lowest revenue, with expenses consisting of fair expense, special design, and setup.

Clearly, the chain stores are the most profitable, followed by the independent toy stores. The fairs are unprofitable. An activity-based analysis can give Barton's management a better idea of which activities to emphasize and where cost cutting might occur. For example, the fairs are money losers on the basis of sales. Perhaps management might consider them a promotional activity and not a customer class at all. In fact, the fairs' major objective is to stimulate interest in the entire Barton line, not merely to sell 10,000 models. Therefore, the entire cost of the fairs could be added to overall marketing expense.

These activity-based data can also give management a good idea of the cost of expanding into one area and away from another. For example, should Barton sell to one more chain outlet if it is at capacity? Each chain outlet averages sales of 4,200 models (315,000/75 outlets). These 4,200 models would not be sold to the independent toy stores. The analysis is as follows:

Profit from Adding One More Chain Outlet:

Revenue from additional outlet	$63,000
Less: discount	5,250
Net additional revenue	$57,750
Less: Cost of goods sold	37,800
Shipping	2,100
Shelf space	1,500
Profit from added outlet	$16,350

Profit from Selling 4,200 Models to Independent Toy Stores:

Revenue	$63,000
Less: Cost of goods sold	37,800
Special packaging	840
Commission	3,150
Profit from independents	$21,210

Barton should continue to sell to the independent toy stores, because the chain outlets are less profitable.

Activity-based accounting can provide data on these marketing activities, which are important in customer profitability analysis. However, it is important to remember that activities alone do not cause costs. Other factors—such as time, business volumes, and earlier decisions—may lead to efficiencies or inefficiencies.

VARIABLE COSTING FOR PLANNING AND CONTROL

Financial planning requires managers to estimate future sales, future production levels, future costs, and so on. Sales forecasts determine production plans, which in turn determine the level of expenditures required for raw materials, direct labour, and manufacturing overhead. Because sales forecasts are not certain, management may wish to look at several different levels of sales to assess the range of possibilities facing the firm. Knowledge of cost behaviour is fundamental to achieving this outcome. Fixed costs do not vary with volume changes, so distinguishing between fixed and variable costs is essential to making an accurate cost assessment at the different possible sales and production volumes.

Once management has chosen one expected sales and production level for the coming year, the costs that should occur can also be determined. The financial plan, then, consists of the expected activity levels and the associated expected costs. This plan can be used to monitor the actual performance as it unfolds.

If actual performance is different from what was expected, corrective action may be necessary. By comparing actual outcomes with the expected outcomes and taking corrective action when necessary, managers exercise control. For the control process to work, though, cost behaviour must be known.

Suppose the financial plan called for 12,000 units to be produced for the year, and the utility cost planned for the year is $18,000. At the end of the first month, the company has produced 3,000 units and spent $4,500 on utilities. Are utility costs being incurred as planned?

Under an absorption-costing approach, the planned utility cost per unit produced is $1.50 ($18,000/12,000). Therefore, for 3,000 units, the firm should spend $4,500 ($1.50 × 3,000). Since the expected utility cost for 3,000 units was $4,500, and the actual cost was $4,500, the plan appears to be unfolding as expected. Unfortunately, this calculation ignores cost behaviour. It assumes that all costs are variable. In reality, the utility cost is a flat fee of $1,000 per month plus $0.50 per kilowatt-hour. If it takes 1 kilowatt-hour to produce 1 unit of output, the expected cost for the 3,000 units produced in one month is $2,500 ($1,000 + $0.50 × 3,000 units). The company should have spent $2,500 on utilities to produce 3,000 units, but it spent $4,500. The plan is not unfolding as it should.

The correct signal about the planned utility cost is given when cost behaviour is considered. Once again, we see the importance of the distinction between fixed and variable costs. Since this distinction is basic to variable costing, we must conclude that variable costing is superior to absorption costing for internal purposes.

SUMMARY OF LEARNING OBJECTIVES

1. Explain the differences between variable and absorption costing.

Variable and absorption costing differ in their treatment of fixed overhead. Variable costing treats fixed overhead as a period expense. Thus, unit production cost under variable costing consists of direct materials, direct labour, and variable overhead. Absorption costing treats fixed overhead as a product cost. Thus, unit production cost under absorption costing consists of direct materials, direct labour, variable overhead, and a share of fixed overhead.

A variable-costing income statement divides expenses according to cost behaviour. First, variable expenses of manufacturing, marketing, and administration are subtracted from sales to yield the contribution margin. Then all fixed expenses are subtracted from the contribution margin to yield variable-costing net income. An absorption-costing income statement divides expenses according to function. First, the cost of goods sold is subtracted from sales to yield gross profit (or gross margin). Then marketing and administrative expenses are subtracted from gross profit to yield absorption-costing net income.

2. Explain how variable costing is useful in evaluating the performance of managers.

By separating costs according to behaviour, variable costing enhances the traceability and controllability of costs. Variable costing preserves the correspondence between effort and outcome that is necessary for good evaluation of management performance.

3. Prepare a segmented income statement based on a variable-costing approach, and explain how this format can be used with activity-based costing to assess customer profitability.

A segmented income statement takes the following form:

	Segment X	Segment Y	Company
Sales	XXX	YYY	CCC
Less variable expenses	XX	YY	CC
Contribution margin	XXX	YYY	CCC
Less direct fixed expenses	XX	YY	CC
Product margin	XX	YY	CC
Less common fixed expenses			CC
Net income (loss)			CC

The use of variable costing emphasizes the cost behaviour of each segment so that management can properly evaluate each segment's contribution to the firm's overall performance. Activity-based costing can be used with the segmented income statement to provide more insight into unit-level, batch-level, and product-level costs. Customer profitability can be assessed by treating each customer group as a segment and determining the activities associated with each group.

4. Explain how variable costing can be used in planning and control.

Variable costing requires management to distinguish between fixed and variable costs. This distinction is important in determining budgeted costs.

KEY TERMS

Absorption costing, 289
Common fixed expenses, 299
Direct fixed expenses, 299

Segment, 297
Segmented reporting, 297
Segment margin, 299

Variable costing, 289

REVIEW PROBLEMS

I. ABSORPTION AND VARIABLE COSTING, SEGMENTED INCOME STATEMENTS

Fine Leathers Company produces a women's wallet and a men's wallet. Selected data for the past year follow:

	Women's Wallets	Men's Wallets
Production (units)	100,000	200,000
Sales (units)	90,000	210,000
Selling price	$5.50	$4.50
Direct labour hours	50,000	80,000
Manufacturing costs:		
Direct materials	$ 75,000	$100,000
Direct labour	250,000	400,000
Variable overhead	20,000	24,000
Fixed overhead:		
Direct	50,000	40,000
Common[a]	20,000	20,000
Nonmanufacturing costs:		
Variable selling	$ 30,000	$ 60,000
Direct fixed selling	35,000	40,000
Common fixed selling[b]	25,000	25,000

[a] Common overhead totals $40,000 and is divided equally between the two products.
[b] Common fixed selling cost totals $50,000 and is divided equally between the two products.

Budgeted fixed overhead for the year, $130,000, equalled the actual fixed overhead. Fixed overhead is assigned to products using a plantwide rate based on expected direct labour hours, which were 130,000. The company had 10,000 men's wallets in inventory at the beginning of the year. These wallets had the same unit cost as the men's wallets produced during the year.

Required:

1. Compute the unit cost for the women's and men's wallets using the variable-costing method. Compute the unit cost using absorption costing.
2. Prepare an income statement using absorption costing.
3. Prepare an income statement using variable costing.
4. Reconcile the difference between the two income statements.
5. Prepare a segmented income statement using products as segments.

Solution

1. The unit cost for a women's wallet is as follows:

Direct materials ($75,000/100,000)	$0.75
Direct labour ($250,000/100,000)	2.50
Variable overhead ($20,000/100,000)	0.20
Variable cost per unit	$3.45
Fixed overhead (50,000 × $1.00)/100,000	0.50
Absorption cost per unit	$3.95

The unit cost for a men's wallet is as follows:

Direct materials ($100,000/200,000)	$0.50
Direct labour ($400,000/200,000)	2.00
Variable overhead ($24,000/200,000)	0.12
Variable cost per unit	$2.62
Fixed overhead (80,000 × $1.00)/200,000	0.40
Absorption cost per unit	$3.02

Notice that the only difference between the variable and absorption unit costs is the assignment of the fixed overhead cost. Notice also that the fixed overhead unit cost is assigned using the predetermined fixed overhead rate ($130,000/130,000 hours = $1 per hour). For example, the women's wallets used 50,000 direct labour hours, so they receive $1 × 50,000, or $50,000, of fixed overhead. This total, when divided by the units produced, gives the $0.50 per unit fixed overhead cost. Finally, observe that variable nonmanufacturing costs are not part of the unit cost under variable costing. For both approaches, only manufacturing costs are used to compute the unit costs.

2.   The income statement under absorption costing is as follows:

Sales [($5.50 × 90,000) + ($4.50 × 210,000)]	$1,440,000
Less: Cost of goods sold [($3.95 × 90,000) + ($3.02 × 210,000)]	989,700
Gross margin	$ 450,300
Less: Selling expenses*	215,000
Net income	$ 235,300

* This is the sum of selling expenses for both products.

3.   The income statement under variable costing is as follows:

Sales [($5.50 × 90,000) + ($4.50 × 210,000)]	$1,440,000
Less variable expenses:	
Variable cost of goods sold	
[($3.45 × 90,000) + ($2.62 × 210,000)]	860,700
Variable selling expenses	90,000
Contribution margin	$ 489,300
Less fixed expenses:	
Fixed overhead	130,000
Fixed selling	125,000
Net income	$ 234,300

4.   Reconciliation is as follows:

$$I_A - I_V = \$235{,}300 - \$234{,}300 = \$1{,}000$$

Thus, variable-costing income is $1,000 less than absorption-costing income. This difference can be explained by the net change in fixed overhead found in inventory under absorption costing.

Women's wallets:	
Units produced	100,000
Units sold	90,000
Increase in inventory	10,000
Unit fixed overhead	× $0.50
Increase in fixed overhead	$5,000

Men's wallets:	
Units produced	200,000
Units sold	210,000
Decrease in inventory	(10,000)
Unit fixed overhead	× $0.40
Decrease in fixed overhead	$ (4,000)

The net change is a $1,000 ($5,000 – $4,000) increase in fixed overhead in inventories. Thus, under absorption costing, there is a net flow of $1,000 of the current period's fixed overhead into inventory. Since variable costing recognized all of the current period's fixed overhead as an expense, variable-costing income should be $1,000 lower than absorption costing, as it is.

5.   Segmented income statement:

	Women's Wallets	Men's Wallets	Total
Sales	$495,000	$945,000	$1,440,000
Less variable expenses:			
Variable cost of goods sold	310,500	550,200	860,700
Variable selling expenses	30,000	60,000	90,000
Contribution margin	$154,500	$334,800	$ 489,300
Less direct fixed expenses:			
Direct fixed overhead	50,000	40,000	90,000
Direct selling expenses	35,000	40,000	75,000
Segment margin	$ 69,500	$254,800	$ 324,300
Less common fixed expenses:			
Common fixed overhead			40,000
Common selling expenses			50,000
Net income			$ 234,300

II. ABSORPTION AND VARIABLE COSTING WITH OVER- AND UNDERAPPLIED OVERHEAD

Bellingham, Inc., has just completed its first year of operations. The unit costs on a normal costing basis are as follows:

Manufacturing costs (per unit):
Direct materials (2 kilograms × $2)	$ 4.00
Direct labour (1.5 hours × $9)	13.50
Variable overhead (1.5 hours × $2)	3.00
Fixed overhead (1.5 hours × $3)	4.50
Total	$25.00

Selling and administrative costs:
Variable	$5/unit
Fixed	$190,000

During the year, the company had the following activity:

Units produced	24,000
Units sold	21,500
Unit selling price	$42
Direct labour hours worked	36,000

Actual fixed overhead was $12,000 less than budgeted fixed overhead. Budgeted variable overhead was $5,000 less than actual variable overhead. The company used an expected actual activity level of 36,000 direct labour hours to compute the predetermined overhead rates. Any overhead variances are closed to Cost of Goods Sold.

Required:

1.   Compute the unit cost using (a) absorption costing, and (b) variable costing.
2.   Prepare an absorption-costing income statement.
3.   Prepare a variable-costing income statement.
4.   Reconcile the difference between the two income statements.

Solution

1.

Absorption Unit Cost		Variable Unit Cost	
Direct materials	$ 4.00	Direct materials	$ 4.00
Direct labour	13.50	Direct labour	13.50
Variable overhead	3.00	Variable overhead	3.00
Fixed overhead	4.50	Total	$20.50
Total	$25.00		

2.

Bellingham, Inc.
Absorption-Costing Income Statement

Sales (21,500 × $42)		$903,000
Cost of goods sold (21,500 × $25.00)	$537,500	
Less: Overapplied overhead*	7,000	530,500
Gross margin		$372,500
Less: Selling and administrative expenses		297,500
Net income		$ 75,000

* The budgeted fixed overhead rate of $3 per direct labour hour was computed based on 36,000 direct labour hours. Therefore, budgeted fixed overhead must have been $108,000. Since actual fixed overhead was $12,000 less than budgeted, actual fixed overhead must be $96,000. Similarly, the variable overhead rate of $2 per direct labour hour implies budgeted variable overhead of $72,000 ($2 × 36,000 direct labour hours). Since actual variable overhead was $5,000 higher than budgeted overhead, actual variable overhead must be $77,000. Both variable and fixed overhead were applied on the basis of direct labour hours. Since 36,000 hours were worked, total applied overhead amounts to $180,000. Actual overhead was $173,000 (actual fixed cost of $96,000 plus actual variable cost of $77,000). Applied overhead $180,000 less actual overhead $173,000 equals overapplied overhead $7,000.

3.

Bellingham, Inc.
Variable-Costing Income Statement

Sales (21,500 × $42)		$903,000
Variable cost of goods sold (21,500 × $20.50)	$440,750	
Add: Underapplied variable overhead	5,000	445,750
Variable selling expenses (21,500 × $5)		107,500
Contribution margin		$349,750
Less: Fixed overhead	$ 96,000	
Selling and administrative expenses	190,000	286,000
Net income		$ 63,750

Note that the underapplied variable overhead is simply the actual variable overhead of $77,000 minus the applied variable overhead of $72,000 ($2 × 36,000 direct labour hours). Note also that actual fixed factory overhead is charged on the income statement, not applied fixed overhead.

4.

$$I_A - I_V = \text{Fixed overhead rate} \times (\text{Production} - \text{Sales})$$
$$\$75,000 - \$63,750 = \$4.50 \times (24,000 - 21,500)$$
$$\$11,250 = \$4.50 \times (2,500)$$
$$\$11,250 = \$11,250$$

QUESTIONS FOR WRITING AND DISCUSSION

1. What is the only difference between the way costs are assigned under variable and absorption costing?

2. A company's variable manufacturing costs are $10 per unit, its variable selling expenses are $2 per unit, and its fixed overhead rate is $5 per unit. What is the per-unit inventory cost of the product under absorption costing? under variable costing?

3. Why is variable costing a more descriptive term for the product-costing method popularly known as direct costing?

4. When production is greater than sales, absorption-costing income is greater than variable-costing income. Why?

5. When sales are greater than production, variable-costing income is greater than absorption-costing income. Why?

6. Assume that a company has a fixed overhead rate of $8 per unit produced. During the year, the company produced 10,000 units and sold 8,000. What is the difference in income generated according to absorption costing and to variable costing?

7. The fixed overhead expense recognized on an income statement was $100,000. The fixed overhead for the period was $80,000. Was the income statement prepared using absorption costing or variable costing? Explain.

8. Why is variable costing better than absorption costing for the evaluation of managerial performance?

9. Why is variable costing better than absorption costing for the evaluation of segment performance?

10. Why is variable costing better than absorption costing for planning and controlling costs?

11. What is the difference between a direct fixed cost and a common fixed cost? Why is this difference important?

12. What is the difference between segment margin and contribution margin?

13. Explain how income under absorption costing can increase from one period to the next even though selling prices and costs have remained the same.

14. How would a segment be identified within a firm?

15. How is activity-based costing applied to segmented reporting?

16. Explain how treating customer groups as segments can be useful to a firm.

17. What is a direct fixed expense? Why is it useful for segment performance evaluation?

EXERCISES

8–1

Unit Costs, Inventory Valuation, Variable and Absorption Costing

LO1

Richard Company produced 25,000 units during its first year of operations and sold 21,500 units at $16 per unit. The company chose to use practical activity—at 25,000 units—to compute its predetermined overhead rate. Manufacturing costs are as follows:

Expected and actual fixed overhead	$65,000
Expected and actual variable overhead	26,500
Direct labour	132,500
Direct materials	162,500

Required:

1. Calculate the unit cost and the cost of finished goods inventory under absorption costing.
2. Calculate the unit cost and the cost of finished goods inventory under variable costing.
3. What is the dollar amount that would be used to report the cost of finished goods inventory to external parties? Why?

8–2

Income Statements, Variable and Absorption Costing

LO1

Spreadsheet

The following information pertains to Morina, Inc., for 2000:

Beginning inventory, units	—
Units produced	15,000
Units sold	13,800
Ending inventory, units	1,200
Variable costs per unit:	
Direct materials	$9.00
Direct labour	4.00
Variable overhead	1.50
Variable selling expenses	3.50
Fixed costs per year:	
Fixed overhead	$48,000
Fixed selling and administrative	22,000

There are no work-in-process inventories. Normal activity is 15,000 units. Expected and actual overhead costs are the same.

Required:

1. Without preparing an income statement, indicate what the difference will be between variable-costing income and absorption-costing income.
2. Assume that the selling price per unit is $30. Prepare an income statement (a) using variable costing and (b) using absorption costing.

8–3

Income Statements and Firm Performance, Variable and Absorption Costing

LO1, LO2

Spreadsheet

Irvine Company had the following operating data for its first two years of operations:

Variable cost per unit:	
Direct materials	$4
Direct labour	2
Variable overhead	1
Fixed costs per year:	
Fixed overhead	$120,000
Selling and administrative	24,300

Irvine produced 20,000 units in the first year and sold 16,000. In the second year, it produced 16,000 units and sold 20,000 units. The selling price per unit each year was $24. Irvine uses an actual-cost system for product costing.

Required:

1. Prepare income statements for both years using absorption costing. Has firm performance, as measured by income, improved or declined from Year 1 to Year 2?
2. Prepare income statements for both years using variable costing. Has firm performance, as measured by income, improved or declined from Year 1 to Year 2?

8–4

Absorption Costing, Variable Costing, Reconciliation with Fixed Overhead Variance

LO1

Denham Company uses a predetermined overhead rate based on normal capacity expressed in units of output. Normal capacity is 75,000 units, and the expected fixed overhead cost for the year is $225,000. During the year, Denham produced 74,000 units and sold 71,000 units. There was no beginning finished goods inventory. The variable-costing income statement for the year follows:

Sales (71,000 units × $20)	$1,420,000
Less variable costs:	
Variable cost of goods sold	710,000
Variable selling expenses	355,000
Contribution margin	$ 355,000
Less fixed costs:	
Fixed overhead	225,000
Fixed selling and administrative	75,000
Net income	$ 55,000

Any under- or overapplied overhead is closed to Cost of Goods Sold. Variable cost of goods sold is already adjusted for any variable overhead variance.

Required:

1. Denham Company needs an income statement based on absorption costing for external reporting. Using the provided information, prepare this statement.
2. Explain the difference between the income reported by variable costing and by absorption costing.

8–5

Segmented Income Statements, Product-Line Analysis

LO3, LO4

Cocino Company produces blenders and coffee makers. During the past year, 100,000 blenders and 25,000 coffee makers were produced and sold. Fixed costs for Cocino totalled $250,000, of which $90,000 can be avoided if the blenders are not produced and $45,000 can be avoided if the coffee makers are not produced. Revenue and variable-cost information follow:

	Blenders	Coffee Makers
Variable expenses per appliance	$20	$43
Selling price per appliance	$22	$45

Required:

1. Prepare product-line income statements. Segregate direct and common fixed costs.
2. What would be the effect on Cocino's profit if the coffee-maker line were dropped? the blender line?
3. What would be the effect on firm profits if an additional 10,000 blenders could be produced (using existing capacity) and sold for $20.50 on a special-order basis? Assume that existing sales would be unaffected by the special order.

8–6

Product-Line Analysis with Complementary Effects

LO3, LO4

FunTime Company produces three lines of greeting cards: scented, musical, and regular. A segmented income statement for the past year is as follows:

	Scented	Musical	Regular	Total
Sales	$10,000	$15,000	$25,000	$50,000
Less: Variable expenses	7,000	12,000	12,500	31,500
Contribution margin	$ 3,000	$ 3,000	$12,500	$18,500
Less: Direct fixed expenses	4,000	5,000	3,000	12,000
Segment margin	$ (1,000)	$ (2,000)	$ 9,500	$ 6,500
Common fixed expenses				7,500
Net profit (loss)				$ (1,000)

Louise LaFortune, FunTime's president, is concerned about her firm's financial performance and is seriously considering dropping both the scented and musical product lines. However, before making a final decision, she consults Jim Dorn, FunTime's vice-president of marketing.

Required:

1. Jim believes that if FunTime increased advertising by $1,000 ($250 for the scented line and $750 for the musical line), sales of those two lines would increase by 30 percent. If you were Louise, how would you react to this information?
2. Jim warns Louise that eliminating the scented and musical lines would lower the sales of the regular line by 20 percent. Given this information, would it be profitable to eliminate the scented and musical lines?
3. Suppose that eliminating either line reduces sales of the regular cards by 10 percent. Would a combination of increased advertising (the option described in Requirement 1) and eliminating one of the lines be beneficial? Identify the best combination for the firm.

8–7

Absorption Costing, Variable Costing, Income Statements, Inventory Valuation, Income Reconciliation

LO1

Emby Company produces and sells soccer balls. The operating costs for the past year were as follows:

Variable costs per unit:	
Direct materials	$2.10
Direct labour	3.70
Variable overhead	0.30
Variable selling	1.20
Fixed costs per year:	
Fixed overhead	$180,000
Selling and administrative	60,000

During the year, Emby produced 200,000 soccer balls and sold 225,000 at $12.00 each. Emby had 31,000 balls in beginning finished goods inventory; costs have not changed from last year to this year. An actual-cost system is used for product costing.

Required:

1. What is the per-unit inventory cost that will be reported on Emby's balance sheet at the end of the year? What will be the reported income?

2. What would the per-unit inventory cost be under variable costing? Does this differ from the unit cost computed in Requirement 1? Why? What would income be using variable costing?

3. Reconcile the difference between the variable-costing and the absorption-costing income figures.

8–8

Variable Costing, Absorption Costing, Income Statements, Inventory Valuation, Underapplied Fixed Overhead

LO1

During its first year of operations, Sugarsmooth, Inc., produced 55,000 jars of hand cream based on a formula containing 10 percent glycolic acid. Unit sales were 53,500 jars. Fixed overhead was applied at $0.50 per unit produced. Fixed overhead was underapplied by $10,000. This fixed overhead variance was closed to Cost of Goods Sold. There was no variable overhead variance. The results of the year's operations are as follows (on an absorption-costing basis):

Sales (53,500 units × $8.50)	$454,750
Less: Cost of goods sold	170,500
Gross margin	$284,250
Less: Selling and administrative (all fixed)	120,000
Net income	$164,250

Required:

1. Give the cost of the firm's ending inventory under absorption costing. What is the cost of the ending inventory under variable costing?

2. Prepare a variable-costing income statement. Reconcile the difference between the two income figures.

8–9

Customer Profitability

LO3

Refer to 8–8. At the end of the first year of operations, Sugarsmooth is considering expanding its customer base. In its first year, it sold to small drugstores and supermarkets. Now, Sugarsmooth wants to add large discount stores and small beauty shops. Working together, the company controller and marketing manager have accumulated the following information:

a. Anticipated sales to discount stores would be 20,000 units at a discounted price of $6.75 each. Higher costs of shipping and return penalties would be incurred. Shipping would amount to $45,000 per year, and return penalties would average 1 percent of sales. In addition, a clerk would need to be hired solely to handle the discount stores' accounts. The clerk's salary and benefits would be $30,000 per year.

b. Anticipated sales to beauty shops would be 10,000 units, at a price of $9 each. A commission of 10 percent of sales would be paid to the independent jobbers who sell to the shops. In addition, an extra packing expense of $0.50 per unit would be incurred, because the shops require fewer bottles per carton.

c. The fixed overhead expenses and the fixed selling and administrative expenses would remain unchanged; all are treated as common costs.

Required:

1. Prepare a segmented variable-costing income statement for next year. The segments correspond to customer groups: drugstores and supermarkets, discount stores, and beauty shops.

2. Are all three customer groups profitable? Should Sugarsmooth expand its marketing base?

8–10

Variable Costing and Absorption Costing, Net Income and Inventory Valuation

LO1, LO2

During October, the Meerkat Company Ltd. produced 10,000 units. The beginning inventory on October 1 was 4,000 units. During October, 12,000 units were sold for $720,000. October cost information is available on a per-unit basis and is consistent with cost patterns of previous months:

Direct materials	$5.00
Direct labour	9.00
Variable overhead	6.00
Fixed overhead	7.00
Variable selling expense	1.00
Fixed selling and administrative expense	2.00

Required:

1. Using variable costing, produce an income statement for October.
2. If Meerkat switched to absorption costing, would its October net income be higher or lower? By how much?
3. Calculate the cost of ending inventory under (a) variable costing, and (b) absorption costing. (CMA Canada adapted)

8–11

Variable and Absorption Costing, Net Income

LO1

The Summerside Company uses absorption costing and has heard about variable costing. The appropriate data for Summerside Company and its industrial product are:

Selling price per unit	$20.00
Costs per unit:	
Direct labour	$3.00
Direct materials	5.00
Variable overhead	4.00
Monthly expenses:	
Fixed overhead	$480,000
Administrative expenses	280,000
Selling expenses	250,000

The denominator used in arriving at the fixed overhead rate was 300,000 units. The company's cost behaviour pattern is consistent. In November, Summerside Company reports the following:

Sales	315,000 units
Beginning inventory	25,000 units
Production	300,000 units

Required:

1. Using absorption costing, prepare a November income statement.
2. Using variable costing, prepare a November income statement.
3. Reconcile and explain the reason for any difference in net income between Requirements 1 and 2. (CMA Canada adapted)

8–12

Variable and Absorption Costing, Overhead Variances

LO1

During its first year of operations, Rose Company produced a product with the following variable costs per unit:

Direct materials	$15.00
Direct labour	20.00
Variable overhead	8.00

These variable costs are from the firm's normal costing system. The budgeted fixed overhead was $260,000. Practical capacity is 20,000 units, but expected production was 13,000 units. Rose's predetermined overhead rate is based on expected annual production. During the year, 14,000 units were produced and 10,500 units were sold. Actual manufacturing costs included $115,000 of variable overhead costs and $265,000 of fixed overhead costs. Rose assigns any overhead variance to Cost of Goods Sold at the end of the year.

Required:

1. Compute the amount of Cost of Goods Sold for the year if Rose used absorption costing.
2. Compute the amount of Cost of Goods Sold for the year if Rose used variable costing.
3. Explain the difference in net income reported by variable costing and absorption costing. (CGA Canada adapted)

8–13

Variable-Costing and Absorption-Costing Income Statement Net Income

LO1

The Grenada Company is comparing its traditional absorption costing with variable costing. An examination of its records provides the following information about 2001:

Budgeted production (units)	40,000
Actual production (units)	42,000
Sales (units)	45,000
Inventory, January 1, 2001 (6,000 units)	$33,000
Sales price per unit	$10.00
Variable manufacturing cost per unit	4.00
Variable selling expenses per unit	1.00
Fixed overhead (actual and budgeted)	$60,000
Fixed selling and administrative expenses	20,000

Any overhead variance is treated as a period cost and is closed to cost of goods sold.

Required:

1. Prepare a variable-costing income statement for 2001.
2. Prepare an absorption-costing income statement for 2001.
3. Reconcile the variable-costing net income with the absorption-costing net income. (CGA Canada adapted)

8–14

Variable-Costing and Absorption-Costing, Income Statements

LO1

The Manning Company manufactures personal time organizers. The following are the firm's operating data for 2000 and 2001:

	2000	2001
Units produced	60,000	50,000
Units sold	54,000	54,000
Selling price per unit	$250	$250
Variable costs per unit:		
Direct materials	$80	$80
Direct labour	40	40
Variable overhead	35	35
Variable selling expenses	30	30
Fixed overhead (total)	$2,500,000	$2,500,000
Fixed selling and administrative expenses (total)	300,000	300,000

There was no finished goods inventory on January 1, 2000. The company uses actual costing and the FIFO method for inventories.

Required:

1. Prepare income statements for 2000 and 2001 using absorption costing.
2. Prepare income statements for 2000 and 2001 using variable costing.
3. Reconcile the absorption-costing and variable-costing net income amounts for 2000 and 2001. (CGA Canada adapted)

8–15

Segmented Income Statements, Absorption Costing, Variable Costing, Regional Analysis

LO3, LO4

Copper Company sells its products in eastern and western Canada. Major plants are located in each region. Based on a recent quarterly income statement, the company's president has expressed some concern regarding performance in the Eastern Region. The income statement (prepared on an absorption-costing basis) follows:

Spreadsheet

Copper Company
Income Statement
(dollars in thousands)

	Western Region	Eastern Region	Total
Sales	$15,000	$12,000	$27,000
Less: Cost of goods sold	8,000	10,000	18,000
Gross margin	$ 7,000	$ 2,000	$ 9,000
Less: Selling and administrative	2,000	2,500	4,500
Net income (loss)	$ 5,000	$ (500)	$ 4,500

Copper sold all of the units produced during the quarter. There were no beginning or ending finished goods inventories. Twenty percent of the cost of goods sold represents fixed overhead costs. Of total fixed overhead costs, 30 percent are traceable directly to the Western Region and 20 percent to the Eastern Region. The remaining fixed overhead costs, common to both regions, are allocated equally between them. All selling and administrative costs are fixed. Of the total, $2 million representing common costs are divided equally between the two regions. Of the remaining selling and administrative fixed costs, 40 percent are traceable directly to the Western Region and 60 percent to the Eastern Region.

Required:

1. Prepare a variable-costing segmented income statement for the quarter ended. Should Copper consider eliminating the Eastern Region?
2. Express the contribution margin and the segment margin computed in Requirement 1 as a percentage of sales. Now assume that each region increases its sales activity in the next quarter by 10 percent. Assuming the same cost relationships, prepare a new variable-costing segmented income statement. Recompute the contribution margin and segment margin ratios. What happened? Explain.

8–16

Unit Cost, Inventory Valuation, Absorption and Variable Costing, Contribution Margin

LO1, LO4

Wetzel Company manufactures yo-yos. In January 2000, Wetzel began producing neon-coloured yo-yos. During the month of January, 8,000 were produced and 7,700 were sold at $6.20 each. The following costs were incurred:

Materials (plastic, string, axles)	$ 5,600
Direct labour	4,400
Variable overhead	4,800
Fixed overhead	24,000

A selling commission of 10 percent of sales price was paid. Administrative expenses, all fixed, amounted to $12,000.

Required:

1. Calculate the unit cost and cost of ending inventory under absorption costing.
2. Calculate the unit cost and cost of ending inventory under variable costing.
3. What is the contribution margin per unit?
4. Wetzel believes that neon-coloured yo-yos will take off after one year of sales. They think January 2001 sales should be twice as high as January 2000 sales. Costs are estimated to remain unchanged. What is the planned net income for Wetzel for January 2000? Did you use variable or absorption costing to determine it?

8–17

Net Income, Absorption and Variable Costing

LO1

Refer to 8–16.

Required:

1. Prepare an absorption-costing income statement for Wetzel Company for January 2000.

2. Prepare a variable-costing income statement for Wetzel Company for January 2000.
3. Reconcile the difference between the two net incomes.

8–18

Inventory Valuation under Absorption and Variable Costing, Variable-Costing Net Income

LO1

Frost Company manufactured 12,000 units during the year and sold 13,000. Frost's accountant prepared the following income statement:

Sales (13,000 × $26)		$338,000
Cost of goods sold (13,000 × $18)		234,000
Gross profit		$104,000
Marketing expense	$26,000	
Administrative expense	15,000	41,000
Net income		$ 63,000

Marketing expenses are strictly variable. Administrative expenses are entirely fixed. The fixed overhead rate is $3 per unit. Beginning inventory was 3,000 units, with a cost of $18 per unit.

Required:

1. Prepare a variable-costing income statement for Frost Company.
2. What was the value of ending inventory under absorption costing?
3. What was the value of ending inventory under variable costing?

8–19

Calculating Unit and Total Costs under Absorption Costing

LO1

Each of the following independent companies, Company A, Company B, and Company C, uses absorption costing. There are no overhead variances. Prices have stayed constant for all relevant time periods.

	A	B	C
Unit information:			
Price	$22	$?	$?
Direct materials	4	2	6
Direct labour	3	4	1
Variable overhead	1	1	1
Fixed overhead	?	3	1
Contribution margin	14	?	?
Gross profit	9	?	?
Units sold	2,000	7,600	?
Units produced	2,000	8,000	?
Beginning inventory, units	500	0	3,000
Total information:			
Sales	$?	$114,000	$136,000
Cost of goods sold	?	?	72,000
Gross profit	?	38,000	?
Variable marketing	?	9,500	24,000
Fixed marketing	5,000	8,000	?
Fixed administrative	3,000	?	8,300
Net income	?	500	16,700
Value of ending inventory	6,500	?	9,000

Required:

Replace each question mark with the correct amount.

8–20

Inventory Valuation and Net Income under Variable Costing

LO1

Refer to 8–19.

Required:

1. What are the net incomes for Companies A, B, and C using variable costing?
2. What are the values of ending inventory for Companies A, B, and C using variable costing?

8–21

**Variable and
Absorption Costing**

LO1

Camrareddy Company manufactures 35mm cameras. The cameras are sold for $25 each. Cost of goods sold is $18; of that amount, $5 is for direct materials. Variable overhead is applied at twice the rate of direct labour. Total fixed overhead is $48,000. Production was 12,000 units for this year due to the need to increase inventory by 2,000 units. Selling and administrative costs, all fixed, amounted to $37,000.

Required:

1. What was absorption-costing net income for Camrareddy Company for the year? What was variable-costing net income?
2. If beginning inventory was zero, what was the value of ending inventory under absorption costing?

8–22

**Variable and
Absorption Costing,
Performance
Evaluation**

LO1, LO4

Selwyn Shroode was hired in early 2000 to manage the Mixed Manufacturing Division and improve its profit picture. His appointment specified a 10 percent bonus of income as well as a promotion to corporate vice-president if profits in 2000 exceeded $1,000,000. The following are partial 1999 and 2000 income statements (in thousands):

		1999		2000
Sales (1,000,000 units)		$10,000		$10,000
Cost of goods sold:				
Beginning inventory	$ 0		$ 0	
Manufacturing costs	7,000		10,000	
Ending inventory	0	7,000	5,000	5,000
Gross margin		$ 3,000		$ 5,000
Selling and administrative expenses		3,000		3,000
Net income before income tax		$ 0		$ 2,000

Assume that manufacturing costs were under control in each of the two years.

Required:

1. How many units were produced in 1999? in 2000?
2. Applying the high–low method, determine the fixed and variable components of manufacturing costs.
3. Prepare variable-costing statements for each year.
4. Comment on Shroode's performance. Should Shroode get a bonus?

8–23

**Customer
Profitability**

LO3

Woolywear, Inc., manufactures knitted gloves, hats, and scarves. For several years, Woolywear sold its products to small specialty shops. Recently, the company landed a large contract (amounting to half of its output) with Giga-Mart. Cost information for Woolywear is as follows:

Units produced and sold	100,000
Average selling price (per unit)	$ 9.00
Manufacturing costs:	
Direct material (per unit)	$ 1.75
Direct labour (per unit)	1.50
Overhead (per unit)	3.00
Marketing expenses:	
Commissions (per unit)	$ 0.90
Special design (per unit)	2.00
Delivery expense	80,000
Shipping expense	20,000
Return penalties	3,000

The specialty stores require special designs, forcing Woolywear to incur additional setup and materials costs. These amount to about $2 per unit. The shipping expense is for shipment to the specialty stores, as are the commissions. Giga-Mart orders do not incur any commissions; however, the discount giant does require a $1 discount on the unit price and just-in-time deliveries. The delivery expense averages $80,000 per year. Also, Giga-Mart levies return penalties if any order does not meet its specifications. These penalties are incurred on about 15 percent of the orders and amount to 5 percent of sales price.

Required:

Compute the profit earned by Woolywear for the specialty shops and for Giga-Mart.

PROBLEMS

8–24

Variable-Costing and Absorption-Costing Income Statements

LO1

Eckel Company manufactures heavy-duty motors. Sales for last year totalled $643,200. Cost of goods sold amounted to 45 percent of sales. Of the total, 20 percent represented fixed overhead costs. Selling expenses were equally split between fixed and variable components. Administrative expenses, all fixed, totalled $60,000. Net income for last year was $170,400. Eckel produced and sold 53,600 motors last year.

Required:

1. Prepare an absorption-costing income statement for Eckel Company for last year.
2. Prepare a variable-costing income statement for Eckel Company for last year.
3. What is the variable cost per motor? What is the variable production cost per motor?

8–25

Variable Costing, Budgeted Income

LO1, LO4

Nguyen Inc. manufactures medical equipment. Nguyen's income statement is as follows:

Sales	$2,340,700
Variable cost of goods sold	1,076,722
Variable selling expense	117,035
Contribution margin	$1,146,943
Fixed overhead	550,000
Fixed selling and administrative	244,000
Net income	$ 352,943

Nguyen believes that it can increase the average price of its products by 8 percent next year. No change in quantity of products sold is forecast. Variable selling expenses will increase by 2 percent, and administrative expenses will increase by $10,500. Variable production costs will decrease by 4 percent; fixed production costs will be unchanged.

Required:

1. Prepare a budgeted variable-costing income statement for next year.
2. Suppose that Nguyen's controller believes that a more conservative estimate of the coming year's activity is a 6 percent increase in prices, no change in variable production costs, an increase in variable selling expenses of 5 percent, and an increase in administrative expenses of $15,000. Prepare a budgeted variable-costing income statement based on the more conservative figures.

8–26

Variable Costing, Targeted Net Income

LO1, LO4

Madengrad Company manufactures a single electronic product called Precisionmix. This unit is a batch-density monitoring device that attaches to the large industrial mixing machines used in flour, rubber, petroleum, and chemical manufacturing. Precisionmix sells for $900 per unit. The following variable costs are incurred to produce each Precisionmix device:

Direct labour	$180
Direct materials	240
Variable overhead	105
Variable product cost	$525
Marketing cost	75
Total variable cost	$600

Madengrad's annual fixed costs are $6,600,000. Except for an operating loss incurred in the year of incorporation, the firm has been profitable over the last five years. Madengrad is forecasting sales of 21,500 units for next year and has budgeted production at that level.

Required:

1. Prepare a pro forma variable-costing income statement for Madengrad Company for next year.
2. Madengrad has just learned of a significant change in production technology that will cause a 10 percent increase in total annual fixed costs and a 20 percent unit labour cost increase as a result of needing higher-skilled direct labour. However, this change permits the replacement of a costly imported component with a domestic component. The effect is to reduce unit material costs and variable overhead costs by 25 percent. No change in selling price is forecast. Prepare a variable-costing income statement for Madengrad Company for next year assuming that it invests in the new production technology. (US CMA adapted)

8–27

Segment Analysis, Addition of a New Product

LO3

Sandia Company currently produces two products, A and B. The company has sufficient floor space to manufacture an additional product, with two (C and D) currently under consideration. Only one of the two products can be chosen. The expected annual sales and associated costs for each product are as follows:

	Product C	Product D
Sales	$100,000	$125,000
Variable costs as a percentage of sales:		
Production	54%	65%
Selling and administrative	12%	5%
Direct fixed expenses	$15,000	$11,250

The company's common fixed costs are allocated to each product line on the basis of sales revenues. The following income statement for last year's operations is also available:

	Product A	Product B	Total
Sales	$250,000	$375,000	$625,000
Less variable expenses:			
Cost of goods sold	100,000	250,000	350,000
Selling and administrative	20,000	65,000	85,000
Contribution margin	$130,000	$ 60,000	$190,000
Less: Direct fixed expenses	10,000	55,000	65,000
Segment margin	$120,000	$ 5,000	$125,000
Less: Common fixed expenses			75,000
Net income			$ 50,000

Required:

1. Prepare an income statement that reflects the impact on the firm's profits of adding Product C. Repeat for Product D. Which of the two would you recommend adding?

2.   Suppose that both Products C and D could be added if either A or B were dropped. Would you drop one of the current products to add both C and D? If so, which would you drop? Why?

8–28

Variable-Costing and Absorption-Costing Income Statements

LO1, LO2, LO4

The following information was taken from the records of Jarrett Company Ltd. during its first six months of operations, which ended May 31, 2001:

Production	27,000 units
Sales	22,000 units
Selling price	$15 per unit
Production costs incurred:	
Direct materials used	$ 67,500
Direct labour	101,250
Variable overhead	54,000
Fixed overhead	189,000
Selling and administrative expenses:	
Variable (commissions)	5% of sales
Fixed	$ 30,000

All ending inventories are complete. Since Jarrett is a new company, its president is interested in installing a proper costing system. He is aware of two alternatives available to him: a full (absorption-based) system, or a variable-costing-based system.

Required:

1.   To assist the president in his decision, prepare two income statements for the six months ended May 31, 2001.
2.   Reconcile the two net incomes, showing your calculations.
3.   Advise the president on which statement approach you feel he should use, pointing out the advantages and disadvantages of each. (CMA Canada adapted)

8–29

Variable Costing, Absorption Costing

LO1

The Moonbeam Company used absorption costing in producing the following income statement for 2001:

Sales (6,000 units)		$240,000
Cost of goods sold:		
Inventory, January 1 (1,500 units)	$ 42,000	
Cost of goods manufactured (6,700 units)	187,600	
Cost of goods available for sale	$229,600	
Less: inventory, December 31	61,600	
Cost of goods sold		168,000
Gross profit		$ 72,000
Operating expenses:		
Selling	$ 24,000	
Administrative	43,000	67,000
Net Income		$ 5,000

An analysis of the costs indicates the following:
- the selling costs are all variable;
- 85% of the administrative costs are fixed; and
- 40% of all manufacturing costs are fixed.

Required:

1.   Produce an income statement using variable costing.
2.   Under what circumstances would a difference arise between net income under absorption costing and net income under variable costing? Reconcile the two net incomes, showing your calculations. (CMA Canada adapted)

8–30

**Absorption Costing
and Inventory
Changes**

LO1, LO2, LO4

B. T. Company Ltd. prepared the following budgeted income statement based on production and sales estimates of 20,000 units:

Sales		$400,000
Cost of goods sold:		
Direct materials	$ 80,000	
Direct labour	60,000	
Variable overhead	40,000	
Fixed overhead*	100,000	
Total cost of goods sold		280,000
Gross profit		$120,000
Selling and administrative expenses:		
Variable	$ 30,000	
Fixed	40,000	
Total selling and administration		70,000
Net income		$ 50,000

* Relevant range of 15,000 to 50,000 units.

During 2001, the company produced 25,000 units and sold 20,000 units. All costs and revenues behaved precisely as expected, but net income was $70,000 instead of the $50,000 expected.

Required:

1. Prepare B. T. Company's income statement for 2001.
2. Why is net income different from that expected? Explain the difference using the actual figures given.
3. What costing system or method would avoid this change in net income? Explain. (CMA Canada adapted)

8–31

**Variable Costing,
Absorption Costing**

LO1

Blades Products was organized as a new division of Amalgamated Stuff, Inc., to produce in-line roller skates. With the continuing popularity of physical fitness, the divisional manager expected a good response to the product. In the first year of operations, Blades reported the following net income to its shareholders:

**Blades Products
Income Statement
For the Year Ended December 31, 2000**

Sales (@ $85)	$42,500,000
Less: Cost of goods sold (@ $65)[a]	32,500,000
Gross margin	$10,000,000
Less: Selling and administrative[b]	5,125,000
Net income	$ 4,875,000

[a] Direct materials $24
  Direct labour 12
  Variable overhead 15
  Fixed overhead 14
  Total $65

[b] $6.25 per unit variable; $2,000,000 fixed

In 2000, Blades produced 100,000 units more than it sold, because sales were less than expected. The divisional manager believed the sales slump was due to a soft economy and was confident that second-year sales would be 20 percent higher. Overhead is applied on the basis of units produced using expected actual activity. Any under- or overapplied overhead is closed to Cost of Goods Sold. For 2000, there was no under- or overapplied overhead.

For 2001, fixed costs and unit variable costs remained the same; the selling price also remained unchanged. Budgeted fixed costs equalled actual fixed costs. In 2001,

Blades produced 500,000 units and sold 600,000 units. Production was 100,000 less than expected, because of unanticipated equipment problems. However, the divisional manager was not displeased: the 20 percent sales increase had been achieved, and production costs were completely in line with plans.

Required:

1. Prepare the 2001 income statement required for shareholders. Did income increase or decrease? What do you think the reaction of the parent company, Amalgamated Stuff, Inc., would be to this income statement? What would the divisional manager's reaction be?
2. Prepare variable-costing income statements for 2000 and 2001. How do you suppose Amalgamated Stuff, Inc., would react now?
3. Reconcile and explain the differences between the variable-costing and absorption-costing income figures for 2000 and 2001.
4. Which type of income statement (variable- or absorption-costing) do you think the divisional manager would prefer? Why?

8–32

Variable Costing, Absorption Costing, Income Statements, Inventory Valuations

LO1

Beldar Company produces and sells a single product. Cost data for the product follow:

Unit variable costs:	
Direct materials	$4
Direct labour	2
Variable overhead	2
Variable selling	1
Total	$9
Fixed costs per year:*	
Overhead	$ 960,000
Selling and administrative	300,000
Total	$1,260,000

* Fixed costs are incurred uniformly throughout the year.

During the first three months, the company produced and sold the following units:

	Units Produced	Units Sold
Month 1	50,000	40,000
Month 2	40,000	40,000
Month 3	40,000	30,000

The company uses an actual-cost system to assign the costs of production. The selling price of the product is $14 per unit. A FIFO inventory system is used.

Required:

1. What is the unit cost for each month under absorption costing? under variable costing?
2. Without preparing income statements, determine the difference between absorption-costing and variable-costing income for each of the three months.
3. Prepare income statements using absorption costing and variable costing for each of the three months. Reconcile the net income figures.

8–33

Segmented Income Statements, Analysis of Proposals to Improve Profits

LO2, LO3

Harris, Inc., has two divisions. One produces and sells paper diapers; the other produces and sells paper napkins and paper towels. A segmented income statement for the most recent quarter follows:

	Diaper Division	Paper Napkin and Towel Division	Total
Sales	$500,000	$750,000	$1,250,000
Less: Variable expenses	425,000	460,000	885,000
Contribution margin	$ 75,000	$290,000	$ 365,000
Less: Direct fixed expenses	85,000	110,000	195,000
Segment margin	$ (10,000)	$180,000	$ 170,000
Less: Common fixed expenses			130,000
Net income			$ 40,000

On seeing the quarterly statement, Rebekkah Cornfield, the president of Harris, Inc., was distressed. "The Diaper Division is killing us," she complained. "It's not even covering its own fixed costs. I'm beginning to believe that we should shut down that division. This is the seventh consecutive quarter it has failed to provide a positive segment margin. I was certain that Fran Simmons could turn it around. But this is her third quarter, and she hasn't done much better than the previous divisional manager."

"Well, before you get too excited about the situation, perhaps you should evaluate Fran's most recent proposals," remarked Tom Ferguson, the company's vice-president of finance. "She wants to lease some new production equipment and at the same time increase the advertising budget by $25,000 per quarter. She has made some improvements in the design of the diaper and wants to let the public know about them. According to her marketing people, sales should increase by 10 percent if the right advertising is done—and done quickly. The new production machinery will increase the rate of production, decrease labour costs, and reduce the division's waste of materials. Fran claims that variable costs will be reduced by 30 percent. The cost of the lease is $105,000 per quarter."

Upon hearing this news, Rebekkah calmed down considerably: in fact, she was somewhat pleased. After all, she was the one who had selected Fran, and she had a great deal of confidence in Fran's judgment and abilities.

Required:

1. Assuming that Fran's proposals are sound, do you think Rebekkah Cornfield should be pleased with the prospects for the Diaper Division? Prepare a segmented income statement for the next quarter that reflects the implementation of Fran's proposals. Assume that the Napkin and Towel Division's sales increase by 5 percent for the next quarter and that the same cost relationships hold.
2. Suppose that everything materializes as Fran projected except for the 10 percent increase in sales—no change in sales revenues take place. Are the proposals still sound? What if the variable costs are reduced by 40 percent instead of 30 percent with no change in sales?

8–34

Variable-Costing, Absorption-Costing, Income Statements, Reconciliation

LO1

The Epsol Company has the following average revenues and costs based on the production and sale of 30,000 units per year:

Selling price	$25.00 per unit
Manufacturing costs:	
Direct materials	$4.00
Direct labour	5.00
Variable overhead	2.00
Fixed overhead	3.00
Total manufacturing costs	$14.00 per unit
Selling and administrative:	
Variable selling	$1.00
Fixed administrative	6.00
Total selling and administrative	$7.00 per unit

The company actually produced 32,000 units but sold only 29,000 units in the year ended February 28, 2001. They did not have a beginning inventory of Finished Goods. All revenues and costs behaved as expected during the year ended February 28, 2001.

Required:

1. Prepare an income statement for the year ended February 28, 2001, assuming that Epsol uses normal absorption costing, with any overhead variances closed to Cost of Goods Sold.
2. Prepare an income statement for the year ended February 28, 2001, assuming the company uses variable costing.
3. Explain why there is, or should be, a difference in the net operating income between the two systems (use the data given to explain the dollar amount of the difference as fully as possible). (CMA Canada adapted)

8–35

Variable and Absorption Costing, Overhead Variances

LO1, LO2

The Woods Company uses a normal absorption-costing system, with overhead being applied based on the expected capacity to be used in the year. Any overhead variances are closed to Cost of Goods Sold at the end of the year. The company has the following income statement for the year ending December 31, 2001, based on the production and sales of 20,000 units:

Sales (20,000 units × $40)		$800,000
Cost of goods sold (40% fixed)	$550,000	
Add: Underapplied overhead for the year	55,000	
Adjusted cost of goods sold		605,000
Gross profit margin		$195,000
Selling and administrative expenses (80% fixed)		180,000
Operating income		$ 15,000

The company expected to produce and sell 22,000 units in 2002, but a change in demand resulted in actual production of 23,000 units and sales of 22,500 units. All revenues and expenses behaved as expected for the year (the same as in 2001).

Required:

1. What was the company's expected production level in 2001, assuming that all revenues and expenses behaved as expected in that year?
2. What is the company's actual operating income for 2002 if they use their present costing system? variable costing?
3. Explain why operating income would normally be different between the two systems, and state exactly how much the difference should be.
4. What advantages would there be in using variable costing instead of normal absorption costing? (CMA Canada adapted)

8–36

Performance Evaluation, Absorption Costing Compared with Variable Costing

LO1, LO2

Reread the opening scenario for this chapter. The following represent three years of operating data and income statements that Kathy Wise received.

	Operating Data		
	Year 1	Year 2	Year 3
Production	10,000	11,000	9,000
Sales (in units)	8,000	10,000	12,000
Unit selling price	$10	$10	$10
Unit costs:			
Fixed overhead*	$2.90	$3.00	$3.00
Variable overhead	1.00	1.00	1.00
Direct materials	1.90	2.00	2.00
Direct labour	1.00	1.00	1.00
Variable selling	0.40	0.50	0.50
Actual fixed overhead	$29,000	$30,000	$30,000
Other fixed costs	$9,000	$10,000	$10,000

* The predetermined fixed overhead rate is based on expected actual units of production and expected fixed overhead. Expected production each year was 10,000 units. Any under- or overapplied fixed overhead is closed to Cost of Goods Sold.

Income Statements

	Year 1	Year 2	Year 3
Sales revenue	$80,000	$100,000	$120,000
Less: Cost of goods sold*	54,400	67,000	86,600
Gross margin	$25,600	$ 33,000	$ 33,400
Less: Selling and administrative	12,200	15,000	16,000
Net income	$13,400	$ 18,000	$ 17,400

* Assume a LIFO inventory flow.

Recall that Kathy was pleased with the operating data, but she was dismayed and perplexed by the income statements. Instead of seeing a significant increase in income for the third year, she saw a small decrease. Kathy's initial reaction was that the accounting department had made an error.

Required:

1. Explain to Kathy why she lost her $5,000 bonus.
2. Prepare variable-costing income statements for each of the three years. Reconcile the differences between the absorption-costing and variable-costing incomes.
3. If you were the vice-president of Kathy's company, which income statement (variable-costing or absorption-costing) would you prefer to use for evaluating Kathy's performance? Why?

8–37

Absorption Costing and Performance Evaluation

LO1, LO2

Wilmont Company's executive committee was meeting to select a new vice-president of operations. The leading candidate was Howard Kimball, manager of Wilmont's largest division. Howard had been divisional manager for three years. The president of Wilmont, Gus Olsen, was impressed with the significant improvements in the division's profits since Howard had assumed command. In the first year of operations, divisional profits had increased by 20 percent. They had shown significant improvements for the following two years as well. To bolster support for Howard, the company's president circulated the following divisional income statements (dollars in thousands):

	1999	2000	2001
Sales	$30,000	$32,000	$34,000
Less: Cost of goods sold[a]	26,250	26,900	27,900
Gross margin	$ 3,750	$ 5,100	$ 6,100
Less: Selling and administrative expenses[b]	3,000	3,600	3,800
Net income	$ 750	$ 1,500	$ 2,300

[a] Assumes a FIFO inventory flow.
[b] All costs are fixed.

"As you can see," Gus observed at a meeting, "Howard has increased profits by a factor of three since 1999. That's by far the most impressive performance of any divisional manager. We could certainly use someone with that kind of drive. I definitely believe that Howard should be the new vice-president."

"I'm not quite as convinced that Howard's performance is as impressive as it appears," responded Theo Petrou, the vice-president of finance. "I could hardly believe that Howard's division could show the magnitude of improvement revealed by the income statements, so I asked the division's controller to supply some additional information. As the data suggest, the profits realized by Howard's division may be attributable to a concerted effort to produce for inventory. In fact, I believe it can be shown that the division is actually showing a loss each year and that real profits have declined by as much as 15 percent since 1999." Theo then presented the following information:

	1999	2000	2001
Sales (units)	150,000	160,000	170,000
Production*	200,000	250,000	300,000
Actual (and budgeted) fixed overhead	$15,000,000	$15,000,000	$15,000,000
Fixed overhead rate	$75	$60	$50
Unit variable production costs	$100	$105	$110

* Represents both expected and actual production. Fixed overhead rates are computed using expected actual production.

Required:

1. Explain what Theo Petrou meant by "producing for inventory."
2. Recast the income statements in a variable-costing format. Now how does the division's performance appear?
3. Reconcile the differences in the income figures using the two methods for each of the three years.
4. If you were a shareholder, how could you detect income increases that are caused mainly by production for inventory?

8–38

Inventory Changes and Absorption-Costing Net Income, Comparison to Variable Costing

LO1, LO4

The Lion Company has prepared the following income statements at two levels of sales:

	10,000 units	15,000 units
Units produced and sold	10,000 units	15,000 units
Sales	$120,000	$180,000
Direct material	14,000	21,000
Direct labour	37,500	56,250
Variable overhead	18,750	28,125
Fixed overhead*	12,000	12,000
Sales salaries	30,000	30,000
Sales commissions (2% of sales)	2,400	3,600
Administrative costs*	25,000	25,000
Net income (loss)	$ (19,650)	$ 4,025

* Relevant range of 5,000 units to 40,000 units.

Required:

1. During 2001, the company actually sold 15,000 units, and all revenues and costs behaved as expected: but the company's net income was actually $7,025 using absorption costing. How many units did the company produce during 2001?
2. If the company used a variable-costing system, would the discrepancy between expected and actual net income occur? Explain why or why not. (CMA Canada adapted)

8–39

Variable and Absorption Costing, Overhead Variances

LO1

During November 2001, the Canberra Company produced 7,000 units. Inventory at November 1, 2001, was 3,000 units. During November, 9,000 units were sold for $450,000. Canberra uses a normal absorption-costing system with the following costs per unit:

Direct materials	$ 6.00
Direct labour	14.00
Variable overhead	7.00
Fixed overhead	5.00
	$32.00

Other information available for November 2001 is as follows:

- Variable selling expenses were $2.00 per unit.
- Fixed selling and administrative expenses were $20,000.
- The activity base for the predetermined rate was 8,000 units.
- Actual overhead was $91,000.
- Overhead variances are closed to Cost of Goods Sold each month.

Required:

1. Prepare an income statement for November 2001, using variable costing.
2. Reconcile the variable-costing net income with the reported net income, using absorption costing. (CGA Canada adapted)

8–40

Variable and Absorption Costing, Overhead Variances

LO1

Shown below is the income statement for Lampton Green Industries for 2001, when 12,000 units of product were sold:

Lampton Green Industries		
Income Statement		
For the Year Ended December 31, 2001		
Sales		$540,000
Cost of goods sold:		
Materials	$102,000	
Direct labour	84,000	
Variable overhead	75,000	
Fixed overhead	85,800	346,800
Unadjusted gross margin		$193,200
Underapplied overhead		8,580
Gross margin		$184,620
Variable selling and administration	$ 63,000	
Fixed selling and administration	80,000	143,000
Net income		$ 41,620

During 2001, 12,800 units were produced. On January 1, 2001, there were 950 units in finished goods and no units in process. On December 31, 2001, there were no units in process. Lampton Green uses a normal absorption-costing system to value inventories. There was no underapplied variable overhead in 2001. All overhead variances are closed to cost of goods sold on the income statement.

Required:

1. Determine the total amount of fixed manufacturing overhead incurred in 2001.
2. What was the total contribution margin for 2001?
3. If Lampton Green has used variable costing, what would net income be for 2001?
4. Explain the difference in net income under absorption costing from that calculated using variable costing. Show your calculations.
5. What is the value of ending inventory under absorption costing? under variable costing? (CMA Canada adapted)

8–41

Variable-Costing and Absorption-Costing Net Income

LO1

On January 1, 2000, Jaskyl Company started operations. For the first two years, Jaskyl used an absorption-costing system. The following are condensed income statements for 2000 and 2001.

	2000	2001
Sales revenue	$1,000,000	$1,200,000
Expenses (including cost of goods sold and		
administrative expenses)	850,000	950,000
Income before income taxes	$ 150,000	$ 250,000
Number of units sold	20,000	30,000

The variable costs consisted of 50 percent direct materials, 25 percent direct labour, and 25 percent variable overhead. Selling and administrative expenses were all fixed. There were 8,000 units in finished goods inventory at December 31, 2000 and 10,000 units at December 31, 2001. In 2000 and 2001, actual fixed overhead was $180,000 and $260,000, respectively. Overhead is applied on the basis of direct labour.

In 2000, there was overapplied overhead of $30,000; in 2001, there was underapplied overhead of $20,000. These amounts were due entirely to fixed overhead and were closed to Cost of Goods Sold.

Required:

1. What would be the reported net income for 2000 and 2001 if variable costing were used?
2. For 2001, prepare a variable-costing income statement (break down expenses in as much detail as possible). (CGA Canada adapted)

8–42

Comparison of Variable and Absorption Costing, Predetermined Overhead Rates

LO1

Camilleri, Inc., has just completed its first year of operations. The unit costs on a normal costing basis are as follows:

Manufacturing costs (per unit):

Direct materials (1.5 kilograms × $2)	$ 3.00
Direct labour (2 hours × $9)	18.00
Variable overhead (2 hours × $2.50)	5.00
Fixed overhead (2 hours × $3.25)	6.50
Total	$32.50

Nonmanufacturing costs:

Variable	15% of sales
Fixed	$230,000

During the year, the company had the following activity:

Units produced	30,000
Units sold	27,400
Unit selling price	$50
Direct labour hours worked	60,000

Actual fixed overhead was $10,000 greater than budgeted fixed overhead. Actual variable overhead was $5,000 greater than budgeted variable overhead. The company used an expected actual activity level of 60,000 direct labour hours to compute the predetermined overhead rates. Any overhead variances are closed to Cost of Goods Sold.

Required:

1. Compute the unit cost using (a) absorption costing, and (b) variable costing.
2. Prepare an absorption-costing income statement.
3. Prepare a variable-costing income statement.
4. Reconcile the difference between the two income statements.

8–43

Segmented Income Statements, Adding and Dropping Product Lines

LO3, LO4

Nancy Henderson has just been appointed manager of Palmroy's Glass Products Division. She has two years to make the division profitable. If the division is still showing a loss after two years, it will be eliminated, and Nancy will be reassigned as an assistant manager in another division. The divisional income statement for the most recent year is given below.

Sales	$5,350,000
Less: Variable expenses	4,750,000
Contribution margin	$ 600,000
Less: Direct fixed expenses	750,000
Divisional margin	$(150,000)
Less: Common fixed expenses (allocated)	200,000
Divisional profit (loss)	$(350,000)

Upon arriving at the division, Nancy requested the following data on the division's three products:

	Product A	Product B	Product C
Sales (units)	10,000	20,000	15,000
Unit selling price	$150	$140	$70
Unit variable costs	$100	$110	$103
Direct fixed costs	$100,000	$500,000	$150,000

She also gathered data on a proposed new product (Product D). If this product were added, it would displace one of the current products. The quantity that could be produced and sold would equal the quantity sold of the product it displaced, although demand would limit the maximum quantity that could be sold to 20,000 units. Because of specialized production equipment, it is not possible for the new product to displace part of the production of a second product. The information on Product D is as follows:

Unit selling price	$70
Unit variable cost	$30
Direct fixed costs	$640,000

Required:

1. Prepare segmented income statements for Products A, B, and C.
2. Determine the products that Nancy should produce for the coming year. Prepare segmented income statements that prove your combination is the best for the division. By how much will profits improve given the combination that you selected? (Hint: Your combination may include one, two, or three products.)

8–44

Comprehensive Review Problem: Variable Costing, Absorption Costing, Segmented Reporting

LO1, LO3

The Clock Division of Thurmond Company produces both wall clocks and table clocks. The clocks are sold in two regions, the West and the East. The table below gives the division's sales (in units) during 2000.

	West	East	Total
Wall clocks	100,000	250,000	350,000
Table clocks	250,000	520,000	770,000

Production data for 2000 are as follows (there were no beginning or ending work-in-process inventories):

	Wall Clocks	Table Clocks
Production	300,000	800,000
Direct labour hours	30,000	40,000
Manufacturing costs:		
Direct materials	$450,000	$720,000
Direct labour	210,000	200,000
Variable overhead	60,000	90,000
Fixed overhead*	360,000	540,000

* Common fixed overhead of $280,000 has been allocated to the two products on the basis of actual direct labour hours and is included in each total.

The selling prices are $4.50 for wall clocks and $3 for table clocks. Variable nonmanufacturing costs are 20 percent of the selling price for wall clocks and 30 percent of the selling price for table clocks. Total fixed nonmanufacturing costs are $300,000, with one-third common to both products and one-third traceable directly to each product. Of the fixed costs (both manufacturing and nonmanufacturing), 20 percent are common to both sales regions, 40 percent are traceable directly to the West, and 40 percent are traceable directly to the East.

Overhead is applied on the basis of direct labour hours. Normal volume is 75,000 hours (300,000 wall clocks, 900,000 table clocks), and the preceding actual overhead figures correspond to the budgeted figures used to compute the predetermined overhead rate. Any under- or overapplied overhead is closed to Cost of Goods Sold. Assume that any beginning finished goods inventory has the same unit costs as current production. The company uses FIFO to value inventories.

Required:

1. Compute the unit costs for each product using (a) absorption costing, and (b) variable costing.
2. Prepare absorption-costing and variable-costing income statements for 2000. Reconcile the difference between the two income figures.
3. Prepare a segmented income statement on a variable-costing basis where segments are defined as products.
4. Prepare a segmented income statement on a variable-costing basis where segments are defined as sales regions.

MANAGERIAL DECISION CASES

8–45

Choice of Costing System

LO1, LO2, LO4

Lougheed Custom Furniture Manufacturers Ltd. has been expanding rapidly over the past two years. During that time, the company's accounting staff consisted of one bookkeeper who was assisted frequently by the company's auditors. Because of the recent expansion, Lougheed's president, Ron Stokes, believes that it is necessary to hire a controller and also to expand the accounting staff by two additional clerks. At the same time, Stokes believes that the current accounting system should be revised to make it more flexible for planning and control purposes.

The current system at Lougheed is simple. Actual costs of material, labour, and overhead items are accumulated as incurred. Periodic inventory counts are made annually for financial statement preparation. Inventories are costed at average annual cost.

Furniture production at Lougheed is a combination of standard frames and springs and custom covering. The furniture design (that is, frame, springs, and so on) is limited to several types, whereas the upholstery for the furniture is custom-made to order.

Stokes believes that some form of job-order costing, perhaps with a predetermined overhead rate, may be advisable. Also, he wonders whether the company could benefit from a variable-costing system of the sort described to him at a recent managerial seminar. Since Stokes is considering entering the institutional market (that is, hotels, hospitals) on a special-order basis, he believes that a new system that would give him a better idea of his costs would be beneficial.

Stokes discussed the subject with his bookkeeper, Ravi Singh, who was not as enthusiastic about the changes. Singh argued that variable costing provided results as arbitrary as absorption costing and, moreover, did not give the full cost of products, something that was needed for pricing and financial reporting. Job-order costing, Singh felt, was too time consuming.

Stokes decided to hire a consultant to recommend a new accounting system for Lougheed.

Required:

As the consultant, prepare a short report analyzing the costs and benefits of an appropriate accounting system for Lougheed, considering the nature of the business described. (CMA Canada adapted)

8–46

Ethical Issues, Absorption Costing, Performance Measurement

LO1, LO2

Ruth Swazey, division controller and CMA, was upset by a recent memo she had received from the divisional manager, Anton Grebov. Ruth was scheduled to present the division's financial performance at headquarters in one week. In the memo, Anton had given Ruth some instructions for this upcoming report. In particular, she had been told to emphasize the significant improvement in the division's profits over last year. Ruth, however, didn't believe that there was any real underlying improvement in the division's performance and was reluctant to say otherwise. She knew that the increase in profits was a result of Anton's conscious decision to produce for inventory.

In an earlier meeting, Anton had convinced his plant managers to produce more than they knew they could sell. He argued that if they deferred some of this period's fixed costs, reported profits would jump. He pointed out two significant benefits. First, by increasing profits, the division could exceed the minimum level needed so that all the managers would qualify for the annual bonus. Second, by meeting the budgeted profit level, the division would be better able to compete for much-needed capital. Ruth had objected but had been overruled. The most persuasive counterargument was that the increase in inventory could be liquidated in the coming year as the economy improved. Ruth, however, considered this event unlikely. From past experience, she knew that it would take at least two years of improved market demand before the division's productive capacity was exceeded.

Required:

1. Discuss the behaviour of Anton Grebov, the divisional manager. Was the decision to produce for inventory an ethical one?
2. What should Ruth Swazey do? Should she comply with the directive to emphasize the increase in profits? If not, what options does she have?
3. In Chapter 1, ethical standards for management accountants were discussed. Identify any standards that apply in this situation.

8–47

Variable Costing versus Absorption Costing

LO1, LO2, LO4

Norma Richardson, manager of a division specializing in concrete pipe and concrete blocks, had just been rebuffed by Eric Hipple, the company's president. Eric had called a meeting of all divisional managers to discuss the downturn in business the company had been experiencing during the past two years. Eric had come down hard on the managers, pointing out that their jobs would be on the line if some immediate improvements were not forthcoming.

Norma, acting as spokesperson for the divisional managers, had tried to explain to Eric why revenues and profits were declining. In the divisional managers' view, business was suffering because residential and commercial construction was down. With the slump in the construction business, competition had intensified. Norma indicated that her division had lost several bids to competitors who were bidding below the full cost of the product. Since company policy prohibited divisional managers from accepting any jobs below full cost, these bids were lost. Norma, on behalf of the managers, requested a change in the company policy concerning bids. She proposed that the floor for bids be changed to variable cost rather than full cost. In times of economic distress, bids that covered at least their variable costs would make a positive contribution toward covering fixed costs and help maintain the divisions' profits.

Norma also proposed that divisional income statements be changed to a variable-costing basis so that a better picture of divisional performance would be available. Additionally, income statements for individual products, organized on a variable-costing basis, would provide better information concerning product performance and would facilitate bidding.

Upon hearing the request, Eric Hipple flatly turned it down. Eric was convinced that all costs must be covered or the company would go under. "It's impossible to sell a product for less than what it costs and stay in business. Those companies that do so will be the first ones to go bankrupt. Also, I want to see the income produced by your divisions when all costs are considered—not just variable costs. I don't believe in variable costing. If any of you can prove to me that variable costing is a better approach, I would consider changing."

Upon returning home, Norma decided to prepare more formal arguments to convince Eric of the value of variable costing. To help in building her case, she had the divisional controller supply the following information concerning the concrete block line.

Last quarter's production (and sales)	100,000
Productive capacity	140,000
Unit manufacturing cost:	
Direct materials	$0.22
Direct labour	0.14
Variable overhead	0.09
Fixed overhead*	0.10
Total	$0.55

Nonmanufacturing costs:	
Selling costs:	
Fixed	$10,000
Variable	5% of sales
Administrative (all fixed)	$20,000

* Based on the productive capacity of 140,000 units.

Total fixed overhead costs were $14,000 (budgeted and actual). Variable overhead was incurred as expected. Overhead variances are closed to Cost of Goods Sold. The average selling price for the 100,000 units sold was $0.90.

Required:

1. Prepare absorption-costing and variable-costing income statements for the last quarter's results. Will this information help Norma in building her case?
2. Suppose that Norma consults her marketing manager and finds that the division could have produced and sold 30,000 more concrete blocks with a unit selling price of $0.54. Compute the gross margin on the sale of these additional 30,000 blocks, assuming a price of $0.54. Now compute the total contribution margin on the 30,000 blocks. Discuss why the two figures differ.
3. Prepare absorption-costing and variable-costing income statements that reflect the sale of the additional 30,000 units at $0.54. Which figure in Requirement 2, gross margin or contribution margin, gave the best indication of the impact of the 30,000 additional units on the division's profits? Explain.
4. What approach would you take to convince Eric that variable costing is a useful managerial tool? Does he have any basis for his contention that a company must cover its full costs and that income statements should reflect all costs, not just variable costs? Explain.

RESEARCH ASSIGNMENT

8–48

Cybercase

LO1, LO2, LO3

Choose one or more of the following Web sites:

- **www.generalmills.com**
- **www.pepsico.com**
- **www.ual.com**
- **www.deere.com**
- **www.ahp.com**

Identify the types of segments for which it would be useful for the company to have income information. Now, check the company's annual report. Is the income statement reported by segment? Do the segments match your earlier identification? Why or why not? Next check the format of the income statement given in the annual report. Is it an absorption-costing or variable-costing income statement?

CHAPTER 9

Cost–Volume–Profit Analysis: A Managerial Planning Tool

Learning Objectives

After studying Chapter 9, you should be able to:

1. Determine the number of units that must be sold to break even or to earn a targeted profit.

2. Determine the amount of revenue required to break even or to earn a targeted profit.

3. Apply cost–volume–profit analysis in a multiple-product setting.

4. Prepare a profit–volume graph and a cost–volume–profit graph, and explain the meaning of each.

5. Explain the impact of risk, uncertainty, and changing variables on cost–volume–profit analysis.

6. Discuss the impact of activity-based costing on cost–volume–profit analysis.

Scenario

For years, Janet McFarland's friends and family raved about her homemade jellies and salsas. Janet traditionally canned several litres of salsa, ladled it into decorative small jars, wrapped them, and sent them as gifts. Her friends said, "You ought to sell this stuff—you'd make a fortune!" So Janet decided to give it a try.

First, she decided to concentrate on one product, a green cactus salsa that had gotten rave reviews. She scouted sources of jars, lids, and labels. In addition, Janet got in touch with her local agricultural extension office and learned a considerable amount about laws regulating food sales. One source of surprise was that she was required to obtain an expert confirmation of the ingredients in her salsa. Usually, Janet added a little of this and a little of that until it tasted right. She found out that this casual approach would not work. Foods were required to be labelled with the name of each ingredient, in order of amount. Suddenly, it mattered whether ancho or poblano chilis were used, and in what proportion. Janet needed a standardized recipe. She located a professional food chemist to analyze the recipe and certify the proportion of ingredients.

Janet travelled to a number of grocery stores and gift shops in the area. Several were willing to stock her product on consignment, placing a few jars by the cash register; others guaranteed shelf space but required a shelf charge for it. She figured that travelling to the stores, checking on sales and stock, and visiting prospective customers would take about one day a week.

Before starting production, Janet consulted with her family accountant, Bob Ryan.

Janet: "Bob, I'm really excited about this opportunity—it all seems to be falling into place."

Bob: "I'm happy for you, too, Janet. But first let's do some planning. I need to look at the costs and selling price you anticipate."

Janet: "I think I can charge $3.50 per jar. It's a new product, and I want to build a market for it. The costs I've come up with are on this sheet. They aren't as high as they could be, since I'm going to start slowly and cook small batches at a time in our kitchen."

Bob (after a couple of minutes of figuring): "Janet, do you realize that at a price of $3.50, and with the variable costs you described, you'll lose money? You can't do that."

Janet: "What if I sell more jars? Will that help?"

Bob: "No, that will just make it worse. Let's go back to the drawing board and see if there's a way to decrease those variable costs and/or increase the price. Otherwise, you would be better off never getting involved with this business."

Questions to Think About

1. What kinds of variable and fixed costs do you think Janet will incur?

2. Give Bob's initial assessment that the variable costs are higher than the price, what is wrong with Janet's thought that selling more is the way to go?

3. How important is breakeven analysis to a firm? Do you suppose that large companies as well as small companies do breakeven analysis?

4. Why is the concept of breaking even important? Doesn't Janet want to make a profit?

5. Janet doesn't know what price to charge. How could she get a better idea?

Cost–volume–profit analysis (CVP analysis) is a powerful tool for planning and decision making. Because CVP analysis emphasizes the interrelationships of costs, quantity sold, and price, it brings together all of the firm's financial information. CVP analysis can be a valuable tool for identifying the extent and magnitude of the economic trouble a division is facing and for helping to pinpoint the necessary solution. For example, SAAB was on the brink of collapse in 1990 when General Motors bought a 50 percent share in the company. Over the last few years, SAAB has cut costs dramatically and lowered its breakeven point from 130,000 cars to 80,000 cars.[1]

CVP analysis can address many other issues as well—such as the number of units that must be sold to break even; the impact of a given reduction in fixed costs on the breakeven point; and the impact of an increase in price on profit. Additionally, CVP analysis allows managers to do a sensitivity analysis by examining the impact of various price or cost levels on profit.

While this chapter deals with the mechanics and terminology of CVP analysis, you should keep in mind that CVP analysis is an integral part of financial planning and decision making. Every accountant and manager should be thoroughly conversant with its concepts, not just the mechanics.

BREAKEVEN POINT IN UNITS

Objective 1

Determine the number of units that must be sold to break even or to earn a targeted profit.

Since we are interested in how revenues, expenses, and profits behave as volume changes, it is natural to begin by finding the firm's breakeven point in units sold. The **breakeven point** is the point at which total revenue equals total cost—the point of zero profit. To find the breakeven point in units, we focus on operating income. We will first discuss the way to find the breakeven point, and then see how our approach can be expanded to determine the number of units that must be sold to earn a targeted profit.

The firm's initial decision in implementing a units-sold approach to CVP analysis is the determination of just what a unit is. For manufacturing firms, the answer is

---

1. James Bennet, "Eurocars: On the Road Again," *New York Times*, 20 August 1995, sec. 3, pp. 1, 10.

obvious. Procter & Gamble may define a unit as a bar of Ivory soap. Service firms face a more difficult choice. Air Canada may define a unit as a passenger kilometre, or as a one-way trip. The Jacksonville Naval Supply Center, which provides naval, industrial, and general supplies to U.S. Navy ships stationed in northeastern Florida and the Caribbean, defines "productive units" to measure the activities involved in delivering services. In this way, more complicated services are assigned more productive units than less complicated services are assigned, thereby standardizing service effort.[2]

A second decision centres on the separation of costs into fixed and variable components. CVP analysis focuses on the factors that effect a *change* in the components of profit. Because we are looking at CVP analysis in terms of units sold, we need to determine the fixed and variable components of cost and revenue with respect to units. This assumption will be relaxed when we incorporate activity-based costing into CVP analysis. It is important to realize that we are focusing on the firm as a whole. Therefore, the costs we are talking about are *all* of the company's costs—manufacturing, marketing, and administrative. Thus, variable costs refer to all costs that increase as more units are sold, including direct materials, direct labour, variable overhead, and variable selling and administrative costs. Similarly, fixed costs include fixed overhead and fixed selling and administrative expenses.

Using Operating Income in CVP Analysis

The income statement is a useful tool for organizing the firm's costs into fixed and variable categories. The income statement can be expressed as a narrative equation:

Operating income = Sales revenues − Variable expenses − Fixed expenses

Note that the term **operating income** is used to denote income or profit *before* income taxes. Operating income includes only revenues and expenses from the firm's normal operations. We will use the term **net income** to mean operating income minus income taxes.

Once we have a measure of units sold, the operating-income equation can be expanded by expressing sales revenues and variable expenses in terms of unit dollar amounts and number of units. Specifically, sales revenue is expressed as the unit selling price multiplied by the number of units sold, and total variable costs are the unit variable cost multiplied by the number of units sold. With these expressions, the operating-income equation takes the following form:

Operating income = (Price × Units) − (Variable cost per unit × Units) − Total fixed cost

The number of units that must be sold to break even or earn a zero profit can be determined by setting operating income to zero and then solving the operating-income equation for the number of units.

We will use the following example to illustrate how to solve for the breakeven point in units. Assume that Whittier Company manufactures a mulching lawn mower. For the coming year, the controller has prepared the following projected income statement:

Sales (1,000 units × $400)	$ 400,000
Less: Variable expenses	325,000
Contribution margin	$ 75,000
Less: Fixed expenses	45,000
Operating income	$ 30,000

2.   David J. Harr, "How Activity Accounting Works in Government," *Management Accounting*, September 1990, pp. 36–40.

We see that for Whittier Company, the price is $400 per unit, and the variable cost is $325 ($325,000/1,000 units). Fixed cost is $45,000. At the breakeven point, then, the operating-income equation would take the following form:

$$0 = (\$400 \times \text{Units}) - (\$325 \times \text{Units}) - \$45,000$$
$$0 = (\$75 \times \text{Units}) - \$45,000$$
$$\$75 \times \text{Units} = \$45,000$$
$$\text{Units} = 600$$

Therefore, Whittier must sell 600 lawn mowers to just cover all fixed and variable expenses. A good way to check this answer is to formulate an income statement based on 600 units sold.

Sales (600 units × $400)	$240,000
Less: Variable expenses	195,000
Contribution margin	$ 45,000
Less: Fixed expenses	45,000
Operating income	$ 0

Indeed, selling 600 units does yield a zero profit.

An important advantage of the operating-income approach is that all further CVP equations are derived from the variable-costing income statement. Any CVP problem can be solved by using this approach.

Shortcut to Calculating Breakeven Units

We can more quickly calculate breakeven units by focusing on the contribution margin. The **contribution margin** is sales revenue minus total variable cost. At breakeven, the contribution margin equals the fixed expenses. If we substitute the unit contribution margin for price minus unit variable cost in the operating-income equation and solve for the number of units, we obtain the following fundamental breakeven equation:

Number of units = Fixed cost/Unit contribution margin

Using Whittier Company as an example, we can see that the contribution margin per unit can be computed in one of two ways. One way is to divide the total contribution margin by the units sold for a result of $75 per unit ($75,000/1,000). A second way is to compute price minus variable cost per unit. Doing so yields the same result, $75 per unit ($400 − $325). To calculate the breakeven number of units for Whittier Company, the fundamental breakeven equation is as follows:

$$\text{Number of units} = \$45,000/(\$400 - \$325)$$
$$= \$45,000/\$75 \text{ per unit}$$
$$= 600 \text{ units}$$

Of course, the answer is identical to that computed using the income statement.

Unit Sales Needed to Achieve Targeted Profit

While the breakeven point is useful information, most firms would like to earn an operating income greater than zero. CVP analysis gives us a way to determine how many units must be sold to earn a particular targeted income. Targeted operating income can be expressed as a dollar amount (for example, $20,000) or as a percentage of sales revenue (for example, 15 percent of revenue). Both the operating-income approach and the contribution margin approach can be easily adjusted to allow for targeted income.

Targeted Income as a Dollar Amount   Assume that Whittier Company wants to earn an operating income of $60,000. How many mulching mowers must be sold to achieve this result? The income statement can be used to find out:

$$\$60,000 = (\$400 \times \text{Units}) - (\$325 \times \text{Units}) - \$45,000$$
$$\$105,000 = \$75 \times \text{Units}$$
$$\text{Units} = 1,400$$

If instead the fundamental breakeven equation is used, targeted profit of $60,000 is added to the fixed cost before solving for the number of units.

$$\text{Units} = (\$45,000 + \$60,000)/(\$400 - \$325)$$
$$\text{Units} = \$105,000/\$75$$
$$\text{Units} = 1,400$$

Whittier must sell 1,400 lawn mowers to earn a before-tax profit of $60,000. The following income statement verifies this outcome:

Sales (1,400 units × $400)	$560,000
Less: Variable expenses	455,000
Contribution margin	$105,000
Less: Fixed expenses	45,000
Operating income	$ 60,000

Another way to check this number of units is to use the breakeven point. As just shown, Whittier must sell 1,400 lawn mowers, or 800 more than the break-even volume of 600 units, to earn a profit of $60,000. The contribution margin per lawn mower is $75. Multiplying $75 by the 800 lawn mowers *above* breakeven produces the targeted profit: $60,000 ($75 × 800). This outcome demonstrates that contribution margin per unit for each unit above breakeven is equivalent to profit per unit. Since the breakeven point had already been computed, the number of lawn mowers to be sold to yield a $60,000 operating income could have been calculated by dividing the unit contribution margin into the target profit and adding the resulting amount to the breakeven volume.

In general, assuming that fixed costs remain the same, the impact on a firm's profits resulting from a change in the number of units sold can be assessed by multiplying the unit contribution margin by the change in units sold. For example, if 1,500 lawn mowers instead of 1,400 are sold, how much more profit will be earned? The change in units sold is an increase of 100 lawn mowers, and the unit contribution margin is $75. Thus, profits will increase by $7,500 ($75 × 100).

Targeted Income as a Percentage of Sales Revenue   Assume that Whittier Company wants to know the number of lawn mowers that it must sell to earn a profit equal to 15 percent of sales revenue. Sales revenue is price multiplied by the quantity sold. Thus, the targeted operating income is 15 percent of price times quantity. Using the income statement (which is simpler in this case), we have the following:

$$0.15 \times (\$400) \times (\text{Units}) = (\$400 \times \text{Units}) - (\$325 \times \text{Units}) - \$45,000$$
$$\$60 \times \text{Units} = (\$400 \times \text{Units}) - (\$325 \times \text{Units}) - \$45,000$$
$$\$60 \times \text{Units} = (\$75 \times \text{Units}) - \$45,000$$
$$\$15 \times \text{Units} = \$45,000$$

Does a volume of 3,000 lawn mowers achieve a profit equal to 15 percent of sales revenue? For 3,000 lawn mowers, the total revenue is $1.2 million ($400 × 3,000). The profit can be computed without preparing a formal income statement. Remember that above breakeven, the contribution margin per unit is the profit per unit. The breakeven volume is 600 lawn mowers. If 3,000 lawn mowers are sold, then 2,400 (3,000 – 600) lawn mowers above the breakeven point are sold. Operating income, therefore, is $180,000 ($75 × 2,400), which is 15 percent of sales ($180,000/$1,200,000).

After-Tax Profit Targets

When calculating the breakeven point, income taxes play no role. This is because the taxes paid on zero income are zero. However, when the company needs to know how many units it must sell to earn a particular net income, some additional consideration is needed. Recall that net income is operating income after income taxes, and that our targeted income figure was expressed in before-tax terms. As a result, when the income target is expressed as net income, we must add back the income taxes to obtain operating income.

In general, assume taxes are computed as a percentage of income. The after-tax profit is computed by subtracting the tax from the operating income (or before-tax profit).

$$\text{Net income} = \text{Operating income} - \text{Taxes}$$
$$= \text{Operating income} - (\text{Tax rate} \times \text{Operating income})$$
$$= \text{Operating income} (1 - \text{Tax rate})$$

or

$$\text{Operating income} = \text{Net income}/(1 - \text{Tax rate})$$

Thus, to convert the after-tax profit to before-tax profit, simply divide the after-tax profit by (1 – Tax rate).

Suppose that Whittier Company wants to achieve a net income of $48,750 and that the firm's tax rate is 35 percent. To convert the after-tax profit target into a before-tax profit target, complete the following steps:

$$\$48,750 = \text{Operating income} - (0.35 \times \text{Operating income})$$
$$\$48,750 = 0.65 \times (\text{Operating income})$$
$$\text{Operating income} = \$75,000$$

In other words, with a tax rate of 35 percent, Whittier Company must earn $75,000 before taxes to have $48,750 after taxes.[3] With this conversion, we can now calculate the number of units that must be sold:

$$\text{Units} = (\$45,000 + \$75,000)/\$75$$
$$\text{Units} = \$120,000/\$75$$
$$\text{Units} = 1,600$$

This answer can be checked by preparing an income statement based on sales of 1,600 lawn mowers.

Sales (1,600 × $400)	$640,000
Less: Variable expenses	520,000
Contribution margin	$120,000
Less: Fixed costs	45,000
Operating income	$ 75,000
Less: Taxes (35% tax rate)	26,250
Net income	$ 48,750

BREAKEVEN POINT IN SALES DOLLARS

Objective 2

Determine the amount of revenue required to break even or to earn a targeted profit.

In some cases when using CVP analysis, managers may prefer to use sales revenues as the measure of sales activity instead of units sold. A units-sold measure can be converted to a sales revenue measure simply by multiplying the unit selling price by the units sold. For example, the breakeven point for Whittier Company was computed at 600 mulching mowers. Since the selling price for each lawn mower is $400, the break-even volume in sales revenue is $240,000 ($400 × 600).

---

3. To practise the after-tax to before-tax conversion, calculate how much before-tax income Whittier would need to have $48,750 after-tax income if the tax rate were 40 percent. [Answer: $81,250]

Any answer expressed in units sold can be easily converted to one expressed in sales revenues, but the answer can be computed more directly by developing a separate formula for the sales revenue case. In this case, the important variable is sales dollars, so both the revenue and the variable costs must be expressed in sales dollars instead of units. Since sales revenue is always expressed in dollars, measuring that variable is no problem. Let's look more closely at variable costs and see how they can be expressed in terms of sales dollars.

To calculate the breakeven point in sales dollars, variable costs are defined as a percentage of sales rather than as an amount per unit sold. Exhibit 9–1 illustrates the division of sales revenue into variable cost and contribution margin. In this exhibit, price is $10; variable cost is $6. Of course, the remainder is contribution margin of $4 ($10 − $6). If 10 units are sold, total variable costs are $60 ($6 × 10 units). Alternatively, since each unit sold earns $10 of revenue and has $6 of variable cost, we could say that 60 percent of each dollar of revenue earned is attributable to variable cost ($6/$10). Thus, focusing on sales revenue, we would expect total variable costs of $60 for revenues of $100 (0.60 × $100).

This 60 percent is the **variable-cost ratio**. It is simply the proportion of each sales dollar that must be used to cover variable costs. The variable-cost ratio can be computed by using either total data or unit data. Of course, the percentage of sales dollars remaining after variable costs are covered is the **contribution margin ratio**. The contribution margin ratio is the proportion of each sales dollar available to cover fixed costs and provide for profit. In Exhibit 9–1, if the variable-cost ratio is 60 percent of sales, then contribution margin must be the remaining 40 percent of sales. It makes sense that the complement of the variable-cost ratio is the contribution margin ratio. After all, the proportion of the sales dollar left after variable costs are covered should be the contribution margin component.

Just as the variable-cost ratio can be computed using total or unit figures, the contribution margin ratio, 40 percent in our exhibit, can also be computed in these two ways. That is, one can divide the total contribution margin by total sales ($40/$100), or one can use the unit contribution margin divided by price ($4/$10). Naturally, if the variable-cost ratio is known, it can be subtracted from 1 to yield the contribution margin ratio (1 − 0.60 = 0.40).

Where do fixed costs fit into this? Since the contribution margin is revenue remaining after variable costs are covered, it must be the revenue available to cover fixed costs and contribute to profit. Exhibit 9–2 uses the same price and variable-cost data from Exhibit 9–1 to show the impact of fixed cost on profit. There are three possibilities: fixed cost can equal contribution margin; fixed cost can be less than

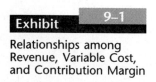

Exhibit   9–1

Relationships among Revenue, Variable Cost, and Contribution Margin

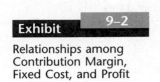

Exhibit 9–2

Relationships among
Contribution Margin,
Fixed Cost, and Profit

Panel A: Fixed Cost = Contribution Margin

Fixed Cost

Revenue {
  Contribution Margin
  Total Variable Cost
}

Panel B: Fixed Cost < Contribution Margin

Fixed Cost | Profit

Revenue {
  Contribution Margin
  Total Variable Cost
}

Panel C: Fixed Cost > Contribution Margin

Fixed Cost | Loss

Revenue {
  Contribution Margin
  Total Variable Cost
}

contribution margin; or fixed cost can be greater than contribution margin. Panel A of Exhibit 9–2 shows fixed cost equal to contribution margin. Of course, profit is zero (the company is at breakeven). Panel B shows fixed cost less than contribution margin. In this case, the company earns a profit. Finally, Panel C shows fixed cost greater than contribution margin. Here, the company faces an operating loss.

Let's turn to some examples based on Whittier Company to illustrate the sales revenue approach. Whittier Company's variable-costing income statement for 1,000 lawn mowers follows:

	Dollars	Percent of Sales
Sales	$400,000	100.00%
Less: Variable expenses	325,000	81.25%
Contribution margin	$ 75,000	18.75%
Less: Fixed expenses	45,000	
Operating income	$ 30,000	

Note that sales revenue, variable costs, and contribution margin have been expressed as a percent of sales. The variable cost ratio is 0.8125 ($325,000/$400,000); the contribution margin ratio is 0.1875 (computed either as 1 − 0.8125, or $75,000/$400,000). Fixed costs are $45,000. Given the information in this income statement, how much sales revenue must Whittier earn to break even?

$$\text{Operating income} = \text{Sales} - \text{Variable costs} - \text{Fixed costs}$$
$$0 = \text{Sales} - (\text{Variable cost ratio} \times \text{Sales}) - \text{Fixed costs}$$
$$0 = \text{Sales} \times (1 - \text{Variable cost ratio}) - \text{Fixed costs}$$
$$0 = \text{Sales} \times (1 - 0.8125) - \$45,000$$
$$\text{Sales} \times (0.1875) = \$45,000$$
$$\text{Sales} = \$240,000$$

Thus, Whittier must earn revenues totalling $240,000 in order to break even. To check this answer, prepare an income statement based on revenue of $240,000 and verify that it yields zero profit. Note that (1 − 0.8125) is the contribution margin ratio. We can skip a couple of steps by recognizing that *Sales − (Variable cost ratio × Sales)* is equal to *Sales × Contribution margin ratio*.

What about the fundamental breakeven equation used to determine the breakeven point in units? That approach can be used here as well. Recall that the formula for the breakeven point in units is:

$$\text{Break-even units} = \text{Fixed cost}/(\text{Price} - \text{Unit variable cost})$$

If we multiply both sides of this equation by price, the left-hand side will equal sales revenue at breakeven:

$$\text{Break-even units} \times \text{Price} = \text{Price} \times \text{Fixed cost}/(\text{Price} - \text{Unit variable cost})$$
$$\text{Break-even sales} = \text{Fixed cost} \times \text{Price}/(\text{Price} - \text{Unit variable cost})$$
$$\text{Break-even sales} = \text{Fixed cost} \times (\text{Price}/\text{Unit contribution margin})$$
$$\text{Break-even sales} = \text{Fixed cost}/\text{Contribution margin ratio}$$

Again using Whittier Company data, the breakeven sales dollars would be computed as ($45,000/0.1875) or $240,000. This is the same answer, arrived at by a slightly different approach.

Profit Targets and Sales Revenue

Consider the following question: How much sales revenue must Whittier generate to earn a before-tax profit of $60,000? This question is similar to the one asked earlier with regard to units, but this time the question is phrased directly in terms of sales revenue. To answer the question, add the targeted operating income of $60,000 to the $45,000 of fixed cost, and divide the total by the contribution margin ratio:

$$\text{Sales} = (\$45,000 + \$60,000)/0.1875$$
$$= \$105,000/0.1875$$
$$= \$560,000$$

Whittier must earn revenues equal to $560,000 to achieve a profit target of $60,000. Since breakeven is $240,000, additional sales of $320,000 ($560,000 − $240,000) must be earned above breakeven. Note that multiplying the contribution margin ratio by revenues above breakeven yields the profit of $60,000 (0.1875 × $320,000). Above breakeven, the contribution margin ratio is a profit ratio; therefore, it represents the proportion of each sales dollar assignable to profit. In this example, every sales dollar earned above breakeven increases profits by $0.1875.

In general, assuming that fixed costs remain unchanged, the contribution margin ratio can be used to find the profit impact of a change in sales revenue. To obtain the total change in profits from a change in revenues, simply multiply the contribution margin ratio times the change in sales. For example, if sales revenues are $540,000 instead of $560,000, how will the expected profits be affected? A decrease in sales revenues of $20,000 will cause a decrease in profits of $3,750 (0.1875 × $20,000).

Comparison of the Two Approaches

For a single-product setting, converting the breakeven point in units to breakeven in sales revenue is simply a matter of multiplying the unit selling price by the units sold. Then why bother with a separate formula for the sales revenue approach? There are two reasons. First, the formula for sales revenue allows us to solve directly for revenue if that is what is desired. Second, the sales revenue approach is much simpler to use in a multiple-product setting, as we will see in the next section.

MULTIPLE-PRODUCT ANALYSIS

Objective 3

Apply cost–volume–profit analysis in a multiple-product setting.

Cost–volume–profit analysis is fairly simple in the single-product setting. However, most firms produce and sell a number of products or services. Even though the conceptual complexity of CVP analysis does increase with multiple products, the operation is reasonably straightforward. The formulas used in a single-product setting can be adapted to the multiple-product setting, as illustrated by expanding the Whittier Company example.

Suppose Whittier Company has decided to offer two models of lawn mowers: a mulching mower that will sell for $400, and a riding mower that will sell for $800. The marketing department is convinced that 1,200 mulching mowers and 800 riding mowers can be sold during the coming year. The controller has prepared the following projected income statement based on the sales forecast:

	Mulching Mower	Riding Mower	Total
Sales	$480,000	$640,000	$1,120,000
Less: Variable expenses	390,000	480,000	870,000
Contribution margin	$ 90,000	$160,000	$ 250,000
Less: Direct fixed expenses	30,000	40,000	70,000
Product margin	$ 60,000	$120,000	$ 180,000
Less: Common fixed expenses			26,250
Operating income			$ 153,750

Note that the controller has separated direct fixed expenses from common fixed expenses. Direct fixed expenses are those fixed costs that can be traced to each segment and that would be avoided if the segment did not exist. Common fixed expenses are the fixed costs that are not traceable to the segments and that would remain even if one of the segments was eliminated.

Breakeven Point in Units

Whittier's owner is somewhat apprehensive about adding a new product line and wants to know how many of each model must be sold to break even. One possible response to this question is to use the equation we developed earlier in which fixed costs were divided by the contribution margin. This equation presents some immediate problems, however. It was developed for a single-product analysis. For two products, there are two unit contribution margins. The mulching mower has a contribution margin per unit of $75 ($400 − $325), and the riding mower has one of $200 ($800 − $600).[4]

One possible solution is to apply the analysis separately to each product line. It is possible to obtain individual breakeven points when income is defined as product margin. Breakeven for the mulching mower is as follows:

$$\text{Mulching mower breakeven units} = \text{Fixed cost}/(\text{Price} - \text{Unit variable cost})$$
$$= \$30,000/\$75$$
$$= 400 \text{ units}$$

Breakeven for the riding mower can be computed as well:

$$\text{Riding mower breakeven units} = \text{Fixed cost}/(\text{Price} - \text{Unit variable cost})$$
$$= \$40,000/\$200$$
$$= 200 \text{ units}$$

Thus, 400 mulching mowers and 200 riding mowers must be sold to achieve a breakeven product margin. But a breakeven product margin covers only direct fixed costs; the common fixed costs remain to be covered. Selling these numbers of lawn mowers would result in a loss equal to the common fixed costs. No breakeven point for the firm as a whole has yet been identified. Somehow the common fixed costs must be factored into the analysis.

Allocating the common fixed costs to each product line before computing a breakeven point may resolve this difficulty. The problem with this approach is that allocation of the common fixed costs is arbitrary. Thus, no meaningful breakeven volume is readily apparent.

Another possible solution is to convert the multiple-product problem into a single-product problem. If this can be done, then all of the single-product CVP methodology can be applied directly. The key to this conversion is to identify the expected *sales mix*, in units, of the products being marketed. **Sales mix** is the relative combination of products being sold by a firm.

Determining the Sales Mix The sales mix can be measured either in units sold or in proportion of revenue. For example, if Whittier plans on selling 1,200 mulching mowers and 800 riding mowers, then the sales mix in units is 1,200:800. Usually, the sales mix is reduced to the smallest possible whole numbers. Thus, the relative mix 1,200:800 can be reduced to 12:8 and further to 3:2. That is, for every three mulching mowers sold, two riding mowers are sold.

Alternatively, the sales mix can be represented by the percentage of total revenue contributed by each product. In that case, the mulching mower revenue is $480,000 ($400 × 1,200), and the riding mower revenue is $640,000 ($800 × 800). The mulching mower accounts for 42.86 percent of total revenue, and the riding mower accounts for the remaining 57.14 percent. It may seem as though the two sales mixes are different. The sales mix in units is 3:2; that is, of every five mowers sold, 60 percent are mulching mowers and 40 percent are riding mowers. However, the revenue-based sales mix is 42.86 percent for the mulching mowers. What is the difference? The sales mix in revenue takes the sales mix in units and weights it by price. Therefore, even though the underlying proportion of mowers sold remains 3:2, the lower-priced mulching mowers are weighted less heavily when price is factored in. For CVP analysis, we will use the sales mix expressed in units.

---

4. The variable cost per unit is derived from the income statement. For the riding mower, total variable costs are $480,000 based on sales of 800 units. This yields a per-unit variable cost of $600 ($480,000/800). A similar computation produces the per-unit variable cost for the mulching mower.

A number of different sales mixes can be used to define the breakeven volume. For example, a sales mix of 2:1 will define a breakeven point of 550 mulching mowers and 275 riding mowers. The total contribution margin produced by this mix is $96,250 [($75 × 550) + ($200 × 275)]. Similarly, if 350 mulching mowers and 350 riding mowers are sold (corresponding to a 1:1 sales mix), the total contribution margin is also $96,250 [($75 × 350) + ($200 × 350)]. Since total fixed costs are $96,250, both sales mixes define breakeven points. Fortunately, every sales mix need not be considered. Can Whittier really expect a sales mix of 2:1 or 1:1? For every two mulching mowers sold, does Whittier expect to sell a riding mower? Or for every mulching mower, can Whittier really sell one riding mower?

According to Whittier's marketing study, a sales mix of 3:2 can be expected. That is the ratio that should be used; others can be ignored. The sales mix that is expected to prevail should be used for CVP analysis.

Sales Mix and CVP Analysis Defining a particular sales mix allows us to convert a multiple-product problem into a single-product CVP format. Since Whittier expects to sell three mulching mowers for every two riding mowers, it can define the single product it sells as a *package* containing three mulching mowers and two riding mowers. Defining the product as a package converts the multiple-product problem into a single-product one. To use the breakeven-point-in-units approach, the package selling price and variable cost per package must be known. To compute these package values, the sales mix, the individual product prices, and the individual variable costs are needed. Given the individual product data found in the projected income statement, the package values can be computed as follows:

Product	Price	Unit Variable Cost	Unit Contribution Margin	Sales Mix	Package Unit Contribution Margin
Mulching	$400	$325	$ 75	3	$225[a]
Riding	800	600	200	2	400[b]
Package total					$625

a This is found by multiplying the number of these units in the package (3) by this unit contribution margin ($75).
b This is found by multiplying the number of these units in the package (2) by this unit contribution margin ($200).

Given the package contribution margin, the fundamental breakeven equation can be used to determine the number of packages that need to be sold to break even. From Whittier's projected income statement, we know that the total fixed costs for the company are $96,250. Thus, the breakeven point is as follows:

$$\text{Breakeven packages} = \text{Fixed cost}/\text{Package contribution margin}$$
$$= \$96,250/\$625$$
$$= 154 \text{ packages}$$

Whittier must sell 462 mulching mowers (3 × 154) and 308 riding mowers (2 × 154) to break even. An income statement verifying this solution is presented in Exhibit 9–3.

Exhibit 9–3

Breakeven Solution Income Statement

	Mulching Mower	Riding Mower	Total
Sales	$184,800	$246,400	$431,200
Less: Variable expenses	150,150	184,800	334,950
Contribution margin	$ 34,650	$ 61,600	$ 96,250
Less: Direct fixed expenses	30,000	40,000	70,000
Segment margin	$ 4,650	$ 21,600	$ 26,250
Less: Common fixed expenses			26,250
Operating income			$ 0

For a given sales mix, CVP analysis can be used as if the firm were selling a single product. However, actions that change the prices of individual products can affect the sales mix because consumers may buy relatively more or less of the product. Accordingly, pricing decisions may involve a new sales mix and must reflect this possibility. Keep in mind that a new sales mix will affect the units of each product that need to be sold in order to achieve a desired profit target. If the sales mix for the coming period is uncertain, it may be necessary to look at several different mixes. In this way, a manager can gain some insight into the possible outcomes facing the firm.

The complexity of the breakeven-point-in-units approach increases dramatically as the number of products increases. Imagine performing this analysis for a firm with several hundred products. Fortunately, this task seems more overwhelming than it actually is. Computers can easily handle a problem with this much data. Furthermore, many firms simplify the problem by analyzing product groups rather than individual products. Another way to handle the increased complexity is to switch from the units-sold approach to the sales revenue approach. The latter approach can accomplish a multiple-product CVP analysis using only the summary data found in an organization's income statement. The computational requirements are much simpler.

Sales Dollars Approach

To illustrate the breakeven point in sales dollars, the same examples will be used. However, the only information needed is the projected income statement for Whittier Company as a whole.

Sales	$1,120,000
Less: Variable expenses	870,000
Contribution margin	$ 250,000
Less: Fixed expenses	96,250
Operating income	$ 153,750

Notice that this income statement corresponds to the total column of the more detailed income statement examined previously. The projected income statement rests on the assumption that 1,200 mulching mowers and 800 riding mowers will be sold (a 3:2 sales mix). The breakeven point in sales revenue also rests on the expected sales mix. (As with the units-sold approach, a different sales mix will produce different results.)

With the income statement, the usual CVP questions can be addressed. For example, how much sales revenue must be earned to break even? To answer this question, we divide the total fixed cost of $96,250 by the contribution margin ratio of 0.2232 ($250,000/$1,120,000):

$$\text{Breakeven sales} = \text{Fixed cost/Contribution margin ratio}$$
$$= \$96,250/0.2232$$
$$= \$431,228[5]$$

The breakeven point in sales dollars implicitly uses the assumed sales mix but avoids the requirement of building a package contribution margin. No knowledge of individual product data is needed. The computational effort is similar to that used in the single-product setting. Moreover, the answer is still expressed in sales revenue. Unlike the breakeven point in units, the answer to CVP questions using sales dollars is still expressed in a single summary measure. The sales revenue approach, however, does sacrifice information concerning individual product performance.

---

5. Because of rounding error in the contribution margin ratio, the sales volume is slightly overstated. The correct answer is $431,200 (obtained by multiplying the package selling price by the packages needed to break even: [$2,800 × 154]).

GRAPHICAL REPRESENTATION OF CVP RELATIONSHIPS

Objective 4

Prepare a profit–volume graph and a cost–volume–profit graph, and explain the meaning of each.

It may further our understanding of CVP relationships to see them portrayed visually. A graphical representation can help managers see the difference between variable cost and revenue. It may also help them understand quickly what impact an increase or decrease in sales will have on the breakeven point. Two basic graphs, the *profit–volume graph* and the *cost–volume–profit graph*, are presented here.

The Profit–Volume Graph

A **profit–volume graph** visually portrays the relationship between profits and sales volume. The profit–volume graph is the graph of the operating-income equation:

Operating income = (Price × Units) – (Unit variable cost × Units) – Fixed cost

In this graph, operating income is the dependent variable; units is the independent variable. Usually, the values of the independent variable are measured along the horizontal axis and the values of the dependent variable along the vertical.

To make this discussion more concrete, a simple set of data will be used. Assume that Tyson Company produces a single product with the following cost and price data:

Total fixed costs	$100
Variable costs per unit	5
Selling price per unit	10

Using these data, operating income can be expressed as follows:

$$\text{Operating income} = (\$10 \times \text{Units}) - (\$5 \times \text{Units}) - \$100$$
$$= (\$5 \times \text{Units}) - \$100$$

Exhibit 9–4

Profit–Volume Graph

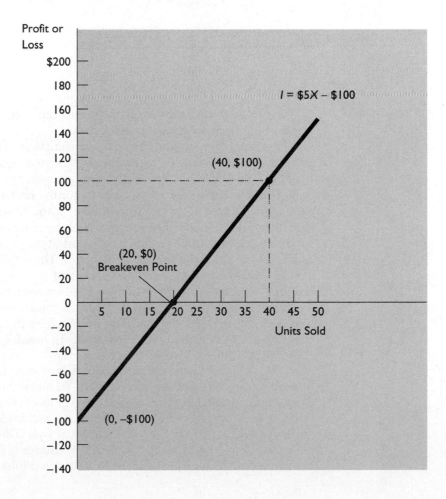

We can graph this relationship by plotting units along the horizontal axis and operating income (or loss) along the vertical axis. Two points are needed to graph a linear equation. While any two points will do, two points often chosen are those that correspond to zero sales volume and zero profits. When units sold are zero, Tyson experiences an operating loss of $100 (or a profit of –$100). The point corresponding to zero sales volume, therefore, is (0, –$100). In other words, when no sales take place, the company suffers a loss equal to its total fixed costs. When operating income is zero, the units sold are equal to 20. The point corresponding to zero profits (breakeven) is (20, $0). These two points, plotted in Exhibit 9–4, define the profit–volume graph.

The graph in Exhibit 9–4 can be used to assess Tyson's profit (or loss) at any level of sales activity. For example, the profit associated with the sale of 40 units can be read from the graph by (1) drawing a vertical line from the horizontal axis to the profit line, and (2) drawing a horizontal line from the profit line to the vertical axis. As we see in Exhibit 9–4, the profit associated with sales of 40 units is $100. But the profit–volume graph, while easy to interpret, fails to reveal how costs change as sales volume changes. An alternative approach to graphing can provide this detail.

The Cost–Volume–Profit Graph

The **cost–volume–profit graph** depicts the relationships among cost, volume, and profits. To obtain the more detailed relationships, it is necessary to graph two separate lines: the total revenue line and the total cost line. These two lines are represented, respectively, by the following two equations:

$$\text{Revenue} = \text{Price} \times \text{Units}$$
$$\text{Total cost} = (\text{Unit variable cost} \times \text{Units}) + \text{Fixed cost}$$

Using the Tyson Company example, we see that the revenue and cost equations are as follows:

$$\text{Revenue} = \$10 \times \text{Units}$$
$$\text{Total cost} = (\$5 \times \text{Units}) + \$100$$

To portray both equations in the same graph, the vertical axis is measured in dollars and the horizontal axis in units sold.

Two points are needed to graph each equation. The same x-coordinates are used as in the profit–volume graph. For the revenue equation, setting number of units equal to 0 results in revenue of $0; setting number of units equal to 20 results in revenue of $200. Therefore, the two points for the revenue equation are (0, $0) and (20, $200). For the cost equation, units sold of 0 and units sold of 20 produce the points (0, $100) and (20, $200). The graph of each equation appears in Exhibit 9–5.

Note that the total revenue line begins at the origin and rises with a slope equal to the selling price per unit (a slope of 10). The total cost line intercepts the vertical axis at a point equal to total fixed costs and rises with a slope equal to the variable cost per unit (a slope of 5). When the total revenue line lies below the total cost line, a loss region is defined. Similarly, when the total revenue line lies above the total cost line, a profit region is defined. The point where the total revenue line and the total cost line intersect is the breakeven point. To break even, Tyson Company must sell 20 units and thus receive $200 total revenues.

Now let's compare the information available from the CVP graph with that available from the profit–volume graph. To make this comparison, consider the sale of 40 units. Recall that the profit–volume graph in Exhibit 9–4 revealed that this sale will produce profits of $100. Now examine Exhibit 9–5 again. The CVP graph also shows profits of $100, but it reveals more as well. The CVP graph discloses that total revenues of $400 and total costs of $300 are associated with the sale of 40 units. Furthermore, the total costs can be broken down into fixed costs of $100 and variable

Exhibit 9–5

Cost–Volume–Profit
Graph

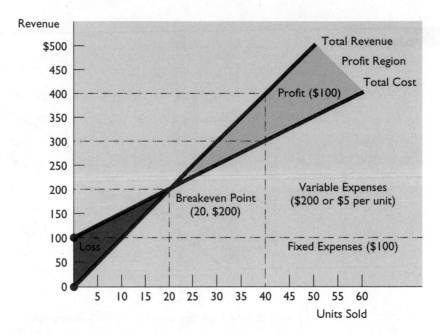

costs of $200. The CVP graph provides revenue and cost information not provided by the profit–volume graph. Unlike the profit–volume graph, some computation is needed to determine the profit associated with a given sales volume. Nonetheless, because of the greater information content, managers are likely to find the CVP graph a more useful tool.

Assumptions of Cost–Volume–Profit Analysis

The profit–volume and cost–volume–profit graphs just illustrated rely on some important assumptions. Some of these assumptions are as follows:

1. The analysis assumes a linear revenue function and a linear cost function.
2. The analysis assumes that price, total fixed costs, and unit variable costs (a) can be accurately identified, and (b) remain constant over the relevant range.
3. The analysis assumes that all production is sold.
4. For multiple-product analysis, the sales mix is assumed to be known.
5. The selling prices and costs are assumed to be known with certainty.

Linear Functions The first assumption, linear cost and revenue functions, deserves additional consideration. Let's look at the underlying total revenue and total cost functions identified in economics. In Exhibit 9–6, Panel A portrays curvilinear revenue and cost functions. As quantity sold increases, revenue also increases, but eventually it begins to rise less steeply than before. This pattern is explained quite simply by the need to decrease price for more units to be sold. The total cost function is more complicated, rising steeply at first, then levelling off somewhat (as increasing returns to scale develop), and then rising steeply again (as decreasing returns to scale develop). How can we deal with these complicated relationships?

Relevant Range Fortunately, we do not need to consider all possible ranges of production and sales for a firm. Remember that CVP analysis is a short-run decision-making tool. (It is short run in orientation because some costs are fixed.) It is only necessary to determine the current operating range, or relevant range, for which the linear cost and revenue relationships are valid. In Exhibit 9–6, Panel B illustrates a relevant range from 5,000 to 15,000 units. Note that the cost and revenue relationships are roughly linear in this range, allowing us to use our linear CVP equations.

Exhibit   9–6

The Relevant Range

Panel A: Curvilinear CVP Relationships

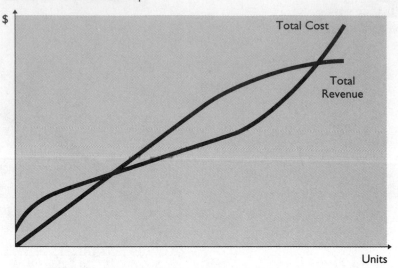

Panel B: Relevant Range and Linear CVP Relationships

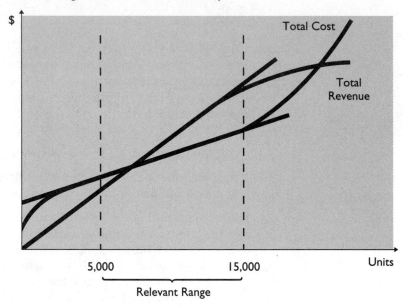

Of course, if the relevant range changes, different fixed and variable costs and different prices must be used.

The second assumption is linked to the definition of relevant range. Once a relevant range has been identified, the cost and price relationships are assumed to be known and constant.

Production Equal to Sales The third assumption is that all production is sold. There is no change in inventory over the period. That inventory has no impact on breakeven analysis makes sense. Breakeven analysis is a short-run decision-making technique, so it is concerned with covering all costs related to a particular time period. Inventory embodies costs from a previous period and is therefore not considered.

Constant Sales Mix In single-product analysis, the sales mix is obviously constant—the one product is 100 percent of sales. Multiple-product breakeven analysis also requires a constant sales mix. However, it is virtually impossible to predict the sales mix with certainty. Typically, this constraint is handled in practice through sensitivity analysis. By using the capabilities of spreadsheet analysis, the sensitivity of variables to a variety of sales mixes can be readily assessed. There will be a different breakeven point (or a specific target profit volume) for each sales mix assumption. Thus, there are multiple breakeven points (or target profit volumes), but only one for each possible sales mix. This emphasizes the importance of correctly estimating and actively planning the sales mix. It is also noteworthy that breakeven points are only incidental.[6] CVP analysis is used to obtain insight into the relationships among crucial variables that affect profitability. This kind of insight helps the manager in planning, budgeting, and decision making.

Prices and Costs Known with Certainty   In actuality, firms seldom know prices, variable costs, and fixed costs with certainty. A change in one variable usually affects the value of others. Often there is a probability distribution to contend with. Furthermore, there are formal ways of explicitly building uncertainty into the CVP model. Exploration of these issues is introduced in the next section.

CHANGES IN THE CVP VARIABLES

Objective 5

Explain the impact of risk, uncertainty, and changing variables on cost–volume–profit analysis.

Because firms operate in a dynamic world, they must be aware of changes in prices, variable costs, and fixed costs. They must also account for the effect of risk and uncertainty. We will now examine the effect of changes in price, unit contribution margin, and fixed cost on the breakeven point and look at how managers can handle risk and uncertainty within the CVP framework.

Suppose that Whittier Company recently conducted a market study that revealed three different alternatives:

1. Alternative 1: An $8,000 increase in advertising expenditures will increase sales from 1,600 units to 1,725 units.
2. Alternative 2: A price decrease from $400 to $375 per lawn mower will increase sales from 1,600 units to 1,900 units.
3. Alternative 3: Decreasing prices to $375 and increasing advertising expenditures by $8,000 will increase sales from 1,600 units to 2,600 units.

Should Whittier maintain its current price and advertising policies, or should it select one of the three alternatives described by the marketing study?

Consider the first alternative. What is the effect on profits if advertising costs increase by $8,000 and sales increase by 125 units? This question can be answered without using the equations but by employing the contribution margin per unit. We know that the unit contribution margin is $75. Since units sold increase by 125, the incremental increase in total contribution margin is $9,375 ($75 × 125 units). However, since fixed costs increase by $8,000, the incremental increase in profits is only $1,375 ($9,375 − $8,000). Exhibit 9–7 summarizes the effects of the first alternative. Note that we need to look only at the incremental increase in total contribution margin and fixed expenses to compute the increase in total profits.

For the second alternative, fixed expenses do not increase. Thus, it is possible to answer the question by looking only at the effect on total contribution margin. For the current price of $400, the contribution margin per unit is $75. If 1,600 units are sold, the total contribution margin is $120,000 ($75 × 1,600). If the price is dropped to $375, then the contribution margin drops to $50 per unit ($375 − $325). If 1,900 units are sold at the new price, then the new total contribution margin is $95,000 ($50 × 1,900). Dropping the price results in a profit decline of $25,000 ($120,000 − $95,000). The effects of the second alternative are summarized in Exhibit 9–8.

---

6. An accounting professor once told his students that they are breaking even on every possible business that they have not invested in. The point is that investors and managers do not wish to break even except in the case of not-for-profit organizations.

Exhibit 9–7

Summary of the Effects
of Alternative 1

	Before the Increased Advertising	With the Increased Advertising
Units sold	1,600	1,725
Unit contribution margin	× $75	× $75
Total contribution margin	$120,000	$129,375
Less: Fixed expenses	45,000	53,000
Profit	$ 75,000	$ 76,375
		Difference in Profit
Change in sales volume		125
Unit contribution margin		× $75
Change in contribution margin		$9,375
Less: Increase in fixed expenses		8,000
Increase in profit		$1,375

Exhibit 9–8

Summary of the Effects
of Alternative 2

	Before the Proposed Price Change	With the Proposed Price Decrease
Units sold	1,600	1,900
Unit contribution margin	× $75	× $50
Total contribution margin	$120,000	$95,000
Less: Fixed expenses	45,000	45,000
Profit	$ 75,000	$50,000
		Difference in Profit
Change in contribution margin ($95,000 − $120,000)		$(25,000)
Less: Change in fixed expenses		0
Decrease in profit		$(25,000)

Exhibit 9–9

Summary of the Effects
of Alternative 3

	Before the Proposed Price and Advertising Change	With the Proposed Price Decrease and Advertising Increase
Units sold	1,600	2,600
Unit contribution margin	× $75	× $50
Total contribution margin	$120,000	$130,000
Less: Fixed expenses	45,000	53,000
Profit	$ 75,000	$ 77,000
		Difference in Profit
Change in contribution margin ($130,000 − $120,000)		$10,000
Less: Change in fixed expenses ($53,000 − $45,000)		8,000
Increase in profit		$ 2,000

The third alternative calls for a decrease in the unit selling price and an increase in advertising costs. As with the first alternative, this alternative's profit impact can be assessed by looking at the incremental effects on contribution margin and fixed expenses. The incremental profit change can be found by (1) computing the incremental change in total contribution margin, (2) computing the incremental change in fixed expenses, and (3) adding the two results.

As shown, the current total contribution margin (for 1,600 units sold) is $120,000. Since the new unit contribution margin is $50, the new total contribution margin is $130,000 ($50 × 2,600 units). Thus, the incremental increase in total contribution margin is $10,000 ($130,000 – $120,000). However, to achieve this incremental increase in contribution margin, an incremental increase of $8,000 in fixed costs is needed. The net effect is an incremental increase in profits of $2,000. The effects of the third alternative are summarized in Exhibit 9–9.

Of the three alternatives identified by the marketing study, the one that promises the most benefit is the third. It increases total profits by $2,000. The first alternative increases profits by only $1,375, and the second actually decreases profits by $25,000.

These examples are all based on a units-sold approach. However, we could just as easily have applied a sales revenue approach. The answers would be the same.

Introducing Risk and Uncertainty

An important assumption of CVP analysis is that prices and costs are known with certainty. But this is seldom the case. Risk and uncertainty are unavoidable in business decision making and must be dealt with somehow. Formally, risk differs from uncertainty: under risk, the probability distributions of the variables are known, whereas under uncertainty, they are not known. For our purposes, however, the terms will be used interchangeably.

How do managers deal with risk and uncertainty? There are a variety of methods. First, of course, is that management must realize the uncertain nature of future prices, costs, and quantities. Next, managers move from considering a breakeven point to considering what might be called a breakeven band. In other words, given the uncertain nature of the data, a firm might break even, for example, when 1,800 to 2,000 units are sold instead of at the point estimate of 1,900 units. Further, managers may engage in sensitivity or what-if analysis. In this, a computer spreadsheet is helpful, allowing managers to set up the breakeven (or targeted profit) relationships and then check to see the impact that varying costs and prices have on quantity sold. Two concepts useful to management are *margin of safety* and *operating leverage*. Both of these may be considered measures of risk. Each requires knowledge of fixed and variable costs.

Margin of Safety The **margin of safety** is the units sold (or expected to be sold) or the revenue earned (or expected to be earned) above the breakeven volume. For example, if a company's breakeven volume is 200 units and the company is currently selling 500 units, then the margin of safety is 300 units (500 – 200). The margin of safety can be expressed in sales revenue as well. If the breakeven volume is $200,000 and current revenues are $350,000, then the margin of safety is $150,000.

The margin of safety can be viewed as a crude measure of risk. There are always events, unknown when plans are made, that can lower sales below the original expected level. If a firm's margin of safety is large given the expected sales for the coming year, the risk of suffering losses should sales take a downward turn is less than if the margin of safety is small. Managers who face a low margin of safety may wish to consider actions to increase sales or decrease costs. These steps will increase the margin of safety and lower the risk of incurring losses.

Operating Leverage In physics, a lever is a simple machine used to multiply force. Basically, the lever multiplies the effort applied, thereby creating more work. The larger the load moved by a given amount of effort, the greater the mechanical advantage. In financial terms, operating leverage is concerned with the relative mix of fixed costs and variable costs in an organization. It is sometimes possible to trade off fixed costs for variable costs. As variable costs decrease, the unit contribution margin increases, making the contribution of each unit sold that much greater. In such a case, the effect of fluctuations in sales on profitability increases. Thus, firms that have achieved lower variable costs by increasing the proportion of fixed costs will benefit with greater increases in profits as sales increase than will firms with a lower proportion of fixed costs. Fixed costs are being used as leverage to increase profits. Unfortunately, it is also true that firms with a higher operating leverage will also experience greater reductions in profits if sales decrease. Therefore, **operating leverage** is the use of fixed costs to extract higher percentage changes in profits as sales activity changes.

The greater the degree of operating leverage, the greater will be the effect of changes in sales activity on profits. Because of this phenomenon, the mix of costs that an organization chooses can have a considerable influence on its operating risk and profit level.

The **degree of operating leverage (DOL)** is measured for a given level of sales by taking the ratio of contribution margin to operating income, as follows:

$$\text{Degree of operating leverage} = \text{Contribution margin}/\text{Operating income}$$

If fixed costs are used to lower variable costs such that contribution margin increases and profit decreases, then the degree of operating leverage increases—signalling an increase in risk.

To illustrate the application of these concepts, consider Cedilla Company, a firm which is planning to add a new product line. In adding the line, Cedilla can choose to rely heavily on automation or on labour. If the firm chooses to emphasize automation rather than labour, fixed costs will be higher and unit variable costs will be lower. Relevant data for a sales level of 10,000 units follow:

	Automated System	Manual System
Sales	$1,000,000	$1,000,000
Less: Variable expenses	500,000	800,000
Contribution margin	$ 500,000	$ 200,000
Less: Fixed expenses	375,000	100,000
Operating income	$ 125,000	$ 100,000
Unit selling price	$100	$100
Unit variable expense	50	80
Unit contribution margin	50	20

The degree of operating leverage for the automated system is 4.0 ($500,000/$125,000). The degree of operating leverage for the manual system is 2.0 ($200,000/$100,000). What happens to profit in each system if sales increase by 40 percent? The following income statements show the resulting change:

	Automated System	Manual System
Sales	$1,400,000	$1,400,000
Less: Variable expenses	700,000	1,120,000
Contribution margin	$ 700,000	$ 280,000
Less: Fixed expenses	375,000	100,000
Operating income	$ 325,000	$ 180,000

Profits for the automated system would increase by $200,000 ($325,000 − $125,000), a 160 percent increase. In the manual system, profits increase by only

Exhibit   9–10

Differences between
Manual and Automated
Systems

	Manual System	Automated System
Price	Same	Same
Variable cost	Relatively higher	Relatively lower
Fixed cost	Relatively lower	Relatively higher
Contribution margin	Relatively lower	Relatively higher
Breakeven point	Relatively lower	Relatively higher
Margin of safety	Relatively higher	Relatively lower
Degree of operating leverage	Relatively lower	Relatively higher
Downside risk	Relatively lower	Relatively higher
Upside potential	Relatively lower	Relatively higher

$80,000 ($180,000 – $100,000), an 80 percent increase. The automated system has a greater percentage increase because it has a higher degree of operating leverage.

In choosing between the two systems, the effect of operating leverage is a valuable piece of information. As the 40 percent increase in sales illustrates, this effect can bring a significant benefit to Cedilla. However, the effect is a two-edged sword. As sales decrease, the automated system will also show much higher percentage decreases. Moreover, the increased operating leverage is available under the automated system because of the presence of increased fixed costs. The breakeven point for the automated system is 7,500 units ($375,000/$50), whereas the breakeven point for the manual system is 5,000 units ($100,000/$20). Thus, the automated system has greater operating risk. The increased risk, of course, provides a potentially higher profit level (as long as units sold exceed 9,167).[7]

In choosing between the automated and the manual systems, Cedilla's manager must assess the likelihood that sales will exceed 9,167 units. If, after careful study, there is a strong belief that sales will easily exceed this level, the choice is obvious: the automated system. On the other hand, if sales are unlikely to exceed 9,167 units, the manual system is preferable. Exhibit 9–10 summarizes the relative difference between the manual and the automated systems in terms of some of the CVP concepts.

Sensitivity Analysis and CVP

The pervasiveness of personal computers and spreadsheets has placed sensitivity analysis within reach of most managers. An important tool, **sensitivity analysis** is a "what-if" technique that examines the impact of changes in underlying assumptions on an answer. It is relatively simple to input data on prices, variable costs, fixed costs, and sales mix and to set up formulas to calculate breakeven points and expected profits. Then the data can be varied as desired to see what impact changes have on the expected profit.

In the preceding example on operating leverage, the Cedilla Company analyzed the impact on profit of using an automated versus a manual system. The computations were done by hand, an approach that makes it cumbersome to introduce much variation. Using the power of a computer, it would be an easy matter to change the sales price in $1 increments between $75 and $125, with related assumptions about quantity sold. At the same time, variable and fixed costs could be adjusted. For example, suppose that the automated system has fixed costs of $375,000, but that those costs could easily range up to twice as much in the first year, coming back down in the second and third year as bugs are worked out of the system and workers learn to use it. Again, a spreadsheet can effortlessly handle the many computations.

Finally, while the spreadsheet is wonderful for cranking out numerical answers, it cannot do the most difficult job in CVP analysis. That job is determining the data

---

7. This benchmark is computed by setting the profit equations of the two systems equal and solving for units: $50 × units – $375,000 = $20 × units – $100,000; units = 9,167.

to be entered in the first place. The accountant must be cognizant of the firm's cost and price distributions, as well as of the impact of changing economic conditions on these variables. The fact that variables are seldom known with certainty is no excuse for ignoring the impact of uncertainty on CVP analysis. Fortunately, sensitivity analysis can also give managers a feel for the degree to which a poorly forecasted variable will affect an answer. That is also an advantage.

CVP ANALYSIS AND ACTIVITY-BASED COSTING

Objective 6

Discuss the impact of activity-based costing on the cost–volume–profit analysis.

Conventional CVP analysis assumes that all costs of the firm can be divided into two categories: those that vary with sales volume (variable costs) and those that do not (fixed costs). Further, costs are assumed to be a linear function of sales volume. However, many companies now realize that this fixed-versus-variable distinction is too simplistic. For example, is the cost of life rafts on airplanes a fixed cost or a variable cost? In terms of passenger kilometres, the rafts ($7,400 each, carried in sets of three or four—enough to handle all the passengers on a jet) are a fixed cost. In terms of the number of jets, the rafts are a variable cost. And finally, fuel consumption is determined by weight as well as by kilometres flown. The rafts weigh 150 to 200 kilograms each, and together they add approximately $26,000 per plane in annual fuel costs. As a result, some U.S. airlines—among them Delta, Continental, Northwest, and American Airlines—have cut back on the number of planes that carry life rafts.[8]

In an activity-based costing system, costs are divided into unit- and nonunit-based categories. Activity-based costing admits that some costs vary with units produced and some costs do not. However, while activity-based costing acknowledges that nonunit-based costs are fixed with respect to production volume changes, it also argues that many nonunit-based costs vary with respect to other activity drivers.

The use of activity-based costing does not mean that CVP analysis is less useful. In fact, it becomes more useful, since it provides more accurate insights concerning cost behaviour. These insights produce better decisions. However, within an activity-based framework, CVP analysis must be modified. To illustrate, assume that Serif Company's costs can be explained by three variables: a unit-level activity driver (units sold), a batch-level activity driver (number of setups), and a product-level activity driver (engineering hours). The ABC cost equation can then be expressed as follows:

Total cost = Fixed cost + (Unit variable cost × Number of units) + (Setup cost × Number of setups) + (Engineering cost × Number of engineering hours)

Operating income, as before, is total revenue minus total cost. This is expressed as:

Operating income = Total revenue − [Fixed cost + (Unit variable cost × Number of units) + (Setup cost × Number of setups) + (Engineering cost × Number of engineering hours)]

The contribution margin approach is used to calculate the breakeven point in units. At breakeven, operating income is zero, and the number of units that must be sold to achieve breakeven is as follows:

Breakeven units = [Fixed cost + (Setup cost × Number of setups) + (Engineering cost × Number of engineering hours)]/ (Price − Unit variable cost)

A comparison of the ABC breakeven point with the conventional breakeven point reveals two significant differences. First, the fixed costs differ. Some costs previously identified as being fixed may actually vary with nonunit-level drivers—in this case, setups and engineering hours. Second, the numerator of the ABC breakeven equation has two nonunit-level variable-cost terms: one for batch-related activities and one for product-sustaining activities.

Example Comparing Conventional and ABC Analysis

To make this discussion more concrete, a comparison of conventional cost–volume–profit analysis with activity-based costing is useful. Assume that Galliard Company wants to compute the units that must be sold to earn a before-tax income of $20,000. The analysis is based on the following data:

Activity Driver	Unit Variable Cost	Level of Activity Driver
Units sold	$ 10	—
Setups	1,000	20
Engineering hours	30	1,000
Other data:		
Total fixed costs (conventional)		$100,000
Total fixed costs (ABC)		50,000
Unit selling price		20

Using CVP analysis, the units that must be sold to earn an operating income of $20,000 are computed as follows:

Number of units = (Targeted income + Fixed cost)/(Price − Unit variable cost)
$$= (\$20,000 + \$100,000)/(\$20 - \$10)$$
$$= \$120,000/\$10$$
$$= 12,000 \text{ units}$$

Using the ABC equation, the units that must be sold to earn an operating income of $20,000 are computed as follows:

Number of units = [$20,000 + $50,000 + ($1,000 × 20) + ($30 × 1,000)]/($20 − $10)
$$= 12,000 \text{ units}$$

The number of units that Galliard Company must sell is identical under both approaches. The reason is simple. The total fixed-cost pool under conventional costing consists of nonunit-based variable costs plus costs that are fixed regardless of the activity driver. ABC breaks out the nonunit-based variable costs. These costs are associated with certain levels of each activity driver. For the batch-level activity driver, the level is 20 setups; for the product-level variable, the level is 1,000 engineering hours. As long as the activity levels for the nonunit-based cost drivers remain the same, the results for the conventional and ABC computations will be the same. But these levels can change; as a result, the information provided by the two approaches can be significantly different. The ABC equation for CVP analysis is a richer representation of the underlying cost behaviour and can provide important strategic insights. To see this, let's use the same data to look at a different application.

Strategic Implications: Conventional CVP Analysis versus ABC Analysis

Suppose that after the conventional CVP analysis, Galliard Company's marketing department indicates that selling 12,000 units is not possible. In fact, only 10,000 units can be sold. The firm's president then directs its product design engineers to find a way to reduce the cost of making the product. The engineers have also been told that the conventional cost equation, with fixed costs of $100,000 and unit variable costs of $10, holds. The variable cost of $10 per unit consists of the following: direct labour, $4; direct materials, $5; and variable overhead, $1. To comply with the request to reduce the breakeven point, engineering produces a new design that requires less labour. The new design would reduce the direct labour cost by $2 per unit, but would not affect materials or variable overhead. Thus, the new variable cost is $8 per unit, and the breakeven point is calculated as follows:

$$\text{Number of units} = \text{Fixed cost}/(\text{Price} - \text{Unit variable cost})$$
$$= \$100,000/(\$20 - \$8)$$
$$= 8,333 \text{ units}$$

And the projected income if 10,000 units are sold is as follows:

Sales ($20 × 10,000)	$200,000
Less: Variable expenses ($8 × 10,000)	80,000
Contribution margin	$120,000
Less: Fixed expenses	100,000
Operating income	$ 20,000

Excited, Galliard's president approves the new design. A year later, she discovers that the expected increase in income did not materialize. In fact, a loss is realized. Why? The answer is provided by an ABC approach to CVP analysis.

The original ABC cost relationship for the Galliard example follows:

$$\text{Total cost} = \$50,000 + (\$10 \times \text{Units}) + (\$1,000 \times \text{Setups})$$
$$+ (\$30 \times \text{Engineering hours})$$

Suppose that the new design requires a more complex setup, increasing the cost per setup from $1,000 to $1,600. Also suppose that the new design, because of increased technical content, requires a 40 percent increase in engineering support (from 1,000 hours to 1,400 hours). The new cost equation, including the reduction in unit-level variable costs, follows:

$$\text{Total cost} = \$50,000 + (\$8 \times \text{Units}) + (\$1,600 \times \text{Setups})$$
$$+ (\$30 \times \text{Engineering hours})$$

The breakeven point, setting operating income equal to zero and using the ABC equation, is calculated as follows (assume that 20 setups are still performed):

$$\text{Number of units} = [\$50,000 + (\$1,600 \times 20) + (\$30 \times 1,400)]/(\$20 - \$8)$$
$$= \$124,000/\$12$$
$$= 10,333 \text{ units}$$

And the income for 10,000 units is as follows (recall that a maximum of 10,000 can be sold):

Sales ($20 × 10,000)		$200,000
Less: Unit-based variable expenses ($8 × 10,000)		80,000
Contribution margin		$120,000
Less: Nonunit-based variable expenses:		
Setups ($1,600 × 20)	$32,000	
Engineering support ($30 × 1,400)	42,000	74,000
Traceable margin		$ 46,000
Less: Fixed expenses		50,000
Operating income (loss)		$ (4,000)

How could the engineers have been off by so much? Didn't they know that the new design would increase setup cost and engineering support? Yes and no. They were probably aware of the increases in these two variables, but the conventional cost equation diverted attention from figuring out just how much impact changes in those variables would have. The information conveyed by the conventional equation to the engineers gave the impression that any reduction in labour cost—as long as it didn't affect materials or variable overhead—would reduce total costs, since changes in the level of labour activity would not affect the fixed costs. The ABC equation, however, indicates that a reduction in labour input that adversely affects setup activity or engineering support might be undesirable. With more insight, better design decisions can be made. Providing ABC cost information to the design engineers would probably have led them down a different path—one that would have been more advantageous to the company.

CVP Analysis and JIT

If a firm has adopted JIT, the variable cost per unit sold is reduced and fixed costs are increased. Direct labour, for example, is now viewed as fixed instead of variable. Direct materials, on the other hand, is still a unit-based variable cost. In fact, the emphasis on total quality and long-term purchasing renders the assumption that direct materials cost is strictly proportional to units produced even more true, because waste, scrap, and quantity discounts are eliminated. Other unit-based variable costs, such as power and sales commissions, also persist. Additionally, the batch-level variable is gone (in JIT, the batch is one unit). Thus, the cost equation for JIT can be expressed as follows:

$$\text{Total cost} = \text{Fixed cost} + (\text{Unit variable cost} \times \text{Number of units})$$
$$+ (\text{Engineering cost} \times \text{Number of engineering hours})$$

Since its application is a special case of the ABC equation, no example is provided.

SUMMARY OF LEARNING OBJECTIVES

1. Determine the number of units that must be sold to break even or to earn a targeted profit.
In a single-product setting, the breakeven point can be computed in units by dividing the total fixed costs by the contribution margin per unit. In essence, sufficient units must be sold to just cover all fixed and variable costs of the firm.

2. Determine the amount of revenue required to break even or to earn a targeted profit.
Breakeven revenue is computed by dividing the total fixed costs by the contribution margin ratio. Targeted profit is added to fixed costs in determining the amount of revenue needed to yield the targeted profit.

3. Apply cost–volume–profit analysis in a multiple-product setting.
Multiple-product analysis requires that an assumption be made concerning the expected sales mix. Given a particular sales mix, a multiple-product problem can be converted into a single-product analysis. However, it should be remembered that the answers change as the sales mix changes. If the sales mix changes in a multiple-product firm, the breakeven point will also change. In

general, increases in the sales of products with high contribution margins will decrease the breakeven point, while increases in the sales of products with low contribution margins will increase the breakeven point.

4. Prepare a profit–volume graph and a cost–volume–profit graph, and explain the meaning of each.
CVP is based on several assumptions that must be considered when applying it to business problems. The analysis assumes linear revenue and cost functions, no finished goods ending inventories, and a constant sales mix. CVP analysis also assumes that selling prices and fixed and variable costs are known with certainty. These assumptions form the basis for simple graphical analysis using the profit–volume graph and the cost–volume–profit graph.

5. Explain the impact of risk, uncertainty, and changing variables on cost–volume–profit analysis.
Measures of risk and uncertainty, such as the margin of safety and operating leverage, can be used to give managers more insight into CVP answers. Sensitivity analysis gives still more insight into the effect of changes in underlying variables on CVP relationships.

6. Discuss the impact of activity-based costing on cost–volume–profit analysis.

CVP can be used with activity-based costing, but the analysis must be modified. Under ABC, a type of sensitivity analysis is used. Fixed costs are separated from a variety of costs that vary with particular cost drivers. At this stage, it is easiest to organize variable costs as unit-level, batch-level, and product-level. Then the impact of decisions on batches and products can be examined within the CVP framework.

The subject of cost–volume–profit analysis naturally lends itself to the use of numerous equations. Some of the more common equations used in this chapter are summarized in Exhibit 9–11.

Exhibit 9–11

Summary of Important Equations

1. Sales revenue = Price × Units
2. Operating income = (Price × Units) − (Unit variable cost × Units) − Fixed cost
3. Breakeven point in units = Fixed cost/(Price − Unit variable cost)
4. Contribution margin ratio = Contribution margin/Sales
   or = (Price − Unit variable cost)/Price
5. Variable cost ratio = Total variable cost/Sales
   or = Unit variable cost/Price
6. Breakeven point in sales dollars = Fixed cost/Contribution margin ratio
   or = Fixed cost/(1 − Variable cost ratio)
7. Margin of safety = Sales − Breakeven sales
8. Degree of operating leverage = Total contribution margin/Operating income
9. Percentage change in profits = Degree of operating leverage × % change in sales
10. Income taxes = Tax rate × Operating income
11. After-tax income = Operating income − (Tax rate × Operating income)
12. Before-tax income = After-tax income/(1 − Tax rate)
13. ABC total cost = Fixed cost + (Unit variable cost × Number of units) + (Batch-level cost × Batch driver) + (Product-level cost × Product driver)
14. ABC breakeven units = [Fixed cost + (Batch-level cost × Batch driver) + (Product-level cost × Product driver)]/(Price − Unit variable cost)

KEY TERMS

Breakeven point, 335
Contribution margin, 337
Contribution margin ratio, 340
Cost–volume–profit graph, 348
Degree of operating leverage (DOL), 354

Margin of safety, 353
Net income, 336
Operating income, 336
Operating leverage, 354
Profit–volume graph, 347
Sales mix, 344

Sensitivity analysis, 355
Variable-cost ratio, 340

REVIEW PROBLEMS

I. BREAKEVEN ANALYSIS
Cutlass Company's projected profit for the coming year is as follows:

	Total	Per Unit
Sales	$200,000	$20
Less: Variable expenses	120,000	12
Contribution margin	$ 80,000	$ 8
Less: Fixed expenses	64,000	
Operating income	$ 16,000	

Required:

1. Compute the breakeven point in units.
2. How many units must be sold to earn an operating income of $30,000?
3. Compute the contribution margin ratio. Using that ratio, compute the additional operating income that Cutlass would earn if sales were $25,000 more than expected.
4. Suppose Cutlass would like to earn operating income equal to 20 percent of sales revenue. How many units must be sold for this goal to be realized? Prepare an income statement to prove your answer.
5. For the projected level of sales, compute the margin of safety.

Solution

1. The breakeven point is computed as follows:

$$\text{Units} = \text{Fixed cost}/(\text{Price} - \text{Unit variable cost})$$
$$= \$64{,}000/(\$20 - \$12)$$
$$= \$64{,}000/\$8$$
$$= 8{,}000 \text{ units}$$

2. The number of units that must be sold to earn an operating income of $30,000 is computed as follows:

$$\text{Units} = (\$64{,}000 + \$30{,}000)/\$8$$
$$= \$94{,}000/\$8$$
$$= 11{,}750 \text{ units}$$

3. The contribution margin ratio is $8/$20 = 0.40. With additional sales of $25,000, the additional operating income would be 0.40 × $25,000 = $10,000.
4. To find the number of units that must be sold to generate an operating income equal to 20 percent of sales, let target income equal (0.20 × Price × Units) and solve for units:

$$\text{Operating income} = (\text{Price} \times \text{Units}) - (\text{Unit variable cost} \times \text{Units}) - \text{Fixed cost}$$
$$0.2 \times \$20 \times \text{Units} = (\$20 \times \text{Units}) - (\$12 \times \text{Units}) - \$64{,}000$$
$$\$4 \times \text{Units} = \$64{,}000$$
$$\text{Units} = 16{,}000$$

The income statement is as follows:

Sales (16,000 × $20)	$320,000
Less: Variable expenses (16,000 × $12)	192,000
Contribution margin	$128,000
Less: Fixed expenses	64,000
Operating income	$ 64,000

5. The margin of safety is 10,000 – 8,000 = 2,000 units, or $40,000 in sales revenues.

II. BREAKEVEN ANALYSIS WITH ABC

Dory Manufacturing Company produces T-shirts screen-printed with the logos of various sports teams. Each shirt is priced at $10. Costs are as follows:

Cost Driver	Unit Variable Cost	Level of Cost Driver
Units sold	$ 5	—
Setups	450	80
Engineering hours	20	500

Other data:	
Total fixed costs (conventional)	$96,000
Total fixed costs (ABC)	50,000

Required:

1. Compute the breakeven point in units using conventional analysis.
2. Compute the breakeven point in units using activity-based analysis.
3. Suppose that Dory could reduce the setup cost by $150 per setup and the number of engineering hours needed to 425. How many units must be sold to break even in this case?

Solution

1. Breakeven units = Fixed cost/(Price − Unit variable cost)
   = $96,000/($10 − $5)
   = 19,200 units
2. Breakeven units = [Fixed cost + (Setups × Setup cost) + (Engineering hours × Engineering cost)]/(Price − Unit variable cost)
   = [$50,000 + ($450 × 80) + ($20 × 500)]/($10 − $5)
   = 19,200 units
3. Breakeven units = [$50,000 + ($300 × 80) + ($20 × 425)]/($10 − $5)
   = $82,500/$5
   = 16,500 units

QUESTIONS FOR WRITING AND DISCUSSION

1. Explain how CVP analysis can be used for managerial planning.

2. Describe the difference between the units-sold approach to CVP analysis and the sales revenue approach.

3. Define the term *breakeven point*.

4. Explain why contribution margin per unit becomes profit per unit above the breakeven point.

5. If the contribution margin per unit is $7 and the breakeven point is 10,000 units, how much profit will a firm make if 15,000 units are sold?

6. What is the variable cost ratio? the contribution margin ratio? How are the two ratios related?

7. Suppose a firm has fixed costs of $20,000 and a contribution margin ratio of 0.4. How much sales revenue must the firm have in order to break even?

8. Suppose a firm with a contribution margin ratio of 0.3 increased its advertising expenses by $10,000 and found that sales increased by $30,000. Was it a good decision to increase advertising expenses?

9. Define the term *sales mix* and give an example to support your definition.

10. Explain how CVP analysis developed for single products can be used in a multiple-product setting.

11. Assume that a firm has two products—A and B.

Last year, 2,000 units of A and 1,000 units of B were sold. The same sales mix is expected for the coming year. Total fixed expenses are $30,000, and the unit contribution margins are $10 for A and $5 for B. How many units of A and how many units of B must be sold to break even?

12. Makeba Company has a contribution margin ratio of 0.6. The breakeven point is $100,000. During the year, Makeba earned total revenues of $200,000. What was Makeba's profit?

13. Explain how a change in sales mix can change a company's breakeven point.

14. Define the term *margin of safety*. Explain how it can be used as a crude measure of operating risk.

15. Explain what is meant by the term *operating leverage*. What impact does increased leverage have on risk?

16. How can sensitivity analysis be used in conjunction with CVP analysis?

17. Why does the activity-based costing approach to CVP analysis offer more insight than the conventional approach?

18. How does JIT affect the firm's cost equation? CVP analysis?

19. A company has a positive profit, p, at a given volume of sales, x. If x doubles (within the relevant range), would profit be equal to $2p$, greater than $2p$, or less than $2p$? Explain.

EXERCISES

9–1
Breakeven in Units
LO1

The controller of Dorian Company prepared the following projected income statement:

Sales (2,000 units × $25)	$50,000
Less: Variable expenses	30,000
Contribution margin	$20,000
Less: Fixed expenses	18,000
Operating income	$ 2,000

Required:

1. Calculate the breakeven number of units.
2. Prepare an income statement for Dorian at breakeven.
3. How many units must Dorian sell to earn operating income equal to $15,000?

9–2
Targeted Income as a Function of Sales, After-Tax Profit
LO1

Refer to 9–1 for data.

Required:

1. How many units must Dorian sell to earn operating income equal to 20 percent of revenue?
2. Assuming a tax rate of 40 percent, how many units must Dorian sell to earn after-tax income equal to $15,000?

9–3
Contribution Margin Ratio, Variable-Cost Ratio, Breakeven in Sales Revenue
LO2

Refer to 9–1 for data.

Required:

1. What is the contribution margin per unit for Dorian Company? What is the contribution margin ratio?
2. What is the variable-cost ratio for Dorian Company?
3. Calculate the breakeven revenue.
4. How much revenue must Dorian make to earn operating income equal to $15,000?

9–4
Multiple-Product Breakeven
LO3

Lacy Company manufactures two products. In the coming year, Lacy expects to sell 1,000 units of Product A and 3,000 units of Product B. A budgeted income statement for next year follows:

	Product A	Product B	Total
Sales	$10,000	$ 36,000	$ 46,000
Less: Variable expenses	6,000	27,000	33,000
Contribution margin	$ 4,000	$ 9,000	$ 13,000
Less: Direct fixed expenses	1,500	3,200	4,700
Product margin	$ 2,500	$ 5,800	$ 8,300
Less: Common fixed expenses			3,100
Operating income			$ 5,200

Required:

1. What is the sales mix for Lacy Company?
2. Calculate the number of units of Product A and the number of units of Product B that Lacy must sell to break even.
3. Without forming a package, calculate the breakeven revenue for Lacy Company.

9–5
Margin of Safety and Degree of Operating Leverage
LO5

Anjou Company has prepared the following income statement for the year:

Sales ($50 × 8,000 units)	$400,000
Less: Variable expenses	140,000
Contribution margin	$260,000
Less: Fixed expenses	119,925
Operating income	$140,075

Required:

1. What is the margin of safety in sales dollars? in units?
2. What is the degree of operating leverage for Anjou Company?

9–6

CVP and Activity-Based Costing

LO6

The controller of Fremont Company collected the following data for one of Fremont's plants:

Activity Driver	Unit Variable Cost	Level of Activity Driver
Units sold	$ 10	—
Setups	$600	50
Engineering hours	60	500

Other data:

Total fixed costs (conventional)	$100,000
Total fixed costs (ABC)	40,000
Unit selling price	20

Required:

1. Calculate the breakeven point in units using the traditional approach.
2. Calculate the breakeven point in units using the ABC approach.
3. If Fremont's engineers can reduce the variable cost of a setup by $100, what will the new breakeven point in units be under the ABC approach? under the traditional approach?

9–7

Units Sold to Break Even, Targeted Income

LO1

Loewen Company produces and sells multivitamins to retailers for $2.72 per bottle. The variable costs per bottle are as follows:

Ingredients	$0.45
Bottle and cap	0.10
Direct labour	0.58
Variable overhead	0.62
Selling	0.17

Fixed manufacturing costs total $136,000 per year. Administrative costs (all fixed) total $14,000.

Required:

1. Compute the number of bottles that Loewen must sell to break even.
2. How many bottles must Loewen sell to earn an operating income of $12,600?
3. What is the unit variable cost? What is the unit variable manufacturing cost? Which is used in cost–volume–profit analysis and why?

9–8

After-Tax Profit, Margin of Safety

LO2, LO5

Refer to 9–7.

Required:

1. Assuming a tax rate of 40 percent, how many bottles must be sold to earn an after-tax profit of $25,200?
2. Assuming a tax rate of 30 percent, how many bottles have to be sold to earn an after-tax profit of $25,200?
3. Assuming a tax rate of 50 percent, how many bottles have to be sold to earn an after-tax profit of $25,200?
4. Suppose that Loewen expects to sell 215,000 bottles. What is the margin of safety in bottles? What is the margin of safety in dollars?

9–9

Units Sold, After-Tax Profit, Margin of Safety

LO2, LO5

Popfresh, Inc., manufactures and sells packaged prepopped popcorn to retailers and movie theatres. The popcorn is packaged in 500-gram bags and sold to retailers for $1.25 per bag. The variable costs per bag are as follows:

Corn	$0.65
Vegetable oil	0.10
Miscellaneous ingredients	0.03
Selling	0.17

Fixed manufacturing costs total $250,000 per year. Administrative costs (all fixed) total $50,000.

Required:

1. Compute the number of bags of popcorn that must be sold for Popfresh to break even.
2. How many bags of popcorn must be sold for Popfresh to earn an operating income of $150,000?
3. Assume a tax rate of 40 percent. How many bags of popcorn must be sold to earn an after-tax profit of $324,000?
4. Suppose that Popfresh expects to sell 1.2 million bags of popcorn. What is the margin of safety?

9–10

Contribution Margin, Unit Amounts

LO1, LO2

Information on four independent companies follows. Calculate the correct amount for each question mark.

	A	B	C	D
Sales	$5,000	$?	$?	$9,000
Total variable expenses	4,000	11,700	9,750	?
Contribution margin	$1,000	$ 3,900	$?	$?
Total fixed costs	?	4,000	?	750
Operating income (loss)	$ 500	$?	$ 400	$2,850
Units sold	?	1,300	125	90
Price per unit	$5	?	$130	?
Variable cost per unit	?	$9	?	?
Contribution margin per unit	?	$3	?	?
Contribution margin ratio	?	?	40%	?
Breakeven in units	?	?	?	?

9–11

CVP, Margin of Safety

LO2, LO5

Daley Company had revenues of $720,000 last year, with total variable costs of $324,000 and fixed costs of $275,000.

Required:

1. What is the variable-cost ratio for Daley? What is the contribution margin ratio?
2. What is the breakeven point in sales revenue?
3. What was the margin of safety for Daley last year?
4. Daley is considering starting a multimedia advertising campaign that is supposed to increase sales by $7,500 per year. The campaign will cost $5,000. Is the advertising campaign a good idea? Explain.

9–12

CVP

LO1, LO2

Solve the following independent problems.

Required:

1. Thiessen Company's breakeven point is 1,500 units. Variable cost per unit is $300; total fixed costs are $120,000 per year. What price does Thiessen charge?
2. Jesper Company charges a price of $3.50; total fixed costs are $160,000 per year; and the breakeven point is 128,000 units. What is the variable cost per unit?

9–13

Breakeven, Targeted Operating Income

LO2

The Heidleweiss Co. Ltd. has a maximum capacity of 210,000 units per year. Variable manufacturing costs are $11 per unit. Fixed overhead is $540,000 per year. Variable selling costs are $3 per unit; fixed selling costs are $252,000 per year. Sales price is $20 per unit.

Required:

1. What is the breakeven point expressed in dollar sales?
2. How many units must be sold to earn a targeted operating income of $60,000 per year?
3. How many units must be sold to earn a targeted operating income of 10 percent of sales? (CGA Canada adapted)

9–14

Contribution Margin, CVP, Margin of Safety

LO1, LO2, LO5

Spreadsheet

Candyland, Inc., produces a particularly rich praline fudge. Each 250-gram box sells for $5.60. Variable unit costs are as follows:

Pecans	$0.70
Sugar	0.35
Butter	1.85
Other ingredients	0.34
Box, packing material	0.76
Selling commission	0.20

Fixed overhead cost is $32,300 per year. Fixed selling and administrative costs are $12,500 per year. Candyland sold 35,000 boxes last year.

Required:

1. What is the contribution margin per unit for a box of praline fudge? What is the contribution margin ratio?
2. How many boxes must be sold to break even? What is the breakeven sales revenue?
3. What was Candyland's operating income last year?
4. What was the firm's margin of safety?
5. Suppose that Candyland raises the price to $6.20 per box, but anticipated sales will drop to 31,500 boxes. What will the new breakeven point in units be? Should Candyland raise the price? Explain.

9–15

After-Tax Profit Target

LO1

The Wencam Company Ltd. produced and sold 55,000 units during 2001. The following amounts were obtained from the financial statements for the year ended December 31, 2001:

Sales	$2,475,000
Direct materials used	476,500
Direct labour costs	805,750
Variable overhead incurred	269,500
Fixed overhead incurred*	347,600
Variable selling and administrative costs	129,250
Fixed selling and administrative costs	187,200

* The relevant range for fixed costs is 10,000 units to 85,000 units.

Expectations for 2002 include the following:

- Variable and fixed costs are expected to behave in the same manner as indicated above, but costs are expected to increase in general by 8 percent.
- The selling price will be raised by 6 percent.
- The company's 2002 income tax rate is expected to be 35 percent.

Required:

How many units must Wencam sell in 2002 in order to earn after-tax income of $211,250? Show all calculations. (CMA Canada adapted)

9–16

CVP, Prices

LO1

The Brisbane Company Ltd. has budgeted the following costs for 2001:

	Total Cost	Unit Cost
Direct materials	$ 160,000	$ 2.00
Direct labour	320,000	4.00
Variable overhead	80,000	1.00
Fixed overhead	400,000	5.00
Variable selling	240,000	3.00
Fixed administrative	600,000	7.50
	$1,800,000	$22.50

Required:

1. What price would Brisbane have to charge in order to produce an after-tax profit of $144,000 if the firm's tax rate is 40 percent?
2. At a sales price of $25.00, what is Brisbane's breakeven point in units?
3. If 70,000 units were produced and sold, what price would Brisbane have to charge in order to have an operating income equal to 10 percent of sales? (CGA Canada adapted)

9–17

Sales Revenue Approach, Variable-Cost Ratio, Contribution Margin Ratio, Margin of Safety

LO2, LO5

Lane Company produces and sells an economy line of ski parkas. The budgeted income statement for the coming year is as follows:

Sales	$450,000
Less: Variable expenses	202,500
Contribution margin	$247,500
Less: Fixed expenses	90,000
Operating income	$157,500
Less: Taxes	47,250
Net income	$110,250

Required:

1. What is Lane's variable-cost ratio? What is its contribution margin ratio?
2. Suppose Lane's actual revenues are $50,000 more than budgeted. By how much will operating income increase? Give the answer without preparing a new income statement.
3. How much sales revenue must Lane earn in order to break even? What is the expected margin of safety?
4. How much sales revenue must Lane generate to earn an operating income of $75,000?
5. How much sales revenue must Lane generate to earn an after-tax profit of $63,000? Prepare a contribution income statement to verify the accuracy of your answer.

9–18

CVP Analysis with Target Profits

LO1, LO2

Tom Flannery has developed a new recipe for fried chicken and plans to open a take-out restaurant in Edmundston. His father-in-law has agreed to invest $500,000 in the operation, provided Tom can convince him that profits will be at least 20 percent of sales revenues. Tom estimated that total fixed expense would be $24,000 per year and that variable expense would be approximately 40 percent of sales revenues.

Required:

1. How much sales revenue must be earned to produce operating income equal to 20 percent of sales revenue? Prepare a contribution income statement to verify your answer.
2. If Tom plans on selling 12-piece buckets of chicken for $10 each, how many buckets must he sell to earn an operating income equal to 20 percent of sales? 25 percent of sales? Prepare a contribution income statement to verify the second answer.
3. Suppose Tom's father-in-law meant that the after-tax profit had to be 20 percent of sales revenue. Under this assumption, how much sales revenue must be generated by Tom's chicken business? (Assume that the tax rate is 40 percent.)

9–19

CVP, Margin of Safety

LO1, LO2, LO5

Commonwealth Computer Company manufactures and sells a line of computers to computer retail stores across Canada. The company has experienced a moderate but steady growth in sales for the last three years. In order to compete with major computer manufacturers and increase market share, Commonwealth's president is planning to cut the unit selling price by 15 percent, effective January 1, 2001.

The following are actual cost data and projected sales volumes for 2000 and 2001:

Selling price per unit for 2000	$ 4,200
Actual sales units (January 1 to September 30, 2000)	35,000
Forecasted sales units (October 1 to December 31, 2000)	10,000
Unit variable costs:	
Direct materials	$ 950
Direct labour	450
Variable overhead	360
Selling expenses	275
Total variable cost per unit	$ 2,035
Fixed cost per year:	
Manufacturing	$15,000,000
Selling	12,800,000
Administrative	8,750,000
Income tax rate	45%

It is anticipated that sales units for 2001 will increase by 5 percent to 47,250 units. The cost structure will remain the same, with no changes in inventory levels.

Required:

1. Determine the following for 2000:
   a. Contribution margin ratio
   b. Breakeven point in units and sales dollars
   c. Projected net income (after tax)
   d. Margin of safety
2. Determine the following for 2001:
   a. Contribution margin ratio
   b. Breakeven point in units and sales dollars
   c. Projected net income (after tax)
   d. Margin of safety (CGA Canada adapted)

9–20

Operating Leverage

LO5

Spreadsheet

Income statements for two different companies in the same industry are as follows:

	Company A	Company B
Sales	$500,000	$500,000
Less: Variable costs	400,000	200,000
Contribution margin	$100,000	$300,000
Less: Fixed costs	50,000	250,000
Operating income	$ 50,000	$ 50,000

Required:

1. Compute the degree of operating leverage for each company.
2. Compute the breakeven point for each company. Explain why Company B's breakeven point is higher.
3. Suppose that both companies experience a 50 percent increase in revenues. Compute the percentage change in profits for each company. Explain why the percentage increase in Company B's profits is so much larger than that in Company A's.

9–21

CVP Analysis with Multiple Products

LO3

Spreadsheet

Gernon Company produces scientific and business calculators. For the coming year, Gernon expects to sell 20,000 scientific calculators and 100,000 business calculators. A segmented income statement for the two products is given below.

	Scientific	Business	Total
Sales	$500,000	$2,000,000	$2,500,000
Less: Variable costs	240,000	900,000	1,140,000
Contribution margin	$260,000	$1,100,000	$1,360,000
Less: Direct fixed costs	120,000	960,000	1,080,000
Segment margin	$140,000	$ 140,000	$ 280,000
Less: Common fixed costs			145,000
Operating income			$ 135,000

Required:

1. Compute the number of scientific calculators and the number of business calculators that Gernon must sell in order to break even.
2. Using information from only the "Total" column of the income statement, compute the sales revenue that must be generated for the company to break even.

9–22

Multiple Product Breakeven, Breakeven Sales Revenue, Margin of Safety

LO1, LO2, LO3, LO5

Serenity Products Incorporated produces and sells yoga-related training products: how-to videotapes; a basic equipment set (a nonskid mat, blocks, a strap, and a small pillow); and an advanced yoga handbook. Last year, Serenity sold 10,000 videos, 5,000 equipment sets, and 2,000 handbooks. Information on the three products is as follows:

	Videotape	Equipment Set	Handbook
Price	$12.00	$15.00	$9.00
Variable cost per unit	4.00	6.00	6.50

Total fixed costs are $69,420.

Required:

1. What is the sales mix of videotapes, equipment sets, and handbooks?
2. Compute the breakeven quantity of each product.
3. Prepare an income statement for Serenity for last year. What is the overall contribution margin ratio? the overall breakeven sales revenue?
4. Compute the margin of safety for last year.

9–23

Changes in Breakeven Points with Changes in Unit Prices

LO1, LO5

The income statement for Roy, Inc., is as follows:

Sales	$600,000
Less: Variable expenses	228,000
Contribution margin	$372,000
Less: Fixed expenses	295,000
Operating income	$ 77,000

Roy produces and sells a single product. The above income statement is based on sales of 100,000 units.

Required:

1. Compute the breakeven point in units and in revenues.
2. Suppose that the selling price increases by 10 percent. Will the breakeven point increase or decrease? Recompute it.
3. Ignoring Requirement 2, suppose that the variable cost per unit increases by $0.35. Will the breakeven point increase or decrease? Recompute it.

4. Can you predict whether the breakeven point will increase or decrease if both the selling price and the unit variable cost increase? Recompute the breakeven point incorporating both of the changes in Requirements 2 and 3.
5. Assume that total fixed costs increase by $50,000. (Assume no other changes from the original data.) Will the breakeven point increase or decrease? Recompute it.

9–24

CVP and Profit–Volume Graphs

LO4, LO5

Bryant Company produces and sells one product. The selling price is $10, and the unit variable cost is $6. Total fixed costs are $10,000.

Required:

1. Prepare a CVP graph with units sold as the horizontal axis and dollars as the vertical axis. Label the breakeven point on the horizontal axis.
2. Prepare CVP graphs for each of the following independent scenarios:
   a. Fixed costs increase by $5,000.
   b. Unit variable cost increases to $7.
   c. Unit selling price increases to $12.
   d. Fixed costs increase by $5,000, and variable cost is $7.
3. Prepare a profit–volume graph using the original data. Repeat, following the scenarios in Requirement 2.
4. Which of the two graphs do you think provides the most information? Why?

9–25

Basic CVP Concepts

LO1, LO2, LO5

Suriname Company produces a single product. The projected income statement for the coming year is as follows:

Sales (50,000 units × $45)	$2,250,000
Less: Variable costs	1,305,000
Contribution margin	$ 945,000
Less: Fixed costs	812,700
Operating income	$ 132,300

Required:

1. Compute the unit contribution margin and the units that must be sold to break even. Suppose that 30,000 units are sold above breakeven. What is the operating income?
2. Compute the contribution margin ratio and the breakeven point in dollars. Suppose that revenues are $200,000 more than expected. What would the total operating income be?
3. Compute the margin of safety.
4. Compute the operating leverage. Compute the new operating income if sales are 20 percent higher than expected.
5. How many units must be sold to earn an operating income equal to 10 percent of sales?
6. Assume that the tax rate is 40 percent. How many units must be sold to earn an after-tax profit of $180,000?

9–26

Multiple-Product Breakeven

LO3

Parker Pottery produces a line of vases and a line of ceramic figurines. Each line uses the same equipment and labour; hence, there are no traceable fixed costs. Common fixed costs equal $30,000. Parker's accountant has begun to assess the profitability of the two lines and has gathered the following data for last year:

	Vases	Figurines
Price	$40	$70
Variable cost	30	42
Contribution margin	$10	$28
Number of units	1,000	500

Required:

1. Compute the number of vases and the number of figurines that must be sold for the company to break even.
2. Parker Pottery is considering upgrading its factory to improve the quality of its product. If the upgrade—which will cost $5,260—is successful, the projected sales of vases will be 1,500; figurine sales will increase to 1,000 units. What is the new breakeven point in units for each of the products?

PROBLEMS

9–27

Basic CVP Concepts

LO1, LO2, LO3

Fisper Company produces a variety of industrial products. One division makes solvents. The division's projected income statement for the coming year is as follows:

Sales (128,000 units × $50)	$6,400,000
Less: Variable expenses	4,480,000
Contribution margin	$1,920,000
Less: Fixed expenses	1,000,000
Operating income	$ 920,000

Required:

1. Compute the contribution margin per unit, and calculate the breakeven point in units (round to the nearest unit). Calculate the contribution margin ratio and the breakeven sales revenue.
2. The divisional manager has decided to increase the advertising budget by $100,000. This change will increase sales revenues by $1 million. By how much will operating income increase or decrease as a result of this action?
3. Suppose sales revenues exceed the estimated amount on the income statement by $315,000. Without preparing a new income statement, by how much is operating income underestimated?
4. Refer to the original data. How many units must Fisper sell to earn an after-tax profit of $630,000? Assume a tax rate of 40 percent.
5. Compute the margin of safety based on the original income statement.
6. Compute the operating leverage based on the original income statement. If sales revenues are 20 percent greater than expected, what is the percentage increase in operating income?

9–28

Multiple-Product Analysis, Change in Sales Mix

LO3

Unicorn Enterprises produces two strategy games, Mystical Wars and Magical Dragons. The projected income for the coming year, segmented by product line, follows:

	Wars	Dragons	Total
Sales	$300,000	$2,500,000	$2,800,000
Less: Variable expenses	100,000	500,000	600,000
Contribution margin	$200,000	$2,000,000	$2,200,000
Less: Direct fixed expenses	28,000	1,500,000	1,528,000
Product margin	$172,000	$ 500,000	$ 672,000
Less: Common fixed expenses			100,000
Operating income			$ 572,000

The selling prices are $30 for Mystical Wars and $50 for Magical Dragons.

Required:

1. Compute the number of games of each kind that must be sold for Unicorn Enterprises to break even.

2. Compute the revenue that Unicorn must earn to produce an operating income of 10 percent of sales revenues.
3. Assume that the marketing manager changes the sales mix of the two games so that the ratio is three Mystical Wars games to five Magical Dragons games. Repeat Requirements 1 and 2.
4. Refer to the original data. Suppose that Unicorn can increase the sales of Magical Dragons with increased advertising. The extra advertising would cost an additional $45,000, and some of the potential purchasers of Mystical Wars would switch to Magical Dragons. In total, sales of Magical Dragons would increase by 15,000 units and sales of Mystical Wars would decrease by 5,000 units. Would Unicorn be better off with this strategy?

9–29

CVP Equation, Basic Concepts, Solving for Unknowns

LO1, LO2

Azucar Company produces combination shampoos and conditioners in individual-use bottles for hotels. Each bottle sells for $0.36. The variable costs for each bottle (materials, labour, and overhead) total $0.27. The total fixed costs are $54,000. During the most recent year, 830,000 bottles were sold. The president of Azucar, not fully satisfied with the product's profit performance, was considering the following options to increase profitability: (1) increase promotional spending; (2) increase the quality of the ingredients and, simultaneously, increase the selling price; (3) increase the selling price; (4) combinations of the three.

Required:

1. The sales manager is confident that an advertising campaign could increase sales volume by 50 percent. If the company president's goal is to increase this year's profits by 50 percent over last year's, what is the maximum amount that can be spent on advertising?
2. Assume that the company has a plan to imprint the name of the purchasing hotel on each bottle. This will increase variable costs to $0.30. How much must the selling price be increased to maintain the same breakeven point?
3. Azucar increases its selling price to $0.40. Sales volume drops from 830,000 to 700,000 bottles. Was the decision to increase the price a good one? Compute the sales volume that would be needed at the new price for the company to earn the same profit as last year.

9–30

CVP, Target Income, Prices

LO1, LO2

Laraby Company produces a single product in its Halifax factory. It sold 25,000 units last year with the following results:

Sales	$625,000
Variable costs	375,000
Contribution margin	$250,000
Fixed costs	150,000
Operating income	$100,000
Income taxes	45,000
Net income	$ 55,000

In an attempt to improve its product in the coming year, Laraby is considering replacing a component part that has cost $2.50 with a new and better part costing $4.50 per unit. A new machine will also be needed to increase plant capacity. The machine, which would cost $18,000, would have a useful life of six years and no salvage value. The company uses straight-line amortization for both financial statements and tax purposes.

Required:

1. What was Laraby Company's breakeven point in number of units last year?
2. How many units of product would Laraby have had to sell last year to earn $77,000 in net income after taxes?

3. If Laraby holds the sales price constant and makes the suggested changes, how many units of product must be sold in the coming year to break even?
4. If Laraby holds the sales price constant and makes the suggested changes, how many units of product must be sold in the coming year to make the same net income after taxes as last year?
5. If Laraby wishes to maintain the same contribution margin ratio after implementing the changes, what selling price per unit of product must it charge next year to cover the increased materials costs? (CGA Canada adapted)

9–31

CVP, Changes in Price and Costs

LO1, LO2, LO5

Nico's Pizza, Inc., is a new company currently studying various alternatives in regard to opening pizza outlets. The only available data was formulated by a hired consultant who, unfortunately, died quite suddenly. A summary of the information that the consultant developed follows:

Average selling price per pizza: $7.50

Normal monthly costs*	Fixed	Variable
Cost of pizzas sold	$ 0	$5,500
Manager's salary	2,000	0
Wages	2,000	0
Rent	1,500	500
Utilities	500	200
Insurance and commissions	1,000	0
Total cost	$7,000	$6,200

* Note: Costs are based on budgeted sales of 2,000 pizzas per month.

The above information represents estimates for the operation of a pizza outlet. Nico's is interested in opening the outlets as soon as possible and has asked you to comment on various points and alternatives.

Required:

1. Compute the breakeven point for a pizza outlet in terms of both sales dollars and number of pizzas sold each month.
2. As a promotion to attract business, the company is considering whether to offer a special price during the first month of operations. This move would, in effect, reduce the average selling price to $5 per pizza. How many additional pizzas will have to be sold by a pizza outlet at the promotional selling price compared with the normal average selling price to earn operating income of $2,500 during the first month?
3. As a potential incentive program for the outlet manager, Nico's is considering a change in the consultant's proposed method of compensation. Instead of paying the outlet manager a fixed wage of $2,000 per month, the company is considering an incentive plan of $1,000 per month plus 8 percent of monthly revenue. Under this alternative compensation method and using the normal average selling price per pizza, calculate how many pizzas will have to be sold to achieve operating income of $2,000 per month.
4. Originally, Nico's planned to set the business hours for each pizza outlet at 11:00 a.m. to 2:00 a.m. (that is, open 15 hours per day), 7 days per week. Management is now considering a decrease in business hours by opening each outlet five hours later (at 4:00 p.m.). With these hours, management feels it would save an average of $1,000 per month (primarily from utilities and wages). The average number of pizzas sold between 11:00 a.m. and 4:00 p.m. was estimated to be 15 per day. (Note: Assume a 30-day month.) Should the company change the outlets' business hours? Support your answer. (CMA Canada adapted)

9–32

CVP, Multiple Products

LO3, LO5

Klamic Ceramics (KC) manufactures and sells ceramic flowerpots. As a result of competitive forces (for example, plastic substitutes), KC has been selling its only product at a price of $10 each. In 2000, its first year of operations, KC determined that at a normal volume of 80,000 units per year, the following costs would apply:

Materials	$2.00
Direct labour	3.50
Applied overhead	2.50
Total cost	$8.00

Annual fixed overhead costs total $180,000. Annual fixed selling and administrative costs total $20,000.

Klamic's owners, Jack and Katie Brown, have recently been offered positions in other companies, which would commence in January 2001. Consequently, Jack and Katie have spent much of the current month (December 2000) attempting to determine whether they could jointly have a higher income by working for other companies. Their salaries would total $70,000 before taxes.

For 2001, Jack considered introducing a new product. After some research, he established that an increasing demand for ceramic lawn ornaments existed in the community. Average variable costs for the ornaments would total $7, and the average selling price would be $12. Additional moulds and a part-time worker would increase total fixed costs to $245,000 per year.

Required:

1. Calculate the breakeven point for the ceramic flowerpot production for 2000.
2. Jack estimated that production and sales in 2001 would be 80,000 flowerpots. Determine whether Jack and Katie would be better off by remaining self-employed by comparing KC's operating income to the couple's joint salaries while working elsewhere. Show supporting calculations.
3. If the company plans to produce and sell 50,000 flowerpots and 30,000 lawn ornaments in 2001, what is the breakeven revenue for both products combined?
4. After some discussions with a local advertising agency, Katie determined that if KC spent $15,000 on additional marketing efforts, it would be able to increase sales of lawn ornaments in 2001 to 40,000 units. However, KC could expect a drop in flowerpot sales to 40,000 units. Assuming KC decides to go ahead with the above marketing plan, determine the impact this decision would have on the company's breakeven point in dollar sales in 2001. (CMA Canada adapted)

9–33

CVP Analysis with Multiple Services

LO3

We-Care Lawn Service is a lawn-care company operating in Kelowna. We-Care offers chemical fertilization, insect control, and weed and crabgrass control for its customers' lawns and foundations. Four chemical applications are given per growing period, which lasts from April through October. Four chemicals are used in the applications: dacthal for crabgrass control, trimel for weed control, urea fertilizer, and Dursban insecticide. In the first application, dacthal accounts for 75 percent of the chemical cost, followed by 10 percent for trimel, 10 percent for urea, and 5 percent for Dursban; in the remaining three applications, dacthal is not used—it is ineffective after May 31.

We-Care offers two services: residential and commercial. The price charged per residential application is $13.50. The average residential area is 0.1 hectares. Commercial applications are for any area larger than a hectare and are priced at $40 per hectare per application.

We-Care's variable costs consist of chemicals, direct labour, operating expenses for its truck, and operating supplies. For the first application, the cost of chemicals is $40 per hectare; for the remaining applications, chemicals cost $10 per application per hectare. We-Care has one employee, who is classified as direct labour. He is paid $6 per hour. Residential lawns should be sprayed at a rate of three lawns per hour (including travel time). Commercial applications are sprayed at a rate of 45 minutes per hectare. Operating expenses for the truck average $13.78 per hectare per residential application and $5 per hectare per commercial application. Operating supplies average $4.13 per hectare per application, regardless of the type of service. Fixed costs for the year follow:

Truck lease	$12,337
Amortization, equipment	1,747
Truck insurance	1,339
Telephone	1,200
Tax and licence	1,085
Advertising	10,000
Salary of supervisor	12,000
Total	$39,708

Based on last year's experience, We-Care services two hectares of residential property for every hectare of commercial property. The owner expects the same sales mix for the coming year.

Required:

1. Assume that every customer receives all four applications. Compute the hectares of residential applications and the hectares of commercial applications that must be serviced for We-Care to break even. Given the hectares of residential servicing, compute the average number of residential customers.
2. Given the breakeven point computed in Requirement 1, determine the labour hours needed to service the breakeven volume. Is one employee sufficient? Assume that the employee works 8 hours per day and a total of 140 days during the 7-month growing season. What volume is needed before a second employee is hired? Discuss the effect on CVP analysis if additional employees are needed.
3. Assume that 60 percent of all residential customers receive only the first application, with the remaining 40 percent receiving all four. All commercial customers receive all four applications. Redo the breakeven analysis. (Hint: There are now two types of residential customers, producing a mix of three services.)

9–34

Basics of the Sales Revenue Approach

LO2, LO5

Dalhart Company produces plastic mailboxes. A projected income statement follows:

Sales	$560,400
Less: Variable costs	257,784
Contribution margin	$302,616
Less: Fixed costs	150,000
Operating income	$152,616

Required:

1. Compute the contribution margin ratio for the mailboxes.
2. How much revenue must Dalhart earn in order to break even?
3. What volume of sales must be earned if Dalhart wants to earn an after-tax income equal to 8 percent of sales? Assume that the tax rate is 34 percent.
4. What is the effect on the contribution margin ratio if the unit selling price and unit variable cost each increase by 10 percent?
5. Suppose that management has decided to give a 3 percent commission on all sales. The projected income statement does not reflect this commission. Recompute the contribution margin ratio assuming that the commission will be paid. What effect does this change have on the breakeven point?

6. If the commission is paid as described in Requirement 5, management expects sales revenues to increase by $80,000. Is it a sound decision to implement the commission? Support your answer with appropriate computations.

9–35

CVP Analysis, Sales Revenue Approach, Pricing, After-Tax Profit Target

LO2

Kline Consulting is a service organization that specializes in the design, installation, and servicing of mechanical, hydraulic, and pneumatic systems. For example, some manufacturing firms, with machinery that cannot be turned off for servicing, need some type of system for lubricating the machinery during use. To deal with this type of problem for a client, Kline designed a central lubricating system that pumps lubricants intermittently to bearings and other moving parts.

Kline's operating results for last year are as follows:

Sales	$802,429
Less: Variable expenses	430,000
Contribution margin	$372,429
Less: Fixed expenses	154,750
Operating income	$217,679

Next year, the firm expects variable costs to increase by 5 percent and fixed costs by 4 percent.

Required:

1. What is the contribution margin ratio for last year?
2. Compute Kline's breakeven point for last year in dollars.
3. Suppose that Kline would like to see a 6 percent increase in operating income next year. What percentage (on average) must Kline raise its bids to cover the expected cost increases and obtain the desired operating income? Assume that Kline expects the same mix and volume of services in each year.
4. Next year, how much revenue must be earned for Kline to earn an after-tax profit of $175,000? Assume a tax rate of 34 percent.

9–36

CVP with Multiple Products, Sales Mix Changes, Changes in Fixed and Variable Costs

LO3, LO5

Artistic Woodcrafting, Inc., began in 1997 as a one-person cabinetmaking operation. Business soon expanded, and employees were added. By 2000, sales volume totalled $850,000. Volume for the first five months of 2001 totalled $600,000, and sales were expected to be $1.6 million for the entire year. Unfortunately, the cabinetmaking business is highly competitive. More than 200 cabinetmaking shops in the area are all competing for the same business.

Artistic currently offers two different quality grades of cabinets: Grade I and Grade II, with Grade I being of higher quality. The average unit selling prices, unit variable costs, and direct fixed costs are as follows:

	Unit Price	Unit Variable Cost	Direct Fixed Costs
Grade I	$3,400	$2,686	$95,000
Grade II	1,600	1,328	95,000

Common fixed costs (fixed costs not traceable to either cabinet) are $35,000. Currently, for every three Grade I cabinets sold, seven Grade II cabinets are sold.

Required:

1. Calculate the number of Grade I and Grade II cabinets that are expected to be sold during 2001.
2. Calculate the number of Grade I and Grade II cabinets that must be sold for the company to break even.
3. Artistic Woodcrafting can buy computer-controlled machines that will make doors, drawers, and frames. If the machines are purchased, the variable costs for each type

of cabinet will decrease by 9 percent, but common fixed costs will increase by $44,000. Compute the effect on net income in 2001, and calculate the new breakeven point. Assume that the machines are purchased at the beginning of the sixth month. Fixed costs for the company are incurred uniformly throughout the year.

4. Refer to the original data. Artistic Woodcrafting is considering adding a retail outlet. This change will increase common fixed costs by $70,000 per year. As a result of adding the retail outlet, the additional publicity and emphasis on quality will allow the firm to change the sales mix to 1:1. The retail outlet is also expected to increase sales by 30 percent. Assume that the outlet is opened at the beginning of the sixth month. Calculate the effect on the company's expected profits for 2001, and calculate the new breakeven point. Assume that fixed costs are incurred uniformly throughout the year.

9–37

CVP, Product Decision

LO1

Junior's Executive Jet Service is planning to run commuter flights between Toronto and Ottawa from Monday through Friday each week. Junior believes that he can charge $150 per customer (round trip) per flight and earn a profit of $2,000 per round trip if he can fill 80 percent of each 70-seat aircraft. At 100 percent capacity, his total profit would be $3,750 per round trip. Junior can schedule his flights either every hour or every two hours between 7:00 a.m. and 6:00 p.m. (thus making either 6 or 12 round-trip flights per day). Junior believes that he will operate at 70 percent capacity if he schedules flights hourly and 85 percent capacity if he schedules flights every two hours.

Required:

1. What is the breakeven point per round-trip flight?
2. What is the breakeven point per week if 6 round-trip flights are scheduled per day?
3. What is the breakeven point per week if 12 round-trip flights are scheduled per day?
4. Should Junior schedule flights every hour or every two hours? Provide appropriate analysis. (CGA Canada adapted)

9–38

Multiple Products, Breakeven Analysis, Operating Leverage

LO3, LO5

Carlyle Lighting Products produces two different types of lamps: a floor lamp and a desk lamp. Floor lamps sell for $30, desk lamps for $20. The projected income statement for the coming year follows:

Sales	$600,000
Less: Variable expenses	400,000
Contribution margin	$200,000
Less: Fixed expenses	150,000
Operating income	$ 50,000

Carlyle's owner estimates that 60 percent of the sales revenues will be produced by floor lamps, with the remaining 40 percent by desk lamps. Floor lamps are also responsible for 60 percent of the variable expenses. Of the fixed expenses, one-third are common to both products, and one-half are directly traceable to the floor lamp product line.

Required:

1. Compute the sales revenue that Carlyle must earn to break even.
2. Compute the number of floor lamps and desk lamps that Carlyle must sell to break even.
3. Compute the degree of operating leverage for Carlyle Lighting Products. Now assume that the actual revenues will be 40 percent higher than the projected revenues. By what percentage will profits increase with this change in sales volume?

9–39

Multiple-Product Breakeven

LO3

Polaris, Inc., manufactures two types of metal stampings for the automobile industry: door handles and trim kits. Fixed costs equal $146,000. Each door handle sells for $12 and has variable costs of $9; each trim kit sells for $8 and has variable costs of $5.

Required:

1. What are the contribution margin per unit and the contribution margin ratio for door handles and for trim kits?
2. If Polaris sells 20,000 door handles and 40,000 trim kits, what is its operating income?
3. How many door handles and how many trim kits must Polaris sell to break even?
4. Assume that Polaris has the opportunity to rearrange its plant to produce only trim kits. If this is done, fixed costs will decrease by $35,000, and 70,000 trim kits can be produced and sold in a year. Is this a good idea? Explain.

9–40

CVP, Margin of Safety

LO1, LO2, LO5

Victoria Company produces a single product. Last year's income statement is as follows:

Sales (29,000 units)	$1,218,000
Less: Variable expenses	812,000
Contribution margin	$ 406,000
Less: Fixed expenses	300,000
Operating income	$ 106,000

Required:

1. Compute the breakeven point in units and sales dollars.
2. What was the margin of safety for Victoria Company last year?
3. Suppose that Victoria Company is considering an investment in new technology that will increase fixed costs by $250,000 per year but will lower variable costs to 45 percent of sales. Units sold will remain unchanged. Prepare a budgeted income statement, assuming that Victoria makes this investment. What is the new breakeven point in units and sales dollars, assuming that the investment is made?

9–41

Multiplant Breakeven

LO2, LO3

The PTO Division of the Galva Manufacturing Company produces power take-off units for the farm equipment business. The PTO Division, headquartered in Neepawa, Manitoba, has a newly renovated plant in Neepawa and an older, less automated plant in Yorkton, Saskatchewan. Both plants produce the same power take-off units for farm tractors that are sold to most domestic and foreign tractor manufacturers.

The PTO Division expects to produce and sell 192,000 power take-off units during the coming year. The divisional production manager has the following data available regarding the unit costs, unit prices, and production capacities for the two plants.

	Neepawa	Yorkton
Selling price	$150.00	$150.00
Variable manufacturing cost	$72.00	$88.00
Fixed manufacturing cost	30.00	15.00
Commission (5%)	7.50	7.50
General and administrative expense	25.50	21.00
Total unit cost	$135.00	$131.50
Unit profit	$ 15.00	$ 18.50
Production rate per day	400 units	320 units

All fixed costs are based on a normal year of 240 working days. When the number of working days exceeds 240, variable manufacturing costs increase by $3 per unit in Neepawa and $8 per unit in Yorkton. Capacity for each plant is 300 working days.

Galva Manufacturing charges each of its plants a per-unit fee for administrative services such as payroll, general accounting, and purchasing, because Galva considers these services to be a function of the work performed at the plants. For each of the plants, a fee of $6.50 represents the variable portion of the general and administrative expense.

Wishing to maximize the higher unit profit at Yorkton, PTO's production manager has decided to manufacture 96,000 units at each plant. This production plan results in Yorkton's operating at capacity and Neepawa's operating at its normal volume. Galva's corporate controller is not happy with this plan; he wonders if it might be better to produce relatively more at the automated plant in Neepawa.

Required:

1. Determine the annual breakeven units for each of PTO's plants.
2. Calculate the operating income that would result from the division production manager's plan to produce 96,000 units at each plant.
3. Calculate the operating income that would result from sales of 192,000 power take-off units if 120,000 of them were produced at the Neepawa plant and the remainder at the Yorkton plant. (US CMA adapted)

9–42

CVP Analysis, Assumptions

LO2, LO6

Marston Corporation manufactures pharmaceutical products that are sold through a network of sales agents located in Canada and the United States. The agents are currently paid an 18 percent commission on sales; this percentage was used when Marston prepared the following pro forma income statement for the fiscal year ending June 30, 2001.

Marston Corporation Pro Forma Income Statement For the Year Ending June 30, 2001 (dollars in thousands)		
Sales		$26,000
Cost of goods sold		
Variable	$11,700	
Fixed	2,870	14,570
Gross profit		$11,430
Selling and administrative costs		
Commissions	$ 4,680	
Fixed advertising cost	750	
Fixed administrative cost	1,850	7,280
Operating income		$ 4,150
Fixed interest cost		650
Income before income taxes		$ 3,500
Income taxes (40%)		1,400
Net income		$ 2,100

Since the completion of the above statement, Marston has learned that its agents are requesting an increase in the commission rate to 23 percent for the upcoming year. As a result, Marston's president has decided to investigate the possibility of hiring its own sales staff in place of the network of sales agents and has asked Tom Ross, Marston's controller, to gather information on the costs associated with this change.

Ross estimates that Marston will have to hire eight salespeople to cover the current market area, and the annual payroll cost for each of these employees will average $80,000, including fringe benefit expense. Travel and entertainment expense is expected to total $600,000 for the year, and the annual cost of hiring a sales manager and sales secretary will be $150,000. In addition to their salaries, the eight salespeople will each earn commissions at the rate of 10 percent on the first $2 million in sales and 15 percent on all sales over $2 million. For planning purposes, Ross expects that all eight salespeople will exceed the $2 million mark and that sales will be at the level previously projected. Ross believes that Marston should also increase its advertising budget by $500,000.

Required:

1. Calculate Marston Corporation's breakeven point in sales dollars for the fiscal year ending June 30, 2001, if the company hires its own sales force and increases its advertising costs.
2. If Marston Corporation continues to sell through its network of sales agents and pays the higher commission rate, determine the estimated volume in sales dollars for the fiscal year ending June 30, 2001, that would be required to generate the same net income as that projected in the pro forma income statement presented above.
3. Describe the general assumptions underlying breakeven analysis that might limit its usefulness in this case. (US CMA adapted)

MANAGERIAL DECISION CASES

9–43

Ethics and a CVP Application

LO1

Danna Lumus, the marketing manager for a division that produces a variety of paper products, was considering the divisional manager's request for a sales forecast for a new line of paper napkins. The divisional manager was gathering data so that he could choose between two different production processes. The first process would have a variable cost of $10 per case produced and fixed costs of $100,000. The second process would have a variable cost of $6 per case and fixed costs of $200,000. The selling price would be $30 per case. Danna had just completed a marketing analysis that projected annual sales of 30,000 cases.

Danna was reluctant to report the 30,000 forecast to the divisional manager. She knew that the first process was labour-intensive, whereas the second was largely automated, with little labour and no requirement for an additional production supervisor. If the first process were chosen, Jerry Jovanovic, a good friend, would be appointed as the line supervisor. If the second process were chosen, Jerry and an entire line of labourers would be laid off. After some consideration, Danna revised the projected sales downward to 22,000 cases.

She believed that the revision downward was justified. Since it would lead the divisional manager to choose the manual-oriented system, it showed a sensitivity to the needs of current employees—a sensitivity that she was afraid her divisional manager did not possess. He was too focused on quantitative factors in his decision making and usually ignored the qualitative aspects.

Required:

1. Compute the breakeven point for each process.
2. Compute the sales volume for which the two processes are equally profitable. Identify the range of sales for which the manual process is more profitable than the automated process. Identify the range of sales for which the automated process is more profitable than the manual process. Why did the divisional manager want the sales forecast?
3. Discuss Danna's decision to alter the sales forecast. Do you agree with it? Did she act ethically? Was her decision justified since it helped a number of employees keep their jobs? Should the impact on employees be factored into decisions? In fact, is it unethical *not* to consider the impact of decisions on employees?
4. Even though Danna is not a management accountant, do any of the ethical standards for management accountants listed in Chapter 1 apply? Explain.

9–44

Service Organization, Multiple Products, Breakeven, Pricing and Scheduling Decisions

LO1, LO2, LO3

Utah Metropolitan Ballet is located in Salt Lake City. The company is housed in the Capitol Theater, one of three buildings that make up the Bicentennial Arts Center in downtown Salt Lake City. The ballet company features five different ballets per year. For the upcoming season, the five ballets to be performed are *The Dream, Petrushka, The Nutcracker, Sleeping Beauty*, and *Bugaku*.

The president and general manager has tentatively scheduled the following number of performances for each ballet for the coming season:

Dream	5
Petrushka	5
Nutcracker	20
Sleeping Beauty	10
Bugaku	5

To produce each ballet, costs must be incurred for costumes, props, rehearsals, royalties, guest artist fees, choreography, salaries of production staff, music, and wardrobe. These costs are fixed for a particular ballet regardless of the number of performances. These direct fixed costs are given below for each ballet.

Dream	Petrushka	Nutcracker	Sleeping Beauty	Bugaku
$275,500	$145,500	$70,500	$345,000	$155,500

Other fixed costs are incurred as follows:

Advertising	$ 80,000
Insurance	15,000
Administrative salaries	222,000
Office rental, phone, and so on	84,000
Total	$401,000

For each performance of each ballet, the following costs also are incurred:

Utah Symphony	$3,800
Auditorium rental	700
Dancers' payroll	4,000
Total	$8,500

The auditorium in which the ballet is presented has 1,854 seats, which are classified as A, B, and C. The A seats offer the best viewing, followed by the B seats and then the C seats. Information concerning the different types of seats is given below:

	A Seats	B Seats	C Seats
Quantity	114	756	984
Price	$35	$25	$15
Percentage sold for each performance:*			
Nutcracker	100%	100%	100%
All others	100%	80%	75%

* Based on past experience, the same percentages are expected for the coming season.

Required:

1. Compute the expected revenues from the performances that have been tentatively scheduled. Prepare a variable-costing income statement for each ballet.
2. Calculate the number of performances of each ballet required to produce the revenues needed to cover each ballet's direct fixed expenses.
3. Calculate the number of performances of each ballet required for the company as a whole to break even. If you were the president and general manager, how would you alter the tentative schedule of performances?

4. Suppose that it is possible to offer a matinee of the popular *Nutcracker*. Seats would sell for $5 less than in the evening, and the auditorium rental would cost $200 less. The president and general manager believes that five matinee performances are feasible and that 80 percent of each type of seat can be sold. What effect will the matinee have on the company's profitability? on the overall breakeven point?
5. Suppose that no additional evening performances can be offered beyond those tentatively scheduled. Assume that the company will offer five matinee performances of *The Nutcracker*. Also, the company expects to receive $60,000 in government grants and contributions from supporters of the fine arts. Will the company break even? If not, what actions would you take to bring revenues in line with costs? Assume that no additional performances of *The Nutcracker* are feasible.

9–45

Cost Behaviour, Breakeven Analysis, CVP Analysis for Evaluation and Decision Making
LO2, LO5

Reinert Moving and Storage was established in 1962 by Allen Reinert in New Westminster, British Columbia. In 1978, the company achieved million-dollar booking status. The company experienced modest growth for the next two years; however, after the deregulation of the transportation industry in 1980, the company's growth accelerated significantly for several years. Unfortunately, by the end of 1998, the company actually experienced a drop in revenues. During the next two years, the revenues earned matched those of 1998. The revenues reported at the end of 2000 totalled $5.493 million. An income statement for 2000 follows:

Revenues:
Local	$1,433,500	
Intraprovince	510,000	
Interprovince	2,490,500	
Containers	333,000	
Packing	437,000	
Storage	289,000	
Total revenues		$5,493,000

Less expenses:
Outside vehicle repair	$ 220,000	
Fuel	352,000	
Sales commissions	102,000	
Tires, oil, lube	20,500	
Wages (driver and helper)	1,584,000	
Internal maintenance	293,000	
Advertising	88,000	
Equipment rental	422,000	
Packing materials	557,000	
Salaries	821,000	
Cargo loss claims	234,000	
Utilities	16,700	
Insurance	44,000	
Fuel taxes and tariffs	132,000	
Bad debt	193,000	
Amortization	205,000	
Total expenses		5,284,200
Operating income		$ 208,800
Less: Taxes (42%)		87,696
Net income		$ 121,104

Upon reviewing the income statement for 2000, Allen Reinert called a meeting to discuss the company's financial status. He invited sales manager Heidi Roos and controller Gaetan Bilodeau.

Allen: "Our before-tax income has dropped from a high of 12 percent of sales to about 4 percent this last year. I know that both of you are aware of our problem and have some suggestions on how we can improve the situation."

Heidi: "Allen, competition has become quite intense in our industry. I have two suggestions to help improve sales. First, we need to increase our advertising budget. We have a good reputation, and I think we need to capitalize on it. I suggest that we emphasize our expertise in crating electronic equipment and other sensitive instruments. Our losses in this area are minuscule. We have a much better record than any of our competitors, and we need to let customers and potential customers know about the quality of our services."

Allen: "That sounds good. How much more do you need for advertising, and what kind of increase in sales would you predict?"

Heidi: "To do it right, I would need to double our current advertising budget. I would guess that sales would increase by 20 percent. I also have another suggestion. I think we should look at the international goods and freight-moving market. Many firms ship goods internationally, and I believe that they would switch to us if we entered that market. My preliminary analysis reveals that we could pick up $500,000 of sales during the first year."

Allen: "Both suggestions seem to offer some potential for improving our profitability. Gaetan, would you gather the data needed to estimate the effect of each of these two alternatives on our profits?"

Gaetan: "Sure. I have a suggestion also—I plan to install a cost accounting system. At this point, we have no real idea how much each of our services is costing. I believe that there is some hope of reducing costs without affecting the quality of our services."

Allen: "I'm all for reducing costs where possible. However, keep in mind that I don't want to lay off any employees yet. I like the idea of providing security to our employees. I would rather see everyone take a pay cut before we reduce our workforce. So far, we have been able to keep everyone despite the drop in our sales. I think it's a good policy. If these two ideas of Heidi's work out, no new hires may be necessary, and we have trained, loyal employees ready for the new business."

Required:

1. Classify all expenses in the 2000 income statement as either variable or fixed. Assume that each expense is strictly variable or strictly fixed with respect to sales revenue. Once the classification is completed, prepare a variable-costing income statement.

2. Using the information obtained in Requirement 1, compute the revenue that Reinert Moving and Storage needs to generate to break even. Now compute the revenue that is needed to earn operating income equal to 12 percent of sales revenue.

3. What is the maximum amount that Reinert can spend on additional advertising assuming that profits remain unchanged for 2001 and sales will increase by 20 percent, as predicted by Heidi? Suppose that Heidi spends the amount she requested and sales increase by 20 percent—what will be the change in profits? Should Heidi's suggestion be adopted?

4. Suppose that the directly traceable fixed expenses associated with entry into the international market are $200,000. Assume that the variable-cost ratio for this segment is the same as that computed in the 2000 income statement prepared in Requirement 1. How much revenue must be generated from international shipping for this segment to break even? What is the expected margin of safety? Would you recommend entry into the international market? Why?

5. Suppose that Allen Reinert decides both to increase advertising and enter the international market. Assume that actual sales increase by 10 percent, with $340,000 of the increase coming from international sales and the remainder from the increased advertising. Using data from Requirements 1 and 4, answer the following questions:
   a. How much did operating income change because of these two decisions?

b. What is the profit change attributable to the advertising campaign? the international market? What is your recommendation for the coming year? Should the company continue these two strategies? Or should it do only one or neither? Explain.

c. Suppose that the company achieved its target profit of 12 percent of sales in spite of the less-than-expected increase in profits from the advertising campaign and the international market. The remaining increase in profits was achieved by cutting variable costs. What is the new variable-cost ratio?

RESEARCH ASSIGNMENT

9–46

Research Assignment
LO1, LO3

Interview the owner of a small business (for example, dry cleaners, shoe repair, CA firm) about the revenue he or she needs to break even. Has the business owner calculated this amount? Does he or she have a feel for the business's variable and fixed costs? Write up the results of your interview.

CHAPTER 10

Tactical Decision Making: Relevant Cash-Flow Analysis

Learning Objectives

After studying Chapter 10, you should be able to:

1. Describe and explain the tactical decision-making model.

2. Explain how the activity resource usage model is used in assessing relevancy.

3. Apply the tactical decision-making concepts in a variety of business situations.

4. Choose the optimal product mix when faced with one constrained resource.

5. Explain the impact of cost on pricing decisions.

6. Explain why decision makers sometimes appear to use sunk costs in making decisions.

7. Use linear programming to find the optimal solution to a problem of multiple constrained resources. (Appendix)

Scenario

Gunn Products, Inc., manufactures potentiometers. A potentiometer is a device that adjusts electrical resistance. Potentiometers are used in switches and knobs, for example, to control the volume on a radio or to raise or lower the lights using a dimmer switch. Currently, all parts necessary for the assembly of the products are produced internally. The firm, in operation for five years, has a single plant located in Penticton, British Columbia. The facilities for the manufacture of potentiometers are leased, with five years remaining on the lease. All equipment is owned by the company. Because of increases in demand, production has been expanded significantly over the five years of operation, straining the capacity of the leased facilities. Currently, the company needs more warehousing and office space, as well as more space for the production of plastic mouldings. The current output of these mouldings, used to make potentiometers, needs to be expanded to accommodate the increased demand for the main product.

Len Gunn, owner and president of Gunn Products, has asked his vice-president of marketing, John Gunn, and his vice-president of finance, Linda Thayn, to meet and discuss the problem of lim-ited capacity. This is the second meeting the three have had concerning the problem. In the first meeting, Len rejected Linda's proposal to build the company's own plant. He believed that it was too risky to invest the capital necessary to build a plant at this stage of the company's development. The combination of leasing a larger facility and subleasing the current plant was also considered but was rejected; subleasing would be difficult, if not impossible. At the end of the first meeting, Len asked John to explore the possibility of leasing another facility comparable to the current one. He also assigned Linda the task of identifying other possible solutions. As the second meeting began, Len asked John to give a report on the leasing alternative.

"After some careful research," John responded, "I'm afraid that the idea of leasing an additional plant is not a very good one. Although we have some space problems, our current level of production doesn't justify another plant. In fact, I expect it will be at least five years before we need to be concerned about expanding into another facility like the one we have now. My market studies reveal a modest growth in sales over the next five years. All this growth can be absorbed by our current production capacity. The large increases in demand that we experienced for the past five years are not likely to be repeated. Leasing another plant would be an overkill solution."

"Even modest growth will aggravate our current space problems," Len observed. "As you both know, we are already operating three production shifts. But, John, you are right—except for plastic mouldings, we could expand production, particularly during the

graveyard shift. Linda, I hope that you have been successful in identifying some other possible solutions. Some fairly quick action is needed."

"Fortunately," Linda replied, "I believe that I have two feasible alternatives. One is to rent an additional building to be used for warehousing. By transferring our warehousing needs to the new building, we will free up internal space for offices and for expanding the production of plastic mouldings. I have located a building within two kilometres of our plant that we could use. It has the capacity to handle our current needs and the modest growth that John mentioned. The second alternative may be even more attractive. We currently produce all the parts that we use to manufacture potentiometers, including shafts and bushings. In the last several months, the market has been flooded with these two parts. Prices have tumbled as a result. It might be better to buy shafts and bushings instead of making them. If we stop internal production of shafts and bushings, that would free up the space we need. Well, Len, what do you

think? Are these alternatives feasible? Or should I continue my search for additional solutions?"

"I like both alternatives," responded Len. "In fact, they are exactly the types of solutions we are looking for. All we have to do now is choose the one that's best for our company. A key factor that must be examined is the cost of each alternative. Linda, you're the financial chief—prepare a report that details the costs that have an impact on this decision."[1]

1. This scenario is based on a company whose name and the names of its executives were changed to preserve confidentiality.

Questions to Think About

1. Describe the decision to be made by Gunn; is it a strategic or a tactical decision?

2. What cost do you think Len is referring to in the last paragraph of the scenario? Give examples.

3. Assume that Gunn Products accepts Linda's first alternative. Are there any noncost factors that should be considered? What about her second alternative?

One of the major roles of the management information system is supplying cost and revenue data that serve as the basis for user actions. Although a variety of user actions are possible, one of the more important actions that can be taken by users is tactical decision making. How cost and revenue data can be used to make tactical decisions is the focus of this chapter.

TACTICAL DECISION MAKING

Objective 1

Describe and explain the tactical decision-making model.

Tactical decision making consists of choosing among alternatives with an immediate or limited end in view. Accepting a special order for less than the normal selling price to utilize idle capacity and increase this year's profits is an example. Thus, some tactical decisions tend to be *short run* in nature; however, it should be emphasized that short-run decisions often have long-run consequences. Consider a second example. Suppose that a company is considering producing a component instead of buying it from suppliers. The immediate objective may be to lower the cost of making the main product. Yet this tactical decision may be a small part of the overall strategy of establishing a cost leadership position for the firm. Thus, tactical decisions are often *small-scale actions* that serve a larger purpose.

The overall objective of **strategic decision making** is to select among alternative strategies so that a long-term competitive advantage is established. Tactical decision making should support this overall objective, even if the immediate objective is short run (accepting a one-time order to increase profits) or small scale (making instead of buying a component). Thus, *sound* tactical decision making means that the decisions made not only achieve the limited objective but also serve a larger purpose. In fact, no tactical decision should be made that does not serve the overall strategic goals of an organization. A good example of a company that has made tactical decisions that are in accordance with its strategic goals is Hyatt Hotels Corporation.[2] In the early 1990s, steep costs jeopardized a number of Hyatt's management contracts. It was necessary to reduce the cost structure fast. However, Hyatt attacked only the costs that guests did not particularly care about (for example, turndown service, in which the bedcovers are turned down at night and a mint is left on the pillow). Services that were important to business travellers, whom Hyatt courted, were expanded (for example, in-room fax machines).

Model for Making Tactical Decisions

How does a company go about making good tactical decisions? We can describe a general approach to making tactical decisions. The six[3] steps describing the recommended decision-making process are as follows:

1. Recognize and define the problem.
2. Identify alternatives as possible solutions to the problem; eliminate alternatives that are clearly not feasible.
3. Identify the costs and benefits associated with each feasible alternative. Classify costs and benefits as relevant or irrelevant, and eliminate irrelevant ones from consideration.
4. Total the relevant costs and benefits for each alternative.
5. Assess the qualitative factors.
6. Select the alternative with the greatest overall benefit.

These six steps define a simple decision model. A **decision model** is a set of procedures that, if followed, will lead to a decision. Exhibit 10–1 depicts the sequence of steps to be followed.

Step 1: Define the Problem The first step is to recognize and define a specific problem. For example, the members of Gunn's management team all recognized the need for additional space for warehousing, offices, and the production of plastic mouldings. The amount of space needed, the reasons for the need, and how the additional space would be used are all important dimensions of the problem. However, the central question is *how* to acquire the additional space.

Step 2: Identify the Alternatives Step 2 is to list and consider possible solutions. Gunn Products identified the following possible solutions:

1. Build its own facility, with sufficient capacity to handle current and immediately foreseeable needs.

---

2. Richard A. Melcher, "Why Hyatt Is Toning Down the Glitz," *Business Week* (27 February 1995): 92, 94.

3. The decision-making model described here has six steps. There is nothing special about this particular listing. You may find it more useful to break down the steps into eight or ten segments. Alternatively, you may find it useful to aggregate them into a shorter list. For example, you could use a three-step model: (1) identify the decision; (2) identify alternatives and their associated relevant costs; and (3) make the decision. The key point is to find a comfortable way for you to remember the important steps in the decision-making model.

Exhibit   10–1

Tactical Decision-Making
Model for Gunn
Products' Space Problem

Step 1	Define the problem.	Increase capacity for warehousing and production.
Step 2	Identify the alternatives.	1. Build new facility. 2. Lease larger facility; sublease current facility. 3. Lease additional facility. 4. Lease warehouse space. 5. Buy shafts and bushings; free up needed space.

Step 3	Identify the costs and benefits associated with each feasible alternative.	Alternative 4:
		   Variable production costs $345,000
		   Warehouse lease 135,000
		 Alternative 5:
		   Purchase price $460,000

Step 4	Total the relevant costs and benefits for each feasible alternative.	Alternative 4: $480,000 Alternative 5: 460,000 Differential cost $ 20,000
Step 5	Assess the qualitative factors.	1. Quality of external supplier 2. Reliability of external supplier 3. Price stability 4. Labour relations and community image
Step 6	Make the decision.	Continue to produce shafts and bushings internally; lease warehouse.

2. Lease a larger facility, and sublease its current facility.
3. Lease an additional, similar facility.
4. Lease an additional building that would be used for warehousing only, thereby freeing up space for expanded production.
5. Buy shafts and bushings externally, and use the space made available (previously used for producing these parts) to solve the space problem.

As part of this step, Gunn must eliminate alternatives that are not feasible. The first alternative was eliminated because it carried too much risk for the company. The second alternative was rejected because subleasing was not a viable option. The third was eliminated because it went too far in solving the space problem, and, presumably, was too expensive. The fourth and fifth alternatives were feasible; they were within the cost and risk constraints and solved the space needs of the company. Notice that Len linked the tactical decision (find more space) to the company's overall growth strategy by rejecting alternatives that involved too much risk at this stage of the company's development.

Step 3: Identify the Costs and Benefits Associated with Each Feasible Alternative In Step 3, the costs and benefits associated with each feasible alternative are identified. At this point, clearly irrelevant costs can be eliminated from consideration.[4] The management accountant is responsible for gathering necessary data.

Assume that Gunn Products determines that the costs of making the shafts and bushings include the following:

---

4. It is fine to include irrelevant costs and benefits in the analysis as long as they are included for *all* alternatives. The reason we usually do not is that focusing only on the relevant costs and benefits reduces the amount of data to be collected.

Direct materials	$130,000
Direct labour	150,000
Variable overhead	65,000
Total variable production cost	$345,000

In addition, a warehouse must be leased to solve the space problem if Gunn continues to manufacture the shafts and bushings internally. An appropriate warehouse has been located for $135,000 per year. The second alternative is to purchase the shafts and bushings externally and use the freed-up production space. An outside supplier has offered to supply sufficient product for $460,000 per year.

It should be mentioned that when the cash-flow patterns become complicated for competing alternatives, it becomes difficult to produce a stream of equal cash flows for each alternative. In such a case, more sophisticated procedures can and should be used for the analysis. These procedures are discussed in Chapter 11, which deals with the long-run investment decisions referred to as *capital expenditure decisions*.

Step 4: Total the Relevant Costs and Benefits for Each Feasible Alternative It is clear now that Alternative 4 (continue producing internally, and lease more space) costs $480,000, whereas Alternative 5 (purchase outside, and use internal space) costs $460,000. The comparison follows:

Alternative 4		Alternative 5	
Variable cost of production	$345,000	Purchase price	$460,000
Warehouse lease	135,000		
Total	$480,000		

The differential cost is $20,000 in favour of Alternative 5.

Step 5: Assess the Qualitative Factors Decision making is based on an evaluation of quantitative and qualitative factors. Typically, the quantitative factors are determined by the differences in net cash flows that would result from different decisions (differential cash flows). In addition to this financial criterion, there are other factors that bear upon the decision and that are usually referred to as qualitative. But qualitative factors can also be measured. Examples of qualitative factors that can be quantified are a ranking of suppliers that is based on quality and service, a rating of customer acceptance of different new products, and an opinion poll that clarifies whether a community prefers jobs or ecological preservation when considering a new logging or mining operation. Although it is more difficult and perhaps undesirable to attempt to measure these factors strictly in dollar terms,[5] in some cases, qualitative factors can be far more important than cash-flow considerations in decision making.

While the costs and revenues associated with the alternatives are important, they do not tell the whole story. Qualitative factors can significantly affect the manager's decision. Qualitative factors are simply those factors that are hard to put a number on.

5. Four measurement scales can be utilized in an attempt to quantify qualitative factors: (a) nominal (such as high, low; male, female; acceptable, unacceptable); (b) ordinal, where it is possible to rank but impossible to say that the difference between Rank 1 and Rank 2 is equal to the difference between Rank 2 and Rank 3 (such as highly acceptable, acceptable, neutral, unacceptable, and highly unacceptable); (c) interval, where the measurement scale assigns equal value to intervals between assigned numbers (such as temperature, IQ scores, aptitude scores); and (d) ratio, where there is a natural zero (as, for example, $0). In that case, $2,000 signifies twice as much money as $1,000. (Other examples would include accounts receivable, quantity of inventories, area affected by a pollutant, and distance or time travelled to transport an important raw material.) The choice to quantify or not to quantify a qualitative factor should be based on cost and benefit considerations of the quantification.

Factors considered in decision making can thus be classified into those that are in cash-flow terms (dollar measures), those that are quantified in nonmonetary terms (nondollar measures), and those that are not quantified. Attempts at quantification should be tempered by good judgment. At the same time as many qualitative factors are quantified, estimates and assumptions surrounding measurement require that good judgment qualifies quantitative measures (quantifying the qualitative, and qualifying the quantitative).

For example, in the make-or-buy decision facing Gunn Products, Len Gunn would likely be concerned with such qualitative considerations as the quality of the shafts and bushings purchased externally, the reliability of supply sources, the expected stability of prices over the next several years, labour relations, community image, and so on. To illustrate the possible impact of qualitative factors on the make-or-buy decision, consider the first two factors, quality and reliability of supply.

If the quality of shafts and bushings is significantly less if purchased externally than what is available internally, then the quantitative advantage from purchasing may be more fictitious than real. Settling for lower-quality materials may reduce the quality of the potentiometers, thus harming sales. Because of this, Gunn Products may choose to continue to produce the parts internally.

Similarly, if supply sources are not reliable, production schedules could be interrupted, and customer orders could arrive late. These factors can increase labour costs and overhead and hurt sales. Again, depending on the perceived tradeoffs, Gunn Products may decide that producing the parts internally is better than purchasing them, even if relevant cost analysis gives the initial advantage to purchasing.

How should qualitative factors be handled in the decision-making process? First, they must be identified. Second, the decision maker should try to quantify them. Often, qualitative factors are simply more difficult to quantify—not impossible. For example, possible unreliability of the outside supplier might be quantified as the probable number of days late multiplied by the labour cost of downtime in Gunn's plant. Finally, truly qualitative factors, such as the impact of late orders on customer relations, must be taken into consideration in the final step of the decision-making model—the selection of the alternative with the greatest overall benefit. It is relatively easy to select an alternative when both quantitative and qualitative factors support that choice. It is also easy not to select an alternative when both quantitative and qualitative factors do not support that choice. However, it is quite difficult to make a decision when the quantitative and qualitative factors lead to different conclusions. Here, as in most cases requiring managerial decisions, judgment is crucial in making the appropriate tradeoffs between the quantitative and qualitative aspects of the decision. This boils down to juxtaposing the financial criterion versus the non-financial factors.

Step 6: Make the Decision Once all relevant costs and benefits for each alternative have been assessed, and the qualitative factors weighed, a decision can be made. What did Len decide for Gunn Products? Given the relatively small difference in costs of the two alternatives, and the weight Gunn Products assigns to ensuring quality and full employment, the decision was made to make the shafts and bushings internally and lease the warehouse.

Relevant Cash-Flow Analysis The tactical decision-making approach just described emphasized the importance of identifying and using relevant future cash inflows and outflows that differ across alternatives. The treatment of relevant future cash inflows does not present any particular problems that require explanation, but the treatment of relevant future cash outflows does. Relevant future cash outflows reflect relevant costs.

Relevant Costs Defined[6] **Relevant costs** are future costs that differ across alternatives. All decisions relate to the future; accordingly, only future costs can be relevant to decisions. However, to be relevant, a cost not only must be a future cost, but must

6. "Relevant cost analysis" is a widely used term, but its use connotes a narrower meaning than is intended. Relevant cash-flow analysis, or differential cash-flow analysis, captures the essence of this analysis, because it includes not only costs but also benefits. Since qualitative factors may not necessarily be measurable in cash-flow terms, differential cash-flow analysis is also somewhat restrictive. Some prefer to use the term "differential analysis" because it is less restrictive. "Relevant cost," "relevant cost and benefit," and "differential cash flow" are often used interchangeably. Differential analysis applies to the qualitative factors as well.

also differ from one alternative to another. If a future cost is the same for more than one alternative, it has no effect on the decision. Such a cost is an *irrelevant cost*. The ability to identify relevant and irrelevant costs is an important decision-making skill.

Relevant Costs Illustrated   To illustrate the concept of relevant costs, consider Gunn's make-or-buy alternatives. The cost of direct labour used to produce shafts and bushings is $150,000 per year (based on normal volume). Should this cost be a factor in the decision? Is the direct labour cost a future cost that differs across the two alternatives? It is certainly a future cost. To produce the shafts and bushings for another year requires the services of direct labourers, who must be paid. But does it differ across the two alternatives? If shafts and bushings are purchased from an external supplier, no internal production is needed. The services of the direct labourers can be eliminated, reducing the direct labour cost for shafts and bushings under this alternative to $0. Thus, the cost of direct labour differs across alternatives ($150,000 for the make alternative and $0 for the buy alternative). It is, therefore, a relevant cost. Implicit in this analysis is the use of a past cost to estimate a future cost. The most recent cost of direct labour for normal activity was $150,000. This past cost was used as the estimate of next year's cost. Although past costs are never relevant, they are often used to predict what future costs will be.

Illustration of an Irrelevant Past Cost   Gunn Products uses machinery to manufacture shafts and bushings. This machinery was purchased five years ago and is being depreciated at an annual rate of $125,000. Is this $125,000 a relevant cost? In other words, is depreciation a future cost that differs across the two alternatives?

Depreciation represents an allocation of a cost already incurred. It is a **sunk cost**, a cost that cannot be affected by any future action. Although we allocate this sunk cost to future periods and call that allocation *depreciation*, none of the original cost is avoidable. Sunk costs are past costs. They are always the same across alternatives and are therefore always irrelevant.

In choosing between the two alternatives, the original cost of the machinery used to produce shafts and bushings and its associated depreciation are not factors. However, it should be noted that the machinery's salvage value (what Gunn could receive for selling the machinery now) would be relevant and would be included as a benefit of purchasing from outside suppliers. To simplify the example, assume that the salvage value of the machinery is zero.

Illustration of an Irrelevant Future Cost   Assume that the cost to lease the entire factory, $340,000, is allocated to different production departments, including the department that produces shafts and bushings, which receives $12,000 of the cost. Is this $12,000 cost relevant to the make-or-buy decision facing Gunn?

The lease payment is a future cost, since it must be paid during each of the next five years. But does the cost differ across the make-and-buy alternatives? Whatever option Gunn chooses, the factory lease payment must be made—it is the same across both alternatives. The amount of the payment allocated to the remaining departments may change if production of shafts and bushings is stopped, but the level of the total payment is unaffected by the decision. It is therefore an irrelevant cost.

The example illustrates the importance of identifying allocations of common fixed costs. Allocations of common fixed costs can be safely classified as irrelevant since any choice usually does not affect the level of cost. The only effect may be a reallocation of those common fixed costs to fewer cost objects or segments.

Examine all three cost examples for the production of shafts and bushings to see which are relevant in deciding whether or not to continue production. Of the three, only direct labour cost is relevant, since it is the only one that occurs if production continues but stops if production stops.

	Cost to Make	−	Cost Not to Make	=	Differential Cost
Direct labour	$150,000		—		$150,000
Depreciation	125,000		$125,000		—
Allocated lease	12,000		12,000		—
	$287,000		$137,000		$150,000

The same concepts apply to benefits. One alternative may produce an amount of future benefits different from another alternative (for example, differences in future revenues). If future benefits differ across alternatives, then they are relevant and should be included in the analysis.

Ethics in Tactical Decision Making

In tactical decision making, ethical concerns revolve around the way in which decisions are implemented, and the possible sacrifice of long-run objectives for short-run gain. Relevant costs are used in making tactical decisions—decisions that have an immediate view or limited objective in mind. However, decision makers should always maintain an ethical framework. Reaching objectives is important, but how you get there is perhaps more important. Unfortunately, many managers have the opposite view. Part of the reason for the problem is the extreme pressure to perform that many managers feel. Often the individual who is not a top performer may be laid off or demoted. Under such conditions, the temptation is often great to engage in questionable behaviour today and let the future take care of itself.

For example, laying off employees to increase profits in the short run could loosely qualify as a tactical decision. However, if the only benefit is an increase in short-run profits, and there is no evidence that the decision supports the firm's longer-term strategic objectives, then the decision can be questioned. In fact, the workload may not decrease at all, but the number of people available to carry out the work has decreased. Pressure may then be exerted by managers on the remaining employees to work unreasonable amounts of overtime. Is this right?

There should be a consistent message throughout the company on its mission and goals. For example, if marketing enthusiastically touts the product's high quality and reliability while engineering and production are busily reducing the quality of the materials and reliability of the design, problems are sure to surface. Customers will see this inconsistency as an ethical lapse.

There can be endless debates about what is right and what is wrong. As was pointed out in Chapter 1, ethical standards have been developed to provide guidance for individuals. Additionally, many companies are hiring full-time ethics officers. Often these officers set up "hot lines" so that employees can call and register complaints or ask about the propriety of certain actions. However, some ethical problems can be avoided simply by using common sense and not focusing solely on the short term at the expense of the long term. Consider two examples of cost cutting at Ford Motor Company. Recently, Ford decided to delete the rubber moulding on the side of the Sable, saving about $100 per car. Years earlier, Ford had saved approximately $7 per car by installing thin-walled gas tanks on the Pinto. Which decision do you think has ethical ramifications?

RELEVANCY, COST BEHAVIOUR, AND THE ACTIVITY RESOURCE USAGE MODEL

Objective 2

Explain how the activity resource usage model is used in assessing relevancy.

The Gunn Products space problem was a very simple example of tactical decision making. Most tactical decisions require more complicated analysis—in particular, they require more extensive consideration of cost behaviour. Earlier work on relevant costing emphasized the importance of variable versus fixed costs. Usually, variable costs were relevant and fixed costs were not. For example, the variable costs of production were relevant to the Gunn Products make-or-buy decision. The depreciation expense and factory lease were not relevant. However, activity-based costing allows further consideration of variable costs with respect to both unit-based and nonunit-based cost drivers.

The key point is that changes in supply and demand for activity resources must be considered when assessing relevance. If changes in demand and supply for resources across alternatives bring about changes in resource spending, then the changes in resource spending are the relevant costs that should be used in assessing the relative desirability of the two alternatives.

Recall from Chapter 3 that the activity-based resource usage model reminds us to consider both flexible and committed resources. These categories can help us to identify relevant costs, thereby facilitating relevant cash-flow analysis.

Flexible Resources

Some resources can be easily purchased in the amount needed and at the time of use. For example, electricity used to run stoves that boil fruit in the production of jelly is a resource acquired as used and needed. Thus, for this resource category, if the demand for an activity changes across alternatives, then resource spending will change and the cost of the activity is relevant to the decision. This type of resource spending is typically referred to as a variable cost. The key point is that the amount of resource demanded by the firm equals the amount of resource supplied.

Now suppose that the jelly producer is asked by a customer to produce a special order of jelly for promotional purposes. The jelly producer must consider the following two alternatives: (1) accept the special, one-time order, and (2) reject the special order. If accepting the order increases the demand for kilowatt-hours (electricity's cost driver), then the cost of electricity will differ across alternatives. Thus, electricity is relevant to the decision.

Committed Resources

Committed resources are purchased before they are used. Therefore, there may or may not be unused capacity that will affect tactical decision making. We will consider two types of committed resources: those that can be altered in the short run and those that provide capacity for multiple periods.

Committed Resources for the Short Run Some committed resources are acquired in advance of usage through implicit contracting; they are usually acquired in lumpy amounts. (Graphically, we usually think of this cost as step-variable or step-fixed.) This category often represents resource spending associated with an organization's salaried and hourly employees. The implicit understanding is that the organization will maintain employment levels even though there may be temporary downturns in the quantity of an activity used. This means that an activity may have unused capacity available. Thus, an increase in demand for an activity across alternatives may not mean that the activity cost will increase (because all the increased demand is absorbed by the unused activity capacity). For example, assume that a company has five manufacturing engineers who supply a capacity of 10,000 engineering hours (2,000 hours each). The cost of this activity capacity is $250,000, or $25 per hour. Suppose that this year, the company expects to use only 9,000 engineering hours for its normal business. This means that the engineering activity has 1,000 hours of unused capacity. In deciding to reject or accept a special order that requires 500 engineering hours, the cost of engineering would be irrelevant. The order can be filled using unused engineering capacity, and the resource spending is the same for each alternative ($250,000 will be spent whether the order is accepted or not).

However, if a change in demand across activities produces a change in resource supply, then the activity cost will change and, thus, be relevant to the decision. A change in resource supply means a change in resource spending and, consequently, a change in activity cost. A change in resource spending can occur in one of two ways: (1) the demand for the resource exceeds the supply (increasing resource spending); or (2) the demand for the resource drops permanently, and supply exceeds demand enough so that activity capacity can be reduced (decreasing resource spending).

To illustrate the first change, consider once again the engineering activity and the special-order decision. Suppose that the special order requires 1,500 engineering hours. This exceeds the resource supply. To meet the demand, the organization would need to hire a sixth engineer or perhaps use a consulting engineer. Either way, resource spending increases if the order is accepted; thus, the cost of engineering is now a relevant cost.

To illustrate the second type of change, suppose that the company's manager is considering purchasing a component used for production instead of making it. Assume the same facts about engineering capacity: 10,000 hours available and 9,000 used. If the component is purchased, then the demand for engineering hours will drop from 9,000 to 7,000. This is a permanent reduction, because engineering support will no longer be needed for manufacturing the component. Unused capacity is now 3,000 hours: 2,000 permanent and 1,000 temporary. Furthermore, since engineering capacity is acquired in chunks of 2,000, this means that the company can reduce activity capacity and resource spending by laying off one engineer or reassigning the engineer to another plant where the services are in demand. Either way, the resource supply is reduced to 8,000 hours. If an engineer's salary is $50,000, then engineering cost would differ by $50,000 across the make-or-buy alternatives. This cost is therefore relevant to the decision. However, if the demand for the engineering activity drops by less than 2,000 hours, the increase in unused capacity is not enough to reduce resource supply and resource spending; in this case, the cost of the engineering activity would not be relevant.

Committed Resources for Multiple Periods   Often resources are acquired in advance for multiple periods, before the resource demands are known. Leasing or buying a building is an example. Buying multiperiod activity capacity is often done by paying cash up front. In this case, an annual expense may be recognized, but no additional resource spending is needed. Up-front resource spending is a sunk cost and, thus, never relevant. Periodic resource spending, such as leasing, is essentially independent of resource usage. Even if a permanent reduction of activity usage is experienced, it is difficult to reduce resource spending because of formal contractual commitments.

For example, assume that a company leases a plant for $100,000 per year for ten years. The plant is capable of producing 20,000 units of a product—the level expected when the plant was leased. After five years, suppose that the demand for the product drops and the plant needs to produce only 15,000 units each year. The lease payment of $100,000 still must be paid each year, even though production activity has decreased. Now suppose that demand increases beyond the 20,000-unit capability. In this case, the company may consider acquiring or leasing an additional plant. Here, resource spending could change across alternatives. The decision, however, to acquire long-term activity capacity is not in the realm of tactical decision making. This is not a short-term or small-scale decision. Decisions involving multiperiod capabilities are called *capital investment decisions* and are discussed in Chapter 11.

Thus, for the multiperiod resource category, changes in activity demands across alternatives rarely affect resource spending and are therefore not usually relevant for tactical decision making. When resource spending does change, it means assessing the prospect of a multiperiod commitment, which is properly treated using capital investment decision models. A good example of the rising importance of resources requiring

Resource Category	Demand and Supply Relationships	Relevancy
Flexible Resources	Supply = Demand	
	a. Demand Changes	a. Relevant
	b. Demand Constant	b. Not Relevant
Committed Resources (Short-Term)	Supply − Demand = Unused Capacity	
	a. Demand Increase < Unused Capacity	a. Not Relevant
	b. Demand Increase > Unused Capacity	b. Relevant
	c. Demand Decrease (Permanent)	
	1. Activity Capacity Reduced	1. Relevant
	2. Activity Capacity Unchanged	2. Not Relevant
Committed Resources (Multiperiod Capacity)	Supply − Demand = Unused Capacity	
	a. Demand Increase < Unused Capacity	a. Not Relevant
	b. Demand Decrease (Permanent)	b. Not Relevant
	c. Demand Increase > Unused Capacity	c. Capital Decision

Exhibit 10–2

Activity Resource Usage Model and Assessing Relevancy

multiperiod commitments is the technology required for design. Black & Decker Corporation's design budget in North America reached $1 million in 1995 (up from $300,000 in 1990). Companies are trying to turn this expense back into the category of a resource acquired in advance (short-term) by outsourcing much of the design work.[7] Exhibit 10–2 summarizes the activity resource usage model's role in assessing relevancy.

ILLUSTRATIVE EXAMPLES OF RELEVANT COST APPLICATIONS

Objective 3

Apply the tactical decision-making concepts in a variety of business situations.

Relevant costing is of value in solving many different types of problems. Traditionally, these applications include decisions to make or buy a component; keep or drop a segment or product line; accept a special order at less than the usual price; and process a joint product further or sell it at the split-off point. Of course, this is not an exhaustive list. However, many of the same decision-making principles apply to a variety of problems.

Make-or-Buy Decisions

Managers are often faced with the decision of whether to make or buy components used in manufacturing. Indeed, management should periodically evaluate past decisions concerning production. Conditions upon which prior decisions were based may have changed, and as a result, a different approach may be required. Periodic evaluations, of course, are not the only source of these **make-or-buy decisions**. Frequently, as with Gunn Products, the decision is motivated by an indirectly related, underlying problem.

To illustrate more fully the cost analysis of a make-or-buy problem, assume that Kopp Manufacturing currently produces an electronic component used in one of its printers. In one year, Kopp will switch production to another type of printer, and the electronic component will no longer be used. However, for the coming year, Kopp must produce 10,000 of these parts to support the production requirements for the old printer.

Kopp has been approached by a potential supplier of the component. The supplier will build the electronic component to Kopp's specifications for $4.75 per unit. The offer sounds very attractive, since the full manufacturing cost per unit is $8.20. Should Kopp Manufacturing make or buy the component?

---

7. Bruce Nussbaum, "Is In-House Design on the Way Out?" *Business Week* (25 September 1995): p. 130.

The problem and the feasible alternatives are both readily identifiable. Since the horizon for the decision is only one period, there is no need to be concerned about periodically recurring costs. Relevant costing is particularly useful for short-run analysis. We simply need to identify the relevant costs, total them, and make a choice (assuming no overriding qualitative concerns).

The full absorption costs associated with the production of these 10,000 parts is computed as follows:

	Total Cost	Unit Cost
Rental of equipment	$12,000	$1.20
Equipment depreciation	2,000	0.20
Direct materials	10,000	1.00
Direct labour	20,000	2.00
Variable overhead	8,000	0.80
General fixed overhead	30,000	3.00
Total	$82,000	$8.20

Most of the equipment is rented. However, one specialized piece of machinery had to be custom-made and was purchased. Rental equipment can be returned at any time without penalty; the company is charged only for the time the equipment is held. The specialized machinery will not be fully depreciated at the end of the year; however, the company plans to scrap it, since it cannot be sold. The company recently purchased sufficient materials for 5,000 components. There is no alternative use for the materials. Variable overhead is applied to the electronic component at $0.40 per direct labour dollar. General fixed overhead for the plant totals $1 million. General fixed overhead is assigned to products based on the space occupied by each product. The manufacturing facilities for the component under consideration occupy 6,000 of the plant's 200,000 square metres. Thus, $30,000 of the general fixed overhead is allocated to the electronic component (0.03 × $1,000,000).

Of these cost items, depreciation can be eliminated from the analysis; it is a sunk cost. Since the direct materials already purchased have no alternative use, half of the total cost of direct materials is also a sunk cost. General overhead is not relevant either. The $30,000 is an allocation of a common fixed cost that will continue even if the component is purchased externally.

All other costs are relevant. The cost of renting the equipment is relevant, since it will not be needed if the part is bought externally. Similarly, direct labour, the remaining 5,000 units of direct materials, and variable overhead are all relevant; they would not be incurred if the component were bought externally.

Now consider the purchase of the component. Of course, the purchase cost is relevant. If the component were made, this cost would not be incurred. Are there any other costs associated with an outside purchase? A check with the receiving dock elicits the information that the receiving and inspecting crew is at capacity. An additional purchase of this magnitude would require hiring an additional half-time employee for the year at a cost of $8,500. The purchasing department has sufficient excess capacity to handle the purchase of the component, so no additional cost would be incurred there.

A listing of the total relevant costs for each alternative follows:

	Alternatives Make	Buy	Differential Cost to Make
Rental of equipment	$12,000	—	$12,000
Direct materials	5,000	—	5,000
Variable overhead	8,000	—	8,000
Direct labour	20,000	—	20,000
Purchase cost	—	$47,500	(47,500)
Half-time employee	—	8,500	(8,500)
Total relevant cost	$45,000	$56,000	$(11,000)

The analysis shows that making the product is $11,000 cheaper than buying it. The supplier's offer should be rejected.

The same analysis can be done on a unit-cost basis. Once the relevant costs are identified, relevant unit costs can be compared. For this example, these costs are $4.50 ($45,000/10,000) for the make alternative and $5.60 ($56,000/10,000) for the buy alternative.

Keep-or-Drop Decisions

Often a manager needs to determine whether or not a segment, such as a product line, should be kept or dropped. Segmented reports prepared on a variable-costing basis provide valuable information for these **keep-or-drop decisions**. Both the segment's contribution margin and its segment margin are useful in evaluating a segment's performance. However, while segmented reports provide useful information for keep-or-drop decisions, relevant costing describes how the information should be used to arrive at a decision.

To illustrate, consider Norton Materials, Inc., which produces concrete blocks, bricks, and roofing tile. The firm's controller has prepared the following estimated income statement for 2001 (in thousands of dollars):

	Blocks	Bricks	Tile	Total
Sales revenue	$ 500	$800	$150	$1,450
Less: Variable expenses	250	480	140	870
Contribution margin	$ 250	$320	$ 10	$ 580
Less direct fixed expenses:				
Salaries	$ 37	40	35	112
Advertising	10	$ 10	$ 10	$ 30
Depreciation	53	40	10	103
Total	$100	$ 90	$ 55	$ 245
Segment margin	$ 150	$230	$ 45	$ 335
Less: Common fixed expenses				125
Net income				$ 210

The projected performance of the roofing tile line shows a negative segment margin. This would represent the third consecutive year of poor performance for that line. The president of Norton Materials, Tilman Blackburn, concerned about this poor performance, is trying to decide whether to drop or keep the roofing tile line.

Tilman's first reaction is to take steps to increase the sales revenue of roofing tiles. He is considering an aggressive sales promotion coupled with an increase in the selling price. The company's marketing manager thinks that this approach would be fruitless, however: the market is saturated and the level of competition too keen to hold out any hope for increasing the firm's market share. An increase in the selling price would almost certainly result in a decrease in sales revenue.

Increasing the product line's profitability through cost cutting is not feasible either. Costs were cut during the past two years to reduce the loss to its current anticipated level. Any further reductions would lower the product's quality and adversely affect sales.

With no hope for improving the line's profit performance beyond its projected level, Tilman has decided to drop it. He reasons that the firm will lose a total of $10,000 in contribution margin but save $45,000 by dismissing the line's supervisor and eliminating its advertising budget. (The depreciation cost of $10,000 is not relevant, since it represents an allocation of a sunk cost.) Thus, dropping the product line has a $35,000 advantage over keeping it. Before finalizing the decision, Tilman decides to notify the marketing manager and the production supervisor. The following memo is sent to both individuals:

MEMO

TO: Debora Sachs, Marketing, and Trevor Molinaro, Production
FROM: Tilman Blackburn, President
SUBJECT: Tentative Decision Concerning the Production of Roofing Tiles
DATE: March 14, 2001

Since there is no realistic expectation of improving the profitability of the roofing tile line, I have reluctantly decided to discontinue its production. I realize that this decision will have a negative impact on the community, since our workforce will need to be reduced. I am also sympathetic to the disruption this may cause in the personal lives of many employees.

However, we must be prepared to take actions that are in the best interests of the firm. By eliminating the roofing tile line, we can improve the firm's cash position by $35,000 per year. To support this decision, I am including the following analysis (focusing only on the tile segment):

	Keep	Drop	Differential Amount to Keep
Sales	$150	$—	$150
Less: Variable expenses	140	—	140
Contribution margin	$ 10	$—	$ 10
Less: Advertising	10	—	10
Cost of supervision	35	—	35
Total relevant benefit (loss)	$ 35	$ 0	$ 35

I have included only future costs and benefits that differ across the two alternatives. Depreciation on the tile equipment is not relevant, since it is simply an allocation of a sunk cost. Also, the level of common fixed costs is unchanged regardless of whether we keep or drop the tile line.

At this point, I view the decision as tentative and welcome any response. Perhaps I am overlooking something that would affect the decision. Please respond as soon as possible.

Keep or Drop with Complementary Effects   In response to the memo, the marketing manager writes that dropping the roofing tile line would lower sales of blocks by 10 percent and of bricks by 8 percent. She explains that many customers buy roofing tile at the same time they purchase blocks or bricks. Some will go elsewhere if they cannot buy both products at the same location.

Shortly after receiving this response, Tilman decides to repeat the analysis, factoring in the effect that dropping the tile line would have on the sales of the other two lines. He decides to use total firm sales and total costs for each alternative. As before, depreciation and common fixed costs are excluded from the analysis on the basis of irrelevancy.

Dropping the product line reduces total sales by $264,000: $50,000 ($0.10 \times $500,000) for blocks, $64,000 ($0.08 \times $800,000) for bricks, and $150,000 for roofing tiles. Similarly, total variable expenses are reduced by $203,400: $25,000 ($0.10 \times $250,000) for blocks, $38,400 ($0.08 \times $480,000) for bricks, and $140,000 for tiles. Thus, total contribution margin is reduced by $60,600 ($264,000 − $203,400). Since dropping the tile line saves only $45,000 in supervision costs and advertising, the net effect is a disadvantage of $15,600 ($45,000 − $60,600). The following is a summary of the analysis using the new information (in thousands):

	Keep	Drop	Differential Amount to Keep
Sales	$1,450	$1,186.0	$ 264.0
Less: Variable expenses	870	666.6	203.4
Contribution margin	$ 580	$ 519.4	$ 60.6
Less: Advertising	30	20.0	10.0
Less: Cost of supervision	112	77.0	35.0
Total	$ 438	$ 422.4	$ 15.6

Tilman is pleased to find the outcome favouring production of the roofing tile. The unpleasant task of dismissing some of his workforce is no longer necessary. However, just as he is preparing to write a second memo announcing his new decision, he receives Trevor Molinaro's written response to his first memo.

Keep or Drop with Alternative Use of Facilities   The production supervisor's response is somewhat different. He agrees that roofing tile should be eliminated but suggests that it be replaced with the production of floor tile. He gives assurances that existing machinery could be converted to produce this new product with little or no cost. He has also contacted the marketing manager about the marketability of floor tile, and he includes this assessment in his response.

The marketing manager sees the market for floor tile as stronger and less competitive than that for roofing tile. However, the other two lines would still lose sales at the same rate; producing floor tile would not change that result. The following estimated financial statement for floor tile is also submitted (in thousands of dollars):

Sales	$100
Less: Variable expenses	40
Contribution margin	$ 60
Less: Direct fixed expenses	55
Segment margin	$ 5

Tilman Blackburn is now faced with a third alternative: replacing the roofing tile with floor tile. Should the roofing tile line be kept, or should it be dropped and replaced with the floor tile?

From his prior analysis, Tilman knows that dropping the roofing tile would decreases the firm's contribution margin by $60,600. Producing the floor tile would generate $60,000 more in contribution margin, according to the estimate. Dropping the roofing tile line and replacing it with floor tile, then, would cause a $600 net decrease in total contribution margin ($60,600 – $60,000). The same outcome can be developed by directly comparing the relevant benefits and costs of the two alternatives (dollars expressed in thousands).

	Keep	Drop and Replace	Differential Amount to Keep
Sales	$1,450	$ 1,286.0[a]	$ 164.0
Variable expenses	(870)	(706.6)[b]	(163.4)
Contribution margin	$ 580	$ 579.4	$ (0.6)

[a] ($1,450 – $150 – $50 – $64) + $100
[b] ($870 – $140 – $25 – $38.4) + $40

The Norton Materials example again illustrates the tactical decision-making process. First, a problem was identified and defined (the poor performance of the roofing tile product line). Next, possible solutions were listed, and those that were not feasible were eliminated. For example, increasing sales or further decreasing costs were both rejected as feasible solutions. Three feasible solutions were examined: (1) keeping the product line, (2) dropping it, and (3) dropping the product line and replacing it with another product. An analysis of the costs and benefits of the feasible alternatives led to the selection of the preferred alternative (keeping the product line).

The example provides some insights beyond the simple application of the decision model. The initial analysis, which focused on two feasible alternatives, led to a tentative decision to drop the product line. Additional information provided by the marketing manager led to a reversal of the first decision. Before that decision could be implemented, the manager was made aware of a third feasible alternative, which required additional analysis.

Often managers do not have all the information necessary to make the best decision. They also may not be able to identify all feasible solutions. Managers benefit from gathering all the information available before finalizing a decision. They should attempt to identify as many feasible solutions as possible. As the example clearly illustrates, limited information can result in poor decisions. If the set of feasible solutions is too narrow, the best solution may never be selected simply because the manager has not thought of it. Managers can benefit from obtaining input from others who are familiar with the problem. By doing so, they can expand both the set of information and the set of feasible solutions. The result is improved decision making.

Special-Order Decisions

Price discrimination laws require that firms sell identical products at the same price to competing customers in the same market. These restrictions do not apply to competitive bids or to noncompeting customers. Bid prices can vary to customers in the same market, and firms often have the opportunity to consider special orders from potential customers in markets not ordinarily served. **Special-order decisions** focus on whether a specially priced order should be accepted or rejected. These orders can often be attractive, especially when the firm is operating below its maximum productive capacity.

Suppose, for example, that an ice-cream company is operating at 80 percent of its productive capacity. The company has a capacity of 20 million one-litre units. The company produces only premium ice cream. The total costs associated with producing and selling 16 million units are as follows (in thousands of dollars):

	Total	Unit Cost
Variable costs:		
Dairy ingredients	$11,200	$0.70
Sugar	1,600	0.10
Flavourings	2,400	0.15
Direct labour	4,000	0.25
Packaging	3,200	0.20
Commissions	320	0.02
Distribution	480	0.03
Other	800	0.05
Total variable costs	$24,000	$1.50
Fixed costs:		
Salaries	$ 960	$0.060
Depreciation	320	0.020
Utilities	80	0.005
Taxes	32	0.002
Other	160	0.010
Total fixed costs	$ 1,552	$0.097
Total costs	$25,552	$1.597
Wholesale selling price	$32,000	$2.000

An ice-cream distributor from a geographic region not normally served by the company has offered to buy 2 million units at $1.55 per unit, provided that its own label can be attached to the product. The distributor has also agreed to pay the transportation costs. Since the distributor approached the company directly, there is no sales commission. As the manager of the ice-cream company, would you accept this order or reject it?

The offer of $1.55 is well below the normal selling price of $2.00; in fact, it is even below the total unit cost. Even so, accepting the order may be profitable. The company does have idle capacity, and the order will not displace other units being produced to sell at the normal price. Additionally, many of the costs are not relevant; fixed costs will continue regardless of whether the order is accepted or rejected.

If the order is accepted, a benefit of $1.55 per unit will be realized that otherwise wouldn't be. However, all of the variable costs except for distribution ($0.03) and commissions ($0.02) will also be incurred, producing a cost of $1.45 per unit. The net benefit is $0.10 ($1.55 – $1.45) per unit. The relevant cost analysis can be summarized as follows:

	Accept	Reject	Differential Benefit to Accept
Revenues	$3,100,000	$—	$3,100,000
Dairy ingredients	(1,400,000)	—	(1,400,000)
Sugar	(200,000)	—	(200,000)
Flavourings	(300,000)	—	(300,000)
Direct labour	(500,000)	—	(500,000)
Packaging	(400,000)	—	(400,000)
Other	(100,000)	—	(100,000)
Total	$ 200,000	$ 0	$ 200,000

We see that for this company, accepting the special order will increase profits by $200,000 ($0.10 × 2,000,000).

Decisions to Sell or Process Further

Joint products have common processes and costs of production up to a split-off point. At that point, they become distinguishable. For example, certain minerals such as copper and gold may both be found in a given ore. The ore must be mined, crushed, and treated before the copper and gold are separated. The point of separation is called the **split-off point**. The costs of mining, crushing, and treatment are common to both products.

Often joint products are sold at the split-off point. Sometimes it is more profitable to process a joint product further, beyond the split-off point, prior to selling it. Determining whether to **sell or process further** is an important decision that a manager must make.

To illustrate, consider Appletime Corporation. Appletime is a large corporate farm that specializes in growing apples. Each plot produces approximately 1,000 kilograms of apples. The trees in each plot must be sprayed, fertilized, watered, and pruned. When the apples are ripened, workers are hired to pick them. The apples are then transported to a warehouse, where they are washed and sorted. The approximate cost of all these activities (including processing) is $300 per 1,000 kilograms per year.

Apples are sorted into three grades (A, B, and C), which are determined by size and blemishes. Large apples without blemishes (bruises, cuts, wormholes, and so on) are sorted into one bin and classified as Grade A. Small apples without blemishes are sorted into a second bin and classified as Grade B. All remaining apples are placed in a third bin and classified as Grade C. Every 1,000 kilograms of apples produce 400 kilograms of Grade A, 300 kilograms of Grade B, and 300 kilograms of Grade C.

Grade A apples are sold to large supermarkets for $0.80 per kilogram. Grade B apples are packaged in 2.5-kilogram bags and sold to supermarkets for $1.30 per bag. (The cost of each bag is $0.05.) Grade C apples are processed further and made into applesauce. The sauce is sold in 500-millilitre cans for $0.75 each. The cost of processing is $0.20 per kilogram of apples. The final output is 500 cans. Exhibit 10–3 summarizes the process. Keep in mind that the processing costs occur only if further processing takes place. Hence, processing costs are relevant.

A large supermarket chain recently requested that Appletime supply 500-millilitre cans of apple pie filling, for which the chain was willing to pay $0.90 per can. Appletime determined that the Grade B apples would be suitable for this purpose and estimated that it would cost $0.40 per kilogram to process the apples into pie filling. The output would be 500 cans.

In deciding whether to sell Grade B apples at split-off or to process them further and sell them as pie filling, the common costs of spraying, pruning, and so on are not relevant. The company must pay the $300 per 1,000 kilograms for these activities regardless of whether it sells at split-off or processes further. However, the revenues earned at split-off are likely to differ from the revenues that would be received if the Grade B apples were sold as pie filling. Therefore, revenues are a relevant consideration.

Since there are 300 kilograms of Grade B apples at split-off, Appletime sells 120 2.5-kilogram bags at a net per-unit price of $1.25 ($1.30 – $0.05). Thus, the total net revenues at split-off are $150 ($1.25 × 120). If the apples are processed into pie filling, the total revenues are $450 ($0.90 × 500). Therefore, the incremental revenues from processing further are $300 ($450 – $150). The incremental costs of processing are $120 ($0.40 × 300 kilograms). Since revenues increase by $300 and costs by only $120, the net benefit of processing further is $180. Thus, Appletime should process the Grade B apples into pie filling. The analysis is summarized as follows:

	Sell	Process Further	Differential Amount to Process Further
Revenues	$150	$ 450	$ 300
Processing cost	—	(120)	(120)
Total	$150	$ 330	$ 180

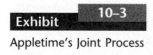

Exhibit **10–3**

Appletime's Joint Process

Yield at Split-Off   *Further Processing*

Grade A
400 kg
Sell for $0.80/kg

Joint Cost $300

Grade B (300 kg)

Bagged
120 2.5-kg bags
Cost $0.05/bag
Sell for $1.30 each

Grade C (300 kg)

Applesauce
500 500-ml cans
Cost $0.20/kg
Sell for $0.75/can

PRODUCT-MIX DECISIONS

In the example above, of every 1,000 kilograms of apples harvested, 400 were Grade A, 300 were Grade B, and 300 were Grade C. Although the relative amounts of each type of apple can be influenced to some extent by the procedures followed in spraying, watering, fertilizing, and so on, the mix of apples is largely beyond Appletime's control. However, many organizations have total discretion in choosing their product mix. Moreover, decisions about product mix can have a significant impact on an organization's profitability.

Each mix represents an alternative that carries with it an associated profit level. A manager should choose the alternative that maximizes total profits. Since fixed costs do not vary with activity level, the total fixed costs of a firm would be the same for all possible mixes and therefore are not relevant to the decision. Hence, a manager needs to choose the alternative that maximizes total contribution margin.

Assume, for example, that Jorgenson Company produces two types of gears: X and Y, with unit contribution margins of $25 and $10, respectively. If the firm possesses unlimited resources and the demand for each product is unlimited, the product-mix decision is simple—produce an infinite number of each product. Unfortunately, every firm faces limited resources and limited demand for each product. These limitations are called **constraints**. A manager must choose the optimal mix given the constraints found within the firm.

Assuming that Jorgenson can sell all that is produced, some may argue that only Gear X should be produced and sold—it has the larger contribution margin. However, this solution is not necessarily the best. The selection of the optimal mix can be significantly affected by the relationships of the constrained resources to the individual products. These relationships affect the quantity of each product that can be produced, and consequently the total contribution margin that can be earned. This point is most vividly illustrated with one resource constraint.

One Constrained Resource

Assume that each gear must be notched by a special machine. The firm owns eight machines that together provide 40,000 hours of machine time per year. Gear X requires two hours of machine time, and Gear Y requires half an hour of machine time. Assume that there are no other constraints. What is the optimal mix of gears? Since each unit of Gear X requires two hours of machine time, 20,000 units of Gear X can be produced per year (40,000/2). At $25 per unit, Jorgenson can earn a total contribution margin of $500,000. On the other hand, Gear Y requires only 0.5 hours of machine time per unit; therefore, 80,000 (40,000/0.5) gears can be produced. At $10 per unit, the total contribution margin is $800,000. Producing only Gear Y yields a higher profit level than producing only Gear X—even though the unit contribution margin for Gear X is 2.5 times larger than that for Gear Y.

The contribution margin per unit of each product is not the critical concern. The contribution margin per unit of *scarce resource* is the deciding factor. The product yielding the highest contribution margin per machine hour should be selected. Gear X earns $12.50 per machine hour ($25/2), but Gear Y earns $20 per machine hour ($10/0.5). Thus, the optimal mix is 80,000 units of Gear Y and none of Gear X.

Multiple Constrained Resources

The presence of only one constrained resource is unrealistic. All organizations face multiple constraints: limitations of raw materials, limitations of labour inputs, limited demand for each product, and so on. Solving the product-mix problem in the presence of multiple constraints is considerably more complicated and requires the use of a specialized mathematical technique known as *linear programming*, which is defined and illustrated in the Appendix to this chapter.

PRICING

One of the more difficult decisions faced by a company is pricing. This section examines the impact of cost on price, and the accountant's role in gathering the needed information.

Cost-Based Pricing

Demand is one side of the pricing equation; supply is the other side. Since revenue must cover cost for the firm to make a profit, many companies start with cost to determine price. That is, they calculate product cost and add the desired profit. The mechanics of this approach are straightforward. Usually, there is some base cost and a markup. The **markup** is a percentage applied to the base cost; it includes desired profit and any costs not included in the base cost. Companies that bid for jobs routinely base bid price on cost.

Consider Elvin Company, owned and operated by Clare Elvin, which assembles and installs computers to customer specifications. Costs of the components and other direct materials are easy to trace. Direct labour cost is similarly easy to trace to each job. Assemblers receive, on average, $12 per hour, and the company pays benefits of approximately 25 percent of that wage. Last year, Elvin Company worked on 650 jobs, which averaged 5 hours each. Overhead, consisting of utilities, small tools, building space, and so on, amounted to $80,000. Elvin Company's income statement for last year is as follows:

Revenues		$856,500
Cost of goods sold:		
Direct materials	$585,000	
Direct labour	48,750	
Overhead	80,000	713,750
Gross profit		$142,750
Selling and administrative expenses		25,000
Operating income		$117,750

Suppose that Clare wants to earn about the same amount of profit on each job as was earned last year. She could calculate a markup on cost of goods sold by summing selling and administrative expenses and operating income, then dividing by cost of goods sold:

$$\text{Markup on COGS} = \text{(Selling and administrative expenses}$$
$$+ \text{ Operating income)/COGS}$$
$$= (\$25,000 + \$117,750)/\$713,750$$
$$= 0.20$$

The markup on cost of goods sold is 20 percent. Notice that the 20 percent markup covers both profit and selling and administrative costs. The markup is not pure profit.

The markup can be calculated using a variety of bases. Clearly for Elvin Company, the cost of purchased materials is the largest component. Last year, the markup on materials amounted to 46.4 percent of all other costs and profit:

$$\text{Markup on direct materials} = \text{(Direct labour + Overhead + Selling and}$$
$$\text{administrative expenses + Operating income)/}$$
$$\text{Direct materials}$$
$$= (\$48,750 + \$80,000 + \$25,000 + \$117,750)/\$585,000$$
$$= 0.464$$

A markup percentage of 46.4 percent of direct materials cost would also yield the same amount of profit, assuming the level of operations and other expenses remained stable. The choice of base and markup percentage generally rests on convenience. If Clare finds that the labour varies in rough proportion to the cost of materials (for example, more expensive components take more time to set up) and that the cost of materials is easier to track than the cost of goods sold, then materials might be the better base.

To see how the markup can be used in bidding, suppose that Clare has the opportunity to bid on a job for a local insurance company. The job requires Elvin Company to assemble 100 computers according to certain specifications. She estimates the following costs:

Direct materials (computer components, software, cables)	$100,000
Direct labour (100 × 6 hours × $15)	9,000
Overhead (@ 60 percent of direct labour cost)	5,400
Estimated cost of goods sold	$114,400
Plus 20 percent markup on COGS	22,880
Bid price	$137,280

Thus, Elvin Company's initial bid price is $137,280. Note that this is the first pass at a bid. Clare can adjust the bid based on her knowledge of competition for the job and other factors. The markup is a guideline, not an absolute rule.

If Elvin Company bids every job at cost plus 20 percent, is it guaranteed a profit? No, not at all. If very few jobs are won, the entire markup will go toward selling and administrative expenses, the costs not explicitly included in the bidding calculations.

Markup pricing is often used by retail stores, and their typical markup is 100 percent of cost. Thus, if a sweater is purchased by Graham Department Store for $24, the retail price marked is $48 [$24 + (1.00)($24)]. Of course, the 100 percent markup is not pure profit. It goes toward the salaries of the clerks, payment for space and equipment (cash registers and so on), utilities, advertising, and so on. A major advantage of markup pricing is that standard markups are easy to apply. Consider the difficulty of setting a price for every piece of merchandise in a hardware or department store. It is much simpler to apply a uniform markup to cost and then adjust prices as needed if less is demanded than anticipated.

Target Costing and Pricing

We just examined the way in which companies use cost to determine price. Working backward shows how price can determine cost. **Target costing** is a method of determining the cost of a product or service based on the price (target price) that customers are willing to pay. This is also referred to as *price-driven costing*.

Most North American companies, and nearly all European firms, set the price of a new product as the sum of the costs and the desired profit. The rationale is that the company must earn sufficient revenues to cover all costs and yield a profit. Peter Drucker writes, "This is true but irrelevant: Customers do not see it as their job to ensure manufacturers a profit. The only sound way to price is to start out with what the market is willing to pay."[8]

Target costing is a method of working backward from price to find cost. The marketing department determines what characteristics and price for a product are most acceptable to consumers. Then it is the job of the company's engineers to design and develop the product such that cost and profit can be covered by that price. Japanese firms have been doing this for years; North American companies are beginning to use target costing. For example, Borland International, Inc., used target costing in developing its 1993 version of Quattro Pro for Windows spreadsheet software.

8.　Peter Drucker, "The Five Deadly Business Sins," *The Wall Street Journal* (21 October 1993): A22.

Priced at $69 (compared with $695 for Lotus and Microsoft versions), it was designed to appeal to new spreadsheet users. "When we were developing the product, we anticipated the pricing and the people it would attract. We thought of features for that audience."[9] Those features included clear instructions, preformatted spreadsheets for 50 common tasks, and interactive on-screen tutorials. Soothing first-time users wasn't the only reason for Quattro Pro's inclusion of built-in help. At $69, the company could not afford numerous calls for technical advice.

Returning to the Elvin Company example, suppose that Clare finds that the insurance company will not consider any bid over $100,000. Her cost-based bid was $137,280. Is she out of the running? No: not if she can tailor her bid to the customer's desired price. Recall that the original bid called for $100,000 of direct materials and $9,000 of direct labour. Clearly, adjusting the materials will yield the greatest savings. Working with the customer specifications, Clare must determine whether or not a less expensive set of components will achieve the insurance company's objectives. Suppose that the insurance company has specified sufficient hard-disk space on each drive to accommodate particular software, and that the minimum required is 1.2 gigabytes. Clare's original bid specified 3-gigabyte hard drives. If she reduces the hard-disk space to 1.5 gigabytes and uses a marginally slower drive, she could save $25,000. Substituting a slightly more expensive monitor (a $20 increase) that does not require the installation of screensaver software would result in saving $30 per computer on software and 15 minutes of direct labour time (at $15 per hour) to install it. The net reduction is $13.75 [($30 + $3.75) − $20] for each of the 100 computers. So far, Clare has developed the following costs:

Direct materials ($100,000 − $25,000)	$75,000
Direct labour (100 × 5.75 hours × $15)	8,625
Total prime cost	$83,625

Recall that Elvin Company applies overhead at the rate of 60 percent of direct labour cost. However, Clare must think carefully about this job. Perhaps somewhat less overhead will be incurred, because purchasing is reduced (no need to purchase screensaver software) and testing is reduced (the smaller hard drives require fewer hours of testing). Perhaps overhead for this job will amount to $4,313 (50 percent of direct labour). That would make the cost of the job $87,938 ($4,313 + $83,625).

Still, not all costs have been covered. There is the administrative cost and desired profit. If the standard markup of 20 percent is applied, the bid would be $105,526. This is still too high. Now Clare must determine if further cuts are possible, or if she wants to decrease desired profit and administrative expenses. As you can see, target costing is an iterative process. Clare will go through the cycle until she either achieves the target cost or determines that she cannot. Note, however, that given the customer's price ceiling, Clare now has a chance of winning the bid.

A further issue might cause concern. Is there anything ethically wrong with changing the components from the initial bid to the target-costed bid? No: the new components meet customer specifications and are clearly described in the bid. In fact, Clare's initial bid was overspecified. If the customer wants a Chevrolet, the bidder need not provide a Rolls-Royce, especially at Chevrolet prices. However, if in Clare's professional opinion the insurance company should upgrade its specifications, she could point that out. For example, if she knows that the insurance company's word-processing program is due for an upgrade that will take more hard-disk space, she could inform the company of that and encourage an increase in specified disk space.

---

9.   Quotation by Joe Ammirato, group manager of the spreadsheet business unit at Borland, as reported by Lawrence M. Fisher, "Using 'Usability' to Sell Spreadsheets to the Masses," *New York Times* (6 February 1994): 12F.

Target costing involves much more up-front work than cost-based pricing. However, additional work must be done if the cost-based price turns out to be higher than what customers will accept. Then the arduous task of bringing costs into line to support a lower price, or the opportunity cost of missing the market altogether, begins. For example, the North American consumer electronics market is virtually nonexistent because cost-based pricing led to increasingly higher prices. Japanese (and later Korean) firms practising target costing offered lower prices and won the market.

Target costing can be used most effectively in the design and development stage of the product life cycle. At that point, the product's features as well as its costs are still fairly easy to adjust.

Legal Aspects of Pricing

Customers and costs are important economic determinants of price. The Canadian government also has an important impact on pricing. The basic principle behind much pricing regulation is that competition is good and should be encouraged. Therefore, collusion by companies to set prices and the deliberate attempt to drive competitors out of business are prohibited. In general, cost is an important justification for price.

Predatory pricing   The practice of setting prices below cost for the purpose of injuring competitors and eliminating competition is called **predatory pricing**. It is important to note that pricing below cost is not necessarily predatory pricing. Companies frequently price an item below cost—loss leaders or weekly specials in a grocery store, for example. In the United States, laws on predatory pricing create a patchwork of legal definitions. Twenty-two states have laws against predatory pricing, each state differing somewhat in definition and rules. Oklahoma, for example, requires retailers to sell products at a price at least 6.75 percent above cost, unless the store is having a sale or matching a competitor's price. A 1937 Arkansas law forbids companies to sell or advertise "any article or product . . . at less than the cost thereof to the vendor . . . for the purpose of injuring competitors and destroying competition." In Canada, the 1986 Competition Act culminated a process of revisions of laws that were put in motion in 1888. Paragraph 34(1)(c) of the Competition Act deals directly with predatory pricing:

> *34(1) Every one engaged in a business who . . .*
> *(c) engages in a policy of selling products at prices unreasonably low, having the effect or tendency of substantially lessening competition or eliminating a competitor, or designed to have such effect; is guilty of an indictable offence and is liable to imprisonment for two years.*

A conviction under this paragraph is based on two conditions—prices must be unreasonably low, and such prices have the effect of reducing competition. Because price competition is so highly valued, it is usually difficult to prove predatory pricing.

An example of the application of state predatory pricing laws is the lawsuit filed by three Conway, Arkansas, drugstores against Wal-Mart.[10] The druggists contended that Wal-Mart engaged in predatory pricing by selling more than 100 products below cost. One difficulty is showing exactly what cost is. Wal-Mart has low overhead and phenomenal buying power. Suppliers are regularly required to shave prices to win Wal-Mart's business. Smaller concerns cannot win such price breaks.

---

10. Wal-Mart lost the suit in October 1993 and won the case on appeal.

Thus, the fact that Wal-Mart prices products below competitors' costs does not necessarily mean that those products are priced below Wal-Mart's cost. (Although in this case, the CEO of Wal-Mart did concede that Wal-Mart on occasion prices products below its own cost.)

Predatory pricing on the international market is called dumping, and occurs when companies sell below cost in other countries. For years, U.S. automobile manufacturers have accused Japanese companies of dumping. Companies found guilty of dumping products in the United States and Canada are subject to trade restrictions and stiff tariffs—which act to increase the price of the good. The defence against a charge of dumping is demonstrating that the price is indeed above or equal to cost.

Price Discrimination   The 1986 Competition Act also includes provisions that outlaw price discrimination. Price discrimination refers to the charging of different prices to different customers for essentially the same product.

Paragraph 34(1)(a) states:

34(1) Every one engaged in a business who
(a) is a party or privy to, or assists in, any sale that discriminates to his knowledge, directly or indirectly, against competitors of a purchaser of articles from him in that any discount, rebate, allowance, price concession or other advantage that, at the time the articles are sold to such purchaser, is not available to such competitors in respect of a sale of articles of like quality and quantity; is guilty of an indictable offence and is liable to imprisonment for two years.

It should be noted that not all price discrimination is an offence. For example, price discrimination based on quantities of goods purchased is not an offence. Unlike the United States, where cost justification can be used as a defence against price discrimination, Canada does not require a seller demonstrate a cost difference to support quantity discounts if the discount pricing structures are available to competing buyers.[11]

Fairness and Pricing

Community standards of fairness have an important effect on prices. For example, should toy stores raise the price of sleds the morning after a heavy snowfall? They could, but generally they do not. Their customers believe that a price increase at such a time would be taking unfair advantage. Whether we characterize the store's reluctance to raise prices in this situation as fairness or as an act in the long-term best interests of the company, the result is the same.

Price gouging is said to occur when firms with market power price products "too high." How high is too high? Surely cost is a consideration. Any time price just covers cost, gouging does not occur. This is why so many firms go to considerable trouble to explain their cost structure and point out costs consumers may not realize exist. Pharmaceutical companies, for example, emphasize the research and development costs associated with new drugs. When a high price is clearly not supported by cost, buyers take offence. For example, after Hurricane Andrew in 1992, some companies and individuals sold ice for very high prices. Floridians faced by those prices were outraged that some suppliers would take advantage of the disaster to profiteer.

It is easy to see that cost as a justification for price underlies community standards of fairness. Ethics are founded on a sense of fairness. So unethical behaviour in pricing is related to taking unfair advantage of customers. Cost-related price increases are the best defence against customer rebellion.

---

11. Montrose Sommers, James Barnes, William Stanton, and Charles Futrell, *Fundamentals of Marketing*, Fifth Canadian Edition (Toronto: McGraw-Hill Ryerson Limited, 1989), 326–329.

SUNK COSTS AND DECISION MAKING

Objective 6

Explain why decision makers sometimes appear to use sunk costs in making decisions.

It is important to repeat here that in all the above examples, as well as in examples that follow in Chapter 11, sunk (past) costs *should not* affect decisions. It would be expected, therefore, that rational decision makers would not use sunk costs in decision making. There is some evidence, however, that decision makers do in fact use sunk costs in their decisions.[12] Typically, the evidence is that decision makers continue their commitment to a project even in the face of negative feedback, presumably because of the sunk cost. Is it necessary to conclude that decision makers are economically irrational? Possible rational reasons for the use of sunk costs in decision making include the following:[13]

1. Performance evaluation systems tend to be oriented toward the short term. This accentuates the desire of managers to cover up previously made but failing investment decisions (now seen as past mistakes) in the hope that they would advance or be promoted before the full effects of these decisions become manifest.
2. Closely linked to the above is the idea that performance evaluation systems are typically retrospective in their outlook. This means that managers are often too concerned about how past costs or performance will appear to their superiors.
3. The generally accepted accounting principles (including accrual accounting) in financial performance measurement are primarily based on historical (sunk) cost accounting. Externally reported results may affect management's performance bonuses and influence management's objectives. Sunk costs can therefore play a role in managerial decisions.
4. Sunk costs represent costs incurred in the past. The evidence that someone else in the organization incurred a certain expenditure as an investment may provide assurance that a decision maker made probabilistic assessments about future outcomes and that the decision was justified in terms of expected future benefits.
5. When sunk costs are justifiably used by decision makers as inputs in cost prediction models, this use may give the appearance that sunk costs are being used in decision models as well.
6. Even when it becomes obvious that a previous course of action was misguided, there is sometimes good reason to believe that not abandoning it can still be rationally justified on the grounds that future benefits may exceed any future expenditures.
7. Not changing a course of action in the face of negative feedback is sometimes seen as being unreasonably influenced by sunk costs. However, it may also reflect commitment, which is a highly regarded attribute in many organizations.
8. The reasons for a failed course of action may be due to noncontrollable (exogenous) factors like bad luck that management expects to change.
9. The size of sunk costs invested in a particular business entity quite often serves as a barrier to entry, since it discourages competitors from entering the marketplace. Competitors' decisions may thus be influenced by a company's sunk costs.

While the above list is not exhaustive, it provides a variety of reasons why, in specific situations, the use of sunk costs in decision making may be explained on rational grounds. In fact, perhaps the term "sunk cost" is a misnomer in these situations. Research in this area suggests that of all the above reasons, the primary factor explaining concern with a sunk cost is self-justification: that is, decision makers seek whenever possible to justify their own previous decisions (1, 2, 3, and 8 above).

---

12. For example, see Barry M. Staw, "Knee-Deep in the Big Muddy: A Study of Escalating Commitment to a Chosen Course of Action," *Organizational Behaviour and Human Performance*, 1976 (16): 27–44; Arkes and Blumer, "The Psychology of Sunk Costs," *Organizational Behaviour and Human Decision Processes*, 1985 (35): 124–140.

13. For more detail on this topic, see Nabil Elias, "Entrapment and the Sunk Cost Phenomenon: More than Self-Justification," Working Paper, Faculty of Management, University of Manitoba, 1988; and Nabil Elias and Mohamed Ibrahim, "Entrapment, Sunk Cost, and Marginal Analysis: An Identification of Issues," Paper Presented at the 15th Congress of the European Accounting Association, Madrid, Spain, April 1992.

APPENDIX: LINEAR PROGRAMMING

Objective 7

Use linear programming to find the optimal solution to a problem of multiple constrained resources.

Linear programming is a method that searches among possible solutions until it finds the optimal solution. The theory of linear programming permits many solutions to be ignored. In fact, all but a finite number of solutions are eliminated by the theory, with the search then limited to the resulting finite set.

To illustrate how linear programming can be used to solve a problem of multiple constrained resources, consider the earlier example of the product mix for Jorgenson Company. Assume that there are demand constraints for both Gear X and Gear Y. For Gear X, no more than 15,000 units can be sold and for Gear Y no more than 40,000 units. As before, the objective is to maximize Jorgenson's total contribution margin subject to the constraints faced by Jorgenson.

The objective can be expressed mathematically. Let X be the number of units produced and sold of Gear X, and let Y stand for Gear Y. Since the unit contribution margins are $25 and $10 for X and Y, respectively, the total contribution margin (Z) can be expressed as:

$$Z = \$25X + \$10Y \tag{10.1}$$

Equation 10.1 is called the **objective function**.

Jorgenson also has three constraints. One is the limited machine hours available for production, and the other two reflect the demand limitations for each product. Consider the machine-hour constraint first. Two machine hours are used for each unit of Gear X, and 0.5 machine hours are used for each unit of Gear Y. Thus, the total machine hours used can be expressed as $2X + 0.5Y$. The maximum of 40,000 machine hours available can be expressed mathematically as follows:

$$2X + 0.5Y \leq 40,000 \tag{10.2}$$

The two demand constraint limitations can also be expressed mathematically:

$$X \leq 15,000 \tag{10.3}$$
$$Y \leq 40,000 \tag{10.4}$$

Jorgenson's problem is to select the number of units of X and Y that maximize total contribution margin subject to the constraints in Equations 10.2, 10.3, and 10.4. This problem can be expressed in the following way, which is the standard formulation for a linear programming problem (often referred to as a *linear programming model*):

$$\text{Max. } Z = \$25X + \$10Y$$

subject to

$$2X + 0.5Y \leq 40,000$$
$$X \leq 15,000$$
$$Y \leq 40,000$$
$$X \geq 0$$
$$Y \geq 0$$

The last two constraints are called *nonnegativity constraints* and simply reflect the reality that negative quantities of a product cannot be produced. All constraints, taken together, are referred to as the **constraint set.**

A **feasible solution** is a solution that satisfies the constraints in the linear programming model. The collection of all feasible solutions is called the **feasible set of solutions.** For example, producing and selling 10,000 units of Gear X and 20,000 units of Gear Y would be a feasible solution and a member of the feasible set. This product mix uses 30,000 machine hours [$(2 \times 10,000) + (0.5 \times 20,000)$], which is under the limit for machine hours. Additionally, the company can sell the indicated amounts, since they do not exceed the demand constraints for each product. If this mix is selected, the company would earn a contribution margin totalling $450,000 [($25 × 10,000) + ($10 × 20,000)].

However, the mix of 10,000 units of X and 20,000 units of Y is not the best mix. One better solution would be to produce and sell 12,000 units of X and 30,000 units of Y. This mix uses 39,000 machine hours [(2 × 12,000) + (0.5 × 30,000)] and produces a total contribution margin of $600,000 [($25 × 12,000) + ($10 × 30,000)]. This feasible solution is better than the first, because it produces $150,000 more in contribution margin and profits. There are, however, even better feasible solutions. The objective is to identify the best. The best feasible solution—the one that maximizes the total contribution margin—is called the **optimal solution**.

When there are only two products, the optimal solution can be identified by graphing. Since solving the problem by graphing provides considerable insight into the way linear programming problems are solved, the Jorgenson problem will be solved in this way.

Four steps are followed in solving the problem graphically.

1. Graph each constraint.
2. Identify the feasible set of solutions.
3. Identify all corner-point values in the feasible set.
4. Select the corner point that yields the largest value for the objective function.

The graph of each constraint for the Jorgenson problem is shown in Exhibit 10–4. The nonnegativity constraints put the graph in the first quadrant. The other constraints are graphed by assuming that equality holds. Since each constraint is a linear equation, the graph is obtained by identifying two points on the line, plotting those points, and connecting them.

A feasible area for each constraint (except for the nonnegativity constraints) is determined by everything that lies below (or to the left) of the resulting line. The

Graphical Solution
(Coordinates represent
thousands)

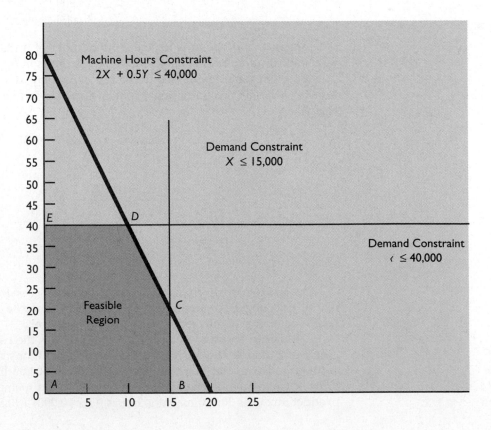

feasible set or *region* is the intersection of each constraint's feasible area. The feasible set is shown by the figure *ABCDE*; it includes the boundary of the figure.

There are five corner points: *A*, *B*, *C*, *D*, and *E*. Their values, obtained directly from the graph, are (0,0) for *A*, (15,0) for *B*, (15,20) for *C*, (10,40) for *D*, and (0,40) for *E*. The impact of these values on the objective function is as follows (expressed in thousands):

Corner Point	X-value	Y-value	$Z = \$25X + \$10Y$
A	0	0	$ 0
B	15	0	375
C	15	20	575
D	10	40	650*
E	0	40	400

* Optimal solution

The optimal solution calls for producing and selling 10,000 units of Gear X and 40,000 units of Gear Y. No other feasible solution will produce a larger contribution margin. It has been shown in the literature on linear programming that the optimal solution will always be one of the corner points. This is because if a solution other than a corner point is considered, there will be always a corner-point solution that includes more of at least one of the products and at least the same amount of the other. Accordingly, the corner-point solution has a larger total contribution margin. Once the graph is drawn and the corner points are identified, finding the solution is simply a matter of computing the value of each corner point and selecting the one with the greatest value.

Graphical solutions are not practical with more than two or three products. Fortunately, an algorithm called the **simplex method** can be used to solve larger linear programming problems. This algorithm is available for use on computers to solve these larger problems.

The linear programming model is an important tool for making product-mix decisions, though it requires very little independent managerial decision making. The mix decision is made by the linear programming model itself. Assuming that the linear programming model is a reasonable representation of reality, the main role for management is to ensure that accurate data are used as input to the model. This includes the ability to recognize the irrelevancy of fixed costs for this type of decision and the ability to assess the accounting and technological inputs accurately (for example, the unit selling prices, the unit costs, and the amount of resource consumed by each product as it is produced).

Objectives that include more than one goal (goal programming) and applications where constraints are nonlinear (nonlinear programming) are beyond the scope of this book.

SUMMARY OF LEARNING OBJECTIVES

1. Describe and explain the tactical decision-making model.
The decision-making model described in this chapter consists of six steps: recognizing and defining the problem, identifying alternatives, determining the costs and benefits of each alternative, comparing relevant costs and benefits for each alternative, assessing qualitative factors, and making the decision. In using cost analysis to choose among alternatives, managers

should take steps to ensure that all important feasible alternatives are being considered.

2. Explain how the activity resource usage model is used in assessing relevancy.
The activity resource usage model breaks costs into two groups: flexible resources and committed resources. Flexible resources are acquired as used and needed: supply equals demand. If demand changes,

the cost is relevant. Committed resources are acquired in advance; therefore, they may have unused capacity. The cost may or may not be relevant. If committed resources have sufficient unused capacity, their cost is not relevant. If there is not sufficient excess capacity, the additional cost is relevant.

3. Apply the tactical decision-making concepts in a variety of business situations.

Several examples illustrating the application of the relevant-costing model were given within the chapter. Applications were illustrated for make-or-buy decisions, keep-or-drop decisions, special-order decisions, and sell-or-process-further decisions. Product-mix decisions were also discussed. The list of applications is by no means exhaustive but was given to illustrate the scope and power of relevant-costing analysis.

4. Choose the optimal product mix when faced with one constrained resource.

In dealing with a resource constraint, it is important to phrase the product contribution margin in terms of contribution margin per unit of constrained resource.

5. Explain the impact of cost on pricing decisions.

Costs are important inputs into the pricing decision. Cost-based pricing uses a markup based on a subset of costs. Target costing works backward from a price acceptable to consumers to find the cost necessary to manufacture the product. The Competition Act prohibits price discrimination.

6. Explain why decision makers sometimes appear to use sunk costs in making decisions.

While normative models indicate that sunk costs should not be used for decision-making purposes, there is some evidence that decision makers appear to be influenced by sunk costs. The main reason for this is managers' concern over their performance evaluation, which is typically based on the past rather than the future.

7. Use linear programming to find the optimal solution to a problem of multiple constrained resources.

Linear programming is a method that locates the optimal solution in a set of feasible solutions. The graphical method may be used with two products. When more than two products are involved, the simplex method is used. (Appendix)

KEY TERMS

Constraints, 404	Make-or-buy decisions, 396	Simplex method, 413
Constraint set, 411	Markup, 405	Special-order decisions, 401
Decision model, 388	Objective function, 411	Split-off point, 402
Feasible set of solutions, 411	Optimal solution, 412	Strategic decision making, 388
Feasible solution, 411	Predatory pricing, 408	Sunk cost, 392
Joint products, 402	Price gouging, 409	Tactical decision making, 387
Keep-or-drop decisions, 398	Relevant costs, 391	Target costing, 406
Linear programming, 411	Sell-or-process further decision, 402	

PROBLEM REVIEW

Rianne Company produces a light fixture with the following unit cost:

Direct materials	$2
Direct labour	1
Variable overhead	3
Fixed overhead	2
Unit cost	$8

The production capacity is 300,000 units per year. Because of a depressed housing market, the company expects to produce only 180,000 fixtures for the coming year. The company also has fixed selling costs totalling $500,000 per year and variable selling costs of $1 per unit sold. The fixtures normally sell for $12 each.

At the beginning of the year, a customer from a geographic region outside the area normally served by the company offered to buy 100,000 fixtures for $7 each. The customer also offered to pay all transportation expenses. Since there would be no sales commissions involved, this order would not have any variable selling expenses.

Required:

Should the company accept the order? Provide both qualitative and quantitative justification for your decision. Assume that no other orders are expected beyond the regular business and the special order.

Solution

The company is faced with a problem of idle capacity. Accepting the special order would bring production up to near capacity. There are two options: accept or reject the order. If the order is accepted, the company could avoid laying off employees and would enhance and maintain its community image. However, the order is considerably below the normal selling price of $12. Because the price is so low, the company needs to assess the potential impact of the sale on its regular customers and on the firm's profitability. Considering the fact that the customer is located in a region not usually served by the company, the likelihood of creating an adverse impact on regular business is not high. Thus, the qualitative factors seem to favour acceptance.

The only remaining consideration is the profitability of the special order. To assess profitability, the firm should identify the relevant costs and benefits of each alternative. This analysis is as follows:

	Accept	Reject
Revenues	$700,000	$—
Direct materials	(200,000)	—
Direct labour	(100,000)	—
Variable overhead	(300,000)	—
Total benefits	$100,000	$ 0

Accepting the order would increase profits by $100,000 (the fixed overhead and selling expenses are all irrelevant since they are the same across both alternatives). Conclusion: The order should be accepted since both qualitative and quantitative factors favour it.

QUESTIONS FOR WRITING AND DISCUSSION

1. What is the difference between tactical and strategic decisions?

2. Explain why depreciation on an existing asset is always irrelevant.

3. Give an example of a future cost that is not relevant.

4. Explain why relevant costs need to be expressed on a periodically recurring basis.

5. Relevant costs always determine which alternative should be chosen. Do you agree? Explain.

6. Give an example of a fixed cost that is relevant.

7. What is the difference, if any, between a relevant cost and a differential cost?

8. When, if ever, is depreciation a relevant cost?

9. What role do past costs play in relevant-costing decisions?

10. Can direct materials ever be irrelevant in a make-or-buy decision? Explain.

11. Discuss the importance of complementary effects in a keep-or-drop decision.

12. What are some ways a manager can expand his or her knowledge of the feasible set of alternatives?

13. Should joint costs be considered in a sell-or-process-further decision? Explain.

14. Suppose that a product can be sold at split-off for $5,000 or processed further at a cost of $1,000 and then sold for $6,400. Should the product be processed further?

15. Why are fixed costs never relevant in a product-mix decision?

16. Suppose that a firm produces two products. Should the firm always place the most emphasis

on the product with the largest contribution margin per unit? Explain.

17. Why would a firm ever offer a price on a product that is below its full cost?

18. When can a firm legally offer different prices for the same product?

19. "Rational managers are not influenced by sunk costs," said the economics professor. "But managers are influenced by sunk costs," responded his organizational behaviour colleague—whereupon the economics professor asked, "Do you mean that managers are irrational? There goes the whole foundation of economics!" Briefly answer the economics professor.

20. Discuss the purpose of linear programming.

21. What is an objective function? a constraint? a constraint set?

22. What is a feasible solution? a feasible set of solutions?

23. Explain the procedures for graphically solving a linear programming problem. What solution method is usually used when the problem includes more than two or three products?

EXERCISES

10–1

Make-or-Buy Decision

LO3

Zorro Manufacturing had always made its components in-house. However, Simpson Component Works had recently offered to supply one component, P7-43, at a price of $5 each. Zorro uses 3,850 units of Component P7-43 each year. The absorption cost per unit of this component is as follows:

Direct materials	$1.30
Direct labour	0.65
Variable overhead	2.50
Fixed overhead	3.00
Total	$7.45

The fixed overhead is an allocated expense; none of it would be eliminated if production of Component P7-43 stopped.

Required:

1. What are the alternatives facing Zorro Manufacturing with respect to production of Component P7-43?
2. List the relevant costs for each alternative. Which alternative is better?

10–2

Keep-or-Drop Decision

LO3

Uintah Company produces three products: A, B, and C. A segmented income statement, with amounts given in thousands, follows:

	A	B	C	Total
Sales revenue	$700	$1,800	$200	$2,700
Less: Variable expenses	350	1,000	140	1,490
Contribution margin	$350	$ 800	$ 60	$1,210
Less: Direct fixed expenses	100	300	70	470
Segment margin	$250	$ 500	$(10)	$ 740
Less: Common fixed expenses				340
Operating income				$ 400

Direct fixed expenses include depreciation on equipment dedicated to the product lines of $20,000 for A, $120,000 for B, and $30,000 for C. None of the equipment can be sold.

Required:

1. What impact on profit would result from dropping Product C?
2. Now suppose that 10 percent of the customers for Product B choose to buy from Uintah because it offers a full range of products, including Product C. If C were no longer available from Uintah, these customers would go elsewhere to purchase B. Now what is the impact on profit if Product C is dropped?

10–3

Special-Order Decision; Flexible and Committed Resources

LO3

Dexter Company has been approached by a new customer with an offer to purchase 1,400 units of Dexter's product at a price of $3 each. The new customer is geographically separated from Dexter's other customers, and there would be no effect on existing sales. Dexter normally produces 10,000 units, but plans to produce and sell only 8,000 in the coming year. The normal sales price is $5 per unit. Unit-cost information is as follows:

Direct materials	$0.75
Direct labour	0.80
Variable overhead	0.40
Fixed overhead	2.00
Total	$3.95

If Dexter accepts the order, no fixed manufacturing activities will be affected, because there is sufficient excess capacity. However, the distribution centre at the warehouse is operating at full capacity and would need to add capacity costing $1,000 for every 5,000 units to be packed and shipped.

Required:

Should Dexter accept the special order? By how much will profit increase or decrease if the order is accepted?

10–4

Keep or Buy Decision; Sunk Costs

LO1, LO3

Heather Alburty purchased a two-year-old previously owned Grand Am for $8,900. Since purchasing the car, she has spent the following amounts on parts and labour:

New stereo system	$1,200
Trick paint	400
New wide racing tires	800
Total	$2,400

Unfortunately, the new stereo doesn't completely drown out the sounds of a grinding transmission. Apparently, the Grand Am needs a considerable amount of work to make it reliable transportation. Heather estimates that the needed repairs include the following:

Transmission overhaul	$2,000
Water pump	400
Master cylinder work	1,100
Total	$3,500

In a visit to a used car dealer, Heather has found a one-year-old Neon in mint condition for $9,400. Heather has advertised and found that she can sell the Grand Am for only $6,400. If she buys the Neon, she will pay cash, but she would need to sell the Grand Am.

Required:

1. In trying to decide whether to restore the Grand Am or buy the Neon, Heather is distressed because she already has spent $11,300 on the Grand Am. The investment seems too much to give up. How would you react to her concern?

2. Assuming that Heather would be equally happy with the Grand Am or the Neon, should she buy the Neon or should she restore the Grand Am?

10–5

Make-or-Buy Decision

LO1, LO2, LO3

Spreadsheet

Fontaro Company is currently manufacturing Part K96, producing 50,000 units annually. The part is used in the production of several products made by Fontaro. The cost per unit for K96 is as follows:

Direct materials	$ 7.00
Direct labour	3.00
Variable overhead	1.50
Fixed overhead	2.50
Total	$14.00

Of the total fixed overhead assigned to K96, $90,000 is direct fixed overhead (the lease of production machinery and salary of a production line supervisor—neither of which will be needed if the line is dropped). The remaining fixed overhead is common fixed overhead. An outside supplier has offered to sell the part to Fontaro for $13. There is no alternative use for the facilities currently used to produce the part.

Required:

1. Should Fontaro Company make or buy Part K96?
2. What is the most Fontaro would be willing to pay an outside supplier?
3. If Fontaro bought the part, by how much would income increase or decrease?

10–6

Make-or-Buy Decision

LO1, LO2, LO3

Refer to Exercise 10–5. Now suppose that *all* of the fixed overhead is common fixed overhead.

Required:

1. Should Fontaro Company make or buy Part K96?
2. What is the most Fontaro would be willing to pay an outside supplier?
3. If Fontaro bought the part, by how much would income increase or decrease?

10–7

Make-or-Buy Decision

LO2, LO3, LO4

The Rocky Company Ltd. currently produces 10,000 units per year of XL500, which is a component of the company's major products. XL500 has the following unit costs:

Direct materials	$ 16.50
Direct labour	37.80
Indirect costs:	
Indirect labour (variable)	12.60
Heat and power (variable)	3.20
Fixed overhead	53.50
Total cost per unit	$123.60

The company expects future annual demand for XL500 to increase to 15,000 units starting next year, which is within present capacity. A supplier has offered to supply 15,000 units of XL500 at $105 per unit.

If the company decided to purchase the required XL500, fixed costs of $13.75 per unit could be avoided based on current production of 10,000 units per year. The vacant area resulting from discontinuing production of XL500 could be rented out for $200,000 per year plus heat and power.

Required:

1. How much could the company gain or lose per year if it purchased the required XL500? Show all calculations.
2. Briefly explain three qualitative factors that would be relevant to the decision to make or buy. (CMA Canada adapted)

10–8

Make-or-Buy Decision; Flexible and Committed Resources; Common and Direct Fixed Overhead

LO1, LO2, LO3

Currently, Pomona Company manufactures and sells a variety of small power tools for households. One of these tools is a low-end power drill. Pomona makes 200,000 of these drills per year at a full cost of $18.75 each. The breakdown of the manufacturing cost is as follows:

Direct materials	$5.00
Direct labour	3.60
Variable overhead	4.20
Fixed overhead	5.95

Schering Company offered to sell Pomona the drill for $14.00. Schering will imprint Pomona's name on the drill, and Pomona can continue to sell the drill as part of its full line of products.

Required:

1. If Pomona buys the drill from Schering, by how much will income increase or decrease?
2. Now suppose that Pomona's controller has completed an activity-based costing study of the factory. He has calculated the following activity rates: materials handling, $25 per move; purchasing, $15 per purchase order; setups, $200 per setup; engineering, $50 per engineering hour; and maintenance, $5 per maintenance hour. The drill line uses 3,200 moves, 5,000 purchase orders, 800 setups, 1,000 engineering hours, and 7,000 maintenance hours. If Pomona buys the drill from Schering, by how much will income increase or decrease?

10–9

Keep-or-Drop Decision; Product Substitutes

LO1, LO2, LO3

Spreadsheet

Willem Vanderburg, president of Vanderburg Corporation, had just received the following variable-costing income statement:

	Product A	Product B
Sales	$100,000	$250,000
Less: Variable expenses	50,000	145,000
Contribution margin	$ 50,000	$105,000
Less: Fixed expenses	80,000	110,000
Operating income (loss)	$ (30,000)	$ (5,000)

Willem was distressed, since this was the fifth consecutive quarter in which both products had shown a loss. Upon careful review, Willem discovered that $70,000 of the total fixed costs were common to both products; the common fixed costs are allocated to the individual products on the basis of sales revenues. He was also told that the products are substitutes for each other. If either product is dropped, the sales of the other product will increase: Product A's by 50 percent if B is dropped and B's by 10 percent if A is dropped.

Required:

1. Prepare a segmented income statement in proper form for the past quarter.
2. Assume that Willem will choose among one of the following alternatives:
   a. Keep both products.
   b. Drop both products.
   c. Drop Product A.
   d. Drop Product B.

Which is the best alternative? Provide supporting computations.

10–10

Special-Order Decision; Flexible and Committed Resources; Qualitative Aspects

LO1, LO2, LO3

Randy Stone, the manager of Specialty Paper Products Company, was agonizing over an offer for an order requesting 5,000 calendars. Specialty Paper Products was operating at 70 percent of its capacity and could use the extra business; unfortunately, the order's offering price of $4.20 per box was below the cost of producing the calendars. Louis Nadeau, the firm's controller, was opposed to taking a loss on the deal. But Yatika Isaacs, the company's personnel manager, argued in favour of accepting the order even though a loss would be incurred: it would avoid the problem of layoffs and would help maintain the company's community image. The full cost to produce a calendar follows:

Direct materials	$1.15
Direct labour	2.00
Variable overhead	1.10
Fixed overhead	1.00
Total	$5.25

Later that day, Louis and Yatika met over coffee. Louis sympathized with Yatika's concerns and suggested that the two of them rethink the special-order decision. He offered to determine relevant costs if Yatika would list the activities to be affected by a layoff. Yatika eagerly agreed and came up with the following activities: a loss of productivity equivalent to 1 percent of total payroll; notification costs to lay off approximately 20 employees; increased costs of rehiring and retraining workers when the downturn was over. Louis determined that these activities would cost the following amounts:

- Total payroll is $1,460,000 per year.
- Layoff paperwork is $25 per laid-off employee.
- Rehiring and retraining is $150 per new employee.

Required:

1. Assume that the company would accept the order only if it increases total profits. Should the company accept or reject the order? Provide supporting computations.
2. Consider the new information on activity costs associated with the layoff. Should the company accept or reject the order? Provide supporting computations.

10–11

Sell-or-Process-Further Decision; Basic Analysis

LO1, LO2, LO3

Shenista, Inc., produces three products (Alpha, Beta, and Gamma) from a common input. The joint costs for a typical quarter follow:

Direct materials	$50,000
Direct labour	36,000
Overhead	72,000

The revenues from each product are as follows: Alpha, $100,000; Beta, $93,000; and Gamma, $30,000.

Management is considering processing Alpha beyond the split-off point, which would increase the sales value of Alpha to $120,000. However, to process Alpha further means that the company must rent some special equipment costing $15,400 per quarter. Additional materials and labour also needed would cost $8,500 per quarter.

Required:

1. What is the operating profit earned by the three products for one quarter?
2. Should the division process Product Alpha further or sell it at split-off? What is the effect of the decision on quarterly operating profit?

10–12

Product-Mix Decision; Single Constraint

LO4

Spreadsheet

Kohata Company produces two products (Juno and Hera) that use the same material input. Juno uses 2 kilograms of the material for every unit produced, and Hera uses 5 kilograms. Currently, Kohata has 16,000 kilograms of the material in inventory. All of the material is imported. For the coming year, Kohata plans to import an additional 8,000 kilograms to produce 2,000 units of Juno and 4,000 units of Hera. The unit contribution margin is $30 for Juno and $60 for Hera.

Kohata Company has received word that the source of the material has been shut down by embargo. Consequently, the company will not be able to import the 8,000 kilograms it planned to use in the coming year's production. There is no other source of the material.

Required:

1. Compute the total contribution margin that the company would earn if it could manufacture 2,000 units of Juno and 4,000 units of Hera.
2. Determine the optimal usage of the company's inventory of 16,000 kilograms of the material. Compute the total contribution margin for the product mix that you recommend.

10–13

**Appendix Required:
Product Mix; Multiple Constraints**

LO5, LO7

Zanbrow Company produces two products that use the same material input. Product A uses 2 kilograms of the material for every unit produced, and Product B uses 5 kilograms. Currently, Zanbrow has 6,000 kilograms of the material in inventory and will not be able to obtain more for the coming year. The maximum demand (sales) for A is estimated at 1,000 units, and for B it is estimated at 2,000 units. The detail of each product's unit contribution margin follows:

	Product A	Product B
Selling price	$81	$139
Less variable expenses:		
Direct materials	20	50
Direct labour	21	14
Variable overhead	10	15
Contribution margin	$30	$ 60

Assume that Product A uses 3 direct labour hours for every unit produced and that Product B uses 2 hours. A total of 6,000 direct labour hours is available for the coming year.

Required:

1. Formulate the linear programming problem faced by Zanbrow Company. To do so, you must derive mathematical expressions for the objective function and for the material and labour constraints.
2. Solve the linear programming problem using the graphical approach.
3. Compute the total contribution margin produced by the optimal mix developed in Requirement 2.

10–14

Machine Replacement

LO2, LO4

The Cord Company currently sells 25,000 units a year at a price of $90 per unit. These units are produced using a machine that was purchased five years ago at a cost of $600,000. It currently has a book value of $300,000; however, due to its specialized nature, it has a market value today of only $35,000. The machine—which is expected to last another five years, after which it will have no expected salvage value—gives rise to the following costs:

Direct materials (5 kilograms @ $1.50/kilogram)	$ 7.50
Direct labour (4 hours @ $15.00/hour)	60.00
Variable overhead (4 hours @ $1.20/hour)	4.80
Fixed overhead (4 hours @ $1.60/hour)*	6.40
Total cost per unit	$78.70

* Based on an annual activity of 100,000 direct labour hours.

The company expects the following changes for next year:

- The unit selling price will increase by 10 percent.
- Direct labour rates will increase by 15 percent.
- Sales are expected to increase to 26,000 units (within the capacity of present facilities) and remain at that level.

Management is currently considering the replacement of the firm's old machine with a new one that would cost $750,000. The new machine is expected to last five years, with a salvage value of $30,000 expected at that time (straight-line depreciation used). By using the new machine, management expects to cut variable direct labour hours to 3.5 hours per unit, but the company will have to hire an operator for the machine at $45,000 per year.

Required (ignore income taxes):

1. Determine whether or not the company should purchase the new machine.
2. How many units would the company have to sell to earn annual profits of $230,000 (before taxes) if it were to purchase the new machine? Ignore any gain or loss on the sale of the old machine. (CMA Canada adapted)

10–15

Special-Order Decision; Capacity Constraint

LO2, LO3, LO4

The Bruning Company has the following budgeted income statement for the month of May, 2001:

Sales (40,000 units)		$2,000,000
Cost of goods sold:		
Direct materials	$300,000	
Direct labour	400,000	
Variable overhead	200,000	
Fixed overhead	600,000	
Total cost of goods sold		1,500,000
Gross profit margin		500,000
Selling and administrative costs:		
Sales commissions (2% of sales)	$ 40,000	
Delivery costs	20,000	
Sales salaries	120,000	
Administrative salaries	100,000	
Office rental	70,000	
Total selling and administrative		350,000
Operating income		$ 150,000

The plant has a maximum capacity of 50,000 units; this capacity can be increased at a cost of $60,000 per increment of 2,000 units.

A company salesperson has brought an offer from a new customer to purchase the product at a price of $35 per unit. The customer will pick up the order at Bruning's factory.

Required:

1. Analyze the consequences for Bruning if it accepts the new order and:
   a. the customer wishes to purchase only 8,000 units.
   b. the customer wishes to purchase only 14,000 units.
2. What qualitative factors should the company consider in making this type of decision? (CMA Canada adapted)

10–16

Keep-or-Buy Decision; Identification of Relevant Costs and Benefits

LO2, LO3

Foster Company is currently using manufacturing machinery that some company officers believe is outdated. They are urging the president to acquire the latest computerized equipment, maintaining that output will increase and operating costs decrease. The company president has commissioned a report that compares costs and revenues of the existing equipment with that of the new equipment. The report is as follows:

	Old	New
Cost of acquisition	$280,000	$540,000
Accumulated depreciation[a]	$100,000	—
Annual operating cost	$63,000	$50,000
Annual maintenance	$8,500	$4,000
Salvage value[b]	—	—
Output	100,000 units	120,000 units
Output selling price	$100	$100

[a] Using the straight-line method. Expected life for both machines is six years.
[b] At the end of the six years. Currently, the old machinery does have market value, and if it is sold now, a six-year note will be paid off, saving the company annual payments of $16,500.

Required:

Identify all costs and benefits relevant to the decision to keep or buy. Ignore taxes.

10–17

Sell-or-Process-Further Decision

LO3

Lastivika Company produces two products from a joint process. Joint costs are $70,000 for one batch, which yields 1,000 litres of cavasol and 4,000 litres of perosol. Cavasol can be sold at the split-off point for $26 or can be processed further, into cavasette, at a manufacturing cost of $2,300 (for the 1,000 litres) and sold for $32 per litre.

If cavasette is sold, additional distribution costs of $0.90 per litre and sales commission of 10 percent of sales will be incurred. In addition, Lastivika's legal department is concerned about potential liability issues with cavasette—issues that do not arise with cavasol.

Required:

1. Considering only gross profit, should cavasol be sold at the split-off point or processed further?
2. Taking a value-chain approach (by considering distribution, marketing, and after-the-sale costs), determine whether or not cavasol should be processed into cavasette.

10–18

Product-Mix Decision with One Constrained Resource

LO4

O'Connor Company produces two models of machine housings that require the use of a special lathe. The six lathes owned by the firm provide a total of 12,000 hours per year. Model 14-D requires 4 hours of machine time, and Model 33-P requires 2 hours of machine time. Model 14-D has a contribution margin of $12 per unit, and Model 33-P has a contribution margin of $10.

Required:

1. Calculate the optimal number of units of each model that should be produced, assuming that an unlimited number of each model can be sold.
2. Calculate the optimal number of units of each model that should be produced, assuming that no more than 5,000 units of each model can be sold.

10–19

Appendix Required: Linear Programming Decision

LO7

Refer to Exercise 10–18. Assume that no more than 2,000 units of Model 14-D can be sold and that no more than 5,000 units of Model 33-P can be sold.

Required:

1. Formulate the linear programming problem faced by O'Connor Company. To do so, you must derive mathematical expressions for the objective function and for the lathe constraints.
2. Solve the linear programming problem using the graphical approach.
3. Compute the total contribution margin produced by the optimal mix developed in Requirement 2.

10–20

Cost-Based Pricing Decision

LO5

Jamil Khan, owner of Khan, Inc., is preparing a bid on a job that requires $1,200 of direct materials, $600 of direct labour, and $250 of overhead. Jamil normally applies a standard markup based on cost of goods sold to arrive at an initial bid price. He then adjusts the price as necessary in view of other factors (for example, competitive pressure). Last year's income statement is as follows:

Sales	$100,000
Cost of goods sold	45,000
Gross margin	$ 55,000
Selling and administrative expenses	24,500
Operating income	$ 30,500

Required:

1. Calculate the markup Jamil will use.
2. What is Jamil's initial bid price?

10–21

Product-Mix Decision; Single Constraint

LO4

Sealing Company manufactures three types of floppy disk storage units. Each of the three types requires the use of a special machine that has a total operating capacity of 15,000 hours per year. Information on the three types of storage units is as follows:

	Basic	Standard	Deluxe
Selling price	$9.00	$30.00	$35.00
Variable cost	$6.00	$20.00	$10.00
Machine hours required	0.10	0.50	0.75

Sealing Company's marketing director has assessed demand for the three types of storage units and believes that the firm can sell as many units as it can produce.

Required:

1. How many of each type of unit should be produced and sold to maximize the company's contribution margin? What is the total contribution margin for your selection?
2. Now suppose that Sealing Company believes that it can sell no more than 12,000 of the deluxe model but up to 50,000 each of the basic and standard models at the selling prices estimated. What product mix would you recommend, and what would be the total contribution margin?

10–22

Relevant Costs; Cash Flows

LO1, LO2

A company invested in Equipment A at a cost of $40,000. It was expected that operating expenses would decrease by $15,000 (from $100,000 to $85,000) annually for four years. Salvage value for Equipment A was estimated at zero throughout its useful life of four years. At the end of the second year, Equipment B became available on the market. To acquire it, the company had to make a further investment of $50,000. Equipment B was expected to decrease operating costs further from $85,000 to $50,000 per year annually for two years. Salvage value for Equipment B was also estimated at zero throughout its useful life of two years.

Required:

Ignore interest and income tax. Was the acquisition of Equipment A a good decision? Was the acquisition of Equipment B a good decision? Would the company have been better off not to acquire Equipment A? Explain.

10–23

Relevant Costs

LO1

Discuss the costs that would be relevant to decision making in each of the following independent situations:

1. in pricing a special one-time-only order, where the order would make use of idle capacity for a firm operating below its breakeven point.
2. in pricing a special one-time-only order, where the order would make use of capacity that would normally be required for regular production.
3. in pricing regular production orders for a company where production is fully automated and therefore has a very high proportion of fixed costs.
4. in making a decision on whether to produce or buy a component for the company's main product line. (CMA Canada adapted)

PROBLEMS

10–24

Comparison of Alternatives

LO2, LO3

Alice Knapp is the director of the Newkirk Drug Counselling Centre. She and her staff design programs to assist clients to become and stay drug-free. Most clients are referred to the centre through their probation officers. The centre is funded through a combination of provincial and federal grants. Alice anticipates that funding will last for another two to three years. After that, the Centre will in all probability cease to exist.

The centre has just been informed that it will lose the lease on its office in two months. Alice is considering three other sites. Information on the sites is as follows:

Site 1: This site is a 160-square-metre office in downtown Newkirk. Other lessees include a law firm, a bail bond agency, and two insurance agencies. Monthly rent is $475. The office has no interior walls, and permanent partitions cannot be installed. However, private meetings between caseworker and client are crucial. Therefore, Alice believes that she must rent movable partitions to surround each caseworker's desk for $85 per month.

Site 2: This site is a 200-square-metre office in a strip mall in a suburban area of Newkirk. It is close to caseworkers' homes but relatively farther from clients' homes. The monthly rent is $500. The office has been subdivided into three smaller offices. One would be suitable for the reception area, another would serve as Alice's office, and the third would accommodate the caseworkers. Permanent partitions could be installed in the caseworkers' office at a cost of $1,500.

Site 3: A former client's parents have heard about the Centre's need for space. They have offered to donate a house that they previously used as a rental home. This site is an older house in Newkirk that is located in a rapidly commercializing district. The house provides plenty of space and privacy for all caseworkers. However, the plumbing and electrical work are not up to standard and must be repaired before the Centre can move in. Additionally, city regulations on handicapped access must be followed, so ramps and handrails must be built. Alice has received estimates on the work needed and figures that the total cost will be $15,000.

Required:

1. Determine the relevant costs associated with each site. Does it matter whether the centre will exist for two or three years? Explain.
2. Write a memo to Alice summarizing the qualitative and quantitative aspects of each site.

10–25

Make-or-Buy Decision; Qualitative Considerations

LO1, LO2, LO3

Hetrick Dentistry Services operates in a large metropolitan area. Currently, Hetrick has its own dental laboratory to produce porcelain and gold crowns. The unit costs to produce the crowns are as follows:

	Porcelain	Gold
Raw materials	$ 70	$130
Direct labour	27	27
Variable overhead	8	8
Fixed overhead	22	22
Total	$127	$187

Fixed overhead is detailed as follows:

Salary (supervisor)	$26,000
Depreciation	5,000
Rent (lab facility)	32,000

Overhead is applied on the basis of direct labour hours. These rates were computed using 5,500 direct labour hours.

A local dental laboratory has offered to supply Hetrick with all the crowns it needs. Its price is $125 for porcelain crowns and $150 for gold crowns; however, the offer is conditional on supplying both types of crowns—it will not supply just one type for the price indicated. If the offer is accepted, the equipment used by Hetrick's laboratory will be scrapped (it is old and has no market value), and the lab facility will be closed. Hetrick uses 2,000 porcelain crowns and 600 gold crowns per year.

Required:

1. Should Hetrick continue to make its own crowns, or should they be purchased from the external supplier? What is the effect of purchasing (in dollars)?
2. What qualitative factors should Hetrick consider in making this decision?
3. Suppose that the lab facility is owned rather than rented and that the $32,000 is depreciation rather than rent. What effect does this have on the analysis in Requirement 1?
4. Refer to the original data. Assume that the volume of crowns used is 3,400 porcelain and 600 gold. Should Hetrick make or buy the crowns? Explain the outcome.

10–26

Sell-or-Process Further Decision

LO1, LO2, LO3

Zanda Drug Corporation buys three chemicals that are processed to produce two type of analgesics used as ingredients for popular over-the-counter drugs. The purchased chemicals are blended for two to three hours and then heated for fifteen minutes. The results of the process are two separate analgesics, depryl and pencol, which are sent to a drying room until their moisture content is reduced to 6 to 8 percent. For every 1,300 kilograms of chemicals used, 600 kilograms of depryl and 600 kilograms of pencol are produced. After drying, depryl and pencol are sold to companies that process them into their final form. The selling prices are $12 per kilogram for depryl and $30 per kilogram for pencol. The costs to produce 600 kilograms of each analgesic are as follows:

Chemicals	$8,500
Direct labour	6,735
Overhead	9,900

The analgesics are packaged in 20-kilogram bags and shipped. The cost of each bag is $1.30. Shipping costs are $0.10 per kilogram.

Zanda could process depryl further by grinding it into a fine powder and then moulding the powder into tablets. The tablets can be sold directly to retail drug stores as a generic brand. If this route were taken, the revenue received per bottle of tablets would be $4, with 10 bottles produced by every kilogram of depryl. The costs of grinding and tableting total $2.50 per kilogram of depryl. Bottles cost $0.40 each. Bottles are shipped in boxes that hold 25 at a shipping cost of $1.60 per box.

Required:

1. Should Zanda sell depryl at split-off, or should depryl be processed and sold as tablets?
2. If Zanda normally sells 265,000 kilograms of depryl per year, what will be the difference in profits if depryl is processed further?

10–27

Keep-or-Drop Decision

LO1, LO2, LO3

AudioMart is a retailer of radios, stereos, and televisions. The store carries two portable sound systems that have radios, tape players, and speakers. System A, of slightly higher quality than System B, costs $20 more. With rare exceptions, the store also sells a headset when a system is sold. The headset can be used with either system. Variable-costing income statements for the three products follow:

	System A	System B	Headset
Sales	$45,000	$ 32,500	$8,000
Less: Variable expenses	20,000	25,500	3,200
Contribution margin	$25,000	$ 7,000	$4,800
Less: Fixed costs*	10,000	18,000	2,700
Operating income	$15,000	$(11,000)	$2,100

* This includes common fixed costs totalling $18,000, allocated to each product in proportion to its revenues.

The owner of the store is concerned about the profit performance of System B and is considering dropping it. If the product is dropped, sales of System A will increase by 30 percent and sales of headsets will drop by 25 percent.

Required:

1. Prepare segmented income statements for the three products using a better format.
2. Prepare segmented income statements for System A and the headsets assuming that System B is dropped. Should B be dropped?
3. Suppose that a third system, System C, with a similar quality to System B, could be acquired. Assume that with C, the sales of A would remain unchanged; however, C would produce only 80 percent of the revenues of B, and sales of the headsets would drop by 10 percent. The contribution margin ratio of C is 50 percent, and its direct fixed costs would be identical to those of B. Should System B be dropped and replaced with System C?

10–28

Dropping a Product

LO2, LO4

The president of Hoboe Company Ltd. has been presented with the following summary of the three products Hoboe manufactures:

	Product A	Product B	Product C	Total
Sales	$15,750	$12,500	$22,500	$50,750
Cost of goods sold	17,460	6,225	10,450	34,135
Gross profit	$1,710	$6,275	$12,050	$16,615
Selling and administrative	5,090	3,125	4,050	12,265
Net income	$ (6,800)	$ 3,150	$ 8,000	$ 4,350
Sales price per unit	$3.50	$5.00	$7.50	
Variable cost of goods sold per unit	3.25	1.25	1.50	
Variable selling and administrative				
expense per unit	0.35	0.20	0.30	

The president is thinking of discontinuing the production and sale of Product A.

Required:

1. Advise the president whether Product A should be discontinued. Show appropriate calculations to support your recommendation.
2. If Product A is discontinued, Hoboe's sales department predicts that the sales of Product C will decrease. At what point would your recommendation in Requirement 1 change? Explain. (CGA Canada adapted)

10–29

Accept or Reject a Special Order

LO2, LO3

Merv Murningham, manager of an electronics division, is considering an offer by Jaya Sellers, manager of a sister division. Jaya's division is operating below capacity and has just been given an opportunity to produce 8,000 units of one of its products for a customer in a market not normally served. The opportunity involves a product that uses an electrical component produced by Merv's division. Each unit that Jaya's department produces requires two of the components. However, the price that the customer is willing to pay is well below the price usually charged; to make a reasonable profit on the order, Jaya needs a price concession from Merv's division. Jaya has offered to pay full manufacturing cost for the parts. So that Merv will know that everything is aboveboard, Jaya has supplied the following unit-cost and price information concerning the special order, excluding the cost of the electrical component:

Selling price	$32
Less costs:	
Direct materials	17
Direct labour	7
Variable overhead	2
Fixed overhead	3
Operating profit	$ 3

The normal selling price of the electrical component is $2.30 per unit. Its full manufacturing cost is $1.85 ($1.05 variable and $0.80 fixed). Jaya has argued that paying $2.30 per component would wipe out the operating profit and result in her division's showing a loss. Merv is interested in the offer because his division is also operating below capacity (the order would not use all the excess capacity).

Required:

1. Should Merv accept the order at a selling price of $1.85 per unit? By how much will his division's profits be changed if the order is accepted? By how much will the profits of Jaya's division change if Merv agrees to supply the part at full cost?
2. Suppose that Merv offers to supply the component at $2. In offering the price, Merv says that it is a firm offer not subject to negotiation. Should Jaya accept this price and produce the special order? If Jaya accepts the price, what is the change in profits for Merv's division?
3. Assume that Merv's division is operating at full capacity and that Merv refuses to supply the part for less than the full price. Should Jaya still accept the special order? Explain.

10–30

Special Order
LO2, LO4

Small Bear Ltd. has its operations in Vancouver manufacturing teddy bears. Small Bear currently produces 45,000 teddy bears a year but has the capacity to produce 50,000. Small Bear has received a special order from a retailer in Seattle for 8,000 teddy bears that will be sold in Seattle.

Small Bear's 1998 income statement is as follows:

Sales (45,000 teddy bears)		$900,000
Cost of goods sold:		
Direct materials	$270,000	
Direct labour	225,000	
Manufacturing overhead	210,000	705,000
Gross profit		$195,000
Selling expenses	$125,000	
Administrative expenses	20,000	145,000
Net income		$ 50,000

Small Bear's variable manufacturing overhead is $3 per bear, and its variable selling expense is $2 per bear. The administrative expense is fixed and will increase by $1,000 if the special order is accepted. There will be no variable selling expense associated with the special order, and the variable manufacturing overhead per bear will remain constant.

Small Bear's direct labour cost per bear for the special order will increase by 5 percent, while its direct materials cost per bear for the special order will increase 10 percent. Fixed manufacturing overhead and fixed selling expenses will not change.

Required:

If the Seattle retailer has offered to pay $18 per bear for the special order, should Small Bear accept the order? Show all calculations. Note: All funds are in Canadian dollars. (CGA Canada adapted)

10–31

Pricing of Special Orders

LO2, LO4

Altaco Ltd. manufactures one product in its Edmonton factory. The firm's general manager, Ellen Ismail, has just received a special request from a customer for 10,000 units of this product to be produced and delivered this month. The customer has suggested a selling price of $3 per unit. Ellen is unsure whether she should accept this offer. The company normally produces and sells 50,000 units per month, and capacity is at 70,000 units per month. The normal selling price is $4 per unit.

Ellen approached Oscar Giterman, the plant accountant, with the issue. Oscar was unable to provide a proper analysis at that time because he had a meeting to attend. However, after quickly reviewing his files, he provided the following schedule of cost information:

Level of Activity (units of production per month)	Average Unit Cost
40,000	$3.675
50,000	3.500
60,000	3.383
70,000	3.400

As he rushed off for his meeting, Oscar indicated that if production exceeds 62,000 units per month, an additional supervisor must be hired and costs will increase by $7,700 per month.

Required:

Note: All requirements are independent situations. Expected activity levels do not include the 10,000 units in the special order that Ellen is considering.

1. Assume that Altaco already expects to be working at a level of 50,000 units for the month. Calculate the minimum price that the company could charge for this special order without reducing its expected net income.
2. If the company expects to produce and sell 55,000 units this month, calculate the minimum price that the company could charge the customer for this special-order job without reducing its expected net income.
3. Assume that the company expects to produce and sell 65,000 units this month. Should Ellen accept the customer's order? Support your decision with appropriate calculations. (CMA Canada adapted)

10–32

Special Order

LO2, LO4

Home Security, Inc., manufactures cabinets in a separate plant for its home security systems and for sale to outsiders. Management expects that during the third quarter of 2001—the three months ending September 30—the cabinet facility will be operating at 80 percent of normal capacity. Because management desires a higher utilization of capacity, it would consider accepting a special order. Data for Home Security cabinets now being manufactured are as follows:

Regular selling price to outsiders	$18.00
Cost per unit:	
Raw materials	$ 5.00
Direct labour—1/2 hour at $12	6.00
Overhead—1/4 machine hour at $8	2.00
Total costs	$13.00

Home Security has received special-order inquiries from two companies, as follows:

a. First Alarm Ltd. would like to order a cabinet similar to that of Home Security. The First Alarm cabinet requirement is for 25,000 to be shipped by October 1,

2001, for a price of $12 each. The cost data for this order would be similar to that for the Home Security cabinets, with one exception. According to the specifications provided by First Alarm, the special cabinet requires raw materials that will cost only $4.50 per cabinet. Management estimates that the remaining costs, labour time and machine time, will be the same as for the Home Security cabinet.

b.   Bar-the-Door, Inc., has submitted another special order to Home Security for 8,000 cabinets at $15 per cabinet. These too would have to be shipped by October 1, 2001. However, the Bar-the-Door cabinet is different from any cabinet in the Home Security line. The estimated unit costs of this cabinet are as follows:

Raw materials	$ 6.50
Direct labour—1/2 hour at $12.00	6.00
Overhead—1/2 hour at $8.00	4.00
Total costs	$16.50

In addition, Home Security will incur $3,600 in additional setup costs and will have to purchase a special device costing $5,200 to manufacture these cabinets; this device would be discarded once the special order is completed.

Home Security's manufacturing capabilities are limited to the total machine hours available. The maximum plant capacity available under normal operating conditions is 87,000 machine hours per year or 7,250 machine hours per month. Home Security has firm orders for 80 percent of the available capacity. The budgeted fixed overhead for 2001 amounts to $417,600. All manufacturing overhead costs are applied to production at the predetermined rate of $8 per hour based on plant capacity.

Home Security will have the entire third quarter—July 1, 2001, to September 30, 2001—to work on the special orders. It is not expected that any repeat business will be generated from either special order. It is Home Security's policy not to subcontract any portion of an order when special orders are not expected to generate repeat sales.

Required:

Should Home Security accept either special order? Justify your answe, and show your calculations. (CMA Canada adapted)

10–33

Pricing of a Special Order

LO2, LO3

The General Rubber Tire Company Ltd. has been approached by a volume buyer with an offer to purchase 50,000 tires at $43 per tire. Delivery must be made within 30 days and variable selling costs will be $2 per tire. The productive capacity of General Rubber is 320,000 tires per month, and 10,000 tires are currently on hand. At the regular price, sales of 300,000 tires are expected for this month. The sales manager believes that 40 percent of sales lost during this month could be recovered later in the year.

Unit price and cost data of regular tires are as follows:

Selling price	$66.00
Product costs	45.00
Gross margin	$21.00
Selling and administration	15.00
Profit per unit	$ 6.00

A recent analysis has shown that regular sales have a variable selling cost of $12 per unit and that the contribution margin is $18 per unit.

Required:

1. Determine whether General Rubber Tire should accept or reject the special order. (Support your answer with an appropriate analysis.)
2. What price could General Rubber Tire charge if the order is sold for zero profits?
3. What other factor should be considered before accepting the order?
4. Assume that the company has 500 defective tires on hand that could be sold as scrap for $2 each. The company has decided instead to retread these tires at a cost of $6 each and then attempt to sell them as "seconds." What is the lowest

price that General Rubber Tire should accept for the retread tires? Explain your answer. (CMA Canada adapted)

10–34

Special Order; Product Deletion

LO1, LO2, LO4

Anji Shah, the president of Whole Company, which manufactures and sells several products, is asking your advice on two issues related to Product A: the first deals with two special orders, and the second deals with dropping the product. Anji has provided you with the following typical annual income statement, and supplementary information:

Annual Income Statement

	Whole Company	Product A Total	Product A Per Unit
Sales	$10,000,000	$1,000,000	$ 50
Cost of goods sold	5,500,000	780,000	39
Gross margin	$ 4,500,000	$ 220,000	$ 11
Selling and administrative expenses	3,800,000	380,000	19
Income (loss) before income tax	$700,000	$ (160,000)	$ (8)
Income tax (30%)	210,000		
Income (loss)	$ 490,000		

Anji has provided supplementary information:

a. Included in Whole Company's income statement above are the results of several products, including Product A. Product A is manufactured in Division A. Currently, Product A sells for $50 per unit.

b. At the current volume of production, the average fixed manufacturing overhead cost is $15 per unit of Product A ($300,000 in total), all of which is incurred in Division A. The average fixed selling and administrative expenses are $10 per unit of Product A ($200,000 in total), $4 of which is incurred in Division A and $6 of which represents an allocation of Whole Company's overhead.

c. There are no work-in-process or finished goods inventories for Product A.

d. Current production capacity for Product A is 30,000 units per year.

The Situation: A special order is received from an organization in Poland for 12,000 units of Product A, at a special price of $38 per unit. The customer in Poland has two conditions: the entire order has to be filled, and the price cannot be higher than $38 per unit. Another special order is received from a customer in Iowa for 5,000 units of Product A at a price of $40 per unit. Regular sales are not expected to be affected by sales to either Iowa or Poland, and are affected only by the decisions that management makes regarding the issues raised by Anji.

Anji exclaims: "At a selling price of $50 per unit, we are losing $160,000 on Product A. Instead of expanding our sales of A at reduced selling prices, which would aggravate the profit picture, we should drop Product A altogether. Am I right in reaching this conclusion?"

Required:

1. Should any or both of the special offers from Poland and Iowa be accepted? Show your calculations. What would Whole Company's after-tax income (loss) be if your recommendation were implemented and no other changes occurred?

2. Refer back to the original data, and ignore the special offers from Poland and Iowa. Should Product A be dropped? If Product A is dropped, it is expected that only 70 percent of the fixed manufacturing, and fixed selling and administrative expenses, that are incurred in Division A can be eliminated. Show your calculations. What would Whole Company's new before-tax income (loss) be if Product A is dropped and no other changes occurred?

3. Based on your analysis in Requirements 1 and 2 above, comment on Anji's remarks as quoted in the last paragraph in the case.

10–35

Keep or Drop a Division

LO2, LO4

Ira Shumard, president and general manager of Danbury Company, is concerned about the future of one of the company's largest divisions. The division's most recent quarterly income statement is as follows:

Sales	$3,751,500
Less: Cost of goods sold	2,722,400
Gross profit	$1,029,100
Less: Selling and administrative	1,100,000
Net profit (loss)	$ (70,900)

Ira is giving serious consideration to shutting down the division, since this is the ninth consecutive quarter that it has shown a loss. To help him in his decision, the following additional information has been gathered:

a. The division produces one product at a selling price of $100 to outside parties.
b. The division sells 50 percent of its output to another division within the company for $83 (full manufacturing cost plus 25 percent). The internal price is set by company policy. If the division were shut down, the user division would buy the part externally for $100 per unit.
c. The fixed overhead assigned per unit is $20.
d. There is no alternative use for the facilities if shut down. The facilities and equipment would be sold and the proceeds invested to produce an annuity of $100,000 per year.
e. Of the fixed selling and administrative expenses, 30 percent represent allocated expenses from corporate headquarters.
f. Variable selling expenses are $5 per unit sold for units sold externally. These expenses are avoided for internal sales. There are no variable administrative expenses.

Required:

1. Prepare an income statement that more accurately reflects the division's profit performance.
2. Should Ira shut down the division? What would be the effect on the company's profits if the division were closed?

10–36

Plant Shutdown or Continue to Operate; Qualitative Considerations

LO2, LO3, LO4

GianAuto Corporation manufactures automobiles, vans, and trucks. Among the various GianAuto plants around Canada and the United States is the Denver cover plant, where vinyl covers and upholstery fabric are sewn. These are used to cover interior seating and other surfaces of GianAuto products.

Oriana Vosilo is the plant manager for the Denver cover plant. The plant was the first GianAuto plant in the region. As other area plants were opened, Oriana, in recognition of her management ability, was given the responsibility of managing them. Oriana functions as a regional manager, although the budget for her and her staff is charged to the Denver plant.

Oriana has just received a report indicating that GianAuto could purchase the entire annual output of the Denver cover plant from outside suppliers for $30 million. Oriana was astonished at the low outside price, because the budget for the Denver plant's operating costs was set at $52 million. Oriana believes that the Denver plant will have to close down operations in order to realize the $22 million in annual cost savings.

The budget (in thousands) for the Denver plant's operating costs for the coming year follows:

Materials		$12,000
Labour:		
Direct	$13,000	
Supervision	3,000	
Indirect plant	4,000	20,000

Overhead:

Depreciation—Equipment	$ 5,000	
Depreciation—Building	3,000	
Pension expense	4,000	
Plant manager and staff	2,000	
Corporate allocation	6,000	20,000
Total budgeted costs		$52,000

Additional facts regarding the plant's operations are as follows:

a.   Due to the Denver plant's commitment to using high-quality fabrics in all its products, the purchasing department was instructed to place blanket orders with major suppliers to ensure the receipt of sufficient materials for the coming year. If these orders were cancelled as a consequence of the plant closing, termination charges would amount to 15 percent of the cost of direct materials.

b.   Approximately 700 plant employees will lose their jobs if the plant is closed. This includes all direct labourers and supervisors as well as the plumbers, electricians, and other skilled workers classified as indirect plant workers. Some would be able to find new jobs, but many others would have difficulty. All employees would have difficulty matching the Denver plant's base pay of $9.40 per hour, the highest in the area. A clause in the Denver plant's contract with the union may help some employees: the company must provide employment assistance to its former employees for 12 months after a plant closing. The estimated cost of administering this service would be $1 million for the year.

c.   Some employees would probably elect to take early retirement, because the Denver plant has an excellent pension plan. In fact, $3 million of next year's pension expense would continue whether the Denver plant is open or not.

d.   Oriana and her staff would not be affected by the closing of the Denver plant. They would still be responsible for administering three other area plants.

e.   The Denver cover plant considers equipment depreciation to be a variable cost and uses the units-of-production method to depreciate its equipment; the Denver plant is the only GianAuto plant to use this depreciation method. However, the Denver plant uses the customary straight-line method to depreciate its building.

Required:

1.   Prepare a quantitative analysis to help in deciding whether or not to close the Denver cover plant. Explain how you treated the nonrecurring relevant costs.

2.   Consider the analysis in Requirement 1 and add to it the qualitative factors that you believe are important to the decision. What is your decision? Would you close the plant? Explain. (US CMA adapted)

10–37

Equipment Purchase; Drop Product

LO1, LO2, LO4

Triangle Ltd. manufactures and sells three different products: Isosceles, Equilateral, and Scalene. Projected income statements by production line for the next year are presented below:

	Isosceles	Equilateral	Scalene	Total
Unit sales	10,000	500,000	125,000	635,000
Revenue	$925,000	$1,000,000	$575,000	$2,500,000
Variable cost of units sold	(285,000)	(350,000)	(150,000)	(785,000)
Fixed cost of units sold	(304,200)	(289,000)	(166,800)	(760,000)
Gross margin	$335,800	$ 361,000	$258,200	$ 955,000
Variable general and administrative expenses	(270,000)	(200,000)	(80,000)	(550,000)
Fixed general and administrative expenses	(125,800)	(136,000)	(78,200)	(340,000)
Net income (loss) before income taxes	$ (60,000)	$ 25,000	$100,000	$ 65,000

The fixed general and administrative expenses are allocated to products in proportion to revenues. The fixed cost of units sold is allocated to products by various allocation bases, such as square metres for factory rent, machine hours for repairs, and so on.

Triangle's management is concerned about the loss for the Isosceles product and is considering two alternative courses of corrective action:

Alternative A. The company would purchase some new machinery for the production of Isosceles. This new machinery would involve an immediate cash outlay of $650,000. Management expects that the new machinery would reduce variable production costs so that the total variable costs (production, and general and administrative) for Isosceles would be 52 percent of Isosceles revenues. The new machinery would increase the total fixed costs and expenses (production, and general and administrative) allocated to Isosceles to $480,000 per year. There would be no additional fixed costs and expenses allocated to the Equilateral and Scalene products.

Alternative B. The company would discontinue the manufacture of Isosceles. Selling prices for Equilateral and Scalene would remain constant. Management expects that Scalene's production and revenues would increase by 50 percent. Some of the production machinery devoted to Isosceles could be sold at scrap value, which would equal its removal cost. The removal of this machinery would reduce the fixed costs and expenses allocated to Isosceles by $30,000 per year. The remaining fixed costs and expenses allocated to Isosceles include $155,000 of rent expense per year. The space previously used for Isosceles can be rented to an outside organization for $157,500 per year.

Required:

1. Prepare a schedule analyzing the effects of Alternative A and Alternative B on projected net income before income taxes.
2. Assume that the immediate cash outlay for the new machine in Alternative A is $700,000 and that all other data remain unchanged. What effect will this have on your analysis? Explain.
3. Explain the term *relevant costs*. How do historical (sunk) costs pertain to decision making when using the relevant cost approach? (CMA Canada adapted)

10–38

Appendix Required: Product-Mix Decision; Single and Multiple Constraints; Basics of Linear Programming

LO4, LO7

Paper Products, Inc., produces table napkins and facial tissues. The manufacturing process is highly mechanized; both products are produced by the same machinery by using different settings. For the coming period, 200,000 machine hours are available. Management is trying to decide on the quantities of each product to produce. The following data are available (for napkins, one unit is one package of napkins; for facial tissue, one unit is one box of tissue):

	Napkins	Tissue
Machine hours per unit	1.00	0.50
Unit selling price	$2.50	$3.00
Unit variable cost	$1.50	$2.25

Required:

1. Determine the units of each product that should be produced in order to maximize profits.
2. Because of market conditions, the company can sell no more than 150,000 packages of napkins and 300,000 boxes of tissue. Do the following:
   a. Formulate the problem as a linear programming problem.
   b. Determine the optimal product mix using a graph.
   c. Compute the maximum profit given the optimal product mix.

10–39

Keep or Drop; Product Mix

LO2, LO4

Olat Corporation produces three gauges. These gauges measure density, permeability, and thickness and are known as *D-gauges*, *P-gauges*, and *T-gauges*, respectively. For many years, Olat has been profitable and has operated at capacity (which is 82,000 direct labour hours). In the last two years, however, prices on all gauges were reduced and selling expenses increased to meet competition and keep the plant operating at full capacity. Third-quarter results (in thousands), as shown below, are representative of recent experience.

	D-gauge	P-gauge	T-gauge	Total
Sales	$900	$1,600	$900	$3,400
Less: Cost of goods sold	770	1,048	950	2,768
Gross profit	$130	$ 552	$ 50	$ 632
Less: Selling and administrative	185	370	135	690
Net income (loss)	$ 55	$ 182	$185	$ 58

Mel Carlo, Olat's president, is concerned about the results of the firm's pricing, selling, and production policies. After reviewing the third-quarter results, he asked his management staff to consider the following three-point course of action:

a. Discontinue production of the T-gauge. T-gauges would not be returned to the line of products unless the problems with the gauge can be identified and resolved.

b. Increase quarterly sales promotion by $100,000 on the P-gauge to increase sales volume by 25 percent.

c. To accommodate the increased demand for P-gauges, cut production of the D-gauge by 50 percent and reduce traceable advertising and promotion costs for this line by $20,000 each quarter.

Kirk Spears, Olat's controller, suggested that a more careful study of the financial relationships be made to determine the possible effects on the company's operating results as a consequence of these proposed actions. Mel agreed, and JoAnn Brower, the firm's assistant controller, was given the assignment. She gathered the following information:

a. All three gauges are manufactured with common equipment and facilities.

b. The quarterly general selling and administrative expenses are allocated to the three product lines in proportion to their dollar sales volumes.

c. Special selling expenses (advertising and shipping) are incurred on each gauge as follows:

	Advertising[a]	Shipping[b]
D-gauge	$100,000	$ 4
P-gauge	210,000	10
T-gauge	40,000	10

[a] Per quarter
[b] Per unit

d. The unit manufacturing costs for the three products are as follows:

	D-gauge	P-gauge	T-gauge
Raw materials	$17	$ 31	$ 50
Direct labour*	20	40	60
Variable overhead	30	45	60
Fixed overhead	10	15	20
Total	$77	$131	$190

* The wage rate averages $10 per hour.

The unit sales prices for the three products are $90 for the D-gauge, $200 for the P-gauge, and $180 for the T-gauge.

The company is manufacturing at capacity and selling all that it produces.

Required:

1. Prepare a variable-costing segmented income statement for the three product lines. Make sure that you separate direct fixed expenses from common fixed expenses.
2. Should the T-gauge line be dropped as Mel suggests? Explain.
3. Evaluate Mel's remaining two suggestions (combined with his first). Was Mel correct in promoting the P-gauge rather than the D-gauge? Explain.
    (US CMA adapted)

10–40

Appendix: Product-Mix Decisions

LO7

Calen Company manufactures and sells three products in a factory with three departments. Both labour and machine time are applied to the products as they pass through each department. The nature of the machine processing and of the labour skills required in each department is such that neither machines nor labour can be switched from one department to another.

Calen's management is attempting to plan its production schedule for the next several months. The planning is complicated by the fact that labour shortages exist in the community and some machines will be down several months for repairs.

Following is information regarding available machine and labour time by department and the machine hours and direct labour hours required per unit of product. These data should be valid for at least the next six months.

	Department		
Monthly Capacity	**1**	**2**	**3**
Labour hours available	3,700	4,500	2,750
Machine hours available	3,000	3,100	2,700

Product	Input per Unit Produced			
401	Labour hours	2	3	3
	Machine hours	1	1	2
402	Labour hours	1	2	—
	Machine hours	1	1	—
403	Labour hours	2	2	2
	Machine hours	2	2	1

Sales believes that the monthly demand for the next six months will be as follows:

Product	Units Sold
401	500
402	400
403	1,000

Inventory levels will not be increased or decreased during the next six months. The unit cost and price data for each product are as follows:

	Product		
	401	**402**	**403**
Unit costs:			
Direct materials	$ 7	$ 13	$ 17
Direct labour	66	38	51
Variable overhead	27	20	25
Fixed overhead	15	10	32
Variable selling	3	2	4
Total unit cost	$118	$ 83	$129
Unit selling price	$196	$123	$167

Required:

1. Calculate the monthly requirement for machine hours and direct labour hours for producing Products 401, 402, and 403 to determine whether the factory can meet the monthly sales demand.
2. Determine the quantities of 401, 402, and 403 that should be produced monthly to maximize profits. Prepare a schedule that shows the contribution to profits of your product mix.
3. Assume that the machine hours available in Department 3 are 1,500 instead of 2,700. Calculate the optimal monthly product mix using the graphing approach to linear programming. Prepare a schedule that shows the contribution to profits from this optimal product mix. (US CMA adapted)

10–41

Appendix: Product-Mix Decision with Multiple Constraints

LO7

Hull Manufacturing Company produces two types of display boards: one is a marking board and the other is a tack board. Both boards pass through two manufacturing departments. All of the raw material—board bases, board coverings, and aluminum frames—are cut to size in the cutting department. Both types of boards are the same size and use the same frames. They are assembled in one of two departments—the automated assembly department or the labour assembly department.

The automated assembly department is a capital-intensive operation that has been in operation for 18 months and was intended to replace the labour assembly department. However, the business has expanded so rapidly that both assembly operations are needed and used. The final results of the two assembly operations are identical. The only difference between the two is the proportion of machine time versus direct labour in each department; thus, they have different costs. Workers have been trained for both operations so that they can be switched between the two operations.

Data regarding the two products and their manufacture are presented in the following schedules:

Sales Data

	Marking Board	Tack Board
Selling price per unit	$60	$45
Variable selling expenses per unit	3	3
Annual fixed selling and administrative expenses*	$900,000	$900,000

* Allocated equally between the two products.

Unit Variable Manufacturing Costs

	Cutting Department		Labour Assembly Department*	Automated Assembly Department*
	Marking Board	Tack Board		
Raw materials				
Base	$ 6.00	$6.00	$ —	$ —
Covering	14.50	7.75	—	—
Frame	8.25	8.25	—	—
Direct labour				
@ $10/DLH	2.00	2.00	—	—
@ $12/DLH	—	—	3.00	0.60
Manufacturing overhead				
Supplies	1.25	1.25	1.50	1.50
Power	1.20	1.20	0.75	1.80

* The unit costs for the marking board and the tack board are the same in each of the two assembly departments. (DLH = Direct Labour Hours.)

Machine-Hour Data

	Cutting Department	Labour Assembly Department	Automated Assembly Department
Machine hours required per board	0.15	0.02	0.05
Monthly machine hours available	25,000	1,500	5,000
Annual machine hours available	300,000	18,000	60,000

All production is to customer specification, made to order, and shipped as produced—that is, no inventory is maintained. Hull produced and sold 600,000 marking boards and 900,000 tack boards last year. Management estimates that total unit sales for the coming year could increase 20 percent if the units can be produced. It has contracts to produce and sell 30,000 units of each board each month. Sales, production, and costs are incurred uniformly throughout the year. There is a maximum labour capacity of 30,000 hours in the cutting department and a total of 40,000 hours in the two assembly departments.

Required:

1. Formulate the problem as a linear programming problem.
2. Can you determine the optimal product mix using a graph? If you can, what is the optimal product mix? If you cannot, explain why. (CGA Canada adapted)

10–42

Appendix: Product Mix with Multiple Constraints and Alternative Objectives

LO7

Toronto Frames Manufacturing makes three types of frames: adjustable, breakable, and collapsible. The frames sell for $25, $45, and $50, respectively. The firm's salesperson is paid $400 per month plus a sales commission of 10 percent of the selling price of the products sold. Each product requires processing on each of two machines. The cutting machine can be operated 8 hours per day for 25 days per month. The adjustable frame requires 2 hours of cutting, the breakable frame requires 3 hours, and the collapsible requires 6 hours. The finishing machine can be operated 8 hours a day for 25 days per month, but the company loses 25 percent of this time due to breakdowns. The adjustable frame uses 2 hours of finishing time, the breakable uses 4 hours, and the collapsible uses 2 hours. Final assembly is done by hand. Four units of adjustable frames can be assembled in an hour, while it takes 2 hours to put together a breakable frame, and 30 minutes to assemble a collapsible frame. All three frames require the same raw material. The adjustable frame needs 6 metres, the breakable frame requires 10 metres, and the collapsible frame needs 16 metres. Labour is paid $7 per hour, and raw material costs $1.50 per metre. The company has determined that overhead cost varies with direct labour according to the following cost equation: Manufacturing overhead = $100 + $3 per direct labour hour. Assume that any other manufacturing, selling, and administrative costs are fixed. Assume that the company has no inventories of work in process or finished goods.

Required:

1. Set up a linear programming model to determine the optimal product mix if management's goal is to maximize net income. Do not solve the model.
2. Set up a linear programming model to determine the optimal product mix if the salesperson's objective is to maximize her or his compensation. Do not solve the model.
3. Assume that Toronto Frames has limited labour available to operate the cutting and finishing machines and to do the final assembly. Three workers are available, and each worker is able to operate either machine and to do the final assembly. Each worker has 160 hours available per month but can work on only a single activity at a time. Set up a linear programming model to determine the optimal product mix if management's goal is to maximize net income. Do not solve the model. (CGA Canada adapted)

10–43

Appendix: Product Mix with Multiple Constraints

LO7

Among its many products, Phylex Corporation manufactures three types of electrical components, designated A, B, and C. From its records, it has determined that the three products use two types of materials (metal and plastic) that are purchased at the cost of $0.40 for one unit of metal and $0.50 for each unit of plastic. Because of contracts with its suppliers, Phylex can obtain up to 18,000 units of metal and 15,000 units of plastic per month at these prices. The three products require machining, inspection, and some final assembly. Available capacity for electrical component production includes 1,420 direct labour hours (at a cost of $15.60 per hour) and 168 machine hours per month (at a cost of $570 per machine hour). Supervisors undertake inspections on a sampling basis as part of their duties. Inspection time is not considered to be part of direct labour cost. All labour used in producing the electrical components is part of the permanent skilled labour force at Phylex, and therefore is considered a fixed cost.

An engineering study developed the following requirements for Products A, B, and C:

	A	B	C
Materials:			
Metal	3 units	6 units	8 units
Plastic	4 units	2 units	2 units
Direct labour	4 minutes	6 minutes	6.5 minutes
Machining	4 minutes	6 minutes	10 minutes

Under a recently negotiated contract, Phylex has agreed to supply 400 units per month of Product C for the next six months. The company's sales staff estimated that at a price of $62 per unit, 2,800 units of Product A could be sold; at a price of $84, 2,100 units of Product B could be sold; and at $120 (the same as the contract price), up to 300 units of Product C (excluding the contract sale) could be sold. Selling costs are 5 percent of the product selling price.

The production manager and the controller met to determine the most profitable sales and production mix for Phylex for the next six months. They decided to use linear programming.

Required:

Formulate the objective function and constraint functions for the linear program. Be sure to define your variables. Do not solve the linear program. (CGA Canada adapted)

10–44

Make-or-Buy Decision

LO2, LO4

Seung Company produces two products, A and B. The segmented income statement for a typical quarter is given below.

	Product A	Product B	Total
Sales	$150,000	$80,000	$230,000
Less: Variable expenses	80,000	46,000	126,000
Contribution margin	$ 70,000	$34,000	$104,000
Less: Direct fixed expenses*	20,000	38,000	58,000
Segment margin	$ 50,000	$ 4,000	$ 46,000
Less: Common fixed expenses			30,000
Net income			$ 16,000

* Includes depreciation.

Product A uses a subassembly that is purchased from an external supplier for $25 per unit. Each quarter, 2,000 subassemblies are purchased. All units produced are sold, and there are no ending inventories of subassemblies. Seung is considering making the subassembly rather than buying it. Unit variable manufacturing costs are as follows:

Direct materials $2
Direct labour   3
Variable overhead   2

Two alternatives exist to supply the productive capacity:

a. Lease the needed space and equipment at a cost of $27,000 per quarter for the space and $10,000 per quarter for a supervisor. There are no other fixed expenses.
b. Drop Product B. The equipment could be adapted with virtually no cost and the existing space utilized to produce the subassembly. The direct fixed expenses, including supervision, would be $38,000, $8,000 of which is depreciation on equipment. If Product B is dropped, there will be no effect on the sales of Product A.

Required:

1. Should Seung Company make or buy the subassembly? If it makes the subassembly, which alternative should be chosen? Explain and provide supporting computations.
2. Suppose that dropping Product B will decrease sales of Product A by 6 percent. What effect does this have on the decision?
3. Assume that dropping Product B decreases sales of Product A by 6 percent and that 2,800 subassemblies are required per quarter. As before, assume that there are no ending inventories of subassemblies and that all units produced are sold. Assume also that the per-unit sales price and variable costs are the same as in Requirement 1. Include the leasing alternative in your consideration. Now what is the correct decision?

10–45

Make-or-Buy Decision

LO2, LO3, LO4

Sportway, Inc., is a wholesale distributor supplying a wide range of moderately priced sporting equipment to large chain stores. About 60 percent of Sportway's products are purchased from other companies, while the remainder of the products are manufactured by Sportway. The company's plastics department is currently manufacturing moulded fishing tackle boxes. Sportway is able to manufacture and sell 8,000 tackle boxes annually, making full use of its direct labour capacity at available work stations. Presented below are the selling price and costs associated with Sportway's tackle boxes:

Selling price per box		$86.00
Costs per box:		
Moulded plastic	$ 8.00	
Hinges, latches, handle	9.00	
Direct labour ($15/hour)	18.75	
Manufacturing overhead	12.50	
Selling and administrative	17.00	65.25
Profit per box		$20.75

Because Sportway believes that it could sell 12,000 tackle boxes if it had sufficient manufacturing capacity, the company has looked into the possibility of purchasing the tackle boxes for distribution. Maple Products, a steady supplier of quality products, would be able to provide up to 9,000 tackle boxes per year at a price of $68 per box delivered to Sportway's facility.

Bart Orazem, Sportway's product manager, has suggested that the company could make better use of its plastics department by manufacturing skateboards. To support his position, Bart has a market study that indicates an expanding market for skateboards and a need for additional suppliers. Bart believes that Sportway could expect to sell 17,500 skateboards annually at a price of $45 per skateboard. His estimate of the costs to manufacture the skateboards is presented below:

Selling price per skateboard		$45.00
Costs per skateboard:		
Moulded plastic	$5.50	
Wheels, hardware	7.00	
Direct labour ($15/hour)	7.50	
Manufacturing overhead	5.00	
Selling and administrative	9.00	34.00
Profit per skateboard		$11.00

In the plastics department, Sportway uses direct labour hours as the application base for manufacturing overhead. Included in the manufacturing overhead for the current year is $50,000 of factorywide fixed manufacturing overhead that has been allocated to the plastics department. For each unit of product that Sportway sells, regardless of whether the product has been purchased or is manufactured by Sportway, an allocated $6 fixed cost per unit for distribution is included in the selling and administrative costs for all products. Total selling and administrative costs for the purchased tackle boxes would be $10 per unit.

Required:

1. In order to maximize the company's profitability, prepare an analysis based on the data presented that will show which product or products Sportway should manufacture and/or purchase and will also show the associated financial impact. Support your answer with appropriate calculations.

2. Discuss some qualitative factors that might have an impact on Sportway's decision. (US CMA adapted)

10–46

Make-or-Buy Decision
LO2, LO4

Sarbec Company needs a total of 125 tonnes of sheet steel (50 tonnes of 5-centimetre width and 75 tonnes of 10-centimetre width) for a customer's job. Sarbec can purchase the sheet steel in these widths directly from Jensteel Corporation, a steel manufacturer, or it can purchase sheet steel from Jensteel that is 60 centimetres wide and have it slit into the desired widths by Precut, Inc. Both vendors are local and have previously supplied materials to Sarbec.

Precut specializes in slitting sheet steel that is provided by a customer into any desired width. When negotiating a contract, Precut tells its customers that there is a scrap loss in the slitting operation but that this loss has never exceeded 2.5 percent of input tonnes. Precut recommends that if a customer has a specific tonnage requirement, it should supply an adequate amount of steel to yield the desired quantity. Precut's charges for steel slitting are based on good output, not input handled.

The 60-centimetre-wide sheet steel is one of Jensteel's regular stock items and can be shipped to Precut within 5 days after receipt of Sarbec's purchase order. If Jensteel is to do the slitting, shipment to Sarbec would be scheduled for 15 days after receipt of the order. Precut has quoted delivery at 10 days after receipt of the sheet steel. In prior dealings, Sarbec has found both Jensteel and Precut to be reliable vendors with high-quality products.

Sarbec has received the following price quotations from Jensteel and Precut:

JENSTEEL CORPORATION RATES

Size	Gauge	Quantity	Cost per Tonne
5 centimetres	14	50 tonnes	$210
10 centimetres	14	75 tonnes	200
60 centimetres	14	125 tonnes	180

PRECUT, INC., STEEL-SLITTING RATES

Size	Gauge	Quantity	Price per Tonne
5 centimetres	14	50 tonnes	$18
10 centimetres	14	75 tonnes	15

FREIGHT AND HANDLING CHARGES

Destination	Cost per Tonne
Jensteel to Sarbec	$10.00
Jensteel to Precut	5.00
Precut to Sarbec	7.50

In addition to the above information, Precut has informed Sarbec that if it purchases 100 output tonnes of each width, the per-tonne slitting rates would be reduced 12 percent. Sarbec knows that the same customer will be placing a new order in the near future for the same material and estimates that it would have to store the additional tonnage for an average of two months at a carrying cost of $1.50 per month for each tonne. There would be no change in Jensteel's prices for additional tonnes delivered to Precut.

Required:

1. Prepare an analysis that will show whether Sarbec Company should:
   a. Purchase the required slit steel directly from Jensteel Corporation.
   b. Purchase the 60-centimetre-wide sheet steel from Jensteel and have it slit by Precut, Inc., into 50 output tonnes 5 centimetres wide and 75 output tonnes 10 centimetres wide.
   c. Take advantage of Precut's reduced slitting rates by purchasing 100 output tonnes of each width.
2. Ignoring your answer to Requirement 1, present three qualitative reasons why Sarbec Company may favour the purchase of the slit steel directly from Jensteel Corporation. (US CMA adapted)

10–47

Make-or-Buy Decision

LO2, LO3, LO4

ABC Company is considering an offer to purchase Component XL, which it requires in the manufacture of most of its products. This component is currently being manufactured by Division Z of ABC Company. The potential supplier of this component is offering a price of $60 per unit for 20,000 units per year, which is the volume ABC requires. ABC's accounting department estimates the average cost of manufacturing this component at $80 per unit, based on the following cost figures for the year just ended:

Annual production of 20,000 units of XL	
Material A (20,000 kilograms)	$ 200,000
Material B (10,000 kilograms)	270,000
Direct labour	416,000
Variable manufacturing overhead	150,000
Division manager's salary	77,000
Depreciation	220,000
Allocated other manufacturing overhead	267,000
Total costs	$1,600,000

Additional information:

a. Direct materials information:
   Material A: 60,000 kilograms already exist in inventories, with a book value of $720,000. The replacement cost is expected to be $11 per kilogram. Its net realizable (resale) value is estimated to be $8 per kilogram.
   Material B: There are no inventories on hand. Replacement cost is estimated to be $28 per kilogram. Net realizable value is estimated to be $25 per kilogram.
b. No change is expected in direct labour or variable overhead rates over the next three years.

    c. If the component is purchased, Division Z will be closed. However, the manager of Division Z will be transferred at the same salary to head office in the organization's research and development unit. Head office is currently searching for someone of the same calibre as the manager of Division Z, but at a salary of about $50,000 per year.

    d. Equipment currently has a book value of $660,000, and three years of useful life remaining (zero salvage value at the end of three years). It has no alternative use if Division Z is closed. Currently, the equipment can be sold for about $300,000. Its replacement cost "new," however, is $1,900,000.

    e. The accounting department does not think that it is fair to allocate the other manufacturing overhead to other products if Component XL is purchased from the supplier, so it will continue to allocate $110,000 to the cost of the purchased components.

    f. For simplicity, assume that annual cash flows occur at the end of each year, while *lump-sum* cash flows occur at the beginning of the related year.

Required:

1. Ignore income taxes. Assuming a three-year planning horizon, calculate the relevant *pre-tax* cash flows that would result from purchasing XL from the supplier rather than continuing to manufacture it, identifying the *individual amounts* and their *timing*. Place your answers on a three-year time chart. Show your calculations.

2. Assume that income tax is based on accounting income and that the applicable income tax rate is 30 percent. The company as a whole is expected to be profitable regardless of the outcome of this make-or-buy decision. Calculate all the *after-tax* cash flows related to Material A and Material B, identifying for each amount whether it occurs in one lump sum (S) or annually (A).

3. What other factors should be considered in making this decision?

MANAGERIAL DECISION CASES

10–48

Make or Buy; Ethical Considerations

LO1, LO2, LO3

Valerie McDonald, CMA and controller for Murray Manufacturing, Inc., was having lunch with Quentin Branch, manager of the company's power department. Over the past six months, Valerie and Quentin had developed a romantic relationship and were making plans for marriage. To keep company gossip at a minimum, Valerie and Quentin had kept the relationship very quiet, and no one in the company was aware of it. The topic of the luncheon conversation centred on a decision concerning the company's power department that Pascal Dallaire, the company's president, was about to make.

Valerie: "Quentin, in our last executive meeting, we were told that a local utility company offered to supply power and quoted a price per kilowatt-hour that they said would hold for the next three years. They even offered to enter into a contractual agreement with us."

Quentin: "This is news to me. Is the bid price a threat to my area? Can they sell us power cheaper than we make it? And why wasn't I informed about this matter? I should have some input. This burns me. I think I should give Pascal a call this afternoon and lodge a strong complaint."

Valerie: "Calm down, Quentin. The last thing I want you to do is call Pascal. He made us all promise to keep this whole deal quiet until a decision has been made. He did not want you involved, because he wanted to make an unbiased decision. You know that the company is struggling somewhat, and it is looking for ways to save money."

Quentin: "Yeah, but at my expense? And at the expense of my department's workers? At my age, I doubt that I could find a job that pays as well and has the same benefits. How much of a threat is this offer?

Valerie: "Colin Lacy, my assistant controller, prepared an analysis while I was on vacation. It showed that internal production is cheaper than buying, but not by much. Pascal asked me to review the findings and submit a final recommendation for next Wednesday's meeting. I've reviewed Colin's analysis, and it's faulty. He overlooked the interactions between your department and other service departments. When these are considered, the analysis is overwhelmingly in favour of purchasing the power. The savings are about $300,000 per year."

Quentin: "If Pascal hears that, my department's gone. Valerie, you can't let this happen. I'm three years away from having a vested retirement. And my workers—they have home mortgages, kids in college, families to support. No, it's not right. Valerie, just tell him that your assistant's analysis is on target. He'll never know the difference."

Valerie: Quentin, what you're suggesting doesn't sound right either. Would it be ethical for me to fail to disclose this information?

Quentin: "Ethical? Do you think it's right to lay off employees who have been loyal, faithful workers simply to fatten the pockets of the owners of this company? The Murrays are already so rich that they don't know what to do with their money. I think that it's even more unethical to penalize me and my workers. Why should we have to bear the consequences of some bad marketing decisions? Anyway, the effects of those decisions are nearly gone, and the company should be back to normal within a year or so."

Valerie: "You may be right. Perhaps the well-being of you and your workers is more important than saving $300,000 for the Murrays."

Required:

1. Should Valerie have told Quentin about the impending decision concerning the power department? In revealing this information, did Valerie violate any of the ethical standards described in Chapter 1?
2. Should Valerie provide Pascal with the correct data concerning the power department? Or should she protect its workers? What would you do if you were Valerie?

10–49

Centralize versus Decentralize

LO1, LO2, LO3

Central University, a Saskatchewan university with approximately 13,000 students, is in the middle of a budget crisis. For the third consecutive year, government funding for higher education has remained essentially unchanged (the university is currently in its 1997–98 academic year). Yet utilities, employee benefits, insurance, and other operating expenses have increased. Moreover, the faculty are becoming restless, and some members have begun to leave for higher-paying opportunities elsewhere.

The president and the academic vice-president have announced their intention to eliminate some academic programs and to reduce others. The savings that result would be used to cover the increase in operating expenses and for raises for the remaining faculty. Needless to say, the possible dismissal of tenured faculty has aroused a great deal of concern throughout the university.

With this background, the president and academic vice-president called a meeting of all deans and department heads to discuss the budget for the coming year. As the budget was presented, the academic vice-president noted that Continuing Education, a separate, centralized unit, has accumulated a deficit of $504,000 over the past several years, which must be eliminated during the coming fiscal year. The vice-president noted that allocating the deficit equally among the seven faculties would create a hardship on some of the faculties, wiping out all of their operating budget except for salaries.

After some discussion of alternative ways to allocate the deficit, the head of the accounting department suggested an alternative solution: decentralize Continuing

Education, allowing each faculty to assume responsibility for its own continuing education programs. In this way, the overhead of a centralized continuing education unit could be avoided.

The academic vice-president responded that the suggestion would be considered, but it was received with little enthusiasm. The vice-president observed that Continuing Education was now generating more revenues than costs—and that the trend was favourable.

A week later, at a meeting of the Deans' Council, the vice-president reviewed the role of Continuing Education. He pointed out that only the dean of Continuing Education holds tenure. If Continuing Education were decentralized, her salary ($50,000) would continue; however, she would return to her academic department, and the university would save $20,000 of instructional wages, since fewer temporary faculty would be needed in her department. All other employees in the unit are classified as staff. Continuing Education has responsibility for all noncredit offerings. Additionally, it has nominal responsibility for credit courses offered in the evening on campus and for credit courses offered off-campus. However, all scheduling and staffing of these evening and off-campus courses is done by the heads of the academic departments. What courses are offered and who staffs them must be approved by the head of each department. According to the vice-president, one of the main contributions of the Continuing Education Department to the evening and off-campus programs is advertising. He estimates that $30,000 per year is being spent.

After reviewing this information, the vice-president made available the following information pertaining to the department's performance for the past several years (the 2000–2001 data were projections). He once again defended keeping a centralized department, emphasizing the favourable trend revealed by the accounting data. (All numbers are expressed in thousands.)

	1997–98	1998–99	1999–2000	2000–2001
Tuition revenues:				
Off-campus	$ 300	$ 400	$ 400	$ 410
Evening	—[a]	525	907	1,000
Noncredit	135	305	338	375
Total	$ 435	$ 1,230	$ 1,645	$ 1,785
Operating costs:				
Administration	$(132)	$ (160)	$ (112)	$ (112)
Off-campus:				
Direct[b]	(230)	(270)	(270)	(260)
Indirect	(350)	(410)	(525)	(440)
Evening	(—)[a]	(220)	(420)	(525)
Noncredit	(135)	(305)	(338)	(375)
Total	$(847)	$(1,365)	$(1,665)	$(1,712)
Income (loss)	$(412)	$ (135)	$ (20)	$ 73

[a] In 1997–98, the department had no responsibility for evening courses. Beginning in 1998, it was given the responsibility to pay for any costs of instruction incurred when temporary or adjunct faculty were hired to teach evening courses. Tuition revenues earned by evening courses also began to be assigned to the department at the same time.
[b] Instructional wages.

The dean of the Faculty of Management is unimpressed by the favourable trend identified by the academic vice-president. The dean maintains that decentralization would still be in the university's best interests. He argues that although decentralization would not fully solve the deficit, it would provide a sizable contribution each year to the operating budgets for each of the seven faculties.

The academic vice-president disagrees vehemently. He is convinced that Continuing Education is now earning its own way and will continue to produce additional resources for the university.

Required:

You have been asked by the president of Central University to assess which alternative, centralization or decentralization, is in the best interests that of the university. The president is willing to decentralize provided that significant savings can be produced and that the mission of the Continuing Education Department will still be carried out. Prepare a memo to the president that details your analysis and reasoning and recommends one of the two alternatives. Provide both qualitative and quantitative reasoning in the memo.

10–50

Sunsilver Mines Company:[14] Decision on Whether to Meet Striking Workers' Demands

LO1, LO2, LO3

"We do not believe that the union demands for unconstitutional surrender constitute collective bargaining. The union's position is not beneficial to the company, the ongoing prosperity of the community, or to the miners themselves. The company offer was $1.50 more than that approved by Valley Mine workers last year." These were Sunsilver Mines President Hal Brown's words in an address to the local stock and bond club. At the time of the speech, October 21, seven and a half months had passed since the beginning of the Sunsilver strike, a bitterly fought strike fraught with violence.

Strikes were not unfamiliar to Sunsilver Mines. Within the past 56 months, the union had struck a total of 20 months. The following conversation took place in corporate offices one week before the current strike began.

Director of Mining Operations: "We have offered the workers an immediate $1-per-hour raise. With the fall in silver prices, we cannot afford anything more. In fact, we cannot afford that amount! The union is griping about weekend work. We cannot afford to pay time-and-a-half on weekends."

Director of Finance: "The silver market has collapsed for the moment. Based on my supply–demand predictions for the world market over the next 10 years, our silver is more valuable underground than mined at the wages the union is demanding. The price of silver is projected to be $100 per ounce by 1985."

President: "I agree with what you both have said, but I have an additional point to add. Because of our legal agreements with other firms that have stakes in the Sunsilver unit area, the other firms are absorbing part of our losses. They lose profits that they would have made and pay standby fees during the strike."

Accountant: "It seems that we are speaking in generalities. We lost a lot of money during our last strike, and our position among firms in the region has been declining. We need a 25 percent return on our capital to hold our position. I believe we need to develop some projections to show what impact your ideas would actually have on the firm."

Percent Income Statement for Sunsilver Mining Co.

Sales	100%
Less direct labour	20%
Less other direct variable costs including:	
Smelting fees to ACLA	15%
Gross profit	65%
Less overhead and administrative expenses	20%
Profit before tax	45%
Tax (.48)	21.6%
Profit after tax	23.4%
Sunsilver profit share (.57)	13.34%

14. Mary Z. Soulier and Roderick Ustanik, "Sunsilver Mines," in *Management Accounting: A Decision Analysis*, 3rd ed. (New York: John Wiley & Sons, 1985). Copyright © 1985, John Wiley & Sons. Reprinted by permission of John Wiley & Sons.

Sales Breakdown:
Percentage of Total Sales Revenues
Attributed to Each Metal

Metal	Average Price During Survey Month	Percentage of Total Revenues
Silver	$15/ounce	98.7%
Copper	$1/pound	0.5%
Antimony	$1.50/pound	0.7%

Projected Silver Prices for 19—
Projections Made 1 Week Before the Strike

Month	Price	Month	Price
March	$11/ounce	August	$22/ounce
April	$12/ounce	September	$23/ounce
May	$13/ounce	October	$23/ounce
June	$16/ounce	November	$24/ounce
July	$20/ounce	December	$24/ounce

The meeting broke up shortly after this discussion. The accountant and financial manager were given one week to study the impact of the strike on the firm.

The Sunsilver Mines Company has been a major silver producer in the country for many years. The firm is diversified, owning both a chain-link fence company and an electronics company. Each of these operations is run as a profit centre and has little or no operating contact with the others. Controlling interest of the corporation has changed hands several times during the past seven years, but the operations managers at the Sunsilver mine have changed very little during that time.

In the Sunsilver unit area, where all of the firm's mining operations are carried out, two other mining firms have a 43 percent interest in the production. All direct costs and certain indirect costs are deducted from any gross income rising out of production and operations in the unit area. The remaining profit is divided among the firms in proportion to their ownership share. These firms pay standby costs of $2,000 per month for each 1 percent interest in the Sunsilver unit area during strikes.

The mining operation involves bringing ore to the surface from one of two shafts and running the ore through a concentrator. The concentrated ore, which contains silver, copper, and antimony, is processed through the firm's antimony plant. The firm has current capacity of 180,000 mined tons of ore per year. It is estimated that this capacity will be unchanged in the foreseeable future. After the antimony is removed from the concentrate, the remaining concentrate is shipped to Tacoma, Washington, where it is refined by the ACLA Company. The average yield per ton of ore extracted is:

Silver	18 ounces per ton
Copper	20 pounds per ton
Antimony	16 pounds per ton

Sunsilver employs 500 miners under the union contract. The cost information shown above was calculated by the accountant several months ago, when silver was priced at $15 per ounce and revenues were $3,900,000 per month. The firm's costs have not changed since this statement was made, and copper and antimony prices have not changed significantly over the period.

The miners are demanding $12 per hour and time-and-a-half for weekend work. The firm has offered the workers an increase from their current wage of $9 per hour to $10 per hour and has refused to pay a time-and-a-half weekend premium.

Required:

1. Prepare a report concerning the issues discussed at the managers' meeting.
2. Make a recommendation with respect to meeting the union's wage demands. (For simplicity, assume that the dollar sales of copper and antimony are so trivial that all sales are from silver only.)

10–51

Decision to Drop a Department; Estimation of Cash Flows

LO1, LO2, LO3

The Liquid Chemical Company (LCC)[15] sells a range of high-grade products that, because of their chemical properties, call for careful packing. The company has always made a feature of the special properties of the containers used. LCC had a special patented lining made from a material known as GHL, and the firm operated a department specially to maintain its containers in good condition and to make new ones to replace those that were past repair.

Mr. Walsh, LCC's general manager, had for some time suspected that the firm might save money and get equally good service by buying its containers outside. After careful inquiries, he approached Packages, Inc., a firm specializing in containing production, and obtained quotations from them. At the same time, he asked Mr. Dyer, the controller, to let him have an up-to-date statement of the cost of operating the containing department.

Within a few days, the quotation from Packages came in. Packages was prepared to supply all the new containers required—at that time running at the rate of 3,000 a year—for $300,000 per annum, the contract to run for a term of five years certain and thereafter to be renewable from year to year. If the number of containers required increased, the contract price would be increased proportionately. Additionally, and irrespective of whether the above contract was concluded or not, Packages undertook to carry out purely maintenance work on containers, short of replacement, for a sum of $87,500 per annum on the same contract terms.

Mr. Walsh compared these figures with the cost figures prepared by Mr. Dyer covering a year's operations of the container department, as follows:

Materials		$100,000
Labour		175,000
Departmental overheads:		
Manager's salary	$40,000	
Rent	7,500	
Depreciation of machinery	30,000	
Maintenance of machinery	6,750	
Other expenses	31,500	115,750
		390,750
Proportion of general administrative overhead		33,750
Total cost of department for year		$424,500

Walsh's conclusion was that no time should be lost in closing down the department, and in entering into the contracts offered by Packages. However, he felt bound to give the manager of the department, Mr. Duffy, an opportunity to question this conclusion before he acted on it. He therefore called him in and put the facts before him, at the same time making it clear that Duffy's own position was not in jeopardy, even if his department were closed down. There was another managerial position shortly becoming vacant to which he could be moved without loss of pay or prospects.

Mr. Duffy looked thoughtful and asked for time to think the matter over. The next morning he asked to speak to Mr. Walsh again, and said that he thought there were a number of considerations that ought to be borne in mind before his department was closed down.

"For instance," he said, "what will you do with the machinery? It cost $240,000 four years ago, but you'd be lucky if you got $40,000 for it now, even though it's good for another four years at least. And then there's the stock of GHL we bought a year ago. That cost us $187,500, and at the rate we're using it now, it'll last us another four years or so. We used up about a fifth of it last year. Dyer's figure of $100,000 for materials probably includes about $37,500 for GHL. But it'll be tricky stuff to handle

15. This case, here slightly adapted, was prepared by the late Professor David Solomons of the University of Pennsylvania and is reprinted by permission he had granted.

if we don't use it up. We bought it well—$750 a tonne we paid for it, and you couldn't buy it today for less than $900. But you wouldn't have more than $600 a tonne left if you sold it, after you'd covered all the handling expenses."

Walsh thought that Dyer ought to be present during this discussion. He called him in and put Duffy's points to him.

"I don't much like all this conjecture," Dyer said. "I think my figures are pretty conclusive. Besides, if we are going to have all this talk about 'what will happen if,' don't forget the problem of space we're faced with. We're paying $13,750 a year in rent for a warehouse a couple of miles away. If we closed Duffy's department, we'd have all the warehouse space we need without renting."

"That's a good point," said Walsh. "Though I must say, I'm a bit worried about the workers if we close the department. I don't think we can find room for any of them elsewhere in the firm. I could see whether Packages can take any of them. But some of them are getting on. There's Walters and Hines, for example. They've been with us since they left school 40 years ago. I'd feel bound to give them a small pension—$5,000 a year, say."

Duffy showed some relief at this. "But I still don't like Dyer's figures," he said. "What about this $33,750 for general administrative overhead? You surely don't expect to fire anyone in the general office if I'm closed down, do you?"

"Probably not," said Dyer, "but someone has to pay for these costs. We can't ignore them when we look at an individual department. If we did that with each department in turn, we'd finish up by convincing ourselves that general managers, accountants, typists, stationery, and the like don't have to be paid for. And they do, believe me."

"Well, I think we've thrashed this out pretty fully," said Walsh, "but I've been turning over in my mind the possibility of perhaps keeping on the maintenance work ourselves. What are your views on that, Duffy?"

"I don't know," said Duffy, "but it's worth looking into. We shouldn't need any machinery for that, and I could hand the supervision over to a foreperson. You'd save $10,000 a year there, say. You'd only need about a fifth of the workers, but you could keep on the oldest. You wouldn't save any space, so I suppose the rent would be the same. I shouldn't think the other expenses would be more than $13,000 a year."

"What about materials?" asked Walsh.

"We use about 10 percent of the total on maintenance," Duffy replied.

"Well, I've told Packages that I'd let them know my decision within a week," said Walsh. "I'll let you know what I decide to do before I write to them."

Required:

Assume a four-year horizon and no inflation.

1. What is the cheapest alternative among the four possible courses of action?
2. As Mr. Walsh, what action would you take? Explain.

RESEARCH ASSIGNMENTS

10–52

Research Assignment
LO1, LO2, LO5

"Dumping" is an accusation that is often made against foreign companies. Japanese automobile companies, for example, have been accused of this practice.

Required:

Go to the library and find out the following:

1. What is dumping?
2. Why do international trade agreements usually prohibit dumping? Do you agree that its prohibition is good for the domestic consumer? Explain.

3. Explain how the relevant-costing principles learned in this chapter relate to dumping.

4. Provide several examples of companies accused of dumping. See if you can determine the outcome of an accusation made against some company. Why do you suppose that international companies pursue dumping even though it's prohibited? What are the ethical implications?

10–53

Cybercase

LO1, LO3

After the acquisition of Canadian Airlines by Air Canada in 2000, Air Canada announced several new routes that neither airline had serviced before. Check Air Canada's web site (**www.aircanada.ca**) for recent examples of tactical decisions. Write a brief paper discussing the types of cost and revenue information that would go into making this sort of tactical decision.

CHAPTER 11
Capital Investment Decisions

Learning Objectives

After studying Chapter 11, you should be able to:

1. Explain what a capital investment decision is, and distinguish between independent and mutually exclusive capital investment projects.

2. Compute the payback period and accounting rate of return for a proposed investment and explain their roles in capital investment decisions.

3. Use net present value (NPV) analysis for capital investment decisions involving independent projects.

4. Use the internal rate of return (IRR) to assess the acceptability of independent projects.

5. Explain why NPV is better than IRR for capital investment decisions involving mutually exclusive projects.

6. Explain the role and value of postaudits.

7. Convert gross cash flows to after-tax cash flows.

8. Describe capital investment in the advanced manufacturing environment.

Scenario

TastyFood Corporation, a large food-store chain, is considering investing in an automated deposit processing system for all of its stores.[1] An investment of $2 million would provide the system for all 150 existing stores as well as for the 30 stores to be opened by the beginning of the following year. The president of TastyFood has assigned the responsibility of assessing the investment to a special capital acquisitions committee. The committee's first act was to design a pilot study to test such a system in seven stores for a nine-month period.

At the end of the nine months, Maryanne Weiss, chair of the capital acquisitions committee and vice-president of finance, scheduled a committee meeting to evaluate the outcome of the pilot study. Besides Maryanne, the committee included Sandor Tokaj, controller; Noah Kimball, vice-president of operations; and Paula Summers, area supervisor for the seven stores where the pilot study was conducted.

"As you recall," Maryanne remarked, "we met more than nine months ago and agreed to implement a pilot study before committing ourselves to an automated deposit system. Because of her close scrutiny of the project, Paula has agreed to give us a summary of the benefits observed in the pilot study."

"I'm extremely pleased with the results of the pilot study," Paula replied, "as I think you will be. To quantify the financial impact of this project, I have classified the benefits into four categories: immediate, near-term, indirect, and potential for future. Immediate benefits are those that are available in a store as soon as the equipment is operational. Near-term benefits are those that will be realized only after the local system is connected to the store computer. Indirect benefits are those that accrue from the project but are more difficult to quantify. Potential future benefits can result from the system's ability to interface directly with the accounting system. Here is a handout that describes some of the specific benefits found in each category."

SPECIFIC BENEFITS BY CATEGORY
Immediate Benefits:
Bank Charge Reduction. An automated deposit processing system reduces the charges for processing cheques, since it encodes the dollar amount on all cheques prior to depositing them.
Productivity Gains. Automation of the system reduces the amount of additional payroll required during the busy season.
Forms Cost Reduction. Automation of the system eliminates nearly 3 million documents used per year to process deposits manually.

Near-Term Benefits:
Reduction of Cash Shortages. Once the system is connected to the store computer, a cash variance analysis can be provided the next day. Currently, this analysis is performed manually at headquarters and is several weeks old by the time it arrives in the store. The ability to respond more quickly to cash shortages should reduce annual losses.

Indirect Benefits:
Greater Data Integrity. Reducing manual calculations will result in greater data integrity. This will decrease time spent on making corrections to incorrect deposit information.
Lower Training Costs. Since the system is simpler and has fewer forms, new cashiers and new store openings should require less training time.

Potential Future Benefits:
Interfacing Abilities. By processing data through the store computer to the host computer in headquarters, an interface program at the host can save time in both the sales audit and cash/banking calculations by eliminating manual entries and expediting bank reconciliations.

"After seeing these benefits, I'm convinced that automatic deposits are a good idea," observed Noah Kimball. "In fact, I wonder why we weren't smart enough to do this years ago. Since I'm also convinced that committees are notorious for wasting time and resources, I move that we attach Paula's handout to a recommendation to implement the automated system for the entire company. Then we can get back to more pressing matters."

"Wait a minute!" interjected Sandor. "While the description of the benefits of the automated system is impressive, we shouldn't be too hasty in our decisions. After all, we are talking about investing $2 million. We need to be certain that this is a sound investment."

"But that's the whole point, Sandor. The benefits make it clear that the investment is sound. Why waste any more time deliberating over an obvious conclusion? We could spend hours discussing a matter that is already clearly decided. What do you say, Maryanne? Can we vote on this matter and adjourn?"

"Well, Noah, we can—if you will first answer the following questions. How much will this investment increase the firm's profits? What effect will it have on our overall value? Will the investment earn at least the return required by company policy? How long will it take us to recover the investment through the savings alluded to in Paula's handout? Only when we know the answers to some of those questions can we accurately assess the investment's soundness. The pilot study provides us with the fundamental information we need to estimate the future cash savings associated with automation. Once we have these estimates, we can use some financial models to assess the merits of the proposed investment. Sandor, for our next meeting, please bring estimates of the cash flows over the life of the proposed system. I will come prepared to discuss some of the financial models that will help us assess the financial merits of the investment."

1. The facts of this case are based on an actual food-store chain; however, the name of the chain has been changed.

Questions to Think About
1. What role should qualitative factors play in capital investment decisions?
2. How do we measure the financial benefits of long-term investments?
3. Why are cash flows important for assessing an investment's financial merits?
4. What role do taxes play in assessing cash flows? What role does inflation play?
5. Should the cash flows of intangible factors be estimated?

TYPES OF CAPITAL INVESTMENT DECISIONS

Objective 1

Explain what a capital investment decision is, and distinguish between independent and mutually exclusive capital investment decisions.

Capital investment decisions are concerned with the process of planning, setting goals and priorities, arranging financing, and using certain criteria to select long-term assets. Capital investment decisions are similar to the decisions discussed in previous chapters, but with a major difference: a longer planning horizon (since capital investment decisions usually provide benefits over a number of years). Differential cash-flow analysis, which summarizes the decision's financial effects, has to take into account the time value of money. How cash flows can be used to evaluate the merits of a proposed capital investment project is the focus of this chapter. The financial models, some incorporating the time value of money, that Maryanne was planning to discuss in her next committee meeting are introduced and explained.

Because capital investment decisions place large amounts of resources at risk for long periods of time and simultaneously affect the firm's future development, they are among the most important decisions that managers make. Every organization has limited resources, which should be used to maintain or enhance its long-run profitability. Poor capital investment decisions can be disastrous. For example, if a company fails to invest in automated manufacturing when competitors do, it may suffer significant losses in market share because of being unable to compete on the basis of quality, cost, and delivery time. Competitors with more modern facilities may produce more output at lower cost and higher quality. Thus, making the right capital investment decision is absolutely essential for long-term survival.

The process of making capital investment decisions is often referred to as **capital budgeting.** Two types of capital budgeting projects will be considered: independent projects and mutually exclusive projects. **Independent projects** are projects that, if accepted or rejected, do not affect the cash flows of other projects. Suppose that the managers of the marketing and the research and development departments jointly propose the addition of a new product line that would require significant outlays for working capital and equipment. If no other new product lines are being considered and if the new product line is not complementary with existing product lines, the decision involving the new product line stands alone. Since it is independent of other proposals, the project can be evaluated on its own merits.

The second type of capital budgeting project requires a firm to choose among several alternatives that will provide the same basic service. Acceptance of one option precludes the acceptance of another. Thus, **mutually exclusive projects** are those projects that, if accepted, preclude the acceptance of all other competing projects. For example, TastyFood was considering replacing its existing manual deposit processing system with an automated system. Part of the company's deliberation would concern different types of automated systems. If three different automated systems were being considered, there are four alternatives in all—the current system plus the three potential new systems. Once one system is chosen, the other three are excluded; they are mutually exclusive.

Notice that one of the competing alternatives in the scenario is maintaining the status quo (the manual system). Of course, at times replacing the old system is mandatory and not discretionary if the firm wishes to remain in business (for example, equipment in the old system may be worn out). In such a situation, going out of business could be a viable alternative, especially if none of the new investment alternatives is profitable.

Capital investment decisions are often concerned with investments in long-term capital assets. With the exception of land, these assets depreciate over their lives, and the original investment is used up as the assets are employed. In general terms, a sound capital investment will earn back its original capital outlay over its life and will at the same time provide a reasonable return on the original investment. Thus, one task of a manager is to decide whether or not a capital investment will earn back its original outlay and provide a reasonable return. By making this assessment, a manager can decide on the acceptability of independent projects and compare competing projects on the basis of their economic merits.

But what is meant by "reasonable return"? It is generally agreed that any new project must cover the opportunity cost of the funds invested. For example, if a company takes money from a money market fund that is earning 6 percent and invests it in a new project, then the project must provide at least a 6 percent return (the return that could have been earned had the money been left in the money market account). Of course, in reality, funds for investment come from different sources—each representing a different opportunity cost. The return that must be earned is a blend of the opportunity costs of the different sources. Thus, if a company uses two sources of funds, one with an opportunity cost of 4 percent and the other with an opportunity cost of 6 percent, then the return that must be earned is somewhere between 4 percent and 6 percent, depending on the relative amounts used from each source. Furthermore, it is usually assumed that managers should select projects that promise to maximize the wealth of the firm's owners.

To make a capital investment decision, a manager must estimate the quantity and timing of cash flows, assess the risk of the investment, and consider the project's expected impact on the firm's profits. One of the most difficult tasks is estimating the cash flows. Projections must be made years into the future, and forecasting is far from a perfect science. Obviously, as the accuracy of cash-flow forecasts increases, the reliability of the decision improves.

In making projections, managers must identify and quantify the benefits associated with the proposed project(s). For example, an automated cash deposit system can produce the following benefits (relative to a manual system): reduced bank charges, productivity gains, reduced cost of forms, greater data integrity, lower training costs, and savings in time required for bank/cash reconciliations. The dollar amount of these benefits must be assessed.

Although forecasting future cash flows is a critical part of the capital investment decision process, we won't consider forecasting methods here. Consequently, cash flows are assumed to be known; our focus will be on making capital investment decisions *given* these cash flows.

Managers must set goals and priorities for capital investments and identify some basic criteria for the acceptance or rejection of proposed investments. In this chapter, we will study four basic methods to guide managers in accepting or rejecting potential investments. The methods include both nondiscounting and discounting decision approaches (two methods are discussed for each approach). The discounting models are applied to both independent and mutually exclusive capital investment decisions.

NONDISCOUNTING MODELS

Objective 2

Compute the payback period and accounting rate of return for a proposed investment, and explain their roles in capital investment decisions.

The basic capital investment decision models can be classified into two major categories: nondiscounting models and discounting models. Nondiscounting models ignore the time value of money,[2] whereas discounting models explicitly consider it. Although many accounting theorists disparage the nondiscounting models because they ignore the time value of money, many firms continue to use these models in making capital investment decisions. However, the use of discounting models has increased over the years, and few firms use only one model—indeed, many firms

2. The time value of money is the notion that a dollar now is worth more than a dollar one period from now. Basic concepts are discussed in Appendix 11A of this chapter.

seem to use both types of models.[3] This suggests that both approaches supply useful information to managers as they struggle to make a capital investment decision.

Payback Period

One nondiscounting model is the payback period. The **payback period** is the time required for a firm to recover its original investment. When a project's annual cash flows are expected to be the same each year, the following formula can be used to compute its payback period:

Payback period = Original investment/Annual cash inflow

For example, if the original investment is $80,000, and the firm expects the project to generate uniform annual cash flows of $40,000, the payback period is two years [$80,000/$40,000].

If, however, the cash flows are uneven, the payback period is computed by adding the annual cash flows until the original investment is recovered. If a fraction of a year is needed, we will assume that cash flows occur evenly within each year. For example, suppose that a car wash facility requires an investment of $100,000 and has a life of five years, with the following expected annual cash flows:

	Year 1	Year 2	Year 3	Year 4	Year 5
Cash flow	$30,000	$40,000	$50,000	$60,000	$70,000

The payback period for the project is 2.6 years, as shown in Exhibit 11–1. Notice that in Year 3, when only $30,000 is needed and $50,000 is available, the amount of time required to earn the $30,000 is found by dividing the amount needed by the annual cash flow.

Exhibit 11–1

Payback Analysis: Uneven Cash Flows

Year	Unrecovered Investment (beginning of year)	Annual Cash Flow
1	$100,000	$30,000
2	70,000	40,000
3	30,000*	50,000
4	—	60,000
5	—	70,000

* At the beginning of Year 3, $30,000 is needed to recover the investment. Since a net cash flow of $50,000 is expected, only 0.6 year ($30,000/$50,000) is needed to recover the $30,000. Thus, the payback is 2.6 years (2.0 + 0.6).

3. In the mid-1950s, Robichek and McDonald reported that only 9 percent of large firms used discounting models; by 1975, Petry reported that 66 percent of large firms were using these techniques. Also in 1975, Petty, Scott, and Bird surveyed Fortune 500 firms and found that 63.4 percent of the respondents used discounting models as their primary evaluation techniques, and that most of the remaining firms used them as secondary techniques. The same study also found that more than half of the firms used nondiscounting models as either a primary or a secondary evaluation technique. By 1988, Klammer, Koch, and Wilner reported that discounting models were used by over 80 percent of surveyed firms as their primary evaluation technique for expansion decisions. In a 1985 Canadian study, Blazouske, Carlin, and Kim reported that 65 percent of Financial Post firms they surveyed used a discounting model as their primary capital investment technique, while 28 percent used a nondiscounting model as their primary technique (53 percent used such a model as a secondary technique). For additional detail, see A. A. Robichek and J. G. McDonald, "Financial Planning in Transition, Long Range Planning Service," Report No. 269 (Menlo Park, Calif.: Stanford Research Institute, January 1966); G. H. Petry, "Effective Use of Capital Budgeting Tools," Business Horizons, Vol. 18, No. 5 (October 1975): 57–65; J. W. Petty, D. F. Scott, and M. M. Bird, "The Capital Budgeting Decision Process at Large Corporations," The Engineering Economist, Vol. 20, No. 3 (Spring 1975): 159–186; J. D. Blazouske, I. Carlin, and S. H. Kim, "Current Capital Budgeting Practices in Canada," CMA Magazine, Vol. 62, No. 2 (March 1988), 51–54; T. Klammer, B. Koch, and N. Wilner, "Capital Budgeting Practices—A Survey of Corporate Use," working paper, University of North Texas.

One way to use the payback period is to set a maximum payback period for all projects and to reject any project that exceeds this level. Why would a firm use the payback period in this way? Some analysts suggest that the payback period can be used as a rough measure of risk, with the notion that the longer it takes for a project to pay for itself, the riskier it is. Also, firms with riskier cash flows could require a shorter payback period for investment projects. Firms with liquidity problems may be more interested in projects with quick paybacks. Another critical concern is obsolescence. In some industries, the risk of obsolescence is high; firms within these industries would be interested in recovering funds rapidly.

Another reason, less beneficial to the firm, may also be at work. Many managers in a position to make capital investment decisions may choose investments with short payback periods out of self-interest. If a manager's performance is measured using such short-run criteria as annual net income, he or she may choose projects with quick paybacks to show improved net income as quickly as possible. For example, divisional managers are often responsible for making capital investment decisions and are evaluated on divisional profits. The tenure of divisional managers, however, is typically short—three to five years would be common. Consequently, such managers have an incentive to shy away from investments that promise healthy long-run returns but relatively meagre returns in the short run. These problems can be eliminated by appropriate capital budgeting policies and a budget review committee.

The payback period can be used to choose among competing alternatives. Under this approach, the investment with the shortest payback period is preferred over investments with longer payback periods. However, this use of the payback period is less defensible, because this measure suffers from two major deficiencies: (1) it ignores the investments' performance beyond the payback period, and (2) it ignores the time value of money.

These two significant deficiencies are easily illustrated. Assume that an engineering firm is considering two different types of CAD (computer-aided design) systems, CAD-A and CAD-B. Each system requires an initial outlay of $150,000, has a five-year life, and displays the following annual cash flows:

Investment	Year 1	Year 2	Year 3	Year 4	Year 5
CAD-A	$90,000	$ 60,000	$50,000	$50,000	$50,000
CAD-B	40,000	110,000	25,000	25,000	25,000

Both investments have payback periods of two years. Thus, for a manager who uses the payback period to choose among competing investments, the two investments would be equally desirable. In reality, however, CAD-A should be preferred over CAD-B, for two reasons. First, CAD-A provides a much larger dollar return for the years beyond the payback period ($150,000 versus $75,000). Second, CAD-A returns $90,000 in the first year, while CAD-B returns only $40,000. The extra $50,000 that CAD-A provides in the first year could be put to productive use, such as investing it in another project. It is better to have a dollar now than to have it a year from now, because the dollar on hand can be invested to provide a return one year from now.

In summary, the payback period provides managers with information that can be used:

1. to help control the risks associated with the uncertainty of future cash flows,
2. to help minimize an investment's impact on a firm's liquidity problems,
3. to help control the risk of obsolescence, and
4. to help control the investment's effect on performance measures.

However, the method suffers significant deficiencies: it ignores a project's total profitability and the time value of money. While computing the payback period may be useful to a manager, relying on it alone for a capital investment decision would be unwise.

Accounting Rate of Return

The accounting rate of return is a second, common, nondiscounting model. The **accounting rate of return** measures the return on a project in terms of income, rather than cash flow. The accounting rate of return is computed by the following formula:

Accounting rate of return = Average income/Original investment (or average investment)

Income is not equivalent to cash flows, because we use accounting accruals and deferrals in computing it. A project's average income is calculated by adding the net income for each year of the project and then dividing this total by the number of years. Average net income can be approximated by subtracting average amortization from average cash flow. The approximation is exact if we assume that all revenues earned in a period are collected and that amortization is the only noncash expense.

Investment can be defined as original investment or as average investment. Letting I equal original investment and S equal salvage value, and assuming that investment is uniformly consumed, we can define average investment as follows:[4]

$$\text{Average investment} = (I + S)/2$$

To illustrate how the accounting rate of return is computed, assume that an investment requires an initial outlay of $100,000. The life of the investment is five years, with the following cash flows:

	Year 1	Year 2	Year 3	Year 4	Year 5
Cash flow	$30,000	$30,000	$40,000	$30,000	$50,000

Assume that the asset has no salvage value after these five years and that all revenues earned within a year are collected in that year. Total cash flow for the five years is $180,000, making average cash flow $36,000 ($180,000/5). Average amortization is $20,000 ($100,000/5). Average net income is the difference between these two amounts: $16,000 ($36,000 − $20,000). Using average net income and original investment, we see that the accounting rate of return is 16 percent ($16,000/$100,000). If average investment is used instead of original investment, the accounting rate of return is 32 percent ($16,000/$50,000).

Debt contracts often require that a firm maintain certain financial accounting ratios, which can be affected by the income reported and by the level of long-term assets. Accordingly, the accounting rate of return may be used as a screening measure to ensure that any new investment will not adversely affect these ratios. Additionally, because bonuses to managers are often based on accounting income or return on assets, managers may have a personal interest in seeing that any new investment contributes significantly to net income. A manager seeking to maximize personal income will select investments that return the highest net income per dollar invested.

Unlike the payback period, the accounting rate of return does consider a project's profitability; like the payback period, it ignores the time value of money. Ignoring the time value of money is a critical deficiency in this method: doing so can lead a manager to choose investments that do not maximize profits. It is because the payback period and the accounting rate of return ignore the time value of money that they are referred to as **nondiscounting models**. Discounting models use **discounted cash flows**, which are future cash flows expressed in terms of their present value. The use of discounting models requires an understanding of present value concepts, which are reviewed in Appendix 11A. Review these concepts and make

---

4. The average investment formula is derived from the definition of the average value of a function and requires the use of calculus.

sure that you understand them before studying the discounting capital investment models. Present value tables (Exhibits 11B–1 and 11B–2) are presented in Appendix 11B. We will use these tables throughout the rest of the chapter.

DISCOUNTING MODELS: THE NET PRESENT VALUE METHOD

Discounting models explicitly consider the time value of money, and therefore incorporate the concept of discounting cash inflows and outflows. Two discounting models will be considered: net present value (NPV) and internal rate of return (IRR). The net present value method will be discussed first; the internal rate of return method is discussed in the following section.

NPV Defined

Net present value (NPV) is the difference in the present value of the cash inflows and outflows associated with a project:

$$\text{NPV} = [\sum CF_t/(1 + i)^t] - I$$
$$= [\sum CF_t \times df_t] - I \tag{11.1}$$
$$= P - I$$

where

I = The present value of the project's cost (usually the initial outlay)
CF_t = The net cash flow to be received in period t, with $t = 1 \ldots n$.
n = The useful life of the project
I = The rate of return
t = The time period
P = The present value of the project's future cash flows
df_t = $1/(1 + i)^t$, the discount factor

NPV measures an investment's profitability. If NPV is positive, it measures the increase in wealth. For a firm, this means that the size of a positive NPV measures the increase in the value of the firm resulting from an investment. To use the NPV method, a *required rate of return* must be defined. The required rate of return is the minimum acceptable rate of return. It is also referred to in certain contexts as the **discount rate**, the *hurdle rate*, and the *cost of capital*.

A positive net present value signals that (1) the initial investment has been recovered, (2) the required rate of return has been achieved, and (3) a return in excess of (1) and (2) has been received. Thus, if NPV is greater than zero, the investment is profitable and acceptable. If NPV equals zero, the decision maker is indifferent between accepting or rejecting the investment proposal. If NPV is less than zero, the investment should be rejected. In this case, it is earning less than the required rate of return.

An Example Illustrating Net Present Value

Majestic Company has developed new earphones for portable CD and tape players that it believes are superior to anything on the market. The firm's marketing manager is excited about the new product's prospects after completing a detailed market study that revealed expected annual revenues of $300,000. The earphones have a projected life cycle of five years. The equipment for producing the earphones would cost $320,000. After five years, that equipment could be sold for $40,000. In addition to equipment, working capital is expected to increase by $40,000 because of increases in inventories and receivables. The firm expects to recover the investment in working capital at the end of the project's life. Annual cash operating expenses are estimated at $180,000. Assuming that the required rate of return is 12 percent, should the company manufacture the new earphones?

Exhibit 11–2

Cash Flows and NPV
Analysis

STEP 1. CASH-FLOW IDENTIFICATION		
Year	Item	Cash Flow
0	Equipment	$(320,000)
	Working capital	(40,000)
	Total	$(360,000)
1–4	Revenues	$ 300,000
	Operating expenses	(180,000)
	Total	$ 120,000
5	Revenues	$ 300,000
	Operating expenses	(180,000)
	Salvage	40,000
	Recovery of working capital	40,000
	Total	$ 200,000

STEP 2A. NPV ANALYSIS			*(continued)*
Year	Cash Flow[a]	Discount Factor[b]	Present Value
0	$(360,000)	1.000	$(360,000)
1	120,000	0.893	107,160
2	120,000	0.797	95,640
3	120,000	0.712	85,440
4	120,000	0.636	76,320
5	200,000	0.567	113,400
Net present value			$ 117,960

STEP 2B. NPV ANALYSIS			
Year	Cash Flow	Discount Factor	Present Value
0	$(360,000)	1.000	$(360,000)
1–4	120,000	3.037	364,440
5	200,000	0.567	113,400
Net present value			$ 117,840[c]

[a] From Step 1
[b] From Exhibit 11B–1 and 11B–2, pages 484–485
[c] The NPV differs because of rounding.

In order to answer this question, two steps must be taken: (1) the cash flows for each year must be identified, and (2) the NPV must be computed using the cash flows from Step 1. The solution to the problem is given in Exhibit 11–2. Notice that two approaches can be used in Step 2 to compute NPV. Step 2A computes NPV by using discount factors from Exhibit 11B–1. Step 2B simplifies the computation by using a single discount factor from Exhibit 11B–2 for the even cash flows occurring in Years 1 to 4.

DISCOUNTING MODELS: INTERNAL RATE OF RETURN

Objective 4

Use the internal rate of return (IRR) to assess the acceptability of independent projects.

The **internal rate of return** (IRR) method is another discounting model. The internal rate of return is defined as the interest rate that sets the present value of a project's net cash flows equal to the present value of the project's cost. In other words, it is the interest rate that sets the project's NPV at zero. The following equation can be used to determine a project's IRR:

$$I = \sum CF_t/(1 + i)^t \qquad (11.2)$$

The left-hand side of Equation 11.2 is the initial investment, and the right-hand side is the present value of the future net cash flows. We know the values for I, CF_t, and t. Thus, we can find the IRR (the interest rate, i, in the equation) by trial and error. Once a project's IRR is computed, it is compared with the firm's required rate of return. If the IRR is greater than the required rate, the project is deemed acceptable; if the IRR is equal to the required rate of return, acceptance or rejection of the investment is equal; if the IRR is less than the required rate of return, the project is rejected.

The internal rate of return is the most widely used of the capital investment techniques.[5] One reason for its popularity may be that it is a rate of return, a concept that managers are comfortable in using. Another possibility is that managers may believe (in most cases, incorrectly) that the IRR is the true or actual compounded rate of return being earned by the initial investment. Whatever the reasons for its popularity, a basic understanding of the IRR is necessary.

Example: Multiple-Period Setting with Uniform Cash Flows

To illustrate how to compute the IRR in a multiple-period setting, assume that a company has an opportunity to invest $120,000 in new equipment that will produce net cash flows of $49,950 at the end of each year for the next three years. The IRR is the interest rate that equates the present value of the three equal receipts of $49,950 to the investment of $120,000. Since the series of cash flows is uniform, a single discount factor from Exhibit 11B–2 can be used to compute the annuity's present value. Letting df be this discount factor and CF be the annual cash flow, Equation 11.2 assumes the following form:

$$I = CF(df)$$

Solving for df, we obtain the following:

$$df = I/CF$$
$$= \text{Investment/Annual cash flow}$$

Once the discount factor is computed, go to Exhibit 11B–2 and find the row corresponding to the life of the project; then move across that row until the computed discount factor is found. The interest rate corresponding to this discount factor is the IRR.

For example, the discount factor for the company's investment is 2.402 [$120,000/$49,950]. Since the life of the investment is three years, we use the third row in Exhibit 11B–2, moving across this row until 2.402 is found. The interest rate corresponding to 2.402 is 12 percent, which is the IRR.

Exhibit 11B–2 does not provide discount factors for every possible interest rate. To illustrate, assume that the annual cash inflows expected by the company are $51,000 instead of $49,950. The new discount factor is 2.353 [$120,000/$51,000]. Going once again to the third row in Exhibit 11B–2, we find that the discount factor— and thus the IRR—is between 12 and 14 percent. We can approximate the IRR by interpolation. Interpolation approximates the actual IRR by assuming that the IRR is the same proportionate distance between 12 percent and 14 percent as the discount factor of 2.353 is between the tabled discount factors. Of course, business calculators or spreadsheet programs can provide a direct calculation of the IRR, making both interpolation and the use of tables unnecessary. For our purposes, we will simply identify the range for the IRR as indicated by the table values.

---

5. Blazouske, Carlin, and Kim (see footnote 3) found that IRR was used as the primary technique by 61.5 percent of the firms that used a discounting method.

Multiple-Period Setting: Uneven Cash Flows

If the cash flows are not uniform, then Equation 11.2 must be solved by trial and error (or by using a business calculator or a software package). To illustrate solution by trial and error, assume that a $10,000 investment in a computer system produces clerical savings of $6,000 and $7,200 over two years. The IRR is the interest rate that sets the present value of these two cash inflows equal to $10,000:

$$P = \$6,000/(1 + i) + \$7,200/(1 + i)^2$$
$$= \$10,000$$

To solve the above equation by trial and error, we start by selecting a possible value for i. Given this first guess, we compute the present value of the future cash flows and then compare the present value to the initial investment. If the present value is greater than the initial investment, the interest rate is too low; if the present value is less than the initial investment, the interest rate is too high. Our next guess is adjusted accordingly.

Assume that our first guess is 18 percent. Using i equal to 0.18, we use Exhibit 11B–1 to find the discount factors for Years 1 and 2: 0.847 and 0.718, respectively. These discount factors produce the following present value for the two cash inflows:

$$P = \$6,000 \times 0.847 + \$7,200 \times 0.718 = \$10,252$$

Since P is greater than $10,000, the interest rate selected is too low. A higher guess is needed. If our next guess is 20 percent, we obtain the following:

$$P = \$6,000 \times 0.833 + \$7,200 \times 0.694 = \$9,995$$

Since this value is reasonably close to $10,000, we can say that the IRR is approximately 20 percent. (The IRR is, in fact, exactly 20 percent: the present value is slightly less than the investment because of rounding in the discount factors found in Exhibit 11B–1.)

MUTUALLY EXCLUSIVE PROJECTS

Objective 5

Explain why NPV is better than IRR for capital investment decisions involving mutually exclusive projects.

Up to this point, we have focused on independent projects. Many capital investment decisions, however, involve mutually exclusive projects. How NPV and IRR analysis are used to choose among competing projects is, of course, an interesting question. An even more interesting question to consider is whether NPV and IRR differ in their ability to help managers make wealth-maximizing decisions in the presence of competing alternatives. For example, we already know that nondiscounting models can produce erroneous choices because they ignore the time value of money. Because of this deficiency, the discounting models are judged superior. Similarly, it can be shown that the NPV model is generally preferred over the IRR model when choosing among mutually exclusive alternatives.

NPV Compared with IRR

NPV and IRR both yield the same decision for independent projects: for example, if the NPV is greater than zero, then the IRR is also greater than the required rate of return—both models signal the correct decision. However, for competing projects, the two models can produce different results. Intuitively, we believe that for mutually exclusive projects, the project with the highest NPV or the highest IRR should be chosen. Since it is possible for the two models to produce different rankings of mutually exclusive projects, the model that consistently reveals the wealth-maximizing project should be preferred.

NPV differs from IRR in two major ways. First, NPV assumes that each cash inflow received is reinvested at the required rate of return, whereas IRR assumes that each cash inflow is reinvested at the computed IRR. Assuming that cash inflows will be reinvesting at the required rate of return is more realistic and produces more reliable results when comparing mutually exclusive projects. Second, NPV measures profitability in absolute terms, whereas IRR measures it in relative terms. NPV measures the amount by which the firm's value changes.

Because NPV measures the impact that competing projects have on the firm's value, choosing the project with the largest NPV is consistent with maximizing the wealth of shareholders. On the other hand, IRR does not consistently result in choices that maximize wealth. As a relative measure of profitability, IRR has the virtue of accurately measuring the rate of return of funds that remain internally invested. However, maximizing IRR will not necessarily maximize the wealth of firm owners, because IRR cannot, by nature, consider the absolute dollar contributions of projects. In the final analysis, what counts are the total dollars earned—the absolute profits—not the relative profits. Accordingly, NPV, not IRR, should be used for choosing among competing, mutually exclusive projects, or among competing projects when capital funds are limited.

An independent project is acceptable if its NPV is positive. For mutually exclusive projects, the project with the largest NPV is chosen. There are three steps in selecting the best project from several competing projects: (1) assessing the cash-flow pattern for each project, (2) computing the NPV for each project, and (3) identifying the project with the greatest NPV. We will use the following example to illustrate NPV analysis for competing projects.

Example: Mutually Exclusive Projects

Hintley Games Corporation has decided to market a game that will allow players to display and develop their knowledge of the geography of Canada, Mexico, and the United States. Given the widespread interest in trivia games, the company is certain that this product will prove successful. The marketing department has selected *Travel North America* as the game's name. Two different board designs are being considered. Design B is more elaborate than Design A and will require a larger investment and greater annual operating costs; however, it will also generate greater annual revenues. The projected annual revenues, annual costs, capital outlays, and project life for each design (in after-tax cash flows) follow:

	Design A	Design B
Annual revenues	$179,460	$239,280
Annual operating costs	119,460	169,280
Equipment (purchased before Year 1)	180,000	210,000
Project life	5 years	5 years

The firm must decide which design to choose. Assume that the company's cost of capital is 12 percent.

Design A requires an initial outlay of $180,000 and has an annual net cash flow of $60,000 (revenues of $179,460 minus costs of $119,460). Design B, with an initial outlay of $210,000, has an annual net cash flow of $70,000 ($239,280 – 169,260). With this information, we can describe the cash-flow pattern for each project and compute NPV. These are shown in Exhibit 11–3. Based on NPV analysis, Design B is more profitable; it has the larger NPV. Accordingly, the company should select Design B over Design A.

Interestingly, Designs A and B have identical internal rates of return. As shown in Exhibit 11–3, both designs have a discount factor of 3.000. From Exhibit 11B–2, it is easily seen that a discount factor of 3.000 and a life of five years give an IRR of about 20 percent. Even though both projects have an IRR of 20 percent, the firm should not consider the two designs equally desirable. The analysis above has just

Exhibit 11-3

Cash-Flow Pattern and
NPV and IRR Analysis:
Designs A and B

CASH-FLOW PATTERN		
Year	Design A	Design B
0	$(180,000)	$(210,000)
1	60,000	70,000
2	60,000	70,000
3	60,000	70,000
4	60,000	70,000
5	60,000	70,000

DESIGN A: NPV ANALYSIS

Year	Cash Flow	Discount Factor*	Present Value
0	$(180,000)	1.000	$(180,000)
1–5	60,000	3.605	216,300
Net present value			$ 36,300

DESIGN A: IRR ANALYSIS

$$\text{Discount factor} = \frac{\text{Initial investment}}{\text{Annual cash flow}}$$

$$= \frac{\$180,000}{60,000}$$

$$= 3.000$$

From Exhibit 11B–2, df = 3.000 for five years implies that IRR = 20% (approximately).

DESIGN B: NPV ANALYSIS

Year	Cash Flow	Discount Factor*	Present Value
0	$(210,000)	1.000	$(210,000)
1–5	70,000	3.605	252,350
Net present value			$ 42,350

DESIGN B: IRR ANALYSIS

$$\text{Discount factor} = \frac{\text{Initial investment}}{\text{Annual cash flow}}$$

$$= \frac{\$210,000}{70,000}$$

$$= 3.000$$

From Exhibit 11B–2, df = 3.000 for five years implies that IRR = 20% (approximately).

[a] From Exhibit 11B–2, page 485

shown that Design B produces a larger NPV, and will therefore increase the firm's value more than Design A will. Hence, Design B should be chosen. This illustrates the conceptual superiority of NPV over IRR for analysis of competing projects.

Capital Investment and Ethical Issues

Capital investment decisions often offer great temptations for misrepresentations. Divisional mangers must often compete for scarce resources. With this competition comes the temptation to engage in deceptive behaviour. Examples of such behaviour are numerous. Managers have been guilty of deliberately overestimating cash inflows and underestimating cash outlays so that a pet project might have the NPV or IRR necessary to be approved. This is particularly tempting when the project's early cash flows are expected to be good, whereas its later cash flows are expected to be poor. Adjusting the estimates of the poor cash flows upward may produce an approved project that has good performance in its early years and poor performance in its later years. Other possibilities also exist. For example, a manager may need approval for any capital expenditure above a certain level. Suppose that a manager acquired a computer system by purchasing it in pieces, where the cost of each piece was less than the manager's capital expenditure approval limit. Was this right?

Managers need to realize that how objectives are reached is almost as important as (and maybe more important than) merely reaching the objectives. Furthermore, companies should structure their performance evaluation systems so that the reward system does not provide strong incentives for unethical behaviour. As observed in an article on ethics, "No code of ethics and no amount of cajolery by the chief executive will have much effect if promotions go regularly to the people who pile up big numbers by cutting corners."[6] In the same article, another interesting observation was made—one that is particularly appropriate for the capital expenditure framework. A positive net present value means that the firm's value should increase. According to the article, James Burke, CEO for Johnson & Johnson, identified a group of firms that paid a lot of attention to ethical standards. From 1950 to 1990, the market value of this group of firms grew at 11.3 percent annually, compared with 6.2 percent growth in the Dow Jones industrials. Perhaps ethical behaviour pays off on the bottom line!

POSTAUDIT OF CAPITAL PROJECTS

Objective 6

Explain the role and value of postaudits.

A key element in the capital investment decision process is a follow-up analysis of a capital project once it is implemented. This analysis is called a *postaudit*. A **postaudit** compares the actual benefits with the estimated benefits and compares the actual operating costs with estimated operating costs; it evaluates the investment's overall outcome and proposes corrective action if any is needed.[7] The following real-world case illustrates the usefulness of a postaudit.

Honley Medical Company: An Illustrative Application

Allen Manesfield and Jenny Winters were discussing a persistent and irritating problem present in the process of producing intravenous needles (IVs). Both Allen and Jenny are employed by Honley Medical, which specializes in the production of medical products and has three divisions: the IV Products Division, the Critical Care Monitoring Division, and the Specialty Products Division. Allen and Jenny both are associated with the IV Products Division—Allen as the senior production engineer and Jenny as the marketing manager.

The IV Products Division produces needles of five different sizes. During one stage of the manufacturing process, the needle itself is inserted into a plastic hub and bonded using epoxy glue. According to Jenny, the use of epoxy to bond the needles was causing the division all kinds of problems. In many cases, the epoxy was not bonding correctly. Rejects were high, and the division was receiving a large number of complaints from its customers. Corrective action was needed to avoid losing sales.

After some discussion and analysis, a recommendation was made to use induction welding in lieu of epoxy bonding. In induction welding, the needles are inserted into the plastic hub, and an RF generator is used to heat the needles. The RF generator works on the same principle as a microwave oven. As the needles get hot, the plastic melts and the needles are bonded.

---

6.   Kenneth Labich, "The New Crisis in Business Ethics," *Fortune* (20 April 1992): 167–176.

7.   Postaudits of capital projects are the subject of the Society of Management Accountants of Canada's Management Accounting Guideline 1, *Post Appraisal of Capital Expenditure*, 1984.

Switching to induction welding required an investment in RF generators and the associated tooling; the IV Division justified the investment based on the savings associated with the new system. Induction welding promised to reduce the cost of direct materials by eliminating the need to buy and use epoxy. Savings of direct labour costs were also predicted, because the new process was much more automated. Adding to these savings were the avoidance of daily cleanup costs and the reduction in rejects. Allen presented a formal NPV analysis showing that the welding system was superior to the epoxy system. The purchase was approved by headquarters.

One Year Later

Jenny: "Allen, I'm quite pleased with induction welding for bonding needles. In the year since the new process was implemented, we've had virtually no complaints from our customers. The needles are firmly bonded."

Allen: "I wish that positive experience were true for all other areas as well. Unfortunately, implementing the process has uncovered some rather sticky and expensive problems that I simply didn't anticipate. The Internal Audit Department recently completed a postaudit of the project, and now my feet are being held to the fire."

Jenny: "That's too bad. What's the problem?"

Allen: "You mean problems. Let me list a few for you. One is that the RF generators interfered with the operation of other equipment. To eliminate this interference, we had to install filtering equipment. But that's not all. We also discovered that the average maintenance person doesn't know how to maintain the new equipment. Now we are faced with the need to initiate a training program to upgrade the skills of our maintenance people. Upgrading skills also implies higher wages. Although the RF bonding process is less messy, it is also more complex. The manufacturing people complained to the internal auditors about that. They maintain that a simple process, even if it's messy, is to be preferred—especially now that demand for the product is increasing by leaps and bounds."

Jenny: "What did the internal auditors conclude?"

Allen: "They observed that many of the predicted savings did take place, but that some significant costs were not foreseen. Because of some of the unforeseen problems, they have recommended that I look carefully at the possibility of moving back to using epoxy. They indicated that NPV analysis using actual data appears to favour that process. With production expanding, the acquisition of additional RF generators and filtering equipment plus the necessary training is simply not as attractive as returning to epoxy bonding. This conclusion is reinforced by the fact that the epoxy process is simpler and by the auditors' conclusion that the mixing of the epoxy can be automated, avoiding the quality problem we had in the first place."

Jenny: "Well, Allen, you can't really blame yourself. You had a real problem and took action to solve it. It's difficult to foresee all the problems and hidden costs of a new process."

Allen: "Unfortunately, the internal auditors don't totally agree. In fact, neither do I. I probably jumped too quickly. In the future, I intend to think through new projects more carefully."

Benefits of a Postaudit

In the case of the RF bonding decision, some of the estimated benefits did materialize: complaints from customers decreased, rejects were fewer, and direct labour and materials costs decreased. However, the investment was greater than expected because filtering equipment was needed, and actual operating costs were much higher because of the increased maintenance cost and the increased complexity of the process. Overall, the internal auditors concluded that the investment was a poor decision. The corrective action they recommended was to abandon the new process and return to epoxy bonding.[8]

Firms that perform postaudits of capital projects experience a number of benefits. First, by evaluating profitability, postaudits ensure that resources are used wisely. If the project is doing well, it may call for additional funds and additional attention. If the project is not doing well, corrective action may be needed to improve performance, or perhaps the project may even be abandoned.

A second benefit of the postaudit is its impact on the behaviour of managers. If managers are held accountable for the results of a capital investment decision, they are more likely to make such decisions in the firm's best interests. Additionally, postaudits supply feedback to managers that should help improve future decision making. Consider Allen's reaction to the postaudit of the RF bonding process. Certainly, he would be expected to be more careful and more thorough in making future investment recommendations. In the future, Allen will probably consider more than one alternative, such as automating the mixing of the epoxy. Also, for those alternatives being considered, he will probably be especially alert to the possibility of hidden costs, such as increased training requirements for a new process.

The case also reveals that the postaudit was performed by the internal audit staff. Generally, more objective results are obtainable if the postaudit is done by an independent party. Since considerable effort is expended to ensure as much independence as possible for the internal audit staff, that group is usually the best choice for this task.

Postaudits, however, are costly. Moreover, even though they may provide significant benefits, they have other limitations. Most obvious is the fact that the assumptions driving the original analysis may often be invalidated by changes in the actual operating environment. Accountability must be qualified to some extent by the impossibility of foreseeing every possible eventuality.

COMPUTATION AND ADJUSTMENT OF CASH FLOWS

Objective 7

Convert gross cash flows to after-tax cash flows.

An important step in capital investment analysis is determining the cash-flow pattern for each project being considered. In fact, the computation of cash flows may be the most critical step in the capital investment process.[9] Erroneous estimates may result in erroneous decisions, regardless of the sophistication of the decision models being used. The Honley Medical Company case described in the previous section illustrates this point vividly. If the cash flows associated with the inductive welding process had been more accurately forecast, a better decision could have been made.

Two steps are needed to compute cash flows: (1) forecasting revenues, expenses, and capital outlays; and (2) adjusting these gross cash flows to after-tax cash flows through a careful analysis of the relevant tax factors. Of the two steps, the more challenging is the first. Forecasting is technically demanding, and its methodology is typically studied in market research and management science courses. Once gross cash flows are estimated, they should be adjusted for significant inflationary effects. Finally, straightforward applications of tax law can be used to compute the after-tax flows. At this level of analysis, we assume that gross cash flows are available, and focus on adjusting forecasted cash flows to improve their accuracy and relevance.

8. The firm did abandon inductive welding and returned to epoxy bonding, which was improved by automating the mixing. The simplicity of the epoxy process was a major qualitative factor in deciding to return to the old, but improved, process.

9. There is a detailed discussion of determining cash-flow patterns in the Society of Management Accountants of Canada's Management Accounting Guideline 2, *Estimating Cash Flows for Capital Expenditure Decisions*, 1985.

Adjusting Forecasts for Inflation

In recent years, inflation in Canada has been relatively modest, so the need to adjust cash flows for inflation may not be as critical. However, firms that operate in the international environment may face different circumstances: inflation can be very high in some countries, and its effect on capital investment decisions can be dramatic. Mexico, for example, has experienced double-digit inflation rates for years. Thus, it is important to know how to adjust the capital investment models for inflationary effects—particularly given the fact that many Canadian firms make capital investment decisions within many different national environments. In an inflationary environment, financial markets react by increasing the cost of capital to reflect inflation. Thus, the **cost of capital** is composed of two elements:

1. the real rate,
2. the inflationary element (investors demand a premium to compensate for the loss in general purchasing power of the dollar or local currency).

Since the required rate of return used in capital investment analysis reflects an inflationary component at the time NPV analysis is performed, inflation must also be considered in predicting the operating cash flows. If the operating cash flows are not adjusted to account for inflation, an erroneous decision may result. In adjusting predicted cash flows, specific price change indexes should be used if possible. If that is not possible, a general price index should be used.

Note, however, that cash inflows due to the tax effects of amortization, which are discussed later in this section, need *not* be adjusted for inflation as long as the national tax law for the country in question requires that amortization (or its equivalent) be based on the *original* dollar investment.

To illustrate, assume that a subsidiary of a Canadian company operating in Hungary is considering a project that requires an investment of 5,000,000 forints (the Hungarian currency) and is expected to produce annual cash inflows of 2,900,000 forints for the coming two years. The required rate of return is 20 percent, which includes an inflationary component. The general inflation rate is expected to average 15 percent for the next two years. Net present value analysis with and without the adjustment of predicted cash flows for inflation is given in Exhibit 11–4. As the analysis shows, not adjusting predicted cash flows for inflation leads to a decision to reject the project, whereas adjusting for inflation leads to a decision to accept it. Thus, failure to adjust the predicted cash flows for inflationary effects can lead to an incorrect conclusion.

Exhibit 11–4

The Effects of Inflation on Capital Investment

WITHOUT INFLATIONARY ADJUSTMENT			
Year	Cash Flow	Discount Factor[a]	Present Value
0	(5,000,000)	1.000	(5,000,000)
1–2	2,900,000	1.528	4,431,200
Net present value			(568,800)

WITH INFLATIONARY ADJUSTMENT			
Year	Cash Flow[b]	Discount Factor[c]	Present Value
0	(5,000,000)	1.000	(5,000,000)
1	3,335,000	0.833	2,778,055
2	3,835,250	0.694	2,661,664
Net present value			439,719

[a] From Exhibit 11B–2, page 485
[b] Adjustment for one year of inflation: $1.15 \times 2,900,000$: adjustment for two years of inflation $1.15 \times 1.15 \times 2,900,000$
[c] From Exhibit 11B–1, page 484
Note: All cash flows are expressed in forints.

Conversion of Gross Cash Flows to After-Tax Cash Flows

Once gross cash flows are predicted with the desired degree of accuracy, the analyst must adjust these cash flows for taxes. To analyze tax effects, cash flows are usually broken into two categories: (1) the initial cash outflows needed to acquire the assets of the project, and (2) the cash flows produced over the life of the project. Cash outflows and cash inflows adjusted for tax effects are called after-tax cash outflows and inflows. After-tax cash flow includes provisions for after-tax revenues, after-tax operating expenses, and the tax implications of amortization.

After-Tax Cash Flows: Year 0 The after-tax cash flow in Year 0 (the initial out-of-pocket outlay) is simply the difference between the initial cost of the project and any cash inflows directly associated with it. The project's gross cost includes such things as the cost of land, the cost of equipment (including transportation and installation), taxes on gains from the sale of assets, and increases in working capital. Cash inflows occurring at the time of acquisition include cash from the sale of assets and tax savings from losses on the sale of assets.

Under current Canadian tax law, all costs relating to the acquisition of assets other than land must be capitalized and written off over the useful life of the assets. In Canada, a capital cost allowance (similar to the accounting amortization concept) based on this capitalized cost is used to write off a portion each year. Capital cost allowance and operating expenses (other than amortization) are deducted from revenues when computing taxable income during each year of the asset's life. However, at the point of acquisition, there is no taxable income related to the asset, so the principal tax implications are related to the recognition of gains or losses on the sale of existing assets.

The sale of assets may produce additional tax payable because of a taxable gain, and the cash inflow from the sale would be reduced accordingly. Losses on the sale of assets are noncash expenses that may reduce taxable income. More details about the tax implications from the sale of assets are discussed later in this section.

After-Tax Cash Flows: Life of the Project In addition to determining the initial out-of-pocket outlay, managers must also estimate the annual after-tax cash flows expected over the life of the project. If the project generates revenue, the principal source of cash flows is from operations. Operating cash flows can be assessed from the project's income statement. The annual after-tax flows are the sum of the project's after-tax profits and its noncash expenses. In terms of a simple formula, this computation can be represented as follows:

$$\text{After-tax cash flows} = \text{After-tax net income} + \text{Noncash expenses}$$
$$CF = NI + NC$$

where CF = After-tax cash flows
NI = After-tax net income
NC = Noncash expenses

The most common examples of noncash expenses are amortization and losses. For income tax purposes in Canada, amortization is not allowed as a deduction in determining taxable income: **capital cost allowances** (CCAs) are used instead. For the purposes of our current discussion, we will treat CCA and amortization as the same for now. We will cover the special features of the CCA system later in this section.

At first glance, it may seem odd that after-tax cash flows are computed including noncash expenses. Noncash expenses are not cash flows, but will affect cash flows by reducing cash tax payments. Shielding income from taxation creates actual cash savings. The use of the income statement to determine after-tax cash flows is illustrated in the following example. We also use the example to show how noncash expenses can increase cash inflows by saving taxes.

Assume that Spear Corporation plans to purchase a machine that costs $300,000. The machine will produce a new product that is expected to increase the firm's annual revenues (and cash inflows) by $300,000. Expenses (and cash outflows) for materials, labour, and other operating costs will be $125,000 per year. The machine has a life of three years and will be amortized on a straight-line basis for accounting and tax purposes. The machine will have no salvage value at the end of three years. The project's projected income statement is as follows:

Revenues	$300,000
Less: Cash operating expenses	125,000
Less: Amortization (or CCA)	100,000
Income before taxes	$ 75,000
Less: Taxes (@ 40%)[10]	30,000
Net income	$ 45,000

Cash flow can be computed from the income statement as follows:

$$CF = NI + NC$$
$$= \$45,000 + \$100,000$$
$$= \$145,000$$

The income approach to determining operating cash flows can be used to assess the after-tax cash flows for each item on the income statement. This is known as the decomposition approach:

$$CF = [(1 - \text{Tax rate}) \times \text{Revenues}] - [(1 - \text{Tax rate}) \times \text{Cash expenses}]$$
$$+ [\text{Tax rate} \times \text{Noncash expenses}]$$

The first term, $[(1 - \text{Tax rate}) \times \text{Revenues}]$, gives the after-tax cash flows from cash revenues. For our example, cash revenues are projected to be $300,000. The firm can therefore expect to keep $180,000 of the revenues received $[(1 - 0.4) \times \$300,000]$. Tax of $120,000 would have to be paid on those cash revenues.

The second term, $[(1 - \text{Tax rate}) \times \text{Cash expenses}]$, is the after-tax cash flows from cash operating expenses. Because cash expenses can be deducted from revenues to arrive at taxable income, the effect is to shield part of the revenues from taxation. This shielding saves taxes and reduces the effective cash outflows associated with a given expenditure. In our example, the firm has cash operating expenses of $125,000. The after-tax cash outflow is $75,000 $[(1 - 0.4) \times \$125,000]$. The deductibility of the operating expenses shields revenue of $125,000 from tax and produces tax savings of $50,000.

The third term, $[\text{Tax rate} \times \text{Noncash expenses}]$, is the cash inflow from tax savings produced by the noncash expenses. Noncash expenses, such as amortization, shield revenues from taxation. In our example, amortization (or CCA) shields revenues of $100,000 from being taxed and thus saves taxes of $40,000; this effect is known as the *amortization (or CCA) tax shield*.

A summary of the three items is given below:

After-tax revenues	$180,000
After-tax cash expenses	(75,000)
Amortization (or CCA) tax shield	40,000
After-tax cash flow	$145,000

10. An important element of adjusting for taxes is the appropriate rate to apply. In Canada, the corporate tax rate is a combination of federal and provincial rates (along with other factors). In Ontario, combined federal and provincial corporate income tax rates (including surcharges) for 2000 ranged from 21.1 percent to 44.6 percent. Other provinces have similar rates. For illustration purposes, we will assume a simple tax rate. An accurate determination of the applicable tax rate is essential for sound capital investment analysis. For a detailed discussion of tax rates, see, for example, W. J. Buckwold, *Canadian Income Taxation, Planning and Decision Making*, Third Edition, 1999, McGraw-Hill.

The decomposition approach yields the same outcome as the income approach but more directly demonstrates the cash-flow consequences of the noncash expenses. Remember that in this section, we have assumed that amortization (for accounting net income) and the capital cost allowance (for taxable income) are determined in the same way. Next, we will consider how our analysis changes when the particulars of the CCA system are included.

Cash-Flow Consequences of Capital Cost Allowances (CCAs)

The capital cost allowance provisions of the Canadian income tax system are different from accounting amortization in some significant ways. When a capital property asset is acquired, it is assigned to a capital asset class along with other assets of a similar type. The CCA that is allowed for a particular class in a tax year is calculated by multiplying the balance of capital cost in the class, after adding new purchases of assets and deducting disposals of assets during the tax year, by the appropriate CCA rate. There are currently more than 40 separate classes, each with a specific maximum rate. A sample of CCA classes and the applicable maximum CCA rates is given in Exhibit 11–5.

Two features of the capital cost allowance system are important for determining the appropriate after-tax or net cash flows for capital investment purposes. Firstly, the capital cost allowance system is generally a declining-balance system: a constant percentage or rate is applied to the remaining balance in the capital cost allowance class.[11] Therefore, unlike the uniform amount under straight-line amortization, the size of the tax shield will change each year, and separate calculations of CCA tax shield are required for each year.

Secondly, the capital costs of each class are combined in a single cost pool. As a consequence, if there are other asset items in the class, a particular project may continue to affect the firm's cash flows even after the project is completed (and its associated assets are retired). This effect is caused because the balance in the cost pool for the class determines the allowable CCA. When an asset item is retired, the cost pool is reduced by the proceeds from its retirement, to a maximum of the asset item's original capital cost. A project will continue to have a tax shield effect if the proceeds are less than the original cost and if some other asset remains in the class.[12]

	Class	Examples of Assets Included	Maximum Rate
Exhibit 11–5	Class 1	Buildings and other structures	4%
	Class 7	Boats, ships	15%
Sample of Capital Cost Allowance Classes and Maximum Rates	Class 8	Equipment and machinery	20%
	Class 9	Aircraft	25%
	Class 10	Computer equipment, trucks	30%
	Class 12	Small tools, computer software	100%
	Class 33	Timber resource property	15%
	Class 37	Amusement park buildings and equipment	15%

11. There are a few exceptions to this general discussion (for example, lease improvements and passenger vehicles), but a more detailed discussion is beyond the scope of this book.

12. If the proceeds from disposal are less than the asset's "unamortized" cost, there will be a tax shield effect from the remaining capital cost (after the proceeds are deducted). If there are other assets in the class, the remaining capital cost will result in a higher CCA tax shield in future years. If the asset was the only one in the class, the remaining capital cost is a terminal loss and would be deducted from taxable income (an immediate tax shield would be realized). If the proceeds on disposal are greater than the "unamortized" capital cost of the asset, the balance in the cost pool may become negative. This is a recapture of CCA and is added to taxable income for the year. If there are other assets in the class, the balance in the pool may still be positive, but the CCA tax shield in future years is reduced. If the proceeds from disposal exceed the original capital cost of the asset, there will also be a taxable capital gain.

To illustrate these factors, we will again consider Spear Corporation's plan to purchase a machine with a capital cost of $300,000, but now we will calculate CCA using a 30 percent rate instead of straight-line amortization. We need to calculate CCA and tax payable for each of the three years. Remember that annual cash flows are $300,000, and cash operating expenses are $125,000. The calculation of after-tax cash flows is shown in Exhibit 11–6.[13]

Exhibit 11–6

After-Tax Cash Flow with CCA

CCA Calculation	Year 1	Year 2	Year 3
Capital cost, beginning of year	$300,000	$210,000	$147,000
Less CCA, 30% × capital cost, beginning of year	90,000	63,000	44,100
Capital cost, end of year	$210,000	$147,000	$102,900

After-Tax Income Calculation	Year 1	Year 2	Year 3
Revenues	$300,000	$300,000	$300,000
Less operating expenses	125,000	125,000	125,000
Less CCA (from above)	90,000	63,000	44,100
Taxable income	$ 85,000	$112,000	$130,900
Less tax payable (40%)	34,000	44,800	52,360
After-tax income	$ 51,000	$ 67,200	$ 78,540

After-Tax Cash-Flow Calculation	Year 1	Year 2	Year 3
After-tax income (from above)	$ 51,000	$ 67,200	$ 78,540
Plus noncash expense (CCA)	90,000	63,000	44,100
After-tax cash flow	$141,000	$130,200	$122,640

Now assume that Spear Corporation has a required rate of return of 10 percent and that the machine will have a zero salvage value after three years. The net present value analysis for the project, based on the after-tax cash flows from Exhibit 11–6, is given below:

Year	Cash Flow[a]	Discount Factor[b]	Present Value
0	$(300,000)	1.000	$(300,000)
1	141,000	0.909	128,169
2	130,200	0.826	107,545
3	122,640	0.751	92,103
Net Present Value			$ 27,817

[a] From Exhibit 11–6
[b] From Exhibit 11B–1, page 484

We can find the amount of the CCA tax shield by comparing the project's NPV with CCA to the project's NPV without CCA. The NPV without CCA is shown in Exhibit 11–7.

13. A further complication of the CCA system is that in the year of acquisition, allowable CCA is limited to one-half the normal amount. We will ignore this requirement here but consider it later in this section.

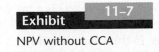

Exhibit 11–7

NPV without CCA

CASH FLOWS—WITHOUT CCA			
	Year 1	Year 2	Year 3
Operating cash flow[a]	$175,000	$175,000	$175,000
Less tax payable (40%)	70,000	70,000	70,000
After-tax cash flow	$105,000	$105,000	$105,000

NET PRESENT VALUE			
Year	Cash Flow	Discount Factor	Present Value
0	$(300,000)	1.000	$(300,000)
1–3	105,000	2.487[b]	261,135
Net Present Value			$ (38,865)

[a] $300,000 − $125,000 = $175,000
[b] From Exhibit 11B–2, page 485

The project's NPV is $(38,865) without CCA, but its NPV with CCA is $27,817. The difference, $66,682, is the present value of the CCA tax shield. We can calculate this amount directly, as shown below:

Year	CCA[a]	Tax Savings[b]	Discount Factor[c]	Present Value
1	$90,000	$36,000	0.909	$32,724
2	63,000	25,200	0.826	20,815
3	44,100	17,640	0.751	13,248
Net Present Value				$66,787[d]

[a] From Exhibit 11–6
[b] CCA × 40%
[c] From Exhibit 11B–1, page 484
[d] The small difference from $66,682 is due to rounding in the discount factors in Exhibit 11B–1.

However, our analysis is still not complete, because there is unused (for CCA purposes) capital cost related to the project of $102,900 at the end of Year 3, as shown in Exhibit 11–6. We need to consider two cases:

The first case is when there are no other assets in the CCA class. This case will result in a terminal loss of $102,900 in Year 3. The calculation of after-tax cash flow for Year 3 will change, because the tax payable will be lower as shown below:

Taxable operating income (from Exhibit 11–6)	$130,900
Less terminal loss	102,900
Taxable income	$ 28,000
Tax payable (@ 40%)	$ 11,200

The after-tax cash flow in Year 3 will be as follows:

$$\text{After-tax cash flow} = \text{Gross cash flow} - \text{Tax payable}$$
$$= \$175,000 - \$11,200$$
$$= \$163,800$$

The complete NPV analysis, including the terminal loss, is given below:

Year	Cash Flow[a]	Discount Factor[b]	Present Value
0	$(300,000)	1.000	$(300,000)
1	141,000	0.909	128,169
2	130,200	0.826	107,545
3	163,800	0.751	123,014
Net Present Value			$ 58,728

[a] From Exhibit 11–6, modified in Year 3
[b] From Exhibit 11B–1, page 484

NPV increases to $58,728 from $27,817, because the terminal loss in Year 3 is a tax shield and reduces the tax payable by $41,160, which has a present value of $30,911.

The second case is when there are other assets in the class. In this case, the allowable CCA in future years (and the associated tax shield) will be higher. We can calculate the present value of the remaining tax shield as follows:

Year	CCAª	Tax Shieldᵇ	Discount Factorᶜ	Present Value
4	$30,870	$12,348	0.683	$ 8,434
5	21,609	8,644	0.621	5,368
6	15,126	6,051	0.564	3,413
...	...	...	...	...
18	209	84	0.180	15
19	147	59	0.164	10
20	103	41	0.149	6
etc.	...	...	...	...
Present Value of Remaining CCA Tax Shield				$23,190

ª 30% × Capital Cost, Beginning of Year
ᵇ 40% × CCA
ᶜ From Exhibit 11B–1

Notice that very little is added to the tax shield in Year 20 and beyond. The present value of the remaining CCA tax shield is $23,190, for a total NPV for the project of $51,007 [$27,817 + 23,190].

We can use an alternative analysis based on the decomposition of the operating cash flows illustrated in the previous section. This approach, the formula method, highlights the present value of the CCA tax shield and offers a simpler calculation.[14] From Exhibit 11–7, the NPV of the after-tax cash flows, ignoring the tax shield effect of CCA, is $(38,865) and represents the first two terms of the after-tax cash-flow equation. The present value of the CCA tax shield, the third term, is calculated using the following formula.

$$\text{Present value of CCA tax shield} = (R \times C \times T)/(R + i)$$

where R = the CCA rate
  C = the original capital cost of the project
  T = the tax rate
  i = required rate of return

For our example, the CCA tax shield is as follows:

$$\text{Present value of CCA tax shield} = (30\% \times \$300,000 \times 40\%)/(30\% + 10\%)$$
$$= \$90,000$$

The machine's NPV, calculated using the CCA tax shield formula, is $(38,865) + $90,000 = $51,135. Rounding accounts for the small difference between this answer and the NPV of $51,007 that we calculated using the direct method.

As we have seen, CCA will affect the amount of tax payable and, therefore, the after-tax cash flows of projects with investments in capital assets. We have looked at two ways to account for the tax shield effect of CCA. In our first analysis, the direct method, we include the tax shield effect of CCA directly when determining the after-tax cash flows over the life of the project. We need to make adjustments for any continuing tax shield after the project ends. In our second analysis, the formula method, we decompose the operating cash flows and prepare an NPV analysis of the project ignoring CCA, and then use the CCA tax shield formula to calculate the present value of the CCA tax shield for the project. So far, our focus has been on the fundamental impact of CCA on capital investment decisions. There are other features of Canadian income tax rules that affect our analysis. We will modify our example for Spear Corporation to illustrate two of these features, the *one-half rule* and the *nonzero salvage value*.

---

14. With the widespread use of spreadsheet programs or customized capital budgeting programs, the major benefit of the formula approach is separating out the CCA tax shield. Simplifying the calculation is now less important.

The One-Half Rule The **one-half rule** restricts the amount of CCA that can be claimed in the year of acquisition to one-half of the CCA rate for the class. In our previous analyses, whether calculating the CCA effect on NPV directly or employing the tax shield formula, we used a full amount of CCA in the first year. If the one-half rule is applied, however, we must adjust our analyses. If we use the direct method, the adjustment is straightforward: reduce the amount of CCA in the first year, and adjust the following years accordingly. We see the adjustment in the CCA amounts, after-tax cash flows, and NPV for our Spear Corporation example in Exhibit 11–8. Note that the total NPV of

Exhibit 11-8

NPV Effect of CCA One-Half Rule

CCA Calculation	Year 1	Year 2	Year 3
Capital cost, beginning of year	$300,000	$255,000	$178,500
Less CCA, 30% × capital cost, beginning of year	45,000	76,500	53,550
Capital cost, end of year	$255,000	$178,500	$124,950

Tax Payable Calculation	Year 1	Year 2	Year 3
Operating cash flow	$175,000	$175,000	$175,000
Less CCA	45,000	76,500	53,500
Taxable income	$130,000	$ 98,500	$121,450
Tax payable (40%)	$ 52,000	$ 39,400	$ 48,580

Cash-Flow Calculation	Year 1	Year 2	Year 3
Cash flow	$175,000	$175,000	$175,000
Less tax payable	52,000	39,400	48,580
After-tax cash flow	$123,000	$135,600	$126,420

NET PRESENT VALUE CALCULATION

Year	Cash Flow[a]	Discount Factor[b]	Present Value
0	$(300,000)	1.000	$(300,000)
1	123,000	0.909	111,807
2	135,600	0.826	112,006
3	126,420	0.751	94,941
Net Present Value			$ 18,754

PRESENT VALUE OF CCA TAX SHIELD AFTER DISPOSAL OF ASSET[b]

Year	CCA	Tax Shield	Discount Factor	Present Value
4	$37,485	$14,994	0.683	$10,241
5	26,240	10,496	0.621	6,517
6	18,368	7,347	0.564	4,144
...	...	...	...	...
18	254	102	0.180	18
19	178	71	0.164	12
20	125	50	0.149	7
etc.	...	...	...	...
Present Value				$28,150

Summary of NPV

NPV (Years 0 – 3)	$18,754
NPV (Years 4 – ∞)	28,150
Total NPV	$46,904

[a] From Exhibit 11B–1, page 484
[b] Assuming other assets in class and zero salvage value

$46,904 is less than the NPV of $51,007 that we calculated without the one-half rule. The effect of the one-half rule is to decrease the project's NPV, because some of the tax shield is deferred during the first year.

If we use the formula approach, the CCA tax shield formula must be adjusted to include the one-half rule. The formula including the one-half rule is given below:

$$\text{Present value of CCA tax shield} = [(R \times C \times T)/(R + i)] \times [(1 + 0.5 \times i)/(1 + i)]$$

where R = the CCA rate
$\quad\quad C$ = the original capital cost of the project
$\quad\quad T$ = the tax rate
$\quad\quad i$ = required rate of return

The formula includes a second term that accounts for the fact that only half of the acquisition cost is taken into the pool in the first year. The calculation of the present value of the CCA tax shield using this formula is shown below:

$$PV = [(30\% \times \$300,000 \times 40\%)/(30\% + 10\%)] \times [(1 + 0.5 \times 10\%)/(1 + 10\%)] = \$85,909$$

The net present value of the after-tax cash flows (excluding the CCA tax shield effect) was $(38,865) (see Exhibit 11–7). Adding the present value of the tax shield gives a total NPV for the project of $47,044 (the small difference between the approaches is due to rounding).

Nonzero Salvage Value   In our examples so far, we have assumed that salvage value is zero. Zero salvage value is also implicit in the CCA tax shield formulas. A nonzero salvage value generates a cash flow at the time of disposal and will have to be included in the NPV analysis. A nonzero salvage value also has three potential tax effects:

1. When a capital asset is sold, the balance in the capital cost pool is reduced by the lesser of the salvage value or the original capital cost. The effect is to reduce the amount of the CCA tax shield, because the remaining CCA pool is reduced.
2. Deducting the salvage value may cause the pool's balance to be negative, triggering a recapture of CCA and an immediate tax payable.
3. If the salvage value is greater than the original capital cost, a capital gain results, generating an additional tax payable.

We can include the tax effects of (2) and (3) by adjusting the cash flows in the year in which the asset is retired. If we use the direct approach, the reduction in tax shield from (1) is automatically accomplished when the CCA pool is reduced. If we use the formula approach, the following adjustment must be subtracted from the present value of the CCA tax shield (calculated with our original assumption of a zero salvage value):

$$[(R \times S \times T)/(R + i)] \times [1/(1 + i)^n]$$

where R = the CCA rate
$\quad\quad S$ = the salvage value of the project
$\quad\quad T$ = the tax rate
$\quad\quad i$ = required rate of return
$\quad\quad n$ = the period of sale on retirement

This adjustment is the tax shield related to the salvage value (the first term) discounted from the time of sale to the present (the second term). For our example, assume that on January 1 of Year 4, Spear Corporation will sell the machine for a salvage value of $40,000. Assume also that there are other assets in the class and that the one-half rule is applied. Because the salvage value is less than the remaining capital cost, there is no capital gain or recapture of capital cost allowance. The salvage value creates a cash flow of $40,000 at the beginning of Year 4. The adjustment to the CCA tax shield for salvage value is shown as follows:

$$[(30\% \times \$40,000 \times 40\%)/(30\% + 10\%)] \times [1/(1 + 10\%)^3] = \$9,016$$

The project's NPV is calculated from the NPV of net cash flows (excluding the CCA tax shield), the present value of the salvage value, and the present value of the CCA tax shield with an adjustment for the salvage value. A summary of the NPV calculation follows:

NPV of net cash flows (from Exhibit 11–7)	$(38,865)
PV of salvage value ($40,000 × 0.751)	30,040
PV of CCA tax shield (unadjusted)	85,909
PV of salvage value adjustment to CCA tax shield	(9,016)
Total NPV	$ 68,068

Income tax rules have a profound effect on capital investment decisions, and it is important to correctly incorporate tax effects into the analysis. In this section we have illustrated the common effects due to CCA, but as tax rules with respect to capital property change, it will be necessary to alter the analysis and consult with tax professionals to ensure that future cash-flow implications are accounted for correctly.

CAPITAL INVESTMENT: THE ADVANCED MANUFACTURING ENVIRONMENT

Objective 8

Describe capital investment in the advanced manufacturing environment.

In the advanced manufacturing environment, long-term investments are generally concerned with the automation of manufacturing. Before any commitment to automation is made, however, a company should first make the most efficient use of existing technology. Many benefits can be realized by redesigning and simplifying the current manufacturing process. An example often given to support this thesis is automation of material handling. Automation of this operation can cost millions—and it is usually unnecessary, because greater efficiency can be achieved by eliminating inventories and simplifying material transfers through the implementation of a JIT system.

Once the benefits from redesign and simplification are achieved, however, it becomes apparent where automation can generate additional benefits. Many companies can improve their competitive positions by adding such features as robotics, flexible manufacturing systems, and completely integrated manufacturing systems. The ultimate commitment to automation is the construction of greenfield factories. Greenfield factories are new factories designed and built from scratch; they represent a strategic decision by a company to completely change the way it manufactures.

Although discounted cash-flow analysis (using net present value and internal rate of return) remains preeminent in capital investment decisions, the new manufacturing environment demands that more attention be paid to the inputs used in discounted cash-flow models. How investment is defined, how operating cash flows are estimated, how salvage value is treated, and how the discount rate is chosen are all different in nature from the traditional approach.[15]

There is also another important dimension. Contemporary investment management involves both financial and nonfinancial criteria. It is critical that a company's investment management process be linked with the organization's strategies. Analyses involving advanced manufacturing technology should consider the contributions made by such technologies toward supporting such strategies as product enhancement, diversification, and risk reduction. For example, advanced technology may contribute to product enhancement by allowing a firm more flexibility in

---

15. Thomas Klammer, "Improving Investment Decisions," *Management Accounting* (July 1993): 35–43; and David Sinason, "A Dynamic Model for Present Value Analysis," *Journal of Cost Management* (Spring 1991): 40–45.

responding to fluctuating demand. Improving quality is also a product enhancement feature. Some product enhancement features are readily quantified. It may be possible to estimate the cost savings attributable to improved quality. Other factors may be more difficult to quantify. Assessing the cost savings or increased revenues from increased flexibility may be quite difficult. Yet the increased flexibility may be as critical for the company as the improved quality. Thus, consideration of nonfinancial factors is important. Of course, every possible effort should be made to quantify all factors affecting the investment decision.

How Investment Differs

Investment in automated manufacturing processes is much more complex than investment in the standard manufacturing equipment of the past. For standard equipment, the direct costs of acquisition represent virtually the entire investment. For automated manufacturing, the direct costs can represent as little as 50 or 60 percent of the total investment; software, engineering, training, and implementation are a significant percentage of the total costs. Thus, great care must be exercised to assess the actual cost of an automated system. It is easy to overlook the peripheral costs, which can be substantial.

How Estimates of Operating Cash Flows Differ

Estimates of operating cash flows from investments in standard equipment have typically relied on directly identifiable benefits, such as direct savings from labour, power, and scrap. Indirect benefits and savings were ignored because they were viewed as immaterial. In the new manufacturing environment, however, the indirect benefits can be material and critical to the project's viability. Greater quality, more reliability, reduced lead time, improved customer satisfaction, and an enhanced ability to maintain market share are all important benefits of an advanced manufacturing system. Reduction of labour in support areas, such as production scheduling and stores, is another indirect benefit. More effort is needed to measure these indirect benefits in order to assess the potential value of investments more accurately.

   We can illustrate the importance of considering indirect benefits with an example. Suppose that a company is evaluating a potential investment in a flexible manufacturing system (FMS). The choice facing the company is to continue producing with its conventional equipment, which is expected to last 10 years, or to switch to the new system, which is also expected to have a useful life of 10 years. The company's discount rate is 12 percent. The data pertaining to the investment are presented in Exhibit 11–9.

   Using these data, we can compute the net present value of the proposed system as follows:

PV ($4,000,000 × 5.650[a])	$22,600,000
Less investment	18,000,000
NPV	$ 4,600,000

[a] Discount factor for an interest rate of 12 percent and a life of 10 years (see Exhibit 11B–2)

   The net present value is positive and large in magnitude, and it clearly signals the acceptability of the FMS. This outcome, however, is strongly dependent on explicit recognition of indirect benefits. If those benefits are eliminated, then the direct savings total $2.2 million, and the NPV is negative:

PV ($2,200,000 × 5.650)	$12,430,000
Less investment	18,000,000
NPV	$ (5,570,000)

Exhibit 11–9

Investment Data: Direct
and Indirect Benefits

	FMS	Status Quo
Investment (current outlay):		
Direct costs	$10,000,000	—
Software, engineering	8,000,000	—
Total current outlay	$18,000,000	$ 0
Net after-tax cash flow	$ 5,000,000	$1,000,000
Less: After-tax cash flow for status quo	1,000,000	n/a
Incremental benefit	$ 4,000,000	n/a
Incremental Benefit Explained		
Direct benefits:		
Direct labour	$1,500,000	
Scrap reduction	500,000	
Setups	200,000	$2,200,000
Indirect benefits:		
Quality savings:		
Rework	$ 200,000	
Warranties	400,000	
Maintenance of competitive position	1,000,000	
Production scheduling	110,000	
Payroll	90,000	1,800,000
Total		$4,000,000

The rise of activity-based costing has made identifying indirect benefits easier with the use of cost drivers. Once they are identified, they can be included in the analysis if they are material.

Exhibit 11–9 reveals the importance of measuring all indirect benefits. One of the most important indirect benefits is maintaining or improving a firm's competitive position. A key question that needs to be asked is what will happen to the firm's cash flows if the investment is not made? That is, if the company chooses to forgo an investment in technologically advanced equipment, will it be able to continue to compete with other firms on the basis of quality, delivery, and cost? This question becomes especially relevant if competitors choose to invest in advanced equipment. If a firm's competitive position deteriorates, the company's current cash flows will decrease.

If cash flows will decrease if the investment is not made, this decrease should show up as an incremental benefit for the advanced technology. In Exhibit 11–9, the company estimates this competitive benefit as $1,000,000. Estimating this benefit requires some serious strategic planning and analysis, but its effect can be critical. If this benefit had been ignored or overlooked, then the net present value would have been negative, and the investment alternative rejected. This calculation is shown below:

PV ($3,000,000 × 5.650)	$16,950,000
Less investment	18,000,000
NPV	$(1,050,000)

Salvage Value

Earlier in this chapter, we saw that salvage value can have a number of tax implications for a firm. But terminal or salvage value is often ignored in investment decisions. The usual reason offered is the difficulty of estimating this value. Because of this uncertainty, the effect of salvage value is often ignored or heavily discounted.

This approach may be unwise, however, because salvage value could make the difference between investing or not investing. Given a highly competitive environment, companies cannot afford to make incorrect decisions. A much better approach to dealing with uncertainty is to use sensitivity analysis. Sensitivity analysis (often referred to as **what-if analysis**) changes the assumptions on which the capital investment analysis relies and assesses their effect on the cash-flow pattern. This approach can be used to address such questions as what is the effect if cash receipts are 5 percent less? 5 percent more? Although sensitivity analysis is time consuming if done manually, it can be done rapidly and easily using many common computer programs.

To illustrate the potential effect of terminal value, assume that the after-tax annual operating cash flow of the project shown in Exhibit 11–9 is $3.1 million instead of $4 million. The net present value without salvage value is as follows:

PV ($3,100,000 × 5.650)	$17,515,000
Less investment	18,000,000
NPV	$ (485,000)

Without the terminal value, the project would be rejected. The net present value with a salvage value of $2 million, however, is a positive result, meaning that the investment should be made.

PV ($3,100,000 × 5.650)	$17,515,000
PV salvage value ($2,000,000 × 0.322[a])	644,000
Total PV	$18,159,000
Less investment	18,000,000
NPV	$ 159,000

[a] Discount factor, 12 percent and 10 years (Exhibit 11B–1)

But what if the salvage value is less than expected? Suppose that the worst possible salvage value is $1,600,000. What is the effect of this information on the decision? The NPV can be recalculated under this new (what-if) scenario:

PV ($3,100,000 × 5.650)	$17,515,000
PV salvage value ($1,600,000 × 0.322)	515,200
Total PV	$18,030,200
Less investment	18,000,000
NPV	$ 30,200

Thus, under a pessimistic scenario the NPV is still positive. This example illustrates how sensitivity analysis can be used to deal with the uncertainty surrounding salvage value. It can also be used for other uncertain cash-flow variables.

Discount Rates

Being overly conservative with discount rates can prove even more damaging. In theory, if future cash flows are known with certainty, the correct discount rate is a firm's cost of capital. In practice, future cash flows are uncertain, and managers often choose a discount rate higher than the cost of capital to deal with that uncertainty. If the rate chosen is excessively high, it will bias the selection process toward short-term investments.

To illustrate the effect of an excessive discount rate, consider the project in Exhibit 11–9 once again. Assume that the correct discount rate is 12 percent but that the firm uses 18 percent. The net present value using an 18 percent discount rate is calculated as follows:

PV ($4,000,000 × 4.494ᵃ)	$17,976,000
Less investment	18,000,000
NPV	$ (24,000)

ᵃ Discount rate for 18 percent and 10 years (Exhibit 11B–2)

The project would be rejected. With a higher discount rate, the discount factor decreases in magnitude more rapidly than does the discount factor for a lower rate (compare the discount factor for 12 percent, 5.650, with the factor for 18 percent, 4.494). The effect of a higher discount factor is to place more weight on earlier cash flows and less weight on later cash flows, thereby favouring short-term over long-term investments. This outcome makes it more difficult for automated manufacturing systems to appear as viable projects, since the cash returns required to justify the investment are received over a longer period of time.

APPENDIX 11A: FUTURE VALUE AND PRESENT VALUE

An important feature of money is that it can be invested and can earn interest. A dollar today is not the same as a dollar tomorrow. This fundamental principle is the backbone of discounting models. Discounting models rely on the relationships between current and future dollars. Thus, to use discounting models, we must understand these relationships.

Future Value

Suppose that a bank advertises a 4 percent annual interest rate. If a customer invests $100 at this rate, then after one year she will receive the original $100 plus $4 interest, or $104. This result can be expressed by the following equation, where F is the future amount, P is the initial or current outlay, and i is the interest rate:

$$F = P(1 + i) \tag{11A.1}$$

For our example, $F = \$100(1 + 0.04) = \$100(1.04) = \$104$.

Now suppose that the same bank offers a 5 percent rate if the customer leaves the original deposit, plus any interest, on deposit for two years. How much will the customer receive at the end of the two years? Again, assume that she invests $100. Using Equation 11A.1, she will earn $105 at the end of Year 1 [$F = \$100(1 + 0.05) = \$105$]. If she leaves this amount in the account for a second year, we can use Equation 11A.1 again, with P now equal to $105. At the end of the second year, then, the total is $110.25 [$F = \$105(1 + 0.05) = \$110.25$]. In the second year, she earns interest on both the original deposit and the interest earned in the first year. The earning of interest on interest is referred to as the **compounding of interest**. The value that accumulates by the end of an investment's life, assuming a specified compound return, is the future value. The future value of the $100 deposit in our second example is $110.25.

We have a more direct way to compute the **future value**. Since the first application of Equation 11A.1 can be expressed as $F = \$105 = \$100(1.05)$, the second application can be expressed as $F = \$105(1.05) = \$100(1.05)(1.05) = \$100(1.05)^2 = P(1 + i)^2$. This suggests the following formula for computing amounts for n periods into the future:

$$F = P(1 + i)^n \tag{11A.2}$$

Present Value

Often a manager needs to compute not the future value but the amount that must be invested *now* in order to earn some given future value. The amount that must be invested now to produce the future value is known as the **present value** of the future amount. For example, how much must be invested now in order to earn $363 two years from now, assuming that the interest rate is 10 percent? Or, put another way, what is the present value of $363 to be received two years from now?

In this example, the future value, the years, and the interest rate are all known; the problem is to find the current outlay that will produce that future amount. In Equation 11A.2, the variable representing the current outlay (the present value of F) is P. Thus, to compute the present value of a future outlay, we need only solve Equation 11A.2 for P:

$$P = F/(1 + i)^n \tag{11A.3}$$

Using Equation 11A.3, we can compute the present value of $363 as follows:

$$P = \$363/(1 + 0.1)^2 = \$363/1.21 = \$300$$

The present value, $300, is what the future amount of $363 is worth today. All other things being equal, having $300 today is the same as having $363 two years from now. Put another way, if a firm requires a 10 percent rate of return, $300 is the most the firm will be willing to pay today for any investment that yields $363 two years from now.

The process of computing the present value of future cash flows is referred to as **discounting**; thus, we say we have discounted the future value of $363 to its present value of $300. The interest rate used to discount the future cash flow is the discount rate. The expression

$$1/(1 + i)^n$$

in Equation 11A.3 is the **discount factor**. Calling the discount factor df, Equation 11A.3 can be expressed as follows:

$$P = F(df)$$

To simplify the computation of present value, a table of discount factors is given for various combinations of i and n (see Exhibit 11B–1 in Appendix 11B). For example, the discount factor for $i = 10$ percent and $n = 2$ is 0.826 (simply go to the 10 percent column of the table and move down to the second row). With the discount factor, the present value of $363 is computed as follows:

$$P = F(df) = \$363 \times 0.826 = \$300 \text{ (rounded)}$$

Present Value of an Uneven Series of Cash Flows   We can use the discount factors from Exhibit 11B–1 to compute the present value of any future cash flow or series of future cash flows. A series of future cash flows is called an **annuity**. The present value of an annuity is found by computing the present value of each future cash flow and then summing these values. For example, suppose that an investment is expected to produce the following annual cash flows: $110, $121, and $133.10. Assuming a discount rate of 10 percent, we can compute the present value of this series of cash receipts as in Exhibit 11A–1.

Exhibit 11A–1	Year	Cash Receipt	Discount Factor	Present Value
Present Value of an Uneven Series of Cash Flows	1	$110.00	0.909	$100.00
	2	121.00	0.826	100.00
	3	133.10	0.751	100.00
				$300.00

Exhibit 11A–2	Year	Cash Receipt*	Discount Factor	Present Value
Present Value of Uniform Series of Cash Flows	1	$100	0.909	$ 90.90
	2	100	0.826	82.60
	3	100	0.751	75.10
			2.486	$248.60

* The annual cash flow of $100 can be multiplied by the sum of the discount factors (2.486) to obtain the present value of the uniform series.

Present Value of a Uniform Series of Cash Flows   If the series of cash flows is even, the computation of the annuity's present value is simplified. Assume, for example, that an investment is expected to return $100 per year for three years. Using Exhibit 11B–1 and assuming a discount rate of 10 percent, we can compute the annuity's present value as in Exhibit 11A–2.

As with the uneven series of cash flows, the present value in Exhibit 11A–2 was computed by calculating the present value of each cash flow separately and then summing them. However, in the case of an annuity that displays uniform cash flows, the computations can be reduced from three to one, as described in the note to Exhibit 11A–2. The sum of the individual discount factors can be thought of as a discount factor for an annuity of uniform cash flows. A table of discount factors that can be used for an annuity of uniform cash flows is available in Exhibit 11B–2.

SUMMARY OF LEARNING OBJECTIVES

1. Explain what a capital investment decision is, and distinguish between independent and mutually exclusive capital investment projects.
Capital investment decisions are concerned with the acquisition of long-term assets and usually involve a significant outlay of funds. There are two types of capital investment projects: independent and mutually exclusive. Independent projects are projects whose acceptance or rejection does not affect the cash flows of other projects. Mutually exclusive projects are projects that, if accepted, preclude the acceptance of all other competing projects.

2. Compute the payback period and accounting rate of return for a proposed investment, and explain their roles in capital investment decisions.
Managers make capital investment decisions by using formal models to decide whether to accept or reject proposed projects. These decision models are classified as nondiscounting and discounting, depending on whether they address the question of the time value of money. There are two nondiscounting models: the payback period and the accounting rate of return.

The payback period is the time required for a firm to recover its initial investment. For even cash flows, it is calculated by dividing the investment by the annual cash flow. For uneven cash flows, the cash flows are summed until the investment is recovered. If only a fraction of a year is needed, then it is assumed that the

cash flows occur evenly within each year. The payback period ignores the time value of money and the profitability of projects, because it does not consider the cash inflows available beyond the payback period. However, it does supply some useful information. The payback period is useful in assessing and controlling risk, minimizing an investment's impact on a firm's liquidity, and controlling the risk of obsolescence.

The accounting rate of return is computed by dividing the average income expected from an investment by either the original investment or the average investment. Unlike the payback period, it does consider the profitability of a project; however, it too ignores the time value of money. Managers may find the accounting rate of return useful for screening new investments to ensure that certain financial accounting ratios (specifically, any accounting ratios that may be monitored to ensure compliance with debt contracts) are not adversely affected.

3. Use net present value (NPV) analysis for capital investment decisions involving independent projects.
NPV is the difference between the present value of future cash flows and the initial investment outlay. To use this model, a required rate of return (usually the cost of capital) must be identified. The NPV method uses the required rate of return to compute the present value of a project's cash inflows and outflows. If the present value of the inflows is greater than the

APPENDIX B: PRESENT VALUE TABLES

Exhibit 11B–1

Present Value of $1[a]

Periods	2%	4%	6%	8%	10%	12%	14%	16%	18%	20%	22%	24%	26%	28%	30%	32%	40%
1	0.980	0.962	0.943	0.926	0.909	0.893	0.877	0.862	0.847	0.833	0.820	0.806	0.794	0.781	0.769	0.758	0.714
2	0.961	0.925	0.890	0.857	0.826	0.797	0.769	0.743	0.718	0.694	0.672	0.650	0.630	0.610	0.592	0.574	0.510
3	0.942	0.889	0.840	0.794	0.751	0.712	0.675	0.641	0.609	0.579	0.551	0.524	0.500	0.477	0.455	0.435	0.364
4	0.924	0.855	0.792	0.735	0.683	0.636	0.592	0.552	0.516	0.482	0.451	0.423	0.397	0.373	0.350	0.329	0.260
5	0.906	0.822	0.747	0.681	0.621	0.567	0.519	0.476	0.437	0.402	0.370	0.341	0.315	0.291	0.269	0.250	0.186
6	0.888	0.790	0.705	0.630	0.564	0.507	0.456	0.410	0.370	0.335	0.303	0.275	0.250	0.227	0.207	0.189	0.133
7	0.871	0.760	0.665	0.583	0.513	0.452	0.400	0.354	0.314	0.279	0.249	0.222	0.198	0.178	0.159	0.143	0.095
8	0.853	0.731	0.627	0.540	0.467	0.404	0.351	0.305	0.266	0.233	0.204	0.179	0.157	0.139	0.123	0.108	0.068
9	0.837	0.703	0.592	0.500	0.424	0.361	0.308	0.263	0.225	0.194	0.167	0.144	0.125	0.108	0.094	0.082	0.048
10	0.820	0.676	0.558	0.463	0.386	0.322	0.270	0.227	0.191	0.162	0.137	0.116	0.099	0.085	0.073	0.062	0.035
11	0.804	0.650	0.527	0.429	0.350	0.287	0.237	0.195	0.162	0.135	0.112	0.094	0.079	0.066	0.056	0.047	0.025
12	0.788	0.625	0.497	0.397	0.319	0.257	0.208	0.168	0.137	0.112	0.092	0.076	0.062	0.052	0.043	0.036	0.018
13	0.773	0.601	0.469	0.368	0.290	0.229	0.182	0.145	0.116	0.093	0.075	0.061	0.050	0.040	0.033	0.027	0.013
14	0.758	0.577	0.442	0.340	0.263	0.205	0.160	0.125	0.099	0.078	0.062	0.049	0.039	0.032	0.025	0.021	0.009
15	0.743	0.555	0.417	0.315	0.239	0.183	0.140	0.108	0.084	0.065	0.051	0.040	0.031	0.025	0.020	0.016	0.006
16	0.728	0.534	0.394	0.292	0.218	0.163	0.123	0.093	0.071	0.054	0.042	0.032	0.025	0.019	0.015	0.012	0.005
17	0.714	0.513	0.371	0.270	0.198	0.146	0.108	0.080	0.060	0.045	0.034	0.026	0.020	0.015	0.012	0.009	0.003
18	0.700	0.494	0.350	0.250	0.180	0.130	0.095	0.069	0.051	0.038	0.028	0.021	0.016	0.012	0.009	0.007	0.002
19	0.686	0.475	0.331	0.232	0.164	0.116	0.083	0.060	0.043	0.031	0.023	0.017	0.012	0.009	0.007	0.005	0.002
20	0.673	0.456	0.312	0.215	0.149	0.104	0.073	0.051	0.037	0.026	0.019	0.014	0.010	0.007	0.005	0.004	0.001
21	0.660	0.439	0.294	0.199	0.135	0.093	0.064	0.044	0.031	0.022	0.015	0.011	0.008	0.006	0.004	0.003	0.001
22	0.647	0.422	0.278	0.184	0.123	0.083	0.056	0.038	0.026	0.018	0.013	0.009	0.006	0.004	0.003	0.002	0.001
23	0.634	0.406	0.262	0.170	0.112	0.074	0.049	0.033	0.022	0.015	0.010	0.007	0.005	0.003	0.002	0.002	0.000
24	0.622	0.390	0.247	0.158	0.102	0.066	0.043	0.028	0.019	0.013	0.008	0.006	0.004	0.003	0.002	0.001	0.000
25	0.610	0.375	0.233	0.146	0.092	0.059	0.038	0.024	0.016	0.010	0.007	0.005	0.003	0.002	0.001	0.001	0.000
26	0.598	0.361	0.220	0.135	0.084	0.053	0.033	0.021	0.014	0.009	0.006	0.004	0.002	0.002	0.001	0.001	0.000
27	0.586	0.347	0.207	0.125	0.076	0.047	0.029	0.018	0.011	0.007	0.005	0.003	0.002	0.001	0.001	0.001	0.000
28	0.574	0.333	0.196	0.116	0.069	0.042	0.026	0.016	0.010	0.006	0.004	0.002	0.002	0.001	0.001	0.000	0.000
29	0.563	0.321	0.185	0.107	0.063	0.037	0.022	0.014	0.008	0.005	0.003	0.002	0.001	0.001	0.000	0.000	0.000
30	0.552	0.308	0.174	0.099	0.057	0.033	0.020	0.012	0.007	0.004	0.003	0.002	0.001	0.001	0.000	0.000	0.000

$$^{a}P_n = \frac{A}{(1+i)^n}$$

Exhibit 11B–2

Present Value of an Annuity of $1 in Arrears[a]

Periods	2%	4%	6%	8%	10%	12%	14%	16%	18%	20%	22%	24%	26%	28%	30%	32%	40%
1	0.980	0.962	0.943	0.926	0.909	0.893	0.877	0.862	0.847	0.833	0.820	0.806	0.794	0.781	0.769	0.758	0.714
2	1.942	1.886	1.833	1.783	1.736	1.690	1.647	1.605	1.566	1.528	1.492	1.457	1.424	1.392	1.361	1.331	1.224
3	2.884	2.775	2.673	2.577	2.487	2.402	2.322	2.246	2.174	2.106	2.042	1.981	1.923	1.868	1.816	1.766	1.589
4	3.808	3.630	3.465	3.312	3.170	3.037	2.914	2.798	2.690	2.589	2.494	2.404	2.320	2.241	2.166	2.096	1.849
5	4.713	4.452	4.212	3.993	3.791	3.605	3.433	3.274	3.127	2.991	2.864	2.745	2.635	2.532	2.436	2.345	2.035
6	5.601	5.242	4.917	4.623	4.355	4.111	3.889	3.685	3.498	3.326	3.167	3.020	2.885	2.759	2.643	2.534	2.168
7	6.472	6.002	5.582	5.206	4.868	4.564	4.288	4.039	3.812	3.605	3.416	3.242	3.083	2.937	2.802	2.677	2.263
8	7.325	6.733	6.210	5.747	5.335	4.968	4.639	4.344	4.078	3.837	3.619	3.421	3.241	3.076	2.925	2.786	2.331
9	8.162	7.435	6.802	6.247	5.759	5.328	4.946	4.607	4.303	4.032	3.786	3.566	3.366	3.184	3.019	2.868	2.379
10	8.983	8.111	7.360	6.710	6.145	5.650	5.216	4.833	4.494	4.192	3.923	3.682	3.465	3.269	3.092	2.930	2.414
11	9.787	8.760	7.887	7.139	6.495	5.938	5.453	5.029	4.656	4.327	4.035	3.776	3.543	3.335	3.147	2.978	2.438
12	10.575	9.385	8.384	7.536	6.814	6.194	5.660	5.197	4.793	4.439	4.127	3.851	3.606	3.387	3.190	3.013	2.456
13	11.348	9.986	8.853	7.904	7.103	6.424	5.842	5.342	4.910	4.533	4.203	3.912	3.656	3.427	3.223	3.040	2.469
14	12.106	10.563	9.295	8.244	7.367	6.628	6.002	5.468	5.008	4.611	4.265	3.962	3.695	3.459	3.249	3.061	2.478
15	12.849	11.118	9.712	8.559	7.606	6.811	6.142	5.575	5.092	4.675	4.315	4.001	3.726	3.483	3.268	3.076	2.484
16	13.578	11.652	10.106	8.851	7.824	6.974	6.265	5.668	5.162	4.730	4.357	4.033	3.751	3.503	3.283	3.088	2.489
17	14.292	12.166	10.477	9.122	8.022	7.120	6.373	5.749	5.222	4.775	4.391	4.059	3.771	3.518	3.295	3.097	2.492
18	14.992	12.659	10.828	9.372	8.201	7.250	6.467	5.818	5.273	4.812	4.419	4.080	3.786	3.529	3.304	3.104	2.494
19	15.678	13.134	11.158	9.604	8.365	7.366	6.550	5.877	5.316	4.843	4.442	4.097	3.799	3.539	3.311	3.109	2.496
20	16.351	13.590	11.470	9.818	8.514	7.469	6.623	5.929	5.353	4.870	4.460	4.110	3.808	3.546	3.316	3.113	2.497
21	17.011	14.029	11.764	10.017	8.649	7.562	6.687	5.973	5.384	4.891	4.476	4.121	3.816	3.551	3.320	3.116	2.498
22	17.658	14.451	12.042	10.201	8.772	7.645	6.743	6.011	5.410	4.909	4.488	4.130	3.822	3.556	3.323	3.118	2.498
23	18.292	14.857	12.303	10.371	8.883	7.718	6.792	6.044	5.432	4.925	4.499	4.137	3.827	3.559	3.325	3.120	2.499
24	18.914	15.247	12.550	10.529	8.985	7.784	6.835	6.073	5.451	4.937	4.507	4.143	3.831	3.562	3.327	3.121	2.499
25	19.523	15.622	12.783	10.675	9.077	7.843	6.873	6.097	5.467	4.948	4.514	4.147	3.834	3.564	3.329	3.122	2.499
26	20.121	15.983	13.003	10.810	9.161	7.896	6.906	6.118	5.480	4.956	4.520	4.151	3.837	3.566	3.330	3.123	2.500
27	20.707	16.330	13.211	10.935	9.237	7.943	6.935	6.136	5.492	4.964	4.524	4.154	3.839	3.567	3.331	3.123	2.500
28	21.281	16.663	13.406	11.051	9.307	7.984	6.961	6.152	5.502	4.970	4.528	4.157	3.840	3.568	3.331	3.124	2.500
29	21.844	16.984	13.591	11.158	9.370	8.022	6.983	6.166	5.510	4.975	4.531	4.159	3.841	3.569	3.332	3.124	2.500
30	22.396	17.292	13.765	11.258	9.427	8.055	7.003	6.177	5.517	4.979	4.534	4.160	3.842	3.569	3.332	3.124	2.500

[a] $P_n = \left(\frac{1}{i}\right)\left[1 - \frac{1}{(1+i)^n}\right]$

present value of the outflows, the net present value is greater than zero, and the project is profitable; if the NPV is less than zero, the project is not profitable and should be rejected.

4. Use the internal rate of return (IRR) to assess the acceptability of independent projects.

The IRR is computed by finding the interest rate that equates the present value of a project's cash inflows with the present value of its cash outflows. If the IRR is greater than the required rate of return (cost of capital), the project is acceptable; if the IRR is less than the required rate of return, the project should be rejected.

5. Explain why NPV is better than IRR for capital investment decisions involving mutually exclusive projects.

In evaluating mutually exclusive or competing projects, managers have a choice of using NPV or IRR. When managers must choose among competing projects, the NPV model correctly identifies the best investment alternative. Using IRR, on the other hand may at times lead to choosing an inferior project. Thus, since NPV always provides the correct signal, it should be used.

6. Explain the role and value of postaudits.

A postaudit of a capital project is an important step in the capital investment decision process. Postaudits evaluate a project's actual performance in relation to its expected performance. A postaudit may lead to corrective action to improve the project's performance, or the project may even be abandoned. Postaudits also serve as an incentive for managers to make capital investment decisions prudently.

7. Convert gross cash flows to after-tax cash flows.

Accurate and reliable cash-flow forecasts are absolutely critical for capital investment decisions. Managers should assume responsibility for the accuracy of cash-flow projections. All cash flows in a capital investment analysis should be after-tax cash flows. There are two different but equivalent ways to compute after-tax cash flows: the income method and the decomposition method. Although amortization is not a cash flow, it does have cash-flow implications, because tax laws allow capital cost allowances (CCAs) to be deducted in computing taxable income, and this has the effect of shielding revenue from taxation. There are two ways to calculate the tax shield effect of CCA: the direct method and the formula method. To reflect income tax more accurately, the one-half rule and nonzero salvage value must also be considered when calculating the effect of CCA on a project's net present value.

8. Describe capital investment in the advanced manufacturing environment.

Capital investment in the advanced manufacturing environment is affected by the way in which inputs are determined. Much greater attention must be paid to the investment outlays, because peripheral items can require substantial resources. Furthermore, in assessing benefits, indirect items such as quality and maintaining competitive position can be deciding factors. Choice of the required rate of return is also critical. The tendency of firms to use required rates of return that are much greater than the cost of capital should be discontinued. Also, since the salvage value of an automated system can be considerable, that value should be estimated and included in the analysis.

KEY TERMS

Accounting rate of return, 458	Discount rate, 459	Net present value, 459
Annuity, 482	Discounted cash flows, 458	Nondiscounting models, 458
Capital budgeting, 454	Discounting, 482	One-half rule, 475
Capital cost allowance (CCA), 469	Discounting models, 459	Payback period, 456
Capital investment decisions, 454	Future value, 481	Postaudit, 465
Compounding of interest, 481	Independent projects, 454	Present value, 482
Cost of capital, 468	Internal rate of return, 460	What-if analysis, 480
Discount factor, 459	Mutually exclusive projects, 454	

REVIEW PROBLEMS

I. BASICS OF CAPITAL INVESTMENT DECISIONS (IGNORE TAXES FOR THIS PROBLEM.)

Sebastian Ebro is investigating the possibility of acquiring an ice-cream franchise. To acquire the franchise requires an initial outlay of $300,000 (the purchase includes building and equipment). To raise the capital, Sebastian will sell stock valued at $200,000 (the stock pays dividends of $24,000 per year) and borrow $100,000. The loan for $100,000 would carry an interest rate of 6 percent. Sebastian figures that his cost of capital is 10 percent $[(2/3 \times 0.12) + (1/3 \times 0.06)]$. This weighted cost of capital is the discount rate that he will use for capital investment decisions.

The franchise will produce an annual cash inflow of $50,000. Sebastian expects to operate the business for 20 years, after which he will turn it over to one of his children.

Required:

1. Compute the payback period.
2. Assuming that amortization is $14,000 per year, compute the accounting rate of return (on total investment).
3. Compute the NPV of the franchise.
4. Compute the IRR of the franchise.
5. Should Sebastian acquire the franchise?

Solution

1. The payback period is $300,000/$50,000, or six years.
2. The accounting rate of return is ($50,000 – $14,000)/$300,000, or 12 percent.
3. From Exhibit 11B–2, the discount factor for an annuity with i at 10 percent and n at 20 years is 8.514. Thus, the NPV is (8.514 × $50,000) – $300,000, or $125,700.
4. The discount factor associated with the IRR is 6.00 ($300,000/$50,000). From Exhibit 11B–2, the IRR is between 14 and 16 percent (using the row corresponding to Period 20); with a calculator, the IRR is 15.8 percent.
5. Since the NPV is positive and the IRR is greater than Sebastian's cost of capital, the franchise is a sound investment. This conclusion, of course, assumes that the cash-flow projections are accurate.

II. CAPITAL INVESTMENT WITH COMPETING PROJECTS (CCA TAX SHIELD)

Blalock Manufacturing has decided to acquire a new parcel van to transport packages from its warehouse to the airport. The choice has been narrowed to two models. The following information has been gathered for each model:

	Model A	Model T
Acquisition cost	$20,000	$25,000
Annual operating costs	$3,500	$2,000
Capital cost allowance rate	30%	30%
Expected salvage value	$4,000	$5,000

Blalock's cost of capital is 14 percent. The company plans to use the van for five years and then sell it for its salvage value. Assume that the tax rate is 40 percent and that Blalock has other assets in the same capital cost class.

Required:

1. Compute the after-tax operating cash flows for each model.
2. Compute the NPV for each model, and make a recommendation.

Solution

1. First, we will calculate the capital cost allowance for each model:

Year	Model A	Model T
1[a]	3,000	3,750
2	5,100	6,375
3	3,570	4,463
4	2,499	3,124
5	1,749	2,187

[a] CCA is calculated at 50% of the usual rate in the first year.

We can calculate after-tax operating cash flows as follows:

MODEL A

Year	(1 – Tax rate) × Revenue	–	(1 – Tax rate) × Cash expenses	+	Tax rate × Noncash expenses	=	After-tax cash flows
1	n/a		$(2,100)[a]		$1,200[b]		$ (900)
2	n/a		(2,100)		2,040		(60)
3	n/a		(2,100)		1,428		(672)
4	n/a		(2,100)		1,000		(1,100)
5	n/a		(2,100)		700		(1,400)

[a] $(1 – 0.4) \times 3,500$
[b] $0.4 \times 3,000$

MODEL T

Year	(1 – Tax rate) × Revenue	–	(1 – Tax rate) × Cash expenses	+	Tax rate × Noncash expenses	=	After-tax cash flows
1	n/a		$(1,200)[a]		$1,500[b]		$ 300
2	n/a		(1,200)		2,550		1,350
3	n/a		(1,200)		1,785		585
4	n/a		(1,200)		1,250		50
5	n/a		(1,200)		874		(326)

[a] $(1 – 0.4) \times 2,000$
[b] $0.4 \times 3,750$

2. NPV computation (direct from net cash flows):
   Given the after-tax operating cash flows from Requirement 1, we can calculate the present value of each model directly.

Year	Discount Factor	MODEL A Cash Flow	MODEL A Present Value	MODEL T Cash Flow	MODEL T Present Value
0	1.000	$(20,000)	$(20,000)	$(25,000)	$(25,000)
1	0.877	(900)	(789)	300	263
2	0.769	(60)	(46)	1,350	1,038
3	0.675	(672)	(454)	585	395
4	0.592	(1,100)	(651)	50	30
5	0.519	(1,400)	(727)	(326)	(169)
Salvage Value[a]	0.519	4,000	2,076	5,000	2,595
Remaining CCA[b]	–	82	11	102	13
NPV			$(20,580)		$(20,835)

[a] Assume that salvage value is received at the beginning of Year 6.
[b] Because there are other assets in the cost pool, any remaining capital cost after the asset is sold will continue as a tax shield. The remaining capital cost for Model A is $20,000 – $15,918 – $4,000 = $82, and that for Model T is $25,000 – $19,898 – $5,000 = $102. The present value is calculated by determining the CCA for years beyond Year 5 and then discounting.

Model A should be chosen, since it has the highest (least negative) NPV, indicating that it is the least costly of the two parcel vans. Note also that the net present values are negative, so that this choice is the least costly investment.

NPV computation: an alternative analysis (using CCA tax shield formula):

We can calculate the NPV for each model by analyzing the direct cash flows and tax shield effects separately. The NPV for each model, without the CCA tax shield, is calculated as follows:

Year	Discount Factor	MODEL A		MODEL T	
		Cash Flow	Present Value	Cash Flow	Present Value
0	1.000	$(20,000)	$(20,000)	$(25,000)	$(25,000)
1	0.877	(2,100)	(1,842)	(1,200)	(1,052)
2	0.769	(2,100)	(1,615)	(1,200)	(923)
3	0.675	(2,100)	(1,418)	(1,200)	(810)
4	0.592	(2,100)	(1,243)	(1,200)	(710)
5	0.519	(2,100)	(1,090)	(1,200)	(623)
Salvage Value[a]	0.519	4,000	2,076	5,000	2,595
NPV			$(25,132)		$(26,523)

[a] Assume that salvage value will be received at the beginning of Year 6.

The present value of the CCA tax shield is calculated by using a formula that includes the adjustment for salvage value and the one-half rule.

Present value of CCA tax shield – Present value of salvage value adjustment:

$$[(R \times C \times T)/(R + i)] \times [(1 + 0.5i)/(1 + i)] - [(R \times S \times T)/(R + i)] \times [1/(1 + i)^n]$$

where R = the CCA rate
C = the original capital cost
T = the tax rate
i = the discount rate
n = the period of sale
S = the salvage value

For Model A, the CCA tax shield has a present value of $4,553, calculated as follows:

$[0.3 \times \$20,000 \times 0.4]/[0.3 + 0.14] \times [(1 + 0.5 \times 0.14)/(1 + 0.14)] =$	$5,120
less $[0.3 \times \$4,000 \times 0.4]/[0.3 + 0.14] \times [1/(1 + 0.14)^5] =$	$ 567
Present value of CCA tax shield	$4,553

For Model T, the CCA tax shield has a present value of $5,692, calculated as follows:

$[0.3 \times \$25,000 \times 0.4]/[0.3 + 0.14] \times [(1 + 0.5 \times 0.14)/(1 + 0.14)] =$	$6,400
less $[0.3 \times \$5,000 \times 0.4]/[0.3 + 0.14] \times [1/(1 + 0.14)^5] =$	$ 708
Present value of CCA tax shield	$5,692

To summarize, the NPV of each model is as follows:

	Model A	Model T
NPV without CCA tax shield	$(25,132)	$(26,523)
PV of CCA tax shield	4,553	5,692
NPV	$(20,579)[a]	$(20,831)[a]

[a] The differences between these answers and those for the previous analysis are due to rounding.

QUESTIONS FOR WRITING AND DISCUSSION

1. Explain the difference between independent projects and mutually exclusive projects.

2. Explain why the timing and quantity of cash flows are important in capital investment decisions.

3. The time value of money is ignored by both the payback period and the accounting rate of return. Explain why this is a major deficiency in these two models.

4. What is the payback period? Compute the payback period for an investment requiring an initial outlay of $80,000 with expected annual cash inflows of $30,000.

5. Name and discuss three possible reasons why the payback period is used to help make capital investment decisions.

6. What is the accounting rate of return? Compute the accounting rate of return for an investment that requires an initial outlay of $300,000 and promises an average net income of $100,000.

7. What is meant by the term *future value*?

8. What are discounted cash flows? What is the discount rate? the discount factor?

9. What is meant by the term *present value*?

10. Compute the present value of an annuity that has uniform cash inflows if the discount rate is 8 percent and the annual cash inflow produced by the annuity is $32,000. The expected life of the annuity is four years.

11. The net present value is the same as the profit of a project expressed in present dollars. Do you agree? Explain.

12. What is the cost of capital? What role does it play in capital investment decisions?

13. What role does the required rate of return play for the NPV model? for the IRR model?

14. The IRR is the true or actual rate of return being earned by the project. Do you agree or disagree? Discuss.

15. Explain how the NPV is used to determine whether a project should be accepted or rejected.

16. Explain the relationship between NPV and a firm's value.

17. Compute the IRR for a project that requires an investment of $299,100 and provides a return of $100,000 per year for four years.

18. What methods would you choose to use to make a capital investment decision? Why?

19. Explain what a postaudit is and how it can provide useful input for future capital investment

decisions, especially those involving advanced technology.

20. Explain why NPV is generally preferred over IRR when choosing among competing or mutually exclusive projects. Why would managers continue to use IRR to choose among mutually exclusive projects?

21. Suppose that a firm must choose between two mutually exclusive projects, both of which have negative NPVs. Explain how a firm can legitimately choose between two such projects.

22. Why is it important to have accurate projections of cash flows for potential capital investments?

23. Describe why it is important for a manager to conduct a careful review of the assumptions and methods used in forecasting cash flows.

24. Why is it necessary to adjust future cash flows for inflation?

25. Explain what sensitivity analysis is. How can it help in capital investment decisions?

26. What are the main tax implications that should be considered in Year 0?

27. Assume that a project's annual after-tax net income is $40,000. Annual amortization for the project is $10,000. What is the project's annual after-tax operating cash inflow?

28. Assume that a project has annual cash expenses of $20,000 and annual amortization of $10,000. The tax rate is 34 percent. Using the decomposition method, compute the project's annual after-tax cash flow. (Assume that the project has no direct revenues and that straight-line amortization is used for tax purposes.)

29. Discuss the differences between amortization (for accounting purposes) and capital cost allowance (for tax purposes).

30. Why is a formula useful for calculating the present value of the CCA tax shield?

31. What is the one-half rule? What is the effect of this rule on the CCA tax shield?

32. What effect does salvage value have on the CCA tax shield?

33. Explain the important factors to consider for capital investment in the advanced manufacturing environment.

EXERCISES

11–1

Payback Period; Accounting Rate of Return

LO2

A new laundromat facility costs $200,000 and has a life of five years with no salvage value. The facility will generate the following annual cash flows:

Year	1	2	3	4	5
Cash flow	$ 60,000	$80,000	$100,000	$120,000	$140,000

Required:

1. Compute the payback period.
2. Compute the accounting rate of return using the original investment.

11–2

NPV

LO3

A new product is expected to produce annual revenues of $500,000. The product has a life cycle of five years. Equipment for producing the product will cost $550,000. After five years, this equipment can be sold for $80,000. Working capital will increase by $60,000, because inventories and receivables will increase. Annual cash operating expenses are estimated at $380,000. The required rate of return is 12 percent. Assume that there are no income taxes.

Required:

1. Compute the annual cash flows.
2. Calculate the NPV for the project.

11–3

IRR; Uniform Cash Flows

LO4

A proposed project requires an investment of $300,000 and will produce annual after-tax cash flows of $124,875. The project life is three years.

Required:

Compute the IRR.

11–4

Mutually Exclusive Projects

LO5

A firm is considering two different product designs: Design A and Design B. The after-tax cash flows for each design follow:

	Design A	Design B
Annual revenues	$300,000	$400,000
Operating expenses	210,000	295,000
Investment	269,190	314,055
Product life	5 years	5 years

The required rate of return is 12 percent.

Required:

1. Compute the NPV for each project.
2. Compute the IRR for each project.
3. Which design should be chosen? Explain.

11–5

After-Tax Cash Flows

LO7

A company has revenues of $900,000, cash expenses of $500,000, and annual amortization of $100,000. The tax rate is 40 percent. (Assume that amortization is used for tax purposes.)

Required:

1. Compute the annual after-tax cash flow using an income statement approach.
2. Compute the annual after-tax cash flows for each item on the income statement.

11–6

Basic Concepts

LO1, LO2, LO3, LO4

Each of the following parts is independent (ignore taxes).

1. Leif Alton has just invested $200,000 as a part owner of a funeral home. He expects to receive an income of $60,000 per year from the investment. What is the payback period for Leif?
2. Cora Javier placed $40,000 in a three-year savings plan. The plan pays 6 percent, and she cannot withdraw the money early without a penalty. Assume that Cora leaves the money in the plan for the full three years. How much money will she have?
3. King Manufacturing is considering the purchase of a robotics material-handling system. The cash benefits will be $240,000 per year. The system costs $1,360,000 and will last 10 years. Compute the NPV assuming a discount rate of 12 percent. Should the company buy the robotics system?
4. Perry Rowe has just invested $100,000 in a company. He expects to receive $16,100 per year for the next eight years. His cost of capital is 6 percent. Compute the internal rate of return. Did Perry make a good decision?

11–7

Present Value Computations

LO3

Complete the following cases, each independent of the others (ignore taxes).

1. Two independent projects have the following cash flows:

	Year 1	Year 2	Year 3	Year 4
Project I	$ 5,000	$ 5,000	$5,000	$5,000
Project II	30,000	20,000	5,000	5,000

Compute the present value of each project, assuming a discount rate of 16 percent.

2. Suppose that two parents want to have $50,000 in a fund six years from now to provide support for their daughter's university education. How much must they invest now in order to have the desired amount if the investment can earn 8 percent? 12 percent? 16 percent?
3. Some new equipment promises to save $40,000 per year in operating expenses. The life of the machine is 10 years. Assume that the company's cost of capital is 12 percent. What is the most the company should pay for the new equipment?
4. A seller is asking $343,300 for some flexible manufacturing equipment, which is expected to last five years and to generate equal annual savings (because of reductions in labour costs, material waste, and so on). What is the minimum savings in operating expenses that must be earned each year to justify the acquisition? Assume that the buyer's cost of capital is 14 percent.

11–8

Payback; Accounting Rate of Return; NPV; IRR

LO1, LO2, LO3, LO4

Kimmer Optical is considering an investment in equipment that will be used to grind lenses. The outlay required is $800,000. The equipment will last five years, with no salvage value. The expected cash flows associated with the project are given below:

	Year 1	Year 2	Year 3	Year 4	Year 5
Cash revenues	$1,300,000	$1,300,000	$1,300,000	$1,300,000	$1,300,000
Cash expenses	1,000,000	1,000,000	1,000,000	1,000,000	1,000,000

Assume that there are no taxes.

Required:

1. Compute the project's payback period.
2. Compute the project's accounting rate of return (a) on initial investment, and (b) on average investment.
3. Compute the project's net present value, assuming a required rate of return of 10 percent.
4. Compute the project's internal rate of return.

11–9

Payback; Accounting Rate of Return; NPV; IRR

LO1, LO2, LO3, LO4

Note: The first two parts are related; each of the last three is independent of all other parts. Ignore taxes.

1. Kwon Wei is considering investing in one of the two following projects. Either project will require an investment of $10,000. The expected cash flows are given below.

	Year 1	Year 2	Year 3	Year 4	Year 5
Project A	$3,000	$4,000	$5,000	$10,000	$10,000
Project B	3,000	4,000	6,000	3,000	3,000

What is the payback period for each project? If rapid payback is important, which project should be chosen? Which would you choose?
2. Calculate the accounting rate of return for each project in Requirement 1. Which project should be chosen based on the accounting rate of return?
3. Wilma Geisler is retiring and has two options: she can take her retirement pension as a lump sum of $225,000, or she can receive $24,000 per year for 20 years. Wilma's required rate of return is 8 percent. Assume that Wilma will live for another 20 years. Should she take the lump sum or the annuity?
4. Darryl Bowen is interested in investing in some tools and equipment so that he can do independent drywalling. The cost of the tools and equipment is $20,000. Darryl estimates that the return from owning his own equipment will be $6,000 per year. The tools and equipment will last six years. Assuming a required rate of return of 8 percent, calculate the NPV of the investment. Should Darryl invest?
5. Zara Folson, the owner of a small manufacturing company, is evaluating what appears to be an attractive opportunity. She has been offered the chance to acquire another small company's equipment that would allow her company to produce a part currently purchased externally. Zara estimates that the savings from internal production would be $25,000 per year. She estimates that the equipment would last 10 years. The owner is asking $130,400 for the equipment. Her company's cost of capital is 10 percent. Calculate the project's internal rate of return. Should Zara acquire the equipment?

11–10

Accounting Rate of Return; NPV

LO2, LO3

The Delta Company is planning a project that is expected to last for six years. During that time, the project is expected to generate net cash flows of $85,000 per year. The project will require the purchase of a machine for $310,000. This new machine is expected to have a salvage value of $20,000 at the end of six years. (Amortization will be calculated on a straight-line basis.) In addition to its annual operating costs, the machine will require an overhaul costing $55,000 at the end of Year 4. The company currently has a minimum desired rate of return of 12 percent. Using this information, the firm's accountant has prepared the following analysis:

Annual cash inflow		$85,000
Less: Annual amortization	$48,333	
Annual average cost of overhaul	9,167	57,500
Average annual net income		$27,500

Return on investment = 27,500/310,000 = 8.87%

Therefore, the accountant recommends that the project be rejected, because it does not meet the company's minimum desired rate of return. Assume that there are no taxes.

Required:

1. What criticism(s) would you make of the accountant's evaluation of the project?
2. Use present value analysis to determine whether or not the project should be accepted. (CMA Canada adapted)

11–11

NPV; Accounting
Rate of Return;
Payback

LO1, LO2, LO3

Timtell Transport is considering investment in two independent loading and pack-aging equipment projects. Each project would require an investment of $200,000. In both cases, assume that the equipment would last five years with no salvage value. The cash inflows associated with each project are given below:

	Year 1	Year 2	Year 3	Year 4	Year 5
Project A	$120,000	$60,000	$ 80,000	$ 40,000	$ 20,000
Project B	20,000	20,000	120,000	160,000	180,000

Assume that there are no taxes.

Required:

1. Assuming a discount rate of 12 percent, compute the net present value of each project.
2. Compute the payback period for each project. Assume that Timtell's manager accepts only projects with a payback period of three years or less. Offer some reasons why this may be a rational strategy, even though the NPV computed in Requirement 1 may indicate otherwise.
3. Compute the accounting rate of return for each project using (a) initial invest-ment and (b) average investment.

11–12

NPV Basic Concepts

LO3

Drury Legal Services is considering an investment that requires an outlay of $200,000 and promises a cash inflow one year from now of $231,000. The company's cost of capital is 10 percent. Ignore taxes.

Required:

1. Break the $231,000 future cash inflow into three components: (a) the return of the original investment, (b) the cost of capital, and (c) the profit earned on the investment. Now compute the present value of the profit earned on the investment.
2. Compute the NPV of the investment. Compare this result with the present value of the profit computed in Requirement 1. What does this comparison tell you about the meaning of NPV?

11–13

NPV; Cost of Capital;
Basic Concepts

LO3

Spreadsheet

Royal Electronics Company has an opportunity to invest in a new product line that will have a three-year life cycle. The investment requires a current $100,000 outlay. The capital will be raised by borrowing $60,000 and by issuing new stock for $40,000. The $60,000 loan will have interest payments of $3,000 at the end of each of the three years, with the principal being repaid at the end of Year 3. The stock issue carries with it an expectation of a 17.5 percent return, expressed in the form of dividends at the end of each year ($7,000 in dividends will be paid each of the next three years). The sources of capital for this investment represent the same proportion and costs that the company typically has. Finally, the project will produce cash inflows of $70,000 per year for the next two years. Ignore taxes.

Required:

1. Compute the cost of capital for the project.
2. Compute the NPV for the project. Explain why it is not necessary to subtract the interest payments and the dividend payments from the annual inflow of $70,000 in carrying out this computation.

11–14

Solving for
Unknowns

LO3, LO4

Solve each of the following independent cases (ignore taxes).

1. Romas Company is investing $120,000 in a project that will yield a uniform series of cash inflows over the next four years. If the internal rate of return is 14 percent, how much cash inflow per year can be expected?

2. Daw's Video Repair has decided to invest in some new electronic equipment. The equipment will have a three-year life and will produce a uniform series of cash savings. The net present value of the equipment is $1,750, using a discount rate of 8 percent. The internal rate of return is 12 percent. Determine the investment and the amount of cash savings realized each year.

3. A new lathe costing $60,096 will produce savings of $12,000 per year. How many years must the lathe last if an IRR of 18 percent is realized?

4. The NPV of a project is $3,927. The project has a life of four years and produces the following cash flows:

Year 1	Year 2	Year 3	Year 4
$10,000	$12,000	$15,000	$?

The cost of the project is two times the cash flow produced in Year 4. The discount rate is 10 percent. Find the cost of the project and the cash flow for Year 4.

11–15

Flexible Manufacturing System; Payback; NPV

LO2, LO3, LO8

Isabel Anders, president of Torront Company, is considering the purchase of a flexible manufacturing system. The benefits/savings associated with the system are described below:

Increased quality	$80,000
Decrease in operating costs	90,000
Increase in on-time deliveries	30,000

The system will cost $1,229,000 and will last 10 years. The company's cost of capital is 12 percent. Ignore taxes.

Required:

1. Calculate the payback period for the system. Assume that Torront has a policy of accepting only projects with a payback of five years or less. Should the system be acquired?

2. Calculate the project's NPV. Should the system be purchased—even if it does not meet the payback criterion?

3. The project manager has reviewed the projected cash flows. He points out that two items have been missed. First, the system would have a salvage value of $100,000 at the end of 10 years. Second, the increased quality and delivery performance would allow Torront to increase its market share by 20 percent. This would produce an additional annual benefit of $50,000. Recalculate the payback period and NPV given this new information. Does the decision change?

11–16

Implementation of an ABC System; Payback; NPV

LO2, LO3

Keith Yearwood was certain that the current cost system was costing the company money. Over time, the cost system had become less useful. Products had been added, and overhead had become a much greater percentage of total manufacturing costs. Keith believed that overhead costs were not being accurately assigned to products, thereby causing distorted product costs. In harmony with these views, Keith had hired a consultant to review the company's accounting system. The consultant recommended the installation of an activity-based costing system. The justification was straightforward. The cost of errors from the current system was high. The consultant estimated the following annual cost of inaccurate cost information:

Special studies	$ 50,000
Lost bids	150,000
Suboptimal product mix	60,000
Poor marketing (mostly related to new products)	140,000
Total	$400,000

These costs, the consultant explained, can be avoided with the installation of a more accurate cost system. The consultant recommended an ABC system. The cost of implementing the system was estimated as follows:

Acquisition of PCs and associated software	$ 425,000
Mainframe upgrade and software development	500,000
System redesign	375,000
Training	450,000
Total investment	$1,750,000

The company's cost of capital is 14 percent. The ABC system is projected to have a life of 10 years. Ignore taxes.

Required:

1. Compute the payback period for the ABC system.
2. Compute the NPV of the ABC system. Should the system be implemented?

11–17

NPV versus IRR

LO5

Spreadsheet

A company is considering two different modifications to its current manufacturing process. The cash flows associated with the two investments are shown below:

Year	Project I	Project II
0	$(100,000)	$(100,000)
1	—	63,857
2	134,560	63,857

The company's cost of capital is 10 percent. Ignore taxes.

Required:

1. Compute the NPV and the IRR for each investment.
2. Show that the project with the larger NPV is the correct choice for the company.

11–18

After-Tax Cash Flows

LO7

Steiner Corporation is evaluating two independent projects. One involves recycling, and the other involves the acquisition of some maintenance equipment. The projects' expected annual operating revenues and expenses are given below.

Project A (recycling project):

Revenues	$180,000
Less cash expenses	90,000
Less amortization	30,000
Income before taxes	$ 60,000
Less taxes	24,000
Net income	$ 36,000

Project B (maintenance equipment):

| Cash expenses | $ 40,000 |
| Amortization | 40,000 |

Required:

Compute the after-tax cash flows for each project. Assume that the tax rate is 40 percent and that amortization is deductible for tax purposes.

11–19

NPV; CCA Tax Shield

LO7

A trucking company is planning to buy special equipment for its maintenance operation. The cost of the equipment is $12,000, and the equipment will have a five-year life and a zero salvage value. The CCA rate is 20 percent, and there are other assets in the class. The tax rate is 38 percent; the cost of capital is 12 percent.

Required:

1. Calculate the present value of the CCA tax shield (including the one-half rule).
2. Calculate the present value of the CCA tax shield, assuming that the equipment has a $2,500 salvage value when sold at the beginning of Year 6.

11–20

Lease or Buy; NPV; CCA

LO5, LO7

Megan Emond, owner of a small company, has decided that she needs to have regular access to a car for local errands and occasional business trips. Megan is trying to decide between buying or leasing the car. The purchase cost is $30,000. The annual operating costs are estimated at $5,000. If the car is leased, a five-year lease will be acquired. The lease requires a refundable deposit of $1,000 and annual lease payments of $8,000. Operating costs, in addition to the lease payment, total $4,500 per year. The company's cost of capital is 10 percent, and its tax rate is 40 percent. If the car is purchased, it will be included with other assets in a class with a maximum CCA rate of 30 percent. Ignore the one-half rule.

Required:

Using NPV analysis, determine whether the car should be leased or purchased.

11–21

NPV; Inflation

LO7

Thistle Bus Company is planning to undertake a project that will have a two-year life. The project requires an initial outlay of $40,000; it will generate cash inflows of $22,000 and $24,000, respectively, in the two years. The company's cost of capital is 12 percent. During the coming two years, inflation is expected to average 5 percent per year. The cash flows have not been adjusted for inflation. The cost of capital, however, reflects an inflationary component. Ignore taxes.

Required:

1. Compute the NPV using the unadjusted cash flows.
2. Compute the NPV using cash flows adjusted for inflationary effects.

11–22

After-Tax Cash Flows; CCA

LO7

As vice-president of Irwin Ltd., you must decide whether or not the following investment proposal should be accepted. Irwin has the opportunity to invest in a new auto-painting business that would require the purchase of a paint-sealing machine for $120,000. The machine is expected to last four years, with a salvage value of $10,000. Your staff has prepared the following budgeted income statement for each of the four years, based on expected contracts for 450 cars per year:

Revenues: Paint-sealing fees earned		$90,000
Operating expenses:		
Machine operator's salary	$22,000	
Variable machine supplies expense	6,000	
Building rental expenses	3,300	
Variable sealant expense	7,000	
Amortization expense	27,500	
Variable machine cleaning (after sealing)	9,000	
Total operating expenses		74,800
Net operating income		$15,200

Your analysis of the above shows the following:

- The machine has a capacity of 2,000 paint jobs per year.
- The machine will be included in a class with other assets. The maximum CCA rate is 20 percent.
- An inventory of supplies and parts costing $5,000 will have to be maintained.
- All cash flows occur at the end of the year.
- The company has an income tax rate of 45 percent.

Required:

Should Irwin purchase the machine assuming a minimum rate of return of 12 percent? Support your answer with calculations. (CMA Canada adapted)

11–23

After-Tax Cash Flows; CCA

LO7

The Craddock Company is considering the purchase of a machine costing $780,000. This machine has an expected useful life of five years and an expected salvage value of $30,000. It will be amortized for accounting purposes using the straight-line method. A CCA rate of 25 percent will be used for tax purposes. Assume that there are other assets in the CCA class. The machine is expected to reduce variable costs of production by 20 percent; however, a machine operator costing $30,000 per year would be required. The machine will increase the company's production capacity to 50,000 units per year (from the present capacity of 30,000 units). The company's income statement for last year, when the company produced 30,000 units and sold 25,000 units, was as follows:

Sales	$950,000
Less: Cost of goods sold (20% of which are fixed)	575,000
Gross profit	$375,000
Less: Operating expenses:	
Variable selling and administration	250,000
Fixed selling and administration	100,000
Net income	$ 25,000

The income tax rate is 38 percent.

Required:

Using the net present value method, determine whether or not the company should purchase the machine, assuming that sales demand is expected to be 50,000 units per year for the next five years and that the company's minimum desired rate of return is 10 percent. (CMA Canada adapted)

11–24

Discount Rates; Advanced Manufacturing Environment

LO8

A company is considering two competing investments. The first is for a standard piece of production equipment; the second is for some computer-aided manufacturing (CAM) equipment. The investment and after-tax operating cash flows are shown below.

Year	Standard Equipment	CAM
0	$(500,000)	$(2,000,000)
1	300,000	100,000
2	200,000	200,000
3	100,000	300,000
4	100,000	400,000
5	100,000	400,000
6	100,000	400,000
7	100,000	500,000
8	100,000	1,000,000
9	100,000	1,000,000
10	100,000	1,000,000

The company uses a discount rate of 18 percent for all of its investments. The company's cost of capital is 10 percent.

Required:

1. Calculate the net present value for each investment using a discount rate of 18 percent.
2. Calculate the net present value for each investment using a discount rate of 10 percent.
3. Which rate should the company use to compute the net present value? Explain.

11–25

Quality; Market Share; Advanced Manufacturing Environment

LO8

Refer to 11–24. Assume that the company's cost of capital is 14 percent.

Required:

1. Calculate the NPV of each alternative using the 14 percent rate.
2. Now assume that if the standard equipment is purchased, the firm's competitive position will deteriorate because of lower quality (relative to competitors who have automated). Marketing estimates that the loss in market share will decrease

the projected after-tax cash inflows by 50 percent for Years 3 through 10. Recalculate the NPV of the standard equipment given this outcome. What is the decision now? Discuss the importance of assessing the effect of indirect benefits.

PROBLEMS

11–26

Basic NPV Analysis

LO1, LO3

Ross Liddel, marketing manager, was arguing for the introduction of a new product— a stair stepper. The company was already a major player in the exercise equipment market, and he felt that the new product bearing the company's brand name would be well accepted. He knew, however, that the acceptance of the new product would depend on the economic feasibility of acquiring the equipment needed to produce the product. The equipment would cost $300,000, and its cash operating expenses would total $60,000 per year. The equipment would last for seven years but would need a major overhaul costing $20,000 at the end of the fifth year. At the end of seven years, the equipment would be sold for $24,000. An increase in working capital totalling $30,000 would also be needed at the beginning of the project. This would be recovered at the end of the seven years.

The stair steppers would sell for $170 per unit and would cost $80 per unit to produce (in addition to the operating expenses of the equipment). Ross expects to sell 1,500 units per year. The cost of capital is 10 percent. Ignore taxes.

Required:

1. Prepare a schedule of cash flows for the proposed project.
2. Compute the NPV of the project. Should the new product be produced?

11–27

Cash Flows; Basic NPV Analysis

LO3

The Cone Company currently sells 25,000 units a year at a price of $90 per unit. These units are produced using a machine that was purchased five years ago at a cost of $600,000. It currently has a book value of $300,000; however, due to its specialized nature, it has a market value today of only $35,000. The machine, expected to last another five years, after which it will have no expected salvage value, gives rise to the following production costs:

Direct materials (5 kilograms @ $1.50/kilogram)	$ 7.50
Direct labour (4 hours @ $15.00/hour)	60.00
Variable overhead (4 hours @ $1.20/hour)	4.80
Fixed overhead (4 hours @ $1.60/hour)[a]	6.40
Total cost per unit	$78.70

[a] Based on an annual activity of 100,000 direct labour hours

The company expects the following changes for next year:

- The selling price will increase by 10 percent.
- Direct labour rates will increase by 15 percent.
- Sales are expected to increase to 26,000 units (within the capacity of present facilities) and remain at that level.

Management is currently considering the replacement of Cone's old machine with a new one that would cost $750,000. The new machine is expected to last five years, with a salvage value of $30,000 expected at that time (straight-line amortization used). By using the new machine, management expects to cut variable direct labour hours to 3.5 hours per unit, but the firm will have to hire an operator for the machine at $45,000 per year. The company has a minimum desired rate of return of 10 percent. Ignore taxes.

Required:

1. Determine the cash flows associated with the machine replacement decision.
2. Determine, by using the net present value approach, whether or not the company should purchase the new machine. (CMA Canada adapted)

11–28

NPV Analysis

LO1, LO3

Box Elder Communications Company is considering the production and marketing of a communications system that will increase the efficiency of messaging for small businesses or branch offices of large companies. Each unit hooked into the system is assigned a mailbox number, which can be matched to a telephone extension number, providing access to messages 24 hours a day. Up to 20 units can be hooked into the system, allowing the delivery of the same message to as many as 20 people. Personal codes can be used to make messages confidential. Furthermore, messages can be reviewed, recorded, cancelled, replied to, or deleted, all during the same phone call. Indicators wired to the telephone blink whenever new messages are present.

To produce this product, a $1.1 million investment in new equipment is required. The equipment would last 10 years but would need major maintenance costing $100,000 at the end of its sixth year. The salvage value of the equipment at the end of 10 years is estimated to be $40,000. If this new system is produced, working capital must also be increased by $50,000. This capital will be restored at the end of the product's life cycle, estimated to be 10 years. Revenues from the sale of the product are estimated at $1.5 million per year; cash operating expenses are estimated at $1.26 million per year.

Required:

1. Prepare a schedule of cash flows for the proposed project. Ignore taxes.
2. Assuming that Box Elder's cost of capital is 12 percent, compute the project's NPV. Should the product be produced?

11–29

Payback; NPV; Managerial Incentives; Ethical Behaviour

LO2, LO3

Dominic Ferrara, manager of a credit union branch, was pleased with his branch's performance over the past three years. Each year the branch's profits had increased, and he had earned a sizable bonus (bonuses are a linear function of the branch's reported income). He had also received considerable attention from higher management. A vice-president had told him in confidence that if his performance over the next three years matched that of his first three, he would be promoted.

Determined to fulfill these expectations, Dominic made sure that he personally reviewed every capital request. He wanted to be certain that any funds invested would provide good, solid returns (the branch's cost of capital is 10 percent). At the moment, he is reviewing two independent requests. Proposal A involves automating a cheque-processing operation that is currently labour-intensive. Proposal B centres on developing and marketing several new electronic tellers. Proposal A requires an initial outlay of $90,000, and Proposal B requires $130,000. Both projects could be funded given the status of the branch's capital budget. Both have an expected life of six years, and the two projects have the following projected cash flows after implementation:

Year	Proposal A	Proposal B
1	$60,000	$(15,000)
2	50,000	(10,000)
3	20,000	(5,000)
4	15,000	85,000
5	10,000	110,000
6	5,000	135,000

After careful consideration of each investment, Dominic approves the funding of Proposal A and rejects B. Ignore taxes.

Required:

1. Compute the NPV for each proposal.
2. Compute the payback period for each proposal.
3. According to your analysis, which proposal(s) should be accepted? Explain.
4. Explain why Dominic accepted only Proposal A. Considering the possible reasons for rejection, would you judge his behaviour to be ethical? Explain.

11–30

Basic IRR Analysis

LO1, LO4

Leshow Company was approached by a local furnace company with the proposition of replacing its old heating system with a modern, more efficient unit. The cost of the new system was quoted at $96,660, but it would save $20,000 per year in fuel costs. The estimated life of the new system is 10 years, with no salvage value. Excited over the possibility of saving $20,000 per year and having a more reliable unit, Leshow's president requested an analysis of the project's economic viability. All capital projects are required to earn at least the firm's cost of capital, which is 10 percent. Assume that there are no tax effects.

Required:

1. Calculate the project's internal rate of return. Should Leshow acquire the new furnace?
2. Suppose that fuel savings are less than claimed. Calculate the minimum annual cash savings that must be realized for the project to earn a rate equal to the firm's cost of capital.
3. Suppose that the life of the furnace is overestimated by two years. Repeat Requirements 1 and 2 under this assumption.
4. Explain the implications of the answers for Requirements 1, 2, and 3.

11–31

NPV; Uncertainty

LO1, LO3

PrairieJet Airlines is interested in acquiring a new aircraft to service a new route. The route would be from Winnipeg to Chicago. The aircraft would fly one round trip daily, except for scheduled maintenance days. There are 15 maintenance days scheduled each year. The aircraft's seating capacity is 150. Flights are expected to be fully booked. The average revenue per passenger per flight (one-way) is $200. Annual operating costs of the aircraft are given below:

Fuel	$1,400,000
Flight personnel	500,000
Food and beverages	100,000
Maintenance	400,000
Other	100,000
Total	$2,500,000

The aircraft will cost $100,000,000 and has an expected life of 20 years. The company requires a 14 percent return. Ignore taxes.

Required:

1. Calculate the NPV for the aircraft. Should PrairieJet buy it?
2. In management discussions regarding the proposal, PrairieJet's marketing manager states his belief that the assumption of 100 percent booking is unrealistic. He believes that the actual booking rate will be somewhere between 70 percent and 90 percent, with the most likely rate being 80 percent. Recalculate the NPV using an 80 percent seating capacity. Should the aircraft be purchased?
3. Calculate the average seating rate that would be needed so that NPV = 0.
4. Suppose that the price per passenger could be increased by 10 percent without any effect on demand. What is the average seating rate now needed to achieve an NPV = 0? What would you now recommend?

11–32

Review of Capital Investment Procedures

LO1, LO2, LO3, LO4

Dr. Hanna White, a dentist, had just returned from a conference at which she learned about a new procedure for performing root canals, which reduces the time for them by 50 percent. Given her patient-load pressures, Hanna was anxious to try out the new technique. By decreasing the time she spent on root canals, she could increase her total revenues by performing more services within a work period. Unfortunately, in order to implement the new procedure, some special equipment costing $74,000 was needed. The equipment had an expected life of four years, with a salvage value of $6,000. Hanna estimated that her cash revenues would increase by the following amounts:

	Year 1	Year 2	Year 3	Year 4
Revenue increase	$19,800	$27,000	$32,400	$32,400

She also expected additional cash expenses amounting to $3,000 per year. Her cost of capital is 12 percent. Ignore taxes.

Required:

1. Compute the payback period for the new equipment.
2. Compute the accounting rate of return using both original investment and average investment.
3. Compute the NPV and IRR for the project. Should Hanna purchase the new equipment? Should she be concerned about payback or the accounting rate of return in making this decision?
4. Before finalizing her decision, Hanna decided to call two dentists who had been using the new procedure for the past six months. These conversations revealed a somewhat less glowing report than she had received at the conference. The new procedure turned out to reduce the required time by about 25 percent, rather than the advertised 50 percent. Hanna estimated that the net operating cash flows of the procedures would be cut by 33 percent because of the extra time and cost involved. Using this information, recompute the NPV and the IRR of the project. What would you now recommend?

11–33

Replacement Decision; NPV; CCA

LO1, LO5, LO7

Dinocare Travel Agency is considering replacing its existing computer system with a new one manufactured by a different company. The old computer was acquired three years ago, has a remaining life of five years, and will have a salvage value of $10,000. The old computer is one of many assets included in a class with a maximum CCA rate of 30 percent. The unamortized capital cost of the old computer is $200,000. The cash operating costs of the existing computer (including software, personnel, and other supplies) total $100,000 per year. The new computer system has an initial cost of $500,000 and will have cash operating costs of $50,000 per year. The new computer system will have a life of five years and will have a salvage value of $100,000 at the end of the fifth year. If the new computer is purchased, the old one will be sold for $50,000. Dinocare needs to decide whether to keep the old computer or buy the new one. The cost of capital is 12 percent. The tax rate is 40 percent.

Required:

Compute the NPV of each alternative. Should Dinocare keep the old computer or buy the new one?

11–34

Machine Replacement; After-Tax Cash Flows

LO7

The Tyler Company Ltd. had the following income statement for the year ended December 31, 2000, when the company produced and sold 18,000 units:

Sales	$720,000
Less: Cost of goods sold	576,000
Gross profit	$144,000
Less: Operating expenses:	
Variable selling	$ 14,400
Fixed selling	23,000
Variable administrative	21,600
Fixed administrative	43,800
Net income (before taxes)	$ 41,200

Cost of goods sold can be broken down as follows:

Direct materials	35%
Direct labour	42%
Variable overhead (incurred in relationship to direct labour costs)	14%
Fixed overhead (relevant range of 8,000 to 25,000 units)	9%

The company is considering the purchase of a machine costing $150,000 with an expected useful life of five years and a salvage value at that time of $25,000. The machine would have a maximum capacity of 25,000 units per year and is expected to reduce direct labour costs by 25 percent; however, it would require an additional supervisor at a cost of $40,000 per year. The machine would be amortized over the five years using the straight-line method for both accounting and tax purposes. Production and sales for the next five years are expected to be as follows:

	2001	2002	2003	2004	2005
Units produced	18,000	18,000	20,000	20,000	20,000

Required:

Assume that Tyler has a minimum desired rate of return of 16 percent and an income tax rate of 38 percent. Should the company purchase the machine? Round amounts to the nearest dollar, and show all calculations. (CMA Canada adapted)

11–35

Lease versus Buy; CCA

LO1, LO5, LO7

Moore Company is trying to decide whether it should purchase or lease a new piece of equipment to be used in manufacturing a new product. If purchased, the new machine will cost $100,000 and will be used for 10 years. Its salvage value is estimated at $20,000. The machine will be added to existing assets in a CCA class with a maximum CCA rate of 20 percent. The annual maintenance and operating costs will be $20,000. Annual revenues are estimated at $55,000.

If the machine is leased, the company will need to make annual lease payments of $20,700. The first lease payment and a deposit of $5,000 are due immediately. The last lease payment is to be paid at the beginning of Year 10. The deposit is refundable at the end of the tenth year. In addition, under a normal contract, the company must pay for all maintenance and operating costs, although the leasing company does offer a service contract that will provide annual maintenance (on leased machines only). The contract must be paid up front and costs $30,000. Moore estimates that the contract will reduce its annual maintenance and operating costs by $10,000. Moore's cost of capital is 14 percent. The tax rate is 40 percent.

Required:

1. Prepare schedules showing the after-tax cash flows for each alternative. (Prepare schedules for the lease alternative with and without the service contract; assume that the service contract is amortized on a straight-line basis for the 10 years and that the annual lease payments are deductible for tax purposes.) Include all revenues and costs associated with each alternative.
2. Compute the NPV for each alternative, assuming that Moore does not purchase the service contract. Should the machine be purchased or leased? For this analysis, was it necessary to include all of the costs and revenues for each alternative? Explain.
3. Compute the NPV for the lease alternative assuming that the service contract is purchased. Does this change your decision about leasing? What revenues and costs could be excluded without affecting the conclusion?

11–36

Advanced Manufacturing Environment

LO7, LO8

"I know that it's the thing to do," insisted Latifah Kincaid, vice-president of finance for Colgate Manufacturing. "If we are going to be competitive, we need to build this completely automated plant."

"I'm not so sure," replied Greg Vitkus. "The savings from labour reductions and increased productivity are only $4 million per year. The price tag for this factory—and it's a small one—is $45 million. That gives a payback period of more than 11 years. That's a long time to put the company's money at risk."

"Yeah, but you're overlooking the savings that we'll get from the increase in quality," interjected Cameron Bay, production manager. "With this system, we can decrease our waste and our rework time significantly. Those savings are worth another million dollars per year."

"Another million will only cut the payback to nine years," retorted Greg. "Raffi, you're the marketing manager—do you have any insights?"

"Well, there are other factors to consider, such as service quality and market share. I think that increasing our product quality and improving our delivery service will make us a lot more competitive. I know for a fact that two of our competitors have decided against automation. That'll give us a shot at their customers, provided that our product is of higher quality and we can deliver it faster. I estimate that it'll increase our net cash benefits by another $6 million."

"Wow! Now that's impressive," Greg exclaimed, nearly convinced. "The payback is now getting down to a reasonable level."

"I agree," said Latifah, "but we do need to be sure that it's a sound investment. I know that estimates for construction of the facility have gone as high as $49.8 million. I also know that the expected residual value, after the 20 years of service we expect to get, is $5 million. Also, you're using before-tax cash flows. We need after-tax cash flows. I think I had better see if this project can cover our 14 percent cost of capital."

"Now wait a minute, Latifah," Greg demanded. "You know that I usually insist on a 20 percent rate of return, especially for a project of this magnitude."

Required:

1. Compute the NPV of the project using the original savings and investment figures. Do the calculation for discount rates of 14 percent and 20 percent. Assume that straight-line amortization is used for tax purposes. The tax rate is 40 percent.
2. Compute the NPV of the project using the additional benefits noted by the production and marketing managers. Also, use the original cost estimate of $45 million. Again, do the calculation for both possible discount rates.
3. Compute the NPV of the project using all estimates of cash flows, including the possible initial outlay of $49.8 million. Do the calculation using discount rates of 14 percent and 20 percent.
4. If you were making the decision, what would you do? Explain.

11–37

After-Tax Cash Flows; NPV

LO7

Thayn Thompson, divisional manager, has been pushing headquarters to grant approval for the installation of a new flexible manufacturing system. Finally, in the last executive meeting, Thayn was told that if he could show how the new system would increase the firm's value, it would be approved. Thayn gathered the following information:

	Old System	Flexible System
Initial investment	—	$1,250,000
Annual operating costs	$350,000	$95,000
Annual amortization	$100,000	?
Tax rate	34%	34%
Cost of capital	12%	12%
Expected life	10 years	10 years
Salvage value	none	none

With the exception of the cost of capital, the above information ignores the rate of inflation, which has been 4 percent per year and is expected to continue at this level for the next decade. (Assume that straight-line amortization is deductible for tax purposes.)

Required:

1. Compute the NPV for each system.
2. Compute the NPV for each system adjusting the future cash flows for the rate of inflation.
3. Comment on the importance of adjusting cash flows for inflationary effects.

11–38

After-Tax Cash Flows; NPV

LO7

The Roofer Company produces a product with the following unit costs based on a level of 5,000 units per year (present capacity):

Direct materials (3 kilograms @ $2.80/kilogram)	$ 8.40
Direct labour (8 hours @ $15/hour)	120.00
Variable overhead (8 hours @ $4/hour)	32.00
Fixed overhead (8 hours @ $2.50/hour)	20.00
Total cost per unit	$180.40

The product's selling price is $270.00 per unit, and the company incurs the following additional costs:

Variable selling and administrative	$3.00 per unit
Fixed selling and administrative	$60,000 per year

Roofer is considering the purchase of a machine that would cost $650,000 and would last for four years, with an expected salvage value of $20,000. If purchased, the machine would reduce direct labour hours by 20 percent per unit and would increase the company's capacity by 2,000 units per year. However, the machine would require an inventory of spare parts and supplies costing $13,000 to be maintained and would require additional power costs of $1.50 per direct labour hour of use. The investment in spare parts and supplies would be fully recoverable at the end of the machine's useful life. The machine would be amortized using the straight-line method. The company's tax rate is 38 percent.

Required:

Assume that Roofer has a minimum desired rate of return of 12 percent, and sales demand is expected to be 6,000 units per year for the next four years. Should the company purchase the new machine? (CMA Canada adapted)

11–39

NPV; CCA; Postaudit; Sensitivity Analysis

LO5, LO6, LO7

Rutherford Products, Inc., is evaluating a new design for one of its manufacturing processes. The new design will eliminate the production of a toxic solid residue. The system's initial cost is estimated at $860,000, including computerized equipment and installation. There is no expected salvage value. The new system has a useful life of eight years and is projected to produce cash operating savings of $270,000 per year over the old system (reducing labour costs and the costs of processing and disposing of toxic waste). In addition to the operating savings, the new system will produce a CCA tax shield that is absent under the old system. The equipment will be in a CCA class with other assets of a similar type. The maximum CCA rate is 30 percent. The tax rate is 34 percent, and the cost of capital is 16 percent

Required:

1. Compute the NPV of the new system.
2. One year after implementation, Rutherford's internal audit staff notes the following about the new system: (1) the cost of acquiring the system was $60,000 more than expected, due to higher installation costs; and (2) the annual cost savings were $20,000 less than expected, because labour cost was higher than expected. Using the changes in expected costs and benefits, compute the NPV as if this information had been available one year ago. Did the company make the right decision?
3. After the results mentioned in the postaudit were reported, Rutherford's marketing manager responded in a memo that revenues had increased by $100,000 per year because of increased purchases by environmentally sensitive customers. Describe the effect this information has on the analysis in Requirement 2.
4. Why would a postaudit be beneficial to Rutherford Products?

11–40

NPV; Competing Projects

LO5

Tamara Snipes, the mayor of the City of Gotham, has recently turned her attention to the apparent problem of a shortage of public transportation in the city. The city has a population of over 350,000. In the last few years, more and more complaints have surfaced with regard to inadequate bus services or difficulties in obtaining taxi services in the suburbs.

To operate a taxi in the city, a special licence is required; these licences are issued by the city council's Taxi Commission. No new licences have been issued since a freeze was instituted in 1957, at which time 3,500 licences were outstanding. Since that time, a number of licences have been returned to the Commission after their owners have retired. There are currently only 1,750 licences still in use. The freedom exists, however, to transfer ownership of a licence. Such transactions have been recently quoted at $1,750 on the open market.

The addition of an airport on the outskirts of the city and three hotels in the city has created an apparent shift by taxi drivers to the core of the city and to the airport routes, resulting in deficient services in the suburban areas. This in turn has led to an increase in the number of uninsured, unlicensed "gypsy" taxi operations and more expensive limousine services. In contemplating this situation, Tamara recognizes two viable alternatives to correct the problem. Either the city can increase the number of buses serving the suburban areas, or it can issue additional taxi licences.

Taxi fares are regulated by the Commission. Tamara recognizes the potential for all taxi drivers to join forces and increase fares, thereby significantly decreasing the number of people using such services. Tax revenues are currently being collected from taxi drivers at a rate of 3 percent of gross revenues. The average trip is estimated to be 10 kilometres. This year, the fare consists of a $1.10 flat rate plus $0.50 for every kilometre. It has been determined that each taxi driver collects revenues from 19,200 trips per year. Tamara estimates that in order to get the desired results, 85 licences would have to be issued at the given open market price. In addition, an incentive of $0.10 per kilometre would have to be placed on the flat rate trips originating in the suburban areas to attract taxi drivers. Accordingly, the ratio of suburban to core city and airport trips would be 1:4.

The other alternative cited above is to increase the number of buses serving the suburban areas. Public transit fares are $1.00 per ride. Tamara has been told that if the number of buses were increased by three, costing a total of $1,400,000, the number of single trips would increase by 1,500,000 per year. The buses would have an expected life of five years, at which time their combined salvage value would equal $100,000. The buses would be amortized on a straight-line basis. For the duration of five years, six additional workers would have to be employed, each at an annual salary of $25,000, and maintenance costs would increase by $36,000 per year.

So far, investigation of these alternatives has revealed that if additional taxi licences are issued, the public transit revenues will drop by $350,000 per year.

Under the pressure of an upcoming municipal election, Tamara feels that the community is anxiously awaiting a decision regarding the transportation issue.

Required:

1. Tamara Snipes has asked you to evaluate the two proposals and provide a recommendation. In your analysis, assume that the rates charged for public transit and taxi fares will remain constant for the five-year period and that all cash flows occur at year-end. The City of Gotham currently has a 12 percent required rate of return.
2. Briefly identify four qualitative factors affecting the recommendation in Requirement 1. (CMA Canada adapted)

11–41

Make or Buy; After-Tax Cash Flows

LO7

The Springster Company manufactures a product called Radids, a major component of which is called Rads. Currently, the company purchases 20,000 units per year of Rads from a supplier at a cost of $53 per unit. The company is considering manufacturing the Rads that it now purchases and has compiled the following data:

- This process would require the purchase of a special machine costing $40,000. This machine would be used for four years, at which time it would be sold for $8,000, and it would be amortized using the straight-line method for financial accounting purposes. The machine would be included with other assets in a class with a CCA rate of 25 percent.
- Direct materials for the Rads would consist of 5 kilograms at a cost of $3 per kilogram. The manufacture of Radids, the major product, currently uses this same material, and the scrap from this production, which would fill 10 percent of the amount required for Rads, is presently sold for $1 per kilogram.
- Direct labour would be two hours per unit of Rads, with an average labour rate of $8 per hour (fringe benefit costs average 10 percent).
- Supervision of the production of Rads would be handled by a manager who is currently paid $30,000 per year. He would continue with his present duties as well as supervising the production of Rads (expected to occupy 15 percent of his time) and would therefore be paid an additional $5,000 per year.
- Variable overhead costs for the production of Rads are expected to total $3.50 per direct labour hour.
- The main factory is rented for $80,000 per year for 5,000 square metres. The production of Rads should require an area of 500 square metres that is presently idle.
- Other fixed overhead costs (all cash) would be applied at the rate of $6 per labour hour.
- In order to fulfill fluctuations in demand, an initial inventory of 1,000 units of Rads would have to be purchased and maintained.
- Springster's minimum desired rate of return is 12 percent, and the income tax rate is 38 percent.

Required:

Use present value analysis to determine whether Springster should continue to purchase the required Rads or manufacture them, assuming that demand is expected to increase by 10 percent annually from Years 2 through 4. Show all calculations to the nearest dollar. (CMA Canada adapted)

11–42

CCA; Competing Projects

LO5, LO7

Nigel Day, owner of a repair shop, has unused space in the building he purchased several years ago. Initially, Nigel offered only the basic auto repair services, but since the business has grown, he is now considering the possibility of using the empty space to offer one of two additional services. Specifically, he is planning to add either an engine overhaul service or a diesel engine repair service. In either case, equipment must be purchased and skilled labour hired. The revenues and costs associated with each alternative are shown below.

	Overhaul Service	Diesel Service
Revenues	$120,000	$250,000
Labour costs	24,000	30,000
Material costs	20,190	100,000
Tax rate	40%	40%

To set up the overhaul service, an initial investment of $280,000 in equipment is required. The equipment investment for the diesel service is $420,000. In each case, the useful life of the equipment is 10 years, with no salvage value expected. Assume that straight-line amortization is used for tax purposes. The cost of capital is 16 percent.

Required:

1. Prepare a schedule of after-tax cash flows for each alternative.
2. Compute the NPV and the IRR for each alternative. Which alternative would you recommend? Do the NPV and the IRR measures recommend the same investment? Will this always be the case?
3. Someone tells Nigel that he should be using CCA instead of straight-line amortization in the analysis. Recompute the NPV for the diesel service alternative using a CCA rate of 20 percent. By how much did the NPV change?

11–43

Alternative Use of Space; CCA; After-Tax Cash Flows

LO5, LO7

The Eagle Crest Company is considering alternative uses for the unused basement area in its plant. One alternative is to sublet the area to a third party at a rate of $6,000 per year. But Eagle Crest's president is hesitant to do this, since the basement represents a third of the total building. The building costs the company $60,000 per year to rent; therefore, the firm would be losing money on the sublet rental. An alternative use for the area is to start up production and sales of a new product line. This option would require the purchase of new machinery at a cost of $250,000. The company's lease expires in five years, at which time the company expects to move to its own premises.

The new product line is expected to be obsolete in five years, at which time the machinery would have an expected salvage value of $30,000. Demand is expected to remain constant for the first four years, but is expected to drop by 60 percent in the final year. Eagle Crest's president has prepared the following income statement for the new product line for the first year, when the department must establish and maintain a finished goods inventory of 5,000 units:

Sales (20,000 units)			$260,000
Cost of goods sold:			
Finished goods—January 1, 2001		$ 0	
Cost of goods manufactured:			
Direct materials	$60,000		
Direct labour	80,000		
Supervisor	30,000		
Plant rental	20,000		
Amortization of machinery	44,000		
Cost of goods manufactured		234,000	
Cost of goods available for sale		$234,000	
Less: Finished goods—December 31, 2001		46,800	
Total cost of goods sold			187,200
Gross profit			$ 72,800
Operating costs:			
Variable selling		$ 26,000	
Head office cost allocation (20% of sales)		52,000	
Total operating costs			78,000
Department income (loss)			$ (5,200)

Required:

1. Use the net present value method to determine the company's optimal course of action assuming that its minimum desired rate of return is 14 percent. Assume also that Eagle Crest will have other assets in the CCA class (at a rate of 25 percent) and that the company's income tax rate is 38 percent.
2. What annual rental rate would be required for subletting the basement area to make the company indifferent as to whether or not it should purchase the machine? (CMA Canada adapted)

11–44

Advanced Manufacturing Environment

LO7, LO8

Meikle Manufacturing, Inc., produces trash compactors, microwave ovens, and electric ranges. Because of increasing competition, Meikle is considering making an investment in a computer-aided manufacturing (CAM) system. Since competition is most keen for microwaves, the microwave production line has been selected for initial evaluation. The CAM system for the microwave line would replace an existing system (purchased a year ago for $6 million). Although the existing system will be fully amortized in nine years, it is expected to last another ten years. The CAM system would also have a useful life of ten years.

The existing system is capable of producing 100,000 microwave ovens per year. The following sales and production data for the existing system have been provided by the accounting department:

Sales per year (units)	100,000
Selling price	$300
Costs per unit:	
Direct materials	$ 80
Direct labour	90
Volume-related overhead	20
Direct fixed overhead	40[a]

[a] All cash expenses with the exception of amortization, which is $6 per unit.
The existing equipment is being amortized using straight-line with no salvage value.

The CAM system will cost $34 million to purchase, plus an estimated $20 million in software and implementation. (Assume that all investment outlays occur at the beginning of the first year.) If the CAM equipment is purchased, the old equipment can be sold for $3 million.

The CAM system will require fewer parts for production and will produce with less waste. Because of this, the direct materials cost per unit will be reduced by 25 percent. Automation will also require fewer support activities; as a consequence, volume-related overhead will be reduced by $5 per unit, and direct fixed overhead (other than amortization) will decrease by $17 per unit. Direct labour will be reduced by 66 2/3 percent. Assume, for simplicity, that the new investment will be amortized on a pure straight-line basis for tax purposes with no salvage value.

Meikle's cost of capital is 12 percent, but management chooses to use 18 percent as the required rate of return when evaluating investments. The tax rate is 40 percent.

Required:

1. Compute the net present value for the old system and the CAM system. Which system should Meikle choose?
2. Repeat the net present value analysis of Requirement 1 using 12 percent as the discount rate.
3. Upon seeing the projected sales for the old system, Meikle's marketing manager comments, "Sales of 100,000 units per year cannot be maintained in the current competitive environment for more than one year unless we buy the CAM system. The CAM system will allow us to compete on the basis of quality and lead time. If we keep the old system, our sales will drop by 10,000 units per year." Repeat the net present value analysis using this new information and a 12 percent discount rate.
4. An industrial engineer for Meikle noticed that salvage value for the CAM equipment had not been included in the analysis. He estimated that the equipment could be sold for $4 million at the end of 10 years. He also estimated that the equipment of the old system would have no salvage value at the end of 10 years. Repeat the net present value analysis using this information, the information in Requirement 3, and a 12 percent discount rate.
5. Given the outcomes of the previous four Requirements, comment on the importance of providing accurate inputs for assessing investments in CAM systems.

MANAGERIAL DECISION CASES

11–45

Payback; NPV; IRR
LO2, LO3, LO4

Shaftel Ready Mix is a processor and supplier of concrete, aggregate, and rock products. One division of the company operates in the intermountain western United States. Currently, Shaftel has 14 cement-processing plants and a labour force of more than 375 employees. With the exception of cement powder, all raw materials (for example, aggregates and sand) are produced internally by the company. U.S. demand for concrete and aggregates has been growing steadily, and in the west, the growth rate has been above the national average. Because of this growth, Shaftel has more than tripled its gross revenues over the past 10 years.

Of the intermountain states, Arizona has been experiencing the most growth. Processing plants have been added over the past several years, and the company is considering the addition of yet another plant (to be located in Scottsdale). A major advantage of having another plant in Arizona is the ability to operate year-round, a feature not found in such states as Utah and Wyoming.

In setting up the new plant, land would have to be purchased and a small building constructed. Equipment and furniture would not need to be purchased; these items would be transferred from a plant that had been opened in Wyoming during the oil-boom period and closed a few years after the end of that boom. However, the equipment needs some repair and modifications before it can be used. It has a book value of $200,000, and the furniture has a book value of $30,000. Neither has any outside market value. Other costs—such as those related to the installation of a silo, a well, electrical hookups, and so on—will be incurred. No salvage value is expected. The summary of the initial investment costs by category is as follows:

Land	$ 20,000
Building	135,000
Equipment:	
Book value	200,000
Modifications	20,000
Furniture (book value)	30,000
Silo	20,000
Well	80,000
Electrical hookups	27,000
General setup	50,000
Total initial outlay	$582,000

Estimates concerning the operation of the Scottsdale plant are given below:

Life of plant and equipment	10 years
Expected annual sales (in cubic yards)	35,000
Selling price (per cubic yard)	$45.00
Variable costs (per cubic yard):	
Cement	$12.94
Sand/gravel	6.42
Fly ash	1.13
Admixture	1.53
Driver labour	3.24
Mechanics	1.43
Plant operations (batching and cleanup)	1.39
Loader operator	0.50
Truck parts	1.75
Fuel	1.48
Other	3.27
Total variable cost	$35.08
Fixed costs (annual):	
Salaries	$135,000
Insurance	75,000
Telephone	5,000
Amortization	58,200*
Utilities	25,000
Total fixed cost	$298,200

* Straight-line amortization is calculated using all initial investment costs over a 10-year period, assuming no salvage value.

After reviewing the above data, Karl Flemming, vice-president of operations, argues against the proposed plant. Karl is concerned because the plant would earn significantly less than the normal 8.3 percent return on sales. All other plants in the company are earning between 7.5 and 8.5 percent on sales. Karl also notes that it would take more than five years to recover the total initial outlay of $582,000. In the past, Shaftel has always insisted that an investment's payback period be no more than four years. The company's cost of capital is 10 percent. Ignore tax effects.

Required:

1. Prepare a variable-costing income statement for the proposed plant. Compute the ratio of net income to sales. Is Karl correct that the return on sales is significantly lower than the company average?
2. Compute the payback period for the proposed plant. Is Karl right that the payback period is greater than four years? Explain. Suppose that you were told that the equipment being transferred from Wyoming could be sold for its book value. Would this affect your answer?
3. Compute the NPV and the IRR for the proposed plant. Would your answer be affected if you were told that the furniture and equipment could be sold for their book values? If so, repeat the analysis with this effect considered.
4. Compute the cubic yards of cement that must be sold for the new plant to break even. Using this breakeven volume, compute the NPV and the IRR. Would the investment be acceptable? If so, explain why an investment that promises to do nothing more than break even can be viewed as acceptable.
5. Compute the volume of cement that must be sold for the IRR to equal Shaftel's cost of capital. Using this volume, compute the firm's expected annual income. Explain this result.

11–46

International Expansion

LO3, LO5

Henry Nassau, owner and manager of the Nassau Sporting Goods Company, is currently reviewing the success of his business and the possibility of expanding into the U.S. market in the coming year. Despite the company's name, only one product is now manufactured in its single factory in Owen Sound. The product is a football helmet primarily sold to university and high-school teams across Canada. At the moment, Nassau is selling 4,000 helmets annually at $120 each, which represents 25 percent of the total Canadian market. This production level is 500 units below the capacity of Nassau's current plant facilities.

With the current low inflation rate and a generally stable economic environment in Canada, Henry does not anticipate many significant changes in the near future. However, he is still reasonably pleased with the $50 contribution margin earned on each helmet. Fixed costs are only $155,000 per year. These costs include his rent payments on the factory, selling and administration costs, and $50,000 amortization on his equipment, which is expected to last another five years. Salvage values in this industry are negligible. Selling costs are low, since Nassau does not deal directly with the public but rather with a small number of wholesalers and a couple of major national sporting goods retailers.

A fair amount of customer loyalty to Nassau's product has been built up over the past few years. As a result, Henry is reluctant to consider shipping his product to the United States to take advantage of the current selling price there of $210 (all dollar amounts in this question are in Canadian dollars). Such a move could result in Henry cutting himself off from his existing customers permanently.

An opportunity has arisen that involves renting a new facility and buying the equipment needed to manufacture his product from a U.S. firm located in Oklahoma. This company is closing its operations and is willing to sell its equipment for $300,000. The facility would be rented; a five-year rental contract, matching the remaining life of the equipment, is available on favourable terms. An annual output of 5,000 helmets would be possible. With his experience in quality control and the availability of inexpensive labour (resulting from the depressed oil industry), Henry estimates that he could keep the variable manufacturing costs down to $75 per helmet.

Henry is also pleased that his rent and selling and administrative costs will be only $85,000 per year. Despite the low costs, however, he is greatly disturbed by the liability insurance premium of $425,000, which is apparently not unusual in this industry in the United States. In fact, the U.S. company is closing down because of the increased number of lawsuits and the size of recent settlements. It has settled all previous claims, and Henry's lawyer has advised him that he would probably not be liable for future claims on the product made by that company in the past.

Henry's bank manager, Neil Fowler, has assured him that the $300,000 needed could be arranged at the usual borrowing rate of 10 percent. Neil has also mentioned that another bank client has expressed interest in buying Nassau's Owen Sound operation for $400,000.

Required:

1. Prepare income statements for the coming year for the current Canadian operation and the prospective U.S. operation.
2. Recommend which of the following actions Henry Nassau should take:
    a. continue operations in Canada, and/or
    b. begin operations in the United States.
3. Briefly list and explain any qualitative factors that Henry should consider in making his decision. (CMA Canada adapted)

11–47

Capital Investment and Ethical Behaviour

LO3

Manny Correia, CMA and controller of Wakeman Enterprises, had been given permission to acquire a new computer and software for the company's accounting system. The capital investment analysis had shown an NPV of $100,000; however, the initial estimates of acquisition and installation costs had been made on the basis of tentative costs without any formal bids. Manny now has two formal bids—one that would allow the firm to meet or beat the original projected NPV, and one that would reduce the projected NPV by $50,000. The second bid involves a system that would increase both the initial cost and the operating cost.

Normally, Manny would take the first bid without hesitation. However, Todd Downing, the owner of the firm presenting the second bid, was a close friend. Manny had called Todd and explained the situation, offering Todd an opportunity to alter his bid and win the job. Todd thanked Manny and then made a counteroffer.

Todd: "Listen, Manny, this job at the original price is the key to a successful year for me. The revenues will help me gain approval for the loan I need for renovation and expansion. If I don't get that loan, I see hard times ahead. The financial stats for loan approval are so marginal that reducing the bid price may blow my chances."

Manny: "Losing the bid altogether would be even worse, don't you think?"

Todd: "True. However, I have a suggestion. If you grant me the job, I will have the capability of adding personnel. I know that your son is looking for a job, and I can offer him a good salary and a promising future. Additionally, I'll be able to take you and your wife on that vacation to Hawaii that we've been talking about."

Manny: "Well, you have a point. My son is having an awful time finding a job, and he has a wife and three kids to support. My wife is tired of having them live with us. She and I could use a vacation. I doubt that the other bidder would make any fuss if we turned it down. Its offices are out of province, after all."

Todd: "Out of province? All the more reason to turn it down. Given the province's economy, it seems almost criminal to take business outside. Those are the kinds of business decisions that cause problems for people like your son."

Required:

Evaluate Manny's ethical behaviour. Should Manny have called Todd in the first place? What if Todd had agreed to meet the lower bid price—would there have been any problems? Identify the standards of ethical conduct (refer to Chapter 1) that Manny may be violating, if any.

11–48

Cash Flows; CCA;
NPV; Advanced
Manufacturing
Environment
LO1, LO5, LO7, LO8

Charles Bradshaw, president and owner of Wellington Metal Works, had just returned from a trip to Europe.[16] While there, he had toured several plants using robotic manufacturing. Seeing the efficiency and success of these companies, Charles became convinced that robotic manufacturing is the wave of the future and that Wellington could gain a competitive advantage by adopting the new technology.

Based on this vision, Charles requested an analysis detailing the costs and benefits of robotic manufacturing for Wellington's material handling and merchandising equipment group. This group of products consists of such items as cooler shelving, stocking carts, and bakery racks. The products are sold directly to supermarkets.

A committee consisting of the controller, the marketing manager, and the production manager was given the responsibility of preparing the analysis. As a starting point, the controller provided the following information on expected revenues and expenses for the existing manual system:

		Percentage of Sales
Sales	$400,000	100%
Less: Variable expenses[a]	228,000	57%
Contribution margin	$172,000	43%
Less: Fixed expenses[b]	92,000	23%
Income before taxes	$ 80,000	20%

[a] Variable cost detail (as a percentage of sales):
Direct materials 16
Direct labour 20
Variable overhead 9
Variable selling 12
[b] $20,000 is amortization; the rest are cash expenses.

Given the current competitive environment, the marketing manager thought that the above level of profitability would not likely change for the next decade.

After some investigation into various robotic equipment, the committee settled on an Aide 900 system, a robot that has the capability of welding stainless steel or aluminum. It can be programmed to adjust the path, angle, and speed of the torch. The production manager was excited about the robotic system because it would eliminate the need to hire welders—an attractive prospect given that the market for welders seemed perpetually tight. By reducing the dependence on welders, better production scheduling and fewer late deliveries would result. Moreover, the robot's production rate is four times that of a person.

It was also discovered that robotic welding is superior in quality to manual welding. Consequently, some of the costs of poor quality could be reduced. The marketing manager was convinced that by providing better-quality products and avoiding late deliveries, the company would have such a competitive edge that it would increase sales by 50 percent for the affected product group by the end of Year 4. The marketing manager provided the following projections for the next 10 years, the useful life of the robotic equipment:

	Year 1	Year 2	Year 3	Years 4–10
Sales	$400,000	$450,000	$500,000	$600,000

Currently, the company employs four welders, who work 40 hours per week and 50 weeks per year at an average wage of $10 per hour. If the robot is acquired, Wellington will need one operator, who will be paid $10 per hour.

Because of improved quality, the robotic system will also reduce the cost of direct materials by 25 percent, the cost of variable overhead by 33.33 percent, and

16. This case is based in part on David A. Greenberg, "Robotics: One Small Company's Experience," in *Cost Accounting for the '90s* (Montvale, N.J.: National Association of Accountants, 1986), 57–63.

variable selling expenses by 10 percent. All of these reductions will take place immediately after the robotic system is in place and operating. Fixed costs will be increased by the amortization associated with the robot. If the robotic system is acquired, the old system will be sold for $40,000.

The robotic system requires the following initial investment:

Purchase price	$380,000
Installation	70,000
Training	30,000
Engineering	40,000

At the end of 10 years, the robot will have a salvage value of $20,000. Assume that the company's cost of capital is 12 percent. The tax rate is 34 percent.

Required:

1. Compute the NPV for each system (assume that the old system has an unamortized capital cost of $200,000 and that both systems are in a CCA class with a rate of 25 percent). Should Wellington invest in the robotic system?
2. In practice, many financial officers tend to use a higher discount rate than is justified by the firm's cost of capital. For example, a firm may use a discount rate of 20 percent when its cost of capital is or could be 12 percent. Offer some reasons for this practice. Assume that the annual after-tax cash benefit of adopting the robotic system is $80,000 per year more than the manual system. The initial outlay for the robotic system is $340,000. Compute the NPV using 12 percent and 20 percent. Would the robotic system be acquired if 20 percent is used? Could this conservative approach have a negative impact on the firm's ability to stay competitive?

RESEARCH ASSIGNMENT

11–49

Analytical Hierarchy
LO1, LO8

The capital expenditure approach you have studied in this chapter relies on quantitative financial measures such as payback, net present value, and the internal rate of return. Some have argued that these traditional capital expenditure models should be only a starting point in the analysis. Other criteria, such as cycle time (the time it takes to convert materials into a finished good) and flexibility, may be important considerations in a capital expenditure decision, yet such factors are not captured by IRR or NPV. In fact, there have been efforts to build formal frameworks that allow explicit consideration of multiple criteria. One of these frameworks is an analytical hierarchy process. This approach is described in the following article: David E. Stout, Matthew J. Liberatore, and Thomas F. Monahan, "Decision Support Software for Capital Budgeting," *Management Accounting* (July 1991): 50–53.

Required:
Read the above article, and write a paper that describes how the method works. In your paper, offer a critique of the method. What is your opinion of the approach? Is it better than the traditional models, or do you think there are ways that the traditional models can capture such criteria as cycle time and flexibility? Do you think that managers would really use this methodology? Explain.

CHAPTER 12

Inventory Management

Learning Objectives

After studying Chapter 12, you should be able to:

1. Describe the traditional inventory management model.

2. Describe JIT inventory management.

3. Describe the theory of constraints and explain how it can be used to manage inventory.

Scenario

Michelle Anderson, president and owner of Anderson Parts, Inc., had just finished reading the report prepared by Henry Jensen, a special consultant attached to the management advisory section of a national public accounting firm. The recommendations in the report were somewhat surprising, and Michelle was looking forward to her meeting with him to discuss them. Her thoughts were interrupted by Henry's arrival.

Michelle: "Have a seat, Henry. I have to confess that your recommendations are intriguing. If you can convince me that they'll work, you'll have more than earned your fee."

Henry: "I think I can provide a lot of support for those recommendations. When we first met, you mentioned that your company had lost 20 percent of its market share over the past five years. In your industry, as in many others, much of that loss is because of the gains made by foreign competitors. Foreign producers are offering a higher-quality product at a lower price and with better delivery performance."

Michelle: "I am aware of that. You remember that in our first meeting I said as much. I was certain at that time that the solution was automation and was prepared to sink millions into that approach. I was convinced that automating would improve quality, lower

manufacturing costs, and cut down our lead time for production. Because so much money was involved, I hired you to tell us how to automate and exactly what type of equipment to buy. Instead you're telling me that I shouldn't automate—at least not right away—but instead simplify our purchasing and manufacturing by installing something called a just-in-time system. Your report also mentions that I should look at the theory of constraints. Do you really believe that this will bring the benefits I'm seeking? Are you speaking from experience or experiment?"

Henry: "Experience. You're certainly not a guinea pig for something we haven't tried before.

Case after case has shown us that 80 percent of the competitive benefits from automation can be achieved by implementing JIT—and at a significantly decreased cost. First implement JIT; then you can see where automation will be of the most benefit. The strategy we recommend is first simplify, automate, integrate, and continuously seek ways of improving. Continuous improvement is essential. A method called the theory of constraints offers an ongoing way of improving performance. One of its major byproducts is inventory reduction."

Michelle: "It sounds promising. But can you be more specific? What benefits have other companies experienced?"

Henry: "Well, Michelle, your firm manufactures machine parts. Another firm in your same line of business was having a difficult time competing. It needed 24 weeks to produce one of its products from start to finish, whereas a Japanese competitor produced and delivered the same part in 6 weeks. After installing a JIT system, the firm was able to produce the part in only 20 days. In some cases, however, the theory of constraints can offer even

more. An electronic division of Ford used JIT to reduce its lead time from 10.6 to 8.5 days. But after one year of using the theory of constraints, lead time was reduced to 2.2 days. And currently the lead time is less than two shifts.[1] Boeing is another example. Using the theory of constraints, it managed to reduce its lead time by 75 percent."[2]

Michelle: "Henry, that's hard to believe. Yet I know that a lot of the business we have lost is because we have such poor delivery performance compared with that of some of our competitors. You're telling me that we can make dramatic improvements in our lead time with our existing technology?"

Henry: "Yes, but that isn't all. Reducing lead time leads to other benefits. Methods like JIT purchasing and manufacturing and the theory of constraints can reduce your inventories—raw materials, work in process, and finished goods—to much lower levels. Firms often tie up as much as 40 percent of their assets in inventory.[3] That's a lot of nonproductive capital. As you might imagine, decreasing lead time allows a

company to reduce its inventories, freeing up a lot of capital to be used elsewhere. Other inventory-related costs are also avoided, and reducing or avoiding these costs can make your company more competitive."

Michelle: "Intriguing. I would like to know more."

1. As reported at **www.goldratt.com/ford.htm**, December 26, 1998.

2. As reported at **www.goldratt.com/boeing. htm**, December 26, 1998.

3. Assuming an average inventory of $Q/2$ is equivalent to assuming that inventory is consumed uniformly.

Questions to Think About

1. Why do firms carry inventory?

2. What are inventory costs?

3. What can be done to minimize inventory costs?

4. How does JIT reduce inventories?

5. What are the weaknesses of JIT?

6. How does the theory of constraints reduce inventories?

7. Why is effective management of inventory so important?

TRADITIONAL INVENTORY MANAGEMENT

Objective 1

Describe the traditional inventory management model.

Managing the levels of inventory is fundamental to establishing a long-term competitive advantage. Quality, product engineering, prices, overtime, excess capacity, ability to respond to customers (due-date performance), lead times, and overall profitability are all affected by inventory levels. In general, firms that maintain higher inventory levels than their competitors maintain tend to be in a worse competitive position. Inventory and how it is managed is strongly related to a firm's ability to obtain the necessary competitive edge to make money now and in the future. Inventory management policy has become a competitive weapon.

How inventory policy can be used to aid in establishing a competitive advantage is the focus of this chapter. First, we review the traditional inventory management model—the model that has been the mainstay of manufacturing firms for decades. Learning the basics of this model and its underlying conceptual foundation will help us understand where it can still be appropriately applied. Understanding traditional inventory management also provides the necessary background for grasping the advantages of inventory management methods that are used in the advanced manufacturing environment, such as JIT and the theory of constraints.

Inventory Costs

In a world of certainty—a world in which the demand for a product or material is known with certainty for a given period of time (usually a year)—two major costs are associated with inventory. If the inventory is a material or good purchased from an outside source, then these inventory-related costs are known as *ordering costs* and *carrying costs*. If the material or good is produced internally, then the costs are called *setup costs* and *carrying costs*.

Ordering costs are the costs of placing and receiving an order. Examples include the costs of processing an order (clerical costs and documents), the cost of insurance for shipment, and unloading costs.

Setup costs are the costs of preparing equipment and facilities so that they can be used to produce a particular product or component. Examples are wages of idled production workers, the cost of idled production facilities (lost income), and the costs of test runs (labour, materials, and overhead).

Carrying costs are the costs of carrying inventory. Examples include insurance, obsolescence, the opportunity cost of funds tied up in inventory, handling costs, and storage space.

Ordering costs and setup costs are similar in nature—both represent costs that must be incurred to acquire inventory. They differ only in the nature of the prerequisite activity (filling out and placing an order versus configuring equipment and facilities). Thus, in the discussion that follows, any reference to ordering costs can be viewed as a reference to setup costs.

If demand is not known with certainty, a third category of inventory costs—called *stock-out costs*—exists. **Stock-out costs** are the costs of not having a product available when demanded by a customer. Examples are lost sales (both current and future), the costs of expediting (increased transportation charges, overtime, and so on), and the costs of interrupted production.

Traditional Reasons for Holding Inventory

Maximizing profits requires that inventory-related costs be minimized. But minimizing carrying costs favours ordering or producing in small lot sizes, whereas minimizing ordering costs favours large, infrequent orders (minimization of setup costs favours long, infrequent production runs). Thus, minimizing carrying costs encourages small or no inventories, and minimizing ordering or setup costs encourages larger inventories. The need to balance these two sets of costs so that the *total* cost of carrying and ordering can be minimized is one reason organizations choose to carry inventory.

Dealing with uncertainty in demand is a second major reason for holding inventory. Even if the ordering or setup costs were negligible, organizations would still carry inventory because of stock-out costs. If the demand for materials or products is greater than expected, inventory can serve as a buffer, giving organizations the ability to meet delivery dates (thus keeping customers satisfied). Although balancing conflicting costs and dealing with uncertainty are the two most frequently cited reasons for carrying inventories, other reasons also exist.

Inventories of parts and raw materials are often viewed as necessary because of supply uncertainties. That is, inventory buffers of parts and materials are needed to keep production flowing in case of late deliveries or no deliveries (strikes, bad weather, and bankruptcy are examples of uncertain events that can cause an interruption in supply). Unreliable production processes may also create a demand for producing extra inventory. For example, a company may decide to produce more units than needed to meet demand because the production process usually yields a large number of nonconforming units. Similarly, buffers of inventories may be required to continue supplying customers or processes with goods even if a process goes down because of a failed machine. Finally, organizations may acquire larger inventories

Exhibit   12–1

Traditional Reasons for
Carrying Inventory

1. To balance ordering or setup costs and carrying costs
2. To satisfy customer demand (for example, meet delivery dates)
3. To avoid shutting down manufacturing facilities because of
    a. machine failure
    b. defective parts
    c. unavailable parts
    d. late delivery of parts
4. To buffer against unreliable production processes
5. To take advantage of discounts
6. To hedge against future price increases

than normal to take advantage of quantity discounts or to avoid anticipated price increases. Exhibit 12–1 summarizes the reasons typically offered for carrying inventory. It's important to realize that these are reasons that are given to justify carrying inventories. There are a host of other reasons that can be offered that encourage the carrying of inventories. For example, performance measures, such as measures of machine and labour efficiency, may promote the buildup of inventories.

Economic Order Quantity: The Traditional Inventory Model

In developing an inventory policy, two basic questions must be addressed:

1. How much should be ordered (or produced)?
2. When should the order be placed (or the setup done)?

The first question needs to be addressed before the second can be answered.

Order Quantity and Total Ordering and Carrying Costs Assume that demand is known. In choosing an order quantity or a lot size for production, managers need be concerned only with ordering (or setup) and carrying costs. The total ordering (or setup) and carrying cost can be described by the following equation:

$$TC = PD/Q + CQ/2 \qquad\qquad (12.1)$$
$$= \text{Ordering cost} + \text{Carrying cost}$$

where TC = The total ordering (or setup) and carrying costs
  P = The cost of placing and receiving an order (or the cost of setting up a production run)
  D = The known annual demand
  Q = The number of units ordered each time an order is placed (or the lot size for production)
  C = The cost of carrying one unit of stock for one year

The cost of carrying inventory can be computed for any organization that carries inventories, including retail, service, and manufacturing organizations. Of course, the inventory cost model using setup costs and lot size as inputs pertains only to those organizations that produce their own inventories (parts or finished goods). To illustrate the application for a service organization, assume that the following values apply for a part used in the repair of refrigerators (the part is purchased from external suppliers):

$$P = \$25 \text{ per order}$$
$$D = 10,000 \text{ units}$$
$$Q = 1,000 \text{ units}$$
$$C = \$2 \text{ per unit}$$

Dividing D by Q produces the number of orders per year, which is 10 (10,000/1,000). Multiplying the number of orders per year by the cost of placing and receiving an order $[(D/Q) \times P]$ yields the total ordering cost of $250 (10 × $25).

The total carrying cost for the year is given by $(CQ/2)$; this expression is equivalent to multiplying the average inventory on hand $(Q/2)$ by the carrying cost per unit (C). For an order of 1,000 units with a carrying cost of $2 per unit, the average inventory is 500 (1,000/2) and the carrying cost for the year is $1,000 ($2 × 500).[3]

With the applications of Equation 12.1, the total cost is $1,250 ($250 + $1,000). An order quantity of 1,000 with a total cost of $1,250, however, may not be the best choice. Some other order quantity may produce a lower total cost. The objective is to find the order quantity that minimizes the total cost. This order quantity is called the **economic order quantity (EOQ)**. The EOQ model is an example of a push inventory system. In a push system, the acquisition of inventory is initiated in anticipation of future demand—not in reaction to present demand. Fundamental to the analysis is the assessment of D, the future demand.

Computing EOQ

Since EOQ is the quantity that minimizes Equation 12.1, a formula for computing this quantity is easily derived:[4]

$$Q = EOQ = \sqrt{2PD/C} \tag{12.2}$$

Use the data from the preceding example, and the EOQ can be computed using Equation 12.2:

$$EOQ = \sqrt{(2 \times 25 \times 10,000)/2}$$
$$= \sqrt{250,000}$$
$$= 500$$

Substituting 500 as the value of Q into Equation 12.1 yields a total cost of $1,000. The number of orders placed would be 20 (10,000/500); thus, the total ordering cost is $500 (20 × $25). The average inventory is 250 (500/2), with a total carrying cost of $500 (250 × $2). Notice that the carrying cost equals the ordering cost. This is always true for the simple EOQ model described by Equation 12.2. Also notice that an order quantity of 500 is less costly than an order quantity of 1,000 ($1,000 versus $1,250).

Reorder Point

The EOQ answers the question of how much to order (or produce). Knowing when to place an order (or initiate a setup for production) is also an essential part of any inventory policy. The **reorder point** is the point in time when a new order should be placed (or setup started). It is a function of the EOQ, the lead time, and the rate at which inventory is depleted. **Lead time** is the time required to receive the economic order quantity once an order is placed or a setup is initiated.

To avoid stock-out costs and to minimize carrying costs, an order should be placed so that it arrives just as the last item in inventory is used. Knowing the rate of usage and lead time allows us to compute the reorder point (ROP) that accomplishes these objectives:

$$ROP = \text{Rate of usage} \times \text{Lead time} \tag{12.3}$$

To illustrate Equation 12.3, we will continue to use the refrigerator part example. Assume that the producer uses 50 parts per day and that the lead time is four days.

---

3. Assuming an average inventory of $Q/2$ is equivalent to assuming that inventory is consumed uniformly.

4. $d(TC)/dQ = C/2 - DP/Q^2 = 0$, which implies that $Q^2 = 2DP/C$ and $Q = \sqrt{2DP/C}$

If so, an order should be placed when the inventory level of the refrigerator part drops to 200 units (4 × 50). Exhibit 12–2 provides a graphical illustration. Note that the inventory is depleted just as the order arrives and that the quantity on hand jumps back up to the EOQ level.

Demand Uncertainty and the Reorder Point   If the demand for the part or product is not known with certainty, the possibility of stock-out exists. For example, if the refrigerator part were used at a rate of 60 parts a day instead of 50, the firm would use 200 parts after three and one-third days. Since the new order would not arrive until the end of the fourth day, repair activity requiring this part would be idled for two-thirds of a day. To avoid this problem, organizations often choose to carry safety stock. **Safety stock** is extra inventory carried to serve as insurance against fluctuations in demand. Safety stock is computed by multiplying the lead time by the difference between the maximum rate of usage and the average rate of usage. For example, if the maximum usage of the refrigerator part is 60 units per day, the average usage is 50 units per day, and the lead time is four days, the safety stock is computed as follows:

Maximum usage	60
Average usage	50
Difference	10
Lead time	×4
Safety stock	40

With the presence of safety stock, the reorder point is computed as follows:

$$ROP = (\text{Average rate of usage} \times \text{Lead time}) + \text{Safety stock} \qquad (12.4)$$

For the refrigerator part example, the reorder point with safety stock is computed as follows:

$$ROP = (50 \times 4) + 40$$
$$= 240 \text{ units}$$

Thus, an order is automatically placed whenever the inventory level drops to 240 units.

A Manufacturing Example   The service repair setting involved the purchase of inventory. The same concepts can be applied to settings where inventory is manufactured. To illustrate, consider Benson Company, a large manufacturer of farm

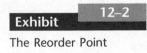

Exhibit   12–2

The Reorder Point

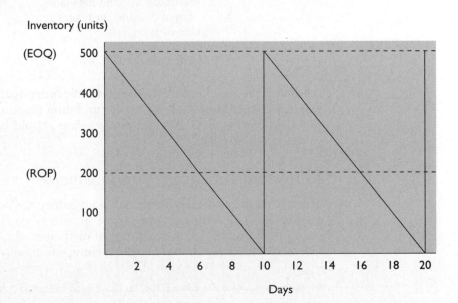

Exhibit   **12–3**

EOQ and Reorder Point
Illustrated

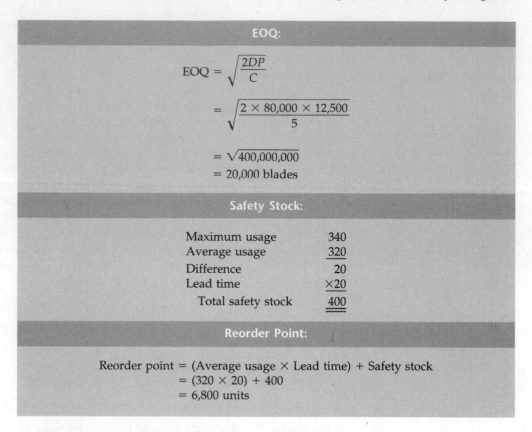

EOQ:

$$EOQ = \sqrt{\frac{2DP}{C}}$$

$$= \sqrt{\frac{2 \times 80{,}000 \times 12{,}500}{5}}$$

$$= \sqrt{400{,}000{,}000}$$

$$= 20{,}000 \text{ blades}$$

Safety Stock:

Maximum usage	340
Average usage	320
Difference	20
Lead time	×20
Total safety stock	400

Reorder Point:

Reorder point = (Average usage × Lead time) + Safety stock

$$= (320 \times 20) + 400$$

$$= 6{,}800 \text{ units}$$

implements with several plants throughout Canada. Each plant produces all sub-assemblies necessary to assemble a particular farm implement. One large plant in Saskatchewan produces plows. The manager of this plant is trying to determine the size of the production runs for the blade fabrication area. He is convinced that the current lot size is too large and wants to identify the quantity that should be produced to minimize the sum of the carrying and setup costs. He also wants to avoid stock-outs, since any stock-out would shut down the assembly department.

To help him in his decision, the controller has supplied the following information:

Average demand for blades	320 per day
Maximum demand for blades	340 per day
Annual demand for blades	80,000
Unit carrying cost	$5
Setup cost	$12,500
Lead time	20 days

Based on this information, the economic order quantity and the reorder point are computed in Exhibit 12–3. As the computation illustrates, the blades should be produced in batches of 20,000 and a new setup should be started when the supply of blades drops to 6,800.

EOQ and Inventory Management

The traditional approach to managing inventory has been referred to as a *just-in-case system*.[5] In some settings, a just-in-case inventory system is entirely appropriate. For example, hospitals need inventories of medicines, drugs, and other critical supplies on hand at all times so that life-threatening situations can be handled. Using an eco-

---

5. Eliyahu M. Goldratt and Robert E. Fox, *The Race* (Croton-on-Hudson, N.Y.: North River Press, 1986).

nomic order quantity coupled with safety stock would seem eminently sensible in such an environment. Relying on a critical drug to arrive just in time to save a heart attack victim is simply not practical. Furthermore, many smaller retail stores, manufacturers, and services may not have the buying power to command alternative inventory management systems, such as just-in-time purchasing.

As the plow blade example illustrates (Exhibit 12–3), the EOQ model is very useful in identifying the optimal tradeoff between inventory carrying costs and setup costs. It is also useful in helping to deal with uncertainty by using safety stock. The historical importance of the EOQ model in many industries can be better appreciated by understanding the nature of the traditional manufacturing environment. This environment has been characterized by the mass production of a few standardized products that typically have a very high setup cost. The production of the plow blades fits this pattern. The high setup cost encouraged a large batch size: 20,000 units. The annual demand of 80,000 units can be satisfied using only four batches. Thus, production runs for these firms tended to be quite long. Furthermore, diversity was viewed as being costly and was avoided. Producing variations of the product can be quite expensive, especially since additional, special features would usually demand even more expensive and frequent setups—the reason for the standardized products.

JIT INVENTORY MANAGEMENT

Objective 2

Describe JIT inventory management.

The manufacturing environment for many of these traditional large-batch, high-setup-cost firms has changed dramatically in the past 10 to 20 years. For one thing, the competitive markets are no longer defined by national boundaries. Advances in transportation and communication have contributed significantly to the creation of global competition. Advances in technology have contributed to shorter life cycles for products, and product diversity has increased. Foreign firms offering higher-quality, lower-cost products *with specialized features* have created tremendous pressures for large-batch, high-setup-cost firms to increase both quality and product diversity while simultaneously reducing total costs. These competitive pressures have led many firms to abandon the EOQ model in favour of a JIT approach. JIT has two strategic objectives: to increase profits and to improve a firm's competitive position. These two objectives are achieved by controlling costs (enabling better price competition and increased profits), improving delivery performance, and improving quality. JIT offers increased cost efficiency and simultaneously has the flexibility to respond to customer demands for better quality and more variety. Quality, flexibility, and cost efficiency are foundation principles for world-class competition.

JIT manufacturing and purchasing represent the continual pursuit of productivity through the elimination of waste. Nonvalue-added activities are a major source of waste. Nonvalue-added activities are either unnecessary, or necessary but inefficient and improvable. Necessary activities are essential to the business and/or are of value to customers. Eliminating nonvalue-added activities is a major thrust of JIT, but it is also a basic objective of any company following the path of continuous improvement—regardless of whether or not JIT is being used. Clearly, JIT is much more than an inventory management system. Inventories, however, are particularly viewed as representing waste. They tie up resources such as cash, space, and labour. They also conceal inefficiencies in production and increase the complexity of a firm's information system. Thus, even though JIT focuses on more than inventory management, control of inventory is an important ancillary benefit. In this chapter, the inventory dimension of JIT is emphasized. In Chapter 4, other benefits and features of JIT were described.

A Pull System

JIT is a manufacturing approach that maintains that goods should be pulled through the system by present demand rather than pushed through the system on a fixed schedule based on anticipated demand. Many fast-food restaurants, like McDonald's, use a pull system to control their finished goods inventory. When a customer orders a hamburger, it is taken from the rack. When the number of hamburgers gets too low, then the cooks make new hamburgers. Customer demand pulls the materials through the system. This same principle is used in manufacturing settings. Each operation produces only what is necessary to satisfy the demand of the succeeding operation. The material or subassembly arrives just in time for production to occur so that demand can be met.

One effect of JIT is to reduce inventories to very low levels. The pursuit of insignificant levels of inventories is vital to the success of JIT. This idea of pursuing insignificant inventories, however, necessarily challenges the traditional reasons for holding inventories (see Exhibit 12–1). These reasons are no longer viewed as valid.

According to the traditional view, inventories solve some underlying problem related to each of the reasons listed in Exhibit 12–1. For example, the problem of resolving the conflict between ordering or setup costs and carrying costs is solved by selecting an inventory level that minimizes the sum of these costs. If demand is greater than expected or if production is reduced by breakdowns and production inefficiencies, then inventories serve as buffers, providing customers with products that might otherwise have been unavailable. Similarly, inventories can prevent shutdowns caused by late delivery of material, defective parts, and failures of machines used to produce subassemblies. Finally, inventories are often the solution to the problem of buying the best raw materials for the least cost through the use of quantity discounts.

JIT refuses to use inventories as the solution to these problems. In fact, inventories are not only viewed as wasteful but are also viewed as being directly associated with a firm's ability to compete. High inventories signal the existence of problems that need to be addressed. High inventories often mean poor quality, long lead times, and poor due-date performance (among other things). JIT inventory management offers alternative solutions that do not require high inventories.

Setup and Carrying Costs: The JIT Approach

JIT takes a radically different approach to minimizing total carrying and setup costs. The traditional approach accepts the existence of setup costs and then finds the order quantity that best balances the two categories of costs. JIT, on the other hand, does not accept setup costs (or ordering costs) as a given; rather, JIT attempts to drive these costs to zero. If setup costs and ordering costs become insignificant, the only remaining cost to minimize is carrying cost, which is accomplished by reducing inventories to very low levels. This approach explains the push for zero inventories in a JIT system.

Long-Term Contracts, Continuous Replenishment, and Electronic Data Interchange

Ordering costs are reduced by developing close relationships with suppliers. Negotiating long-term contracts for the supply of outside materials will obviously reduce the number of orders and the associated ordering costs. Retailers have found a way to reduce ordering costs by adopting an arrangement known as *continuous replenishment*. With **continuous replenishment,** a manufacturer assumes the inventory management function for the retailer. The manufacturer tells the retailer when and how much stock to reorder. The retailer reviews the recommendation and approves the order if it makes sense. Wal-Mart and Procter & Gamble, for example, use this arrangement.[6] The arrangement has reduced inventories for Wal-Mart, and it has also reduced stock-out problems. Additionally, Procter & Gamble's goods are often sold before Wal-Mart has to pay for them. Procter & Gamble, on the other

6. Michael Hammer and James Champy, *Reengineering the Corporation* (New York: HarperBusiness, 1993).

hand, has become a preferred supplier, has more and better shelf space, and also has less demand uncertainty. The ability to project demand better allows Procter & Gamble to produce and deliver continuously in smaller lots—a goal of JIT manufacturing. Similar arrangements can be made between manufacturers and suppliers.

The process of continuous replenishment is facilitated by electronic data interchange. **Electronic data interchange (EDI)** allows suppliers access to a buyer's on-line database.[7] By knowing the buyer's production schedule (in the case of a manufacturer), the supplier can deliver the needed parts where they are needed just in time for their use. EDI involves no paper—no purchase orders or invoices. The supplier uses the production schedule that is in the database to determine its own production and delivery schedules. When the parts are shipped, an electronic message is sent from the supplier to the buyer that a shipment is en route. When the parts arrive, a bar code is scanned with an electronic wand; this action initiates payment for the goods. Clearly, EDI requires a close working arrangement between the supplier and the buyer—they almost operate as one company rather than two separate companies. General Motors' Saturn plant uses an EDI arrangement with its component suppliers. This approach has enabled both suppliers and Saturn to reduce overhead.[8]

Reducing Setup Times   Reducing setup times requires a company to search for new, more efficient ways to accomplish setup. Fortunately, experience has indicated that dramatic reductions in setup times can be achieved. Upon adopting a JIT system, Harley-Davidson reduced setup times by more than 75 percent on the machines evaluated.[9] In some cases, Harley-Davidson was able to reduce the setup times from hours to minutes. Other companies have experienced similar results. Generally, setup times can be reduced by at least 75 percent.[10]

Due-Date Performance: The JIT Solution

Due-date performance is a measure of a firm's ability to respond to customer needs. In the past, finished goods inventories have been used to ensure that a firm is able to meet a requested delivery date. JIT solves the problem of due-date performance not by building inventory but by dramatically reducing lead times. Shorter lead times increase a firm's ability to meet requested delivery dates and to respond quickly to the demands of the market. Thus, the firm's competitiveness is improved. JIT cuts lead times by reducing setup times, improving quality, and using cellular manufacturing.

Manufacturing cells reduce travel distance between machines and inventory; they can also have a dramatic effect on lead time. For example, in a traditional manufacturing system, one company took two months to manufacture a valve. Grouping the lathes and drills used to make the valves into U-shaped cells reduced the lead time to two or three days. Oregon Cutting Systems, a chain saw manufacturer, was able to reduce travel distance by more than 90 percent and lead times from 21 days to 3 days. Because of the reduced lead time and plans for even further reduction, the company now fills orders directly from the factory rather than from finished goods warehouses.[11] These reductions in lead time are not unique—most companies experience at least a 90 percent reduction in lead times when they implement JIT.[12]

7. For more discussion on EDI, see *Implementing Electronic Data Exchange*, Management Accounting Guideline 24, The Society of Management Accountants of Canada (Hamilton, Ontario, 1994) and *The Role of Management Accounting in Electronic Data Interchange*, The Society of Management Accountants of Canada, 1992. See also John W. Yu, "The Paperless EDI Environment," *CGA Magazine*, September 1993, 40–42, 74–75.

8. Hammer and Champy, 90–91.

9. Gene Schwind, "Man Arrives Just in Time to Save Harley-Davidson," *Materials Handling Engineering* (August 1984): 28–35.

10. William J. Stoddard and Nolan W. Rhea, "Just-in-Time Manufacturing: The Relentless Pursuit of Productivity," *Materials Handling Engineering* (March 1985): 70–76.

Avoidance of Shutdown and Process Reliability: The JIT Approach

Most shutdowns occur for one of three reasons: machine failure, defective material or subassembly, or unavailability of a raw material or subassembly. Holding inventories is one traditional solution to all three problems. Those espousing the JIT approach claim that inventories do not solve the problems but cover up or hide them. JIT proponents use the analogy of rocks in a lake. The rocks represent the three problems, and the water represents inventories. If the lake is deep (that is, if inventories are high), then the rocks are never exposed, and managers can pretend that they do not exist. Once inventories are reduced to zero, the rocks are exposed and can no longer be ignored. JIT solves the three problems by emphasizing total preventive maintenance and total quality control and by building the right kind of relationship with suppliers.

Total Preventive Maintenance Zero machine failures is the goal of **total preventive maintenance.** By paying more attention to preventive maintenance, a firm can avoid most machine breakdowns. This objective is easier to attain in a JIT environment because of the interdisciplinary labour philosophy. It is not uncommon for a cell worker to be trained in maintenance for the machines he or she operates. Because of the pull-through nature of JIT, it is also not unusual for a cell worker to have idle manufacturing time. Some of this time can be used productively by having the cell workers involved in preventive maintenance.

Total Quality Control The problem of defective parts is solved by striving for zero defects. Because JIT manufacturing does not rely on inventories to replace defective parts or materials, the emphasis on quality for both internally produced and externally purchased materials increases significantly. The outcome is impressive: the number of rejected parts tends to fall by 75 to 90 percent.[13] Decreasing defective parts also diminishes the justification for inventories based on unreliable processes.

The Kanban System To ensure that parts or materials are available when needed, the **Kanban system** is employed. This information system controls production through the use of markers or cards. The Kanban system is responsible for ensuring that the necessary products (or parts) are produced (or acquired) in the necessary quantities at the necessary time. It is the heart of the JIT inventory management system.

The cards or markers used in a Kanban system are plastic, cardboard, or metal plates measuring 10 centimetres by 20 centimetres. The Kanban card is usually placed in a vinyl sack and attached to the part or a container holding the needed parts.

A basic Kanban system uses three cards: a withdrawal Kanban, a production Kanban, and a vendor Kanban. The first two control the movement of work among the manufacturing processes, while the third controls the movement of parts between the processes and outside suppliers. A **withdrawal Kanban** specifies the quantity that a subsequent process should withdraw from the preceding process. A **production Kanban** specifies the quantity that the preceding process should produce. **Vendor Kanbans** are used to notify suppliers to deliver more parts; they also specify when the parts are needed. The three Kanbans are illustrated in Exhibits 12–4, 12–5, and 12–6.

11. Richard Schonberger, "Just-in-Time Production Systems: Replacing Complexity with Simplicity in Manufacturing Management," *Industrial Engineering* (October 1984): 52–63. For an excellent description of the savings realized by Oregon Cutting Systems, read the article by Jack Bailes and Ilene K. Kleinsorge, "Cutting Waste with JIT," *Management Accounting* (May 1992): 28–32.

12. See Stoddard and Rhea, "Just-in-Time Manufacturing," 76.

13. Stoddard and Rhea, "Just-in-Time Manufacturing," 70–76.

Exhibit 12–4

Withdrawl Kanban

Item No.	**15670T07**		Preceding Process
Item Name	**Circuit Board**		**CB Assembly**
Computer Type	**TR6547 PC**		
Box Capacity	**8**		Subsequent Process
Box Type	**C**		**Final Assembly**

Exhibit 12–5

Production Kanban

Item No.	**15670T07**		Process
Item Name	**Circuit Board**		**CB Assembly**
Computer Type	**TR6547 PC**		
Box Capacity	**8**		
Box Type	**C**		

Exhibit 12–6

Vendor Kanban

Item No.	**15670T08**		Name of Receiving Company
Item Name	**Computer Casing**		**Electro PC**
Box Capacity	**8**		Receiving Gate
Box Type	**A**		**75**
Time to Deliver	**8:30 A.M., 12:30 P.M., 2:30 P.M.**		
Name of Supplier	**Gerry Supply**		

How Kanban cards are used to control the work flow can be illustrated with a simple example. Assume that two processes are needed to manufacture a product. The first process (CB Assembly) builds and tests printed circuit boards (using a U-shaped manufacturing cell). The second process (Final Assembly) puts eight circuit boards into a subassembly purchased from an outside supplier. The final product is a personal computer.

Exhibit 12–7 provides the plant layout corresponding to the manufacture of the personal computers. Refer to this exhibit as the steps involved in using Kanbans are outlined.

Consider first the movement of work between the two processing areas. Assume that eight circuit boards are placed in a container and that one such container is located in the CB stores area. Attached to this container is a production Kanban (P-Kanban).

Exhibit 12–7

Kanban Process

A second container with eight circuit boards is located near the Final Assembly line (the withdrawal store) with a withdrawal Kanban (W-Kanban). Now assume that the production schedule calls for the immediate assembly of a computer.

The Kanban setups can be described as follows:

1.   A worker from the Final Assembly line goes to the withdrawal store, removes the eight circuit boards, and places them into production. The worker also removes the withdrawal Kanban and places it on the withdrawal post.
2.   The withdrawal Kanban on the post signals that the Final Assembly unit needs an additional eight circuit boards.
3.   A worker from Final Assembly (or a material handler called a carrier) removes the withdrawal Kanban from the post and carries it to CB stores.
4.   At the CB stores area, the carrier removes the production Kanban from the container of eight circuit boards and places it on the production-ordering post.
5.   The carrier next attaches the withdrawal Kanban to the container of parts and carries the container back to the Final Assembly area. Assembly of the next computer can begin.
6.   The production Kanban on the production-ordering post signals the workers of the CB Assembly to begin producing another lot of circuit boards. The production Kanban is removed and accompanies the units as they are produced.
7.   When the lot of eight circuit boards is completed, the units are placed in a container in the CB stores area with the production Kanban attached. The cycle is then repeated.

The use of Kanbans ensures that the subsequent process (Final Assembly) withdraws the circuit boards from the preceding process (CB Assembly) in the necessary quantity at the appropriate time. The Kanban system also controls the preceding process by allowing it to produce only the quantities withdrawn by the subsequent process. In this way, inventories are kept at a minimum, and the components arrive just in time to be used.

Essentially, the same steps are followed for a purchased subassembly. The only difference is the use of a vendor Kanban in place of a production Kanban. A vendor Kanban on a vendor post signals to the supplier that another order is needed. As with the circuit boards, the subassemblies must be delivered just in time for use. A JIT purchasing system requires the supplier to deliver small quantities on a frequent basis. These deliveries could be weekly, daily, or even several times a day. This system calls for a close working relationship with suppliers. Long-term contractual agreements tend to ensure supply of materials.

Discounts and Price Increases: JIT Purchasing versus Holding Inventories

Traditionally, inventories are carried so that a firm can take advantage of quantity discounts and hedge against future price increases of the items purchased. The objective is to lower the cost of inventory. JIT achieves the same objective without carrying inventories. The JIT solution is to negotiate long-term contracts with a few chosen suppliers located as close to the production facility as possible and to establish more extensive supplier involvement. Suppliers are not selected on the basis of price alone. Performance—the quality of the component and the supplier's ability to deliver as needed—and commitment to JIT purchasing are vital considerations. Other benefits of long-term contracts exist. They stipulate prices and acceptable quality levels. Long-term contracts also dramatically reduce the number of orders placed, which helps drive down the ordering cost. Another effect of JIT purchasing is to lower the cost of purchased parts by 5 to 20 percent.[14]

JIT's Limitations

JIT is not an approach that can simply be purchased and plugged in with immediate results. Its implementation should be more of an evolutionary process than a revolutionary process. Patience is needed. JIT is often referred to as a program of simplification—yet this does not imply that it is simple or easy to implement. Time is required, for example, to build sound relationships with suppliers. Insisting on immediate changes in delivery times and quality may not be realistic and may cause difficult confrontations between a company and its suppliers. Partnership, not coercion, should be the basis of supplier relationships. To achieve the benefits that are associated with JIT purchasing, a company may be tempted to unilaterally redefine its supplier relationships. Unilaterally redefining supplier relationships by extracting concessions and dictating terms may create supplier resentment and may actually cause suppliers to retaliate. In the long run, suppliers may seek new markets, find ways to charge higher prices than those that would exist with a preferred supplier arrangement, or seek regulatory relief. These actions may destroy many of the JIT benefits extracted by the impatient company.

Workers also may be affected by JIT. Studies have shown that sharp reductions in inventory buffers may cause a regimented work flow and high levels of stress among production workers.[15] Some have suggested a deliberate pace of inventory reduction to allow workers to develop a sense of autonomy and to encourage their participation in broader improvement efforts. Forced and dramatic reductions in inventories may indeed reveal problems—but it may also cause problems: lost sales and stressed workers. If the workers perceive JIT as a way of simply squeezing more out of them, then JIT efforts may be doomed. Perhaps a better strategy for JIT implementation is one under which inventory reductions follow the process improvements that JIT offers. Implementing JIT is not easy, and it requires careful and thorough planning and preparation. Companies should expect some struggle and frustration.

The most glaring deficiency of JIT is the absence of inventory to buffer production interruptions. Current sales are constantly being threatened by an unexpected interruption in production. In fact, if a problem occurs, JIT's approach consists of trying to find and solve the problem before any further production activity occurs. Retailers who use JIT tactics also face the possibility of shortages (JIT retailers order what they need now, not what they expect to sell; the idea is to flow goods through the channel as late as possible, keeping inventories low and decreasing the need for markdowns). If demand increases well beyond the retailer's supply of inventory, the retailer may be unable to make order adjustments quickly enough to avoid lost sales

14. Stoddard and Rhea, "Just-in-Time Manufacturing," 70–76.

15. For a more complete discussion of JIT's supplier and worker effects, see Paul L. Zipkin, "Does Manufacturing Need a JIT Revolution?" *Harvard Business Review* (January/February 1991): 40–50.

and irked customers. For example, during the 1993 Christmas shopping season, many retailers (for example, Toys "R" Us) that were using a JIT approach lost millions in sales because of their inability to accurately forecast demand for Mighty Morphin Power Rangers.[16] It was estimated that shipments of the Power Ranger action figures would be around 600,000 units before December 25, compared with an actual demand that was estimated at 12 million units. Yet despite the downside, retailers seem to be strongly committed to JIT. Apparently, losing sales on surprise hits is less costly than carrying high levels of inventory.

The JIT manufacturing company is also willing to place current sales at risk to achieve assurance of future sales. This assurance comes from higher quality, faster response time, and lower operating costs. Even so, we must recognize that a sale lost today is a sale lost forever. Installing a JIT system so that it operates with very little interruption is not a short-run project. Thus, losing sales is a real cost of installing a JIT system.

An alternative and perhaps complementary approach is the theory of constraints (TOC). In principle, TOC can be used in conjunction with JIT manufacturing; after all, JIT manufacturing environments also have constraints. Furthermore, the TOC approach has the very appealing quality of protecting current sales while also striving to increase future sales by increasing quality, lowering response time, and decreasing operating costs.

THEORY OF CONSTRAINTS

Objective 3

Describe the theory of constraints and explain how it can be used to manage inventory.

Every firm faces limited resources and limited demand for each product. These limitations are called *constraints*. The theory of constraints recognizes that the performance of any organization is limited by its constraints. The theory of constraints then develops a specific approach to managing constraints in a way that supports the objective of continuous improvement. According to TOC, if performance is to be improved, an organization must identify its constraints, exploit the constraints in the short run, and, in the longer term, find ways to overcome the constraints.

Basic Concepts

TOC focuses on three measures of organizational performance: *throughput, inventory,* and *operating expenses*. **Throughput** is the rate at which an organization generates money through sales.[17] In operational terms, throughput is the difference between sales revenue and unit-level variable costs such as materials and power. Direct labour is typically viewed as a fixed unit-level expense and is not usually included in the definition. With this understanding, throughput corresponds to contribution margin. **Inventory** is all the money the organization spends in turning raw materials into throughput. **Operating expenses** are defined as all the money the organization spends in turning inventories into throughput. Based on these three measures, the objectives of management can be expressed as increasing throughput, minimizing inventory, and decreasing operating expenses.

Increasing throughput, minimizing inventory, and decreasing operating expenses will affect three financial measures of performance: net income and return on investment will increase, and cash flow will improve. Increasing throughput and decreasing operating expenses have always been emphasized as key elements in improving these three financial measures of performance. However the role of minimizing inventory in achieving these improvements has been traditionally regarded as less important than throughput and operating expenses.

---

16. Joseph Pereira, "Tough Game: The Power Rangers Surprise," *The Wall Street Journal* (21 December 1993): A1, A5.

17. This follows the definition offered by Eliyahu Goldratt and Robert Fox in *The Race*. Other definitions and basic concepts of the theory of constraints are also based upon the developments of Goldratt and Fox.

Like JIT, the theory of constraints, assigns inventory management a much more prominent role than the traditional viewpoint does. TOC recognizes that lowering inventory decreases carrying costs—and therefore decreases operating expenses and improves net income. TOC, however, argues that lowering inventory helps produce a competitive edge through better products, lower prices, and faster response to customer needs.

Better Products   Better products mean higher quality. It also means that the company is able to improve products and provide these improved products quickly to the market. The relationship between low inventories and quality has been described in the JIT section. Essentially, low inventories allow defects to be detected more quickly and the cause of the problem to be assessed. Improving products is also a key competitive element. New or improved products need to reach the market quickly—before competitors can provide similar features. This goal is facilitated with low inventories. Low inventories allow new product changes to be introduced more quickly because the company has fewer old products (in stock or in process) that would need to be scrapped or sold before the new product is introduced.

Lower Prices   High inventories mean that more productive capacity is needed and thus more investment in equipment and space. Since lead time and high work-in-process inventories are usually correlated, high inventories may often be the cause of overtime. Overtime, of course, increases operating expenses and lowers profitability. Lower inventories reduce carrying costs, per-unit investment costs, and other operating expenses such as overtime and special shipping charges. Lowering investment and operating costs increases the unit margin of each product, providing more flexibility in pricing decisions. Lower prices are possible or higher product margins occur if competitive conditions do not require prices to be lowered.

Responsiveness   Delivering goods on time and producing goods with shorter lead times than the market dictates are important competitive tools. Delivering goods on time is related to a firm's ability to forecast the time required to produce and deliver goods. If a firm has higher inventories than its competitors have, then the firm's production lead time is higher than the industry's forecast horizon. High inventories may obscure the actual time required to produce and fill an order. Lower inventories allow actual lead times to be more carefully observed, and more accurate delivery dates can then be provided. Shortening lead times is also crucial. Shortening lead times is equivalent to lowering work-in-process inventories. A company carrying 10 days of work-in-process inventories has an average production lead time of 10 days. If the company can reduce lead time from 10 days to 5 days, then the company should now be carrying only 5 days' worth of work-in-process inventories.

As lead times are reduced, it is also possible to reduce finished goods inventories. For example, if a product's lead time is 10 days and the market requires delivery on demand, then the firm must carry, on average, 10 days of finished goods inventory (plus some safety stock to cover demand uncertainty). Suppose that the firm is able to reduce lead time to 5 days. In this case, finished goods inventory should also be reduced to 5 days. Thus, the levels of inventories signal the organization's ability to respond. High levels relative to those of competitors translate into a competitive disadvantage. TOC thus emphasizes reduction of inventories by reducing lead times.

TOC Steps

The theory of constraints uses five steps to achieve its goal of improving organizational performance:

1.   Identify the organization's constraint(s).
2.   Exploit the binding constraint(s).

3. Subordinate everything else to the decisions made in Step 2.
4. Elevate the binding constraint(s).
5. Repeat the process.

Step 1: Identify the Organization's Constraint(s) Constraints can be classified as *external* or *internal*. **External constraints** are limiting factors imposed on the firm from external sources (such as market demand). **Internal constraints** are limiting factors found within the firm (such as machine-time availability). Although resources and demands may be limited, certain product mixes may not meet all the demand or use all of the available resources. Constraints whose limited resources are not fully used by a product mix are **loose constraints. Binding constraints** are those constraints whose available resources are fully utilized.

In Step 1 of the TOC process, then, internal and external constraints are identified. The optimal product mix is identified as the mix that maximizes throughput subject to all the organization's constraints. The optimal mix reveals how much of each constrained resource is used and which of the organization's constraints are binding.

Decisions about product mix can have a significant impact on an organization's profitability. Each mix represents an alternative that carries with it an associated profit level. A manager should choose the alternative that maximizes total profits. The usual approach is to assume that only unit-based variable costs are relevant to the product-mix decision. Thus, assuming that nonunit-level costs are the same for different mixes of products, we ascertain that the optimal mix is the one that maximizes total contribution margin.

A manager must choose the optimal product mix given the constraints faced by his or her firm. Assume, for example, that Confer Company produces two types of machine parts: X and Y, with unit contribution margins of $300 and $600, respectively. Assuming that Confer can sell all that is produced, some may argue that only Part Y should be produced and sold, because it has the larger contribution margin. However, this solution is not necessarily the best. The selection of the optimal mix can be significantly affected by the relationships of the constrained resources to the individual products. These relationships affect the quantity of each product that can be produced and, consequently, the total contribution margin that can be earned. This point is most vividly illustrated by looking at a situation where there is one binding internal resource constraint.

One Binding Internal Constraint Assume that each part must be drilled by a special machine. The firm owns three machines, which together provide 120 drilling hours per week. Part X requires 1 hour of drilling, and Part Y requires 3 hours of drilling. Assuming no other binding constraints, what is the optimal mix of parts? Since each unit of X requires 1 hour of drilling, 120 units of X can be produced per week (120/1). At $300 per unit, Confer can earn a total contribution margin of $36,000 per week. On the other hand, Y requires 3 hours of drilling per unit; therefore, 40 (120/3) parts can be produced. At $600 per unit, the total contribution margin is $24,000 per week. Producing only X yields a higher profit level than producing only Y—even though the unit contribution margin for Y is two times larger than that for X. The contribution margin per unit of each product is not the critical concern. The contribution margin per unit of *scarce resource* is the deciding factor. The product yielding the highest contribution margin per drilling hour should be selected. Part X earns $300 per machine hour ($300/1), while Part Y earns only $200 per machine hour ($600/3). Thus, the optimal mix is 120 units of Part X and none of Part Y, producing a total contribution margin of $36,000 per week. Notice that since this product mix uses up all 120 machine hours, the machine-hour constraint is binding.

Internal Binding Constraint and External Binding Constraint The contribution margin per unit of scarce resource can also be used to identify the optimal product mix when an external binding constraint exists. For example, assume the same internal constraint of 120 drilling hours, but also assume that Confer can sell at most 30 units of Part X and 100 units of Part Y. The internal constraint allows Confer to produce 120 units of Part X, but this is no longer a feasible choice, because only 30 units of X can be sold. Thus, we now have a binding external constraint, one that affects the earlier decision to produce and sell only Part X. Since the contribution per unit of scarce resource (machine hour) is $300 for Part X and $200 for Part Y, it still makes sense to produce as much of X as possible before producing any of Y. Confer should first produce 30 units of X, using 30 machine hours. This leaves 90 machine hours, allowing the production of 30 units of Y. The optimal mix is now 30 units of X and 30 units of Y, producing a total contribution margin of $27,000 per week ($300 × 30 + $600 × 30).

Step 2: Exploit the Binding Constraint(s)   One way to make the best use of binding constraints is to ensure that the optimal product mix is produced. Making the best use of binding constraints, however, is more extensive than simply ensuring production of the optimal mix. This step is the heart of TOC's philosophy of short-run constraint management and is directly related to TOC's goal of reducing inventories and improving performance.

In most organizations, there are only a few binding resource constraints. The major binding constraint is defined as the drummer. Assume, for example, that there is only one internal binding constraint. By default, this constraint becomes the drummer. The drummer constraint's production rate sets the production rate for the entire plant. Downstream processes fed by the drummer constraint are naturally forced to follow its rate of production. Scheduling for downstream processes is easy. Once a part is finished at the drummer process, the next process begins its operation. Similarly, each subsequent operation begins when the prior operation is finished. Upstream processes that feed the drummer constraint are scheduled to produce at the same rate as the drummer constraint. Scheduling at the drummer rate prevents the production of excessive upstream work-in-process inventories.

For upstream scheduling, there are two additional features that TOC uses in managing constraints to lower inventory levels and improve organizational performance: buffers and ropes. First, an inventory buffer is established in front of the major binding constraint. The inventory buffer is referred to as the time buffer. A **time buffer** is the inventory needed to keep the constrained resource busy for a specified time interval. The purpose of a time buffer is to protect the organization's throughput from any disruption that can be overcome within the specified time interval. For example, if it takes one day to overcome most interruptions that occur upstream from the drummer constraint, then a two-day buffer should be sufficient to protect throughput from any interruptions. Thus, in scheduling, the operation immediately preceding the drummer constraint should produce the parts needed by the drummer resource two days in advance of their planned usage. Any other preceding operations are scheduled backward in time to produce so that their parts arrive just in time for subsequent operations.

Ropes are actions taken to tie the rate at which raw material is released into the plant (at the first operation) to the production rate of the constrained resource. The objective of a rope is to ensure that the work-in-process inventory will not exceed the level needed for the time buffer. Thus, the drummer rate is used to limit the rate of raw material release and effectively controls the rate at which the first operation produces. The rate of the first operation then controls the rates of subsequent operations. The TOC inventory system is often called the **Drum–Buffer–Rope (DBR) System**. Exhibit 12–8 illustrates the DBR structure for a general setting.

The Confer Company example can be expanded to provide a specific illustration of the DBR system. Assume that there are three sequential processes: grinding, drilling, and polishing. Each of these processes has a limited amount of resources. Demand for each type of machine part produced is also limited (30 for Part X and 100 for Part Y, as indicated earlier). Assume that the only internal binding constraint is drilling and that the optimal product mix consists of 30 units of Part X and 30 units

Exhibit   **12–8**

Drum–Buffer–Rope
System: General
Description

of Part Y (per week). This is the most that the drilling process can handle. The other two processes represent loose constraints and are therefore capable of producing more per week of each part than the optimal mix calls for. Since the drilling process feeds the polishing process, we can define the drilling constraint as the drummer for the plant. Assume that the demand for each part is uniformly spread out over the week. This means that the production rate should be 6 per day of each part (for a 5-day workweek). A 2-day time buffer would require 24 completed parts from the grinding process: 12 for Part X and 12 for Part Y. To ensure that the time buffer does not increase at a rate greater than 6 per day for each part, raw materials should be released to the grinding process in such a way that only 6 of each part can be produced each day (this is the rope—tying the release of materials to the production rate of the drummer constraint). Exhibit 12–9 summarizes the specific DBR details for the Confer Company.

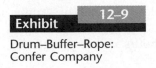

Exhibit 12–9

Drum–Buffer–Rope:
Confer Company

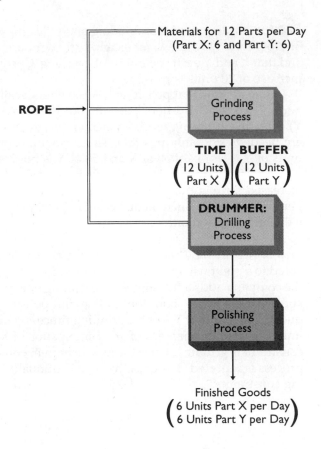

Materials for 12 Parts per Day
(Part X: 6 and Part Y: 6)

ROPE ⟶

Grinding
Process

TIME | BUFFER
$\left(\begin{array}{c}12\ \text{Units}\\ \text{Part X}\end{array}\right)\left(\begin{array}{c}12\ \text{Units}\\ \text{Part Y}\end{array}\right)$

DRUMMER:
Drilling
Process

Polishing
Process

Finished Goods
$\left(\begin{array}{c}6\ \text{Units Part X per Day}\\ 6\ \text{Units Part Y per Day}\end{array}\right)$

Step 3: Subordinate Everything Else to the Decisions Made in Step 2   The drummer constraint essentially sets the capacity for the entire plant. All remaining departments should be subordinated to the needs of the drummer constraint. This principle requires many companies to change the way they view things. For example, the use of efficiency measures at the departmental level may no longer be appropriate. Consider the Confer Company once again. Encouraging maximum productive efficiency for the grinding department would produce excess work-in-process inventories. For example, assume that the capacity of the grinding department is 80 units per week. Assuming that the two-day buffer is in place, we soon find out that if it worked at capacity, the grinding department would add 20 units per week to the buffer in front of the drilling department. Over a period of a year, the potential exists for building very large work-in-process inventories (1,000 units of the two parts would be added to the buffer over a 50-week period). Polishing, of course, must produce at the rate of drilling, because it follows drilling in the sequential production process. Thus, the only concern for polishing is that it can handle the output of drilling.

Step 4: Elevate the Binding Constraint(s)   Once actions have been taken to make the best possible use of the existing constraints, the next step is to embark on a program of continuous improvement by reducing the limitations that the binding constraint(s) place on the organization's performance. Suppose, for example, that Confer Company adds a half shift for the drilling department, increasing the drilling hours from 120 to 180 per week. With 60 additional drilling hours, Confer can increase production of Part Y from 30 to 50 units, an additional 20 units per week (recall that Part Y uses 3 hours per unit, yielding the 20 additional units (60/3)). Since Part Y has a unit contribution margin of $600, this will increase throughput by $12,000 per week

($600 × 20), assuming that grinding and polishing can handle an increase of 20 units of Y per week. We know, for example, that grinding has 80 hours per week available and that X and Y each use 1 hour of grinding. Currently, 60 hours are being used. An increase of 20 units is possible.

Now assume that polishing has 160 hours available and that Part X uses 2 hours per unit and Part Y 1 hour per unit. For the current product mix (30 of X and 30 of Y), 90 hours are being used. To increase production of Y by 20 units, 20 more hours are needed—certainly possible. Thus, moving from a mix of 30 units of X and 30 units of Y to a mix of 30 of X and 50 of Y is possible. Is the half shift worth it? This question is answered by comparing the cost of adding the half shift with the increased throughput of $12,000 per week. If the cost of adding the half shift is $50 per hour, then the incremental cost is $3,000 per week, and the decision to add the half shift is a good one.

Step 5: Repeat the Process Eventually, the drilling resource constraint will be elevated to a point where the constraint is no longer binding. Suppose, for example, that the company adds a full shift for the drilling operation, increasing the resource availability to 240 hours. Both the drilling and polishing constraints are capable of producing more of Part Y, but the grinding process cannot (grinding can produce a maximum of 80 units per week of any combination of X and Y). Thus, the new drummer constraint is grinding. Once the new drummer constraint is identified, then the TOC process is repeated. The objective is to continually improve performance by managing constraints.

SUMMARY OF LEARNING OBJECTIVES

1. Describe the traditional inventory management model.
The traditional approach uses inventories to manage the tradeoffs between ordering (setup) costs and carrying costs. The optimal tradeoff defines the economic order quantity. Other reasons for inventories are also offered: due-date performance, avoiding shutdowns (protecting sales), hedging against future price increases, and taking advantage of discounts. JIT and TOC, on the other hand, argue that inventories are costly and are used to cover up fundamental problems that need to be corrected so that the organization can become more competitive.

2. Describe JIT inventory management.
JIT uses long-term contracts, continuous replenishment, and EDI to reduce or even eliminate ordering costs. Engineering efforts are made to reduce setup times drastically. Once ordering costs and setup costs are reduced to minimal levels, it becomes possible to reduce carrying costs by reducing inventory levels. JIT carries small buffers in front of each operation and uses a Kanban system to regulate production. Production is tied to market demand. If an interruption occurs, throughput tends to be lost because of the small buffers. Yet future throughput tends to increase, because efforts are being made to improve such things as quality, productivity, and lead time.

3. Describe the theory of constraints and explain how it can be used to manage inventory.
TOC identifies an organization's constraints and exploits them so that throughput is maximized, and inventories and operating costs are minimized. Identifying the optimal product mix is part of this process. The major binding constraint is identified and is used to set the plant's productive rate. Release of raw materials into the first process (operation) is regulated by the drummer constraint. A time buffer is located in front of critical constraints. This time buffer is sized so that it protects throughput from any interruptions. As in JIT, the interruptions are used to locate and correct the problem. However, unlike JIT, the time buffer serves to protect throughput. Furthermore, because buffers are located only in front of critical constraints, TOC may actually produce smaller inventories than JIT does.

KEY TERMS

REVIEW PROBLEMS

I. INVENTORY COSTS; EOQ; REORDER POINT

A local TV repair shop uses 36,000 units of a part each year (an average of 100 units per working day). It costs $20 to place and receive an order. The shop orders in lots of 400 units. It cost $4 to carry one unit per year in inventory.

Required:

1. Calculate the total annual ordering cost.
2. Calculate the total annual carrying cost.
3. Calculate the total annual inventory cost.
4. Calculate the EOQ.
5. Calculate the total annual inventory cost using the EOQ inventory policy.
6. How much is saved per year using the EOQ versus an order size of 400 units?
7. Compute the reorder point, assuming that the lead time is three days.
8. Suppose that the usage of the part can be as much as 110 units per day. Calculate the safety stock and the new reorder point.

Solution

1. Ordering cost $= PD/Q$
    $$= \$20 \times 36{,}000/400$$
    $$= \$1{,}800$$

2. Carrying cost $= CQ/2$
    $$= \$4 \times 400/2$$
    $$= \$800$$

3. Total cost $=$ Ordering cost $+$ Carrying cost
    $$= \$1{,}800 + \$800$$
    $$= \$2{,}600$$

4. EOQ $= \sqrt{2PD/C}$
    $$= \sqrt{(2 \times 20 \times 36{,}000/4)}$$
    $$= \sqrt{360{,}000}$$
    $$= 600$$

5. Total cost $= (PD/Q) + (CQ/2)$
    $$= (\$20 \times 36{,}000/600) + (\$4 \times 600/2)$$
    $$= \$1{,}200 + \$1{,}200$$
    $$= \$2{,}400$$

6. Savings $= \$2{,}600 - \$2{,}400 = \$200$
7. Reorder point $= 100 \times 3 = 300$ units
8. Safety stock $= (110 - 100) \times 3 = 30$ units
    Reorder point $= 300 + 30 = 330$ units (or $110 \times 3 = 330$ units)

II. OPTIMAL MIX

Two types of gears are produced: A and B. Gear A has a unit contribution margin of $200, and Gear B has a unit contribution margin of $400. Gear A uses 2 hours of grinding time, and Gear B uses 5 hours of grinding time. There are 200 hours of grinding time available per week. This is the only constraint.

Required:

1. Is the grinding constraint an internal constraint or an external constraint?
2. Determine the optimal product mix. What is the total contribution margin?
3. Suppose that there is an additional demand constraint: market conditions will allow the sale of only 80 units of each gear. Now what is the optimal product mix? the total contribution margin?

Solution

1. It's an internal constraint.
2. Gear A: $200/2 = $100 per grinding hour
   Gear B: $400/5 = $80 per grinding hour

   Since Gear A earns more contribution margin per unit of scarce resource than Gear B does, only Gear A should be produced and sold (based on the fact that the firm can sell all it wants of either product).

   Optimal product mix: Gear A: 100 units (200/2); Gear B: 0 units

   Total contribution margin = $200 × 100 + $400 × 0 = $20,000 per week

3. Now the firm should produce and sell 80 units of Gear A using 160 hours (80 × 2) and 8 units of Gear B ((200 − 160)/5)). The total contribution margin = $200 × 80 + $400 × 8 = $19,200 per week.

III. DRUMMERS AND INVENTORY MANAGEMENT SYSTEMS

Traditional and JIT inventory management systems also have drummers—factors that determine the plant's production rate. For a traditional just-in-case system, the drummer is the excess capacity of the first operation. For JIT, the drummer is market demand.

Required:

1. Explain why the drummer of a just-in-case system is identified as the excess capacity of the first operation.
2. Explain how market demand drives the JIT production system.
3. Explain how a drummer constraint is used in the TOC approach to inventory management.
4. What are the advantages and disadvantages of the three types of drummers?

Solution

1. In a traditional inventory system, local efficiency measures encourage the manager of the first operation to keep the department's workers busy. Raw materials are therefore released to satisfy this objective. This practice is justified because the inventory may be needed just in case the demand is greater than expected, or just in case the first operation has downtime or other problems.
2. In a JIT system, when the final operation delivers its goods to a customer, a backward-rippling effect triggers the release of raw materials into the factory. First, the last process removes the buffer inventory from the withdrawal store; this leads to a P-Kanban being placed on the production post of the preceding operation. That operation then begins production, withdrawing the parts that it needs from its withdrawal store, leading to a P-Kanban being placed on the production post of its preceding operation. This process repeats itself all the way back to the first operation.

3. A drummer constraint sets the factory's production rate to match its own production rate. This is automatically true for succeeding operations. For preceding operations, the rate is controlled by tying the drummer constraint's production rate to that of the first operation. A time buffer is also set in front of the drummer constraint to protect throughput in the event of interruptions.

4. The excess capacity drummer will typically build excess inventories. This serves to protect current throughput. However, it ties up a lot of capital and tends to cover up problems such as poor quality, bad delivery performance, and inefficient production. Because it is costly and covers up certain critical production problems, the just-in-case approach may threaten future throughput by damaging a firm's competitive position. JIT reduces inventories dramatically—using only small buffers in front of each operation as a means of regulating production flow and signalling when production should occur. JIT has the significant advantage of uncovering problems and eventually correcting them. However, discovering problems usually means that current throughput will be lost while the problems are being corrected. Future throughput tends to be protected, however, because the firm is taking actions to improve its operations. TOC uses time buffers in front of the critical constraints. These buffers are large enough to keep the critical constraints operating while other operations may be down. Once the problem is corrected, the other resource constraints usually have sufficient excess capacity to catch up. Thus, current throughput is protected. Furthermore, future throughput is also protected, because TOC uses the same approach as JIT—namely, uncovering and correcting problems. TOC can be viewed as an improvement on JIT methods—correcting the lost-throughput problem while maintaining the other JIT features.

QUESTIONS FOR WRITING AND DISCUSSION

1. What are ordering costs? Provide examples.

2. What are setup costs? Illustrate with examples.

3. What are carrying costs? Illustrate with examples.

4. What are stock-out costs?

5. Explain why, in the traditional view of inventory, carrying costs increase as ordering costs decrease.

6. Discuss the traditional reasons for carrying inventory.

7. What is the economic order quantity?

8. Suppose that a raw material has a lead time of three days and that the average usage of the material is 12 units per day. What is the reorder point? If the maximum usage is 15 units per day, what is the safety stock?

9. Explain how safety stock is used to deal with demand uncertainty.

10. What approach does JIT take to minimize total inventory costs?

11. Explain how long-term contractual relationships with suppliers can reduce the acquisition cost of raw materials.

12. What is EDI, and what relationship does it have to continuous replenishment?

13. One reason for inventory is to prevent shutdowns. How does the JIT approach to inventory management deal with this potential problem?

14. Explain how the Kanban system helps reduce inventories.

15. What is a constraint? an internal constraint? an external constraint?

16. What are loose constraints? binding constraints?

17. Define and discuss the three measures of organizational performance used by the theory of constraints.

18. Explain how lowering inventory produces better products, lower prices, and better responsiveness to customer needs.

19. What are the five steps that TOC uses to improve organizational performance?

20. What is a Drum–Buffer–Rope System?

EXERCISES

12–1

Ordering and Carrying Costs

LO1

Snowgo Company uses 24,000 carburetors each year in its production of snowmobiles. The cost of placing an order is $125. The cost of holding one unit of inventory for one year is $6. Currently, Snowgo places twelve orders of 2,000 carburetors each year.

Required:

1. Compute the annual ordering cost.
2. Compute the annual carrying cost.
3. Compute the cost of Snowgo's current inventory policy.

12–2

Economic Order Quantity

LO1

Refer to the data in 12–1.

Required:

1. Compute the economic order quantity.
2. Compute the ordering cost and the carrying cost for the EOQ.
3. How much money does using the EOQ policy save the company over the policy of purchasing 2,000 carburetors per order?

12–3

Economic Order Quantity

LO1

Spreadsheet

Quito Mining Company uses 720,000 litres of sulphuric acid each year. The cost of placing an order is $5, and the carrying cost for 1 litre of acid is $0.05.

Required:

1. Compute the economic order quantity for sulphuric acid.
2. Compute the carrying cost and the ordering cost for the EOQ.

12–4

Reorder Point

LO1

Spreadsheet

Nissan Company manufactures radios. One part that it orders from an outside supplier is a potentiometer. Information pertaining to the potentiometer is as follows:

Economic order quantity	60,000 units
Average daily usage	4,000 units
Maximum daily usage	6,000 units
Lead time	3 days

Required:

1. What is the reorder point, assuming that no safety stock is carried?
2. What is the reorder point, assuming that safety stock is carried?

12–5

EOQ with Setup Costs; Reorder Point; Production Scheduling

LO1

Power Manufacturing produces two different types of engines: one for riding lawn mowers and one for jet skis. In order to produce the different engines, equipment must be set up. Each setup configuration corresponds to a particular type of engine. The setup cost per batch of lawn mower engines is $2,000; the setup cost for the jet-ski engines is $2,400 per batch. The cost of carrying lawn mower engines in inventory is $2 per engine per year; for jet-ski engines, this cost is $3 per engine per year. During the coming year, the company expects to produce 162,000 lawn mower engines and 250,000 jet-ski engines. The company hopes to sell an average of 648 lawn mower engines per workday and an average of 500 jet-ski engines per workday. It takes Power two days to set up the equipment for production of either engine. Once the equipment is set up, Power can produce 2,000 engines per workday. There are 250 workdays available per year. The lead time is 11 days for lawn mower engines and 12 days for jet-ski engines.

Required:

1. Compute the number of lawn mower engines that should be produced per setup to minimize total setup and carrying costs for this product.
2. Compute the total setup and carrying costs associated with the economic order quantity for lawn mower engines.
3. What is the reorder point for lawn mower engines?
4. Repeat Requirements 1 through 3 for jet-ski engines.
5. Using the economic order batch size, find out whether it is possible for Power to produce the amount that can be sold of each engine. Does scheduling have a role here? Explain. Is this a push- or pull-system approach to inventory management? Explain.

12–6

EOQ; Setup Cost; Setup Time

LO1, LO2

Refer to 12–5. Suppose that Power was able to reduce the setup time from 2 days to 0.5 days and that, as a consequence, setup cost are reduced to 25 percent of their current level (for both products). Engineering predicts that within one year, setup time and costs can be further reduced (0.5 days to 0.05 days, and costs to $100).

Required:

1. Calculate the EOQ for lawn mower engines for the new setup time (0.5 days). Repeat for the projected setup time and costs.
2. How is reducing the setup time to 0.05 days (and setup costs to $100) associated with JIT?

12–7

Safety Stock

LO1

Pinegar Manufacturing produces a component used in its production of answering machines. The time required to set up and produce a batch of the components is six days. The average daily usage is 300 components, and the maximum daily usage is 350 components.

Required:

Compute the reorder point, assuming that Pinegar carries safety stock. How much safety stock does the company carry?

12–8

Reasons for Carrying Inventory

LO1, LO2, LO3

The following reasons have been offered for holding inventories:

a. To balance ordering or setup costs and carrying costs.
b. To satisfy customer demand (for example, to meet delivery dates).
c. To avoid shutting down manufacturing facilities because of
    (i)   machine failure,
    (ii) defective parts,
    (iii) unavailable parts, or
    (iv) late delivery of parts.
d. To buffer against unreliable production processes.
e. To take advantage of discounts.
f. To hedge against future price increases.

Required:

1. Explain how the JIT approach responds to each of these reasons and, consequently, argues for maintaining insignificant levels of inventories.

2. The theory of constraints (TOC) criticizes the JIT approach to inventory management, arguing that it fails to protect throughput. Explain what this means, and describe how TOC addresses this issue.

12–9

Kanban Cards

LO2

Explain the use of each of the following cards in the Kanban system:

1. The withdrawal Kanban
2. The production Kanban
3. The vendor Kanban

12–10

JIT Limitations

LO2

Many companies have viewed JIT as a panacea—a knight in shining armour promising rescue from sluggish profits, poor quality, and productive inefficiency. JIT is often lauded for its beneficial effects on employee morale and self-esteem. Yet JIT may also cause a company to struggle and may produce a good deal of frustration. In some cases, JIT appears to deliver less than its reputation warrants.

Required:

Discuss some of the limitations and problems that companies may encounter when implementing a JIT system.

12–11

Product-Mix Decisions; Single Constraint

LO3

Marvel Company has the capability of producing three types of rods used in the manufacture of different kinds of hydraulic cylinders. All three rods can be shaped and cut on the same machine. Marvel owns one of these machines, which has a total operating capacity of 20,000 hours per year. Information on each of the three rods follows:

	Type I	Type II	Type III
Selling price	$20.00	$30.00	$50.00
Unit variable cost	$10.00	$14.00	$24.00
Machine hours required	0.20	0.50	1.50

Marvel's marketing manager has determined that the company can sell all that it can produce of each of the three products.

1. How many of each product should be sold to maximize total contribution margin? What is the total contribution margin for this product mix?
2. Suppose that Marvel can sell no more than 50,000 units of each type at the prices indicated. What product mix would you recommend, and what would be the total contribution margin?

12–12

Drum–Buffer–Rope System

LO3

Goicoechea, Inc., manufactures two models of bows: regular and deluxe. The firm sells all the bows it produces. Bows are produced in three processes: laminating, moulding, and finishing. In laminating, limbs are created by laminating layers of wood. In moulding, the limbs are heat-treated, under pressure, to form a strong, resilient limb. In finishing, any protruding glue is removed, and the limbs are cleaned with acetone, dried, and sprayed with final finishes. Recently, Goicoechea implemented a TOC approach for its Kelowna plant. One binding constraint was identified, and the optimal product mix was determined. The diagram on page 543 reflects the TOC outcome.

Required:

1. What is the daily production rate? What process sets this rate?
2. How many days of buffer inventory is Goicoechea carrying? How is this time buffer determined?
3. Explain what the letters A, B, and C represent in the diagram. Discuss each of their roles in the TOC system.

Materials for 800 Bows per Day
(Regular Bow: 600, Deluxe Bow: 200)

A →

Laminating
Process

B

(300 Units
Regular Bow) (100 Units
Deluxe Bow)

C
Moulding
Process

Finishing
Process

Finished Goods
(600 Regular Units per Day
200 Deluxe Units per Day)

PROBLEMS

12–13

EOQ and Reorder Point

LO1

Italia Pizzeria is a popular pizza restaurant near a college campus. Brandon Thayn, an accounting student, works for Italia Pizzeria. After several months at the restaurant, Brandon began to analyze the efficiency of the business, particularly its inventory practices. He noticed that the owner had more than 50 items regularly carried in inventory. Of these items, the most expensive to buy and carry was cheese. Cheese was ordered in blocks at $17.50 per block. Annual usage totals 14,000 blocks.

Upon questioning the owner, Brandon discovered that the owner did not use any formal model for ordering cheese. It took five days to receive a new order when placed, which was done whenever the inventory of cheese dropped to 200 blocks. The size of the order was usually 400 blocks. The cost of carrying one block of cheese is 10 percent of its purchase price. It costs $40 to place and receive an order.

Italia Pizzeria stays open seven days a week and operates fifty weeks a year. The restaurant closes for the last two weeks of December.

Required:

1. Compute the total cost of ordering and carrying the cheese inventory under the current policy.
2. Compute the total cost of ordering and carrying cheese if the restaurant were to change to the economic order quantity. How much would the restaurant save per year by switching policies?
3. If the restaurant uses the economic order quantity, when should it place an order? (Assume that the amount of cheese used per day is the same throughout the year.) How does this timing compare with the current reorder policy?

4. Suppose that storage space allows a maximum of 600 blocks of cheese. Discuss the inventory policy that should be followed under this restriction.

5. Suppose that the maximum storage is 600 blocks of cheese and that cheese can be held for a maximum of 10 days. The owner will not hold cheese any longer, since doing so can interfere with the pizzas' flavour and quality. Under these conditions, evaluate the owner's current inventory policy.

12–14

EOQ with Safety Stock

LO1

Parry Chiropractic Clinic uses an EOQ model to order supplies. Lately, several chiropractors have been complaining about the availability of X-ray film. During the past three months, the clinic has had to place five rush orders because of stock-outs. Because of the problem, the supply officer has decided to review the current inventory policy. The following data have been gathered:

Cost of placing and receiving an order	$90
Cost of carrying one package	$1.825
Average usage per day	10 packages
Maximum usage per day	15 packages
Lead time for an order	4 days
Annual demand	3,650 packages

The clinic currently does not carry any safety stock. The clinic operates 250 days each year.

Required:

1. Compute the economic order quantity and the reorder point. What is the total ordering and carrying cost for the clinic's current inventory policy?

2. Assume that the clinic has decided to carry safety stock. Compute how much should be carried to ensure no stock-outs. Compute the total ordering and carrying cost for this policy. Will the reorder point change? If so, what will it be?

12–15

EOQ; Safety Stock; Setup Costs

LO1, LO2

Geneva Company produces safety goggles for coal miners. Goggles are produced in batches according to model and size. Although the setup and production times vary for each model, the smallest lead time is 6 days. The most popular model, Model SG4, takes 2 days for setup; its production rate is 750 units per day. The expected annual demand for the model is 36,000 units. However, demand for this model can reach 45,000 units. The cost of carrying one SG4 unit is $3 per unit. The setup cost is $6,000. Geneva chooses its batch size based on the economic order quantity criterion. Expected annual demand is used to compute the EOQ.

Recently, Geneva has encountered some stiff competition—especially from foreign sources. Some of the firm's foreign competitors have been able to produce and deliver the goggles to retailers in half the time it takes Geneva to do so. For example, a large retailer recently requested a delivery of 12,000 SG4 goggles with the stipulation that delivery occur within 7 working days. Geneva had 3,000 units of SG4 in stock. It informed the potential customer that it could deliver 3,000 units immediately and the other 9,000 units in about 14 working days—with the possibility of interim partial orders being delivered. The customer declined the offer, indicating that the total order had to be delivered within 7 working days so that its stores could take advantage of some special local conditions. The customer expressed regret and indicated that it would place this order with one of Geneva's competitors, a firm that could satisfy the time requirements.

Required:

1. Calculate the optimal batch size for Model SG4 using the EOQ model. Was Geneva's response to the customer right? Would it take the time indicated to produce the number of units wanted by the customer? Explain with supporting computations.

2. Upon learning of the lost order, Geneva's marketing manager grumbled about the company's inventory policy. "We lost the order because we didn't have suf-

ficient inventory. We need to carry more units in inventory to deal with unexpected orders like these." Do you agree? How much additional inventory would have been needed to meet the customer's requirements? In the future, should Geneva carry more inventory? Can you think of other solutions?

3. Fenton Gray, Geneva's head of industrial engineering, reacted differently to the lost order. "Our problem is more complex than insufficient inventory. I know that our foreign competitors carry much less inventory than we do. What we need to do is decrease the lead time. I have been studying this problem, and my staff has found a way to reduce the setup time for Model SG4 from 2 days to 1.5 hours. Using this new procedure, we can reduce setup cost to about $94. Also, by rearranging the plant layout for this product—creating what are called manufacturing cells—we can increase the production rate from 750 units per day to about 2,000 units per day. This is done simply by eliminating a lot of move time and waiting time—both nonvalue-added activities."

Assume that Fenton's estimates are on target. Compute the new optimal batch size (using the EOQ formula). What is the new lead time? Given this new information, find out whether Geneva would have been able to meet the customer's time requirements. Assume that there are 8 hours available in each workday.

4. Suppose that the setup time and cost are reduced to 0.5 hour and $10, respectively. What is the batch size now? As setup time approaches zero and the setup cost becomes negligible, what does this imply? Assume, for example, that it takes 5 minutes to set up and costs about $0.864 per setup.

12–16

Kanban System; EDI

LO2

Packer Company produces a product that requires two processes. In the first process, a subassembly is produced (Subassembly A); in the second process, this subassembly and a subassembly purchased from outside (Subassembly B) are assembled to produce the final product. For simplicity, assume that the assembly of one unit takes the same time as the production of Subassembly A. Subassembly A is placed in a container and sent to an area called the subassembly stores (SB stores) area. A production Kanban is attached to this container. A second container, also with one subassembly, is located near the assembly line (this second container is called the withdrawal store). This container has attached to it a withdrawal Kanban.

Required:

1. Explain how withdrawal and production Kanban cards are used to control the work flow between the two processes. How does this approach minimize inventories?
2. Explain how vendor Kanban cards can be used to control the flow of the purchased subassembly. What implication does this have for supplier relationships? What role, if any, do continuous replenishment and EDI play in this process?

12–17

Product-Mix Decision; Single and Multiple Constraints

LO3

Morning Beverages, Inc., produces two instant breakfast drinks: Rich Instant and Diet Instant. Rich Instant has more ingredients and therefore requires more machine time for grinding and mixing. The manufacturing process is highly mechanized; the same equipment produces both products by using different settings. For the coming period, 800,000 machine hours are available. Management is trying to decide on the quantities of each product to produce. The following data are available:

	Rich Instant	Diet Instant
Machine hours per unit	2.00	1.00
Unit selling price	$5.00	$6.00
Unit variable cost	$3.00	$4.50

Required:

1. Determine the units of each product that should be produced in order to maximize profits. What is the total contribution margin earned by this optimal product mix?

2. Because of market conditions, the company can sell no more than 500,000 pack-
    ages of Rich Instant and 600,000 packages of Diet Instant. Now what is the opti-
    mal product mix? the total contribution margin?

12–18

Optimal Product Mix

LO3

Wilson Company manufactures and sells three components in a factory of three
departments. The components are used as replacement parts in jet aircraft. After
machining in each department, the components are subjected to stress tests. The nature
of the machine processing and of the labour skills required for stress testing is such that
neither machines nor test labour can be switched from one department to another.
Wilson's management is planning its production schedule for the next several months.
Planning is complicated by the facts that labour shortages exist in the community and
that some machines will be down for several months while undergoing repairs.

Following is information regarding available machine and test time by department, along with the machine hours and test hours required for each component.
These data are valid for at least the next six months.

	Department		
Monthly Capacity	**A**	**B**	**C**
Test hours available	7,400	9,000	5,500
Machine hours available	6,000	6,200	5,400

Component	**Input per Unit Produced**			
12-L	Test hours	2	3	3
	Machine hours	1	1	2
16-M	Test hours	1	2	—
	Machine hours	1	1	—
40-S	Test hours	2	2	2
	Machine hours	2	2	1

The monthly demand for the next six months will be as follows:

Component	**Units Sold**
12-L	1,000
16-M	800
40-S	2,000

Inventory levels will not be increased or decreased during the next six months.
The unit cost and price data for each component are as follows:

	Component		
	12-L	**16-M**	**40-S**
Unit costs:			
Direct material	$ 14	$ 26	$ 34
Test labour	66	38	51
Variable overhead	27	20	25
Fixed overhead	15	10	32
Variable selling	3	2	4
Total unit cost	$125	$ 96	$146
Unit selling price	$203	$136	$184

Required:

1. Calculate the monthly requirement for machine hours and test hours for pro-
    ducing components 12-L, 16-M, and 40-S to determine whether the factory can
    meet the monthly sales demand.

2. Determine the quantities of each component that should be produced monthly to maximize profits. Prepare a schedule that shows the contribution to profits of your recommended product mix. (US CMA adapted)

12–19

Identifying and Exploiting Constraints; Constraint Elevation

LO3

Covey Company produces two metal parts used in industrial equipment (Part A and Part B). The company has three processes: moulding, grinding, and finishing. In moulding, moulds are created and molten metal is poured into the shell. Grinding removes the gates that allowed the molten metal to flow into the mould's cavities. In finishing, rough edges caused by the grinders are removed by small handheld pneumatic tools. In moulding, the setup time is 1 hour. The other two processes require no setup time. The demand for Part A is 300 units per day, and the demand for Part B is 500 units per day. The minutes required per unit for each product follow:

	Minutes Required per Unit of Product		
Product	Moulding	Grinding	Finishing
Part A	10	20	30
Part B	20	30	40

The company operates one 8-hour shift. The moulding process employs 24 workers (who each work 8 hours). Two hours of their time, however, is used for setups (assuming that both products are being produced). The grinding process has sufficient equipment and workers to provide 24,000 grinding minutes per shift.

The finishing department is labour-intensive and employs 70 workers, who each work 8 hours per day. The only significant unit-level variable costs are materials and power. For Part A, the variable cost per unit is $80; for Part B, it is $100. Selling prices for A and B are $180 and $220, respectively. Covey's policy is to use two setups per day: an initial setup to produce all that is scheduled for A and a second setup (changeover) to produce all that is scheduled for B. The amount scheduled does not necessarily correspond to each product's daily demand.

Required:

1. Calculate the time (in minutes) needed each day to meet the daily market demand for Part A and Part B. What is the major internal constraint facing Covey Company?
2. Describe how Covey should exploit its major binding constraint. Specifically, identify the product mix that will maximize daily throughout.
3. Assume that manufacturing engineering has found a way to reduce the moulding setup time from 1 hour to 10 minutes. Explain how this improvement affects the optimal product mix and the daily throughput.

12–20

Theory of Constraints; Internal Constraints

LO3

Young Company produces two subassemblies used by aircraft manufacturers: Sub A and Sub B. Sub A is made up of two components, one manufactured internally and one purchased from external suppliers. Sub B is made up of three components, one manufactured internally and two purchased from suppliers. The company has two processes: fabrication and assembly. In fabrication, the internally produced components are made. Each component takes 20 minutes to produce. In assembly, it takes 30 minutes to assemble the components for Sub A and 40 minutes to assemble the components for Sub B. Young Company operates one shift per day. Each process employs 100 workers, each of whom works 8 hours per day.

Sub A earns a unit contribution margin of $20, and Sub B earns a unit contribution margin of $24 (calculated as the difference between revenue and the cost of materials and energy). Young can sell all that it produces of either part. There are no other constraints. Young can add a second shift of either process. Although a second shift would also work 8 hours, there is no mandate that it must employ the same number of workers. The labour cost per hour for fabrication is $8, and the labour cost per hour for assembly is $7.

Required:

1. Identify the constraints facing Young. How many binding constraints are possible? What is Young's optimal product mix? What daily contribution margin is produced by this mix?
2. What is the drummer constraint? How much excess capacity does the other constraint have? Assume that a 1.5-day buffer inventory is needed to deal with any production interruptions. Describe the drummer–buffer–rope concept, using the Young data to illustrate the process.
3. Explain why the use of local labour efficiency measures will not work in Young's TOC environment.
4. Suppose that Young decides to elevate the binding constraint by adding a second shift of 50 workers (for assembly only). Would elevation of Young's binding constraint improve its system performance? Explain with supporting computations.

12–21

TOC; Internal and External Constraints

LO3

Bountiful Manufacturing produces two types of bike frames (X and Y). Both frames pass through four processes: cutting, welding, polishing, and painting. With the exception of polishing, each of the processes employs 20 workers, each of whom works 8 hours each day. Polishing employs 26 workers. Frame X sells for $80 per unit, and Frame Y sells for $110 per unit. Raw materials cost is the only unit-level variable cost. The materials cost for Frame X is $40 per unit, and the materials cost for Frame Y is $50 per unit. Bountiful's accounting system has provided the following additional information about its operations and products:

Resource Name	Resource Available	Frame X Resource Usage (per unit)	Frame Y Resource Usage (per unit)
Cutting labour	9,600 minutes	30 minutes	20 minutes
Welding labour	9,600 minutes	30 minutes	60 minutes
Polishing labour	12,480 minutes	30 minutes	30 minutes
Painting labour	9,600 minutes	20 minutes	30 minutes
Market demand:			
Frame X	200 per day	1 unit	—
Frame Y	100 per day	—	1 unit

Bountiful's management has determined that any production interruptions can be corrected within two days.

Required:

1. Assuming that Bountiful can meet daily market demand, compute the potential daily profit. Now compute the minutes needed for each process to meet the daily market demand. Can Bountiful meet daily market demand? If not, where is the bottleneck?
2. Determine the optimal product mix and the maximum daily contribution margin (throughput).
3. Explain how a DBR system would work for Bountiful.
4. Suppose that Bountiful's engineering department has proposed a process design change that will increase the polishing time for Frame X from 30 to 46 minutes per unit and decrease its welding time from 30 to 20 minutes per unit. The cost of process redesign would be $20,000. Evaluate this proposed change. What step in the TOC process does this proposal represent?

MANAGERIAL DECISION CASES

12–22

Ethical Issues

LO2

Mac Ericson and Tammy Ferguson met at a conference two months ago and began dating. Mac is the controller of Longley Enterprises, and Tammy is a marketing manager for Sharp Products. Longley is a major supplier for Piura Products, a major competitor of Sharp's. Longley has entered into a long-term agreement to supply certain materials to Piura. Piura has been developing a JIT purchasing and manufacturing system. As part of its development, Piura and Longley have established EDI capabilities. The following conversation took place during a luncheon engagement:

Tammy: "Mac, I understand that you have EDI connections with Piura. Is that right?"

Mac: "Sure. It's part of the partners-in-profit arrangement that we've worked so hard to get. It's working real well. Knowing Piura's production schedule helps us stabilize our own schedule. It has actually cut some of our overhead costs. It has also decreased Piura's costs. I estimate that both firms have decreased their production costs by about 7 to 10 percent."

Tammy: "That's interesting. You know, I have a real chance of getting promoted to VP of marketing ..."

Mac: "Hey, that's great. When will you know?"

Tammy: "It all depends on this deal that I am trying to cut with Balboa—if I win the contract, then I think I have it. My main problem is Piura. If I knew what their production schedule was, I could get a pretty good idea as to how long it would take them to deliver. I could then make sure that we beat their delivery offer—even if we had to work overtime and do all kinds of expediting. I know that how fast we can deliver is very, very important to Balboa. Our quality is as good as Piura's, but they tend to beat us on delivery time. My boss would love to kick Piura. They have beaten us too many times recently. I'm wondering if you'd be willing to help me out."

Mac: "Tammy, you know that I'd help if I could, but Piura's production schedule is confidential information. If word got out that I had leaked that kind of stuff to you, I would be history."

Tammy: "Well, no one would ever know. Besides, I have already had a chat with Tom Anderson, who is our CEO. Our VP of finance is retiring. He knows about you and your capabilities. I think he'd be willing to hire you—especially if he knew that you had helped swing this Balboa deal. You could increase your salary by 40 percent."

Mac: "I don't know. I have my doubts about the propriety of all this. It might look kind of funny if I were to take over as VP of finance not long after Piura loses the Balboa deal. But a VP position and a big salary increase are tempting. It's unlikely that I'll ever have a shot at the VP position in my company."

Tammy: "Think it over. If you are interested, I'll arrange a dinner with Tom. He said that he'd like to meet you. He knows a little about this. I'm sure that he has the ability to keep it quiet. I don't think there is much risk."

Required:

1. Based on this information, do you think Mac has violated any of the standards of ethical conduct outlined in Chapter 1?
2. Suppose that Mac decides to provide information in exchange for the VP position. What ethical standards has he violated?

RESEARCH ASSIGNMENT

12–23

Cybercase

LO3

The theory of constraints is a method for bringing about continuous improvement (the five TOC steps are a continuous improvement loop). In effect, TOC addresses three questions: (1) what to change, (2) what to change to, and (3) how to cause the change. The answers to these questions have to do with what is called the "thinking process." There are specific thinking process tools suggested: the current reality tree, the evaporative cloud, the future reality tree, the negative branches, the prerequisite tree, and the transition tree. Supporters of TOC claim that the method can bring about significant improvements in lead time, inventory, and financial performance. Furthermore, some advocate changing to what is called "constraint accounting." These issues create some significant opportunities for TOC-related Internet research.

Required:

1. Search the Internet for definitions of the thinking process and of the thinking process tools listed above.
2. Search the Internet and find examples of three companies that have successfully used the theory of constraints. List some of the benefits achieved by these companies. Is TOC more than an inventory management method?
3. Search the Internet and find information on constraint accounting. What is constraint accounting? Is it an alternative to activity- and functional-based accounting? Explain.

PART 3

Planning and Control

Topics dealing with managerial decision making were covered in Part 2. The discussion was based on the assumption that a company always makes an optimal decision after examining the differential cash flow effects of the decision. This assumption, however, ignores the fact that decisions are made by many different people throughout the organization, and that the total differential cash flow calculus, from the corporate point of view, may not be known to each decision maker. Even when decision makers have company wide information, they may still be motivated to make decisions in their own best interest. Sometimes such decisions might also be good for the company, but at other times the interests of the decision maker and the organization conflict. Suboptimization of corporate interests could be the result.

It is also important to keep in mind that different parts of the organization often have different objectives. Different managers sometimes have different views as to what is most crucial or most pressing. For example, a marketing manager may be less concerned about the effects of accepting a rush order on production cost than a production manager. The latter would have the responsibility of changing the production schedule and incurring additional costs for setup and overtime. On the other hand, a production manager may be less concerned with the effects on customer relations of failing to satisfy a request for immediate delivery. The coordination of such conflicting objectives and the communication of the necessary information are achieved through company policies and through planning and budgeting. Once plans are drawn up, it is also important to check periodically to see if actual performance is on target, and if not, why not. This calls for the possibility of taking appropriate corrective action. All these activities involve the design and implementation of managerial planning and control systems, typically referred to as management control systems.

Management Control Systems

A management control system is a planning and control system that is aimed at the effective and efficient allocation and use of resources within an organization. Any system can be thought of in terms of a structure and a process. To understand a transportation system, for example, requires an understanding of both structure (highways, freeways, and bridges) and process (the types of vehicles travelling, the flow of traffic, and bottlenecks). Understanding planning and control systems requires a knowledge of the structures within which planning and control processes take place. Organizational structure and the assignment of responsibility for decisions are primary determinants of the management control system structure.

Assignment of responsibility for cost, revenue, profit, or investment performance are examples of structure issues.

Since planning and control occur within given structures in the organization, their study requires an examination of the processes used in setting goals, objectives, targets, and budgets. The budgeting process is typically a major component of a management control system, but the control process does not stop when the budget is approved. Actual performance is tracked and compared to the budget, differences between actual and budgeted amounts are analyzed, and appropriate corrective action, if warranted, is taken. A myriad of financial, other quantifiable, and nonquantifiable information measuring or reflecting aspects of effectiveness and efficiency are also part of the management control process. While it is conceptually helpful to think of structure and process separately, particularly when the system is being designed, evaluated, or changed, it is difficult to maintain that distinction in practice.

Conflicting Interests and Management Incentives

The potential for conflict between corporate interests and an individual manager's interests requires close examination of the effect of the management control system on individual managers. Management control is more complicated than control of a mechanical process because managers have the freedom to make choices. Although it is possible that some of these choices may be suboptimal from a corporate perspective, it is also possible that on closer examination, the apparently suboptimal corporate behaviour may turn out to be the most efficient way of balancing the interests of the different constituencies of an organization. *Agency theory* is a useful way to examine these issues. Agency theory is the general study of economic behaviour related to the agency relationships. Many agency relationships exist within organizations, and conflict management is a rich area of study. The conflicts between manager and manager, and manager and owner (or shareholders), are studied in several chapters in this section of the book. How to coordinate the conflicting objectives of different managers, how to measure performance in accordance with predetermined targets, and the possible suboptimization that could occur because of the delegation of decisions are topics that are covered in this section.

The typical agency relationship is between, for example, the owners or shareholders of the business (known as the principal) and management (called the agent). Both parties are assumed to be self-interested and the managers are assumed to be effort averse. Effort aversion implies that managers prefer to work less, other things being equal, and must be compensated for additional effort. This reflects a basic conflict of interest. In addition, because managers know the level of their effort, while the owners do not and cannot directly or indirectly observe managerial effort, there is information asymmetry in the agency relationship that causes problems for management control. Information asymmetry results in what is known as the "moral hazard" problem, where the manager has an incentive to "shirk" and expend less effort than would be desirable from the company's point of view. Agency theory considers a variety of control processes to overcome this fundamental problem by a better alignment of the manager's interests with those of the owners. Bonus plans that are contingent on observed results (even though the manager lacks total control over the company's level of performance) and relative performance evaluations are examples of the topics examined in this literature. The details and derivation of these conclusions are beyond the scope of this text.

Part 3 of the book examines both the management control structure and its processes. Chapter 13 deals with the process of budgeting. One of the major uses of budgets is as a tool to coordinate conflicting objectives. The chapter addresses this role as well as the behavioural dimensions of budgeting, which are inextricably linked to the assignment of responsibilities for performance (an issue of structure) and appropriate incentives. Chapter 14 focuses on the process of comparison between actual performance and budgets. The process results in the analysis of variances between actual peformance and budgets and an examination of these variances to discover causes in order to take corrective action. Chapters 13 and 14 assume responsibility allocations either for an entire firm or for a specific cost or revenue centre. Chapter 15 deals with activity- and strategic-based responsibility accounting. Chapters 16 and 17 deal with two strategic cost management issues. Chapter 16 addresses the strategic issues of quality, quality costs, and productivity. Chapter 17 deals with issues related to environmental cost management. Chapter 18 addresses issues of profit and investment centres and examines structural issues; in particular, it deals with the problems of decentralization, profit centres, and investment centres. The question of internal pricing between divisions that have profit responsibility involves a number of difficult but interesting and crucial issues that arise because of the conflict of objectives of different managers. Thus a good portion of Chapter 18 deals with the issue of transfer pricing. Finally, the last chapter of the book, Chapter 19, treats managerial accounting issues from an international perspective.

Examples of the Importance of Planning and Control

The importance of planning and control is illustrated by the following examples:

1. Over 80 percent of new small businesses fail within the first three years, primarily due to poor planning and, particularly, poor cash flow planning.
2. The price charged by a profit division of a particular company included its variable and fixed costs and a profit mark-up. This price was seen as a strictly variable cost by another division that was a "customer." Decisions made by the buying division did not take into account the behaviour of costs from the corporate point of view (the consequence of the joint actions of the selling and buying divisions) but only from the divisional point of view. Short-term suboptimization was the consequence.
3. A company had an excellent process in place for setting up its budget. However, the company's management was incapable of making decisions based on an analysis of actual results against the budget whenever disputes arose regarding whose fault it was that the budget targets were not achieved. In other words, the company succeeded in using the budget as a planning tool but not as a control tool.
4. A company was determined to cut the fat in its budget (budgetary slack). It found out the hard way that it was not easy to cut the slack from the budget. Most employees were so unhappy with the process of budget cutting that in the end this effort cost the company (and the employees) the sense of commitment that had previously prevailed. Employees felt more secure in a budget environment that allowed some slack to exist, and felt threatened when their actions were more transparent to management in the absence of this slack. The company lost its competitive edge and many employees lost their jobs.
5. A company discovered that its environmental costs were not as low as originally perceived. The company not only adopted pollution prevention policies but also embarked on a product stewardship program and is now grappling with the issues of how to provide environmental solutions beyond its traditional role.

The above examples suggest the type of problems that might exist when some aspects of the management control system are not well understood. Understanding the challenges and the problems posed by management control systems is the best way to ensure that the effects of such problems are minimized.

CHAPTER 13

Budgeting for Planning and Control

Learning Objectives

After studying Chapter 13, you should be able to:

1. Define *budgeting* and discuss its role in planning, control, and decision making.

2. Define and prepare the *master budget*, identify its major components, and explain the interrelationships of its various components.

3. Describe flexible budgeting and identify the features that a budgetary system should have to encourage managers to engage in goal-congruent behaviour.

4. Describe activity-based budgeting.

Scenario[1]

By all outward appearances, Dr. Roger Jones was a successful dentist. He owned his own office building, which he leased to the professional corporation housing his dental practice. The revenues from his practice exceeded $750,000 each year, providing him with a salary of $150,000 a year. He and his family lived in a large home in a well-regarded neighbourhood.

However, Roger had just received a registered letter from Canada Customs and Revenue Agency threatening to impound his business and sell its assets for failure to remit income tax withholdings and pay employment insurance premiums for the past six months. Furthermore, the professional corporation was also having difficulty paying its suppliers. The corporation owed one supplier more than $200,000 and had made arrangements to pay interest payments on the bill, but was missing even those payments. The corporation had experienced these kinds of difficulties repeatedly for the past five years.

In the past, Roger had solved similar problems by borrowing money on the equity in either his personal residence or his office building. Sufficient equity still existed in his office building to solve the employment insurance problem. A visit to a local bank resulted in a refinancing agreement that produced sufficient capital to pay the overdue taxes and premiums and the associated penalties and interest.

This time, however, Roger was not satisfied with the short-run solution to his financial difficulties. His latest loan had exhausted his personal financial resources; further difficulties simply couldn't be tolerated. His first action was to dismiss his receptionist/bookkeeper, reasoning that part of the blame was hers for failing to properly manage his financial resources. He called Lawson, Johnson, and Day, a local CA firm, and requested that a consultant determine the cause of his recurring financial difficulties.

Jeanette Day, a partner in the CA firm, spent a week examining the records of the practice and extensively interviewing Roger. She delivered the following report:

Dr. Roger Jones
1091 West Apple Avenue
Cambridge, Ontario

Dear Dr. Jones:

The cause of your current financial difficulties is the absence of proper planning and control. Currently, many of your expenditure decisions are made in a haphazard and arbitrary manner. Affordability is seldom, if ever, considered. Because of this, resources are often committed beyond the capabilities of the practice. To meet these additional commitments, your bookkeeper has been forced to postpone payments for essential operating expenses, such as employment insurance premiums, supplies, and laboratory services.

The following examples illustrate some of the decisions that have contributed to your financial troubles:

1. *Salary decisions.* You have been granting 5 percent increases each year whether or not the business could successfully absorb these increases. Also, your salary is 10 percent higher than those of dentists with comparable practices.

2. *Withdrawal decisions.* For the past five years, you have withdrawn from cash receipts approximately $1000 per month. These withdrawals have been treated as a loan from the corporation to you, the president of the corporation.

3. *Equipment acquisition decisions.* During the past five years, the corporation has acquired a van, a video recorder, a refrigerator, and a microcomputer system. Some of these items were cash acquisitions, and some are being paid for on an installment basis. None of them was essential to the mission of your corporation.

These decisions, and others like them, have adversely affected both your personal financial status and the financial well-being of the corporation. The mortgage payments for your personal residence and your office building have increased by 50 percent over the past five years. Additionally, the liabilities of the corporation have increased by 200 percent for the same period of time.

To solve your financial problems, I recommend the installation of a formal budgetary system. A comprehensive financial plan is needed so that you know where you are going and what you are capable of doing.

My firm would be pleased to assist you in designing and imple-

menting the recommended system. For it to be successful, you and your staff need to be introduced to the elementary principles of budgeting. As a part of this implementation, we will offer three two-hour seminars on budgeting. The first will describe the basic philosophy of budgeting, the second will teach you how to prepare budgets, and the third will explore the use of budgets for planning, control, and performance evaluation.

Sincerely,
Jeanette Day, CA

---

1. This scenario is based on the experience of a real company. The names have been changed to preserve confidentiality.

Questions to Think About

1. Why did Roger fire his bookkeeper? Were his financial problems her fault? Why or why not?

2. How would a formal budgeting system help Roger get out of his financial difficulties?

3. Many small businesses do not budget, reasoning that they are small enough to keep track of all revenues and expenditures mentally. Comment on this idea.

4. Do you budget? Explain why or why not.

DESCRIPTION OF BUDGETING

Objective 1

Define *budgeting* and discuss its role in planning, control, and decision making.

All businesses should prepare budgets; all large businesses do. As the scenario for Dr. Jones shows, budgeting is vital for small businesses, too. Every for-profit and not-for-profit entity can benefit from the planning and control provided by budgets.

Budgeting and Planning and Control

Planning and control are inextricably linked. Planning involves looking ahead and determining what actions should be taken to realize particular goals. Control involves looking backward, determining what actually happened and comparing it with the previously planned outcomes. This comparison can then be used to adjust the budget, looking forward once more. Exhibit 13–1 illustrates the cycle of planning, results, and control. Let's look further at the planning component of this exhibit.

A key component of planning, **budgets** are financial plans for the future; they identify objectives and the actions needed to achieve them. Before a budget is prepared, an organization should develop a strategic plan. The **strategic plan** identifies strategies for future activities and operations, generally covering at least five years. The organization can translate the overall strategy into long-term and short-term objectives. These objectives form the basis of the budget. Notice that there should be a tight linkage between the budget and the strategic plan. In developing this linkage, however, management should ensure that all attention is not focused on the short run. This is important because budgets that are one-period plans are short run in nature.

To illustrate the process, consider again the case of Dr. Roger Jones. (Refer to Exhibit 13–1 as you read this illustration.) Assume that Roger's strategic plan is to increase the size and profitability of his business by building a practice that has a reputation for quality and timely service. A key element in achieving this strategy is the addition of a dental laboratory to his building so that crowns, bridges, and dentures can be made in house. This is his long-term objective. In order to add the laboratory, he needs additional money. His financial status dictates that the capital must be obtained by increasing revenues. After some careful calculation, Roger concludes that annual revenues must be increased by 10 percent; this is a short-term objective.

How are these long-term and short-term objectives to be achieved? Suppose that Roger finds that his fees for fillings and crowns are below the average in his community and decides that the 10 percent increase can be achieved by increasing these fees. He now has a short-term plan. A sales budget would outline the quantity of fillings and crowns expected for the coming year, the new per-unit fee, and the total fees expected. Thus, the sales budget becomes the concrete plan of action needed to

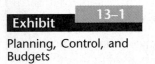

Exhibit 13–1

Planning, Control, and Budgets

achieve the 10 percent increase in revenues. As the year unfolds, Roger can compare the actual revenues received with the budgeted revenues (monitoring and comparing). If actual revenues are less than planned, he should figure out why (investigation). Then he can act to remedy the shortfall—for example, by working longer hours or by increasing fees for other dental services (corrective action). The reasons for the shortfall may also lead to an alteration of future plans (feedback).

Purposes of Budgeting

A budgetary system gives an organization several advantages:

1. It forces managers to plan.
2. It provides resource information that can be used to improve decision making.
3. It provides a standard for performance evaluation.
4. It improves communication and coordination.

Budgeting forces management to plan for the future. It encourages managers to develop an overall direction for the organization, foresee problems, and develop future policies. If Roger had spent time planning, he would have known the capabilities of his practice and where the resources of the business should be used.

Budgets improve decision making. For example, if Roger had known the expected revenues and the costs of supplies, lab fees, utilities, salaries, and so on, he might have lowered the rate of salary increases, avoided borrowing money from the corporation, and limited the purchase of nonessential equipment. These better decisions might in turn have prevented the problems that arose and resulted in a better financial status for both the business and Roger.

Budgets also set standards that can control the use of a company's resources and motivate employees. A vital part of the budgetary system, **control** is achieved by comparing actual results with budgeted results on a periodic basis (for example, monthly). A large difference between actual and planned results is feedback revealing that the system is out of control. Steps should be taken to find out why, and then to correct the situation. For example, if Roger knows how much amalgam should be used in a filling and what the cost should be, he can evaluate his use of this resource. If more amalgam is being used than expected, Roger may discover that he is often careless in its use and that extra care will produce savings. The same principle applies to other resources used by the corporation. In total, the savings could be significant.

Budgets also serve to communicate and coordinate. Budgets formally communicate the organization's plans to each employee. Accordingly, all employees can be aware of their role in achieving those objectives. Since budgets for the organization's various areas and activities must all work together to achieve organizational objectives, coordination is promoted. Managers can see the needs of other areas and are encouraged to subordinate their individual interests to those of the organization. The role of communication and coordination becomes more significant as an organization increases in size.

Two Dimensions of Budgeting

There are two dimensions to budgeting: (1) how the budget is prepared, and (2) how the budget is used to implement the organization's plans. The first dimension concerns the mechanics of budget preparation. The second involves how individuals within an organization react to a budgetary system. The use of budgets to exercise control, evaluate performance, communicate, and encourage coordination suggests that budgeting is a human activity. As such, budgeting carries a strong behavioural dimension, and the success or failure of budgeting depends on how well management considers its behavioural implications. The remainder of this chapter focuses on these two dimensions.

PREPARING THE BUDGET

Objective 2

Define and prepare the *master budget*, identify its major components, and explain the interrelationships of its various components.

Most organizations prepare the budget for the coming year during the last four or five months of the current year. However, some organizations have developed a continuous budgeting philosophy. A **continuous budget** is a moving 12-month budget. As a month expires in the budget, an additional month in the future is added so that the company always has a 12-month plan on hand. Proponents of continuous budgeting maintain that it forces managers to plan ahead constantly.

Typically, a budget covers a one-year period corresponding to the company's fiscal year. Yearly budgets are broken down into quarterly budgets, and quarterly budgets are broken down into monthly budgets. The use of smaller time periods allows managers to compare actual data with budgeted data more frequently, so that problems may be noticed and solved sooner.

Directing and Coordinating

Someone must be responsible for directing and coordinating an organization's overall budgeting process. This **budget director**, usually the controller, works under the direction of the budget committee. The **budget committee** reviews the budget, provides policy guidelines and budgetary goals, resolves differences that arise as the budget is prepared, approves the final budget, and monitors the organization's actual performance as the year unfolds. The organization's president appoints the committee members, who are usually the president, the vice-presidents, and the controller.

The Master Budget

The **master budget** is the comprehensive financial plan for the organization as a whole; it is made up of various individual budgets. A master budget can be divided into operating and financial budgets. **Operating budgets** describe the firm's income-generating activities: sales, production, and finished goods inventories. The ultimate outcome of the operating budgets is a pro forma or budgeted income statement. **Financial budgets** detail the inflows and outflows of cash and the overall financial position. Planned cash inflows and outflows appear in the cash budget. Expected financial position at the end of the budget period is shown in a budgeted, or pro forma, balance sheet. Since many of the financing activities are not known until the operating budgets are known, the operating budget is prepared first.

Preparing the Operating Budget

The operating budget consists of a budgeted income statement accompanied by the following supporting schedules:

1. Sales budget
2. Production budget
3. Direct materials purchases budget
4. Direct labour budget
5. Overhead budget
6. Selling and administrative expenses budget
7. Ending finished goods inventory budget
8. Cost of goods sold budget

The sales forecast is the basis for the sales budget, which in turn is the basis for all of the other operating budgets and most of the financial budgets. Accordingly, the accuracy of the sales forecast strongly affects the soundness of the entire master budget.

Creating the sales forecast is usually the responsibility of the marketing department. One approach to forecasting sales is the *bottom-up approach*, which requires individual salespeople to submit sales predictions. These are aggregated to form a total sales forecast. The accuracy of this sales forecast may be improved by considering other factors such as the general economic climate, competition, advertising, pricing policies, and so on. Some companies supplement the bottom-up approach with other, more formal approaches, such as time-series analysis, correlation analysis, and econometric modelling.

An example illustrating the effect that these factors can have on sales forecasting can be found in the market for personal computers. That market has exploded globally. Consider two producers: Compaq and Dell.[2] In 1998, Compaq was the world's number one personal computer maker. It operated in over one hundred countries and had four times as many employees as Dell. Dell, however, was a significant player in the PC market and was viewed by some as a major challenger to Compaq. For example, comparing the results for the quarter ending August 2, 1998, with the results for the same quarter a year earlier, Dell's revenues grew by 53 percent (from $2.8 billion to $4.3 billion). On the other hand, Compaq's revenues grew by 5 percent for the comparable quarter (from $5.52 billion to $5.8 billion). Yet according to one expert, there was enough new market growth potential that each company could have doubled or tripled revenue without taking market share from the other. At the same time, the Asian economic crisis of 1998 dampened sales, and prices for PCs and computer chips fell. With the market slowing down, one analyst foresaw Compaq and Dell bidding against each other, with Dell winning because of its lower cost structure. It is easy to see how this kind of information could affect the sales forecast. In making a sales forecast for the comparable quarter of the following year, Compaq's management had to consider the competitive threat from Dell, the Asian economic crisis, and the long-run market potential for PCs.

Sales Budget The sales forecast is merely the initial estimate. The **sales budget** is the projection approved by the budget committee that describes expected sales in units and dollars. The sales forecast is presented to the budget committee for consideration. The budget committee may decide that the forecast is too pessimistic or too optimistic and revise it appropriately. For example, if the budget committee decides that the forecast is too pessimistic and not in harmony with the organization's strategic plan, it may recommend specific actions to increase sales beyond the forecast level, such as increasing promotional activities and hiring additional salespeople.

To illustrate the master-budgeting process, let's look at the activities of Canblock, Inc., which manufactures concrete blocks and pipes in plants located in several western Canadian cities. Schedule 1 illustrates the sales budget for Canblock's concrete block line. For simplicity, we assume that Canblock has only one product: a standard block, measuring $20 \times 20 \times 40$ centimetres. (For a multiple-product firm, the sales budget reflects sales for each product in units and sales dollars.)

Schedule 1 (in thousands)
Canblock, Inc.
Sales Budget
For the Year Ended December 31, 2002

| | Quarter | | | | |
	1	2	3	4	Year
Units	2,000	6,000	6,000	2,000	16,000
Unit selling price	× $0.70	× $0.70	× $0.80	× $0.80	× $0.75
Sales	$1,400	$4,200	$4,800	$1,600	$12,000

2. The information about the demand for Compaq and Dell PCs is taken from Doug Levy, "Lone Star State Rivals Duke It Out," *USA Today*, 19 October 1998: pp. 1B and 2B.

Notice that the sales budget reveals that Canblock's sales fluctuate seasonally. Most sales (75 percent) take place in the spring and summer quarters. Also note that the budget reflects an expected increase in selling price beginning in the summer quarter (from $0.70 to $0.80). Because of the price change within the year, an average price must be used for the column that describes the total year's activities ($0.75 = $12,000/16,000 units).

Production Budget The **production budget** describes how many units must be produced in order to meet sales needs and satisfy ending inventory requirements. From Schedule 1, we know how many concrete blocks are needed to satisfy sales demand for each quarter and for the year. If there were no beginning or ending inventories, the concrete blocks to be produced would exactly equal the units to be sold. In a JIT firm, for example, units sold equal units produced, since a customer order triggers production. Usually, however, the production budget must consider the existence of beginning and ending inventories, since traditional manufacturing firms use inventories as a buffer against uncertainties in demand or production. Assume that company policy requires 100,000 concrete blocks to be available in inventory at the beginning of the first and fourth quarters and 500,000 blocks at the beginning of the second and third quarters. This policy is equivalent to budgeting 100,000 concrete blocks as ending inventory for the third and fourth quarters and 500,000 concrete blocks as ending inventory for the first and second quarters.

To compute the units to be produced, both unit sales and units of beginning and ending finished goods inventory are needed:

Units to be produced = Expected unit sales + Units in ending inventory
− Units in beginning inventory

This formula is the basis for the production budget in Schedule 2. Let's go through the first column of Schedule 2, the production needs for the first quarter. We see that Canblock anticipates sales of 2 million concrete blocks. In addition, the company wants 500,000 blocks in ending inventory at the end of the first quarter. Thus, 2.5 million blocks are needed during the first quarter. Where will these 2.5 million blocks come from? Beginning inventory can provide 100,000 blocks, leaving 2.4 million blocks to be produced during the quarter. Notice that the production budget is expressed in terms of units.

Schedule 2 (in thousands)
Canblock, Inc.
Production Budget
For the Year Ended December 31, 2002

| | Quarter | | | | |
	1	2	3	4	Year
Sales (Schedule 1)	2,000	6,000	6,000	2,000	16,000
Desired ending inventory	500	500	100	100	100
Total needs	2,500	6,500	6,100	2,100	16,100
Less: Beginning inventory	100	500	500	100	100
Units to be produced	2,400	6,000	5,600	2,000	16,000

Direct Materials Budget After the production budget is completed, the budgets for direct materials, direct labour, and overhead can be prepared. The **direct materials purchases budget** depends on the expected use of materials in production and the firm's raw materials inventory needs.

The amount of direct materials needed for production depends on the number of units to be produced. Suppose that a lightweight concrete block (a single unit of output) requires cement, sand, gravel, shale, pumice, and water. For simplicity, we will treat all raw materials jointly (as if there were only one raw material input) and assume that 13 kilograms of raw material are needed per block. Then if Canblock wants to produce 2.4 million blocks in the first quarter, it will need 31.2 million kilograms of raw material (13 kilograms × 2.4 million blocks).

Once expected usage is computed, the purchases (in units) can be computed as follows:

Purchases = Direct materials needed for production + Desired direct materials in ending inventory − Direct materials in beginning inventory

The quantity of direct materials in inventory is determined by the firm's inventory policy. Canblock's policy is to have 2,500 metric tons (2.5 million kilograms) of raw materials in ending inventory for the third and fourth quarters and 4,000 metric tons (4 million kilograms) of raw materials in ending inventory for the first and second quarters.

The direct materials purchases budget for Canblock is presented in Schedule 3. Notice how similar the direct materials purchases budget is to the production budget. Again, let's go through the first quarter of Schedule 3. The 2.4 million blocks to be produced are multiplied by 13 kilograms to yield the total raw materials needed for production. Then the desired ending inventory of 4 million kilograms is added. We see that 35.2 million kilograms of raw materials are required during the first quarter. Of these total needs, 2.5 million kilograms are provided by beginning inventory, meaning that the remaining 32.7 million kilograms must be purchased. Multiplying the 32.7 million kilograms by the cost of $0.02 gives Canblock the $654,000 expected cost of raw materials purchases for the first quarter of the year. Of course, there would be a separate direct materials purchases budget for each type of raw material used by a firm.

Schedule 3 (in thousands)
Canblock, Inc.
Direct Materials Purchases Budget
For the Year Ended December 31, 2002

	Quarter				
	1	2	3	4	Year
Units to be produced (Schedule 2)	2,400	6,000	5,600	2,000	16,000
Direct materials per unit (kg)	× 13	× 13	× 13	× 13	× 13
Production needs (kg)	31,200	78,000	72,800	26,000	208,000
Desired ending inventory (kg)	4,000	4,000	2,500	2,500	2,500
Total needs	35,200	82,000	75,300	28,500	210,000
Less: Beginning inventory[a]	(2,500)	(4,000)	(4,000)	(2,500)	(2,500)
Direct materials to be purchased (kg)	32,700	78,000	71,300	26,000	208,000
Cost per kilogram	× $0.02	× $0.02	× $0.02	× $0.02	× $0.02
Total purchase cost	$654	$1,560	$1,426	$520	$4,160

[a] Canblock follows the inventory policy of having 4 million kilograms of raw material on hand at the end of the first and second quarters and 2.5 million kilograms on hand at the end of the third and fourth quarters.

Direct Labour Budget The **direct labour budget** shows the total direct labour hours needed and the associated cost for the number of units in the production budget. As with direct materials, the budgeted hours of direct labour are determined by the relationship between labour and output. For example, if a batch of 100 concrete blocks requires 1.5 direct labour hours, then the direct labour time per block is 0.015 hours.

Given the direct labour used per unit of output and the units to be produced from the production budget, the direct labour budget is computed as shown in Schedule 4.

Schedule 4 (in thousands)
Canblock, Inc.
Direct Labour Budget
For the Year Ended December 31, 2002

	Quarter				
	1	2	3	4	Year
Units to be produced (Schedule 2)	2,400	6,000	5,600	2,000	16,000
Direct labour time per unit (hr.)	× 0.015	× 0.015	× 0.015	× 0.015	× 0.015
Total hours needed	36	90	84	30	240
Average wage per hour	× $10	× $10	× $10	× $10	× $10
Total direct labour cost	$360	$900	$840	$300	$2,400

In the direct labour budget, the wage rate ($10 per hour in this example) is the *average* wage paid to the direct labourers associated with the production of the concrete blocks. Since it is an average, it allows for the possibility of differing wage rates paid to individual labourers.

Overhead Budget The **overhead budget** shows the expected cost of all indirect manufacturing items. Unlike direct materials and direct labour, overhead items display no readily identifiable input–output relationship. Instead, there are a series of activities and related drivers. In order to focus on budgeting issues, we will simplify by ignoring the various activities, cost pools, and cost drivers. Instead, we will use traditional overhead rates, classified into variable and fixed components. At the end of the chapter, we will revisit the activity-based budgeting issues.

Past experience can be used as a guide to determine how overhead costs vary. Individual items that will vary are identified (for example, supplies and utilities), and the amount that is expected to be spent for each item per unit of activity is estimated. Individual rates are then totalled to obtain a variable overhead rate. For our example, let's assume that two overhead cost pools are created: one for overhead activities that vary with direct labour hours, and one for all other activities, which are fixed. The variable overhead rate is $8 per direct labour hour; fixed overhead is budgeted at $1.28 million ($320,000 per quarter). Using this information and the budgeted direct labour hours from the direct labour budget (Schedule 4), the overhead budget in Schedule 5 is prepared.

Selling and Administrative Expenses Budget The next budget to be prepared, the **selling and administrative expenses budget**, outlines planned expenditures for

Schedule 5 (in thousands)
Canblock, Inc.
Overhead Budget
For the Year Ended December 31, 2002

	Quarter				
	1	2	3	4	Year
Budgeted direct labour hours (Schedule 4)	36	90	84	30	240
Variable overhead rate	× $8	× $8	× $8	× $8	× $8
Budgeted variable overhead	$288	$ 720	$672	$240	$1,920
Budgeted fixed overhead[a]	320	320	320	320	1,280
Total overhead	$608	$1,040	$992	$560	$3,200

[a] Includes $200,000 of depreciation in each quarter.

nonmanufacturing activities. As with overhead, selling and administrative expenses can be broken down into fixed and variable components. Such items as sales commissions, freight, and supplies vary with sales activity. The selling and administrative expenses budget is illustrated in Schedule 6.

Schedule 6 (in thousands)
Canblock, Inc.
Selling and Administrative Expenses Budget
For the Year Ended December 31, 2002

	Quarter				
	1	2	3	4	Year
Planned sales in units (Schedule 1)	2,000	6,000	6,000	2,000	16,000
Variable selling and administrative expenses per unit	× $0.05	× $0.05	× $0.05	× $0.05	× $ 0.05
Total variable expenses	$100	$300	$ 300	$100	$800
Fixed selling and administrative expenses:					
Salaries	$ 35	$ 35	$ 35	$ 35	$ 140
Advertising	10	10	10	10	40
Depreciation	15	15	15	15	60
Insurance	4	4	4	4	16
Travel	5	5	5	5	20
Total fixed expenses	$ 69	$ 69	$ 69	$ 69	$ 276
Total selling and administrative expenses	$ 169	$ 369	$ 369	$ 169	$1,076

Ending Finished Goods Inventory Budget The **ending finished goods inventory budget** supplies information needed for the balance sheet and also serves as an important input for the preparation of the cost of goods sold budget. To prepare this budget, the unit cost of producing each concrete block must be calculated using information from Schedules 3, 4, and 5. The unit cost of a concrete block and the cost of the planned ending inventory are shown in Schedule 7.

Schedule 7 (in thousands)
Canblock, Inc.
Ending Inventory Budget
For the Year Ended December 31, 2002

Unit-cost computation:
  Direct materials (13 kilograms @ 0.02) $0.26
  Direct labour (0.015 hours @ $10)   0.15
Overhead:
  Variable (0.015 hours @ $8)   0.12
  Fixed (0.015 hours @ $5.33[a])   0.08
  Total unit cost $0.61

[a] $\frac{\text{Budgeted fixed overhead (Schedule 5)}}{\text{Budgeted direct labour hours (Schedule 4)}} = \frac{\$1,280}{240} = \$5.33$

	Units	Unit Cost	Total
Finished goods: Concrete block	100,000	$0.61	$61,000

Cost of Goods Sold Budget Assuming that the beginning finished goods inventory is valued at $55,000, we can prepare the **cost of goods sold budget** using Schedules 3, 4, 5, and 7. The cost of goods sold budget (Schedule 8) is the last schedule needed before the budgeted income statement can be prepared.

Schedule 8 (in thousands) Canblock, Inc. Cost of Goods Sold Budget For the Year Ended December 31, 2002	
Direct materials used (Schedule 3)[a]	$4,160
Direct labour used (Schedule 4)	2,400
Overhead (Schedule 5)	3,200
Budgeted manufacturing costs	$9,760
Beginning finished goods	55
Goods available for sale	$9,815
Less: Ending finished goods (Schedule 7)	61
Budgeted cost of goods sold	$9,754

[a] Production needs $\times$ $0.02 = 208,000 $\times$ $0.02.

Budgeted Income Statement   With the completion of the cost of goods sold budget, Canblock has all the operating budgets needed to prepare an estimate of operating income. This budgeted income statement is shown in Schedule 9. The eight schedules already prepared, along with this budgeted operating-income statement, define Canblock's operating budget .

Schedule 9 (in thousands) Canblock, Inc. Budgeted Income Statement For the Year Ended December 31, 2002	
Sales (Schedule 1)	$12,000
Less: Cost of goods sold (Schedule 8)	9,754
Gross margin	$ 2,246
Less: Selling and administrative expenses (Schedule 6)	1,076
Operating income	$ 1,170
Less: Interest expense (Schedule 10, p. 567)	54
Income before taxes	$ 1,116
Less: Income taxes	650
Net income	$ 466

Operating income is *not* equivalent to the net firm's income. To yield net income, interest expenses and taxes must be subtracted from operating income. The interest expense deduction is taken from the cash budget shown in Schedule 10 (see p. 567). The taxes owed depend on the current tax laws.

Preparing the Financial Budget

The remaining budgets found in the master budget are the financial budgets. The usual financial budgets prepared are as follows:

1. the cash budget
2. the budgeted balance sheet
3. the budget for capital expenditures

The master budget also contains a plan for acquiring long-term assets—assets that have a time horizon that extends beyond the one-year operating period. Some of these assets may be purchased during the coming year; plans to purchase others may be detailed for future periods. This part of the master budget is typically referred to as the *capital budget*. Decision making for capital expenditures is considered in

Chapter 11. Accordingly, only the cash budget and the budgeted balance sheet will be illustrated here.

Cash Budget Knowledge of cash flows is critical to managing a business. Often a business is successful in producing and selling a product but fails because of timing problems associated with cash inflows and outflows. By knowing when cash deficiencies and surpluses are likely to occur, a manager can plan to borrow cash when needed and to repay the loans during periods of excess cash. Bank loan officers use a company's **cash budget** to document the firm's need for cash, as well as its ability to repay. Because cash flow is an organization's lifeblood, the cash budget is one of the most important budgets in the master budget. The cash budget is illustrated in Exhibit 13–2.

Cash available consists of the beginning cash balance and the expected cash receipts. Expected cash receipts include all sources of cash for the period being considered. The principal source of cash is from sales. Because a significant proportion of sales is usually on account, a major task of an organization is to determine the pattern of collection for its accounts receivable.

If a company has been in business for a while, it can use past experience in creating an accounts receivable aging schedule. In other words, the company can determine, on average, what percentages of its accounts receivable are paid in the months following sale. For example, suppose that Patton Hardware Store has the following accounts receivable payment experience:

Percentage paid in the month of sale	30%
Percentage paid in the month after the sale	60%
Percentage paid in the second month after the sale	10%

If Patton sold $100,000 worth of goods on account in the month of May, then it would expect to receive $30,000 cash from May credit sales in the month of May; $60,000 cash from May credit sales in June; and $10,000 from May credit sales in July. (Notice that Patton expects to receive all of its accounts receivable. This is not typical. If a company experiences, let's say, 3 percent uncollectible accounts, then this 3 percent of sales is ignored for the purpose of cash budgeting—it is simply not received.)

The cash disbursements section lists all planned cash outlays for the period. All expenses not resulting in a cash outlay are excluded from the list (depreciation, for example, is never included in the disbursements section). A disbursement that is typically not included in this section is interest on short-term borrowing. This interest expenditure is reserved for the section on loan repayments.

The cash surplus or deficiency line compares the cash available with the cash needed. Cash needed is the total cash disbursements plus the minimum cash balance required by company policy. The minimum cash balance is simply the lowest amount of cash on hand that the firm finds acceptable. Consider your own chequing account. You probably try to keep at least some cash in the account, perhaps because a minimum balance avoids service charges, or because a minimum balance allows you to

Exhibit	13–2

The Cash Budget

Beginning cash balance	xxx
Add: Cash receipts	xxx
Cash available	xxx
Less: Cash disbursements	xxx
Less: Minimum cash balance	xxx
Cash surplus (deficiency)	xxx
Add: Cash from loans	xxx
Less: Loan repayments	xxx
Add: Minimum cash balance	xxx
Ending cash balance	xxx

make an unplanned purchase. Similarly, companies also require minimum cash balances. The amount varies from firm to firm and is determined by each company's particular needs and policies. If the total cash available is less than the cash needs, a deficiency exists. In such a case, a short-term loan will be needed. On the other hand, with a cash surplus (cash available is greater than the firm's cash needs), the firm has the ability to repay loans and perhaps make some temporary investments.

The final section of the cash budget consists of borrowings and repayments. If there is a deficiency, this section shows the necessary amount to be borrowed. When surplus cash is available, this section shows planned repayments, including interest expense.

The last line of the cash budget is the planned ending cash balance. Remember that the minimum cash balance was subtracted to find the cash surplus or deficiency. However, the minimum cash balance is not a disbursement, so it must be added back to yield the planned ending balance.

To illustrate the cash budget, assume the following for Canblock:

a.   A $100,000 minimum cash balance is required for the end of each quarter.
b.   Money can be borrowed and repaid in multiples of $100,000. Interest is 12 percent per year. Interest payments are made only for the amount of the principal being repaid. All borrowing takes place at the beginning of a quarter, and all repayment takes place at the end of a quarter.
c.   Half of all sales are for cash, 70 percent of credit sales are collected in the quarter of sale, and the remaining 30 percent are collected in the following quarter. The sales for the fourth quarter of 2001 were $2 million.
d.   Purchases of raw materials are made on account; 80 percent of purchases are paid for in the quarter of purchase. The remaining 20 percent are paid for in the following quarter. The purchases for the fourth quarter of 2001 were $500,000.
e.   Budgeted depreciation is $200,000 per quarter for overhead and $15,000 per quarter for selling and administration (see Schedules 5 and 6).
f.   The capital budget for 2002 reveals plans to purchase additional equipment to handle increased demand at a small plant in British Columbia. The cash outlay for the equipment, $600,000, will take place in the first quarter. The company plans to finance the acquisition of the equipment with operating cash, supplementing it with short-term loans as necessary.
g.   Corporate income taxes are approximately $650,000 and will be paid at the end of the fourth quarter (Schedule 9).
h.   Beginning cash balance equals $120,000.

Given this information, we can show the cash budget for Canblock in Schedule 10 (all figures are rounded to the nearest thousand). Much of the information needed to prepare the cash budget comes from the operating budgets. In fact, Schedules 1, 3, 4, 5, and 6 contain important input. However, these schedules by themselves do not supply all of the needed information. The collection pattern for revenues and the payment pattern for materials must be known before the cash flow for sales and purchases on credit can be found.

Exhibit 13–3 displays the pattern of cash inflows from both cash and credit sales. Let's look at the cash receipts for the first quarter of 2002. Cash sales during the quarter are budgeted for $700,000 (0.50 × $1,400,000; Schedule 1). Collections on account for the first quarter relate to credit sales made during the last quarter of the previous year and the first quarter of 2002. Quarter 4, 2001, credit sales equalled $1,000,000 (0.50 × $2,000,000) and $300,000 of those sales (0.30 × $1,000,000) remain to be collected in Quarter 1, 2002. Quarter 1, 2002, credit sales are budgeted at $700,000, and 70 percent will be collected in that quarter. Therefore, $490,000 will be collected on account for credit sales made in that quarter. Similar computations are made for the remaining quarters.

Similar computations are done for purchases. In both cases, patterns of collection and payment are needed in addition to the information supplied by the schedules. Additionally, all noncash expenses, such as depreciation and insurance, need to be removed from the total amounts reported in the expense budgets. Overhead expenses

Source	Quarter 1	Quarter 2	Quarter 3	Quarter 4
Cash sales	$ 700,000	$2,100,000	$2,400,000	$ 800,000
Received on account from:				
Quarter 4, 2001	300,000			
Quarter 1, 2002	490,000	210,000		
Quarter 2, 2002		1,470,000	630,000	
Quarter 3, 2002			1,680,000	720,000
Quarter 4, 2002				560,000
Total cash receipts	$1,490,000	$3,780,000	$4,710,000	$2,080,000

Exhibit 13–3

Canblock's Cash Receipts Pattern for 2002

in Schedule 5 were reduced by depreciation of $200,000 per quarter. Selling and administrative expenses in Schedule 6 were reduced by depreciation of $15,000 and insurance of $4,000 per quarter. In addition, cash payments for insurance of $16,000 are made in the third quarter. The net amounts are what appear in the cash budget.

The cash budget shown in Schedule 10 underscores the importance of breaking down the annual budget into smaller time periods. The cash budget for the year

Schedule 10 (in thousands)
Canblock, Inc.
Cash Budget
For the Year Ended December 31, 2002

	Quarter 1	Quarter 2	Quarter 3	Quarter 4	Year	Source[a]
Beginning cash balance	$ 120	$ 169	$ 162	$ 985	$ 120	
Collections:						
Cash sales	700	2,100	2,400	800	6,000	c, 1
Credit sales:						
Current quarter	490	1,470	1,680	560	4,200	c, 1
Prior quarter	300	210	630	720	1,860	c, 1
Total cash available	$1,610	$3,949	$4,872	$3,065	$12,180	
Less disbursements:						
Raw materials:						
Current quarter	$ 523	$1,248	$1,141	$ 416	$ 3,328	d, 3
Prior quarter	100	131	312	285	828	d, 3
Direct labour	360	900	840	300	2,400	4
Overhead	408	840	792	360	2,400	e, 5
Selling and administrative	150	350	366	150	1,016	e, 6
Income taxes	—	—	—	650	650	g, 9
Equipment	600	—	—	—	600	f
Total disbursements	$2,141	$3,469	$3,451	$2,161	$11,222	
Minimum cash balance	100	100	100	100	100	a
Total cash needs	$2,241	$3,569	$3,551	$2,261	$11,322	
Excess (deficiency) of cash available over needs	$ (631)	$ 380	$1,321	$ 805	$ 858	
Financing:						
Borrowings	700	—	—	—	700	
Repayments	—	(300)	(400)	—	(700)	b
Interest[b]	—	(18)	(36)	—	(54)	b
Total financing	$ 700	$ (318)	$ (436)	—	$ (54)	
Ending cash balance[c]	$ 169	$ 162	$ 985	$ 904	$ 904	

[a] Letters refer to the information on page 566. Numbers refer to schedules already developed.
[b] Interest payments are 6/12 × 0.12 × $300 and 9/12 × 0.12 × $400, respectively. Since borrowings occur at the beginning of the quarter and repayments at the end of the quarter, the first principal repayment takes place after six months, and the second principal repayment takes place after nine months.
[c] Total cash available minus total disbursements plus (or minus) total financing.

gives the impression that sufficient operating cash will be available to finance the acquisition of the new equipment. Quarterly information, however, shows the need for short-term borrowing ($700,000) because of both the acquisition of the new equipment and the timing of the firm's cash flows. Most firms prepare monthly cash budgets, and some even prepare weekly and daily budgets.

Another significant piece of information emerges from Canblock's cash budget. By the end of the third quarter, the firm has a considerable amount of cash ($986,000). It is certainly not wise to allow this much cash to sit idly in a bank account. Canblock's management should consider paying dividends and making long-term investments. At the very least, the excess cash should be invested in short-term marketable securities. Once plans are finalized for use of the excess cash, the cash budget should be revised to reflect those plans. Budgeting is a dynamic process. As the budget is developed, new information becomes available, so better plans can be formulated.

Budgeted Balance Sheet   The budgeted balance sheet depends on information contained in the current balance sheet and in the other budgets in the master budget. The balance sheet for the beginning of the year is given in Exhibit 13–4. The budgeted balance sheet for December 31, 2002, is given in Schedule 11. Explanations for the budgeted figures follow the schedule.

As we have described the individual budgets that make up the master budget, the interdependencies of the component budgets have become apparent. A diagram displaying these interrelationships is shown in Exhibit 13–5.

Schedule 11 (in thousands)		
Canblock, Inc.		
Budgeted Balance Sheet		
December 31, 2002		
Assets		
Current assets:		
Cash	$ 904[a]	
Accounts receivable	240[b]	
Raw materials inventory	50[c]	
Finished goods	61[d]	
Total current assets		$1,255
Property, plant, and equipment:		
Land	$2,500[e]	
Building and equipment	9,600[f]	
Accumulated depreciation	(5,360)[g]	
Total property, plant, and equipment		6,740
Total assets		$7,995
Liabilities and Stockholders' Equity		
Current liabilities:		
Accounts payable		$ 104[h]
Stockholders' equity:		
Common stock, no par	$ 600[i]	
Retained earnings	7,291[j]	
Total shareholders' equity		7,891
Total liabilities and stockholders' equity		$7,995

[a] Ending balance from Schedule 10.
[b] 30 percent of fourth-quarter credit sales (0.30 × $800,000)—see Schedules 1 and 10.
[c] From Schedule 3.
[d] From Schedule 7.
[e] From the December 31, 2001, balance sheet.
[f] December 31, 2001, balance ($9,000,000) plus new equipment acquisition of $600,000 (see the 2001 ending balance sheet and Schedule 10).
[g] From the December 31, 2001, balance sheet, Schedule 5, and Schedule 6 ($4,500,000 + $800,000 + $60,000).
[h] 20 percent of fourth-quarter purchases (0.20 × $520,000)—see Schedules 3 and 10.
[i] From the December 31, 2001, balance sheet.
[j] $6,825,000 + $467,000 (December 31, 2001, balance plus net income from Schedule 9).

Exhibit 13–4

Canblock, Inc., Balance Sheet—December 31, 2001

Canblock, Inc.
Balance Sheet
December 31, 2001
(in thousands)

Assets

Current assets:		
Cash	$ 120	
Accounts receivable	300	
Raw materials inventory	50	
Finished goods	55	
Total current assets		$ 525
Property, plant, and equipment:		
Land	$2,500	
Building and equipment	9,000	
Accumulated depreciation	(4,500)	
Total property, plant, and equipment		7,000
Total assets		$7,525

Liabilities and Stockholders' Equity

Current liabilities:		
Accounts payable		$ 100
Stockholders' equity:		
Common stock, no par	$ 600	
Retained earnings	6,825	
Total stockholders' equity		7,425
Total liabilities and stockholders' equity		$7,525

Exhibit 13–5

The Master Budget and Its Interrelationships

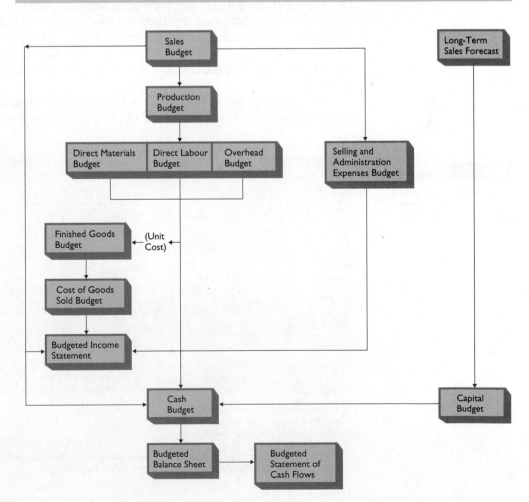

USING BUDGETS FOR PERFORMANCE EVALUATION

Objective 3

Describe flexible budgeting and identify the features that a budgetary system should have to encourage managers to engage in goal-congruent behaviour.

Budgets are useful control measures. To use them in performance evaluation, however, two major considerations must be addressed. The first is to determine how budgeted amounts should be compared with actual results. The second consideration involves the impact of budgets on human behaviour.

Static Budgets versus Flexible Budgets

Budgets can be used for both planning and control. In planning, companies prepare a master budget based on their best estimate of the level of activity to be achieved in the coming year. However, typically the actual level of activity does not equal the budgeted level. As a result, budgeted amounts cannot be compared with actual results. Therefore, companies may also prepare flexible budgets to be used for performance evaluation.

Static Budgets The master budget developed for Canblock is an example of a static **budget**. A **static budget** is a budget for a particular level of activity. For Canblock, budgets were developed based on expected annual sales of 16 million units. Because static budgets depend on a particular level of activity, they are not very useful when it comes to preparing performance reports.

To illustrate, suppose that Canblock's first-quarter sales were greater than expected: 2.6 million concrete blocks were sold instead of the 2 million budgeted in Schedule 1. Because of increased sales activity, production was increased over the planned level. Instead of producing 2.4 million units (Schedule 2), Canblock produced 3 million units.

A performance report comparing the actual production costs for the first quarter with the original planned production costs is given in Exhibit 13–6. In contrast to Schedule 5, budgeted amounts for individual overhead items are provided. Thus, the individual budgeted amounts for each overhead item constitute new information (except for depreciation). Usually, this information would be detailed in an overhead budget.

According to the report, unfavourable variances occurred for direct materials, direct labour, supplies, indirect labour, and rent. However, there is something fun-

Exhibit 13–6

Performance Report: Quarterly Production Costs (in thousands)

	Actual	Budget	Variance
Units produced	3,000	2,400	600 F[a]
Direct materials cost	$ 927.30	$ 624.00[b]	$303.30 U[c]
Direct labour cost	450.00	360.00[d]	90.00 U
Overhead:[e]			
Variable:			
Supplies	80.00	72.00	8.00 U
Indirect labour	220.00	168.00	52.00 U
Power	40.00	48.00	(8.00) F
Fixed:			
Supervision	90.00	100.00	(10.00) F
Depreciation	200.00	200.00	0.00
Rent	30.00	20.00	10.00 U
Total	$2,037.30	$1,592.00	$445.30

[a] F means that the variance is favourable.
[b] From Schedule 3 (31,200 kilograms × $0.02).
[c] U means that the variance is unfavourable.
[d] From Schedule 4.
[e] Schedule 5 provides the aggregate amount of budgeted overhead (e.g., the aggregate variable overhead is 0.015 × 2,400,000 × $8 = $288,000, and the total budgeted fixed overhead is $320,000).

damentally wrong with the report. Actual costs for production of 3 million concrete blocks are being compared with planned costs for production of 2.4 million. Because direct materials, direct labour, and variable overhead are variable costs, we would expect them to be greater at a higher activity level. Thus, even if cost control were perfect for the production of 3 million units, unfavourable variances would be produced for at least some of the variable costs. To create a meaningful performance report, actual costs and expected costs must be compared at the *same* level of activity. Since actual output often differs from planned output, some method is needed for computing what the costs should have been for the actual output level.

Flexible Budgets   A budget that provides a firm with the capability of computing expected costs for a range of activity is called a **flexible budget**. Flexible budgeting has three major uses:

1. The flexible budget can be used to prepare the budget before the fact for the expected level of activity.
2. Because flexible budgeting can determine what costs should be at various levels of activity, the budget can be used after the fact to compute what costs should have been for the actual level of activity. Once expected costs are known for the actual level of activity, a performance report that compares those expected costs to actual costs can be prepared.
3. Flexible budgeting can help managers deal with uncertainty by allowing them to see the expected outcomes for a range of activity. It can be used to generate financial results for a number of plausible scenarios.

Flexible budgeting is the key to providing the frequent feedback that managers need in order to exercise control and effectively carry out the organization's plans.

To compute the expected cost at different levels of activity, we need to know the cost behaviour pattern of each item in the budget. That is, we need to know the variable cost per unit of activity, and the fixed cost per item. Let's prepare a flexible budget for Canblock where activity level is measured by the number of concrete blocks produced. From Schedule 7, we know the variable costs for direct materials ($0.26 per unit), direct labour ($0.15 per unit), and variable overhead ($0.12 per unit). To increase the detail of the flexible budget, let's assume that supplies, indirect labour, and power have variable costs per unit of $0.03, $0.07, and $0.02, respectively. These three individual variable overhead amounts sum to $0.12. From Schedule 5, we also know that fixed overhead is budgeted at $320,000 per quarter. Exhibit 13–7 displays a flexible budget for production costs at three levels of activity.

Exhibit 13–7

Flexible Production Budget (in thousands of dollars)

Production Costs	Variable Cost per Unit	2,400	3,000	3,600
Variable:				
Direct materials	$0.26	$ 624	$ 780	$ 936
Direct labour	0.15	360	450	540
Variable overhead:				
Supplies	0.03	72	90	108
Indirect labour	0.07	168	210	252
Power	0.02	48	60	72
Total variable costs	$0.53	$1,272	$1,590	$1,908
Fixed overhead:				
Supervision		$ 100	$ 100	$ 100
Depreciation		200	200	200
Rent		20	20	20
Total fixed costs		$ 320	$ 320	$ 320
Total production costs		$1,592	$1,910	$2,228

Range of Production (units)

Exhibit   13–8

Actual versus Flexible Performance Report: Quarterly Production Costs (in thousands)

	Actual	Budget*	Variance
Units produced	3,000	3,000	—
Production costs:			
Direct materials	$ 927.30	$ 780.00	$147.30 U
Direct labour	450.00	450.00	0.00
Variable overhead:			
Supplies	80.00	90.00	(10.00) F
Indirect labour	220.00	210.00	10.00 U
Power	40.00	60.00	(20.00) F
Total variable costs	$1,717.30	$1,590.00	$127.30 U
Fixed overhead:			
Supervision	$ 90.00	$ 100.00	$(10.00) F
Depreciation	200.00	200.00	0.00
Rent	30.00	20.00	10.00 U
Total fixed costs	$ 320.00	$ 320.00	0.00
Total costs	$2,037.30	$1,910.00	$127.30 U

* From Exhibit 13–7.

Notice in Exhibit 13–7 that total budgeted production costs increase as the activity level increases. Budgeted costs change because of variable costs. Because of this, flexible budgets are sometimes referred to as **variable budgets**. Flexible budgets are powerful control tools because they allow management to compute what the costs should be for any level of activity. Exhibit 13–7 reveals what the costs should have been for the actual level of activity (3 million units). Now we can provide management with a useful performance report—one that compares actual and budgeted costs for the actual level of activity. This report is given in Exhibit 13–8.

The revised performance report in Exhibit 13–8 paints a much different picture than does the one in Exhibit 13–6. By comparing budgeted costs for the actual level of activity with actual costs for the same level, a problem area can be immediately identified—expenditures for direct materials are excessive. (The other unfavourable variances seem relatively small.) With this knowledge, management can search for the causes of the excess expenditures and take action to prevent the same problems from occurring in future quarters.

A difference between the actual amount and the flexible budget amount is the **flexible budget variance**. The flexible budget provides the capability to assess a manager's efficiency. In addition to measuring the efficiency of a manager, it is often desirable to measure whether a manager accomplishes his or her goals. The static budget is important for this, since it represents certain goals that the firm wants to achieve. A manager is *effective* if the goals described by the static budget are achieved or exceeded. Any differences between the flexible budget and the static budget are attributable to differences in volume. They are called *volume variances*. A five-column performance report that reveals both the flexible budget variances and the volume variances can be used. Exhibit 13–9 provides an example of such a report using the Canblock data.

As the report in Exhibit 13–9 reveals, production volume was 600,000 units greater than the original budgeted amount. Thus, the manager exceeded the original budgeted goal. This volume variance is labelled *favourable* because it exceeds the original production goal. (Recall that the *reason* for the extra production was the fact that the demand for the product was greater than expected. Thus, the increase in production over the original amount was truly favourable.) On the other hand, the budgeted variable costs are greater than expected because of the increased production. This difference is labelled *unfavourable* because the costs are greater than expected; however, the increase in costs is a result of an increase in production. For this particular exam-

| | | | Flexible | | |
Exhibit 13–9	Actual Results	Flexible Budget	Budget Variances[a]	Static Budget	Volume Variance[b]
Units produced	3,000	3,000	—	2,400	600 F
Production costs:					
Direct materials	$ 927.30	$ 780.00	$147.30 U	$ 624.00	$156.00 U
Direct labour	450.00	450.00	—	360.00	90.00 U
Supplies	80.00	90.00	(10.00) F	72.00	18.00 U
Indirect labour	220.00	210.00	10.00 U	168.00	42.00 U
Power	40.00	60.00	(20.00) F	48.00	12.00 U
Supervision	90.00	100.00	(10.00) F	100.00	—
Depreciation	200.00	200.00	—	200.00	—
Rent	30.00	20.00	10.00 U	20.00	—
Total costs	$2,037.30	$1,910.00	$127.30 U	$1,592.00	$318.00 U

Managerial Performance Report: Quarterly Production (in thousands)

[a] Actual results minus flexible budget.
[b] Flexible budget minus static budget.

ple, the manager's effectiveness is not in question: the main issue is how well the manager controls costs, as revealed by the flexible budget variances.

Flexible Revenue and Expense Budgets The discussion above highlights the usefulness of using flexible budgets to evaluate manufacturing and nonmanufacturing cost performance, but an operating budget encompasses revenues as well as costs. Flexible budgets assist in the process of evaluating not only cost performance but also profit performance. Exhibit 13–10 is an example of a profit performance report for Canblock's second quarter, when actual sales and production were 5.4 million concrete blocks at an average selling price of $0.75. Actual income results for the second quarter are provided in Exhibit 13–10.

The last column in Exhibit 13–10 shows that in the second quarter, the effect of sales volume on profit, other things remaining constant, is $72,000 unfavourable. That can be verified by multiplying the decrease in sales (5,400,000 – 6,000,000) times the budgeted contribution margin ($0.70 – $0.58 = $0.12). In Exhibit 13–10, this is shown in two steps: the decrease in revenue resulting from the decrease in volume (600,000 units × $0.70 = $420,000 unfavourable), less the decrease in variable costs resulting from the decrease in volume (600,000 units × $0.58 = $348,000 favourable), or a total of $72,000 unfavourable.[3]

The middle column of Exhibit 13–10 shows that the effect of the selling price increase on profits, other things remaining constant, is $270,000 favourable. This can be verified by multiplying the increase in selling price ($0.75 – $0.70) by the actual volume sold (5,400,000 units). The middle column also shows cost performance effects. For variable production expenses, this amounts to $88,000 unfavourable, since the actual variable costs exceeded the flexible budget amount;[4] for variable selling and administrative expenses, the flexible budget variance is $10,000 unfavourable. Finally, the middle column also shows a variance in the amount of $23,000 unfavourable for fixed costs; this consists of a $20,000 unfavourable variance in production and a $3,000

3. A variance's effect on profit can be determined by the sign of the variance. Comparing actual amounts minus budget, and assigning positive signs to revenues and negative signs to expenses, the profit volume variance = (5,400,000 – 6,000,000) × ($0.70 – $0.58) = 600,000 × $0.12 = – $72,000, or $72,000U. The flexible budget variance for variable expenses is –$3,230,000 – (–$3,132,000) = –$98,000, or $98,000U. It is more direct to use common sense to determine the direction of the effect on profit without formally following mathematical signs.

4. The variable production cost variance is a total amount that can be broken down further into material, labour, and variable manufacturing overhead variances. Each of these variances can be decomposed even further to isolate the effect of input price, efficiency, etc. This analysis is the subject of Chapter 14.

Exhibit　13–10

Profit Performance
Report (in thousands)

	Actual Results	Flexible Budget	Flexible Budget Variances[a]	Static Budget	Volume Variance[b]
Sales (units)	5,400	5,400	—	6,000	600 U
Sales revenue	$4,050[c]	$3,780[d]	$270 F	$4,200[e]	$420 U
Variable expenses:					
Production	$2,950	$2,862[f]	$ 88 U	$3,180[f]	$318 F
Selling and administrative	$ 280	$ 270[g]	$ 10 U	$ 300[g]	$ 30 F
Total variable expenses	$3,230	$3,132	$ 98 U	$3,480	$348 F
Contribution margin	$ 820	$ 648	$172 F	$ 720	$ 72 U
Fixed expenses:					
Production	$ 340	$ 320[h]	$ 20 U	$ 320[h]	$ —
Selling and administrative	72	69[i]	$ 3 U	69[i]	—
Total fixed expenses	$ 412	$ 389	$ 23 U	$ 389	$ —
Net income	$ 408	$ 259	$149 F	$ 331	$ 72 U

[a] Actual results minus flexible budget.
[b] Flexible budget minus static budget.
[c] 5,400 × $0.75.
[d] 5,400 × $0.70.
[e] From Schedule 1.
[f] From Exhibit 13–7; 5,400 × $0.53; 6,000 × $0.53.
[g] From Schedule 6; 5,400 × $0.05; 6,000 × $0.05.
[h] From Schedule 5.
[i] From Schedule 6.

unfavourable variance in selling and administrative expenses. The total of the last column and the middle column of Exhibit 13-10 is equal to the difference between the actual profit ($408,000) and the static budget profit ($331,000), a difference of $77,000 favourable. A summary of these variances is provided below.

Summary of variances:	
Profit volume variance	$ 72,000 U
Sales price variance	270,000 F
Variable-cost variances	98,000 U
Fixed-cost variances	23,000 U
Total variance from static budget[a]	$ 77,000 F

[a] Also called static budget variance, or master budget variance.

Note that the flexible budget is important in separating the effects of sales (and production) volume from the effects of price and cost performance. The above example illustrates variance analysis as an analytical tool that can be used to separate the effects of each factor on planned outcome (budgeted profit), thereby gaining insight into its relative impact on that outcome. The results of this analysis will help in determining the appropriate corrective action.[5]

The Behavioural Dimension of Budgeting

Budgets are often used to judge the actual performance of managers. Bonuses, salary increases, and promotions are all affected by a manager's ability to achieve or beat budgeted goals. Since a manager's financial status and career can be affected, budgets can have a significant behavioural effect. Whether that effect is positive or negative depends to a large extent on how budgets are used.

5.　A more detailed discussion of cost and revenue variance analysis is the subject of Chapter 14.

Positive behaviour occurs when the goals of individual managers are aligned with the goals of the organization, and the manager has the drive to achieve them. The alignment of managerial and organizational goals is often referred to as **goal congruence**. In addition to goal congruence, however, a manager must also exert effort to achieve the organization's goals. If the budget is improperly administered, subordinate managers may subvert the organization's goals. **Dysfunctional behaviour** is individual behaviour that is in basic conflict with the organization's goals.

A theme underlying the behavioural dimension of budgeting is ethics. The importance of budgets in performance evaluation and managers' pay raises and promotions leads to the possibility of unethical action. All of the dysfunctional actions that can be taken regarding budgets can have an unethical aspect. For example, a manager who deliberately underestimates sales and overestimates costs for the purpose of making the budget easier to achieve is engaging in unethical behaviour. It is the company's responsibility to create budgetary incentives that do not encourage unethical behaviour. It is the manager's responsibility to refrain from engaging in such behaviour.

An ideal budgetary system is one that achieves complete goal congruence and simultaneously creates a drive in managers to achieve the organization's goals in an ethical manner. While an ideal budgetary system probably does not exist, research and practice have identified some key features that promote a reasonable degree of positive behaviour. These features include frequent feedback on performance; monetary and nonmonetary incentives; participative budgeting; realistic standards; controllability of costs; and multiple measures of performance.

Frequent Feedback on Performance Managers need to know how they are doing as the year unfolds. Providing them with frequent, timely performance reports allows them to know how successful their efforts have been, to take corrective actions, and to change plans as necessary.

The use of flexible budgets allows management to see if actual costs and revenues are in accord with budgeted amounts. Selective investigation of significant variances allows managers to focus only on areas that need attention. This process is called *management by exception*.

Monetary and Nonmonetary Incentives A sound budgetary system encourages goal-congruent behaviour. The means used by an organization to influence a manager to exert effort to achieve the organization's goal are called **incentives**. Traditional organizational theory assumes that individuals are motivated primarily by monetary rewards, will resist work, and are inefficient and wasteful. Thus, **monetary incentives** are used in an attempt to control a manager's tendency to shirk and waste resources by relating budgetary performance to salary increases, bonuses, and promotions. The threat of dismissal is the ultimate economic sanction for poor performance. But in reality, individuals are motivated by more than economic factors. Individuals are also motivated by intrinsic psychological and social factors, such as the satisfaction of a job well done, recognition, responsibility, self-esteem, and the nature of the work itself. Thus, **nonmonetary incentives**—including job enrichment, increased responsibility and autonomy, nonmonetary recognition programs, and so on—can be used to enhance a budgetary control system.

Participative Budgeting Rather than imposing budgets on subordinate managers, **participative budgeting** allows subordinate managers considerable say in how the budgets are established. Typically, overall objectives are communicated to the manager, who helps develop a budget that will accomplish these objectives. Participative budgeting communicates a sense of responsibility to subordinate managers and fosters creativity. Since the subordinate manager creates the budget, it is more likely that the budget's goals will become the manager's personal goals, resulting in greater goal congruence. The increased responsibility and challenge inherent in the process provide nonmonetary incentives that lead to a higher level of performance.

Participative budgeting has three potential problems:

1. setting standards that are either too high or too low;
2. building slack into the budget (often referred to as *padding the budget*); and
3. pseudoparticipation.

Some managers may tend to set the budget either too loose or too tight. Since budgeted goals tend to become the manager's goals when participation is allowed, making this mistake in setting the budget can result in decreased performance levels. If goals are too easily achieved, a manager may lose interest, and performance may actually drop. Challenge is important to aggressive and creative individuals. Similarly, setting the budget too tight ensures failure to achieve the standards and frustrates the manager. This frustration, too, can lead to poorer performance. The trick is to get managers in a participative setting to set high but achievable goals.

The second problem with participative budgeting is the opportunity for managers to build slack into the budget. **Budgetary slack** (or *padding the budget*) exists when a manager deliberately underestimates revenues or overestimates costs. Either approach increases the likelihood that the manager will achieve the budget and consequently reduces the risk that the manager faces. Top management should carefully review budgets proposed by subordinate managers, providing input where needed in order to decrease the effects of building slack into the budget.

The third problem with participation occurs when top management assumes total control of the budgeting process, seeking only superficial participation from lower-level managers. This practice is termed **pseudoparticipation**. Top management is simply obtaining formal acceptance of the budget from subordinate managers, not seeking real input. Accordingly, none of the behavioural benefits of participation will be realized.

Realistic Standards Budgeted objectives are used to gauge performance; accordingly, they should be based on realistic conditions and expectations. Budgets should reflect operating realities such as actual levels of activity, seasonal variations, efficiencies, and general economic trends. Flexible budgets are used to ensure that budgeted costs can be realistically compared to costs for actual levels of activity. Interim budgets should reflect seasonal effects. Toys "R" Us, for example, would expect much higher sales in the quarter that includes Christmas than in other quarters. Budgetary cuts should be based on *planned* increases in efficiency and not simply on arbitrary across-the-board reductions. Across-the-board cuts without any formal evaluation may impair the ability of some units to carry out their missions. General economic conditions also need to be considered. Budgeting for a significant increase in sales when a recession is projected is not only foolish but potentially dangerous.

Controllability of Costs Managers should be held accountable only for costs over which they have control. **Controllable costs** are costs whose level a manager can influence. For example, divisional managers have no power to authorize such corporate-level costs as research and development and the salaries of top managers. Therefore, they should not be held accountable for the incurrence of those costs. If noncontrollable costs are put in the budgets of subordinate managers to help them understand that these costs also need to be covered, then they should be separated from controllable costs and labeled *noncontrollable*.

Multiple Measures of Performance Organizations often make the mistake of using budgets as their only measure of managerial performance. While financial measures of performance are important, overemphasis can lead to a form of dysfunctional behaviour called *milking the firm* or *myopia*. **Myopic behaviour** occurs when a manager takes actions that improve budgetary performance in the short run but bring long-run harm to the firm. For example, to meet budgeted cost objectives or profits, managers can fail to promote promotable employees, or they can reduce expenditures for preventive maintenance, for advertising, and for new product development. Using measures that are both financial and nonfinancial and that take into account both the long term and the short term can alleviate this problem. Budgetary measures by themselves are inadequate. The use of an integrated multiple-measures system known as the *Balanced Scorecard* is explored in Chapter 15.

ACTIVITY-BASED BUDGETING

Objective 4

Describe activity-based budgeting.

Companies that have implemented an ABC system may also wish to install an **activity-based budgeting system.** A budgetary system at the activity level can be a useful approach to support continuous improvement and process management. Furthermore, because activities are what consume resources—and therefore are the causes of costs—activity-based budgeting may prove to be a much more powerful planning and control tool than the traditional functional-based budgeting approach. An activity-based budgetary approach can be used to emphasize cost reduction through the elimination of wasteful activities and to improve the efficiency of necessary activities.

Static Activity Budgets

Activities cause costs by consuming resources; however, the amount of resources consumed depends on the demand for the activity's output. Thus, to build an activity-based budget, three steps are needed: (1) the activities within an organization must be identified, (2) the demand for each activity's output must be estimated, and (3) the cost of resources required to produce this activity output must be assessed. If an organization has implemented an ABC or ABM system, then Step 1 will already have been accomplished. Assuming that ABC has been implemented, the major emphasis for activity-based budgeting is estimating the workload (demand) for each activity and then budgeting the resources required to sustain this workload. The workload for each activity must be set to support the sales and production activities expected for the coming period.

Thus, as with traditional functional-based budgeting, activity-based budgeting begins with sales and production budgets. Direct materials and direct labour budgets are also compatible with an ABC framework, because these production inputs are directly traceable to the individual products. The major differences between functional and activity-based budgeting are found within the overhead and selling and administration expenses categories. In a functional-based approach, budgets within these categories are typically detailed by cost elements (see Exhibit 13–6 for an example of a detailed overhead budget). These cost elements are classified as variable or fixed, using production or sales output measures as the basis for determining cost behaviour. Furthermore, these budgets are usually constructed by budgeting for a cost item within a department (function) and then rolling these items up into the master overhead budget. For example, the cost of supervision in the overhead budget of Exhibit 13–6 is the sum of all the supervision costs of the various departments. Activity-based budgeting, on the other hand, identifies the overhead, selling, and administrative *activities* and then builds a budget for each activity, based on the resources needed to provide the required activity output levels. Costs are classified as variable or fixed with respect to the *activity* of output measure.

Consider, for example, the activity, purchasing materials. The demand for this activity is a function of the materials requirements for the various products and services produced. An activity driver, such as number of purchase orders, measures the activity output demand. Suppose that materials requirements as expressed by the materials purchases budget create a demand for 15,000 purchase orders. To execute the purchasing activity, resources such as purchasing agents, supplies (forms, paper, stamps, envelopes, and so on), desks, computers, and office space are needed. Assuming that a purchasing agent can process 3,000 orders per year, then five agents are needed. Similarly, five desks, five computers, and office space for five agents are required. A budget for the purchasing activity is given below (depreciation is on the desk and computers, and occupancy is the cost of the office space).

Salaries	Depreciation	Supplies	Occupancy	Total
$200,000	$5,000	$15,000	$6,000	$226,000

Of the resources consumed by the purchasing activity, supplies is a flexible resource (and therefore a variable cost), whereas the other resources consumed are committed resources (and therefore display a fixed-cost behaviour—a step-fixed cost behaviour in the case of salaries and depreciation). However, there is an important difference that should be mentioned: fixed and variable purchasing costs are defined with respect to the *number of purchase orders* and not direct labour hours or units produced or other measures of production output. The cost behaviour of each activity is defined with respect to *its* output measure (which is often different from the production-based drivers used in functional-based budgeting). Knowing the output measure provides significant insights for controlling activity costs. In an activity framework, controlling costs translates into managing activities. For example, by redesigning products so that they use more common components, the number of purchase orders can be decreased. By decreasing the number of purchase orders demanded, flexible resource demand is reduced; furthermore, decreasing the number of purchase orders demanded also reduces the activity capacity needed. Thus, activity costs will decrease. This is an example of activity-based management and is more fully discussed in Chapter 15.

Activity Flexible Budgeting

The ability to identify changes in activity costs as activity output changes allows managers to more carefully plan and monitor activity improvements. **Activity flexible budgeting** is the prediction of what activity costs will be as activity output changes. Variance analysis within an activity framework makes it possible to improve traditional budgetary performance reporting. It also enhances the ability to manage activities.

In a functional-based approach, budgeted costs for the actual level of activity are obtained by assuming that a single unit-based driver (units of product or direct labour hours) drives all costs. A cost formula is developed for each cost item as a function of units produced or direct labour hours. Exhibit 13–7 illustrates a traditional flexible budget using units of product as the driver. Exhibit 13–11 presents a flexible budget based on direct labour hours. If, however, costs vary with respect to more than one driver and the drivers are not highly correlated with direct labour hours, then the predicted costs can be misleading.

The solution, of course, is to build flexible budget formulas for more than one driver. Cost estimation procedures (the high–low method, the method of least squares, and so on) can be used to estimate and validate the cost formulas for each activity. In principle, the variable-cost component for each activity should correspond to resources acquired as needed (flexible resources), and the fixed-cost component should correspond to resources acquired in advance of usage (committed resources). This multiple-formula approach allows managers to predict more accurately what costs ought to be for different levels of activity usage, as measured by the activity output measure. These costs can then be compared with the actual costs to

Exhibit 13–11	Cost Formula		Direct Labour Hours	
Flexible Budget: Direct Labour Hours	Fixed	Variable	10,000	20,000
Direct materials	—	$10	$100,000	$200,000
Direct labour	—	8	80,000	160,000
Maintenance	$ 20,000	3	50,000	80,000
Machining	15,000	1	25,000	35,000
Inspections	120,000	—	120,000	120,000
Setups	50,000	—	50,000	50,000
Purchasing	220,000	—	220,000	220,000
Total	$425,000	$22	$645,000	$865,000

help assess budgetary performance. Exhibit 13–12 illustrates an activity flexible budget. Notice that the budgeted amounts for materials and labour are the same as those reported in Exhibit 13–11: they use the same activity output measure. The budgeted amounts for the other items differ significantly from the traditional amounts, because their activity output measures differ.

Assume that the first activity level for each driver in Exhibit 13–12 corresponds to the actual activity usage levels. Exhibit 13–13 compares the budgeted costs for the actual activity usage levels with the actual costs. One item is on target, and the other seven items are mixed. The net outcome is a favourable variance of $21,500.

The performance report in Exhibit 13–13 compares total budgeted costs for the actual level of activity with the total actual costs for each activity. It is also possible to compare the actual fixed activity costs with the budgeted fixed activity costs and the actual variable activity costs with the budgeted variable activity costs. For

Exhibit 13–12	DRIVER: DIRECT LABOUR HOURS			
Activity Flexible Budget	Formula		Level of Activity	
	Fixed	Variable	10,000	20,000
Direct materials	$ —	$10	$100,000	$200,000
Direct labour	—	8	80,000	160,000
Subtotal	$ 0	$18	$180,000	$360,000
	DRIVER: MACHINE HOURS			
	Fixed	Variable	8,000	16,000
Maintenance	$20,000	$5.50	$64,000	$108,000
Machining	15,000	2.00	31,000	47,000
Subtotal	$35,000	$7.50	$95,000	$155,000
	DRIVER: NUMBER OF SETUPS			
	Fixed	Variable	25	30
Inspections	$80,000	$2,100	$132,500	$143,000
Setups	—	1,800	45,000	54,000
Subtotal	$80,000	$3,900	$177,500	$197,000
	DRIVER: NUMBER OF ORDERS			
	Fixed	Variable	15,000	25,000
Purchasing	$211,000	$1	$226,000	$236,000
Total			$678,500	$948,000

Exhibit 13-13		Actual Costs	Budgeted Costs	Budget Variance
Activity-Based Performance Report*	Direct materials	$101,000	$100,000	$ 1,000 U
	Direct labour	80,000	80,000	—
	Maintenance	55,000	64,000	9,000 F
	Machining	29,000	31,000	2,000 F
	Inspections	125,500	132,500	7,000 F
	Setups	46,500	45,000	1,500 U
	Purchasing	220,000	226,000	6,000 F
	Total	$657,000	$678,500	$21,500 F

* Actual levels of drivers: 10,000 direct labour hours, 8,000 machine hours, 25 setups, and 15,000 orders.

example, assume that the actual fixed inspection costs are $82,000 (due to a midyear salary adjustment, reflecting a more favourable union agreement than anticipated) and that the actual variable inspection costs are $43,500. The variable and fixed budget variances for the inspection activity are computed as follows:

Activity	Actual Cost	Budgeted Cost	Variance
Inspection:			
Fixed	$ 82,000	$ 80,000	$2,000 U
Variable	43,500	52,500	9,000 F
Total	$125,500	$132,500	$7,000 F

Breaking each variance into fixed and variable components provides more insight into the source of the variation in planned and actual expenditures. Other kinds of variance analysis are useful for activity management; however, consideration of these types of analyses is deferred to Chapter 15.

SUMMARY OF LEARNING OBJECTIVES

1. Define *budgeting* and discuss its role in planning, control, and decision making.
Budgeting is the creation of a plan of action expressed in financial terms. Budgeting plays a key role in planning, control, and decision making. Budgets also serve to improve communication and coordination, a role that becomes increasingly important as organizations grow in size.

2. Define and prepare the *master budget*, identify its major components, and explain the interrelationships of its various components.
The master budget, an organization's comprehensive financial plan, consists of the operating and financial budgets. The operating budget is the budgeted income statement and all supporting schedules. The sales budget (Schedule 1) consists of the anticipated quantity and price of all products to be sold. The production budget (Schedule 2) gives the expected production in units to meet forecasted sales and desired ending inventory goals; expected production is supplemented by beginning inventory. The direct materials purchases

budget (Schedule 3) gives the necessary purchases during the year for every type of raw material to meet production and desired ending inventory goals. The direct labour budget (Schedule 4) and overhead budget (Schedule 5) give the amounts of these resources necessary for the coming year's production. The overhead budget may be broken down into fixed and variable components to facilitate preparation of the budget. The selling and administrative expenses budget (Schedule 6) gives the forecasted costs for these functions. The finished goods inventory budget (Schedule 7) and the cost of goods sold budget (Schedule 8) detail production costs for the expected ending inventory and the units sold, respectively. The budgeted income statement (Schedule 9) outlines the net income to be realized if budgeted plans come to fruition.

The financial budget includes the cash budget, the capital expenditures budget, and the budgeted balance sheet. The cash budget (Schedule 10) is simply the beginning balance in the cash account, plus anticipated receipts, minus anticipated disbursements, plus or minus any necessary borrowing. The budgeted (or pro forma) balance sheet (Schedule 11) gives the anticipated ending balances of the asset, liability, and equity accounts if budgeted plans hold.

3. Describe flexible budgeting and identify the features that a budgetary system should have to encourage managers to engage in goal-congruent behaviour.

The success of a budgetary system depends on how seriously human factors are considered. To discourage dysfunctional behaviour, organizations should avoid overemphasizing budgets as a control mechanism. Other areas of performance should be evaluated in addition to budgets. Budgets can be improved as performance measures by using participative budgeting and other nonmonetary incentives, providing frequent feedback on performance, using flexible budgeting, ensuring that the budgetary objectives reflect reality, and holding managers accountable for only controllable costs.

4. Describe activity-based budgeting.

Activity-based budgeting identifies activities, demands for activity output, and the cost of resources needed to support the activity output demanded. The principal difference in an activity-based approach is a detailed listing of activities and their expected costs within the overhead, selling, and administrative categories. Activity-based budgeting has the potential of being more accurate than traditional budgeting, because it focuses on output measures for each activity and thus allows a manager to understand cost behaviour at a much more detailed level. Activity flexible budgeting is also more accurate because it uses cost formulas that depend on each activity's output measures.

KEY TERMS

Activity-based budgeting system, 577	Direct materials purchases budget, 560	Nonmonetary incentives, 575
Activity flexible budgeting, 578	Dysfunctional behaviour, 575	Operating budgets, 558
Budget committee, 558	Ending finished goods inventory	Overhead budget, 562
Budget director, 558	budget, 563	Participative budgeting, 575
Budgetary slack, 576	Financial budgets, 558	Production budget, 560
Budgets, 556	Flexible budget, 571	Pseudoparticipation, 576
Cash budget, 565	Flexible budget variance, 572	Sales budget, 559
Continuous budget, 558	Goal congruence, 575	Selling and administrative expenses
Control, 557	Incentives, 575	budget, 562
Controllable costs, 576	Master budget, 558	Static budget, 570
Cost of goods sold budget, 563	Monetary incentives, 575	Strategic plan, 556
Direct labour budget, 561	Myopic behaviour, 577	Variable budgets, 572

REVIEW PROBLEMS

1. SELECTED OPERATIONAL BUDGETS

Young Products produces coat racks. The projected sales for the first quarter of the coming year and the beginning and ending inventory data are as follows:

Unit sales	100,000
Unit price	$15
Units in beginning inventory	8,000
Units in targeted ending inventory	12,000

The coat racks are moulded and then painted. Each rack requires 4 kilograms of metal, which costs $2.50 per kilogram. The beginning inventory of raw materials is 4,000 kilograms. Young Products wants to have 6,000 kilograms of metal in inventory at the end of the quarter. Each rack produced requires 30 minutes of direct labour time, which is billed at $9 per hour.

Required:

1. Prepare a sales budget for the first quarter.
2. Prepare a production budget for the first quarter.

3. Prepare a direct materials purchases budget for the first quarter.
4. Prepare a direct labour budget for the first quarter.

Solution

1.
Young Products
Sales Budget
For the First Quarter

Units	100,000
Unit price	× $15
Sales	$1,500,000

2.
Young Products
Production Budget
For the First Quarter

Sales (in units)	100,000
Desired ending inventory	12,000
Total needs	112,000
Less: Beginning inventory	8,000
Units to be produced	104,000

3.
Young Products
Direct Materials Purchases Budget
For the First Quarter

Units to be produced	104,000
Direct materials per unit (kg)	× 4
Production needs (kg)	416,000
Desired ending inventory (kg)	6,000
Total needs (kg)	422,000
Less: Beginning inventory (kg)	4,000
Materials to be purchased (kg)	418,000
Cost per kilogram	× $2.50
Total purchase cost	$1,045,000

4.
Young Products
Direct Labour Budget
For the First Quarter

Units to be produced	104,000
Labour: Hours per unit	× 0.5
Total hours needed	52,000
Cost per hour	× $9
Total direct labour cost	$468,000

2. CASH BUDGETING

Rogier, Inc., expects to receive cash from sales of $45,000 in March. In addition, Rogier expects to sell property worth $3,500. Payments for materials and supplies are expected to total $10,000, direct labour payroll will be $12,500, and other cash expenditures are budgeted at $14,900. On March 1, the cash account balance is $1,230.

Required:

1. Prepare a cash budget for Rogier, Inc., for the month of March.
2. Assume that Rogier, Inc., wanted a minimum cash balance of $15,000 and that it

could borrow from the bank in multiples of $1,000 at an interest rate of 12 percent per year. What would Rogier's adjusted ending balance for March be? How much interest would Rogier owe in April assuming that the entire amount borrowed in March would be paid back?

Solution:

1.

Rogier, Inc.
Cash Budget for the Month of March

Beginning cash balance	$ 1,230
Cash sales	45,000
Sale of property	3,500
Total cash available	$49,730
Less disbursements:	
Materials and supplies	$10,000
Direct labour payroll	12,500
Other expenditures	14,900
Total disbursements	$37,400
Ending cash balance	$12,330

2.

Unadjusted ending balance	$12,330
Plus borrowing	3,000
Adjusted ending balance	$15,330

In April, interest owed would be (1/12 × 0.12 × $3,000) = $30.

QUESTIONS FOR WRITING AND DISCUSSION

1. Define the term *budget*. How are budgets used in planning?

2. Define *control*. How are budgets used to control?

3. Explain how both small and large organizations can benefit from budgeting.

4. Discuss some of the reasons for budgeting.

5. What is a master budget? an operating budget? a financial budget?

6. Explain the role of a sales forecast in budgeting. What is the difference between a sales forecast and a sales budget?

7. All budgets depend on the sales budget. Is this true? Explain.

8. How do master budgets differ among manufacturing, merchandising, and service organizations?

9. Discuss the differences between static and flexible budgets. Why are flexible budgets superior to static budgets for performance reporting?

10. Explain why mixed costs must be broken down into their fixed and variable components before a flexible budget can be developed.

11. Why is goal congruence important?

12. Why is it important for a manager to receive frequent feedback on his or her performance?

13. Discuss the roles of monetary and nonmonetary incentives. Do you believe that nonmonetary incentives are needed? Why or why not?

14. What is participative budgeting? Discuss some of its advantages.

15. A budget too easily achieved will lead to diminished performance. Do you agree? Explain.

16. What is the role of top management in participative budgeting?

17. Explain why a manager has an incentive to build slack into the budget.

18. Explain how a manager can "milk the firm" to improve budgetary performance.

19. Identify performance measures other than budgets that can be used to discourage myopic behaviour. Discuss how you would use these measures.

20. How important are the behavioural aspects of a budgetary control system? Explain.

21. In an era of budgetary cuts, across-the-board cuts harm good programs more than bad programs.

Do you agree? What approach would you recommend? Why?

22. Explain how an activity-based budget is prepared.

23. What is the difference between an activity flexible budget and a functional-based (traditional) flexible budget?

EXERCISES

13–1

Sales Budget

LO1, LO2

Benson Sporting Goods sells a variety of sporting goods and clothing, including custom screen-printed T-shirts. Benson produces one of the T-shirts for a popular singing group. (The group goes on tour and sells various T-shirts and merchandise imprinted with its name and the name of the tour.) In the coming summer, the group plans an 18–city tour and will require screen-printed T-shirts in the following quantities:

June	40,000
July	30,000
August	20,000

Benson sells each shirt for $23.50.

Required:

1. Prepare a sales budget for June, July, and August.
2. How will Benson use this sales budget?

13–2

Production Budget

LO2

Refer to Exercise 13–1. To meet its sales commitment for the T-shirts, Benson plans to begin production during the last half of May. At that time, there will be no T-shirts in beginning inventory. Benson requires that ending inventory for one month be equal to 50 percent of sales for the next month (this requirement was met on June 1). But, desired ending inventory for August is zero, since once the concerts are over, demand for the T-shirts will be minimal.

Required:

Prepare a production budget for May, June, July, and August. Show the number of units that should be produced each month as well as for the four-month period in total.

13–3

Direct Materials Purchases Budget

LO2

Refer to 13–2. Suppose that each T-shirt requires, on average, 40 grams of a special ink that costs $0.03 per gram. The ending inventory policy for ink is that there must be a sufficient amount on hand to meet 20 percent of the next month's production requirement. The ending inventory of ink for August is zero. The beginning inventory of ink May 1 is 85 kilograms.

Required:

Prepare a direct materials purchases budget for May, June, July, and August.

13–4

Production Budget

LO2

Spreadsheet

Carson, Inc., produces office supplies, including pencils. Pencils are bundled in packages of four and sold for $0.50. The sales budget for the first four months of the year follows for this product.

	Unit Sales	Dollar Sales
January	200,000	$100,000
February	240,000	120,000
March	220,000	110,000
April	200,000	100,000

Company policy requires that ending inventories for each month be 15 percent of next month's sales. However, at the beginning of January, due to greater sales in December than anticipated, the beginning inventory of pencils is only 18,000 packages.

Required:

Prepare a production budget for the first quarter of the year. Show the number of units that should be produced each month as well as for the quarter in total.

13–5

Direct Materials Purchases Budget

LO2

Lester Company produces a variety of labels, including iron-on name labels that are sold to parents of camp-bound children. (The camps require campers to have their name on every article of clothing.) The labels are sold in a roll of 1,000, which requires about 25 metres of paper strip. Each metre of paper strip costs $0.17. Lester has budgeted production of the label rolls for the next four months as follows:

	Units
March	5,000
April	25,000
May	35,000
June	6,000

Inventory policy requires that sufficient paper strip be in ending monthly inventory to satisfy 20 percent of the following month's production needs. Inventory of paper strip at the beginning of March equals exactly the amount needed to satisfy the inventory policy.

Required:

Prepare a direct materials purchases budget for March, April, and May showing purchases in units and in dollars for each month and in total.

13–6

Direct Labour Budget

LO2

Refer to the production budget in 13–5. Each roll of labels produced requires (on average) 0.03 direct labour hours. The average cost of direct labour is $8 per hour.

Required:

Prepare a direct labour budget for March, April, and May showing the hours needed and the direct labour cost for each month and in total.

13–7

Sales Budget

LO2

Garland, Inc., manufactures six models of moulded plastic waste containers. Garland's budgeting team is finalizing the sales budget for the coming year. Sales in units and dollars for last year follow:

Model	Number Sold	Price	Revenue
W–1	16,800	$ 9	$151,200
W–2	18,000	15	270,000
W–3	25,200	13	327,600
W–4	16,200	10	162,000
W–5	2,400	22	52,800
W–6	1,000	26	26,000
Total			$989,600

In looking over the previous year's sales figures, Garland's sales budgeting team recalled the following:

a. Model W–1's costs were rising faster than its price could rise. Preparatory to phasing out this model, Garland, Inc., planned to slash advertising for this model and raise its price by 50 percent. The number of units of Model W–1 to be sold were forecast at 20 percent of the previous year's units.

b. Models W–5 and W–6 were introduced on November 1 last year. They are brightly coloured, heavy-duty wheeled garbage containers designed for household use. Garland estimates that demand for both models will continue at the previous year's rate.

c. A competitor has announced plans to introduce an improved version of Model W–3. Garland believes that the Model W–3 price must be cut 20 percent to maintain unit sales at the previous year's level.

586 Chapter Thirteen Budgeting for Planning and Control

d. It was assumed that unit sales of all other models would increase by 10 percent, prices remaining constant.

Required:

Prepare a sales budget by product and in total for Garland, Inc., for the coming year.

13–8

Production Budget; Direct Materials Purchases Budget

LO2

Spreadsheet

Jenna Mitchell, owner of Jenna's Jams and Jellies, produces homemade-style jellies using fruits indigenous to her local area. Jenna has estimated the following sales of 500-gram jars of fruit jelly for the rest of the year and January of next year.

September	100
October	150
November	170
December	225
January	100

Jenna likes to have 20 percent of the next month's sales needs on hand at the end of each month. This requirement was met on August 31.

Materials needed for each jar of fruit jelly are as follows:

Fruit	0.5 kilograms
Sugar	0.5 kilograms
Pectin	100 grams
Jar sets	1

The materials inventory policy is to have 5 percent of the next month's fruit needs on hand as well as 50 percent of the next month's production needs for all other materials. (The relatively low inventory amount for fruit is designed to prevent spoilage.) Materials inventory on September 1 met this company policy.

Required:

1. Prepare a production budget for September, October, November, and December for fruit jelly.
2. Prepare a direct materials purchases budget for all materials used in the production of fruit jelly for the months of September, October, and November. (Round all answers to the nearest whole unit.)
3. Why can't you prepare a direct materials purchases budget for December?

13–9

Direct Materials Purchases Budget; Budgeted Income Statement

LO2

The following data relate to the operation of David Company Ltd., a retail store:

Sales Forecast 2002	
April	$ 70,000
May	60,000
June	80,000
July	100,000
August	120,000

a. Cost of sales averages 40 percent of sales. Other variable costs are 20 percent of sales.
b. Inventory is maintained at twice the budgeted sales requirements for the following month.
c. Fixed costs are $20,000 per month.
d. The income tax rate is estimated to be 40 percent.

Required:

1. Prepare a direct materials purchases budget in dollars for June 2002.
2. Prepare a budgeted income statement for June 2002. (CGA Canada adapted)

13–10

Cash Receipts Budget

LO2

Andrea's Shop sells china, silverware, and kitchenware. A popular feature is her wedding registry service, which includes free gift wrapping and delivery of gifts to local brides. Andrea accepts cash, cheques, and Visa, MasterCard, and American Express charges. These methods of payment have the following characteristics:

Cash	Payment is immediate; no fee is charged.
Cheque	Payment is immediate; the bank charges $0.25 per cheque; 1 percent of cheque revenue is from "bad" cheques that Andrea cannot collect.
Visa/MasterCard	Andrea accumulates these credit card receipts throughout the month and submits them in one bundle for payment on the last day of the month. The money is credited to Andrea's account by the fifth day of the following month. A fee of 1.5 percent is charged by the credit card company.
American Express	Andrea accumulates these receipts throughout the month and mails them in for payment on the last day of the month. American Express credits Andrea's account by the sixth day of the following month. A fee of 3.5 percent is charged by American Express.

During a typical month, Andrea has sales of $24,000, broken down as follows:

American Express	20%
VISA/MasterCard	50%
Cheque	5% (checks average $37.50 each)
Cash	25%

Required:

If Andrea estimates sales of $30,000 in April and $60,000 in May, what are her planned net cash receipts for May?

13–11

Cash Budget

LO2

Spreadsheet

The owner of a small mining supply company has requested a cash budget for June. After examining the company's records, you find the following:

a. Cash balance on June 1 is $345.
b. Actual sales for April and May are as follows:

	April	May
Cash sales	$10,000	$15,000
Credit sales	25,000	35,000
Total sales	$35,000	$50,000

c. Credit sales are collected over a three-month period: 50 percent in the month of sale, 30 percent in the second month, and 15 percent in the third month. The sales collected in the third month are subject to a 1.5 percent late fee, but only half of the affected customers pay the late fee, and the firm's owner does not think that it is worth his while to try to collect from the other half. The remaining sales are uncollectible.
d. Inventory purchases average 60 percent of a month's total sales. Of those purchases, 40 percent are paid for in the month of purchase. The remaining 60 percent are paid for in the following month.
e. Salaries and wages total $8,700 a month, including a $4,500 salary paid to the owner.
f. Rent is $1,200 per month.
g. Taxes to be paid in June are $5,500.

The owner also tells you that he expects cash sales of $20,000 and credit sales of $40,000 for June. There is no minimum cash balance required. The company's owner does not have access to short-term loans.

Required:

1. Prepare a cash budget for June. Include supporting schedules for cash collections and cash payments.
2. Did the business show a negative cash balance for June? Assuming that the owner has no hope of establishing a line of credit for the business, what recommendations would you give the owner for dealing with a negative cash balance?

13–12

Overhead Budget; Functional-Based Flexible Budget

LO2, LO3

Lyman, Inc., manufactures machine parts in its Blackwell plant. Lyman has developed the following flexible budget for overhead for the coming year. Activity level is measured in direct labour hours.

		Activity Level (hours)		
	Variable-Cost Formula	20,000	30,000	40,000
Variable costs:				
Maintenance	$1.00	$ 20,000	$ 30,000	$ 40,000
Supplies	0.50	10,000	15,000	20,000
Power	0.10	2,000	3,000	4,000
Total variable costs	$1.60	$ 32,000	$ 48,000	$ 64,000
Fixed costs:				
Depreciation		$ 7,200	$ 7,200	$ 7,200
Salaries		64,800	64,800	64,800
Total fixed costs		$ 72,000	$ 72,000	$ 72,000
Total overhead costs		$104,000	$120,000	$136,000

The Blackwell plant produces two different types of parts. The production budget for October is 48,000 units for Part 301 and 18,000 units for Part 414. Part 301 requires 15 minutes of direct labour time, and Part 414 requires 20 minutes. Fixed overhead costs are incurred uniformly throughout the year.

Required:

Prepare an overhead budget for October.

13–13

Activity-Based Budgeting: Static and Flexible

LO4

Jamison, Inc., uses three forklifts to move materials from Receiving to Stores. The forklifts are also used to move materials from Stores to the production area. The forklifts are obtained through an operating lease that costs $8,000 per year per forklift. Jamison employs 10 forklift operators, who receive an average salary of $40,000 per year, including benefits. Each move requires the use of a crate. The crates are used to store the parts and are emptied only when the parts are used in production. Crates are disposed of after one cycle (two moves), where a cycle is defined as Receiving to Stores to Production. Each crate costs $2. Fuel for a forklift costs $1.20 per litre. A litre of gas is used every 20 moves. Forklifts can make three moves per hour and are available for 280 days per year, 24 hours per day (the remaining time is downtime for various reasons). Each operator works 40 hours per week and 50 weeks per year.

Required:

1. Prepare an annual budget for the activity of moving materials, assuming that all of the capacity of the activity is used. Identify which resources you would treat as fixed costs and which would be viewed as variable costs.
2. Assume that Jamison uses only 90 percent of the activity capacity. What is the budget for this level of activity?
3. Suppose that a redesign of the plant layout reduces the demand for moving materials by 75 percent. What would be the budget for this new activity level?

13–14

Overhead Budget; Flexible Budget

LO2, LO3

Regina Johnson, controller for Pet-Care Company, has been instructed to develop a flexible budget for overhead costs. The company produces two types of dog food. One, BasicDiet, is a standard mixture for healthy dogs. The second, SpecDiet, is a reduced-protein formulation for older dogs with health problems. The two dog foods use common raw materials in different proportions. The company expects to produce 100,000 twenty-kilogram bags of each product during the coming year. BasicDiet requires 0.25 direct labour hours per bag, and SpecDiet requires 0.30. Regina has developed the following fixed and variable costs for each of the four overhead items:

Overhead Item	Fixed Cost	Variable Rate per DLH
Maintenance	$17,000	$0.40
Power		0.50
Indirect labour	26,500	1.60
Rent	18,000	

Required:

1. Prepare an overhead budget for the expected activity level for the coming year.
2. Prepare an overhead budget that reflects production that is 10 percent higher than expected (for both products), and another one for production that is 20 percent lower than expected.

13–15

Performance Report

LO3

Refer to the information given in Exercise 13–14. Assume that Pet-Care actually produced 120,000 bags of BasicDiet and 100,000 of SpecDiet. The actual overhead costs incurred were as follows:

Maintenance	$ 40,500
Power	31,700
Indirect labour	119,000
Rent	18,000

Required:

1. Prepare a performance report for the period.
2. Based on the report, would you judge any of the variances to be significant? Can you think of some possible reasons for the variances?

13–16

Budgeted Cash Collections; Budgeted Cash Payments

LO2

Information pertaining to Noskey Corporation's sales revenue follows:

	November 2001 (Actual)	December 2001 (Actual)	January 2002 (Budgeted)
Cash sales	$ 80,000	$100,000	$ 60,000
Credit sales	240,000	360,000	180,000
Total sales	$320,000	$460,000	$240,000

Management estimates that 5 percent of credit sales are uncollectible. Of the credit sales that are collectible, 60 percent are collected in the month of sale and the remainder in the month following the sale. Purchases of inventory each month are 70 percent of the next month's projected total sales. All purchases of inventory are on account; 25 percent are paid in the month of purchase, and the remainder are paid in the month following the purchase.

Required:

1. What are Noskey's budgeted cash collections in December 2001 from November 2001 credit sales?
2. What are total budgeted cash receipts in January 2002?
3. What is Noskey budgeting for total cash payments in December 2001 for inventory purchases? (US CMA adapted)

13–17

Participative versus Imposed Budgeting

LO3

An effective budget converts an organization's goals and objectives into data. The budget serves as a blueprint for management's plans. The budget is also the basis for control. Management performance can be evaluated by comparing actual results with the budget.

Thus, creating the budget is essential for the successful operation of an organization. Finding the resources to implement the budget—that is, getting from the starting point to the ultimate goal—requires the extensive use of human resources. How managers perceive their roles in the budgeting process is important to the successful use of the budget as an effective tool for planning, communicating, and controlling.

Required:

1. Discuss the behavioural implications of planning and control when a company's management employs:
   a. An imposed budgetary approach.
   b. A participative budgetary approach.
2. Communications plays an important role in the budgetary process whether a participative or an imposed budgetary approach is used.
   a. Discuss the differences between communication flows in these two budgetary approaches.
   b. Discuss the behavioural implications associated with the communication process for each of the budgetary approaches. (US CMA adapted)

13–18

Flexible Budgeting

LO3

Budgeted overhead costs for two different levels of activity follow.

	Direct Labour Hours	
	1,000	**2,000**
Maintenance	$10,000	$16,000
Depreciation	5,000	5,000
Supervision	15,000	15,000
Supplies	1,400	2,800
Power	750	1,500
Other	8,100	8,200

Required:

Prepare a flexible budget for an activity level of 1,650 direct labour hours.

13–19

Cash Receipts Budget

LO2

Kendall Law Firm has found from past experience that 30 percent of its services are for cash. The remaining 70 percent are on credit. An aging schedule for accounts receivable reveals the following pattern:

- Ten percent of fees on credit are paid in the month service is rendered.
- Seventy percent of fees on credit are paid in the month following legal service.
- Seventeen percent of fees on credit are paid in the second month following the legal service.
- Three percent of fees on credit are never collected.

Fees on credit that have not been paid until the second month following performance of the legal service are considered overdue and are subject to a 2 percent late charge. Kendall has developed the following forecast of fees:

May	$228,000
June	255,000
July	204,000
August	240,000
September	300,000

Required:

Prepare a schedule of cash receipts for August and September.

13–20

Cash Payments Schedule

LO2

Barrett's Department Store purchases a wide variety of merchandise. Purchases are made evenly throughout the month and all are on account. On the first of every month, the firm's accounts payable clerk pays for all of the previous month's purchases. Terms are 2/10, n/30 (that is, a 2 percent discount can be taken if the bill is paid within 10 days; otherwise, the entire amount is due within 30 days).

The forecast purchases for the months of May through September are as follows:

May	$40,000
June	50,000
July	42,000
August	60,000
September	66,000

Required:

1. Prepare a cash payments (disbursements) schedule for inventory for the months of August and September.
2. Now suppose that the store manager wants to see what difference it would make to have the accounts payable clerk pay for any purchases that have been made three times per month, on the 1st, the 11th, and the 21st. Prepare a cash payments schedule for the months of August and September assuming this new payment schedule.
3. Suppose that Barrett's accounts payable clerk does not have time to make payments on two extra days per month and that a temporary employee is hired on the 11th and 21st at $22 per hour, for four hours on each of those two days. Is this a good decision? Explain.

13–21

Static and Flexible Profit Budgets

LO3

MBA Ltd. had the following two alternative budgets prepared at two different volume levels. The company eventually adopted the higher budget for 2001. The actual performance for 2001 is also shown. MBA Ltd. uses variable costing.

	Low-Volume Budget	High-Volume Budget	Actual
Sales (units)	18,000	20,000	19,200
Sales revenue	$1,800,000	$2,000,000	$1,950,000
Expenses	$1,504,000	$1,600,000	$1,596,000
Net Income	$ 296,000	$ 400,000	$ 354,000

1. Using the high–low method, determine the flexible budget formula.
2. Determine the reasons for not attaining the $400,000 budgeted income, and quantify the effects of each of these factors.
3. Identify the major assumptions that are necessary to make your answers in Requirements 1 and 2 valid.

PROBLEMS

13–22

Operating Budget; Comprehensive Analysis

LO2

Woodruff Manufacturing produces a subassembly used in the production of jet aircraft engines. The assembly is sold to engine manufacturers and to aircraft maintenance facilities. Projected sales for the coming four months follow:

January	40,000
February	50,000
March	60,000
April	60,000

The following data pertain to production policies and manufacturing specifications followed by Woodruff Manufacturing:

a. Finished goods inventory on January 1 is 32,000 units, each costing $148.71. The desired ending inventory for each month is 80 percent of the next month's sales.

b.   The data on materials used are as follows:

Direct Materials	Per-Unit Usage	Unit Cost
Metal	10 kilograms	$8
Components	6	2

Inventory policy dictates that sufficient materials be on hand at the beginning of the month to produce 50 percent of that month's estimated sales. This is exactly the amount of material on hand on January 1.

c.   The direct labour used per unit of output is four hours. The average direct labour cost per hour is $9.25.

d.   Overhead each month is estimated using a flexible budget formula. (Activity is measured in direct labour hours.)

	Fixed-Cost Component	Variable-Cost Component
Supplies	—	$1.00
Power	—	0.50
Maintenance	$ 30,000	0.40
Supervision	16,000	—
Depreciation	200,000	—
Taxes	12,000	—
Other	80,000	1.50

e.   Monthly selling and administrative expenses are also estimated using a flexible budgeting formula. (Activity is measured in units sold.)

	Fixed Costs	Variable Costs
Salaries	$50,000	—
Commissions	—	$2.00
Depreciation	40,000	—
Shipping	—	1.00
Other	20,000	0.60

f.   The unit selling price of the subassembly is $180.

g.   All sales and purchases are for cash. The cash balance on January 1 equals $400,000. If the firm develops a cash shortage by the end of the month, sufficient cash is borrowed to cover the shortage. Any cash borrowed is repaid at the end of the quarter, as is the interest due (cash borrowed at the end of the quarter is repaid at the end of the following quarter). The interest rate is 12 percent per annum. There is no money owed at the beginning of January.

Required:

Prepare a monthly operating budget for the first quarter with the following schedules:

1. Sales budget
2. Production budget
3. Direct materials purchases budget
4. Direct labour budget
5. Overhead budget
6. Selling and administrative expenses budget
7. Ending finished goods inventory budget
8. Cost of goods sold budget
9. Budgeted income statement
10. Cash budget

13–23

Cash Budget; Pro Forma Balance Sheet

LO2

Spreadsheet

Ryan Richards, controller for Grange Retailers, has assembled the following data to assist in the preparation of a cash budget for the third quarter of 2002:

a. Sales:

May (actual)	$100,000
June (actual)	120,000
July (estimated)	90,000
August (estimated)	100,000
September (estimated)	135,000
October (estimated)	110,000

b. Each month, 30 percent of sales are for cash and 70 percent are on credit. The collection pattern for credit sales is 20 percent in the month of sale, 50 percent in the following month, and 30 percent in the second month following the sale.

c. Each month, the ending inventory exactly equals 50 percent of the cost of next month's sales. The markup on goods is 25 percent of cost.

d. Inventory purchases are paid for in the month following the purchase.

e. Recurring monthly expenses are as follows:

Salaries and wages	$10,000
Depreciation on plant and equipment	4,000
Utilities	1,000
Other	1,700

f. Property taxes of $15,000 are due and payable on July 15, 2002.

g. Advertising fees of $6,000 must be paid on August 20, 2002.

h. A lease on a new storage facility is scheduled to begin on September 2, 2002. Monthly payments are $5,000.

i. The company has a policy of maintaining a minimum cash balance of $10,000. If necessary, it will borrow to meet its short-term needs. All borrowing is done at the beginning of the month. All payments on principal and interest are made at the end of a month. The annual interest rate is 9 percent. The company must borrow in multiples of $1,000.

j. A partly completed balance sheet as of June 30, 2002, follows. (Accounts payable is for inventory purchases only.)

Cash	$?	
Accounts receivable	?	
Inventory	?	
Plant and equipment	425,000	
Accounts payable		$?
Common stock		210,000
Retained earnings		268,750
Total	$?	$?

Required:

1. Complete the balance sheet given in (j).

2. Prepare a cash budget for each month in the third quarter and for the quarter in total (the third quarter begins on July 1). Provide a supporting schedule of cash collections.

3. Prepare a pro forma balance sheet as of September 30, 2002.

13–24

Cash Budget

LO2

The Mosquito Net Company has the following data.

Part of the trial balance at April 1 showed the following:

	Debits	Credits
Cash	$ 6,000	
Accounts receivable	19,500	
Allowance for bad debts		$2,400
Merchandise inventory	12,000	
Accounts payable (merchandise)		9,000

The company's purchases are payable within 10 days. Assume that one-third of the purchases of any month are due and paid in the following month.

The unit invoice cost of the merchandise purchased is $10. At the end of each month, the company's policy is to have an inventory equal to 50 percent of the following month's unit sales.

Sales terms include a 1 percent discount if payment is made by the end of the calendar month in which the sales took place. Past experience indicates that 60 percent of the billings will be collected during the month of sale, 30 percent in the following month, and 6 percent in the next following month; the remaining 4 percent will be uncollectible.

Sales data are as follows:

Selling price per unit	$ 15
February actual sales revenue	15,000
March actual sales revenue	45,000
April estimated sales revenue	36,000
May estimated sales revenue	27,000
Total sales expected for the year	450,000

The company's fiscal year begins February 1. Exclusive of bad debts, the total budgeted selling and administrative expenses for the year are estimated at $70,500, of which $21,000 is fixed expense (inclusive of a $9,000 annual depreciation charge). These fixed expenses are incurred uniformly throughout the year. The balance of the selling and administrative expenses varies with sales. Expenses are paid as incurred.

Required:

Prepare a cash budget for April. (CGA Canada adapted)

13–25

Cash Budget; Budgeted Income Statement

LO2

The balance sheet of Victoria Company on December 31, 2001, is as follows:

Cash	$ 25,600
Accounts receivable (net of allowance for doubtful accounts of $6,400)	121,600
Inventory	51,200
Fixed assets (net of accumulated depreciation of $192,000)	128,000
Total assets	$326,400
Accounts payable (for inventory purchases)	$264,000
Common shares	40,000
Retained earnings	22,400
Total liabilities and shareholders' equity	$326,400

Projected sales for January are $352,000 and $384,000 for February. The gross profit percentage is 25 percent. Cash collections for accounts receivable are estimated to be 50 percent in the month of sale, and 48 percent in the following month; the remaining 2 percent are uncollectible. Purchases of inventory each month are 75 percent of the next month's projected sales and are paid for in full in the following month. Depreciation is $16,000 per month. Other expenses, amounting to $52,800 per month, are paid in cash in the month incurred.

Required:

Prepare a cash budget and budgeted income statement for January 2002. (CGA Canada adapted)

13–26

Cash Collections; Cash Disbursements

LO2

The following information concerning Laurel Ltd. is available to develop a cash budget and other budget information for the months of July, August, and September 2002.

a. Balances at July 1 are expected to be as follows:

Cash	$5,500
Accounts receivable	437,000
Inventories	309,400
Accounts payable	133,055

b. The budget is based on the following assumptions:
  • Each month's sales are billed on the last day of the month.
  • Customers are allowed a 3 percent discount if payment is made within 10 days after the billing date. Receivables are booked at the gross amount.
  • Sixty percent of the billings are collected within the discount period, 25 percent are collected by the end of the month after the date of sale, 9 percent are collected by the end of the second month after the date of sale, and 6 percent prove uncollectible.
  • Fifty-four percent of all purchases of material and selling and administrative expenses are paid in the month incurred. The remainder is paid in the following month.
  • Each month's units of ending inventory are equal to 130 percent of the next month's sales in units.
  • The cost of each unit of inventory is $20.
  • Selling and administrative expenses, of which $2,000 is depreciation, are equal to $16,000 plus 9 percent of the month's sales.

c. Actual and projected sales are as follows:

	Sales	Units
May	$354,000	11,800
June	363,000	12,100
July	357,000	11,900
August	342,000	11,400
September	360,000	12,000
October	366,000	12,200

Required:

Calculate the following:

1. Budgeted cash disbursements during the month of August 2002.
2. Budgeted cash collections during the month of July 2002.
3. Budgeted number of units of inventory to be purchased during the month of September 2002. (CMA Canada adapted)

13–27

**Cash Budget;
Budgeted Income
Statement**

LO2

The CF Supply Company buys and sells a product line with a current average selling price of $20 per unit. All sales are on account, with a 2 percent discount available to those customers who settle their accounts by the end of the month of purchase. On average, 80 percent of the customers take advantage of this arrangement, 4 percent never pay their account, and the rest remit their payment in the month following the sale. CF's accountant recognizes the estimated bad debts at the end of each month.

Purchases of the product line (at an average cost of $9 per unit) take place evenly throughout the month, with a target of maintaining an end-of-month inventory of 200 units. Purchases are also on account, but are due in 10 days with no discounts available. As a result, two-thirds of the cost of purchases is paid in the month of purchase.

Other information:

1. Rent and utilities amounting to $1,200 are paid on the 20th of each month, and employee salaries of $6,700 are paid on the 28th.
2. Office supplies are purchased in January, April, July, and October for use in each quarter. The quarterly outlays have been $4,200.
3. Office equipment, with an expected five-year life, was purchased at the beginning of 2000. Its net book value is currently $9,350. CF uses straight-line depreciation.
4. Monthly sales in units were as follows:

	Estimated	Actual
December 2001	1,300	1,400
January 2002	1,600	1,400
February 2002	1,200	1,200
March 2002	850	—
April 2002	900	—

It is now March 1, 2000, and you have been asked to prepare estimates for the activities during the coming month. The company's cash balance is $2,350. The company has a good credit rating, so a loan from its bank is possible to obtain.

Required:

1. Prepare a schedule of projected cash receipts and disbursements for March 2002. Will CF have to take out a loan?
2. Prepare a projected income statement for March 2002. (CMA Canada adapted)

13–28

Participative Budgeting; Not-for-Profit Setting

LO3

Scott Weidner, the controller in his province's division of social services, recognizes the importance of the budgetary process for planning, control, and motivation. He believes that a properly implemented process of participative budgeting and management by exception will motivate his subordinates to improve productivity within their particular departments. Based upon this philosophy, Scott has implemented the following budgetary procedures:

1. An appropriation target figure is given to each department manager. This amount represents the maximum funding that each department can expect to receive in the next fiscal year.
2. Department managers develop their individual budgets within the following spending constraints as directed by the controller's staff:
   a. Requests for spending cannot exceed the appropriated target.
   b. All fixed expenditures should be included in the budget. Fixed expenditures include such items as contracts and salaries at current levels.
   c. All government projects directed by higher authority should be included in the budget in their entirety.
3. The controller's staff consolidates the requests from the various departments into one budget for the entire division.
4. Upon final budget approval by the legislature, the controller's staff allocates the appropriation to the various departments on instructions from the division manager. However, a specified percentage of each department's appropriation is held back in anticipation of potential budget cuts and special funding needs. The amount and use of this contingency fund is left to the discretion of the division manager.
5. Each department is allowed to adjust its budget when necessary to operate within the reduced appropriation level. However, as stated in the original directive, specific projects authorized by higher authority must remain intact.
6. The final budget is used as the basis of control for a management-by-exception form of reporting. Excessive expenditures by account for each department are highlighted on a monthly basis. Department managers are expected to account for all expenditures over budget. Fiscal responsibility is an important factor in the overall performance evaluation of department managers. Scott believes that his policy of allowing the department managers to participate in the budget process and then holding them accountable for the final budget is essential, especially in times of limited resources. He further believes that the department managers will be motivated to increase the efficiency and effectiveness of their departments because they have provided input into the initial budgetary process and are required to justify any unfavourable performances.

Required:

1. Discuss the advantages and limitations of participative budgeting.

2. Identify deficiencies in Scott Weidner's outline for a budgetary process. Recommend how each deficiency identified can be corrected. (US CMA adapted)

13-29

Cash Budget

LO2

The controller of Manoba Company is gathering data to prepare the cash budget for July 2002. She plans to develop the budget from the following information:

a. Of all sales, 30 percent are cash sales.
b. Of credit sales, 60 percent are collected within the month of sale. Half of the credit sales collected within the month receive a 2 percent cash discount (for accounts paid within 10 days). Twenty percent of credit sales are collected in the following month; remaining credit sales are collected the month thereafter. There are virtually no bad debts.
c. Sales for the second two quarters of the year follow. (The first three months are actual sales, and the last three months are estimated sales.)

Sales	
April	$ 460,000
May	600,000
June	1,000,000
July	1,140,000
August	1,200,000
September	1,134,000

d. The company sells all that it produces each month. The cost of raw materials equals 24 percent of each sales dollar. The company requires a monthly ending inventory equal to the coming month's production requirements. Of raw materials purchases, 50 percent are paid for in the month of purchase. The remaining 50 percent is paid for in the following month.
e. Wages total $110,000 each month and are paid in the month incurred.
f. Budgeted monthly operating expenses total $336,000, of which $50,000 is depreciation and $6,000 is expiration of prepaid insurance (the annual premium of $72,000 is paid on January 1).
g. Dividends of $140,000, declared on June 30, will be paid on July 15.
h. Old equipment will be sold for $25,200 on July 4.
i. On July 13, new equipment will be purchased for $168,000.
j. The company maintains a minimum cash balance of $20,000.
k. The cash balance on July 1 is $27,000.

Required:

Prepare a cash budget for July. Give a supporting schedule that details the cash collections from sales.

13-30

Revision of Operating Budget; Pro Forma Statements of Income and Cost of Goods Sold

LO2

Mary Dalid founded Molid Company three years ago. The company produces a modem for use with minicomputers and microcomputers. Business has expanded rapidly since the company's inception. Bob Wells, the company's general accountant, prepared a budget for the fiscal year ending August 31, 2002. The budget was based on the prior year's sales and production activity, because Mary believed that the sales growth experienced during the prior year would not continue at the same pace. The pro forma statements of income and cost of goods sold that were prepared as part of the budgetary process follow:

Molid Company
Pro Forma Statement of Income (in thousands)
For the Year Ending August 31, 2002

Net sales	$ 31,248
Less: Cost of goods sold	20,765
Gross margin	$ 10,483
Less: Operating expenses	5,400
Income before taxes	$ 5,083

Molid Company
Pro Forma Statement of Cost of Goods Sold (in thousands)
For the Year Ending August 31, 2002

Direct materials:		
Materials inventory, September 1, 2001	$ 1,360	
Materials purchased	14,476	
Available for use	15,836	
Less: Materials inventory, August 31, 2002	1,628	
Direct materials used		$14,208
Direct labour		1,134
Overhead:		
Indirect materials	$1,421	
General	3,240	4,661
Cost of goods manufactured		$20,003
Finished goods, September 1, 2001		1,169
Total goods available		$21,172
Less: Finished goods, August 31, 2002		407
Cost of goods sold		$20,765

On December 10, 2001, Mary and Bob met to discuss the first-quarter operating results. Bob believed that several changes should be made to the budget assumptions that had been used to prepare the pro forma statements. He prepared the following notes summarizing the changes, which had not become known until the first quarter results were compiled. He submitted the following data to Mary:

a. Actual first-quarter production was 35,000 units. The estimated production for the fiscal year should be increased from 162,000 to 170,000, with the balance of production being scheduled in equal segments over the last nine months of the fiscal year.

b. The planned ending inventory for finished goods of 3,300 units at the end of the fiscal year remains unchanged. The finished goods inventory of 9,300 units as of September 1, 2001, had dropped to 9,000 units by November 30, 2002. The finished goods inventory at the end of the fiscal year will be valued at the average manufacturing costs for the year.

c. Direct materials sufficient to produce 16,000 units were on hand at the beginning of the fiscal year. The plan to have the equivalent of 18,500 units of production in direct materials inventory at the end of the fiscal year remains unchanged. Direct materials inventory is valued on a LIFO basis. Direct materials equivalent to 37,500 units of output were purchased for $3.3 million during the first quarter of the fiscal year. Molid's suppliers have informed the company that direct materials prices will increase 5 percent on March 1, 2002. Direct materials needed for the rest of the fiscal year will be purchased evenly through the last nine months.

d. On the basis of historical data, indirect materials cost is projected at 10 percent of the cost of direct materials consumed.

e. Half of general factory overhead, and all selling and general and administrative expenses, are considered fixed.

Required:

Based on the revised data presented by Bob Wells, prepare new pro forma statements for income and cost of goods sold for the year ending August 31, 2002.
(US CMA adapted)

13–31

**Performance
Reporting; Behavioural
Considerations**

LO1, LO3

Berwin, Inc., is a manufacturer of small industrial tools with annual sales of approximately $3.5 million. Sales growth has been steady during the year, and there is no evidence of cyclical demand. Production has increased gradually during the year and has been evenly distributed throughout each month. The company has a sequential processing system. The four manufacturing departments—casting, machining, finishing, and packaging—are all located in the same building. Fixed overhead is assigned using a plantwide rate.

Berwin has always been able to compete with other manufacturers of small tools. However, its market has expanded only in response to product innovation. Thus, research and development is very important and has helped Berwin to expand as well as maintain demand.

Carla Viller, Berwin's controller, has designed and implemented a new budget system in response to concerns voiced by George Berwin, the firm's president. Carla prepared an annual budget that has been divided into 12 equal segments; this budget can be used to assist in the timely evaluation of monthly performance. George was visibly upset upon receiving the May performance report for the machining department. He exclaimed, "How can they be efficient enough to produce nine extra units every working day and still miss the budget by $300 per day?" Gene Jordan, supervisor of the machining department, could not understand "all the red ink" when he knew that the department had operated more efficiently in May than it had in months. Gene stated, "I was expecting a pat on the back, and instead the boss tore me apart. What's more, I don't even know why!"

Berwin, Inc.
Machining Department Performance Report
For the Month Ended May 31, 2001

	Budgeted	Actual	Variance
Volume in units	3,000	3,185	185 F
Variable manufacturing costs:			
Direct materials	$24,000	$ 24,843	$ 843 U
Direct labour	27,750	29,302	1,552 U
Variable overhead	33,300	35,035	1,735 U
Total variable costs	$85,050	$ 89,180	$4,130 U
Fixed manufacturing costs:			
Indirect labour	$ 3,300	$ 3,334	$ 34 U
Depreciation	1,500	1,500	—
Taxes	300	300	—
Insurance	240	240	—
Other	930	1,027	97 U
Total fixed costs	$ 6,270	$ 6,401	$ 131 U
Corporate costs:			
Research and development	$ 2,400	$ 3,728	$1,328 U
Selling and administrative	3,600	4,075	475 U
Total corporate costs	$ 6,000	$ 7,803	$1,803 U
Total costs	$97,320	$103,384	$6,064 U

Required:

1. Review the May performance report. Use the information given in the report and elsewhere.
   a. Discuss the strengths and weaknesses of the new budgetary system.
   b. Identify the weaknesses of the performance report, and explain how it should be revised to eliminate each weakness.
2. Prepare a revised report for the machining department using the May data.
3. What other changes would you make to improve Berwin's budgetary system? (US CMA adapted)

13–32

Functional versus Flexible Budgeting

LO3, LO4

Amy Bunker, a production manager, was upset with the latest performance report, which indicated that she was $100,000 over budget. Given the efforts that she and her workers had made, she was confident that they had met or beat the budget. Now she was not only upset but also genuinely puzzled over the results. Three items—direct labour, power, and setups—were over budget. The actual costs for these three items follow:

Direct labour	$210,000
Power	135,000
Setups	140,000
Total	$485,000

Amy knew that her operation had produced more units than originally had been budgeted, so that more power and labour had naturally been used. She also knew that the uncertainty in scheduling had led to more setups than planned. When she pointed this out to Gary Grant, the firm's controller, he assured her that the budgeted costs had been adjusted for the increase in productive activity. Curious, Amy questioned Gary about the methods used to make the adjustment."

Gary: "If the actual level of activity differs from the original planned level, we adjust the budget by using budget formulas—formulas that allow us to predict the costs for different levels of activity."

Amy: "The approach sounds reasonable. However, I'm sure something is wrong here. Tell me exactly how you adjusted the costs of direct labour, power, and setups."

Gary: "First, we obtain formulas for the individual items in the budget by using the method of least squares. We assume that cost variations can be explained by variations in productive activity, where activity is measured by direct labour hours. Here is a list of the cost formulas for the three items you mentioned. The variable X is the number of direct labour hours."

$$\text{Direct labour cost} = \$10X$$
$$\text{Power cost} = \$5,000 + \$4X$$
$$\text{Setup cost} = \$100,000$$

Amy: "I think I see the problem. Power costs don't have a lot to do with direct labour hours. They have more to do with machine hours. As production increases, machine hours increase more rapidly than direct labour hours do. Also, …"

Gary: "You know, you have a point. The coefficient of determination for power cost is only about 50 percent. That leaves a lot of unexplained cost variation. The coefficient for labour, however, is much better—it explains about 96 percent of the cost variation. Setup costs, of course, are fixed."

Amy: "Well, as I was about to say, setup costs also have very little to do with direct labour hours. And I might add that they are certainly not fixed—at least not all of them. Because of the scheduling changes, we had to do more setups than our original plan called for. And we have to pay our people when they work extra hours. It seems like we are always paying overtime. I wonder if we simply do not have enough people for the setup activity. Also, there are supplies that are used for each setup, and these are not cheap. Did you build these extra costs of increased setup activity into your budget?"

Gary: "No, we assumed that setup costs were fixed. I see now that some of them could vary as the number of setups increases. Amy, let me see if I can develop some cost formulas based on better explanatory variables. I'll get back to you in a few days."

Assume that after a few days' work, Gary developed the following cost formulas, all with a coefficient of determination greater than 90 percent:

$$\text{Direct labour cost} = \$10X, \text{ where } X = \text{Direct labour hours}$$
$$\text{Power cost} = \$68,000 + 0.9Y, \text{ where } Y = \text{Machine hours}$$
$$\text{Setup cost} = \$98,000 + \$400Z, \text{ where } Z = \text{Number of setups}$$

The actual measures of each of the activity drivers are as follows:

Direct labour hours	20,000
Machine hours	90,000
Number of setups	110

Required:

1. Prepare a performance report for direct labour, power, and setups using the direct-labour-based formulas.
2. Prepare a performance report for direct labour, power, and setups using the multiple-cost-driver formulas that Gary developed.
3. Of the two approaches, which provides the more accurate picture of Amy's performance? Why?

13–33

Activity Flexible Budgeting

LO4

Billy Adams, controller for Westcott, Inc., prepared the following budget for manufacturing costs at two different levels of activity for 2002:

DIRECT LABOUR HOURS

	Level of Activity	
	50,000	100,000
Direct materials	$ 300,000	$ 600,000
Direct labour	200,000	400,000
Depreciation (plant)	100,000	100,000
Subtotal	$ 600,000	$1,100,000

MACHINE HOURS

	Level of Activity	
	200,000	300,000
Maintaining equipment	$ 360,000	$ 510,000
Machining	112,000	162,000
Subtotal	$ 472,000	$ 672,000

MATERIAL MOVES

	Level of Activity	
	20,000	40,000
Materials handling	$ 165,000	$ 290,000

NUMBER OF BATCHES INSPECTED

	Level of Activity	
	100	200
Inspecting products	$ 125,000	$ 225,000
Total	$1,362,000	$2,287,000

During 2002, Westcott worked a total of 80,000 direct labour hours, used 250,000 machine hours, made 32,000 moves, and performed 120 batch inspections. The following actual costs were incurred:

Direct materials	$440,000
Direct labour	355,000
Depreciation	100,000
Maintenance	425,000
Machining	142,000
Materials handling	232,500
Inspecting products	160,000

Westcott applies overhead using rates based on direct labour hours, machine hours, number of moves, and number of batches. The second level of activity (the far-right column in the preceding table) is the practical level of activity (the available activity for resources acquired in advance of usage) and is used to compute predetermined overhead pool rates.

Required:

1. Prepare a performance report for Westcott's manufacturing costs in 2002.
2. Assume that one of the products produced by Westcott is budgeted to use 10,000 direct labour hours, 15,000 machine hours, and 500 moves and will be produced in five batches. A total of 10,000 units will be produced during the year. Calculate the budgeted unit manufacturing cost.
3. One of Westcott's managers said the following: "Budgeting at the activity level makes a lot of sense. It really helps us manage costs better. But the above budget really needs to provide more detailed information. For example, I know that the materials-handling activity involves the usage of forklifts and operators, and this information is lost with simply reporting the total cost of the activity for various levels of output. We have four forklifts, each capable of providing 10,000 moves per year. We lease these forklifts for five years, at $10,000 per year. Furthermore, for our two shifts, we need up to eight operators if we run all four forklifts. Each operator is paid a salary of $30,000 per year. Also, I know that fuel costs us about $0.25 per move."

   Based on these comments, explain how this additional information may help Wescott better manage its costs. Also, assuming that these are the only three items, expand the detail of the flexible budget for materials handling to reveal the cost of these three resource items for 20,000 moves and 40,000 moves, respectively. You may wish to review the concepts of flexible, committed, and discretionary resources found in Chapter 3.

13–34

Master Budget; Comprehensive Review

LO2

Optima Company is a high-technology organization that produces a mass-storage system. The design of Optima's system is unique and represents a breakthrough in the industry. The units Optima produces combine the positive features of both floppy and hard disks. The company is completing its fifth year of operations and is preparing to build its master budget for the coming year (2002). The budget will detail each quarter's activity and the activity for the year in total. The master budget will be based on the following information:

a. Fourth-quarter sales for 2001 are 55,000 units.
b. Unit sales by quarter (for 2002) are projected as follows:

First quarter	65,000
Second quarter	70,000
Third quarter	75,000
Fourth quarter	90,000

The selling price is $400 per unit. All sales are credit sales. Optima collects 85 percent of all sales within the quarter in which they are realized; the other 15 percent are collected in the following quarter. There are no bad debts.

c. There is no beginning inventory of finished goods. Optima is planning the following ending finished goods inventories for each quarter:

First quarter	13,000 units
Second quarter	15,000 units
Third quarter	20,000 units
Fourth quarter	10,000 units

d. Each mass-storage unit uses five hours of direct labour and three units of direct materials. Labourers are paid $10 per hour, and one unit of direct materials costs $80.

e. There are 65,700 units of direct materials in beginning inventory as of January 1, 2002. At the end of each quarter, Optima plans to have 30 percent of the direct materials needed for next quarter's unit sales. Optima will end the year with the same level of direct materials found in this year's beginning inventory.

f. Optima buys direct materials on account. Half of the purchases are paid for in the quarter of acquisition, and the remaining half are paid for in the following quarter. Wages and salaries are paid on the 15th and 30th of each month.

g. Fixed overhead totals $1 million each quarter. Of this total, $350,000 represents depreciation. All other fixed expenses are paid for in cash in the quarter incurred. The fixed overhead rate is computed by dividing the year's total fixed overhead by the year's expected actual units produced.

h. Variable overhead is budgeted at $6 per direct labour hour. All variable overhead expenses are paid for in the quarter incurred.

i. Fixed selling and administrative expenses total $250,000 per quarter, including $50,000 depreciation.

j. Variable selling and administrative expenses are budgeted at $10 per unit sold. All selling and administrative expenses are paid for in the quarter incurred.

k. The balance sheet as of December 31, 2001, is as follows:

Assets

Cash	$ 250,000
Direct materials inventory	5,256,000
Accounts receivable	3,300,000
Plant and equipment	33,500,000
Total assets	$42,306,000

Liabilities and Stockholders' Equity

Accounts payable	$ 7,248,000*
Capital stock	27,000,000
Retained earnings	8,058,000
Total liabilities and stockholders' equity	$42,306,000

* For purchase of direct materials only

l. Optima will pay quarterly dividends of $300,000. At the end of the fourth quarter, $2 million of equipment will be purchased.

Required:

Prepare a master budget for Optima Company for each quarter of 2002 and for the year in total. The following component budgets must be included:

a. Sales budget
b. Production budget
c. Direct materials purchases budget
d. Direct labour budget
e. Overhead budget
f. Selling and administrative expenses budget
g. Ending finished goods inventory budget
h. Cost of goods sold budget
i. Cash budget
j. Pro forma income statement (using absorption costing)
k. Pro forma balance sheet

13–35

Flexible Budgeting

LO3, LO4

Patterson Company employs flexible budgeting techniques to evaluate the performance of several of its activities. The selling expenses flexible budgets for three representative monthly activity levels follow.

Representative Monthly Flexible Budgets for Selling Expenses

Activity measures:			
Unit sales volume	400,000	425,000	450,000
Dollar sales volume	$10,000,000	$10,625,000	$11,250,000
Number of orders	4,000	4,250	4,500
Number of salespersons	72	72	72
Monthly expenses:			
Advertising and promotion	$ 1,200,000	$ 1,200,000	$ 1,200,000
Administrative salaries	57,000	57,000	57,000
Sales salaries	75,600	75,600	75,600
Sales commissions	300,000	318,750	337,500
Salesperson travel	170,000	175,000	180,000
Sales office expense	490,000	498,750	507,500
Shipping expense	675,000	712,500	750,000
Total	$ 2,967,600	$ 3,037,600	$ 3,107,600

The following assumptions were used to develop the selling expenses flexible budgets:

a. The average size of Patterson's sales force during the year was planned to be 72 people.
b. Salespersons are paid a monthly salary plus commission on gross dollar sales.
c. The travel costs are best characterized as a step-variable cost. The fixed portion is related to the number of salespersons; the variable portion tends to fluctuate with gross dollar sales.
d. Sales office expense is a mixed cost, with the variable portion related to the number of orders processed.
e. Shipping expense is a mixed cost, with the variable portion related to the number of units sold.

A sales force of 80 persons generated a total of 4,300 orders resulting in a sales volume of 420,000 units during November. The gross dollar sales amounted to $10.9 million. The selling expenses incurred for November were as follows:

Advertising and promotion	$1,350,000
Administrative salaries	57,000
Sales salaries	84,000
Sales commissions	327,000
Salesperson travel	185,000
Sales office expense	497,200
Shipping expense	730,000
Total	$3,230,200

Required:

1. Explain why the selling expenses flexible budgets presented would not be appropriate for evaluating Patterson Company's November selling expenses; indicate how the flexible budget would have to be revised.
2. Prepare a selling expenses report for November that Patterson Company can use to evaluate its control over selling expenses. The report should have a line for each selling expense item showing the appropriate budgeted amount, the actual selling expense, and the monthly dollar variation. (US CMA adapted)

13–36

Importance of Cash Budget; Cash Budget

LO1, LO2

CrossMan Corporation, a rapidly expanding crossbow distributor to retail outlets, is in the process of formulating plans for 2002. Joan Caldwell, firm's marketing director, has completed her 2002 forecast and is confident that sales estimates will be met or exceeded. The following sales figures show the growth expected and will provide the planning basis for other corporate departments.

Month	Forecasted Sales
January	$1,800,000
February	$2,000,000
March	$1,800,000
April	$2,200,000
May	$2,500,000
June	$2,800,000
July	$3,000,000
August	$3,000,000
September	$3,200,000
October	$3,200,000
November	$3,000,000
December	$3,400,000

George Brownell, CrossMan's assistant controller, has been given the responsibility for formulating the cash-flow projection, a critical element during a period of rapid expansion. The following information will be used in preparing the cash analysis.

CrossMan has experienced an excellent record in accounts receivable collection and expects this trend to continue. Sixty percent of billings are collected in the month after the sale and 40 percent in the second month after the sale. Uncollectible accounts are nominal and will not be considered in the analysis.

The purchase of the crossbows is CrossMan's largest expenditure; the cost of these items equals 50 percent of sales. Sixty percent of the crossbows are received one month prior to sale, and 40 percent are received during the month of sale.

Prior experience shows that 80 percent of accounts payable are paid by CrossMan one month after receipt of the purchased crossbows, and the remaining 20 percent are paid the second month after receipt.

Hourly wages, including fringe benefits, are a factor of sales volume and are equal to 20 percent of the current month's sales. These wages are paid in the month incurred.

General and administrative expenses are projected to be $2,640,000 for 2002. The composition of the expenses follows. All of these expenses are incurred uniformly throughout the year except the property taxes, which are paid in four equal installments in the last month of each quarter.

Salaries	$ 480,000
Promotion	660,000
Property taxes	240,000
Insurance	360,000
Utilities	300,000
Depreciation	600,000
Total	$2,640,000

Income tax payments are made by CrossMan in the first month of each quarter based on the income for the prior quarter. CrossMan's income tax rate is 40 percent. CrossMan's net income for the first quarter of 2002 is projected to be $612,000.

CrossMan has a corporate policy of maintaining an end-of-month cash balance of $100,000. Cash is invested or borrowed monthly, as necessary, to maintain this balance. CrossMan uses a calendar-year reporting period.

Required:

1. Prepare a pro forma schedule of cash receipts and disbursements for CrossMan Corporation, by month, for the second quarter of 2002. Be sure that all receipts, disbursements, and borrowing and investing amounts are presented on a monthly basis. Ignore the interest expense and/or interest income associated with the borrowing and investing activities.

2. Discuss why cash budgeting is particularly important for a rapidly expanding company such as CrossMan Corporation. (US CMA adapted)

13–37

Static Budget Variances

LO3

The following condensed performance report showing budget, actual, and variances for a recent three-month period in one firm's Transportation Division is an example of performance reports produced by a multinational company.

		(in thousands)	
	Master Budget	Actual	Variance
Revenue	$50,000	$47,000	$3,000U
Fuel and energy	$ 5,000	$ 4,600	$400F
Repairs and maintenance	1,000	1,000	—
Supplies and miscellaneous	3,000	2,800	200F
Variable payroll	30,000	29,000	1,000F
Total variable expenses[a]	39,000	37,400	1,600F
Supervision	$1,000	$1,200	$200U
Rent	2,000	2,000	—
Depreciation	1,000	1,000	—
Other fixed costs	3,000	2,000	1,000F
Total fixed expenses	7,000	6,200	800F
Total expenses	$46,000	$43,600	$2,400F
Net operating income	$ 4,000	$ 3,400	$ 600U

[a] For purposes of this analysis, assume that all these expenses are strictly variable. In an actual situation, many costs are mixed and are subdivided between variable and fixed.

Although the division manager was disappointed about not attaining the budgeted revenue level, he was quite happy about his cost performance. Otherwise net operating income would have been even worse. But his newly appointed immediate superior, the executive vice-president, was totally unhappy. She addressed her remarks to the company's chief financial officer: "I can see some merit in comparing actual performance with the budget, in the sense that we can see whether actual revenue coincided with our best estimate for budget purposes. But I can't see how this type of performance report can help me or the divisional manager evaluate the division's cost performance."

Required:

1. Express the budget in a flexible budget formula.
2. The chief financial officer has asked you, the corporate controller, how you could improve the performance report. How would you answer her?
3. Assuming that sales prices were exactly as budgeted, prepare a performance report that should provide better insight into the division's performance.
4. Identify the major assumptions that are necessary to make the answers in Requirements 1 and 3 valid.

13–38

Profitability Analysis; Variance Analysis as an Analytical Tool

LO3

Thorne Ltd. manufactures two types of appliances that are sold in national markets. The budget for one of these appliances for the past year and the company's actual performance appear below:

	Budget	Actual
Units	12,000	13,000
Selling price per unit	$200	$210
Variable cost per unit	$140	$130
Total direct fixed cost	$400,000	$420,000

Required:

1. Prepare actual and budgeted operating income statements.
2. Analyze, by cause, the effect of each variable on profit.
3. Comment on the performance of Thorne, Ltd.
4. Identify any assumptions that are necessary to make your answers in Requirement 2 valid.

13–39

Profitability Analysis; Variance Analysis as an Analytical Tool

LO3

Toyworld manufactures and sells a line of toys. The toys are distributed primarily through department stores. As president of Toyworld, you wanted to analyze Toyworld's profitability. Your capable assistant has provided you with the following data for 2002 related to one of your major product lines.

	Master Budget	Actual
Selling price, per unit	$20.00	$21.00
Variable manufacturing cost, per unit	$11.00	$12.00
Variable marketing and administrative expenses, per unit	$1.00	$1.10
Fixed manufacturing cost, total	$17,250	$18,000
Fixed marketing and administrative expenses, total	$20,000	$22,000
Sales volume, in units	9,000	10,000

Required:

1. Analyze, in as much detail as the data permit, the difference between budgeted and actual operating income for 2002.
2. Comment on Toyworld's performance based on your analysis.

13–40

Profitability Analysis; Variance Analysis as an Analytical Tool

LO3

Smieliauskas Ltd. had the following budgeted and actual income statements:

	(in thousands)	
	Budget	Actual
Sales	$2,100	$2,000
Variable expenses	1,260	1,500
Contribution margin	$ 840	$ 500
Fixed expenses	580	620
Operating income (loss)	$ 260	$ (120)

Additional information:

a. Sales prices were exactly as budgeted.
b. The budgeted fixed expenses included discretionary amounts of $180,000. Of the actual fixed expenses, $560,000 were committed fixed expenses.

Required:

1. Analyze, in as much detail as the data permit, the difference between budgeted and actual operating income.
2. Comment on the performance of Smieliauskas Ltd. based on your analysis.

13–41

Profitability Analysis; Variance Analysis as an Analytical Tool

LO2

Feltham Ltd. had the following budgeted and actual income statements:

	(in thousands)	
	Budget	Actual
Sales	$4,200	$4,400
Variable expenses	2,520	2,700
Contribution margin	$1,680	$1,700
Fixed expenses	1,160	1,240
Operating income (loss)	$ 520	$ 460

Additional information:

a. Actual sales at budgeted prices were $4,000,000.
b. The budgeted fixed expenses included discretionary amounts of $360,000. Of the actual fixed expenses, $1,120,000 were committed fixed expenses.

Required:

1. Calculate the following variances in terms of their effect on profit:
   a. sales price variance
   b. profit volume variance
   c. flexible budget variable expenses variance
   d. discretionary fixed expenses variance
   e. committed fixed expenses variance
2. Reconcile actual and budgeted operating income.
3. Is there any significance for control purposes to breaking down fixed expenses into discretionary and committed amounts? Explain, using the provided information.
4. Comment on the performance of Feltham Ltd.
5. Identify the major assumptions that are necessary to make your answers above valid.

13–42

Cash Budget

LO2

Jennifer Johnson decided to start a business that would require the purchase of assets at a total cost of $200,000. She started her business with a cash investment of $50,000 and on January 1, 2001, took out a loan for $150,000. The terms of the loan stipulated that interest of 9 percent (annual) would be paid at the end of each month, and a payment of $30,000 of principal would be payable at the end of each quarter. The company manufactures a product with the following budgeted revenues and expenses, based on a monthly volume of 5,000 units:

Selling price per unit		$150
Manufacturing costs per unit:		
Direct materials		$20
Direct labour		30
Variable overhead:		
Utilities	$ 5	
Supplies	6	
Indirect labour	4	15
Fixed overhead:		
Factory rent	10	
Depreciation	15	25
Total manufacturing cost		$90

Selling and administrative costs:	
Sales commissions	$8 per unit
Bad debt expenses	$3 per unit
Office rentals	$12,000 per month
Equipment depreciation	$5,000 per month

Other information:

a. Expected sales:

January 2001	$360,000
February 2001	450,000
March 2001	480,000
April 2001	600,000

b. All sales are on credit; terms are 2/10, net 30 days. Collection of accounts receivable are expected to display the following pattern:
   • 30 percent will be collected in the month of sale (80 percent of these customers will take the discount).
   • 30 percent will be collected in the month after the sale.
   • 38 percent will be collected two months after the sale.
   • 2 percent will be uncollectible.
c. A direct materials inventory of $2,000 will have to be maintained at all times. All direct materials purchases are expected to be incurred uniformly throughout the month, with payments made in the month of purchase.

d. In order to meet fluctuations in customer demand, a finished goods inventory equal to 100 units plus 10 percent of the demand expected for the following month (in units) will be maintained.

e. Wages payable at the end of each month are expected to average $7,500.

f. A minimum cash balance of $10,000 is to be maintained at all times.

Required:

Prepare a cash budget for the first quarterly period ending on March 31, 2001. Include any supporting schedules and budgets that are appropriate, and indicate what financing (if any) may be required. (CMA Canada adapted)

13–43

Cash Disbursements

LO2

The Hoskins Company has the following policies with regard to inventory levels; these policies have been adhered to in the past:

Finished goods: 200 units plus 20 percent of the units expected to be sold in the next month

Direct materials: 1,000 kilograms plus 10 percent of the materials required for production in the next month

The company also expected the following costs:

Direct materials: 2 kilograms @ $3 per kilogram
Direct labour: $12 per unit

Factory overhead:
• Factory supplies of $6,000 used each month.
• Depreciation of factory equipment of $15,000 per month.
• Factory supervision of $14,000 per month.
• Insurance on factory of $1,000 per month (an annual policy paid on January 1 of each year).

Selling and administrative expenses:
• Bad debt expense of $2 per unit sold.
• Salaries of $40,000 per month.

Required:

Calculate the total budgeted cash disbursements for the month of January 1, 2001, assuming the following:
• All purchases of direct materials are paid for in the month of purchase.
• Accrued salaries and wages payable are expected to increase by $2,400 in the month.
• Factory supplies on hand are expected to increase by $900 in the month.
• Sales are expected to be 30,000 units in January, 25,000 units in February, and 20,000 units in March. (CMA Canada adapted)

MANAGERIAL DECISION CASES

13–44

Budgetary Performance; Rewards; Ethical Behaviour

LO3

Linda Ellis, a division manager, is evaluated and rewarded on the basis of budgetary performance. She, her assistants, and the plant managers are all eligible to receive a bonus if actual divisional profits are between budgeted profits and 120 percent of budgeted profits. The bonuses are based on a fixed percentage of actual profits. Profits above 120 percent of budgeted profits earn a bonus at the 120 percent level (in other words, there is an upper limit on possible bonus payments). If the actual profits are less than budgeted profits, no bonuses are awarded. Now consider the following actions taken by Linda:

a. Linda tends to overestimate expenses and underestimate revenues. This approach facilitates the divison's ability to attain budgeted profits. Linda believes that the action is justified because it increases the likelihood of receiving bonuses and helps keep the managers' morale high.

b. Suppose that toward the end of the fiscal year, Linda saw that the division would not achieve budgeted profits. Accordingly, she instructed the sales department to defer the closing of a number of sales agreements to the following fiscal year. She also decided to write off some inventory that was nearly worthless. Deferring revenues to next year and writing off the inventory in a no-bonus year increased the chances of a bonus for next year.

c. Assume that toward the end of the year, Linda saw that actual profits would likely exceed the 120 percent limit. She took actions similar to those described in (b).

Required:

1. Comment on the ethics of Linda's behaviour. Are her actions right or wrong? What role does the company play in encouraging her actions?

2. Suppose that you were the division's marketing manager, and you received instructions to defer the closing of sales until the next fiscal year. What would you do?

3. Suppose that you were a plant manager, and you knew that your budget had been padded by the division manager. Further suppose that the padding is common knowledge among the plant managers, who support it because it increases the ability to achieve the budget and receive a bonus. What would you do?

4. Suppose that you were the division controller, and you received instructions from the division manager to accelerate the recognition of some expenses that legitimately belonged to a future period. What would you do?

13–45

Cash Budget

LO2

According to the analysis of a local consultant, the financial difficulties facing Dr. Roger Jones have been caused by the absence of proper planning and control.[6] Budgetary control is sorely needed. To assist you in preparing a plan of action that will help his dental practice regain financial stability, Roger has made available the following financial information, that describes a typical month:

	Revenues	
	Average Fee	**Quantity**
Fillings	$ 50	90
Crowns	300	19
Root canals	170	8
Bridges	500	7
Extractions	45	30
Cleaning	25	108
X-rays	15	150

Costs		
Salaries:		
Two dental assistants	$1,900	
Receptionist/bookkeeper	1,500	
Hygienist	1,800	
Public relations (Meseah Jones*)	1,000	
Personal salary	6,500	
Total salaries		$12,700

* Roger's wife.

6. Review the introduction to this chapter for a description of the financial difficulties that Roger faces on a recurring basis.

Benefits	1,344
Building lease	1,500
Dental supplies	1,200
Janitorial	300
Utilities	400
Phone	150
Office supplies	100
Lab fees	5,000
Loan payments	570
Interest payments	500
Miscellaneous	500
Depreciation	700
Total costs	$24,964

Benefits include Roger's share of employment insurance and a supplemental health insurance premium for all employees. Although all revenues billed in a month are not collected, the cash flowing into the business is approximately equal to the month's billings because of collections from prior months. The dental office is open on Monday through Thursday from 8:30 a.m. to 4:00 p.m. and on Friday from 8:30 a.m. to 12:30 p.m. A total of 32 hours are worked each week. Additional hours could be worked, but Roger is reluctant to do so because of other personal endeavours that he enjoys.

Roger has noted that the two dental assistants and the receptionist are not fully utilized. He estimates that they are busy about 65 to 70 percent of the time. Roger's wife, Meseah, spends about five hours each week on a monthly newsletter that is sent to all patients; she also maintains a birthday list and sends cards to the patients on their birthdays.

Roger spends about $2,400 yearly on informational seminars. These seminars, designed especially for dentists, teach them how to increase their revenues. It was as a result of one of these seminars that Roger decided to invest in promotion and public relations (the newsletter and the birthday list).

Required:

1. Prepare a monthly cash budget for Roger. Does he have a significant cash-flow problem? How would you use the budget to show Roger why he is having financial difficulties?
2. Using the cash budget prepared in Requirement 1 and the information given in the case, recommend actions to solve Roger's financial problems. Prepare a cash budget that reflects these recommendations and demonstrates to Roger that the problems can be corrected. Do you think that Roger will accept your recommendations? Do any of the behavioural principles discussed in this chapter have a role in this type of setting? Explain.

RESEARCH ASSIGNMENTS

13–46

Cybercase

LO1, LO2

Just as companies must, the government of Canada must prepare a budget each year. However, unlike the budgets of private, for-profit companies, the government's budget and its details are available to the public. The entire budgetary process is established by law. The government makes available a considerable amount of information concerning the federal budget. Most of this information can be found on the Internet. Using Internet resources, answer the following questions:

1. When is the federal budget prepared?
2. Who is responsible for preparing the federal budget?

3. How is the final federal budget determined? Explain in detail how the government creates its budget.
4. What percentage of the gross domestic product (GDP) is represented by the federal budget?
5. What are the revenue sources for the federal budget? Indicate the percentage contribution from each of the major sources.
6. How does our spending as a percentage of GDP compare to spending by other countries?
7. How are deficits financed?

13–47

Research Assignment
LO1, LO2

A formal master-budgeting process is important to many companies. Locate a manufacturing plant in your community that has its headquarters elsewhere. Interview the plant's controller regarding the master-budgeting process. Ask when the process starts each year, what schedules and budgets are prepared at the plant level, how the controller forecasts the amounts, and how those schedules and budgets fit in with the overall corporate budget.

CHAPTER 14

Standard Costing: A Managerial Control Tool

Learning Objectives

After studying Chapter 14, you should be able to:

1. Explain how unit standards are set and why standard cost systems are adopted.

2. Explain the purpose of a standard cost sheet.

3. Describe the basic concepts underlying variance analysis, and explain when variances should be investigated.

4. Compute the materials and labour variances, and explain how they are used for control.

5. Compute the variable and fixed overhead variances, and explain their meanings.

6. Prepare journal entries for materials and labour variances, and describe the accounting for overhead variances. (Appendix A)

7. Use variance analysis as an analytical tool for profitability analysis. (Appendix B)

Scenario

Millie Anderson, manager of Honley Medical's IV Products Division, was more than satisfied with her division's performance last year. At the start of the year, the division had introduced a new line of polyurethane catheters, replacing the old teflon catheters, and sales had more than tripled. The market reaction to the new catheter was a virtual replay of the company's history: Honley Medical was establishing a dominant position in the IV market.

Nearly 30 years ago, Lindell Honley, the founder of Honley Medical, had perceived the need for something other than a metal needle for long-term insertion into veins. Metal needles were irritating and could damage the vein. Based on this, Honley had developed a catheter using teflon, a lubricated plastic that was easy to insert into the vein. The development was well received by the medical community and produced a new and successful company, which gradually expanded its activities into a variety of medical products.

For years, the new technology allowed Honley to dominate the market, but when the patent expired, other companies entered the market with their own teflon catheters, increasing competition. Prices were driven down, and profit margins began eroding.

The eroding profit margins had prompted Millie and other high-level managers to examine the continued viability of the teflon catheters. After many years, the medical profession had noted that after 24 hours of catheter use, an infection tended to develop around the point of insertion. Researchers at Honley Medical had discovered that the problem was one of incompatibility between the teflon and the patient's blood and tissue. Further studies showed that different plastics produced different reactions. Research began immediately on finding a material that was more biocompatible than teflon. The outcome was polyurethane catheters. The new catheter could be left in for 72 hours, compared to 24 hours for the teflon catheters.

Millie also knew that history would repeat itself in the later stages—the time would come when other firms would produce catheters with the same degree of biocompatibility. In fact, Honley's research scientists estimated that competitors would have a competing catheter on the market within three years. This time, however, Millie was determined to protect the division's market share. Since most patients have little need for a catheter beyond 72 hours, further improvements in biocompatibility were not likely to yield the same market benefits as in the past. Price competition would become more important. Competing on price meant that cost control would become critical. In the past, because of its dominant position, the division had not been too concerned with manufacturing costs. Millie believed that by implementing cost control measures now, the division could better compete on price when competition resurfaced in a few years. She consulted with Reed McCourt, the division's controller.

Millie: "Reed, is our budgetary system the only attempt we make to control manufacturing costs?"

Reed: "Yes. But it really isn't a very good effort. Budgets are based on last year's costs plus some allowance for inflation. We have never tried to identify what the costs ought to be. Nor have we held managers responsible for cost control. Our profitability has always been good and resources plentiful. My guess is that we spend more than necessary simply because we have been so successful."

Millie: "Well, resources wouldn't be so plentiful now if we hadn't developed the polyurethane catheter. And I'm afraid that resources won't be plentiful in the future unless we take actions now to control our manufacturing costs. If we can be more profitable now by using better cost control, we ought to use it. I want my plant and production managers to recognize their responsibilities in this area. Any suggestions?"

Reed: "We need to inject more formality into the budgetary system. First, budgets should reflect what costs should be, not what they have been. Second, we can encourage managers to be cost conscious by having them help identify efficient levels of cost on which the budget will be based and tying bonuses and promotions into the system. However, I think we can gain cost control by going one step further and establishing a standard cost system."

Millie: "Doesn't that entail the specification of unit price and quantity standards for materials and labour?"

Reed: "That's essentially correct. Using the unit price and quantity standards, budgeted costs for labour, materials, and overhead are established for each unit produced. The standards are based on efficiency expectations and will demand less resource usage than our traditional incremental budgetary approach. The unit price and quantity standards are used to develop budgets—and then, once actual costs are in, to break down the budgetary variances into price and efficiency variances. A standard cost system provides more detailed control information than a budgetary system using normal costing. We can hold our managers responsible for meeting the established standards."

Millie: "I think our division needs this type of system. It's about time that our managers become cost conscious."

Questions to Think About

1. What was motivating Millie to implement a more formal cost control system?

2. Why does a standard cost system provide more detailed control information?

3. What type of control is being exercised with the use of standards?

4. How can standards be used to control costs?

UNIT STANDARDS

Objective 1

Explain how unit standards are set and why standard cost systems are adopted.

Millie and Reed both recognized the need to encourage operating managers to control costs. Cost control often means the difference between success and failure or between above-average profits and average or below-average profits. Millie was convinced that cost control meant that her managers had to be cost conscious and they had to assume responsibility for this important objective. Reed suggested that the way to control costs and involve managers is through the use of a formal budgetary system.

In Chapter 13, we saw how budgets provide standards that are used to control and evaluate managerial performance. However, budgets are aggregate measures of performance; they identify the revenues and costs that an organization should experience in total if plans are executed as expected. By comparing the actual costs and actual revenues with the corresponding budgeted amounts at the same level of activity, budgetary performance reporting firms measure managerial efficiency.

Although the process just described provides significant information for control, control can be enhanced by developing standards for *unit* amounts as well as for total amounts. In fact, the groundwork for unit standards already exists within the framework of flexible budgeting. For flexible budgeting to work, the budgeted variable cost per unit of input for each unit of output must be known for every item in the budget. The budgeted variable input cost per unit of output is a unit standard. Unit standards are the basis or foundation on which a flexible budget is built.

To determine the unit standard cost for a particular input, two decisions must be made: (1) how much of the input should be used per unit of output (the *quantity decision*), and (2) how much should be paid for the quantity of the input to be used (the *pricing decision*). The quantity decision produces **quantity standards**, and the pricing decision produces **price standards**. The unit standard cost can be computed by multiplying these two standards.

For example, a soft-drink company may decide that 0.1 litres of fructose should be used for every 355-millilitre can of cola (the quantity standard) and that the price of the fructose should be $2.50 per litre (the price standard). The standard cost of the fructose per can of cola is then $0.25 (0.1 × $2.50). The standard cost per unit of fructose can be used to predict what the total cost of fructose should be as the activity level varies; it thus becomes a flexible budget formula. Thus, if 10,000 cans of cola are produced, the total expected cost of fructose is $2,500 ($0.25 × 10,000); if 15,000 cans are produced, the total expected cost of fructose is $3,750 ($0.25 × 15,000).

How Standards Are Developed

Historical experience, engineering studies, and input from operating personnel are three potential sources of quantitative standards. Although historical experience may provide an initial guideline for setting standards, it should not be used without caution. Often, processes are operating inefficiently; adopting input–output relationships from the past merely perpetuates these inefficiencies. The IV division of Honley Medical, for example, had never emphasized cost control and had operated in a resource-rich environment. Both the divisional manager and the controller were convinced that significant inefficiencies existed. Engineering studies can determine the most efficient way to operate and can provide very rigorous guidelines; however, engineered standards are often too rigorous. They may not be achievable by operating personnel. Since operating personnel are accountable for meeting the standards, they should have significant input in setting standards. The same principles pertaining to participative budgeting also pertain to setting unit standards.

Price standards are the joint responsibility of operations, purchasing, personnel, and accounting. Operations determines the quality of the inputs required; personnel and purchasing are responsible for acquiring the input quality requested at the lowest price. Market forces, trade unions, and other external forces limit the range of choices for price standards. In setting price standards, purchasing must consider discounts, freight, and quality; personnel, on the other hand, must consider payroll taxes, fringe benefits, and qualifications. Accounting is responsible for recording the price standards and preparing reports that compare actual performance to the standard.

Types of Standards

Standards are generally classified as either *ideal* or *currently attainable*. **Ideal standards** are standards that demand maximum efficiency and can be achieved only if everything operates perfectly. No machine breakdowns, slack, or lack of skill (even momentarily) are allowed. **Currently attainable standards** can be achieved under efficient operating conditions. Allowance is made for normal breakdowns, interruptions, less-than-perfect skill, and so on. These standards are demanding but achievable.

Of the two types, currently attainable standards offer the most behavioural benefits. If standards are too tight and never achievable, workers become frustrated, and performance levels decline. However, challenging but achievable standards tend to extract higher performance levels—particularly when the individuals who are subject to the standards have participated in their creation.

Why Standard Cost Systems Are Adopted

Two reasons for adopting a standard cost system are frequently mentioned: to improve planning and control and to facilitate product costing.

Planning and Control   Standard cost systems enhance planning and control and improve performance measurement. Unit standards are a fundamental requirement for a flexible budgeting system, which is a key feature of a meaningful planning and control system. Budgetary control systems compare actual costs with budgeted costs by computing variances—the differences between the actual and planned costs for the actual level of activity. By developing unit price and quantity standards, an overall variance can be decomposed into two components: a *price variance* and a *usage or efficiency variance*.

By performing this decomposition, a manager acquires more information. If the variance is unfavourable, the manager can tell whether it is attributable to discrepancies between planned prices and actual prices, to discrepancies between planned usage and actual usage, or to both. Since managers have more control over the usage of inputs than over their prices, efficiency variances provide specific signals regarding the need for corrective action and where that action should be focused. Thus, in principle, the use of efficiency variances enhances operational control. Additionally, by breaking out the price variance, over which managers have little control, the system provides an improved measure of managerial efficiency.

The benefits of operational control, however, may not extend to the advanced manufacturing environment. The use of a standard cost system for operational control in an advanced manufacturing environment can produce dysfunctional behaviour. Thus, the detailed computation of variances—at least at the operational level—is discouraged in this new environment. Nonetheless, standards are still useful for planning in the advanced manufacturing environment—for example, in the creation of bids. Also, variances may still be computed and presented in reports to higher-level managers so that the financial dimension can be monitored.

Finally, it should be mentioned that there are many firms operating with conventional manufacturing systems. Standard cost systems are widely used. In a 1991 survey, 87 percent of the firms responding used a standard cost system.[1] Furthermore, the survey revealed that significant numbers of the respondents were calculating variances at the operational level. For example, about 40 percent of the firms using a standard cost system reported labour variances for small work crews or individual workers.

Product Costing   In a standard cost system, costs are assigned to products using quantity and price standards for all three manufacturing costs: direct materials, direct labour, and overhead. In contrast, a normal cost system predetermines over-

1. Bruce R. Gaumnitz and Felix P. Kollaritsch, "Manufacturing Variances: Current Practice and Trends," *Journal of Cost Management* (Spring 1991): 58–64.

Exhibit 14–1

Cost Assignment Approaches

	Manufacturing Costs		
	Direct Materials	Direct Labour	Overhead
Actual cost system	Actual	Actual	Actual
Normal cost system	Actual	Actual	Budgeted
Standard cost system	Standard	Standard	Standard

head costs for the purpose of product costing but assigns direct materials and direct labour to products by using actual costs. Overhead is assigned using a budgeted rate and actual activity. At the other end of the cost assignment spectrum, an actual cost system assigns the actual costs of all three manufacturing inputs to products. Exhibit 14-1 summarizes these three cost assignment approaches. Standard product costing has several advantages over both normal costing and actual costing. One, of course, is the greater capacity for control. Standard cost systems also provide readily available unit-cost information that can be used for pricing decisions. This is particularly helpful for companies that do a significant amount of bidding and for those paid on a cost-plus basis.[2]

Other simplifications are also possible. For example, if a process-costing system uses standard costing to assign product costs, there is no need to compute a unit cost for each equivalent unit-cost category. A standard unit cost would exist for each category.[3] Additionally, there is no need to distinguish between the FIFO and weighted average methods of accounting for beginning inventory costs. Usually, a standard process-costing system will follow the equivalent unit calculation of the FIFO approach. That is, current equivalent-units of work are calculated. By calculating current equivalent work, firms can compare current actual production costs with standard costs for control purposes.

STANDARD PRODUCT COSTS

Objective 2

Explain the purpose of a standard cost sheet.

Standard costs can also be used in service organizations. Canada Customs and Revenue Agency (CCRA), for example, could set standard processing times for different categories of tax returns. If the standard processing time is 3 minutes for a simple return, and the standard price of labour is $9 per hour, then the standard cost of processing a simple return is $0.45 ($9 × 3/60). Other examples exist. Provincial governments classify illnesses into diagnostic related groups (DRGs), and hospital costs that should be incurred for an average case are predetermined. (The costs include patient days, food, medicine, supplies, use of equipment, and so on.) A government pays the hospital the standard cost of the DRG. If the cost of the patient's treatment is greater than the DRG allows, the hospital suffers a deficit. If the cost of the patient's treatment is less than the DRG reimbursement, the hospital gains a surplus. On average, the hospital supposedly breaks even. Although service organizations can and do make use of standard costing, these applications are more common in manufacturing organizations. Furthermore, the concepts are more easily illustrated in manufacturing settings.

In manufacturing firms, standard costs are developed for materials, labour, and overhead. Using these costs, we can compute the **standard cost per unit**. The **standard cost sheet** provides detail underlying the standard unit cost. To illustrate, consider a standard cost sheet for a 400-gram bag of corn chips produced by

---

2. For example, the concrete and pipe company (Canblock, Inc.) mentioned in Chapter 13 conducts the vast majority of its business through bidding and uses a standard cost system primarily to facilitate the bidding process.

3. If you have not yet read Chapter 5, the example illustrating the simplifications made possible by standard costing will not be as meaningful. However, the point being made is still relevant. Standard costing can bring useful computational savings.

Crunchy Chips Company. The production of corn chips begins by steaming and soaking corn kernels overnight in a lime solution. This process softens the kernels so that they can be shaped into a sheet of dough. The dough is then cut into small triangular chips. Next, the chips are toasted in an oven and dropped into a deep fryer. After cooking, the chips pass under a salting device and are inspected for quality. Substandard chips are sorted and discarded; the chips that pass inspection are bagged by a packaging machine. The bagged chips are manually packed into boxes for shipping.

Four materials are used to process corn chips: yellow corn, cooking oil, salt, and lime. The package into which the chips are placed is also classified as a direct material. Crunchy Chips has two types of direct labourers: machine operators and inspectors (or sorters). Variable overhead is made up of three costs—gas, electricity, and water—and is applied using direct labour hours. Fixed overhead is also applied using direct labour hours. The standard cost sheet is given in Exhibit 14–2. Note that it should cost $0.56 to produce a 400-gram package of corn chips. Also notice that the company uses 500 grams of corn to produce a 400-gram package of chips. There are two reasons. First, some chips are discarded during the inspection process. The company plans on a normal amount of waste. Second, the company wants to have more than 400 grams in each package to increase customer satisfaction with its product and avoid any problems with fair packaging laws.

Exhibit 14–2 also reveals other important insights. The standard usage for variable and fixed overhead is tied to the direct labour standards.[4] For variable overhead, the rate is $3.85 per direct labour hour. Since one package of corn chips uses 0.0078 direct labour hours, the variable overhead cost assigned to a package of corn chips is $0.03 ($3.85 × 0.0078). For fixed overhead, the rate is $32.05 per direct labour hour, making the fixed overhead cost per package of corn chips $0.25 ($32.05 × 0.0078). Nearly half of the cost of production is fixed, indicating a capital-intensive production effort. Indeed, much of the operation is mechanized.

The standard cost sheet also reveals the quantity of each input that should be used to produce one unit of output. The unit quantity standards can be used to compute the total amount of inputs allowed for the actual output. This computation is an essential component in computing efficiency variances. A manager should be able to compute

Exhibit 14–2	Description	Standard Price	Standard Usage	Standard Cost[a]	Subtotal
Standard Cost Sheet for Corn Chips	Direct materials:				
	Yellow corn	$0.216/kilogram	500 grams	$0.108	
	Cooking oil	$1.00/litre	62 millilitres	0.062	
	Salt	$0.20/kilogram	25 grams	0.005	
	Lime	$4.00/litre	1 millilitre	0.004	
	Bags	$0.044/bag	1 bag	0.044	
	Total direct materials				$0.223
	Direct labour:				
	Inspection	$7/hour	0.0070 hours	$0.049	
	Machine operators	$10/hour	0.0008 hours	0.008	
	Total direct labour				0.057
	Overhead:				
	Variable overhead	$3.85/hour	0.0078 hours	$0.030	
	Fixed overhead	$32.05/hour	0.0078 hours	0.250	
	Total overhead				0.280
	Total standard unit cost				$0.560

[a] Calculated by multiplying price times usage.

4. We revert here to a conventional costing environment only for simplicity to focus on issues of standard costing. Most standard costing systems exist in a conventional costing environment.

the **standard quantity of materials allowed** (*SQ*) and the **standard hours allowed** (*SH*) for the actual output. This computation must be done for every class of direct material and every class of direct labour. Assume, for example, that 100,000 packages of corn chips are produced during the first week of March. How much yellow corn should have been used for the actual output of 100,000 packages? The unit quantity standard is 500 grams of yellow corn per package (see Exhibit 14–2). For 100,000 packages, the standard quantity of yellow corn allowed is computed as follows:

$$SQ = \text{Unit quantity standard} \times \text{Actual output}$$
$$= 500 \times 100{,}000$$
$$= 50{,}000{,}000 \text{ grams} = 50{,}000 \text{ kilograms}$$

The computation of standard direct labour hours allowed can be illustrated using machine operators. From Exhibit 14-2, the unit quantity standard is 0.0008 hours per package produced. Thus, if 100,000 packages are produced, the standard hours allowed is computed as follows:

$$SH = \text{Unit quantity standard} \times \text{Actual output}$$
$$= 0.0008 \times 100{,}000$$
$$= 80 \text{ direct labour hours}$$

VARIANCE ANALYSIS: GENERAL DESCRIPTION

Objective 3

Describe the basic concepts underlying variance analysis, and explain when variances should be investigated.

A flexible budget can be used to identify the costs that should have been incurred for the actual level of activity. This figure is obtained by multiplying the amount of input allowed for the actual output by the standard unit price. Letting *SP* be the standard unit price of an input and *SQ* the standard quantity of inputs allowed for the actual output, the planned or budgeted input cost is $SP \times SQ$. The actual input cost is $AP \times AQ$, where *AP* is the actual price per unit of the input and *AQ* is the actual quantity of input used.

Price and Efficiency Variances

The **total flexible budget variance** is simply the difference between the actual cost of the input and the planned cost for the actual output. For all variable-cost items, it is easier to refer to the total flexible budget variance as the *budget variance* or the *total variance*.

$$\text{Total variance} = (AP \times AQ) - (SP \times SQ)$$

In a standard cost system, the total variance is broken down into price and usage variances. **Price (rate) variance** is the difference between the actual and standard unit price of an input multiplied by the number of inputs used. **Usage (efficiency) variance** is the difference between the actual and the standard quantity of inputs multiplied by the input's unit price. As mentioned earlier, by breaking the total flexible budget variance down into these two components, managers can better analyze and control the total variance. They are able to identify the origin of cost increases and take appropriate corrective action.

Dividing the total variance into price and efficiency components is accomplished by subtracting and adding $SP \times AQ$ to the right-hand side of the total variance equation:

$$\begin{aligned}
\text{Total variance} &= \text{Price variance} + \text{Usage variance} \\
&= (AP - SP)AQ + (AQ - SQ)SP \\
&= [(AP \times AQ) - (SP \times AQ)] + [(SP \times AQ) - (SP \times SQ)] \\
&= (AP \times AQ) - (SP \times AQ) + (SP \times AQ) - (SP \times SQ) \\
&= (AP \times AQ) - (SP \times SQ)
\end{aligned}$$

Exhibit 14–3 presents a three-pronged diagram that describes this process.

Variance Analysis:
General Description

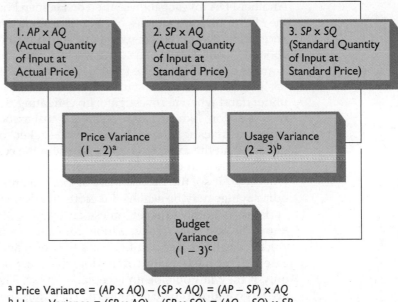

[a] Price Variance = $(AP \times AQ) - (SP \times AQ) = (AP - SP) \times AQ$
[b] Usage Variance = $(SP \times AQ) - (SP \times SQ) = (AQ - SQ) \times SP$
[c] Budget Variance = $(AP \times AQ) - (SP \times SQ)$

Usually, the total variance is divided into price and efficiency components for direct materials and direct labour. The treatment of overhead is discussed later in the chapter.

Unfavourable (U) variances occur whenever actual prices or usage of inputs is greater than standard prices or usage. When the opposite occurs, **favourable (F) variances** are obtained. Favourable and unfavourable variances are not equivalent to good and bad variances. The terms merely indicate the relationship of the actual prices or quantities to the standard prices and quantities. Whether or not the variances are good or bad depends on *why* they occurred. Determining why requires managers to do some investigation.

The Decision to Investigate

Rarely will actual performance exactly meet the established standards, nor does management expect it to. Random variations around the standard are expected. Because of this, management should have in mind an acceptable range of performance. When variances are within this range, they are assumed to have been caused by random factors. When a variance falls outside this range, the deviation is likely to have been caused by nonrandom factors, either factors that managers can control or factors that they cannot control. In the noncontrollable case, managers need to revise the standard.

An example from the pharmaceutical industry may drive home the importance of variance investigation.[5] Drugs must contain a certain amount of the active ingredient, plus or minus a small percent (for example, aspirin claiming to have 5 grains per tablet must really have somewhere between 90 and 110 percent of the specified amount). The U.S. Food and Drug Administration (FDA) is responsible for ensuring the safety and efficacy of drugs sold in the United States, whether manufactured at home or abroad. In 1991, an anonymous letter alerted the FDA to manufacturing problems with an antibiotic produced by a Canadian firm, Novopharm Ltd. Basically, the drug was too strong, and could possibly destroy beneficial bacteria along with the harmful bacteria. Upon investigation, the FDA found the blending process to be "out of control." The result was that the firm stopped shipping that drug until the process could be corrected.

5. The examples given here are taken from an article by Christopher Drew, "Medicines from Afar Raise Safety Concerns," *The New York Times*, 29 October 1995, A1 and A16.

Another FDA investigation centred on Haimen Pharmaceutical Factory in China. There, the FDA found the samples of an antileukemia drug to be too weak. Again, large variances from standard triggered an investigation. Interestingly, the question of what to do about the company and the drug was not clear-cut. In this case, the FDA did not withdraw its approval, because the drug was in short-supply.

Now that we understand why variance investigation is important, we need to understand when to investigate. Investigating the cause of variances and taking corrective action, like all activities, have a cost associated with them. As a general principle, an investigation should be undertaken only if the anticipated benefits are greater than the expected costs. Assessing the costs and benefits of a variance investigation is not an easy task, however. A manager must consider whether a variance will recur. If so, the process may be permanently out of control, meaning that periodic savings may be achieved if corrective action is taken. But how can we tell if the variance is going to recur unless an investigation is conducted? And how do we know the cost of corrective action unless the cause of the variance is known?

Because it is difficult to assess the costs and benefits of variance analysis on a case-by-case basis, many firms adopt the general guideline of investigating variances only if they fall outside an acceptable range. They are not investigated unless they are large enough to be of concern. They must be large enough to have been caused by something other than random factors and large enough (on average) to justify the costs of investigating and taking corrective action.

How do managers determine whether variances are significant? How is the acceptable range established? The acceptable range is the standard plus or minus an allowable deviation. The top and bottom measures of the allowable range are called the **control limits**. The upper control limit is the standard plus the allowable deviation, and the lower control limit is the standard minus the allowable deviation. Current practice sets the control limits subjectively: using past experience, intuition, and judgment, management determines the allowable deviation from standard.[6] Exhibit 14–4 graphically illustrates the concept of control limits. The assumed standard is $100,000, and the allowable deviation is plus or minus $10,000. The upper limit is $110,000, and the lower limit is $90,000. Investigation occurs whenever an observation falls outside these limits (as would be the case for the sixth observation). Trends can also be important.

Exhibit 14–4

Control Chart

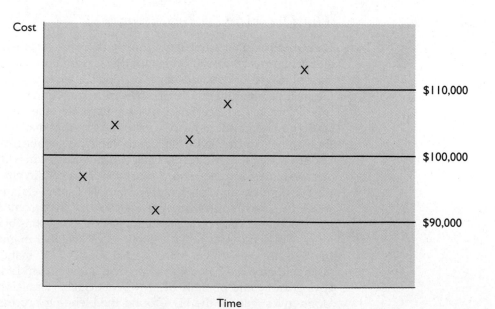

6. Gaumnitz and Kollaritsch, "Manufacturing Variances: Current Practices and Trends," report that about 45–47 percent of the firms that responded to one survey use dollar or percentage control limits. Most of the remaining use judgment rather than any formal identification of limits.

The control limits are often expressed both as a percentage of the standard and as an absolute dollar amount. For example, the allowable deviation may be expressed as the lesser of (a) 10 percent of the standard amount, or (b) $10,000. In other words, management will not accept a deviation of more than $10,000 even if that deviation is less than 10 percent of the standard. Alternatively, even if the dollar amount is less than $10,000, an investigation is required if the deviation is more than 10 percent of the standard amount.

Formal statistical procedures can also be used to set the control limits. This approach involves less subjectivity and allows a manager to assess the likelihood that the variance was caused by random factors. At this time, the use of such formal procedures has gained little acceptance.[7]

VARIANCE ANALYSIS: MATERIALS AND LABOUR

Objective 4

Compute the materials and labour variances, and explain how they are used for control.

The total variance measures the difference between the actual cost of materials and labour and their budgeted costs for the actual level of activity. To illustrate, consider these selected data for Crunchy Chips from the first week of March:[8]

Actual production: 48,500 bags of corn chips
Actual corn usage: 20,500 kilograms
Actual price paid per kilogram of corn: $0.252
Actual hours of inspection: 360 hours
Actual wage rate: $7.35 per hour

Using the above actual data and the unit standards from Exhibit 14–2, we can develop a performance report for the first week of March (see Exhibit 14–5). As has been mentioned, the total variance can be divided into price and usage variances, providing more information to the manager. This will be done in the following sections.

Direct Materials Variances

The three-pronged columnar approach or formula approaches may be used to calculate materials price and usage variances.

The Columnar Approach   Applying this approach to the Crunchy Chips example is illustrated in Exhibit 14–6. Only the price and usage variances for corn are shown. Many find this graphical approach to be easier than the use of variance formulas.

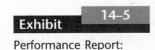
Exhibit   14–5

Performance Report:
Total Variances

	Actual Costs	Budgeted Costs[a]	Total Variance
Corn	$5,166.00	$5,238.00	$ 72.00 F[b]
Inspection labour	2,646.00	2,376.50	269.50 U[b]

[a] The standard quantities for materials and labour are computed as follows, using unit quantity standards from Exhibit 14–2:

Materials: 500 × 48,500 = 24,250,000 grams = 24,250 kilograms
Labour: 0.007 × 48,500 = 339.5 hours

Multiplying these standard quantities by the unit standard prices given in Exhibit 14–2 produces the budgeted amounts appearing in this column.

[b] F = Favourable; U = Unfavourable

---

7. According to Gaumnitz and Kollaritsch, only about 1 percent of the responding firms used formal statistical procedures.

8. To keep the example simple, only one material (corn) and one type of labour (inspection) are illustrated. A complete analysis for the company would include all types of materials and labour categories.

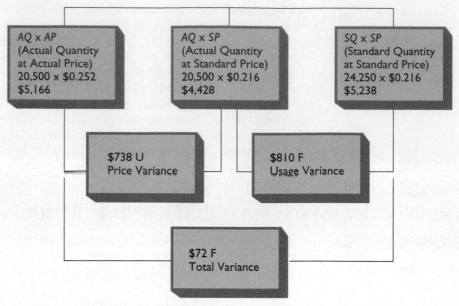

SP = $0.216 (from Exhibit 14–2)
SQ = 24,250 kg (from Exhibit 14–5, footnote a)

Materials Price Variance: Formula Approach   The materials price variance can be calculated separately. The **materials price variance** (*MPV*) measures the difference between what should have been paid for raw materials and what was actually paid. A simple formula for computing this variance is as follows:

$$MPV = (AP \times AQ) - (SP \times AQ)$$

or, after factoring, as follows:[9]

$$MPV = (AP - SP) \times AQ$$

where

AP = the actual price per unit
SP = the standard price per unit
AQ = the actual quantity of material used

Computation of the Materials Price Variance   Crunchy Chips purchased and used 20,500 kilograms of yellow corn for the first week of March. The purchase price was $0.252 per kilogram. Thus, *AP* is $0.252, *AQ* is 20,500 kilograms, and *SP* (from Exhibit 14–2) is $0.261. Using this information, we can compute the materials price variance as follows:

$$
\begin{aligned}
MPV &= (AP - SP) \times AQ \\
&= (\$0.252 - \$0.216) \times 20,500 \\
&= \$0.036 \times 20,500 \\
&= \$738 \text{ U}
\end{aligned}
$$

Percentage of $SP \times AQ$ = $738/$4,428 = 17%

9. The materials price variance that is usually calculated includes a component that combines the effect of both price and usage deviations. It is possible to compute a pure price variance as $(AS - SP) \times SQ$ and a combined or joint price-usage variance as $(AP - SP) \times (AQ - SQ)$. Together they add up to the price variance described here.

Responsibility for the Materials Price Variance The responsibility for controlling the materials price variance is usually the purchasing agent's. Admittedly, the price of materials is largely beyond his or her control; however, the price variance can be influenced by such factors as quality, quantity discounts, distance of the source from the plant, and so on. These factors are often under the control of the agent.

Using the price variance to evaluate the performance of purchasing has some limitations. Emphasis on meeting or beating the standards can produce some undesirable outcomes. For example, if the purchasing agent feels pressured to produce favourable variances, materials of lower quality than desired may be purchased or too much inventory may be acquired to take advantage of quantity discounts.

Analysis of the Materials Price Variance The first step in variance analysis is deciding whether or not the variance is significant. If it is judged to be immaterial, no further steps are needed. Assume that an unfavourable materials price variance of $738 (17 percent of the standard cost) is judged to be material. The next step is to find out why it occurred.

For the Crunchy Chips example, the investigation revealed that a higher-quality corn was purchased because of a shortage of the usual grade in the market. Once the reason is known, corrective action can be taken if necessary—and if possible. In this case, no corrective action is needed. The firm has no control over the supply shortage; it will simply have to wait until market conditions improve.

Timing of the Price Variance Computation The materials price variance can be computed at one of two points: (1) when the raw materials are issued for use in production, or (2) when they are purchased. Computing the price variance at the point of purchase is preferable. It is better to have information on variances earlier than later. The more timely the information, the more likely proper managerial action can be taken. Old information is often useless information.

Materials may sit in inventory for weeks or months before they are needed in production. By the time the materials price variance is computed, signalling a problem, it may be too late to take corrective action. And even if corrective action is still possible, the delay may cost the company thousands of dollars. For example, suppose a new purchasing agent is unaware of the availability of a quantity discount on a raw material. If the materials price variance that ignores the discount is computed when a new purchase is made, the resulting unfavourable signal would lead to quick corrective action. (In this case, the action would be to use the discount for future purchases.) If the materials price variance is not computed until the material is issued to production, it may be several weeks or even months before the problem is discovered.

If the materials price variance is computed at the point of purchase, AQ needs to be redefined as the actual quantity of materials *purchased*, or AQP, rather than actual materials used. The materials price variance on materials purchased is called the **materials purchase price variance**. Since the materials purchased may differ from the materials used, the overall materials budget variance is not necessarily the sum of the materials price variance and the materials usage variance. When the materials purchased are all used in production for the period in which the variances are calculated, the two variances will equal the total variance.

Recognizing the materials purchase price variance at the point of purchase also means that the raw materials inventory is carried at standard cost. The journal entry associated with the purchase of raw materials for a standard cost system is illustrated in Appendix A of this chapter.

Direct Materials Usage Variance: Formula Approach The **materials usage variance** (MUV) measures the difference between the direct materials actually used and the direct materials that should have been used for the actual output. The formula for computing this variance is as follows:

$$MUV = (SP \times AQ) - (SP \times SQ)$$

or, after factoring, as follows:[10]

$$MUV = (AQ - SQ) \times SP$$

where AQ = the actual quantity of materials used
SQ = the standard quantity of materials allowed for the actual output
SP = the standard price per unit

Computation of the Materials Usage Variance   Crunchy Chips used 20,500 kilograms of yellow corn to produce 48,500 bags of corn chips. Therefore, AQ is 20,500. From Exhibit 14-2, SP is $0.216 per kilogram of yellow corn. Although standard materials allowed (SQ) has already been computed in Exhibit 14-5 (footnote a), the details underlying the computation need to be reviewed. Recall that SQ is the product of the unit quantity standard and the actual units produced. From Exhibit 14-2, the unit standard is 500 grams of yellow corn for every bag of corn chips. Thus, SQ is $500 \times 48,500$, or 24,250,000 grams, or 24,250 kilograms. Thus, the materials usage variance is computed as follows:

$$
\begin{aligned}
MUV &= (AQ - SQ) \times SP \\
&= (20,500 - 24,250) \times (\$0.216) \\
&= (-3,750 \times \$0.216) \\
&= \$810 \text{ F}
\end{aligned}
$$

Percentage of $SQ \times SP = \$810/\$5,238 = 15\%$

When materials are issued, the materials quantity variance can be calculated. Accounting for the issuance of materials in a standard cost system is illustrated in Appendix A of this chapter.

Responsibility for the Materials Usage Variance   The production manager is generally responsible for materials usage. Minimizing scrap, waste, and rework are all ways in which the manager can ensure that the standard is met. However, at times the cause of the variance is attributable to others outside the production area, as the next section shows.

As with the price variance, using the usage variance to evaluate performance can lead to undesirable behaviour. For example, a production manager feeling pressure to produce a favourable variance might allow a defective unit to be transferred to finished goods. While this action avoids the problem of wasted materials, it may create customer-relations problems.

Analysis of the Materials Usage Variance   Investigation at Crunchy Chips revealed that the favourable materials usage variance was the result of the higher-quality corn acquired by the purchasing department. In this case, the favourable variance is essentially assignable to purchasing. Since the materials usage variance is favourable—and larger than the unfavourable price variance—the overall result of the change in purchasing is favourable.

If management expects the favourable usage variance to persist, the higher quality of corn should be purchased regularly and the price and quantity standards revised to reflect the decision to do so. As this example reveals, standards are not static. As improvements in production take place and conditions change, standards may need to be revised to reflect the new operating environment.

---

10. The usage variance calculated this way is a pure variance, because it is affected only by deviations in quantity.

Direct Labour Variances

The rate (price) and efficiency (usage) variances for labour can be calculated using either the columnar approach of Exhibit 14–3 or a formula approach.

Columnar Approach The three-pronged calculation for inspection labour at the Crunchy Chips plant is illustrated in Exhibit 14–7. The calculation using formulas is discussed next.

Labour Rate Variance: Formula Approach The **labour rate variance** (*LRV*) computes the difference between what was paid to direct labourers and what should have been paid:

$$LRV = (AR \times AH) - (SR \times AH)$$

or, after factoring:

$$LRV = (AR - SR) \times AH$$

where *AR* = the actual hourly wage rate
   SR = the standard hourly wage rate
   AH = the actual direct labour hours used

Computation of the Labour Rate Variance Direct labour activity for Crunchy Chips's inspectors will be used to illustrate the computation of the labour rate variance. For inspection during the first week in March, 360 hours were used. The actual hourly wage paid for inspection was $7.35. From Exhibit 14-2, the standard wage rate is $7. Thus, *AH* is 360, *AR* is $7.35, and *SR* is $7. The labour rate variance is computed as follows:

$$
\begin{aligned}
LRV &= (AR - SR)\, AH \\
&= (\$7.35 - \$7)360 \\
&= \$0.35 \times 360 \\
&= \$126 \text{ U}
\end{aligned}
$$

Percentage of *SR* × *AH* = $126/$2,520 = 5%

Exhibit 14–7

Labour Variances:
Columnar Approach

Responsibility for the Labour Rate Variance   Labour rates are largely determined by such external forces as labour markets and union contracts. The actual wage rate rarely departs from the standard rate. When labour rate variances do occur, they usually do so because an average wage rate is used for the rate standard or because more skilled and more highly paid labourers are used for less skilled tasks. Unexpected overtime can also be the cause of a labour rate variance.

Wage rates for a particular labour activity often differ among workers because of differing levels of seniority. Rather than selecting labour rate standards reflecting those different levels, an average wage rate is often chosen. As the seniority mix changes, the average rate changes. This will give rise to a labour rate variance; it also calls for a new standard to reflect the new seniority mix. Controllability is not assignable for this cause of a labour rate variance.

However, the *use* of labour is controllable by the production manager. The use of more skilled workers to perform less skilled tasks (or vice versa) is a decision that a production manager makes consciously. For this reason, responsibility for the labour rate variance is generally assigned to the individuals who decide how labour will be used.

Analysis of the Labour Rate Variance   Although a 5 percent variance is not likely to be judged significant, for illustrative purposes assume that an investigation is conducted. The cause of the variance at Crunchy Chips is found to be the use of more highly paid and skilled machine operators as inspectors, which occurred because two inspectors quit without formal notice. The corrective action is to hire and train two new inspectors.

Labour Efficiency Variance: Formula Approach   The **labour efficiency variance** (*LEV*) measures the difference between the labour hours that were actually used and the labour hours that should have been used:

$$LEV = (AH \times SR) - (SH \times SR)$$

or, after factoring:

$$LEV = (AH - SH)SR$$

where AH = The actual direct labour hours used
            SH = The standard direct labour hours that should have been used
            SR = The standard hourly wage rate

Computation of the Labour Efficiency Variance   Crunchy Chips used 360 direct labour hours for inspection while producing 48,500 bags of corn chips. From Exhibit 14–2, 0.007 hours per bag of chips at a cost of $7 per hour should have been used. The standard hours allowed for inspection or sorting are 339.5 (0.007 × 48,500). Thus, *AH* is 360, *SH* is 339.5, and *SR* is $7. The labour efficiency variance is computed as follows:

$$
\begin{aligned}
LEV &= (AH - SH)SR \\
&= (360 - 339.5) \times \$7 \\
&= 20.5 \times \$7 \\
&= \$143.50 \text{ U}
\end{aligned}
$$

Percentage of $SH \times SR$ = $143.50/$2,376.50 = 6%

Responsibility for the Labour Efficiency Variance   Generally speaking, production managers are responsible for the productive use of direct labour. However, as is true of all variances, once the cause is discovered, responsibility may be assigned elsewhere. For example, frequent breakdowns of machinery may cause interruptions and nonproductive use of labour. But the responsibility for these breakdowns may be faulty maintenance. If so, the maintenance manager should be charged with the unfavourable labour efficiency variance.

Production managers may be tempted to engage in dysfunctional behaviour if too much emphasis is placed on the labour efficiency variance. For example, to avoid losing hours and avoid using additional hours because of possible rework, a production manager could deliberately transfer defective units to finished goods.

Analysis of the Labour Efficiency Variance Assume that the $143.50 unfavourable variance was judged to be significant and its cause was investigated. The investigation revealed that more shutdowns of the process occurred because the duties of the machine operators were split between machine operations and inspection. (Recall that this reassignment was necessary because two inspectors quit unexpectedly.) This resulted in more idle time for inspection. Also, the machine operators were unable to meet the standard output per hour for inspection because of their lack of experience with the sorting process. The corrective action needed to solve the problem is the same as that recommended for the unfavourable rate variance—hire and train two new inspectors.

Sum of LRV and LEV From Exhibit 14–7, the total labour variance is $269.50 unfavourable. This total variance is the sum of the unfavourable labour rate variance and the unfavourable labour efficiency variance ($126.00 + $143.50).

VARIANCE ANALYSIS: OVERHEAD COSTS

Objective 5

Compute the variable and fixed overhead variances, and explain their meanings.

For direct materials and direct labour, total variances are broken down into price and efficiency variances. The total overhead variance—the difference between applied and actual overhead—is also broken down into component variances. How many component variances are computed depends on the method of variance analysis used. One method divides overhead into categories—fixed and variable—and isolates component variances for each category. The total variable overhead variance is divided into two components: the variable overhead spending variance and the variable overhead efficiency variance. Similarly, the total fixed overhead variance is divided into two components: the fixed overhead spending variance (also called the fixed overhead flexible budget variance) and the fixed overhead denominator variance.[11]

Variable Overhead Variances[12]

To illustrate the variable overhead variances, consider one week of activity for Crunchy Chips Company (the first week in March). The following data were gathered for this time period:

Variable overhead rate (standard)	$3.85 per direct labour hour
Actual variable overhead costs	$1,600
Actual hours worked	400[a]
Bags of chips produced	48,500
Hours allowed for production	378.3[b]
Applied variable overhead	$1,456[c]

[a] includes both inspection and machine operator labour
[b] .0078 (from Exhibit 14–2) × 48,500
[c] $3.85 × 378.3 (rounded to nearest dollar; overhead is applied using hours allowed in this standard cost system)

---

11. The denominator variance is often called the volume variance. In this book, we discourage the use of the expression "volume variance" without a qualifier. The denominator variance refers to the production (or manufacturing) volume variance and measures the effect of the denominator volume, used to allocate fixed manufacturing overhead, on the under- or overallocation of fixed manufacturing costs. The profit volume variance measures the effect of sales volume on profit, as discussed in Chapter 13.

12. The analysis provided here assumes a traditional costing environment with labour hours as the cost driver for variable overhead items. The implications of ABC for flexible budgeting and overhead variances were discussed in Chapter 13.

Total Variable Overhead Flexible Budget Variance The total variable overhead flexible budget variance (also called the total variable overhead variance) is the difference between the actual and the applied variable overhead. The total variable overhead variance is computed as follows:

$$\text{Total variable overhead variance} = \$1,600 - \$1,456$$
$$= \$144 \text{ U}$$

This total variance can be divided into spending and efficiency variances. This computation is illustrated using a three-pronged approach in Exhibit 14–8.

Variable Overhead Spending Variance The **variable overhead spending variance** measures the aggregate effect of differences in the actual variable overhead rate (*AVOR*) and the standard variable overhead rate (*SVOR*). The actual variable overhead rate is simply actual variable overhead divided by actual hours. For our example, this rate is $4 ($1,600/400 hours). The formula for computing the variable overhead spending variance is given below:

$$\text{Variable overhead spending variance} = (AVOR \times AH) - (SVOR \times AH)$$
$$= (AVOR - SVOR) \times AH$$
$$= (\$4 - \$3.85) \times 400$$
$$= (\$0.15) \times 400$$
$$= \$60 \text{ U}$$

Comparison to the Materials and Labour Price Variances The variable overhead spending variance is similar but not identical to the materials and labour price variances; there are some conceptual differences. Variable overhead is not a homogeneous input—it is made up of a large number of individual items, such as indirect materials, indirect labour, electricity, maintenance, and so on. The standard variable overhead rate represents the weighted cost per direct labour hour that should be incurred for all variable overhead items. The difference between what should have been spent per hour and what actually was spent per hour is a type of price variance.

A variable overhead spending variance can arise because prices for individual variable overhead items have increased or decreased. Assume, for the moment, that the price changes of individual overhead items are the only cause of the spending

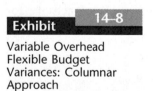

Exhibit 14–8

Variable Overhead
Flexible Budget
Variances: Columnar
Approach

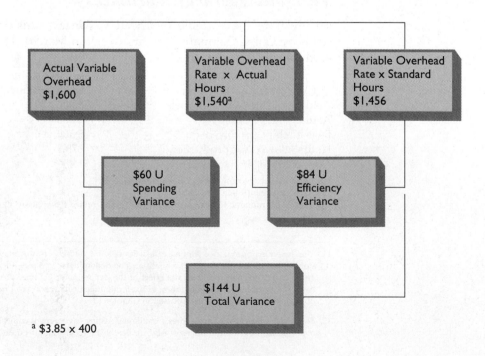

a $3.85 x 400

variance. If the spending variance is unfavourable, price increases for individual variable overhead items are the cause; if the spending variance is favourable, price decreases are dominating.

If price changes were the only source of the variable overhead spending variance, then it would be completely analogous to the materials and labour price variances. Unfortunately, the spending variance is also affected by how efficiently overhead is used. Waste or inefficiency in the use of variable overhead increases the actual variable overhead cost. This increased cost, in turn, is reflected in an increased actual variable overhead rate. Thus, even if the actual prices of the individual overhead items were equal to the budgeted or standard prices, an unfavourable variable overhead spending variance could still take place. For example, more kilowatt-hours of power may be used than should be, yet this variance is not captured by any change in direct labour hours. Insead, the additional kilowatt-hours show up as an increase in the total cost of power—and thus an increase in the total cost of variable overhead. Similarly, efficiency can decrease the actual variable overhead cost and decrease the actual variable overhead rate. Efficient use of variable overhead items contributes to a favourable spending variance. If the waste effect dominates, the net contribution will be unfavourable; if efficiency dominates, the net contribution is favourable. Thus, the variable overhead spending variance is the result of both price and efficiency.

Responsibility for the Variable Overhead Spending Variance Many variable overhead items are affected by several responsibility centres. For example, utilities are a joint cost.[13] To the extent that consumption of variable overhead can be traced to a responsibility centre, responsibility can be assigned. Consumption of indirect materials is an example of a traceable variable overhead cost.

Controllability is a prerequisite for assigning responsibility. Price changes of variable overhead items are essentially beyond the control of supervisors. If price changes are small (as they often are), the spending variance is primarily a matter of the efficient use of overhead in production, which is controllable by production supervisors. Accordingly, responsibility for the variable overhead spending variance is generally assigned to production departments.

Analysis of the Variable Overhead Spending Variance The $60 unfavourable variance simply reveals that in the aggregate, Crunchy Chips spent more on variable overhead than expected. Even if the variance were insignificant, it would reveal nothing about how well costs of individual variable overhead items were controlled. Control of variable overhead requires line-by-line analysis for each individual item. Exhibit 14–9 presents a performance report that supplies the line-by-line information essential for proper control of variable overhead.

From Exhibit 14–9, it is clear that two of the three items present no control problems for the firm. Electricity is the only item showing an unfavourable variance; in fact, it is the cause of the overall variable overhead spending variance. If the variance is significant, an investigation may be warranted. This investigation may reveal that the power company raised the price of electricity. If so, the cause of the variance is beyond the company's control. The correct response is to revise the budget formula to reflect the increased cost of electricity. However, if the price of electricity has remained unchanged, the usage of electricity is greater than expected. For example, the company may find that there were more startups and shutdowns of machinery than normal, causing an increased consumption of electricity.

13. If a company installs meters to measure consumption of utilities for each responsibility centre, responsibility can be assigned. However, the cost of assigning responsibility can sometimes exceed any potential benefit. The alternative is allocation. Unfortunately, allocations can be arbitrary, and it is often difficult to identify accurately the amount actually consumed.

Exhibit   14–9

Flexible Budget
Performance Report

	Cost Formula[a]	Actual Costs	Budget[b]	Spending Variance
Gas	$3.00	$1,190	$1,200	$10 F
Electricity	0.78	385	312	73 U
Water	0.07	25	28	3 F
Total cost	$3.85	$1,600	$1,540	$60 U

Crunchy Chips Company
Flexible Budget Performance Report
For the Week Ended March 8, 2001

[a] Per direct labour hour
[b] Computed using the cost formula and an activity level of 400 actual direct labour hours

Variable Overhead Efficiency Variance   Variable overhead is assumed to vary as the production volume changes. Thus, variable overhead changes in proportion to changes in the direct labour hours used. The **variable overhead efficiency variance** measures the change in variable overhead consumption that occurs because of efficient (or inefficient) use of direct labour. The efficiency variance is computed using the following formula:

$$\text{Variable overhead efficiency variance} = (AH - SH) \times SVOR$$
$$= (400 - 378.3) \times \$3.85$$
$$= 21.7 \times \$3.85$$
$$= \$84U \text{ (rounded)}$$

Responsibility for the Variable Overhead Efficiency Variance   The variable overhead efficiency variance is directly related to the direct labour efficiency or usage variance. If variable overhead is truly proportional to direct labour consumption, then like the labour usage variance, the variable overhead efficiency variance is caused by efficient or inefficient use of direct labour. If more (or fewer) direct labour hours are used than the standard calls for, the total variable overhead cost will increase (or decrease). The validity of the measure depends on the validity of the relationship between variable overhead costs and direct labour hours. In other words, do variable overhead costs *really* change in proportion to changes in direct labour hours? If so, responsibility for the variable overhead efficiency variance should be assigned to the individual who has responsibility for the use of direct labour: the production manager.

Analysis of the Variable Overhead Efficiency Variance   At Crunchy Chips, the reasons for the unfavourable variable overhead efficiency variance are the same as those offered for the unfavourable labour usage variance. More hours were used than the standard called for because of excessive idle time for inspectors and because the machine operators used as substitute inspectors were inexperienced in sorting. More information concerning the effect of labour usage on variable overhead is available in a line-by-line analysis of individual variable overhead items. This can be accomplished by comparing the budget allowance for the actual hours used with the budget allowance for the standard hours allowed for each item. A performance report that makes this comparison for all variable overhead costs is shown in Exhibit 14–10.

From Exhibit 14–10, the cost of gas is affected most by inefficient use of labour. This can be explained by the need to keep the cooking oil hot (assuming that gas is used for cooking), even though the cooking process is slowed down by the subsequent sorting process.

The column labelled "Budget for Standard Hours" gives the amount that should have been spent on variable overhead for the actual output. The total of all items in this column is the applied variable overhead, the amount assigned to production in a standard cost system. Note that in a standard cost system, variable overhead is

Exhibit   14–10

Performance Report—
Variable Overhead

**Crunchy Chips Company
Performance Report
For the Week Ended March 8, 2001**

Cost	Cost Formula[a]	Actual Costs	Budget for Actual Hours	Spending Variance[b]	Budget for Standard Hours[c]	Efficiency Variance[d]
Gas	$3.00	$1,190	$1,200	$10 F	$1,135	$65 U
Electricity	0.78	385	312	73 U	295	17 U
Water	0.07	25	28	3 F	26	2 U
Total	$3.85	$1,600	$1,540	$60 U	$1,456	$84 U

[a] Per direct labour hour
[b] Spending variance = Actual costs − Budget for actual hours
[c] Computed using the cost formula and an activity level of 378.3 standard hours. Rounded to the nearest dollar.
[d] Efficiency variance = Budget for actual hours − Budget for standard hours

applied using the hours allowed for the actual output (*SH*), while in normal costing, variable overhead is applied using actual hours (see Chapter 4). Although not shown in Exhibit 14–10, the difference between actual costs and this column is the total variable overhead variance (underapplied by $144). Thus, the underapplied variable overhead variance is the sum of the spending and efficiency variances.

Fixed Overhead Variances

The Crunchy Chips example will illustrate the computation of the fixed overhead variances. The data needed for the example are given below:

Budgeted/Planned Items

Budgeted fixed overhead	$749,970
Practical activity	23,400 direct labour hours[a]
Standard fixed overhead rate	$32.05[b]

[a] Hours allowed to produce 3,000,000 bags of chips: 0.0078 × 3,000,000
[b] $749,970/23,400

Actual Results

Actual production	2,750,000 bags of chips
Actual fixed overhead cost	$749,000
Standard hours allowed for actual production	21,450[a]

[a] 0.0078 (from Exhibit 14–2) × 2,750,000

Total Fixed Overhead Variance

The total fixed overhead variance is the difference between actual fixed overhead and applied fixed overhead, when applied fixed overhead is obtained by multiplying the standard fixed overhead rate times the standard hours allowed for the actual output. Thus, the applied fixed overhead is as follows:

$$\text{Applied fixed overhead} = \text{Standard fixed overhead rate} \times \text{Standard hours}$$
$$= \$32.05 \times 21,450$$
$$= \$687,473 \text{ (rounded)}$$

The total fixed overhead variance is the difference between the actual fixed overhead and the applied fixed overhead:

$$\text{Total fixed overhead variance} = \$749,000 - \$687,473$$
$$= \$61,527 \text{ underapplied}$$

To help managers understand why fixed overhead was underapplied by $61,527, the total variance can be broken into two variances: the fixed overhead spending variance and the fixed overhead denominator (or volume) variance. The calculation of the two variances is illustrated in Exhibit 14–11.

Fixed Overhead Spending Variance   The **fixed overhead spending variance** is defined as the difference between the actual fixed overhead and the budgeted fixed overhead. For Crunchy Chips, the spending variance is favourable, because less was spent on fixed overhead items than was budgeted.

Responsibility for the Fixed Overhead Spending Variance   Fixed overhead is made up of a number of individual items, such as salaries, depreciation, taxes, and insurance. Many fixed overhead items result from long-run investments and are not subject to change in the short run; consequently, fixed overhead costs are often beyond the immediate control of management. Since many fixed overhead costs are affected primarily by long-run decisions, not by changes in production levels, the budget variance is usually small. For example, depreciation, salaries, taxes, and insurance costs are not likely to be much different than planned.

Analysis of the Fixed Overhead Spending Variance   Because fixed overhead is made up of many individual items, a line-by-line comparison of budgeted costs with actual costs provides more information concerning the causes of the spending variance. Exhibit 14–12 provides such a report. The report reveals that the fixed overhead spending variance is essentially in line with expectations. The fixed overhead spending variances, both on a line-item basis and in the aggregate, are relatively small.

Fixed Overhead Denominator Variance   The **fixed overhead denominator variance** is the difference between budgeted fixed overhead and applied fixed overhead. The denominator variance measures the effect of the actual output departing from the output used at the beginning of the year to compute the predetermined standard fixed overhead rate. To see this, let $SH(D)$ represent the standard hours allowed for the denominator volume (the volume used at the beginning of the year to compute the predetermined fixed overhead rate). The standard fixed overhead rate ($SFOR$) is computed in the following way:

$$SFOR = (\text{Budgeted fixed overhead})/SH(D)$$

Exhibit 14–11

Fixed Overhead Variances

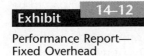

Exhibit 14–12

Performance Report—
Fixed Overhead

Fixed Overhead Items	Actual Cost	Budgeted Cost	Variance
	Crunchy Chips Company		
	Performance Report		
	For the Year Ended 2001		
Depreciation	$530,000	$530,000	$ —
Salaries	159,370	159,970	600 F
Taxes	50,500	50,000	500 U
Insurance	9,130	10,000	870 F
Total fixed	$749,000	$749,970	$970 F

From Exhibit 14–11, the fixed overhead denominator variance can be computed as follows:

Fixed overhead denominator variance = Budgeted fixed overhead – Applied fixed overhead

$$= SFOR \times SH(D) - SFOR \times SH$$
$$= SFOR \times (SH(D) - SH)$$
$$= \$32.05 \times (23{,}400 - 21{,}450)$$
$$= \$62{,}497 \text{ U (rounded)}$$

Thus, for a fixed overhead denominator variance to occur, the denominator hours, $SH(D)$, must differ from the standard hours allowed for the actual volume, SH. At the beginning of the year, Crunchy had the capacity to produce 3,000,000 bags of chips, using 23,400 direct labour hours. The actual outcome was 2,750,000 bags produced, using 21,450 standard hours. Thus, less was produced than expected, so an unfavourable fixed overhead denominator variance arises.

But what is the meaning of this variance? The variance occurs because the actual output differs from predicted output volume. At the beginning of the year, if management had used 2,750,000 bags of corn chips as the denominator volume, the denominator variance would not have existed. In this view, the denominator variance is seen as prediction error—a measure of management's inability to select the correct volume over which to spread fixed overhead.

If, however, the denominator volume represented the amount that management believed *could* be produced and sold, the denominator variance conveys more significant information. If the actual volume is less than the denominator volume, the denominator variance signals management that a loss in volume has occurred. That loss is not equivalent, however, to the dollar value of the denominator variance. The loss is equal to the lost contribution margin on the units that were not produced and sold. However, the denominator variance is positively correlated with the loss. For example, suppose that the contribution margin per standard direct labour hour is $40. By producing only 2.75 million bags of chips instead of 3 million bags, the company lost sales of 250,000 bags. This is equivalent to 1,950 hours (0.0078 × 250,000). At $40 per hour, the loss is $78,000. This variance was called the profit volume variance in Chapter 13. The unfavourable denominator variance of $62,497 signals this loss but in this case understates it. In this sense, the denominator variance is a measure of utilization of capacity, but is clearly less useful than the profit volume variance. The demoninator variance is analogous to the cost of unused capacity described in Chapter 3. Unlike the profit volume variance, its management does not reflect opportunity costs.

Responsibility for the Denominator Variance Assuming that denominator variance measures capacity utilization implies that the general responsibility for this variance should be assigned to the production department. At times, however, investigation into the reasons for a significant denominator variance may reveal the cause to be factors beyond the control of production. In this instance, specific responsibility may be assigned elsewhere. For example, if purchasing acquires a raw material of lower quality than usual, significant rework time may result, causing lower production and an unfavourable denominator variance. In this case, responsibility for the variance rests with purchasing, not production.

Summary of Manufacturing Cost Flexible Budget Variances

Below is a summary of the flexible budget variances discussed in this chapter, with common alternative names found in practice. Each variable cost has a price dimension and an input quantity dimension:

Cost Item	Price Dimension	Quantity Dimension
Materials	Price variance (based on usage)	Quantity variance
	Purchase price variance (based on purchases)	Usage variance
		Efficiency variance
Labour	Price variance	Quantity variance
	Rate variance	Usage variance
		Efficiency variance
Variable overhead	Rate variance	Quantity variance
	Spending variance	Usage variance
		Efficiency variance
Fixed overhead	Price variance	Not applicable
	Spending variance	Not applicable
	Flexible budget variance	Not applicable

The fixed overhead denominator variance is not a flexible budget variance and is unique to fixed overhead. The denominator variance results from the difference between the flexible budget and applied fixed overhead, and is solely due to the denominator used in prorating fixed overhead on the basis of some output measure (such as units produced) or input measure (such as labour hours or machine hours).

APPENDIX A: ACCOUNTING FOR VARIANCES

Objective 6

Prepare journal entries for materials and labour variances, and describe the accounting for overhead variances.

To illustrate recording variances, assume that the materials price variance is computed at the time materials are purchased. With this assumption, a general rule for a firm's inventory accounts is that all inventories are carried at standard cost. Actual costs are never entered into an inventory account. In recording variances, unfavourable variances are always debits, and favourable variances are always credits.

Entries for Direct Materials Variances

Materials Purchase Price Variance The entry to record the purchase of materials is given below (assuming an *unfavourable MPV* and that *AQP* is materials purchased).

Materials	$SP \times AQ$	
Materials purchase price variance	$(AP - SP) \times AQ$	
Accounts payable		$AP \times AQ$

For example, if *AP* is \$0.252 per kilogram of corn, *SP* is \$0.216, and 20,500 kilograms are purchased, the entry would be as follows:

Materials	\$4,428	
Materials purchase price variance	738	
Accounts payable		\$5,166

Notice that the raw materials are carried in the inventory account at standard cost.

Materials Usage Variance   The general form for the entry to record the issuance and usage of materials, assuming a *favourable MUV*, is as follows:

Work in process	$SQ \times SP$	
Materials usage variance		$(AQ - SQ) \times SP$
Materials		$AQ \times SP$

Here *AQ* is the materials issued and used, not necessarily equal to the materials purchased. Notice that only standard quantities and standard prices are used to assign costs to Work in Process; no actual costs enter this account.

    For example, if *AQ* is 20,500 kilograms of corn, *SQ* is 24,250 kilograms, and *SP* is \$0.216 per kilogram, then the entry would be as follows:

Work in process	\$5,238	
Materials usage variance		\$ 810
Materials		4,428

Notice that the favourable usage variance appears as a credit entry.

Entries for Direct Labour Variances

Unlike the direct materials variances, both types of labour variances are recorded in a single entry. The general form of this entry is given below (assuming a *favourable* labour rate variance and an *unfavourable* labour efficiency variance).

Work in Process	$SH \times SR$	
Labour efficiency variance	$(AH - SH) \times SR$	
Labour rate variance	$(AR - SR) \times AH$	
Accrued payroll		$AH \times AR$

Notice again that only standard hours and standard rates are used to assign costs to Work in Process. Actual prices or quantities are not used.

    To give a specific example, assume that *AH* is 360, *SH* is 339.5, *AR* is \$7.35, and *SR* is \$7. The following general ledger entry would be made:

Work in process	\$2,376.50	
Labour efficiency variance	143.50	
Labour rate variance	126.00	
Accrued payroll		\$2,646.00

Disposition of Materials and Labour Variances

At the end of the year, the variances for materials and labour are usually closed to Cost of Goods Sold. (This practice is acceptable provided that variances are not material in amount.) With the use of the above data, the entries would take the following form:

Cost of goods sold	$1007.50	
Materials purchase price variance		$738.00
Labour efficiency variance		143.50
Labour rate variance		126.00
Materials usage variance	810.00	
Cost of goods sold		810.00

If the variances are material, they should be prorated among various accounts if management desires to maintain the firm's financial statements on an actual costing basis. The materials purchase price variance is prorated among Materials Inventory, Materials Usage Variance, Work in Process, and Cost of Goods Sold. The remaining materials and labour variances are prorated among Work in Process, Finished Goods, and Cost of Goods Sold. Typically, materials variances are prorated on the basis of the cost of materials balances in each of these accounts and labour variances on the basis of the labour balances in the accounts.

Overhead Variances

Although overhead variances can be recorded following a pattern similar to that described for labour and materials, these variances are more generally treated as part of a periodic overhead analysis. Applied overhead is accumulated in the applied accounts, and actual overhead is accumulated in the control accounts. Periodically (for example, monthly), performance reports that provide overhead variance information are prepared. At the end of the year, the applied accounts and control accounts are closed out and the variances isolated. The overhead variances are then disposed of by closing them to Cost of Goods Sold if they are not material, or by prorating them among Work in Process, Finished Goods, and Cost of Goods Sold if they are material.

APPENDIX B: PROFITABILITY ANALYSIS

Objective 7

Use variance analysis as an analytical tool for profitability analysis.

In Chapter 13, the discussion of flexible budgeting was followed by an example of profitability analysis where the effects of sales volume, selling prices, and cost performance were identified. This appendix expands on the idea of analyzing actual profit against a static profit budget. The purpose is to show an example of the information that variance analysis can provide as an analytical tool that is adaptable to different situations.

Consider the following example for Virtuality Ltd., a manufacturer of two types of helmets used in virtual reality architectural design and other applications. Virtuality sells these products in the Canadian market. Exhibit 14–13 shows selected

Exhibit 14–13

Virtuality Ltd.

	Budgeted	Actual
Sales of product A (in units)	360	390
Sales of product B (in units)	240	225
Total sales (in units)	600	615
Selling price per unit of A	$ 10,000	$ 10,500
Variable cost per unit of A	7,000	6,500
Contribution margin per unit of A	$ 3,000	$ 4,000
Selling price per unit of B	$ 5,000	$ 4,500
Variable cost per unit of B	2,500	2,000
Contribution margin per unit of B	$ 2,500	$ 2,500
Total fixed costs	$450,000	$462,000

information about the company's annual budget and actual results for its two products. Assume that Virtuality has no inventories and that it uses variable costing.

Budgeted sales volume was based on an expected industry volume for Products A and B (combined) of 4,500 units. Actual industry volume was 4,950 units. Although Products A and B serve different needs, they are considered to be substitute products, in the sense that a customer is likely to buy either a unit of A or a unit of B, but not both.

This example provides an analysis of variances that identifies the effect of each factor on profit. Using the data provided in Exhibit 14–13, Exhibit 14–14 shows that budgeted operating profit was $1,230,000, and actual profit was $1,660,500. This results in a **total profit variance**, the difference between actual and budgeted profit (using the static budget), in the amount of $430,500F. The concepts of cost variance analysis can be used to provide insight into the effect of various changes on profit. It is obvious that the actual sales volume was higher for A by 30 units but lower for B by 15 units. This raises the question of the sales volume effect on revenues and variable costs. Furthermore, selling prices were higher by $500 for A but lower for B by $500. Unit variable costs were lower for A by $500 and lower for B by $500. Finally, fixed costs were higher than budgeted by $12,000. Each of these factors has an effect on profits. To show more clearly the impact of each of these factors or causes on the bottom line, a series of variances are computed to measure each factor's effects on profits while holding other factors constant. The first stage of this analysis is shown in Exhibit 14–14.

The following is a breakdown of the effect of each factor on profit as shown in Exhibit 14–14.

1. *Sales Price Variance* The **sales price variance** measures the direct effect of the change in selling prices on profit. Actual selling prices were $500 higher than budget for A and $500 lower for B. Based on the actual units sold, this is a variance in profit of $82,500F (390 × $500 = $195,000F for A and 225 × $500 = $112,500U for B).
2. *Profit Volume Variance (Gross)* This variance measures the effect on profits of the increase from budget in sales of A by 30 units and the decrease in the sales of B by 15 units, other things remaining constant. The sales volume changes affect both revenue and variable cost. The profit volume variance for revenue is $225,000F (30 × $10,000 = $300,000F for A, and 15 × $5,000 = $75,000U for B), and the profit volume variance for variable cost is $172,500U (30 × $7,000 = $210,000U for A, and 15 × $2,500 = $37,500F for B). Together the effect is $52,500F. This variance can be calculated directly from the standard unit contribution margins (30 × $3,000 = $90,000F for A, and 15 × $2,500 = $37,500U for B, for a total of $52,500 F).

Exhibit 14–14

Comparison of Actual and Budget Profits

	Actual Results	Flexible Budget[a]	Flexible Budget Variance[b]	Static Budget	Profit Volume Variance[c]
Sales revenue	$5,107,500[d]	$5,025,000[e]	(1)$ 82,500 F	$4,800,000[f]	$225,000 F
Variable costs	2,985,000[g]	3,292,500[h]	(3) 307,500 F	3,120,000[i]	172,500 U
Contribution margin	$2,122,500	$1,732,500	$390,000 F	$1,680,000	(2)$ 52,500 F
Fixed costs	462,000	450,000	(4) 12,000 U	450,000	—
Profit	$1,660,500	$1,282,500	$378,000 F	$1,230,000	$ 52,500 F

[a] Based on actual sales and budgeted prices and costs
[b] Actual results minus flexible budget
[c] Flexible budget minus static budget
[d] (390 × $10,500) + (225 × $4,500)
[e] (390 × $10,000) + (225 × $5,000)
[f] (360 × $10,000) + (240 × $5,000)
[g] (390 × $6,500) + (225 × $2,000)
[h] (390 × $7,000) + (225 × $2,500)
[i] (360 × $7,000) + (240 × $2,500)

3. *Variable Cost Flexible Budget Variance* Actual unit variable costs were $500 lower than budget for A, and $500 lower for B. These unit-cost differences account for a profit variance of $307,500F (390 × $500 = $195,000F for A, and 225 × $500 = $112,500F for B).
4. *Fixed Cost Flexible Budget Variance* Because fixed costs are not affected by sales volume, the variance is the difference between the actual fixed costs and the budgeted fixed costs, or $12,000U.

These variances account for the $430,500F profit variance as shown in the following summary:

Sales price variance	$ 82,500 F
Profit volume variance (gross)	52,500 F
Variable cost flexible budget variance	307,500 F
Fixed cost flexible budget variance	12,000 U
Total profit variance	$430,500 F

The variances can be analyzed in greater detail. Variable cost variances can be decomposed into manufacturing and nonmanufacturing; manufacturing cost variances can be decomposed into material, labour, and overhead; each can be further decomposed into price and quantity variances, as detailed in this chapter. In the same way, it is possible to analyze the profit volume variance (gross) in more detail. The concept is the same; isolate the effect of one factor, such as total sales volume, while holding the other factors, such as sales mix or selling price, constant. An application of this analysis is illustrated in the next section.

Detailed Analysis of the Profit Volume Variance

The **profit volume variance (gross)** can be broken down into a **profit volume variance (net)** and a **sales mix variance** as follows:

1. *Profit Volume Variance (Net)* This variance measures the effect on profit of the increase in total sales volume from the budget of 600 units to the actual volume of 615 units, with other factors (including sales mix and contribution margin per unit) being held constant. From Exhibit 14–14, the average standard contribution margin for the budgeted sales mix is $1,680,000/600 = $2,800. The net effect on profit of sales volume changes is (615 – 600) × $2,800 = $42,000F.
2. *Sales Mix Variance* This variance measures the effect of the change from the budgeted sales mix. From Exhibit 14–14, the average standard contribution margin for the actual sales mix is $1,732,500/615 = $2,817.07. The effect on profit of the change from the budgeted sales mix is ($2,817.07 – $2,800) × 615 = $10,500F.

The total of these two components is equal to the profit volume variance (gross) ($42,000F + $10,500F = $52,500F).

Another level of analysis is possible. The profit volume variance (net) can be broken into an **industry volume variance** and a **market share variance** as follows:

1. *Industry Volume Variance* Virtuality Ltd. based its sales budget on an industry volume of 4,500 units and expected to sell a total of 600 units. The actual industry sales were 4,950 units, or 10 percent higher than expected. All other factors being held constant, the increase in industry sales should increase Virtuality's sales by 600 × 10 percent = 60 units. The effect on profit of the increase in industry sales is 60 × $2,800 = $168,000F.
2. *Market Share Variance* Virtuality's actual market share was 12.4 percent (615/4,950) and not the expected 13.3 percent (600/4,500). Had Virtuality maintained its market share, it would have obtained 660 units (4,950 × 13.3 percent) instead of 615 units. The effect on profit of the decrease in the company's share of the market is (660 – 615) × $2,800 = $126,000U.

Profit Variance Analysis

Industry volume variance	$168,000 F		
Market share variance	126,000 U		
Profit volume variance (net)		$42,000 F	
Sales mix variance		10,500 F	
Profit volume variance (gross)			$ 52,500 F
Sales price variance			82,500 F
Variable cost flexible budget variance			12,000 U
Fixed cost flexible budget variance			307,500 F
Total profit variance			$430,500 F

The total of industry volume and market share variances is equal to the profit volume variance (net) ($168,000F + $126,000U = $42,000F).

This example illustrates how variance analysis can be used as an analytical tool to obtain more information on the economic effects on income of the various factors that varied from the budget. The results are summarized in Exhibit 14–15.

Exhibit 14–16 starts with the static profit budget on the left and adjusts the budget in successive steps, one factor at a time, ending with the actual profit performance. This generates a series of variances that account for the difference between budgeted and actual profit.

The sequence of changing factors can affect the resulting variances. It is important to isolate exogenous factors first: volume, mix, and price, in that order. After that, the cost variances will reflect actual volume, mix, and price. As another illustration, the change in industry volume is less controllable than the change in market share. Thus the sequence of variance calculations to decompose the profit volume variance (net) will begin with industry volume and end with market share variances. As stated before, this is an illustration of using profitability variance analysis for Virtuality. Other companies can create their own tailor-made approach to profitability variance analysis.

Exhibit 14-16   Virtuality Profitability Analysis

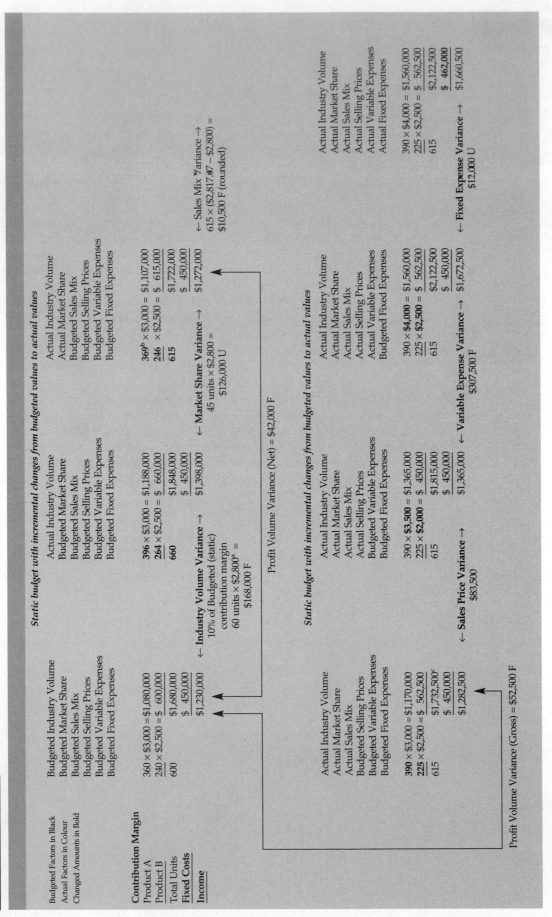

[a] Average budgeted contribution margin based on standard mix = $1,680,000 / 600 = $2,800

[b] Actual volume of 615: 60% from A and 40% from B

[c] Average budgeted contribution margin based on actual mix = $1,732,500 / 615 = $2,817

SUMMARY OF LEARNING OBJECTIVES

1. Explain how unit standards are set and why standard cost systems are adopted.
A standard cost system budgets quantities and costs on a unit basis. These unit budgets are for labour, material, and overhead. Standard costs, therefore, are the amount that should be expended to produce a product or service. Standards are set using historical experience, engineering studies, and input from operating personnel, marketing, and accounting. Currently attainable standards are those that can be achieved under efficient operating conditions. Ideal standards are those achievable under maximum efficiency—under ideal operating conditions. Standard cost systems are adopted to improve planning and control and to facilitate product costing. By comparing actual outcomes with standards, and breaking the variance into price and quantity components, this approach provides detailed feedback to managers. This information allows managers to exercise a greater degree of cost control than that found in a normal or actual cost system. Decisions such as those related to bidding are also made more easily when a standard cost system is in place.

2. Explain the purpose of a standard cost sheet.
The standard cost sheet provides the detail for the computation of the standard cost per unit. It shows the standard costs for materials, labour, variable, and fixed overhead. It also reveals the quantity of each input that should be used to produce one unit of output. Using these unit quantity standards, the standard quantity of materials allowed and the standard hours allowed can be computed for the actual output. These computations play an important role in variance analysis.

3. Describe the basic concepts underlying variance analysis, and explain when variances should be investigated.
The budget variance is the difference between the actual costs and the planned costs. In a standard cost system, the budget variance is broken down into price and usage variances. By breaking the budget variances into price and usage variances, managers have more ability to analyze and control the total variance. Variances should be investigated if they are material and if the benefits of corrective action are greater than the costs of investigation. Because of the difficulty of assessing costs and benefits on a case-by-case basis, many firms set up formal control limits—either a dollar amount, a percentage, or both. Others use judgment to assess the need to investigate.

4. Compute the materials and labour variances, and explain how they are used for control.
The materials price and usage variances are computed using either a three-pronged approach or formulas. The three-pronged approach for materials is illustrated in Exhibit 14–6. The materials price variance is the difference between what should have been paid for materials and what was paid (generally associated with the purchasing activity). The materials usage variance is the difference between the standard cost of the materials that should have been used and the amount that was used (generally associated with the production activity). When a significant variance is signalled, an investigation occurs to find the cause. Corrective action is taken, if possible, to put the system back in control. The labour variances are computed using either a three-pronged approach or formulas. The three-pronged approach for labour is illustrated in Exhibit 14–7. The labour rate variance is caused by the actual wage rate differing from the standard wage rate. It is the difference between the wages that were paid and those that should have been paid. The labour efficiency variance is the difference between the cost of the labour that was used and the cost of the labour that should have been used. When a significant variance is signalled, investigation is called for and corrective action should be taken, if possible, to put the system back in control.

5. Compute the variable and fixed overhead variances, and explain their meanings.
The variable overhead spending variance is the difference between the actual variable overhead cost and the budgeted variable overhead cost for actual hours worked. It is therefore a budget variance, resulting from price changes and efficient or inefficient use of variable overhead inputs. The variable efficiency variance is the difference between budgeted variable overhead at actual hours and applied variable overhead. It is strictly attributable to the efficiency of labour usage and assumes that the variable overhead items are all driven by direct labour hours.

The fixed overhead spending variance is the difference between the actual fixed overhead costs and the budgeted fixed overhead costs. Therefore, it is simply a budget variance. The denominator variance is the difference between the budgeted fixed overhead and the applied fixed overhead. It occurs whenever the actual production volume is different from the expected production volume used to determine the fixed overhead rate, and is thus a measure of capacity utilization.

6. Prepare journal entries for materials and labour variances, and describe the accounting for overhead variances. (Appendix A)
Assuming that the materials price variance is computed at the point of purchase, all inventories are carried

at standard cost. Actual costs are never entered into an inventory account. Accounts are created for materials price and usage variances and for labour rate and efficiency variances. Unfavourable variances are always debits; favourable variances are always credits. Overhead variances are generally not journalized. Instead, periodic overhead reports are prepared that provide overhead variance information.

7. Use variance analysis as an analytical tool for profitability analysis. (Appendix B)

The same concepts used to analyze cost variances can be used to identify the effects of different factors on profit. Variances related to sales volume and price factors, variable costs, and fixed costs can be isolated. In turn, theses variances can be decomposed into components. For example, the profit volume variance may be decomposed into profit volume (net) and sales mix variances (for multiproduct firms), and the profit volume variance (net) may be decomposed into industry volume and market share components. This analysis allows managers to identify the factors that have contributed significantly to profit performance.

KEY TERMS

Control limits, 622
Currently attainable standards, 617
Efficiency variance, 620
Favourable (F) variances, 621
Fixed overhead denominator variance, 634
Fixed overhead spending variance, 634
Ideal standards, 616
Industry volume variance, 640
Labour efficiency variance, 628
Labour rate variance, 627
Market share variance, 640

Materials price variance, 624
Materials purchase price variance, 625
Materials usage variance, 625
Price (rate) variance, 620
Price standards, 616
Profit volume variance (gross), 640
Profit volume variance (net), 640
Quantity standards, 616
Rate variance, 620
Sales mix variance, 640
Sales price variance, 639
Standard cost per unit, 618

Standard cost sheet, 618
Standard hours allowed, 620
Standard quantity of materials allowed, 620
Total flexible budget variance, 620
Total profit variance, 639
Unfavourable (U) variances, 621
Usage (efficiency) variance, 620
Variable overhead efficiency variance, 632
Variable overhead spending variance, 630

REVIEW PROBLEMS

MATERIALS, LABOUR, AND OVERHEAD VARIANCES

Wangsgard Manufacturing has the following standard cost sheet for one of its products:

Direct materials (2 metres @ $5)	$10
Direct labour (0.5 hours @ $10)	5
Variable overhead (0.5 hours @ $4)	2
Fixed overhead (0.5 hours @ $2[a])	1
Standard unit cost	$18

[a] Rate based on expected activity of 2,500 hours

During the most recent year, the following actual results were recorded:

Production	6,000 units
Direct materials (11,750 metres purchased and used)	$61,100
Direct labour (2,900 hours)	29,580
Variable overhead	10,500
Fixed overhead	6,000

Required:

Compute the following variances:

1. Materials price and usage variances
2. Labour rate and efficiency variances
3. Variable overhead spending and efficiency variances
4. Fixed overhead spending and denominator variances

Solution

1. Materials variances:

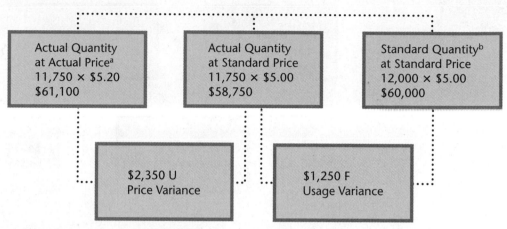

^{a} $61,100/11,750 = $5.20 = Actual price
^{b} 2 × 6,000 = 12,000 metres = Standard quantity

Or, using formulas:

$$MPV = (AP - SP) \times AQ$$
$$= (\$5.20 - \$5.00) \times 11,750$$
$$= \$2,350 \text{ U}$$

$$MUV = (AQ - SQ) \times SP$$
$$= (11,750 - 12,000) \times \$5.00$$
$$= \$1,250 \text{ F}$$

2. Labour variances:

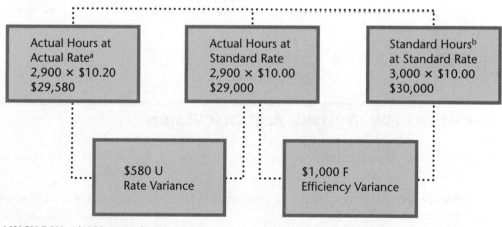

^{a} $29,580/2,900 = $10.20 = Actual price
^{b} 0.5 × 6,000 = 3,000 = Standard hours

Or, using formulas:

$$LRV = (AR - SR) \times AH$$
$$= (\$10.20 - \$10.00) \times 2,900$$
$$= \$580 \text{ U}$$

$$LEV = (AH - SH) \times SR$$
$$= (2,900 - 3,000) \times \$10.00$$
$$= \$1,000 \text{ F}$$

3. Variable overhead variances:

4. Fixed overhead variances:

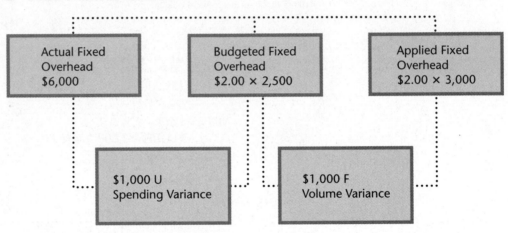

QUESTIONS FOR WRITING AND DISCUSSION

1. Discuss the difference between budgets and standard costs.

2. Describe the relationship that unit standards have with flexible budgeting.

3. What is the *quantity decision*? The *pricing decision*?

4. Why is historical experience often a poor basis for establishing standards?

5. Should standards be set by engineering studies? Why or why not?

6. What are ideal standards? currently attainable standards? Of the two, which is usually adopted? Why?

7. Explain why standard cost systems are adopted.

8. How does standard costing improve the control function?

9. Discuss the differences among actual costing, normal costing, and standard costing.

10. What is the purpose of a standard cost sheet?

11. The budget variance for variable production costs is broken down into quantity and price variances. Explain why the quantity variance is more useful for control purposes than the price variance.

12. When should a standard cost variance be investigated?

13. What are control limits and how are they set?

14. Explain why the materials price variance is often computed at the point of purchase rather than at the point of issuance.

15. The materials usage variance is always the responsibility of the production supervisor. Do you agree or disagree? Why?

16. The labour rate variance is never controllable. Do you agree or disagree? Why?

17. Suggest some possible causes of an unfavourable labour efficiency variance.

18. Explain why the variable overhead spending variance is not a pure price variance.

19. The variable overhead efficiency variance has nothing to do with efficient use of variable overhead. Do you agree or disagree? Why?

20. Explain why the fixed overhead spending variance is usually very small.

21. What is the cause of an unfavourable denominator variance? Does the denominator variance convey any meaningful information to managers?

22. Which do you think is more important for control of fixed overhead costs: the spending variance or the denominator variance? Explain.

EXERCISES

14–1

Setting Standards and Assigning Responsibility

LO1

Associated Media Graphics (AMG) is a rapidly expanding company involved in the mass reproduction of instructional materials. Ralph Boston, AMG's owner and manager, has made a concerted effort to provide a quality product at a fair price with delivery on the promised due date. Expanding sales have been attributed to this philosophy. As the business grows, however, Ralph is finding it increasingly difficult to personally supervise the operations of AMG. As a result, he is beginning to institute an organizational structure that would facilitate management control.

One recent change was to designate the operating departments as cost centres, with control over departmental operations transferred from Ralph to each departmental manager. However, quality control still reports directly to Ralph, as do the finance and accounting functions. A materials manager was hired to purchase all raw materials and to oversee inventory handling (receiving, storage, and so on) and recordkeeping. The materials manager is also responsible for maintaining an adequate inventory based upon planned production levels.

The loss of personal control over AMG's operations caused Ralph to look for a method to evaluate performance efficiently. Dave Cress, a new cost accountant, proposed the use of a standard cost system. Variances for material, labour, and overhead could then be calculated and reported directly to Ralph.

Required:

1. Assume that AMG is going to implement a standard cost system and establish standards for materials, labour, and overhead.
   a. Who should be involved in setting the standards for each cost component?
   b. What factors should be considered in establishing the standards for each cost component?
2. Describe the basis for assignment of responsibility under a standard cost system. (US CMA adapted)

14–2

Computation of Inputs Allowed; Materials and Labour

LO2

During the year, Marsing Company produced 45,000 mechanical components for a tractor manufacturer. Marsing's materials and labour standards are as follows:

Direct materials (3 components @ $8) $24.00
Direct labour (0.8 hours @ $12)   9.60

Required:

1. Compute the standard hours allowed for the production of 45,000 units.
2. Compute the standard number of components allowed for the production of 45,000 units.

14–3

Materials and Labour Variances

LO4

Spreadsheet

Jus Company produces fruit juices that are sold in litres. Recently, the company adopted the following standards for each litre of its cranberry juice:

Direct materials (1 litre @ $1.28)	$1.28
Direct labour (0.03 hours @ $7)	0.21
Standard prime cost	$1.49

During the first week of operation, the company experienced the following actual results:

a. Units produced: 8,000 litres
b. Litres of materials purchased: 8,400 litres at $1.15
c. There are no beginning or ending inventories of raw materials
d. Direct labour: 250 hours at $7.50

Required:

1. Compute price and usage variances for direct materials.
2. Compute the rate and efficiency variances for direct labour.

14–4

Overhead Variances

LO5

Spreadsheet

Anderson, Inc. has gathered the following data on last year's operations:

a. Units produced: 28,000
b. Direct labour: 20,000 hours @ $9
c. Actual fixed overhead: $280,000
d. Actual variable overhead: $92,000

Anderson employs a standard cost system. During the year, the following rates were used: standard fixed overhead rate, $12 per hour; standard variable overhead rate, $4.05 per hour. The labour standard requires 0.75 hours per unit produced. (These rates were based on a standard normal volume of 22,500 direct labour hours.)

Required:

1. Compute the fixed overhead spending and denominator variances.
2. Compute the variable overhead spending and efficiency variances.

14–5

Decomposition of Budget Variances; Materials and Labour

LO4

Cordero Corporation produces high-quality leather purses. The company uses a standard cost system and has set the following standards for materials and labour:

Leather (6 strips @ $8)	$48
Direct labour (1.5 hours @ $12)	18
Total prime cost	$66

During the year, Cordero produced 10,000 leather purses. Actual leather purchased was 61,000 strips at $7.96 per strip. There were no beginning or ending inventories of leather. Actual direct labour was 15,600 hours at $12.50 per hour.

Required:

1. Compute the costs of leather and direct labour that should have been incurred for the production of 10,000 leather purses.
2. Compute the total budget variances for materials and labour.
3. Break down the total materials variance into a price variance and a usage variance.
4. Break down the total labour variance into a rate variance and an efficiency variance.

14–6

Materials and Labour Variances; Journal Entries; Appendix A

LO4, LO6

Mawani Products produces instructional aids. Among the company's products are whiteboards, which use coloured markers instead of chalk. They are particularly popular for conference rooms in educational institutions and at the executive offices of large corporations. The standard costs of materials and labour for this product are given below.

Direct materials: 10 kilograms @ $8.25
Direct labour: 3.5 hours @ $9.65

During the first month of the year, 3,200 boards were produced. Information concerning actual costs and usage of materials and labour is given below.

Materials purchased: 36,000 kilograms @ $8.35
Material used: 31,800 kilograms
Direct labour: 11,520 hours; total cost: $112,896

Required:

1. Compute the materials price and usage variances.
2. Compute the labour rate and efficiency variances.
3. Prepare journal entries for all activity relating to materials and labour for the month.

14-7

Overhead Application; Overhead Variances

LO5

Warsami Company is planning to produce 2,400,000 power drills for the coming year. Each drill requires 0.5 standard hours of labour for completion. The company uses direct labour hours to assign overhead to products. The total overhead budgeted for the coming year is $2,700,000, and the standard fixed overhead rate is $0.55 *per unit produced*. Actual results for the year follow:

Actual production (units)   2,360,000
Actual direct labour hours   1,190,000
Actual variable overhead $1,410,000
Actual fixed overhead $1,260,000

Required:

1. Compute the applied fixed overhead.
2. Compute the fixed overhead spending and volume variances.
3. Compute the applied variable overhead.
4. Compute the variable overhead spending and efficiency variances.

14-8

Investigation of Variances

LO3

Underwood Company uses the following rule to determine whether materials usage variances ought to be investigated. A materials usage variance will be investigated any time the amount exceeds the lesser of $8,000 or 10 percent of the standard cost. Reports for the past five weeks provided the following information:

Week	MUV	Standard Materials Cost
1	$7,000 F	$80,000
2	7,800 U	75,000
3	6,000 F	80,000
4	9,000 U	85,000
5	7,000 U	69,000

Required:

1. Using the rule provided, identify the cases that will be investigated.
2. Suppose that investigation reveals that the cause of an unfavourable materials usage variance is the use of lower-quality materials than are usually used. Who is responsible? What corrective action would likely be taken?
3. Suppose that investigation reveals that the cause of a significant unfavourable materials usage variance is attributable to a new approach to manufacturing that takes less labour time but causes more material waste. Upon examining the labour efficiency variance, you discover that it is favourable and that it is larger than the unfavourable materials usage variance. Who is responsible? What action should be taken?

14–9

Overhead Application; Overhead Variances; Journal Entries; Appendix A

LO5, LO6

Tavera Company uses a standard cost system. The direct labour standard indicates that for every unit produced, 4 direct labour hours should be used. Tavera produces one product. The normal production volume is 120,000 units of this product. The budgeted overhead for the coming year (2002) is given below.

Fixed overhead	$1,440,000
Variable overhead	960,000[a]

[a] At normal volume

Tavera applies overhead on the basis of direct labour hours.

During 2002, Tavera produced 119,000 units, worked 487,900 direct labour hours, and incurred actual fixed overhead costs of $1,500,000 and actual variable overhead costs of $950,000.

Required:

1. Calculate the standard fixed overhead rate and the standard variable overhead rate.
2. Compute the applied fixed overhead and the applied variable overhead. What is the total fixed overhead variance? the total variable overhead variance?
3. Break the total fixed overhead variance into a spending variance and a denominator variance. Discuss the significance of each.
4. Compute the variable overhead spending and efficiency variances. Discuss the significance of each.
5. Prepare the journal entries that would be related to fixed and variable overhead at the end of the year. Assume variances are closed to Cost of Goods Sold.

14–10

Basic Variance Calculations

LO4, LO5

The Shank Company Ltd. uses a costing system with standard costs developed for each of its various products. One product, X–29, has the following standard costs:

Direct materials (6 kilograms @ $2.40/kilogram)	$14.40
Direct labour (3 hours @ $16/hour)	48.00
Variable overhead (3 hours @ $4.50/hour)	13.50
Fixed overhead (3 hours @ $2.80/hour[a])	8.40
Total cost per unit of X–29	$84.30

[a] Based on an annual activity of 7,500 direct labour hours

The company identifies the material purchase price variance when materials are purchased and calculates all possible variances for overhead.

Actual results for X–29 production in 2001 were as follows:

- Started and completed 2,450 units of X-29 (no beginning or ending inventories of work in process).
- Direct material purchases totalled 15,000 kilograms at a cost of $38,250. A total of 14,680 kilograms were issued to production in 2001.
- Direct labour costs totalled $122,430 (for 7,420 hours).
- Variable overhead costs were $33,675 in 2001.
- Fixed overhead costs were $22,500 in 2001.

Required:

Calculate all cost variances. (CMA Canada adapted)

14–11

Materials, Labour, and Overhead Variances

LO4, LO5

At the beginning of 1998, Kanaan Company had the following standard cost sheet for one of its products:

Direct materials (5 kilograms @ $1.60)	$ 8
Direct labour (2.0 hours @ $9)	18
Fixed overhead (2.0 hours @ $2)	4
Variable overhead (2.0 hours @ $1.50)	3
Standard cost per unit	$33

Spreadsheet

Kanaan computes its overhead rates using practical volume, which is 72,000 units. The actual results for 1998 are as follows:

a. Units produced: 70,000
b. Materials purchased: 372,000 kilograms at $1.55
c. Materials used: 369,000 kilograms
d. Direct labour: 145,000 hours at $8.95
e. Fixed overhead: $240,000
f. Variable overhead: $220,000

Required:

1. Compute price and usage variances for materials.
2. Compute the labour rate and efficiency variances.
3. Compute the fixed overhead spending and denominator variances.
4. Compute the variable overhead spending and efficiency variances.

14–12

Appendix A; Journal Entries

LO6

Refer to the data in 14–11. Prepare journal entries for the following:

1. The purchase of raw materials
2. The issuance of raw materials to production (Work in Process)
3. The addition of labour to Work in Process
4. The addition of overhead to Work in Process
5. The closing out of variances to Cost of Goods Sold

14–13

Basic Variance Analysis

LO4, LO5

The Carberg Company manufactures and sells a single product for $20. The company uses a standard costing system, with all variances being separated as soon as possible. The standards, which are updated each month, were as follows on November 1:

Direct materials (1 kilogram @ $2/kilogram)	$ 2.00
Direct labour (1.6 hours @ $8/hour)	12.80
Variable factory overhead ($2/hour)	3.20
Fixed factory overhead ($1/hour[a])	1.60
Total standard cost per unit	$19.60

[a] Overhead is applied on the basis of direct labour hours. The combined overhead application rate amounts to $3 per direct labour hour.

Normal production capacity has been established as 60,000 units per year, or 96,000 direct labour hours.

Actual operating results for the month of November are as follows:

Actual units produced	5,100
Direct materials purchased (@ $2.10/kilogram)	$10,920
Kilograms of direct materials used in production	5,300
Actual cost of direct labour (8,200 hours)	$67,240
Variable factory overhead	$16,560
Fixed factory overhead	$ 8,190

Required:

Determine all standard cost variances for the month of November. (CMA Canada adapted)

14–14

Variances, Evaluation, and Behaviour

LO1

Jackie Iverson was furious. She was nearly ready to fire Tom Rich, her purchasing agent. Just a month ago, she had given him a salary increase and a bonus for his performance. She had been especially pleased with his ability to meet or beat the price standards. But now she finds out that he was able to do so only because of a huge purchase of raw materials. It'll take months to use that inventory, and there is hardly space to store it. In the meantime, where can the other materials supplies that will be ordered and processed on a regular basis be put? Additionally, she knows it was a lot of capital to tie up in inventory—money that could have been used to help finance the cash needs of the new product just coming on line.

Her interview with Tom proved frustrating. He was defensive—arguing that he had thought that she wanted those standards met and that the means were not that important. He also pointed out that quantity purchases were the only way to meet the price standards. Otherwise, an unfavourable variance would have been realized.

Required:

1. Why did Tom Rich purchase the large quantity of raw materials? Do you think that this behaviour was the objective of the price standard? If not, what is or are the objective(s)?
2. Suppose that Tom is right and that the only way to meet the price standards is through the use of quantity discounts. Also assume that using quantity discounts is not a desirable practice for this company. What would you do to solve this dilemma?
3. Should Tom be fired? Explain.

14–15

Straightforward Computation of Variances: Materials and Labour

LO4

Basura Company produces plastic garbage cans. The following standards for producing one unit have been established:

Direct material (5 kilograms @ $0.90)	$ 4.50
Direct labour (1.5 hours @ $7.00)	10.50
Standard prime cost	$15.00

During December, 53,000 kilograms of material were purchased and used in production. There were 10,000 cans produced, with the following actual prime costs:

Direct materials	$ 42,000
Direct labour	$102,000 (for 14,900 hours)

Required:

Compute the materials and labour variances, labelling each variance as favourable or unfavourable.

14–16

Appendix A

LO6

Refer to 14–15. Prepare journal entries for the following:

1. The purchase of raw materials
2. The issuance of raw materials
3. The addition of labour to Work in Process
4. Closing of variances to Cost of Goods Sold

14–17

Incomplete Data; Variance Analysis

LO4, LO5

Layner Company uses a standard costing system. During the past quarter, the following variances were computed:

Variable overhead efficiency variance	$ 8,000 U
Labour efficiency variance	20,000 U
Labour rate variance	6,000 U

Layner applies variable overhead using a standard rate of $2 per direct labour hour allowed. Four direct labour hours are allowed per unit produced (only one type of product is manufactured). During the quarter, Layner used 20 percent more direct labour hours than should have been used.

Required:

1. What were the actual direct labour hours worked? the total hours allowed?
2. What is the standard hourly rate for direct labour? the actual hourly rate?
3. How many actual units were produced?

PROBLEMS

14–18 ✶

Basic Variance Calculations and Interpretation
LO1, LO4, LO5

The Stay Dry Company Ltd. manufactures an internationally known line of umbrellas. Management has recently established a standard cost system in order to control costs and to set the selling price of its umbrellas at 150 percent of standard cost.

The standard costs per unit based on a monthly production of 1,200 units are as follows:

Raw materials	12 parts per unit at $1.12 per part
Direct labour	2 hours per unit at $5.50 per hour
Manufacturing overhead:	
Variable	$1.40 per direct labour hour
Fixed	$4.10 per direct labour hour

During the month of June 2001, 1,000 units were put into production and completed. The following additional information was gathered concerning production:

a. Inventory: at June 1: none

                at June 30: none

b. Raw materials: 14,000 parts used at a total cost of $14,280

c. Direct labour cost for the month of June: $16,000

d. Actual direct labour hours: 2,500 hours

e. Manufacturing overhead incurred for the month of June:

    Variable: $3,600

    Fixed: $10,000

Required:

1. Determine the following:
   a. the unit selling price.
   b. all the variances resulting from production for the month of June 2001, including direct materials, direct labour, and overhead.
2. Comment on the possible causes of each manufacturing overhead variance.
3. Explain why it is preferable to compare actual data to standards rather than historical data. (CMA Canada adapted)

14–19

Basics of Variance Analysis; Materials, Labour, and Overhead
LO4, LO5

You have been given the following information for the Carr Company Ltd.:

Standard material price	$5 per kilogram
Direct labour costs incurred	$65,570 for 7,900 hours
Variable overhead applied	$2 per direct labour hour
Finished goods produced	4,000 units
Standard direct labour hours per unit	2 hours
Actual fixed overhead	$29,000
Materials purchased	15,000 kilograms for $73,500
Denominator activity	10,000 direct labour hours
Standard direct labour rate	$8 per hour
Materials used	12,300 kilograms
Fixed overhead spending variance	$1,000 favourable
Standard quantity of material in one unit	3 kilograms
Variable overhead costs incurred	$16,200

Required:

Compute variances for materials, labour, and overhead. (CGA Canada adapted)

14–20

Basics of Variance Analysis; Variable Inputs

LO3, LO4

Kascara Company manufactures plastic football helmets. The following standards have been established for the helmet's variable inputs:

	Standard Quantity	Standard Price (Rate)	Standard Cost
Direct materials	1.20 kilograms	$ 6.00	$ 7.20
Direct labour	0.32 hours	10.00	3.20
Variable overhead	0.32 hours	2.50	0.80
Total			$11.20

During the first week of July, the company had the following actual results:

Units produced	40,000
Actual labour costs	$140,000
Actual labour hours	13,200
Materials purchased and used	46,000 kilograms @ $6.10
Actual variable overhead costs	$53,000

Other information includes the following. The purchasing agent located a new source of slightly higher-quality plastic, and this material was used during the first week in July. Also, a new manufacturing process was implemented on a trial basis. The new process required a slightly higher level of skilled labour. The higher-quality material has no effect on labour utilization. However, the new manufacturing process was expected to reduce materials usage by 0.025 kilograms per helmet.

Required:

1. Compute the materials price and usage variances. Assume that the 0.025-kilogram reduction of materials occurred as expected and that the remaining effects are all attributable to the higher-quality material. Would you recommend that the purchasing agent continue to buy this quality? Or should the usual quality be purchased? Assume that the quality of the end product is not affected significantly.
2. Compute the labour rate and efficiency variances. Assuming that the labour variances are attributable to the new manufacturing process, should it be continued or discontinued? In answering, consider the new process's materials reduction effect as well. Explain.
3. Refer to Requirement 2. Suppose that the industrial engineer argued that the new process should not be evaluated after only one week. His reasoning was that it would take at least a week for the workers to become efficient with the new approach. Suppose that the production was the same the second week and that the actual labour hours were 12,000 and the labour cost was $124,000. Should the new process be adopted? Assume that the variances are attributable to the new process. Assuming production of 40,000 units per week, what would be the projected annual savings? (Include the materials reduction effect.)

14–21

Setting Standards; Materials and Labour Variances

LO1, LO2, LO4

Osgood Company is a small manufacturer of wooden household items. Ellen Acland, the firm's controller, plans to implement a standard cost system for Osgood. She has the information needed to develop standards for Osgood's products.

One of Osgood's products is a wooden cutting board. Each cutting board requires 0.4 metres of lumber and 12 minutes of direct labour time to prepare and cut the lumber. The cutting boards are inspected after they are cut. Because the cutting boards are made of a natural material that has imperfections, one board is normally rejected for each five that are accepted (the rejected boards are totally scrapped). Four rubber footpads are attached to each good cutting board. A total of 15 minutes of direct labour time is required to attach all four footpads and finish each cutting board. The lumber for the cutting boards costs $9.50 per metre, and each footpad costs $0.05. Direct labour is paid at the rate of $8 per hour.

Required:

1. Develop the standard costs for the cutting board's direct cost components. The standard cost should identify the standard quantity, standard rate, and standard cost per unit for each direct cost component of the cutting board.
2. Identify the advantages of implementing a standard cost system.
3. Explain the role of each of the following persons in developing standards:
   a. Purchasing manager
   b. Industrial engineer
   c. Cost accountant
4. Assume that the standards have been set and that the following actual results occur during the first month under the new standard cost system:
   a. Actual good units produced: 10,000
   b. Lumber purchased: 4,800 metres @ $10.10
   c. Lumber used: 4,800 metres
   d. Rubber footpads purchased (and used): 51,000 @ $0.048
   e. Direct labour cost: 5,550 hours @ $8.05
   Compute price and usage variances for materials and labour. (US CMA adapted)

14–22

Basic Variance Analysis

LO4, LO5

The Cuvier Company manufactures a product that has the following unit costs:

Direct materials (2.5 kilograms @ $4)	$10.00
Direct labour (3 hours @ $8)	24.00
Variable factory overhead (3 hours @ $1.50)	4.50
Fixed factory overhead (3 hours @ $2.50)	7.50

The denominator activity for 2001 was 16,000 units (or 48,000 hours). During 2001, the company produced 15,750 units and incurred the following costs:

Direct materials purchased (40,000 kilograms)	$164,000
Direct materials used in production (39,000 kilograms)	156,000
Direct labour (48,200 hours)	385,600
Manufacturing overhead incurred:	
Variable overhead	73,500
Fixed overhead	121,600

Required:

1. Calculate variances for direct materials, direct labour, variable overhead, and fixed overhead.
2. Provide some possible causes for the variable overhead spending variance, and explain the fixed overhead denominator variance. (CGA Canada adapted)

14–23

Setting a Direct Labour Standard; Learning Effects

LO1, LO2

Norris Company produces customized parts for industrial equipment. Although the parts are cus\tom-made, most follow a fairly standard pattern. Recently, a potential new customer has approached the company and requested a new part, one that is significantly different from the usual parts manufactured by Norris. New equipment and some new labour skills will be needed to manufacture the part. The customer is placing an initial order of 15,000 units and has indicated that if the part is satisfactory, several additional orders of the same size will be placed over the next two to three years.

Norris uses a standard cost system and wants to develop a set of standards for the new part. The usage standard for direct materials is 4 kilograms per part; the materials price standard is $3 per kilogram. Management has also decided on standard rates for labour and overhead: the standard labour rate is $11 per hour, the standard variable overhead rate is $6 per hour, and the standard fixed overhead rate is $2 per hour. The only remaining decision is the standard for labour usage. To assist in developing this standard, the Production Engineering Department has estimated the following relationship between units produced and average direct labour hours used:

Cumulative Average	
Units Produced	**Time per Unit**
20	1.00 hour
40	0.80 hours
80	0.64 hours
160	0.512 hours
320	0.448 hours

As the workers learn more about the production process, they become more efficient in manufacturing the part, and the average time needed to produce one unit declines. Engineering estimates that all of the learning effects will be achieved by the time 160 units are produced. No further improvement will therefore be realized past this level.

Required:

1. Assuming no further improvement in labour time per unit is possible past 160 units, explain why the cumulative average time per unit at 320 is lower than the time at 160 units.
2. What standard would you set for the per-unit usage of direct labour? Explain.
3. Using the standard you set in Requirement 2, prepare a standard cost sheet that details the standard cost per unit for the new part.
4. Given the standard you set in Requirement 2, would you expect favourable or unfavourable labour and variable overhead efficiency variances for production of the first 160 units? Explain.

14–24

Variance Analysis; Materials, Labour, and Overhead

LO2, LO4, LO5

The Keywiz Electrical Company manufactures specialized electrical equipment. The standard costs to assemble one multiplex Whoozit are:

Direct materials:
  8 sheets soft iron @ $1.50 a sheet
  2 spools copper wire @ $2.50 a spool
Direct labour rate: $16 per hour
Factory overhead rate (variable and fixed combined): $4.25 per direct labour hour

Overhead is applied to the Whoozit on the basis of standard direct labour hours. From Keywiz's flexible budget, you notice that when 1,000 units are produced, total overhead is $17,000; when 1,200 units are produced, total overhead is $19,000. The production budget for the past month called for 4,400 direct labour hours and $11,000 variable overhead costs.

During the past month 1,050 Whoozits were produced at the costs listed below:

Direct materials purchased:	
9,000 sheets soft iron	$13,050
2,200 spools copper wire	5,566
Direct materials used:	
8,000 sheets soft iron	
2,150 spools copper wire	
Direct labour (4,100 hours)	66,010
Overhead:	
Variable	10,750
Fixed	7,850

Required:

1. What is the standard time for assembling a Whoozit?
2. What is the standard absorption cost?
3. Calculate the following variances during the past month:
   a. Materials price
   b. Materials efficiency

c. Direct labour rate
d. Direct labour efficiency
e. Variable overhead spending
f. Variable overhead efficiency
g. Fixed overhead spending
h. Fixed overhead denominator (CGA Canada adapted)

14–25

Appendix Problem: Variance Analysis; Revision of Standards; Journal Entries

LO4, LO5, LO6

The Windor plant of Morril's Small Motor Division produces a major subassembly for a 6.0-horsepower motor for lawn mowers. The plant uses a standard costing system for production costing and control. The standard cost sheet for the subassembly follows:

Direct materials (3.0 kilograms @ $10)	$30.00
Direct labour (1.6 hours @ $12)	19.20
Variable overhead (1.6 hours @ $10)	16.00
Fixed overhead (1.6 hours @ $6)	9.60
Standard unit cost	$74.80

During the year, the Windsor plant had the following actual production activity:

a. Production of motors totalled 50,000 units.
b. A total of 130,000 kilograms of raw materials was purchased at $9.40 per kilogram.
c. There were 30,000 kilograms of raw materials in beginning inventory (carried at $10 per kilogram). There was no ending inventory.
d. The company used 82,000 direct labour hours at a total cost of $1,066,000.
e. Actual fixed overhead totalled $556,000.
f. Actual variable overhead totalled $860,000.

The Windsor plant's practical activity is 60,000 units per year. Standard overhead rates are computed based on practical activity measured in standard direct labour hours.

Required:

1. Compute the materials price and usage variances. Of the two materials variances, which is viewed as the most controllable? To whom would you assign responsibility for the usage variance in this case? Explain.
2. Compute the labour rate and efficiency variances. Who is usually responsible for the labour efficiency variance? What are some possible causes for this variance?
3. Compute the variable overhead spending and efficiency variances.
4. Compute the fixed overhead spending and volume variances. Interpret the volume variance. What can be done to reduce this variance?
5. Assume that the purchasing agent for the small-motors plant purchased a lower-quality raw material from a new supplier. Would you recommend that the plant continue to use this cheaper raw material? If so, what standards would likely need revision to reflect this decision? Assume that the end product's quality is not significantly affected.
6. Prepare all possible journal entries.

14–26

Fixed Overhead Spending and Denominator Variances; Capacity Management

LO5

Drury Company, a producer of recreational vehicles, recently decided to begin producing a major subassembly for jet skis. The subassembly would be used by Drury's jet-ski plants and would also be sold to other producers. The decision was made to lease two large buildings in two different locations: Ste-Foy, Québec, and Calgary, Alberta. The company agreed to a 10-year renewable lease contract. The plants were both the same size, and each had 10 production lines. New equipment was purchased for each line and workers were hired to operate the equipment. The company also hired production line supervisors for each plant. A supervisor is capable of directing up to two production lines per shift. Two shifts are run for each plant. The practical production capacity of each plant was 300,000 subassemblies per year. There are two standard direct labour hours allowed for each subassembly. The costs for leasing, equipment depreciation, and supervision are given below for a single plant (the costs are assumed to be the same for each plant).

Supervision (10 supervisors @ $50,000)	$ 500,000
Building lease (annual payment)	800,000
Equipment depreciation (annual)	1,100,000
Total fixed overhead costs*	$2,400,000

* For simplicity, assume these are the only fixed overhead costs.

After beginning operations, Drury discovered that demand for the product in the region covered by the Ste-Foy plant was less than anticipated. At the end of the first year, only 240,000 units were sold. The Calgary plant sold 300,000 units as expected. The actual fixed overhead costs at the end of the first year were $2,500,000 (for each plant).

Required:

1. Calculate a fixed overhead rate based on standard direct labour hours.
2. Calculate the fixed overhead spending and denominator variances for the Ste-Foy and Calgary plants. What is the most likely cause of the spending variance? Why are the denominator variances different for the two plants?
3. Suppose that from now on, the sales for the Ste-Foy plant are expected to be no more than 240,000 units. What actions would you take to manage the capacity costs (fixed overhead costs)?
4. Calculate the fixed overhead cost per subassembly for each plant. Do they differ? Should they differ? Explain. Do activity-based costing concepts help in analyzing this issue?

14–27

Unit Costs; Multiple Products; Variance Analysis; Journal Entries; Appendix A

LO2, LO4, LO5, LO6

Koolkare Company manufactures two types of icemakers, small and regular. The standard quantities of labour and materials per unit for 2001 are as follows:

	Small	Regular
Direct materials (grams)	340	560
Direct labour (hours)	0.2	0.30

The standard price paid per kilogram of direct materials is $3.20. The standard rate for labour is $8. Overhead is applied on the basis of direct labour hours. A plantwide rate is used. Budgeted overhead for the year is given below.

Budgeted fixed overhead	$720,000
Budgeted variable overhead	960,000

The company expects to work 24,000 direct labour hours in 2001; standard overhead rates are computed using this activity level. For every small icemaker produced, the company produces two regular icemakers.

Actual operating data for 2001 are as follows:

a. Units produced: small icemakers, 35,000; regular icemakers, 70,000.
b. Direct materials purchased and used: 56,000 kilograms @ $3.10: 13,000 for the small icemaker and 43,000 for the regular icemaker. There were no beginning or ending raw materials inventories.
c. Direct labour: 29,600 hours: 7,200 hours for the small icemaker, and 22,400 hours for the regular. Total cost of labour: $229,400.
d. Variable overhead: $1,215,000.
e. Fixed overhead: $700,000.

Required:

1. Prepare a standard cost sheet showing the unit cost for each product.
2. Compute the materials price and usage variances for each product. Prepare journal entries to record materials activity.
3. Compute the labour rate and efficiency variances. Prepare journal entries to record labour activity.
4. Compute the variances for fixed and variable overhead. Prepare journal entries to record overhead activity. All variances are closed to Cost of Goods Sold.
5. Assume that you know only the total direct materials used for both products and the total direct labour hours used for both products. Can you compute the total materials and labour usage variances? Explain.

14–28

Incomplete Data; Variance Calculation

LO4, LO5

The Hendrix Company Ltd. uses a standard costing system in accounting for its production, with all variances being separated as soon as possible. The company's standard costs for 2001 were as follows:

Direct materials (5 kilograms @ $17/kilogram)	$ 85
Direct labour (10 hours @ $14/hour)	140
Variable overhead (10 hours @ $2.50/hour)	25
Fixed overhead (10 hours @ $3.80/hour)	38
Total standard cost per unit	$288

Unfortunately, a fire destroyed most of the company's records on December 31, 2001, and only the following information was available:

a. Purchases of materials totalled 95,000 kilograms at a cost of $1,726,000.
b. Production for the year totalled 16,000 units.
c. Variable overhead totalled $403,620, with an efficiency variance of $3,625 (favourable).
d. The fixed manufacturing overhead actually totalled $515,000, and there was a production denominator variance of $95,000 (favourable).
e. The direct materials usage variance was $4,318 (favourable).
f. There were no beginning or ending work-in-process inventories.
g. Direct labour actually averaged $14.30 per hour.

Required:

1. Calculate all variances not given.
2. What was the company's denominator level of activity? (CMA Canada adapted)

14–29

Incomplete Data; Overhead Analysis

LO2, LO4, LO5

Watts Company produces surge protectors. To help control costs, Watts employs a standard cost system and uses a flexible budget to predict overhead costs at various levels of activity. For the most recent year, Watts used a standard overhead rate equal to $18 per direct labour hour. The rate was computed using practical activity. Budgeted overhead costs are $396,000 for 18,000 direct labour hours and $540,000 for 30,000 direct labour hours. During the past year, Watts generated the following data:

a. Actual production: 100,000 units
b. Fixed overhead denominator variance: $20,000 U
c. Variable overhead efficiency variance: $18,000 F
d. Actual fixed overhead costs: $200,000
e. Actual variable overhead costs: $310,000

Required:

1. Calculate the fixed overhead rate.
2. Determine the fixed overhead spending variance.
3. Determine the variable overhead spending variance.
4. Determine the standard hours allowed per unit of product.
5. If the standard labour rate is $9.50 per hour, compute the labour efficiency variance.

14–30

**Comprehensive
Variance Analysis;
Incomplete Data
LO4, LO5**

The Auward Company, Inc., uses a flexible budget and standard costs to aid in planning and control. At a level of 50,000 direct labour hours, budgeted variable overhead is $40,000. The company uses a variable overhead rate of 16 percent of standard direct labour hour cost for flexible budgeting purposes.

The following are selected results for March:

Variable overhead flexible budget variance	$ 9,000 U
Variable overhead efficiency variance	2,400 U
Actual direct labour costs incurred	330,000
Direct materials purchase price variance	12,000 F
Direct materials efficiency variance	19,000 U

The standard price per kilogram of direct material is $0.95. The standard allowance is 1 kilogram of direct material for each unit of finished product. Eighty thousand finished units were produced during March. There was no beginning or ending work in process. In March, the purchase price variance was $0.08 per kilogram. The actual wage rate in March exceeded the standard average wage rate by $0.50 per hour.

Required:

Determine the following amounts:

1. Standard direct labour cost per hour.
2. Total number of kilograms of material purchased.
3. Total number of kilograms of excess material usage.
4. Price paid per kilogram for March direct materials purchases.
5. Variable overhead spending variance.
6. Actual cost per hour of labour.
7. Actual number of hours worked.
8. Total number of standard hours allowed for the finished units produced.
9. Actual variable overhead cost. (CGA Canada adapted)

14–31

**Control Limits;
Variance
Investigation
LO2, LO3, LO4, LO5**

Demismell Company produces a well-known cologne. The standard manufacturing cost of the cologne is described by the following standard cost sheet:

Direct materials:	
Liquids (125 millilitres @ $8.40 per litre)	$1.05
Bottles (1 @ $0.05)	0.05
Direct labour (0.2 hours @ $12.50)	2.50
Variable overhead (0.2 hours @ $4.70)	0.94
Fixed overhead (0.2 hours @ $1)	0.20
Standard cost per unit	$4.74

Management has decided to investigate only those variances that exceed the lesser of 10 percent of the standard cost for each category or $20,000.

During the past quarter, 250,000 bottles of cologne were produced. Actual activity for the quarter is described below.

a. A total of 34,000 litres of liquids were purchased, mixed, and processed. Evaporation was higher than expected (no inventories of liquids are maintained). The price paid per litre averaged $9.15.
b. Exactly 250,000 bottles were used. The price paid for each bottle was $0.048.
c. Direct labour hours totalled 48,250, with a total cost of $622,425.
d. Variable overhead costs totalled $239,000.
e. Fixed overhead costs were $50,500.

Normal production volume for Demismell is 250,000 bottles per quarter. The standard overhead rates are computed using normal volume. All overhead costs are incurred uniformly throughout the year.

Required:

1. Calculate the upper and lower control limits for each manufacturing cost category.
2. Compute the total materials variance and then break it into price and usage variances. Would these variances be investigated?
3. Compute the total labour variance and break it into rate and efficiency variances. Would these variances be investigated?
4. Compute all overhead variances. Would any of them be investigated? Would you recommend a different approach to deal with overhead? Explain.

14–32

Flexible Budget: Overhead Variances

LO3, LO4, LO5

Kelly Company produces a single product in its manufacturing plant. Overhead is applied to production on the basis of standard direct labour hours (DLH). The following schedule has been prepared as a flexible budget for overhead review purposes:

DLH in Month	Overhead Cost
3,000	$30,000
4,000	35,000
5,000	40,000
6,000	45,000

The standard costs of one unit of product have been determined as follows:

Direct labour, 4 hours @ $25	$100.00
Direct materials, 10 kilograms @ $6	60.00
Overhead	32.00
Total standard costs	$192.00

During the month of May, the company produced 1,200 units, actually worked 5,100 direct labour hours, and incurred overhead costs of $40,400, of which $15,100 were fixed.

Required:

1. Prepare an analysis of overhead variances for the month of May to the extent possible with the information provided.
2. As controller of the company, prepare a brief report to the president discussing how well control over overhead costs was maintained during May. Indicate who should be held responsible for the variances you have calculated. (CMA Canada adapted)

14–33

Flexible Budget; Standard Cost Variances; T-Accounts; Appendix A

LO1, LO4, LO5

Shumaker Company manufactures a line of high-top basketball shoes. At the beginning of the year, the following plans for production and costs were revealed:

Pairs of shoes to be produced and sold	55,000
Standard cost per unit:	
Direct materials	$15
Direct labour	12
Variable overhead	6
Fixed overhead	3
Total unit cost	$36

During the year, 50,000 units were produced and sold. The following actual costs were incurred:

Direct materials	$775,000
Direct labour	590,000
Variable overhead	310,000
Fixed overhead	180,000

There were no beginning or ending inventories of raw materials. The materials price variance was $5,000 unfavourable. In producing the 50,000 units, 63,000 hours were worked, 5 percent more hours than the standard allowed for the actual output. Overhead costs are applied to production using direct labour hours.

Required:

1. Using a flexible budget, prepare a performance report comparing expected costs for the actual production with actual costs.
2. Determine the following:
   a. Materials usage variance
   b. Labour rate variance
   c. Labour usage variance
   d. Fixed overhead spending and denominator variances
   e. Variable overhead spending and efficiency variances
3. Use T-accounts to show the flow of costs through the system.

14–34

Control Limits; Variance Investigation

LO3, LO4

The management of Golding Company has determined that the cost to investigate a variance produced by its standard cost system ranges from $2,000 to $3,000. If a problem is discovered, the average benefit from taking corrective action usually outweighs the cost of investigation. Past experience from the investigation of variances has revealed that corrective action is rarely needed for deviations within 8 percent of the standard cost. Golding produces a single product, which has the following standards for materials and labour:

Direct materials (8 kilograms @ $0.25) $2
Direct labour (0.4 hours @ $7.50)   3

Actual production for the past three months, along with the associated actual usage and costs for materials and labour, are given below. There were no beginning or ending raw material inventories.

	April	May	June
Production (units)	90,000	100,000	110,000
Direct materials:			
Cost	$189,000	$218,000	$230,000
Usage (kilograms)	723,000	870,000	885,000
Direct labour:			
Cost	$270,000	$323,000	$360,000
Usage (hours)	36,000	44,000	46,000

Required:

1. What upper and lower control limits would you use for materials variances? For labour variances?
2. Compute the materials and labour variances for April, May, and June. Identify those that would require investigation.
3. Let the horizontal axis be time and the vertical axis be variances measured as a percentage deviation from standard. Draw horizontal lines that identify upper and lower control limits. Plot the labour and materials variances for April, May, and June. Prepare a separate graph for each type of variance. Explain how you would use these graphs (called control charts) to assist you in analyzing variances.

14–35

Standard Process Costing; Cost Variance Analysis

LO4, LO5

The Laval Company manufactures a single product. The standard unit cost information for the product is shown below:

Direct materials:
  Material Y (10 kilograms @ $0.50) $ 5.00
  Material W (5 metres @ $0.75)   3.75
Direct labour (3 hours @ $6)   18.00
Variable overhead (3 hours @ $1.50)   4.50
Fixed overhead (3 hours @ $1)   3.00

The company has chosen 10,000 units (30,000 standard direct labour hours) as the denominator activity level for the month of August 2001. The following are the operating data for August 2001:

a. There were no units in process at the beginning of August 2001.
b. The number of units completed during the month was 9,000 units.
c. There were 500 units in work in process at the end of the month. These 500 units were 60 percent complete with respect to their conversion costs. All of Material Y had been issued for these work-in-process units, while only 60 percent of Material W had been issued.
d. Actual direct labour cost was $195,000 at a rate of $6.50 per hour.
e. Materials issued to production were as follows:

    Material Y (95,000 kilograms @ $0.55)
    Material W (55,000 metres @ $0.75)

f. The company incurred $43,000 in variable overhead and $31,000 in fixed overhead during the month.

Required:

1. Determine the following variances from standard costs:
    a. Direct materials price variances for Materials Y and W
    b. Direct materials quantity variances for Materials Y and W
    c. Direct labour rate variance
    d. Direct labour efficiency variance
    e. Variable overhead spending variance
    f. Variable overhead efficiency variance
    g. Fixed overhead spending variance
    h. Fixed overhead denominator variance
2. Explain the relationship between direct labour efficiency variance and variable overhead efficiency variance. (CGA Canada adapted)

14–36

Standard Costing; Planned Variances

LO2, LO4

As part of its cost control program, Hepler Company uses a standard cost system for all manufactured items. The standard cost for each item is established at the beginning of the fiscal year, and the standards are not revised until the beginning of the next fiscal year. Changes in costs, caused during the year by changes in material or labour inputs or by changes in the manufacturing process, are recognized as they occur by the inclusion of planned variances in Hepler's monthly operating budgets.

Presented below is the labour standard that was established for one of Hepler's products effective June 1, 2001, the beginning of the fiscal year:

Assembler A labour (5 hours @ $10 per hour)	$ 50
Assembler B labour (3 hours @ $11 per hour)	33
Machinist labour (2 hours @ $15 per hour)	30
Standard cost per 100 units	$113

The standard was based on the labour being performed by a team consisting of five workers with Assembler A skills, three workers with Assembler B skills, and two workers with machinist skills; this team represents the most efficient use of the company's skilled employees. The standard also assumed that the quality of materials that had been used in prior years would be available for the coming year.

For the first seven months of the fiscal year, actual manufacturing costs at Hepler have been within the standards established. However, the company has received a significant increase in orders, and there is an insufficient number of skilled workers to meet the increased production. Therefore, beginning in January, the production teams will consist of eight workers with Assembler A skills, one worker with Assembler B skills, and one worker with machinist skills. The reorganized teams will work more slowly than the normal teams do; as a result, only 80 units will be produced in the same time period in which 100 units would normally be produced. Faulty work has never been a cause for units to be rejected in the final inspection process, and it is not expected to be a cause for rejection with the reorganized teams.

Furthermore, Hepler has been notified by its material supplier that lower-quality materials will be supplied beginning January 1. Normally, one unit of raw materials is required for each good unit produced, and no units are lost due to defective material. Hepler estimates that 10 percent of the units manufactured after January 1 will be rejected in the final inspection process due to defective material.

Required:

1. Determine the number of units of lower-quality material that Hepler Company must enter into production in order to produce 54,000 good finished units.
2. How many hours of each class of labour must be used to manufacture 54,000 good finished units?
3. Determine the amount that should be included in Hepler's January operating budget for the planned labour variance caused by the reorganization of the labour teams and the lower-quality material. (US CMA adapted)

14–37

Variance Analysis; Incomplete Data

LO4, LO5

The KleenAir Company Ltd. uses a standard costing system and manufactures a product, DustTrap. The standard unit manufacturing and selling and administrative costs are as follows:

Manufacturing:

Direct materials (15 metres @ $2/metre)	$30
Direct labour (4 hours @ $8/hour)	32
Total factory overhead[a]	20
	$82

[a] Applied at 5/8 of a direct labour hour, the ratio of variable to fixed overhead is 3:1.

Selling and administrative:

Variable	$10
Fixed	0
	$10

The following information relates to the month of June:

Normal volume (in direct labour hours)	2,500
Actual cost of 20,000 metres of direct materials	$39,500.00
Material usage variance	$900.00 F
Actual direct labour cost	$22,620.50
Actual production (units)	700
Total factory overhead	$13,287.50
Actual cost per direct labour hour	$8.05

Required:

1. What is the standard cost of one unit of DustTrap?
2. Compute the standard variable overhead rate per direct labour hour.
3. Compute the total budgeted fixed factory overhead for June.
4. Compute the following:
   a. Purchase price variance
   b. Labour rate variance
   c. Actual metres of direct material used
   d. Labour efficiency variance
   e. Variable overhead efficiency variance
   f. Fixed overhead denominator variance (CGA Canada adapted)

14–38

Overhead Variances; Incomplete Data

LO5

Alyce Kooper has been hired as the cost accountant for the Widget Department of Global Corporation. Only one product is manufactured in the Widget Department. It requires a standard direct labour input of 2.5 hours per unit. Total overhead is applied to production using a predetermined rate per standard direct labour hour.

It is now the beginning of February. Alyce has been asked to prepare an analysis of total overhead costs for January. However, she is not aware of the basis for the analysis, and her supervisor in the accounting department is on vacation. All that she has available is the following analysis for November and December:

	December	November
Actual overhead costs	$27,500	$25,100
Standard direct labour hours allowed	8,250	7,000
Overhead variances:		
Spending	$400 U	$200 F
Efficiency	100 U	800 U
Denominator	1,050 F	700 U

Required:

1. Calculate the following items:
   a. the predetermined overhead rate.
   b. the flexible budget formula.
   c. the denominator volume.
2. Prepare an analysis of overhead costs during January, in as much detail as possible, assuming that 3,100 units were actually produced in the department and that $25,850 of total overhead costs were incurred. (CMA Canada adapted)

14–39

Incomplete Data; Variance Analysis; Standard Cost Sheet

LO2, LO4, LO5

Emerson Company had recently acquired Madera, Inc., a small manufacturing firm. Unfortunately, Madera had very poor internal controls, and a master disk with some fundamental cost data for the past year was accidentally erased. No backup existed. Kathy Shorts, an internal auditor for Emerson, was assigned to Madera and given the task of reconstructing some of the cost records. At first she was discouraged with the assignment, but she became excited when she discovered part of a computer printout that contained some information about last year's operations. The information pertained to Madera's cost accounting system and is presented below.

Selected Actual Results

- Direct materials: 5,000 kilograms purchased and used, costing $51,000
- Production: 20,000 units
- Labour cost: 4,400 hours totalling $34,320
- Fixed overhead cost: $23,000
- Variable overhead: $46,000

Variances	
MPV	$ 1,000 U
MUV	10,000 F
LEV	3,200 U
Variable overhead efficiency	4,000 U
Variable overhead spending	2,000 U
Underapplied fixed overhead	3,000 U
Denominator variance	4,000 U

Kathy also interviewed Madera's controller and discovered that overhead rates are based on expected actual activity. Madera calculates two variances for variable overhead and two for fixed overhead. However, before Kathy could analyze the information she had gathered, she had to take emergency leave because of a family crisis. You have been given the task of performing the analysis described by the following requirements.

Required:

1. Prepare a standard cost sheet in good form. Show fixed and variable overhead as separate items.
2. Compute the fixed overhead spending variance.
3. Compute the labour rate variance.
4. Determine the expected actual activity used to compute the predetermined fixed overhead rate.

14–40

**Incomplete Data;
Overhead Variances**

LO4, LO5

For the production of Magic-Glue, the Stick-Tile Company uses the following standards based on producing 100,000 cases and using 300,000 direct labour hours for its 2001 fiscal year:

Direct materials (4 litres for each case)		$ 300,000
Direct labour		2,700,000
Manufacturing overhead:		
Variable	$300,000	
Fixed	600,000	900,000
Total standard cost (100,000 cases)		$3,900,000

Other information:

a. Manufacturing overhead is applied on the basis of direct labour hours. The denominator activity is 300,000 direct labour hours.
b. During 2001, Stick-Tile produced 97,000 cases of Magic-Glue and used 293,000 direct labour hours and 394,000 litres of direct materials.
c. There was no beginning inventory of direct materials.
d. Based on the purchase of 440,000 litres of direct materials, the purchase price variance was $5,500 unfavourable.
e. The direct labour rate variance was $29,300 favourable.

Required:

1. What is the actual price per litre paid for the direct materials purchased?
2. What is the actual prime cost of a case of Magic-Glue during 2001?
3. Actual overhead during 2001 was $937,600, of which $316,000 was variable. Calculate the overhead variances. (CGA Canada adapted)

14–41

**Variance Analysis;
Incomplete Data**

LO4, LO5

Mission Bay Boat Manufacturers was recently hit by an extremely high tide that destroyed many of the records in the accounting office. As an assistant cost accountant for the company, you have been able to reconstruct the following information from the variance analysis for the month of February:

Standard Costs:	
Direct materials (4 metres @ $4.50 per metre)	$18
Direct labour (3 hours @ $12 per hour)	36
Variable overhead (3 hours @ $2 per hour)	6
Fixed overhead (3 hours @ $5 per hour)	15

Other information that you were able to piece together includes the following:

a. The direct materials price variance is $4,750F. The price variance is isolated when material is issued to production. The average actual cost of material issued was $4.40 per metre. The direct materials standard cost of the units produced in February was $207,000.
b. The actual direct labour rate was $12.20 per hour, and 33,400 hours were worked during February.
c. Actual variable overhead was $67,400, and actual fixed overhead was $156,200. The fixed overhead spending variance was $1,300F.

Required:

1. What is the company's denominator activity level for February?
2. Determine the remaining variances for direct materials, direct labour, and overhead.
3. Describe an alternative method of calculating the direct materials price variance, and explain why that method would be preferable to the company's present method. (CMA Canada adapted)

14–42 ✳

Incomplete Data; Variance Analysis

LO4, LO5

You have the following information about Awesome Company Ltd., which uses a standard costing system for its one product.

a. In November 2001, 5,000 units were produced.
b. The annual overhead budget includes $750,000 for variable and $1,050,000 for fixed overhead items. Budgeted production for the year is 50,000 units. Overhead is applied on the basis of direct labour hours.
c. The materials standard per unit is 5 litres at $4.
d. The direct labour standard per unit is 3 hours at $10.
e. The actual price paid for material was $3.98.
f. The actual direct labour rate was $10.50.
g. Actual fixed overhead costs totalled $88,000.
h. The following variances have already been computed:

Materials price	$ 600 F
Materials quantity	1,600 U
Labour rate	7,400 U
Variable overhead spending	1,800 U

Required:

Calculate the following:

1. The quantity of material purchased
2. The quantity of material used
3. The actual direct labour hours worked
4. Labour efficiency variance
5. Variable overhead efficiency variance
6. Actual variable overhead
7. Fixed overhead spending variance
8. Fixed overhead denominator variance (CGA Canada adapted)

14–43

Variance Analysis; Incomplete Data

LO4, LO5

The Marsh Company recently had a small fire in its accounting office that destroyed part of the firm's accounting records for the month of July. The company uses a standard cost system, with the direct materials purchase price variance being isolated when the materials are purchased. A search of the remaining records has turned up a few useful bits of information.

The following standards (per unit) were used for the month of July:

Direct materials (15 kilograms @ $4 per kilogram)	$60
Direct labour (3 hours @ $9 per hour)	27
Variable overhead (3 hours @ $5 per hour)	15
Fixed overhead (3 hours @ $10 per hour)	30

The file with the variance analysis for July was partly destroyed, but it was possible to make out the following information:

a. The direct materials average actual price was $4.20 per kilogram.
b. The direct materials usage variance was $3,080 unfavourable.
c. Direct materials inventories decreased by 3,500 kilograms in the month of July.
d. The standard direct labour cost was $324,000.
e. The direct labour rate variance was $3,800 favourable.
f. The actual variable overhead costs amounted to $197,000, and the associated spending variance was $7,000 favourable.

g. The actual fixed overhead costs were the same as budgeted.
h. Total overhead was $77,000 underapplied for July.

Required:

Calculate the following for the month of July:

1. the total units produced in the month
2. the direct materials purchase price variance
3. the average actual rate of pay for direct labour
4. the direct labour efficiency variance
5. the variable overhead efficiency variance
6. the denominator variance
7. the denominator activity level used to establish the standards for July
(CMA Canada adapted)

14–44

Profitability Analysis; Variance Analysis as an Analytical Tool; Appendix B

LO7

(*Note:* This problem is an extension of 13–38.) Thorne Ltd. manufactures two types of appliances that are sold in national markets. The budgets for these two products for the past year, and the actual figures recorded, appear below:

	Thorne Ltd.		Industry	
	Budgeted	Actual	Budgeted	Actual
Units of Product A	12,000	13,000	100,000	120,000
Units of Product B	8,000	7,500	50,000	45,000
Selling price per unit of A	$200	$210		
Variable cost per unit of A	$140	$130		
Selling price per unit of B	$100	$90		
Variable cost per unit of B	$50	$40		
Total fixed cost	$600,000	$620,000		

Required:

1. Prepare actual and budgeted operating income statements.
2. Analyze, by cause, the effect of each variable on profit. (*Hint:* Calculate a variance for each of the following: industry volume, market share, sales mix, sales price, variable cost, and fixed cost.)
3. Comment on the performance of Thorne Ltd.

14–45

Profitability Analysis; Variance Analysis as an Analytical Tool; Appendix B

LO7

(*Note:* This problem is an extension of 13–39.) Toyworld manufactures and sells a variety of toys that can be classified in two types in terms of costs and selling prices: Type A and Type B. The toys are primarily distributed through department stores. Toyworld's master budget for 2001 showed an expected variable costing operating income of $69,000. At the end of the year, its actual variable-costing operating income was $64,400. As president of Toyworld, you decided to analyze Toyworld's profitability. Your capable assistant provided you with the following data:

	Master Budget			Actual		
	A	B	Total	A	B	Total
Selling price, per unit	$20	$30	—	$21	$32	—
Variable manufacturing cost, per unit	$11	$18	—	$12	$20	—
Variable marketing and administrative expenses, per unit	$1	$1	—	$1.10	$1.10	—
Fixed manufacturing cost, total	—	—	$34,500	—	—	$36,000
Fixed marketing and administrative expenses, total	—	—	$40,000	—	—	$44,000
Sales volume, in units	9,000	6,500	15,500	10,000	6,000	16,000
Industry volume of similar toys	—	—	77,500	—	—	64,000

Required:

1. Calculate the profit volume variance (gross).
2. Calculate the effect of the change in sales mix and the profit volume variance (net).
3. Separate the profit volume variance (net) into two components, one due to the decrease in industry volume and another due to a change in the market share.
4. Calculate the sales price variance.
5. Calculate the variable cost flexible budget variances.
6. Calculate the fixed cost flexible budget variances.
7. Based on Requirements 1–6 above, reconcile budgeted and actual operating income.
8. Comment on Toyworld's performance based on your reconciliation in Requirement 7 above.

14–46

Profitability Analysis;
Variance Analysis as
an Analytical Tool;
Appendix B
LO7

(*Note:* This problem is an extension of 13–40.) Smieliauskas Ltd., a multiproduct firm, had the following budgeted and actual income statements:

(in thousands of dollars)

	Budget	Actual
Sales	$2,100	$2,000
Variable expenses	1,260	1,500
Contribution margin	$ 840	$ 500
Fixed expenses	580	620
Operating income (loss)	$ 260	$ (120)

Additional information:

a. Sales prices were exactly as budgeted.
b. Industry volume was higher than initially estimated by 10 percent (of original estimate).
c. The budgeted contribution margin per dollar of sales based on the actual sales mix was $0.38.
d. The budgeted fixed expenses included discretionary amounts of $180,000. Of the actual fixed expenses, $560,000 were committed fixed expenses.

Required:

1. Calculate the profit volume variance (gross).
2. Calculate the effect of the change in sales mix and the profit volume variance (net).
3. Separate the profit volume variance (net) into two components, one due to the decrease in industry volume and another due to a change in the market share.
4. Calculate the sales price variance.
5. Calculate the variable cost flexible budget variances.
6. Calculate the fixed cost flexible budget variances.
7. Based on Requirements 1–6 above, reconcile budgeted and actual operating income.
8. Comment on the performance of Smieliauskas Ltd. based on your reconciliation in Requirement 7 above.

14–47

Profitability Analysis;
Variance Analysis as
an Analytical Tool;
Appendix B
LO7

(*Note:* This problem is an extension of 13–41.) Feltham Ltd., a multiproduct firm, had the following budgeted and actual income statements:

(in thousands of dollars)

	Budget	Actual
Sales	$4,200	$4,400
Variable expenses	2,520	2,700
Contribution margin	$1,680	$1,700
Fixed expenses	1,160	1,240
Operating income (loss)	$ 520	$ 460

Additional information:

1. Actual sales at budgeted prices were $4,000,000.
2. The budgeted contribution margin per dollar of sales based on the actual sales mix was $0.43.
3. The budgeted fixed expenses included discretionary amounts of $360,000. Of the actual fixed expenses, $1,120,000 were committed fixed expenses.

Required:

1. Calculate the following variances in terms of their effect on profit:
   a. Sales price variance
   b. Profit volume variance (net)
   c. Sales mix variance (the effect of the change in sales mix on budgeted contribution margins)
   d. Flexible budget variable expenses variance
   e. Discretionary fixed expenses variance
   f. Committed fixed expenses variance
2. Reconcile actual and budgeted operating income.
3. Is there any significance for control purposes to breaking down fixed expenses into discretionary and committed amounts? Explain, using the provided information.
4. Comment on the performance of Feltham Ltd.

MANAGERIAL DECISION CASES

14–48

Standard Costing
LO1, LO2, LO3

Mark Wright Inc. (MWI) is a specialty frozen-food processor located in the Atlantic provinces. Since its founding in 1982, MWI has enjoyed a loyal clientele willing to pay premium prices for the high-quality frozen food it prepares from specialized recipes. In the last two years, the company has experienced rapid sales growth in its operating region and has had many inquiries about supplying its products on a national basis. To meet this growth, MWI expanded its processing capabilities, which resulted in increased production and distribution costs. Furthermore, MWI has been encountering pricing pressure from competitors outside its normal marketing region.

Because MWI desires to continue its expansion, Jim Condon, the CEO, has engaged a consulting firm to assist MWI in determining its best course of action. The consulting firm recommended the institution of a standard cost system that would also facilitate a flexible budgeting system to better accommodate the changes in demand that can be expected when serving an expanding market area.

Jim met with his management team and explained the consulting firm's recommendations. He then assigned the task of establishing standard costs to his management team. After discussing the situation with their respective staffs, the management team met to review the matter.

Jane Morgan, MWI's purchasing manager, advised that meeting expanded production would necessitate obtaining basic food supplies from sources other than MWI's traditional suppliers. This change would entail increased raw material and shipping costs and might result in lower-quality supplies. Consequently, these increased costs would need to be made up by the processing department if current costs were to be maintained or reduced.

Stan Walters, MWI's processing manager, countered that the need to accelerate processing cycles to increase production, coupled with the possibility of receiving lower-grade supplies, could be expected to result in a slip in quality and a greater product rejection rate. Under these circumstances, per-unit labour utilization could not be maintained or reduced, and forecasting future unit labour content would become very difficult.

Tom Lopez, MWI's production engineer, advised that the equipment would have to be properly maintained and thoroughly cleaned at prescribed daily intervals; otherwise, the quality and unique taste of the frozen-food products would almost certainly be affected. Jack Reid, MWI's vice president of sales, stated that if quality could not be maintained, MWI could not expect to increase sales to the levels projected.

When Jim was apprised of the problems encountered by his management team, he advised them that if agreement could not be reached on the appropriate standards, he would arrange to have them set by the consulting firm, and everyone would have to live with the results.

Required:

1. List the major advantages of using a standard cost system.
2. List disadvantages that can result from the use of a standard cost system.
3. Identify those who should participate in setting standards, and describe the benefits of their participation in the standard-setting process.
4. What characteristics of a standard cost system make it an effective tool for cost control?
5. What could be the consequences if Jim has the standards set by the outside consulting firm? (US CMA adapted)

14–49

Establishment of Standards; Variance Analysis

LO1, LO2, LO4

Crunchy Chips was established in 1938 by Paul Golding and his wife Nancy (Nancy sold her piano to help raise capital to start the business). Paul assumed responsibility for buying potatoes and selling chips to local grocers; Nancy assumed responsibility for production. Since Nancy was already known for her delicious, thin potato chips, the business prospered.

Over the past 60 years, the company has established distribution channels in five provinces, with production facilities in New Brunswick, Ontario, and Manitoba. In 1980, Paul Golding died, and his son, Edward, took control of the business. By 2001, the company was facing stiff competition from national snack-food companies. Edward was advised that the company's plants needed to gain better control over production costs; to assist in achieving this objective, he hired a consultant to install a standard cost system. To help the consultant in establishing the necessary standards, Edward sent her the following memo:

To: Diana Craig, CMA
From: Edward Golding, President, Crunchy Chips
Subject: Description and Data Relating to the Production of Our Plain Potato Chips
Date: September 28, 2001

The manufacturing process for potato chips begins when the potatoes are placed into a large vat, in which they are automatically washed. After washing, the potatoes flow directly to an automatic peeler. The peeled potatoes then pass by inspectors, who manually cut out deep eyes or other blemishes. After inspection, the potatoes are automatically sliced and dropped into the cooking oil. The frying process is closely monitored by an employee. After they are cooked, the chips pass under a salting device and then travel past more inspectors, who sort out the unacceptable finished chips (those that are discoloured or too small). The chips then continue on the conveyor belt to a bagging machine, which bags them in 454-gram bags. After bagging, the bags are placed in a box and shipped. Each box holds 15 bags.

The raw potato pieces (eyes and blemishes), peelings, and rejected finished chips are sold to animal feed producers for $0.35 per kilogram. The company uses this revenue to reduce the cost of potatoes; we would like this reflected in the price standard relating to potatoes.

Crunchy Chips purchases high-quality potatoes at a cost of $0.54 per kilogram. Each potato averages 120 grams. Under efficient operating conditions, it takes four potatoes to produce one 454-gram bag of plain chips. Although we label bags as containing 454 grams, we actually place 460 grams in each bag. We plan to continue this policy to ensure customer satisfaction. In addition to potatoes, other raw materials are the cooking oil, salt, bags, and boxes. Cooking oil costs $1.35 per litre, and we use 100 millilitres of oil per bag of chips. The cost of salt is so small that we add it to overhead. Bags cost $0.11 each, and boxes $0.52.

Our plant produces 8.8 million bags of chips per year. A recent engineering study revealed that we would need the following direct labour hours to produce this quantity if our plant is operating at peak efficiency:

Raw potato inspection	3,200
Finished chip inspection	12,000
Frying monitor	6,300
Boxing	16,600
Machine operators	6,300

I'm not sure that we can achieve the level of efficiency advocated by the study. In my opinion, the plant is operating efficiently for the level of output indicated if the hours allowed are about 10 percent higher.

The hourly labour rates agreed upon with the union are as follows:

Raw potato inspectors	$8.60
Finished chip inspectors	6.15
Frying monitor	8.00
Boxing	6.50
Machine operators	7.50

Overhead is applied on the basis of direct labour dollars. We have found that variable overhead averages about 116 percent of our direct labour cost. Our fixed overhead is budgeted at $1,135,216 for the coming year.

Required:

1. Discuss the benefits of a standard cost system for Crunchy Chips.
2. Discuss the president's concern about using the result of the engineering study to set the labour standards. What standard would you recommend?
3. Develop a standard cost sheet for Crunchy Chips's plain potato chips.
4. Suppose that the level of production was 8.8 million bags of potato chips for the year as planned. If 4.3 million kilograms of potatoes were used, compute the materials usage variance for potatoes.

14–50

Standard Costing and Ethical Behaviour

Pat James, the purchasing agent for a local plant of the Oakden Electronics Division, was considering the possible purchase of a component from a new supplier. The component's purchase price, $0.90, compared favourably with the standard price of $1.10. Given the quantity that would be purchased, Pat knew that the favourable price variance would help offset an unfavourable variance for another component. By offsetting the unfavourable variance, it would make his overall performance report look impressive—good enough to help him qualify for the annual bonus. More importantly, a good performance rating this year would help him secure a position at divisional headquarters at a significant salary increase.

Purchase of the part, however, presented Pat with a dilemma. Consistent with his past behaviour, Pat made inquiries regarding the reliability of the new supplier and the part's quality. Reports were basically negative. The supplier had a reputation for making the first two or three deliveries on schedule but being unreliable from then on. Worse, the part itself was of questionable quality. The number of defective units was only slightly higher than that for other suppliers, but the life of the component was 25 percent less than what normal sources provided.

If the part was purchased, no problems with deliveries would surface for several months. The problem of shorter life would cause eventual customer dissatisfaction and perhaps some loss of sales, but the part would last at least 18 months after the final product began to be used. If all went well, Pat expected to be at headquarters within 6 months. He saw very little personal risk associated with a decision to purchase the part from the new supplier. By the time any problems surfaced, they would belong to his successor. With this rationalization, Pat decided to purchase the component from the new supplier.

Required:

1. Do you agree with Pat's decision? Why or why not? How important do you think Pat's assessment of his personal risk was in the decision? Should it be a factor?
2. Do you think that the use of standards and the practice of holding individuals accountable for their achievement played major roles in Pat's decision?
3. Review the ethical standards for management accountants in Chapter 1. Even though Pat is not a management accountant, identify the standards that might apply to his situation. Should every company adopt a set of ethical standards that apply to its employees, regardless of their specialty?

RESEARCH ASSIGNMENT

14–51

Research Assignment: Usefulness of Standard Costing

LO1, LO3, LO4, LO5

The usefulness of standard costing has been challenged in recent years. Some claim that its use is an impediment to the objective of continuous improvement (an objective that many feel is vital in today's competitive environment). Write a short paper that analyzes the role and value of standard costing in today's manufacturing environment. In writing this paper, address the following questions:

1. What are the major criticisms of standard costing?
2. Will standard costing disappear? Or is there still a role for it in the new manufacturing environment? If so, what is the role?
3. Given the criticisms, can you explain why its use continues to be so prevalent? Will this use eventually change?
4. If standard costing is no longer completely suitable for some manufacturing environments, what control approaches are being used to supplement (replace?) the traditional control model?

In preparing your paper, you may find the following references useful; however, do not restrict your literature search to these references. They are provided simply to help you get started.

1. Robin Cooper and Robert S. Kaplan, "Activity-Based Systems: Measuring the Costs of Resource Usage," *Accounting Horizons* (September 1992): 1–13.
2. Forrest B. Green and Felix E. Amenkhienan, "Accounting Innovations: A Cross-Sectional Survey of Manufacturing Firms," *Journal of Cost Management* (Spring 1992): 58–64.
3. Bruce R. Gaumnitz and Felix P. Kollaritsch, "Manufacturing Variances: Current Practice and Trends," *Journal of Cost Management* (Spring 1991): 58–64.
4. Robert S. Kaplan, "Limitations of Cost Accounting in Advanced Manufacturing Environments," in Robert S. Kaplan (ed.), *Measures for Manufacturing Excellence* (Boston: Harvard Business School Press, 1990).
5. George Foster and Charles Horngren, "JIT: Cost Accounting and Cost Management Issues," *Management Accounting* (June 1987): 19–25.

CHAPTER 15

Activity- and Strategic-Based Responsibility Accounting

Learning Objectives

After studying Chapter 15, you should be able to:

1. Compare and contrast functional-based, activity-based, and strategic-based responsibility accounting systems.

2. Explain process value analysis.

3. Describe activity performance measurement.

4. Explain the basic features of the Balanced Scorecard.

Scenario

Michelle Anderson, president and owner of Anderson Parts, Inc., was looking forward to her meeting with Henry Jensen, a consultant from a national public accounting firm. Anderson Parts was in desperate need of ways to improve its competitive position. About six months previously, Michelle had approved the implementation of a JIT purchasing and manufacturing system. At the same time, Anderson Parts had begun emphasizing total quality management. Early results were respectable, but well below Michelle's expectations. Inventories had been reduced, but they were still well above desired levels.

Furthermore, although lead times had been reduced, they too were still higher than projected. Significant problems with quality, delivery, excessive scrap, and machine performance were persisting. Before Michelle became too concerned, however, she wanted to hear what Henry had to say. He had come to provide a progress report and additional recommendations for changes. In particular, he had mentioned to her that Anderson needed to consider implementing both activity-based management and the Balanced Scorecard methodologies.

Michelle: "Glad to see you again, Henry. I'm eager to hear what you

have to say about this activity-based management system and the Balanced Scorecard. It appears that we still haven't realized many of the benefits from JIT that my manufacturing engineers had predicted six months ago."

Henry: "Well, that's certainly true. Change does take time, but your company is actually making the transition from traditional manufacturing to JIT much more easily than other firms I've had as clients. You've already shown some significant improvement—more so than usual for this stage of development."

Michelle: "That's encouraging. How much longer will it take to realize the full benefits? What else do we need to do?"

Henry: "The levels of improvement that I predicted should be achieved within a year. After that, I would expect to see additional improvement each year. You should focus your efforts to improve on more than just manufacturing activities. For example, improving your overall competitive position means focusing your attention on processes. Process improvement and process innovation are fundamental to your objective of continuous improvement. Since processes are defined by activities, activity management is needed. But you need to understand that activity-based management involves a totally different way of looking at things. You need to know what activities you are performing, why you are doing them, and how well you are performing them. Good evaluation and control are critical for the success of activity-based management."

Michelle: "Henry, we do have a good system for evaluating and controlling our operations. We have a standard costing system and budgetary control of all our major responsibility centres. We also have good incentive pay schemes in place to encourage both labour and managerial productivity."

Henry: "Michelle, measuring and controlling performance is fundamental—but performance measurement must be compatible with the concept of continuous improvement. Otherwise, the measures used can actually limit the efficiency made possible by such improvement programs as JIT and total quality management. Unfortunately, some of the functional-based control measures you mentioned are no longer suitable for your new environment."

Michelle: "Explain. I don't see why our performance measures are so bad. They've worked well for years."

Henry: "The functional-based approach concerns managing costs, but costs can't be managed—only the activities that cause the costs can be. The typical accounting report produces variances, and these variances are supposed to signal problems, if any exist. This approach encourages reactive decision making and is essentially backward-looking management. After all, the events that caused the costs are past, and we can't change those events. Also, I might add, it is important that performance measurement be an integrated approach—one that supports the organization's overall mission and strategy. Your improvement programs need to be linked to your overall strategy. At this point, your improvement efforts are fragmented and not linked to specific financial outcomes. The Balanced Scorecard approach offers the integration and linkages that you need."

Questions to Think About

1. What is meant by continuous improvement?

2. Why are functional-based evaluation and control measures not suitable for a continuous improvement environment?

3. Why are process innovation and improvement key to continuous improvement?

4. How can we measure activity performance?

5. Why is activity-based management compatible with continuous improvement?

6. What role, if any, do cost accounting reports play in a continuous improvement environment?

7. How can an organization achieve an integrated performance measurement system?

RESPONSIBILITY ACCOUNTING SYSTEMS

Objective 1

Compare and contrast functional-based, activity-based, and strategic-based responsibility accounting systems

The type of environment in which a firm operates can have a significant effect on the type of control and communication system chosen and implemented. Consider, for example, a firm that produces concrete pipes and blocks. The products and production processes are well defined and relatively stable. Functional skills are specialized to gain operating efficiencies. Interactions with suppliers and customers are mainly limited to arm's-length transactions. Competition tends to be local or regional, as opposed to national or international. A successful firm operating in this type of environment would tend to emphasize maintaining the status quo: preservation of market share, stable growth, and continuation of efficient production. On the other hand, a firm involved in producing computers and computer-related products operates in an environment where change is rapid. Products and processes are constantly being redesigned and improved, and stiff national and international competition are always present. The competitive environment demands that firms offer customized products and services to diverse customer segments. This, in turn, means that firms must find cost-efficient ways of producing high-variety, low-demand products. This requirement usually means that more attention is paid to linkages between the firm and its suppliers and customers, with the goal of improving cost, quality, and response times for all parties in the value chain. Furthermore, for many industries, product life cycles are shrinking, placing greater demands on the need for innovation. Thus, organizations operating in a dynamic, rapidly changing environment are finding that adaptation and change are essential to survival. To find ways to improve performance, firms in this kind of environment are forced to re-evaluate how they do things. Improving performance translates into constantly searching for ways to eliminate waste—a process known as *continuous improvement*. Waste reduction, the theme of continuous improvement, is made possible through the use of various waste reduction tools, such as JIT purchasing and manufacturing, re-engineering, total quality management, employee empowerment, and computer-aided manufacturing. These tools and methods all attempt to eliminate waste, which appears in the form of such things as inventories, unnecessary activities, defective products, rework, setup time, and underutilization of employee talents and skills.

Regardless of whether the environment is stable or dynamic, an organization needs to exercise control over its operations so that its objectives are achieved. However, what is measured and rewarded can have an important effect on an organization's efforts to achieve its objectives. The adages "You get what you measure and reward" and "If you don't measure it, it won't improve, and if you don't monitor it, it will get worse" are both relevant when designing and selecting a control system. Consider, for example, an employment agency that wanted to increase the number of applicants placed in the workplace. To encourage achievement of this objective, management selected "number of persons interviewed" as the performance measure and rewarded the agency's employees based on this measure. What the agency got was an increase in the number of interviews—and even fewer placements. When it changed the measure to "number of applicants placed" instead of number of persons interviewed, behaviour and results changed. This anecdotal example suggests that the control system for firms operating in a stable environment ought to be different from those operating in a continuous improvement environment. After all, maintaining status quo is a very different objective from that of continuous improvement. In other words, the control system selected is contingent on the environment in which the firm operates. A recent study found that JIT firms in Canada had different management control characteristics than non-JIT firms.[1]

The management accounting system plays a key role in measuring actions and outcomes and in defining the rewards to be received by individuals. This role is referred to as *responsibility accounting* and is a fundamental tool of managerial control. The responsibility control model is defined by four essential elements: (1) assigning responsibility, (2) establishing performance measures or benchmarks, (3) evaluating performance, and (4) assigning rewards. The objective of this model is to influence behaviour in such a way that individual and organizational initiatives are aligned to achieve a common goal or goals.

Management accounting offers three types of responsibility accounting systems: *functional-based, activity-based,* and *strategic-based*. In accordance with the contingency argument, a firm should choose the system that is compatible with the requirements and economics of its business operating environment. Firms that operate in a stable environment with standardized products and processes and low competitive pressures will likely find the less complex functional-based responsibility accounting systems to be quite adequate. As organizational complexity increases and the competitive environment becomes more dynamic, the activity-based and strategic-based

1.   See Murray Lindsay and Suresh Kalagnanam, *The Adoption of Just-In-Time Production Systems in Canada and Their Association with Management Control Practices,* A Research Publication of the Society of Management Accountants of Canada, 1992.

systems are likely to be more suitable. Since the natural evolutionary progression has been from functional-based to activity-based to strategic-based systems, we will first compare functional-based with activity-based responsibility accounting. Next, activity-based and strategic-based systems will be compared. These comparisons are designed to provide an overview and conceptual framework for the three systems.

Functional-Based versus Activity-Based Responsibility Accounting

The responsibility accounting system for a stable environment is referred to as **functional-based responsibility accounting**. A functional-based responsibility accounting system assigns responsibility to organizational units and expresses performance measures in financial terms. It emphasizes a financial perspective. The functional-based system was developed when most firms were operating in relatively stable environments. **Activity-based responsibility accounting**, on the other hand, is the responsibility accounting system developed for those firms operating in continuous improvement environments. Activity-based responsibility accounting assigns responsibility to processes and uses both financial and nonfinancial measures of performance. This approach emphasizes both financial and process perspectives. Exhibits 15–1 and 15–2 illustrate the four responsibility elements for each of the two approaches. An element-by-element comparison of these two approaches provides some key insights into the differences between the two environments.

Exhibit 15–1

Elements of a
Functional-Based
Responsibility
Accounting System

Assigning Responsibility Exhibit 15–1 reveals that functional-based responsibility accounting focuses on functional organizational units and individuals. First, a responsibility centre is identified. This centre is typically an organizational unit, such as a department or production line. Whatever the functional unit is, responsibility is assigned to the individual in charge of that unit. Responsibility is defined in financial terms (for example, costs). Exhibit 15–2 reveals that in an activity- or process-based responsibility accounting system, the focal point changes from units and individuals to processes and teams. However, financial responsibility continues to be vital. The reasons for the change in focus are simple. In a continuous improvement environment, the financial perspective translates into continuously *enhancing revenues, reducing costs*, and *improving resource utilization*. To create this continuous growth and improvement, an organization must constantly improve its capabilities of delivering value to customers and shareholders. Processes are chosen as the focus because they are the key to achieving an organization's financial objectives. The customer can be internal or external to the organization. Procurement, product development, customer acquisition, and customer service are examples of processes.

Since processes are the way things are done, changing the way things are done means changing processes. There are three methods of changing the way things are done: *process improvement*, *process innovation*, and *process creation*.

Process improvement refers to incremental and constant increases in the efficiency of an existing process. For example, Alpargatas, the largest manufacturer of textiles and sports shoes in Argentina, focused on improving the quality of the heels in its sports shoes by improving the cutting, stitching, and back-part moulding processes. These efforts produced savings of $225,000 per year.[2]

Process innovation (business re-engineering) refers to performing a process in a radically new way, with the objective of achieving dramatic improvements in response time, quality, and efficiency. IBM Credit, for example, radically redesigned its credit approval process and reduced its time for preparing a quote for leasing or buying a computer from seven days to one day. Similarly, Federal-Mogul, a parts manufacturer, used process innovation to reduce development time for part prototypes from 20 weeks to 20 days.[3]

Process creation refers to installing an entirely new process, with the objective of meeting customer and financial objectives. Chemical Bank, for example, identified three new internal processes: understanding customer segments, developing new products, and cross-selling the product line.[4] These new internal processes were viewed as critical by the bank's management for improving the customer and profit mix and creating an enabled organization. It should be mentioned that process creation does not mean that the process has to be original to the organization. It must merely be *new* to the organization. For example, developing new products is a process common to many organizations, but evidently was new to Chemical Bank.

Many processes cut across functional boundaries. This facilitates an integrated approach that emphasizes the firm's value-chain activities. It also means that cross-functional skills are needed for effective process management. Teams are the natural outcome of this process management requirement. Teams also improve the quality of work life by fostering friendships and a sense of belonging. Process improvement, innovation, and creation require significant group activity (and support) and cannot be carried out effectively by individuals. General Electric, Xerox, Martin Marietta, and Aetna Life Insurance have all begun to use teams as their basic work unit.[5]

Establishing Performance Measures   Performance measures must be identified and standards set to serve as benchmarks for performance measurement. According to Exhibit 15–1, budgeting and standard costing are the cornerstones of the benchmark activity for a functional-based system. This, of course, implies that performance measures are objective and financial in nature. Furthermore, they tend to support the status quo and are relatively stable over time. Exhibit 15–2 suggests some striking differences for firms operating in a continuous improvement environment. First, performance measures are process-oriented, and thus must be concerned with process attributes such as process time, quality, and efficiency. Second, performance measurement standards are structured to support change. Thus, standards are dynamic in nature. They need to change to reflect new conditions and new goals and to help maintain any progress that has been realized. For example, standards can be set that reflect some desired level of improvement for a process. Once the desired level is achieved, the standard is changed to encourage an additional increment of improvement. In an environment where constant improvement is sought, standards cannot be static. Third, optimal standards assume a vital role. They set the ultimate achievement target and thus identify the potential for improvement. Finally, standards should reflect the value added by individual activities and processes.

2.   Masaaki Imai, *Gemba Kaizen: A Commonsense Low-Cost Approach to Management* (New York: McGraw-Hill, 1997), 285–293.

3.   Thomas H. Davenport, *Process Innovation* (Boston: Harvard Business School Press, 1993), 2.

4.   Norman Klein and Robert Kaplan, *Implementing the Balanced Scorecard*, Harvard Business School, Case 125-210, 1995, 5–6.

5.   Davenport, *Process Innovation*, 97.

Evaluating Performance In a functional-based framework (see Exhibit 15–1), performance is measured by comparing actual outcomes with budgeted outcomes. In principle, individuals are held accountable only for those items over which they have control. Cost performance is strongly emphasized. In a continuous improvement framework (see Exhibit 15–2), performance is concerned with more than just the functional perspective. Time, quality, and efficiency are all critical dimensions of performance. Decreasing the time a process takes to deliver its output to customers is viewed as basic. Thus, such measures as cycle time and on-time deliveries become important. Performance measures relating to quality and efficiency are also vital. Productivity and cost measures are emphasized for assessing changes in efficiency. Improving a process should translate into better financial results. Thus, measures of cost reductions achieved, cost trends, and cost per unit of output are all useful indicators of whether a process has improved. Progress toward achieving optimal standards and interim standards needs to be measured. The objective is to provide low-cost, high-quality products, delivered on a timely basis.

Assigning Rewards In both systems, individuals are rewarded or penalized according to the policies and discretion of higher management. Of course, as Exhibit 15–1 reveals, the functional-based reward system is designed to encourage individuals to manage costs—to meet or beat budgetary standards. In the activity-based continuous improvement system illustrated in Exhibit 15–2, rewarding individuals is more complicated than in a functional-based setting. Individuals simultaneously have accountability for team and individual performance. Since process-related improvements are mostly achieved through team efforts, group-based rewards are more suitable than individual rewards. In one company (a producer of electronic components), for example, optimal standards have been set for unit costs, on-time delivery, quality, inventory turns, scrap, and cycle time.[6] Bonuses are awarded to a team whenever performance is maintained on all measures and improves on at least one measure. Note the multidimensional nature of this measurement and reward system. Another difference concerns the notion of gain-sharing versus profit-sharing. Profit-sharing is a global incentive designed to encourage employees to contribute to the overall well-being of the organization. Gain-sharing is more specific. Employees are allowed to share in gains related to specific improvement projects. Gain-sharing helps obtain the necessary "buy-in" for specific improvement programs such as total quality management.

Activity-Based versus Strategic-Based Responsibility Accounting

Activity-based responsibility accounting represents a significant change in how responsibility is assigned, measured, and evaluated. Effectively, the activity-based system added a process perspective to the financial perspective of the functional-based responsibility accounting system. It also altered the financial perspective by changing the point of view from that of cost control by maintaining the status quo to that of cost reduction by continuous learning and change. Thus, responsibility accounting changed from a one-dimensional system to a two-dimensional system and from a control system to a learning and cost management system. Adding the process perspective was necessary to operate in an environment that required continuous improvement. Although these changes were dramatic and were headed in the right direction, it was soon discovered that the new approach also had some limitations. The most significant shortcoming was the fact that the continuous improvement efforts were often fragmented and failed to connect with an organization's

---

6. C. J. McNair, "Responsibility Accounting and Controllability Networks," *Handbook of Cost Management* (Boston: Warren Gorham Lamont, 1993), E4-1–E4-33.

overall mission and strategy. A navigational system was lacking, and the result was undirected and rudderless continuous improvement. Consequently, the expected competitive successes sometimes did not materialize.

What was needed was *directed continuous improvement*. However, a formal guidance system for continuous improvement meant that managers of an organization needed to carefully specify a mission and strategy for their organization and also to identify the objectives, performance measures, and initiatives necessary for accomplishing this overall mission and strategy. In other words, a *strategic-based responsibility accounting system* was the next step in the evolution of responsibility accounting. A **strategic-based responsibility accounting (Balanced Scorecard)** system translates an organization's mission and strategy into operational objectives and measures for four different perspectives: the financial perspective, the customer perspective, the process perspective, and the infrastructure (learning and growth) perspective.[7] Exhibit 15–3 illustrates the four responsibility elements for the strategic-based responsibility system.

Assigning Responsibility Exhibit 15–3 reveals that the strategic-based responsibility accounting system maintains the process and financial perspectives of the activity-based approach but adds a customer perspective and a learning and growth (infrastructure) perspective. Although more perspectives could be allowed, these four

Exhibit 15–3

Elements of a Strategic-Based Responsibility Accounting System

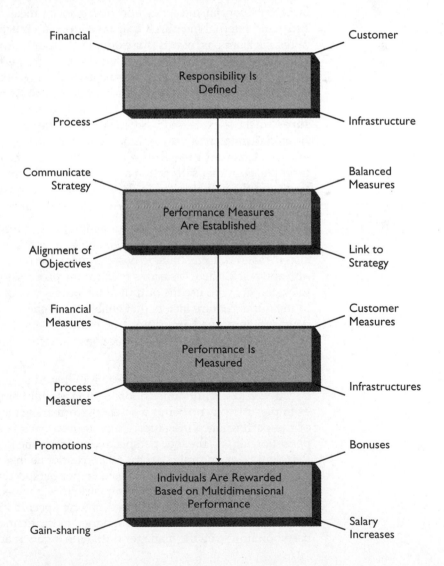

7.   Robert S. Kaplan and David P. Norton, *The Balanced Scorecard* (Boston: Harvard Business School Press, 1996).

perspectives are essential for creating a competitive advantage and allowing managers to articulate and communicate the organization's mission and strategy. Only perspectives that serve as a potential source for a competitive advantage should be included. This leaves open the possibility of expanding the number of perspectives. Notice that the two additional perspectives consider the interest of customers and employees, interests that were not fully considered by the activity-based responsibility system.

Establishing Performance Measures   Exhibit 15–3 indicates that the performance measures are perspective-oriented. The strategic-based approach thus includes the process orientation of the activity-based system. None of the advantages developed in an activity-based approach are lost, but the strategic-based approach adds some important refinements. In a strategic-based responsibility accounting system, performance measures must be integrated so that they are mutually consistent and reinforcing. In effect, the organization's mission, strategy, and objectives should drive the organization's performance measures. In fact, performance measures should be designed so that they communicate the strategy of the business and help align individual and organizational goals and initiatives. Thus, the measures must be balanced and linked to the organization's strategy.

Balanced measures means that the measures selected are balanced between lag measures and lead measures, between objective measures and subjective measures, between financial measures and nonfinancial measures, and between external measures and internal measures. **Lag measures** are outcome measures—that is, measures of results from past efforts (for example, customer profitability). **Lead measures (performance drivers)** are factors that drive future performance (for example, hours of employee training). **Objective measures** are those that can be readily quantified and verified (for example, market share), whereas **subjective measures** are less quantifiable and more judgment-based (for example, employee capabilities). **Financial measures** are those expressed in monetary terms (for example, cost per unit), whereas **nonfinancial measures** use nonmonetary units (for example, number of dissatisfied customers). **External measures** are those that relate to customers and shareholders (for example, customer satisfaction and return on investment, respectively). **Internal measures** are those that relate to the processes and capabilities that create value for customers and shareholders (for example, process efficiency and employee satisfaction).

Performance Measurement   In an activity-based responsibility system, performance measures are process-oriented. Financial consequences of improving processes are also measured. In a strategic-based system, performance measurement has been significantly expanded. Measures relate to the processes (for example, process efficiency); to customers who use the output of the processes (for example, customer satisfaction); to the infrastructure factors that enable the organization to learn, change, and execute new and improved processes (for example, employee satisfaction and employees' skills); and finally, to the economic consequences of executing processes (for example, cost trends).

Assigning Rewards   As with the activity-based system, how to assign rewards most effectively in a multidimensional setting is still being explored. One possibility, for example, is to pay no bonus if actual performance is less than a minimum value on any of the performance measures. Another approach is to distribute the incentive compensation among the four perspectives using some kind of weighting scheme. Pioneer Petroleum, for example, assigns 60 percent of its incentive compensation to the financial perspective, 10 percent to the customer perspective, 10 percent to the process perspective, and 20 percent to the infrastructure perspective.[8] Within each category, the bonus compensation is distributed among specific measures. For example, of the 60 percent incentive compensation assigned to the financial perspective, 3 percent is paid based on how well the manager does with a new market growth measure.

---

8.   Kaplan and Norton, *The Balanced Scorecard*, 218–219.

Operational Details: Overview

Exhibits 15–1, 15–2, and 15–3 provide the conceptual framework for the three responsibility accounting systems. Chapters 13, 14, and 18 provide significant operational details for the functional-based responsibility accounting system. Operational details for the strategic-based responsibility accounting system are presented in the last section of this chapter. Chapter 17 includes operational details for the strategic-based approach when an environmental perspective is added.

The emergence of activity accounting is the key factor required for operationalizing a continuous improvement responsibility accounting system. Processes are the source of many of the improvement opportunities that exist within an organization. Processes are made up of activities that are linked to perform a specific objective. Improving processes means improving the way activities are performed. Thus, managing activities, not costs, is the key to successful control for firms operating in continuous improvement environments. The realization that activities are crucial to both improved product costing and effective control has led to a new view of business process called *activity-based management*.

Activity-based management (ABM) is a systemwide integrated approach that focuses management's attention on activities with the objective of improving customer value and the profit achieved by providing this value.[9] Activity-based management encompasses both product costing and process value analysis. Thus, the activity-based management model has two dimensions: a cost dimension and a process dimension. This two-dimensional model was first introduced in Chapter 2 (Exhibit 2–9) and for convenience is updated in Exhibit 15–4. The cost dimension provides cost information about resources, activities, products, and customers (and other cost objects that may be of interest). The objective of the cost dimension is improving the accuracy of cost assignment. As the model suggests, the cost of resources is traced to activities, and then the cost of activities is assigned to products and customers. This activity-based costing dimension is useful for product costing, strategic cost management, and tactical analysis. The second dimension, the process dimension, provides information about what activities are performed, why they are performed, and how

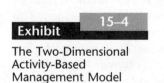

Exhibit 15–4

The Two-Dimensional Activity-Based Management Model

---

9. For a discussion of the implementation of ABM in Canada, see *Activity-Based Management*, Management Accounting Issues Paper 10, The Society of Management Accountants of Canada, 1995.

well they are done. This dimension's objective is cost reduction. It is this dimension that provides the ability to engage in and measure continuous improvement. To understand how the process view connects with continuous improvement, we need to have a more explicit understanding of process value analysis.

PROCESS VALUE ANALYSIS

Objective 2

Explain process value analysis.

Process value analysis is fundamental to activity-based responsibility accounting, focuses on accountability for activities rather than costs, and emphasizes the maximization of systemwide performance instead of individual performance. Process value analysis helps convert the concepts of activity-based responsibility accounting from a conceptual to an operational basis. As the model in Exhibit 15–4 illustrates, process value analysis is concerned with (1) *driver analysis*, (2) *activity analysis*, and (3) *performance measurement.*

Driver Analysis: The Search for Root Causes

Managing activities requires an understanding of what causes activity costs. Every activity has inputs and outputs. **Activity inputs** are the resources consumed by the activity in producing its output. **Activity output** is the result or product of an activity. For example, if the activity is writing a computer program, the inputs would be such things as a programmer, a computer, a printer, computer paper, and disks. The output would be a computer program. An **activity output measure** is the number of times the activity is performed. It is the quantifiable measure of the output. For example, the number of programs is a possible output measure for writing programs.

The output measure is effectively a measure of the demands placed on an activity and is what we have been calling an *activity driver*. As the demands for an activity change, the cost of the activity can change. For example, as the number of programs written increases, the activity of writing programs may need to consume more inputs (labour, disks, paper, and so on). However, output measures, such as the number of programs, may not (and usually don't) correspond to the *root causes* of activity costs; rather, they are the consequences of the activity being performed. The purpose of driver analysis is to reveal the root causes. Thus, **driver analysis** is the effort expended to identify those factors that are the root causes of activity costs. For example, an analysis may reveal that the root cause of the cost of moving materials is plant layout. Once the root cause is known, action can then be taken to improve the activity. Specifically, reorganizing plant layout can reduce the cost of moving materials.

Often the root cause of one activity's cost is also the root cause of the costs for other related activities. For example, the costs of inspecting purchased parts (output measure = number of inspection hours) and reordering (output measure = number of reorders) may both be caused by poor supplier quality. By implementing total quality management and a supplier evaluation program, companies may improve both activities and the procurement process itself.

Activity Analysis: Identifying and Assessing Value Content

The heart of process value analysis is activity analysis. **Activity analysis** is the process of identifying, describing, and evaluating the activities that an organization performs. Activity analysis should produce four outcomes: (1) what activities are done, (2) how many people perform the activities, (3) the time and resources required to perform the activities, and (4) an assessment of the value of the activities to the organization, including a recommendation to select and keep only those that add value. Steps 1 to 3 have been discussed in Chapter 4. These steps were critical for assigning costs. Step 4, determining the value-added content of activities, is concerned with cost reduction rather than cost assignment. Thus, some feel that this is the most important part of activity analysis. Activities can be classified as *value-added* or *nonvalue-added*.[10]

Value-Added Activities   Those activities that are necessary to keep the company in business are **value-added activities**. Some activities, *required activities*, are necessary to comply with legal mandates. The remaining activities in the firm are *discretionary*. A discretionary activity is classified as value-added when it simultaneously satisfies three conditions: (1) the activity produces a change of state, (2) the change of state was not achievable by preceding activities, and (3) the activity enables other activities to be performed.

For example, consider the production of rods used in hydraulic cylinders. The first activity, cutting rods, cuts long rods into the correct lengths for the cylinders. Next, the cut rods are welded to cut plates. The rod-cutting activity is value-added because (1) it causes a change of state—uncut rods become cut rods, (2) no prior activity was supposed to create this change of state, and (3) it enables the welding activity to be performed. Though the value-added properties are easy to see for an operational activity like cutting rods, what about a more general activity like supervising production workers? A managerial activity is specifically designed to manage other value-added activities—to ensure that they are performed in an efficient and timely manner. Supervision certainly satisfies the enabling condition. Is there a change in state? There are two ways of answering in the affirmative. First, supervising can be viewed as an enabling resource that is consumed by the operational activities that do produce a change of state. Thus, supervising is a secondary activity that serves an input that is needed to help bring about the change of state expected for value-added primary activities. Second, it could be argued that the supervision brings order by changing the state from uncoordinated activities to coordinated activities. Once value-added activities are identified, we can define value-added costs. **Value-added costs** are the costs of performing value-added activities with perfect efficiency.

Nonvalue-Added Activities   All activities, other than those that are absolutely essential to remain in business, and therefore considered unnecessary, are referred to as **nonvalue-added activities**. A nonvalue-added activity can be identified by its failure to satisfy any one of the three previous defining conditions. Violation of the first two is the usual case for nonvalue-added activities. Inspecting cut rods (for correct length), for example, is a nonvalue-added activity. Inspection is a state-detection activity, not a state-changing activity (that is, it tells us the state of the cut rod— whether it is the right length or not). Thus, it fails the first condition. Consider the activity of reworking goods or subassemblies. Rework is designed to bring a good from a nonconforming state to a conforming state. Thus, a change of state occurs. Yet the activity is nonvalue-added, because it repeats work: it involves doing something that should have been done by preceding activities (thus, it violates Condition 2). **Nonvalue-added costs** are costs that are caused either by nonvalue-added activities or by the inefficient performance of valued-added activities. Because of increased competition, many firms are attempting to eliminate nonvalue-added activities because they add unnecessary cost and impede performance; firms are also striving to optimize value-added activities. Thus, activity analysis attempts to identify and eventually eliminate all unnecessary activities, while simultaneously increasing the efficiency of necessary activities.

10. See *Value Chain Analysis for Assessing Competitive Advantage*, Management Accounting Guideline 41, The Society of Management Accountants of Canada, 1996.

The theme of activity analysis is waste elimination. As waste is eliminated, costs are reduced. The cost reduction *follows* the elimination of waste. Note the value of managing the *causes* of the costs rather than the costs themselves. Managing costs may increase an activity's efficiency, but if the activity is unnecessary, what does it matter if it's performed efficiently? An unnecessary activity is wasteful and should be eliminated. For example, moving raw materials and partly finished goods is often cited as a nonvalue-added activity. Installing an automated material-handling system may increase the efficiency of this activity—but changing to cellular manufacturing, with on-site, just-in-time delivery of raw materials, could virtually eliminate the activity. It's easy to see which approach is preferable.

Examples of Nonvalue-Added Activities Reordering parts, expediting production, and rework because of defective parts are examples of nonvalue-added activities. Other examples include warranty work, handling customer complaints, and reporting defects. Nonvalue-added activities can exist anywhere in the organization. In a manufacturing operation, five major activities are often cited as wasteful and unnecessary:

1. *Scheduling* An activity that uses time and resources to determine when different products have access to processes (or when and how many setups must be done) and how much will be produced.
2. *Moving* An activity that uses time and resources to move raw materials, work in process, and finished goods from one department to another.
3. *Waiting* An activity in which raw materials or work in process use time and resources by waiting on the next process.
4. *Inspecting* An activity in which time and resources are spent ensuring that the product meets specifications.
5. *Storing* An activity that uses time and resources while a good or raw material is held in inventory.

None of these activities adds any value for the customer. (Note that inspection would not be necessary if the product were produced correctly the first time, and therefore adds no value for the customer.) The challenge of activity analysis is to find ways to produce the good without using any of these activities.

Cost Reduction Continuous improvement carries with it the objective of cost reduction. Efforts to reduce the costs of existing products and processes are referred to as **kaizen costing**. Competitive conditions dictate that companies must deliver products the customers want, on time, and at the lowest possible cost. An organization must therefore continually strive for cost improvement. Kaizen costing is characterized by constant, incremental improvements to existing processes and products. Activity analysis is a key element of kaizen costing. Activity analysis can reduce costs in four ways:[11]

1. Activity elimination
2. Activity selection
3. Activity reduction
4. Activity sharing

Activity elimination focuses on nonvalue-added activities. Once activities that fail to add value are identified, measures must be taken to rid the organization of these activities. For example, the activity of inspecting incoming parts seems necessary to ensure that the product using the parts functions according to specifications. Use of a bad part can produce a bad final product. Yet this activity is necessary only because of the poor quality performance of the supplying firms. Selecting suppliers

---

11. Peter B. B. Turney, "How Activity-Based Costing Helps Reduce Cost," *Journal of Cost Management* (Winter 1991): 29–35.

who are able to supply high-quality parts or who are willing to improve their quality performance to achieve this objective will eventually allow the elimination of incoming inspection. Cost reduction then follows.

Activity selection involves choosing among different sets of activities that are caused by competing strategies. Different strategies cause different activities. Different product design strategies, for example, can require significantly different activities. Activities, in turn, cause costs. Each product design strategy has its own set of activities and associated costs. All other things being equal, the lowest-cost design strategy should be chosen. In a kaizen cost framework, *redesign* of existing products and processes can lead to a different, cheaper set of activities. Thus, activity selection can have a significant effect on cost reduction.

Activity reduction decreases the time and resources required by an activity. This approach to cost reduction should be primarily aimed at improving the efficiency of necessary activities or at implementing a short-term strategy for improving nonvalue-added activities until they can be eliminated. Setup activity is a necessary activity that is often cited as an example for which less time and fewer resources need to be used. Finding ways to reduce setup time—and thus lower the cost of setups—is another example of the kaizen costing concept.

Activity sharing increases the efficiency of necessary activities by using economies of scale. Specifically, the quantity of the cost driver is increased without increasing the total cost of the activity itself. This lowers the cost driver's per-unit cost and the amount of cost traceable to the products that consume the activity. For example, a new product can be designed to use components already being used by other products. By using existing components, the company takes advantage of the activities already associated with those components and avoids having to create a whole new set of activities.

Activity Performance Measurement

Assessing how well activities (and processes) are performed is fundamental to management's efforts to improve profitability. Activity performance measures exist in both financial and nonfinancial forms. These measures are designed to assess how well an activity was performed and the results achieved. They are also designed to reveal whether constant improvement is being realized. Measures of activity performance centre on three major dimensions: efficiency, quality, and time.

Efficiency focuses on the relationship between activity inputs and activity outputs. For example, one way to improve activity efficiency is to produce the same activity output with lower cost for the inputs used. *Quality* is concerned with doing the activity right the first time it is performed. If the activity output is defective, then the activity may need to be repeated, causing unnecessary cost and reducing efficiency. The *time* required to perform an activity is also critical. Longer times usually mean more resource consumption and less ability to respond to customer demands. Time measures of performance tend to be nonfinancial, whereas efficiency and quality measures are both financial and nonfinancial.

MEASURES OF ACTIVITY PERFORMANCE

Objective 3

Describe activity performance measurement.

Knowing how well we are currently performing an activity should disclose the potential for doing better. Since many of the nonfinancial measures that apply at the activity level will be discussed for the process perspective of the Balanced Scorecard, this section will emphasize financial measures of activity performance. Financial measures of performance should also provide specific information about the dollar effects of activity performance changes. Thus, financial measures should indicate both potential and actual savings. Financial measures of activity efficiency include (1) value-added and nonvalue-added activity cost reports, (2) trends in activity cost reports, (3) kaizen standard costing, (4) benchmarking, and (5) life-cycle costing.

Value-Added and Nonvalue-Added Cost Reporting

Reducing nonvalue-added costs is one way to increase activity efficiency. A company's accounting system should distinguish between value-added costs and nonvalue-added costs, because improving activity performance requires eliminating nonvalue-added activities and optimizing value-added activities. Thus, a firm should identify and formally report the value-added and nonvalue-added costs of each activity. Highlighting nonvalue-added costs reveals the magnitude of the waste the company is currently experiencing, thus providing some information about the potential for improvement. This information encourages managers to place more emphasis on controlling nonvalue-added activities. Progress can then be assessed by preparing trend and cost reduction reports. Tracking these costs over time lets managers assess the effectiveness of their activity management programs.

Knowing the amount of costs saved is important for strategic purposes. For example, if an activity is eliminated, then the costs saved should be traceable to individual products. These savings can produce price reductions for customers, making the firm more competitive. Changing the pricing strategy, however, requires knowledge of the cost reductions created by activity analysis. A cost-reporting system is therefore an important ingredient in an activity-based responsibility accounting system.

Value-added costs are the only costs that an organization should incur. A *value-added standard* calls for the complete elimination of nonvalue-added activities; for these activities, the optimal output is zero—with zero cost. A value-added standard also calls for completely eliminating the inefficiency of activities that are necessary but inefficiently carried out. Thus, value-added activities also have an optimal output level. A **value-added standard**, therefore, identifies the optimal activity output. Identifying the optimal activity output requires activity output measurement.

Setting value-added standards does not mean that they will be (or should be) achieved immediately. The idea of continuous improvement is to move toward the ideal, not to achieve it immediately. Workers (teams) can be rewarded for improvement. Moreover, nonfinancial operational performance measures can be used to supplement and support the goal of eliminating nonvalue-added costs (such measures are discussed later in the chapter). Finally, measuring the efficiency of individual workers and supervisors is not the way to eliminate nonvalue-added activities. Remember, activities cut across departmental boundaries and are part of processes. Focusing on activities and providing incentives to improve processes is a more productive approach. Improving the process should lead to improved results.

By comparing actual activity costs with value-added activity costs, management can assess the level of activity inefficiency and determine the potential for improvement. To identify and calculate value- and nonvalue-added costs, output measures for each activity must be identified. Once output measures are identified, then value-added standard quantities (SQ) for each activity can be defined. Value-added costs can be computed by multiplying the value-added standard quantities by the price standard (SP). Nonvalue-added costs can be calculated as the difference between the actual level of the activity's output (AQ) and the value-added level, multiplied by the unit standard cost. These formulas are presented in Exhibit 15–5. Some further explanation is needed.

Exhibit   **15–5**

Formulas for Value-Added and Nonvalue-Added Costs

Value-added costs $= SQ \times SP$
Nonvalue-added costs $= (AQ - SQ) \times SP$

Where $SQ =$ The value-added output level for an activity
  $SP =$ The standard price per unit of activity output measure
  $AQ =$ The actual quantity used of flexible resources or practical activity capacity acquired for committed resources

For flexible resources (resources acquired as needed), AQ is the actual quantity of activity used. For committed resources (resources acquired in advance of usage), AQ represents the actual quantity of activity capacity acquired, as measured by the activity's practical capacity. This definition of AQ allows the computation of nonvalue-added costs for both variable and fixed activity costs. For fixed activity costs, SP is the budgeted activity costs divided by AQ, where AQ is practical activity capacity.

To illustrate the power of these concepts, let's focus on the following four production activities for a JIT firm: welding, reworking defective products, setting up equipment, and inspecting purchased components. Of the four activities, two—welding and setups—are viewed as necessary; inspection and rework are unnecessary. The following data pertain to the four activities:

Activity	Activity Driver	SQ	AQ	SP
Welding	Welding hours	10,000	12,000	$40
Rework	Rework hours	0	10,000	9
Setups	Setup hours	0	6,000	60
Inspection	Number of inspection	0	4,000	15

Notice that the value-added standards (SQ) for rework and inspection call for their elimination; the value-added standard for setups calls for a zero setup time. Ideally, there should be no defective products; by improving quality, changing production processes, and so on, companies can eventually eliminate inspection. Setups are necessary, but in a JIT environment, efforts are made to drive setup times to zero.

Exhibit 15–6 classifies the costs for the four activities as value-added or nonvalue-added. For simplicity, and to show the relationship to actual costs, the actual price per unit of the cost driver is assumed to be equal to the standard price. In this case, the value-added cost plus the nonvalue-added cost equals actual cost. Normally, it might be necessary to add a price variance column.

The cost report in Exhibit 15–6 allows managers to see the nonvalue-added costs; consequently, it emphasizes the opportunity for improvement. By redesigning the products, the company can reduce welding time. By training welders and improving labour skill, management can reduce rework. Reducing setup time and implementing a supplier evaluation program are actions that can be taken to improve performance for the setup and inspection activities.

Thus, reporting value- and nonvalue-added costs at a given point in time may trigger actions to manage activities more effectively. Seeing the amount of waste may induce managers to search for ways to reduce, select, share, and eliminate activities to bring about cost reductions. Reporting these costs may also help managers improve planning, budgeting, and pricing decisions. For example, lowering the selling price to meet a competitor's price may be seen as possible if a manager can see the potential for reducing nonvalue-added costs to absorb the effect of the price reduction.

Exhibit 15–6 Value-Added and Nonvalue-Added Cost Report for the Year Ended December 31, 2000		Costs	
Activity	**Value-Added**	**Nonvalue-Added**	**Actual**
Welding	$400,000	$ 80,000	$480,000
Rework	0	90,000	90,000
Setups	0	360,000	360,000
Inspection	0	60,000	60,000
Total	$400,000	$590,000	$990,000

Trend Reporting

As managers take actions to improve activities, do the cost reductions follow as expected? One way to answer this question is to compare the costs for each activity over time. The goal is activity improvement as measured by cost reduction, so we should see a decline in nonvalue-added costs from one period to the next—provided that the activity analysis is effective. For example, assume that at the beginning of 2000, four major activity management decisions were implemented: the use of statistical process control, product redesign, a labour training program, and a supplier evaluation program. How effective were these decisions? Did a cost reduction occur as expected? Exhibit 15–7 provides a cost report that compares the nonvalue-added costs of 2001 with those that occurred in 2000. The 2001 costs are assumed, but would be computed the same way as shown for 2000. We assume that *SQ* is the same for both years. Comparing 2001's nonvalue-added costs directly with those in 2000 requires *SQ* to be the same for both years. If *SQ* changes, prior-year nonvalue-added costs are adjusted by simply assuming the same percentage deviation from standard in the current year as was realized in the prior year.

The trend report reveals that cost reductions followed, as expected. More than half of the nonvalue-added costs have been eliminated. There is still ample room for improvement, but activity improvement so far has been successful. As a note of interest, comparing the actual costs of the two periods would have revealed the same reduction. Reporting nonvalue-added costs, however, not only reveals the reduction but also provides managers with information on how much potential for cost reduction remains. But there is an important qualification. Value-added standards, like other standards, are not cast in stone. New technology, new designs, and other innovations can change the nature of the activities performed. Value-added activities can be converted to nonvalue-added activities, and value-added levels can change as well. Thus, as new ways for improvement surface, value-added standards can change. Managers should not become complacent, but should continually seek higher levels of efficiency.

Activity	Nonvalue-Added Costs		
	2000	2001	Change
Welding usage	$ 80,000	$ 50,000	$ 30,000 F
Rework	90,000	70,000	20,000 F
Setups	360,000	200,000	160,000 F
Inspection	60,000	35,000	25,000 F
Total	$590,000	$355,000	$235,000 F

The Role of Kaizen Standards

Kaizen costing is concerned with reducing the costs of existing products and processes. This translates into reducing nonvalue-added costs. Controlling this cost reduction process is accomplished through the repetitive use of two major subcycles: (1) the kaizen or continuous improvement cycle, and (2) the maintenance cycle. The kaizen subcycle is defined by a Plan–Do–Check–Act sequence. Thus, if a company emphasizes reducing nonvalue-added costs, the amount of improvement planned for the coming period (month, quarter, year, etc.) can be set (the *Plan* step). A **kaizen standard** reflects the planned improvement for the upcoming period. The planned improvement is assumed to be attainable; kaizen standards are therefore a type of currently attainable standard. Actions are taken to implement the planned improvements (the *Do* step). Next, actual results (for example, costs) are compared with the

Exhibit 15–8

Kaizen Cost Reduction
Process

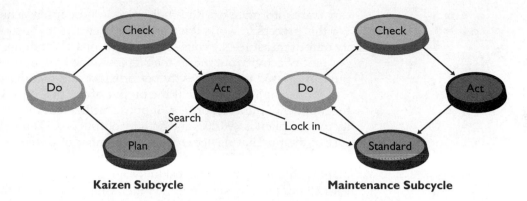

Kaizen Subcycle   **Maintenance Subcycle**

kaizen standard to provide a measure of the amount of improvement attained (the *Check* step). Setting this new level as the minimum standard for future performance locks in the realized improvements and simultaneously initiates the maintenance cycle and a search for additional improvement opportunities (the *Act* step). The maintenance cycle follows a traditional Standard–Do–Check–Act sequence. A *standard* is set based on prior improvements (locking in these improvements). Next, actions are taken (the *Do* step) and the results checked to ensure that performance conforms to this new level (the *Check* step). If not, then corrective actions are taken to restore performance (the *Act* step). The kaizen cost reduction process is summarized in Exhibit 15–8.

For example, assume that a medical products division inspects every unit produced of a particular surgical instrument. The unit-level value-added standard for this product calls for zero inspection hours per unit and a value-added inspection cost of $0 per unit. Assume that in the prior year, the company used 15 minutes to inspect each instrument at a cost of $15 per inspection hour. Thus, the actual inspection cost per unit is $3.75 ($15 × 0.25 hours). This is also the nonvalue-added cost. For the coming quarter, the company is installing a new production process that is expected to increase the precision with which the instrument is produced. These changes are expected to reduce the inspection time from 15 minutes to 10 minutes. Thus, the planned cost reduction is $1.25 per unit. The kaizen standard is defined as 10 minutes per unit, with a standard inspection cost of $2.50 per unit—the actual prior-year cost less the targeted reduction ($3.75 – $1.25). Now suppose that the actual cost after implementing the new production process is $2.50. The expected improvements did materialize, and the new minimum standard is $2.50, locking in the improvements. Until further improvements are developed, inspection costs should be no more than $2.50. For subsequent periods, additional improvements would be sought and a new kaizen standard defined. For example, in the third quarter, the company is planning to install a statistical process control system that will increase the reliability of the process even more, so that inspection time can be further reduced. This shift will then produce a different standard from the one for the current year.

Benchmarking

Another approach to standard setting that is used to help identify opportunities for activity improvement is called *benchmarking*. **Benchmarking** uses best practices as the standard for evaluating activity performance. Within an organization, different units (for example, different plant sites) that perform the same activities are compared. The unit with the best performance for a given activity sets the standard. Other units then have a target to meet or exceed. Furthermore, the best practices unit can share information with other units on how it has achieved its superior results. For this process to work, it is necessary to ensure that activity definitions and activity output measures are consistent across units. Such things as activity rates, the cost per unit of activity output, or the amount of activity output per unit of process output can be used to rank activity performance and identify the best performer.[12]

For example, assume that the output of the purchasing activity is measured by the number of purchase orders. Suppose further that the cost of the purchasing activity for one plant is $90,000, and activity output is 4,500 purchase orders. Dividing the cost of the purchasing activity by the number of purchase orders prepared gives a unit cost of $20 per order. If the best unit cost is $15 per purchase order, then the plant with the $20-per-unit cost knows that it could improve activity efficiency by at least $5 per unit. By studying the purchasing practices of the best plant, other plants should be able to increase their activity efficiency.

The objective of this approach is to become the best at performing activities and processes. Ideally, benchmarking should involve comparisons with competitors or other industries. However, it is often difficult to obtain the necessary data for external benchmarking to work. In some cases, it may be possible to study best practices of noncompetitors. There are certain activities and processes that are common to all organizations. If superior external best practices can be identified, then they can be used as standards to motivate internal improvements.

Drivers and Behavioural Effects

Activity output measures are needed to compute and track nonvalue-added costs. Reducing nonvalue-added activity should produce a reduction in the demand for the activity and a consequent reduction in the activity output measures. If a team's performance is affected by its ability to reduce nonvalue-added costs, then the selection of activity drivers (as output measures), and how they are used, can affect behaviour. For example, by choosing setup time as the output measure for setup costs, management creates an incentive for workers to reduce setup time. Since the value-added standard for setup costs calls for their complete elimination, the incentive to drive setup time to zero is compatible with the company's objectives, and the induced behaviour is beneficial.

Suppose, however, that the objective is to reduce the number of unique parts a company processes, thus reducing the demand for such activities as purchasing and incoming inspection. If the costs of these activities are assigned to products based on the number of parts, then the incentive created is to reduce the number of parts in a product. While this behaviour may be desirable to a point, it can also have negative consequences. Design teams may actually reduce the product's marketability by reducing the number of parts too greatly and adversely affecting its functionality.

This type of behaviour can be discouraged by the proper use of standards. Functional analysis can be used to identifying the value-added standard number of parts for each product.[13] Designers can then be encouraged to reduce the nonvalue-added costs by designing to reach the value-added standard number of parts. The standard has provided a concrete objective and defined the kind of behaviour that the incentive allows.

12. For more discussions of benchmarking, see the following publications from The Society of Management Accountants of Canada: *Implementing Benchmarking*, Management Accounting Guideline 16, 1993; *Benchmarking: A Survey of Canadian Practice*, Management Accounting Issues Paper 7, 1994; *Tools and Techniques for Effective Benchmarking Studies*, Management Accounting Guideline 35, 1995.

13. Functional analysis compares the price customers are willing to pay for a particular product function with the cost of providing that function.

Activity Capacity Management

Activity capacity is the number of times an activity can be performed. Activity drivers measure activity capacity. For example, consider inspecting finished goods as the activity. A sample of each batch is taken to determine the batch's overall quality. The demand for the inspection activity determines the amount of activity capacity that is required. For instance, suppose that the activity output is measured by the number of batches inspected. Now suppose that 60 batches are scheduled for production. Thus the required capacity is 60 batches. Finally, assume that a single inspector can inspect 20 batches per year. Thus, three inspectors must be hired to provide the necessary capacity. If each inspector is paid $40,000, the budgeted cost of the activity capacity is $120,000. This is the cost of the resources (labour) acquired in advance of usage. The budgeted activity rate is $2,000 per batch ($120,000/60).

There are several questions relating to activity capacity and its cost. First, what *should* the activity capacity be? The answer to this question provides the ability to measure the amount of improvement possible. Second, how much of the capacity acquired was actually used? The answer to this question signals a nonproductive cost and, at the same time, an opportunity for capacity reduction and cost savings.

Capacity Variances   Exhibit 15–9 illustrates the calculation of two capacity variances: the *activity volume variance* and the *unused capacity variance.*[14] The **activity volume variance** is the difference between the actual activity level acquired (practical capacity, AQ) and the value-added standard quantity of activity that should be used (SQ). Assuming that inspection is a nonvalue-added activity, $SQ = 0$ is the value-added standard. The volume variance in this framework has a useful economic interpretation: it is the nonvalue-added cost of the inspection activity. It measures the amount of improvement that is possible through analysis and management of activities ($120,000 in this example). However, since the supply of the activity in question (inspections) must be acquired in blocks (one inspector at a time), it is also important to measure the current demand for the activity (actual usage).

When supply exceeds demand by a large enough quantity, management can take action to reduce the quantity of the activity provided. Thus the **unused capacity variance**, the difference between activity availability (AQ) and activity usage (AU), is important information that should be provided to management. The goal is to reduce the demand for the activity until unused capacity equals the activity volume variance. Why? Because the activity volume variance is a nonvalue-added cost, and the unused capacity variance measures the progress in reducing this nonvalue-added cost. Notice

Exhibit 15–9

Activity Capacity Variances

AQ = Activity capacity acquired (practical capacity)
SQ = Activity capacity that should be used
AU = Actual usage of the activity
SP = Fixed activity rate

$SP \times SQ$	$SP \times AQ$	$SP \times AU$
$2,000 × 0	$2,000 × 60	$2,000 × 40
$0	$120,000	$80,000

Activity Volume Variance	Unused Capacity Variance
$120,000 U	$40,000 F

14. See Y. T. Mak and Melvin L. Roush, "Flexible Budgeting and Variance Analysis in an ABC Environment," *Accounting Horizons* (June 1994): 93–103; and Robin C. Cooper and Robert Kaplan, "Activity-Based Systems: Measuring the Costs of Resource Usage," *Accounting Horizons* (September 1992): 1–13.

that Exhibit 15–9 shows an unused capacity of 20 batches, valued at $40,000. Assume that this unused capacity exists because management has developed a quality-improvement program that has reduced the need to inspect certain batches of products. This difference between the supply of inspection resources and their usage should affect future spending plans (reduction of a nonvalue-added activity is labelled as favourable).

For example, we know that the supply of inspection resources is greater than its usage. Furthermore, because of the quality improvement program, we can expect this difference to persist and even become greater (with the ultimate goal of reducing the cost of inspection activity to zero). Management must now be willing to exploit the unused capacity that has been created. Activity availability can be reduced, and the spending on inspection can be decreased. A manager has several options to use to achieve this outcome. Since the inspection demand has been reduced by 20 batches, the company needs only two full-time inspectors. The extra inspector could be permanently reassigned to an activity where resources are in short supply. If reassignment is not feasible, the company should lay off the extra inspector.

This example illustrates an important feature of activity improvement. Activity improvement can create unused capacity, but managers must be willing and able to make the tough decisions to reduce resource spending on the redundant activities to gain the potential profit increase. Profits can be increased by reducing resource spending or by transferring the resources to other activities that will generate more revenues.

Life-Cycle Cost Budgeting

The product design stage can have a significant effect on costs. In fact, 90 percent or more of the costs associated with a product are committed during the development stage of the product's life cycle.[15] **Product life cycle** is simply the time a product exists, from conception to abandonment. **Life-cycle costs** are all the costs associated with the product for its entire life cycle. These include the costs of development (planning, design, and testing), production (conversion activities), and logistics support (advertising, distribution, warranty, and so on). The product life cycle and the associated cost commitment curve are illustrated in Exhibit 15–10.[16]

Because total customer satisfaction has become a vital issue in the new business setting, whole-life cost has emerged as the central focus of life-cycle cost management. **Whole-life cost** is the life-cycle cost of a product plus postpurchase costs that consumers incur, including operation, support, maintenance, and disposal.[17] Since the costs a purchaser incurs after buying a product can be a significant percentage of whole-life costs, and thus an important consideration in the purchase decision, managing activities so that whole-life costs are reduced can provide an important competitive advantage. Note that cost reduction, not cost control, is the emphasis. Moreover, cost reduction is achieved by judicious analysis and management of activities. Whole-life costing emphasizes managing the entire value chain. The value chain is the set of activities required to design, develop, produce, market, and service a product (or service). Thus, **life-cycle cost management** focuses on managing value-

15. John P. Campi, "Corporate Mindset: Strategic Advantage or Fatal Vision," *Journal of Cost Management* (Spring 1991): 53–57; Callie Berliner and James A. Brimson (eds.), *Cost Management for Today's Advanced Manufacturing* (Boston: Harvard Business School Press, 1988). The section on life-cycle costing is based on these two sources, with particular emphasis on the second source.

16. Life cycle can be viewed from a production perspective or from a marketing perspective. We have adopted a production perspective, with stages of the life cycle defined by changes in the types of activities performed: development, production, and logistical. The marketing perspective, on the other hand, focuses on sales demand and has the following four stages: startup, growth, maturity, and decline.

17. It can be argued that whole-life cost is an alternative definition of life-cycle cost—one that includes the customer's perspective as well as the production viewpoint. For an excellent treatment of life-cycle costing, see Michael D. Shields and S. Mark Young, "Managing Product Life Cycle Costs: An Organizational Model," *Journal of Cost Management* (Fall 1991): 39–52.

Exhibit 15–10

Life-Cycle Cost
Commitment Curve

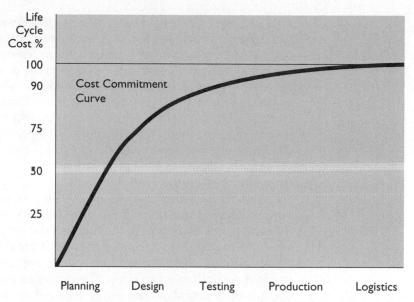

By the end of the development stage, at least 90 percent of the life-cycle costs are committed (but not incurred).

chain activities so that a long-term competitive advantage is created. To achieve this goal, managers must balance a product's whole-life cost, method of delivery, innovativeness, and various product attributes including performance, features offered, reliability, conformance, durability, aesthetics, and perceived quality.

Cost Reduction Since 90 percent or more of a product's costs are committed during the development stage, it makes sense to emphasize management of activities during this phase of a product's existence. Studies have shown that every dollar spent on premanufacturing activities saves $8 to $10 on manufacturing and postmanufacturing activities.[18] The real opportunities for cost reduction occur before manufacturing begins! Managers need to invest more in premanufacturing assets and dedicate more resources to activities in the early phases of the product life cycle so that overall whole-life costs can be reduced.

Yet despite this observation, the traditional emphasis has been on controlling costs during the production stage (when much less can be done to influence them). Furthermore, product cost has been narrowly defined as production costs; development and logistics costs have been treated as period costs and have been virtually ignored when computing product profitability. Additionally, little attention has been given to the effect of the customer's postpurchase costs. While this practice may be acceptable for external reporting, it is not acceptable for managerial product costing. In today's highly competitive environment, world-class competitors need comprehensive product cost information.

Whole-Life Product Cost From a whole-life viewpoint, product cost is made up of four major elements: (1) nonrecurring costs (planning, designing, and testing), (2) manufacturing costs, (3) logistics costs, and (4) the customer's postpurchase costs. Measuring, accumulating, and reporting all of a product's whole-life costs allow managers to better assess the effectiveness of life-cycle planning and build more effective and sophisticated marketing strategies. Life-cycle costing also increases their ability to make good pricing decisions and improve the assessment of product profitability.

18. Mark D. Shields and S. Mark Young, "Managing Product Life Cycle Costs: An Organizational Model"; R. L. Engwall, "Cost Management Systems for Defense Contractors," *Cost Accounting for the 90s, Responding to Technological Change* (Montvale, N.J.: National Association of Accountants, 1988).

Role of Target Costing   Life-cycle cost management emphasizes cost reduction, not cost control. Thus, target costing becomes a particularly useful tool for establishing cost reduction goals. A **target cost** is the difference between the sales price needed to capture a predetermined market share and the desired per-unit profit. The sales price reflects the product specifications or functions valued by the customer (referred to as *product functionality*). If the target cost is less than what is currently achievable, then management tries to budget cost reductions that move the actual cost toward the target cost. Finding these cost reductions is the principal challenge of target costing.

There are three cost reduction methods typically used: (1) reverse engineering, (2) value analysis, and (3) process improvement. Reverse engineering tears down competitors' products with the objective of discovering design features that create cost reductions. Value analysis attempts to assess the value that customers place on various product functions. If the price customers are willing to pay for a particular function is less than its cost, the function is a candidate for elimination. Anther possibility is to find ways to reduce the cost of providing the function—for example, by using common components. Both reverse engineering and value analysis focus on product design to reduce costs. The processes used to produce and market a product are also potential sources of reduced costs. Thus, redesigning processes to improve efficiency can also contribute to achieving the needed cost reductions. The target-costing model is summarized in Exhibit 15–11.

Exhibit 15–11

Target-Costing Model

The concepts described by Exhibit 15–11 can be illustrated by a simple example. Assume that a company is considering the production of a new trencher. Current product specifications and the targeted market share call for a sales price of $250,000. The required profit is $50,000 per unit. The target cost is computed as follows:

$$\text{Target cost} = \$250,000 - \$50,000$$
$$= \$200,000$$

The current product and process designs are estimated to produce a cost of $225,000 per unit. Thus the cost reduction required in order to achieve the target cost and desired profit is $25,000 ($225,000 – $200,0000). A tear-down analysis of a competitor's trencher reveals a design improvement that promises to save $5,000 per unit. Given that the required cost reduction is $25,000, additional effort is called for. A marketing study of customer reactions to product functions shows that the extra trenching speed in the new design is relatively unimportant. Changing the design to yield a lower trenching speed saves $10,000. The company's supplier also proposes the use of a standardized component, reducing costs by another $5,000. Finally, the design team is able to change the process design and reduce the test time by 50 percent. This saves $6,000 per unit. The last change reaches the threshold value, and production for the new model is approved.

Target costs are a type of currently attainable standard. But they are conceptually different from the modified standards discussed earlier. What makes them different is the motivating force. The initial modified definition of currently attainable standards was motivated by the objective of moving toward a value-added standard generated internally by industrial engineers and production managers. Target costs, on the other hand, are externally driven, generated by an analysis of markets and competitors.[19]

Short Life Cycles   Although life-cycle cost management is important for all manufacturing firms, it is particularly important for firms that have products with short life cycles. Products must recover all life-cycle costs and provide an acceptable profit. If a firm's products have long life cycles, profit performance can be increased by such actions as redesigning, changing prices, cost reduction, and altering the product mix. In contrast, firms that have products with short life cycles usually do not have time to react in this way, so their approach must be proactive. For short life cycles, good life-cycle planning is critical, and prices must be set properly so as to recover all the life-cycle costs and provide a good return. Activity-based costing can be used to encourage good life-cycle planning. Careful selection of cost drivers can motivate design engineers to choose cost-minimizing designs.

Life-Cycle Costing: An Example   Murphy Company produces electronic products that typically have about a 27-month life cycle. At the beginning of the last quarter of 2000, a new component was proposed. Design engineering believed that the product would be ready to produce by the beginning of 2001. To produce this and other similar products, resistors had to be inserted into a circuit board. Management had discovered that the cost of the circuit board was driven by the number of insertions. Knowing this, design engineering produced the new component using fewer insertions than the products in the past had employed.

The budgeted costs and profits for the product over its two-year life cycle are illustrated in Exhibit 15–12. Notice that the life-cycle unit cost is $10, compared with the conventional definition of $6 (which includes only the production costs) and the whole-life cost of $12. To be viable, of course, the product must cover all of its life-cycle costs and produce an acceptable profit (the target profit). The $15 target price can be compared with the target profit to obtain the target cost. Suppose the target profit is $6.50 per unit. The *life-cycle target cost* is then $8.50. Focusing only on the $6 cost could have led to a suboptimal design and production decision. Changing the focus requires managers to move away from the traditional, financially driven definition of product cost. Conventional cost systems do not directly identify development costs with the product being developed. The whole-life cost provides even

---

19. Also see *Implementing Target Costing*, Management Accounting Guideline 28, The Society of Management Accountants of Canada, 1994.

more information—information that could prove vital for the company's life-cycle strategy. For example, if competitors sell a similar product for the same price but with postpurchase costs of only $1 per unit, the company could be at a competitive disadvantage. Given this information, management can consider actions aimed at eliminating the disadvantage (for example, redesigning the product to lower the postpurchase costs).

Feedback on the effectiveness of life-cycle planning is also helpful. This information can help future new product planning and can also be useful for assessing how design decisions affect operational and support costs. Comparing actual costs with the budgeted costs can provide useful insights. Exhibit 15–13 illustrates a simple life-cycle cost performance report. As can be seen, production costs were greater than expected. Investigation revealed that costs are driven by total number of insertions, not just insertions of resistors. Further analysis also revealed that reducing the total number of insertions would reduce postpurchase costs. Thus, future design work on similar products can benefit from this assessment.

Exhibit 15–12

Life-Cycle Costing: Budgeted Costs and Income

Unit Cost and Price Information	
Unit production cost	$ 6
Unit life-cycle cost	10
Unit whole-life cost	12
Budgeted unit selling price	15

	Budgeted Costs			
Item	2000	2001	2002	Item Total
Development costs	$200,000	—	—	$ 200,000
Production costs	—	$240,000	$360,000	600,000
Logistics costs	—	80,000	120,000	200,000
Annual subtotal	$200,000	$320,000	$480,000	$1,000,000
Postpurchase costs*	—	80,000	120,000	200,000
Annual total	$200,000	$400,000	$600,000	$1,200,000
Units produced		40,000	60,000	

Budgeted Product Income Statements				
Year	Revenues	Costs	Annual Income	Cumulative Income
2000	—	$(200,000)	$(200,000)	$(200,000)
2001	$600,000	(320,000)	280,000	80,000
2002	900,000	(480,000)	420,000	500,000

* Because postpurchase costs are costs incurred by the customer, these costs would not be included in the budgeted income statements.

Exhibit 15–13

Performance Report: Life-Cycle Costs

Year	Item	Actual Costs	Budgeted Costs	Variance
2000	Development	$190,000	$200,000	$10,000 F
2001	Production	300,000	240,000	60,000 U
	Logistics	75,000	80,000	5,000 F
2002	Production	435,000	360,000	75,000 U
	Logistics	110,000	120,000	10,000 F

Analysis: Production costs were higher than expected because insertions of diodes and integrated circuits also drive costs (both production and postpurchase costs). *Conclusion:* The design of future products should try to minimize total insertions.

THE BALANCED SCORECARD: BASIC CONCEPTS

The *Balanced Scorecard* is a strategic management system that defines a strategic-based responsibility accounting system. The **Balanced Scorecard** *translates* an organization's mission and strategy into operational objectives and performance measures for four different perspectives: the financial perspective, the customer perspective, the internal business perspective, and the learning and growth (infrastructure) perspective. The **financial perspective** describes the economic consequences of actions taken in the other three perspectives. The **customer perspective** defines the customer and market segments in which the business unit will compete. The **internal business perspective** describes the internal process required to provide value for customers and owners. Finally, the **learning and growth (infrastructure) perspective** defines the capabilities that an organization needs in order to create long-term growth and improvement. This last perspective is concerned with three *enabling factors*: employee capabilities, information system capabilities, and employee attitudes (motivation, empowerment, and alignment).

Strategy Translation

Strategy, according to the creators of the Balanced Scorecard framework, is defined as follows:

> *choosing the market and customer segments the business intends to serve, identifying the critical internal and business processes that the unit must excel at to deliver the value propositions to customers in the targeted market segments, and selecting the individual and organizational capabilities required for the internal, customer, and financial objectives.*[20]

Strategy, then, specifies management's desired relationships among the four perspectives. *Strategy translation*, on the other hand, means specifying objectives, measures, targets, and initiatives for each perspective. Exhibit 15–14 illustrates the strategy translation process. Consider, for example, the financial perspective. For the financial perspective, a company may specify an *objective* of increasing revenues by introducing new products. The *performance measure* may be the percentage of revenues from the sale of new products. The *target* or *standard* for the measure for the coming year may be 20 percent (that is, 20 percent of the total revenue for the coming year must be from the sale of new products). The *initiative* describes how this will be accomplished. The "how," of course, involves the other three perspectives. The company must now identify the customer segments, internal process, and individual and organizational capabilities that will permit the realization of the growth objective. This illustrates the fact that the financial objectives serve as the focus for the objectives, measures, and initiatives of the three other perspectives.

The Role of Performance Measures

In Exhibit 15–14, we can see clearly that the Balanced Scorecard is not simply a collection of critical performance measures. The performance measures are derived from the company's vision, strategy, and objectives. These measures must be *balanced* between outcome measures and lead measures (performance drivers), between objective and subjective measures, between external and internal measures, and between financial and nonfinancial measures. Performance measures must also be *linked* to the company's strategy.

---

20. Kaplan and Norton, *The Balanced Scorecard*, 37.

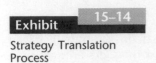

Exhibit   15–14

Strategy Translation
Process

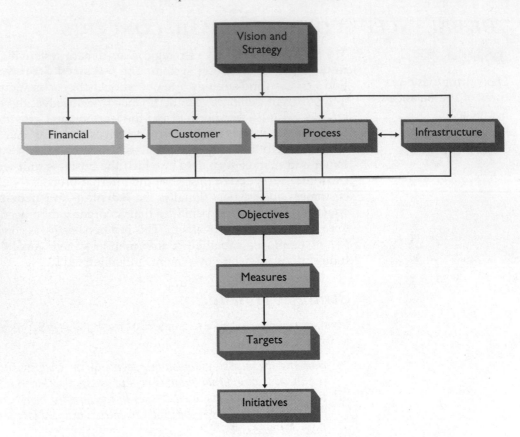

Linking Performance Measures to Strategy   Balancing measures helps link measures to the organization's strategy. For example, balancing outcome measures with performance drivers is essential to linking with the organization's strategy. Performance drivers are the measures that make things happen; consequently, they are indicators of how the outcomes are going to be realized. They tend to be unique to a particular strategy. Outcome measures are also important, because they reveal whether the strategy is being implemented successfully with the desired economic outcomes. For example, if the number of defective products is decreased, does this change indeed produce a greater market share? And does that, in turn, produce more revenues and profits? These questions suggest that the most important principle of linkage is the use of cause-and-effect relationships. In fact, a **testable strategy** can be defined as a set of linked objectives aimed at an overall goal. A strategy's testability is established by restating the strategy as a set of cause-and-effect hypotheses that are expressed by a sequence of if–then statements.[21] For example, consider the following sequence of if–then statements that link quality training with increased profitability:

> *If design engineers receive quality training, then they can redesign products to reduce the number of defective units; if the number of defective units is reduced, then customer satisfaction will increase; if customer satisfaction increases, then market share will increase; if market share increases, then sales will increase; if sales increase, then profits will increase.*

The quality improvement strategy, as a sequence of if–then statements, is summarized in Exhibit 15–15. There are a number of interesting points in this exhibit. First, notice how each of the four perspectives is present. The learning and growth

---

21. Kaplan and Norton, *The Balanced Scorecard*, 149. Kaplan and Norton describe the sequence of if–then statements only as a strategy. Calling it a testable strategy distinguishes it from the earlier, more general definition offered—and, in our opinion, properly so.

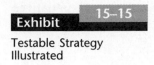

Exhibit 15–15

Testable Strategy
Illustrated

perspective is present through the training dimension; the process perspective is represented by the redesign and manufacturing processes; the customer perspective is represented by customer satisfaction and market share; and finally, revenues and profits represent the financial perspective. All four perspectives are linked through the cause-and-effect relationships hypothesized. Second, the strategy's viability is testable. Strategic feedback is available that allows managers to test the strategy's reasonableness. Hours of training, the number of products redesigned, the number of defective units, customer satisfaction, market share, revenues, and profits are all observable measures. The claimed relationships can be checked to see whether the strategy produces the expected results. If not, it could be due to one of two causes: (1) implementation problems, or (2) an invalid strategy. First, it is possible that key *performance drivers* such as training and redesign of products did not achieve their targeted levels (that is, fewer hours of training occurred and fewer products were redesigned than had been planned). In this case, an implementation shortfall accounts for the failure to produce the targeted outcomes for defects, customer satisfaction, market share, revenues, and profits. On the other hand, if the targeted levels of performance drivers were achieved and the expected outcomes did not materialize, then the problem could well lie with the strategy itself. This is an example of *double-loop feedback*. **Double-loop feedback** occurs whenever managers receive information about both the *effectiveness* of strategy implementation and the *validity* of the assumptions underlying the strategy. In a functional-based responsibility accounting system, typically only *single-loop feedback* is provided. **Single-loop feedback** emphasizes only the effectiveness of implementation. In single-loop feedback, actual results that deviate from planned results are a signal to take corrective action so that the plan (strategy) can be executed as intended. Typically, the validity of the assumptions underlying the plan is not explicitly considered.

The Four Perspectives and Performance Measures   The four perspectives define the organization's strategy. Furthermore, the example of if–then statements illustrates that the four perspectives provide the structure or framework for developing an integrated, cohesive set of performance measures. Once developed, these measures become the means for articulating the organization's strategy and communicating that strategy to its employees and managers. The measures also contribute to aligning individual objectives and actions with organizational objectives and initiatives. Given the role that the four perspectives play in developing performance measures, a more detailed examination of the perspectives is warranted.

The Financial Perspective

The financial perspective establishes the long- and short-term financial performance objectives. The financial perspective is concerned with the global financial consequences of the three other perspectives. The objectives and measures of the other perspectives must be linked to the financial objectives. The financial perspective has three strategic themes: revenue growth, cost reduction, and asset utilization. These themes are the building blocks for the development of specific operational objectives and measures.

Revenue Growth   There are several possible objectives associated with revenue growth. Among these possibilities are the following: increase the number of new products, create new applications for existing products, develop new customers and markets, and adopt a new pricing strategy. Once operational objectives are known, performance measures can be designed. For example, possible measures for the above list of objectives, in the order given, are percentage of revenue from new products, percentage of revenue from new applications, percentage of revenue from new customers and market segments, and profitability by product or customer.

Cost Reduction   Cost reduction objectives could include reducing the cost per unit of product, per customer, or per distribution channel. The appropriate measures are obvious: the cost per unit of the particular cost object. Trends in these measures will tell whether the costs are being reduced or not. The accuracy of cost assignment is particularly important. Activity-based costing can play an essential measurement role, especially for selling and administration costs—costs not usually assigned to cost objects like customers and distribution channels.

Asset Utilization   Improving asset utilization is the principal objective. Financial measures such as return on investment and economic value added are used. These are discussed in detail in Chapter 17. The objectives and measures for the financial perspective are summarized in Exhibit 15–16.

Exhibit 15–16

Summary of Objectives and Measures: Financial Perspective

Objectives	Measures
Revenue growth:	
Increase the number of new products	Percentage of revenue from new products
Create new applications	Percentage of revenue from new applications
Develop new customers and markets	Percentage of revenue from new sources
Adopt a new pricing strategy	Product and customer profitability
Cost reduction:	
Reduce unit product cost	Unit product cost
Reduce unit customer cost	Unit customer cost
Reduce distribution channel cost	Cost per distribution channel
Asset utilization:	
Improve asset utilization	Return on investment
	Economic value added

Customer Perspective

The customer perspective is the source of the revenue component for the financial objectives. This perspective defines and selects the customer and market segments in which the company chooses to compete.

Core Objectives and Measures Customers and segments are defined, and *core objectives and measures* are developed. **Core objectives and measures** are those that are common across all organizations. There are five key core objectives: increase market share, increase customer retention, increase customer acquisition, increase customer satisfaction, and increase customer profitability. Possible core measures for the objectives, respectively, are market share (percentage of market), percentage growth of business from existing customers and percentage of repeating customers, number of new customers, ratings from customer satisfaction surveys, and individual and segment profitability. Activity-based costing is a key tool in assessing customer profitability. Notice that customer profitability is the only financial measure among the core measures. This measure, however, is critical because it emphasizes the importance of the *right* kind of customers. What good is it to have customers if they are not profitable? The obvious answer spells out the difference between being customer-focused and customer-obsessed.

Customer Value In addition to the core objectives and measures, measures are needed that drive the creation of *customer value,* and thus drive the core outcomes. For example, increasing customer value builds customer loyalty (increases retention) and increases customer satisfaction. **Customer value** is the difference between realization and sacrifice. Realization is what the customer receives. Sacrifice is what the customer gives up. Realization includes such things as product functionality (features), product quality, reliability of delivery, delivery response time, image, and reputation. Sacrifice includes product price, time to learn to use the product, operating cost, maintenance cost, and disposal cost. The costs incurred by the customer *after* purchase are called **postpurchase costs**.

The realization and sacrifice value propositions provide the basis for the objectives and measures that will lead to improving the core outcomes. The objectives for the sacrifice value proposition are the simplest: decrease price and decrease postpurchase costs. Selling price and postpurchase costs are important measures of value creation. Decreasing these customer costs decreases customer sacrifice and increases customer value. Increasing customer value should have a favourable impact on most of the core objectives.

Similar favourable effect can be obtained by increasing realization. Realization objectives, for example, would include the following: improve product functionality, improve product quality, increase delivery reliability, improve delivery response time, and improve product image and reputation. Possible measures for these objectives include feature satisfaction ratings, percentage of returns, on-time delivery percentage, and product recognition rating.

Delivery reliability will be used to illustrate how measures can affect managerial behaviour, indicating the need to be careful in the choice and use of performance measures. Delivery reliability means that the product is delivered on time. On-time delivery is a commonly used operational measure of reliability. To measure on-time delivery, a firm sets delivery dates and then finds on-time delivery performance by dividing the orders delivered on time by the total number of orders delivered. The goal, of course, is to achieve a ratio of 100 percent. Some, however, have found that this measure by itself may produce unfavourable behavioural consequences.[22] Specifically, plant managers were giving priority to orders not yet late over orders that were already late. The performance measure encouraged managers to have one

---

22. Joseph Fisher, "Nonfinancial Performance Measures," *Journal of Cost Management* (Spring 1992): 31–38.

	Objectives	Measures
	Core:	
	Increase market share	Market share (percentage of market)
	Increase customer retention	Percentage growth of business from existing customers
		Percentage of repeating customers
	Increase customer acquisition	Number of new customers
	Increase customer satisfaction	Ratings from customer surveys
	Increase customer profitability	Customer profitability
	Customer value:	
	Decrease price	Price
	Decrease postpurchase costs	Postpurchase costs
	Improve product functionality	Ratings from customer surveys
	Improve product quality	Percentage of returns
	Improve delivery reliability	On-time delivery percentage
		Aging schedule
	Improve product image and reputation	Ratings from customer surveys

Exhibit 15–17

Summary of Objectives and Measures: Customer Perspective

very late shipment rather than several moderately late shipments! A chart showing the age of late deliveries could help mitigate this problem. Exhibit 15–17 summarizes the objectives and measures for the customer perspective.

Internal Business Perspective

Processes are the means for creating customer and shareholder value. Thus, the internal business perspective entails identifying the processes needed to achieve the customer and financial objectives. A *process value chain* provides the framework needed for this perspective. The **process value chain** is made up of three processes: the *innovation process*, the *operations process*, and the *postsales service process*. The **innovation process** anticipates customers' emerging and potential needs and creates new products and services to satisfy those needs. It represents what is called the *long-wave* of value creation. The **operations process** produces and delivers existing products and services to customers. It begins with a customer order and ends with the delivery of the product or service. It is the *short-wave* of value creation. The **postsales service process** provides critical and responsive services to customers after the product or service has been delivered.

Innovation Process: Objectives and Measures Objectives for the innovation process include the following: increase the number of new products, increase the percentage of revenue from proprietary products, and decrease the time to develop new products. Associated measures are actual new products developed versus planned products, percentage of total revenues from new products, percentage of revenue from proprietary products, and development cycle time (market to market).

Operations Process: Objectives and Measures There are three operations process objectives that are almost always emphasized: increase process quality, increase process efficiency, and decrease process time. Examples of process quality measures are quality costs, output yields (good output/good input), and percentage of defective units (good output/total output). Quality costing and control are discussed in detail in Chapter 16. Process efficiency measures are concerned with process cost and process productivity. Measuring and tracking process costs is facilitated by activity-based costing and process value analysis. These issues are explored later in this chapter. Productivity measurement is discussed in Chapter 16. Common process time measures are cycle time, velocity, and manufacturing cycle effectiveness (MCE).

Cycle Time and Velocity The time taken by a firm to respond to a customer's order is referred to as the firm's *responsiveness. Cycle time* and *velocity* are two operational measures of responsiveness. **Cycle time** is the length of time it takes to produce a unit of activity output from the time raw materials are received (the cycle's starting point) until the good is delivered to finished goods inventory (the cycle's finishing point).[23] Cycle time is the time required to manufacture a product (time/units produced). **Velocity** is the number of units of output that can be produced in a given period of time (units produced/time).

Incentives can be used to encourage operational managers to reduce manufacturing cycle time or to increase velocity, thus improving delivery performance. A natural way to accomplish this objective is to tie product costs to cycle time and reward operational managers for reducing product costs. For example, in a JIT firm, cell conversion costs can be assigned to products on the basis of the time that it takes a product to move through the cell. Using the theoretical productive time available for a period (in minutes), we can compute a value-added standard cost per minute.

$$\text{Standard cost per minute} = \text{Cell conversion costs/Minutes available}$$

To obtain the conversion cost per unit, we multiply this standard cost per minute by the actual cycle time used to produce the units during the period. By comparing the unit cost computed using the actual cycle time with the unit cost possible using the theoretical or optimal cycle time, a manager can assess the potential for improvement. Note that the more time it takes a product to move through the cell, the greater the unit product cost will be. With incentives to reduce product cost, this approach to product costing encourages operational managers and cell workers to find ways to decrease cycle time or increase velocity.

An example will illustrate the concepts. Assume that a company has the following data for one of its manufacturing cells:

Theoretical velocity: 12 units per hour
Productive minutes available (per year): 400,000
Annual conversion costs: $1,600,000
Actual velocity: 10 units per hour

The actual and theoretical conversion costs per unit are shown in Exhibit 15–18. Note from Exhibit 15–18 that decreasing cycle time from 6 minutes per unit to 5 minutes per unit (or increasing velocity from 10 units per hour to 12 units per hour) reduces the per-unit conversion cost from $24 to $20. At the same time, the objective of improving delivery performance is achieved.

Exhibit 15–18	
Conversion Cost Computations	

Actual Conversion Cost per Unit	
Standard costs per minute	= $1,600,000/400,000
	= $4 per minute
Actual cycle time	= 60 minutes/10 units
	= 6 minutes per unit
Actual conversion costs	= $4 × 6
	= $24 per unit
Theoretical Conversion Cost per Unit	
Theoretical cycle time	= 60 minutes/12 units
	= 5 minutes per unit
Theoretical conversion costs	= $4 × 5
	= $20 per unit

23. There are other definitions of cycles; for example, a cycle's starting point could be when a customer's order is received, and its finishing point could be when the goods are delivered to the customer. For a JIT firm, delivery to the customer is a reasonable finishing point. Another possibility for the finishing point is when the customer receives the goods. Cycle time measures the time elapsed from start to finish, regardless of how the starting and finishing points are defined.

Manufacturing Cycle Efficiency Another time-based operational measure calculates manufacturing cycle efficiency (MCE), as follows:

$$MCE = \text{Processing time}/(\text{Processing time} + \text{Move time} + \text{Inspection time} + \text{Waiting time})$$

where processing time is the time it takes to convert raw materials into a finished good. The other activities and their times are viewed as wasteful, and the goal is to reduce those times to zero. If this is accomplished, the value of MCE would be 1.0. As MCE improves (that is, as it moves toward 1.0), cycle time decreases. Furthermore, since the only way MCE can improve is by decreasing the nonvalue-added activities, cost reduction must also follow.

To illustrate MCE, let's use the data from Exhibit 15–18. The actual cycle time is 6 minutes, and the theoretical cycle time is 5 minutes. Thus, the time wasted is 1 minute (6 – 5), and MCE is computed as follows:

$$MCE = 5/6$$
$$= 0.83$$

Actually, this is a fairly efficient process, as measured by MCE. Many manufacturing companies have MCEs that are less than 0.05.[24]

Postsales Service Process: Objectives and Measures

Increasing quality, increasing efficiency, and decreasing process time are also objectives that apply to the postsales service process. Service quality, for example, can be measured by first-pass yields, where first-pass yields are defined as the percentage of customer requests resolved with a single service call. Efficiency can be measured by cost trends and productivity measures. Process time can be measured by cycle time, where a cycle's starting point is defined as the receipt of a customer's request, and its finishing point is defined as when the customer's problem is solved. The objectives and measures for the internal business perspective are summarized in Exhibit 15–19.

Exhibit 15–19

Summary of Objectives and Measures: Internal Business Perspective

Objectives	Measures
Innovation:	
Increase the number of new products	Number of new products versus planned
Increase proprietary products	Percentage revenue from proprietary products
Decrease new product development time	Time to market (from start to finish)
Operations:	
Increase process quality	Quality costs
	Output yields
	Percentage of defective units
Increase process efficiency	Unit cost trends
	Output/input(s)
Decrease process time	Cycle time and velocity
	MCE
Postsales Service:	
Increase service quality	First-pass yields
Increase service efficiency	Cost trends
	Output/input
Decrease service time	Cycle time

24. Kaplan and Norton, *The Balanced Scorecard*, 117.

Learning and Growth Perspective

The learning and growth perspective is the source of the capabilities that *enable* the accomplishment of the other three perspectives' objectives. This perspective has three main objectives: increase employee capabilities; increase motivation, empowerment, and alignment; and increase information systems capabilities.

Employee Capabilities   Three core *outcome* measurements for employee capabilities are employee satisfaction ratings, employee turnover percentages, and employee productivity (for example, revenue per employee). Examples of lead measures or performance drivers for employee capabilities are hours of training and strategic job coverage ratios (percentage of critical job requirements filled). As new processes are created, this often demands new skills. Training and hiring are sources of these new skills. Furthermore, the percentage of employees needed in certain key areas with the requisite skills signals the organization's capability to meet the objectives of the other perspectives.

Motivation, Empowerment, and Alignment   Employees must not only have the necessary skills, they must also have the freedom, motivation, and initiative to use these skills effectively. The number of suggestions per employee and the number of suggestions implemented per employee are possible measures of motivation and empowerment. Suggestions per employee provide a measure of the *degree* of employee involvement, whereas suggestions implemented per employee signals the *quality* of employee participation. The second measure also signals to employees whether or not their suggestions are taken seriously.

Information Systems Capabilities   Increasing information system capabilities means providing more accurate and timely information to employees so that they can improve processes and effectively execute new processes. Possible measures include percentage of processes with real-time feedback capabilities and percentage of customer-facing employees with on-line access to customer and product information. Exhibit 15–20 summarizes the objectives and measures for the learning and growth perspective.

Exhibit 15–20	Objectives	Measures
Summary of Objectives and Measures: Learning and Growth Perspective	Increase employee capabilities	Employee satisfaction ratings Employee turnover percentages Employee productivity (revenue/employee) Hours of training Strategic job coverage ratio (percentage of critical job requirements filled)
	Increase motivation and alignment	Suggestions per employee Suggestions implemented per employee
	Increase information systems capabilities	Percentage of processes with real-time feedback capabilities Percentage of customer-facing employees with on-line access to customer and product information

SUMMARY OF LEARNING OBJECTIVES

1. Compare and contrast functional-based, activity-based, and strategic-based responsibility accounting systems.

Functional-based responsibility accounting focuses on organizational units such as departments and plants, uses financial outcome measures and static standards and benchmarks to evaluate performance, and emphasizes the status quo and organizational stability. On the other hand, activity-based responsibility accounting focuses on process, uses both operational and financial measures and dynamic standards, and emphasizes and supports continuous improvement. Activity-based responsibility accounting adds a process perspective. Strategic-based responsibility accounting expands the number of responsibility dimensions from two to four. The customer perspective and the learning and growth perspective are added. Furthermore, the performance measures become an integrated set of measures linked to an organization's mission and strategy. Functional-based responsibility accounting works best for organizations that operate in a stable environment, whereas activity- and strategic-based responsibility accounting work best for firms that operate in dynamic environments.

2. Explain process value analysis.

Process value analysis provides information about why work is done and how well it is done. It involves cost driver analysis, activity analysis, and performance measurement. It is this latter dimension that connects process value analysis to the concept of continuous improvement. A key element of activity-based control is activity analysis—the process of identifying and describing a firm's activities, assessing their value to the organization, and selecting only those that are of value. Cost reduction is realized by decreasing, eliminating, selecting, and sharing activities. Emphasis is placed on identifying and eliminating nonvalue-added costs. These costs are the result of unnecessary activities and of inefficiencies found in necessary activities.

3. Describe activity performance measurement.

Activity performance is evaluated on three dimensions: efficiency, quality, and time. Financial measures of efficiency allow managers to identify the dollar values for potential improvement and for improvements achieved. Value- and nonvalue-added cost reports, trends in costs, benchmarking, kaizen standards, capacity management, and life-cycle budgeting are examples of financial measures of activity efficiency.

4. Explain the basic features of the Balanced Scorecard.

The Balanced Scorecard is a strategic management system that translates an organization's vision and strategy into operational objectives and measures. Objectives and measures are developed for each of four perspectives: the financial perspective, the customer perspective, the process perspective, and the learning and growth perspective. The objectives and measures of the four perspectives are linked by a series of cause-and-effect hypotheses. This produces a testable strategy that provides strategic feedback to managers. The Balanced Scorecard is compatible with activity-based responsibility accounting because it focuses on processes and requires the use of activity-based information to implement many of its objectives and measures.

KEY TERMS

REVIEW PROBLEMS

I. FUNCTIONAL-BASED RESPONSIBILITY ACCOUNTING VERSUS ACTIVITY-BASED RESPONSIBILITY ACCOUNTING

The labour standard for a company is 2 hours per unit produced, which includes setup time. At the beginning of the last quarter, 20,000 units had been produced and 44,000 hours used. The firm's production manager was concerned about the prospect of reporting an unfavourable labour efficiency variance at the end of the year. Any unfavourable variance in excess of 9 to 10 percent of the standard usually meant a negative performance rating. Bonuses were adversely affected by negative ratings. Accordingly, for the last quarter, the production manager decided to reduce the number of setups and use longer production runs. He knew that his production workers were usually within 5 percent of the standard. The real problem was with setup times. Reducing the setups would bring the actual hours used within 7 to 8 percent of the standard hours allowed.

Required:

1. Explain why the production manager's behaviour is unacceptable for a continuous improvement environment.
2. Explain how an activity-based responsibility accounting approach would discourage the kind of behaviour described.

Solution

1. In a continuous improvement environment, efforts are made to reduce inventories and eliminate nonvalue-added costs. The production manager is focusing on meeting the labour usage standard and is ignoring the impact on inventories that longer production runs may have.
2. Activity-based responsibility accounting focuses on activities and activity performance. For the setup activity, the value-added standard would be zero setup time and zero setup costs. Thus, avoiding setups would not save labour time, and it would not affect the labour variance. Of course, labour variances themselves would not be computed—at least not at the operational level.

II. ACTIVITY VOLUME VARIANCE; UNUSED ACTIVITY CAPACITY; VALUE- AND NONVALUE-ADDED COST REPORTS; KAIZEN STANDARDS; BALANCED SCORECARD

Pollard Manufacturing has developed value-added standards for its activities, three of which are material usage (in this case, using lumber), purchasing, and inspecting. The value-added output levels for each of these activities, their actual levels achieved, and the standard prices are as follows:

Activity	Activity Driver	SQ	AQ	SP
Using lumber	Board feet	24,000	30,000	$10
Purchasing	Purchase orders	800	1,000	50
Inspecting	Inspection hours	0	4,000	12

Assume that material usage and purchasing costs correspond to flexible resources (acquired as needed) and that inspection uses resources that are acquired in blocks, or steps, of 2,000 hours. The actual prices paid for the inputs equal the standard prices.

Required:

1. Assume that continuous improvement efforts reduce the demand for inspection by 30 percent during the year (that is, actual usage drops by 30 percent). Calculate the activity volume and unused capacity variances for the inspection activity. Explain their meaning. Also explain why there is no activity volume or unused capacity variance for the other two activities.
2. Prepare a cost report that details value-added and nonvalue-added costs.
3. Suppose that Pollard wants to reduce nonvalue-added costs by 30 percent in the coming year. Prepare kaizen standards that can be used to evaluate the company's progress toward this goal. How much will this approach save in resource spending?
4. Suppose that Pollard has implemented the Balanced Scorecard. Explain how nonvalue-added cost reduction, nonvalue-added cost reports, and kaizen standards might fit into the Balanced Scorecard framework.

Solution

1. Actual usage = $4,000 \times (1 - 0.3) = 2,800$

$SP \times SQ$	$SP \times AQ$	$SP \times AU$
12×0	$12 \times 4,000$	$12 \times 2,800$
$0	$48,000	$33,600

Activity Volume Variance	Unused Capacity Variance
$48,000 U	$14,400 F

The activity volume variance is the nonvalue-added cost. The unused capacity variance measures the cost of the unused activity capacity. The two other activities have no volume variance and no unused capacity variance because they use only flexible resources. There is no activity capacity acquired in advance of usage. Thus, there cannot be an unused capacity variance or an activity volume variance.

2.

	Costs		
	Value-Added	**Nonvalue-Added**	**Total**
Using lumber	$240,000	$ 60,000	$300,000
Purchasing	40,000	10,000	50,000
Inspection	0	48,000	48,000
Total	$280,000	$118,000	$398,000

3.

	Kaizen Standards	
	Quantity	**Cost**
Using lumber	28,200	$282,000
Purchasing	940	47,000
Inspection	2,800	33,600

If the standards are met, then the savings are as follows:

Using lumber: $10 \times 1,800 = $18,000
Purchasing: $50 \times 60 =   3,000
Savings $21,000

There is no reduction in resource spending for inspections, because this resource must be purchased in steps of 2,000 hours, and only 1,200 hours were saved—another 800 hours must be reduced before any reduction in resource spending is possible. The unused capacity variance must reach $24,000 (2,000 × $12) before resource spending can be reduced.

4. The Balanced Scorecard has four perspectives: financial, customer, internal business, and learning and growth. One of the objectives of the financial perspective is reducing the unit costs of products. Reducing nonvalue-added costs should produce a reduction in the company's product costs. The most direct connection to the Balanced Scorecard is with the internal business perspective of the Balanced Scorecard. Value-added and nonvalue-added cost reports are financial measures that relate to internal process efficiency. Similarly, kaizen standards deal with improving internal process efficiency. Activity volume variances and unused capacity measures are also concerned with process efficiency. Finally, the value of the Balanced Scorecard relative to these measures is that the Balanced Scorecard will integrate these measures into the overall strategic framework. The learning and growth perspective provides the enabling factors needed to reduce nonvalue-added costs. What good are nonvalue-added cost reports if nobody has the capability of finding ways to improve activities and processes? As process efficiency increases and costs are reduced, customer value can then be increased by reducing prices. As customer value increases, market share may increase, and this in turn may increase revenues and profits.

QUESTIONS FOR WRITING AND DISCUSSION

1. Describe a functional-based responsibility accounting system.

2. Describe an activity-based responsibility accounting system. How does it differ from functional-based responsibility accounting?

3. Describe a strategic-based responsibility accounting system. How does it differ from activity-based responsibility accounting?

4. What are the two dimensions of the activity-based management (ABM) model? How do they differ?

5. What is driver analysis? What role does it play in process value analysis?

6. What is meant by "activity inputs"? "activity output"? "activity output measurement"?

7. What is activity analysis? Why is this approach compatible with the goal of continuous improvement?

8. What are value-added activities? value-added costs?

9. What are nonvalue-added activities? nonvalue-added costs? Give an example of each.

10. Identify and define four different ways to manage activities so that costs can be reduced.

11. Explain how value-added standards are used to identify value-added and nonvalue-added costs.

12. Explain how trend reports of nonvalue-added costs can be used.

13. What is a kaizen standard? Describe the kaizen and maintenance subcycles.

14. Explain how benchmarking can be used to improve activity performance.

15. In controlling nonvalue-added costs, explain how activity output measures (activity drivers) can induce behaviour that is either beneficial or harmful. How can value-added standards be used to reduce the possibility of dysfunctional behaviour?

16. What is the meaning of the activity volume variance? Explain how the unused capacity variance is useful to managers.

17. Describe the benefits of life-cycle cost budgeting.

18. What is target costing? Describe how costs are reduced so that the target cost can be met.

19. What is the purpose of a Balanced Scorecard?

20. According to the Balanced Scorecard, what is a strategy?

21. Explain the differences between lead measures and lag measures.

22. What is a testable strategy?

23. What is meant by double-loop feedback?

24. What are the three strategic themes of the financial perspective?

25. Identify the five core objectives of the customer perspective.

26. Explain what is meant by the long-wave and the short-wave of value creation.

27. What is cycle time? velocity?

28. What is manufacturing cycle efficiency?

29. Identify three objectives of the learning and growth perspective.

EXERCISES

15–1

Functional-Based versus Activity-Based Responsibility Accounting

LO1

For each situation below, two scenarios are described, labelled A and B. Choose which scenario is descriptive of a setting corresponding to activity-based responsibility accounting and which is descriptive of functional-based responsibility accounting. Provide a brief commentary on the differences between the two systems for each situation, addressing the possible advantages of the activity-based view over the functional-based view.

Situation 1
A: The purchasing manager, receiving manager, and accounts payable manager are given joint responsibility for procurement. The charge given to the group of managers is to reduce costs of acquiring materials, decrease the time required to obtain materials from outside suppliers, and reduce the number of purchasing mistakes (for example, wrong type of materials or the wrong quantities ordered).
B: The plant manager commended the manager of the grinding department for increasing his department's machine utilization rates—and doing so without exceeding the department's budget. The plant manager then asked other department managers to make an effort to obtain similar efficiency improvements.

Situation 2
A: Delivery mistakes had been reduced by 70 percent, saving over $40,000 per year. Furthermore, delivery time to customers had been cut by two days. According to company policy, the team responsible for the savings was given a bonus equal to 25 percent of the savings attributable to improving delivery quality. Company policy also provided a salary increase of 1 percent for every day saved in delivery time.
B: Bill Johnson, manager of the product development department, was pleased with his department's performance on the last quarter's projects. It had managed to complete all projects under budget, virtually assuring Bill of a fat bonus, just in time to help with this year's Christmas purchases.

Situation 3
A: "Harvey, don't worry about the fact that your department is producing at only 70 percent capacity. Increasing your output would simply pile up inventory in front of the next production department. That would be costly for the organization as a whole. Sometimes one department must reduce its performance so that the performance of the entire organization can improve."
B: "Susan, I am concerned about the fact that your department's performance measures have really dropped over the past quarter. Labour usage variances are unfavourable, and I also see that your machine utilization rates are down. Now, I know that yours is not a bottleneck department, but I get a lot of flak when my managers' efficiency ratings drop."

Situation 4

A: Colby was muttering to himself. He had just received last quarter's budgetary performance report. Once again, he had managed to spend more than budgeted for both materials and labour. The real question now was how to improve his performance for the next quarter.

B: Great! Cycle time had been reduced, and at the same time, the number of defective products had been cut by 35 percent. Cutting the number of defects reduced production costs by more than planned. Trends were favourable for all three performance measures.

Situation 5

A: Cambry was furious. An across-the-board budget cut! "How can they expect me to provide the computer services required on less money? Management is convinced that costs are out of control, but I would like to know where—at least in my department!"

B: After a careful study of the accounts payable department, it was discovered that 80 percent of an accounts payable clerk's time was spent resolving discrepancies between the purchase order, receiving document, and supplier's invoice. Other activities, such as recording and preparing cheques, consumed only 20 percent of a clerk's time. A redesign of the procurement process eliminated virtually all discrepancies and produced significant cost savings.

Situation 6

A: Five years ago, the management of Breeann Products commissioned an outside engineering consulting firm to conduct a time-and-motion study so that labour efficiency standards could be developed and used in production. These labour efficiency standards are still in use today and are viewed by management as an important indicator of productive efficiency.

B: Janet was quite satisfied with this quarter's labour performance. When compared with the same quarter of last year, labour productivity had increased by 23 percent. Most of the increase was due to a new assembly approach suggested by production line workers. She was also pleased to see that materials productivity had increased. The increase in materials productivity was attributed to reducing scrap because of improved quality.

Situation 7

A: "The system converts materials into products, not people at work stations. Therefore, process efficiency is more important than labour efficiency—but we also must pay particular attention to those who use the products we produce, whether inside or outside the firm."

B: "I was quite happy to see a revenue increase of 15 percent over last year, especially when the budget called for a 10 percent increase. However, after reading the recent copy of our trade journal, I now wonder whether we are doing so well. I found out that the market expanded by 30 percent, and our leading competitor increased its sales by 40 percent."

15–2

Activity-Based Responsibility Accounting versus Strategic-Based Responsibility Accounting

LO1

Cambry Day, president of DayTime Novelties, was considering a memo sent to her by Colby Sorensen, the firm's vice-president of operations. The memo argued that DayTime needed to change its responsibility accounting system from an activity-based approach to a strategic-based approach. Colby was convinced that the change would enhance DayTime's overall competitiveness. He had requested a meeting to explain the similarities and differences between the two approaches. Cambry agreed to the meeting, but asked Colby to prepare a memo in advance listing the most important similarities and differences between the activity-based and strategic-based approaches to responsibility accounting.

Required:

Prepare the memo requested by Cambry.

15–3

Functional-Based versus Activity-Based or Strategic-Based Responsibility Accounting; Ethical Issues; Incentives

LO1

David Christensen, plant manager, was given the charge to produce 120,000 bolts used in the manufacture of small twin-engine aircraft. Directed by his divisional manager to give the bolt production priority over other jobs, he had two weeks to produce the units. Meeting the delivery date was crucial for renewal of a major contract with a large airplane manufacturer. Each bolt requires 20 minutes of direct labour and 150 grams of metal. After the production of a batch of bolts, each bolt is subjected to a stress test. Those that pass are placed in a carton, which is stamped "Inspected by Inspector No. _____" (the inspector's identification number is inserted). Defective units are discarded, having no salvage value. Because of the nature of the process, rework is not possible.

At the end of the first week, the plant had produced 60,000 acceptable units and used 24,000 direct labour hours, 4,000 hours more than the standard allowed. Furthermore, a total of 65,000 bolts had been produced and 5,000 had been rejected, creating an unfavourable materials usage variance of 750 kilograms. David knew that a performance report would be prepared when the 120,000 bolts were completed. This report would compare the labour and materials used with that allowed. Any variance in excess of 5 percent of standard would be investigated. David expected the same or worse performance for the coming week and was worried about a poor performance rating for himself. Accordingly, at the beginning of the second week, David moved his inspectors to the production line (all inspectors had production experience). However, for reporting purposes the production hours provided by inspectors would not be counted as part of direct labour. They would still appear as a separate budget item on the performance report. Additionally, David instructed the inspectors to pack the completed bolts in the cartons and stamp them as inspected. One inspector objected; David reassigned the inspector temporarily to material handling and gave an inspection stamp with a fabricated identification number to a line worker who was willing to stamp the cartons of bolts as inspected.

Required:

1. Explain why David stopped inspections on the bolts and reassigned inspectors to production and material handling. Discuss the ethical ramifications of this decision.
2. What features in the functional-based responsibility accounting system provided the incentives(s) for David to take the actions described? Would an activity-based or strategic-based responsibility system have provided incentives that discourage this kind of behaviour? Explain.
3. What likely effect would David's actions have on the quality of the bolts? Was the decision justified by the need to obtain renewal of the contract, particularly if the plant returns to a normal inspection routine after the rush order is completed? Do you have any suggestions about the quality approach taken by this company? Explain why activity-based or strategic-based responsibility accounting might play a useful role in this setting.

15–4

Calculation of Nonvalue-Added Costs

LO2, LO3

Six independent situations are presented below:
A. It takes 45 minutes and 6 kilograms of material to produce a product using a traditional manufacturing process. A process re-engineering study provided a new manufacturing process design (using existing technology) that would take 15 minutes and 4 kilograms of material. The cost per labour hour is $12, and the cost per kilogram of materials is $8.
B. With its original design, a product requires 15 hours of setup time. Redesigning the product could reduce the setup time to an absolute minimum of 30 minutes. The cost per hour of setup time is $200.
C. A product currently requires eight moves. By redesigning the manufacturing layout, the firm can reduce the number of moves from eight to zero. The cost per move is $10.
D. Inspection time for a plant is 8,000 hours per year. The cost of inspection consists of the salaries of four inspectors, totalling $120,000. Inspection also uses

supplies costing $2 per inspection hour. A supplier evaluation program, product redesign, and process redesign reduced the need for inspection by creating a zero-defect environment.

E. Each unit of a product requires 5 components. The average number of components used is actually 5.3, due to component failure that requires rework and extra components. By developing relationships with the right suppliers and increasing the quality of the purchased component, the firm can reduce the average number of components used to 5 components per unit. The cost per component is $600.

F. A plant produces 100 different electronic products. Each product requires an average of eight components that are purchased externally. The components are different for each part. Redesigning the products will make it possible to produce the 100 products so that they all have four components in common. This change will reduce the demand for purchasing, receiving, and paying bills. Estimated savings from the reduced demand are $900,000 per year.

Required:

Provide the following information for each of the six situations presented above:

1. An estimate of the nonvalue-added cost caused by each activity.
2. The root causes of the activity cost (such as plant layout, process design, and product design).
3. The cost reduction measure: activity elimination, activity reduction, activity sharing, or activity selection.

15–5

Calculation of Value-Added and Nonvalue-Added Costs; Activity Volume and Unused Capacity Variances

LO2, LO3

Spreadsheet

Maurice Entertainment Products produces a variety of plastic toys. Because of competitive pressures, the company has been making an effort to reduce costs. As part of this effort, management has implemented an activity-based management system and has begun focusing its attention on processes and activities. Purchasing is among the processes that have been carefully studied. The study has revealed that the number of purchase orders is a good cost driver for purchasing costs. During the last year, the company incurred fixed purchasing costs of $140,000 (the combined salaries of four employees). The fixed costs provide a capacity of processing 16,000 orders (4,000 per employee at practical capacity). Management has decided that the value-added standard number of purchase orders is 8,000. The actual orders processed in the most recent period were 14,000.

Required:

1. Calculate the activity volume and unused capacity variances for the purchasing activity. Explain what each variance means.
2. Prepare a report that presents value-added, nonvalue-added, and actual costs. Explain why highlighting the nonvalue-added costs is important.
3. Explain why purchasing would be viewed as a value-added activity. List all possible reasons. Also list some possible reasons that explain why the demand for purchasing is more than the value-added standard.
4. Assume that management is able to improve the purchasing activity and reduce the demand for purchasing from 14,000 orders to 12,000 orders. What actions should now be taken regarding activity capacity management?

15–6

Cost Report; Value-Added and Nonvalue-Added Costs

LO3

Lemmons Company has developed value-added standards for four activities: purchasing parts, assembling parts, administering parts, and inspecting parts. The activities, the activity driver, the standard and actual quantities, and the price standards follow for 2000:

Activities	Activity Driver	SQ	AQ	SP
Purchasing parts	Orders	500	700	$300
Assembling parts	Labour hours	60,000	66,500	12
Administering parts	Number of parts	6,000	8,600	110
Inspecting parts	Inspection hours	0	25,000	15

The actual prices paid per unit of each activity driver were equal to the standard prices.

Required:

1. Prepare a cost report that lists the value-added costs, nonvalue-added costs, and actual costs for each activity.
2. Which activities are nonvalue-added? Explain why. Explain why value-added activities can have nonvalue-added costs.

15–7

Trend Report; Nonvalue-Added Costs

LO3

Refer to 15–6. Suppose that Lemmons Company used an activity analysis program during 2001 in an effort to reduce nonvalue-added costs. The value-added standards, actual quantities, and prices for 2001 follow:

Activity	Activity Driver	SQ	AQ	SP
Purchasing parts	Orders	500	600	$300
Assembling parts	Labour hours	60,000	62,000	12
Administering parts	Number of parts	6,000	8,000	110
Inspecting parts	Inspection hours	0	15,000	15

Required:

1. Prepare a trend report that compares the nonvalue-added costs for 2000 with those of 2001.
2. Comment on the value of a trend report.

15–8

Activity Analysis; Activity Drivers; Driver Analysis; Behavioural Effects

LO3

Kenzie Sorensen, controller of Riqueza Company, has been helping an outside consulting group install an activity-based cost management system. This new accounting system is designed to support Riqueza's efforts to become more competitive (by creating a competitive advantage). For the past two weeks, Kenzie has been identifying activities, associating workers with activities, and assessing the time and resources consumed by individual activities. Now she and the consulting group have entered into the fourth phase of activity analysis: assessing value content. At this stage, Kenzie and the consultants also plan to identify drivers for assigning costs to cost objects. Furthermore, as a preliminary step to improving activity efficiency, they have decided to identify the potential root causes of activity costs. Kenzie's assignment for today is to assess the value content of five activities, choose a suitable activity driver for each, and identify the possible root causes of the activities. Following are the five activities she is investigating, along with possible activity drivers:

Activity	Possible Activity Drivers
Setting up equipment	Setup time, number of setups
Creating scrap*	Kilograms of scrap, number of defective units
Welding subassemblies	Welding hours, subassemblies welded
Material handling	Number of moves, distance moved
Inspecting parts	Hours of inspection, number of defective parts

* Scrap is defined as a bad product or subassembly that cannot be reworked and must therefore be discarded.

Kenzie runs a regression analysis for each potential activity driver, using the method of least squares to estimate the variable- and fixed-cost components. In all five cases, costs are highly correlated with the potential drivers. Thus, all of the drivers listed appear to be good candidates for assigning costs to products. The company plans to reward production managers for reducing product costs.

Required:

1. For each activity, assess the value content and classify each activity as value-added or nonvalue-added (justify the classification). Identify some possible root

causes of each activity, and describe how this knowledge can be used to improve activity management. For purposes of discussion, assume that the value-added activities are not performed with perfect efficiency.
2.   Describe the behaviour that each activity driver will encourage, and evaluate the suitability of that behaviour for the company's objective of creating a sustainable competitive advantage.

15–9

Kaizen Costing

LO3

Nabors Motors Division has been given the charge to reduce the delivery time of its tractor motors from three days to one day. To help achieve this goal, engineering and production workers have made a commitment to reduce setup times. Current setup times are 12 hours. Setup cost is $50 per setup hour. For the first quarter, engineering develops a new process design that it believes will reduce setup time from 12 hours to 8 hours. After the design is implemented, the actual setup time dropped from 12 to 7 hours—an hour more than expected. In the second quarter, production workers suggest a new setup procedure. Engineering's evaluation of the suggestion is positive, and it projects that the new approach will save an additional hour of setup time. Setup labour is trained to perform new setup procedures. The actual reduction in setup time based on the suggested changes is 1.5 hours.

Required:

1.   What is the kaizen setup standard that would be used at the beginning of each quarter?
2.   Describe the kaizen subcycle using the two quarters of data provided by Nabors.
3.   Describe the maintenance subcycle using the two quarters of data provided by Nabors.
4.   How much nonvalue-added cost has been eliminated by the end of two quarters?
5.   How does kaizen costing differ from standard costing?

15–10

Life-Cycle Costing; Target Costing

LO3

The product development department at Metcalf Electronics is in the process of developing a new model for its cellular phone line. The product life cycle is estimated at 27 months. Estimated sales over its life cycle are 200,000 units. For the current design, the development, production, and logistics costs for the life cycle are estimated at $12,000,000. The product specifications and the targeted market share call for a price of $90 per unit. The target profit per unit is $40. Postpurchase costs for the current design are estimated to be $5 per unit.

Required:

1.   What is the total life-cycle profit desired for the new model?
2.   What is the projected life-cycle profit for the new model?
3.   What is the target cost? How much must costs be reduced per unit and in total for this target to be met? Describe three approaches available for reducing costs so that the target cost is met.
4.   Should postpurchase costs be included in life-cycle costing? target costing? Explain.

15–11

Balanced Scorecard; Strategy Translation; Single- and Double-Loop Feedback

LO4

NBH Company, a small electronics firm, buys circuit boards and manually inserts various electronic devices into the printed circuit board. NBH sells its products to original equipment manufacturers. Profits for the last two years have been less than expected. Natalie Henson, NBH's owner, is convinced that her firm needs to adopt a revenue growth strategy to increase overall profits. To help in building a viable strategy, Natalie hires a local consultant. After a careful review, the consultant tells Natalie that the main obstacle for increasing revenues is the high defect rate of her products (which have a 5 percent reject rate). She is told that revenues would grow if the defect rate were reduced dramatically. By decreasing the defect rate, NBH will increase customer satisfaction. With increased customer satisfaction, the company's market share should increase. The following suggestions are made to help ensure the success of the revenue growth strategy:

- Improve the soldering capabilities by sending employees to an outside course.
- Redesign the insertion process to eliminate some of the common mistakes.
- Improve the procurement process by selecting suppliers that provide higher-quality circuit boards.

Required:

1. State the revenue growth strategy using a series of cause-and-effect relationships expressed as if–then statements. It is possible to have a compound if–then statement (more than one cause for one effect).
2. Illustrate the strategy using a flow diagram like the one shown in Exhibit 15–15.
3. Explain how the revenue growth strategy can be tested. In your explanation, discuss the role of lead and lag measures, targets, and double-loop feedback.

15–12

Balanced Scorecard; Classification of Performance Measures

LO4

Listed below are a number of scorecard measures. Classify each performance measure according to the following: Perspective (for example, customer or learning and growth), Financial or Nonfinancial, Subjective or Objective, External or Internal, and Lead or Lag.

a. Number of new customers
b. Percentage of customer complaints resolved with one contact
c. Unit product cost
d. Cost per distribution channel
e. Suggestions per employee
f. Quality costs
g. Product functionality ratings (from surveys)
h. Cycle time for solving a customer's problem
i. Strategic job coverage ratio
j. On-time delivery percentage
k. Percentage of revenues from new products

15–13

Cycle Time and Conversion Cost per Unit

LO4

The theoretical cycle time for a product is 20 minutes per unit. The budgeted conversion costs for the manufacturing cell are $1,800,000 per year. The total labour minutes available are 400,000. During the year, the cell was able to produce two units of the product per hour. Suppose also that production incentives exist to minimize unit product costs.

Required:

1. Compute the theoretical conversion cost per unit.
2. Compute the applied conversion cost per minute (the amount of conversion cost actually assigned to the product).
3. Discuss how this approach to assigning conversion cost can improve delivery-time performance.

15–14

Cycle Time and Velocity; MCE

LO4

Spreadsheet

A manufacturing cell has the theoretical capability to produce 30,000 stereo speakers per quarter. The conversion cost per quarter is $60,000. There are 5,000 production hours available within the cell per quarter.

Required:

1. Compute the theoretical velocity (per hour) and the theoretical cycle time (minutes per unit produced).
2. Compute the ideal amount of conversion cost that will be assigned per speaker.
3. Speaker production uses two minutes of move time, one minute of wait time, and two minutes of inspection time. Compute the amount of conversion cost actually assigned to each speaker. Now calculate MCE.
4. Based on your analysis in Requirements 2 and 3, how much nonvalue-added time is being used? How much is it costing per speaker?

PROBLEMS

15–15

**Continuous
Improvement;
Balanced Scorecard;
Performance
Measurement**

LO4

At the beginning of 1999, Wilson Company implemented a low-cost strategy to improve its competitive position. Its objective was to become the lowest-cost producer in its industry. To lower costs, Wilson undertook a number of improvement activities, such as JIT production, total quality management, and activity-based management. Now, after two years of operating under this new system, Wilson's president wants some assessment of the system's achievements. To help provide this assessment, the following information on one product has been gathered:

	1999	2001
Theoretical annual capacity[a]	96,000	96,000
Actual production[b]	76,000	88,000
Production hours available (20 workers)	40,000	40,000
Postpurchase costs per unit	$20	$10
Scrap (kilograms)	10,000	8,000
Materials used (kilograms)	100,000	100,000
Actual cost per unit	$125	$100
Days of inventory	6	3
Number of defective units	4,500	2,000
Suggestions per employee	2	6
Hours of training	100	400
Selling price per unit	$150	$140
Number of new customers	2,000	8,000

[a] Amount that could be produced given the available production hours.
[b] Amount that was produced given the available production hours.

Required:

1. Compute the following measures for 1999 and 2001:
   a. Theoretical velocity and cycle time
   b. Actual velocity and cycle time
   c. Percentage change in postpurchase costs (for 2001 only)
   d. Labour productivity (output/hours)
   e. Scrap as a percentage of total material issued
   f. Percentage change in actual product cost (for 2001 only)
   g. Percentage change in days of inventory (for 2001 only)
   h. Defective units as a percentage of total units produced
   i. New customers
   j. Hours of training
   k. Selling price per unit (as given)
   l. Total employee suggestions
2. For the measures listed in Requirement 1, list likely strategic objectives, classified according to the Balanced Scorecard perspectives. Next classify each measure as a lead or lag measure. Finally, evaluate the strategy's success. Would you like any additional information to carry out the evaluation? Explain.
3. Based on the results in Requirement 2, express Wilson's strategy as a series of if–then statements. What does this tell you about Balanced Scorecard measures?

15–16

**Activity-Based
Management;
Nonvalue-Added
Costs; Target Costs**

LO1, LO2, LO3

Danna Martin, president of Mays Electronic, was concerned about the end-of-the-year marketing report that she had just received. According to Larry Savage, marketing manager, a price decrease for the coming year was again needed to maintain the company's annual sales volume of integrated circuit boards (CBs). This would make a bad situation worse. The current selling price of $18 per unit was producing a $2-per-unit profit—half the customary $4-per-unit profit. Foreign competitors kept reducing their prices. To match the latest reduction would reduce the price from $18 to $14. This would put the price below the cost of producing and selling each unit.

How could Mays's competitors sell for such a low price? Determined to find out if there were problems with the company's operations, Danna decided to hire a consultant to evaluate the way in which the CBs were produced and sold. After two weeks, the consultant had identified the following activities and costs:

Batch-level activities:	
Setting up equipment	$ 125,000
Material handling	180,000
Inspecting products	122,000
Product-sustaining activities:	
Engineering support	120,000
Handling customer complaints	100,000
Filling warranties	170,000
Storing goods	80,000
Expediting goods	75,000
Unit-level activities:	
Using materials	500,000
Using power	48,000
Manual insertion labour[a]	250,000
Other direct labour	150,000
Total costs	$1,920,000[b]

[a] Diodes, resistors, and integrated circuits are inserted manually into the circuit board.
[b] This total cost produces a unit cost of $16 for last year's sales volume.

The consultant indicated that some preliminary activity analysis shows that per-unit costs can be reduced by at least $7. Since the marketing manager had indicated that the market share (sales volume) for the boards could be increased by 50 percent if the price could be reduced to $12, Danna became quite excited.

Required:

1. What is activity-based management? What phases of activity analysis did the consultant provide? What else remains to be done?
2. Identify as many nonvalue-added costs as possible. Compute the cost savings per unit that would be realized if these costs were eliminated. Was the consultant correct in his preliminary cost reduction assessment? Discuss actions that the company can take to reduce or eliminate the nonvalue-added activities.
3. Compute the target cost required to maintain current market share while earning a profit of $4 per unit. Now compute the target cost required to expand sales by 50 percent. How much cost reduction would be required to achieve each target?
4. Assume that further activity analysis revealed the following: switching to automated insertion would save $60,000 of engineering support and $90,000 of direct labour. Now what is the total potential cost reduction per unit available from activity analysis? With these additional reductions, can Mays achieve the target cost to maintain current sales? to increase them by 50 percent? What form of activity analysis is this: reduction, sharing, elimination, or selection?
5. Calculate income based on current sales, prices, and costs. Now calculate the income using a $14 price and a $12 price, assuming that the maximum cost reduction possible is achieved (including Requirement 4's reduction). What price should be selected?

15–17

Value-Added and Kaizen Standards; Nonvalue-Added Costs; Volume Variance; Unused Capacity

LO3

Clement Mallet, vice-president of Suegros Company (a producer of a variety of plastic products), has been supervising the implementation of an activity-based cost management system. One of Clement's objectives is to improve process efficiency by improving the activities that define the processes. To illustrate the new system's potential to the firm's president, Clement has decided to focus on two processes: production and customer service.

Within each process, one activity will be selected for improvement: materials usage for production, and sustaining engineering for customer service (sustaining engineers are responsible for redesigning products based on customer needs and feedback). Value-added standards are identified for each activity. For materials usage, the value-added standard calls for 6 kilograms per unit of output (although the plastic products differ in shape and function, their size, as measured by weight, is uniform). The value-added standard is based on the elimination of all waste due to defective moulds. The standard price of materials is $5 per kilogram. For sustaining engineering, the standard is 58 percent of current practical activity capacity. This standard is based on the fact that about 42 percent of the complaints have to do with design features that could have been avoided or anticipated by the company.

Current practical capacity (at the end of 2000) is defined by the following requirements: 6,000 engineering hours for each product group that has been on the market or in development for five years or less, and 2,400 hours per product group of more than five years. Four product groups have less than five years' experience, and ten product groups have more. There are 24 engineers, each paid a salary of $60,000. Each engineer can provide 2,000 hours of service per year. There are no other significant costs for the engineering activity.

Actual materials usage for 2000 was 25 percent above the level called for by the value-added standard; engineering usage was 46,000 hours. There were 80,000 units of output produced. Clement and the company's operational managers have selected some improvement measures that promise to reduce nonvalue-added activity usage by 40 percent in 2001. Selected annual results achieved for 2001 are as follows:

Units produced	80,000
Materials used	584,800
Engineering hours	35,400

The actual prices paid for materials and engineering hours are identical to the standard or budgeted prices.

Required:

1. For 2000, calculate the nonvalue-added usage and costs for material usage and sustaining engineering. Also, calculate the cost of unused capacity for the engineering activity.
2. Using the targeted reduction, establish kaizen standards for materials and engineering (for 2001).
3. Using the kaizen standards prepared in Requirement 2, compute the 2001 usage variances, expressed in both physical and financial measures for materials and engineering (for engineering, compare actual resource usage with the kaizen standard). Comment on the company's ability to achieve its targeted reductions. In particular, discuss what measures the company must take to capture any realized reductions in resource usage.

15–18

**Target Costing;
Benchmarking;
Nonvalue-Added
Costs**

LO3, LO4

Arequipa Products has two plants that manufacture a line of recliners. One plant is located in Edmonton and the other in Calgary. Each plant is set up as a profit centre. During the past year, both plants sold the regular model for $450. Sales volume averages 20,000 units per year in each plant. Recently, the Calgary plant reduced the price of the regular model to $400. Discussion with the Calgary manager revealed that the price reduction was possible because the plant had reduced its manufacturing and selling costs by reducing what was called "nonvalue-added costs." The Calgary plant's manufacturing and selling costs for the regular chair were $350 per unit. The Calgary manager offered to loan the Edmonton plant his cost accounting manager to help them achieve similar results. The Edmonton plant's manager readily agreed, knowing that his plant must keep pace, not only with the Calgary plant but also with the firm's competitors. A local competitor had also reduced its price on a similar model, and the Edmonton plant's marketing manager had indicated that the price must be matched or sales would drop dramatically. In fact, the marketing manager suggested that if the price were dropped to $390 by the end of the year, the plant could expand its share of the market by 20 percent. The plant manager agreed, but insisted that the current profit per unit must be maintained and now wants to know if the plant can at least match the Calgary plant's $350-per-unit cost. He also wants to know if the plant can achieve the cost reduction using the Calgary plant's approach.

The Edmonton plant's controller and the Calgary plant's cost accounting manager have assembled the following data from the Edmonton plant for the most recent year. The actual cost of inputs, their value-added (ideal) quantity levels, and the actual quantity levels are provided (for production of 20,000 units). Assume that there is no difference between actual prices of activity units and standard prices.

	SQ	AQ	Actual Cost
Materials (kilograms)	237,500	250,000	$5,250,000
Labour (hours)	57,000	60,000	750,000
Setups (hours)	—	4,000	300,000
Material handling (moves)	—	10,000	700,000
Warranties (number repaired)	—	10,000	1,000,000
Total			$8,000,000

Required:

1. Calculate the target cost for expanding the Edmonton market share by 20 percent, assuming that the per-unit profitability is maintained as requested by the plant manager.
2. Calculate the nonvalue-added cost per unit. Assuming that nonvalue-added costs can be reduced to zero, do you think the Edmonton plant can match the Calgary plant's per-unit cost? Can the target cost for expanding market share be achieved? What actions would you take if you were the Edmonton plant's manager?
3. Describe the role that benchmarking played in the Edmonton plant's effort to protect and improve its competitive position.

15–19

Life-Cycle Cost Management

LO3

Boyce Products manufactures products with life cycles that average three years. The first year involves product development, and the remaining two years emphasize production and sales. A budgeted life-cycle income statement developed for two proposed products follows. Each product will sell 200,000 units. The price has been set to yield a 50 percent gross margin ratio.

	Product A	Product B	Total
Sales	$4,000,000	$5,000,000	$9,000,000
Cost of goods sold	2,000,000	2,500,000	4,500,000
Gross margin	$2,000,000	$2,500,000	$4,500,000
Period expenses:			
Research and development			2,000,000
Marketing			1,150,000
Life-cycle income			$1,350,000

Upon seeing the budget, Rick Moss, the president of Boyce Products, called in LeeAnn Gordon, the firm's marketing manager, and Art Cummings, its design engineer.

Rick: "These two products are earning only a 15 percent return on sales. We need 20 percent to earn an acceptable return on our investment. Can't we raise prices?"
LeeAnn: "I doubt that the market would bear any increase in prices. However, I will do some additional research and see what's possible. The gross profit ratio is already high. The problem appears to be with R & D. Those expenses seem higher than normal."
Art: "These products are more complex than usual, and we need to have the extra resources—at least if you want to have a product that functions as we are claiming it will. Also, we are charting some new waters with the features these products are offering. Specifically, our design is intended to reduce the postpurchase costs that

consumers incur, including operation, support, maintenance, and disposal. LeeAnn, if you'll recall, you mentioned to us a year ago that our competitors were providing products that had lower postpurchase costs. This new design was intended to make us market leaders in this area. At any rate, in the future we can probably get by on less—after we gain some experience. But it wouldn't be much less— perhaps $50,000."

Rick: "That would still allow us to earn only about 15.6 percent—even after you get more proficient. Maybe we ought to stay with our more standard features."

LeeAnn: "Before we abandon these new lines, perhaps we ought to look at each product individually. Maybe one could be retained. These new features will give us an edge in the market. Also, I'll bet that if Art knew what was driving those costs, he could redesign the product so that production costs could be lowered. I'm concerned that our competitors will exploit their postpurchase cost advantage. We really need to be leaders in this postpurchase area: —our reputation is at stake. If we're not careful, we'll begin losing market share."

Required:

1. What specific improvements would you suggest to Rick to improve Boyce's life-cycle cost management system?
2. Assume that the "period" expenses are traceable to each product. Product A is responsible for 60 percent of research and development costs and 50 percent of marketing costs. Prepare a revised income statement for each product. Based on this analysis, do you think that either product should be produced?
3. Based on the revised income statements from Requirement 2, how much do you think production costs must be reduced to make each product acceptable? Discuss how activity analysis can help achieve this outcome. Explain why this analysis should occur now, not after the products are in production.
4. According to Art, the motivation for the new design was to reduce the postpurchase costs of the new products. Explain why whole-life cost should be the focus of life-cycle cost management

15–20

Cycle Time; Conversion Cost per Unit; MCE

LO4

A manufacturing cell has the theoretical capability to produce 60,000 space heaters per quarter. The conversion cost per quarter is $600,000. There are 20,000 production hours available within the cell per quarter.

Required:

1. Compute the theoretical velocity (per hour) and the theoretical cycle time (minutes per unit produced).
2. Compute the ideal amount of conversion cost that will be assigned per heater.
3. Suppose that the actual time required to produce a heater is 30 minutes. Compute the amount of conversion cost actually assigned to each heater. Discuss how this approach to assigning conversion cost can improve delivery time.
4. Calculate MCE. How much nonvalue-added time is being used? How much is it costing per heater?
5. Cycle time, velocity, MCE, conversion cost per unit (theoretical conversion rate × actual conversion time), and nonvalue-added costs are all measures of performance for the cell process. Discuss the incentives provided by these measures.

15–21

MCE

LO2, LO4

Anderson Company makes a product that experiences the following activities (and times):

	Hours
Processing (two departments)	30
Inspecting	2
Rework	5
Moving (three moves)	8
Waiting (for the second process)	24
Storage (before delivery to customer)	31

Required:

1. Compute the MCE for this product.
2. Discuss how process value analysis can help improve this efficiency measure.
3. Is this a lead measure or a lag measure? If it is a lag measure, what would be some lead measures that would affect this measure?

15–22

Functional-Based versus Activity-Based Responsibility Accounting; Strategic-Based Measures

LO1

Continuous improvement is the governing principle of an activity-based responsibility accounting system. Following are several performance measures. Some of these measures would be associated with a functional-based responsibility accounting system, and some would be associated with an activity-based responsibility accounting system.

a. Materials price variances
b. Cycle time
c. Comparison of actual product costs with target costs
d. Materials quantity or efficiency variances
e. Comparison of actual product costs over time (trend reports)
f. Comparison of actual overhead costs, item by item, with the corresponding budgeted costs
g. Comparison of product costs with competitors' product costs
h. Percentage of on-time deliveries
i. Quality reports
j. Reports of value-added and nonvalue-added costs
k. Labour efficiency variances
l. Machine utilization rates
m. Days of inventory
n. Downtime
o. Manufacturing cycle efficiency (MCE)
p. Unused capacity variance
q. Labour rate variance
r. Using a sister plant's best practices as a performance standard

Required:

1. Classify each measure as functional-based or activity-based. If functional-based, discuss the measure's limitations for an activity-based environment. If activity-based, describe how the measure supports the objectives of an activity-based environment.
2. Classify the measures into operational (nonfinancial) and financial categories. Explain why operational measures are better for control at the shop level (on the production floor) than financial measures are. Should any financial measures be used at the operational level?
3. Discuss how strategic-based responsibility accounting differs from activity-based responsibility accounting. Provide examples of measures that would be added to the above list if a strategic-based system were used.

15–23

Cycle Time; Velocity; Product Costing

LO4

Silverman Company has a JIT system in place. Each manufacturing cell is dedicated to the production of a single product or major subassembly. One cell, dedicated to the production of paint guns, performs four operations: machining, finishing, assembly, and qualifying (testing). The machining process is automated, using computers. In this process, the paint gun's body, cup, and nozzle are machined. In finishing, sandblasting, buffing, and anodizing are done. In assembly, the three parts of the paint gun are assembled. Finally, each paint gun is tested using 20 millilitres of paint.

For the past year, the paint gun cell had the following budgeted costs and cell time (both at theoretical capacity):

Budgeted conversion costs	$2,500,000
Budgeted raw materials	$3,000,000
Cell time	4,000 hours
Theoretical output	30,000 paint guns

During the year, the following actual results were obtained:

Actual conversion costs	$2,500,000
Actual materials	$2,600,000
Actual cell time	4,000 hours
Actual output	25,000 paint guns

Required:

1. Compute the velocity (number of paint guns per hour) that the cell can theoretically achieve. Now compute the theoretical cycle time (number of hours or minutes per paint gun) that it takes to produce one paint gun.
2. Compute the actual velocity and the actual cycle time.
3. Compute MCE. Comment on the efficiency of the operation.
4. Compute the budgeted conversion cost per minute. Using this rate, compute the conversion cost per paint gun if theoretical output is achieved. Using this measure, compute the conversion cost per paint gun for actual output. Does this product-costing approach provide an incentive for the cell manager to reduce cycle time? Explain.

15–24

Balanced Scorecard; Nonvalue-Added Activities; Strategy Translation; Kaizen Costing

LO2, LO3, LO4

At the beginning of the last quarter of 1999, Microcom, Inc., a large consumer products firm, hired Leming Imai to take over one of its divisions. The division manufactured small home appliances and was struggling to survive in a very competitive market. Leming immediately requested a projected income statement for 1999. In response, the controller provided the following statement:

Sales	$25,000,000
Variable expenses	20,000,000
Contribution margin	$ 5,000,000
Fixed expenses	6,000,000
Projected loss	$(1,000,000)

After some investigation, Leming soon realized that the products being produced had a serious problem with quality. He once again requested a special study by the controller's office to supply a report on the level of quality costs. By the middle of November, Leming received the following report from the controller:

Inspection costs, finished product	$ 400,000
Rework costs	2,000,000
Scrapped units	600,000
Warranty costs	3,000,000
Sales returns (quality-related)	1,000,000
Customer complaint department	500,000
Total estimated quality costs	$7,500,000

Leming was surprised at the level of quality costs. They represented 30 percent of sales, certainly excessive. He knew that to survive, the division had to produce high-quality products. The number of defective units produced needed to be reduced dramatically. Thus, Leming decided to pursue a quality-driven turnaround strategy. Revenue growth and cost reduction could both be achieved if quality could be improved. By increasing revenues and decreasing costs, a firm can increase profitability.

After Leming met with the managers of production, marketing, purchasing, and human resources, the following decisions were made, effective immediately (end of November 1999):

1. More will be invested in employee training. Workers will be trained to detect quality problems and empowered to make improvements. Workers will be allowed a bonus of 10 percent of any cost savings produced by their suggested improvements.

2. Two design engineers will be hired immediately, with expectations of hiring one or two more within a year. These engineers will be in charge of redesigning processes and products with the objective of improving quality. They will also be given the responsibility of working with selected suppliers to help improve the quality of their products and processes. Design engineers were considered a strategic necessity.

3. A new process, the evaluation and selection of suppliers, will be implemented, with the objective of selecting a group of suppliers that are willing to provide (and capable of providing) nondefective components.

4. Effective immediately, the division will begin inspecting purchased components. According to production, many of the quality problems are caused by defective components purchased from outside suppliers. Incoming inspection was viewed as a transitional activity. Once the division has developed a group of suppliers capable of delivering nondefective components, this activity will be eliminated.

5. Within three years, the goal is to produce products with a defect rate of less than 0.1 percent. Marketing is confident that reducing the defect rate to this level will increase market share by at least 50 percent (as a consequence of increased customer satisfaction). Products with better quality will help establish an improved product image and reputation, allowing the division to capture new customers and increase market share.

6. Accounting will be given the charge to install a quality information reporting system. Daily reports on operational quality data (for example, percentage of defective units), weekly updates of trend graphs (posted throughout the division), and quarterly cost reports are the types of information required.

7. To help direct the improvements in quality activities, kaizen costing is to be implemented. For example, for the year 2000, rework costs, a kaizen standard of 6 percent of the selling price per unit was set, a 25 percent reduction from the current actual cost.

To ensure that the quality improvements were directed and translated into concrete financial outcomes, Leming also began to implement a Balanced Scorecard for the division. By the end of 2000, progress was being made. Sales had increased to $26,000,000, and the kaizen improvements were meeting or beating expectations. For example, rework costs had dropped to $1,500,000.

At the end of 2001, two years after the turnaround quality strategy was implemented, Leming received the following quality cost report:

Quality training	$ 500,000
Supplier evaluation	230,000
Incoming inspection costs	400,000
Inspection costs, finished product	300,000
Rework costs	1,000,000
Scrapped units	200,000
Warranty costs	750,000
Sales returns (quality-related)	435,000
Customer complaint department	325,000
Total estimated quality costs	$4,140,000

Leming also received an income statement for 2001:

Sales	$30,000,000
Variable expenses	22,000,000
Contribution margin	$ 8,000,000
Fixed expenses	5,800,000
Income	$2,200,000

Leming was pleased with the outcomes. Revenues had grown, and costs had been reduced by at least as much as he had projected for the two-year period. He believed that next year's growth would be even greater, because he was beginning to observe a favourable effect from the higher-quality products. Also, further quality cost reductions should materialize, because incoming inspections were showing much higher-quality purchased components.

Required:

1. Identify the strategic objectives, classified by Balanced Scorecard perspectives. Next, suggest measures for each objective. Classify the measures as lead and lag measures.
2. Using the results from Requirement 1, describe Leming's strategy using a series of if–then statements. Next, prepare a visual diagram of the strategy similar to (although more complex than) the one shown in Exhibit 15–15.
3. Explain how you would evaluate the success of the quality-driven turnaround strategy. What additional information would you like to have for this evaluation?
4. Explain why Leming felt that the Balanced Scorecard would increase the likelihood that the turnaround strategy would actually produce good financial outcomes.
5. The kaizen standard for rework was 6 percent of sales for 2000. Was the standard met? What would be the maintenance standard at the end of 2000? Describe the role for kaizen costing in Leming's strategy.
6. Of the quality activities listed in the 2001 report, which ones are nonvalue-added? By eliminating all nonvalue-added activities, how much further cost reduction is possible?

MANAGERIAL DECISION CASES

15–25

Ethical Considerations

LO1

Tim Ireland, controller of Roberts Electronics Division, was having lunch with Jimmy Jones, the division's chief design engineer. Tim and Jimmy were good friends, having belonged to the same fraternity during their university days. The luncheon, however, was more business than pleasure.

Jimmy: "Well, Tim, you indicated this morning that you have something important to tell me. I hope this isn't too serious. I don't want my weekend ruined."

Tim: "Well, the matter is important. You know that at the beginning of this year, I was given the charge to estimate postpurchase costs for new products. This is not an easy task."

Jimmy: "Yeah, I know. That's why I had our department supply you with engineering specs on the new products—stuff like expected component life."

Tim: "This new product you've been developing has a problem. According to your reports, there are two components that will wear out within about fourteen months. According to your test runs, the product starts producing subpar performance during the thirteenth month."

Jimmy: "Long enough to get us past the twelve-month warranty. So why worry? There are no warranty costs for us to deal with."

Tim: "Yes, but the customer must then incur substantial repair costs. And the product will have to be repaired once again before its useful life is ended. The estimated repair costs, when added to the normal life-cycle costs, put the whole-life cost above the target cost. According to the new guidelines, we are going to have to scrap this new product—at least using its current design. Perhaps you can find a new design that avoids the use of these two components—or find ways that they won't be so stressed so that they last much longer."

Jimmy: "Listen, Tim, I don't have the time or the budget to redesign this product. I have to come in under budget, and I have to meet the targeted production date—otherwise, I'll have the divisional manager down my throat. Besides, you know that I'm up for the engineering management position at headquarters. If this project goes well, then it'll give me what I need to edge out Thompson Division's chief engineer. If I do the redesign, my opportunity for the job is gone. Help me out on this. You know how much this opportunity means to me."

Tim: "I don't know what I can do. I have to file the whole-life cost report, and I'm required to supply supporting documentation from marketing and engineering."

Jimmy: "Well, that's easy to solve. Linda, the engineer who ran the tests on this product, owes me a favour. I'll get her to redo the tests so that the data produce a twenty-four-month reliability period for the components. That should cut your estimated repair costs in half. Would that be enough to meet the targeted whole-life costs?"

Tim: "Yes, but ..."

Jimmy: "Hey, don't worry. If I tell Linda that I'll push her for chief divisional engineer, she'll cooperate. No sweat. This is a one-time thing. How about it? Are you a player?"

Required:

1. What pressures does Tim have to comply with Jimmy's requests? Do you think he should comply? Would you, if you were Tim? If not, how would you handle the situation?
2. Assume that Tim cooperates with Jimmy and covers up the design deficiency. What standards of ethical conduct for management accountants are being violated? (See the code of ethics described in Chapter 1.)
3. Suppose that Tim refuses to cooperate. Jimmy then gets Linda to rerun the tests anyway, with the new, more optimistic results. He then approaches Tim with the tests and indicates that he is sending a copy of the latest results to the divisional manager. Jimmy indicates that he will challenge any redesign recommendations that Tim makes. What should Tim do?

RESEARCH ASSIGNMENT

15–26

Research Assignment LO4

You are a newly employed accountant working for a medium-sized manufacturing firm. This firm is facing intense competition from foreign and domestic competitors. Your supervisor, Kathy Bumstead, has asked you to research the use of nonfinancial performance measures. Use your library's resources, paying particular attention to articles appearing in the following journals: *Management Accounting, Journal of Cost Management,* and *Harvard Business Review.* Once you have collected what you can on the topic, write a memo to Kathy that addresses the following issues:

1. What has brought about the rise of nonfinancial measures?
2. What are the deficiencies of the traditional accounting performance measures?
3. What nonfinancial measures should be used and why? In particular, what is the firm trying to measure?
4. How can control be achieved through the use of nonfinancial measures?
5. What problems or limitations are associated with nonfinancial measures?
6. What is your recommendation concerning the use of nonfinancial measures?

Kathy wants you to list the sources for the views that you articulate in your memo. She is also willing for you to address any other substantive issues that you encounter in your research. However, the memo must be no longer than two pages.

CHAPTER 16

Quality Costs and Productivity: Measurement, Reporting, and Control

Learning Objectives

After studying Chapter 16, you should be able to:

1. Identify and describe the four types of quality costs.

2. Prepare a quality cost report, and explain the difference between the conventional view of acceptable quality level and the view espoused by total quality control.

3. Explain why quality cost information is needed and how it is used.

4. Explain what productivity is, and calculate the impact of productivity changes on profits.

Scenario

Russell Walsh, president of Ladd Lighting Corporation, had just returned from a productivity seminar, excited and encouraged by what he had heard. He immediately called a meeting with Sarah Burke, the company's production quality manager, and Dennis Schmitt, the company's controller and financial vice-president.

Russell: "I am convinced that we can become more competitive by increasing productivity and improving quality. Something needs to be done given the direction our profits have been heading over the past several years."

Dennis: "I agree that we need to do something. Improving quality will cost, and I am not sure that

spending more on quality will help much. After all, right now we spend a lot on quality-related activities. Pouring more money into quality may not be the answer."

Russell: "I don't intend to spend more on quality—just the opposite. According to experts and backed up by the experience of numerous cases, improving quality *decreases* quality costs. Most quality-related costs are incurred because of poor quality. It costs us when we do things wrong, in terms of rework, scrap, repairs, and so on. By controlling quality costs, profitability can be improved and we become more competitive.

"Ford Motor Company, for example, as part of a 1994 Ford

2000 initiative, made a commitment to reduce the vehicle defects per car by a significant percentage. And, according to a 1997 JD Power Initial Quality Study, Ford's quality performance had taken a dramatic leap. Using a quality metric expressed as problems per 100 cars, Ford scored an 81, which placed it above the industry average of 86 and beat both General Motors and Chrysler. The score also represented a 28 percent improvement. Ford also had two plants that won Power's Platinum award, an award given to vehicle assembly plants with the fewest reported problems of all facilities serving U.S. customers."[1]

Sarah: "I can see how this would make Ford more competitive. As I have always maintained, it costs us when we do things wrong."

Russell: "Exactly. I now understand what you were saying. Poor quality is what costs. Several cases were discussed at the conference. One example given was that of Tennant Company, a manufacturer of industrial floor maintenance products. Tennant's quality improvement efforts have been remarkable. The most exciting thing about Tennant's experience, however, is the effect of the improved quality on its profitability. When the quality improvement program began, Tennant estimated that its cost of doing things wrong was as high as 17 percent of sales. Within a six-year period, this cost had dropped to 8 percent of sales. Based on annual sales of $136 million, savings from improved quality totalled $12.24 million."[2]

Dennis: "I'm impressed by the potential savings through improved quality. I'm not sure, however, what role you envision for me, other than being aware of the

importance of a quality improvement program. Sarah's department has been responsible for quality cost reporting."

Russell: "I envision your role as being much more extensive than simple awareness. We need a solid, reliable quality cost-reporting system, and I expect you to assume responsibility for its development and operation. Our company needs quality information to help our managers make quality improvement decisions. We also need to monitor and control the programs that we implement. Sarah, do you have any problem with this arrangement?"

Sarah: "None at all. It seems sensible that the controller's office be responsible for collecting and reporting quality costs. I know that other companies have this arrangement. The quality department should be responsible for analyzing and controlling these costs. Besides, I have a feeling that given the increased emphasis on quality, my department will have

plenty to do without worrying about a cost-reporting system."

1. Melissa Larson, "Ford Puts Quality Data in Human Hands," *Quality Magazine* (December 1997) (an on-line article, see **www.qualitymag.com/1297f3.html**).

2. Lawrence Carr and Thomas Tyson, "Planning Quality Cost Expenditures," *Management Accounting* (October 1992): pp. 52–56.

Questions to Think About

1. Why has measurement of productivity and quality become so important?

2. What are quality costs?

3. How can improving quality reduce quality costs?

4. What kind of quality cost reports should be prepared by the accounting department?

5. What is meant by "productivity"?

6. How is productivity measured?

MEASURING THE COSTS OF QUALITY

Objective 1

Identify and describe the four types of quality costs.

By attending a productivity seminar, Russell Walsh discovered that paying more attention to quality can increase profitability. Quality improvement can increase profitability in two ways: (1) by increasing customer demand, and (2) by decreasing costs. In a tightly competitive market, increased demand, and cost savings can mean the difference between surviving and thriving. The Baldrige National Quality Award was created by law in the United States to recognize U.S. companies that excel in quality management and achievement.[3] The award categories include manufacturing, small business, service, educational, and health entities. Past winners have included 3M Dental Products Division, Solectron Corporation, Xerox Business Services, Motorola, Inc., Federal Express, General Motors' Cadillac Division, Zytec, Globe Metallurgical, Inc., Texas Instruments, Inc., and the Ritz-Carlton Hotel Company.

The costs of quality can be substantial and a source of significant savings. Studies indicate that costs of quality for American companies are typically 20 to 30 percent of sales.[4] Yet, quality experts maintain that the optimal quality level should

3. The Malcolm Baldrige National Quality Award was created by U.S. Public Law 100-107 in 1987. The first awards were given in 1988.

4. Michael R. Ostrenga, "Return on Investment Through the Costs of Quality," *Journal of Cost Management* (Summer 1991): pp. 37–44.

be about 2 to 4 percent of sales. This difference between actual and optimal figures represents a veritable gold mine of opportunity. Improving quality can produce significant improvements in profitability. Xerox, for example, saved more than $200 million over a four-year period by improving quality.[5]

In the last two decades, quality has become an important competitive dimension for both service and manufacturing organizations. Quality is an integrating theme for all organizations. Foreign firms' ability to sell higher-quality products at lower prices has cost many North American firms market share. In an effort to combat this stiff competition, North American firms have increasingly paid more attention to quality and productivity, especially given the potential to reduce costs and improve product quality simultaneously. The senior management of IBM, for example, identified poor quality as the root cause of problems that it was having. In an effort to solve some of these problems, the company implemented a quality program called "Market-Driven Quality." According to former IBM chairman John Akers, quality improvement is a survival issue for today's businesses.[6] Other North American companies are following suit and are striving to meet consumer quality expectations. Standard Aero of Winnipeg embarked on an impressive quality management program.[7] Standard Aero recognized that airplane owners routinely sent their engines to be overhauled, a process that took two months in the shop and required a stock of spare engines at a cost of more than a million dollars each. The company decided to cut the overhaul time from two months to 15 days as one of the features of its comprehensive quality programs. As a result of increased productivity and the implementation of total quality management, Standard Aero's 4.5 percent sales increase produced 45 percent higher earnings.[8] Some have called this push for increased quality a "second industrial revolution."[9] Thus, the quality revolution has been in process for sufficient time so that some believe that quality has shifted from that of being a source of strategic advantage to that of a competitive necessity.[10]

In response to the globalization of markets, the International Organization for Standardization (ISO), comprising 96 member nations (the Canadian Standards Association [CSA] is the Canadian member), has developed the ISO 9000 series of quality assurance and quality management standards. ISO 9000 has gained wide acceptance internationally, particularly in Europe. An increasing number of North American companies that sell products internationally now follow ISO 9000. The Society of Management Accountants of Canada issued a Management Accounting Guideline to provide practical guidance for the implementation of required quality systems and for becoming ISO 9000 registered.[11]

As companies implement quality improvement programs, a need arises to monitor and report on the progress of these programs.[12] Managers need to know what

5. Lawrence P. Carr, "How Xerox Sustains the Cost of Quality," *Management Accounting* (August 1995): pp. 26–32.

6. Lawrence Carr and Thomas Tyson, "Planning Quality Expenditures," *Management Accounting* (October 1992): pp. 52–56.

7. Paul Sharman, "World-Class Productivity at Standard Aero," *CMA Magazine*, April 1991, 7–12.

8. These results are also found for other industries. For example, J. M. Schneider, Inc., responded to declining demand in the meat-packing industry by adopting a program of continuous improvement. Costs were reduced by $8.1 million, customer returns were down by 45 percent, and rework was down by 43 percent. See Douglas Dodds, "Making It Better ... and Better," *CMA Magazine*, February 1992, 16–21. An examination of service organizations can be found in H. David Sherman, *Service Organization Productivity Management*, A Research Monograph, The Society of Management Accountants of Canada, 1988.

9. James P. Simpson and David L. Muthler, "Quality Costs: Facilitating the Quality Initiative," *Journal of Cost Management* (Spring 1987): pp. 25–34.

10. Robert S. Kaplan and David P. Norton, *The Balanced Scorecard* (Boston: Harvard Business Press, 1996): pp. 87–88.

11. The Society of Management Accountants of Canada, *Becoming ISO 9000 Registered*, Management Accounting Guideline 25, Hamilton, Ontario, 1994.

12. The Society of Management Accountants of Canada, *Managing Quality Improvements*, Management Accounting Guideline 14, Hamilton, Ontario, 1992, provides guidance for implementing a quality management process.

quality costs are and how they are changing over time. Reporting and measuring quality performance is absolutely essential to the success of an ongoing quality improvement program. A fundamental prerequisite for this reporting is measuring the costs of quality. But to measure those costs, an operational definition of *quality* is needed.

Quality Defined

The typical dictionary definition of *quality* refers to the "degree or grade of excellence"; in this sense, quality is a relative measure of goodness. But defining quality as goodness is so general that it offers no operational content. How do we build an operational definition? The answer is, "Adopt a customer focus." Operationally, a **quality product or service** is one that meets or exceeds customer expectations. In effect, quality is customer satisfaction. But what is meant by "customer expectations"? Customer expectations can be described by quality attributes, or what are often referred to as "dimensions of quality."[13] Thus, a quality product or service is one that meets or exceeds customer expectations on the following eight dimensions:

1. Performance
2. Aesthetics
3. Serviceability
4. Features (quality of design)
5. Reliability
6. Durability
7. Quality of conformance
8. Fitness for use

The first four dimensions describe important quality attributes, but are difficult to measure. **Performance** refers to how consistently and how well a product functions. For services, the inseparability principle means that the service is performed in the presence of the customer. Thus, the performance dimension for services can be further defined by the attributes of responsiveness, assurance, and empathy. *Responsiveness* is simply the willingness to help customers and provide prompt, consistent service. *Assurance* refers to the knowledge and courtesy of employees and their ability to convey trust and confidence. *Empathy* means providing caring, individualized attention to customers. **Aesthetics** is concerned with the appearance of tangible products (for example, style and beauty) as well as the appearance of the facilities, equipment, personnel, and communication materials associated with services. **Serviceability** measures the ease of maintaining and/or repairing the product. **Features (quality of design)** refer to characteristics of a product that differentiate functionally similar products. For example, the function of automobiles is to provide transportation. Yet one auto may have a four-cylinder engine, a manual transmission, vinyl seats, room to seat four passengers comfortably, and front disk brakes; another may have a six-cylinder engine, an automatic transmission, leather seats, room to seat six passengers comfortably, and antilock brakes. Similarly, first-class air travel and economy air travel reflect different design qualities. First-class air travel, for example, offers more legroom, better meals, and more luxurious seats. Obviously, in both cases the product features are different. Higher design quality is usually reflected in higher manufacturing costs and in higher selling prices. Quality of design helps a company determine its market. There is a market for both the four-cylinder and the six-cylinder cars as well as for both economy air travel and first-class air travel.

---

13. These dimensions are based on Edwin S. Schecter, *Managing for World Class Quality* (Milwaukee: ASQC Quality Press, 1992) and Leonard L. Berry and A. Parasurman, *Marketing Services: Competing Through Quality* (New York: The Free Press, Macmillan, 1991), 16.

Reliability is the probability that the product or service will perform its intended function for a specified length of time. **Durability** is defined as the length of time a product functions. **Quality of conformance** is a measure of how a product meets its specifications. For example, the specifications for a machined part may be a drilled hole that is 5 centimetres in diameter, plus or minus 0.25 centimetres. Parts that fall within this range are defined as conforming parts. **Fitness of use** is the suitability of the product for carrying out its advertised functions. If there is a fundamental design flaw, the product may fail in the field even if it conforms to its specifications. Product recalls are frequently the result of fitness-of-use failures.

Improving quality, then, means improving one or more of the eight quality dimensions while maintaining performance on the remaining dimensions. Providing a higher-quality product than a competitor provides means outperforming the competitor on at least one dimension while matching performance on the remaining dimensions. Although all eight dimensions are important and can affect customer satisfaction, the quality attributes that are measurable tend to receive more emphasis. Conformance, in particular, is strongly emphasized. In fact, many quality experts believe that "quality is conformance" is the best operational definition. There is some logic to this position. Product specifications should explicitly consider such things as reliability, durability, fitness of use, and performance. Implicitly, a conforming product is reliable, durable, and fit for use, and performs well. The product should be produced as the design specifies it; specifications should be met. Conformance is the basis for defining what is meant by a nonconforming, or defective, product.

A **defective product** is one that does not conform to specifications. **Zero defects** means that all products conform to specifications. But what is meant by "conforming to specifications"? The *traditional view* of conformance assumes that there is an acceptable range of values for each specification or quality characteristic. A target value is defined, and upper and lower limits are set that describe acceptable product variation for a given quality characteristic. Any unit that falls within the limits is deemed nondefective. For example, losing or gaining zero minutes per month may be the target value for a watch, and any watch that keeps time correctly within plus or minus two minutes per month is judged acceptable. On the other hand, the *robust quality view* of conformance emphasizes fitness of use. *Robustness* means hitting the target value every time. There is no range in which variation is acceptable. A nondefective watch in the robust setting would be one that does not gain or lose any minutes during the month. Since evidence exists that product variation can be costly, the robust quality definition of conformance is superior to the traditional definition.

Costs of Quality Defined

Quality-linked activities are those activities performed because poor quality may or does exist. The costs of performing these activities are referred to as costs of quality. Thus, the **costs of quality** are the costs that exist because poor quality may or does exist.[14] This definition implies that quality costs are associated with two subcategories of quality-related activities: control activities and failure activities. **Control activities** are performed by an organization to prevent or detect poor quality (because poor quality *may* exist). Thus, control activities are made up of prevention and appraisal activities. **Control costs** are the costs of performing control activities. **Failure activities** are performed by an organization or its customers in response to poor quality (because poor quality *does* exist). If the response to poor quality occurs before delivery of a bad (nonconforming, unreliable, not durable, and so on) product to a customer, the activities are classified as internal failure activities; otherwise, they are classified as external failure activities. **Failure costs** are the costs incurred by an organization because failure activi-

---

14. This is the definition in Wayne J. Morse, Harold P. Roth, and Kay M. Poston, *Measuring, Planning, and Controlling Quality Costs* (Montvale, NJ: National Association of Accountants, 1987), 19. Another way of looking at the cost of quality involves determining how much is spent on discovering, scrapping, and correcting errors. See Mohammed Beheiry, "New Thoughts on an Old Concept: The Cost of Quality," *CMA Magazine*, June 1991, 24–25.

ties are performed. Note that the definitions of failure activities and failure costs imply that customer response to poor quality can impose costs on an organization. The definitions of quality-related activities also imply four categories of quality costs: (1) prevention costs, (2) appraisal costs, (3) internal failure costs, and (4) external failure costs.

Prevention costs are incurred to prevent poor quality in the products or services being produced. As prevention costs increase, we would expect the costs of failure to decrease. Examples of prevention costs are quality engineering, quality training programs, quality planning, quality reporting, supplier evaluation and selection, quality audits, quality circles, field trials, and design reviews.

Appraisal costs are incurred to determine whether products and services are conforming to their requirements or customer needs. Examples include inspecting and testing raw materials, packaging inspection, supervising appraisal activities, product acceptance, process acceptance, measurement (inspection and test) equipment, and outside endorsements. Two of these terms require further explanation.

Product acceptance involves sampling from batches of finished goods to determine whether they meet an acceptable quality level; if so, the goods are accepted. *Process acceptance* involves sampling goods while in process to see if the process is in control and producing nondefective goods; if not, the process is shut down until corrective action can be taken. The main objective of the appraisal function is to prevent nonconforming goods from being shipped to customers.

Internal failure costs are incurred because products and services do not conform to specifications or customer needs. This nonconformance is detected prior to being shipped or delivered to outside parties. These are the failures detected by appraisal activities. Examples of internal failure costs are scrap, rework, downtime (due to defects), reinspection, retesting, and design changes. These costs disappear if no defects exist.

External failure costs are incurred because products and services fail to conform to requirements or satisfy customer needs after being delivered to customers. Of all the costs of quality, this category can be the most devastating. Costs of recalls, for example, can run into the hundreds of millions. Other examples include lost sales because of poor product performance, returns and allowances because of poor quality, warranties, repair, product liability, customer dissatisfaction, lost market share, and complaint adjustment. External failure costs, like internal failure costs, disappear if no defects exist.

Measuring Quality Costs

Quality costs can also be classified as observable or hidden. **Observable quality costs** are those that are available from an organization's accounting records. **Hidden quality costs** are opportunity costs resulting from poor quality (opportunity costs are not usually recognized in accounting records). Consider, for example, all the examples of quality costs listed in the previous section. With the exception of lost sales, customer dissatisfaction, and lost market share, all the quality costs are observable and should be available from the accounting records. Note also that the hidden costs are all in the external failure category. These hidden quality costs can be significant and should be estimated. Although estimating hidden quality costs is not easy, three methods have been suggested: (1) the multiplier method, (2) the market research method, and (3) the Taguchi quality loss function.

The Multiplier Method   The multiplier method assumes that the total failure costs are simply some multiple of measured failure costs:

$$\text{Total external failure costs} = k(\text{Measured external failure costs})$$

where k is the multiplier effect. The value of k is based on experience. For example, Westinghouse Electric reports a value of k between 3 and 4.[15] Thus, if the measured

15. T. L. Albright and P. R. Roth, "The Measurement of Quality Costs: An Alternative Paradigm," *Accounting Horizons* (June 1992): 15–27. This article also describes the three approaches to measuring hidden quality costs.

external failure costs are $2 million, the actual external failure costs are between $6 million and $8 million. Including hidden costs in assessing the amount of external failure costs allows management to more accurately determine the appropriate level of resource spending for prevention and appraisal activities. Specifically, with an increase in failure costs, we would expect management to increase its investment in control costs.

The Market Research Method   Formal market research methods are used to assess the effect of poor quality on sales and market share. Customer surveys and interviews with members of a company's sales force can provide significant insights into the magnitude of a company's hidden costs. Market research results can be used to project future profit losses attributable to poor quality.

The Taguchi Quality Loss Function   The traditional zero-defects definition assumes that hidden quality costs exist only for units that fall outside the upper and lower specification limits. The **Taguchi loss function** assumes that any variation from the target value of a quality characteristic causes hidden quality costs. Furthermore, the hidden quality costs increase quadratically as the actual value deviates from the target value. The Taguchi quality loss function, illustrated in Exhibit 16–1, can be described by the following equation:

$$L(y) = k(y - T)^2 \qquad\qquad (16.1)$$

where

k = A proportionality constant dependent upon the organization's external failure cost structure
y = Actual value of quality characteristic
T = Target value of quality characteristic
L = Quality loss

Exhibit 16–1

The Taguchi Quality Loss Function

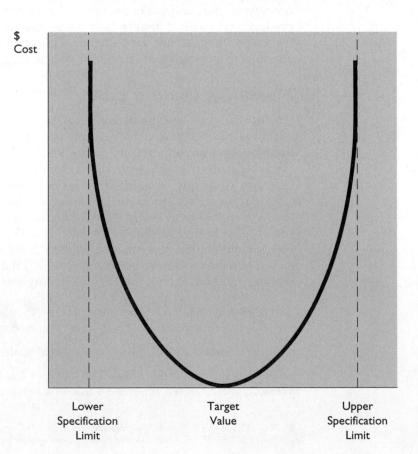

$ Cost

Lower
Specification
Limit

Target
Value

Upper
Specification
Limit

Unit	Actual Diameter (y)	$y - T$	$(y - T)^2$	$k(y - T)^2$
1	9.9	−0.10	0.010	$ 4
2	10.1	0.10	0.010	4
3	10.2	0.20	0.040	16
4	9.8	−0.20	0.040	16
Total			0.100	$40
Average			0.025	$10

Exhibit 16–2

Quality Loss
Computation Illustrated

Exhibit 16–1 demonstrates that the quality cost is zero at the target value and increases symmetrically, at an increasing rate, as the actual value varies from the target value. Assume, for example, that $k = \$400$ and $T = 10$ centimetres in diameter. Exhibit 16–2 illustrates the computation of the quality loss for four units. Note that the cost quadruples when the deviation from the target doubles (from units 2 to 3). Note also the average deviation squared and the average loss per unit can be computed. These averages can be used to compute the total expected hidden quality costs for a product. If, for example, the total units produced are 2,000 and the average squared deviation is 0.025, then the expected cost per unit is $10 (0.025 × $400), and the total expected loss for the 2,000 units would be $20,000 ($10 × 2,000).

To apply the Taguchi loss function, k must be estimated. The value for k is computed by dividing the estimated cost at one of the specification limits by the squared deviation of the limit from the target value:

$$k = c/d^2$$

where

c = Loss at the lower or upper specification limit
d = Distance of limit from target value

This means that we must still estimate the loss for a given deviation from the target value. The first two methods, the multiplier method or the market research method, may be used to help in this estimation (a one-time assessment need). Once k is known, the hidden quality costs can be estimated for any level of variation from the target value.

REPORTING QUALITY COST INFORMATION

Objective 2

Prepare a quality cost report, and explain the difference between the conventional view of acceptable quality level and the view espoused by total quality control.

A quality cost-reporting system is essential for an organization that is serious about improving and controlling quality costs. The first and simplest step in creating such a system is assessing current actual quality costs. A detailed listing of actual quality costs by category can provide two important insights. First, it reveals the magnitude of the quality costs in each category, allowing managers to assess their financial impact. Second, it shows the distribution of quality costs by category, allowing managers to assess the relative importance of each category.

Quality Cost Reports

The financial significance of quality costs can be assessed more easily by expressing these costs as a percentage of actual sales. Exhibit 16–3, for example, reports the quality costs of Jensen Products for fiscal 2001.[16] According to the report, quality costs

---

16. The quality cost report given in Exhibit 16–3 parallels the format used by ITT, except for several minor differences. First, the ITT report combines the internal and external categories into one failure category. Second, the ITT report has a third column allowing the reporting unit to express quality costs as a percentage of a measure other than sales. For more detail, see Morse, Roth, and Poston, *Measuring, Planning, and Controlling Quality Costs*, 78–81.

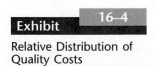

Exhibit 16–3

Quality Cost Report

	Quality Costs		Percentage (%) of Sales[a]
Prevention costs:			
Quality training	$35,000		
Reliability engineering	80,000	$115,000	4.11
Appraisal costs:			
Materials inspection	$20,000		
Product acceptance	10,000		
Process acceptance	38,000	68,000	2.43
Internal failure costs:			
Scrap	$50,000		
Rework	35,000	85,000	3.04
External failure costs:			
Customer complaints	$25,000		
Warranty	25,000		
Repair	15,000	65,000	2.32
Total quality costs		$333,000	11.90[b]

Jensen Products
Quality Cost Report
For the Year Ended March 31, 2001

[a] Actual sales of $2,800,000.
[b] $333,000/$2,800,000 = 11.89 percent; difference is rounding error.

represent almost 12 percent of sales. Given the rule of thumb that quality costs should be no more than about 2.5 percent, Jensen Products has ample opportunity to improve profits by decreasing quality costs. Understand, however, that reduction in costs should come through improvement of quality. Reducing quality costs without any effort to improve quality could prove to be a disastrous strategy.

Additional insight concerning the relative distribution of quality costs can be realized by constructing a pie chart. Exhibit 16–4 provides such a chart, using the quality costs reported in Exhibit 16–3. Managers, of course, have the responsibility of assessing the optimal level of quality and determining the relative amount that should be spent in each category. There are two views concerning optimal quality costs: the traditional view, which calls for an *acceptable quality level*; and the contem-

Exhibit 16–4

Relative Distribution of Quality Costs

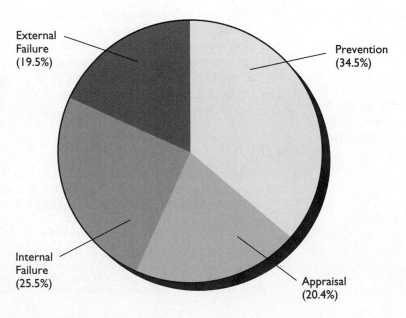

porary view, referred to as *total quality control*. Each view offers managers insights about how quality costs ought to be managed.

Quality Cost Function: Acceptable Quality View

The acceptable quality view assumes that there is a tradeoff between control costs and failure costs. As control costs increase, failure costs should decrease. As long as the decrease in failure costs is greater than the corresponding increase in control costs, a company should continue increasing its efforts to prevent or detect nonconforming units. Eventually, a point is reached at which any additional increase in this effort costs more than the corresponding reduction in failure costs. This point represents the minimum level of total quality costs. It is the optimal balance between control costs and failure costs and defines what is known as the **acceptable quality level (AQL)**. This theoretical relationship is illustrated in Exhibit 16–5.

In Exhibit 16–5, two cost functions are assumed: one for control costs and one for failure costs. It is also assumed that the percentage of defective units increases as the amount spent on prevention and appraisal activities decreases; failure costs, on the other hand, increase as the number of defective units increases. From the total quality cost function, we see that total quality costs decrease as quality improves—up to a point. After that, no further improvement is possible. An optimal level of defective units is identified, and the company works to achieve this level. This level of allowable defective units is the *acceptable quality level*.

Exhibit	16–5

AQL Quality Cost Graph

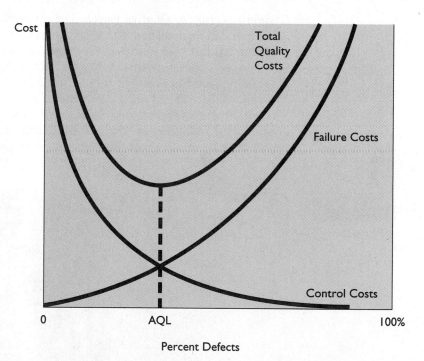

Quality Cost Function: Zero-Defects View

The AQL viewpoint is based on a traditional defective product definition. In the classic sense, a product is defective if it falls outside the tolerance limits for a quality characteristic. Under this view, failure costs are incurred only if the product fails to conform to specifications, and an optimal tradeoff exists between failure and control costs. The AQL view permitted—and, in fact, encouraged—the production of a given number of defective units. This model prevailed in the quality control world until the late 1970s, when the AQL model was challenged by the *zero-defects model*. Essentially, the zero-defects model made the claim that it is cost-beneficial to reduce nonconforming units to zero.

Firms producing increasingly fewer nonconforming units became more competitive relative to firms that continued using the traditional AQL model. In the mid-1980s, the zero-defects model was taken one step further by the *robust quality model*, which challenged the definition of a defective unit. According to the robust view, a loss is experienced from producing products that vary from a target value, and the greater the distance from the target value the greater the loss. Furthermore, the loss is incurred even if the deviation is within the specification limits. In other words, variation from the ideal is costly, and specification limits serve no useful purpose: in fact, they may be deceptive. The zero-defects model understates the quality costs and thus the potential for savings from even greater efforts to improve quality (remember the multiplication factor of Westinghouse Electric). Thus, the robust quality model tightened the definition of a defective unit, refined our view of quality costs, and intensified the quality race.

For firms operating in an intensely competitive environment, quality can offer an important competitive advantage. If the robust quality view is correct, then firms can capitalize on it, decreasing the number of defective units (robustly defined) while simultaneously decreasing their total quality costs. This is what appears to be happening for those firms that are striving to achieve a robust zero-defect state for their products (a robust zero-defect state is one with zero tolerance). The optimal level for quality costs occurs where products are produced that meet their target values. The quest to find ways to achieve the target value creates a dynamic quality world as opposed to the static quality world of AQL.

Dynamic Nature of Quality Costs   The discovery that tradeoffs among quality cost categories can be managed differently from what is implied by the relationships portrayed in Exhibit 16–5 is analogous to the discovery that inventory cost tradeoffs can be managed differently from what the traditional inventory model (EOQ) implied. Essentially, what happens is that as firms increase their prevention and appraisal costs and reduce their failure costs, they discover that they can then cut back on the prevention and appraisal costs. What initially appears to be a tradeoff turns out to be a permanent reduction in costs for all quality cost categories. Exhibit 16–6 displays the changes in quality cost relationships; it shows a total quality cost function con-

Exhibit 16–6

Contemporary Quality
Cost Graph

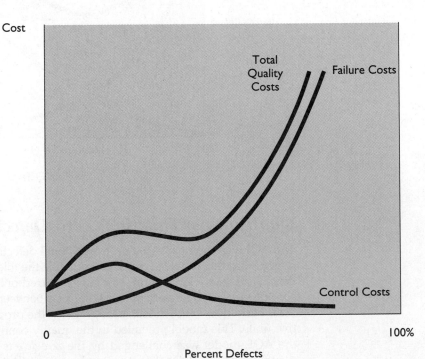

sistent with the quality cost relationships described. There are some key differences. First, control costs do not increase without limit as a robust zero-defect state is approached. Second, control costs may increase and then decrease as the robust state is approached. Third, failure costs can be driven to zero.

Suppose, for example, that a firm has decided to improve the quality of its raw material inputs through the implementation of a supplier selection program. The objective is to identify and use suppliers who are willing to meet certain quality standards. As the firm works to implement this program, additional costs may be incurred (for example, review of suppliers, communication with suppliers, contract negotiations, and so on). And initially, other prevention and appraisal costs may continue at their current levels. However, once the program is fully implemented and evidence is surfacing that the failure costs are being reduced (for example, less rework, fewer customer complaints, and fewer repairs), then the company may decide to cut back on inspections of incoming raw materials, reduce the level of product acceptance activities, and so on. The net effect is a reduction in all quality cost categories. And quality has increased!

This example is consistent with the strategy for reducing quality costs recommended by the American Society for Quality Control:

> The strategy for reducing quality costs is quite simple: (1) take direct attack on failure costs in an attempt to drive them to zero; (2) invest in the "right" prevention activities to bring about improvement; (3) reduce appraisal costs according to results achieved; and (4) continuously evaluate and redirect prevention efforts to gain further improvement.
>
> This strategy is based on the premise that:
> - For each failure there is a root cause.
> - Causes are preventable.
> - Prevention is always cheaper.[17]

This ability to reduce total quality costs dramatically in all categories is borne out by real-world experiences. Tennant, for example, reduced its costs of quality from 17 percent of sales in 1980 to 2.5 percent of sales in 1988, and at the same time significantly altered the relative distribution of the quality cost categories. In 1980, failure costs accounted for 50 percent of the company's total costs of quality (8.5 percent of sales) and control costs 50 percent (8.5 percent of sales). Once the 2.5 percent level was achieved, failure costs accounted for only 15 percent of the total costs of quality (0.375 percent of sales), and control costs had increased to 85 percent of the total (2.125 percent of sales). Tennant increased quality, reduced quality costs in every category and in total, and shifted the distribution of quality costs to the control categories, with the greatest emphasis on prevention. This outcome argues strongly against the traditional quality cost model portrayed in Exhibit 16–5. According to this model, total quality costs can be decreased only by trading off control and failure costs (increasing one while decreasing the other). Further support for the total quality control model is provided by Westinghouse Electric. Like Tennant, Westinghouse Electric found that its profits continued to improve until its control costs accounted for about 70 percent to 80 percent of total quality costs.[18] Based on these two companies' experiences, we know that it is possible to reduce total quality costs significantly—in all categories—and that the process radically alters the relative distribution of the quality cost categories.

Activity-Based Management and Optimal Quality Costs Activity-based management classifies activities as value-added and nonvalue-added and keeps only those that add value. This principle can be applied to quality-related activities. Appraisal and failure activities and their associated costs are nonvalue-added and should therefore be eliminated. Prevention activities—performed efficiently—can be classified as

17. Jack Campanella, ed., *Principles of Quality Costs* (Milwaukee: ASQC Quality Press, 1990), 12.

18. These factual observations are based on those reported by Lawrence P. Carr and Thomas Tyson, "Planning Quality Cost Expenditures."

value-added and should therefore be retained. Initially, however, prevention activities may not be performed efficiently, and activity reduction and activity selection (and perhaps even activity sharing) can be used to achieve the desired value-added state. Grede Foundries Inc. of Milwaukee, the world's largest foundry company, has been tracking all four categories of quality costs for more than 15 years. However, it does not report prevention costs as part of its final cost-of-quality figures, because it does not want its managers to reduce quality costs by cutting prevention activities. It feels strongly that spending money on prevention activities pays off. For example, it has found that a 1 percent reduction in scrap reduces external defects by about 5 percent.[19]

Once the activities are identified for each category, resource drivers can be used to improve cost assignments to the individual activities. Root (cost) drivers can also be identified, especially for failure activities, and used to help managers understand what is causing the costs of the activities. This information can then be used to select ways of reducing quality costs to the level demonstrated in Exhibit 16–6. In effect, activity-based management supports the robust zero-defect view of quality costs. There is no optimal tradeoff between control and failure costs; the latter are nonvalue-added costs and should be reduced to zero. Some control activities are nonvalue-added and should be eliminated. Other control activities are value-added but may be performed inefficiently, and the costs caused by the inefficiency are nonvalue-added. Thus, costs for these categories may also be reduced to lower levels.

Trend Analysis

Quality cost reports reveal the magnitude of quality costs and their distribution among the four categories, thus revealing opportunities for improvement. Once quality improvement measures are undertaken, it is important to determine whether quality costs are being reduced as planned. Quality cost reports will not reveal whether improvement has occurred or not. It would be useful to have a picture of how the quality improvement program has been doing since its inception. Is the multiple-period trend—the overall change in quality costs—moving in the right direction? Are significant quality gains being made each period? Answers to these questions can be given by providing a trend chart or graph that tracks the change in quality costs through time. Such a graph is called a **multiple-period quality trend report**. By plotting quality costs as a percentage of sales against time, the company can access the overall trend in the quality program. The first year plotted is the year prior to the implementation of the quality improvement program. Assume that a company has experienced the following:

	Quality Costs	Actual Sales	Costs as a Percentage (%) of Sales
1997	$440,000	$2,200,000	20.0
1998	423,000	2,350,000	18.0
1999	412,500	2,750,000	15.0
2000	392,000	2,800,000	14.0
2001	280,000	2,800,000	10.0

Let 1997 be Year 0, 1998 be Year 1, and so on; the trend graph is shown in Exhibit 16–7. Periods of time are plotted on the horizontal axis and percentages of sales on the vertical. The ultimate quality cost objective of 3 percent, the target percentage, is represented as a horizontal line on the graph.

The graph reveals that there has been a steady downward trend in quality costs expressed as a percentage of sales. The graph also reveals that there is still ample room for improvement toward the long-run target percentage.

Additional insight can be provided by plotting the trend for each individual quality category. Assume that each category is expressed as a percentage of sales for the same period of time.

19. Nancy Chase, "Counting Costs, Reaping Returns," *Quality Magazine* (October 1998): on-line article, **www.qualitymag.com/articles/oct98/1098fl.html**.

Exhibit 16–7

Exhibit 16–7

Multiple-Period Trend Graph: Total Quality Costs

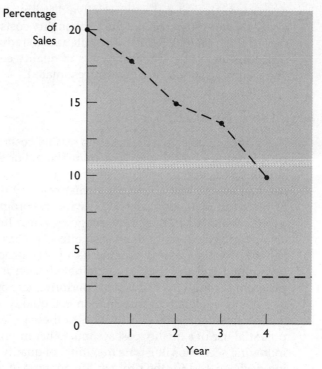

	Prevention	Appraisal	Internal Failure	External Failure
1997	2.0%	2.0%	6.0%	10.0%
1998	3.0%	2.4%	4.0%	8.6%
1999	3.0%	3.0%	3.0%	6.0%
2000	4.0%	3.0%	2.5%	4.5%
2001	4.1%	2.4%	2.0%	1.5%

The graph showing the trend for each category is displayed in Exhibit 16–8. From Exhibit 16–8, we can see that the company has had dramatic success in reducing external and internal failures. More money is being spent on prevention (the amount has doubled as a percentage). Appraisal costs have increased and then

Exhibit 16–8

Multiple-Period Trend Graph: Individual Quality Cost Categories

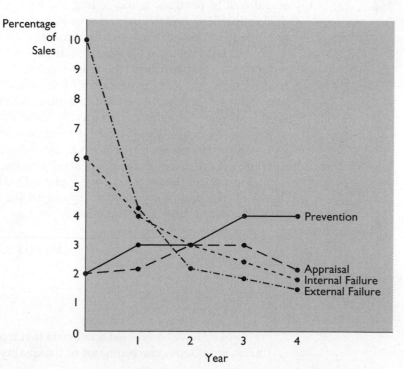

decreased. Note also that the relative distribution of costs has changed. In 1997, failure costs were 80 percent of the total quality costs (0.16/0.20). In 2001, they are 35 percent of the total (0.035/0.10). The potential to reduce quality costs also affects the way decisions are made. The usefulness of quality cost information for decision making and planning should not be underestimated.

USING QUALITY COST INFORMATION

Objective 3

Explain why quality cost information is needed and how it is used.

The principal objective of reporting quality costs is to improve and facilitate managerial planning, control, and decision making. For example, in deciding to implement a supplier selection program to improve the quality of material inputs, a manager will need an assessment of current quality costs by item and by category, an assessment of the additional costs associated with the program, and an assessment of the projected savings by item and by category. When the costs and savings will occur must also be projected. Once these cash effects are projected, a capital budgeting analysis can be done to assess the merits of the proposed program. If the outcome is favourable and the program is initiated, then it becomes important to monitor the program through fairly standard performance reporting.

Using quality cost information for quality program implementation decisions and for evaluating the effectiveness of these programs, once implemented, is just one potential use of a quality cost system. Other important uses can also be identified. The following scenarios illustrate the utility of quality cost information for a strategic pricing decision and for the profitability analysis of a new product design.

Scenario A: Strategic Pricing

Leola Wise, a marketing manager, muttered to herself as she reviewed the latest market share data for her company's low-priced electronic measurement instruments. Once again the share had dropped! The Japanese firms were continuing to put pressure on this product line. Anticipating this outcome, Leola had begun preparing a brief to support a significant price decrease for this line of products. A price decrease of $3 was needed to recapture the lost market share. The new price less the desired profit per unit produced a target cost that was less than the current actual cost of producing and selling the lower-level instruments. To continue producing this line, cost reductions would need to be made. A cost reduction strategy was needed to re-establish its competitive position.

In the last executive meeting, the discussion had focused on how to achieve cost reductions. Ben Blackburn, the chief engineer, had indicated that process redesign could offer about half the needed cost reduction. Leola had suggested that the company adopt a total quality control position and work to reduce the cost of the lower-level instruments by decreasing quality costs. To determine the potential magnitude of the cost reductions, she asked Earl Simpson, the controller, what the quality costs were for the lower-level instruments. Earl admitted that the costs were not tracked separately. For example, the cost of scrap was buried in the Work in Process account. He did promise, however, to have some estimates of the costs—perhaps not complete—by the end of the month. The report for the lower-level instruments (in the form of a memo from Earl Simpson) follows:

MEMO

To: Leola Wise
From: Earl Simpson
Subject: Quality Costs

Leola, I have assembled some data that may be useful to you. As requested, I have provided some estimates of the quality costs associated with this line. I have not included any costs of lost sales due to nonconforming products, as you are probably in a better position to assess this effect.

Quality costs (estimated):

Inspection of raw materials	$ 200,000
Scrap	800,000
Rejects	500,000
Rework	400,000
Product inspection	300,000
Warranty work	1,000,000
Total estimate	$3,200,000

Upon receiving the memo, Leola immediately called the quality control department and arranged a meeting with its manager, Art Smith. Art indicated that implementing total quality initiatives would reduce quality costs by 50 percent within 18 months. He had already begun planning the implementation of a new quality program. With this information and using a volume of 1,000,000 units, Leola calculated that a 50 percent reduction in the quality costs associated with the lower-level instruments would reduce costs by about $1.60 per unit ($1,600,000/1,000,000). This would make up slightly more than half of the $3 reduction in selling price that would be needed (the reduction is 15 percent of $20). Based on this outcome, Leola decided to implement the price reduction in three phases: a $1 reduction immediately, a $1 reduction in 6 months, and the final reduction of $1 in 12 months. This phased reduction would likely prevent any further erosion of market share and would start increasing it sometime into the second phase. Phasing in the price reductions would give the quality department time to reduce costs so that any big losses could be avoided.

Scenario A illustrates that both quality cost information and the implementation of a total quality control program can contribute to a significant strategic decision. It also shows that improving quality is not a panacea. The reductions are not large enough to bear the full price reduction. Other productivity gains, such as those promised by engineering, will be needed to ensure the long-range viability of the product line.

Scenario B: New Product Analysis

Tara Anderson, a marketing manager, and Brittany Fox, a design engineer, were both unhappy. They had been certain that their proposal for a new product was going to be approved. Instead, they received the following report from the controller's office.

Report: New Product Analysis, Project #675

Estimated product life cycle: 2 years
Projected sales potential: 50,000 units (life cycle)
Projected life-cycle income statement:

Sales (50,000 @ $60)	$3,000,000
Cost of inputs:	
Materials	800,000
Labour	400,000
Scrap	150,000
Inspection	350,000
Repair work	200,000
Product development	500,000
Selling	300,000
Life-cycle income	$ 300,000

Decision: Reject
Reason(s): Life-cycle income is less than the company-required 18 percent return on sales.

"You know," Tara remarked, "I can't quite believe this report. Why don't we ask Bob how he came up with these figures?"

"I agree," responded Brittany. "I'll arrange a meeting for tomorrow. I'll ask him to provide more detail than just the aggregate figures shown on the report."

The next day, the following conversation was recorded. Tara and Brittany had just completed a review of the detailed cost projections supplied by Bob Brown, the assistant controller.

Brittany: "Bob, I would like to know why there is a $3-per-unit scrap cost. And the inspection costs—they seem high. Can you explain these costs?"

Bob: "Sure. It's based on the scrap cost that we track for existing, similar products. Also, as you know, we have a 10 percent destructive-sampling requirement for these types of products."

Brittany: "Well, I think you have overlooked the new design features of this new product. Its design virtually eliminates any waste—especially when you consider that the product will be made on a numerically controlled machine."

Tara: "Also, this $2-per-unit charge for repair work should be eliminated. The new design that Brittany is proposing solves the failure problems we have had with related products. It also means that the $100,000 of fixed costs associated with the repair activity can be eliminated. Furthermore, because of the new design, destructive sampling is not required and we need one less inspector than you have budgeted."

Bob: "Brittany, how certain are you that this new design will eliminate some of these quality problems?"

Brittany: "I'm absolutely positive. The early prototypes did exactly as we expected. The results of those tests are included in the proposal. You must not have read the prototype results."

Bob: "Right. I didn't. Eliminating scrap reduces the unit-level variable cost by $3 per unit. I also see where the repair and inspection activities are overcosted. We need only one inspector, who'll cost $50,000. And eliminating the repair activity saves $200,000. That means the projected life-cycle profits are $650,000 more than I have projected, which in turn means the return on sales is more than 30 percent."

Scenario B illustrates the importance of further classifying quality costs by behaviour. The scenario also reinforces the importance of identifying and reporting quality costs separately. The new product was designed to reduce its quality costs, and only by knowing the quality costs assigned could Brittany and Tara have discovered the error in the life-cycle income analysis.

Reporting quality costs so that they can be used for decision making is just one objective of a good quality-costing system. Another objective is controlling quality costs—a factor critical in helping expected outcomes of decisions come to fruition. The pricing decision in Scenario A, for example, depended on the plan to reduce quality costs.

PRODUCTIVITY: MEASUREMENT AND CONTROL

Objective 4

Explain what productivity is, and calculate the impact of productivity changes on profits.

Productivity is concerned with producing output efficiently; specifically, it addresses the relationship between output and the inputs used to produce the output. Usually, different combinations or mixes of inputs can be used to produce a given level of output. **Total productive efficiency** is the point at which two conditions are satisfied: (1) for any mix of inputs that will produce a given output, no more of any one input is used than necessary to produce the output, and (2) given the mixes that satisfy the first condition, the least costly mix is chosen. The first condition is driven by technical relationships, and is therefore referred to as **technical efficiency**. Viewing activities as inputs, the first condition requires eliminating all nonvalue-added activities and performing value-added activities with the minimal quantities needed to produce the given output. The second condition is driven by relative input price relationships, and is therefore referred to as **input tradeoff efficiency**. Input prices determine the relative proportions of each input that should be used. Deviation from these fixed proportions creates input tradeoff inefficiency.

Productivity improvement programs attempt to move toward a state of total productive efficiency. Technical improvements in productivity can be achieved by using less input to produce the same output or by producing more output using the same inputs or more output with relatively less inputs. For example, in 1992, Lantech, a wrapping-machine producer, produced 8 wrapping machines per day with 50 workers, an average of 0.16 machines per worker. By 1998, the output had increased to 14 machines per day using 20 workers—an average of 0.7 machines per worker. By 1992 productivity standards, about 87.5 workers would have been needed to produce 14 machines. Thus, output increased and fewer workers were needed.[20]

Exhibit 16–9 illustrates the three ways to achieve an improvement in technical efficiency. The output is tons of steel, and the inputs are labour (number of workers) and capital (dollars invested in automated equipment). Notice that the relative proportions of the inputs are held constant so that all productivity improvement is attributable to improving technical efficiency.

20. Melissa Larson, "Are You Ready for Kaizen?" *Quality Magazine* (June 1998): on-line article, **www.qualitymag.com/articles/jun98/0698fl.html**.

Exhibit 16–9
Technical Efficiency

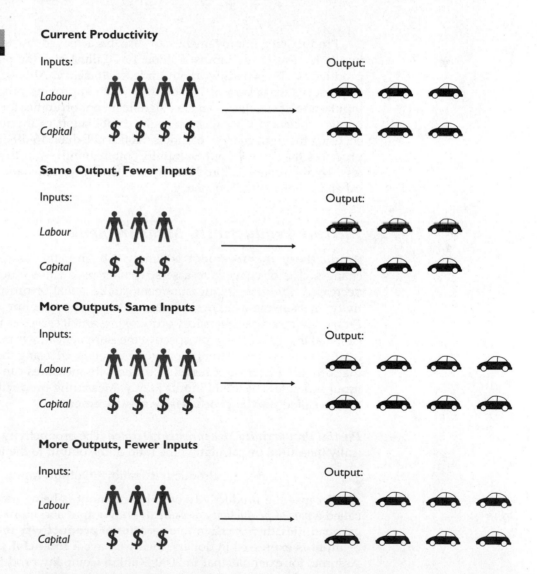

Exhibit 16–10

Input Trade-off Efficiency

Technically Efficient Combination I:
Total Cost of Inputs = $20,000,000

Labour

Capital

Technically Efficient Combination II:
Total Cost of Inputs = $25,000,000

Labour

Capital

Productivity improvement can also be achieved by trading off more costly inputs for less costly inputs. Exhibit 16–10 illustrates the possibility of improving productivity by increasing input tradeoff efficiency. Although improving technical efficiency is what most people think of when improving productivity is mentioned, input tradeoff efficiency can offer significant opportunities for increasing overall economic efficiency. Choosing the right combination of inputs can be as critical as choosing the right quantity of inputs. Notice in Exhibit 16–10 that Input Combination I produces the same output as Input Combination II—but that the cost is $5 million less. Total measures of productivity are usually a combination of changes in technical and input tradeoff efficiency.

Partial Productivity Measurement

Productivity measurement is simply a quantitative assessment of productivity changes. The objective is to assess whether productive efficiency has increased or decreased. Productivity measurement can be actual or prospective. *Actual* productivity measurement allows managers to assess, monitor, and control changes. *Prospective* measurement is forward-looking, and it serves as input for strategic decision making. Specifically, prospective measurement allows managers to compare the relative benefits of different input combinations, choosing the inputs and input mix that provide the greatest benefit. Productivity measures can be developed for each input separately or for all inputs jointly. Measuring productivity for one input at a time is called **partial productivity measurement**.

Partial Productivity Measurement Defined The productivity of a single input is typically measured by calculating the ratio of the output to the input:

$$\text{Productivity ratio} = \text{Output}/\text{Input}$$

Because the productivity of only one input is being measured, the measure is called a *partial productivity measure*. If both output and input are measured in physical quantities, then we have an **operational productivity measure**. If either output or input is expressed in dollars, then we have a **financial productivity measure**. Assume, for example, that in 2000, Kankul Company produced 120,000 motors for small window air-conditioning units and used 40,000 hours of labour. The labour productivity ratio is 3 motors per hour (120,000/40,000). This is an operational measure, since the units are expressed in physical terms. If the selling price of each motor is $50 and the cost of labour is $12 per hour, then output and input can be expressed in dollars. The labour productivity ratio, expressed in financial terms, is $12.50 of revenue per dollar of labour cost ($6,000,000/$480,000).

Partial Measures and Measuring Changes in Productive Efficiency   The labour productivity ratio of 3 motors per hour measures Kankul's 2000 productivity experience. By itself, the ratio conveys little information about productive efficiency or about whether the company's productivity has improved or declined. It is possible, however, to make a statement about increasing or decreasing productive efficiency by measuring changes in productivity. To do so, the actual current productive measure is compared with the productivity measure from a prior period. This prior period is referred to as the **base period** and sets the benchmark, or standard, for measuring changes in productive efficiency. The prior period can be any period desired. It could, for example, be the preceding year, the preceding week, or even the period during which the last batch of products was produced. For strategic evaluations, the base period usually chosen is an earlier year. For operational control, the base period tends to be close to the current period—such as the preceding batch of products or the preceding week.

To illustrate, assume that 2000 is the base period; the labour productivity standard, therefore, is 3 motors per hour. Further assume that late in 2000, Kankul decided to try a new procedure for producing and assembling the motors with the expectation that the new procedure would use less labour. In 2001, there were 150,000 motors produced, using 37,500 hours of labour. The labour productivity ratio for 2001 is 4 motors per hour (150,000/37,500). The *change* in productivity is a 1-unit-per-hour increase in productivity (from 3 units per hour in 2000 to 4 units per hour in 2001). The change is a significant improvement in labour productivity and provides evidence supporting the efficacy of the new process.

Advantages of Partial Measures   Partial measures allow managers to focus on the use of a particular input. Partial operational measures have the advantage of being easily interpreted by all within the organization, so they are easy to use for assessing the productivity performance of operating personnel. Labourers, for instance, can relate to units produced per hour or units produced per kilogram of material. Thus, partial operational measures provide feedback that operating personnel can relate to and understand—measures that deal with the specific inputs over which they have control. This increases the likelihood that the measures will be accepted by operating personnel. Furthermore, for operational control, the standards for performance are often very short term. For example, standards can be the productivity ratios of prior batches of goods. Using this standard, we can track productivity trends within the year.

Disadvantages of Partial Measures   Partial measures, used in isolation, can be misleading. A decline in the productivity of one input may be necessary to increase the productivity of another. Such a tradeoff is desirable if overall costs decline, but the effect would be missed by using either partial measure. For example, changing a process so that direct labourers take less time to assemble a product may increase scrap and waste while leaving total output unchanged. Labour productivity has increased, but productive use of materials has declined. If the increase in the cost of waste and scrap outweighs the savings of the decreased labour, overall productivity has declined.

Two important conclusions can be drawn from this example. First, the possible existence of tradeoffs mandates a total measure of productivity for assessing the merits of productivity decisions. Only by looking at the total productivity effect of all inputs can managers accurately draw any conclusions about overall productivity performance. Second, because of the possibility of tradeoffs, a total measure of productivity must assess the aggregate financial consequences, and should therefore be a financial measure.

Total Productivity Measurement

Measuring productivity for all inputs at once is called **total productivity measurement.** In practice, it may not be necessary to measure the effect of all inputs. Many firms measure the productivity of only those factors that are thought to be relevant indicators of organizational performance and success. Thus, in practical terms, total productivity measurement can be defined as focusing on a limited number of inputs that, in total, indicate organizational success. In either case, total productivity measurement requires the development of a multifactor measurement approach. A common multifactor approach suggested in the productivity literature (but rarely found in practice) is the use of aggregate productivity indexes. Aggregate indexes are complex and difficult to interpret and have not been generally accepted. Two approaches that have gained some acceptance are *profile measurement* and *profit-linked productivity measurement.*

Profile Productivity Measurement Producing a product involves numerous critical inputs, such as labour, materials, capital, and energy. **Profile measurement** provides a series or a vector of separate and distinct partial operational measures. Profiles can be compared over time to provide information about productivity changes. To illustrate the profile approach, we will use only two inputs: labour and materials. Let's return to the Kankul Company example. As before, Kankul implements a new production and assembly process in 2001. Only now let's assume that the new process affects both labour and materials. Initially, let's look at the case for which the productivity of both inputs moves in the same direction. The following data for 2000 and 2001 are available:

	2000	2001
Number of motors produced	120,000	150,000
Labour hours used	40,000	37,500
Materials used (kilograms)	1,200,000	1,428,571

Exhibit 16–11 provides productivity ratio profiles for each year. The 2000 profile is (3, 0.100), and the 2001 profile is (4, 0.105). Comparing profiles for the two years, we can see that productivity increased for both labour and materials (from 3 to 4 for labour and from 0.100 to 0.105 for materials). The profile comparison provides enough information so that a manager can conclude that the new assembly process has definitely improved overall productivity. The *value* of this improvement, however, is not revealed by the ratios.

As just shown, profile analysis can provide managers with useful insights about changes in productivity. However, comparing productivity profiles will not always reveal the nature of the overall change in productive efficiency. In some cases, profile analysis will not provide any clear indication of whether a productivity change is good or bad.

Exhibit 16–11	Partial Productivity Ratios	
Productivity Measurement: Profile Analysis with No Tradeoffs	**2000 Profile[a]**	**2001 Profile[b]**
Labour productivity ratio	3.000	4.000
Materials productivity ratio	0.100	0.105

[a] Labour: 120,000/40,000; materials: 120,000/1,200,000
[b] Labour: 150,000/37,500; materials: 150,000/1,428,571

Exhibit 16–12	Partial Productivity Ratios	
	2000 Profile[a]	2001 Profile[b]
Labour productivity ratio	3.000	4.000
Materials productivity ratio	0.100	0.088

Exhibit 16–12
Productivity
Measurement: Profile
Analysis with Tradeoffs

[a] Labour: 120,000/40,000; materials: 120,000/1,200,000
[b] Labour: 150,000/37,500; materials: 150,000/1,700,000

To illustrate this, let's revise the Kankul data to allow for tradeoffs among the two inputs. Assume that all the data are the same except for materials used in 2001. Let the materials used in 2001 be 1,700,000 kilograms. Using this revised number, we present the productivity profiles for 2000 and 2001 in Exhibit 16–12. The productivity profile for 2000 is still (3, 0.100), but the profile for 2001 has changed to (4, 0.088). Comparing productivity profiles now provides a mixed signal. Productivity for labour has increased, from 3 to 4; but productivity for materials has decreased, from 0.100 to 0.088. The new process has caused a tradeoff in the two productivity measures. Furthermore, while a profile analysis reveals that the tradeoff exists, it does not reveal whether the tradeoff is good or bad. If the economic effect of the productivity changes is positive, then the tradeoff is good; otherwise it must be viewed as bad. Valuing the tradeoffs would allow us to assess the economic effect of the decision to change the assembly process. Furthermore, by valuing the productivity change, we obtain a total measure of productivity.

Profit-Linked Productivity Measurement Assessing the effects of productivity changes on current profits is one way to value productivity changes. Profits change from the base period to the current period. Some of that profit change is attributable to productivity changes. Measuring the amount of profit change attributable to productivity change is defined as **profit-linked productivity measurement**.

Assessing the effect of productivity changes on current-period profits will help managers understand the economic importance of productivity changes. Linking productivity changes to profits is described by the following rule:

Profit-Linkage Rule: For the current period, calculate the cost of the inputs that would have been used in the absence of any productivity change and compare this cost with the cost of the inputs actually used. The difference in costs is the amount by which profits changed due to productivity changes.

To apply the profit-linkage rule, the inputs that would have been used for the current period in the absence of a productivity change must be calculated. Let *PQ* represent this productivity-neutral quantity of input. To determine *PQ* for a particular input, divide the current-period output by the input's base-period productivity ratio:

$$PQ = \text{Current output/Base-period productivity ratio}$$

To illustrate the application of the profit-linked rule, let's return to the Kankul example with input tradeoffs. To these data, we must add some cost information. The expanded Kankul data follow:

	2000	2001
Number of motors produced	120,000	150,000
Labour hours used	40,000	37,500
Materials used (kilograms)	1,200,000	1,700,000
Unit selling price (motors)	$50	$48
Wages per labour hour	$11	$12
Cost per kilograms of material	$2	$3

Current output (2001) is 150,000 motors. From Exhibit 16–12, we know that the base-period productivity ratios are 3 and 0.10 for labour and materials, respectively.

Using this information, the productivity-neutral quantity for each input is computed as follows:

$$PQ \text{ (labour)} = 150,000/3 = 50,000 \text{ hours}$$
$$PQ \text{ (materials)} = 150,000/0.10 = 1,500,000 \text{ kilograms}$$

For our example, PQ gives the labour and materials inputs that would have been used in 2001, assuming no productivity change. What the cost would have been is computed by multiplying each individual input quantity (PQ) by its current price (P) and adding:[21]

Cost of labour (50,000 × $12)	$ 600,000
Cost of materials: (1,500,000 × $3)	4,500,000
Total PQ cost	$5,100,000

The actual cost of inputs is obtained by multiplying the actual quantity (AQ) by current input price (P) for each input and adding:

Cost of labour (37,500 × $12)	$ 450,000
Cost of materials (1,700,000 × $3)	5,100,000
Total current cost	$5,550,000

Finally, the productivity effect on profits is computed by subtracting the total current cost from the total PQ cost.

$$\text{Profit-linked productivity effect} = \text{Total } PQ \text{ cost} - \text{Total current cost}$$
$$= \$5,100,000 - \$5,550,000$$
$$= \$450,000 \text{ decrease in profits}$$

The calculation of the profit-linked effect is summarized in Exhibit 16–13. The summary in Exhibit 16–13 reveals that the net effect of the process change was unfavourable. Profits declined by $450,000 because of the productivity changes. Notice also that profit-linked productivity effects can be assigned to individual inputs. The increase in labour productivity created a $150,000 increase in profits; however, the drop in materials productivity caused a $600,000 decrease in profits. Most of the profit decrease came from an increase in materials usage—apparently, waste, scrap, and spoiled units are much greater with the new process. Thus, the profit-linked measure provides partial measurement effects as well as a total measurement effect. The total profit-linked productivity measure is the sum of the individual partial measures. This property makes the profit-linked measure ideal for assessing tradeoffs. A much clearer picture of the effects of the changes in productivity emerges. Unless waste and scrap can be brought under better control, Kankul

Exhibit 16–13

Profit-Linked Productivity Measurement

Input	(1) PQ^*	(2) $PQ \times P$	(3) AQ	(4) $AQ \times P$	(2) − (4) $(PQ \times P) - (AQ \times P)$
Labour	50,000	$ 600,000	37,500	$ 450,000	$ 150,000
Materials	1,500,000	4,500,000	1,700,000	5,100,000	(600,000)
Total		$5,100,000		$5,550,000	$(450,000)

* Labour: 150,000/3; materials: 150,000/0.10

21. Base-period prices are frequently used to value productivity changes. It has been shown, however, that current input prices should be used for accurate profit-linked productivity measurement. See Don R. Hansen, Maryanne Mowen, and Lawrence Hammer, "Profit-Linked Productivity Measurement," *Journal of Management Accounting Research* (Fall 1992): pp. 79–98.

ought to return to its old assembly process. Of course, it is possible that the learning effects of the new process are not yet fully captured and that further improvements in labour productivity might therefore be observed. As labour becomes more proficient at the new process, it is possible that the materials usage could also decrease.

Price-Recovery Component

The profit-linked measure computes the amount of profit change from the base period to the current period attributable to productivity changes. This generally will not be equal to the total profit change between the two periods. The difference between the total profit change and the profit-linked productivity change is called the **price-recovery component**. This component is the change in revenues less a change in the cost of inputs, assuming no productivity changes. It therefore measures the ability of revenue changes to cover changes in the cost of inputs, assuming no productivity change. To calculate the price-recovery component, we first need to compute the change in profits for each period:

	2001	2000	Difference
Revenues[a]	$7,200,000	$6,000,000	$ 1,200,000
Cost of inputs[b]	5,550,000	2,840,000	2,710,000
Profit	$1,650,000	$3,160,000	$(1,510,000)

[a] $48 × 150,000; $50 × 120,000
[b] ($12 × 37,500) + ($3 × 1,700,000); ($11 × 40,000) + ($2 × 1,200,000)

$$\text{Price recovery} = \text{Profit change} - \text{Profit-linked productivity change}$$
$$= (\$1,510,000) - (\$450,000)$$
$$= (\$1,060,000)$$

The increase in revenues would not have been sufficient to recover the increase in the cost of the inputs. The decrease in productivity simply aggravated the price-recovery problem. Note, however, that increases in productivity can be used to offset price-recovery losses.

Quality and Productivity

Improving quality may improve productivity and vice versa. For example, if rework is reduced by producing fewer defective units, less labour and fewer materials are used to produce the same output. Reducing the number of defective units improves quality; reducing the amount of inputs used improves productivity.

Since most quality improvements reduce the amount of resources used to produce and sell an organization's output, most quality improvements will improve productivity. Thus, quality improvements will generally be reflected in productivity measures. However, there are other ways to improve productivity. A firm may produce a good with few or no defects but still have an inefficient process.

For example, consider a good that passes through two 5-minute processes. (Assume that the good is produced free of defects.) One unit, then, requires 10 minutes to pass through both processes. Currently, units are produced in batches of 1,200. Process 1 produces 1,200 units; the batch is then conveyed by forklift to another location, where the units pass through Process 2. Thus, for each process, a total of 6,000 minutes, or 100 hours, are needed to produce a batch. The 1,200 finished units, then, require a total of 200 hours (100 hours for each process) plus conveyance time; assume that to be 15 minutes.

By redesigning the manufacturing process, the company can improve efficiency. Suppose that the second process is relocated close enough to the first process so that as soon as a unit is completed by the first process, it can be passed to the second process. In this way, the first and second processes can be working at the same time. The second process no longer has to wait for the production of 1,200 units plus conveyance time before it can begin operation. The total time to produce 1,200 units is now 6,000 minutes plus the waiting time for the first unit (5 minutes). Thus, production of 1,200 units has been reduced from 200 hours and 15 minutes to 100 hours and 5 minutes. More output can be produced with fewer inputs (time).

Gain-Sharing

Gain-sharing is providing to a company's entire workforce cash incentives that are keyed to quality and productivity gains. For example, suppose that a company has a target of reducing the number of defective units by 10 percent during the next quarter for a particular plant. If the goal is achieved, the company estimates that $1,000,000 will be saved (through avoiding such activities as reworks and warranty repairs). Gain-sharing provides an incentive by offering a bonus to the employees that will be equal to a percentage of the cost savings, say 20 percent. Palliser, a Winnipeg-based Canadian furniture manufacturer, uses a gain-sharing scheme that applies to workers. Other companies use systems that apply to executives.

Ford Motor Company, for example, has proposed overhauling its compensation program for its top 5,000 executives, implementing a new compensation program that replaces profit-driven bonus structures with performance-based measures such as overall product quality. The size of the bonus pool can grow or shrink depending on how well productivity and quality targets are met. Sun Microsystems provides another example.[22] Bonuses are tied to customer loyalty and customer quality indexes. Sun Microsystems has found that such quality measures as late deliveries and software defects have declined steadily, while customer loyalty measures have increased. Pay-for-performance plans allowing employees to share in the benefits seem to create additional interest and commitment. Interestingly, these gain-sharing plans are entirely complementary, and perhaps even essential, to an integrated measurement system such as the Balanced Scorecard discussed in Chapter 15.

SUMMARY OF LEARNING OBJECTIVES

1. Identify and describe the four types of quality costs.

To understand quality costs, it is first necessary to understand what is meant by quality. There are two types of quality: quality of design and quality of conformance. Quality of design concerns quality differences that arise for products with the same function but different specifications. Quality of conformance, on the other hand, concerns meeting the specifications required by the product. Quality costs are incurred when products fail to meet design specifications (and are therefore associated with quality of conformance). There are four categories of quality costs: prevention, appraisal, internal failure, and external failure. Prevention costs are those incurred to prevent poor quality. Appraisal costs are those incurred to detect poor quality. Internal failure costs are those incurred when products fail to conform to

requirements and this lack of conformity is discovered before an external sale. External failure costs are those incurred when products fail to conform to requirements after an external sale is made.

2. Prepare a quality cost report, and explain the difference between the conventional view of acceptable quality level and the view espoused by total quality control.

A quality cost report is prepared by listing costs for each item within each of the four major quality cost categories. See Exhibit 16–3. There are two views concerning the optimal distribution of quality costs: the AQL view and the zero-defects view. The AQL view holds that there is a tradeoff between costs of failure and prevention and appraisal costs. This tradeoff produces an optimal level of performance called the acceptable quality level. AQL is the level at which the number of

---

22. Both examples come from the following source: Melissa Larson, "Betting Your Bonus on Quality," (May 1998): online article, **www. qualitymag.com/articles/may98/0598f3.html**.

defects allowed minimizes total quality costs. The zero-defects view, on the other hand, espouses total quality control. Total quality control maintains that the conflict between failure and appraisal and prevention costs is more conjectural than real. The actual optimal level of defects is the zero-defect level; companies should be striving to achieve this level of quality. Although quality costs do not vanish at this level, they are much lower than the optimal envisioned by the AQL view.

3. Explain why quality cost information is needed and how it is used.

Quality cost information is needed to help managers control quality performance and to serve as input for decision making. It can be used to evaluate the overall performance of quality improvement programs. It can also be used to help improve a variety of managerial decisions—for example, strategic pricing and new product analysis. Perhaps the most important observation is that quality cost information is fundamental to a company's pursuit of continuous improvement. Quality is one of the major competitive dimensions for world-class competitors.

4. Explain what productivity is, and calculate the impact of productivity changes on profits.

Productivity concerns how efficiently inputs are used to produce the output. Partial measures of productivity evaluate the efficient use of single inputs. Total measures of productivity assess efficiency for all inputs. Profit-linked productivity effects are calculated by using the profit-linkage rule. Essentially, the profit-linked effect is computed by taking the difference between the cost of the inputs that would have been used without any productivity change and the cost of the actual inputs used. Because of the possibility of input tradeoffs, it is essential to value productivity changes. Only in this way can the effect of productivity changes be properly assessed. Finally, gain-sharing can be used as an incentive for managers and workers to look for ways to increase quality and productivity.

KEY TERMS

Acceptable quality level (AQL), 739
Aesthetics, 733
Appraisal costs, 735
Base period, 749
Control activities, 734
Control costs, 734
Costs of quality, 734
Defective product, 734
Durability, 734
External failure costs, 735
Failure activities, 734
Failure costs, 734
Features (quality of design), 733
Financial productivity measure, 748

Fitness of use, 734
Gain-sharing, 754
Hidden quality costs, 735
Input tradeoff efficiency, 747
Internal failure costs, 735
Multiple-period quality trend report, 742
Observable quality costs, 735
Operational productivity measure, 748
Partial productivity measurement, 748
Performance, 733
Prevention costs, 735
Price-recovery component, 753
Productivity, 746
Productivity measurement, 748

Profile measurement, 750
Profit-linked productivity measurement, 751
Quality of conformance, 734
Quality product or service, 733
Reliability, 734
Serviceability, 733
Taguchi loss function, 736
Technical efficiency, 746
Total productive efficiency, 746
Total productivity measurement, 750
Zero defects, 734

REVIEW PROBLEMS

1. QUALITY

At the beginning of 2001, Kare Company initiated a quality improvement program. Considerable effort was expended to reduce the number of defective units produced. By the end of the year, reports from the production manager revealed that scrap and rework had both decreased. The company's president was pleased to hear about the success but wanted some assessment of the financial impact of the improvements. To make this assessment, the following financial data were collected for the preceding and current years:

	2000	2001
Sales	$10,000,000	$10,000,000
Scrap	400,000	300,000
Rework	600,000	400,000
Product inspection	100,000	125,000
Product warranty	800,000	600,000
Quality training	40,000	80,000
Materials inspection	60,000	40,000

Required:

1. Classify the costs as prevention, appraisal, internal failure, and external failure.
2. Compute quality cost as a percentage of sales for each of the two years. By how much has profit increased because of quality improvements? Assuming that quality costs can be reduced to 2.5 percent of sales, how much additional profit is available through quality improvements (assume that sales revenues will remain the same)?
3. Prepare a quality cost report for 2001.

Solution

1. Appraisal costs: product inspection and materials inspection; prevention costs: quality training; internal failure costs: scrap and rework; external failure costs: warranty.
2. For 2000—total quality costs: $2,000,000; percentage of sales: 20 percent ($2,000,000/ $10,000,000). For 2001—total quality costs: $1,545,000; percentage of sales: 15.45 percent ($1,545,000/$10,000,000). Profit has increased by $455,000. If quality costs drop to 2.5 percent of sales, another $1,295,000 of profit improvement is possible ($1,545,000 − $250,000).

3.

Kare Company
Quality Cost Report
For the Year Ended 2001

	Quality Costs		Percentage (%) of Sales
Prevention costs:			
Quality training	$ 80,000	$ 80,000	0.80
Appraisal costs:			
Product inspection	$125,000		
Materials inspection	40,000	165,000	1.65
Internal failure costs:			
Scrap	$300,000		
Rework	400,000	700,000	7.00
External failure costs:			
Product warranty	$600,000	600,000	6.00
Total quality costs		$1,545,000	15.45

2. PRODUCTIVITY

Bearing Company made some changes at the end of 2000 that it hoped would favourably affect the efficiency of the input usage. Now, at the end of 2001, the company's president wants an assessment of the changes in the company's productivity. The data needed for the assessment follow:

	2000	2001
Output	5,000	6,000
Output prices	$10	$10
Materials (kilograms)	4,000	4,200
Materials unit price	$3	$4
Labour (hours)	2,500	2,400
Labour rate per hour	$8	$8
Power (kilowatt-hours)	1,000	1,500
Price per kilowatt-hour	$2	$3

Required:

1. Compute the partial operational measures for each input for both 2000 and 2001. What can be said about productivity improvement?
2. Prepare an income statement for each year, and calculate the total change in profits.
3. Calculate the profit-linked productivity measure for 2001. What can be said about the productivity program?
4. Calculate the price-recovery component. What does this tell you?

Solution

1. Partial measures:

	2000	2001
Materials	5,000/4,000 = 1.25	6,000/4,200 = 1.43
Labour	5,000/2,500 = 2.00	6,000/2,400 = 2.50
Power	5,000/1,000 = 5.00	6,000/1,500 = 4.00

Productive efficiency has increased for materials and labour and decreased for power. The outcome is mixed, and no statement about overall productivity improvement can be made without valuing the tradeoff.

2. Income statements:

	2000	2001
Sales	$50,000	$60,000
Cost of inputs	34,000	40,500
Income	$16,000	$19,500

Total change in profits: $19,500 − $16,000 = $3,500 increase

3. Profit-linked measurement:

	(1)	(2)	(3)	(4)	(2) − (4)
Input	PQ^*	$PQ \times P$	AQ	$AQ \times P$	$(PQ \times P) - (AQ \times P)$
Materials	4,800	$19,200	4,200	$16,800	$2,400
Labour	3,000	24,000	2,400	19,200	4,800
Power	1,200	3,600	1,500	4,500	(900)
		$46,800		$40,500	$6,300

* Materials: 6,000/1.25; labour: 6,000/2; power: 6,000/5

The value of the increases in efficiency for materials and labour more than offsets the increased usage of power. Thus, the productivity program should be labelled successful.

4. Price recovery:

Price-recovery component = Profit change − Profit-linked productivity change
$$= \$3{,}500 - \$6{,}300$$
$$= (\$2{,}800)$$

This says that without the productivity improvement, profits would have declined by \$2,800. The \$10,000 increase in revenues would not have offset the increase in the cost of inputs. From the solution to Requirement 3, the cost of inputs without a productivity increase would have been \$46,800 (Column 2). The increase in the input cost without productivity would have been \$46,800 − \$34,000 = \$12,800. This is \$2,800 more than the increase in revenues. Only because of the productivity increase did the firm show an increase in profitability.

QUESTIONS FOR WRITING AND DISCUSSION

1. Explain what is meant by "quality."

2. What is reliability? durability?

3. What is quality of conformance?

4. Explain the difference between the traditional view of conformance and the robust view.

5. Why are quality costs the costs of doing things wrong?

6. Identify and discuss the four kinds of quality costs.

7. Explain why external failure costs can be more devastating to a firm than internal failure costs.

8. What are hidden quality costs? Provide an example.

9. What are the three methods for estimating hidden quality costs?

10. Discuss the value of a quality cost report.

11. What is the difference between the AQL model and the zero-defects model?

12. What is the difference between the zero-defects model and the robust quality model?

13. Explain the purpose of multiple-period trend analysis for quality costs.

14. Define total productive efficiency.

15. Explain the difference between partial and total measures of productivity.

16. Discuss the advantages and disadvantages of partial measures of productivity.

17. How can a manager measure productivity improvement?

18. What is profit-linked productivity measurement?

19. Explain why profit-linked productivity measurement is important.

20. What is the price-recovery component?

21. Can productivity improvements be achieved without improving quality? Explain.

22. Why is it important for managers to be concerned with both productivity and quality?

23. What are the differences between quality and productivity? the similarities?

24. What is gain-sharing?

EXERCISES

16–1

Quality Cost Classification

LO1

Classify the following quality activities as prevention costs, appraisal costs, internal failure costs, or external failure costs:

1. Customers do not want second-class products. However, if they are sent slightly defective products, they may be willing to keep them, provided that they are given a price reduction.
2. Components from suppliers are carefully inspected.
3. Workers sand and stain a piece of wood, and then it warps. The piece of wood is then discarded as useless.

4. An automobile company recalls a model to repair a defective transmission.
5. A tire manufacturer is sued for deaths caused by a defective tire.
6. Design verification and review to evaluate the quality of new products.
7. New personnel are trained in quality circle methods.
8. Work stoppage to correct process malfunction (discovered using statistical process control procedures).
9. Packaging and shipping for returned products.
10. Reinspection of rework.
11. A defective product is replaced with a good one.
12. An internal audit is done to ensure that quality policies are being followed.
13. A product is redesigned to reduce the number of worker mistakes leading to a defective product.
14. Purchase orders are corrected to reflect the correct items and quantities.
15. Adjustments are made to accounts receivable to compensate for returned goods and price concessions.
16. New products are tested to ensure that they function as intended.
17. Field service personnel are sent to repair products on-site.
18. Software is corrected for defects.
19. Suppliers are evaluated to assess whether they are capable of providing nondefective components.
20. Subassemblies are inspected.
21. Processing of customer complaints.
22. Prototype inspection and testing.
23. A worker accidentally drills a hole in a steel plate, and it must be welded shut for the plate to be useful.

16–2

Quality Cost Improvement and Profitability; Quality Cost Report

LO1, LO2, LO3

During 2000 and 2001, Hunington Company reported sales of $6,000,000 (for each year). Hunington listed the following quality costs for the past two years. Assume that all changes in the quality costs are due to a quality improvement program.

	2000	2001
Design review	$ 150,000	$ 300,000
Recalls	200,000	100,000
Reinspection	100,000	50,000
Materials inspection	60,000	40,000
Quality training	40,000	100,000
Process acceptance	—	50,000
Scrap	145,000	35,000
Lost sales (estimated)	300,000	200,000
Product inspection	50,000	30,000
Returned goods	155,000	95,000
Total	$1,200,000	$1,000,000

Required:

1. Prepare a quality cost report for each year (2000 and 2001).
2. How much were the additional resources invested in prevention and appraisal activities (control costs) from one year to the next? What return did this investment generate? (What reduction in failure costs was achieved?)
3. The management of Hunington believes that it is possible to reduce quality costs to 2.5 percent of sales. Assuming that sales continue at the $6,000,000 level, calculate the additional profit potential facing Hunington. Is the expectation of improving quality and reducing quality costs to 2.5 percent of sales realistic? Explain.

16–3

Quality Costs; Distribution Across Categories; Gain-sharing

LO1, LO2, LO3, LO4

Lakay Company had sales of $40 million in 1994. In 2001, sales had increased to $50 million. A quality improvement program was implemented in 1994. Overall conformance quality was targeted for improvement. The quality costs for 1994 and 2001 follow. Assume that any changes in quality costs are attributable to improvements in quality.

	1994	2001
Internal failure costs	$ 3,000,000	$ 150,000
External failure costs	4,000,000	100,000
Appraisal costs	1,800,000	375,000
Prevention costs	1,200,000	625,000
Total quality costs	$10,000,000	$1,250,000

Required:

1. Compute the quality costs/sales ratio for each year. Is this type of improvement possible?
2. Calculate the relative distribution of quality costs by category for 1994 (quality costs by category/total quality costs). What do you think of the relative cost distribution? How do you think quality costs will be distributed as the company approaches a zero-defects state?
3. Calculate the relative distribution of costs by category for 2001. What do you think of the level and distribution of quality costs? Do you think that further reductions are possible?
4. Suppose that the CEO of Lakay received a bonus equal to 10 percent of the quality cost savings each year. Do you think gain-sharing is a good or bad idea? What risks are there, if any, to gain-sharing?

16–4

Tradeoffs among Quality Cost Categories; Gain-sharing

LO2, LO4

Mendara Company has sales of $4 million and quality costs of $800,000. The company is embarking on a major quality improvement program. During the next three years, Mendara intends to attack prevention costs by increasing its appraisal and prevention costs. The "right" prevention activities will be selected, and appraisal costs will be reduced according to the results achieved. For the coming year, management is considering six specific activities: quality training, process control, product inspection, supplier evaluation, redesign of two major products, and prototype testing. To encourage managers to focus on reducing nonvalue-added quality costs and select the right activities, a bonus pool is established relating to reduction of quality costs. The bonus pool is equal to 10 percent of the total reduction in quality costs.

Current quality costs and the costs of these six activities are given in the following table. Each activity is added sequentially so that its effect on the cost categories can be assessed. For example, after quality training is added, the control costs increase to $160,000, and the failure costs drop to $520,000. Even though the activities are presented sequentially, they are totally independent of each other. Thus, only beneficial activities need be selected.

	Control Costs	**Failure Costs**
Current quality costs*	$ 80,000	$720,000
Quality training	160,000	520,000
Process control	260,000	360,000
Product inspection	300,000	328,000
Supplier evaluation	360,000	100,000
Prototype testing	480,000	60,000
Engineering redesign	500,000	20,000

*All current control costs are appraisal costs.

Required:

1. Identify the control activities that should be implemented, and calculate the total quality costs associated with this selection. Assume that an activity is selected only if it increases the bonus pool.
2. Given the activities selected in Requirement 1, calculate the following:
   a. the reduction in total quality costs
   b. the percentage distribution for control and failure costs
   c. the amount for this year's bonus pool
3. Suppose that a quality engineer complained about the gain-sharing incentive system. Basically, he argued that the bonus should be based only on reductions of failure and appraisal costs. In this way, investment in prevention activities would be encouraged, and failure and appraisal costs would eventually be eliminated. After eliminating the nonvalue-added costs, focus could then be placed on the level of prevention costs. If this approach were adopted, what activities would be selected? Do you agree with this approach? Explain.

16–5

Quality Cost Report;
Taguchi Quality Loss
Function

LO1, LO2

Spreadsheet

At the end of 2001, Minot Metal Works began to focus on its quality costs. As a first step, it identified the following costs in its accounting records as quality-related:

	2001
Sales (50,000 units @ $20)	$1,000,000
Scrap	30,000
Rework	40,000
Training program	12,000
Consumer complaints	20,000
Warranty	40,000
Test labour	30,000
Inspection labour	25,000
Supplier evaluation	3,000

Required:

1. Prepare a quality cost report by quality cost category.
2. Calculate the relative distribution percentages for each quality cost category. Comment on the distribution.
3. Using the Taguchi quality loss function, an average loss per unit is computed at $3. What are the hidden costs of external failure? How does this affect the relative distribution? What effect will the hidden-cost information have on a quality improvement program?

16–6

Taguchi Quality Loss
Function

LO1

Nestten Company manufactures a product that has a target value of 20 grams. Specification limits are 20 grams plus or minus 0.50 grams. The value of K is $80. A sample of five units produced the following measures:

Unit	Measured Weight
1	20.20
2	20.50
3	20.30
4	19.50
5	19.75

During April, 12,500 units were produced.

Required:

1. Calculate the loss for each unit. Calculate the average loss for the sample of five.
2. Using the average loss, calculate the hidden quality costs for April.

16–7

Multiple-Year Trend Reports

LO2

The controller of Golden Company has computed quality costs as a percentage of sales for the past five years (1997 was the first year the company implemented a quality improvement program). This information follows:

	Prevention	Appraisal	Internal Failure	External Failure	Total
1997	2%	3%	8%	12%	25%
1998	3	4	7	10	24
1999	4	5	6	7	22
2000	5	4	3	6	18
2001	6	3	1	2	12

Required:

1. Prepare a trend graph for total quality costs. Comment on what the graph has to say about the success of the quality improvement program.
2. Prepare a graph that shows the trend for each quality cost category. What does the graph indicate about the success of the quality improvement program? Does this graph supply more insight than the total cost trend graph does? What does the graph reveal about the distribution of quality costs in 1997? in 2001?

16–8

Productivity Measurement; Partial Measure

LO4

Doran Company produces a product that uses two inputs, energy and labour. During the past month, 40 units of the product were produced, requiring 32 units of energy and 128 hours of labour. An engineering study revealed that Doran can produce the same output of 40 units using either of the following two combinations of inputs:

	Energy	Labour
Combination A	20	80
Combination B	32	50

Energy costs $12 per unit used; the cost of labour is $10 per hour.

Required:

1. Calculate the output/input ratio for each input of Combination A. Does this represent a productivity improvement over the current use of inputs? What is the total dollar value of the improvement? Classify this as technical or price efficiency improvement.
2. Calculate output/input ratios for each input of Combination B. Does this represent a productivity improvement over the current use of inputs? Now compare these ratios to those of Combination A. What has happened?
3. Compute the cost of producing the 20 units of output using Combination B. Compare this to the cost using Combination A. Does moving from Combination A to Combination B represent a productivity improvement? Explain.

16–9

Interperiod Measure of Productivity; Basic Computations

LO4

Spreadsheet

The following data pertain to the last two years of operation at Chelsey, Inc.:

	2000	2001
Output	16,000	20,000
Power (quantity used)	2,000	2,000
Materials (quantity used)	4,000	4,500
Unit price (power)	$1.00	$2.00
Unit price (materials)	$4.00	$5.00
Unit selling price	$2.00	$2.50

Required:

1. Compute the partial operational productivity ratios for each year. Did productivity improve? Explain.

2. Compute the profit-linked productivity measure. By how much did profits increase due to productivity?

3. Calculate the price-recovery component for 2001. Explain its meaning.

16–10

Productivity Measurement: Tradeoffs

LO4

Spreadsheet

Manson Company decided to install an automated manufacturing system. The decision to automate was made because of the promise to reduce the use of materials and labour inputs. After one year of operation, management wants to evaluate the productivity change. The president is particularly interested in knowing whether the tradeoff among capital, labour, and materials was favourable. Data concerning output, labour, materials, and capital are provided for the year before implementation and the year after.

	Year Before	Year After
Output	200,000	240,000
Input quantities:		
Materials (kilograms)	50,000	40,000
Labour (hours)	10,000	4,000
Capital	$10,000	$600,000
Input prices:		
Materials	$2	$2
Labour	$5	$5
Capital	15%	15%

Required:

1. Compute the partial measures for materials, labour, and capital for each year. What caused the change in labour and materials productivity?

2. Calculate the change in profits attributable to the change in productivity of the three inputs. Assuming that these are the only three inputs, evaluate the decision to automate.

16–11

Productivity Measurement: Technical and Price Efficiency Illustrated

LO4

The manager of Dowson Company was reviewing two competing proposals for the machining department. The fiscal year was coming to a close, and the manager wanted to make a decision concerning the proposed process changes so that they could be used, if beneficial, during the coming year. The process changes would affect the department's input usage. For the year just ended, the accounting department provided the following information about the inputs used to produce 50,000 units of output:

	Quantity	Unit Prices
Materials	90,000 kilograms	$ 8
Labour	40,000 hours	10
Energy	20,000 kilowatt-hours	2

Each proposal offers a process design different from the one currently used. Neither proposal would cost anything to implement. Both proposals project input usage for producing 60,000 units (the expected output for the coming year).

	Proposal A	Proposal B
Materials	90,000 kilograms	100,000 kilograms
Labour	40,000 hours	30,000 hours
Energy	20,000 kilowatt-hours	20,000 kilowatt-hours

Input prices are expected to remain the same for the coming year.

Required:

1. Compute the partial operational productivity measures for the most recently completed year and for each proposal. Does either proposal improve technical efficiency? Explain. Can you make a recommendation about either proposal using only the physical measures?
2. Calculate the profit-linked productivity measure for each proposal. Which proposal offers the best outcome for the company? How does this relate to the concept of price efficiency? Explain.

16–12

Productivity and Quality

LO4

Rington Company is considering the acquisition of an automated system that would decrease the number of units scrapped because of poor quality. (This proposal is part of an ongoing effort to improve quality.) The production manager is pushing for the acquisition, because he believes that productivity will be greatly enhanced—particularly when it comes to labour and material inputs. Output and input data follow. The after-acquisition data are projections.

	Current	After Acquisition
Output (units)	10,000	10,000
Output selling price	$40	$40
Input quantities:		
Materials (kilograms)	40,000	35,000
Labour (hours)	20,000	15,000
Capital	$20,000	$100,000
Energy (kilowatt-hours)	10,000	25,000
Input prices:		
Materials	$4.00	$4.00
Labour	$9.00	$9.00
Capital	10.00%	10.00%
Energy	$2.00	$2.50

Required:

1. Calculate the partial operational ratios for materials and labour under each alternative. Is the production manager right in thinking that materials and labour productivity increases with the automated system?
2. Compute the partial ratios for all four inputs. Does the system improve productivity?
3. Determine the amount by which profits will change if the system is adopted. Are the tradeoffs among the inputs favourable? Comment on the system's ability to improve productivity.

16–13

Basics of Productivity Measurement

LO4

Lau Company gathered the following data for the past two years:

	Base Year	Current Year
Output	150,000	180,000
Output prices	$20	$20
Input quantities:		
Materials (kilograms)	200,000	180,000
Labour (hours)	50,000	90,000
Input prices:		
Materials	$5	$6
Labour	$8	$8

Required:

1. Calculate the partial operational measures for each year.
2. Prepare income statements for each year. Calculate the total change in income.
3. Calculate the change in profits attributable to productivity changes.
4. Calculate the price-recovery component. Explain its meaning.

PROBLEMS

16–14

Classification of Quality Costs

LO1

Classify the following quality costs as prevention, appraisal, internal failure, or external failure.

1. Prototype inspection and testing
2. Reinspection of reworked product
3. Packaging and shipping repaired goods
4. Loss of customer goodwill due to inferior-quality products
5. Grinding bumps off a poorly welded steel plate
6. Maintenance of inspection equipment
7. Design verification and review to evaluate the quality of new products
8. Design and development of quality equipment
9. Quality training program for new personnel
10. Correcting an improperly filled-out purchase order
11. The cost of purchasing replacement parts to repair a product that breaks down while under warranty
12. Internal audit assessing the effectiveness of the quality system
13. Replacing a component that was improperly inserted and damaged
14. Machine jammed and damaged because of an incorrectly sized subassembly
15. Quality reporting
16. Proofreading
17. Cost to incinerate scrap
18. Setup for testing
19. Lending engineers to help improve processes and products of suppliers
20. Cost of developing a new quality improvement program
21. Extra overhead costs incurred due to returned products
22. Supervision of in-process inspection
23. Inspection of parts purchased from suppliers
24. Customer complaint department
25. Outside labouratory evaluation of product quality

16–15

Quality Cost Summary; Gain-sharing

LO1, LO2, LO3, LO4

Linda Wise, the president of Troy Company, has recently returned from a conference on quality and productivity. At the conference, she learned that many North American firms have made significant progress in improving quality and reducing quality costs. Many of these firms have been able to reduce quality costs from between 20 percent and 30 percent of sales to between 2 percent and 3 percent of sales. She was skeptical, however, about this statistic. But even if the quality gurus were right, she was sure that her company's quality costs were much lower—probably less than 5 percent. On the other hand, if she was wrong, she would be passing up an opportunity to improve profits significantly and simultaneously strengthen her competitive position. In fact, she reflected on the comment of one of the quality experts: "Quality has become a condition of entrance to the market. If the product is not good, you will quickly go out of business." The quality issue was at least worth exploring. Moreover, she decided that it might be too risky *not* to assess her company's quality performance. She knew that her company produced most of the information needed for quality cost reporting—but there had never been a need to bother with any formal quality data gathering and analysis.

This conference, however, had convinced her that a firm's profitability can increase significantly by improving quality—provided that the potential for improvement exists. Thus, before committing the company to a quality improvement program, Linda contacted her controller and requested a preliminary estimate of the total quality costs currently being incurred. She also instructed the controller to classify quality costs into four categories: prevention, appraisal, internal failure, and external failure costs. The controller has gathered the following information from the past year, 2001:

a. Sales revenue is $20,000,000; net income is $4,000,000.
b. During the year, customers returned 60,000 units needing repair. Repair cost averages $7 per unit.
c. Ten inspectors are employed, each earning an annual salary of $30,000. These 10 inspectors are involved only with final inspection (product acceptance).
d. Each year, approximately 300,000 units are rejected in final inspection. Of these units, 80 percent can be recovered through rework. The cost of rework is $3 per unit. The remainder is scrap.
e. Total scrap is 60,000 units. All scrap is quality-related. The cost of scrap is about $15 per unit.
f. A customer cancelled an order that would have increased profits by $500,000. The customer's reason for cancellation was poor product performance. The accounting and marketing departments agree that the company loses at least this much each year for the same reason.
g. The company employs eight full-time employees in its complaint department. Each earns $25,000 a year.
h. The company gave sales allowances totalling $250,000 to customers being sent substandard products.
i. The company requires all new employees to take its three-hour quality training program. The estimated annual cost of the program is $160,000.
j. Inspection of the final product requires testing equipment. The annual cost of operating and maintaining this equipment is $240,000.

Required:

1. Prepare a simple quality cost report, classifying costs by category. Comment on the quality costs/sales ratio.
2. Discuss the distribution of quality costs among the four categories. Are they properly distributed? Explain.
3. Discuss how Troy Company can improve its overall quality and at the same time reduce total quality costs. Consider specifically the strategy advocated by the American Society for Quality Control (p. 741).
4. Suppose Troy Company decides that a five-year program will reduce quality costs to 2.5 percent of sales and that control costs will be 80 percent of total quality costs. Calculate the income increase that will occur if sales remain at $20,000,000. Also, calculate the total amount spent on control and failure costs.
5. Refer to Requirements 1 and 4. Suppose that Linda decides to create a bonus pool to allow employees to share in the benefits from quality improvements. The bonus pool is 20 percent of quality cost reductions. How much will be put in the bonus pool for the five-year period? Why establish such a pool? Suppose that Linda's quality manager suggests that the bonus be based only on reductions of appraisal and failure costs. Explain why he might suggest this modification. Do you agree?
6. For Linda's company, hidden quality costs are estimated by using a multiplier of 3. What are the actual external failure costs? What methods are available for estimating hidden quality costs? What effect does this estimation have on a quality improvement strategy? Finally, should reductions in these costs be included in the bonus pool mentioned in Requirement 5? If such reductions were included, what would be the effect on the bonus pool?

16–16

Quality Costs; Pricing Decisions; Market Share

LO3

Tannert Company manufactures furniture. One of its product lines is an economy-line kitchen table. During the last year, Tannert produced and sold 100,000 units for $100 per unit. Sales of the table are on a bid basis, but Tannert has always been able to win sufficient bids using the $100 price. This year, however, Tannert was losing more than its share of bids. Concerned, Larry Franklin, owner and president of the company, called a meeting of his executive committee (Megan Johnson, marketing manager; Fred Davis, quality manager; Kevin Jones, production manager; and Helen Jackson, controller).

Larry: "I don't understand why we're losing bids. Megan, do you have an explanation?"

Megan: "Yes, as a matter of fact. Two competitors have lowered their price to $92 per unit. That's too big a difference for most of our buyers to ignore. If we want to keep selling our 100,000 units per year, we will need to lower our price to $92. Otherwise, our sales will drop to between 20,000 and 25,000 per year."

Helen: "The unit contribution margin on the table is $10. Lowering the price to $92 will cost us $8 per unit. Based on a sales volume of 100,000, we'd make $200,000 in contribution margin. If we keep the price at $100, our contribution margin would be $200,000 to $250,000. If we have to lose, let's just take the lower market share. It's better than lowering our prices."

Megan: "Perhaps. But the same thing could happen to some of our other product lines. My sources tell me that these two companies are on the tail end of a major quality improvement program—one that allows them significant savings. We need to rethink our whole competitive strategy—at least if we want to stay in business. Ideally, we should match the price reduction and work to reduce the costs to recapture the lost contribution margin."

Fred: "I think I have something to offer. We are about to embark on a new quality improvement program of our own. I have brought the following estimates of the current quality costs for this economy line. As you can see on the overhead, these costs run about 16 percent of current sales. That's excessive, and we believe that they can be reduced to about 4 percent of sales over time."

Scrap	$ 700,000
Rework	300,000
Rejects (sold as seconds to discount houses)	250,000
Returns (due to poor workmanship)	350,000
	$1,600,000

Larry: "This sounds good. Fred, how long will it take you to achieve this reduction?"

Fred: "Because all these costs vary with sales level, I'll express their reduction rate in those terms. Our best guess is that we can reduce these costs by about 1 percent of sales per quarter. So it should take about 12 quarters, or three years, to achieve the full benefit. Keep in mind that this is with an improvement in quality."

Megan: "This offers us some hope. If we meet the price immediately, we can maintain our market share. Furthermore, if we can ever reach the point of reducing the price beyond the $92 level, then we can increase our market share. I estimate that we can increase sales by about 10,000 units for every $1 of price reduction beyond the $92 level. Kevin, how much extra capacity for this line do we have?"

Kevin: "We can handle an extra 30,000 or 40,000 tables per year."

Required:

1. Assume that Tannert immediately reduces its bid price to $92. How long will it be before the unit contribution margin is restored to $10, assuming that quality costs are reduced as expected and that sales are maintained at 100,000 units per year (25,000 per quarter)?

2. Assume that Tannert holds the price at $92 until the 4 percent target is achieved. At this new level of quality costs, should the price be reduced? If so, by how much should the price be reduced, and what is the increase in contribution margin? Assume that the price can be reduced only in $1 increments.

3. Assume that Tannert immediately reduces the price to $92 and begins the quality improvement program. Now suppose that Tannert does not wait until the end of the three-year period before reducing prices. Instead, prices will be reduced when profitable to do so. Assume that prices can be reduced only by $1 increments. Identify when the first future price change should occur (if any).

4. Discuss the differences in viewpoints concerning the decision to decrease prices and the short-run contribution margin analysis done by Helen, the controller. Did quality cost information play an important role in the strategic decision making illustrated by the problem?

16–17

**Quality Costs;
Cost–Volume–Profit
Analysis
LO2, LO3**

At the end of 1997, Panguich Company, a large electronics firm, hired Milton Lawson to manage one of its troubled divisions. Milton had a reputation for turning around businesses that were having difficulty. In 1998, the division had sales of $100 million, a unit-level variable cost ratio of 0.8, and total fixed costs of $24 million. The division produced only one product, and all sales were to external customers. Seeking to solve the division's problems, Milton asked for a report on quality costs for 1998 and received the following report:

	Fixed	Variable (unit-level)
Prevention	$ 800,000	—
Appraisal	1,200,000	$ 4,000,000
Internal failure	2,000,000	8,000,000
External failure	4,000,000	20,000,000
Total	$8,000,000	$32,000,000

Milton was astounded at the level of expenditure on quality costs. Although he had heard of companies with quality costs that had reached as high as 60 percent of sales, he had never personally seen any that exceeded 20 to 30 percent of sales. This division's level of 40 percent was clearly out of line. He immediately implemented a program aimed at improving conformance quality. By the end of 1999, the following quality costs were reported:

	Fixed	Variable (unit-level)
Prevention	$ 4,000,000	—
Appraisal	4,000,000	$ 4,000,000
Internal failure	2,000,000	4,000,000
External failure	4,000,000	14,000,000
Total	$14,000,000	$22,000,000

Revenues and other costs were unchanged for 1999.

Milton projects that by 2003, the defective rate will be 0.1 percent, compared to the rate of 2 percent for 1998. He also projects that quality costs will be reduced to $2 million, distributed as follows:

	Fixed	Variable (unit-level)
Prevention	$ 800,000	—
Appraisal	800,000	—
Internal failure	—	$ 80,000
External failure	—	320,000
Total	$1,600,000	$400,000

Required:

1. Calculate the breakeven point in revenues for 1998. How much was the division losing?
2. Calculate the breakeven point in 1999. Explain the change.
3. Calculate the breakeven point in 2003, assuming that revenues and other costs have remained the same. Is it possible to reduce quality costs as dramatically as portrayed?
4. Assume that from 1998 to 2003, the division was forced to cut selling prices so that total revenues dropped to $60 million. Calculate the income (loss) that would be

reported under a 1998 cost structure. Now calculate the income (loss) that would be reported under the 2003 quality cost structure (assuming all other costs remain unchanged). Discuss the strategic significance of quality cost management.

16–18

Quality Cost Report; Quality Cost Categories

LO1, LO2

In September 2000, Olson Company received a report from an external consulting group on its quality costs. The consultants reported that the company's quality costs total about 25 percent of its sales revenues. Somewhat shocked by the magnitude of the costs, Frank Roosevelt, president of Olson Company, decided to launch a major quality improvement program. This program was scheduled for implementation in January 2001. The program's goal was to reduce quality costs to 2.5 percent by the end of the year 2003 by improving overall quality.

In 2001, it was decided to reduce quality costs to 22 percent of sales revenues. Management felt that the amount of reduction was reasonable and that the goal could be realized. To improve the monitoring of the quality improvement program, Frank directed Pamela Golding, the controller, to prepare quarterly performance reports comparing budgeted and actual quality costs. He told Pamela that improving quality should reduce quality costs by 1 percent of sales for each of the first three quarters and 2 percent in the last quarter. Sales are projected at $5 million per quarter. Based on the consulting report and the targeted reductions, Pamela prepared the budgets for the first two quarters of the year:

	Quarter 1	Quarter 2
Sales	$5,000,000	$5,000,000
Quality costs:		
Warranty	$ 300,000	$ 250,000
Scrap	150,000	125,000
Incoming materials inspection	25,000	50,000
Product acceptance	125,000	150,000
Quality planning	40,000	60,000
Field inspection	30,000	0
Retesting	50,000	40,000
Allowances	65,000	50,000
New product review	10,000	10,000
Rework	130,000	100,000
Complaint adjustment	60,000	20,000
Downtime (defective parts)	50,000	40,000
Repairs	50,000	35,000
Product liability	85,000	60,000
Quality training	30,000	70,000
Quality engineering	0	40,000
Design verification	0	20,000
Process control measurement	0	30,000
Total budgeted costs	$1,200,000	$1,150,000
Quality costs/sales ratio	24%	23%

Required:

1. Assume that Olson Company reduces quality costs as indicated. What will quality costs be as a percentage of sales for the entire year? for the end of the fourth quarter? Will the company achieve its goal of reducing quality costs to 22 percent of sales?

2. Reorganize the quarterly budgets so that quality costs are grouped in one of four categories: prevention, appraisal, internal failure, or external failure (effectively, prepare a budgeted cost of quality report). Also, identify each cost as variable or fixed. (Assume that none are mixed costs.)

3. Compare the two quarterly budgets. What do they reveal about the quality improvement plans of Olson Company?

16–19

Distribution of Quality Costs

LO2

Paper Products Division produces paper diapers, paper napkins, and paper towels. The divisional manager has decided that quality costs can be minimized by distributing quality costs evenly among the four quality categories and reducing them to no more than 5 percent of sales. He has just received the following quality cost report:

Paper Products Division
Quality Cost Report
For the Year Ended December 31, 2001

	Diapers	Napkins	Towels	Total
Prevention:				
Quality training	$ 3,000	$ 2,500	$ 2,000	$ 7,500
Quality engineering	3,500	1,000	2,500	7,000
Quality audits	—	500	1,000	1,500
Quality reporting	2,500	2,000	1,000	5,500
Total	$ 9,000	$ 6,000	$ 6,500	$ 21,500
Appraisal:				
Inspection, materials	$ 2,000	$ 3,000	$ 3,000	$ 8,000
Process acceptance	4,000	2,800	1,200	8,000
Product acceptance	2,000	1,200	2,300	5,500
Total	$ 8,000	$ 7,000	$ 6,500	$ 21,500
Internal failure:				
Scrap	$10,000	$ 3,000	$ 2,500	$ 15,500
Disposal costs	7,000	2,000	1,500	10,500
Downtime	1,000	1,500	2,500	5,000
Total	$18,000	$ 6,500	$ 6,500	$ 31,000
External failure:				
Allowances	$10,000	$ 3,000	$ 2,750	$ 15,750
Customer complaints	4,000	1,500	3,750	9,250
Product liability	1,000	—	—	1,000
Total	$15,000	$ 4,500	$ 6,500	$ 26,000
Total quality costs	$50,000	$24,000	$26,000	$100,000

Assume that all prevention costs are fixed and that the remaining quality costs are variable.

Required:

1. Assume that the sales revenue for the year totalled $2 million, with sales for each product as follows: diapers, $1 million; napkins, $600,000; towels, $400,000. Evaluate the distribution of costs for the division as a whole and for each product line. What recommendations do you have for the divisional manager?
2. Now assume a different scenario, where total sales of $1 million have this breakdown: diapers, $500,000; napkins, $300,000; towels, $200,000. Evaluate the distribution of costs for the division as a whole and for each product line in this case. Do you think that it is possible to reduce the quality costs to 5 percent of sales for each product line and for the division as a whole and, simultaneously, achieve an equal distribution of the quality costs? What recommendations do you have?
3. Assume total sales of $1 million with this breakdown: diapers, $500,000; napkins, $180,000; towels, $320,000. Evaluate the distribution of quality costs. What recommendations do you have for the divisional manager?
4. Discuss the value of having quality costs reported by segment.

16–20

Trend Analysis; Quality Costs

LO2

In 1997, Jack Donaldson, president of Thayn Electronics, received a report indicating that quality costs were 21 percent of sales. Faced with increasing pressures from imported goods, Jack resolved to take measures to improve the overall quality of the company's products. After hiring a consultant, the company began, in 1998, an aggressive program of total quality control. At the end of 2001, Jack requested an analysis of the progress the company had made in reducing and controlling quality costs. The accounting department assembled the following data:

	Sales	Prevention	Appraisal	Internal Failure	External Failure
1997	$500,000	$ 5,000	$10,000	$40,000	$50,000
1998	600,000	20,000	20,000	50,000	60,000
1999	700,000	30,000	25,000	30,000	40,000
2000	600,000	35,000	35,000	20,000	25,000
2001	500,000	35,000	15,000	8,000	12,000

Required:

1. Compute the quality costs as a percentage of sales by category and in total for each year.
2. Explain why quality costs increased in total and as a percentage of sales in 1998, the first year of the quality improvement program.
3. Prepare a multiple-year trend graph for quality costs, both by total costs and by category. Using the graph, assess the progress made in reducing and controlling quality costs. Does the graph provide evidence that quality has improved? Explain.

16–21

Profit-Linked Measurement; Price Recovery; Gain-sharing

LO4

Norton Company produces handcrafted leather belts. Virtually all the manufacturing cost consists of materials and labour. Over the past several years, profits have been declining because the cost of the two major inputs has been increasing. Barry Norton, the company's president, has indicated that the price of the belts cannot be increased; thus, the only way to improve or at least stabilize profits is by increasing overall productivity. At the beginning of 2001, Barry implemented a new productivity program. To encourage greater attention to productivity, he established a bonus pool, equal to 10 percent of the productivity gains. He now wants to know how much profits have increased from the previous year because of the productivity program. In order to provide this information to the president, the following data have been gathered:

	2000	2001
Unit selling price	$32	$32
Output produced and sold	100,000	120,000
Materials used (kilograms)	200,000	200,000
Labour used (hours)	50,000	50,000
Unit price of materials	$8	$9
Unit price of labour	$9	$10

Required:

1. Compute the partial productivity ratios for each year. Comment on the effectiveness of the productivity improvement program.
2. Compute the increase in profits attributable to increased productivity, net of gain-sharing.
3. Calculate the price-recovery component, and comment on its meaning. Ignore the bonus cost in this calculation.

16–22

Productivity Measurement

LO4

In 2000, Brindon Products, Inc., used the following input combination to produce 2,000 units of output:

Materials   2,200 kilograms
Labour   2,000 hours

The following combination is optimal for an output of 2,000 units (but unknown to Brindon Products):

Materials   1,000 kilograms
Labour   4,000 hours

The cost of materials is $40 per kilogram, and the cost of labour is $10 per hour. These input prices hold for 2000 and 2001. In 2001, Brindon Products again produced 2,000 units, with the following input combination:

Materials   1,200 kilograms
Labour   5,000 hours

Required:

1. Compute the partial productivity ratios for each of the following:
    a.   The actual inputs used in 2000
    b.   The actual inputs used in 2001
    c.   The optimal input combination
    Did productivity increase in 2001—as measured by the partial productivity ratios?
2. Compute the cost of 2000's productive inefficiency relative to the optimal input combination.
3. By how much did profits increase because of improvements in productive efficiency from 2000 to 2001?
4. How much additional improvement in profits is possible after 2001 (assuming that input costs remain the same and that output doesn't change)?

16–23

Productivity Measurement; Partial and Total Measures; Price Recovery

LO4

The battery division of Chalmur Company recently engaged in a vigorous effort to increase productivity. Over the past several years, competition had intensified, indicating to the divisional manager that a significant price decrease for Chalmur's batteries was in order. Otherwise, the division would lose at least 50 percent of its market share.

To maintain its market share, Chalmur had to decrease its per-unit price by $2.50 by the end of 2001. Decreasing the price by $2.50, however, necessitated a similar increase in cost efficiency. If divisional profits dropped by $2.50 per unit, the division's continued existence would be in question. To assess the outcome of the productivity improvement program, the following data were gathered:

	2000	2001
Output	400,000	500,000
Input quantities:		
Materials (kilograms)	100,000	100,000
Labour (hours)	400,000	200,000
Capital	$4,000,000	$10,000,000
Energy (kilowatt-hours)	100,000	300,000
Input prices:		
Materials	$2	$3
Labour	$8	$10
Capital	15%	10%
Energy	$2	$2

Required:

1. Calculate the partial productivity ratios for each year. Can you say that productivity has improved? Explain.
2. Calculate the profit change attributable to productivity changes.
3. Calculate the cost per unit for 2000 and 2001. Was the division able to decrease its per-unit cost by at least $2.50? Comment on the relationship between competitive advantage and productive efficiency.

16–24

Quality and Productivity; Interaction; Use of Operational Measures

LO4

Andy Confer, production line manager, had arranged a visit with Will Keating, plant manager. He had some questions about the new operational measures that were being used.

Andy: "Will, my questions are more to satisfy my curiosity than anything else. At the beginning of the year, we began some new procedures that require us to work toward increasing our output per kilogram of material and decreasing our output per labour hour. As instructed, I've been tracking these operational measures for each batch we've produced so far this year. Here's a copy of a trend report for the first five batches of this year. Each batch had 10,000 units in it."

Batches	Materials Usage (kilograms)	Ratio	Labour Usage (hours)	Ratio
1	4,000	2.50	2,000	5.00
2	3,900	2.56	2,020	4.95
3	3,750	2.67	2,150	4.65
4	3,700	2.70	2,200	4.55
5	3,600	2.78	2,250	4.44

Will: "Andy, this report is very encouraging. The trend is exactly what we hoped for. I'll bet we meet our goal of getting the batch productivity measures. Let's see, those goals were 3 units per kilogram for materials and 4 units per hour for labour. Last year's figures were 2.50 for materials and 5 for labour. Things are looking good. I guess tying bonuses and raises to improving these productivity stats was a good idea."

Andy: "Maybe so, but I don't understand why you want to make these tradeoffs between materials and labour. The materials cost only $5 per kilogram, and labour costs $10 per hour. It seems like you're simply increasing the cost of making this product."

Will: "Actually, it may seem that way, but it's not so. There are other factors to consider. You know we've been talking about quality improvement. Well, the new procedures that you are implementing are producing products that conform to the product's specification. More labour time is needed to achieve this, and as we take more time, we do waste fewer materials. But the real benefit is the reduction in our external failure costs. Every defect in a batch of 10,000 units costs us $1,000—warranty work, lost sales, a customer service department, and so on. If we can reach the materials and labour productivity goals, our defects will drop from 20 per batch to 5 per batch."

Required:

1. Discuss the advantages of using only operational measures of productivity for controlling shop-level activities.
2. Assume that the batch productivity statistics are met by the end of the year. Calculate the change in a batch's profits between the beginning of the year and the end attributable to changes in materials and labour productivity.
3. Now assume that three inputs are to be evaluated: materials, labour, and quality. Quality is measured by the number of defects per batch. Calculate the change in a batch's profits between the beginning of the year and the end attributable to changes in productivity of all three inputs. Do you agree that quality is an input? Explain.

16–25

Productivity; Tradeoffs

LO4

Connie Baker, president of Fleming Chemicals, had just concluded a meeting with two of her plant managers. She had told each that their product was going to have a 50 percent increase in demand next year over this year's output (which is expected to be 10,000 litres). A major foreign source of the raw material had been shut down because of civil war. It would be years before the source would be available again. The result was twofold. First, the price of the raw material was expected to quadruple. Second, many of Fleming's less efficient competitors would leave the business, creating more demand and higher output prices: in fact, output prices would double.

In discussing the situation with her plant managers, she had reminded them that the automated process now allowed them to increase the productivity of the raw material. By using more machine hours, the plant could decrease evaporation substantially (this was a recent development and would be operational by the beginning of the new fiscal year). There were, however, only two other feasible settings beyond the current setting. The current usage of inputs for the 10,000-litre output (current setting) and the input usage for the other two settings follow. The input usage for the remaining two settings is for an output of 15,000 litres. Inputs are measured in litres for the material and in machine hours for the equipment.

	Current	Setting A	Setting B
Input quantities:			
Materials	25,000	15,000	30,000
Equipment	6,000	15,000	7,500

The current prices for this year's inputs are $3 per litre for materials and $12 per machine hour for the equipment. The materials price will change for next year as explained, but the $12 rate for machine hours will remain the same. The chemical is currently selling for $20 per litre. Based on separate productivity analyses, one plant manager chose Setting A, and the other chose Setting B.

The manager who chose Setting B justified his decision by noting that it was the only setting that clearly signalled an increase in both partial measures of productivity. The other manager agreed that Setting B was an improvement but believed that Setting A was even better.

Required:

1. Calculate the partial measures of productivity for the current year and for the two settings. Which of the two settings signals an increase in productivity for both inputs?
2. Calculate the profits that will be realized under each setting for the coming year. Which setting provides the greatest profit increase?
3. Calculate the profit change for each setting attributable to productivity changes. Which setting offers the greatest productivity improvement? By how much? Explain why this happened. (*Hint:* Look at tradeoffs.)

MANAGERIAL DECISION CASES

16–26

**Quality Cost
Performance Reports**

LO2

Nickles Company, a large printer, is in its fourth year of a five-year quality improvement program. The program began in 1997 with an internal study that revealed the quality costs being incurred. In that year, a five-year plan was developed to lower quality costs to 10 percent of sales by the end of 2001. Sales and quality costs for each year are as follows:

	Sales Revenues	Quality Costs
1997	$10,000,000	$2,000,000
1998	10,000,000	1,800,000
1999	11,000,000	1,815,000
2000	12,000,000	1,680,000
2001*	12,000,000	1,320,000

* Budgeted figures

Quality costs by category are expressed as a percentage of sales as follows:

	Prevention	Appraisal	Internal Failure	External Failure
1997	1.0%	3.0%	7.0%	9.0%
1998	2.0	4.0	6.0	6.0
1999	2.5	4.0	5.0	5.0
2000	3.0	3.5	4.5	3.0
2001	3.5	3.5	2.0	2.0

The detail of the 2001 budget for quality costs is also provided.

Prevention costs:
Quality planning	$ 150,000
Quality training	20,000
Quality improvement (special project)	80,000
Quality reporting	10,000

Appraisal costs:
Proofreading	500,000
Other inspection	50,000

Failure costs:
Correction of typos	150,000
Rework (because of customer complaints)	75,000
Plate revisions	55,000
Press downtime	100,000
Waste (because of poor work)	130,000
Total quality costs	$1,320,000

All prevention costs are fixed; all other quality costs are variable.

During 2001, the company had $12 million in sales. Actual quality costs for 2000 and 2001 are as follows:

	2000	2001
Quality planning	$140,000	$150,000
Quality training	20,000	20,000
Special project	120,000	100,000
Quality reporting	12,000	12,000
Proofreading	580,000	520,000
Other inspection	80,000	60,000
Correction of typos	200,000	165,000
Rework	131,000	76,000
Plate revisions	83,000	58,000
Press downtime	123,000	102,000
Waste	191,000	136,000

Required:

1. Prepare a quality cost performance report for 2001 that compares actual 2001 quality costs with budgeted quality costs. Comment on the firm's ability to achieve its quality goals for the year.
2. Prepare a one-period quality performance report for 2001 that compares the actual costs of 2000 with the actual costs of 2001. How much did profits change because of improved quality?
3. Prepare a graph that shows the trend in total quality costs as a percentage of sales since the inception of the quality improvement program.
4. Prepare a graph that shows the trend for all four quality cost categories for 1997 through 2001. How does this graph show management that the reduction in total quality costs is attributable to quality improvements?

16–27

Quality Performance and Ethical Behaviour

LO1, LO4

Reece Manufacturing rewards its plant managers for their ability to meet budgeted quality cost reductions. The bonus is increased if the productivity goal is met or exceeded. The productivity goal is computed by multiplying the units produced by the prevailing market price and then dividing this measure of output by the total cost of the inputs used. Additionally, if the plant as a whole meets the budgeted targets, the production supervisors and workers receive salary and wage increases. Matt Rasmussen, the manager of a plant in Alberta, feels obligated to do everything he can to provide this increase to his employees. Accordingly, he has decided to take the following actions during the last quarter of the year to meet the plant's budgeted targets and increase the productivity ratio:

a. Decrease inspections of the process and final product by 50 percent and transfer inspectors temporarily to quality training programs. Matt believes that this move will increase the inspectors' awareness of the importance of quality; also, decreasing inspection will produce significantly less downtime and less rework. By increasing the output and decreasing the costs of internal failure, the plant can meet the budgeted reductions for internal failure costs, and simultaneously increase its productivity measure. Also, by showing an increase in the costs of quality training, the plant can meet the budgeted level for prevention costs.

b. Delay replacing and repairing defective products until the beginning of the following year. While this may increase customer dissatisfaction somewhat, Matt believes that most customers expect some inconvenience. Besides, the policy of promptly dealing with dissatisfied customers could be reinstated in three months. In the meantime, the action would significantly reduce the costs of external failure, allowing the plant to meet its budgeted target.

Required:

1. Evaluate Matt's ethical behaviour, taking into account his concern for his employees. Is he justified in pursuing the actions described in the problem? If not, what should he do instead?
2. Assume that the company views Matt's behaviour as undesirable. What can it do to discourage it?
3. Assume that Matt is a CMA. Refer to the ethical code for management accountants in Chapter 1. Are any of these ethical standards being violated?

RESEARCH ASSIGNMENTS

16–28

Library and Cyberspace Research

LO1, LO2, LO3

Listed below are articles that describe some of the quality improvement efforts of five companies, undertaken a number of years ago:

1. Corning Incorporated: Keith H. Hammonds, "Corning's Class Act: How Jamie Houghton Reinvented the Company," *Business Week* (May 13, 1991): pp. 68–73.
2. Federal Express: American Management Association, *Blueprint for Service Quality: The Federal Express Approach*, 1991.
3. Motorola: Keki R. Bhote, "Motorola's Long March to the Malcolm Baldrige National Quality Award," *National Productivity Review*, VIII, 4 (Autumn 1989): pp. 365–375.
4. Solectron: "What Drives Quality?" *Internal Auditor Magazine* (April 1992): pp. 39–45.
5. Southern Pacific: Gus Welty, "Southern Pacific's Quality Comeback," *Railway Age* (November 1992): pp. 30–34.

Required:

Write a three- to five-page paper that compares and contrasts the experiences of any three of the five companies, where at least one of the three is a service company. Include in your discussion the ways in which the companies defined quality. Also, describe how quality was measured, if at all. Were the financial effects measured? Was there any mention of quality costs? Finally, conduct a library and/or Internet search to see if there is anything written that describes how any one of the companies is doing now. As part of this analysis, determine whether or not the quality achievements have been maintained, and assess whether quality continues to be emphasized.

16–29

Cybercase

LO1

Using the Internet, answer the following questions:

1. Go to **www.qualitymag.com** and, using the resources of this site, summarize three cases involving companies that have improved their quality performance during the most recent year.
2. Using library or Internet resources, research "QNet." Write two paragraphs describing QNet's role in promoting quality in Canadian companies.

CHAPTER 17

Environmental Cost Management

Learning Objectives

After studying Chapter 17, you should be able to:

1. Explain the importance of measuring environmental costs.

2. Explain how environmental costs are assigned to products and processes.

3. Describe the life-cycle cost assessment model.

4. Describe activity- and strategic-based environmental control.

Scenario

Robert Artavia, president of Thamus, Inc., had just received the results of an environmental study. The study was concerned with the installation of an effluent treatment system.[1] Thamus's largest plant was located near a river. The plant was dumping liquid residues into the river, and the amount being dumped was exceeding the levels permitted by law. These excessive levels were degrading the quality of the river's water to the point that, on occasion, fish had been killed. The effect on the fish was troublesome, but even more so was the fact that the river was an important resource for a small city. It was the source of drinking water

for over a 200,000 people. To discuss the results of the study and possible solutions, Robert asked his chief engineer, Tammy Burns, and his newly hired environmental manager, Larry Pratt, to meet with him.

Robert: "Tammy, I have just received your report on the effluent treatment system, and I must say that while the proposed treatment system solves the effluent problem, it is an extremely expensive solution. Your report indicates that the benefits are much less than the costs, measured in current dollars."

Tammy: "I understand your concern. If you recall, the study commissioned was one that dealt

strictly with treatment of the effluents currently emitted into the river. This is the cheapest alternative that we could find. And, as you indicate, the investment does cost more than its benefits."

Larry: "Tammy, a question. In assessing the viability of this project, what environmental costs did you use in your studies?"

Tammy: "The only real environmental costs we could identify were the fines that the company is facing. Of course, the costs of building and operating the effluent system itself are environmental costs. By comparing the costs avoided with the costs of building and operating the system, we obtained the negative outcome indicated by Robert."

Larry: "Did you make an effort to estimate any possible cleanup costs and perhaps assess the loss of revenues because of a negative public reaction to our polluting activities?"
Tammy: "No. The point is valid, though. Knowing these costs would make the investment more attractive, because they would increase the benefits of the proposed effluent system. Those costs seemed very difficult to estimate, so we didn't include them."
Larry: "Well, there are other costs, too, that might be avoided, even though we may not be responsible for them financially. For example what about the adverse health effects on the people who use the river as a source of drinking water?"
Robert: "I am not convinced that we should include the latter type of costs in our decision. I doubt we would be financially responsible for them as you mention. Also, any negative health effects would not likely occur for many years into the future, if at all."
Larry: "Well, there are many who believe that costs such as adverse

health effect costs should be considered by socially responsible firms. Furthermore, factoring into our decisions the environmental costs that we cause—but are not financially responsible for—and then advertising the societal benefits may bring an improved image and increased sales. But let me change the subject here. I want to get to the heart of the problem that this study is trying to solve. Do you know what processes and products are the sources of the contaminating effluents? How much of the cost of the pollution is assigned to each of our products? How much of the pollution cost belongs to each of the processes? For example, if most of the cost is attributable to one product, then one possibility is to eliminate that product from our product mix. That could be a very inexpensive solution."
Robert: "Those are good questions, and I am afraid that we do not have the answers to them. Our cost accounting system does not report environmental costs

separately. Perhaps it should. We could possibly save millions of dollars if we had better information."

1. Effluents refer to flows of liquid residues.

Questions to Think About

1. What are environmental costs?

2. Are environmental costs significant enough to track and report to management?

3. Will improving environmental performance increase or decrease total environmental costs?

4. Should environmental costs be assigned to products and processes as a separate item?

5. What is the best way to control environmental costs?

6. Should companies be concerned about environmental costs that they cause but for which they do not have financial responsibility?

MEASURING ENVIRONMENTAL COSTS

Objective 1

Explain the importance of measuring environmental costs.

As the opening scenario revealed, environmental performance can have a significant effect on a firm's financial position. It also revealed a need for sound environmental cost information. In reality, for many organizations, management of environmental costs is becoming a matter of high priority and intense interest. Several reasons can be offered for this increased interest, but two in particular stand out. First, in many countries, environmental regulations have increased significantly, and even more stringent regulations are expected. Often, the regulatory laws carry enormous fines or penalties, creating strong incentives for compliance. Furthermore, the costs for compliance can be significant. Thus, selecting the least costly way of compliance becomes a major objective. To satisfy this objective, compliance costs must be measured and their fundamental causes identified. Second, successful treatment of environmental concerns is becoming a significant competitive issue. Corporations are discovering that meeting sound business objectives and resolving environmental concerns are not mutually exclusive. To understand this critical observation, it is important to examine a concept known as *ecoefficiency*.

The Benefits of Ecoefficiency

Ecoefficiency essentially maintains that organizations can produce more useful goods and services while *simultaneously* reducing negative environmental impacts, resource consumption, and costs. This concept conveys at least three important messages. First, improving ecological and economic performance can and should be complementary. Second, improving environmental performance should no longer be viewed as a matter of charity and goodwill but rather as a matter of competitiveness. Third, ecoefficiency is complementary and supportive of *sustainable development*. **Sustainable development** is defined as development that meets the needs of the present without compromising the ability of future generations to meet their own needs. In addition to this intergenerational dimension of substainable development, there is also the international dimension. Environmental pollution recognizes no boundary, and exporting environmental degraduation is not globally sustainable.[2] Although absolute sustainability may not be attainable, progress toward its achievement certainly seems to have some merit. The Netherlands, for example, set a goal in 1989 and 1990 to attain sustainable development within one generation.[3] The Winnipeg based International Institute for Sustainable Development (IISD) maintains an excellent IISD.com Web site on issues of sustainability.

Ecoefficiency implies that increased efficiency comes from improving environmental performance. Incentives and causes for this increased efficiency have a number of sources. First, customers are demanding cleaner products—products that are produced without degrading the environment and whose use and disposal are environmentally friendly. Second, employees prefer to work for environmentally responsible firms, resulting in greater productivity (that is, clean and safe working conditions attract good workers and stimulate productivity). Third, environmentally responsible firms tend to capture external benefits, such as a lower cost of capital and lower insurance rates. Fourth, better environmental performance can produce significant social benefits, such as benefits to human health. This in turn improves the company's image and enhances its ability to sell its products and services. Fifth, focusing on improving environmental performance awakens within managers a need to innovate and search for new opportunities. For example, this may lead to new markets for outputs that were formerly classified as useless residues. Sixth, reducing environmental costs can maintain or create a competitive advantage. These causes and incentives for ecoefficiency are summarized in Exhibit 17–1.

Exhibit 17–1

Causes and Incentives for Ecoefficiency

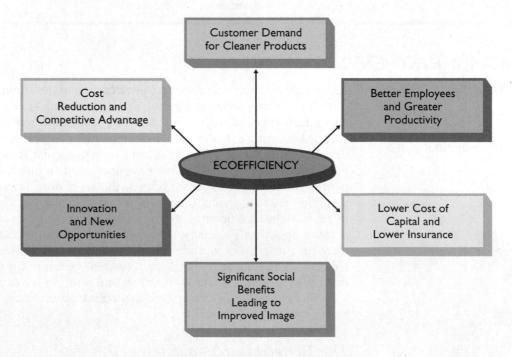

2. T. Anderson, N. Elias, and D. Zéghal, *Environmental Management and Reporting* (Vancouver, BC: CGA-Canada, 1988): pp. 1–10.

3. T. E. Graedel and B. R. Allenby, *Industrial Ecology* (Englewood Cliffs, New Jersey: Prentice-Hall, 1995): pp. 74–75.

The cost reduction and competitiveness incentive is particularly important. Environmental costs can be a significant percentage of total operating costs, and interestingly, many of these costs can be reduced or eliminated through effective management. For example, knowledge of environmental costs and their causes may lead to a redesign of a process that, as a consequence, reduces the raw materials used and the pollutants emitted to the environment (an interaction between the innovation and cost reduction incentives). Thus, current and future environmental costs are reduced, and the firm becomes more competitive. For example, between 1988 and 1994, Baxter International, Incorporated, a producer of medical products, reduced 17 toxic wastes emitted to air, water, and soil by 95 percent and at the same time reduced environmental costs by $74.6 million.[4]

Effective cost management leading to cost reduction like that described for Baxter means that environmental cost information must be provided to management. To provide this financial information, it is necessary to define, measure, classify, and assign environmental costs to processes, products, and other cost objects of interest. Environmental costs should be reported as a separate classification so that managers can assess their impact on firm profitability. Furthermore, assigning environmental costs to products and processes reveals the sources of these costs and helps identify their fundamental causes so that they can be controlled.

Environmental Quality Cost Model

Before environmental cost information can be provided to management, environmental costs must be defined. Various possibilities exist; however, an appealing approach is to adopt a definition consistent with a total environmental quality model. In the total environmental quality model, the ideal state is that of zero damage to the environment (analogous to the zero-defects state of total quality management).[5] Damage is defined as (1) direct degradation of the environment, such as the emission of solid, liquid, or gaseous residues into the environment (for example, water contamination and air pollution; or (2) indirect degradation, such as *unnecessary* usage of materials and energy.

Accordingly, environmental costs can be referred to as *environmental quality costs*.[6] In a similar sense to quality costs, **environmental costs** are costs that are incurred because poor environmental quality *exists* or because poor environmental quality *may* exist. Thus, environmental costs are associated with the creation, detection, remediation, and prevention of environmental degradation. With this definition, environmental costs can be classified into four categories: prevention costs, detection costs, internal failure costs, and external failure costs. External failure costs, in turn, can be subdivided into realized and unrealized categories.

Environmental prevention costs are the costs of activities carried out to prevent the production of contaminants and/or waste that could cause damage to the environment. Examples of prevention activities include the following: evaluating and selecting suppliers, evaluating and selecting equipment to control pollution, designing processes and products to reduce or eliminate contaminants, training employees, studying environmental impacts, auditing environmental risks, undertaking environmental research, developing environmental management systems, recycling products, and obtaining ISO 14001 certification.[7]

---

4. Baxter Environmental Performance Report, 1994.

5. This model of quality costs is based on the following paper: Don R. Hansen and Roberto Mendoza, "Costos de Impacto Ambiental: Su Medición, Asignación, y Control," INCAE Revista, Vol. X, No. 2, 1999. See also Anderson, Elias, and Zéghal, *Environmental Management and Reporting*, pp. 100–102.

6. Also known as 'Legacy Costing'

7. ISO 14001 certification is obtained when an organization installs an environmental management system that satisfies specific, privately set international standards. These standards are concerned with environmental *management* procedures and do not directly indicate acceptable levels of environmental performance. The certification, therefore, functions primarily as a signal that a firm is interested in and willing to improve its environmental performance.

Environmental detection costs are the costs of activities executed to determine whether products, processes, and other activities within the firm are in compliance with appropriate environmental standards. The environmental standards and procedures that a firm seeks to follow are defined in three ways: (1) regulatory laws enacted by governments, (2) voluntary standards (ISO 14001) developed by the International Standards Organization, and (3) environmental policies developed by management. Examples of detection activities are auditing environmental activities, inspecting products and processes (for environmental compliance), developing environmental performance measures, carrying out contamination tests, verifying supplier environmental performance, and measuring levels of contamination.

Environmental internal failure costs are costs of activities performed because contaminants and waste have been produced but not discharged into the environment. Thus, internal failure costs are incurred to eliminate and manage contaminants or waste once produced. Internal failure activities have one of two goals: (1) to ensure that the contaminants and waste produced are not released to the environment, or (2) to reduce the level of contaminants released to an amount that complies with environmental standards. Examples of internal failure activities include operating equipment in ways that minimize or eliminate pollution, treating and disposing of toxic materials, maintaining pollution equipment, licensing facilities for producing contaminants, and recycling scrap.

Environmental external failure costs are the costs of activities performed *after* discharging contaminants and waste into the environment. **Realized external failure costs** are those incurred and directly or indirectly paid for by the firm. These include, for example, the cost of cleaning up an oil spill when that cost is paid directly by the company responsible, but may also include lost profits due to lost sales resulting from customers' switching to other companies or other sources of energy. **Unrealized external failure costs (societal costs)** are caused by the firm but are incurred and paid for by parties outside the firm. Societal costs can be further classified as (1) those resulting from environmental degradation and (2) those associated with an adverse impact on the property or welfare of individuals. In either case, the costs are borne by others and not by the firm, even though they are caused by the firm. Of the four environmental cost categories, the external failure category is the most devastating. For example, Panhandle Eastern, a natural gas transport company, had to pay more than $400 million for cleaning up chemical waste released into the environment.[8] Furthermore, according to a report issued by Standard and Poor's, it is estimated that worldwide cleanup costs during the next 30 years will approach $125 billion.[9] Examples of realized external failure activities are cleaning up a polluted lake, cleaning up oil spills, cleaning up contaminated soil, using materials and energy inefficiently, settling personal injury claims resulting from environmentally unsound practices, settling property damage claims, restoring land to its natural state, and losing sales because of a bad environmental reputation. Examples of societal costs include receiving medical care because of polluted air (individual welfare), losing a lake for recreational use because of contamination (degradation), losing employment because of contamination (individual welfare), and damaging ecosystems from solid waste disposal (degradation).

Exhibit 17–2 summarizes the four environmental cost categories and lists specific activities for each category. Within the external failure cost category, societal costs are labelled with an "S." The costs for which the firm is financially responsible are called **private costs**. All costs without the "S" label are private costs.

---

8. R. Abelson, "Messy Accounting," *Forbes* (14 October 1991): pp. 172–173.

9. Ian Jarret, "Putting Environmental Accounting on the Books," *Asian Business* (October 1996): pp. 6–10.

Exhibit   17–2   Classification of Environmental Costs by Activity

Prevention Activities	Internal Failure Activities
Evaluating and selecting suppliers	Operating pollution control equipment
Evaluating and selecting pollution control equipment	Treating and disposing of toxic waste
Designing processes	Maintaining pollution equipment
Designing products	Licensing facilities for producing contaminants
Carrying out environmental studies	Recycling scrap
Auditing environmental risks	
Developing environmental management systems	**External Failure Activities**
Recycling products	
Obtaining ISO 14001 certification	Cleaning up a polluted lake
	Cleaning up oil spills
Detection Activities	Cleaning up contaminated soil
	Settling environment-related personal injury claims
Auditing environmental activities	Restoring land to its natural state
Inspecting products and processes	Losing sales due to poor environmental reputation
Developing environmental performance measures	Using materials and energy inefficiently
Testing for contamination	Receiving medical care due to polluted air (S)
Verifying supplier environmental performance	Losing employment because of contamination (S)
Measuring contamination levels	Losing a lake for recreational use (S)
	Damaging ecosystems from solid waste disposal (S)

Environmental Cost Report

Environmental cost reporting is essential if an organization is serious about improving its environmental performance and controlling environmental costs. A good first step is a report that details the environmental costs by category. Reporting environmental costs by category reveals two important outcomes: (1) the impact of environmental costs on firm profitability, and (2) the relative amounts expended in each category. Exhibit 17–3 provides an example of a simple environmental cost report.

The report in Exhibit 17–3 highlights the importance of the environmental costs by expressing them as a percentage of total operating costs. In this report, environmental costs are 15 percent of total operating costs, seemingly a significant amount. From a practical point of view, environmental costs will receive managerial attention only if they represent a significant amount. Although environmental managerial cost reporting is in its infancy, some evidence exists concerning this issue. After six months of investigation, Amoco concluded that environmental costs at its Yorktown, Virginia, refinery were at least 22 percent of operating costs.[10] Other evidence from case studies by the World Resources Institute suggests that environmental costs are 20 percent or more of a firm's total operating costs.[11] It appears that environmental costs can significantly affect a firm's profitability.

The cost report also provides information relating to the relative distribution of the environmental costs. Of the total environmental costs, only 20 percent are from the prevention and detection categories. Thus, 80 percent of the environmental costs are failure costs—costs that exist because of poor environmental performance.

---

10. Daniel Baker, "Environmental Accounting's Conflicts and Dilemmas," *Management Accounting* (October 1996): pp. 46–48.

11. Daryl Ditz, Janet Ranganathan, and R. Daryl Banks, *Green Ledgers: Case Studies in Corporate Environmental Accounting*, World Resources Institute (May 1995).

Exhibit   17–3

Environmental Cost
Report

Numade Corporation Environmental Cost Report For the Year Ended December 31, 2001			
		Environmental Costs	Percentage of Operating Costs
Prevention costs:			
Training employees	$ 60,000		
Designing products	180,000		
Selecting equipment	40,000	$ 280,000	1.40%
Detection costs:			
Inspecting processes	$240,000		
Developing measures	80,000	320,000	1.60%
Internal failure costs:			
Operating pollution equipment	$400,000		
Maintaining pollution equipment	200,000	600,000	3.00%
External failure costs:			
Cleaning up lake	$900,000		
Restoring land	500,000		
Property damage claim	400,000	1,800,000	9.00%
Totals		$3,000,000	15.00%

Reducing Environmental Costs

Fortunately, evidence exists that environmental failure costs can be reduced by investing more in prevention and detection activities. Ford Motor Company, for example, has made a commitment to improve its environmental performance. As part of this overall commitment, Ford has resolved to obtain ISO 14001 certification in all its plants throughout the world. Some of its plants in Germany and England have already received this certification. In these certified plants, Ford has already saved hundreds of thousands of dollars in environmental costs.[12] In the organic chemical industrial sector, studies concerned with efforts to prevent toxic waste have shown that for every dollar spent on prevention activities, $3.49 was saved from environmental failure activities (per year).[13] For a typical project, savings were $351,000 per year, and an average of 1.6 million pounds of chemical were eliminated.[14]

It is possible that the environmental cost reduction model will behave in a very similar way to the total quality cost model. Perhaps the lowest environmental costs are attainable at the *zero-damage point,* much like the zero-defects point of the total quality cost model. This point of view is certainly compatible with the notion of eco-efficiency. The idea underlying the zero-damage view is that *prevention is cheaper than the cure.* In Phillips Petroleum, this concept is referred to as the *rule of 1–10–100.*[15] This rule states that if a problem is solved in its own area of work, it costs $1; if the problem is solved outside the originating area but within the company, it costs $10; if the problem is solved outside the company, it costs $100. The rule suggests that zero damage is the lowest cost point for environmental costs.

In reality, it may be that zero degradation is the low cost point for many types of contaminating activities. For example, Numar, a Costa Rican producer of margarines and cooking oils, managed to reduce its emission of contaminated water effluents to

12. Michael Prince, "ISO Now Offering Voluntary Standards," *Business Insurance* (11 November 1996): pp. 21–23.

13. Michael E. Porter and Claus van der Linde, "Green and Competitive: Ending the Stalemate," *Harvard Business Review* (Sept.–Oct. 1995): pp. 120–134.

14. See also *Cutting Chemical Waste* (1985) and *Environmental Dividends: Cutting More Chemical Waste* (1991), INFORM, New York, NY. (INFORM is a not-for-profit group that conducted a study of 29 chemical companies.)

15. Blair W. Feltmate, "Making Sustainable Development a Corporate Reality," *CMA Magazine* (March 1997): pp. 9–16.

zero.[16] The actions taken by Numar were in response to a new environmental law that prohibits the dumping of these effluents into rivers and streams. Numar invested in a new system that treated the water and allowed the firm to recover usable materials and, at the same time, reuse the treated water. The annual costs of the investment, including depreciation, purchase of bacteria, electricity, and maintenance, were $116,350. Three benefits were observed. First, the amount of water required on a daily basis was reduced from 950 cubic metres to 200 cubic metres (because of the ability to recycle water). This produced savings of $391,500 per year. Second, the materials recovered from the treated water were worth $30,000 per year (cost only). Third, the company avoided stiff environmental fines and possible closure costs. Thus, the zero-degradation state for solid residues was achieved at a cost of $116,350 per year, but *benefits* of at least $421,500 were produced. The approach taken to obtain zero emissions actually increased the firm's profitability! It is curious that a legal incentive was required for the company to seek the more efficient approach. Part of the reason can be attributed to the common view that improving environmental performance is a charitable act. It is also true that most firms do not have the necessary environmental cost information. Knowing environmental costs and how they relate to products, for example, can be a strong incentive for innovating and increasing efficiency.

An Environmental Financial Report

Ecoefficiency suggests a possible modification to environmental cost reporting. Specifically, in addition to reporting environmental costs, why not report *environmental benefits?* In a given period, there are three types of benefits: income, current savings, and cost avoidance (ongoing savings). Income refers to revenues that flow into the organization due to environmental actions such as recycling paper, finding new applications for nonhazardous waste (for example, using wood scraps to make wooden chess pieces and boards), and increased sales due to an enhanced environmental image. Cost avoidance refers to ongoing savings produced in prior years. Current savings refer to reductions in environmental costs achieved in the current year. By comparing benefits produced with environmental costs incurred in a given period, a type of environmental financial statement is produced. Managers can use this statement to assess progress (benefits produced) and potential for progress (environmental costs). The environmental financial statement could also form part of an environmental progress report that is provided to shareholders on an annual

Exhibit 17–4

Environmental Financial Statement

Numade Corporation Environmental Financial Statement For the Year Ended December 31, 2001	
Environmental benefits:	
Cost reductions, contaminants	$ 300,000
Cost reductions, hazardous waste disposal	400,000
Recycling income	200,000
Energy conservation cost savings	100,000
Packaging cost reductions	150,000
Total environmental benefits	$1,150,000
Environmental costs:	
Prevention costs	$ 280,000
Detection costs	320,000
Internal failure costs	600,000
External failure costs	1,800,000
Total environmental costs	$3,000,000

16. Arnoldo Rodriguez, "Grupo Numar," *INCAE* (June 1997).

basis. Exhibit 17–4 provides an example of an environmental financial statement. For simplicity, details of the environmental cost categories are not shown. The cost reductions shown are the sum of current savings plus avoidance of environmental costs due to prior-period environmental actions. The benefits reported reveal good progress, but the costs are still nearly three times the benefits, indicating that more improvements are clearly needed.[17]

ASSIGNING ENVIRONMENTAL COSTS

Objective 2

Explain how environmental costs are assigned to products and processes.

Both products and processes are sources of environmental costs. Processes that *produce* products can create solid, liquid, and gaseous residues that are subsequently introduced into the environment. These residues have the potential of degrading the environment. Residues, then, are the causes of both internal and external environmental failure costs (for example, investing in equipment to prevent the introduction of the residues into the environment and cleaning up residues after they are allowed into the environment). Production processes are not the only source of environmental costs. Packaging is also a source of environmental costs. For example, in the United States, 30 percent of all municipal solid waste is packaging material.[18]

Products themselves can be the source of environmental costs. After selling a product, its use and disposal by the customer can produce environmental degradation. These are examples of *environmental postpurchase costs.* Most of the time, environmental postpurchase costs are borne by society and not by the company; thus they are societal costs. On occasion, however, environmental postpurchase costs are converted into realized external costs.

Environmental Product Costs

The environmental costs of processes that produce, market, and deliver products and the environmental postpurchase costs caused by the use and disposal of the products are examples of *environmental product costs.* **Full environmental costing**[19] is the assignment of all environmental costs, both private and societal, to products. **Full private costing** is the assignment of only private costs to individual products. Private costing, then, would assign the environmental costs to products caused by the internal processes of the organization. Private costing is probably a good starting point for many firms. Private costs can be assigned using data created *inside* the firm. Full costs require gathering of data that are produced outside the firm from third parties. As the firm gains experience with environmental costing, it may be well advised to expand product cost assignments and implement an approach called *life-cycle cost assessment*, discussed later in the chapter.

Assigning environmental costs to products can produce valuable managerial information. For example, it may reveal that a particular product is responsible for much more toxic waste than other products. This information may lead to a more efficient and environmentally friendly alternative design for the product or its associated processes. It could also reveal that with the environmental costs correctly assigned, the product is not profitable. This could mean something as simple as dropping the product to achieve significant improvement in environmental performance and economic efficiency. Many opportunities for improvement may exist, but knowledge of the environmental product costs is the key. Moreover, it is critical that environmental costs be assigned accurately.

17. For other forms of environmental reports to external stakeholders, see Canadian Institute of Chartered Accountants, *Environmental Reporting in Canada: a Survey of 1993 Reports* (Toronto: CICA, 1994), and *Reporting on Environmental Performance* (Toronto: CICA, 1994).

18. T. E. Graedel and B. R. Allenby, *Industrial Ecology*, p. 243.

19. For more information on this topic, see Canadian Institute of Chartered Accountants, *Full Cost Accounting from an Environmental Perspective*, CICA Research Report (Toronto: CICA, 1997).

Functional-Based Environmental Cost Assignments

In most cost accounting systems, explicit environmental costs are hidden within overhead.[20] Using the environmental cost definitions and classification framework just developed, environmental costs must first be separated into an environmental cost pool. Once separated into their own pool, functional-based costing would assign these costs to individual products using unit-level drivers such as direct labour hours and machine hours. This approach may work well for a homogeneous product setting; however, in a multiple-product firm with product diversity, a functional-based assignment can produce cost distortions.

Suppose, for example, that a company produces two types of glass: Type A and Type B. There are 50,000 sheets of each type produced, and each sheet of glass requires 0.5 machine hours. Assume that machine hours will be used to assign environmental costs to products. In producing glass products, cadmium emissions occur. To produce cadmium emissions, a special government permit must be purchased that costs $300,000. The permit must be renewed every three years. Thus, the permit cost is $100,000 per year. The permit authorizes a certain level of cadmium emissions. If emissions exceed the allowed level, a fine is imposed. There is one unannounced inspection each quarter. The firm averages $50,000 per year in fines. Thus, the annual cost of cadmium emissions is $150,000 ($100,000 + $50,000). The environmental cost per machine hour is $3 ($150,000/50,000 machine hours). Use of this rate produces an environmental cost per unit of $1.50 for each product ($3 × 0.5 machine hours).

The accuracy of the assignment is critical. For example, what if Type A glass is responsible for all or most of the cadmium emissions? If Type A is responsible for all the emissions, then the environmental cost should be $3 per unit for Type A and $0 per unit for Type B. In this case, Type A was undercosted, and Type B was overcosted. This possibility is not imaginary. Something very similar happened with Spectrum Glass, a producer of specialty glass. It discovered that only one product, "Ruby Red," was responsible for all its cadmium emissions.[21] Yet the firm's cost accounting system was assigning a portion of this cost to every product produced.

Activity-Based Environmental Cost Assignments

The emergence of activity-based costing facilitates environmental costing. Tracing the environmental costs to the products responsible for those costs is a fundamental requirement of a sound environmental accounting system. Costs must be assigned using causal relationships. This approach, of course, is exactly what ABC does.

The Cadmium Example Revisited   Emitting cadmium is the environmental activity (in this case, an external failure activity). The cost of the activity is the cost of the fine and the permit fees: $150,000. Assume now that the quantity of cadmium emissions is the activity output measure, and let that quantity be 20,000 units. The activity rate is $7.50 per unit ($150,000/20,000 units). If Type A produces 20,000 units of emissions and Type B produces 0 units, then the cost assignments are as they should be: $150,000 to Type A ($7.50 × 20,000) and $0 to Type B. This ABC assignment produces a unit environmental cost of $3 for Type A ($150,000/50,000) and $0 for Type B.

All costs assigned in this example are private costs. Societal costs are also possible. If so, and if they can be estimated, then a fuller costing approach can be used. For example, suppose that cadmium emissions cause $150,000 per year in medical expenses for those who live in the community affected by the emissions. In this case, the cost per unit for Type A would double.

---

20. It should be noted that many environmental costs are hidden from the books altogether. This is the case, for example, when a company does not recognize social costs as private costs at a given point in time only to find out that it must pay for its past sins. Superfund liabilities tend to fall into this category. See Anderson, Elias, and Zéghal, Chapter 5.

21. Daniel Baker, "Environmental Accounting's Conflicts and Dilemmas," *Management Accounting* (October 1996): pp. 46–48.

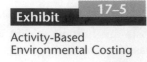

Activity-Based
Environmental Costing

Activities	Cleanser A	Cleanser B
Evaluate and select suppliers	$0.20	$ 0.05
Design processes (to reduce pollution)	0.10	0.10
Inspect processes (for pollution problems)	0.25	0.15
Capture and treat chlorofluorocarbons	0.05	1.00
Maintain environmental equipment	0.00	0.50
Toxic waste disposal	0.10	1.75
Excessive materials usage	0.08	0.25
Environmental cost per unit	$0.78	$ 3.80
Other manufacturing costs (nonenvironmental)	9.02	16.20
Unit cost	$9.80	$20.00
Units produced	100,000	100,000

Example with Multiple Activities The cadmium example had only one activity. In reality, there will be multiple environmental activities. Each activity will be assigned costs, and activity rates will be computed. These rates are then used to assign environmental costs to products based on usage of the activity. Exhibit 17–5 shows the assignment of environmental costs to two products (two different types of industrial cleansers) when there is a variety of activities. This cost assignment allows managers to see the relative environmental economic impact of the two products, and to the extent that environmental costs reflect environmental damage, the unit environmental cost can also act as an index or measure of product cleanliness. The "dirtier" products can then be the focus of efforts to improve environmental performance and economic efficiency. Exhibit 17–5 reveals, for example, that Cleanser B has more environmental problems than Cleanser A does. Cleanser B's environmental costs total $380,000 ($3.80 × 100,000) and are 19 percent of the total manufacturing costs. Furthermore, its environmental failure costs are $350,000, representing 92.1 percent of the total environmental costs. Cleanser A portrays a much better picture. Its environmental costs total $78,000, or 8 percent of the total manufacturing costs, and its failure costs are 29.5 percent of the total environmental costs. It is evident that Cleanser B offers the most environmental and economic potential for improvement.

LIFE-CYCLE COST ASSESSMENT

Objective 3

Describe the life-cycle cost assessment model.

The environmental product costs may reveal a need to improve a company's *product stewardship*. **Product stewardship** is the practice of designing, manufacturing, maintaining, and recycling products to minimize adverse environmental impacts. *Life-cycle assessment* is the means for improving product stewardship. **Life-cycle assessment** identifies the environmental consequences of a product through its entire life cycle and then searches for opportunities to obtain environmental improvements. **Life-cycle cost assessment** assigns costs and benefits to the environmental consequences and improvements.

Product Life Cycle

The U.S. Environmental Protection Agency (EPA) has identified four stages in the life cycle of a product: resource extraction, product manufacture, product use, and recycling and disposal.[22] Another possible stage, not explicitly considered by the EPA guidelines, is that of product packaging. Product life cycle, including packaging, is illustrated in Exhibit 17–6. As shown, the different life-cycle stages can be

22. *Life Cycle Assessment: Inventory Guidelines and Principles*, EPA/600/R-92/245 (February 1993).

Exhibit   17-6

Product Life-Cycle Stages

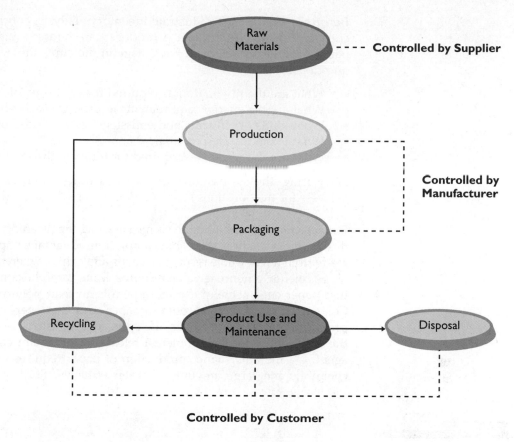

under the control of someone other than the producer of the product. Note that the source of materials for the product can come through extraction (raw materials) or from recycling. If all or some of the product's components cannot be recycled, then disposal is required and waste management becomes an issue.

The life-cycle viewpoint adopted combines supplier, manufacturer, and customer viewpoints. Both internal and external linkages are thus considered important in assessing the environmental consequences of different products, the product designs, and process designs. If the cost accounting system is going to play a role in life-cycle assessment, then the most obvious step is assessing and assigning the environmental costs caused by the producer in each of the life-cycle stages. This then allows managers to compare the economic effects of competing designs. However, before discussing cost assessment, a more detailed understanding of life-cycle analysis is needed.

Assessment Stages

Life-cycle assessment is defined by three formal stages: (1) inventory analysis, (2) impact analysis, and (3) improvement analysis.[23] **Inventory analysis** specifies the types and quantities of materials and energy inputs needed and the resulting environmental releases in the form of solid, liquid, and gaseous residues. Inventory analysis spans the product's life cycle. **Impact analysis** assesses the environmental effects of competing designs and provides a relative ranking of those effects. **Improvement analysis** has the objective of reducing the environmental impacts revealed by the inventory and impact steps.

23. T. E. Graedel and B. R. Allenby, *Industrial Ecology*, pp. 108–121.

Inventory Analysis To illustrate inventory analysis, consider single-use hot-drink cups for fast-food restaurants. A producer can choose to make such cups using either paper or polystyrene foam. Each stage in the cup's life cycle produces certain key questions:

- What are the raw materials required for each type of cup?
- What are the energy requirements to produce each product?
- What kinds of effluents and emissions are produced by each product?
- What is the recycle potential?
- What are the resources required for ultimate disposal?

Answering these questions defines inventory analysis. Exhibit 17–7 provides answers for the questions based on data reported in a study by Martin Hocking.[24]

Impact Analysis Impact analysis next assesses the meaning of the values provided by the inventory analysis step. For example, one advantage of paper cups is that paper is made from a renewable resource (woods and chips), whereas the polyfoam cup relies on petroleum, a nonrenewable resource. More careful examination, however, reveals that paper cups actually use more petroleum than polyfoam cups do! The reason? Converting wood chips to pulp to paper cups uses energy. Effluents and emissions produced during the products' life cycle are also listed in Exhibit 17–7. Interestingly, the only significant environmental release for polyfoam cups is pentane, a blowing agent. On the other hand, production of paper requires extensive use of inorganic chemicals and large amounts of water effluents. Furthermore, recycling seems to

Exhibit 17–7

Inventory Analysis

	Paper Cup	Polyfoam Cup
Materials usage per cup:		
Wood and bark (grams)	33.0	0.0
Petroleum (grams)	4.1	3.2
Finished weight (grams)	10.0	11.5
Utilities per milligram of material:		
Steam (kilogram)	9,000–12,000	5,000
Power (gigajoules)	3.5	0.4–0.6
Cooling water (cubic metres)	50	154
Water effluent per milligram of material:		
Volume (cubic metres)	50–190	0.5–2.0
Suspended solids (kilograms)	35–60	trace
BOD (kilograms)	30–50	0.07
Organochlorides (kilograms)	5–7	0
Metal salts (kilograms)	1–20	20
Air emissions per milligram of material:		
Chlorine (kilograms)	0.5	0
Sulfides (kilograms)	2.0	0
Particulates (kilograms)	5–15	0.1
Pentane (kilograms)	0	35–50
Recycle potential:		
Primary user	Possible	Easy
After use	Low	High
Ultimate disposal:		
Heat recovery (megajoules per kilogram)	20	40
Mass to landfill (grams)	10.1	11.5
Biodegradable	Yes	No

24. M. B. Hocking, "Paper versus Polystyrene: A Complex Choice," *Science,* 251 (1991): pp. 504–505.

favour polyfoam cups. Finally, ultimate disposal, at least in landfills, tends to favour paper cups because of their biodegradability. Yet this advantage is called into question by recent studies indicating that biodegradable materials in anaerobic landfills remain *undegraded* over relatively long periods of time.[25] From the viewpoint of a variety of environmental impacts, perhaps polyfoam cups are better than paper cups!

Cost Assessment Up to this point, the analysis has used only nonfinancial measures and qualitative factors. The hot-drink cup example, however, does offer the opportunity to introduce costs and discuss their value in life-cycle assessment. Life-cycle cost assessment involves determining the financial consequences of the environmental impacts identified in the inventory and improvement steps of life-cycle assessment. Assessing environmental costs for the inventory stage can facilitate impact analysis. In the paper-cup-versus-polyfoam-cup example, the comparisons of operational data were fairly "clean," in the sense that one product's environmental impacts were almost always less than the other product's. But even here there are some questions that can be raised. For example, what is the cost of producing pentane emissions compared to the cost of water effluents and particulates? What are the economic benefits from recycling polyfoam cups? The advantage of assigning costs is that the total environmental costs provide an index that can be used for ranking the competing alternatives. How are costs assigned?

The answer to the cost assignment question has already been given. Materials costs are assigned through direct tracing. We can identify the amount of materials consumed per unit and then multiply by the price paid for the materials. Energy costs and the costs of producing environmental releases are assigned through driver tracing. Thus, for existing products (or processes, if they are the cost object), we simply identify the associated environmental activities and their costs, calculate an activity rate, and assign those costs to the respective products. If some of the energy consumption and environmental releases are associated with the use of the product after purchase, then a full environmental costing analysis requires their inclusion. It is also possible to assign only private costs. Recycling and disposal are separate but important issues. Many of the costs here are societal costs, and their measurement becomes more difficult. Taking only a private costing approach is also possible for recycling and disposal.

For example, assume that the following environmental costs per unit have been determined for the two cups:

	Paper Cups	Polyfoam Cups
Materials usage	$0.010	$0.004
Utilities	$0.012	$0.003
Contaminant-related resources	$0.008	$0.005
Total private costs	$0.030	$0.012
Recycling benefits (societal)	$0.001	$0.004
Environmental cost per unit	$0.029	$0.008

The unit life-cycle costs provide a summary measure of the relative environmental impacts of the two products and serve to support the qualitative interpretations of the operational and subjective environmental data found in Exhibit 17–7.

Improvement Analysis Assessing the environmental impacts in operational and financial terms sets the stage for the final step, that of searching for ways to reduce the environmental impacts of the alternatives being considered or analyzed. It is this step that connects with the organization's control system. Improving the environmental performance of existing products and processes is the overall objective of an environmental control system.

25. T. E. Graedel and B. R. Allenby, *Industrial Ecology*, p. 149.

STRATEGIC-BASED ENVIRONMENTAL RESPONSIBILITY ACCOUNTING

Objective 4

Describe activity- and strategic-based environmental control.

The overall goal of improving environmental performance suggests that a continuous improvement framework for environmental control would be the most appropriate. In fact, an environmental perspective is a possible fifth perspective for the Balanced Scorecard framework that we discussed in Chapter 15. The creators of the Balanced Scorecard mention a specific instance where a company added an environmental perspective to its Balanced Scorecard.[26] If one accepts the ecoefficiency paradigm, then an environmental perspective is legitimate, because improving environmental performance can be the source of a competitive advantage (the criterion for a perspective to be included). A strategic-based environmental management system provides an operational framework for improving environmental performance. For example, linking the environmental perspective to the process perspective is critical for improving environmental performance. Knowledge of root causes for environmental activities is fundamental to any process design changes needed to improve environmental performance. Thus, the Balanced Scorecard framework supplies objectives and measures that are integrated to achieve the overall goal of improving environmental performance.

Environmental Perspective

We can identify at least five core objectives for the environmental perspective: (1) minimize the use of raw or virgin materials; (2) minimize the use of hazardous materials; (3) minimize energy requirements for production and use of the product; (4) minimize the release of solid, liquid, and gaseous residues; and (5) maximize opportunities to recycle.

There are two environmental themes associated with materials and energy (the first three core objectives). First, no more energy and materials should be used than absolutely necessary (conservation issue). Second, means should be sought to eliminate the usage of materials and energy that damage the environment (hazardous substance issue). Performance measures should reflect these two themes. Thus, possible measures would be total and per-unit quantities of the different types of materials and energy (for example, kilograms of toxic chemicals used), productivity measures (output/materials, output/energy), and hazardous materials (energy) costs expressed as a percentage of total materials cost.

The fourth core objective can be realized in one of two ways: (1) using technology and methods to prevent the release of residues, *once produced,* and (2) *avoiding* production of the residues by identifying fundamental causes and redesigning products and processes to eliminate the causes. Of the two methods, the second is preferred. The first method is analogous to obtaining product quality by inspection and rework (*inspecting in quality*). Experience with quality management has revealed that this approach is much more costly than *doing it right the first time.* This same outcome is likely to be true for the control of residues once produced. It makes more sense to avoid residues than to contain them once produced. Performance measures for this objective include kilograms of toxic waste produced, cubic metres of effluents, tonnes of greenhouse gases produced, and percentage reduction of packaging materials.

The fifth objective emphasizes conserving of nonrenewable resources by reusing them. Recycling reduces the demand for extraction of additional raw materials. It also reduces environmental degradation by reducing the waste disposal requirements placed on end users. Measures include kilograms of materials recycled, number of different materials (the fewer, the better), number of different components (the fewer, the better for recycling), percentage of units remanufactured, and energy produced from incineration. Exhibit 17–8 summarizes the objectives and measures for the environmental perspective.

26. Robert S. Kaplan and David P. Norton, *The Balanced Scorecard* (Boston: Harvard Business School, 1996): p. 35.

Exhibit 17–8

Objectives and
Measures: Environmental
Perspective

Objectives	Measures
Minimize hazardous materials	Types and quantities (total and per unit) Percentage of total materials cost Productivity measures (output/input)
Minimize raw or virgin materials	Types and quantities (total and per unit) Productivity measures (output/input)
Minimize energy requirements	Types and quantities (total and per unit) Productivity measures (output/input)
Minimize release of residues	Kilograms of toxic waste produced Cubic metres of effluents Tonnes of greenhouse gases produced Percentage reduction of packaging materials
Maximize opportunities to recycle	Kilograms of materials recycled Number of different components Percentage of units remanufactured Energy produced from incineration

The Role of Activity Management

Analysis of environmental activities is critical for a sound environmental control system. Of course, as we already know, identifying environmental activities and assessing their costs are prerequisites for activity-based environmental costing. Knowing the environmental costs and what products and processes are causing them is absolutely essential as a first step for control. Next, environmental activities must be classified as value-added and nonvalue-added.

Nonvalue-added activities are those that are not necessary if the firm is operating in an optimal environmentally efficient state. Interestingly, Porter and van der Linde claim that environmental pollution is equivalent to economic inefficiency.[27] If production of contaminants is equivalent to economic inefficiency, as they claim, then all failure activities must be labelled nonvalue-added. Adopting an ecoefficiency paradigm implies that there always exist activities that can simultaneously prevent environmental degradation and produce a state of economic efficiency better than the current state. Failure activities, of course, are not the only nonvalue-added activities. Many detection activities, such as inspection, are nonvalue-added as well.

Nonvalue-added environmental costs are the costs of nonvalue-added activities. These costs represent the benefits that can be captured by improving environmental performance. The key to capturing these benefits is identifying root causes for nonvalue-added activities and then redesigning products and processes to minimize and ultimately eliminate these nonvalue-added activities.

Design for the Environment This special design approach is called *design for the environment*. It touches products, processes, materials, energy, and recycling. In other words, the entire product life cycle and its effects on the environment must be considered. Manufacturing processes, for example, are the direct sources of many solid, liquid, and gaseous residues. Many of these end up being released into the environment. Often, redesign of a process can eliminate the production of such residues (the Numar case cited earlier is a good example). Product designs can also reduce environmental degradation. Eastman Kodak, for example, has designed its expendable cameras to facilitate recycling.[28] The expendable cameras have components that are colour-coded. These components can be separated and used to build new cameras.

27. Michael E. Porter and Claus van der Linde, "Green and Competitive: Ending the Stalemate," *Harvard Business Review* (September–October 1995): pp. 120–134.

28. Joseph Fiskel, "Competitive Excellence Through Environmental Excellence," *Corporate Environmental Strategy* (Summer 1997): pp. 55–61.

Exhibit   17–9

Nonvalue-Added Cost
Trends: Environmental
Costs

Nonvalue-Added Environmental Activity	Year	
	2001	2000
Inspecting processes	$ 200,000	$ 240,000
Operating pollution equipment	350,000	400,000
Maintaining pollution equipment	200,000	200,000
Cleaning up water pollution	700,000	900,000
Property damage claim	300,000	400,000
Totals	$1,750,000	$2,140,000

Approximately 86 percent of each new camera is made of recycled materials. It is estimated that 5,000,000 units have been recycled since the introduction of this product, totalling about 700,000 pounds of materials.

Financial Measures   Environmental improvements ought to produce significant and beneficial financial consequences. This means that the firm has achieved a favourable tradeoff among failure activities and prevention activities. If ecoefficient decisions are being made, then total environmental costs should diminish as environmental performance improves. Thus, environmental cost trends are an important performance measure. One possibility is preparing a nonvalue-added environmental cost report for the current period and comparing these costs with the nonvalue-added costs of the prior period. An example of such a report is shown in Exhibit 17–9. Some care is needed in deciding how costs and trends are to be measured. Cost reductions should be attributable to environmental improvements and not simply discharging some environmental liability. Thus, external failure costs should reflect the average annual obligations resulting from current environmental efficiency. Therefore, the cost of cleaning up water pollution in 2000 is the expected annual cost assuming that current environmental performance remains the same. The $900,000 cleanup cost, for example, could be the annual amount that must be set aside to have the total funds necessary to execute a cleanup five years from now. As actions are taken to improve environmental performance, this may mean that the amount of future cleanup will diminish, thus reducing the annual amount to $700,000. The $200,000 trend improvement, then, is attributable to improved environmental performance.

Exhibit   17–10

Environmental Cost
Trend Graph

Environmental Costs/Sales

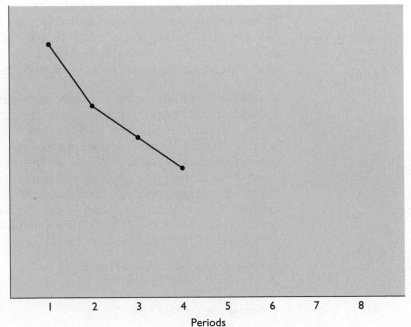

Periods

Another possibility is computing total environmental costs as a percentage of sales and tracking this value over several periods. Exhibit 17–10 illustrates such a trend graph. This graph is of particular interest because it tracks all environmental costs and not just nonvalue-added environmental costs. If ecoefficient decisions are being made, we should observe a reduction in *total* environmental costs. This implies that there is a favourable tradeoff between investments in environmental-related prevention activities and reduction of environmental failure costs. The trend should be downward, as ecoefficient investments are made.

Other graphical illustrations for specific areas can also be used to show progress made. For example, a bar graph can be used to show the total amount of a pollutant emitted on a year-by-year basis. A downward trend would be a favourable indication. Pie charts can also be useful. For example, a pie chart could visually display hazardous waste management by category: percentage of waste incinerated, percentage of waste recycled/reclaimed, percentage of waste landfilled, percentage of waste treated, and percentage of waste deep-well injected. Exhibit 17–11 illustrates a bar graph analysis of CFCs (chlorofluorocarbons) released over a four-year period, and Exhibit 17–12 shows a pie chart for hazardous waste management.

Exhibit 17–11

Bar Graph for Trend Analysis

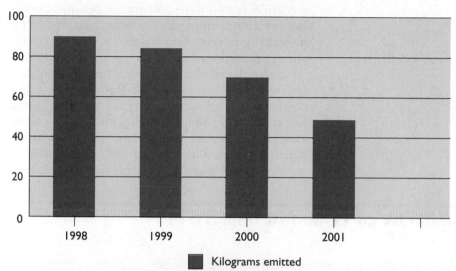

Exhibit 17–12

Hazardous Waste Pie Chart

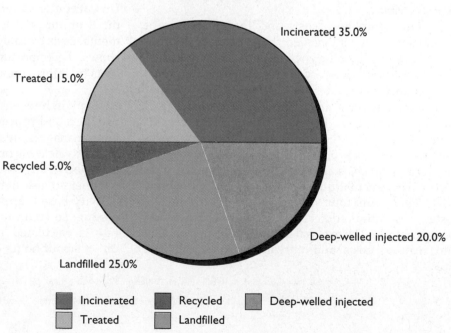

Environmental Strategy and Sustainability[29]

The focus of this chapter is primarily on cost avoidance, pollution prevention, and cost management strategies. This is because most companies are still grappling with these issues. However, it is clear that if all companies follow these strategies, sustainability may not be the outcome. On the other hand, these strategies are not in competition with the sustainability strategy. Rather, they are components of such a strategy. Strategic sustainability has provided valuable business opportunities, but these opportunities will likely multiply geometrically in the near future as business and government worldwide attempt to face insurmountable global environmental challenges.

According to Hart (1997),[30] there are different levels of environmental strategies. Initially, businesses tend to pay attention to compliance with environmental laws and regulations. As a company's environmental strategy develops, it begins to search for ways to avoid unnecessary environmental costs such as fines, penalties, and cost upgrades. The strategy begins to anticipate rather than wait for environmental regulations.

The next stage in the development of an environmental strategy is aimed at long-term cost reduction and prudent cost management. Only a few companies have begun the dialogue on how a sound ecological and sustainable development view can affect not only the cost stream but also the revenue stream. For example, Volvo has begun redefining its business from that of producing cars to that of providing sustainable transportation services. Some exciting opportunities are awaiting innovative corporations that are directing their activities toward creating the future.

Examples of such companies are not many, but the trend is currently being set. A steel company is searching for ways to make a lighter-weight steel that maintains the desirable qualities of heavy steel. An energy company is creating energy resources whose primary residue is clean water. An agricultural products company is developing agricultural product strains that eliminate the need for pesticides. But with each innovation develops a new controversy. Careful and prudent re-examination of corporate strategy and available technologies can provide new paths to sustainable development.

SUMMARY OF LEARNING OBJECTIVES

1. Explain the importance of measuring environmental costs.

Increasing compliance costs and the emergence of ecoefficiency have intensified the interest in environmental costing. Ecoefficiency implies that cost reductions can be achieved by increasing environmental performance. Furthermore, for many companies, environmental costs are a significant percentage of total operating costs. This fact, coupled with ecoefficiency, emphasizes the importance of defining, measuring, and reporting environmental costs. Environmental costs are those costs incurred because poor environmental quality exists or because it may exist. There are four categories of environmental costs: prevention, detection, internal failure, and external failure. The external failure category is divided into realized costs and unrealized costs. Realized costs are those external costs that the firm has to pay. Unrealized or societal costs are those costs caused by the firm but paid for by society. Reporting environmental costs by category reveals their importance and shows the opportunity for reducing environmental costs by improving environmental performance.

2. Explain how environmental costs are assigned to products and processes.

First, managers must decide whether they will assign only private costs or whether they want all costs to be assigned (full costing). Next, they must choose whether to use a functional-based approach or an activity-based approach. Under functional-based costing, an environmental cost pool is created and a rate is calculated using unit-level drivers such as direct labour hours or machine hours. Environmental

---

29. This subsection draws heavily on Anderson, Elias, and Zéghal, pp. 214–215.

30. S.L. Hart, "Beyond Greening: Strategies for a Sustainable World," *Harvard Business Review*, January–February 1997, pp. 67–76.

costs are then assigned to each product based on its usage of direct labour hours or machine hours. This approach is probably satisfactory for firms with little product diversity. For firms with product diversity, activity-based cost assignments are likely to be superior. ABC assigns costs to environmental activities and then calculates activity rates. These rates are then used to assign environmental costs to products.

3. Describe the life-cycle cost assessment model.

Life-cycle cost assessment is a fundamental part of life-cycle assessment. Life-cycle cost assessment assigns costs to the environmental impacts of competing product designs. These costs are a function of the materials used, the energy consumed, and the environmental releases resulting from the manufacture of a product. Thus, before assessing these cost assignments, it is first necessary to do an inventory analysis that details materials, energy, and environmental releases. This analysis is carried out over the life cycle of the product itself. Once completed, the financial and operational impacts can be assessed and steps taken to improve environmental performance.

4. Describe activity- and strategic-based environmental control.

Controlling environmental costs relies on a strategic-based responsibility accounting system. This system has two important features: a strategic component and an operational component. The strategic component uses the Balanced Scorecard framework. The adaptation for environmental control is the addition of a fifth perspective: the environmental perspective. The environmental perspective has five objectives relating to materials and energy usage, production and release of environmental residues, and recycling. Operational measures such as kilograms of hazardous materials and kilograms of recycled materials are developed for each objective. Activity-based management provides the operational system that produces environmental improvements. Nonvalue-added environmental activities and their root causes are identified. Designs for the environmental approaches are then used to eliminate these nonvalue-added activities. Ecoefficient improvements should produce favourable financial consequences that can be measured using trends in nonvalue-added environmental costs and trends in total environmental costs.

KEY TERMS

Ecoefficiency, 779

Environmental costs, 781

Environmental detection costs, 782

Environmental external failure costs, 782

Environmental internal failure costs, 782

Environmental prevention costs, 781

Full environmental costing, 786

Full private costing, 786

Impact analysis, 789

Improvement analysis, 789

Inventory analysis, 789

Life-cycle assessment, 788

Life-cycle cost assessment, 788

Private costs, 782

Product stewardship, 788

Realized external failure costs, 782

Sustainable development, 780

Unrealized external failure costs (societal costs), 782

REVIEW PROBLEMS

1. ENVIRONMENTAL COSTS

At the beginning of 2001, Kleaner Company initiated a program to improve its environmental performance. Efforts were made to reduce the production and emission of contaminating gaseous, solid, and liquid residues. By the end of the year, in an executive meeting, the company's environmental manager indicated that Kleaner had made significant improvement in its environmental performance, reducing the emission of contaminating residues of all types. The company's president was pleased with the reported success, but wanted an assessment of the financial consequences of the environmental improvements. To satisfy this request, the following financial data were collected for 2000 and 2001 (all changes in costs are a result of environmental improvements):

	2000	2001
Sales	$20,000,000	$20,000,000
Evaluating and selecting suppliers	0	600,000
Treating and disposing of toxic materials	1,200,000	800,000
Inspecting processes (environmental objective)	200,000	300,000
Land restoration (annual fund contribution)	1,600,000	1,200,000
Maintaining pollution equipment	400,000	300,000
Testing for contaminants	150,000	100,000

Required:

1. Classify the costs as prevention, detection, internal failure, and external failure.
2. Prepare an environmental cost report for the most recent year, with costs expressed as a percentage of sales (instead of operating costs).

Solution:

1. Prevention costs: evaluating and selecting suppliers; detection costs: testing for contaminants and inspecting processes; internal failure: maintaining pollution equipment and treating and disposing of toxic materials; and external failure: land restoration.

2.

Kleaner Company
Environmental Cost Report
For the Year Ended December 31, 2001

	Environmental Costs	Percentage of Sales
Prevention costs:		
Evaluating and selecting suppliers	$ 600,000	3.00%
Detection costs:		
Inspecting processes	$ 300,000	
Testing for contaminants	100,000	
	$ 400,000	2.00%
Internal failure costs:		
Treating and disposing of toxic materials	$ 800,000	
Maintaining pollution equipment	300,000	
	$1,100,000	5.50%
External failure costs:		
Land restoration	$1,200,000	6.00%
Total environmental costs	$3,300,000	16.50%

2. ASSIGNING ENVIRONMENTAL COSTS; LIFE-CYCLE COST ASSESSMENT; ENVIRONMENTAL COST CONTROL

Pierce Enterprises produces two types of fertilizers: Quikrichen and Longrichen. Pierce has recently received significant criticism from environmental groups, local residents, and the federal government concerning its environmental performance. Henry Hyde, president of Pierce, wants to know how the company's environmental activities affect the cost of each product. He believes that the main source of the environmental problems lies with Quikrichen but would like some evidence to support (or refute) this belief. The controller has assembled the following data to help answer this question:

	Quikrichen	Longrichen
Kilograms of fertilizer produced	1,000,000	2,000,000
Engineering hours (process design)	1,500	4,500
Kilograms of solid residues treated	30,000	10,000
Inspection hours (environmental)	10,000	5,000
Cleanup hours (local lake)	8,000	2,000

Additionally, the following environmental activity costs were reported:

Designing process	$150,000
Treating residues	600,000
Inspecting process	120,000
Cleaning up lake	200,000

Required:

1. Calculate the environmental cost per kilogram of fertilizer for each product.
2. Based on the calculations in Requirement 1, which product appears to be the most environmentally harmful?
3. Would life-cycle cost assessment provide stronger evidence for the environmental suitability of each product? Explain.
4. Explain how a strategic-based responsibility accounting system can be used to help improve Pierce's performance.

Solution:

1. First, calculate activity rates as follows:

Designing process	$150,000/6,000 = $25 per engineering hour
Treating residues	$600,000/40,000 = $15 per kilogram of residue
Inspecting process	$120,000/15,000 = $8 per inspection hour
Cleaning up lake	$200,000/10,000 = $20 per cleanup hour

Second, use rates to assign environmental costs and calculate unit environmental costs:

	Quikrichen
$25 × 1,500	$ 37,500
$15 × 30,000	450,000
$8 × 10,000	80,000
$20 × 8,000	160,000
Total	$ 727,500
	÷ 1,000,000
Unit cost per kilogram	$ 0.7275

	Longrichen
$25 × 4,500	$ 112,500
$15 × 10,000	150,000
$8 × 5,000	40,000
$20 × 2,000	40,000
Total	$ 342,500
	÷ 2,000,000
Unit cost per kilogram	$ 0.17125

2. As measured by the environmental cost per unit, Quikrichen is the product causing the most environmental damage, confirming the president's beliefs.
3. Life-cycle assessment has three steps: inventory analysis, impact analysis, and improvement analysis. Of the three steps, the first two are concerned with identifying the materials and energy requirements, environmental releases, and the environmental effects of competing process and product designs (over the life cycle of the products). Thus, a life-cycle assessment provides a more comprehensive analysis of environmental effects than the environmental cost per unit does (unless the cost per unit is a *life-cycle* environmental cost per unit).
4. The environmental perspective (from the Balanced Scorecard framework) can improve environmental performance by translating an environmental improvement strategy into operational objectives, measures, targets, and initiatives. For example, consider the five core environmental objectives. These objectives, if followed, will reduce the amounts of materials and energy used (including hazardous materials) and will also reduce residues released. Furthermore, the

environmental perspective is tied to the other four perspectives of the Balanced Scorecard. Thus, it is explicitly recognized that improving environmental performance means that capabilities, processes, customers, and financial consequences must be considered.

QUESTIONS FOR WRITING AND DISCUSSION

1. Explain why firms have an increased interest in environmental costing.

2. What is ecoefficiency?

3. What are the six incentives, or causes, for ecoefficiency?

4. What is an environmental cost?

5. What are the four categories of environmental costs? Define each category.

6. What is the difference between a realized external failure (environmental) cost and an unrealized external failure (societal) cost?

7. What does full environmental costing mean? full private costing?

8. Explain how functional-based costing assigns environmental costs to products. What are the problems with this approach?

9. Explain how activity-based costing assigns environmental costs to products.

10. What information is communicated by the unit environmental cost of a product?

11. What is life-cycle assessment?

12. What are the environmentally important life-cycle stages of a product?

13. Define the three steps of life-cycle assessment.

14. How can life-cycle costing improve life-cycle assessment?

15. What is the justification for adding an environmental perspective to the Balanced Scorecard?

16. What are the five core objectives of the environmental perspective?

17. Why is minimizing the use of raw materials an environmental issue?

18. What are some possible performance measures for the objective of minimizing the release of residues?

19. Do you agree that all environmental failure activities are nonvalue-added activities? Explain.

20. What is the meaning of "design for the environment"? What is its role in activity-based management of environmental activities?

21. Describe the possible value of financial measures of environmental performance. Give several examples.

EXERCISES

17–1

Ecoefficiency and Sustainable Development

LO1

There are two views often expounded relative to the environment: (1) greater production means greater pollution (economic and ecological considerations are incompatible), and (2) the state (federal and provincial governments) has the exclusive responsibility to solve environmental problems and see that sustainable development is supported.

Required:

1. Explain why the first view is more of a myth than a reality. In offering this explanation, give explicit reasons for your position.
2. What is sustainable development? Should the state have exclusive environmental responsibility for solving environmental problems and ensuring sustainable development? If not, what role should it play?

17–2

Classification of Environmental Costs

LO1

Classify the following environmental activities as prevention costs, detection costs, internal failure costs, or external failure costs. For external failure costs, classify the costs as societal or private. Also, label as "SD" those activities that are compatible with sustainable development.

1. A company takes actions to reduce the amount of material in its packages.
2. After its useful life, a soft-drink producer returns the activated carbon used for purifying water for its beverages to the supplier. The supplier reactivates the carbon for a second use in nonfood applications. As a consequence, many tonnes of material are prevented from entering landfills.
3. An evaporator system is installed to treat wastewater and to collect usable solids for other uses.
4. The inks used to print snack packages (for chips) contain heavy metals.
5. Processes are inspected to ensure compliance with environmental standards.
6. Delivery boxes are used five times and then recycled. This prevents 50 million kilograms of cardboard from entering landfills and saves 2 million trees per year.
7. Scrubber equipment is installed to ensure that air emissions are less than the level permitted by law.
8. Local residents are incurring medical costs from illnesses caused by air pollution from automobile exhaust pollution.
9. As part of implementing an environmental perspective for the Balanced Scorecard, environmental performance measures are developed.
10. Because of liquid and solid residues being discharged into a local lake, it is no longer fit for swimming, fishing, and other recreational activities.
11. To reduce energy consumption, magnetic ballasts are replaced with electronic ballasts, and more efficient light bulbs and lighting sensors are installed. As a result, 2.3 million kilowatt-hours of electricity are saved per year.
12. Because of a legal settlement, a chemical company must spend $20,000,000 to clean up contaminated soil.
13. A soft-drink company uses the following practice: in all bottling plants, packages damaged during filling are collected and recycled (glass, plastic, and aluminum).
14. Products are inspected to ensure that the gaseous emissions produced during operation follow legal and company guidelines.
15. Costs are incurred to operate pollution control equipment.
16. An internal audit is conducted to verify that environmental policies are being followed.

17–3

Environmental Cost Report

LO1

Spreadsheet

At the end of 2001, Kingston Chemicals began to implement an environmental quality management program. As a first step, it identified the following costs for the year just ended in its accounting records as environment-related:

	2001
Inefficient materials usage	$200,000
Treating and disposing of toxic waste	800,000
Cleanup of chemically contaminated soil	300,000
Testing for contamination	100,000
Operating pollution control equipment	140,000
Maintaining pollution control equipment	60,000
Performing environmental studies	20,000
Verifying supplier environmental performance	10,000
Training (environment-related)	12,500

Required:

1. Prepare an environmental cost report by category. Assume that total operating costs are $10,000,000.

2. Calculate the relative distribution percentages for each environmental cost category (the percentage of the total environmental cost represented by each category). Comment on the distribution.
3. Suppose that the newly hired environmental manager examines the report and makes the following comment: "This report understates the total environmental costs. It fails to consider the costs that we are imposing on the local community. For example, we have polluted the river and lake so much that swimming and fishing are no longer possible. I have heard rumblings from the local citizens, and I'll bet that we will be facing a big cleanup bill in a few years."

Assume that subsequent to the comment, engineering estimates that cleanup costs for the river and lake will amount to $1,000,000, assuming that the cleanup is required within five years. To pay for the cleanup, annual contributions of $175,000 will be invested with the expectation that the fund will grow to $1,000,000 by the end of the fifth year. Assume also that the loss of recreational opportunities is costing the local community $400,000 per year. How would this information alter the report in Requirement 1?

17–4

Environmental Cost Assignment

LO2

Spreadsheet

Lethbridge Chemical produces a number of chemical products, two of which are a dyestuff intermediate and an adhesive for rubber. The controller and environmental manager have identified the following environmental activities and costs associated with the two products.

	Dyestuff Intermediate	Rubber Adhesive
Kilograms produced	2,000,000	5,000,000
Packaging materials (kilograms)	600,000	300,000
Energy usage (kilowatt-hours)	200,000	100,000
Toxin releases (kilograms into air)	500,000	100,000
Pollution control (machine hours)	80,000	20,000
Costs of activities:		
Using packaging materials	$900,000	
Using energy	240,000	
Releasing toxins (fines)	120,000	
Operating pollution control equipment	280,000	

Required:

1. Calculate the environmental cost per kilogram for each product. Which of the two appears to cause the most degradation to the environment?
2. In which environmental category would you classify excessive use of materials and energy?
3. Suppose that the toxin releases cause health problems for those who live near the chemical plant. The costs, due to missed work and medical treatments, are estimated at $540,000 per year. How would assignment of these costs change the unit cost? Should they be assigned?

17–5

Environmental Costing, Ecoefficiency, and Competitive Advantage

LO1, LO2

Refer to the data in Exercise 17–4. Suppose that the CEO of Lethbridge decides to launch an environmental performance improvement program. First, efforts were made to reduce the amount of packaging. The demand for packaging materials was reduced by 10 percent. Second, a way was found to reuse the packaging materials. Usage of packaging materials changed from one time to two times. These two changes together saved $495,000 in packaging costs. Third, the manufacturing processes were redesigned to produce a reduced environmental load. The new processes were able to reduce emissions by 50 percent and private emission costs by 75 percent. The new processes also reduced the demand for energy by one-third. Energy costs were also reduced by the same amount. There was no change in the demand or cost of operating pollution control equipment.

The cost of implementing the changes was $201,000 (salaries of $120,000 for hiring two environmental engineers and $81,000 for treating the packaging materials so they can be reused). Engineering hours used for each process are 3,000 for the intermediate process and 1,000 for the adhesive process.

Required:

1. Calculate the new cost per kilogram for each product. Assume that the environmental reductions for each product are in the same proportions as the total reductions.
2. Calculate the net savings produced by the environmental changes for each product, in total and on a per-unit basis. Does this support the concept of ecoefficiency?
3. Classify the activities as prevention, detection, internal failure, or external failure. What does this tell you about the relationship between the various categories?
4. Describe how the environmental improvements can contribute to improving the firm's competitive position.

17–6

Life-Cycle Cost Assessment

LO3

Thorne Chemical Products Division produces surfactants, ingredients used in producing laundry detergents (surfactants are the components that help release soil from clothing). There are different types of surfactants possible, depending on the nature of the raw material input. One possibility, for example, is the usage of beef tallow as the primary raw material input. Another possibility is to use petrochemical stock as the primary raw material input. The primary input plus other inputs and energy sources are used to produce the surfactants. An inventory analysis produces the following for the production of surfactants:

	Petrochemical	Tallow
Raw materials (kilograms per 1,000 kilograms of surfactant)	900	850
Water usage (kilograms per 1,000 kilograms of surfactants used)	50	500
Energy usage (kilowatt-hours per 1,000 kilograms of surfactants):		
For production of raw materials	55	30
Transportation	10	20
Processing (production of surfactants)	60	60
Residues (emissions per 1,000 kilograms of surfactants):		
Particulates (air contaminant)	2	12
Hydrocarbons (air contaminant)	40	30
Dissolved solids (liquid contaminant)	6	4
Land contamination (solid residue)	80	160

The greater water usage for tallow relates to the requirement that water must be used to produce feed for beef. The cost per kilogram of petrochemical stock is $0.40. The cost per kilogram of tallow is $0.60. Water costs $0.50 per kilogram, and energy is $1.20 per kilowatt-hour. When air contaminants exceed 5 per 1,000 kilograms, pollution control equipment must be purchased and installed. The cost of acquiring and operating this equipment is $500 per five units of contaminants. Liquid contaminants are more trouble. If dumped into local streams over the product's life cycle, the costs are estimated to be $120 per unit of liquid contaminant. If a water treatment system is used, the cost is $60 per unit of contaminant. Finally, soil cleanup is estimated at $20 per unit of solid residue.

Required:

1. Assess the relative environmental impacts of the two approaches to producing surfactants using only operational environmental measures. Which of the two approaches would you recommend? Justify your choice.
2. Use the cost information to calculate an environmental impact cost per 1,000 kilograms of surfactants. Which of the two approaches would you now recommend? Does the life-cycle cost approach have limitations? Explain.

3.   Which parts of the life cycle described by the inventory analysis are controlled by the supplier? by the producer? What part of the inventory analysis is missing?

17–7

**Life-Cycle
Assessment:
Packaging and
Product Use; Impact
Analysis**

LO3

Derby Chips is an international producer of corn chips. At the end of 2001, Mary Hahn, president of Derby, appointed a task force to focus on the packaging and product use segments of its product's life cycle. Since customers consumed the contents of the package (if not consumed, the contents are biodegradable), the main concern was on the ability to conserve, recycle, and dispose of packaging materials. A new packaging proposal was being considered. A partial inventory analysis of the current packaging and the new packaging is given below.

	Current	New
Delivery boxes:		
Recycle potential	Low	High
Times used before disposal	1	5
Paper bags:		
Average package weight		
(in hundreds of grams)	2	1.5
Ink with heavy metals	Yes	No
Ultimate disposal:		
Safe for incineration	No	Yes

Upon seeing the inventory analysis, Mary was pleased to see the apparent environmental benefits of the new packaging. However, she wanted a more detailed analysis of the impact of the new packaging. In response to this request, environmental engineers and cost accounting provided the following estimates:

Annual packages produced and sold	200,000,000
Current demand for delivery boxes	140,000,000 kilograms
Recycle forecast	90% of delivery boxes used
Cost per 100 grams (package)	$0.02
Cost per kilogram (delivery boxes)	$0.60

The company's environmental engineers also indicated that in Europe and Japan, about 75 percent of the packaging will participate in waste–to–energy combustion programs for the generation of steam or electricity. In North America, only about 25 percent of the packaging will participate in such programs. As a footnote, environmental engineering also noted that saving 140 kilograms of paperboard is equivalent to saving one tree.

Required:

1.   Calculate the total kilograms of delivery boxes saved because of the new packaging. How much does this save in dollars? How many trees are saved because of recycling and reduction in demand for boxes? Because of recycling, how many kilograms of cardboard are diverted from landfills?
2.   Calculate the total kilograms of materials saved by reducing packaging (bag) weight. What are the dollar savings? Now assume that a design engineer has indicated that by reducing the packaging seal from 1 centimetre, the industry standard, to 0.5 centimetres, an additional 5 percent reduction in bag packaging can be achieved. How many kilograms of materials are saved? How many dollars are saved?
3.   Explain why the ultimate disposal qualities of packaging are important environmental considerations.
4.   Why emphasize saving a material that comes from a renewable resource (trees)?

17–8

Environmental Performance Measures and Core Objectives

LO4

Identify the *core environmental objective* associated with each of the following measures.

a. Tonnes of greenhouse gas emissions
b. Tonnes of hazardous waste delivered for off-site management
c. Kilograms of plastic recycled
d. British Thermal Units (BTUs)
e. Cars produced/Kilograms of steel used
f. Percentage of vehicles powered by propane gas
g. Percentage of recycled paper used (green purchasing)
h. Kilograms of toxic chemical releases
i. Hazardous waste cost/Total materials cost
j. Kilograms of nonhazardous waste/Kilograms of materials issued
k. Percentage reduction in packaging materials
l. Kilograms of organic chemicals in effluents sent to local river
m. Percentage of nonhazardous waste recycled

17–9

Cost Classification; Environmental Responsibility Accounting

LO1, LO4

At the beginning of 1999, Henderson Company, an international telecommunications company, embarked on an environmental improvement program. The company set a goal to have all its facilities ISO 14001 registered by 2002 (there are 30 facilities worldwide). It also adopted the Balanced Scorecard, with an environmental perspective added as a fifth perspective. To communicate the environmental progress made, management decided to issue, on a voluntary basis, an annual environmental progress report. Internally, the accounting department issued monthly progress reports and developed a number of measures that could be reported even more frequently to assess progress. Henderson also asked Deloitte & Touche, an international CA firm, to prepare an auditor's report that would comment on the reasonableness and fairness of Henderson's approach to assessing and measuring environmental performance.

At the end of 2002, the controller had gathered data that would be used in preparing the environmental progress report. A sample of the data collected is given below.

Year	Number of ISO 14001 Registrations	Energy Consumption (BTUs)*	Greenhouse Gases**
1999	3	3,000	40,000
2000	9	2,950	39,000
2001	15	2,900	38,000
2002	24	2,850	36,000

* in billions (measures electricity, natural gas, and heating oil usage)
** in tonnes

Required:

1. What is the justification for adding an environmental perspective to the Balanced Scorecard?
2. Henderson Company decided to do the following: obtain ISO 14001 registration, prepare an annual environmental progress report, prepare internal environmental progress reports, and procure an audit of the external report. How do these decisions fit within the Balanced Scorecard framework? To what environmental cost categories do these activities belong?
3. Using the data, prepare a bar graph for each of the three environmental variables provided (registrations, energy, and greenhouse gases). Comment on the progress made on these three dimensions. To which core objectives do each of the three measures relate?

17–10

Environmental
Responsibility
Accounting; Cost
Trends

LO4

Refer to Exercise 17–9. As part of its environmental cost-reporting system, Henderson tracks its total environmental costs. Consider the cost and sales data given below.

Year	Total Environmental Costs	Sales Revenue
1999	$30,000,000	$250,000,000
2000	25,000,000	250,000,000
2001	22,000,000	275,000,000
2002	19,250,000	275,000,000

Required:

1. Prepare a bar graph for environmental costs expressed as a percentage of sales. Assuming that environmental performance has improved, explain why environmental costs have decreased.

2. Normalize energy consumption by expressing it as a percentage of sales. Now prepare a bar graph for energy. Comment on the progress made in reducing energy consumption. How does this compare with the conclusion that would be reached using a measure of progress that has not been normalized? Which is the best approach? Explain.

PROBLEMS

17–11

Cost Classification;
Ecoefficiency;
Strategic
Environmental
Objectives

LO1, LO4

The following items are listed in an environmental financial statement (issued as part of an environmental progress report):

Environmental Benefits—savings, income, and cost avoidance:

- Ozone-depleting substances cost reductions
- Hazardous waste disposal cost reductions
- Hazardous waste material cost reductions
- Nonhazardous waste disposal cost reductions
- Nonhazardous waste material cost reductions
- Recycling income
- Energy conservation cost savings
- Packaging cost reductions

Environmental Costs:

- Corporate-level administrative costs
- Auditor fees
- Environmental engineering
- Facility professionals and programs
- Packaging professionals and programs for packaging reductions
- Pollution controls: operations and maintenance
- Pollution controls: depreciation
- Legal fees for cleanup claims, notices of violations (NOVs)
- Settlements of government claims
- Waste disposal
- Environmental taxes for packaging
- Remediation/cleanup: on-site
- Remediation/cleanup: off-site

Required:

1. Classify each item in the statement as prevention, detection, internal failure, or external failure. In classifying the items listed in the environmental savings cat-

egory, first classify the underlying cost item (for example, the cost of hazardous waste disposal). Next, think of how you would classify the cost of the activities that led to the cost reduction. That is, how would you classify the macro activity *reducing hazardous waste cost disposal?*

2. For each item in the environmental benefits category, indicate a possible measure or measures and the core strategic environmental objective that would be associated with the measure. Is it possible that a measure may be associated with more than one objective? Explain.

3. Assuming ecoefficiency, what relationship would you expect to observe over time between the environmental benefits category and the environmental cost category?

17–12

Environmental
Financial Reporting;
Ecoefficiency;
Improving
Environmental
Performance
LO1, LO4

Refer to 17–11. In the Environmental Benefits Section of the report, three types of benefits are listed: savings, income, and cost avoidance. Now consider the following data for selected items over a four-year period:

Year	Engineering Design Costs	Cost of Ozone-Depleting Substances
1999	$100,000	$1,800,000
2000	800,000	1,200,000
2001	400,000	800,000
2002	50,000	200,000

The engineering design costs were incurred to redesign the production processes and products. Redesign of the product allowed the substitution of a raw material that produced less ozone-depleting substances. Modifications in the design of the processes also accomplished the same objective. Because of the improvements, the company was able to reduce the demand for pollution control equipment (with its attendant depreciation and operating costs) and avoid fines and litigation costs. All of the savings generated in a given year represent costs avoided for future years. The engineering costs are investments in design projects. Once the results of the project are realized, design costs can be reduced to lower levels. However, since some ongoing design activity is required for maintaining the system and improving it as needed, the environmental engineering cost will not be reduced lower than the $50,000 reported in 2001.

Required:

1. Prepare a partial environmental financial statement, divided into benefit and cost sections for 2000, 2001, and 2002.

2. Evaluate and explain the outcomes. Does this result support or challenge ecoefficiency? Explain.

17–13

Environmental
Financial Report
LO1

Given below are the environmental cost reports for 2000, 2001, and 2002 for the communications products division of Kartel Company, a telecommunications company. In 2000, Kartel committed itself to a continuous environmental improvement program, which was implemented throughout the company.

Environmental Activity	2000	2001	2002
Disposing of hazardous waste	$200,000	$150,000	$ 50,000
Measuring contaminant releases	10,000	100,000	70,000
Releasing air contaminants	500,000	400,000	250,000
Producing scrap (nonhazardous)	175,000	150,000	125,000
Operating pollution equipment	260,000	200,000	130,000
Designing processes and products	50,000	300,000	100,000
Using energy	180,000	162,000	144,000
Training employees (environmental)	10,000	20,000	40,000
Remediation (cleanup)	400,000	300,000	190,000
Inspecting processes	0	100,000	80,000

At the beginning of 2002, Kartel began a new program of recycling nonhazardous scrap. The effort produced recycling income totalling $25,000. The marketing vice-president and the environmental manager estimated that annual sales revenue had increased $200,000 since 2000 because of an improved public image relative to environmental performance. The company's finance department also estimated that Kartel saved $80,000 in 2002 because of reduced finance and insurance costs, all attributable to improved environmental performance. All reductions in environmental costs from 2000 to 2002 are attributable to improvement efforts. Furthermore, any reductions represent ongoing savings.

Required:

1. Prepare an environmental financial statement for 2002 (for the communications products division). In the cost section, classify environmental costs by category (prevention, detection, and so on.).
2. Evaluate the changes in environmental performance.

17–14

Assignment of Environmental Costs

LO2

Refer to 17–13. In 2000, Jack Carter, Kartel's president, requested that environmental costs be assigned to the two major products produced by the company. He felt that knowledge of the environmental product costs would help guide the design decisions that would be necessary to improve environmental performance. The products represent two different models of a cellular phone (Model XA2 and Model KZ3). The models use different processes and materials. To assign the costs, the following data were gathered for 2000:

Activity	Model XA2	Model KZ3
Disposing of hazardous waste (tonnes)	20	180
Measuring contaminant releases (transactions)	1,000	4,000
Releasing air contaminants (tonnes)	25	225
Producing scrap (kilograms of scrap)	25,000	25,000
Operating pollution equipment (hours)	120,000	400,000
Designing processes and products (hours)	1,500	500
Using energy (BTUs)	600,000	1,200,000
Training employees (hours)	50	50
Remediation (labour hours)	5,000	15,000

During 2000, Kartel's communications products division produced 200,000 units of Model XA2 and 300,000 units of Model KZ3.

Required:

1. Using the activity data, calculate the environmental cost per unit for each model. How will this information be useful?
2. Upon examining the cost data produced in Requirement 1, an environmental engineer made the following suggestions: (1) substitute a new plastic for a raw material that appeared to be the source of much of the hazardous waste (the new material actually cost less than the contaminating material it would replace); (2) redesign the processes to reduce the amount of air contaminants produced.

   As a result of the first suggestion, by 2002, the amount of hazardous waste produced had diminished to 50 tonnes—10 tonnes for Model XA2 and 40 tonnes for Model KZ3. The second suggestion reduced the contaminants released by 50 percent by 2002 (15 tonnes for Model XA2 and 110 tonnes for Model KZ3). The need for pollution control equipment also diminished, and the hours required for producing Model XA2 and Model KZ3 were reduced to 60,000 and 200,000, respectively. Calculate the unit cost reductions for the two models associated with the actions and outcomes described (assume the same production as in 2000). Do you think the efforts to reduce the environmental cost per unit were economically justified? Explain.

17–15

Life-Cycle Assessment

LO3

Thomas Manufacturing produces automobile components used in automobile assembly. One of its divisions manufactures automotive front-end pieces. The division is currently considering two different designs: one using galvanized steel and the other using a polymer composite. Both products are considered equally durable. The main issue being considered is the environmental effects of the designs. To help in this assessment, an inventory analysis and associated cost information for the two designs are given below.

	Polymer	Galvanized Steel
Materials:		
Virgin materials (kilograms)	8	14
Reused production scrap (kilograms)	1	6
Energy:		
During production (kilowatt-hours/kilogram)	15	10
During product use (kilograms of petroleum used per year per unit)	66	110
Contaminants:		
Gaseous residues (kilograms per unit)	0.4	0.2
Solid residues (kilograms per unit)	0.6	2.0
Recycle potential:		
Incineration (kilograms)	7.0	—
Quantity to landfill (kilograms)	1.0	0.5
Recycled (kilograms)	—	8.5
Financial information:		
Cost per kilogram of raw materials	$ 30.00	$ 15.00
Cost per kilowatt-hour	0.50	0.50
Cost per kilogram of petroleum	0.70	0.70
Cost per kilogram of gaseous residue	100.00	100.00
Cost per kilogram of solid residue	40.00	50.00
Incineration benefits per unit	2.00	—
Recyclable benefits per unit	—	20.00

Required:

1. Using the operational measures, assess the environmental impact of each design. What other information would be useful?
2. Using the financial information, calculate an environmental life-cycle cost per unit. Discuss the strengths and weaknesses of this information.
3. Explain why a manager might wish to include product use and disposal information in the assessment of environmental performance. After all, these costs are not incurred by the company. For example, the petroleum consumption per year is a cost incurred by the end user.
4. Based on all the information, what recommendation would you make?

17–16

Environmental Responsibility Accounting; Balanced Scorecard

LO4

Ann Colson, president of Deerstone, Inc., a consumer products firm, has decided to follow an environmental improvement strategy. The goal is to increase profits by increasing revenues and decreasing environmental costs. Ann is convinced that revenues can be increased if she can improve the company's environmental image. Customers are demanding cleaner products, and her marketing manager has indicated that producing "greener" products would definitely lead to an increase in market share. Furthermore, Ann has recently returned from an environmental management seminar where she learned about ecoefficiency. She now believes that costs can be reduced while simultaneously improving environmental performance. She has two objectives in mind: reduce packaging, and reduce the production and release of contaminating residues. Ann has decided on the following actions to achieve the desired improvements:

1. Hire two environmental engineers to provide the capabilities needed to improve environmental performance. One engineer will be responsible for a new

packaging design and reduction process. The other will be given responsibility for redesigning products and processes with the objective of reducing the production of residues. Ann expects these actions to reduce packaging costs and pollution control costs.

2. All employees will be sent to several training seminars to learn about environmental management. They will then be empowered to make improvements in environmental performance (for example, by suggesting ways to reduce contaminants and packaging materials).

3. Once the processes and products are redesigned, she will participate in a third-party environmental certification program so that customers will be assured that the environmental improvements are valid.

Required:

1. Explain why adding an environmental perspective to the Balanced Scorecard is considered to be legitimate.

2. Express the environmental improvement strategy as a series of cause-and-effect relationships expressed as if–then statements.

3. Illustrate the strategy using a flow diagram like the one shown in Exhibit 15–15, with one important modification: add an environmental perspective (the flow diagram should then illustrate five perspectives). Place the environmental perspective in between the processes and customer perspectives.

17–17

Environmental Responsibility Accounting; Trend Measurement

LO1, LO4

During the past four years, Blanding Company has made significant efforts to improve its environmental performance. Two of the strategic objectives that have received considerable attention are those of minimizing hazardous materials and minimizing the release of liquid residues. Actually, there are two objectives associated with hazardous waste. First, the company wants to reduce the amount produced. Second, the company wants to shift its ways of dealing with hazardous waste from landfill and deep-well injections to such methods as incineration, treatment, and recycling. Kim Gladden, president of Blanding, has also required the accounting department to track and report on environmental progress. Internal and external environmental progress reports are prepared. Given below are data pertaining to the two strategic objectives that have been emphasized.

Hazardous waste objective (measure is in tonnes):

Year	Incinerated	Treated	Recycled	Landfilled	Injection	Total
1999	2,000	2,000	1,000	35,000	10,000	50,000
2000	4,000	2,000	2,000	30,000	10,000	48,000
2001	8,000	3,000	3,000	25,000	7,000	46,000
2002	15,000	3,000	3,500	15,000	3,500	40,000

RESEARCH ASSIGNMENT

17–18

Cybercase

LO1, LO2, LO3

A number of firms voluntarily disclose environmental information. Many of these firms are listed at **http://www.greenbiz.com/corpweb.cfm.** Among those listed are PepsiCo, McDonald's, and Baxter. PepsiCo reports some interesting environmental activities. Access this site, select a sample of these firms, and read their environmental disclosures. See how many of the following questions you can answer:

1. How much has been saved due to environmental actions? (Try Baxter.)
2. Describe the packaging reduction efforts and the resulting savings (savings can be expressed in nonfinancial terms).
3. Describe the recycling activities both for their own products as well as for the materials they receive from suppliers.
4. How much reduction in contaminating residues has been reported?
5. Can you find firms that use bar graphs and pie charts to describe their environmental performance?
6. What kinds of performance measures are being used? Can you relate these to the core strategic objectives discussed in this chapter?
7. What reasons do they offer for providing environmental information?
8. How do the environmental reports compare? Select a sample of six to eight reports, and comment on the different approaches. Which report did you like best and why?

17–19

Cybercase

LO2, LO4

Some might argue that environmental reporting is a form of signalling. By voluntarily disclosing environmental information, these firms are indicating that they are superior performers. Go to the same Web site listed in Research Assignment 17–18, and select two or three firms with extensive environmental disclosures. Now go to the EDGAR database[37] and find firms that are in the same industry but that do not disclose environmental performance. Compare the economic performance of the firms with environmental disclosure with that of those with no environmental disclosure. Do you find any evidence that the environmental firms are superior performers?

37. According to **http://www.sec.gov/edaux/wedgar.htm,** "EDGAR," the Electronic Data Gathering, Analysis, and Retrieval system, performs automated collection, validation, indexing, acceptance, and forwarding of submissions by companies and other who are required by [U.S.] law to file forms with the U.S. Securities and Exchange Commission (SEC). Its primary purpose is to increase the efficiency and fairness of the securities market for the benefit of investors, corporations, and the economy by accelerating the receipt, acceptance, dissemination, and analysis of time-sensitive corporate information filed with the agency" (see **http://www.sec.gov/edgarhp.htm**).

CHAPTER 18

Performance Evaluation in the Decentralized Firm, and Transfer Pricing

Learning Objectives

After studying Chapter 18, you should be able to:

1. Define responsibility accounting, and describe four types of responsibility centres.

2. Explain why firms choose to decentralize.

3. Compute and explain return on investment (ROI) and economic value added (EVA).

4. Discuss methods of evaluating and rewarding managerial performance.

5. Explain the role of transfer pricing in a decentralized firm.

Scenario

Ted Munsen was worried. He had founded Technoco in the middle 1990s to manufacture a scrubbing device that cleaned airborne contaminants from industrial smokestacks. Back then, the company consisted of Ted and a few other young engineers who were excited by the potential for the device. They routinely worked 16-hour days, 7 days a week, to see their vision turn into reality. The hard work paid off; the scrubbing device was efficient and effective. Profits at Technoco soared. Through the years, Ted and his associates had purchased several other loosely related companies in the pollution cleanup field, and

had gone public with the conglomerate just a few years ago. Now, as CEO of an established company, Ted faced new problems. He met with Steve Scully, head of Canadian operations, to discuss them.

Ted: "Steve, look at these projected financial statements. Our net income has increased at a barely noticeable rate. Our return on investment has actually declined from last year. Divisional managers are squabbling over transfer prices when they should be cooperating. What's happening here? I remember when working at this company meant something. We shared a vision. We were working not just for ourselves, but for a better

world. It may sound corny, but that vision sure kept me going through some pretty dark days."
Steve (chuckling): "Don't forget the dark nights! Look, Ted: we're older and larger, now; it's harder to keep that culture going when you're a multidivision company. I hardly know some of our newer managers, much less feel sure that we share the same values. What can you do? We just have to accept the inevitable, cut costs, or something. I don't know. What would Nortel, Bell Canada, GM, or IBM do?"
Ted: "I don't care what those companies would do—they have problems enough of their own. I also don't want to throw in the towel just yet. Surely we can struc-

ture an incentive program to get our managers moving in the same direction again, and have some fun doing it. I want you to do some research on management incentive plans. See what's out there; maybe some other company has faced this problem and solved It. Let's meet again on this matter in two weeks."

Two weeks later.

Steve: "Ted, I may have a solution to our problems. I spoke to a friend of mine at Thermo Electro. They make high-tech devices, such as very sensitive bomb and drug detectors, and remediation facilities for cleaning gasoline-contaminated soil. They're a lot like us—a great small company that grew like crazy. They had problems keeping their entrepreneurial spirit alive. They handed out stock options to motivate their managers, but it didn't seem to work. The R&D expenditures were crucial to long-term success, but were dragging down earnings. Anyway, they experimented with splitting up the company. In 1983, they sold 16 percent of one of their divisions, Thermedics. The man-

agers of Thermedics got 3 percent of the shares; it really turned them into entrepreneurs. It also raised more than $5 million."[1]

Ted: "So far, so good. But what happened to return on investment? And what about the other divisions? Did they resent the special deal Thermedics got?"

Steve: "No, the other managers have the same chance. The other Thermo Electro divisions compete to become the new spinoff. Now there are numerous spinoffs, including Thermo Fibertek (equipment and products for papermaking and recycling industries), Thermo TerraTech (industrial outsourcing and manufacturing support), Thermo Laser (maker of the SoftLight Laser hair removal system), and Thermo Cardiosystems (developer of cardiac support devices). Each one is traded publicly and has its own stock symbol. Possible spinoffs are not considered until the business shows the potential to grow 30 percent per year. Thermo Electro has an average annual ROI of about 20 percent in its spinoffs."

Ted: "Sounds good! Let's go through these divisional financial

statements and see what we've got. Maybe we can apply some of Thermo Electro's lessons to our own situation."

1. Jennifer Reese, "How to Grow Big by Staying Small," *Fortune* (28 December 1992): pp. 50, 54.

Questions to Think About

1. What problems does Ted face as the CEO of a large, divisionalized company that he did not face as the head of a small company?

2. What values did Steve and Ted share in the company's early days? What values do you suppose that the division managers hold now? Are these values the same or different?

3. How do managerial values affect profit? Should they affect profit at all?

4. What is a management incentive plan? Can you think of a plan or plans that would help Ted and Steve move their managers in the directions they want?

RESPONSIBILITY ACCOUNTING

Objective 1

Define responsibility accounting, and describe four types of responsibility centres.

In general, a company is organized along the lines of responsibility. The traditional organizational chart, with its pyramid shape, illustrates the lines of responsibility flowing from the CEO down through the vice-presidents to middle- and lower-level managers. As the opening scenario indicates, when organizations increase in size, these lines of responsibility become longer and more numerous. The structure becomes cumbersome. Contemporary practice is moving toward a flattened hierarchy. This structure, emphasizing teams, is consistent with decentralization. Nelson Thomson Learning (a division of International Thomson Publishing), for example, eliminated much of its previous departmental organization and developed cross-functional teams. As a result, it reduced its levels of hierarchy. GE Capital, as another example, is essentially a group of smaller businesses. The head of each sub-business is expected to stay in his or her market area—not at headquarters. If a new opportunity arises, it is approached as a new business; and when it grows to $25 million in earnings, it separates from its creator group.[2]

2. John Curran, "GE Capital: Jack Welch's Secret Weapon," *Fortune* (November 10, 1997): pp. 116–134.

There is a strong link between the structure of an organization and the organization's responsibility accounting system. Ideally, the responsibility accounting system mirrors and supports the organization's structure.

Types of Responsibility Centres

As a firm grows, top management typically creates areas of responsibility, known as responsibility centres, and assigns subordinate managers to those areas. A **responsibility centre** is a segment of the business whose manager is accountable for specified sets of activities. **Responsibility accounting** is a system that measures the results for each responsibility centre according to the information managers need to operate their centres. There are four major types of responsibility centres:

1. **Cost centre**: A responsibility centre in which a manager is financially responsible only for costs.
2. **Revenue centre**: A responsibility centre in which a manager is financially responsible only for sales.
3. **Profit centre**: A responsibility centre in which a manager is financially responsible for both revenues and costs.
4. **Investment centre**: A responsibility centre in which a manager is financially responsible for revenues, costs, and investments.

The way that responsibility centres are assigned mirrors the actual situation and the type of information available to the manager. Exhibit 18–1 displays these centres along with the type of information they need to manage their operations.

A production department within the factory, such as assembly or finishing, is an example of a cost centre. The supervisor of a production department controls manufacturing costs but does not set price or make marketing decisions. Therefore, the production department supervisor is evaluated on the basis of how well costs are controlled.

The marketing department manager sets price and projected sales. Therefore, the marketing department may be evaluated as a revenue centre. Direct costs of the marketing department and overall sales are the responsibility of the sales manager.

In some companies, plant managers are given the responsibility for manufacturing and marketing their products. These plant managers control both costs and revenues, putting them in control of a profit centre. Operating income would be an important performance measure for profit centre managers.

Finally, divisions are often cited as examples of investment centres. In addition to having control over cost and pricing decisions, divisional managers have the power to make investment decisions, such as plant closings and openings, and decisions to keep or drop a product line. As a result, both operating income and some type of return on investment are important performance measures for investment centre managers.

It is important to realize that while the responsibility centre manager has responsibility for only that centre's activities, decisions made by that manager can affect other responsibility centres. For example, the sales force at a floor care products firm

Exhibit 18–1

Types of Responsibility Centres and Accounting Information Used to Measure Performance

	ACCOUNTING INFORMATION USED TO MEASURE PERFORMANCE			
	Cost	Sales	Capital Investment	Other
Cost centre	X			
Revenue centre	Direct cost only	X		
Profit centre	X	X		
Investment centre	X	X	X	X

routinely offers customers price discounts at the end of the month. Sales increase dramatically, and that is good for revenue and the sales force. However, the factory is forced to institute overtime shifts to keep up with demand; this increases the costs of the factory as well as the cost per unit of product.

The Role of Information and Accountability

Information is the key to appropriately holding managers responsible for outcomes. For example, a production department manager is held responsible for departmental costs but not for sales. This is because the production department manager not only controls some of these costs, but knows and understands them. Any difference between actual and expected costs can best be explained at this level. Sales are the responsibility of the sales manager, again because this manager can best explain what is happening regarding price and quantity sold.

Responsibility also entails *accountability*. Accountability implies performance measurement, which means that actual outcomes are compared with expected or budgeted outcomes. This system of responsibility, accountability, and performance evaluation is often referred to as *responsibility accounting* because of the key role that accounting measures and reports play in the process. A key distinction must be made between responsibility and blame. For example, in 1991, Anne Busquet was the general manager of the Optima Card unit at Amercian Express when the company discovered that 5 of her 2,000 employees had deliberately hidden $24 million in losses on the Optima Card accounts. Busquet was held responsible and accountable (she lost her Optima job) despite the fact that she was not personally to blame. Basically, as manager, she was expected to be aware of what was going on in her shop. On a happier note, Busquet accepted the challenge of turning around American Express's merchandise services unit. She was made executive vice-president for consumer-card marketing at American Express.[3] Now, she is the president of American Express Relationship Services, responsible for the company's Fee Services, Merchandise Services, Telecommunications Service, and Educational Finance Group.[4]

DECENTRALIZATION

Objective 2

Explain why firms choose to decentralize.

Firms with multiple responsibility centres usually choose one of two decision-making approaches to manage their diverse and complex activities: *centralized* or *decentralized*. In **centralized decision making**, decisions are made at the very top level, and lower-level managers are charged with implementing these decisions. On the other hand, **decentralized decision making** allows managers at lower levels to make and implement key decisions pertaining to their areas of responsibility. **Decentralization** is the practice of delegating decision-making authority to the lower levels.

Organizations range from highly centralized to strongly decentralized. Most firms fall somewhere in between, with the majority tending toward decentralization. The reasons for the popularity of decentralization and the ways in which a company may choose to decentralize are discussed next.

Reasons for Decentralization

There are many reasons to explain why firms decide to decentralize, including (1) ease of gathering and using local information; (2) focusing of central management; (3) training and motivating segment managers; and (4) enhanced competition through exposing segments to market forces.

3. Patricia Sellers, "So You Fail. Now Bounce Back!" *Fortune* (1 May 1995): pp. 48–66.

4. This is from a Web page announcement by Administaff, Inc., of Busquet's election to its Board of Directors (**www.administaff.com/Press/PR-031098.html**).

Gathering and Using Local Information   The quality of decisions is affected by the quality of information available. As a firm grows in size and operates in different markets and regions, central management may not understand local conditions. Lower-level managers, however, who are in contact with immediate operating conditions (such as the strength and nature of local competition, the nature of the local labour force, and so on) have access to this information. As a result, local managers are often in a position to make better decisions. For example, Kmart practises micromarketing by allowing individual store managers to decide what goods to stock. The result is that each Kmart store can differentiate to meet the needs of its local market. Thus, two stores only, 10 kilometres apart may stock very different items. This advantage of decentralization is particularly applicable to multinational corporations, where far-flung divisions may be operating in a number of different countries, subject to various legal systems and customs. (International issues in management accounting are discussed in Chapter 19.)

A second problem is information overload. In an organization that operates in diverse markets with hundreds or thousands of different products, no one person has all of the expertise and training needed to process and use the information.

Individuals with specialized skills are still needed. Rather than having different individuals at headquarters for every specialized area, why not let these individuals have direct responsibility in the field? For example, a manager with an engineering background may head a factory, while another manager with specialized skills in data analysis may be in charge of the computer centre.

In a centralized setting, time is needed to transmit the local information to headquarters and to transmit the decision back to the local unit. Furthermore, the two transmissions increase the probability that the manager responsible for implementing the decision might misinterpret the instructions. This decreases the effectiveness of the response. In a decentralized organization, where the local manager both makes and implements the decision, this problem does not arise.

Focusing of Central Management   By decentralizing the operating decisions, central management frees itself to engage in strategic planning and decision making. The organization's long-run survival should be of more importance to central management than its day-to-day operations.

Training and Motivating Managers   Organizations always need well-trained managers to replace higher-level managers who leave to take advantage of other opportunities. What better way to prepare a future generation of higher-level managers than by providing them with the opportunity to make significant decisions? These opportunities also enable top managers to evaluate local managers' capabilities. Those who make the best decisions are the ones who can be promoted.

Greater responsibility can produce more job satisfaction and motivate the local manager to exert greater effort. More initiative and more creativity may result. Of course, the extent to which the behavioural benefits can be realized depends to a large degree on how managers are evaluated and rewarded for their performance.

Enhanced Competition   In a highly centralized company, overall profit margins can mask inefficiencies within the various subdivisions. Large companies now find that they cannot afford to keep a noncompetitive division. One of the best ways to improve performance of a division or factory is to expose it more fully to market forces.[5] At Koch Industries, Inc., each unit is expected to act as an autonomous business unit, setting prices both externally and internally. Units whose services are not required by other Koch units will die on the vine.

5.   John W. Verity, "Deconstructing the Computer Industry," *Business Week* (23 November 1992): p. 92.

The Units of Decentralization

Decentralization is usually achieved by creating units called divisions. One way in which divisions are differentiated is by the types of goods or services produced. For example, divisions of PepsiCo include the Snack Ventures Europe division (a joint venture with General Mills), Frito-Lay, Inc., and Tropicana, as well as its flagship soft-drink division. These divisions are organized on the basis of product lines. Notice that some divisions depend on other divisions. For example, PepsiCo spun off its restaurant divisions to Tricon Global Restaurant (YUM). As a result, the cola you drink at Pizza Hut, Taco Bell, and KFC will be Pepsi—not Coke. In a decentralized setting, some interdependencies usually exist; otherwise, a company would merely be a collection of totally separate entities.

Divisions may also be created along geographic lines. For example, UAL, Inc. (parent of United Airlines) has a number of regional divisions: Asia/Pacific, Caribbean, European, Latin American, and North American. The presence of divisions spanning one or more regions creates the need for performance evaluation that can take into account differences in divisional environments.

A third way divisions differ is by the type of responsibility given to the divisional manager. Recall the four major types of responsibility centres: cost centres, revenue centres, profit centres, and investment centres. Investment centres represent the greatest degree of decentralization (followed by profit centres and finally by cost and revenue centres) because their managers have the freedom to make the greatest variety of decisions.

A recent Canadian study of 10 "excellent" companies found that in general, even though they were strongly centralized, there was "talk" about decentralization. Decentralization was found only in "circumscribed areas where delegated decision making occurred within narrow boundaries."[6] The study also concluded that although accountability was often decentralized, control essentially remained centralized.

Organizing divisions as responsibility centres creates the opportunity to control the divisions through the use of responsibility accounting. Control of cost or revenue centres is achieved by evaluating the efficiency and the effectiveness of divisional managers based on control of costs or sales. Profit centres are evaluated on the basis of income. Since performance reports and contribution income statements have been discussed elsewhere, this chapter will not go into the evaluation of managers of cost centres, revenue centres, or profit centres. The focus will be on the evaluation of managers of investment centres.

MEASURING THE PERFORMANCE OF INVESTMENT CENTRES

Objective 3

Compute and explain return on investment (ROI) and economic value added (EVA).

We need to make a distinction between the evaluation of investment centres and the evaluation of the managers who run them. The distinction is sometimes subtle, and often lost. Still, it is clear that a division can do well or poorly irrespective of the efforts of its manager. For this reason, a company tries to separate the evaluations. The evaluation of the segment is examined in this section; the evaluation of the manager is reserved for the section on measuring and rewarding the performance of managers.

Return on Investment

Divisions that are investment centres will have an income statement and a balance sheet. So could we simply rank the divisions on the basis of net income? Suppose, for example, that a company has two divisions—Alpha and Beta. Alpha's net income is $100,000, and Beta's is $200,000. Did Beta perform better than Alpha? What if Alpha

6. Tupper Cawsey, Gene Deszca, and Howard Teall, "Management Control Systems in Excellent Canadian Companies," *Issues Papers*, The Society of Management Accountants of Canada, 1994, 9.

used an investment of $500,000 to produce the contribution of $100,000, while Beta used an investment of $2 million to produce the $200,000 contribution? Does your response change? Clearly, relating the reported operating profits to the assets used to produce them is a more meaningful measure of performance.

One way to relate operating profits to assets employed is to compute the profit earned per dollar of investment. **Return on investment (ROI)** is the most common measure of performance for an investment centre. It can be defined as follows:

$$ROI = \text{Operating income/Average operating assets}$$

First, let's define terms. **Operating income** refers to earnings before interest and taxes. **Operating assets** are all assets acquired to generate operating income, including cash, receivables, inventories, land, buildings, and equipment. The figure for average operating assets is computed as follows:

$$\text{Average operating assets} = (\text{Beginning net book value} + \text{Ending net book value})/2$$

Opinions vary regarding how long-term assets (plant and equipment) should be valued (for example, gross book value versus net book value or historical cost versus current cost). Most firms use historical cost and net book value.[7]

Going back to our example, Alpha's ROI is 0.20 ($100,000/ $500,000), whereas Beta's ROI is only 0.10 ($200,000/$2,000,000). The formula for ROI is quick and easy to use. However, the decomposition of ROI into margin and turnover ratios gives additional information. Let's look at this possibility in more detail.

Margin and Turnover

A second formula for ROI is simply margin times turnover. Thus, the formula for ROI can also be expressed as follows:

$$ROI = \text{Margin} \times \text{Turnover}$$
$$= (\text{Operating income/Sales}) \times (\text{Sales/Average operating assets})$$

Suppose, for example, that Alpha had sales of $400,000. Margin would then be 0.25 ($100,000/$400,000), and turnover would be 0.80 ($400,000/$500,000). Alpha's ROI would still be 0.20 (0.25 × 0.80).

Margin is simply the ratio of operating income to sales. It expresses the portion of sales that is available for interest, taxes, and profit. **Turnover** is a different measure; it is found by dividing sales by average operating assets. The result shows how productively assets are being used to generate sales.

While both approaches yield the same ROI, the calculation of margin and turnover gives a manager valuable information. To illustrate this additional information, consider the data presented in Exhibit 18–2. The Electronics Division improved its ROI from 18 percent in 2000 to 20 percent in 2001. The Medical Supplies Division's ROI, however, dropped from 18 to 15 percent. A better picture of what caused the change in rates is revealed by computing the margin and turnover ratios for each division. These ratios are also presented in Exhibit 18–2.

Notice that the margins for both divisions dropped in 2001 from 2000. In fact, the divisions experienced the *same* percentage of decline (16.67 percent). A declining margin could be explained by increasing expenses, by competitive pressures (forcing a decrease in selling prices), or by both factors.

In spite of the declining margin, the Electronics Division was able to increase its rate of return. The reason is that the increase in turnover more than compensated for the decline in margin. One explanation for the increased turnover could be a deliberate policy to reduce inventories. (Notice that the average assets employed remained the same for the Electronics Division even though sales increased by $10 million.)

7. For a discussion of the relative merits of gross book value, see James S. Reese and William R. Cool, "Measuring Investment Centre Performance," *Harvard Business Review* (May–June 1978): pp. 28–46, 174–176.

Exhibit   18-2

Comparison of Divisional
Performance

COMPARISON OF ROI	Electronics Division	Medical Supplies Division
2000:		
Sales	$30,000,000	$117,000,000
Operating income	1,800,000	3,510,000
Average operating assets	10,000,000	19,500,000
ROI[a]	18%	18%
2001:		
Sales	$40,000,000	$117,000,000
Operating income	2,000,000	2,925,000
Average operating assets	10,000,000	19,500,000
ROI[a]	20%	15%

MARGIN AND TURNOVER COMPARISONS	Electronics Division		Medical Supplies Division	
	2000	2001	2000	2001
Margin[b]	6.0%	5.0%	3.0%	2.5%
Turnover[c]	× 3.0%	× 4.0%	× 6.0%	× 6.0%
ROI	18.0%	20.0%	18.0%	15.0%

[a] Operating income divided by average operating assets
[b] Operating income divided by sales
[c] Sales divided by average operating assets

The experience of the other division was less favourable. Because its turnover rate remained unchanged, its ROI dropped. This division, unlike the other one, could not overcome the decline in margin.

Advantages of ROI

At least three positive results stem from the use of ROI:

1. It encourages managers to focus on the relationship among sales, expenses, and investment, as should be the case for a manager of an investment centre.
2. It encourages managers to focus on cost efficiency.
3. It encourages managers to focus on operating asset efficiency.

These advantages are illustrated by the following three scenarios.

Focus on ROI Relationships Della Barnes, manager of the Plastics Division, is mulling over a suggestion from her marketing vice-president to increase the advertising budget by $100,000. The marketing vice-president is confident that this increase will boost sales by $200,000 and raise the contribution margin by $110,000. Della realizes that an additional $50,000 of operating assets will be needed to support this large an increase in sales. Currently, the division has sales of $2 million, net operating income of $150,000, and operating assets of $1 million.

If advertising increased by $100,000 and the contribution margin by $110,000, operating income would go up by $10,000 ($110,000 − $100,000). The ROI without the additional advertising is 15 percent ($150,000/$1,000,000). With the additional advertising and $50,000 investment in assets, the ROI would be 15.24 percent ($160,000/$1,050,000). Since ROI would be increased by the proposal, Della decides to authorize the increased advertising.

Focus on Cost Efficiency   Kyle Chugg, manager of Turner's Battery Division, groaned as he reviewed the projections for the last half of the current fiscal year. The recession was hurting his division's performance. Adding the projected operating income of $200,000 to the actual operating income of the first half produced expected annual earnings of $425,000. Kyle then divided the expected operating income by the division's average operating assets to obtain an expected ROI of 12.15 percent. "This is awful," muttered Kyle. "Last year our ROI was 16 percent. And I'm looking at a couple more bad years before business returns to normal. Something has to be done to improve our performance."

Kyle directed all operating managers to identify and eliminate nonvalue-added activities. As a result, lower-level managers found ways to reduce costs by $150,000 for the remaining half of the year. This reduction increased the annual operating income from $425,000 to $575,000, increasing ROI from 12.15 percent to 16.43 percent as a result. Interestingly, Kyle found that some of the reductions could be maintained after business returned to normal.

Focus on Operating Asset Efficiency   The Electronic Storage Division prospered during its early years. In the beginning, the division developed a new technology for mass storage of data; sales and return on investment were extraordinarily high. However, during the past several years, competitors had developed competing technology, and the division's ROI had plunged from 30 to 15 percent. Cost cutting had helped initially, but the fat had all been removed, making further improvements from cost reductions impossible. Moreover, any increase in sales was unlikely—competition was too stiff. The divisional manager searched for some way to increase the ROI by at least 3 to 5 percent. Only by raising the ROI so that it compared favourably to that of the other divisions could the division expect to receive additional capital for research and development.

The divisional manager initiated an intensive program to reduce operating assets. Most of the gains were made in the area of inventory reductions; however, one plant was closed because of a long-term reduction in market share. By installing a just-in-time purchasing and manufacturing system, the division was able to reduce its asset base without threatening its remaining market share. Finally, the reduction in operating assets meant that operating costs could be decreased still further. The end result was a 50 percent increase in the division's ROI, from 15 percent to more than 22 percent.

Disadvantages of the ROI Measure

Overemphasis on ROI can produce myopic behaviour. Two negative aspects associated with ROI are frequently mentioned.

1. It can produce a narrow focus on divisional profitability at the expense of profitability for the overall firm.
2. It encourages managers to focus on the short run at the expense of the long run.

These disadvantages are illustrated by the following two scenarios.

Narrow Focus on Divisional Profitability   A cleaning products division has the opportunity to invest in two projects for the coming year. The outlay required for each investment, the dollar returns, and the ROI are as follows:

	Project I	Project II
Investment	$10,000,000	$4,000,000
Operating income	1,300,000	640,000
ROI	13%	16%

The division currently earns ROI of 15 percent, with operating assets of $50 million and operating income on current investments of $7.5 million. The division has approval to request up to $15 million in new investment capital. Corporate head-quarters requires that all investments earn at least 10 percent (this rate represents the corporation's cost of acquiring the capital). Any capital not used by a division is invested by headquarters, and it earns exactly 10 percent.

The divisional manager has four alternatives: (1) invest in Project I, (2) invest in Project II, (3) invest in both Projects I and II, or (4) invest in neither project. The divisional ROI was computed for each alternative.

	Alternatives			
	Select Project I	Select Project II	Select Both Projects	Select Neither Project
Operating income	$ 8,800,000	$ 8,140,000	$ 9,440,000	$ 7,500,000
Operating assets	60,000,000	54,000,000	64,000,000	50,000,000
ROI	14.67%	15.07%	14.75%	15.00%

The divisional manager chose to invest only in Project II, since it would boost ROI from 15 percent to 15.07 percent.

While the manager's choice maximized divisional ROI, it actually cost the company profit. If Project I had been selected, the company would have earned $1.3 million. Because Project I was not selected, the $10 million in capital was invested at 10 percent, earning only $1 million (0.10 × $10,000,000). The single-minded focus on divisional ROI, then, cost the company $300,000 in profits ($1,300,000 − $1,000,000).

Encourages Short-Run Optimization Ruth Lunsford, manager of a small tools division, was displeased with her division's performance during the first three quarters. Given the expected income for the fourth quarter, the ROI for the year would be 13 percent, at least two percentage points below where she had hoped to be. Such an ROI might not be strong enough to justify the early promotion she wanted. With only three months left, drastic action was needed. Increasing sales for the last quarter was unlikely. Most sales were booked at least two to three months in advance. Emphasizing extra sales activity would benefit next year's performance. What was needed were some ways to improve this year's performance.

After careful thought, Ruth decided to take the following actions:

1. Lay off five of the highest-paid salespeople.
2. Cut the advertising budget for the fourth quarter by 50 percent.
3. Delay all promotions within the division for three months.
4. Reduce the preventive maintenance budget by 75 percent.
5. Use cheaper raw materials for fourth-quarter production.

In the aggregate, these steps would reduce expenses, increase income, and raise the ROI to about 15.2 percent.

While Ruth's actions increase the profits and ROI in the short run, they have some negative long-run consequences. Laying off the highest-paid (and possibly the best) salespeople may harm the division's future sales-generating capabilities. Future sales could also be hurt by cutting back on advertising and by using cheaper raw materials. Delaying promotions could hurt employee morale, which could, in turn, lower productivity and future sales. Finally, reducing preventive maintenance will likely increase downtime and decrease the life of the productive equipment.

Economic Value Added

To compensate for ROI's tendency to discourage investments that are profitable for the company but that lower a division's ROI, some companies have adopted an alternative performance measure known as *economic value added (EVA)*. **Economic value added (EVA)** is after-tax operating profit minus the total annual cost of capital.

If EVA is positive, the company is creating wealth. If it is negative, then the company is destroying capital. Over the long term, only those companies creating capital, or wealth, can survive.

EVA is a dollar figure, not a percentage rate of return. However, it does bear a resemblance to rates of return such as ROI, because it links net income (return) to capital employed. The key feature of EVA is its emphasis on *after-tax* operating profit and the *actual* cost of capital. Other return measures may use accounting book value numbers, which may or may not represent the true cost of capital. Residual income, for example, typically uses a minimum expected rate of return. Investors like EVA because it relates profit to the amount of resources needed to achieve it. A number of companies have been evaluated on the basis of EVA. For example, Coca-Cola had economic value added of $2,442 million in 1997. Similarly, General Electric, Microsoft, and Merck experienced significant increases in wealth for 1997[8] according to EVA. Other companies, however, showed decreases in wealth for 1997 according to EVA calculations. These included IBM, Boeing, Disney, and Dupont.

Calculating EVA   EVA is after-tax operating income minus the dollar cost of capital employed. The equation for EVA is expressed as follows:

$$\text{EVA} = \text{After-tax operating income} - (\text{Weighted average cost of capital} \times \text{Total capital employed})$$

The difficulty faced by most companies is computing the cost of capital employed. There are two steps involved: (1) determine the weighted average cost of capital (a percentage figure), and (2) determine the total dollar amount of capital employed.

To calculate the weighted average cost of capital, the company must identify all sources of invested funds. Typical sources are borrowing and equity (stock issued). Any borrowed money usually has an interest rate attached, and that rate can be adjusted for its tax deductibility. For example, if a company has issued 10-year bonds at an annual interest rate of 8 percent and the tax rate is 40 percent, then the after-tax cost of the bonds is 4.8 percent $(0.08 - [0.4 \times 0.08])$. Equity is handled differently. The cost of equity financing is the opportunity cost to investors. Over time, stockholders have received an average return that is 6 percentage points higher than the return on long-term government bonds. If these bond rates are about 6 percent, then the average cost of equity is 12 percent. Riskier stocks command a higher return, while more stable and less risky stocks bring in a somewhat lower return. Finally, the proportionate share of each method of financing is multiplied by its percentage cost and summed to yield a weighted average cost of capital.

Suppose that a company has two sources of financing: $2 million of long-term bonds paying 9 percent interest and $6 million of common stock, which is considered to be of average risk. If the company's tax rate is 40 percent and the rate of interest on long-term government bonds is 6 percent, the company's weighted average cost of capital is computed as follows:

	Amount	Percent	× After-Tax Cost =	Weighted Cost
Bonds	$2,000,000	0.25	0.09(1 − 0.4) = 0.054	0.0135
Equity	6,000,000	0.75	0.06 + 0.06 = 0.120	0.0900
Total	$8,000,000			0.1035

Thus, the company's weighted average cost of capital is 10.35 percent.

The second data point necessary to calculate the dollar cost of capital employed is the amount of capital employed. Clearly, the amount paid for buildings, land, and machinery must be included. However, other expenditures meant to have a long-term payoff, such as research and development, employee training, and so on,

---

8. Richard Teitelbaum, "America's Greatest Wealth Creators," *Fortune* (November 10, 1997): pp. 265–276.

should also be included. Despite the fact that the latter are classified by GAAP as expenses, EVA is an internal management accounting measure, and they can be thought of as the investments that they truly are.

EVA Example Suppose that Mahalo, Inc., had after-tax operating income last year of $1,700,000. Three sources of financing were used by the company: $2 million of mortgage bonds paying 8 percent interest, $3 million of unsecured bonds paying 10 percent interest, and $10 million in common stock, which was considered to be no more or less risky than other stocks. Mahalo pays a marginal tax rate of 40 percent. The after-tax cost of the mortgage bonds is 0.048 ([1 − 0.4] × 0.08). The after-tax cost of the unsecured bonds is 0.06 ([1 − 0.4] × 0.10). There are no tax adjustments for equity, so the cost of the common stock is 12 percent (6 percent return on long-term treasury bonds plus the 6 percent average premium). The weighted average cost of capital is computed by taking the proportion of capital from each source of financing and multiplying it by its cost. The weighted average cost of capital for Mahalo is computed as follows:

	Amount	Percent	×	After-Tax Cost	=	Weighted Cost
Mortgage bonds	$ 2,000,000	0.133		0.048		0.006
Unsecured bonds	3,000,000	0.200		0.060		0.012
Common stock	10,000,000	0.667		0.120		0.080
Total	$15,000,000					
Weighted average cost of capital						0.098

When the weighted average cost of capital is multiplied by total capital employed, the dollar cost of capital is known. For Mahalo, the amount of capital employed is the same amount as long-term capital—$15 million—so the cost of capital is $1,470,000 (0.098 × $15 million).

Mahalo's EVA is calculated as follows:

After-tax operating income	$1,700,000
Less: Cost of capital	1,470,000
EVA	$ 230,000

The positive EVA means that Mahalo earned operating profit over and above the cost of the capital used. It is creating wealth.

Companies such as AT&T and Coca-Cola have found a strong correlation between EVA and stock prices. In fact, stock prices follow EVA better than other accounting measures of return, such as earnings per share or return on equity.[9]

Using EVA for Individual Projects Just as ROI can be computed for individual projects, so can EVA. Let's reconsider the case of the cleaning products division. Recall that the divisional manager rejected Project I because it would have reduced divisional ROI; however, that decision cost the company $300,000 in profits. The use of EVA as the performance measure would have prevented this loss. EVA for each project is computed next.

Project I:

$$\text{EVA} = \text{Project income} - \text{Cost of capital}$$
$$= \$1,300,000 - (0.10 \times \$10,000,000)$$
$$= \$1,300,000 - \$1,000,000$$
$$= \$300,000$$

Note that the cost of capital is simply the company's percent cost of funds multiplied by the assets employed.

9. Shawn Tully, "The Real Key to Creating Wealth," *Fortune* (September 20, 1993): pp. 38–50.

Project II:

$$EVA = \$640,000 - (0.10 \times \$4,000,000)$$
$$= \$640,000 - \$400,000$$
$$= \$240,000$$

Notice that both projects have positive EVA, indicating that both contribute to wealth. For comparative purposes, the divisional EVA for each of the four alternatives identified follows:

	Alternatives			
	Select Project I	Select Project II	Select Both Projects	Select Neither Project
Operating assets	$60,000,000	$54,000,000	$64,000,000	$50,000,000
Operating income	$ 8,800,000	$ 8,140,000	$ 9,440,000	$ 7,500,000
Cost of capital*	6,000,000	5,400,000	6,400,000	5,000,000
EVA	$ 2,800,000	$ 2,740,000	$ 3,040,000	$ 2,500,000

* 0.10 × Operating assets

The table shows that selecting both projects produces the greatest increase in EVA. The use of EVA encourages managers to accept any project that earns above the minimum rate.

Behavioural Aspects of EVA A number of companies have discovered that EVA helps to encourage the right kind of behaviour from their divisions in a way that emphasis on operating income alone cannot. The underlying reason is EVA's reliance on the true cost of capital. In many companies, the responsibility for investment decisions rests with corporate management. As a result, the cost of capital is considered a corporate expense. If a division builds inventories and investment, the cost of financing that investment is passed along to the overall income statement and does not show up as a reduction from the division's operating income. The result is to make investment seem free to the divisions—and of course, they then want more.

A good example of this situation is that of Quaker Oats. Prior to 1991, Quaker Oats evaluated its business segments on the basis of quarterly profits. In order to keep quarterly earnings on an upward march, segment managers offered sharp discounts on products at the end of each quarter. This resulted in huge orders from retailers and sharp surges in production at Quaker's plants at the end of each three-month period. This practice is called *trade loading*, because it "loads up the trade" (retail stores) with product. It is not inexpensive, however, because trade loading requires massive amounts of capital—for example, working capital, inventories, and warehouses to store the quarterly spikes in output. Quaker's plant in Danville, Illinois, produces snack foods and breakfast cereals. Before EVA, the Danville plant ran well below capacity throughout the early part of the quarter. Purchasing, however, bought huge quantities of boxes, plastic wrappers, granola, and chocolate chips. The raw materials purchases buildup was in anticipation of the production surge during the last six weeks of the quarter. As the products were finished, Quaker packed 15 warehouses with finished goods. All costs associated with inventories were absorbed by corporate headquarters. As a result, they appeared to be free to the plant managers, who were encouraged to build ever higher inventories. The advent of EVA and the cancellation of trade loading led to a smoothing of production throughout the quarter, higher overall production (and sales), and lower inventories. Quaker's Danville plant reduced inventories from $15 million to $9 million. Quaker has closed one-third of its 15 warehouses, saving $6 million annually in salaries and capital costs.[10]

10. *Ibid.*

Multiple Measures of Performance

ROI and EVA are important measures of managerial performance. In fact, they are important components of the financial section of the Balanced Scorecard discussed in Chapter 15. As a result, the temptation exists for managers to focus only on dollar figures. This focus may not tell the whole story for the company. In addition, lower-level managers and employees may feel helpless to affect net income or investment. As a result, nonfinancial operating measures have been developed. For example, top management could look at such factors as market share, customer complaints, personnel turnover ratios, and personnel development. By letting lower-level managers know that attention to long-run factors is also vital, the firm reduces their tendency to overemphasize financial measures.

Managers in an advanced manufacturing environment are especially likely to use multiple measures of performance and to include nonfinancial as well as financial measures. For example, GM's Saturn plant measures absenteeism (it averages 2.5 percent versus the 10 to 14 percent experienced by other GM plants).[11] Hewlett-Packard has found that product profitability is higher the sooner a new product reaches the market. Thus, in the design phase of a new product, strict conformance to schedule is one of HP's key performance measures.[12]

MEASURING AND REWARDING THE PERFORMANCE OF MANAGERS

Objective 4

Discuss methods of evaluating and rewarding managerial performance.

While some companies consider the performance of the division to be equivalent to the performance of the manager, there is a compelling reason to separate the two. Often, the performance of the division is subject to factors beyond the manager's control. It is particularly important, then, to link managerial compensation to factors under the manager's control.

Incentive Pay for Managers

The subjects of managerial evaluation and incentive pay would be of little concern if all managers were equally likely to perform to the best of their abilities and if those abilities were known in advance. In the case of a small company, owned and managed by the same person, there is no problem. The owner puts in as much effort as he or she wishes and receives all of the income from the firm as a reward for performance. However, in most companies, the owner hires managers to operate the company on a day-to-day basis and delegates decision-making authority to them. For example, the stockholders of a company hire the CEO through the board of directors. Similarly, divisional managers are hired by the CEO to operate their divisions on behalf of the owners. The owners must then ensure that the managers are providing good service.

Why would managers not provide good service? There are three reasons: (1) they may have low ability, (2) they may prefer to not work as hard as needed, and (3) they may prefer to spend company resources on *perquisites*. The first reason requires the owner to discover information about the manager before hiring him or her. Think back to the reasons for decentralization: one was that it provided training for future managers. This is true, and it also provides signals to higher management about the managerial ability of divisional managers. The second and third reasons require the owner to monitor the manager or to arrange an incentive scheme that will more closely align the manager's goals with those of the owner. In general, it is thought that managers may prefer not to do hard or routine work. Thus, it is necessary to compensate them for this. Closely related is the tendency of some managers to overuse perquisites. **Perquisites** are a type of fringe benefit received over and above salary.

11. David Woodruff, "Where Employees Are Management," *Business Week,* Reinventing America 1992, p. 66.

12. Robert D. Hof, "From Dinosaur to Gazelle," *Business Week,* Reinventing America 1992, p. 65.

Some examples are a nice office, use of a company car or jet, expense accounts, and company-paid country club memberships. While some perquisites are legitimate uses of company resources, they can be abused. A well-structured incentive pay plan can help encourage goal congruence between managers and owners.

Management Compensation: Encouraging Goal Congruence

Management compensation frequently includes incentives tied to performance. The objective is to encourage goal congruence, so that managers will act in the best interests of the firm. As this chapter's opening scenario reveals, arranging managerial compensation to encourage managers to adopt the same goals as the overall firm is an important issue. Managerial rewards include salary increases, bonuses based on reported income, stock options, and noncash compensation.

Cash Compensation   Cash compensation includes salaries and bonuses. A company may reward good managerial performance by granting periodic raises. However, once the raise takes effect, it is usually permanent. Bonuses give a company more flexibility. Many companies use a combination of salary and bonus to reward performance by keeping salaries fairly level and allowing bonuses to fluctuate with reported income. A manager may find the bonus tied to divisional net income or to targeted increases in net income. For example, a divisional manager may receive an annual salary of $75,000 and a yearly bonus of 5 percent of the increase in reported net income. If net income does not rise, the manager's bonus is zero. This incentive pay scheme makes increasing net income—an objective of the owner—important to the manager as well.

Of course, income-based compensation can encourage dysfunctional behaviour. The manager may engage in unethical practices, such as postponing needed maintenance. If the bonus is capped at a certain amount (for example, say the bonus is equal to 1 percent of net income, but cannot exceed $50,000), managers may postpone revenue recognition at the end of a year in which the maximum bonus has already been achieved, preferring to have that revenue recognized in the next year. Those who structure the reward systems need to understand both the positive incentives built into the system and the potential for negative behaviour.

Issues in Structuring Income-Based Compensation   Single measures of performance, which are often the basis of bonuses, may encourage gaming behaviour. That is, managers may increase short-term measures at the expense of the firm's long-term health. For example, a manager may keep net income up by refusing to invest in more modern and efficient equipment. Depreciation expense remains low, but so do productivity and quality. Clearly, the manager has an incentive to understand the computation of the accounting numbers used in performance evaluation. An accounting change in the method of depreciation, for example, will change net income even though sales and costs remain unchanged. Frequently, we see that a new CEO of a troubled corporation will take a number of losses (for example, inventory write-downs) all at once. This is referred to as the "big bath" and usually results in very low (or negative) net income in that year. Then, the books are cleared for a good increase in net income, and a correspondingly large bonus, for the next year.

Cash bonuses can encourage a short-term orientation. To encourage a longer-term orientation, some companies are requiring top executives to purchase and hold a certain amount of company stock to retain employment. Eastman Kodak, Xerox, CSX, Gerber Products, Union Carbide, and Hershey Foods all have stock ownership guidelines for their top management. A survey of companies in which top executives own relatively large amounts of company stock shows that they tend to perform better in terms of share price than low-ownership companies.[13]

---

13. Joann S. Lublin, "Buy or Bye," *The Wall Street Journal* (21 April 1993): p. R9.

Another issue in structuring management compensation plans is that frequently owners and managers are affected differently by risk. When managers have so much of their own capital—both financial and human—invested in the company, they may be less apt to take risks. Owners, because of their ability to diversify away some of the risk, may prefer a more risk-taking attitude. As a result, managers must be somewhat insulated from catastrophic downside risks in order to encourage them to make entrepreneurial decisions.

Noncash Compensation   Noncash compensation is also important. We see this at work for managers, as they may trade off increased salary for improvements in title, office location and trappings, use of expense accounts, and so on. Autonomy in the conduct of their daily business is also an important perquisite. Each of these perquisites signals upper management's approval of lower managers' performance. Use of perquisites is an important feature of management compensation. They can be used well to make the manager more efficient. For example, a busy manager may be able to effectively employ several assistants and may find that use of a corporate jet allows him or her to more efficiently schedule travel in overseeing far-flung divisions. However, perquisites may be abused as well. For instance, one wonders how the shareholders of RJR Nabisco benefited from former CEO F. Ross Johnson's use of corporate jets to fly friends around the country.[14]

TRANSFER PRICING

Objective 5

Explain the role of transfer pricing in a decentralized firm.

In many decentralized organizations, the output of one division is used as the input of another. This raises an accounting issue. How do we value the transferred good? When divisions are treated as responsibility centres, they are evaluated on the basis of operating income and return on investment. As a result, the value of the transferred good is revenue to the selling division and cost to the buying division. This value, or internal price, is called the **transfer price**. Transfer pricing is a complex issue. We will examine the impact of transfer prices on divisions and on the company as a whole, as well as methods of setting transfer prices, in the following sections.

Impact on Performance Measures

Transfer pricing affects both transferring divisions and the firm as a whole. It does this through its impact on (1) divisional performance measures, (2) firmwide profits, and (3) divisional autonomy.

Impact on Divisional Performance Measures   The price charged for the transferred good affects the costs of the buying division and the revenues of the selling division. Thus, the profits of both divisions, as well as the evaluation and compensation of their managers, are affected by the transfer price. Since profit-based performance measures of the two divisions are affected (for example, ROI and EVA), transfer pricing can often be a very emotionally charged issue. Exhibit 18–3 illustrates the effect of the transfer price on two divisions of ABC, Inc. Division A produces a component and sells it to another division of the same company, Division C. The $30 transfer price is revenue to Division A; clearly Division A wants the price to be as high as possible. Conversely, the $30 transfer price is cost to Division C, just like the cost of any raw material. Division C prefers a lower transfer price.

Impact on Firmwide Profits   While the actual transfer price nets out for the company as a whole, transfer pricing can affect the level of profits earned by the company in

---

14. Bryan Burrough and John Helyar, *Barbarians at the Gate: The Fall of RJR Nabisco* (New York: Harper and Row, 1990): p. 95.

Exhibit   18–3

Impact of Transfer Price
on Transferring Divisions
and the Company as a
Whole

ABC, Inc.	
Division A	**Division C**
Produces component and transfers it to C for transfer price of $30 per unit	Purchases component from A at transfer price of $30 per unit and uses it in production of final product
Transfer price = $30 per unit	Transfer price = $30 per unit
Revenue to A	Cost to C
Increases net income	Decreases net income
Increases ROI	Decreases ROI

Transfer price revenue = Transfer price cost
Zero impact on ABC, Inc.

two ways: if it affects divisional behaviour and if it affects income taxes. Divisions, acting independently, may set transfer prices that maximize divisional profits but adversely affect firmwide profits. For example, the buying division may decide to purchase the good from an outside party because the outside price is lower than the transfer price, when, in reality, the cost of producing the good internally is much lower than the transfer price. Suppose that Division A in Exhibit 18–3 sets a transfer price of $30 for a component that costs $24 to produce. If Division C can obtain the component from an outside supplier for $28, it will refuse to buy from Division A. Division C will realize a savings of $2 per component ($30 internal transfer price − $28 external price). However, assuming that Division A cannot replace the internal sales with external sales, the company as a whole will be worse off by $4 per component ($28 external cost − $24 internal cost). This outcome would increase the total cost to the firm.

Transfer pricing can affect overall corporate income taxes. This is particularly true for multinational corporations. As a general rule, however, the corporation may try to set the transfer price so that more revenue is assigned to divisions in low-tax countries and more cost is assigned to divisions in high-tax countries. The international transfer pricing situation is examined in detail in Chapter 19.

Impact on Autonomy   Because transfer pricing decisions can affect firmwide profitability, top management is often tempted to intervene and dictate desirable transfer prices. If such intervention becomes a frequent practice, however, the organization has effectively abandoned decentralization and all of its advantages. Organizations decentralize because the benefits are greater than the associated costs. One of these costs is occasional suboptimal behaviour by divisional managers. Thus, intervention by central management to reduce this cost may actually prove to be more expensive in the long run than nonintervention.

The Transfer Pricing Problem

A transfer pricing system should satisfy three objectives: accurate performance evaluation, goal congruence, and preservation of divisional autonomy.[15] *Accurate performance evaluation* means that no one divisional manager should benefit at the expense of another (in the sense that one division is made better off while the other is made worse off). *Goal congruence* means that divisional managers select actions that maximize firmwide profits. *Autonomy* means that central management should not interfere with the decision-making freedom of divisional managers. The **transfer pricing problem** concerns finding a system that simultaneously satisfies all three objectives.

15. Joshua Ronen and George McKinney, "Transfer Pricing for Divisional Autonomy," *Journal of Accounting Research* (Spring 1970): pp. 100–101.

Although direct intervention by central management to set specific transfer prices may not be advisable, the development of some general guidelines may be appropriate. One such guideline, called the *opportunity cost approach,* can be used to describe a wide variety of transfer pricing practices. Under certain conditions, this approach is compatible with the objectives of performance evaluation, goal congruence, and autonomy.

The Opportunity Cost Approach as a Guide for Transfer Pricing

In establishing a transfer pricing policy, the views of both the selling division and the buying division must be considered. The **opportunity cost approach** achieves this goal by identifying the minimum price that the selling division would be willing to accept and the maximum price that the buying division would be willing to pay. These minimum and maximum prices correspond to the opportunity costs of transferring internally. They are defined for each division as follows:

1. The **minimum transfer price** is the transfer price that would leave the selling division no worse off if the good were sold or the service provided to an internal division than if the good were sold or the service provided to an external party. This is sometimes referred to as the "floor" of the bargaining range.
2. The **maximum transfer price** is the transfer price that would leave the buying division no worse off if an input were purchased from an internal division than if the same good or service were purchased externally. This is sometimes referred to as the "ceiling" of the bargaining range.

The opportunity cost approach guides divisions in determining when internal transfers should occur. Specifically, the good should be transferred or the service provided internally whenever the opportunity cost (minimum price) of the selling division is less than the opportunity cost (maximum price) of the buying division. By its very definition, this approach ensures that neither divisional manager is worse off by transferring internally. But what is meant by indifferent or no worse off? In practical terms, this means that total divisional profits are not decreased by the internal transfer.

Market Price

If there is a perfectly competitive outside market for the transferred product, the correct transfer price is the market price.[16] In such a case, divisional managers' actions will optimize divisional profits and firmwide profits simultaneously. Furthermore, no division can benefit at the expense of another. In this setting, central management will not be tempted to intervene.

The opportunity cost approach also signals that the correct transfer price is the market price. Since the selling division can sell all that it produces at the market price, transferring internally at a lower price would make the division worse off. Similarly, the buying division can always acquire the good at the market price, so it would be unwilling to pay more for an internally transferred good. Since the minimum transfer price for the selling division is the market price, and the maximum price for the buying division is also the market price, the only possible transfer price is the market price.

In fact, moving away from the market price will decrease the firm's overall profitability. This principle can be used to resolve divisional conflicts that may occur, as the following example illustrates.

16. A perfectly competitive market for the intermediate product requires four conditions: (1) the division producing the intermediate product is small relative to the market as a whole and cannot influence the price of the product; (2) the intermediate product is indistinguishable from the same product of other sellers; (3) firms can easily enter and exit the market; and (4) consumers, producers, and resource owners have perfect knowledge of the market.

Tyson Manufacturers is a large, privately held corporation that produces small appliances. The company has adopted a decentralized organizational structure. The Small Parts Division, managed by Ned Kimberly, produces parts that are used by the Small Motor Division, managed by Andrea Ferguson. The parts can also be sold to other manufacturers and to wholesalers. For all practical purposes, the market for the parts is perfectly competitive. Frank Johnston, a vice-president at corporate headquarters and the immediate supervisor of Ned and Andrea, just received the following memo from Andrea.

MEMORANDUM

To: Frank Johnston, Vice-President
From: Andrea Ferguson
Subject: Transfer Price of Component No. 14
Date: October 15, 2001

Frank, as you know, our division is operating at 70 percent capacity. Last week we received a request for 100,000 units of Model 1267 at a price of $30. Detailed below are the costs we incur to produce that particular motor (because of the special arrangements, we avoid any costs of distribution). The full cost includes the component that we usually buy from Ned's division.

Direct materials	$10
Transferred-in component	8
Direct labour	2
Variable overhead	1
Fixed overhead	10
Total cost	$31

As you can see, if we accept the order, we will lose $1 per unit. The purpose of this memo is to register a complaint about the Small Parts Division. I must confess that I am somewhat irritated with Ned. I know that the full cost of the component supplied by his division is $5. Well, I asked for a more favourable transfer price— $6.50 instead of the $8 we normally pay. He absolutely refused, and in fact seemed somewhat put out by my request. I believe that the concession was needed so that I could accept the order and show a small profit. The benefits of this order are appealing. My capacity utilization jumps to 85 percent, and I avoid the need to lay off some skilled workers. Avoiding the layoff will save the company at least $50,000 in training costs next year. Also, the special order may open up some new markets for the company within a year.

Can't you persuade Ned to make this small concession for the good of the company? In my opinion, more teamwork is needed. After all, I have been a faithful customer of Ned's for several years.

If you were Frank Johnston, how would you react to the memo? Should Frank intervene and dictate a lower transfer price? Is the market price guideline for transfer pricing invalid for this particular case? To answer these questions, let's turn to the opportunity cost approach. Since Ned can sell all he produces, the minimum transfer price for his division is the market price of $8. Any lower price would make his division worse off. For Andrea's division, identifying the maximum transfer price that can be paid so that her division is no worse off requires more analysis.

Since the Small Motor Division is under capacity, the $10 of fixed overhead allocated to Model 1267 is not relevant. The relevant costs are those additional costs that will be incurred only if the order is accepted. These costs, excluding for the moment the cost of the transferred-in component, are as follows:

Direct materials	$10
Direct labour	2
Variable overhead	1
Total	$13

Thus, the contribution to profits before considering the cost of the transferred-in component is $17 ($30 − $13). The division could actually pay $17 for the component and still break even on the special order. However, since the component can always be purchased from an outside supplier for $8, the maximum price that the division should pay internally is $8. If the buying division pays $8, the selling division is no worse off. Furthermore, relative to the status quo, the buying division is better off by $9 ($17 − $8). Thus, the transfer price of $8 should be paid and the special order accepted.

There is no reason for central management to intervene; the market price is the correct transfer price. The vice-president could point out the benefits of the special order to Andrea. The need to do so, however, raises some questions about Andrea's managerial abilities or her training in the use of accounting information.

Negotiated Transfer Prices

In reality, perfectly competitive markets seldom exist. In many cases, buyers or sellers can influence price to some degree (for example, through large size, or by selling closely related but differentiated products, or by selling a unique product). When imperfections exist in the market for the intermediate product, market price may no longer be suitable. In this case, negotiated transfer prices may be a practical alternative. Opportunity costs can be used to define the boundaries of the negotiation set.

Example 1: Avoidable Distribution Costs To illustrate, assume that a division produces a circuit board that can be sold in the outside market for $22. The division can sell all that it produces at $22. Currently, the division is selling 1,000 units per day, with a variable manufacturing cost of $12 per unit and a variable distribution cost of $2 per unit. Alternatively, the board can be sold internally to the company's Electronic Games Division. The $2 distribution cost is avoided if the board is sold internally.

The Electronic Games Division is also at capacity, producing and selling 350 games per day. Each game is priced at $45 and has a variable manufacturing cost of $32. Variable selling expenses of $3 per unit are also incurred. Sales and production data for each division are summarized in Exhibit 18–4.

Since the Electronic Games Division was acquired very recently, no transfers between the two divisions have yet taken place. Susan Swift, the manager of the Circuit Board Division, requested a meeting with Randy Schrude, manager of the Electronic Games Division, to discuss the possibility of internal transfers. The following is their conversation:

Exhibit 18–4

Summary of Sales and Production Data

	Board Division	Games Division
Units sold:		
Per day	1,000	350
Per year*	260,000	91,000
Unit data:		
Selling price	$22	$45
Variable costs:		
Manufacturing	$12	$32
Selling	$2	$3
Annual fixed costs	$1,480,000	$610,000

* There are 260 selling days in a year.

Susan: "Randy, I'm excited about the possibility of supplying your division with circuit boards. What is your current demand for the type of board we produce? And how much are you paying for the boards?"

Randy: "We would use one in each of our video games, and our production is about 350 games per day. We pay $22 for each board."

Susan: "We can supply that amount simply by displacing external sales. Furthermore, we would be willing to sell them at the same price we charge outside customers. We can at least meet your price; that way you are no worse off."

Randy: "Actually, I was hoping for a better price than $22. The circuit board is by far our most expensive input. By transferring internally, you can avoid some selling, transportation, and collection expenses. I called corporate headquarters, which estimated these costs at approximately $2 per unit. I'd be willing to pay $20 each for your units. You'd be no worse off, and, with a less expensive component, I can make about $700 per day more profit. This deal would make the company $182,000 more during the coming year."

Susan: "Your information about avoiding $2 per unit is accurate. I also understand how the cheaper component can allow you to increase your profits. However, if you were to purchase the board at $22, I could increase my division's profits, and the corporation's for that matter, by $700 per day—just by selling you the 350 units and saving the $2 per unit I must spend to sell externally. You would be no worse off, and my division and the corporation would be better off by the $182,000 per year that you mentioned. It seems to me that most of the benefits to the corporation come from avoiding the distribution costs incurred when we sell externally. Nonetheless, I'll sweeten the deal. Since we're both members of the same family, I'll let you have the 350 boards for $21.50 each. That price allows you to increase your profits by $175 per day and reflects the fact that most of the savings are generated by my division."

Randy: "I don't agree that most of the savings are generated by your division. You can't achieve those savings unless I buy from you. I'm willing to buy internally, but only if there is a fair sharing of the joint benefits. I think a reasonable arrangement is to split the benefits equally; however, I will grant a small concession. I'll buy 350 units at $21.10 each—that will increase your divisional profits by $385 per day and mine by $315 per day. Deal?"

Susan: "Sounds reasonable. Let's have a contract drawn up."

This dialogue illustrates how the minimum transfer price ($20) and the maximum transfer price ($22) set the limits of the negotiation set. The example also demonstrates how negotiation can lead to improved profitability for each division and for the firm as a whole. Exhibit 18–5 provides income statements for each division before and after the agreement. Notice how the firm's total profits increase by $182,000 as claimed; notice, too, how that profit increase is split between the two divisions.

Example 2: Excess Capacity In a perfectly competitive market, the selling division can sell all that it wishes at the prevailing market price. In a less ideal setting, a selling division may not be able to sell all that it produces, leading to excess capacity.[17]

To illustrate the role of transfer pricing and negotiation in this setting, consider the dialogue between Sharon Bunker, manager of a plastics division, and Carlos Rivera, manager of a pharmaceuticals division:

Carlos: "Sharon, my division has shown a loss for the past three years. When I took over the division at the beginning of the year, I set a goal with headquarters to break even. At this point, projections show a loss of $5,000—but I think I have a way to reach my goal, if I can get your cooperation."

---

17. Output can be increased by decreasing selling price. Of course, decreasing selling price to increase sales volume may not increase profits—in fact, profits could easily decline. We assume in this example that the divisional manager has chosen the most advantageous selling price and that the division is still left with excess capacity.

Exhibit   18–5

Comparative Income Statements

BEFORE NEGOTIATION: ALL SALES EXTERNAL			
	Board Division	Games Division	Total
Sales	$5,720,000	$4,095,000	$9,815,000
Less variable expenses:			
Cost of goods sold	3,120,000	2,912,000	6,032,000
Variable selling	520,000	273,000	793,000
Contribution margin	$2,080,000	$ 910,000	$2,990,000
Less: Fixed expenses	1,480,000	610,000	2,090,000
Net income	$ 600,000	$ 300,000	$ 900,000

AFTER NEGOTIATION: INTERNAL TRANSFERS @ $21.10			
	Board Division	Games Division	Total
Sales	$5,638,100	$4,095,000	$9,733,100
Less variable expenses:			
Cost of goods sold	3,120,000	2,830,100	5,950,100
Variable selling	338,000	273,000	611,000
Contribution margin	$2,180,100	$ 991,900	$3,172,000
Less: Fixed expenses	1,480,000	610,000	2,090,000
Net income	$ 700,100	$ 381,900	$1,082,000
Change in net income	$ 100,100	$ 81,900	$ 182,000

Sharon: "If I can help, I certainly will. What do you have in mind?"

Carlos: "I need a special deal on your plastic bottle Model 3. I have the opportunity to place our aspirin with a large retail chain on the west coast—a totally new market for our product. But we have to give it a real break on price. The chain has offered to pay $0.85 per bottle for an order of 250,000 bottles. My variable cost per unit is $0.60, not including the cost of the plastic bottle. I normally pay $0.40 for your bottle, but if I do that, I'll lose $37,500 on the order. I cannot afford that kind of loss. I know that you have excess capacity. I'll place an order for 250,000 bottles, and I'll pay your variable cost per unit, provided that it's no more than $0.25. Are you interested? Do you have sufficient excess capacity to handle a special order of 250,000 bottles?"

Sharon: "I have enough excess capacity to handle the order easily. The variable cost per bottle is $0.15. Transferring at that price would make me no worse off; my fixed costs will be there whether I make the bottles or not. However, I would like to have some contribution from an order like this. I'll tell you what I'll do. I'll let you have the order for $0.20. That way we both make $0.05 contribution per bottle, for a total contribution of $12,500. That'll put you in the black and help me get closer to my budgeted profit goal."

Carlos: "Great. This is better than I expected. If this west coast chain provides more orders in the future—as I expect it will—and at better prices, I'll make sure you get our business."

Notice the role that opportunity costs play in the negotiation. In this case, the minimum transfer price is the plastics division's variable cost ($0.15), representing the incremental outlay if the order is accepted. Since plastics has excess capacity, only variable costs are relevant to the decision. For the buying division, the maximum transfer price is the purchase price that would allow the division to cover its incremental costs on the special order ($0.25). Adding the $0.25 to the other costs of processing ($0.60), the total incremental costs incurred are $0.85 per unit; since the selling price is also $0.85 per unit, the division is made no worse off. Both divisions, however, can be better off if the transfer price is between the minimum price of $0.15 and the maximum price of $0.25.

Comparative statements showing the contribution margin earned by each division and by the firm as a whole are shown in Exhibit 18–6 for each of the four transfer prices discussed. These statements show that the firm earns the same profit for all four transfer prices; however, different prices do affect the individual divisions' profits differently. Because of the autonomy of each division, however, there is no guarantee that the firm will earn the maximum profit. For example, if Sharon had insisted on maintaining the price of $0.40, no transfer would have taken place, and the $25,000 increase in profits would have been lost.

Disadvantages of Negotiated Transfer Prices Three disadvantages of negotiated transfer prices are commonly mentioned.

1. A divisional manager who has private information may take advantage of another divisional manager.
2. Performance measures may be distorted by the negotiating skills of managers.
3. Negotiation can consume considerable time and resources.

It is interesting to observe that Carlos, the manager of the pharmaceuticals division, did not know the variable cost of producing the plastic bottle. Yet that cost was a key to the negotiation. This lack of knowledge gave Sharon, the plastics division's manager, the opportunity to exploit the situation. For example, she could have claimed that the variable cost was $0.27 and offered to sell for $0.25 per unit as a favor to Carlos, saying that she would be willing to absorb a $5,000 loss in exchange for a promise of future business. In this case, she would capture the full $25,000 benefit of the transfer. Alternatively, she could have misrepresented the figure and used it to turn down the request, thus preventing Carlos from achieving his budgetary goal; after all, she is in competition with Carlos for promotions, bonuses, salary increases, and so on.

Fortunately, Sharon displayed sound judgment and acted with integrity. For negotiation to work, managers must be willing to share relevant information. How can

Exhibit 18–6

Comparative Statements

TRANSFER PRICE OF $0.40	Pharmaceuticals	Plastics	Total
Sales	$212,500	$100,000	$312,500
Less: Variable expenses	250,000	37,500	287,500
Contribution margin	$ (37,500)	$ 62,500	$ 25,000
TRANSFER PRICE OF $0.25			
Sales	$212,500	$ 62,500	$275,000
Less: Variable expenses	212,500	37,500	250,000
Contribution margin	$ 0	$ 25,000	$ 25,000
TRANSFER PRICE OF $0.20			
Sales	$212,500	$ 50,000	$262,500
Less: Variable expenses	200,000	37,500	237,500
Contribution margin	$ 12,500	$ 12,500	$ 25,000
TRANSFER PRICE OF $0.15			
Sales	$212,500	$ 37,500	$250,000
Less: Variable expenses	187,500	37,500	225,000
Contribution margin	$ 25,000	$ 0	$ 25,000

this requirement be satisfied? The answer lies in the use of good internal control procedures. Perhaps the best internal control procedure is to hire managers with integrity. Another possibility would be for top management to give divisional managers access to relevant accounting information of other divisions. This step would minimize the possibility of exploitive behaviour because of differences in information.

The second disadvantage of negotiated transfer prices is that divisional profitability may be affected too strongly by the negotiating skills of managers, masking the actual management of resources entrusted to each manager. Although this argument may have some merit, it ignores the fact that negotiating skill is itself a desirable managerial skill. Perhaps divisional profitability *should* reflect differences in negotiating skills.

The third criticism of this technique is that negotiating can be very time consuming. The time spent in negotiation by divisional managers could be spent managing other activities, which may have a greater bearing on the division's success. Occasionally, negotiations may reach an impasse, forcing top management to spend time mediating the process.[18] Although the use of managerial time may be costly, it may prove to be far more costly if this interaction is not allowed to take place. A mutually satisfactory negotiated outcome can produce increased profits for the firm that easily exceed the cost of the managerial time involved. Furthermore, negotiation does not have to be repeated each time for similar transactions.

Advantages of Negotiated Transfer Prices   Despite the disadvantages, negotiated transfer prices offer some hope of complying with the three criteria of goal congruence, autonomy, and accurate performance evaluation. In addition, negotiated transfer prices have been identified as a means by which goal congruence throughout the entire firm can be achieved.[19] If negotiation helps ensure goal congruence, there is no need for top management to intervene in divisional affairs. Finally, if the negotiating skills of divisional managers are comparable, or if the firm views these skills as an important managerial skill, concerns about motivation and accurate performance measures are avoided.

Cost-Based Transfer Prices

Companies that use cost-based transfer pricing require that all transfers take place at some form of cost. Three forms of cost-based transfer pricing will be considered: (1) full cost, (2) full cost plus markup, and (3) variable cost plus fixed fee. In all three cases, to avoid passing on the inefficiencies of one division to another, standard costs should be used to determine the transfer price. For example, the Micro Products Division of Tandem Computers, Inc., uses a corporate materials overhead rate, rather than the division-specific rate, to facilitate cost-based transfers between divisions.[20] A more important issue, however, is the propriety of cost-based transfer prices. Should they be used? If so, under what circumstances?

Full-Cost Transfer Pricing   Full cost includes the cost of direct materials, direct labour, variable overhead, and a portion of fixed overhead. Possibly the least desirable transfer pricing approach, its only real virtue is simplicity. Its disadvantages are

18. The involvement of top management may be very cursory, however. In the case of a very large oil company that negotiates virtually all transfer prices, two divisional managers could not come to an agreement after several weeks of effort and appealed to their superior. His response: "Either come to an agreement within twenty-four hours, or you are both fired." Needless to say, an agreement was reached within the allotted time.

19. For an excellent discussion of the role of negotiated transfer prices in a decentralized organization, see David Watson and John Baumler, "Transfer Pricing: A Behavioural Context," *The Accounting Review* (July 1975): pp. 466–474.

20. Earl D. Bennett, Sarah A. Reed, and Ted Simmonds, "Learning from a CIM Experience," *Management Accounting* (July 1991): pp. 28–33.

considerable. Full-cost transfer pricing can provide perverse incentives and distort performance measures. As we have seen, the opportunity costs of both the buying and selling divisions are essential for determining the propriety of internal transfers; at the same time, they provide useful reference points for determining a mutually satisfactory transfer price. Only rarely will full cost provide accurate information about opportunity costs.

A full-cost transfer price would have shut down the negotiated prices described in the examples. In the first example, the selling division manager would never have considered transferring internally if the price had had to be full cost. Yet because the transfer took place at selling price less some distribution expenses, both divisions—and the firm as a whole—were better off. In the second example, the manager of the pharmaceuticals division could never have accepted the special order with the west coast chain. Both divisions and the company would have been worse off, both in the short run and in the long run.

Full Cost Plus Markup Full cost plus markup suffers from the same problems as full cost. It is somewhat less perverse, however, if the markup can be negotiated. For example, a full cost plus markup formula could have been used to represent the negotiated transfer price of the first example. In some cases, a full cost plus markup formula may be the outcome of negotiation; if so, it is simply another example of negotiated transfer pricing. In these cases, the use of this method is justified. Using full cost plus markup to represent all negotiated prices, however, is not possible (for example, it could not be used to represent the negotiated price of the second example). The superior approach is negotiation, since more cases can be handled and opportunity costs can be considered.

Variable Cost Plus Fixed Fee Like full cost plus markup, variable cost plus fixed fee can be a useful transfer pricing approach provided that the fixed fee is negotiable. This method has one advantage over full cost plus markup: if the selling division is operating below capacity, variable cost is its opportunity cost. Assuming that the fixed fee is negotiable, the variable-cost approach can be equivalent to negotiated transfer pricing. Negotiation with full consideration of opportunity costs is preferred.

Propriety of Use In spite of the disadvantages of cost-based transfer prices, companies actively use these methods, especially full cost and full cost plus markup.[21] There must be some compelling reasons for their use—reasons that outweigh the benefits associated with negotiated transfer prices and the disadvantages of these methods. The methods do have the virtue of being simple and objective. These qualities alone cannot justify their use, however. Some possible explanations for the use of these methods can be given.

In many cases, transfers between divisions have a small impact on the profitability of either division. For this situation, it may be cost-beneficial to use an easily identifiable, cost-based formula rather than spending valuable time and resources on negotiation.

In other cases, the use of full cost plus markup may simply be the formula agreed upon in negotiations. That is, the full cost plus markup formula is the outcome of negotiation, but the transfer pricing method being used is reported as full cost plus markup. Once established, this formula could be used until the original conditions change to the point where renegotiation is necessary. In this way, the time and resources of negotiation can be minimized. For example, the goods transferred may be custom-made, and the managers may have little ability to identify an outside

21. In a survey of profit centres, Umapathy found that 42 percent used full cost and full cost plus markup. Over 50 percent used either market price or negotiated prices. See Srinivasan Umapathy, "Transfers Between Profit Centers," in *Decentralization: Managerial Ambiguity by Design,* ed. Richard F. Vancil (Homewood, Ill.: Dow Jones-Irwin, 1978).

market price. In this case, reimbursement of full costs plus a reasonable rate of return may be a good surrogate for the transferring division's opportunity costs.

A final note regarding corporate use of transfer prices is that many corporations are moving toward the use of benchmarking and outsourcing. Both of these approaches reduce the need for internal pricing by tying divisional behaviour to the outside market. Benchmarking involves tracking the most effective and efficient provider of a particular activity. For example, USAA, an insurance company, is widely considered to be a world leader in the use of technology to respond to customers; L.L. Bean, Inc. (the Maine catalogue company) is a world leader in fast and accurate order filling. Other companies routinely visit these companies to learn how they do it. The result for transfer pricing is that the company is less interested in setting a transfer price and more interested in getting the cost/price as low as possible. With outsourcing, the internally provided good or service is provided by an external company. Now the price is a true market price.

SUMMARY OF LEARNING OBJECTIVES

1. Define responsibility accounting, and describe four types of responsibility centres.
Responsibility accounting is a system that measures the results of responsibility centres and compares those results with expected outcomes. The four types of responsibility centres are cost centres, revenue centres, profit centres, and investment centres.

2. Explain why firms choose to decentralize.
To increase overall efficiency, many companies choose to decentralize. The essence of decentralization is decision-making freedom. In a decentralized organization, lower-level managers make and implement decisions, whereas in a centralized organization, lower-level managers are responsible only for implementing decisions. Reasons for decentralization are numerous. Companies decentralize because local managers can make better decisions using local information. Local managers can also provide a more timely response to changing conditions. Additionally, decentralization for large, diversified companies is necessary because of cognitive limitations—it is impossible for any one central manager to be fully knowledgeable about all products and markets. Other reasons include training and motivating local managers and freeing top management from day-to-day operating conditions so that they can spend time on more long-range activities, such as strategic planning.

3. Compute and explain return on investment (ROI) and economic value added (EVA).
ROI is the ratio of operating income to average operating assets. This ratio can be broken down into two components: margin (the ratio of operating income to sales) and turnover (the ratio of sales to average operating assets). EVA is the difference between income and the dollar cost of capital.

Return on investment is the most common mea-

sure of performance for managers of decentralized units. Return on investment encourages managers to focus on improving their divisions' profitability by improving sales, controlling costs, and using assets efficiently. Unfortunately, the measure can also encourage managers to increase ROI by sacrificing long-run gains for short-run benefits (for example, it can encourage managers to forgo investments that are profitable for the firm but that would lower the divisional ROI).

Economic value added (EVA) is after-tax operating profit minus the total annual cost of capital. If EVA is positive, the company is creating wealth. If it is negative, then the company is destroying capital. EVA is a dollar figure, not a percentage rate of return. The key feature of EVA is its emphasis on *after-tax* operating profit and the *actual* cost of capital. Investors like EVA because it relates profit to the amount of resources needed to achieve it. EVA rectifies the problem that ROI poses as the effective hurdle rate for investments but it does not resolve the issue of short-term orientation. Multiple performance measurements are required, as per the Balanced Scorecard approach.

4. Discuss methods of evaluating and rewarding managerial performance.
Decentralized firms may encourage goal congruence by constructing management compensation programs that reward managers for taking actions that benefit the firm. Possible reward systems include cash compensation and noncash benefits.

5. Explain the role of transfer pricing in a decentralized firm.
When one division of a company produces a product that can be used in production by another division, transfer pricing exists. The transfer price is revenue to the selling division and cost to the buying division;

thus, the price charged for the intermediate good affects the operating income of both divisions. Since both divisions are evaluated on their profitability, the price charged for the intermediate good can be a point of serious contention.

The transfer pricing problem involves finding a mutually satisfactory transfer price that is compatible with the company's goals of accurate performance evaluation, divisional autonomy, and goal congruence.

Three methods generally are used for setting transfer prices: market-based, negotiated, and cost-based. If a perfectly competitive market exists for the intermediate product, market price is the best transfer price. In this case, the market price reflects the opportunity costs of both the buying and selling divisions. If no perfectly competitive market exists, a negotiated transfer price is preferred. In this case, opportunity costs for the buying and selling divisions differ, and they form the upper and lower boundaries for the transfer price. The use of cost-based transfer prices is not generally recommended; however, if the transfers have little effect on either division's profitability, such an approach is acceptable. Additionally, cost-based pricing formulas may be appropriate if they are set through the process of negotiation.

KEY TERMS

Centralized decision making, 815
Cost centre, 814
Decentralization, 815
Decentralized decision making, 815
Economic value added (EVA), 821
Investment centre, 814
Margin, 818

Maximum transfer price, 829
Minimum transfer price, 829
Operating assets, 818
Operating income, 818
Opportunity cost approach, 829
Perquisites, 825
Profit centre, 814

Responsibility accounting, 814
Responsibility centre, 814
Return on investment (ROI), 818
Revenue centre, 814
Transfer price, 827
Transfer pricing problem, 828
Turnover, 818

REVIEW PROBLEMS

1. TRANSFER PRICING

The Components Division produces a part that is used by the Goods Division. The cost of manufacturing the part follows:

Direct materials	$10
Direct labour	2
Variable overhead	3
Fixed overhead*	5
Total cost	$20

* Based on a practical volume of 200,000 parts

Other costs incurred by the Components Division are as follows:

Fixed selling and administrative	$500,000
Variable selling (per unit)	$1

The part usually sells for between $28 and $30 in the external market. Currently, the Components Division is selling it to external customers for $29. The division is capable of producing 200,000 units of the part per year; however, because of a weak economy, only 150,000 parts are expected to be sold during the coming year. The variable selling expenses are avoidable if the part is sold internally.

The Goods Division has been buying the same part from an external supplier for $28. It expects to use 50,000 units of the part during the coming year. The manager of the Goods Division has offered to buy 50,000 units from the Components Division for $18 per unit.

Required:

1. Determine the minimum transfer price that the Components Division would accept.
2. Determine the maximum transfer price that the manager of the Goods Division would pay.
3. Should an internal transfer take place? Why? If you were the manager of the Components Division, would you sell the 50,000 components for $18 each? Explain.
4. Suppose that the average operating assets of the Components Division total $10 million. Compute the ROI for the coming year, assuming that the 50,000 units are transferred to the Goods Division for $21 each.

Solution

1. The minimum transfer price is $15. The Components Division has idle capacity and so must cover only its incremental costs, which are the variable manufacturing costs. (Fixed costs are the same whether or not the internal transfer occurs; the variable selling expenses are avoidable.)
2. The maximum transfer price is $28. The Goods Division would not pay more for the part than it has to pay an external supplier.
3. Yes, an internal transfer ought to occur; the opportunity cost of the selling division is less than the opportunity cost of the buying division. The Components Division would earn an additional $150,000 profit ($3 × 50,000). The total joint benefit, however, is $650,000 ($13 × 50,000). The manager of the Components Division should attempt to negotiate a more favourable outcome for that division.
4. Income statement:

Sales [($29 × 150,000) + ($21 × 50,000)]	$5,400,000
Less: Variable cost of goods sold ($15 × 200,000)	(3,000,000)
Variable selling expenses ($1 × 150,000)	(150,000)
Contribution margin	$2,250,000
Less: Fixed overhead ($5 × 200,000)	(1,000,000)
Fixed selling and administrative	(500,000)
Operating income	$ 750,000

$$\text{ROI} = \text{Operating income/Average operating assets}$$
$$= \$750,000/\$10,000,000$$
$$= 0.075$$

2. WEIGHTED AVERAGE COST OF CAPITAL AND EVA

One division of El Sueño, Inc., had after-tax income last year of $600,000. Two sources of financing were used by the company: $2.5 million in mortgage bonds paying 8 percent interest and $10 million in common stock, which was considered to be no more or less risky than other stocks. The rate of return on long-term treasury bonds is 6 percent. El Sueño, Inc., pays a marginal tax rate of 40 percent. Total capital employed in the division is $5.3 million.

Required:

1. What is the weighted cost of capital for El Sueño?
2. Calculate EVA for the division.

Solution

1. After-tax cost of the mortgage bonds:
   $[(1 - 0.4)(0.08)] = 0.048$
   Cost of the common stock:

   $$= \text{Return on long-term treasury bonds} + \text{Average premium}$$
   $$= 6\% + 6\%$$
   $$= 12\%$$

	Amount	Percent ×	After-Tax Cost =	Weighted Cost
Common stock	$10,000,000	0.80	0.120	0.0960
Mortgage bonds	2,500,000	0.20	0.048	0.0096
Total	$12,500,000			
Weighted average cost of capital				0.1056

2. Cost of capital = $5,300,000 × 0.1056 = $559,680

After-tax operating income	$600,000
Less: Cost of capital	559,680
EVA	$ 40,320

QUESTIONS FOR WRITING AND DISCUSSION

1. Discuss the differences between centralized and decentralized decision making.

2. What is decentralization?

3. Explain why firms choose to decentralize.

4. Explain how access to local information can improve decision making.

5. One division had operating profits of $500,000, and a second division had operating profits of $3 million. Which divisional manager did the best job? Explain.

6. Assume that a division earned operating profits of $500,000 on average operating assets of $2 million. What is the division's return on investment? Suppose that a second division had operating profits of $3 million and average operating assets of $30 million. Compute this division's ROI. Which division did the better job? Explain.

7. What are margin and turnover? Explain how these concepts can improve the evaluation of an investment centre.

8. What are the three benefits of ROI? Explain how each can lead to improved profitability.

9. What are two disadvantages of ROI? Explain how each can lead to decreased profitability.

10. What is EVA? Explain how EVA overcomes one of ROI's disadvantages.

11. What disadvantage is shared by ROI and EVA? What can be done to overcome this problem?

12. What problems do owners face in encouraging goal congruence of managers?

13. What is a transfer price?

14. Explain how transfer prices can impact performance measures, firmwide profits, and the decision to decentralize decision making.

15. What is the transfer pricing problem?

16. Explain the opportunity cost approach to transfer pricing.

17. If the minimum transfer price of the selling division is less than the maximum transfer price of the buying division, the intermediate product should be transferred internally. Do you agree? Why or why not?

18. If a perfectly competitive outside market exists for the intermediate product, what should the transfer price be? Why?

19. Suppose that a selling division can sell all that it produces for $50 per unit. Of that $50, however, $3 represents the costs of distribution (commissions, freight, collections, and so on). Assuming that the distribution costs are avoidable if the product is sold internally, what is the minimum transfer price? the maximum transfer price?

20. Discuss the advantages of negotiated transfer prices.

21. Discuss the disadvantages of negotiated transfer prices.

22. Identify three cost-based transfer prices. What are the disadvantages of cost-based transfer prices? When might it be appropriate to use cost-based transfer prices?

23. The performance of the divisional manager is equivalent to the performance of a division. Do you agree? Explain.

EXERCISES

18–1

Types of Responsibility Centres

LO1

Consider each of the following scenarios.

A. Terrin Belson, plant manager for the laser printer factory of CompuGear, Inc., brushed his hair back and sighed. December had been a bad month; two machines had broken down, and some direct labourers (all on salary) were idled for part of the month. Materials prices increased, and insurance premiums on the factory increased. No way out of it: costs were going up. He hoped that the marketing vice-president would be able to push through some price increases, but that really wasn't his department.

B. Joanna Pauly was delighted to see that her ROI figures had increased for the third straight year. She was sure that her campaign to lower costs and use machinery more efficiently (enabling her factories to sell several older machines) was the reason why. Joanna planned to take full credit for the improvements at her semiannual performance review.

C. Gil Rodriguez, sales manager for CompuGear, was not pleased with a memo from headquarters detailing the recent cost increases for the laser printer line. Headquarters suggested raising prices. "Great," thought Gil, "An increase in price will kill sales—and revenue will go down. Why can't the plant shape up and cut costs like every other company in Canada is doing? Why turn this into my problem?"

D. Susan Whitehorse looked at the quarterly profit/loss statement with disgust. Revenue was down, and costs were up—what a combination! Then she had an idea. If she cut back on maintenance of equipment and let a product engineer go, expenses would decrease—perhaps enough to reverse the trend in income.

E. Shonna had just been hired to improve the fortunes of the Eastern Division of ABC, Inc. She met with top staff and hammered out a three-year plan to improve the situation. A centrepiece of the plan was the retiring of obsolete equipment and the purchasing of state-of-the-art computer-assisted machinery. The new machinery would take time for the workers to learn to use, but once that was done, waste would be virtually eliminated.

Required:
For each of the above independent scenarios, indicate the type of responsibility centre involved (cost, revenue, profit, or investment) and the accounting numbers on which performance evaluation is likely based.

18–2

Margin; Turnover; ROI

LO3

Seamans Company had sales of $100,000, expenses of $63,000, and operating assets of $62,500.

Required:

1. Compute the margin and turnover ratios.
2. Compute the ROI.

18–3

Margin; Turnover; ROI; Average Operating Assets

LO3

Kaminsky Company provided the following income statement for last year.

Sales	$50,000
Less: Variable expenses	25,000
Contribution margin	$25,000
Less: Fixed expenses	22,250
Operating income	$ 2,750

At the beginning of last year, Kaminsky had $18,650 in operating assets. At the end of the year, Kaminsky had $21,350 in operating assets.

Required:

1. Compute average operating assets.
2. Compute the margin and turnover ratios for last year. Compute ROI.

18–4

ROI; Margin; Turnover

LO3

Spreadsheet

The following data have been collected for the past two years for the Delta Division of Chancellor Company:

	2000	2001
Sales	$30,000,000	$30,000,000
Net operating income	2,400,000	2,220,000
Average operating assets	15,000,000	15,000,000

Required:

1. Compute the margin and turnover ratios for each year.
2. Compute the ROI for each year.
3. Explain why the division experienced decreased ROI from 2000 to 2001.

18–5

ROI; Margin; Turnover

LO3

Data follow for the Theta Division of Chancellor Company (see Exercise 18–4).

	2000	2001
Sales	$50,000,000	$50,000,000
Net operating income	4,000,000	3,700,000
Average operating assets	25,000,000	20,000,000

Required:

1. Compute the margin and turnover ratios for each year.
2. Compute the ROI for the Theta Division for each year.
3. How does the performance of the Theta Division compare with that of the Delta Division?

18–6

ROI and Investment Decisions

LO3

Robin Wayne, division manager of Great Outdoors, Inc., was debating the merits of a new product—a two-person tent capable of withstanding winds of up to 160 kilometres per hour. The tent would be a high-end product, designed for climbers of the world's highest peaks, but was expected to appeal to well-off weekend climbers as well.

The budgeted income of the division was $3,150,000, with operating assets of $17,500,000. The proposed investment would add income of $360,000 and would require an additional investment in equipment of $3,000,000.

Required:

1. Compute the ROI of each of the following:
   a. the division if the tent project is not undertaken.
   b. the tent project alone.
   c. the division if the tent project is undertaken.
2. Do you suppose that Robin will decide to invest in the new tent? Why or why not?

18–7

Weighted Average Cost of Capital; EVA

LO3

Spreadsheet

Bernhardt, Inc., has decided to use EVA to evaluate its performance. Last year, Bernhardt had after-tax operating income of $550,000. Two sources of financing were used by the company: $2.5 million in mortgage bonds paying 6 percent interest and $5 million in common stock, which was considered to be no more or less risky than other stocks. The rate on long-term treasury bonds is 5 percent. Bernhardt, Inc., has $4,000,000 in operating assets and pays a marginal tax rate of 40 percent.

Required:

1. Calculate the weighted average cost of capital for Bernhardt, Inc.
2. Calculate EVA for Bernhardt. Is Bernhardt creating wealth or not?

18–8

Weighted Average Cost of Capital; EVA

LO3

Refer to Exercise 18–7. Now suppose that Bernhardt, Inc., is considering borrowing $2,000,000 in unsecured bonds at a rate of 8 percent. The money will be used to purchase additional operating assets of $1,200,000 (making total operating assets of $5,200,000). This added investment will enable the company to manufacture products that are budgeted to provide $100,000 in after-tax operating income.

Required:

1. Calculate the new weighted average cost of capital for Bernhardt, Inc.
2. Calculate EVA for Bernhardt, Inc., including the new products. Is the new investment a good idea?

18–9

ROI of Two Divisions

LO3

An electronics division has the opportunity to invest in two projects for the coming year: a digital telephone answering machine and a portable video game player. The outlay required for each investment, the dollar returns, and the ROI follow:

	Answering Machine	Video Game Player
Investment	$10,000,000	$4,000,000
Operating income	1,300,000	640,000
ROI	13%	16%

The division is currently earning an ROI of 18 percent, using operating assets of $75 million; operating income on the current investment is $13.5 million. The division has approval to request up to $15 million in new investment capital. Corporate headquarters requires that all investments earn at least 12 percent (this rate represents the amount the corporation must earn to cover the cost of acquiring the capital). The weighted average cost of capital for the company is 12 percent.

Required:

Calculate the ROI for the division for each of the following scenarios: (1) invest in the answering machine; (2) invest in the video game player; (3) invest in both; or (4) invest in neither. Which option would the divisional manager choose?

18–10

EVA

LO3

Refer to Exercise 18–9.

Required:

1. Calculate the EVA for the answering machine.
2. Calculate the EVA for the video game player.
3. Calculate the EVA for the division if neither investment is made. If the manager is evaluated on the basis of EVA, what choice of investments (answering machine, video game player, neither, or both) will be made? Why?

18–11

Transfer Pricing

LO5

Celano, Inc., has a number of divisions, including a mattress division and a furniture division. The Furniture Division manufactures a line of sofa beds, which use a mattress purchased from an outside supplier for $94. Kel Woodburn, manager of the Mattress Division, has approached Brianna Hessler, manager of the Furniture Division, about selling mattresses to the Furniture Division for the sofa beds. Kel has researched the mattress costs and determined the following costs:

Direct materials	$20
Direct labour	18
Variable overhead	17
Fixed overhead	30
Total manufacturing cost	$85

Currently, the Mattress Division has enough capacity to produce 100,000 mattresses but is producing only 50,000. The Furniture Division needs 30,000 mattresses per year.

Required:

1. What is the maximum transfer price? the minimum transfer price? Should the transfer occur?
2. Suppose that Kel and Brianna agree on a transfer price of $75. What is the benefit to each division? What is the benefit to the company as a whole?
3. Suppose that the Mattress Division were operating at capacity. What would be the maximum transfer price? the minimum transfer price? Should the transfer take place in this case? Why or why not?

18–12

Transfer Pricing; Outside Market with Full Capacity

LO5

Delbert Company's Can Division produces a variety of cans that are used for food processing. Delbert's Nut Division buys nuts; deshells, roasts, and salts them; and places them in cans. It sells the cans of roasted nuts to various retailers. The most frequently used can is the 375-gram size. In the past, the Nut Division has purchased these cans from external suppliers for $0.65 each. The manager of the Nut Division has approached the manager of the Can Division and has offered to buy 200,000 375-gram cans each year. The Can Division, which is currently producing at capacity, produces and sells 300,000 375-gram cans to outside customers for $0.65 each.

Required:

1. What is the minimum transfer price for the Can Division? What is the maximum transfer price for the Nut Division? Is it important that transfers take place internally? If transfers do take place, what should the transfer price be?
2. Now assume that the Can Division incurs selling costs of $0.04 per can that could be avoided if the cans are sold internally. Identify the minimum transfer price for the Can Division and the maximum transfer price for the Nut Division. Should the internal transfer take place? If so, what is the benefit to the firm as a whole?
3. Suppose that you are the manager of the Can Division. Selling costs of $0.04 per can are avoidable if the cans are sold internally. Would you accept an offer of $0.63 from the manager of the Nut Division? How much better off (or worse off) would your division be if this price is accepted?

18–13

Transfer Pricing; Idle Capacity

LO5

The Film Division of Photolife, Inc., produces 35mm film that can be sold externally or internally to Photolife's School Photography Division. Sales and cost data per roll of 35mm film follow:

Unit selling price	$2.95
Unit variable cost	1.40
Unit product fixed cost*	1.20
Practical capacity	500,000 units

* $600,000/$500,000

During the coming year, the Film Division expects to sell 350,000 rolls of this film. The School Photography Division currently plans to buy 150,000 rolls of the film on the outside market for $2.95 each. Andrea Harper, manager of the Film Division, has approached Karel Padgett, manager of the School Photography Division, and offered to sell the 150,000 rolls for $2.94 each. Andrea explains to Karel that she can avoid selling costs of $0.02 per film roll and that she will split the savings by offering a $0.01 discount on the usual price.

Required:

1. What is the minimum transfer price that the Film Division would be willing to accept? What is the maximum transfer price that the School Photography Division would be willing to pay? Should an internal transfer take place? What would be the benefit (or loss) to the firm as a whole if the internal transfer took place?
2. Suppose that Karel knew that the Film Division has idle capacity. Do you think that she would agree to the transfer price of $2.94? Suppose she countered with

an offer to pay $2.85? If you were Andrea, would you be interested in this price? Explain with supporting computations.

3. Suppose that Photolife's policy is that all internal transfers take place at full manufacturing cost. What would the transfer price be? Would the transfer take place?

18–14

ROI; Margin; Turnover

LO3

Ready Electronics is facing stiff competition from imported goods. Its operating-income margin has been declining steadily for the past several years; the company has been forced to lower prices so that it can maintain its market share. The operating results for the past three years are as follows:

	Year 1	Year 2	Year 3
Sales	$10,000,000	$ 9,500,000	$ 9,000,000
Net operating income	1,200,000	1,045,000	945,000
Average assets	15,000,000	15,000,000	15,000,000

For the coming year, Ready's president plans to install a JIT purchasing and manufacturing system. She estimates that inventories will be reduced by 70 percent during the first year of operations, producing a 20 percent reduction in the average operating assets of the company, which would remain unchanged without the JIT system. She also estimates that sales and operating income will be restored to Year 1 levels because of simultaneous reductions in operating expenses and selling prices. Lower selling prices will allow Ready to expand its market share.

Required:

1. Compute the ROI, margin, and turnover for Years 1, 2, and 3.
2. Suppose that in Year 4 the sales and operating income were achieved as expected, but inventories remained at the same level as in Year 3. Compute the expected ROI, margin, and turnover. Explain why the ROI increased over the Year 3 level.
3. Suppose that the sales and net operating income for Year 4 remained the same as in Year 3, but inventory reductions were achieved as projected. Compute the ROI, margin, and turnover. Explain why the ROI exceeded the Year 3 level.
4. Assume that all expectations for Year 4 were realized. Compute the expected ROI, margin, and turnover. Explain why the ROI increased over the Year 3 level.

18–15

Transfer Pricing and Autonomy

LO5

The Parts Division supplies Part 678 to the Medical Products Division, which uses it in manufacturing a heart monitor. The Medical Products Division is currently operating below capacity (by 10,000 units), while the Parts Division is operating at capacity. Part 678 sells externally for $50. The cost of producing the heart monitor follows:

Part 678	$ 50
Direct materials	100
Direct labour	20
Variable overhead	30
Fixed overhead	40
Total unit cost	$240

The Medical Products Division has received an order for 1,000 heart monitors from a wholesaler, with an offering price of $230. Since company policy prohibits selling any product below full cost, the divisional manager requested a price concession from the Parts Division. When that manager refused the request, the manager of the Medical Products Division filed an appeal with higher-level management, arguing that a transfer price of full cost should be used so that pricing decisions in his division would not be distorted.

Required:

1. Assume that the full cost of Part 678 is $30. Will the firm as a whole benefit if the part is transferred at $30? Should top management intervene?

2. Is anything wrong with the company policy that a division's selling price cannot be below full cost?
3. Compute the minimum and maximum transfer prices. Is an internal transfer indicated? If a transfer were to take place, what should the transfer price be?

18–16

**Transfer Pricing;
Alternative Prices**

LO5, LO6

International Company is a decentralized company with several divisions. The Component Division currently sells its product to other manufacturers at a price of $50 per unit. The Assembly Division has been purchasing 500,000 units per year from an external source at a price of $48 per unit due to the large number of units purchased. The Component Division has adequate capacity to supply the Assembly Division, and this capacity cannot be used for anything else in the short run. The Component Division would like to supply the Assembly Division, but the Assembly Division is unwilling to pay the $50 price. The Component Division's unit cost is presented below:

Direct materials	$18
Direct labour	14
Variable overhead	6
Fixed overhead*	4
	$42

* Based on a capacity of 4,000,000 units.

Required:

1. What is the market price of the component?
2. What is the full cost price of the component?
3. What price range is appropriate for short-run intracompany transfers?
4. From International Company's perspective, should the Assembly Division purchase from external sources under current circumstances? Why?
5. What pricing concept is appropriate to this situation and benefits both divisions? Why? (CGA Canada adapted)

18–17

**Margin; Turnover;
ROI**

LO3

Calculate the missing data for each of the four independent companies below.

	A	B	C	D
Revenue	$10,000	$45,000	$200,000	$ —
Expenses	7,800	—	188,000	—
Net income	2,200	18,000	—	—
Assets	20,000	—	100,000	9,600
Margin	— %	40%	— %	6.25%
Turnover	—	0.3125	—	2.00
ROI	—	—	—	—

18–18

EVA

LO3

Refer to 18–17. Assume that the cost of capital is 12 percent for each of the four firms.

Required:

Compute the EVA for each of the four firms.

18–19

Transfer Pricing

LO6

Adler Industries is a vertically integrated firm with several divisions that operate as decentralized profit centres. Adler's Systems Division manufactures scientific instruments and uses the products of two of Adler's other divisions. The Board Division manufactures printed circuit boards (PCBs). One PCB model is made exclusively for the Systems Division using proprietary designs, while less complex models are sold in outside markets. The products of the Transistor Division are sold in a well-developed competitive market; however, one transistor model is also used by the Systems Division. The costs per unit of the products used by the Systems Division are presented below:

	PCB	Transistor
Direct material	$2.50	$0.80
Direct labour	4.50	1.00
Variable overhead	2.00	0.50
Fixed overhead	0.80	0.75
Total cost	$9.80	$3.05

The Board Division sells its commercial product at full cost plus a 25 percent markup and believes that the proprietary board made for the Systems Division would sell for $12.25 per unit on the open market. The market price of the transistor used by the Systems Division is $3.70 per unit.

Required:

1. What is the minimum transfer price for the Transistor Division? What is the maximum transfer price of the transistor for the Systems Division?
2. Assume the Systems Division is able to purchase a large quantity of transistors from an outside source at $2.90 per unit. Further assume that the Transistor Division has excess capacity. Can the Transistor Division meet this price?
3. The Board and Systems divisions have negotiated a transfer price of $11 per printed circuit board. Discuss the impact that this transfer price will have on each division. (US CMA adapted)

PROBLEMS

18–20

ROI for Multiple Investments; EVA

LO3

The manager of a division that produces add-on products for the automobile industry has just been presented with the opportunity to invest in two independent projects. The first is an air conditioner for the back seats of vans and minivans. The second is a turbo-charger. Without the investments, the division will have average assets for the coming year of $25.6 million and expected operating income of $3.584 million. The outlay required for each investment and the expected operating incomes are as follows:

	Air Conditioner	Turbocharger
Outlay	$750,000	$540,000
Operating income	67,500	54,000

Corporate headquarters will secure up to $1.3 million in loans for the automotive add-on division for further investments. The company's cost of capital is 9 percent.

Required:

1. Compute the ROI for each investment project.
2. Compute the budgeted *divisional* ROI for each of the following four alternatives:
   a. The air conditioner investment is made.
   b. The turbocharger investment is made.
   c. Both investments are made.
   d. Neither additional investment is made.
   Assuming that divisional managers are evaluated and rewarded on the basis of ROI performance, which alternative do you think the divisional manager will choose?
3. Suppose that the investment must be for the entire $1.3 million. Calculate the EVA of the two investments taken as a package. Based on EVA, are the investments profitable?

18–21

Transfer Pricing with Idle Capacity

LO5

GreenWorld, Inc., is a nursery products firm. It has three divisions that grow and sell plants: the Western Division, the Central Division, and the Eastern Division. Recently, the Central Division of GreenWorld acquired a plastics factory that manufactures green plastic pots. These pots can be sold both externally and internally. Company policy permits each manager to decide whether to buy or sell internally.

Each divisional manager is evaluated on the basis of return on investment and EVA.

The Western Division had previously bought its plastic pots in lots of 100 from a variety of vendors. The average price paid was $75 per box of 100 pots. However, the acquisition made Rosario Sanchez-Ruiz, manager of the Western Division, wonder whether or not a more favourable price could be arranged. She decided to approach Lorne Matthews, manager of the Central Division, to see if he wanted to offer a better price for an internal transfer. She suggested a transfer of 3,500 boxes at $70 per box.

Lorne gathered the following information regarding the cost of a box of 100 pots:

Direct materials	$35
Direct labour	8
Variable overhead	10
Fixed overhead*	10
Total unit cost	$63
Selling price	$75
Production capacity	20,000 boxes

* Fixed overhead is based on $200,000/20,000 boxes.

Required:

1. Suppose that the plastics factory is producing at capacity and can sell all that it produces to outside customers. How should Lorne respond to Rosario's request for a lower transfer price?
2. Now assume that the plastics factory is currently selling 16,000 boxes. What are the minimum and maximum transfer prices? Should Lorne consider the transfer at $70 per box?
3. Suppose that GreenWorld's policy is that all transfer prices be set at full cost plus 20 percent. Would the transfer take place? Why or why not?

18–22

ROI Calculations with Varying Assumptions

LO3

Knitpix Products is a division of Parker Textiles, Inc. During the coming year, it expects to earn a net operating income of $310,000 based on sales of $3.45 million; without any new investments, the division will have average net operating assets of $3 million. The division is considering a capital investment project—adding knitting machines to produce gaiters—that requires an additional investment of $600,000 and increases net operating income by $57,500 (sales would increase by $575,000). If made, the investment would increase beginning net operating assets by $600,000 and ending net operating assets by $400,000. Assume that the minimum rate of return required by the company is 7 percent.

Required:

1. Compute the ROI for the division without the investment.
2. Compute the margin and turnover ratios without the investment. Show that the product of the margin and turnover ratios equals the ROI computed in Requirement 1.
3. Compute the ROI for the division with the new investment. Do you think that the divisional manager will approve the investment?
4. Compute the margin and turnover ratios for the division with the new investment. Compare these with the old ratios.
5. Assume that a JIT purchasing and manufacturing system is installed, reducing average operating assets by $800,000. Compute the ROI with and without the investment under this new scenario. Now do you think that the divisional manager will accept the new investment? Should he accept it? Explain your answer.
6. Refer to Requirement 5. Compute the margin and turnover ratios without the investment. Use these ratios to explain why the ROI increases.

18–23

ROI; EVA; Evaluating
Performance

LO3, LO4

Raddington Industries produces tool and die machinery for manufacturers. The company expanded vertically in 1994 by acquiring one of its suppliers of alloy steel plates, Reigis Steel Company. To manage the two separate businesses, the operations of Reigis are reported separately as an investment centre.

Raddington monitors its divisions on the basis of both unit contribution and return on average investment (ROI), with investment defined as average operating assets employed. Management bonuses are determined on ROI. The average cost of capital is 11 percent of operating investment.

Reigis's cost of goods sold is considered to be entirely variable, while the division's administrative expenses are not dependent on volume. Selling expenses are a mixed cost, with 40 percent attributed to sales volume. Reigis contemplated a capital acquisition with an estimated ROI of 11.5 percent; however, divisional management decided against the investment because it believed that the investment would decrease Reigis's overall ROI. The 2001 operating statement for Reigis follows. The division's operating assets employed were $15,750,000 at November 30, 2001, a 5 percent increase over the 2000 year-end balance.

Reigis Steel Division Operating Statement For the Year Ended November 30, 2001 ($000 omitted)		
Sales revenue		$25,000
Less expenses:		
Cost of goods sold	$16,500	
Administrative expenses	3,955	
Selling expenses	2,700	23,155
Income from operations before income taxes		$ 1,845

Required:

1. Calculate the unit contribution margin for Reigis Steel Division if 1,484,000 units were produced and sold during the year ended November 30, 2001.
2. Calculate the following performance measures for 2001 for the Reigis Steel Division:
    a. Pretax return on average investment in operating assets employed (ROI).
    b. EVA calculated on the basis of average operating assets employed.
3. Explain why the management of the Reigis Steel Division would have been more likely to accept the contemplated capital acquisition if EVA rather than ROI had been used as a performance measure.
4. The Reigis Steel Division is a separate investment centre within Raddington Industries. Identify several items that Reigis should control if it is to be evaluated fairly by either the ROI or EVA performance measures. (US CMA adapted)

18–24

Setting Transfer
Prices—Market Price
versus Full Cost

LO5

Videodays, Inc., manufactures stereo receivers, televisions, and VCRs in its four divisions: Receiver, TV, VCR, and Components. The Components Division produces electronic components that can be used by the other three divisions. All the components that this division produces can be sold to outside customers; however, from the beginning, about 70 percent of its output has been used internally. The current policy requires that all internal transfers of components be transferred at full cost.

Recently, Will Ferguson, the new chief executive officer of Videodays, decided to investigate the transfer pricing policy. He was concerned that the current method of pricing internal transfers might force decisions by divisional managers that would be suboptimal for the firm. As part of his inquiry, he gathered some information concerning Component 12F, used by the Receiver Division in its production of a clock radio, Model 357K.

The Receiver Division sells 100,000 units of Model 357K each year at a unit price of $21. Given current market conditions, this is the maximum price that the division can charge for Model 357K. The cost of manufacturing the radio follows:

Component 12F	$ 6.50
Direct materials	5.50
Direct labour	4.00
Variable overhead	1.00
Fixed overhead	2.00
Total unit cost	$19.00

The radio is produced efficiently, and no further reduction in manufacturing costs is possible.

The manager of the Components Division indicated that she could sell 100,000 units (the division's capacity for this part) of Component 12F to outside buyers at $12 per unit. The Receiver Division could also buy the part for $12 from external suppliers. She supplied the following details on the manufacturing cost of the component:

Direct materials	$2.50
Direct labour	0.50
Variable overhead	1.50
Fixed overhead	2.00
Total unit cost	$6.50

Required:

1. Compute the firmwide contribution margin associated with Component 12F and Model 357K. Also compute the contribution margin earned by each division.
2. Suppose that Will Ferguson abolishes the current transfer pricing policy and gives divisions autonomy in setting transfer prices. Can you predict what transfer price the manager of the Components Division will set? What should the minimum transfer price for this part be? the maximum?
3. Given the new transfer pricing policy, predict how this will affect the production decision for Model 357K of the Receiver Division manager. How many units of Component 12F will the manager of the Receiver Division purchase, either internally or externally?
4. Given the new transfer price set by the Components Division and your answer to Requirement 3, how many units of Component 12F will be sold externally?
5. Given your answers to Requirements 3 and 4, compute the firmwide contribution margin. What has happened? Was Will's decision to grant additional decentralization good or bad?

18–25

Transfer Pricing— Full Cost Plus Policy

LO5

Crownside Aluminum manufactures and installs aluminum products for houses, such as siding, soffit and fascia, and eavestroughs. The company has decentralized, designating Manufacturing as one division and Sales and Installation as another. Company policies require that all aluminum products sold be manufactured internally and that the transfer price to be used is full absorption cost plus a markup of 10 percent on cost.

Recently, the Sales Division negotiated a contract with a local builder to supply 40 lots of a particular style of eavestrough, Model 403, at a price of $900 within the next 30 days. The Manufacturing Division, when asked to supply these units, claimed that it would have to produce the units in overtime because it was already at capacity. The overtime charges would double the cost of labour and overhead components of the item, as shown below.

Cost and Transfer Price of Model 403 (per unit)

	Regular Time	Overtime
Materials	$300	$300
Direct labour	100	200
Variable overhead[a]	100	200
Fixed overhead[a]	80	160
Total cost	$580	$860
Plus 10 percent	58	86
Transfer price	$638	$946

[a] Applied on the basis of direct labour dollars.

The Sales Division does not want to pay the additional $308 per unit and has found that it can obtain the same product from another supplier for $825. Sales has asked Manufacturing to match the $825 price, and Manufacturing has stood its ground, claiming that it must charge the $946 because of company policy. The two divisions have decided to appeal to the company president to settle the dispute.

Required:

1. Should the Sales Division be allowed to purchase Model 403 externally to meet its contract commitments? Provide calculations to support your response, and include any qualitative factors that should be taken into account in making the decision.
2. Evaluate the effectiveness of the transfer-pricing policies and decentralization at Crownside. (CGA Canada adapted)

18–26

Market Price versus Full Cost Plus Markup

LO5

Nashmen Manufacturing Corporation produces lawn mowers, snowblowers, and tillers. The company has six divisions, each set up as an investment centre. Managers of the divisions are evaluated and rewarded on the basis of return on investment and EVA. Company policy dictates that internal transfers must take place whenever possible and that the transfer price will be full cost plus 10 percent. Ken Booth, vice-president of operations, is reevaluating the company's current internal transfer policy in the light of a recent memo received from Dana Lemmons, manager of the Parts Division. The memo follows:

MEMORANDUM

To: Ken Booth, Vice-President of Operations
From: Dana Lemmons, Manager of Parts Division
Subject: Transfer-Pricing Policy

Ken, I must register serious concern about our current transfer-pricing policy of full cost plus 10 percent. First, I believe that this policy creates a significant understatement of my division's ROI. Second, it creates a disincentive for my division to decrease our costs of manufacturing.

For example, consider our production of Part 34 (small carburetors). Currently, we are capable of producing 300,000 of these units each year. Of these 300,000 carburetors, 200,000 are transferred to the Small Motor Division at a price of $16.50 per unit; 100,000 are sold to external customers at $20 each. I know that we can sell every carburetor we make to external customers. By being forced to transfer internally, we are losing income and showing a much smaller ROI than we otherwise could.

But the problem is even greater. My engineers have created a new design that will allow us to decrease our fixed manufacturing costs for carburetors by $5 per unit. However, if we implement this design, our transfer price will drop to $11, and the revenues we receive from internal sales will drop significantly. All the savings and more are transferred to the buying division.

In my opinion, all of these problems can be resolved by allowing each divisional manager to set transfer prices and allowing each of us to buy or sell our products as we see fit.

After reading the memo, Ken gathered production information.

Manufacturing cost of carburetor:

Direct materials	$ 6.00
Direct labour	1.25
Variable overhead	1.50
Fixed overhead	6.25
Total cost	$15.00

Manufacturing cost of small motor:

Carburetor	$16.50
Direct materials	23.50
Direct labour	8.75
Variable overhead	3.25
Fixed overhead	8.40
Total cost	$60.40

Production and sales of small motor:

Production	200,000
Sales	200,000
Unit price	$75

Required:

1. Assume that the Parts Division implements the new design change. Assume also that the internal demand for the carburetors remains constant. Compute the change in profits for the firm as a whole from this decision. Now compute the change in profits for the Parts Division and the Small Motor Division. Was Dana's concern valid? Were all the benefits of the improved design captured by the Small Motor Division?

2. Refer to Requirement 1. Now assume that the reduced cost of the carburetor increases the internal demand from 200,000 to 300,000 units. Evaluate the impact on firmwide profits and on each division's profits. If Dana anticipated this effect, do you think that she would implement the cost-reducing design?

3. Refer to the original data. Ken Booth wants to know the effect of decentralizing the internal pricing decisions. Assuming that the Small Motor Division can buy carburetors of equal quality for $20 from outside suppliers, provide Dana with a complete assessment of the effect. In your assessment, include the change in firmwide and divisional profits. Also, comment on the incentives that Dana would have for implementing the cost-reducing design.

18–27

Full Cost Plus Pricing and Negotiation

LO5

Technovia, Inc., has two divisions: Auxiliary Components and Audio Systems. Divisional managers are encouraged to maximize return on investment and EVA. Managers are essentially free to determine whether goods will be transferred internally and what internal transfer prices will be. Headquarters has directed that all internal prices be expressed on a full cost plus basis. The markup in the full-cost pricing arrangement, however, is left to the discretion of the divisional managers. Recently, the two divisional managers met to discuss a pricing agreement for a sub-woofer that would be sold with a personal computer system. Production of the sub-woofers is at capacity. Subwoofers can be sold for $31 to outside customers. The Audio Systems Division can also buy the subwoofer from external sources for the same price; however, the manager of this division is hoping to obtain a price concession by buying internally. The full cost of manufacturing the subwoofer is $20. If the manager of the Auxiliary Components Division sells the subwoofer internally, $5 of selling and distribution costs can be avoided. The volume of business would be 250,000 units per year, well within the capacity of the producing division.

After some discussion, the two managers agreed on a full cost plus pricing scheme that would be reviewed annually. Any increase in the outside selling price would be added to the transfer price by simply increasing the markup by an appropriate amount. Any major changes in the factors that led to the agreement could initiate a new round of negotiation; otherwise, the full cost plus arrangement would continue in force for subsequent years.

Required:

1. Calculate the minimum and maximum transfer prices.
2. Assume that the transfer price agreed upon between the two managers is halfway between the minimum and maximum transfer prices. Calculate the full cost plus transfer price that would represent this transfer price.
3. Refer to Requirement 2. Assume that in the following year, the outside price of subwoofers increases to $32. What is the new full cost plus transfer price?
4. Assume that two years after the initial agreement, the market for subwoofers has softened considerably, causing excess capacity for the Auxiliary Components Division. Would you expect a renegotiation of the full cost plus pricing arrangement for the coming year? Explain.

18–28

Transfer Pricing; Various Computations

LO5

Courtland Company is a decentralized organization with a divisional structure. Each divisional manager is evaluated on the basis of ROI.

The Plastics Division produces a plastic container that the Chemical Division can use. Plastics can produce up to 100,000 of these containers per year. The variable costs of manufacturing the plastic containers are $4.50. The Chemical Division labels the plastic containers and uses them to store an important industrial chemical, which is sold to outside customers for $50 per container. The division's capacity is 20,000 units. The variable costs of processing the chemical (in addition to the cost of the container itself) are $26.

Required: (Assume that each requirement is independent, unless otherwise indicated.)

1. Assume that all of the plastic containers produced can be sold to external customers for $12 each. The Chemical Division wants to buy 20,000 containers per year. What should the transfer price be?
2. Refer to Requirement 1. Assume $2 of avoidable distribution costs. Identify the maximum and minimum transfer prices. Identify the actual transfer price, assuming that negotiation splits the difference.
3. Assume that the Plastics Division is operating at 75 percent of capacity. The Chemical Division is currently buying 20,000 containers from an outside supplier for $9.50 each. Assume that any joint benefit will be split evenly between the two divisions. What is the expected transfer price? How much will the profits of the firm increase under this arrangement? How much will the profits of the Plastics Division increase, assuming that it sells the extra 20,000 containers internally?
4. Assume that both divisions have excess capacity. Currently, 15,000 containers are being transferred between divisions at a price of $8. The Chemical Division has an opportunity to take a special order for 5,000 containers of chemical at a price of $33.75 per container. The manager of the Chemical Division approached the manager of the Plastics Division and offered to buy an additional 5,000 plastic containers for $5 each. Assuming that the Plastics Division has excess capacity totalling at least 5,000 units, should the manager take the offer? What is the minimum transfer price? the maximum? Assume that the Plastics Division manager counters with a price of $5.50. Would the Chemical Division manager be interested?

18–29

Transfer Pricing;
Custom-Made
Subassembly

LO5

The Industrial Machine Division has requested a specially designed subassembly from the Metal Fabricating Division. Because the subassembly is specially designed, there is no outside market price that can serve as a reference point for establishing an internal transfer price. The estimated cost of manufacturing the subassembly follows:

Direct materials	$100
Direct labour	25
Variable overhead	50
Fixed overhead*	30
Total unit cost	$205

* Representing an allocation of existing fixed overhead.
  The total fixed overhead is the same regardless of whether
  the Metal Fabricating Division produces the subassembly.

The Industrial Machine Division will use 10,000 of the subassemblies per year.

Required:

1. Assume that producing the special subassembly displaces other potential jobs. How should the manager of the Metal Fabricating Division set the transfer price for the custom-made subassembly?
2. Assume that two potential jobs will be displaced by the special subassembly. The expected revenues and the total expected costs of these jobs are as follows:

	Job 1	Job 2
Revenues	$2,600,000	$1,500,000
Variable manufacturing	1,950,000	1,050,000
Fixed overhead	200,000	300,000

   Compute the minimum price that the Metal Fabricating Division should charge.

3. Now assume that the Metal Fabricating Division can produce the special subassembly without displacing any work for outside customers. What is the minimum transfer price that should be charged for the subassembly?
4. Refer to Requirement 3. The manager of the Metal Fabricating Division has offered to supply the subassembly for full cost plus the division's average markup. Assuming that average markup is 35 percent, compute the offered transfer price. What do you think of the pricing scheme suggested by the manager of the selling division?
5. Refer to Requirement 4. The manager of the Industrial Machine Division refuses to pay the average markup. He indicates that an outside supplier has offered to produce the subassembly for $200 per unit. He offers to pay variable costs plus a lump sum of $125,000 to help cover fixed costs and provide some profit. Do you think the manager of the Metal Fabricating Division should accept this last offer? Would she be tempted to do so? Explain.

18–30

Transfer Pricing;
Various
Computations

LO3, LO5

Stamwell Company has two divisions: the Milk Division and the Dairy Products Division. Divisional managers are evaluated on the basis of return on investment. The Milk Division has the capability to produce 1,000,000 litres of milk per year. The Dairy Products Division uses milk to produce ice cream, cheese, and cottage cheese. The following data are available for the Milk Division:

Selling price per litre	$1.20
Variable production cost	.25
Fixed production cost*	.50

* Based on 1,000,000 litres of output.

The Dairy Products Division uses 600,000 litres of milk per year when it is operating at capacity.

Required:

1. (Unless otherwise indicated, assume that the requirements are independent of each other.) Assume that the Milk Division can sell all that it produces. The Dairy Products Division is operating at 90 percent of capacity. It can buy all the milk that it needs for $1 per litre from outside suppliers. What are the minimum and maximum transfer prices? What transfer price would you recommend? How many litres of milk do you think that the Dairy Products Division will buy internally, assuming that it is operating at 90 percent of capacity?

2. Refer to Requirement 1. How would your answers differ if the Milk Division can avoid distribution costs of $0.10 per litre by selling the milk internally?

3. The manager of the Milk Division realizes that excess capacity will exist for the last six months of the current year. He is reluctant to sell any of the milk cows to reduce production, because he expects the market to rebound in the coming year. Accordingly, the cows will continue to be milked, creating excess production of 80,000 litres. Unless a market for the excess milk can be found, it will simply be dumped. Discouraged about the possibility of finding any new outside customers, the manager of the Milk Division approaches the manager of the Dairy Products Division to see if a deal for internal sales can be arranged. The Dairy Products Division has been buying all of its milk from outside suppliers at $1 per litre. Assume that production of milk is spread evenly over the year and that milk sold externally is sold for the normal price. Under these conditions, identify the minimum and maximum transfer prices. Assume that the managers split the difference between the two prices. How many litres will be transferred internally? By how much will the profits of the firm and each division increase?

4. Refer to Requirement 3. Now assume that the Milk Division has an offer to sell the 80,000 litres of extra milk to a government agency for conversion into powdered milk. The offering price is $0.60 per litre. How does this change your answers to Requirement 3?

18–31

Transfer Pricing

LO5

PortCo Products is a divisionalized furniture manufacturer. The divisions are autonomous segments with each responsible for its own sales, costs of operations, working capital management, and equipment acquisition. Each division serves a different market in the furniture industry. Because the markets and products of the divisions are so different, there have never been any transfers between divisions.

The Commercial Division manufactures equipment and furniture that is purchased by the restaurant industry. The division plans to introduce a new line of counter and chair units that feature a cushioned seat for the counter chairs. John Kline, the divisional manager, has discussed the manufacture of the cushioned seat with Russ Fiegel of the Office Division. They both believe that a cushioned seat currently made by the Office Division for use on its deluxe office stool could be modified for use on the new counter chair. Consequently, John has asked Russ for a price for 100-unit lots of the cushioned seat. The following conversation took place about the price to be charged for the cushioned seats.

Russ: "John, we can make the necessary modifications to the cushioned seat easily. The raw materials used in your seat are slightly different and should cost about 10 percent more than those used in our deluxe office stool. However, the labour time (0.5 DLH) should be the same, because the seat fabrication operation is basically the same. I would price the seat at our regular rate—full cost plus 30 percent markup."

John: "That's higher than I expected, Russ. I was thinking that a good price would be your variable manufacturing costs. After all, your capacity costs will be incurred regardless of this job."

Russ: "John, I'm at capacity. If I make the cushioned seats for you, I'll have to cut my production of deluxe office stools. Of course, I can increase my production of economy office stools. The labour time freed by not having to fabricate the frame or assemble the deluxe stool can be shifted to the frame fabrication and assembly of the economy office stool. Fortunately, I can switch my labour force between these two models of stools without any loss of efficiency. As you know, overtime is not a feasible alternative in our community. I'd like to sell it to you at variable cost, but I have excess demand for both products. I don't mind changing my product mix to emphasize the economy model if I get a good return on the seats I make for you. Here are my standard costs for the two stools and a schedule of my manufacturing overhead."

OFFICE DIVISION
STANDARD COSTS AND PRICES

	Deluxe Office Stool	Economy Office Stool
Raw materials, framing	$ 8.15	$ 9.76
Cushioned seat, padding	2.40	—
Vinyl	4.00	—
Molded seat (purchased)	—	6.00
Direct labor:		
1.5 DLH @ $7.50	11.25	
0.8 DLH @ $7.50		6.00
Manufacturing overhead:		
1.5 DLH @ $12.80	19.20	
0.8 DLH @ $12.80		10.24
Total standard cost	$45.00	$32.00
Selling price (30% markup)	$58.50	$41.60

OFFICE DIVISION
MANUFACTURING OVERHEAD BUDGET

Overhead Item	Nature	Amount
Supplies	Variable (at current market prices)	$ 420,000
Indirect labour	Variable	375,000
Supervision	Nonvariable	250,000
Power	Use varies with activity; rates are fixed	180,000
Heat and light	Nonvariable (light is fixed regardless of production, while heat/air conditioning varies with fuel charges)	140,000
Property insurance	Nonvariable (any change in amounts/rates is independent of production)	200,000
Depreciation	Fixed dollar total	1,700,000
Employee benefits	20% of supervision, direct and indirect labour	575,000
Total overhead		$3,840,000
Capacity in DLH		300,000
Overhead rate/DLH		$12.80

John: "I guess I see your point, Russ, but I don't want to price myself out of the market. Maybe we should talk to corporate to see if it can give us any guidance."

Required:

1. John and Russ did ask PortCo's corporate management for guidance on an appropriate transfer price. Corporate management suggested they consider using a transfer price based on variable manufacturing cost plus opportunity cost. Calculate a transfer price for the cushioned seat based on variable manufacturing cost plus opportunity cost.
2. Which alternative transfer pricing system—full cost, variable manufacturing cost, or variable manufacturing cost plus opportunity cost—would be better as the underlying concept for an intracompany transfer price policy? Explain your answer. (US CMA adapted)

18–32

Managerial
Performance
Evaluation

LO3, LO4

Greg Peterson has recently been appointed vice-president of operations for Webster Corporation. Greg has a manufacturing background and previously served as operations manager of Webster's Tractor Division. The business segments of Webster include the manufacture of heavy equipment, food processing, and financial services.

In a recent conversation with Carol Andrews, Webster's chief financial officer, Greg suggested that segment managers be evaluated on the basis of the segment data appearing in Webster's annual financial report. This report presents revenues, earnings, identifiable assets, and depreciation for each segment for a five-year period. Greg believes that evaluating segment managers by criteria similar to those used to evaluate the company's top management would be appropriate. Carol expressed her reservations about using segment information from the annual financial report for this purpose and suggested that Greg consider other ways to evaluate the performance of segment managers.

Required:

1. Explain why the segment information prepared for public reporting purposes may not be appropriate for the evaluation of segment management performance.
2. Describe the possible behavioural impact on Webster Corporation's segment managers if their performance is evaluated on the basis of the information in the annual financial report.
3. Identify and describe several types of financial information that would be more appropriate for Greg Peterson to review when evaluating the performance of segment managers. (US CMA adapted)

18–33

Management
Compensation

LO4

Renslen, Inc., a truck manufacturing conglomerate, has recently purchased two divisions, Meyers Service Company and Wellington Products, Inc. Meyers provides maintenance service on large truck cabs for 12-wheeler trucks, and Wellington produces air brakes for the 12-wheeler trucks.

The employees at Meyers take pride in their work, and Meyers is proclaimed to offer the best maintenance service in the trucking industry. The management of Meyers, as a group, has received additional compensation from a 10 percent bonus pool based on income before taxes and bonus; Renslen plans to continue to compensate the Meyers management team on this basis, since it is the same incentive plan used for all other Renslen divisions.

Wellington offers a high-quality product to the trucking industry and is the premium choice even when compared to foreign competition. The management team at Wellington strives for zero defects and minimal scrap costs; current scrap levels are at 2 percent. The incentive compensation plan for Wellington management has been a 1 percent bonus based on gross profit margin; Renslen plans to continue to compensate the Wellington management team on this basis.

Following are the condensed income statements for both divisions for the fiscal year ended May 31, 2001.

Renslen, Inc.
Divisional Income Statements
For the Year Ended May 31, 2001

	Meyers Service Company	Wellington Products, Inc.
Revenues	$4,000,000	$10,000,000
Cost of product	75,000	4,950,000
Salaries*	2,200,000	2,150,000
Fixed selling expenses	1,000,000	2,500,000
Interest expense	30,000	65,000
Other operating expenses	278,000	134,000
Total expenses	3,583,000	9,799,000
Income before taxes and bonus	$ 417,000	$ 201,000

* Each division has $1,000,000 of management salary expense that is eligible for the bonus pool.

Renslen has invited the management teams of all its divisions to an off-site management workshop in July, where the bonus cheques will be presented. Renslen is concerned that the different bonus plans at the two divisions may cause some heated discussion.

Required:

1. Determine the 2001 bonus pool available for the management team at
   a. Meyers Service Company
   b. Wellington Products, Inc.

2. Identify at least two advantages and at least two disadvantages to Renslen, Inc., of the bonus pool incentive plan at
   a. Meyers Service Company
   b. Wellington Products, Inc.

3. Having two different types of incentive plans for two operating divisions of the same corporation can create problems.
   a. Discuss the behavioural problems that could arise within management for Meyers Service Company and Wellington Products, Inc. as a result of having different types of incentive plans.
   b. Present arguments that Renslen, Inc., can give to the management teams of both Meyers and Wellington to justify having two different incentive plans.

18–34

Management Compensation

LO4

Shehata Enterprises is contemplating the idea of establishing an incentive scheme for its divisional executive group. Shehata is a large public company whose shares trade on the Toronto Stock Exchange. The company is organized into divisions, each of which is headed by a divisional vice-president. Head office is overseen by the president and five senior vice-presidents. Currently, the head office executives are partly compensated by means of a stock option plan based on annual company earnings. For the divisional group, the board of directors has recommended a performance bonus scheme based on the achievement of annual divisional return on investment. The bonus pool will be defined as a percentage (say 6 percent) of the company's net income after taxes. Divisional income is currently defined as net income after all head office charges and taxes, and investment is defined as total assets.

Required:

Evaluate the proposal to establish an incentive plan for the divisions. Include in your answer an assessment of the strengths and weaknesses of the performance evaluation scheme and a discussion of ways in which these weaknesses can be corrected. Briefly comment on the stock option plan already in place. (CGA Canada adapted)

MANAGERIAL DECISION CASES

18–35

ROI and EVA; Ethical Considerations

LO3

Grate Care Company specializes in producing products for personal grooming. The company operates six divisions, including the Hair Products Division. Each division is treated as an investment centre. Managers are evaluated and rewarded on the basis of ROI performance. Only those managers who produce the best ROIs are selected to receive bonuses and to fill higher-level managerial positions. Fred Olsen, manager of the Hair Products Division, has always been one of the top performers. For the past two years, Fred's division has produced the largest ROI; last year, the division earned a net operating income of $2.56 million and employed average operating assets valued at $16 million. Fred was pleased with his division's performance and had been told that if the division does well this year, he would be in line for a headquarters position.

For the coming year, Fred's division has been promised new capital totalling $1.5 million. Any of the capital not invested by the division will be invested to earn the company's cost of capital (9 percent). After some careful investigation, the marketing and engineering staff recommended that the division invest in equipment that could be used to produce a crimping and waving iron, a product currently not produced by the division. The cost of the equipment was estimated at $1.2 million. The division's marketing manager estimated operating earnings from the new line at $156,000 per year.

After receiving the proposal and reviewing the potential effects, Fred turned it down. He then wrote a memo to corporate headquarters, indicating that his division would not be able to employ the capital in any new projects within the next eight to ten months. He did note, however, that he was confident that his marketing and engineering staff would have a project ready by the end of the year. At that time, he would like to have access to the capital.

Required:

1. Explain why Fred Olsen turned down the proposal to add the capability of producing a crimping and waving iron. Provide computations to support your reasoning.
2. Compute the effect that the new product line would have on the profitability of the firm as a whole. Should the division have produced the crimping and waving iron?
3. Suppose that the firm used EVA as a measure of divisional performance. Do you think Fred's decision might have been different? Why?
4. Explain why a firm like Grate Care might decide to use both EVA and return on investment as measures of performance.
5. Did Fred display ethical behaviour when he turned down the investment? In discussing this issue, consider why he refused to allow the investment.

18–36

Transfer Pricing; Behavioural Considerations

LO5

Lynsar Corporation started as a single plant that produced the major components of electric motors, the company's main product, and then assembled them. Lynsar later expanded by developing outside markets for some of the components used in its motors. Eventually, Lynsar reorganized into four manufacturing divisions: Bearing, Casing, Switch, and Motor. Each of the four manufacturing divisions operates as an autonomous unit, and divisional performance is the basis for year-end bonuses.

Lynsar's transfer pricing policy permits the manufacturing divisions to sell externally to outside customers as well as internally to the other divisions. The price for goods transferred between divisions is to be negotiated between the buying and selling divisions without any interference from top management.

Lynsar's profits have dropped for the current year even though sales have increased, and the drop in profits can be traced almost entirely to the Motor Division. Jere Feldon, Lynsar's chief financial officer, has determined that the Motor Division has purchased switches for its motors from an outside supplier during the current year rather than buy them from the Switch Division. The Switch Division is at capacity and has refused to sell the switches to the Motor Division, because it can sell them to outside customers at a price higher than the actual full (absorption) manufacturing cost that has always been negotiated in the past with the Motor Division. When the Motor Division refused to meet the price that the Switch Division was receiving from its outside buyer, the Motor Division had to purchase the switches from an outside supplier at an even higher price.

Jere is reviewing Lynsar's transfer pricing policy because he believes that suboptimization has occurred. While the Switch Division made the correct decision to maximize its divisional profit by not transferring the switches at actual full manufacturing cost, this decision was not necessarily in the best interests of Lynsar. The Motor Division paid more for the switches than the selling price the Switch Division charged its outside customer. The Motor Division has always been Lynsar's largest division and has tended to dominate the smaller divisions. Jere has learned that the Casing and Bearing divisions are also resisting the Motor Division's desires to continue using actual full manufacturing cost as the negotiated price.

Jere has requested that the corporate accounting department study alternative transfer pricing methods that would promote overall goal congruence, motivate divisional management performance, and optimize overall company performance. Three of the transfer pricing methods being considered follow. If one of these methods is selected, it will be applied uniformly across all divisions:

a. Standard full manufacturing costs plus markup.
b. Market selling price of the products being transferred.
c. Outlay (out-of-pocket) costs incurred to the point of transfer plus opportunity cost per unit.

Required:

1. Discuss both the positive and the negative behavioural implications that can arise from employing a negotiated transfer price system for goods that are transferred between divisions. Explain the behavioural problems that can arise from using actual full (absorption) manufacturing costs as a transfer price.
2. Discuss the behavioural problems that could arise if Lynsar Corporation decides to change from its current policy covering the transfer of goods between divisions to a revised transfer pricing policy that would apply uniformly to all divisions.
3. Discuss the likely behaviour of both "buying" and "selling" divisional managers for each of the three transfer pricing methods being considered by Lynsar Corporation:
   a. Standard full manufacturing costs plus markup.
   b. Market selling price of the products being transferred.
   c. Outlay (out-of-pocket) costs incurred to the point of transfer plus opportunity cost per unit. (US CMA adapted)

18–37

Birch Paper Company Case

LO5

"If I were to price these boxes any lower than $480 a thousand," said James Brunner, manager of Birch Paper Company's Thompson Division, "I'd be countermanding my order of last month for our [salespeople] to stop shaving their bids and to bid full-cost quotations. I've been trying for weeks to improve the quality of our business, and if I turn round now and accept this job at $430 or $450 or something less than $480, I'll be tearing down this program I've been working so hard do build up. The division can't very well show a profit by putting in bids that don't even cover a fair share of overhead costs, let alone give us a profit."

Birch Paper Company was [a] medium-sized, partly integrated paper company [that produced] white and kraft papers and paperboard. A portion of its paperboard output was converted into corrugated boxes by the Thompson Division, which also printed and colored the outside surface of the boxes. Including Thompson, the company had four producing divisions and a timberland division, which supplied part of the company's pulp requirements.

For several years, each division had been judged independently on the basis of its profit and return on investment. Top management had been working to gain effective results from a policy of decentralizing responsibility and authority for all decisions except those relating to overall company policy. The company's top officials believed that the past few years, the concept of decentralization had been applied successfully and that the company's profit and competitive position definitely had improved.

The Northern Division had designed a special display box for one of its papers in conjunction with the Thompson Division, which was equipped to make the box. Thompson's staff for package design and development spent several months perfecting the design, production methods, and materials to be used. Because of the unusual color and shape, these were far from standard. According to an agreement between the two divisions, the Thompson Division was reimbursed by the Northern Division for the cost of its design and development work.

When all the specifications were prepared, the Northern Division asked for bids on the box from the Thompson Division and from two outside companies. Each division manger was normally free to buy from whatever supplier he [or she] wished, and even on sales within the company, divisions were expected to meet the going market price if they wanted the business.

During this period, the profit margins of such converters as the Thompson Division were being squeezed. Thompson, as did many other similar converters, bought its paperboard, and its function was to print, cut, and shape it into boxes. Though it bought most of its materials from other Birch divisions, most of Thompson's sales were made to outside customers. If Thompson got the order from Northern, it probably would buy its linerboard and corrugating medium from the Southern Division of Birch. The walls of a corrugated box consist of outside and inside sheets of linerboard sandwiching the fluted corrugating medium. About 70 percent of Thompson's out-of-pocket cost of $400 for the order represented the cost of linerboard and corrugating medium. Though Southern had been running below capacity and had excess inventory, it quoted the market price, which had not noticeably weakened as a result of the oversupply. Its out-of-pocket costs on both liner and corrugating medium were about 60 percent of the selling price.

The Northern Division received bids on the boxes of $480 a thousand from the Thompson Division, $430 a thousand from West Paper Company and $432 a thousand from Eire Paper, Ltd. Eire Papers offered to buy from Birch the outside linerboard with the special printing already on it, but would supply its own inside liner and corrugating medium. The outside liner would be supplied by the Southern Division at a price equivalent of $90 a thousand boxes, and it would be printed for $30 a thousand by the Thompson Division. Of the $30, about $25 would be out-of-pocket costs.

Since this situation appeared to be a little unusual, William Kenton, manager of the Northern Division, discussed the wide discrepancy of bids with Birch's commercial vice president. He told the vice president: "We sell in a very competitive market, where higher costs cannot be passed on. How can we be expected to show a decent profit and return on investment if we have to buy our supplies at more than 10 percent over the going market?"

[Given] that Mr. Brunner on occasion in the past few months had been unable to operate the Thompson Division at capacity, it seemed odd to the vice president that Mr. Brunner would add the full 20 percent overhead and profit charge to his out-of-pocket costs. When asked about this, Mr. Brunner's answer was the statement that appears at the beginning of [this exercise]. He went on to say that having done the developmental work on the box, and having received no profit on that, he felt entitled to a good markup on the production of the box itself.

The vice president explored further the cost structure of the various divisions. He remembered a comment that the controller had made at a meeting the week before, to the effect that costs which were variable for one division could be largely fixed for the company as a whole. He knew that in the absence of specific orders from top management, Mr. Kenton would accept the lowest bid, which was that of the West Paper Company for $430. However, it would be possible for top management to order the acceptance of another bid if the situation warranted such action. And though the volume represented by the transactions in question was less than 5 percent of the volume of any of the divisions involved, other transactions would conceivably raise similar problems later.

Questions:

1. Which bid should Northern Division accept that is in the best interests of Birch Paper Company?
2. Should Mr. Kenton accept this bid? Why or why not?
3. Should the vice president of Birch Paper Company take any action?

4. In the controversy described, how, if at all, is the transfer price system dysfunctional? Does this problem call for some change, or changes, in the transfer pricing policy of the overall firm? If so, what *specific* changes do you suggest?

This case was prepared by William Rotch under the supervision of Neil Harlan, Harvard Business School. Copyright by the President and Fellows of Harvard College. Harvard Business School case 158–001. One-time permission to reproduce granted by Western Business School, under authority from Harvard Business School Publishing.

RESEARCH ASSIGNMENT

18–38

Research Assignment
LO4

Every year *The Financial Post*, *Fortune*, and *Business Week* review current trends in executive compensation. Research this issue in the library, using these three magazines as a starting point, and write a three- to five-page paper on executive compensation. Be sure to give specific examples of the ways in which companies reward executives and the ways in which compensation is tied to performance.

18–39

Cybercase
LO1, LO4, LO5

Go to the Koch Industries Web site (**www.kochind.com**) to read about the philosophy of CEO Charles Koch. Relate the concept of "market-based management" to decentralization and to transfer pricing.

CHAPTER 19

International Issues in Management Accounting

Learning Objectives

After studying Chapter 19, you should be able to:

1. Explain the role of the management accountant in the international environment.

2. Discuss the varying levels of involvement that firms can undertake in international trade.

3. Explain the ways management accountants can manage foreign currency risk.

4. Explain why multinational firms choose to decentralize.

5. Explain how environmental factors can affect performance evaluation in the multinational firm.

6. Discuss the role of transfer pricing in the multinational firm.

7. Discuss ethical issues that affect firms operating in the international environment.

Scenario

Paterson Company is a company based in Canada that manufactures and sells electronic components worldwide. Virtually all of the manufacturing takes place in Canada. The company has marketing divisions located throughout Europe, including one in France. Debbie Kishimoto is manager of this division; she was hired away from a competitor three years ago. Debbie, recently informed of a price increase in one of the major product lines, had requested a meeting with Peter Duhamel, the marketing vice-president.

Debbie: "Peter, I simply don't understand why the price of our main product has increased from $5 to $5.50 per unit. We negotiated an agreement earlier in the year with our manufacturing division in Montreal for a price of $5 for the entire year. I called the manager of that division, and he indicated that the original price was still acceptable—he said that the increase was a directive from

headquarters. That's why I requested a meeting with you. I need some explanations. When I was hired, I was told that pricing decisions were made at the divisional level—that divisions were given a lot of decision-making latitude. This directive not only interferes with this decentralized philosophy but also will lower my division's profits. Given current market conditions, there is no way that we can pass on the cost increase. Profits for my division will drop at least $600,000 if this

864

price is maintained. I think a midyear increase of this magnitude is unfair to my division."

Peter: "Under normal operating conditions, headquarters will not interfere with divisional decisions. As a company, however, we are having some problems. What you just told me is exactly why the price of your product has been increased. We want the profits of all of our European marketing divisions to drop."

Debbie: "What do you mean, you want the profits to drop? That doesn't make any sense. Aren't we in business to make money?"

Peter: "What you lack is corporate perspective. We are in business to make money, and that's why we want European profits to decrease. Let me explain. Our divisions in Canada are not doing well this year. Projections show significant losses. At the same time, projections for European operations show good profitability. By increasing the cost of key products transferred to Europe—to your division, for example—we increase revenues and profits in Canada. By decreasing your profits, we avoid paying taxes in France; with losses on other Canadian operations to offset the corresponding increase in domestic profits, we avoid paying taxes in Canada as well. The net effect is a much-needed increase in our cash flow. Besides, you know how difficult it is in some of these European countries to transfer out capital. This is a clean way of doing it."

Debbie: "I'm not so sure that it's clean. It doesn't seem right to me. I can't imagine the tax laws permitting this type of scheme. There is another problem as well. You know that the company's bonus plans are tied to a division's profitability. This plan could cost all the European managers a lot of money."

Peter: "Debbie, you have no reason to worry about the effect on your bonus—or on our evaluation of your performance, for that matter. Corporate management has already taken steps to ensure no loss of compensation. The plan is to compute what income would have been if the old price had prevailed and base bonuses on that figure. I plan to meet with the other divisional managers and explain the situation to them as well."

Debbie: "The bonus adjustment seems fair, although I wonder if the reasons for the drop in profits will be remembered in a couple of years when I'm being considered for promotion. Anyway, I still have some strong concerns about the propriety of all this. How does this scheme relate to the tax laws?"

Peter: "We will be in technical compliance with the tax laws. In Canada, Section 69 of the *Income Tax Act* and Canada Customs and Revenue Agency's Information Circular 87-2 govern this type of transaction. Not unlike in the United States and most European countries, the key legal point is evidence of an arm's-length price. Since you're a distributor, we can use the resale price method to determine such a price. Essentially, the arm's-length price for the transferred good is backed into by starting with the price at which you sell the product and then adjusting that price for the markup and other legitimate differences, such as tariffs and transportation."

Debbie: "If I were a French tax auditor, I would wonder why the markup dropped from last year to this year. I also wonder if we are being good citizens and meeting the fiscal responsibilities imposed on us by each country in which we operate."

Peter: "Well, a French tax auditor might wonder about the drop in markup. The markup, however, is still within reason, and we can make a good argument for increased costs. In fact, we have already instructed the managers of our manufacturing divisions to find as many costs as they can that can be legitimately reassigned to the European product lines affected by this increase. So far they have been very successful. I think our records will support the increase that you are receiving. Debbie, you really do not need to be concerned with the tax authorities. Our Tax Department assures me that this move has been carefully researched and planned—it's unlikely that a tax audit will create any difficulties. It'll all be legal and aboveboard. We've done this several times in the past with total success. We have some good people in that department."

Note: This scenario is an adaptation based on the experiences of an actual firm. Names and other details have been changed to preserve confidentiality.

Questions to Think About

1. Do you think that the transfer pricing scheme interferes with decentralization? How much autonomy should central headquarters grant to the divisions?

2. What does Peter mean by "corporate perspective"?

3. Discuss Debbie's concerns regarding her bonus and promotion opportunities. To what extent should she be concerned?

4. Peter says that everything is "legal and aboveboard." Do you agree? Is it ethical? (Note: Managerial Decision Case 19–16 addresses this question in more detail.)

MANAGEMENT ACCOUNTING IN THE INTERNATIONAL ENVIRONMENT

Objective 1

Explain the role of the management accountant in the international environment.

Doing business in a global environment requires management to shift perspective. While many aspects of business dealing remain the same, other aspects are quite different. Debbie Kishimoto's conversation with Peter Duhamel shows that she is struggling with one of these differences: the income tax implications of transfer pricing. The company doing business in both its home country and other countries may find that practices that work well in the home country work imperfectly or not at all in another country. Much of the difference can be related to the business environment—that is, the cultural, legal, political, and economic environment of the various countries. Just as a fish supposedly is not aware of water, North Americans take their business environment for granted and have grown accustomed to a market economy and to the concept of private property with a legal system that enforces contracts. A sense of ethics grew in tandem with the underlying environment. When the environment changes, ethical problems may arise. Of course, the case at the beginning of this chapter raises the question of the ethics of the tax-avoidance scheme. While this question is not necessarily common to all divisional structures, evaluating the ethical content of divisional decisions is common.

Where does the management accountant fit into the global business environment? Business looks to the management accountant for financial and business expertise. The management accountant's job is not cut-and-dried. Knowledge, creativity, flexibility, and competence are needed to help managers make decisions. Good training, education, and keeping up with one's field are important to any management accountant. However, the job of the management accountant in the international firm is made more challenging by the ambiguous and ever-changing nature of global business. Since much of the management accountant's job is to provide relevant information to management, staying up to date requires a management accountant to read books and articles in a variety of business areas, including information systems, marketing, management, politics, and economics. In addition, the management accountant must be familiar with the financial accounting rules of the countries in which the firm operates.

The remainder of this chapter will touch on various issues facing the multinational firm. Our focus will be on the management accountant and how he or she must deal with those issues.

LEVELS OF INVOLVEMENT IN INTERNATIONAL TRADE

Objective 2

Discuss the varying levels of involvement that firms can undertake in international trade.

More than two decades ago, one writer asserted that the Canadian economy is more susceptible than most to the effects of international transfer pricing (discussed later in the chapter) because much of Canadian industry is foreign owned and because of the amount of trade between Canadian companies and their foreign counterparts.[1] This statement is even more true in the new millennium.[2] It has been pointed out, for example, that in 1988, General Motors of Canada, Ford Motor Company of Canada, Chrysler Canada, and Imperial Oil (a subsidiary of Exxon) are four of the eleven largest Canadian companies.[3] Another writer observes that the U.S. direct investment position (DIP) in Canada more than tripled between 1970 and 1990, reaching $68.4 billion in 1990. It is true that direct investment in the United States by Canada increased almost ninefold during the same period, reaching $27.7 billion in 1990, but

---

1.   Alex J. Milburn, "International Transfer Transactions: What Price?" *CA Magazine* (December 1976): 22–27.

2.   The ideas in this paragraph draw heavily from Roger Y. W. Tang, *Transfer Pricing in the 1990s: Tax and Management Perspectives* (Quorum Books, 1993), 33–39.

3.   Isaiah A. Litvak, "U.S. Multinationals: Repositioning the Canadian Subsidiary," *Business in the Contemporary World* (Autumn 1990): 111–119.

this figure still represents only 40 percent of the U.S. direct investments in Canada.[4] International investments and trade are thus critical to the economic life of Canada. The North American Free Trade Agreement has intensified the significance of international trade to Canada.

North American Free Trade Agreement (NAFTA)

Prior to the **North American Free Trade Agreement (NAFTA)**, Canada and the United States entered into a Free Trade Agreement (FTA), implementation of which began on January 1, 1989. NAFTA is a free trade agreement between Canada, the United States, and Mexico that is aimed at encouraging trade in goods, commercial services, and investments by removing barriers to trade, particularly tariffs. In anticipation of free trade, some companies have restructured their operations and others continue to do so. For example, in 1990, General Electric opened a gas-range factory in San Luis Potosi in central Mexico aimed at supplying not only the United States, but also Mexico and Canada. General Electric's strategy is to maintain its largest mass-production facilities in the United States, with specialized and flexible lines in Canada. Less sophisticated products (such as gas ranges) will be manufactured in Mexico.[5] Opportunities abound for Canadian businesses to take advantage not only of the huge and well-established U.S. market but also of the fast-developing and unsaturated markets in Mexico. At the same time, however, Canadian companies are facing unparalleled competition from their U.S. counterparts. The General Agreement on Tariffs and Trade (GATT)—and more recently the World Trade Organization (WTO)—is likely to intensify competition from other sources, particularly from companies in Europe, Japan, and the emerging economies of the post-recession Asia–Pacific region. All of this means that businesses, large or small, will inevitably feel the impact of increased opportunities and competitive threats. The management accounting function must therefore be adaptable and less constraining in order to support new strategic directions to meet the global challenges. The topics in the remainder of this chapter are aimed at providing a preliminary familiarization with international aspects of management accounting.

A **multinational corporation (MNC)** is one that "does business in more than one country in such a volume that its well-being and growth rest in more than one country."[6] The involvement of the MNC in international trade may take many forms. On a fairly simple level, the MNC may import raw materials and/or export finished product. On a more complex level, the MNC may be a large firm consisting of a parent company and a number of divisions in various countries.

In the international environment, the choice of company structure goes beyond the issue of centralized versus decentralized firm structure described in Chapter 18. While multinational companies are very often decentralized, with the subsidiaries being wholly owned by the parent firm, the many legal and regulatory systems under which the firm must operate require careful consideration of company structure. Some of the choices are importing/exporting, wholly owned subsidiaries, and joint ventures.

Importing and Exporting

A relatively simple form of multinational involvement is importing and exporting. A company may import parts for production. Similarly, a company may export finished product to foreign countries. Even such simple transactions as importing and exporting can present new risks and opportunities for companies.

4. Roger Y. W. Tang, 34–37.

5. "Inching towards a North American market," *Business Week* (June 25, 1990): 40.

6. Yair Aharoni, "On the Definition of a Multinational Corporation," in A. Kapoor and Phillip D. Grub (eds.), *The Multinational Enterprise in Transition* (Princeton, N.J.: Darwin Press, 1972), 4.

Importing A company may import raw materials for use in production. While this transaction may look identical to the purchase of materials from domestic suppliers, Canadian tariffs add complexity and cost. In accounting for materials in Chapter 3, it was noted that freight-in is a materials cost. An imported part may have **tariff (or duty)** in addition to freight-in cost. A tariff is a tax on imports that is levied by the federal government. This tax is also a cost of materials. Companies look hard for ways to decrease tariffs. They may restrict the amount of imported materials, alter the materials by adding Canadian resources (to increase the domestic content and gain more favourable tariff status), or, as is the case in the United States, utilize foreign trade zones.

U.S. Foreign Trade Zones The U.S. government has set up **foreign trade zones**, areas near a customs port of entry that are physically on U.S. soil but considered to be outside U.S. commerce. San Antonio, Texas, New Orleans, Louisiana, and the Port of Catoosa, Oklahoma, are examples of cities with foreign trade zones. Some U.S. companies have set up manufacturing plants within the foreign trade zones. Goods imported into a foreign trade zone are duty-free until they leave the zone. This has important implications for U.S. manufacturing firms that import raw materials. Since tariffs are not paid until the imported materials leave the zone (as part of a finished product), the company can postpone payment of duty and the associated loss of working capital. Additionally, the company does not pay duty on defective materials or on inventory that has not yet been included in finished product.

An example may help to illustrate the cost advantages of operating a plant in a U.S. foreign trade zone. Suppose that Roadrunner, Inc., operates a petrochemical plant located in a foreign trade zone. The plant imports volatile materials (for example, chemicals that experience substantial evaporation loss during processing) for use in production. Wilycoyote, Inc., operates an identical plant just outside the foreign trade zone. Consider the impact on duty and related expenditures for the two plants for the purchase of $400,000 of crude oil imported from Venezuela. Both Roadrunner and Wilycoyote use the oil in chemical production. Each purchases the oil about three months before use in production, and the finished chemicals remain in inventory about five months before sale and shipment to the customer. About 30 percent of the oil is lost through evaporation during production. Duty is assessed at 6 percent of cost. Each company faces 12 percent carrying cost.

Wilycoyote pays duty, at the point of purchase, of $24,000 (0.06 × $400,000). In addition, Wilycoyote has carrying cost associated with the duty payment of 12 percent per year times the portion of the year that the oil is in raw materials or finished goods inventory. In this case, the months in inventory equal 8 (3 + 5). Total duty-related carrying cost is $1,920 (0.12 × 8/12 × $24,000). Total duty and duty-related carrying cost is $25,920. Roadrunner, on the other hand, pays duty at the time of sale because it is in a foreign trade zone, and imported goods do not incur duty until (unless) they are moved out of the zone. Since 70 percent of the original imported oil remains in the final product, duty equals $16,800 (0.7 × $400,000 × 0.06). There is no carrying cost associated with the duty. A summary of the duty-related costs for the two companies follows:

	Roadrunner	Wilycoyote
Duty paid at purchase	$ 0	$24,000
Carrying cost of duty	0	1,920
Duty paid at sale	16,800	0
Total duty and related cost	$16,800	$25,920

Clearly, Roadrunner has saved $9,120 ($25,920 − $16,800) on just one purchase of imported raw materials by locating its plant in the foreign trade zone.

U.S. foreign trade zones provide additional advantages. For example, goods that do not meet U.S. health, safety, and pollution control regulations are subject to fines.

Foreign goods can be imported into foreign trade zones and modified to comply with the law without being subject to the fines. Another example of the efficient use of foreign trade zones is the assembly of high-tariff component parts into a lower-tariff finished product. In this case, the addition of domestic labour raises the domestic content of the finished product and makes the embedded foreign parts eligible for more favourable tariff treatment.[7]

Canadian companies can benefit from the foreign trade zones to the extent that U.S. importers can delay the payment of U.S. duty on Canadian imports. Similar zones are established in other countries, notably in China.

The management accountant must be aware of the costs to U.S. clients of importing Canadian materials and products. He or she should also be able to evaluate the potential benefits of selling to clients in a foreign trade zone. The management accountant in the United States should evaluate the potential benefits in considering the location of satellite plants in foreign trade zones.

Exporting   Exporting is the sale of a company's products in foreign countries. Canadian exports have traditionally been dominated by agricultural products, lumber, hydroelectricity, crude oil, and natural gas. They have also encompassed a large variety of manufactured consumer and industrial goods, including high-tech products. It is not necessary to have a production facility in the foreign country; finished products can simply be transported to the buyer. However, exporting is usually more complex than the sale of finished goods within the home country. Foreign countries have a variety of import and tariff regulations. The job of complying with the foreign rules and regulations often falls to the controller's office, just as compliance with the Income Tax Act and other Canadian tax regulations is an accounting function. Alternatively, a Canadian company may choose to work with an experienced distributor who is familiar with the legal complexities of the other countries. In some cases the distributor is wholly owned (as is the one headed by Debbie Kishimoto); in other cases the distributor is a separate company.

Treaties and Tariffs   Trade treaties between countries affect the tariffs charged. For example, the North American Free Trade Agreement (NAFTA) allows importers in the United States, Mexico, and Canada to pay reduced tariffs on goods produced in the three countries. However, strict adherence to regulations is required. U.S. Customs has stepped up enforcement of NAFTA regulations by checking for valid certificates of origin on imported goods. A *certificate of origin* is a document summarizing the information that enables companies to qualify for reduced NAFTA duties. The penalties for noncompliance are steep—ranging from twice the revenue lost (in tariffs) to the domestic value of the goods. Management accountants must be aware of the customs regulations and ensure that adequate recordkeeping and internal control mechanisms exist.[8]

Wholly Owned Subsidiaries

A company may choose to purchase an existing foreign company, making the purchased company a wholly owned subsidiary of the parent. This strategy has the virtue of simplicity. The foreign company has established an outlet for the product, and has the production and distribution facilities already set up. For example, in 1989, U.S.-based Whirlpool expanded into the European market by purchasing the appliance business of Philips N.V., Europe's third-largest appliance manufacturer. This purchase gave Whirlpool immediate access to production and distribution facil-

7. These examples are taken from James E. Groff and John P. McCray, "Foreign-Trade Zones: Opportunity for Strategic Development in the Southwest," *Journal of Business Strategies* (Spring 1992): 14–26.

8. "NAFTA and U.S. Customs—The Honeymoon Is Over," *Deloitte & Touche Review* (May 15, 1995): 4–5.

ities, as well as an established brand name. Even so, the approach is not inexpensive. The first three years were spent blending company cultures, before the European operation could be streamlined to cut costs. Finally, more investment was necessary in marketing to replace the Philips name with Whirlpool's and develop a marketing plan for all of Europe, as opposed to the more fragmented country-by-country approach used previously.[9] Examples of acquisitions by Canadian companies in the United States include the following: the Bank of Montreal acquired Harris Bank Corporation of Illinois for $547 million in 1984; Maclean-Hunter Holdings, Ltd., acquired the Houston Post for $100 million in 1983; Inter-City Gas Corporation acquired Whirlpool's Heil-Quaker Home Systems of Tennessee for $176 million in 1987; and John Labatt, Ltd., acquired Pasquale Food Company, Inc., of Alabama for $152 million in 1986. Unsuccessful investments in the United States include those made by Mark's Work Wearhouse, Ltd., and Canadian Tire Corporation, Ltd.

Foreign investments in controlled subsidiaries also abound in Canada. In addition to control of Canadian operations by General Motors, Ford, Chrysler, General Electric, and Exxon, the Canadian operations of John Deere, J. I. Case Canada, and Honeywell are directly owned or controlled by U.S. companies. Japanese, British, and German companies also own or control Canadian operations.

It is noteworthy that in recent years, the many immigrants to Canada from the Asia–Pacific region have increased the level of trade between Canada and countries in that region, particularly Hong Kong, Taiwan, Singapore, Thailand, and South Korea. Although there are examples of this type of business activity throughout Canada, much of it appears to be concentrated in British Columbia. Canadians are paying more attention to the growing economies in the Asia–Pacific region and are exploiting business and trade opportunities through direct investments in these countries.

If the laws of the country permit, an MNC can simply set up a wholly owned subsidiary or branch office in the country. In Ireland, for example, U.S. insurance and software companies have set up branch offices. Quarterdeck Office Systems, a California-based software company, routes customer calls to its second phone-answering operation in Dublin. Scores of multilingual workers take calls from all over Europe—and from North America. When it is 5:00 a.m. on North America's west coast, Irish workers are well into their working day and can answer calls from customers in North America's Eastern Time Zone. The Irish Development Authority provides generous tax and other incentives worth about a year's pay for each job created.[10]

Outsourcing of technical and professional jobs is becoming an important issue for cost-conscious North American firms. **Outsourcing** is the payment by a company for a business function that was formerly performed in-house. For example, some domestic companies outsource their legal needs to outside law firms rather than hiring corporate attorneys. In the context of the MNC, outsourcing refers to moving a business function to another country. For example, U.S.-based Texas Instruments set up an impressive software programming operation in Bangalore, in southern India. The availability of underemployed college graduates in India meant that the area offered a combination of low wage rates and high productivity. However, the underdeveloped Indian infrastructure required considerable capital investment. "Even though [Texas Instruments] had to install its own electrical generators and satellite dishes to operate efficiently, wages are low enough that work still gets done for half what it costs in the U.S."[11]

Outsourcing is done in North America by foreign firms, as well. Toyota Motor outsourced its design needs for the Previa to California. Benefits to Toyota include the greater familiarity California designers have for the North American minivan market as well as the political advantage of having part of the Previa's development in the United States.

9. Barry Rehfeld, "Where Whirlpool Flies, and Maytag Sputters," *The New York Times* (January 3, 1993): 5.

10. "Your New Global Work Force," *Fortune* (December 14, 1992): 52–66.

11. "Your New Global Work Force," op. cit.: 64.

The management accountant must be alert to outsourcing opportunities and be aware of the numerous costs and benefits of outsourcing that would not be available in Canada. The varying tax structures and incentives of local authorities, as well as the country's overall educational level and infrastructure, all play a role in the management accountant's assessment of costs and benefits.

Joint Ventures

Sometimes companies with the expertise needed by MNCs do not exist or are not for sale. In such a case, a joint venture may work. A **joint venture** is a type of partnership in which investors co-own the enterprise. IBM spent much time and money on plasma display technology for portable computers before it realized that the technology was impractical because of excessive power usage. Liquid-crystal displays (LCDs) provided a possible solution. IBM formed a joint venture with Toshiba Corp. to marry its own expertise in materials with Toshiba's superior manufacturing. IBM, Toshiba, and Siemens have also united in manufacturing memory chips.[12] In the 1990s, General Mills formed strategic alliances with the following firms: Nestle, to create Cereal Partners Worldwide; PepsiCo, to form Snack Ventures Europe (now the largest snack foods company in Europe); CPC International, to create International Dessert Partners to serve Mexico and Latin America; and Want Want Holdings Ltd. to form Tong Want—a snack food venture in the People's Republic of China.[13] Other examples of firms that have arranged joint ventures include Hewlett-Packard and Hitachi; Boeing and Mitsubishi; and Apple Computer and Sharp Electronics. Canadian companies such as Northern Telecom and Cominco have established a number of joint ventures internationally.[14] The Halifax-based IMP Group and Aeroflot, an airline operating out of the Commonwealth of Independent States (previously the Soviet Union), have established a joint commercial real estate venture.[15] Examples of joint ventures by Canadian and U. S. corporations involving direct investments in the United States include Garth Drabinsky of Cineplex and the Bronfman family ($65 million) with Universal Studios in Florida in 1986; and Bell Canada Enterprises Ltd. ($43 million) with Inet Company of America, located in Virginia.

Sometimes a joint venture is required because of restrictive laws. In China, for example, MNCs are not free to purchase companies or set up their own subsidiaries. Joint ventures with Chinese firms are recommended if not strictly required. Similarly, India and Thailand demand local ownership. The U.S.-based Loctite Corporation, maker of Super Glue, runs joint ventures in both India and Thailand for that reason.

A special case of joint venture cooperation is the maquiladora. **Maquiladoras** are manufacturing plants located in Mexico that process imported materials and re-export them to the United States or Canada. Originally designed to encourage U.S. firms to invest in Mexico, the program has now expanded to include Canadian firms, such as Northern Telecom (now Nortel), and other foreign firms, such as Nissan and Sony. Basically, the maquiladora enjoys special status in both Mexico, which grants operators an exemption from Mexican laws governing foreign ownership, and in the United States and Canada, which grant exemptions from or reductions in custom duties levied on re-exported goods. Most maquiladoras are located in cities bordering the United States to take advantage of ready access to U.S. transportation and communication facilities. The advantage to foreign companies operating in Mexico

12. John Carey, Neil Gross, Mark Maremont, and Guy McWilliams, "Moving the Lab Closer to the Marketplace," *Business Week* (Reinventing America 1992): 164–171.

13. This information comes from General Mills Web site, **www.generalmills.com/explore/overview**.

14. *Northern Miner*, v. 76 (51) (February 25, 1991): 12.

15. *Halifax Chronicle Herald* (April 28, 1990): D1.

is the abundance of low-cost, high-quality labour. The structure of the maquiladora is flexible. Mexico permits different levels of involvement. The minimal level combines low risk with low cost savings. In this case, the U.S. or Canadian firm transfers materials to an existing Mexican firm and imports them back in finished form. All hiring and operating of the Mexican plant is accomplished by the Mexican owners. The highest level of involvement offers both high risk and high cost savings. At this level, the U.S. or Canadian firm owns the Mexican subsidiary and oversees all the operations.[16]

Maquiladoras are an example of a government program aimed at increasing production that has worked well. Foreign investment has moved well beyond the border cities and into a broad band of northern Mexico. Improvements in Mexican infrastructure (for example, roads, communications) have enticed companies further into the interior, lowering nonlabour costs. While U.S. companies were originally drawn to the maquiladoras for the cheap labour, now both wage rates and other benefits have risen. For example, the GM Delphi plant in Ciudad Juarez teaches new employees to read and write and provides low-cost mortgages. Delphi benefits by having 53 Mexican plants that have not experienced strikes for five years.[17]

U.S. firms have also found other benefits to investment in maquiladoras. For example, Ford's plant in Chihuahua was built to satisfy export requirements for doing business in Mexico. Now it supports Ford's sales to Mexico, establishing a marketing reason for the plant's presence.

No matter which structure the MNC takes, it faces issues of foreign trade. An important issue is foreign currency exchange, which is addressed in the next section.

FOREIGN CURRENCY EXCHANGE

Objective 3

Explain the ways management accountants can manage foreign currency risk.

When a company operates only in its home country, only one currency is used, so exchange issues never arise. However, when a company begins to operate in the international arena, it must use foreign currencies. These foreign currencies can be exchanged for the domestic currency using **exchange rates**. If the exchange rates never changed, problems would not occur. Exchange rates do change, however, often on a daily or more frequent basis. Thus, a Canadian dollar that could be traded for U.S.$0.80 or 100 yen one day might be worth only U.S.$0.72 or 90 yen on another day. Currency rate fluctuations add considerably to the uncertainty of operating in the international arena.

The management accountant plays an important role in managing the company's exposure to currency risk. **Currency risk management** refers to the company's management of its transaction, economic, and translation exposure due to exchange rate fluctuations.[18] **Transaction risk** refers to the possibility that future cash transactions will be affected by changing exchange rates. **Economic risk** refers to the possibility that a firm's present value of future cash flows will be affected by exchange fluctuations. **Translation (or accounting) risk** is the degree to which a firm's financial statements are exposed to exchange rate fluctuation. These three components of currency risk, along with ways in which the accountant can manage the company's exposure to them, are examined more closely in the next section.

16. James E. Groff and John P. McCray, "Maquiladoras: The Mexico Option Can Reduce Your Manufacturing Cost," *Management Accounting* (January 1991): 43–46.

17. Joel Millman, "In Mexico, a GM Worker Sprints into the Middle Class," *The Wall Street Journal* (July 19, 1998): pp. B1 and B4.

18. A good discussion of this topic can be found in Foreign Currency Risk Management, *CMA Management Accounting Guidelines #6*, The Society of Management Accountants of Canada, 1987.

Managing Transaction Risk

Today's MNC deals in many different currencies. These currencies may be traded for one another depending on the exchange rate in effect at the time of the trade. The **spot rate** is the exchange rate of one currency for another for immediate delivery (that is, today). Exhibit 19–1 lists a number of selected currencies and their spot rates as of April 14, 2000. While spot rates change daily, this exhibit provides an idea of relative values. Changes in the spot rates can affect the value of a company's future cash transactions, posing transaction risk. Currency appreciation and depreciation will be examined in this section, followed by a look at exchange gains and losses, and hedging.

Currency Appreciation and Depreciation   When one country's currency strengthens relative to another country's currency, **currency appreciation** occurs, and one unit of the first country's currency can buy more units of the second country's currency. Conversely, **currency depreciation** means that one country's currency has become relatively weaker and buys fewer units of another currency. For example, in mid-1985 the yen was worth Canadian $0.00588 (or the Canadian dollar was worth 170 yen, the unit of Japanese currency symbolized by ¥). By mid-1986, the yen was worth Canadian $0.009091(or the Canadian dollar had weakened to only 110 yen). In 2000, the yen appreciated, so that 75 yen became equal to a Canadian dollar. This fluctuation has an impact on trade between the two countries. Suppose that Fujinon Optical Company sold rubber-coated marine binoculars for ¥93,600. In mid-1985 this meant a price of $550 (93,600/170, or 93,600 × 0.00588) to Canadian importers. In mid-1986, however, the same binoculars, priced at the same ¥93,600, would have cost Canadian importers $851 (93,600/110, or 93,600 × 0.009091). Of course, while the dollar weakened, the yen strengthened. Another example relates to the well-publicized spree of cross-border shopping activities by Canadians in U.S. border towns in the early

Exhibit 19–1				

Spot Rates as of April 14, 2000

Country	Currency Name	Exchange Rate in terms of Canadian Dollars	Exchange Rate in terms of U.S. Dollars
Australia	Australian Dollar	0.8781	0.5968
Canada	Dollar	1.0000	0.6796
China	Renminbi	0.1778	0.1208
Egypt	Pound	0.4275	0.2905
European Union	Euro	1.4047	0.9546
France	Franc	0.2141	0.1455
Germany	Deutsche Mark	0.7182	0.4881
Great Britain	Pound	2.3372	1.5884
Hong Kong	Hong Kong Dollar	0.1889	0.1284
India	Rupee	0.0336	0.0228
Israel	New Shekel	0.3637	0.2472
Italy	Lira	0.000725	0.000493
Japan	Yen	0.013908	0.009452
Mexico	New Peso	0.1561	0.1061
Netherlands	Guilder	0.6336	0.4306
Singapore	Singapore Dollar	0.8577	0.5829
Spain	Peseta	0.00839	0.00570
South Africa	Rand	0.2234	0.1518
South Korea	Won	0.001325	0.00090
Sweden	Krona	0.1683	0.1144
Switzerland	Swiss franc	0.8924	0.6065
Taiwan	Taiwan Dollar	0.04854	0.03299
Thailand	Baht	0.0388	0.0264
United States	Dollar	1.4714	1.0000
Venezuela	Bolivar	0.002182	0.001483

1990s. Cross-border shopping was, at least in part, due to a relatively strong Canadian dollar. As the Canadian dollar weakened vis-à-vis the U.S. dollar in 1993, the level of cross-border shopping dramatically decreased and continued at this low level through 2000. The loss in property value and decline in business in British Columbia in the late 1990s was due in part to the decline in value of Asian currencies during the economic meltdown in Asia as Asian immigrants could no longer invest in British Columbia at the same level as before.

Exchange Gains and Losses   What is the impact of changes in exchange rates on the sale of goods to other countries? Suppose that Super Tubs, Inc., based in Winnipeg, sells its line of whirlpool tubs at home and to foreign distributors. On January 15, Bonbain, a French distributor of luxury plumbing fixtures, orders 100 tubs at a price of $1,000 per tub, to be delivered immediately, and to be paid in French francs on March 15. Has Super Tubs just made a sale of $100,000 (100 × $1,000)? The payment is to be in francs, not dollars, so the exchange rate for francs must be considered. If the exchange rate on January 15 is 4 francs per dollar (or 1 French franc = $0.25), then Bonbain is really promising to pay 400,000 francs (4 × $100,000) on March 15. If the exchange rate remained at 4 francs per dollar on March 15, Super Tubs would receive 400,000 francs convertible to $100,000. But suppose that the exchange rate on March 15 is 4.1 francs per dollar (or 1 French franc = $0.2439). Bonbain still pays 400,000 francs, but Super Tubs can convert that amount into only $97,561 (400,000/4.1), not the $100,000 it anticipated back in January when the sale was made. The difference between the two amounts, $2,439, is the loss on currency exchange. The impact of transaction risk on this example can be summarized as follows:

Receivable in dollars on 1/15	$100,000
Received in dollars on 3/15	97,561
Exchange loss	$ 2,439

In the case of a receivable denominated in a foreign currency, an **exchange loss** is a loss on the exchange of one currency for another due to depreciation of the foreign currency.

Of course, if the franc strengthened against the dollar—say, to an exchange rate of 3.9 francs per dollar (or 1 French franc = $0.25641)—an exchange gain would occur. For a receivable, an **exchange gain** is the gain on the exchange of one currency for another due to appreciation of the foreign currency. In the example, Bonbain again pays 400,000 francs, which Super Tubs is able to convert into $102,564 (400,000/3.9, or 400,000 × 0.25641). In this case, the impact of transaction risk would result in a gain.

Receivable in dollars on 1/15	$100,000
Received in dollars on 3/15	102,564
Exchange gain	$ 2,564

Transaction risk also affects the purchase of commodities from foreign companies. Suppose that on February 20, Timberland, Inc. (based in Big Timber, B.C.) purchases computers from NEC (located in Japan) for $50,000, payable in yen on May 20. Assume that the spot rate for the yen is 130 per dollar (or 1 yen = $0.0076923) on February 20. It is easy to see that Timberland's true payable is for ¥6,500,000 (50,000 × 130). If the spot rate for yen is 135 (or 1 yen = $0.0074074) on May 20, it will cost Timberland only $48,148 (6,500,000/135, or 6,500,000 × 0.0074074) to get enough yen to pay NEC.

Liability in dollars on 2/20	$50,000
Liability in dollars on 5/20	48,148
Exchange gain	$ 1,852

The more favourable May 20 spot rate has resulted in an exchange gain. Clearly, transaction risk caused by the movement of foreign currency against the dollar must be taken into account by managers, because it affects the prices paid and received for goods. Suppose management does not want to be involved in gambling on exchange rates? What then? The following section on hedging explains how a management accountant can manage a company's exposure to exchange gains and losses.

Hedging   One way of insuring against gains and losses on foreign currency exchanges is **hedging**. Typically, a forward exchange contract is used as a hedge. The **forward contract** requires the buyer to exchange a specified amount of a currency at a specified rate (the forward rate) on a specified future date.

Consider again the example of Super Tubs's sale of $100,000 in tubs to the French company. The spot rate on January 15 was 4 francs per dollar (1 French franc = $0.25). Super Tubs's problem is that it does not know what the exchange rate will be on March 15. If the exchange rate is more than 4 francs per dollar (that is, if the French franc < $0.25), Super Tubs will receive less than the $100,000 anticipated in accounts receivable. Of course, if the exchange rate is less than 4 francs per dollar (or the French franc > $0.25), Super Tubs will receive more. But the difficulty is in predicting short-term exchange rate movements. Super Tubs may well decide that it is in the business of manufacturing and selling tubs, not in the business of betting on exchange rate fluctuations. Therefore, it will forgo the opportunity for exchange rate gains by hedging against exchange rate losses. Here is how this might work using forward contracts.

On January 15, Super Tubs purchases a contract to exchange 400,000 francs into dollars on March 15 at a forward rate of 4.02 francs (or a forward rate of 1 French franc = $0.24876). Super Tubs has agreed to sell francs for dollars. At this point, Super Tubs has locked in the exchange rate. The 0.02 difference between the spot rate of 4 and the forward rate of 4.02 (or the difference between $0.25 and $0.24876) is the premium Super Tubs pays the exchange dealer on the transaction. Think of it as an insurance premium.

On March 15, the following transactions will occur. Bonbain pays Super Tubs 400,000 francs, Super Tubs pays the exchange dealer 400,000 francs, and the exchange dealer pays Super Tubs $99,502 (400,000/4.02, or 400,000 × 0.24876). The difference between the $100,000 original account receivable and the $99,502 cash paid is charged to an exchange premium expense account. Remember that in the original example, the exchange rate on March 15 is 4.1 francs per dollar (or 1 French franc = $0.2439). Had Super Tubs not hedged, it would have received only $97,561. Therefore, the exchange premium expense of $498 saved Super Tubs a loss of $2,439.

Receivable in dollars on 1/15	$100,000
Received in dollars on 3/15	99,502
Premium expense	$ 498

Of course, the hedging can also be done by agreeing to exchange dollars for a foreign currency at a future date. Recall the previous example of Timberland's purchase of ¥6,500,000 worth of computer equipment. At a spot rate of 130 (or 1 yen = $0.0076923), Timberland expects to pay $50,000 to satisfy its liability. Timberland may fear that the rate will decline, say to ¥125 (or 1 yen = $0.008). If it did, Timberland would have to pay $52,000 (6,500,000/125, or 6,500,000 × 0.008) for the same ¥6,500,000. A hedging transaction would resolve Timberland's uncertainty. Assuming that the forward rate is ¥128.7 per dollar (or 1 yen = $0.00777), Timberland could purchase a forward contract to purchase ¥6,500,000 on May 20 for $50,505 (6,500,000/128.7, or 6,500,000 × 0.00777).

Liability in dollars on 2/20	$50,000
Payment in dollars on 5/20	50,505
Premium expense	$ 505

Hedging transactions can become much more complex than the foregoing example. Companies with significant transaction exposure may choose to hedge all or part of their exposure. Hedging may also be used as a tool to manage economic risk. That use will be addressed in the following section.

Managing Economic Risk

Dealing in different currencies can introduce an economic dimension into currency exchange transactions. Recall that economic risk was defined as the impact of exchange rate fluctuations on the present value of a firm's future cash flows. The risk can affect the relative competitiveness of the firm, even if it never participates directly in international trade. Take a simple example based on the market for telephone equipment.

Suppose that Canadian customers can choose to purchase telephone equipment from Nortel Networks (based in Canada) or from Nippon (based in Japan). Assume that the price of the product is $120,000 from either manufacturer. However, while Nortel Networks truly means $120,000, Nippon is really interested in 8,400,000 yen, its own currency. At an exchange rate of $1 equals 70 yen (or 1 yen = $0.014286), the price of $120,000 is set. Now suppose that the value of the dollar strengthens against the yen, and the exchange rate becomes $1 equals 80 yen (or 1 yen = $0.0125). To get the same 8,400,000 yen, Nippon requires a price of only $105,000. The cost structures of the two firms have not changed, and neither has customer demand, but because of currency fluctuations, the Japanese firm has become more "competitive." Of course, as the dollar weakens, the position is reversed, and Canadian exports become relatively cheaper to foreign customers.

How does the accountant manage the company's exposure to economic risk? Most importantly, he or she must be aware of it, by understanding the position of the firm in the global economy. As we can see in the Nortel Networks–Nippon example, the two firms were competitors and were linked through their customers' participation in the global marketplace. The accountant provides financial structure and communication for the firm. In preparing the master budget, for example, budgeted sales must take into account potential strengthening or weakening of the currencies of competitors' countries. Often, the controller's office is responsible for forecasting foreign exchange movements.

Hedging can provide another means of managing economic risk. For example, the Toronto Blue Jays baseball team receives its revenues in Canadian dollars but pays most of its expenses in U.S. dollars. In 1985 the team anticipated a loss due to unfavourable exchange rate fluctuations. To prevent this, in 1984 the team purchased forward contracts of U.S. dollars at $1 equals U.S.$0.75 (or U.S.$1 = $1.33). The exchange rate at the end of 1984 was $1 equals U.S.$0.7568 (or U.S.$1 = $1.3214); the exchange rate dropped steadily throughout 1985, to $1 equals U.S.$0.7156 (or U.S.$1 = $1.397) by the end of the fourth quarter of 1985. The depreciation of Canada's currency, carefully hedged against through the purchase of forward contracts, resulted in a profit to the team.[19]

Managing Translation Risk

Often the parent company restates all subsidiaries' income into the home currency. This restatement can result in gain and loss opportunities on the revaluation of foreign currencies and can have an impact on a subsidiary's financial statements and the related ROI and EVA computations.

Suppose that a division based in Mexico earned 320,000 pesos this year, up from 200,000 pesos the year before, a hefty 60 percent increase. Now suppose that the divi-

19. Paul V. Mannino and Ken Milani, "Budgeting for an International Business," *Management Accounting* (February 1992): 36–41.

sion's income is translated into dollars. If the exchange rate last year was 6 pesos per dollar and the exchange rate this year is 10 pesos per dollar, the net income figures translate into $33,333 net income last year and $32,000 net income this year. Suddenly, there is a decrease in net income. Similar unpleasant surprises await ROI and net worth computations. The potential for gain or loss on currency revaluation is particularly relevant for countries whose currencies are volatile—and depreciating relative to the home company's currency.

Foreign currency fluctuations also cause difficulties in evaluating local managers' adherence to company policy. U.S.-based Monsanto faced this problem. The company noticed declining sales in some of its foreign markets. The local managers were instructed to increase promotional expenditures. However, dollar-denominated reports showed no increases. Top management continued to press local managers to carry out instructions. Local managers were frustrated by their inability to persuade higher management that they had increased expenditures, since the reports showed fewer dollars being spent. Eventually local currency statements were placed alongside the dollar-denominated reports. These comparative statements clearly showed that increased expenditures had taken place.

A simple numerical example—based on Monsanto's experience, but not using its figures—may illustrate the problem. Assume that Multinational, Inc., has a foreign division, FD, which has been experiencing eroding sales. Multinational directs FD managers to increase marketing expenditures. FD managers do increase marketing expenditures over the following four quarters, as follows:

Quarter	Expenditures in Local Currency
1	LC 10,000
2	LC 11,000
3	LC 12,100
4	LC 13,310

As shown, marketing expenditures have grown by 10 percent in each quarter. However, Multinational managers do not see the above table. Instead, they see dollar-denominated reports. In order to translate local currency figures into dollars, the exchange rates for each quarter are needed. Suppose that the dollar has strengthened against the local currency and that the quarterly exchange rates of $1 for units of local currency are 1.00, 1.20, 1.35, and 1.50, respectively. Then FD's marketing expenditures in dollars would be as follows:

Quarter	Expenditures in Dollars
1	$10,000
2	$ 9,167
3	$ 8,963
4	$ 8,873

What a difference! Not only have local managers not increased expenditures, it looks as if they have actually decreased expenditures. Only by comparing the dollar-denominated figures with those denominated in local currency can Multinational see the two effects of an increase in marketing expenditures and the strengthening of the dollar. In this case, FD's increase in marketing expenditures was hidden in currency translation.

The objective of dollar-denominated internal reports is to measure all figures on the same basis. While this strategy may work at any one point in time, it may mislead managers when comparisons are made over time. The management accountant must be aware of this source of translation risk.

DECENTRALIZATION

In this chapter's opening scenario, Debbie Kishimoto complained that corporate headquarters was interfering with a pricing arrangement she had negotiated with the manager of the manufacturing division. She complained because Paterson Company had been espousing decentralization. This was her first experience with any interference by headquarters. This is not an unusual complaint. Frequently, firms that are decentralized in the home country may exercise tighter control over foreign divisions, at least until they gain more experience with their overseas operations. Just as decentralization offers advantages for home country divisions, it also offers advantages for foreign divisions.

Advantages of Decentralization in the MNC

The quality of information is better at the local level, and that can improve the quality of decisions. This is particularly true in MNCs, where far-flung divisions may be operating in a number of different countries, subject to various legal systems and customs. As a result, local managers are often in a position to make better decisions. Decentralization allows an organization to take advantage of this specialized knowledge. For example, Loctite Corporation has local managers run their own divisions. In particular, marketing and pricing are under local control. Language is not a problem, as local managers are in control. Similarly, local managers are conversant with their own laws and customs.

Local managers in the MNC are capable of a more timely response in decision making. They are able to respond quickly to customer discount demands, local government demands, and changes in the political climate.

Chapter 18 discussed the need for centralized managers to transmit instructions, and the chance that the manager responsible for implementing the decision might misinterpret the instructions. The different languages native to managers of divisions in the MNC make this an even greater problem. MNCs address this problem in two ways. First, a decentralized structure pushes decision making down to the local manager level, eliminating the need to interpret instructions from above. Second, MNCs are learning to incorporate technology that overrides the language barrier and eases cross-border data transfer. Technology is of great help in smoothing communication difficulties between parent and subsidiary and between one subsidiary and another. Loctite's plant in Ireland uses computerized labelling on adhesives bound for Great Britain or Israel. Bar code technology "reads" the labels, eliminating the need for foreign language translation.

Just as decentralization gives the lower-level managers in the home country a chance to develop managerial skills, foreign subsidiary managers also gain valuable experience. Just as important, home country managers gain broader experience by interacting with managers of foreign divisions. The chance for learning from each other is much greater in a decentralized MNC. Off and on throughout the latter half of the twentieth century, a tour of duty at a foreign subsidiary has been a part of the manager's climb to the top. Now, foreign subsidiary managers may expect to spend some time at headquarters in the home office as well.

Creation of Divisions

The MNC has great flexibility in creating types of divisions. Divisions are often created along geographic lines. IBM, for example, has divisional boundaries that organize production and sales for Asia and the Far East (AFE), North America, Latin and South America, and Europe and Africa.

Product lines may afford a rationale for the creation of divisions. Many MNCs are diversified, manufacturing and selling a number of different products. The MNC may decide that the major difference is the type of product sold, not the country in which it is sold. An oil company, for example, may have an exploration division, a refining division, and a chemicals division. Each of these divisions may include plants or operations in a number of different countries.

Divisions may follow functional management lines. In the early 1970s, Avon Products created three regional marketing and planning centres, one each in New York, London, and Australia. These worked reasonably well for a while and achieved the objective of sharing expertise and training divisional managers. However, national needs and differences caused conflict. So by the late 1980s, Avon had disbanded the regional centres and decentralized to the individual country level.[20]

The presence of divisions in more than one country creates the need for performance evaluation that can take into account differences in divisional environments. The next section examines performance evaluation in the MNC.

MEASURING PERFORMANCE IN THE MULTINATIONAL FIRM

Objective 5

Explain how environmental factors can affect performance evaluation in the multinational firm.

It is important for the MNC to separate the evaluation of the *manager* of a division from the evaluation of the *division*. The manager's evaluation should not include factors over which he or she exercises no control, such as currency fluctuations, taxes, and so on. Instead, managers should be evaluated on the basis of revenues and costs incurred. Once a manager is evaluated, then the subsidiary financial statements can be restated in the home currency and uncontrollable costs can be allocated.[21]

The manager of a foreign division may be assigned responsibility for performance either in the local currency or in dollars. If currencies are managed centrally, currency risk responsibility is normally not assigned to divisional management. The implicit message in this case is that divisional management should be concerned with operational performance in the local currency and should not pay attention to exchange rate changes. Instead, this responsibility is centralized as a corporate function. Only if there are specific directions from the corporation should local management be concerned with dollar performance. If, on the other hand, currency management is decentralized, responsibility will be assigned to divisional management in dollars. The implicit message in this case is that since results will be evaluated in terms of dollars, divisional management should manage its own local currency exposure and continually evaluate operating and financial decisions from the parent's perspective in dollars.

It is particularly difficult to compare the performance of the manager of a division (or subsidiary) in one country with the performance of the manager of a division in another country. Even divisions that appear to be similar in terms of production may face very different economic, social, or political forces. International environmental conditions may be very different from, and more complex than, domestic conditions.[22] Environmental variables facing local managers of divisions include economic, legal, political, social, and educational factors. Some important economic variables are inflation, foreign exchange rates, taxes, and transfer prices. Legal and political actions also have differing impacts. For example, a country may not allow cash outflows, forcing the corporation to find ways to trade for the host country's output.[23] Educational variables vary from country to country, as does the sophistication of the accounting system. Sociological and cultural variables affect how the multinational firm is treated by the subsidiary's country.

The existence of differing environmental factors makes interdivisional comparison of ROI potentially misleading. Suppose that a Canadian-based MNC has three

20. Louis V. Consiglio, "Global Competitive Advantage: Lessons from Avon," Working paper No. 1 (July 1992), Center for Applied Research, Lubin School of Business, Pace University.

21. Gerhard G. Mueller, Helen Gernon, and Gary Meek, *Accounting: An International Perspective* (Homewood, Ill.: Richard D. Irwin, 1987).

22. Wagdy M. Abdallah, "Change the Environment or Change the System," *Management Accounting* (October 1986): 33–36.

23. One MNC faced with Philippine prohibitions on taking cash out of the country decided to hold its annual meeting in Manila. All corporate costs of the meeting (for example, hotel, meals) could then be paid in pesos earned by the MNC's Philippine subsidiary. Example taken from Jeff Madura, *International Financial Management*, 2nd ed. (St. Paul, Minn.: West Publishing Company, 1989), 382.

divisions located in the United States, Brazil, and France with the following information given in millions of dollars:

	Assets	Revenues	Net Income	Margin	Turnover	ROI*
Brazil	$10	$ 6	$ 3	0.50	0.60	0.30
United States	18	13	10	0.77	0.72	0.55
France	15	10	6	0.60	0.67	0.40

* Rounded to two decimal places.

On the basis of ROI, it appears that the manager of the U.S. subsidiary did the best job, while the manager of the Brazilian subsidiary did the worst job. But is this a fair comparison? France and Brazil face very different legal, political, educational, and economic conditions. Inflation has been very high in South America compared to that in North America. Many South American firms have responded by adjusting reported financial amounts for inflation. Suppose in the example that the U.S. firm reports its assets at historical cost and that the Brazilian firm adjusts its assets for inflation. If inflation during the period the assets have been held has averaged 100 percent (not an unreasonable assumption in a country that has faced monthly double-digit inflation rates for years), then the historical cost of the Brazilian assets would be $5 million. The calculation is as follows:

$$x + (100\%)x = \$10$$
$$x + 1.00x = \$10$$
$$2x = \$10$$
$$x = \$5$$

If the Brazilian subsidiary's assets are restated at historical cost, then the ROI becomes 60 percent ($3/5 = .6$). If this computation is used, the Brazilian subsidiary appears to be the most successful, not the least. It should be noted that accounting for inflationary effects on income and assets is very complicated, and that the simple restatement shown above is not a comprehensive approach. Additionally, top management is typically aware of the existence of differential inflation rates. Still, the lack of consistency in internal reporting may obscure interdivisional comparisons, and the management accountant must be aware of this problem.

Other environmental factors can differ between countries. A minimum wage law in one country will restrict the manager's ability to affect labour costs. Another country may prevent the export of cash. Still others may have a well-educated work force but poor infrastructure (transportation and communication facilities). Therefore, the corporation must be aware of and control for these differing environmental factors when assessing managerial performance. Exhibit 19–2 lists some environmental factors that may make interdivisional comparisons misleading.

Political and Legal Factors Affecting Performance Evaluation

On June 3, 1989, the Chinese military opened fire on students in Beijing's Tiananmen Square. The world was stunned, glued to CNN and other media for news of the uprising. Would the Chinese government fall? Would an already repressive regime clamp down even more tightly? Half a world away, the controller of a manufacturer of custom oil field equipment weighed the Chinese events in a business decision. Should he accept a Chinese letter of credit? His company's product was loaded on a ship in Vancouver, set to sail for China within the week. The sale was booked, and it was an important one, worth $3 million dollars (the company's total annual sales revenue was $15 million). But was the letter of credit still good? Ordinarily, the Foreign Credit Insurance Association (which underwrites insurance through the World Bank) guarantees letters of credit drawn on banks in approved countries.

Exhibit 19–2

Environmental Factors
Affecting Performance
Evaluation in the
Multinational Firm*

Economic factors
  Organization of central banking system
  Economic stability
  Existence of capital markets
  Currency restrictions

Political and legal factors
  Quality, efficiency, and effectiveness of legal structure
  Effect of defense policy
  Impact of foreign policy
  Level of political unrest
  Degree of governmental control of business

Educational factors
  Literacy rate
  Extent and degree of formal education and training systems
  Extent and degree of technical training
  Extent and quality of management development programs

Sociological factors
  Social attitude toward industry and business
  Cultural attitude toward authority and persons in subordinate positions
  Cultural attitude toward productivity and achievement (work ethic)
  Social attitude toward material gain
  Cultural and racial diversity

* Adapted from Wagdy M. Abdallah, "Change the Environment or Change the System," *Management Accounting* (October 1986): pp. 33–36. Used with the permission of the Institute of Management Accountants.

After the Tiananmen Square massacre, China was suspended from the FCIA's approved countries list. If the Bank of China refused to pay, there would be no insurance, leaving the controller's company holding $3 million of worthless paper. The controller waited three days, evaluating the constantly changing situation, before cancelling the shipment.[24]

The management accountant in the MNC must be aware of more than business and finance. Political and legal systems have important implications for the company. Sometimes the political system changes quickly, throwing the company into crisis mode, as it did for the controller in the Chinese letter of credit dilemma. Other times, the situation evolves more slowly. The shift in Spain's political system, from Franco's dictatorship to a democracy, is a case in point.

Management accounting has gained increased importance in Spain since the early 1980s. Part of the increased importance is due to the increase in competitive pressures. The profitability of many Spanish firms has eroded, and firms see the need for more formal mechanisms of control, such as budgeting and standard costing. A second reason is the shift from a sheltered economy and political dictatorship to a democratic society. The previous dictatorship favoured external methods of control, reinforcing a coercive political and social structure. The system was isolated from the rest of Europe, with a highly regulated economy. The shift to a more democratic society and a loosening of the regulatory environment has allowed Spanish firms more freedom of action in business and has led to the need for management accounting control.[25]

---

24. Several months later, when China had been reinstated on the approved countries list, the company did make the sale.

25. Joan M. Amat Salas, "Management Accounting Systems in Spanish Firms," in the proceedings of the Second European Management Control Symposium, Volume 1.

Multiple Measures of Performance

Both EVA and ROI are important measures of managerial performance. However, they are both short-term measures. The temptation therefore exists for managers to trade off short-run benefits at the expense of the company's long-run well-being. One way to discourage this myopic behaviour is to use additional measures of performance that relate more closely to the division's long-run health. For example, in addition to ROI and EVA, top management could look at such factors as market share, customer complaints, personnel turnover ratios, and personnel development. By letting lower-level managers know that attention to long-run factors is also vital, a company should be able to diminish its tendency to overemphasize ROI or EVA.

Additionally, the use of ROI and EVA in the evaluation of managerial performance in an MNC's divisions is subject to problems beyond those faced by a decentralized company that operates in only one country. It is particularly important, then, to take a responsibility accounting approach. That is, managers should be evaluated on the basis of factors under their control. This can be facilitated by using multiple measures of performance and the Balance Scorecard approach.

TRANSFER PRICING AND THE MULTINATIONAL FIRM

Objective 6

Discuss the role of transfer pricing in the multinational firm.

For the multinational firm, transfer pricing must accomplish two objectives: performance evaluation and optimal determination of income taxes.

Performance Evaluation

Divisions are frequently evaluated on the basis of net income and return on investment.[26] As is the case for any transfer price, the selling division wants a high transfer price that will raise its net income, and the buying division wants a low transfer price that will raise its net income. But transfer prices in MNCs are frequently set by the parent company (as in this chapter's opening scenario), making the use of ROI and net income suspect. Because they are not under the control of division managers, they can no longer serve as indicators of management performance in such cases.

Income Taxes and Transfer Pricing

If all countries had the same tax structure, then transfer prices would be set independently of taxes. However, as the opening scenario illustrated, this does not happen. Instead, there are high-tax countries (like Canada) and low-tax countries (such as the Cayman Islands). As a result, MNCs may use transfer pricing to shift costs to high-tax countries and shift revenues to low-tax countries.

Exhibit 19–3 illustrates this concept, as two transfer prices are set. The first transfer price is $100 as title for the goods passes from the Belgian subsidiary to the reinvoicing centre in Bermuda. Because the first transfer price is equal to full cost, profit is zero, and taxes on zero profit also equal zero. The second transfer price is set at $200 by the reinvoicing centre in Bermuda. The transfer from Bermuda to Canada does result in profit, but this profit does not result in any tax, because Bermuda has no corporate income taxes. Finally, the Canadian subsidiary sells the product to an external party at the $200 transfer price. Again, price equals cost, so there is no profit on which to pay income taxes. Consider what would have happened without the reinvoicing centre. The goods would have gone directly from Belgium to Canada. If the transfer price was set at $200, the profit in Belgium would have been $100, subject to the 42 percent tax rate. Alternatively, if the transfer price set was $100, no Belgian tax would have been paid, but the Canadian subsidiary would have realized a profit of $100, and

---

26. A study of 70 multinationals revealed that 80 percent used these measures. See Helen Gernon Morsicato, *Currency Translation and Performance Evaluation in Multinationals* (Ann Arbor: UMI Research Press, 1982).

Exhibit 19–3

Use of Transfer Pricing to Affect Taxes Paid

Action	Tax Impact
Belgian subsidiary of Parent Company produces a component at a cost of $100/unit. Title to the component is transferred to a reinvoicing centre* in Bermuda at a transfer price of $100/unit.	42% tax rate $100 revenue − $100 cost = $0 Taxes paid = $0
Reinvoicing centre in Bermuda, also a subsidiary of Parent Company, transfers title of component to Canadian subsidiary of Parent Company at a transfer price of $200/unit.	0% tax rate $200 revenue − $100 cost = $100 Taxes paid = $0
Canadian subsidiary sells component to external company at $200/unit.	46% tax rate $200 revenue − $200 cost = $0 Taxes paid = $0

* A reinvoicing centre takes title to the goods but does not physically receive them. The primary objective of a reinvoicing centre is to shift profits to divisions in low-tax countries.

that would have been subject to the Canadian corporate income tax rate of approximately 46 percent.

Canadian-based multinationals are subject to the *Income Tax Act* (Section 69) and to Canada Customs and Revenue Agency's Information Circular 87–2 on the pricing of intracompany transactions. These give the CCRA the authority to reallocate income and deductions among divisions if it believes that such reallocation will reduce potential tax evasion. Basically, Section 69 requires that sales be made at "arm's length." That is, the transfer price set should match the price that would be set if the transfer were being made by unrelated parties, adjusted for differences that have a measurable effect on the price. Differences include landing costs and marketing costs. Landing costs (freight, insurance, customs duties, and special taxes) can increase the allowable transfer price. Marketing costs are usually avoided for internal transfers and reduce the transfer price. The CCRA allows three pricing methods that approximate arm's-length pricing. In order of preference, these are the comparable uncontrolled price method, the resale price method, and the cost-plus method.

The **comparable uncontrolled price method** essentially uses the market price. If the component has a market price of $50 and shipping costs are $4, then the transfer price will be $54. If any costs are avoided as a result of internal transfer (for example, sales commissions of $5), these costs will be subtracted from the market price. In this case, the eventual transfer price would be calculated as follows:

Market price	$50
Add: Shipping	4
Less: Commissions	5
Transfer price	$49

The **resale price method** is equal to the sales price received by the reseller less an appropriate markup. That is, the subsidiary purchasing a good for resale sets a transfer price equal to the resale price less a gross profit percentage. Suppose that our Canadian division receives a product from the French division that can be resold in Canada for $60. The Canadian division typically receives a markup of 50 percent on cost. The transfer price would be $40 ($60 = cost + 0.5 cost; so, cost is $40).

The **cost-plus method** is simply the cost-based transfer price. The manufacturing cost of the product is adjusted for any other expenses, such as shipping and duty. Suppose that the Canadian division produces a product that costs $25 to manufacture. It ships the product to the Brazilian division at a cost of $3. The transfer price is $28. This price can be adjusted for a markup on goods.

These methods are also adopted in the United States and are an endorsement by the CCRA of a 1979 Organization for Economic Co-operation and Development (OECD) report, "Transfer Pricing and Multinational Enterprises."

The determination of an arm's-length price is a difficult one. Many times, the transfer pricing situation facing a company does not "fit" any of the three preferred methods. Other methods may be used in support of one of the above-mentioned three methods or where none of these methods is appropriate. The method that is used should reflect an attempt to present the price that would have been established in an arm's-length relationship. Recently, the CCRA followed the lead of the Internal Revenue Service (IRS) in the United States to permit a fourth method—a transfer price negotiated between the company and the CCRA. Taxation authorities, taxpayers, and the courts have struggled with negotiated transfer prices for years. However, this type of negotiation occurs after the fact—after income tax returns have been submitted and the company is being audited. More recently, the CCRA has authorized the issuance of **advance pricing agreements** (APAs) to assist tax-paying firms in determining whether or not a proposed transfer price is acceptable to the CCRA in advance of tax filing. "An APA is an agreement between [taxation authorities] and a taxpayer on the pricing method to be applied in an international transaction. It can cover transfers of intangibles (such as royalties on licenses), sales of property, provision of services and other items. An APA is binding on both the [taxation authorities] and the taxpayer for the years specified in the APA and is not made public."[27] Since the APA procedure is still relatively new, neither the taxation authorities nor the firms are sure of the informational requirements. Currently, advance rulings are limited to transactions between Canadian companies and divisions in treaty countries, such as the United States, Australia, Japan, and the United Kingdom. For example, Apple Computer obtained an advance pricing agreement from the IRS in the United States on transfers of Apple products to its Australian subsidiary.[28]

Transfer pricing abuses are illegal in Canada, the United States, and many other countries—if they can be proved to be abuses. Incidents of firms charging unusual transfer prices exist. However, this subject is difficult to research, since managers are reluctant to state overtly that their transfer prices are unusual for fear of prosecution. The primary evidence is therefore case law. For example, the IRS successfully showed that Toyota had been overcharging its U.S. subsidiary for cars, trucks, and parts sold in the United States. The effect was to lower Toyota's reported income substantially in the United States and increase income reported in Japan. The settlement reportedly approached $1 billion.[29]

The arm's-length pricing is the legal basis for intercompany purchases and sales of goods (including raw materials, semifinished products and components, and finished goods). CCRA Information Circular 87–2 stipulates that the same principles apply to the acquisition or disposition of intangible property (for example, the transfer of a patent). Apparently, the CCRA suspected that Canadian companies were transferring their intangibles (patents, copyrights, customer lists, and so on) to foreign subsidiaries at less than fair market value. In the United States, for example, a U.S. pharmaceutical firm would develop a new drug and license its Puerto Rican subsidiary to produce it. The drug would then be purchased by the parent company for sale in the United States, and a royalty would be charged to the Puerto Rican subsidiary. The royalty rate, taxable income to the parent, was low, but was similar to other third-party transactions. Thus, the IRS could not challenge it. The "super royalty" provision of Section 482 of the *Internal Revenue Code* in the United States that was added in 1986 changed this situation by linking the transfer price of the intangible to the income attributable to the

27. "New Intercompany Pricing Rulings Create and Eliminate Tax Uncertainty," *Deloitte & Touche Review* (March 25, 1991): 6.

28. Roger Y. W. Tang, "Transfer Pricing in the 1990s," *Management Accounting* (February 1992): 22–26.

29. "The Corporate Shell Game," *Newsweek* (April 15, 1991): 48–49.

intangible. "A Study on Intercompany Pricing," issued by the IRS in 1990, requires much stricter documentation for the pricing of intangibles.[30]

The CCRA also regulates the transfer pricing of foreign companies with Canadian subsidiaries. A Canadian company that is at least 25 percent foreign owned must keep extensive documentation of arm's-length transfer pricing. Because of the relative size, strength, and resources of the IRS in the United States vis-à-vis the CCRA, exporters to the United States pay more attention to satisfying the IRS than they do to satisfying the CCRA.

Of course, MNCs are also subject to taxation by other countries as well as Canada and the United States. Since income taxes are virtually universal, consideration of income tax effects pervades management decision making. Japan, the European Union, and South Korea have all issued transfer pricing regulations within the past couple of decades.[31] This increased emphasis on transfer price justification may account for the increased use of market prices as the transfer price by MNCs. A survey of transfer pricing methods used by Fortune 500 companies in 1977 and 1990 showed that MNCs had reduced their reliance on cost-based transfer prices in favour of market-based transfer prices over a 13-year-period.[32] Additionally, the most important environmental variable considered by MNCs in setting a transfer-pricing policy is overall profit to the company—with overall profit including the income tax impact of intracompany transfers.

Managers may legally avoid taxes; they may not evade them. The distinction is important. Unfortunately, the difference between avoidance and evasion is less a line than a blurry grey area. While the situation depicted in Exhibit 19–3 is clearly abusive, other tax-motivated actions are not. For example, an MNC may decide to establish a needed research and development centre within an existing subsidiary in a high-tax country, since the costs are deductible. MNCs may have tax-planning information systems that attempt to accomplish global tax minimization. This is not an easy task.[33]

ETHICS IN THE INTERNATIONAL ENVIRONMENT

Objective 7

Discuss ethical issues that affect firms operating in the international environment.

Business ethics pose difficulties in a single-country context. But ethics pose far more problems in a global context. Richard J. Mahoney, CEO of Monsanto Company, wrote, "As Monsanto becomes a global enterprise, we continually face the problem of different cultures and different cultural expectations. A service fee in one country is a bribe in another. Environmental laws can be extraordinarily strict in a country but not be enforced—and your industrial neighbours laugh at you for obeying the laws."[34] Given these difficulties, how does the modern corporation conduct business in an ethical manner? Is each country different? Is there a baseline? Some research indicates that human societies do share an ethical basis. However, there are some prerequisites for the establishment of an ethical business environment. These include basic societal stability; legitimacy and accountability of government; legitimacy of private ownership and personal wealth; confidence in one's own and society's future; confidence in the ability to provide for one's family; and knowledge of how the system works and how to participate in it.[35]

30. Alfred M. King, "The IRS's New Neutron Bomb," *Management Accounting* (December 1992): 35–38.

31. Tang, op. cit.

32. Tang, op. cit.

33. It should be noted here that differences in applicable income tax rates between Canadian provinces may also result in an incentive to locate activities in a given province or territory, and to shift profits from one province to another. The international transfer pricing issue also arises domestically between provinces, except for the absence of duties (customs charges). Canada's provinces have recently embarked on an attempt to dismantle trade barriers between them, particularly by disallowing provincial government contracts from being restricted to businesses operating within a given province's boundaries.

34. Richard J. Mahoney, "Ethics: Doing the Right Thing at Monsanto," *Management Accounting* (June 1991): 24.

35. Cynthia Scharf, "The Wild, Wild East: Everyone's a Capitalist in Russia Today, and Nobody Knows the Rules," *Business Ethics* (November/December 1992): 23.

For example, the Russian equivalent of insider trading or conflict of interest is *blat*. *Blat* is "an informal system of acquiring goods and services based on influence and back-door favors between acquaintances."[36] *Blat* is a natural extension of a culture that emphasized personal relationships over impersonal monetary transactions. Legal contracts are still in a rudimentary phase in Russia, because enforcement is weak. As a result, the personal relationships that characterize *blat* are a stronger basis for business dealings.

A strong underlying system is important for enforcing contracts and also provides the basis for confidence in ethical dealings. For some countries (for example, Canada, the United States, and Western European countries), that system is legal, with deviations punishable by law. For others (for example, Japan and countries in the Middle East), it is cultural, and deviations are punished at least as severely by loss of honour. The importance of a strong underlying social code of conduct is clearly evident in illegal business dealings. For obvious reasons, a buyer of marijuana would be loath to contact the police about its low quality. Similarly in India, where foreign currency exchange is tightly controlled, the black market in currency exchange is rife with unethical conduct. If someone would like to exchange dollars and rupees, he or she can get a markedly better rate from the black market. However, the method of exchange requires that the rupees be first handed to the black marketeer, after which the buyer must wait a minute or two while the black marketeer goes to a back room to get the dollars. Sometimes the black marketeer returns with the requisite number of dollars; sometimes not. If not, then what? The person can hardly go to the police! Such risky situations are not faced in a bank.

Other ethical problems with bribes and differing business laws exist. North American companies that contract with overseas firms may find themselves the target of unfavourable publicity for the use of child labour. They find themselves in a quandary. Do they give foreign companies a minimum age for the workers they hire? U.S. history includes immigrant children aged 10 and 12 at work in the steel mills of Bethlehem, Pennsylvania; and in the United States and Canada there are currently substantial numbers of illegal immigrants employed below the minimum wage. What about bribes to government officials? The stories of rampant bribery of Middle Eastern officials are legendary. In some countries, these bribes are a necessary part of doing business. Similarly, insider trading is not illegal in Europe, but it is definitely illegal in Canada and the United States.

To go back to the original question, what is a company to do when faced with conflicting sets of ethics? What if an action is legally permissible? Early in Monsanto's history, it faced the possibility of bankruptcy. John Queeny, the company's founder, was advised to "close down the plant, lay off all the workers, and then open up with new people at lower wages. 'Since when,' Mr. Queeny asked, 'do we lie to our employees?'" As a result, Monsanto holds that doing the right thing is nonnegotiable.[37] Perhaps the answer is to ask, Is the action right legally? and then, is the action right morally?

SUMMARY OF LEARING OBJECTIVES

1. Explain the role of the management accountant in the international environment.
The management accountant provides financial and business expertise. The job of the management accountant in the international firm is made more challenging by the ambiguous and ever-changing nature of global business. He or she must stay up to date in a variety of business areas ranging from information systems to marketing to management to politics and economics. In addition, the management accountant must be familiar with the financial accounting rules of the countries in which his or her firm operates.

36. Scharf, 22.

37. Scharf, 24.

2. Discuss the varying levels of involvement that firms can undertake in international trade.

Companies involved in international business may structure their activities in three major ways. They may engage in import/export activities; they may purchase wholly owned subsidiaries; or they may participate in joint ventures.

3. Explain the ways management accountants can manage foreign currency risk.

Management accountants must be aware of the potential exposure of their firms to transaction risk, economic risk, and translation risk. They may hedge to limit exposure to these risks.

4. Explain why multinational firms choose to decentralize.

MNCs choose to decentralize for much the same reasons domestic companies choose to decentralize. Reasons for decentralization are numerous. Companies decentralize because local managers can make better decisions using local information. Local managers can also provide a more timely response to changing conditions. Additionally, decentralization is necessary for large, diversified companies because of cognitive limitations—it is impossible for any one central manager to be fully knowledgeable about all products and markets. Other reasons include training and motivating local managers and freeing top management from day-to-day operating conditions so that they can spend time on more long-range activities, such as strategic planning.

5. Explain how environmental factors can affect performance evaluation in the multinational firm.

Environmental factors are those social, economic, political, legal, and cultural factors that differ from country to country and that managers cannot affect. These factors, however, do affect profits and ROI. Therefore, evaluation of the divisional manager should be separated from evaluation of the subsidiary.

6. Discuss the role of transfer pricing in the multinational firm.

When one division of a company produces a product that can be used in production by another division, transfer pricing exists. The transfer price is revenue to the selling division and cost to the buying division. As is the case with domestic companies, MNCs may use transfer prices in performance evaluation. MNCs with subsidiaries in both high-tax and low-tax countries may use transfer pricing to shift costs to the high-tax countries (where their deductibility will lower tax payments) and to shift revenues to low-tax countries.

7. Discuss ethical issues that affect firms operating in the international environment.

MNCs face ethical issues that do not arise for domestic companies. Other countries have business customs and laws that differ from those of the home country. The firm must determine whether a particular custom is merely a different way of doing business or violates the company's own code of ethics.

KEY TERMS

Advance pricing agreements, 884
Comparable uncontrolled price method, 883
Cost-plus method, 883
Currency appreciation, 873
Currency depreciation, 873
Currency risk management, 872
Economic risk, 872
Exchange gain, 874

Exchange loss, 874
Exchange rates, 872
Foreign trade zones, 868
Forward contract, 875
Hedging, 875
Joint venture, 871
Maquiladoras, 871
Multinational corporation (MNC), 867

North American Free Trade Agreement (NAFTA), 867
Outsourcing, 870
Resale price method, 883
Spot rate, 873
Tariff (or duty), 868
Transaction risk, 872
Translation (or accounting) risk, 872

REVIEW PROBLEM

FOREIGN CURRENCY EXCHANGE

Golo, Inc. has two manufacturing plants, one in Singapore and the other in Calgary. On March 1, Golo received a large order from a Japanese customer. The order is for ¥10,000,000 to be paid on receipt of the goods, scheduled for June 1. Golo assigned this order to the Calgary plant; however, one necessary component for the order is to be manufactured by the Singapore plant. The component will be transferred to Calgary on April 1 using a cost-plus transfer price of $10,000 (Canadian dollars). The Canadian tariff on the component parts is 30 percent.

The spot rates for Japanese yen and Singapore dollars, in Canadian dollars, are as follows.

Exchange Rates for	Yen	Singapore Dollars
March 1	0.012461	0.8333
April 1	0.012403	0.8602
June 1	0.012392	0.8889

Required:

1. What is the total cost of the imported parts from Singapore to the Calgary plant in Canadian dollars?
2. How much does Golo expect to receive from the Japanese customer in Canadian dollars using the spot rate at the time of the order?
3. How much does Golo expect to receive from the Japanese customer in Canadian dollars using the spot rate at the time of payment?
4. Suppose that on March 1, the forward rate for June 1 delivery of the Japanese yen is 0.012438. If Golo's policy is to hedge foreign currency transactions, what is the amount Golo expects to receive on June 1 in dollars?

Solution:

1.

Transfer price	$10,000
Tariff ($10,000 × 0.3)	3,000
Total cost	$13,000

The transfer price was set in Canadian dollars, so there is no currency exchange involved for the Calgary plant.

2. On March 1, Golo expects to receive $124,610 (¥10,000,000 × 0.012461).
3. On June 1, Golo expects to receive $123,920 (¥10,000,000 × 0.012392).
4. If Golo hedges, the forward rate is used, and the amount to be received on June 1 is $124,380 (¥10,000,000 × 0.012438).

QUESTIONS FOR WRITING AND DISCUSSION

1. How do international issues affect the role of the management accountant?

2. Define outsourcing, and discuss why companies may outsource various functions.

3. What are joint ventures, and why do companies engage in them?

4. What is an exchange rate for currency? What is the difference between a spot rate and future rate?

5. Define currency appreciation. What impact does currency appreciation have on a company's ability to import goods?

6. What impact does currency appreciation have on a company's ability to export its goods?

7. Mexico is considering devaluing the peso versus the dollar. You are the controller for a company considering production in Mexico. How does this news affect the decision? Now suppose you are a local labour union leader. How do you take the news?

8. What is transaction risk? economic risk? translation risk?

9. What is hedging? If a company imports raw materials, payable in full in 90 days in the foreign currency, why might the company want to hedge?

10. The performance of the subsidiary manager is equivalent to the performance of the subsidiary. Do you agree? Explain.

11. What environmental factors may affect divisional performance in a multinational firm?

12. What is the purpose of Section 69 of the *Income Tax Act* and of the CCRA's Information Circular 87–2? What four methods of transfer pricing are acceptable in Canada?

EXERCISES

19–1

Preparation for Becoming a Management Accountant in an MNC

LO1

A close friend of yours is majoring in accounting and would like to work for a multinational corporation upon graduation. Your friend is unsure just what courses would help prepare him or her for that goal and wants your advice.

Required:

Advise your friend on the kind of courses that might prepare him or her for this goal.

19–2

Exchange Gains and Losses

LO3

On March 1, Scherson Import-Export Company purchased merchandise from a Mexican firm costing 6,000 pesos. Payment was due, in pesos, on June 1. The exchange rates of pesos for $1 were as follows:

March 1 $1 = 6.2 pesos
June 1 $1 = 6.5 pesos

Required:

1. What is the liability in dollars on March 1?
2. What is the liability in dollars on June 1?
3. If Scherson pays on June 1, is there an exchange gain or loss? How much is it?

19–3

Hedging

LO3

Spreadsheet

Refer to Exercise 19–2. Suppose that Scherson also sells to Mexican firms under the same terms—payment is made in pesos three months after purchase. Scherson sells merchandise to Javier, SA, on March 1, for 60,000 pesos. Payment will be made in pesos on June 1. Scherson can purchase a contract to exchange 60,000 pesos into dollars on June 1 at a forward rate of 6.23 pesos.

Required:

1. What is the value of the receivable in dollars on March 1?
2. What is the dollar value of the amount Javier pays Scherson on June 1?
3. What is the exchange loss for Scherson if no hedging occurs?
4. If Scherson purchases the hedging contract on March 1, what is the premium expense?
5. What is the net savings to Scherson by hedging?

19–4

Currency Exchange

LO3

Déjà Vu Distributors, Inc., based in Montreal, is an export–import firm. On June 1, Déjà Vu purchased goods from a British company costing £80,000. Payment is due in pounds on September 1. The spot rate on June 1 was 2.20 dollars per pound, and on September 1 it was 2.15 dollars per pound.

Required:

1. Did the dollar strengthen or weaken against the pound during the three-month period?
2. How much would Déjà Vu have to pay for the purchase (in dollars) if it paid on June 1? How much would Déjà Vu have to pay for the purchase (in dollars) if it paid on September 1?

19–5

Exchange Gains and Losses

LO3

Refer to 19–4. If Déjà Vu paid for the purchase using the September 1 spot rate, what was the exchange gain or loss?

19–6

Hedging

LO3

Kanaan Company engages in many foreign currency transactions. Company policy is to hedge exposure to exchange gains and losses by using forward contracts. On July 1, Kanaan sold merchandise to a German company for 50,000 deutsche marks (DM), payable on September 30. Exchange rates for DM, in Canadian dollars, were as follows:

Spot rate July 1	.7867
Forward rate September 30	.7783
Spot rate September 30	.7600

Required:

1. Did Kanaan Company buy or sell marks for future delivery?
2. According to company policy, how many dollars did Kanaan receive for this sale?

19–7

Currency Exchange Rates

LO3

Suppose you are in the market for a BMW and are considering going to Germany to purchase it, drive it around Europe for a couple of weeks, and then ship it home. The car of your choice costs DM 65,000. When you first looked into the possibility of buying a car in Germany, the rate of exchange for DM, in Canadian dollars, was 0.8343; now the exchange rate is 0.8660.

Required:

Has the dollar appreciated or depreciated against the German mark? Would this news about the exchange rate change please or displease you? Why?

19–8

Divisional Performance Evaluation in the MNC

LO5

Fred Phillips, vice-president of Electronics for Consolidated, Inc., was reviewing the latest results for two divisions. The first, located in Baja California, Mexico, had posted net income of $150,000 on assets of $1,500,000. The second, in Punt-on-Thames, England, showed net income of $230,000 on assets of $2,000,000.

Required:

1. Calculate the ROI for each division.
2. Can a meaningful comparison be made of the British division's ROI with the Mexican division's ROI? Explain.

19–9

Transfer Pricing in the MNC

LO6

Lanfranoni, Inc., manufactures a broad line of industrial and consumer products. One of its plants is located in Madrid, Spain, and another in Singapore. The Madrid plant is operating at 85 percent capacity. Softness in the market for its main product, electric motors, has led to predictions of further softening of the market, leading perhaps to production at 65 percent capacity. If that happens, workers will have to be laid off and one wing of the factory closed. The Singapore plant manufactures heavy-duty industrial mixers that use the motors manufactured by the Madrid plant as an integral component. Demand for the mixers is strong. Price and cost information for the mixers is as follows:

Price	$2,200
Direct materials	630
Direct labour	125
Variable overhead	250
Fixed overhead	100

Fixed overhead is based on an annual budgeted amount of $3,500,000 and budgeted production of 35,000 mixers. The direct materials cost includes the cost of the motor at $200 (market price).

The Madrid plant capacity is 20,000 motors per year. Cost data are as follows:

Direct materials	$ 75
Direct labour	60
Variable overhead	60
Fixed overhead	100

Fixed overhead is based on budgeted fixed overhead of $2,000,000.

Required:

1. What is the maximum transfer price that the Singapore plant would accept?
2. What is the minimum transfer price that the Madrid plant would accept?
3. Consider the following environmental factors.

Madrid Plant	Singapore Plant
Full employment is very important. Local government prohibits layoffs without permission (which is rarely granted).	Cheap labour is plentiful.
Accounting is legalistic and conservative, designed to ensure compliance with government objectives.	Accounting is based on British-American model, oriented toward decision-making needs of creditors and investors.

How might these environmental factors have an impact on the transfer pricing decision?

19–10

Transfer Pricing

LO6

Avery Company has a division in Canada that produces computerized thermostats for heating units. These thermostats are transferred to a division in Sweden. The thermostats can be (and are) sold externally in Canada for $40 each. It costs $2.70 per thermostat for shipping and $5 per thermostat for import duties. When the thermostats are sold externally, Avery spends $4 per thermostat for commissions and an average of $1.50 per thermostat for advertising.

Required:

1. What transfer price method should be used to comply with the requirements of the Canada Customs and Revenue Agency?
2. Calculate the transfer price.

PROBLEMS

19–11

Decentralization in the MNC

LO4

Latest Styles, Inc., (LSI) supplies a limited range of garments to several boutiques in New York. LSI produces these garments in a small factory owned and operated in Nuevo Laredo, Mexico. LSI has been more responsive to the boutiques' needs for delivery of changing styles than the Asian garment producers, whose shipments take 30 days. As a result, several other boutiques have approached LSI as a potential supplier. Victoria Johnson, president of LSI, has decided that expansion will be required to meet the needs of these additional boutiques.

Victoria discussed the situation with her colleagues, Frank Corrigan, controller, and Tom Conway, production and shipping manager, and it was agreed that the expansion should be undertaken. Since Victoria makes most of the decisions that involve day-to-day operations and does the majority of the designing, Frank and Tom are concerned about her ability to manage the expansion at the same time. Frank and Tom expressed this concern in a meeting with Victoria, who agreed that the additional workload resulting from the planned expansion would be too great for her to handle. Accordingly, Victoria has decided to delegate some of these increased functions to Frank and Tom.

During these discussions, Victoria stated that in view of the North American Free Trade Agreement, she is considering even further expansion to increase the range of garments produced and also to supply boutiques in Philadelphia and Boston. As a consequence, she is considering further decentralization of the business, since expanded operations in Mexico, increased product lines, and the need to supply two new geographical areas will require hands-on operational management at these locations to keep up with inventory needs and differing local fashion trends. Both Frank and Tom are capable of handling these operational duties, although they will need to hire new managers to assist them in the expansion and decentralization.

Required:

1. Decentralization is the extent to which power and authority are systematically delegated throughout an organization.
   a. Discuss the factors that generally determine the degree of decentralization in an organization.
   b. Describe several benefits to an organization that can generally be derived from decentralization.
   c. Discuss several disadvantages to an organization from decentralization.
2. How does the NAFTA affect Victoria Victoria's decision? (US CMA adapted)

19–12

Exporting

LO2

Paladin Company manufactures plain-paper fax machines in a small factory in Minnesota. Sales have increased by 50 percent in each of the past three years, as Paladin has expanded its market from the United States to Canada and Mexico. As a result, the Minnesota factory is at capacity. Beryl Adams, president of Paladin, has examined the situation and developed the following alternatives.

1. Add a permanent second shift at the plant. However, the semiskilled workers who assemble the fax machines are in short supply, and the wage rate of $15 per hour would probably have to be increased across the board to $18 per hour in order to attract sufficient workers from out of town. The total wage increase (including fringe benefits) would amount to $125,000. The heavier use of plant facilities would lead to increased plant maintenance and small-tool cost.
2. Open a new plant and locate it in Mexico. Wages (including fringe benefits) would average $3.50 per hour. Investment in plant and equipment would amount to $300,000.

Required:

Advise Beryl of the advantages and disadvantages of each of her alternatives.

19–13

Foreign Currency Exchange; Hedging

LO3

Kalman Shutters, Inc., manufactures custom window shutters on a job-order basis. Kalman has invested heavily in precision woodworking equipment. As a result, the company has a reputation for producing excellent-quality interior shutters. On July 1, Kalman received orders from interior designers in France and Japan. Cynthia Simmons, president and co-owner of Kalman Shutters, was delighted. The French order is for shutters priced at $50,000. The order is due in Marseilles on September 1, with payment due in full on October 1. The Japanese order is for shutters priced at $65,000. It is due in Tokyo on August 1, with payment due in full on October 1. Both orders are to be paid in the customer's currency. The French customer has a reputation in the industry for late payment, and it could take as long as six months. Cynthia has never received payment in foreign currency before. She had her accountant prepare the following table of exchange rates, in Canadian dollars.

Exchange Rate for	French Franc	Yen
Spot rate	0.2458	0.012392
30-day forward	0.2448	0.012390
90-day forward	0.2432	0.012392
180-day forward	0.2411	0.012397

Required:

1. If the price of the shutters is set using the spot rate as of July 1, how many francs does Cynthia expect to be paid on October 1? How many yen does she expect on October 1?

2. Use the number of francs and yen calculated in requirement 1. How many dollars does Cynthia expect to receive on October 1? Will she receive that much? What is the value of hedging in this situation?

19–14

Transfer Pricing

LO6

The Canadian division of MegaBig, Inc., has excess capacity. MegaBig's European division, located in Lisbon, has offered to buy a component that would increase the Canadian division's utilization of capacity from 70 to 80 percent. The component has an outside market in Canada with a unit selling price of $12. The variable costs of production for the component are $6. Landing costs total $2 per unit, and an internal transfer avoids $1.25 per unit of variable marketing costs. The European and Canadian divisions agree on a transfer price of $9. The European division can purchase the component locally for $12.

Required:

Suppose you have scheduled a meeting with a Canada Customs and Revenue Agency representative. What arguments would you make for an advance pricing agreement that would permit the use of the $9 price?

19–15

Transfer Pricing

LO6

Audio-tech, Inc., manufactures stereos and boom boxes at plants in Ontario, Manitoba, and Alberta. It also has distribution centres in Brussels, Belgium, and Minnesota (U.S.). The market price of the Model 655 cd + stereo is $425. The unit costs are as follows:

Variable product costs	$135
Fixed factory overhead	70
Landing costs (U.S.)	20
Landing costs (Belgium)	25
Avoidable marketing costs	35

Audio-tech has set a transfer price of $425 to both the U.S. and Belgian divisions.

Required:

1. Calculate the transfer price under the comparable uncontrolled price method for both the U.S. and Belgian transfers.
2. Will Canada Customs and Revenue Agency be concerned about the transfer price actually set by Audio-tech?

MANAGERIAL DECISON CASES

19–16

Transfer Pricing and Ethical Issues

LO6, LO7

Reread the scenario at the beginning of the chapter.

Required:

1. Do you think that the tax-minimization scheme described to Debbie Kishimoto is in harmony with the ethical behaviour that should be displayed by top corporate executives? Why or why not? What would you do if you were Debbie?
2. Apparently, the Tax Department of Paterson Company has been strongly involved in developing the tax-minimization scheme. Assume that the accountants responsible for the decision are CMAs and are subject to the typical provincial standards of ethical conduct. Review the standards for ethical conduct outlined in Chapter 1 (you may refer either to the IMA standards or to the Code of Ethics of the Society of Management Accountants of Manitoba in the Appendix to Chapter 1). Are any of these standards being violated by the accountants in Paterson's Tax Department? If so, identify them. What should these tax accountants do if asked to develop a questionable tax-minimization scheme?

19–17

**Transfer Pricing;
International Setting;
Tax Implications**

LO6, LO7

Valley Electronics Corporation is a large multinational firm involved in the manufacture and marketing of various electronic components. Recently, Rhonda Cooper, president of Valley Electronics, received some complaints from divisional managers about the company's international transfer pricing practices. Essentially, the managers believed that they had less control than they wished over how prices were set. After reviewing some of the practices, Rhonda found that three different methods were being used: (1) the comparable uncontrolled price method, (2) the resale price method, and (3) the cost-plus method. Unable to determine why there were three methods and exactly how each worked, Rhonda requested a meeting with Wayne Sill, vice-president of finance.

Rhonda: "Wayne, I need to respond to our divisional managers' concerns about the transfer-pricing policies that we apply to goods shipped internationally. It appears that three methods are being used and that they differ across divisions."

Wayne: "The three methods used are the ones allowed by Section 69 of the *Income Tax Act* and by the CCRA's Information Circular 87-2. Which method is applicable depends on the operating circumstances surrounding the transfer of a particular component."

Rhonda: "So the way we price these internal transfers is driven—to some degree, at least—by tax laws. Interesting. Perhaps you can describe for me how each method works and what conditions dictate that we use that method."

Wayne: "The basic concept underlying any transfer price we use is the notion of an arm's-length price. Ideally, an arm's-length price is the price that an unrelated party would pay for the good being transferred. The CCRA allows three methods of determining the arm's-length price, and these are the methods we use. The comparable uncontrolled price method is based on market price. If the good being transferred has an external market, then the transfer price should be the price paid by an unrelated party, adjusted for differences that have a measurable effect on the price."

Rhonda: "What kind of differences? Give me some examples."

Wayne: "Well, the market price can be adjusted for such differences as landing costs (freight, insurance, customs duties, and special taxes) and marketing costs (commissions and advertising can be avoided with internal transfers). Adding landing costs and subtracting avoidable marketing costs are allowable adjustments to the market price."

Rhonda: "I see. What happens if we sell the product to a related buyer who then resells it without any further processing? Or if the transferred good has no outside market at all?"

Wayne: "For the resale scenario, we use the resale price method. We take the resale price realized by our marketing divisions and adjust that price for the markup percentage and any differences like the ones we mentioned for the comparable uncontrolled method. We work back from the third-party selling price to obtain an allowable transfer price."

Rhonda: "How is the markup determined?"

Wayne: "It corresponds to the percentage of gross profit earned by the reseller or the gross profit percentage earned by other parties who buy and resell similar products."

Rhonda: "I'm beginning to understand why we have three different methods. We have divisions that fit both of the first two types. We also have some transfers that have no outside market, nor do they have any potential for resale. These goods are simply used as components of other products that are sold. Is this where cost-plus pricing is used?"

Wayne: "Absolutely. In this case, the transfer price is defined as the costs of production plus an appropriate gross profit percentage, with adjustments for differences such as landing costs."

Rhonda: "How do we define the appropriate gross profit percentage?"

Wayne: "Well, it could be the gross profit percentage earned by the seller on the sale of the final product. Or, if we can obtain the information, it could be the gross profit percentage earned by another party on a similar product."

Rhonda: "Seems to me that the cost-plus method could be used for all three settings. Why don't we do that so that we have some uniformity in the way we compute transfer prices?"

Wayne: "There is a problem. If the requirements are met for any one of the methods, then it must be used—unless we can show that another method is more appropriate. The burden of proof is on us. I doubt that uniformity would be an acceptable justification. If the CCRA audits us and determines that the transfer price does not fairly reflect profits recognized in Canada, it can reallocate corporate income for purposes of taxation."

Required:

1. Assume that Valley Electronics transfers a component from a Canadian division to a German division for $11.70. The landing costs are $2.50 per unit, and the avoidable commissions and advertising total $0.50 per unit. The component has a market price within Canada of $10. Is the company complying with the comparable uncontrolled price method? Would the CCRA be concerned if the transfer price is greater than the market price after adjustments? Why or why not?

2. Assume that a manufacturing division in Canada transfers a component to a marketing division for resale. The resale price is $8, the gross profit percentage (gross profit divided by sales) is 25 percent, and landing costs total $1.20 per unit. Suppose that the actual transfer price (excluding landing costs) is $4.50. Should the company continue transferring at $4.50?

3. Suppose that a Canadian division has excess capacity. A European division has offered to buy a component that would increase the Canadian division's utilization of its capacity. The component has an outside market in Canada with a unit selling price of $12. The variable costs of production for the component are $6. Landing costs total $2 per unit, and an internal transfer avoids $1.25 per unit of marketing costs. The European division can purchase the component locally for $12. If we ignore income taxes, what is the minimum price that the European division should pay for the component (including landing costs)? the maximum price? If we assume that the joint benefit is split equally, what is the transfer price? Now discuss the impact of Section 69 of the *Income Tax Act* and of the CCRA's Information Circular 87–2 on this decision. (*Hint:* Consider Wayne's closing statement.) (US CMA Adapted)

19–18

Universal Data Corporation Transfer Pricing; International Setting*

LO6, LO7

The scene is a conference room in the head office in Geneva of Universal Data Corporation's European operations. The time is shortly after lunch on a winter day in 1997. Three people are finishing cups of coffee.

Seated at the head of the table is Clive Price, age 45, British by nationality and president of UDC-Europe. The other two are Irene Simmons, 39, Swiss and vice-president, finance; and Clinton Salter, 48, American and vice-president in charge of sales. (Two other officers of UDC-Europe mentioned in the conversation that follows are William O'Shaughnessy, general manager of the British Isles subsidiary, and Christine van Rhijn, general manager of the Belgian subsidiary.) UDC—its operations and its management control system—is briefly described at the end of the case.

Clive: "You know why we're here. We've got problems related to pricing at our Belgian subsidiary that require our immediate attention."

Clinton: "What's the story in Belgium?"

Irene: "We received a fax from the controller of the Belgian subsidiary this morning. Here, I made a copy for each of you."

She gives Clive and Clinton each a sheet of paper, which they read. The text of the fax follows.

Attn: I. P. Simmons

Paperwork on first shipment u82/15 enroute from Ireland received today. Five machines enroute to Brussels at f.o.b. $41,000 each.

We do not want to clear these machines through customs, as shipments from France have been arriving at f.o.b. $32,000 and from USA at f.o.b. $35,200.

Please instruct Ireland to issue revised invoices at f.o.b. $32,000 each so that we can clear this shipment without creating very dangerous situation with local customs.

We await urgent reply to request.

Dag Ericsson
UDC-Brussels

Irene: "You see, our Belgian controller is worried about the reaction of the customs authorities. He thinks that they won't understand why the same model is arriving from three different sources at three different prices."

Clive: "Pardon me, Irene, but doesn't the real risk involve dumping? After all, seeing the same model come in at three prices may lead customs to conclude that some of the machines were dumped—particularly the American ones. If that happens, wouldn't we be slapped with higher duty charges on the American machines?"

Irene: "I fear you're right, Clive. They might decide to put higher duty charges on all our American-made imports. With a duty on those imports of 8.4 percent, it would take little change in the assessed value of the goods to rack up a substantial tax bill. And it could get worse. We think that the Belgian officials trade data with their counterparts in other countries. Imagine the mess if all the European Union countries began to investigate our transfer pricing."

Clinton: "Well, the answer to this one seems simple enough. Let's lower the incoming price to the French level. It's only a bookkeeping entry anyway."

Clive: "It's not that simple. The machines were diverted to Brussels at the request of the Belgian subsidiary. Christine van Rhijn agreed to take the machines, at $41,000 each, from the Irish plant."

Clinton: "I'm confused. Why would she do that?"

Irene: "The story goes back several months now. During the spring, Clive received a telephone call from Christine demanding to know whether we actually planned to allow Galway to bill Belgium at an above-budget price for these extra machines. In addition, she complained about the 10 percent premium she had had to pay in order to get several extra machines from the United States."

Clive: "Irene and I explained to her that the high price resulted from three things—the increased demand for this model, higher-than-usual startup costs in Galway, and the favourable tax deal we obtained from the Irish government. As you remember, we have a 16-year exemption from income tax on all export sales."

Irene: "Christine wasn't exactly thrilled with our explanation. She thought the Irish were taking advantage of the tight supply situation. She saw no reason why Belgium should absorb Galway's production inefficiencies. Moreover, she insisted that her reported results and her own annual bonus should not be affected by some quirk in the tax laws."

Clive: "So I rang up William O'Shaughnessy and asked whether he could bring the price down. He mentioned the tax arrangement, saying that it would be sheer folly to transfer any more profit to a high-tax area like Belgium. Then he reminded me that Belgium had no alternative source and that Ireland could place the machines elsewhere. Besides, he said, the Brussels operation would still show a small profit on the transactions."

Irene: "I finally faxed Brussels that the final decision on price was up to them and William's group. I did note, however, that the Irish tax savings were substantial. They settled on the price of $41,000 each, f.o.b. Brussels."

Clinton: "You know, I'm not wild about *your* explanation either. It seems to me that this creative transfer pricing is bound to blow up in our faces. In fact, my eyebrows feel a little warm right now."

Clive: "Now, now, Clint, tax minimization is part of the game. You know very well that the decision to locate in Galway was heavily influenced by its cash-flow advantages."

Irene: "Clive's right, Clint. We all agreed to the Galway plant decision. Besides, we're in business to earn a profit for our shareholders. Contributing corporate cash to the Belgian government is not high on UDC's list of priorities."

Clinton: "Well, I'm still not convinced. Don't you think we ought to forget the fancy footwork and stick to what we know best—building and selling computers?"

Required:

Assume the role of Clive Price. How would you resolve the transfer pricing issue raised in this case?

Facts about UDC-Europe

The company, founded in 1972, is a U.S.-based manufacturer of computers and peripheral hardware. It sells, leases, and services its equipment worldwide. Of its $800 million in revenues, the European operations contribute $185 million.

UDC-Europe, a wholly owned subsidiary, was founded in 1976. It is very profitable and enjoys a great deal of autonomy from the parent company. Its 10 geographically organized subsidiaries, each of which is overseen by a general manager, are administrative umbrellas for two or more legal entities created to meet national legal and tax requirements. Four subsidiaries (the Spanish, the French, the British, and the Irish) have manufacturing as well as marketing operations.

UDC-Europe treats each subsidiary as a profit centre for purposes of managerial control and evaluation. It sets annual budgets in terms of pre-tax profit and judges local managers largely on their ability to meet or beat the targeted figures. UDC-Europe prices intracompany transfers at levels determined at the annual budget meeting, except under special circumstances—such as unexpectedly higher volume or a complex tax situation. In the former case, the subsidiary manager is expected to negotiate a price. In the latter case, management at Geneva may set the price.

Profitability of Belgian Sales*
(estimated per unit of Model U82/15)[a]

	High transfer price	Low transfer price
General data		
Manufactured in	Ireland	Ireland
Sold to customer in	Belgium	Belgium
Selling subsidiary	Belgium	Belgium
UDC-Europe		
Retail price	$60,000	$60,000
Cost of goods sold	27,000	27,000
Gross margin	$33,000	$33,000
All other expenses[b]	18,000	17,700
Profit before tax	$15,000	$15,300
Tax[c]	2,400	6,900
Profit after tax	$12,600	$ 8,400

Continued on next page.

Belgian subsidiary only

Retail price	$60,000	$60,000
Transfer price in	41,000	32,000
Gross margin	$19,000	$28,000
All other expenses[b]	14,000	13,700
Profit before tax	$ 5,000	$14,300
Tax[c]	2,400	6,900
Profit after tax	$ 2,600	$ 7,400

Irish subsidiary only

Transfer price out	$41,000	$32,000
Cost of goods sold	27,000	27,000
Gross margin	$14,000	$ 5,000
All other expenses	4,000	4,000
Profit before tax	$10,000	$ 1,000
Tax[c]	0	0
Profit after tax	$10,000	$ 1,000

N.A. = Not available.

[a] Data are on a per-machine basis. Actual exchange rates and cost figures from most recent monthly operations reports are employed. This shipment involves five machines. The agreement between the two subsidiaries covered a total of 40 machines.

[b] Differences in incoming duty payments account for the disparity between the two columns. The duty payments are based on the invoiced (transfer) price.

[c] Based on local tax rates.

[*] Adapted by permission of *Harvard Business Review*. An excerpt from "Case of the Tangled Transfer Price" by M. Edgar Barrett, May/June 1977. Copyright © 1977 by the President and Fellows of Harvard College; all rights reserved.

RESEARCH ASSIGNMENTS

19–20

Research Assignment

Use the library or the Internet to research the development of the North American Free Trade Agreement (NAFTA). What are the implications of its passage for companies located in Canada? Mexico? the United States?

19–21

Cybercase

LO2

Find five multinational companies with Web sites that describe their type(s) of involvement in international trade. Find at least one overseas joint venture. What proportion of revenues and profit stem from the overseas ventures?

Glossary

A

absorption costing A product-costing method that assigns all manufacturing costs to a product: direct materials, direct labour, variable overhead, and fixed overhead.

absorption-costing (full-costing) income Income computed by following a functionally-based statement. Cost of goods sold includes all variable manufacturing costs and a portion of fixed overhead.

acceptable quality level (AQL) An approach to quality control that permits or allows defects to occur provided that they do not exceed a predetermined level.

accounting rate of return The rate of return obtained by dividing the average accounting net income by the original investment (or by average investment).

Accounting Standards Board Establishes financial accounting standards, including the nature of inputs and the rules and conventions governing financial accounting processes.

activity A basic unit of work performed within an organization. It can also be defined as an aggregation of actions within an organization useful to managers for purposes of planning, controlling, and decision making.

activity analysis The process of identifying, describing, and evaluating the activities an organization performs.

activity attributes Nonfinancial and financial information items that describe individual activities.

activity-based budgeting system In activity-based budgeting, the workload (demand) for each activity is estimated and the resources required to sustain this workload are established.

activity-based costing (ABC) A cost assignment approach that first uses direct and driver tracing to assign costs to activities and then uses drivers to assign costs to cost objects.

activity-based costing (ABC) system A cost system that first traces costs to activities and then traces costs from activities to products.

activity-based management (ABM) A system-wide, integrated approach that focuses management's attention on activities with the objective of improving customer value and the profit achieved by providing this value. It includes driver analysis, activity analysis, and perfor-

mance evaluation, and draws on activity-based costing as a major source of information.

activity-based management (ABM) accounting system An accounting system that emphasizes the use of activities for assigning and managing costs.

activity-based responsibility accounting A control system defined by centring responsibility on processes and teams where activity performance is measured in terms of time, quality, and efficiency.

activity capacity The number of times an activity can be performed.

activity dictionary A list of activities described by specific attributes, such as name, definition, classification as primary or secondary, and activity driver.

activity drivers Factors that measure the consumption of activities by products and other cost objects.

activity elimination The process of eliminating nonvalue-added activities.

activity flexible budgeting The prediction of what activity costs will be as activity usage changes.

activity inputs The resources consumed by an activity in producing its output (they are the factors that enable the activity to be performed).

activity output The result or product of an activity.

activity output measure The number of times an activity is performed. It is the quantifiable measure of the output.

activity rate The average unit cost, obtained by dividing the resource expenditure by the activity's practical capacity.

activity reduction Decreasing the time and resources required by an activity.

activity selection The process of choosing among sets of activities caused by competing strategies.

activity sharing Increasing the efficiency of necessary activities by using economies of scale.

activity volume variance The cost of the actual activity capacity acquired and the capacity that should be used.

actual costing An approach that assigns actual costs for direct materials, direct labour, and overhead to products.

adjusted cost of goods sold The cost of goods sold after all adjustments for overhead variance are made.

administrative costs   All costs associated with the general administration of the organization that cannot be reasonably assigned to either marketing or production.

advance pricing agreements   An agreement between the Canada Customs and Revenue Agency (formerly Revenue Canada) and a taxpayer on the acceptability of a transfer price. The agreement is private and is binding on both parties for a specified period of time.

aesthetics   A quality attribute that is concerned with the appearance of tangible products (for example, style and beauty) as well as the appearance of the facilities, equipment, personnel, and communications materials associated with services.

allocation   Assignment of indirect costs to cost objects.

annuity   A series of future cash flows.

applied overhead   Overhead assigned to production using predetermined rates.

appraisal costs   Costs incurred to determine whether products and services are conforming to requirements.

B

Balanced Scorecard   *See* strategic-based responsibility accounting.

base period   A prior period used to set the benchmark for measuring productivity changes.

batch-level activities   Activities that are performed each time a batch is produced.

benchmarking   An approach that uses the best practices as the standard for evaluating activity performance.

best-fitting line   The line that fits a set of data points the best, in the sense that the sum of the squared deviations of the data points from the line is the smallest.

binding constraints   Constraints whose resources are fully utilized.

break-even point   The point where total sales revenue equals total costs; the point of zero profits.

budget committee   A committee responsible for setting budgetary policies and goals, reviewing and approving the budget, and resolving any differences that may arise in the budgetary process.

budget director   The individual responsible for coordinating and directing the overall budgeting process.

budgetary slack   The process of padding the budget by overestimating costs and underestimating revenues.

budgets   Plans of action expressed in financial terms.

C

capital budgeting   The process of making capital investment decisions.

capital cost allowances (CCAs)   Deduction for Canadian income tax purposes related to the capital cost of fixed assets.

capital investment decisions   The process of planning, setting goals and priorities, arranging financing, and identifying criteria for making long-term investments.

carrying costs   The costs of holding inventory.

cash budget   A detailed plan that outlines all sources and uses of cash.

causal factors   Activities or variables that invoke service costs. Generally, it is desirable to use causal factors as the basis for allocating service costs.

centralized decision making   A system in which decisions are made at the top level of an organization and local managers are given the charge to implement them.

Certified General Accountant (CGA)   An accountant who holds the CGA designation after satisfying the examination and practice requirements. CGAs are found both in public practice and in private- and public-sector organizations.

Certified Internal Auditor (CIA)   A person who has passed a comprehensive examination designed to ensure technical competence and has two years' experience.

Certified Management Accountant (CMA)   An accountant who holds the CMA designation after satisfying the entrance examination, professional program, and experience requirements. CMAs are found primarily in private- and public-sector organizations.

Chartered Accountant (CA)   An accountant who holds the CA designation after satisfying the examination and public practice requirements. CAs are found in both public practice and private and public sector organizations.

coefficient of correlation   The square root of the coefficient of determination, which is used to express not only the degree of correlation between two variables but also the direction of the relationship.

coefficient of determination   The percentage of total variability in a dependent variable (e.g., cost) that is explained by an independent variable (e.g., activity level). It assumes a value between 0 and 1.

committed fixed costs   Costs incurred for the acquisition of long-term activity capacity, usually as the result of strategic planning.

committed resources   Resources that are purchased in advance of usage. These resources may or may not have unused (excess) capacity.

common costs   The costs of resources used in the output of two or more services or products.

common fixed expenses   Fixed expenses that cannot be directly traced to individual segments and that are unaffected by the elimination of any one segment.

comparable uncontrolled price method   The transfer price most preferred by the Canada Customs and Revenue Agency (formerly Revenue Canada). The comparable uncontrolled price is essentially equal to the market price.

compounding of interest   Paying interest on interest.

constraint set   The collection of all constraints that pertain to a particular optimization problem.

constraints   Mathematical expressions that express resource limitations.

consumption ratio The proportion of an overhead activity consumed by a product.

continuous budget A moving 12-month budget with a future month added as the current month expires.

continuous improvement The process of searching for ways of increasing the overall efficiency and productivity of activities by reducing waste, increasing quality, and reducing costs.

continuous replenishment A system where a manufacturer assumes the inventory management function for the retailer.

contribution margin Sales revenue minus total variable cost or price minus unit variable cost.

contribution margin ratio Contribution margin divided by sales revenue. It is the proportion of each sales dollar available to cover fixed costs and provide for profit.

control The process of setting standards, receiving feedback on actual performance, and taking corrective action whenever actual performance has deviated significantly from planned performance.

control activities Activities performed by an organization to prevent or detect poor quality (because poor quality may exist).

control costs Costs incurred from performing control activities.

control limits The maximum allowable deviation from a standard.

controllable costs Costs that managers have the power to influence.

controller The chief accounting officer, who supervises all accounting departments and activities.

controlling The managerial activity of monitoring a plan's implementation and taking corrective action as needed.

conversion cost The sum of direct labour cost and overhead cost.

core objectives and measures Those objectives and measures common to most organizations.

cost The cash or cash equivalent value sacrificed for goods and services that are expected to bring a current or future benefit to the organization.

cost assignment The process of associating the costs, once measured, with the units produced.

cost behaviour The way in which a cost changes in relation to changes in activity usage.

cost centre A responsibility centre in which a manager is responsible only for costs.

cost formula The linear function $Y = F + VX$, where Y = total mixed cost, F = fixed cost, V = variable cost per unit of activity, and X = activity level.

cost measurement The act of determining the dollar amounts of direct materials, direct labour, and overhead used in production.

cost object Any item, such as products, departments, projects, activities, and so on, for which costs are measured and assigned.

cost of capital The cost of investment funds, usually viewed as a weighted average of the cost of funds from all sources.

cost of goods manufactured The total cost of goods completed during the current period.

cost of goods sold The cost of direct materials, direct labour, and overhead attached to the units sold.

cost of goods sold budget The estimated costs for the units sold.

cost-plus method A transfer price acceptable to the Canada Customs and Revenue Agency (formerly Revenue Canada). The cost-plus method is simply a cost-based transfer price.

cost reconciliation The final section of the production report and the section that compares the costs to account for with the costs accounted for to ensure that they are equal.

cost-volume-profit graph A graph that depicts the relationships among costs, volume, and profits. It consists of a total revenue line and a total cost line.

costs of quality Costs incurred because poor quality may exist or because poor quality does exist.

currency appreciation A country's currency becomes stronger and can purchase more units of another country's currency.

currency depreciation A country's currency becomes weaker and can purchase fewer units of another country's currency.

currency risk management A company's management of its transaction, economic, and translation exposure due to exchange rate fluctuations.

currently attainable standards Standards that reflect an efficient operating state; they are rigorous but attainable.

customer perspective A Balanced Scorecard viewpoint that defines the customer and market segments in which the business will compete.

customer value The difference between what a customer receives (customer realization) and what the customer gives up (customer sacrifice).

cycle time The length of time required to produce one unit of a product.

D

decentralization The granting of decision-making freedom to lower operating levels.

decentralized decision making A system in which decisions are made and implemented by lower-level managers.

decision making The process of choosing among competing alternatives.

decision model A specific set of procedures that, when followed, produces a decision.

defective product A product or service that does not conform to specifications.

degree of operating leverage (DOL) A measure of the sensitivity of profit change to changes in sales volume.

It measures the percentage change in profits resulting from a percentage change in sales.

dependent variable A variable whose value depends on the value of another variable. For example, Y in the cost formula $Y = F + VX$ depends on the value of X.

direct costs Costs that can be easily and accurately traced to a cost object.

direct fixed expenses Fixed costs that are directly traceable to a given segment and, consequently, disappear if the segment is eliminated.

direct labour Labour that is traceable to the goods or services being produced.

direct labour budget A budget showing the total direct labour hours needed and the associated cost for the number of units in the production budget.

direct materials Materials that are traceable to the goods or services being produced.

direct materials purchases budget A budget that outlines the expected usage of materials for production and purchases of the direct materials required.

direct method A method that allocates service costs directly to producing departments. This method ignores any interactions that may exist among support departments.

direct tracing The process of identifying costs that are specifically or physically associated with a cost object.

discount factor The factor used to convert a future cash flow to its present value.

discount rate The rate of return used to compute the present value of future cash flows.

discounted cash flows Future cash flows expressed in present value terms.

discounting The act of finding the present value of future cash flows.

discounting models Capital investment models that explicitly consider the time value of money in identifying criteria for accepting or rejecting proposed projects.

discretionary fixed costs Costs incurred for the acquisition of short-term capacity or services, usually as the result of yearly planning.

double-loop feedback Information about both the effectiveness of strategy implementation and the validity of assumptions underlying the strategy.

driver analysis The effort expended to identify those factors that are the root causes of activity costs.

driver tracing The use of drivers to assign costs to cost objects.

drivers Factors that cause changes in resource usage, activity usage, costs, and revenues.

Drum-Buffer-Rope (DBR) System The TOC (theory of constraints) inventory management system that relies on the drum beat of the major constrained resources, time buffers, and ropes to determine inventory levels.

durability The length of time a product functions.

dysfunctional behaviour Individual behaviour that conflicts with the goals of the organization.

E

ecoefficiency A view of environmental management that maintains that organizations can produce more useful goods and services while simultaneously reducing the negative environmental impacts, resource consumption, and costs.

economic order quantity (EOQ) The amount that should be ordered (or produced) to minimize the total ordering (or setup) and carrying costs.

economic risk The possibility that a firm's present value of future cash flows can be affected by exchange rate fluctuations.

economic value added A performance measure that is calculated by taking the after-tax operating profit minus the total annual cost of capital.

efficiency variance *See* usage variance.

electronic data interchange (EDI) An inventory management method that allows suppliers access to a buyer's on-line database.

employee empowerment The authorization of operational personnel to plan, control, and make decisions without explicit authorization from middle and higher-level management.

ending finished goods inventory budget A budget that describes planned ending inventory of finished goods in units and dollars.

environmental costs Costs that are incurred because poor environmental quality exists or may exist.

environmental detection costs Costs incurred to detect poor environmental performance.

environmental external failure costs Costs incurred after contaminants are introduced into the environment.

environmental internal failure costs Costs incurred after contaminants are produced but before they are introduced into the environment.

environmental prevention costs Costs incurred to prevent damage to the environment.

equivalent units of output Complete units that could have been produced given the total amount of manufacturing effort expended during the period.

ethical behaviour Choosing actions that are "right" and "proper" and "just." Our behaviour can be right or wrong, it can be proper or improper, and the decisions we make can be fair or unfair.

exchange gain A gain on the exchange of one currency for another due to appreciation in the home currency.

exchange loss A loss on the exchange of one currency for another due to depreciation in the home currency (for receivables).

exchange rate The rate at which a foreign currency can be exchanged for the domestic currency.

expected activity capacity Expected activity output for the coming year.

expenses Expired costs.

external constraints Limiting factors imposed on the firm from external sources (such as market demand).

external failure costs Costs incurred because products fail to conform to requirements after being sold to outside parties.

external linkages The relationship of a firm's activities within its segment of the value chain with those activities of its suppliers and customers.

external measures Measures that relate to customer and shareholder objectives.

F

facility-level activities Activities that sustain a facility's general manufacturing process.

failure activities Activities performed by an organization or its customers in response to poor quality (poor quality *does* exist).

failure costs The costs incurred by an organization because failure activities are performed.

favourable (F) variances Variances produced whenever the actual amounts are less than the budgeted or standard allowances.

feasible set of solutions The collection of all feasible solutions.

feasible solution A product mix that satisfies all constraints.

features (quality of design) Characteristics of a product that differentiate functionally similar products.

feedback Information that can be used to evaluate or correct the steps being taken to implement a plan.

FIFO costing method A process-costing method that separates units in beginning inventory from those produced during the current period. Unit costs include only current-period costs and production.

financial accounting information system An accounting information subsystem that is primarily concerned with producing outputs for external users and uses well-specified economic events as inputs and processes that meet certain rules and conventions.

financial budgets The portions of the master budget that include the cash budget, the budgeted balance sheet, the budgeted statement of cash flows, and the capital budget.

financial measures Measures expressed in dollar terms.

financial perspective A Balanced Scorecard viewpoint that describes the financial consequences of actions taken in the other three perspectives.

financial productivity measure A productivity measure in which inputs and outputs are expressed in dollars.

fitness of use The suitability of a product for carrying out its advertised functions.

fixed (activity) costs Costs that, *in total*, are constant within the relevant range as the activity output varies.

fixed activity rate The fixed activity cost divided by the total capacity of the activity driver.

fixed overhead denominator variance The difference between budgeted fixed overhead and applied fixed overhead.

fixed overhead spending variance The difference between actual fixed overhead and applied fixed overhead.

flexible budget A budget that can specify costs for a range of activity.

flexible budget variance The sum of price variances and efficiency variances in a performance report comparing actual costs to expected costs predicted by a flexible budget.

flexible resources Resources that are acquired as used and needed. There is no unused or excess capacity for these resources.

foreign trade zones Areas that are physically on U.S. soil but considered to be outside U.S. commerce. Goods imported into a foreign trade zone are duty-free until they leave the zone.

forward contract An agreement that requires the buyer to exchange a specified amount of currency at a specified rate (the forward rate) on a specified future date.

full environmental costing The assignment of all environmental costs, both private and societal, to products.

full private costing The assignment of only private costs to individual products.

functional-based costing (FBC) An approach for assigning costs of shared resources to products and other cost objects using only production or unit-level drivers.

functional-based management (FBM) A managerial approach that attempts to control costs by focusing on the efficiency of organizational subunits.

functional-based management (FBM) accounting system An accounting information system that emphasizes the use of functional organizational units to assign and manage costs.

functional-based responsibility accounting A control system defined by centring responsibility on organizational units and individuals, with traditional budgets and standard costing used to evaluate and monitor performance.

future value The value that will accumulate by the end of an investment's life if the investment earns a specified compounded return.

G

gain-sharing Providing cash incentives for a company's entire workforce that are keyed to quality and productivity gains.

goal congruence The alignment of a manager's personal goals with those of the organization.

goodness of fit The degree of association between Y and X (cost and activity). It is measured by how much of the total variability in Y is explained by X.

H

hedging One way of insuring against gains and losses on foreign currency exchange.

heterogeneity One of the four qualities that distinguish services from products—the fact that there is a greater chance of variation in the performance of services than in the production of products.

hidden quality costs Opportunity costs resulting from poor quality.

high-low method A method for fitting a line to a set of data points using the high and low points in the data set. For a cost formula, the high and low points represent the high and low activity levels. This method is used to break out the fixed and variable components of a mixed cost.

homogeneous cost pool A collection of overhead costs associated with activities that have the same process and the same level, and that can use the same activity driver to assign costs to products.

I

ideal standards Standards that reflect perfect operating conditions.

impact analysis A life-cycle assessment step where the environmental impacts of different product (or process) designs are compared and evaluated.

improvement analysis A life-cycle assessment step where efforts are made to reduce the environmental impacts revealed by the inventory analysis and the impact analysis steps.

incentives The positive or negative measures taken by an organization to induce a manager to exert effort toward achieving the organization's goals.

independent projects Projects that, if accepted or rejected, will not affect the cash flows of another project.

independent variable A variable whose value does not depend on the value of another variable. For example, in the cost formula $Y = F + VX$, the variable X is an independent variable.

indirect costs Costs that cannot be traced to a cost object.

industrial value chain The linked set of value-creating activities from basic raw materials to end-use customers.

industry volume variance A difference in profit due to the difference between budgeted sales volume based on expected industry sales volume and budgeted sales volume based on actual industry sales volume.

innovation process A process that anticipates customers' emerging and potential needs and creates new products and services to satisfy these needs.

input tradeoff efficiency The least-cost, technically efficient mix of outputs.

inseparability One of the four qualities that distinguish services from products—the fact that producers of services and buyers of services must usually be in direct contact for an exchange to take place.

intangibility One of the four qualities that distinguish services from products—the fact that buyers of services cannot see, feel, hear, or taste a service before it is bought.

intercept parameter The fixed cost, representing the point where the cost formula intercepts the vertical axis. In the cost formula $Y = F + VX$, F is the intercept parameter.

internal business perspective A Balanced Scorecard viewpoint that describes the internal processes needed to provide value for customers and owners.

internal constraints Limiting factors found within the firm (such as machine time availability).

internal failure costs Costs incurred because products and services fail to conform to requirements where lack of conformity is discovered prior to external sale.

internal linkages Relationships among activities within a firm's value chain.

internal measures Measures that relate to the processes and capabilities that create value for customers and shareholders.

internal rate of return The rate of return that equates the present value of a project's cash inflows with the present value of its cash outflows (i.e., it sets the net present value equal to zero). Also, the rate of return being earned on funds that remain internally invested in a project.

internal value chain The set of activities required to design, develop, produce, market, distribute, and service a product (the product could be a service).

inventory The money an organization spends in turning raw materials into throughput.

inventory analysis A life-cycle assessment step where the qualities and types of material, energy, and environmental release are described.

investment centre A responsibility centre in which a manager is responsible for revenues, costs, and investments.

J

JIT manufacturing A demand-pull system whose objective is to eliminate waste by producing a product only when it is needed and only in the quantities demanded by customers.

JIT purchasing A purchasing method that requires suppliers to deliver parts and materials just in time to be used in production.

job-order cost sheet A document that is subsidiary to the work-in-process account and on which the total costs of materials, labour, and overhead for a single job are accumulated.

job-order costing system A costing system in which costs are collected and assigned to units of production for each individual job.

joint products Products that are inseparable prior to a split-off point. All manufacturing costs up to the split-off point are joint costs.

joint venture A type of partnership in which investors co-own the enterprise.

K

kaizen costing Efforts to reduce the costs of existing products and processes.

kaizen standard   An interim standard that reflects the planned improvement for a coming period.

Kanban system   An information system that controls production on a demand-pull basis through the use of cards or markers.

keep-or-drop decisions   Relevant cost analyses that focus on keeping or dropping a segment of business.

L

labour efficiency variance (LEV)   The difference between the actual direct labour hours used and the standard direct labour hours allowed multiplied by the standard hourly wage rate.

labour rate variance (LRV)   The difference between the actual hourly rate paid and the standard hourly rate multiplied by the actual hours worked.

lag measures   Outcome measures or measures of results from past efforts.

lead measures (performance drivers)   Factors that drive future performance.

lead time   For purchasing, the time to receive an order after it is placed. For manufacturing, the time to produce a product from start to finish.

learning and growth (infrastructure) perspective   A Balanced Scorecard viewpoint that defines the capabilities that an organization needs to create long term growth and improvements.

life-cycle assessment   An approach that identifies the environmental consequences of a product through its entire life cycle and then searches for opportunities to obtain environmental improvements.

life-cycle cost assessment   A method that assigns costs and benefits to environmental consequences and improvements.

life-cycle cost management   The management of value-chain activities so that a long-term competitive advantage is created.

life-cycle costs   All costs that are associated with the product for its entire life cycle.

line positions   Positions that have direct responsibility for the basic objectives of an organization.

linear programming   A method that searches among possible solutions until it finds the optimal solution.

long run   A period of time in which all costs are variable.

loose constraints   Constraints whose limited resources are not fully used by a product mix.

M

make-or-buy decisions   Relevant cost analyses that focus on whether a component should be made internally or purchased externally.

Management Accounting Guidelines   Document published by CMA-Canada to assist management accountants in fulfilling their responsibilities; however, management accountants are under no obligation to follow any set of standards except as related to external reporting.

management accounting information system   An information system that produces outputs using inputs and processes needed to satisfy specific management objectives.

manufacturing cells   Machines grouped in families, usually in a semicircle, so that they can be used to perform a variety of operations in sequence. Each cell is set up to produce a particular product or product family.

maquiladoras   Manufacturing plants located in Mexico that process imported materials and re-export them to Canada or the United States.

margin   The ratio of net operating income to sales.

margin of safety   The units sold or expected to be sold or sales revenue earned or expected to be earned above the breakeven volume.

market share variance   A difference in profit due to the difference between the budgeted market share and the actual market share.

marketing (selling) costs   The costs necessary to market and distribute a product or service.

markup   The percentage applied to a base cost; it includes desired profit and any costs not included in the base cost.

master budget   The collection of all area and activity budgets representing a firm's comprehensive plan of action.

materials price variance (MPV)   The difference between the actual price paid per unit of materials and the standard price allowed per unit multiplied by the actual quantity of materials purchased.

materials purchase price variance   The materials price variance based on materials purchased.

materials requisition form   A source document that records the type, quantity, and unit price of the direct materials issued to each job.

materials usage variance (MUV)   The difference between the direct materials actually used and the direct materials allowed for the actual output multiplied by the standard price.

maximum transfer price   The transfer price that will make the buying division no worse off if an input is acquired internally.

method of least squares   A statistical method to find a line that best fits a set of data. This method is used to break out the fixed and variable components of a mixed cost.

minimum transfer price   The transfer price that will make the selling division no worse off if an output is sold internally.

mixed cost   A cost that has both a fixed and a variable component.

monetary incentives   The use of economic rewards to motivate managers.

multinational corporation (MNC)   A corporation for which a significant amount of business is done in more than one country.

multiple regression   The use of the least-squares method to determine the parameters in a linear equation involving two or more explanatory variables.

multiple-period quality trend report   A graph that plots quality costs (as a percentage of sales) against time.

mutually exclusive projects   Projects that, if accepted, preclude the acceptance of competing projects.

myopic behaviour   Managerial actions that improve budgetary performance in the short run at the expense of the long-run welfare of the program.

N

net income   Operating income less income taxes.

net present value   The difference between the present value of a project's cash inflows and the present value of its cash outflows.

nondiscounting models   Capital investment models that identify criteria for accepting or rejecting projects without considering the time value of money.

nonfinancial measures   Measures expressed in nonmonetary units.

noninventoriable (period) costs   Costs that are expensed in the period in which they are incurred.

nonmonetary incentives   The use of psychological and social rewards to motivate managers.

nonproduction costs   Costs associated with the functions of selling and administration.

nonunit-level activity drivers   Factors that measure the consumption of nonunit-level activities by products and other cost objects.

nonunit-level drivers   Factors, other than the number of units produced, that measure the consumption of activities by cost objects.

nonvalue-added activities   All activities other than those that are absolutely essential to remain in business.

nonvalue-added costs   Costs that are caused either by nonvalue-added activities or by the inefficient performance of value-added activities.

normal activity capacity   The average activity output for a given period.

normal cost of goods sold   The cost of goods sold before adjustment for any overhead variance.

normal costing   An approach that assigns the actual costs for direct materials and direct labour to products but uses a predetermined rate to assign overhead costs.

North American Free Trade Agreement (NAFTA)   A free trade agreement between Canada, the United States, and Mexico that is aimed at encouraging trade in goods, commercial services, and investments by removing barriers to trade, particularly tariffs.

O

objective function   The function to be optimized, usually a profit function; thus, optimization usually means maximizing profits.

objective measures   Measures that can be readily quantified and verified.

observable quality costs   Quality costs that are available from an organization's accounting records.

one-half rule   The rule that restricts the amount of CCA that can be claimed in the year of acquisition to one-half of the CCA rate for the class.

operating assets   Assets used to generate operating income, usually consisting of cash, inventories, receivables, property, plant, and equipment.

operating budgets   Budgets associated with the income-producing activities of an organization.

operating expenses   The money an organization spends in turning inventories into throughput.

operating income   Revenues minus expenses from the firm's normal operations. Income taxes are excluded.

operating leverage   The use of fixed costs to extract higher percentage changes in profits as sales activity changes. Leverage is achieved by increasing fixed costs while lowering variable costs.

operation costing   A hybrid costing method that assigns material costs to a product using a job-order approach and assigns conversion costs using a process approach.

operations process   A process that produces and delivers existing products and services to customers, beginning with a customer order and ending with the delivery of the product or service.

operational productivity measure   A measure that is expressed in physical terms.

opportunity cost   The benefit sacrificed or forgone when one alternative is chosen over another.

opportunity cost approach   A transfer pricing system that identifies the minimum price that a selling division would be willing to accept and the maximum price that a buying division would be willing to pay.

optimal solution   The feasible solution that produces the best value for the objective function (the largest value if seeking to maximize the objective function; the minimum otherwise).

ordering costs   The costs of placing and receiving an order.

outsourcing   The payment by a company for a business function that was formerly done in-house.

overapplied overhead   The amount by which applied overhead exceeds actual overhead.

overhead   All production costs other than direct materials and direct labour.

overhead budget   A budget that reveals the planned expenditures for all indirect manufacturing items.

overhead variance   The difference between actual overhead and applied overhead.

P

parallel processing   A processing pattern in which two or more sequential processes are required in order to produce a finished good.

partial productivity measurement   A ratio that measures productive efficiency for one input.

participative budgeting An approach to budgeting that allows managers who will be held accountable for budgetary performance to participate in the budget's development.

payback period The time required for a project to return its investment.

performance The measure of how consistent and well a product functions.

performance reports Reports that compare the actual data with planned data.

perishability One of the four qualities that distinguish services from products—the fact that services cannot be stored for future use by the consumer.

perquisites A type of fringe benefit over and above salary that is received by managers.

physical flow schedule A schedule that reconciles units to account for with units accounted for. The physical units are not adjusted for percent of completion.

planning Setting objectives and identifying methods of achieving those objectives.

pool rate The overhead costs for a homogeneous cost pool divided by the practical capacity of the activity driver associated with the pool.

postaudit A follow-up analysis of an investment decision, comparing actual benefits and costs with expected benefits and costs.

postpurchase costs The costs of using, maintaining, and disposing of a product.

postsales service process A process that provides critical and responsive service to customers after the product or service has been delivered.

practical activity capacity The activity output produced when the activity is performed efficiently.

practical capacity The efficient level of activity performance.

predatory pricing The practice of setting prices below cost for the purpose of injuring competitors and eliminating competition.

predetermined overhead rate An overhead rate computed using estimated data.

present value The current value of a future cash flow. It represents the amount that must be invested now if the future cash flow is to be received, assuming compounding at a given rate of interest.

prevention costs Costs incurred to prevent defects in products or services being produced.

price gouging A subjective term referring to the practice of setting an "excessively" high price.

price (rate) variance The difference between the standard price and the actual price multiplied by the actual quantity of inputs used.

price-recovery component The difference between the total profit change and the profit-linked productivity change.

price standard The price that should be paid per unit of input.

primary activity An activity that is consumed by products or customers.

prime cost The sum of direct materials cost and direct labour cost.

private costs Environmental costs that an organization has to pay.

process A series of activities (operations) that are linked to perform a specific objective.

process-costing system A costing system that accumulates production costs by process or by department for a given period of time.

process creation The installation of an entirely new process with the objective of meeting customer and financial objectives.

process improvement Incremental and constant increases in the efficiency of an existing process.

process innovation (business re-engineering) The performance of a process in a radically new way with the objective of achieving dramatic improvements in response time, quality, and efficiency.

process value analysis An approach that focuses on processes and activities and emphasizes systemwide performance instead of individual performance.

process value chain The innovation, operations, and post-sales service processes.

producing departments Units within an organization that are responsible for producing the products or services that are sold to customers.

product cost A cost assignment method that satisfies a well-specified managerial objective.

product diversity The situation present when products consume overhead in different proportions.

product-level (sustaining) activities Activities that are performed to enable the production of each different type of product.

product life cycle The time a product exists, from conception to abandonment.

product stewardship The practice of designing, manufacturing, maintaining, and recycling products to minimize adverse environmental impacts.

production budget A budget that shows how many units must be produced to meet sales needs and satisfy ending inventory requirements.

production costs Costs associated with the manufacture of goods or the provision of services.

production drivers Drivers that are highly correlated with production output (volume).

production Kanban A card or marker that specifies the quantity that the Kanban system should produce.

production report A document that summarizes the manufacturing activity that takes place in a process department for a given period of time.

productivity The efficient production of output, using the least quantity of inputs possible.

productivity measurement The assessment of productivity changes.

profile measurement A series or vector of separate and distinct partial operational measures.

profit centre A responsibility centre in which a manager is responsible for both revenues and costs.

profit–volume graph A graph that depicts the relationship between profits and sales volume.

profit volume variance (gross) Consists of a profit volume variance (net) and a sales mix variance.

profit volume variance (net) Measures the effect on profit of the difference in total sales volume between the budget and the actual volume, with other factors—including sales mix and contribution margin per unit—remaining constant.

profit-linked productivity measurement The assessment of the amount of profit change (from the base period to the current period) attributable to productivity changes.

pseudoparticipation A budgetary system in which top management solicits inputs from lower-level managers and then ignores those inputs. Thus, in reality, budgets are dictated from above.

Q

quality of conformance Conforming to the design requirements of the product.

quality product or service A product that meets or exceeds customer expectations.

quantity standard The quantity of input allowed per unit of output.

R

rate variance *See* price (rate) variance.

realized external failure costs Environmental costs caused by environmental degradation and paid for by the responsible organization.

reciprocal method A method that simultaneously allocates service costs to all user departments. It gives full consideration to interactions among support departments.

relevant costs Future costs that change across alternatives.

relevant range The range over which an assumed cost relationship is valid for the normal operations of a firm.

reliability The probability that the product or service will perform its intended function for a specified length of time.

reorder point The point in time at which a new order (or setup) should be initiated.

resale price method A transfer price acceptable to the Canada Customs and Revenue Agency (formerly Revenue Canada). The resale price method computes a transfer price equal to the sales price received by the reseller less an appropriate markup.

resource drivers Factors that measure the consumption of resources by activities.

responsibility accounting A system that measures the results of each responsibility centre according to the information that managers need in order to operate their centre.

responsibility centre A segment of the business whose manager is accountable for specified sets of activities.

return on investment (ROI) The ratio of operating income to average operating assets.

revenue centre A responsibility centre in which a manager is responsible only for sales.

ropes Actions taken to tie the rate at which raw material is released into the plant (at the first operation) to the production rate of the constrained resource

S

safety stock Extra inventory carried to serve as insurance against fluctuations in demand.

sales budget A budget that describes expected sales in units and dollars for the coming period.

sales mix The relative combination of products (or services) being sold by an organization.

sales mix variance Measures the effect of the change from the budgeted sales mix.

scattergraph A plot of (X, Y) data points. For cost analysis, X is activity usage and Y is the associated cost at that activity level.

scatterplot method A method of fitting a line to a set of data using two points that are selected by judgment. It is used to break out the fixed and variable components of a mixed cost.

secondary activity An activity that is consumed by primary activities and/or other secondary activities.

segment A subunit of a company that is sufficiently important to warrant the production of performance reports.

segment margin The contribution a segment makes to cover common fixed costs and variable costs and provide for profit after direct fixed costs and variable costs are deducted from the segment's sales revenue.

segmented reporting The preparation of financial performance reports for each segment of importance within a firm.

sell or process further Relevant cost analysis that focuses on whether a product should be processed beyond the split-off point.

selling and administrative expenses budget A budget that outlines planned expenditures for nonmanufacturing activities.

selling price variance Measures the direct effect of the change in selling prices on profit.

sensitivity analysis The "what-if" process of altering certain key variables to assess the effect on the original outcome.

sequential (or step) method A method that allocates service costs to user departments in a sequential manner. It gives partial consideration to interactions among support departments.

sequential processing A processing pattern in which units pass from one process to another in a set order.

serviceability The ease of maintaining and/or repairing a product.

services Tasks or activities performed for a customer using an organization's products or facilities.

setup costs The cost of preparing equipment and facilities so that they can be used for production.

short run A period of time in which at least one cost is fixed.

simplex method An algorithm that identifies the optimal solution for a linear programming problem.

single-loop feedback Information about the effectiveness of strategy implementation.

slope parameter The variable cost per unit of activity usage, represented by V in the cost formula $Y = F + VX$.

special-order decisions Relevant cost analyses that focus on whether a specially priced order should be accepted or rejected.

split-off point The point at which products become distinguishable after passing through a common process.

spot rate The exchange rate of one currency for another for immediate delivery.

staff positions Positions that are supportive in nature and have only indirect responsibility for an organization's basic objectives.

standard cost per unit The per-unit cost that should be achieved given materials, labour, and overhead standards.

standard cost sheet A listing of the standard costs and standard quantities of direct materials, direct labour, and overhead that should apply to a single product.

standard hours allowed (*SH*) The direct labour hours that should have been used to produce the actual output (Unit labour standard × Actual output).

standard quantity of materials allowed (*SQ*) The quantity of materials that should have been used to produce the actual output (Unit materials standard × Actual output).

static budget A budget for a particular level of activity.

step cost A cost function in which cost is defined for ranges of activity usage rather than point values. The function has the property of displaying constant cost over a range of activity usage and then changing to a different cost level as a new range of activity usage is undertaken.

stock-out costs The costs of insufficient inventory.

strategic-based responsibility accounting (Balanced Scorecard) Responsibility accounting system objectives and measures for four different perspectives: the financial perspective, the customer perspective, the process perspective, and the learning and growth (infrastructure) perspective.

strategic cost management The use of cost data to develop and identify superior strategies that will produce a competitive advantage.

strategic decision making Choosing among alternative strategies with the goal of selecting the strategy or strategies that provide a company with reasonable assurance for long-term growth and survival.

strategic plan The long-term plan for future activities and operations, usually involving at least five years.

strategy The process of choosing a business's market and customer segments, identifying its critical internal business processes, and selecting the individual and organizational capabilities needed to meet internal, customer, and financial objectives.

subjective measures Measures that are nonquantifiable and whose values are judgmental in nature.

sunk cost A cost for which the outlay has already been made and that cannot be affected by a future decision.

supplies Those materials necessary for production that do not become part of the finished product or that are not used in providing a service.

support departments Units within an organization that provide essential support services for producing departments.

sustainable development Development that meets the needs of the present without compromising the ability of future generations to meet their own needs.

T

tactical decision making Choosing among alternatives with an immediate or limited end in view.

Taguchi loss function A function that assumes that any variation from the target value of a quality characteristic causes hidden quality costs.

tangible products Goods that are produced by converting raw materials through the use of labour and capital inputs such as plant, land, and machinery.

target cost The difference between the sales price needed to achieve a projected market share and the desired per-unit profit.

target costing A method of determining the cost of a product or service based on the price (target price) that customers are willing to pay.

tariff (or duty) The tax on imports levied by the federal government.

technical efficiency The point at which, for any mix of inputs that will produce a given output, no more of any one input is used than is absolutely necessary.

testable strategy A set of linked objectives aimed at an overall goal that can be restated into a sequence of cause-and-effect hypotheses.

theoretical activity capacity The activity output possible if the activity is performed with perfect efficiency.

throughput The rate at which an organization generates money through sales.

time buffer The inventory needed to keep the constrained resource busy for a specified time interval.

time ticket A source document by which direct labour costs are assigned to individual jobs.

total flexible budget variance The difference between the actual cost of the input and the planned cost for the actual output.

total preventive maintenance A program of preventive maintenance that has zero machine failures as its standard.

total product The complete range of tangible and intangible benefits that a customer receives from a purchased product.

total productive efficiency The point at which technical and price efficiency are achieved.

total productivity measurement The assessment of productive efficiency for all inputs combined.

total profit variance The difference between actual and budgeted profit.

total quality management An approach to quality in which manufacturers strive to create an environment that will enable workers to manufacture perfect (zero-defect) products.

traceability The ability to assign a cost directly to a cost object in an economically feasible way using a causal relationship.

tracing Assigning costs to a cost object using an observable measure of the cost object's resource consumption.

transaction risk The possibility that future cash transactions will be affected by changing exchange rates.

transfer price The price charged for goods transferred from one division to another.

transfer pricing problem The problem of finding a transfer pricing system that simultaneously satisfies the three objectives of accurate performance evaluations, goal congruence, and autonomy.

transferred-in costs Costs transferred from a prior process to a subsequent process.

translation (or accounting) risk The degree to which a firm's financial statements are exposed to exchange rate fluctuations.

treasurer The person responsible for the finance function. Specifically, the treasurer raises capital and manages cash and investments.

turnover The ratio of sales to average operating assets.

U

underapplied overhead The amount by which actual overhead exceeds applied overhead.

unfavourable (U) variances Variances produced whenever the actual input amounts are greater than the budgeted or standard allowances.

unit cost The total costs assigned to a product divided by the number of units produced of that product.

unit-level activities Activities that are performed each time a unit is produced.

unit-level activity drivers Factors that measure the consumption of unit-level activities by products and other cost objects.

unit-level drivers *See* production drivers.

unrealized external failure costs (societal costs) Environmental costs caused by an organization but paid for by society.

unused capacity variance The difference between acquired capacity (practical capacity) and actual capacity.

usage (efficiency) variance The difference between standard quantities and actual quantities multiplied by standard price.

V

value-added activities Activities that are necessary to achieve corporate objectives and remain in business.

value-added costs Costs caused by value-added activities.

value-added standard The optimal output level for an activity.

value chain The set of activities required to design, develop, produce, market, and deliver products and services to customers.

variable activity rate The total variable activity cost divided by the amount of activity driver used.

variable budgets *See* flexible budget.

variable cost Costs that, in total, vary in direct proportion to changes in a cost driver.

variable costing A product-costing method that assigns only variable manufacturing costs—direct materials, direct labour, and variable overhead—to production. Fixed overhead is treated as a period cost.

variable-cost ratio Variable costs divided by sales revenues. It is the proportion of each sales dollar needed to cover variable costs.

variable overhead efficiency variance Assuming that direct labour hours are used to apply overhead costs, the difference between the actual direct labour hours used and the standard hours allowed multiplied by the standard variable overhead rate.

variable overhead spending variance The difference between the actual variable overhead and the budgeted variable overhead based on the actual hours used to produce the actual output.

velocity The number of units that can be produced in a given period of time (e.g., output per hour).

vendor Kanbans Cards or markers that signal to a supplier the quantity of materials that need to be delivered and the time of delivery.

W

weighted average costing method A process-costing method that combines beginning inventory costs with current-period costs to compute unit costs. Costs and output from the current period and the previous period are averaged to compute unit costs.

whole-life cost The life-cycle cost of a product plus costs that consumers incur, including operation, support, maintenance, and disposal.

withdrawal Kanban A marker or card that specifies the quantity that a subsequent process should withdraw from a preceding process.

work in process All partly completed units found in production at a given point in time.

work-in-process file A file that is the collection of all job-order cost sheets.

Z

zero defects A quality performance standard that requires all products and services to be produced and delivered according to specifications.

Index

Check Figures

Check figures are given for selected problems.

Chapter 2 Problems

2–15   1. Total service costs added = $930,000
        3. Gross margin = $510,000
2–16   1. Cost of goods manufactured = $652,000
        2. Average cost - $163
        3. Gross margin = $902,100
2–17   1. Cost of goods manufactured = $9,490
        2. Total prime costs = $6,300
        3. Total conversion costs = $6,690
        4. Net income = $2,010
2–18   1. Total manufacturing costs added = $800,000
        2. Total cost of lost inventory = $330,000
2–19   1. Cost of goods manufactured = $2,042,000
        2. Cost of goods available for sale = $2,137,000
2–20   2. Average cost per equipment hour = $144.05
        3. Average traceable cost per equipment hour = $140.20

Chapter 3 Problems

3–16   2. Decrease in resource spending caused by production of rollers = $60,000
        3. Cost of unused capacity, machining = $5,000
3–17   1. Heat, light, and power @ 2,500 hours = $15,000
        3. Heat, light, and power @ 2,500 hours = $15,012
3–18   1. Cost formula = $10,800 + $6.00 Receiving orders
        2. Cost formula = $4,513 + $13.38 Receiving orders
        3. Cost formula = $5,632 + $0.045 Kilograms received
        4. Cost formula = $752 + $7.15 Receiving orders + $0.033 Kilograms received
3–19   1. Total unit variable cost = $210
        3. Total unit variable cost = $222
3–20   1. Variable cost per hour = $51.67
        3. (a) Cost formula = $2,678 + $48.43 Hour
        3. (b) Cost formula = $10,081 + $34.95 Hour
        3. (c) Cost formula = $19,964 + $50.02 Hour
3–21   1. Budgeted setup cost = $9,016
        2. Budgeted setup cost = $9,227
        4. Budgeted setup cost = $9,376
3–22   4. Cost formula = $1,027,385 + $21,479 Administrative staff
        5. Cost formula = $1,275,743 + $1,674 Patient admissions
        6. R^2, Administrative staff = 0.322; R^2, Patient admissions = 0.776
3–23   2. Forecasted sales for 2001 = $2,150,000

Chapter 4 Problems

4–18   1. Accounting cost per backpack = $1.20
        2. Accounting cost per backpack = $0.60
        3. Accounting cost per backpack = $0.60

4–20   1. Overhead cost per unit, Model A = $7.00
        3. Overhead cost per unit, Model A = $5.30

4–21   1. Material handling cost = $120,000
        2. Unit cost, basic model = $87.50
        4. Unit cost, basic model = $84.40

4–22   1. Total manufacturing cost = $1,300,000
        2. Total manufacturing cost = $1,600,000
        3. Total manufacturing cost = $1,840,000

4–23   1. Cost per patient day = $200
        2. Cost per patient day, normal = $150

4–24   1. Unit gross margin, X-12 = $5.25
        2. Unit gross margin, X-12 = $8.30

4–26   1. Overhead cost per modern lamp base = $32
        2. Overhead cost per modern lamp base = $25

4–27   1. Cost per account = $81.40
        2. Cost per medium account = $67.50

4–28   2. Cost per order, category III = $0.03

4–29   2. Shipping and warehousing cost per ton = $770.41

Chapter 5 Problems

5–21   1. Plantwide overhead rate = $9 per machine hour
        2. Bid price, Job 1 = $9,256

5–22   1. Overhead rate = $8 per machine hour
        2. Total cost, Willis job = $17,110

5–23   1. Gross margin = $2,036
        3. Gross margin = $14,852

5–24   1. Total cost, Job 19 = $18,995
        3. Finished goods inventory = $38,840

5–25   1. Production cost traceable to Job 3 = $35,813
        2. Total cost, Job 3 = $46,578
        4. Selling price, Job 3 = $66,329

5–26   1. Product costs, Project 480 = $10,727
        2. Work-in-process = $20,529
        3. Net income = $4,175

5–27   1. Bid price, Job TT = $60.00
        2. Bid price, Job TT = $101.01
        3. Difference in gross margin = $90,923

5–28   1. Cost, Job SS = $126,671
        2. Bid price, Job SS = $13.19

5–29   1. Overhead rate = 60% of direct labour cost
        2. Unit cost, Job 204 = $414.72
        3. Work-in-process inventory = $22,800
        4. Cost of goods manufactured = $83,186
        5. Under-applied overhead = $640

5–30   1. (a) Predetermined overhead rate = $12 per hour
        1. (c) Cost of goods manufactured = $32,400
        3. Under-applied overhead = $23,700

5–31   1. This year's unit-based overhead rate = $10
        2. Total overhead, bike rental = $50,000
        3. Carson rental price = $141.40
        4. Cost, Estes job = $41.55

5–32   1. Predetermined overhead rate = 80% of direct labour cost

2. Actual overhead cost = $1,952
3. Direct materials cost put into production = $3,790
4. Direct labour cost incurred = $3,190
5. Cost of goods manufactured = $9,625

5–34   1. Cost, Job 267 = $26.00
       2. Cost, three surfaces = $34.33
5–35   1. Unit cost = $7.16
       3. Unit cost = $7.54

Chapter 6 Problems

6–28   Cost of goods transferred out = $107,260
6–29   Cost of goods transferred out = $108,881
6–30   1. (b) Equivalent units, pigment = 530,000
       2. Unit cost, pigment = $0.50
       3. Cost of goods transferred out = $1,058,650
6–31   2. Equivalent units, materials = 1,800,000
       3. Unit cost, labour = $2.20
       4. Cost of goods transferred out = $1,365,000
6–32   Cost of goods transferred out = $469,925
6–33   Work-in-process = $104,701
6–34   Cost of goods transferred out = $210,420
6–35   Cost of goods transferred out = $44,258
6–36   Cost of goods transferred out = $44,280
6–37   1. Cost of EWIP = $10,040
       3. Cost of EWIP = $23,400
6–38   1. Cost of EWIP = $10,144
       3. Cost of EWIP = $23,419
6–39   1. Cost of goods transferred out = $17,122
       2. Cost of goods transferred out = $23,192
6–40   1. Cost of goods transferred out = $17,154
       2. Cost of goods transferred out = $23,219
6–41   3. Unit cost, moulding = $11.50
       4. EWIP, moulding = $1,260
6–42   3. Unit cost, moulding = $11.437
       4. EWIP, moulding = $1,257.48
6–43   Cost incurred in December, prior department = $68,000
       Cost of goods transferred out = $68,457
6–44   1. (a) Raw materials = 19,000 kg; $95,000
       2. (b) Equivalent units, conversion costs = 147,700
       4. Cost of EWIP = $225,500
       5. Cost of goods transferred out = $2,800,000
6–46   1. Unit cost = $70.71
       2. Unit cost, Econo model = $48.75

Chapter 7 Problems

7–21   1. Total cost, Western Division = $413,360
       2. Total cost, Western Division = $407,750
       3. Total cost, Western Division = $410,638
7–22   1. (a) Bid price = $2,034.08
       1. (b) Bid price = $2,118.33
7–23   1. (a) Bid price = $2,161.38
       1. (b) Bid price = $1,980.10
7–24   1. Total variable cost, Cooking Department = $77,238
       3. Total variable cost, Cooking Department = $78,711
7–25   1. Unit cost per kilowatt = $0.10
       2. Unit cost per kilowatt = $0.126

7–26   1. Total cost, PD1 = $261,750
        2. Total cost, PD1 = $247,924
7–27   1. Costs allocated to Brandon = $17,776
        2. Costs allocated to Brandon = $23,008
7–29   2. Bid price, Job SS = $14.63
7–30   1. (a) Net income, AC = $16,000
        1. (b) Net income, AC = $14,045
7–32   1. Bid price, 500D = $243.42
        2. Actual loss = $131,538

Chapter 8 Problems

8–24   1. Operating income = $170,400
        2. Operating income = $170,400
        3. Variable production cost per motor = $4.32
8–25   1. Operating income = $570,427
        2. Operating income = $472,533
8–26   1. Contribution margin = $6,450,000
        2. Contribution margin = $7,530,375
8–27   1. Net income, adding Product C = $69,000
8–28   1. Contribution margin = $132,000
8–29   1. Contribution margin = $108,750
8–30   1. Net income = $70,000
8–31   1. Net income decrease from 2000 = $25,000
        2. Net income, 2001 = $6,250,000
8–32   1. Absorption costing unit cost, Month 1 = $9.60
        2. Difference in net income, Month 1 = $16,000
        3. Variable costing net income, month 1 = $95,000
8–33   1. Net income = $72,250
        2. Net income = $37,500
8–34   1. Net operating income = $116,000
        2. Net operating income = $107,000
8–35   1. Expected production = 25,000 units
        2. Variable costing operating income = $69,250
8–36   2. Contribution margin, Year 1 = $45,600
8–37   2. Contribution margin, 1999 = $15,000
8–38   1. Production during 2001 = 20,000 units
8–39   1. Net income = $141,000
8–40   1. Fixed overhead incurred, 2001 = $100,100
        2. Contribution margin = $216,000
        3. Net income = $35,900
        5. Ending inventory, variable costing = $38,062.50
8–41   1. Variable costing net income, 2001 = $235,000
        2. Contribution margin = $1,035,000
8–42   1. Absorption costing unit cost = $32.50
        2. Net income = $29,000
        3. Net income = $12,100
8–43   1. Product margin, Product B = $100
8–44   2. Absorption costing net income = $(177,500)
        3. Product margin, table clocks = $164,500
        4. Segment margin, East region = $255,200
8–47   1. Absorption costing net income = $(3,500)
        2. Contribution margin = $1,890
        3. Contribution margin = $42,390

Chapter 9 Problems

9–27   1. Breakeven point in units = 66,667

    2. Increase in operating income = $200,000
    3. Underestimated operating income = $94,500
    4. Required sales, units = 136,667
    5. Margin of safety = $3,066,667
    6. Percentage increase in operating income = 41.8%
9–28 1. Breakeven point = 7,400 Wars; 37,000 Dragons
    2. Revenue = $2,374,216
    3. Breakeven point = 18,785 Wars; 31,308 Dragons
9–29 1. Maximum advertising spending = $27,000
    2. Increased selling price = $0.39
    3. Required sales volume = 574,615 units
9–30 1. Breakeven point = 15,000 units
    2. Required sales = 29,000 units
    3. Breakeven point = 19,125 units
    4. Required sales = 31,625 units
    5. Required selling price = $28.33
9–31 1. Breakeven point = $11,932
    2. Required additional pizza sales = 2,841
    3. Required sales = 2,105 pizzas
9–32 1. Breakeven point = 47,059 units
    2. 2001 operating income = $140,000
    3. Breakeven point = $581,258
    4. Breakeven point = $618,312
9–33 1. Average number of customers = 1,182
9–34 1. Contribution margin ratio = 0.54
    2. Breakeven point = $277,778
    3. Required sales = $358,176
    4. Contribution margin ratio = 0.54
9–35 1. Contribution margin ratio = 0.464
    2. Breakeven point = $333,513
    3. Increase in bids = 11.6%
    4. Required revenue = $974,593
9–36 1. Grade I = 224 units
    2. Grade II = 392 units
9–37 1. Breakeven point = 40 seats
    2. Breakeven point = 1,200 seats
    3. Breakeven point = 2,400 seats
9–38 1. Breakeven point = $450,000
    2. Breakeven point = 9,000 desk lamps; 9,000 table lamps
    3. Degree of operating leverage = 4.0
9–39 1. Contribution margin ratio, trim kits = 0.375
    2. Contribution margin = $180,000
    3. Breakeven point = 16,222 door handles; 32,444 trim kits
    4. Contribution margin = $210,000
9–40 1. Breakeven point = $900,000
    2. Margin of safety = $318,000
    3. Contribution margin = $669,900
9–41 1. Breakeven point, Neepawa = 73,500 units
    2. Contribution margin = $10,598,400
    3. Contribution margin = $11,064,000
9–42 1. Breakeven point = $18,025,000
    2. Required sales = $30,063,000
9–43 1. Breakeven point, second process = 8,333 cases
9–44 1. Total revenue = $1,507,500
    4. Increase in contribution margin = $72,020
9–45 1. Contribution margin = $1,805,500
    2. Breakeven point = $7,603,333

Chapter 10 Problems

10–24 1. Relevant costs for Site 1, 2 years = $13,440
10–25 1. Cost of making = $367,000
       3. Cost of making = $335,000
       4. Cost of making = $514,000
10–26 1. Margin, process further = $19,716
       2. Additional income per kilogram = $21.025
10–27 1. Segment margin, system B = $(4,158)
       2. Segment margin, headset = $2,584
       3. Segment margin, system C = $1,842
10–28 1. Contribution margin, product A = $(450)
       2. Breakeven point = 79 units of C
10–29 1. Increase in profit, Merv's division = $12,800
       2. Increase in profit, Jaya's division = $16,000
       3. Increase in profit = $11,200
10–30 Increase in profit = $12,200
10–31 1. Minimum price = $2.80
       2. Minimum price = $3.57
       3. Decrease in profit = $4,000
10–32 Excess capacity available = 4,350 machine hours
10–33 1. Increase in profit = $34,000
       2. Price = $42.32
       4. Minimum price = $8.00
10–34 1. Increase in profit, accept Poland order only = $26,000
       2. Decrease in profit, drop product A = $74,000
10–35 1. Net income = $(70,900)
10–36 1. Advantage to buying, first year = $200,000
10–37 1. Net income, alternative A = $89,000
       2. Increase in amortization = $3,846
10–38 1. Tissues = 400,000 packages; Napkins = 0 packages
       2. Maximum profit = $275,000
10–39 1. Segment margin, P-gauge = $382,000
          Segment margin, T-gauge = $(40,000)
       3. Segment margin, D-gauge = $15,000
10–40 1. Required labour hours, Department 1 = 3,400
       2. Contribution margin = $113,250
       3. Contribution margin = $113,250
10–41 1. Objective function = $18.55 ML + $19.90 MA + $10.30 TL + $11.65 TA
10–42 1. Objective function = $11 A + $5.5 B + $16 C
       2. Objective function = $25 A + $45 B + $50 C
10–43 Objective function = $16.66 A + $17.84 B + $12.20 C
10–44 1. Relevant cost, lease and make = $51,000
       3. Relevant cost, lease and make = $56,600
10–45 1. Increase in contribution margin = $236,250
10–46 1. (b) Cost per ton = $213.44
10–47 1. Annual net differential cash flow, years 1–3 = $(304,000)

Chapter 11 Problems

11–26 1. Annual operating cash flows, years 1–7 = $75,000
       2. NPV = $50,382
11–27 1. Annual cash savings = $194,850
       2. NPV = $42,306
11–28 1. Net cash flows, year 10 = $330,000
       2. NPV = $184,250
11–29 1. NPV, Proposal B = $46,855
       2. Payback period, Proposal B = 4.68 years

11–30　1. IRR = 16%
　　　　2. Minimum annual cash savings = $15,730
　　　　3. Minimum annual cash savings = $18,118

11–31　1. Annual cash flow = $18,500,000
　　　　2. Annual cash flow = $14,300,000
　　　　3. Average seating rate = 84%
　　　　4. Average seating rate = 77%

11–32　1. Payback period = 3.13 years
　　　　2. Accounting rate of return, average investment = 19.8%
　　　　3. NPV = $3,577
　　　　4. NPV = $(21,009)

11–33　NPV, old = $(155,109)

11–34　NPV = $(19,353)

11–35　2. NPV, purchase = $35,752
　　　　3. NPV = $39,608

11–36　1. NPV, 14% = $(23,441,400)
　　　　2. NPV, 14% = $4,375,200
　　　　3. NPV, 14% = $211,008

11–37　1. NPV, flexible system = $(1,364,130)
　　　　2. NPV, flexible system = $(1,436,517)

11–38　NPV = $(90,327)

11–39　1. NPV = $91,645
　　　　2. NPV = $(13,309)
　　　　3. NPV = $273,395

11–40　1. NPV, bus = $3,393,670

11–41　Increase in NPV from manufacturing = $47,350

11–42　1. Annual cash flows, overhaul service years 1–10 = $56,686
　　　　2. NPV, overhaul service = $(6,037)
　　　　3. NPV, diesel service = $9,170

11–43　1. NPV, buy machine = $992
　　　　2. Rental rate = $466

11–44　1. NPV, old system = $21,525,000
　　　　2. NPV, old system = $27,042,000
　　　　3. NPV, old system = $13,680,000
　　　　4. NPV, new system = $23,278,800

11–45　1. Net income = $51,000
　　　　2. Payback period = 3.28 years
　　　　3. NPV = $306,744
　　　　4. Breakeven = 29,859 cubic yards
　　　　5. Net income = $1,082

11–46　1. Net income, current Canadian operation = $45,000
　　　　2. NPV, Canadian operations = $360,145

11–48　1. NPV, robotic system = $754,269
　　　　2. NPV, 12% = $112,000

Chapter 12 Problems

12–13　1. Total cost = $1,750
　　　　2. Total cost = $1,400
　　　　3. Reorder point = 200 blocks
　　　　4. Total cost = $1,458

12–14　1. EOQ = 600
　　　　2. Safety stock = 20

12–15　1. Optimal batch size = 12,000
　　　　3. Optimal batch size = 1,502
　　　　4. Optimal batch size, 0.5 hours; $10 = 490

12–17　1. Diet = 800,000; Rich = 0

        2. Total contribution margin = $1,100,000
12–18   1. Monthly machine hours required = 15,600
        2. Total contribution = $226,500
12–19   1. Total requirements, molding = 13,000
        2. Product mix = 300 A; 282 B
        3. Product mix = 300 A; 402 B
12–20   1. Daily contribution margin = $32,000
        2. Excess capacity, fabrication = 266.67 hours
        4. Increase in profit = $13,200
12–21   1. Potential daily contribution = $14,000
        2. Daily contribution = $11,600
        4. Increase in daily contribution = $1,980

Chapter 13 Problems

13–22   1. Total sales = $27,000,000
        2. Production, February = 58,000 units
        3. Metal purchased, January = 530,000 kilograms
        4. Direct labour, January = 192,000 hours
        5. Total overhead, March = $1,154,000
        6. Total selling and administrative expenses, March = $326,000
        7. Ending finished goods = $7,138,080
        8. Cost of goods sold = $22,306,240
        9. Net income = $3,823,760
       10. Cash balance, March 31 = $1,642,076
13–23   1. Cash = $13,550
        2. Cash collections, August = $100,700
        3. Cash = $12,005
13–24   Cash collections = $35,784
13–25   Net income = $12,160
13–26   1. Cash disbursements, August = $280,445
        2. Cash collections, July = $330,384
        3. Purchases = 12,260 units
13–27   1. Net cash flow = $568
        2. Net income = $(1,177)
13–29   Ending cash balance = $113,412
13–30   Cost of goods sold = $22,049
13–31   2. Total cost variance = $984F
13–32   1. Direct labour budget variance = $10,000U
        2. Setup budget variance = $2,000F
13–33   1. Machining budget variance = $5,000U
        2. Unit cost = $15.29
13–34   (a) Total sales = $120,000,000
        (b) Production, Quarter 3 = 80,000
        (c) Direct materials purchase, Quarter 3 = 253,500
        (d) Direct labour, Quarter 3 = 400,000 hours
        (e) Total overhead, Quarter 3 = $3,400,000
        (f) Selling and administrative, Quarter 4 = $1,150,000
        (g) Finished goods = $3,329,000
        (h) Cost of goods sold = $99,871,000
        (i) Ending cash balance = $11,090,000
        (j) Net income = $16,129,000
        (k) Total assets = $58,975,000
13–35   2. Sales office expense variance = $3,300F
13–36   1. Cash receipts, May = $2,040,000
13–37   1. Flexible budget formula = $7,000 + 0.78 Sales
        3. Variable expense variance = $740U

13–38   1. Budgeted net income = $320,000
        2. Variable cost variance = $130,000F
13–39   1. Profit volume variance = $18,000F
13–40   1. Committed fixed cost variance = $160,000U
13–41   1. Profit volume variance = $80,000U
13–42   Budgeted cash collections = $760,608
13–43   Budgeted cash disbursements = $589,500
13–45   1. Cash deficit = $(2,904)

Chapter 14 Problems

14–18   1. (a) Unit standard cost = $35.44
        1. (b) Direct labour rate variance = $2,250U
14–19   Labour efficiency variance = $800F
        Fixed overhead denominator variance = $6,000U
14–20   1. Material usage variance = $12,000F
        2. Labour efficiency variance = $4,000U
        3. Annual savings = $520,000
14–21   1. Unit standard cost = $8.68
        2. Labour efficiency variance = $5,200U
14–22   1. Fixed overhead denominator variance = $1,875U
14–23   2. Standard hours per unit = 0.384
        3. Standard cost per unit = $19.29
14–24   1. Standard time = 4 DLH
        2. Standard cost per unit = $98.00
        3. Variable overhead efficiency variance = $250F
14–25   1. Material usage variance = $100,000U
        2. Labour efficiency variance = $24,000U
        3. Variable overhead efficiency variance = $20,000U
        4. Fixed overhead spending variance = $20,000F
14–26   1. Fixed overhead rate = $4.00 per hour
        2. Fixed overhead denominator variance, Ste-Foy = $480,000U
14–27   1. Unit cost, regular ice maker = $25.19
        2. Materials usage variance, regular = $12,160U
        3. Labour rate variance = $7,400F
        4. Variable overhead spending variance = $31,000U
        5. Materials usage variance = $15,680U
14–28   1. Labour efficiency variance = $20,300F
        2. Denominator activity = 135,000 hours
14–29   1. Fixed overhead rate = $6
        2. Fixed overhead spending variance = $20,000U
        3. Variable overhead spending variance = $7,996U
        4. Standard hours per unit = 0.26667
        5. Labour efficiency variance = $14,250F
14–30   1. Standard direct labour cost = $5.00 per hour
        2. Kilograms of materials purchased = 150,000
        3. Kilograms of excess usage = 20,000
        4. Price per kilogram = $0.87
        5. Variable overhead spending variance = $6,600U
        6. Actual labour rate = $5.50
        7. Actual hours = 60,000
        8. Standard hours allowed = 57,000
        9. Actual variable overhead cost = $54,600
14–31   1. UCL, liquids = $282,500
        2. Liquid material usage variance = $23,100U
        3. Labour efficiency variance = $21,875F
        4. Fixed overhead spending variance = $500U

14–32   1. Variable overhead efficiency variance = $1,500U
14–33   1. Total budget variance = $40,000U
        2. (a) Material usage variance = $20,000U
        2. (d) Fixed overhead denominator variance = $15,000U
        2. (e) Variable overhead spending variance = $5,000F
14–34   1. Labour efficiency UCL, April = $21,600
        2. Material usage variance, June = $1,250U
           Labour efficiency variance, June = $15,000U
14–35   1. (b) Direct material usage variance, Material W = $6,375U
        1. (d) Direct labour efficiency variance = $12,600U
        1. (f) Variable overhead efficiency variance = $3,150U
        1. (h) Fixed overhead denominator variance = $2,100U
14–36   1. Units of material used = 60,000
        2. Assembler B = 750 hours
        3. Planned labour variance = $18,480
14–37   1. Standard cost per unit = $77
        2. Variable overhead rate = $3.75 per DLH
        3. Fixed overhead = $3,125
        4. (b) Labour rate variance = $140.50U
        4. (d) Labour efficiency variance = $80.00U
        4. (f) Fixed overhead denominator variance = $375F
14–38   1. (a) Overhead rate = $8.50 per unit
        1. (b) Flexible budget formula = $10,500 + $2 DLH
        1. (c) Denominator volume = 7,500 DLH
        2. Denominator variance = $350F
14–39   1. Standard cost per unit = $7.60
        2. Fixed overhead spending variance = $1,000F
        3. Labour rate variance = $880F
        4. Expected activity = 4,800 hours
14–40   1. Actual price per litre = $0.75
        2. Actual prime cost per case = $29.9807
        3. Variable efficiency variance = $2,000U
14–41   1. Denominator activity = 31,500 DLH
        2. Direct material usage variance = $6,750U
           Labour efficiency variance = $13,200F
           Variable overhead spending variance = $600U
           Fixed overhead denominator variance = $15,000F
14–42   1. Quantity of materials purchased = 30,000 litres
        2. Quantity of materials used = 24,500 litres
        3. Actual direct labour = 14,800 hours
        4. Labour efficiency variance = $2,000F
        5. Variable overhead efficiency variance = $1,000F
        6. Actual variable overhead = $75,800
        7. Fixed overhead spending variance = $500U
        8. Fixed overhead denominator variance = $17,500F
14–43   1. Units produced = 12,000
        2. Materials purchase price variance = $35,454U
        3. Actual labour rate = $8.907 per hour
        4. Direct labour efficiency variance = $43,200U
        5. Variable overhead efficiency variance = $24,000U
        6. Fixed overhead denominator variance = $60,000U
        7. Denominator activity level = 14,000 units
14–44   1. Actual net income = $795,000
        2. Market share variance = $76,000U; Industry volume variance = $104,000F
14–45   1. Profit volume variance (gross) = $2,500F
        2. Profit volume variance (net) = $4,629F
        3. Industry volume variance = $24,997U

4. Sales price variance = $22,000F
5. Total variable cost flexible budget variance = $23,600U
6. Total fixed cost flexible budget variance = $5,500U

14–46
1. Profit volume variance (gross) = $80U
2. Sales mix variance = $40U
3. Market share variance = $124U
4. Sales price variance = 0
5. Total variable cost flexible budget variance = $260U
6. Total fixed cost flexible budget variance = $40U

14–47
1. (a) Sales price variance = $400,000F
1. (b) Profit volume variance (net) = $80,000U
1. (c) Sales mix variance = $120,000F
1. (d) Flexible budget variable expense variance = $420,000U
1. (e) Discretionary fixed expense variance = $240,000F
1. (f) Committed fixed expense variance = $320,000U

14–49
4. Material usage variance = $39,930U

Chapter 15 Problems

15–15
1. (a) 1999 theoretical cycle time = 25 minutes
1. (b) 1999 actual cycle time = 32 minutes
1. (c) 2001 change in postpurchase costs = 50%
1. (d) 1999 labour productivity = 1.9
1. (e) 1999 scrap = 10%
1. (f) 2001 change in product cost = (20)%
1. (g) 2001 change in days of inventory = (50)%
1. (h) 1999 defective units = 5.9%
1. (i) 1999 new customers = .026
1. (j) 1999 hours of training = 100
1. (l) 1999 total employee suggestions = 40

15–16
2. Potential unit cost reduction = $7.10
3. Target cost to expand sales = $8.00
4. Potential unit cost reduction = $8.35

15–17
1. Nonvalue-added cost, engineering = $604,800
   Cost of unused capacity, engineering = $60,000
2. 2001 Kaizen standard, materials = 552,000 kilograms
3. 2001 usage variance, materials = $164,000U

15–18
1. Target cost = $340
2. Unit nonvalue-added cost = $115

15–19
2. Life-cycle income, Product A = $225,000
3. Target cost, Product A = $3,200,000

15–20
1. Theoretical velocity = 3 per hour
2. Ideal conversion cost = $10.00
3. Applied conversion cost = $15.00
4. MCE = 0.67

15–21
1. MCE = 0.30

15–23
1. Theoretical velocity = 7.5 per hour
2. Actual velocity = 6.25 per hour
3. MCE = 0.83
4. Actual conversion cost per unit = $100.03

15–24
5. Kaizen goal for rework = $1,560,000
6. Potential cost reduction = $3,410,000

Chapter 16 Problems

16–15
1. Total quality costs = $3,690,000
2. Internal failure costs = 43.9%
4. Control costs = $400,000

5. Bonus pool = $638,000
6. Actual external failure costs = $4,110,000

16–16   1. Percentage of sales to regain lost contribution margin = 8.7%
2. Increase in contribution margin = $20,800

16–17   1. Breakeven point = $120,000,000
2. Breakeven point = $100,000,000
3. Breakeven point = $34,108,527
4. Loss = $12,000,000

16–18   1. Quality costs as a percentage of sales = 22.25%
2. External failure costs, Quarter 2 = $415,000

16–19   1. Total internal failure costs = 1.55%
2. Total internal failure costs = 3.10%
3. Internal failure costs, napkins = 3.61%

16–20   1. Appraisal cost, 2000 = 5.83%

16–21   1. Materials partial productivity ratio, 2000 = 0.50
2. Increase in profits due to productivity = $460,000
3. Price recovery component = $(70,000)

16–22   1. (a) Labour partial productivity ratio = 1.00
1. (b) Labour partial productivity ratio = 0.40
1. (c) Labour partial productivity ratio = 0.50
2. Productivity inefficiency, 2000 = $28,000
3. Increase in profits = $10,000
4. Potential increase in profits = $18,000

16–23   1. Capital partial productivity ratio, 2000 = 0.10
2. Productivity induced profit increase = $2,225,000
3. Per unit input cost, 2000 = $10.50

16–24   2. Decrease in profit = $1,665
3. Increase in profit = $13,335

16–25   1. Materials partial productivity, setting B = 0.50
2. Net income, setting B = $150,000
3. Profit change, setting B = $107,784

16–26   1. Total failure cost variance = $27,000U
2. Total failure cost variance = $191,000F

Chapter 17 Problems

17–12   1. Environmental costs, 2000 = $800,000
17–13   1. Total benefits = $1,131,000
17–14   1. Unit cost, XA2 = $2.11
2. Unit cost reduction, XA2 = $0.30
17–15   2. Life-cycle cost per unit, polymer = $445.70
17–17   4. Reduction in environmental costs = $513,000

Chapter 18 Problems

18–20   1. ROI, turbocharger = 10.0%
2. (b) ROI, with turbocharger = 13.92%
2. (d) ROI, neither = 14.0%
3. EVA = $45,450
18–21   2. Minimum transfer price = $53
3. Transfer price = $75.60
18–22   1. ROI = 10.33%
2. Turnover = 1.15
3. ROI = 10.5%
4. Turnover = 1.15
5. ROI, without investment = 14.09%
6. Turnover, without investment = 1.57
18–23   1. Total contribution margin = $7,420,000

2. (a) ROI = 12%
2. (b) EVA = $153,750

18–24   1. Contribution margin, company = $600,000
2. Transfer price = $12
4. External sales = 100,000 units
5. Firmwide contribution margin = $750,000

18–25   1. Change in profit if bought externally = $(5,000)

18–26   1. Total increase in profits = $1,500,000
2. Total increase in profits = $3,450,000
3. Total increase in profits = $1,500,000

18–27   1. Maximum transfer price = $31
3. Full cost plus transfer price = $29.50

18–28   1. Transfer price = $12
2. Minimum transfer price = $10
3. Increase in profits, Plastic Division = $50,000
4. Minimum transfer price = $4.50

18–29   2. Minimum price = $285
3. Minimum price = $175
4. Offered transfer price = $276.75
5. Suggested transfer price = $187.50

18–30   1. Maximum price = $1.00
3. Transfer price = $0.625
4. Transfer price = $0.80

18–31   1. Transfer price = $18.69

18–33   1. Bonus pool, Meyers Service = $41,700

18–35   1. ROI = 13%
2. Increase in company's income = $48,000
3. EVA = $48,000

Chapter 19 Problems

19–13   1. Price, Japanese order = 5,245,320 yen
2. Cash expected, October 1 = $114,471

19–14   Comparable uncontrolled price = $12.75

19–15   1. Transfer price, Belgian = $415

19–17   1. Adjusted market price = $12.00
2. Allowable transfer price = $7.20
3. Transfer price, benefit split equally = $9.38